HANDEL

A DOCUMENTARY BIOGRAPHY

Da Capo Press Music Reprint Series

GENERAL EDITOR
ROLAND JACKSON
UNIVERSITY OF SOUTHERN CALIFORNIA

HANDEL

A DOCUMENTARY BIOGRAPHY

by Otto Erich Deutsch

DA CAPO PRESS • NEW YORK • 1974

Library of Congress Cataloging in Publication Data

Deutsch, Otto Erich, 1883-1967.
   Handel, a documentary biography.

   (Da Capo Press music reprint series)
   Reprint of the 1955 ed. published by W. W. Norton,
New York.
   Bibliography: pp. 863-886
   1. Handel, George Friedrich, 1685-1759.
[ML410.H13D47   1974]   780'.92'4[B]   74-3118
ISBN 0-306-70624-5

This Da Capo Press edition of *Handel: A Documentary Biography*
is an unabridged republication of the first edition published
in New York in 1955. It is reprinted by special arrangement
with W. W. Norton & Company.

Published by Da Capo Press, Inc.
A Subsidiary of Plenum Publishing Corporation
227 West 17th Street, New York, N.Y. 10011

HANDEL

A DOCUMENTARY BIOGRAPHY

I. HANDEL'S MONUMENT IN WESTMINSTER ABBEY

Marble by Louis François Roubiliac, 1760.   (Photograph by Helmut
Gernsheim : Warburg Institute, London)

See page 849

HANDEL

A DOCUMENTARY BIOGRAPHY

BY

OTTO ERICH DEUTSCH

WITH THIRTY-ONE PLATES
AND TEN LINE DRAWINGS

W · W · NORTON & COMPANY · INC

PUBLISHERS   NEW YORK

TO ENGLAND

HIS SECOND FATHERLAND

CONTENTS

ILLUSTRATIONS

ix

The tail-pieces on pages 51, 79, 131, 192, 219, 266, 422, 446 and 532 are reproduced from James Stow's engravings (1825) of the silver tokens designed by William Hogarth and issued in 1738 as "season tickets" to regular visitors to Vauxhall Gardens. The token on page 446 shows Roubiliac's Handel statue, with the inscription *Blandius Orpheo* (Horace, *Odes*, I. xxiv. 13). The tail-piece on page 381 is a reproduction of Hogarth's subscription card for his portrait of David Garrick as Richard III.

PREFACE

THIS book is a companion to *Schubert, a Documentary Biography*, by the same compiler, published by J. M. Dent & Sons, London, in 1946 and, under the title *The Schubert Reader*, by W. W. Norton & Co., New York, in 1947.

The idea of a biography in documents was apparently initiated by the German edition of the same book, entitled *Franz Schubert, die Dokumente seines Lebens*, and published in 1914 by Georg Müller, Munich, which was, however, incomplete.

The present collection of all known and many hitherto unknown or overlooked documents referring to Handel's life was commenced in 1948, although some preliminary work had been done from 1941 onwards. It was inspired by Arthur Henry Mann's Handel collection of music, books, extracts and notes preserved in the Library of King's College, Cambridge, but nearly all the important Handel collections in the British Isles were visited.

In the collecting of Handel documents, including newspaper notices and advertisements, I have had several predecessors. I acknowledge my gratitude to the following :

Horace Townsend, who collected, with the help of George Finlayson, the documents of Handel's visit to Dublin (1852).

Michael Rophino Lacy (1795–1867), of Spanish origin, Schoelcher's collaborator in London.

Victor Schoelcher (1804–1893), the French author of an English biography (1857) and of a Handel catalogue (manuscript), who lived in London from 1851 till 1870.

Friedrich Chrysander (1826–1901), who published the great German Life of Handel (1856–1867, never completed), and who edited, for the *Deutsche Händel-Gesellschaft, Händel's Werke*, here called the Collected Works.

Julian Marshall (1836–1903), who wrote the first Handel article for Grove's *Dictionary of Music and Musicians* (1879).

Arthur Henry Mann (1850–1929), see above.

William C. Smith, of Chislehurst, Kent, who published in 1948 a book, *Concerning Handel*, and in 1954, in Gerald Abraham's *Handel Symposium*, a catalogue of Handel's works.

Jacob Maurice Coopersmith, of Norman, Oklahoma, who compiled a thematic catalogue of Handel's works (manuscript).

Erich H. Mueller von Asow, of Berlin, who first collected Handel's letters (English edition 1935, German edition 1949).

Research during the last hundred years has brought to light a mass of documents referring to Handel's life but, as usual, the biographies, serious and popular, quote only selections of documents, and those in an arbitrary manner. The narrative of a master's life leads to such scraps of quotations, often without exact dates and, therefore, sometimes misleading to the reader. One of several examples, in the case of Handel, is the error mentioned here on page 336, where the year 1741 is given instead of 1733. More often the reader does not know to what exact year an author refers when he only gives the day and month of an event.

The collection of all available documents presents a very different picture of a life from that offered by such random selections. If the collection is properly annotated, and if the compiler in his commentary freely admits any lacunae, the result may be a biography more satisfactory to the true student than the narrative of the most expert essayist.

It is not only the comparative completeness of facts and documents that makes such records a reliable substitute for more entertaining historical representations ; it is the cumulative truth that results from chronological documentation. " Truth is the daughter of Time ", according to Aulus Gellius ; and, by a coincidence, one of Handel's oratorios is entitled *The Triumph of Time and Truth*.

Wherever possible the original manuscripts of printed sources have been used ; but articles or books on Handel in which such sources have first been quoted are mentioned at the beginning of each commentary, in a shortened version referring to the *Bibliography*. Where no such reference is given, the documents are probably new in Handel literature.

In Handel's time the number of newspapers and magazines in Britain, and especially in London, was greater than anywhere else in the world. Not all those periodicals have been preserved, and some papers which were still available in the nineteenth century are no longer traceable. The research of earlier Handelian scholars was of great assistance in finding a way through the maze of periodicals listed in the *Bibliography*, but many additional items have now been traced. The great experience of Mr. William C. Smith in the handling of newspapers of Handel's time enabled him, in his "Catalogue of Works", to quote, if only by date and not by name, advertisements originally not quoted in this book: these are mentioned in the *Addenda*. There are also some German sources added to the text, hitherto not used in Handel biographies and discovered by the compiler after his return to Austria.

Among the printed sources quoted in the book are some in which Handel is not mentioned at all : these are of secondary importance and chosen for their reference to Handel's circle or environment.

The chronological order of the documents is often self-explanatory, and therefore simplifies the necessary commentary.

The *Appendix* gives a selection of Handel documents written or published after his death and before the London Commemoration of 1784, covering the years 1760 till 1780.

The *Bibliography* contains, alphabetically arranged, the manuscript sources used, a list of the periodicals quoted, and the titles of all articles and books which have proved of practical value. It differs considerably from the bibliography in Schoelcher's life, probably collected by Lacy, and from that in Sir Newman Flower's popular biography, provided by William C. Smith, both of which are in chronological order and offer an unequal selection. Kurt Taut's German bibliography, published in book form, is too extensive and at the same time incomplete, especially in English literature. Robert Manson Myers's "Select Bibliography", in his book *Handel's Messiah*, has so far been the most reasonable and reliable.

My thanks are due to all archives, libraries and institutions named in the commentary, especially to the following : The Bank of England ; the British Museum (Departments of Printed Books and of Manuscripts) ; the University Library, Cambridge ; the Bodleian, Oxford ; the National Libraries of Ireland and of Scotland ; the Huntington Library, San Marino, California ; the National Portrait Gallery, London ; the Fitzwilliam Museum, Cambridge ; the Public Record Office, London ; the Library of King's College, Cambridge ; the British Council, London ; the Royal Society of Musicians of Great Britain, London ; the Foundling Hospital, London ; and Mercer's Hospital, Dublin.

The number of people who helped in the compilation of this book is very large, and the following list may not be quite complete. If any have been unwittingly omitted, the compiler offers his apologies and requests forgiveness.

The documents in foreign languages were translated by Maurice J. E. Brown (German) ; Marius Flothuis (Dutch) ; Henry Gilford (Latin) ; Leonardo Pettoello (Italian) ; and Alexis Vlasto (French).

The manuscript was revised by John Nowell. The galley proofs were read by Geoffrey Glaister, of the British Council (Vienna), who checked them with the compiler against the manuscript, and these proofs were revised by Winton Dean. The page proofs were read by C. L. Cudworth and again by Mr. Nowell.

Mr. Gerald Coke, of Bentley, Hants, the owner of the most precious Handel collection in private hands, assisted me in every possible way.

Of special service were : C. H. Collins Baker, R. Harry Beard, Mme Nanie Bridgman (of the Bibliothèque nationale, Paris), J. F. Burnet, Adam Carse, John V. Cockshoot, Dr. J. M. Cooper-smith (of Norman, Oklahoma), Edward Croft-Murray (Department of Prints and Drawings, British Museum), Cyril A. Eland (British Council, Baghdad), Dr. Henry G. Farmer, Frank B. Greatwich, Lord Howe, the Earl of Ilchester, Gilbert S. Inglefield, Miss Cari Johansson (Kungl. Musikaliska Akademiens bibliotek, Stockholm), Dr. A. Kessen (Bibliotheek der Rijksuniversiteit, Leiden), Mrs. Cynthia Legh, Dr. Viktor Luithlen (Vienna), the late Deryck Lynham, G. E. Maby (University Library, Bristol), the late E. H. W. Meyerstein, Robert Manson Myers (New Orleans, Louisiana), Lady Kathleen Oldfield, Cecil B. Oldman, C.B. (Principal Keeper of Printed Books, British Museum), G. F. Osborn, F.L.A. (City of Westminster Libraries), Prof. Emma Pirani (Biblioteca Estense, Modena), Prof. Marco Primerano (Rome), Prof. Dr. Franz Stoessl (Vienna), Frank Walker, G. F. Winternitz (Bologna), Prof. Dr. Hellmuth Christian Wolff (Leipzig), Miss Avril Wood (British Council, London), and the late Alan Yorke-Long. Many of the newspaper extracts were traced and copied in the British Museum by Mr. George Berkovits.

Finally I wish to thank, most sincerely, my publishers for their advice and patience.

O. E. DEUTSCH

VIENNA, Spring 1954

THE DOCUMENTS

The first Handel biography, compiled by John Mainwaring in 1760, will be quoted on appropriate places. This remarkable little book, the first life of a composer ever published, has never been reprinted in its original language. The quotations, printed here in italics, are confined to biographical details as recorded by Handel's contemporaries, mainly by John Christopher Smith, his pupil. On the whole these details are trustworthy, but where dates or names are obviously wrong the necessary corrections are added in square brackets.

1683–1710

FROM THE MARRIAGE REGISTER OF THE CHURCH OF ST. BARTHOLOMEW
IN GIEBICHENSTEIN, 23rd April 1683 (Translated)

The noble, honourable, greatly respected and renowned Herr Georg
Hendel, duly appointed Valet to the Elector of Brandenburg, with the
maiden Dorothea, my daughter, on 23 April at Giebichenstein.

(Chrysander, I. 5.) The entry was written by Pastor Georg Taust, the bride's
father. A facsimile of the entry is to be found on p. 4 of the reproduction of the
funeral sermon for Dorothea Händel ; see 22nd December 1730.

---

*George Frederic Handel was born at Hall, a city in the circle of Upper-Saxony . . . by
a second wife of his father, who was an eminent surgeon and physician of the same place,
and above sixty when his son was born.* (Mainwaring, pp. 1 f.)

The Mainwaring extracts in this book, printed throughout in italics, are taken
from his *Memoirs of the Life of the late George Frederic Handel*, published anonymously
in 1760. Handel was probably born on the 23rd February 1685. His father was
sixty-three years of age and lived at the house " Zum gelben Hirsch " in the Kleine
Klausstrasse, now Nicolaistrasse, in Halle. (Johann Sebastian Bach was born four
weeks later, on 21st March 1685, at Eisenach, Thüringen.)

FROM THE BAPTISMAL REGISTER OF THE CHURCH " ZU UNSER LIEBEN
FRAUEN " AT HALLE-ON-SAAL, 24th February 1685 (Translated)

1685
The week of *Sexagesima.*

Feb. ♂ 24	Father.	Infant receiving baptism.	Godparents.
	Herr Georg Händel, Valet and official Surgeon.	Georg Friederich	Herr Philipp Fehrsdorff, Steward to the Court of Saxony at Langendorff, Anna, Spinster, daughter of the late Herr Georg Taust, Pastor of Giebichenstein, and Herr Zacharias Kleinhempel, Surgeon-Barber in Näumarkt of this locality.

(Chrysander, I. 9.) ♂ is the astronomical sign for Tuesday. Fehrsdorff and
Kleinhempel were Händel's brothers-in-law, Anna Taust his aunt.

H.–1

Handel's elder sister, Dorothea Sophia, born 6th October 1687.
(Chrysander, I. 9.)

———

Handel's father is dangerously ill, September 1689. (Opel,
Mitteilungen.)

———

Handel's younger sister, Johanna Christiana, born 10th January
1690. (Chrysander, I. 9.)

———

While he was yet under seven years of age, he went [*in* 1693 [1]] *with his father to the
Duke of Saxe-Weisenfels. His strong desire to pay a visit to his half-brother, a good
deal older than himself, (for we have before observed that he was the issue of a second
marriage) and at that time* valet de chambre *to the Prince, was the occasion of his going.
His father intended to have left him behind, and had actually set out without him. He
thought one of his age a very improper companion when he was going to the court of a
Prince, and to attend the duties of his profession. The boy finding all his solicitations
ineffectual, had recourse to the only method which was left for the accomplishment of his
wish. Having watched the time of his father's setting out, and concealed his intention
from the rest of the family, he followed the chaise on foot. It was probably retarded by
the roughness of the roads, or some other accident, for he overtook it before it had advanced
to any considerable distance from the town. His father, greatly surprised at his courage,
and somewhat displeased with his obstinacy, could hardly resolve what course to take.
When he was asked, how he could think of the journey, after such a plain refusal had been
given him ; instead of answering the question, he renewed his intreaties in the most pressing
manner, and pleaded in language too moving to be resisted. Being taken into the chaise,
and carried to court, he discovered an unspeakable satisfaction at meeting with his brother
above-mentioned, whom till then he had never seen. . . .*

*From his very childhood Handel had discovered such a strong propensity to Music,
that his father, who always intended him for the study of the Civil Law, had reason to be
alarmed. Perceiving that this inclination still increased, he took every method to oppose
it. He strictly forbad him to meddle with any musical instrument ; nothing of that kind
was suffered to remain in the house, nor was he ever permitted to go to any other, where
such kind of furniture was in use. All this caution and art, instead of restraining, did
but augment his passion. He had found means to get a little clavichord privately convey'd
to a room at the top of the house. To this room he constantly stole when the family was
asleep. He had made some progress before Music had been prohibited, and by his assiduous
practice at the hours of rest, had made such farther advances, as, tho' not attended to at that
time, were no slight prognostics of his future greatness. . . .*

*It happened one morning, that while he was playing on the organ after the service was
over, the Duke was in the church. Something there was in the manner of playing, which
drew his attention so strongly, that his Highness, as soon as he returned, asked his* valet
de chambre *who it was that he had heard at the organ, when the service was over. The
valet replied, that it was his brother. The Duke demanded to see him.*

After he had seen him, and made all the inquiries which it was natural for a man of

---

[1] Percy Robinson(*Music & Letters*, 1939) dates this journey 1696.   (Ed.)

taste and discernment to make on such an occasion, he told his physician, that every father must judge for himself in what manner to dispose of his children ; but that, for his own part, he could not but consider it as a sort of crime against the public and posterity, to rob the world of such a rising Genius !

The old Doctor still retained his prepossessions in favour of the Civil Law. Though he was convinced it was almost become an act of necessity to yield to his son's inclinations (as it seemed an act of duty to the Prince's advice and authority) yet it was not without the utmost reluctance that he brought himself to this resolution. He was sensible of the Prince's goodness in taking such notice of his son, and giving his opinion concerning the best method of education. But he begged leave humbly to represent to his Highness, that though Music was an elegant art, and a fine amusement, yet if considered as an occupation, it had little dignity, as having for its object nothing better than mere pleasure and entertainment : that whatever degree of eminence his son might arrive at in such a profession, he thought that a much less degree in many others would be far preferable.

The Prince could not agree with him in his notions of Music as a profession, which he said were much too low and disparaging, as great excellence in any kind entitled men to great honour. And as to profit, he observed how much more likely he would be to succeed, if suffered to pursue the path that Nature and Providence seemed to have marked out for him ; than if he was forced into another track to which he had no such bias ; nay, to which he had a direct aversion. He concluded with saying, that he was far from recommending the study of Music in exclusion of the Languages, or of the Civil Law, provided it was possible to reconcile them together : what he wished was, that all of them might have fair play ; that no violence might be used, but the boy be left at liberty to follow the natural bent of his faculties, whatever that might be.

All this while he had kept his eyes stedfastly fixed on his powerful advocate ; and his ears were as watchful and attentive to the impressions which the Prince's discourse made upon his father.

The issue of their debate was this : not only a toleration was obtained for Music, but consent for a master to be employed, who should forward and assist him in his advances on his return to Hall. At his departure from Weisenfels, the Prince fill'd his pockets with money, and told him, with a smile, that if he minded his studies, no encouragements should be wanting. . . .

The first thing which his father did at his return to Hall [1694], was to place him under one ZACKAW *[Zachau], who was organist to the cathedral church. This person had great abilities in his profession, and was not more qualified than inclined to do justice to any pupil of a hopeful disposition. Handel pleased him so much, that he never thought he could do enough for him. The first object of his attention was to ground him thoroughly in the principles of harmony. His next care was to cultivate his imagination, and form his taste. He had a large collection of Italian as well as German music : he shewed him the different styles of different nations ; the excellences and defects of each particular author ; and, that he might equally advance in the practical part, he frequently gave him subjects to work, and made him copy, and play, and compose in his stead. Thus he had more exercise, and more experience than usually falls to the share of any learner at his years. . . .*

. . . It may seem strange to talk of an assistant at seven years of age, for he could not be more, if indeed he was quite so much, when first he was committed to the care of this person. But it will appear much stranger, that by the time he was nine he began to compose

the church service for voices and instruments, and from that time actually did compose a service every week for three years successively. . . .[1]

From the few facts just related it is easy to guess, that from the time of Handel's having a master in form, the Civil Law could have had no great share of his attention. . . . Hall was not a place for so aspiring a youth to be long confined to. *During this interval of three or four years, he had made all the improvements that were any way consistent with the opportunities it afforded; but he was impatient for another situation, which would afford him better, and such a one at length presented itself. After some consultations, Berlin was the place agreed on. He had a friend and relation at the court, on whose care and kindness his parents could rely. It was in the year 1698* [2] *that he went to Berlin. The Opera there was in a flourishing condition, under the direction of the King of Prussia,* [Friedrich I] *. . . who, by the encouragement which he gave to singers and composers, drew thither some of the most eminent from Italy, and other parts. Among these were* [Giovanni] BUONONCINI *and* ATTILIO [Ariosti], *the same who afterwards came to England while Handel was here, and of whom the former was at the head of a formidable opposition against him. This person was in high request for his compositions, probably the best which that court had known. But from his natural temper, he was easily elated with success, and apt to be intoxicated with admiration and applause. Though Handel was talk'd of as a most extraordinary player on the harpsichord for one so young, yet on account of his years he had always considered him as a mere child. But as people still persisted in their encomiums, it was his fancy to try the truth of them. For this end he composed a Cantata in the chromatic style, difficult in every respect, and such as even a master, he thought, would be puzzled to play, or accompany without some previous practice. When he found that he, whom he had regarded as a mere child, treated this formidable composition as a mere trifle, not only executing it at sight, but with a degree of accuracy, truth, and expression hardly to be expected even from repeated practice;—then indeed he began to see him in another light, and to talk of him in another tone.*

ATTILIO, *somewhat his inferior as a composer, was a better performer on the harpsichord, and, from the sweetness of his temper, and modesty of his character, was much more beloved as a man. His fondness for Handel commenced at his first coming to Berlin, and continued to the time of his leaving it. He would often take him on his knee, and make him play on his harpsichord for an hour together, equally pleased and surprized with the extraordinary proficiency of so young a person. . . . The kindness of* ATTILIO *was not thrown away; as he was always welcome, he never lost any opportunity of being with him, or of learning from him all that a person of his age and experience was capable of shewing him. It would be injustice to* BUONONCINI *not to mention his civilities to Handel, but they were accompanied with that kind of distance and reserve, which always lessen the value of an obligation, by the very endeavour to enhance it. . . .*

Thus much is certain, that the little stranger had not been long at court before his abilities became known to the King, who frequently sent for him, and made him large presents. Indeed his Majesty, convinc'd of his singular endowments, and unwilling to lose the opportunity of patronizing so rare a genius, had conceived a design of cultivating it at his own expence. His intention was to send him to Italy, where he might be formed under the best masters, and have opportunities of hearing and feeling all that was excellent in the kind. As soon as it was intimated to Handel's friends (for he was yet too young to determine

---

[1] The earliest of Handel's compositions preserved, six sonatas for two oboes and bass, are from 1696. (Ed.)

[2] Chrysander (I. 52) dates this journey 1696, Percy Robinson (1939) 1703. (Ed.)

*for himself) they deliberated what answer it would be proper to return, in case this scheme
should be proposed in form.   It was the opinion of many that his fortune was already
made, and that his relations would certainly embrace such an offer with the utmost alacrity.
Others, who better understood the temper and spirit of the court at Berlin, thought this a
matter of nice speculation, and cautious debate.   For they well knew, that if he once engag'd
in the King's service, he must remain in it, whether he liked it, or not ; that if he continued
to please, it would be a reason for not parting with him ; and that if he happened to
displease, his ruin would be the certain consequence.   To accept an offer of this nature, was
the same thing as to enter into a formal engagement, but how to refuse it was still the
difficulty.   At length it was resolved that some excuse must be found.   It was not long
before the King caused his intentions to be signified, and the answer was, that the Doctor
would always retain the profoundest sense of the honour done to him by the notice which
his Majesty had been graciously pleased to take of his son ; but as he himself was now
grown old, and could not expect to have him long with him, he humbly hoped the King
would forgive his desire to decline the offer which had been made him by order of his
Majesty.*   (Mainwaring, pp. 2-25.)

———

" George Handell " sends his account, for operating on a man who
swallowed a knife, to Oberpräsident Eberhard von Danckelmann :
the Elector grants him fifty Reichsthaler ; 2nd May 1696.

Letter in Geheimes Staatsarchiv, Berlin, published by Ernst Friedlaender.

———

Handel's father dies, 11th February 1697.

———

INSCRIPTION ON THE TOMBSTONE OF HANDEL'S PARENTS, ERECTED
IN 1697 AND DESTROYED BEFORE 1860 (Translated)

For a sure resting-place, the former Valet, Physician-in-ordinary, and
for 40 years Official Surgeon to the Dukes of Saxe-Merseburg and to
the Electors of Brandenburg,

Herr Georg Händel

in 1674 purchased this vault as a family tomb for himself and his own,
and caused this stone to be set here for remembrance.   Born here in
Halle of Herr Valentin Händel, Councillor, on 24th September 1622.
Married, 1643, to Anna, née Katte, who fell asleep on 9th Oct. 1682, and
rests here in her tomb, in God, until the joyful resurrection.   In 40 years
of marriage with her he begat 3 sons and 3 daughters : namely, Dorothea
Elisabet, Gottfried, Licentiate of Medicine [?], Christoph, who died in
youth, Anna Barbara, Karl, Valet to His Grace of Saxe-Weisenfels,
Sophia Rosina ; of these he lived, as grandfather, to see 28 children's
children, and 2 children's children's children.

On 23rd April 1683 married a second time to the maiden Dorothea
Taust, legitimate daughter of Herr Georg Taust, the elder, well-deserved

[of his Parish], Pastor of Giebichenstein, in which marriage he begat 1 son, Georg Friedrich and [2 daughters] Dorothea Sophia, Johanna Christiana.

In true faith in God and in the precious merits of his Redeemer, Jesus Christ, fell asleep on 11th Feb. 1697, and his body rests here till the joyful resurrection of all believers.

For which resurrection also [await] here the buried remains of his widow, Dorothea, née Taust, who, in the spirit, followed her husband into eternity on 27th Dec. 1730, after 33 years of widowhood.

(Chrysander, II. 228.) The inscription was augmented in 1731. Some words were already illegible when the inscription was copied by Chrysander. The still-born son of the second marriage is not mentioned here.

—

FROM JOHANN CHRISTIAN OLEARIUS' FUNERAL SERMON FOR
HANDEL'S FATHER, DELIVERED AT HALLE, 18th February 1697
(Translated)

. . . To you, however, beloved brethren, the deeply afflicted widow and surviving children offer due thanks for your willing attendance in this house of sorrow. For this you can be assured of their prayers for you. . . .

. . . With her [his second wife] he has begotten 3 children, namely a son, Georg Friedrich, a daughter, Dorothea Sophia, and then again a daughter, Johanna Christiana ; may God bless their upbringing and may it powerfully console the sorrowing widow. . . .

This funeral sermon is printed in a booklet the only complete copy of which seems to have been preserved in the *gräfliche Bibliothek* at Stolberg. It contains, in addition to the sermon, a number of mourning poems, as was usual in German countries at that time ; among them one by Olearius himself, *kurfürstlich Branden-burgischer Konsistorialrat im Herzogtum Magdeburg und Erster Pastor in Halle, Stadt und Kreis* (cf. 22nd December 1730) ; three by Pastor Johann Gottfried Taust, of Oppin ; one each by Christoph Andreas Rotth, Pastor at Grosskugel, by Georg Taust, Pastor at Giebichenstein and Crölwitz, by Johann Georg and Johann Christian Taust (minors), by "J.G.", and finally by "Georg Friedrich Händel." The booklet was printed by Salfeld's widow at Halle, on four pages folio. The sermon was delivered in the house of the Handel family. The still-born son, older than Georg Friedrich, is not mentioned. (Opel, *Mitteilungen*, pp. 10 ff.)

—

YOUNG HANDEL'S POEM MOURNING HIS FATHER, 18th February 1697

Ach Herzeleid ! Mein liebstes Vaterherze
Ist durch den Tod von mir gerissen hin.
Ach Traurigkeit ! Ach, welcher großer Schmerze
Trifft mich itzund, da ich ein Waise bin.

Mein alles liegt, mein *Hoffen* ist verschwunden,
  Mein *Rat* und *Schutz* steht mir nicht ferner bei !
Ach ! O Verlust ! Ach ! O der Schmerzenswunden !
  Sagt, ob ein Schmerz wie der zu finden sei.

Wann sich verhüllt der Sonnen güldne Kerze,
  Das Licht der Welt, erschricket Feld und Land,—
So wird ein Kind, wann ihm das Vaterherze
  So früh entweicht, gesetzt in Trauerstand.

Man liebt den Baum, der Schatten uns gegeben,
  Der uns erfrischt mit seiner grünen Nacht,
Viel mehr ein Kind den, der es erst ans Leben
  Und dann mit Sorg' kaum auf die Beine bracht.

Ein Wald erbebt, wann hohe Cedern fallen,
  Die Tanne heult, die schlanke Birk erblaßt,
Und sollt' bei mir kein Angstgeschrei erschallen,
  Weil's Vaters Haupt die Todessichel faßt ?

Ob aber gleich ich wollte ganz verderben
  Mein Augenlicht durch steten Thränenguß,
So könnt' ich doch nicht wiederum erwerben,
  Ach ! den Verlust, den ich empfinden muß.

Gott lebet noch, der itzt mir hat entrissen
  Das Vaterherz durch einen sel'gen Tod,
Der wird hinfort vor mich zu sorgen wissen
  Und helfen mir aus aller Angst und Noth.

Also bethränte den zwar seligen, doch, ihm allzu frühen Hintritt
seines herzlich geliebten Herrn Vaters
                George Friedrich Händel,
            der freien Künste ergebener.

(Translation)

Ah ! bitter grief ! my dearest father's heart
  From me by cruel death is torn away.
Ah ! misery ! and ah ! the bitter smart
  Which seizes me, poor orphan from this day.

My all lies low, my *hopes* to nothing fade,
  And ah ! my loss ! and ah ! my painful wound !
No more his *counsel* and *defence* my aid !
  Say if a grief like this is to be found.

Whene'er the sun's gold candle, earth's own light,
    Is dimm'd, o'er field and hill dark terrors cloud,—
So is a child, when early from his sight
    His father vanishes, with sorrow bowed.

We love the tree which grateful shadow throws,
    And which refreshes us with its green night,
Much more a child loves him, who life bestows,
    And guides his helpless feet to walk aright.

A forest trembles when high cedars fall,
    The fir trees howl, and pale the birches grow,
Shall then my anguish'd cry not sound at all,
    Since Death's keen sickle lays my father low ?

What though the light of mine own eyes should dim
    Through constant welling of my bitter tears ?
Still could I nevermore recover him
    Whose loss I must endure through empty years.

GOD, who bereaves me of a father's care
    By that dear father's death, yet liveth still ;
And henceforth, in mine anguish and despair,
    I find my help and guidance in His Will.

Thus the passing of his dearly beloved father, blessed indeed, yet to his son, all too previous, is mourned by
                    Georg Friedrich Händel,
             dedicated to the liberal arts.
(Opel, *Händel und sein Sohn,* p. 10.)

———

Handel keeps a copybook, marked " G.F.H.", with compositions by Zachau, Alberti, Froberger, Krieger, Kerl, Ebner, Strunck, etc., 1698.
    (Schoelcher, pp. 8 ff.) Handel preserved this book all his life, but it was lost during the nineteenth century.

———

On *Cantata* Sunday Handel takes part in the Communion Service, 24th April 1701.
    (Opel, *Mitteilungen.*) *Cantata* Sunday is the fourth Sunday after Easter.

———

Handel enters the University of Halle, without entering a special faculty, 10th February 1702, and signs himself : Georg Friedrich Händel Hall Magdeburg.
    (Opel, *Mitteilungen* ; Flower, p. 59.) The University was founded in 1694.

———

HANDEL'S APPOINTMENT AS ORGANIST OF THE CATHEDRAL IN
HALLE, 13th March 1702 (Translated)

Appointment
of the organist, Hendel.

Since it is necessary once more to appoint a capable person as organist
of the Royal Palace- and Cathedral-Church here in place of the recently
departed Johann Christoph *Leporin*, and since the student Georg Friedrich
Hendel, who has already at different times acted as deputy to the said
Leporin in his absence, has been praised to us and recommended above all
others for his skilfulness ; so have we, the ordained Pastors and Elders
at the Royal Palace- and Cathedral-Church, and also of the Reformed
Parish of this place, appointed the same as organist at the aforesaid Church,
for one probationary year, on these conditions : that he is to discharge
such offices entrusted to him with loyal and industrious attention, and to
perform such duties in a way that will seem to an upright organist
suitable and fitting, on Sundays, on Thanksgiving Days and on other
Feast Days and also, when called for, *extraordinarié* on any future occasions
which may be outside these days, to play the organ fittingly at Divine
Service, and for this purpose to pre-intone the prescribed Psalms and
Spiritual Songs, and to have due care to whatever might be needful to
the support of beautiful harmony, to take heed to this end, that he be
always in Church in good time and before the pealing of the bells ceases,
and no less to take good care of the preservation of the organ and whatever
appertains to the same, and where anything faulty in it should be found
to report such forthwith, and then to assist and supervise the directed
repair with good counsel, also to render to the Pastors and Elders set over
him due honour and obedience, to live peaceably with the other Church
Officers, and for the rest, to lead a Christian and edifying life.

In return for his trouble and performance he is promised and assigned,
as a stipend for the probationary year, that is to say, from *Reminiscere* of
this year up to the same time in 1703, fifty thalers, which he will draw
from the Royal Purse of this province, against his receipt, in quarterly
instalments of 12 thalers 12 gulden, beginning next Trinity Sunday, and
in addition free lodging in the Moritzburg most generously assigned to
organists by His Royal Highness.

This appointment is given at Halle under the hands and seals of us, the
Pastors and Elders, this 13th day of March in the year 1702.

V. Achenbach.

(Chrysander, pp. 59 f.)   The cathedral was Calvinist, Handel Lutheran.

———

" H[er]r G. F. Händel " takes part in the Communion Service, on
Quasimodo-geniti Sunday, 23rd April 1702.

(Opel, *Mitteilungen*.)   *Quasimodo-geniti* is the first Sunday after Easter.

———

H.-1 *a*

"H[err] Händel" takes part in the Communion Service on Maundy Thursday, 5th April 1703.

(Opel, *Mitteilungen.*)

———

As his fortune was to depend on his skill in profession, it was necessary to consider of some place less distant [than Berlin], where he might employ his time to advantage, and be still improving in knowledge and experience. Next to the Opera of Berlin, that of HAMBURGH *was in the highest request. It was resolved to send him thither on his own bottom, and chiefly with a view to improvement. . . .*

His father's death happened not long after his return from Berlin. This event produced a considerable change for the worse in the income of his mother. That he might not add to her expences, the first thing which he did on his arrival at Hamburgh [spring 1703], was to procure scholars, and obtain some employment in the orchestra. Such was his industry and success in setting out, that the first remittance which his mother sent him he generously returned her, accompanied with a small present of his own. (Mainwaring, pp. 27-9.)

———

Handel meets Johann Mattheson in the organ loft of the Church of St. Mary Magdalene at Hamburg, 9th July 1703.

(Mattheson, *Ehrenpforte*, pp. 29 and 191.) In his *Lebensbeschreibung*, p. 22, Mattheson gives the date as 9th June 1703.

———

Handel and Mattheson make a river excursion together near Hamburg, 15th July 1703.

(Mattheson, *Ehrenpforte*, pp. 93 ff.)

———

Handel and Mattheson play the organ in the Church of St. Mary Magdalene at Hamburg, 30th July 1703.

(Mattheson, *Ehrenpforte*, pp. 93 ff.)

———

Mattheson and Handel visit Dietrich Buxtehude in Lübeck, 17th August 1703.

(Mattheson, *Ehrenpforte*, pp. 93 ff.) Magnus von Wedderkopp, President of the Holstein Privy Council, invited Mattheson to Lübeck, with a view to the possibility of his succeeding Buxtehude as organist at St. Mary's Church in Lübeck, which had a famous organ from the 16th century. Buxtehude, who married the daughter of his predecessor, Franz Tunder, expected the same from his successor. Neither Handel nor J. S. Bach, who visited Buxtehude from Arnstadt in late autumn 1705, fulfilled this condition, but Johann Christian Schiefferdecker married Margreta Buxtehude and, in 1707, became organist in Lübeck.

———

HANDEL'S REPLACEMENT AS ORGANIST OF THE CATHEDRAL IN HALLE, 12th September 1703 (Translated)

. . . Since necessity demands that at the Royal Palace- and Cathedral-Church here, the post of organist, recently vacated by Georg Friedrich Hendel, must once more be filled by a good and skilful person, and since above all others Johann Kohlhardt has been recommended and acclaimed, as much for his pious conduct as for his skill. . . . So have the ordained Court Chaplains, Administrators and Elders appointed the aforesaid Kohlhardt as organist. . . . Halle 12th September 1703.

(Opel, *Händel und sein Sohn*, p. 14 ; Chrysander, I. 61.) Kohlhardt was a teacher at the Gymnasium of the Reformed Church (Lutheran Parish).

———

Mattheson becomes tutor to Cyril, son of John Wyche, since 1702 British Resident at Hamburg, 7th November 1703.

Handel had given the boy a few music lessons before this time. In January 1706 Mattheson became secretary to the Resident, who, in June 1709, was made Envoy Extraordinary to the Courts of Holstein and Mecklenburg and to the Hansa Towns. Mattheson remained secretary under Cyril, who succeeded his father on the latter's death in 1714. He was knighted in 1729. The family of Wyche may have been instrumental in bringing Handel to England.

———

Prince Gian Gastone de' Medici arrives in Hamburg at the end of December 1703.

The Prince, who took a great interest in Handel, became Grand Duke of Tuscany in 1723 on the death of his father, Grand Duke Cosmo III ; his elder brother Ferdinand, the Crown Prince and a true patron of art, having died in 1713.

———

Handel's first oratorio, the Passion according to St. John, is produced at Hamburg on Good Friday, 17th February 1704. The word-book, from the nineteenth chapter of the gospel, is by Christian Heinrich Postel.

Twenty years later, in 1725, Mattheson dealt severely with Handel's work in *Critica Musica*, II. 1-29 and 33-56 (Chrysander, I. 96 ff.), as he did again, in 1739, in his *Vollkommener Capellmeister*, pp. 176-8.

———

HANDEL TO MATTHESON IN AMSTERDAM

[Hamburg,] 18. März 1704

. . . Ich wünsche vielmahl in Dero höchstangenehmen Conversation zu seyn, welcher Verlust bald wird ersetzet werden, indem die Zeit heran kömt, da man, ohne deren Gegenwart, nichts bey den Opern wird vornehmen können. Bitte also gehorsamst, mir Dero Abreise zu notificieren, damit ich Gelegenheit haben möge, meine Schuldigkeit, durch deroselben Einholung, mit Mlle Sbülens, zu erweisen. . . .

(Translation)

. . . I wish very much to have the pleasure of seeing you and talking with you, and this is likely to be achieved soon, for the time is coming when nothing can be done at the Opera in your absence. I beg you respectfully to let me know when you leave, so that with Mlle Sbülens I may perform the pleasurable duty of meeting you. . . .

(Mattheson, *Ehrenpforte*, p. 94.) Mattheson received this letter in Amsterdam, on his way to England, and because of it decided to return to Hamburg. " Mlle Sbülens " may have been the daughter of the merchant Johann Wilhelm Sbuelen, who died in Hamburg in 1738 and is mentioned in Handel's letters of 30th July 1731 and 17th August 1736. Handel was engaged to play in the orchestra of the Hamburg Theater beim Gänsemarkt, a post he had probably held since the autumn of 1703 ; this theatre was then under the direction of Reinhard Keiser, the composer, and Drüsicke, an amateur. This is one of three letters preserved, which Handel wrote in German. He preferred to write in French, even to Mattheson and G. P. Telemann.

——

Before we advance any farther in his history, it is necessary some accounts should be given of the Opera at Hamburgh, as well as some character of the composer and singers.

The principal singers were CONRATINI [*Conradin*] *and* MATHYSON [*Mattheson*]. *The latter was secretary to . . . Wych, who was resident for the English court, had Handel for his [son's] music-master, and was himself a fine player on the harpsichord.*

MATHYSON *was no great singer, for which reason he sung only occasionally ; but he was a good actor, a good composer of lessons, and a good player on the harpsichord. He wrote and translated several treatises. One that he wrote was on Composition. . . .*

CONRATINI *excelled greatly both as an actress and a singer.* KEYSAR [*Keiser*] *did the same as a composer, but being a man of gaiety and expence, involved himself in debts, which forced him to abscond. His Operas, for some time, continued to be performed during his absence. On his disappearing, the person who before had played the second harpsichord, demanded the first. This occasioned a dispute between him and Handel, the particulars of which, partly for the sake of their singularity, and partly on account of their importance, may deserve to be mentioned.*

On what reasons Handel grounded his claim to the first harpsichord I do not understand : he had played a violin in the orchestra, he had a good command on this instrument, and was known to have a better on the other. But the older candidate was not unfit for the office, and insisted on the right of succession. Handel seemed to have no plea but that of natural superiority, of which he was conscious, and from which he would not recede. This dispute occasioned parties in the Opera-house. On the one side it was said, with great appearance of reason, that to set such a boy as Handel over a person so much his senior, was both unjust and unprecedented. On the other, it was urged with some plausibility, that the Opera was not to be ruined for punctilios ; that it was easy to foresee, from the difficulties KEYSAR *was under, that a Composer would soon be wanted, but not so easy to find a person capable of succeeding him, unless it were Handel. In short, matters (they said) were now at that pass, that the question, if fairly stated, was not who should conduct the Opera, but whether there should be any Opera at all.*

These arguments prevailed ; and he, to whom the first place seemed of course to be due, was constrained to yield it to his stripling-competitor. But how much he felt the indignity, may be guessed from the nature and degree of his resentment ; more suited to the glowing temper of an Italian, than to the phlegmatic constitution of a German : For, determined to make Handel pay dear for his priority, he stifled his rage for the present, only to wait an opportunity of giving it full vent. As they were coming out of the orchestra, he made a push at him with a sword, which being aimed full at his heart, would for ever have removed him from the office he had usurped, but for the friendly Score, which he accidentally carried in his bosom ; and through which to have forced it, would have demanded all the might of Ajax himself. . . .

Whatever might be the merits of the quarrel at first, Handel seemed now to have purchased his title to precedence by the dangers he had incurred to support it. What he and his friends expected, soon happened. (Mainwaring, pp. 30-37.)

———

Handel and Mattheson have a fight outside the Theater beim Gänsemarkt in Hamburg, after a quarrel over Handel's playing of the continuo in Mattheson's opera *Cleopatra,* 5th December 1704. (Mattheson, *Ehrenpforte,* pp. 94 and 193.)

Mattheson's opera was first performed on 20th October 1704. The composer sang and conducted alternately. When originally engaged in the orchestra Handel had played one of the two second violins ; he now played the harpsichord, however, and it was his refusal to give up his place at this that led to the fight. (Mattheson, *Lebensbeschreibung.*)

———

Handel and Mattheson, reconciled, dine together and afterwards go to the rehearsal of Handel's opera *Almira,* 30th December 1704. (Mattheson, *Ehrenpforte,* pp. 94 f.)

———

From conducting the performance, he became Composer to the Opera. KEYSAR, *from his unhappy situation, could no longer supply the Manager, who therefore applied to Handel, and furnished him with a drama to set. The name of it was* ALMERIA, *and this was the first Opera which he made. The success of it was so great, that it ran for thirty nights without interruption. He was at this time not much above fourteen : before he was quite fifteen, he made a second, entitled* FLORINDA ; *and soon after, a third called* NERONE, *which were heard with the same applause. It never was his intention to settle at Hamburgh : he told the Manager, on his first application to him, that he came thither only as a traveller, and with a view to improvement : that till the Composer should be at liberty, or till some other successor or substitute could be found, he was willing to be employed, but was resolved to see more of the world before he entered into any engagements, which would confine him long to any particular place. The Manager left that matter for him and his friends to determine ; but so long as he thought proper to be concerned in the Opera, he promised him advantages at least as great as any Composer that had gone before him. This indeed was no more than what interest would readily suggest to a person in his situation : for good houses will always afford good pay, to all who bear a part in the performance ; and especially to that person, whose character and abilities can ensure its success.*

At the time that ALMERIA *and* FLORINDA *were performed, there were many persons of note at Hamburgh, among whom was the Prince of Tuscany, brother to John Gaston de Medicis, Grand Duke. The Prince was a great lover of the art for which his country is so renowned. Handel's proficiency in it, not only procured him access to his Highness, but occasioned a sort of intimacy betwixt them : they frequently discoursed together on the state of Music in general, and on the merits of Composers, Singers, and Performers in particular. The Prince would often lament that Handel was not acquainted with those of Italy ; shewed him a large collection of Italian Music ; and was very desirous he should return with him to Florence. Handel plainly confessed that he could see nothing in the Music which answered the high character his Highness had given it. On the contrary, he thought it so very indifferent, that the Singers, he said, must be angels to recommend it. The Prince smiled at the severity of his censure, and added, that there needed nothing but a journey to Italy to reconcile him to the style and taste which prevailed there. He assured him that there was no country in which a young proficient could spend his time to so much advantage ; or in which every branch of his profession was cultivated with so much care. Handel replied, that if this were so, he was much at a loss to conceive how such great culture should be followed by so little fruit. However, what his Highness had told him, and what he had before heard of the fame of the Italians, would certainly induce him to undertake the journey he had been pleased to recommend, the moment it should be convenient. The Prince then intimated, that if he chose to return with him, no conveniences should be wanting. Handel, without intending to accept of the favour designed him, expressed his sense of the honour done him. For he resolved to go to Italy on his own bottom, as soon as he could make a purse for that occasion. This noble spirit of independency, which possessed him almost from his childhood, was never known to forsake him, not even in the most distressful seasons of his life.* (Mainwaring, pp. 37-41.)

Handel's first opera, *Almira*, is produced at Hamburg, 8th January 1705.

The libretto, by Friedrich Christian Feustking, is based on an Italian word-book by Giulio Pancieri, which had been set to music in 1691 by Giuseppe Boniventi. The full title of Handel's work is *Der in Krohnen erlangte Glücks-Wechsel, oder : Almira, Königin von Castilien*. It contains 42 German and 15 Italian airs. It ran for about twenty nights. An epilogue, called *Der Genius von Europa*, was provided by Keiser who, in 1706, probably out of jealousy, composed the same libretto, altered by Barthold Feind, under the title *Der durchlauchtigste Secretarius, oder Almira, Königin in Castilien*. Handel's work was revived, with alterations, in Hamburg on 7th February 1732, the alterations probably by Georg Philipp Telemann. (Loewenberg, p. 57.) No author's name is given in the librettos. There are three issues of the first edition, the first issue being dated 1704.

CAST OF " ALMIRA ", HAMBURG, 8th January 1705

Almira—soprano
Edilla—soprano
Bellante—soprano
Raymondo—bass

Consalvo—bass
Osman—tenor
Fernando—tenor
Fabarco—tenor

The names of the singers are not recorded.

———

From Mattheson's Hamburg Opera List, 1704 [or rather, 1705]
(Translated)

ALMIRA. Music by Kapellmeister *Händel*. Libretto by Herr *Feustking*.
Attached to it was an epilogue, called the Genius von Europa, composed
by Herr *Keiser*.

(Chrysander, 1877.)   ———

From Feustking's Pamphlet "Der Wegen der 'Almira'
Abgestriegelte Hostilius.   Andere Bastonade" ("Hos-
tilius given a dressing down on account of 'Almira'.
Second Bastonado"), Hamburg, 1705 (Translated)

To censure Almira, which receives *approbation* from reasonable people
as much for its verses as for the artistic music by Herr Hendel, and up
to the present is honoured with such approbation, is a sign of *malicious*
unreasonableness or unreasonable *malice*.

(Chrysander, I. 109 f.)   Copy in the Staats- und Universitäts-Bibliothek,
Hamburg. This, Feustking's second pamphlet attacking his enemies, was probably
published in February 1705. Handel's name is printed here for the first time, if
we do not count the privately printed poem of 1697.

———

From   Christian   Friedrich   Hunold's   ("Menantes")
Pamphlet, " Wohlmeinendes Send-Schreiben An den Herrn
Pastor Friderich Christian Feistking, etc." ("Friendly
communication to Pastor Friedrich Christian Feistking,
etc."), Hamburg, 1705 (Translated)

. . . So we were successful in the music as well as in your poetic work,
and we are sure that if you had been present you would have been more
in debt to us for its *naturelle composition* than to Monsieur Händel. . . .
27th November [1705].

(Chrysander, I. 111.)   Copy in the Staats- und Universitäts-Bibliothek, Hamburg. Hunold was on Feind's side in this struggle with Feustking.

———

Handel's second opera, *Nero*, is produced at Hamburg, six weeks
after *Almira*, 25th February 1705.

The libretto by Feustking is entitled *Die durch Blut und Mord erlangete
Liebe, oder: Nero*. The same subject was treated by Feind in his libretto

Die römische Unruhe, oder Die edelmütige Octavia, set by Keiser and produced, in competition with *Nero*, on 5th August 1705. (Loewenberg,
p. 59.) Mattheson sang in Handel's opera, this being his last part on the
stage. No author's name is given in the libretto. The opera was also
performed on the 26th, and perhaps on the 27th. It was a failure. The
music is lost.

———

FROM MATTHESON'S HAMBURG OPERA LIST, 1705 (Translated)

NERO. Music by Herr *Händel*. Poem by Herr *Feustking*.
(Chrysander, 1877.)

———

FROM HUNOLD'S ("MENANTES") "THEATRALISCHE, GALANTE
UND GEISTLICHE GEDICHTE" ("DRAMATIC, ELEGANT, AND
SPIRITUAL POEMS"), HAMBURG, 1705 (Translated)

How is a musician to create anything beautiful if he has no beautiful
words? Therefore, in the case of the composition of the *Opera Nero*,
someone has not unjustly complained : There is no spirit in the *verse*, and
one feels vexation in setting such to *music*.

(Chrysander, I. 127.) Handel himself is supposed to have made this complaint.

———

*During his continuance at Hamburg, he made a considerable number of Sonatas. But
what became of these pieces he never could learn, having been so imprudent as to let them
go out of his hands.*

*. . . It has already been observed, that instead of being chargeable to his mother, he began
to be serviceable to her before he was well settled in his new situation. Tho' he had
continued to send her remittances from time to time, yet, clear of his own expences, he
had made up a purse of 200 ducats. On the strength of this fund he resolved to set out for
Italy.* (Mainwaring, p. 42.)

———

After the failure of *Nero*, Handel retires from the opera house
and lives by giving music lessons (1705–6).

It is uncertain when Handel left for Italy, but it was probably not
until 1706. The visit was made on the suggestion either of Prince Gian
Gastone de' Medici, or, more probably, of his brother, Crown Prince
Ferdinand of Tuscany. Handel's itinerary through Italy, from 1706 till
the spring of 1710, is not known in detail. He may have visited Venice
for the first time on his way from Florence to Rome at the end of 1706.

———

*We left him just on the point of his removal to Italy ; where he arrived soon after the
Prince of Tuscany [? July 1706]. Florence, as it is natural to suppose, was his first
destination ; for he was too well known to his Highness to need any other recommendations
at the court of the Grand Duke [Cosimo III], to whose palace he had free access at all
seasons, and whose kindness he experienced on all occasions. The fame of his abilities
had raised the curiosity of the Duke and his court, and rendered them very impatient to*

have some performance of his composing. With less experience, and fewer years to mature his judgment, he had hitherto succeeded to the utmost extent of his wishes. But he was now to be brought to the trial in a strange country, where the style was as different from that of his own nation, as the manners and customs of the Italians are from those of the Germans. Sensible as he was of this disadvantage, his ambition would not suffer him to decline the trial to which he was invited . . . He made the Opera of RODRIGO [in 1707], *for which he was presented with* 100 *sequins, and a service of plate. This may serve for a sufficient testimony of its favourable reception.* VITTORIA [Tarquini], *who was much admired both as an Actress, and a Singer, bore a principal part in this Opera. She was a fine woman, and had for some time been much in the good graces of his Serene Highness. But, from the natural restlessness of certain hearts, so little sensible was she of her exalted situation, that she conceived a design of transferring her affections to another person. Handel's youth and comeliness, joined with his fame and abilities in Music, had made impressions on her heart. Tho' she had the art to conceal them for the present, she had not perhaps the power, certainly not the intention, to efface them.* (Mainwaring, pp. 49-51.)

We are now to relate his reception at ROME. *The fame of his musical achievements . . . had reached that metropolis long before him. His arrival therefore was immediately known, and occasioned civil enquiries and polite messages from persons of the first distinction there. Among his greatest admirers was the Cardinal* [Pietro] OTTOBONI, *a person of a refined taste, and princely magnificence. Besides a fine collection of pictures and statues, he had a large library of Music, and an excellent band of performers, which he kept in constant pay. The illustrious* [Arcangelo] CORELLI *played the first violin, and had apartments in the Cardinal's palace. It was a customary thing with his eminence to have performances of Operas, Oratorios, and such other grand compositions, as could from time to time be procured. Handel was desired to furnish his quota ; and there was always such a greatness and superiority in the pieces composed by him, as rendered those of the best masters comparatively little and insignificant. There was also something in his manner so very different from what the Italians had been used to, that those who were seldom or never at a loss in performing any other Music, were frequently puzzled how to execute his.* CORELLI *himself complained of the difficulty he found in playing his Overtures. Indeed there was in the whole cast of these compositions, but especially in the opening of them, such a degree of fire and force, as never could consort with the mild graces, and placid elegancies of a genius so totally dissimilar. Several fruitless attempts Handel had one day made to instruct him in the manner of executing these spirited passages. Piqued at the tameness with which he still played them, he snatched the instrument out of his hand ; and, to convince him how little he understood them, played the passages himself. But* CORELLI, *who was a person of great modesty and meekness, wanted no conviction of this sort ; for he ingenuously declared that he did not understand them ; i.e. knew not how to execute them properly, and give them the strength and expression they required. When Handel appeared impatient,* Ma, caro Sassone (said he) questa Musica é nel stylo Francese, di ch'io non m'intendo. . . .

Hitherto Handel has chiefly been considered, if not wholly, in the quality of Composer. We shall now have occasion to enter into his character as a Player or Performer. And it must not be forgot, that, though he was well acquainted with the nature and management of the violin ; yet his chief practice, and greatest mastery was on the organ and harpsichord.

When he came first into Italy, the masters in greatest esteem were ALESSANDRO SCARLATTI, [Francesco] GASPARINI, *and* [Antonio] LOTTI. *The first of these he became acquainted with at Cardinal* OTTOBONI's. *Here also he became known to* DOMENICO SCARLATTI . . . *author of the celebrated lessons. As he was an exquisite player on the harpsichord, the Cardinal was resolved to bring him and Handel together for a trial of skill. The issue of the trial on the harpsichord hath been differently reported. It has been said that some gave the preference to* SCARLATTI. *However, when they came to the Organ there was not the least pretence for doubting to which of them it belonged.* SCARLATTI *himself declared the superiority of his antagonist, and owned ingenuously, that till he had heard him upon this instrument, he had no conception of its powers. So greatly was he struck with his peculiar method of playing, that he followed him all over Italy, and was never so happy as when he was with him.*

Handel used often to speak of this person with great satisfaction ; and indeed there was reason for it ; for besides his great talents as an artist, he had the sweetest temper, and the genteelest behaviour. On the other hand, it was mentioned . . . by the two PLA[T]s *(the famous Haut-bois) who came from Madrid, that* SCARLATTI, *as oft as he was admired for his great execution, would mention Handel, and cross himself in token of veneration.*

Though no two persons ever arrived at such perfection on their respective instruments, yet it is remarkable that there was a total difference in their manner. The characteristic excellence of SCARLATTI *seems to have consisted in a certain elegance and delicacy of expression. Handel had an uncommon brilliancy and command of finger : but what distinguished him from all other players who possessed these same qualities, was that amazing fulness, force, and energy, which he joined with them. And this observation may be applied with as much justness to his compositions, as to his playing.*

While he was at Rome he was also much and often at the palaces of the two Cardinals, [Carlo] COLONNA, *and* [Benedetto] PAMPHILLI [Panfili]. *The latter had some talents for Poetry, and wrote the drama of* IL TRIONFO DEL TEMPO, *besides several other pieces, which Handel set at his desire, some in the compass of a single evening, and others extempore. One of these was in honour of Handel himself. He was compared to* ORPHEUS, *and exalted above the rank of mortals. Whether his Eminence chose this subject as most likely to inspire him with fine conceptions, or with a view to discover how far so great an Artist was proof against the assaults of vanity, it is not material to determine. Handel's modesty was not however so excessive, as to hinder him from complying with the desire of his illustrious friend.*

As he was familiar with so many of the Sacred Order, and of a persuasion so totally repugnant to theirs, it is natural to imagine that some of them would expostulate with him on that subject. For how could these good catholics be supposed to bear him any real regard, without endeavouring to lead him out of the road to damnation ? Being pressed very closely on this article by one of these exalted Ecclesiastics, he replied, that he was neither qualified, nor disposed to enter into enquiries of this sort, but was resolved to die a member of that communion, whether true or false, in which he was born and bred. No hopes appearing of a real conversion, the next attempt was to win him over to outward conformity. But neither arguments, nor offers had any effect, unless it were that of confirming him still more in the principles of protestantism. These applications were made only by a few persons. The generality looked upon him as a man of honest, though mistaken principles, and therefore concluded that he would not easily be induced to change them. While he was at Rome he made a kind of Oratorio entitled, RESURRECTIONE, *and one hundred and fifty Cantatas, besides Sonatas and other Music.* (Mainwaring, pp. 54-65.)

From the Valesio Diary, Rome, 14th January 1707 (Translated)

A German has arrived in this city who is an excellent player of the harpsichord and composer. Today he exhibited his prowess by playing the organ in the church of St. John [in the Lateran] to the admiration of everybody.

(Flower, p. 82.) The Handel entries in the Valesio Diary (Archivio Storico Capitolino, Rome) were found by Mr. L. A. Sheppard, and published in English translation by Sir Newman Flower, 1923. Handel, like other German musicians, was called *Il Sassone* in Italy.

———

Handel composes his second setting of Psalm 110, " Dixit Dominus ", in Rome, April 1707.

———

Handel composes Psalm 112, " Laudate pueri Dominum ", in D, Rome, 8th July 1707.

———

Handel composes a double chorus, " Gloria Patriae ", Rome, 13th July 1707.

———

From Monsieur de Blainville's Diary, Rome, 14th May 1707
(Translated)

His Eminence [Cardinal Ottoboni] keeps in his pay the best musicians and performers in Rome, and amongst others the famous Arcangelo Corelli and young Paolucci, who is reckoned the finest voice in Europe, so that every Wednesday he has an excellent concert in his palace, and we assisted there this very day. . . .

(Streatfeild, 1917.) Antonio Caldara and Alessandro Scarlatti were also among Ottoboni's *virtuosi*.

———

Annibale Merlini to Prince Ferdinand de' Medici, Rome,
24th September 1707 (Translated)

He [the virtuoso] is a lad of twelve years, a Roman by birth, who, though of so tender an age, plays the *arciliuto* with such science and freedom that, if compositions he has never even seen are put before him, he rivals the most experienced and celebrated professors, and wins great admiration and well-deserved applause. He appears at the concerts and leading academies of Rome, as, for instance, that of His Eminence Cardinal Ottoboni, and at that which continues daily all the year round at the Casa Colonna. . . . And all this can be testified by the famous Saxon, who has heard him in the Casa Ottoboni, and in the Casa Colonna has played with him and plays there continually.

(Archivio Mediceo, filza 5897 ; Streatfeild, 1909.) Merlini was the Prince's correspondent in Rome.

———

Handel composes the opera *Rodrigo* for Florence, 1707 or 1708.

The title rôle, a soprano, was intended for Vittoria Tarquini,[1] called
La Bombace (or Bombragia). Whether this opera was really performed
in Florence has not been established. Cf. p. 287.

———

Handel composes the serenata *Il Trionfo del Tempo e della Verità*,
text by Cardinal Panfili (?), in Rome about 1708. It is performed
at the palace of Cardinal Ottoboni (?).

Percy Robinson (*Music & Letters,* 1939) assumes that the work was
performed in summer 1707. Its original title was *Il Trionfo del Tempo
e del Disinganno.*

———

Handel's opera *Florindo* is performed at Hamburg in two parts, as
Florindo and *Daphne,* January and February 1708.

The full titles of the librettos are : *Der beglückte Florindo,* in three acts,
after an unknown Italian word-book, by Hinrich Hinsch ; and *Die
verwandelte Daphne,* in three acts, also by Hinsch. The second *Singspiel*
shows some arias with Italian, others with German words only. The
names of the authors are not given in either libretto. The music is lost.

———

FROM HINSCH'S PREFACE TO " FLORINDO ", January 1708 (Translated)

Since the admirable *music* with which this *Opera* is adorned has turned
out to be rather long, and might put the audience out of humour, it has
been considered necessary to arrange the complete work in two parts,
of which the *first* presents the feast *Pythia,* arranged to the honour of
Apollo, and, occurring on the same day, the betrothal of *Florindo* with
Daphne ; it receives, therefore, on account of this prominent part of the
plot, the name *Happy* FLORINDO. *The second part* will represent the
stubbornness of *Daphne* against the love of *Phoebus,* and also the repug-
nance she feels for all love, and finally her transformation into a laurel-
tree, and hence it will receive the name *Transformed* DAPHNE.

(Chrysander, I. 138.)

———

FROM MATTHESON'S HAMBURG OPERA LIST, 1708 (Translated)

FLORINDO. Herr *Händel* composed the verses [of the libretto] written
by Herr *Hinsch.*

DAPHNE. By the same authors.

(Chrysander, 1877.)

———

[1] Not Vittoria Tesi (Signora Tramontini) as related by some writers ; she was
born in 1700, and was a contralto. (Ed.)

FROM THE PREFACE OF JOHANN HEINRICH SAURBREY'S "DIE
LUSTIGE HOCHZEIT, UND DABEY ANGESTELLTE BAUREN-MAS-
QUERADE" ("THE MERRY WEDDING, AND THE RUSTIC MAS-
QUERADE PERFORMED WITH IT"), PLAYED AS AN INTERLUDE WITH
MUSIC TO HANDEL'S "DAPHNE", IN HAMBURG, February 1708
(Translated)

For several years many beautiful *operas* have been composed, with
admirable *verse*, as well as with almost unsurpassable *music*, by the
Capellmeister R. Keyser, as well as by the well-beloved and renowned
Mons. Hendel, now in Italy, and by the no less praiseworthy *Mons.*
Graupner and other valiant people, and have been performed here at our
great Hamburg Theatre. . . .

Saurbrey had been manager of the Hamburg Theatre since Easter 1707. It
is uncertain whether he, or his predecessors, commissioned the new opera by
Handel, and when.

———

Handel finishes the cantata, *Lungi del mio bel Nume*, in Rome, 3rd
March 1708.

———

FROM THE HOUSEHOLD BOOKS OF PRINCE RUSPOLI, ROME
(Translated)

18th March [1708]
Payment for transport of the bed and other things for *Monsù* Endel
20 baiocchi.

[*c.* 20th March 1708]
Payment to the Jew for a month's hire of the said bed and linen
coverlets 60 baiocchi.

Flower, p. 91, gives the figures as 10 and 70. The Handel entries in the archives
of the Ruspoli family in Rome were found by Mr. Sheppard and published by
Sir Newman Flower in 1923, in English. The archives are now in the Vatican
Library, Rome. The Marchese Francesco Maria Ruspoli, Principe di Cerveteri,
was a secular competitor of Cardinal Ottoboni as a patron of the arts.

———

Handel finishes the oratorio *La Resurrezione* in Rome, April 1708.

According to Carlo Sigismondo Capece's word-book, it was performed
on Easter Sunday " nella Sala dell' Accademia del Signor Marchese
Ruspoli "; but according to Handel's manuscript it was written for " La
Festa di Pasqua dal Marchese Ruspoli ".

———

FROM THE HOUSEHOLD BOOKS OF PRINCE RUSPOLI, 8th April 1708
(Translated)

As for the decorations in the hall of the most illustrious and excellent
Signor Marchese Ruspoli, for the Oratorio of the Resurrection of Our
Lord, performed on 8th April 1708.

[Here follows a detailed description of the decorations, including a picture of the Resurrection.]
Total cost 44 scudi, 15 baiocchi. The whole settled for 30 scudi.
                                        Angelo Valeri, Master of the Household.

Flower (p. 90) quotes, in English translation, the wording of a bill by the carpenter Crespineo Pavone, but without figures. This entry, however, could not be traced.

———

FROM THE VALESIO DIARY, 8th April 1708 (Translated)

                                        Easter Sunday, 8th April [1708]
This evening the Marchese Ruspoli had a very fine musical oratorio performed in the Bonelli palace at the SS. Apostoli, having set up in the great hall a well-appointed theatre for the audience. Many of the nobility and a few cardinals were present.

(Flower, p. 91.) The Ruspoli family's own palace, in the Corso, was being rebuilt at this time ; the newly created Prince, therefore, hired the palace of the Duke of Bonelli, in the Piazza SS. Apostoli, for a few years.

———

FROM THE VALESIO DIARY, 9th April 1708 (Translated)

Monday, 9th April [1708]. His Beatitude [the Pope] has issued an admonishment for having a female singer perform in the Oratorio of the preceding evening.

(Flower, p. 92.) The Pope was Clement XI.

———

FROM THE HOUSEHOLD BOOKS OF PRINCE RUSPOLI, 11th April 1708
(Translated)

Angelo Valeri, Master of the Household, will pay to Signor Arcangelo Corelli the above mentioned 144 scudi and 50 marks, of these to be paid to the aforesaid musicians, to each his quota, being the complete and final payment for all the services rendered by them, as indicated in the attached list, which sum will be paid to them and a receipt taken therefor only from the said Signor Arcangelo. This day 11th April 1708.
[Receipt :] Scudi 144,50. I, Domenico Castrucci, on behalf of the aforesaid Signor Arcangelo Corelli, have received the aforesaid sum, and by his order have consigned it to Sig. Almerigo Bandiera for the aforesaid payment to be made, as under :
Several payments made by order of His Excellency to the under-mentioned :
To Signor Arcangelo Corelli scudi 20, to Marco 10, to Filippo 10, to Pasqualino 18, to Vittorio 10, to Cristofano 10, to Pastufato for copying 30. [Total :] 108.

The sum for the above-mentioned musicians consigned to Signor Arcangelo : 144,50.

Grand total of payments made by order of His Excellency : 252,50.

In addition, paid to the undermentioned for rings hereunder described, as delivered to His Excellency's Master of the Household : 116.

Rose-diamond Ring, with rubies and diamonds :	12
another ring, with diamonds and aquamarine :	18
another, with diamonds of large size :	38
another, with one large and sixteen small diamonds :	35
another, with emerald and six diamonds :	13
	Scudi 116

[This list of the rings is included in Bill no. 20 of all the Expenses for the Oratorio of the Resurrection, amounting to scudi 528,50.]

(Flower, p. 91.) The order refers to the performance of Handel's oratorio. The Castrucci, in whose name the receipt is made out, must not be confused with Pietro Castrucci, Corelli's pupil, who went to London with Lord Burlington in 1715. The receipt gives the names of all the musicians, except Corelli, the leader of Ottoboni's orchestra, who was paid separately. He received 20 scudi, or a little over four pounds. The other players got from about ten shillings to one pound. The total costs are estimated by Flower at about £110 for the performance.

———

FROM THE HOUSEHOLD BOOKS OF PRINCE RUSPOLI, 24th April 1708
(Translated)

24th April [1708]. Paid to the singers and musicians for the Oratorio of the Resurrection, as individually listed by order of His Excellency : scudi 252,50.

List of the Performers who took part in the Oratorio of the Resurrection of Our Lord Jesus Christ, in the Palace of the most illustrious and Excellent Signor Marchese Ruspoli in the current year 1708.

[There follows a list with the particular fees paid to the 20 violins, 4 violas, 5 bass-viols, 5 double-basses, 2 trumpets, 1 trombone and 4 oboes, for two performances and for three or, for some, two rehearsals.]

(Flower, p. 91.)

———

FROM THE HOUSEHOLD BOOKS OF PRINCE RUSPOLI, 30th April 1708
(Translated)

30th April 1708.

For return of the Jew's bed, hired for *Monsù* Endel [scudi] 20. Paid to the abovementioned Sig. Francesco Maria de Tolla, victualler, for food for *Monsù* Endel and company, as per list and receipt [scudi] 38,75.

Flower (p. 92) gives the second figure as 38 scudi 25 bajocchi.

———

CARDINAL BENEDETTO PANFILI'S POEM ADDRESSED TO HANDEL
AND SET TO MUSIC BY HIM, ROME (? spring) 1708

CANTATA

Recitativo

Handel, non può mia Musa
Cantare in un istante
Versi che degni sian della tua lira,
Ma sento che in me spira
Sì soave armonia che a' tuoi concenti
Son costretto cantare in questi accenti :

Aria

Puote Orfeo, con dolce suono
Arrestar d'angelli il volo
   E fermar di belva il piè,
Si muovèro a un sì bel suono
Tronchi e sassi ancor dal suolo,
   Ma giammai cantar li fè.

Recitativo

Dunque, maggior d'Orfeo, tu sforzi al canto
Mia Musa allor che il plettro appeso avea
A un tronco annoso, e immobile giacea.

Aria

Ognun canti e all'armonia
Di novello Orfeo si dia
Alla destra il moto, al canto
   Voce tal che mai s'udì,
E in sì grata melodia
Tutta gioia l'alma sia :
Ingannando il tempo intanto
   Passi lieto e l'ore e il dì.

(Translation)

Recitative

My Muse, O Handel, is not so wise
Thus instantly to improvise
Verse worthy of thy Muse's art,
Yet now thy harmonies impart
Sounds to me so persuasive sweet, that I
Perforce with words must match thy melody.

Aria

Orpheus with music and with lay
Made pause the prowling beasts of prey
   And charmed birds on the wing ;
Stones, tree-trunks rooted in the ground,
All moved at his Lyre's compelling sound,
   But he never made them sing.

Recitative

O greater, then, than Orpheus, thou
Hast from my Muse such inspiration wrung,
Long after on an aged bough
My harp unused and lifeless I had hung.

Aria

Sing all and raise each voice
To strains of new beauty,
And let your fingers play
To this new Orpheus' tune.
Let every heart rejoice
In so sweet melody,
And make the time of day
Pass happily but not soon.

This poem and its music were apparently improvised at one of the meetings of the " Arcadian Shepherds ", or *Accademia poetico-musicale*, a Roman society of noblemen and artists founded in 1690. Among the members in Handel's time were Ottoboni, Ruspoli, Corelli, Alessandro Scarlatti, Marcello and Bernardo Pasquini, the organist. Handel was too young to be a member. The fact that he set his own praise to music was a precedent for Haydn's songs " What art expresses " and " O tuneful voice " as well as for Schubert's " Geheimnis ". The cantata was first found in the Granville copy, in the British Museum (Eg. 2942, f. 113b), and the text published by Streatfeild in 1911 ; then the autograph was discovered by Edward J. Dent in the Library of the University of Münster, in Westphalia, and the text, slightly differently, printed in the programme of the Handel Festival at Cambridge, held in June 1935 ; another manuscript copy of the cantata is to be found in the Fitzwilliam Museum, Cambridge. The autograph, accompanied by a fair copy (by Domenico Scarlatti ?) came from Ruspoli to Fortunato Santini, whose famous music library is now at Münster. The text, as printed here, was kindly revised by Mr. Decio Pettoello, Cambridge. The second line of the second recitative seems to begin in Handel's setting : " La mia Musa all'ora . . .", but Mr. Pettoello altered it for the sake of the rhythm into " Mia Musa allor . . .", which was probably the original version of the poem. Performed again in Cambridge, at the Guildhall, 10th June 1935.

—

Handel composes a cantata, as a farewell to Rome, entitled *Partenza di G. B. di G. F. Hendel*, (?) May 1708.

(Chrysander, I. 231.) The initials (G. B.) of the author have not been identified. It must have been in or about May 1708 that Handel went from Rome to Naples.

—

From Rome he removed to NAPLES, *where, as at most other places, he had a palazzo at command, and was provided with table, coach, and all other accommodations. While he was at this capital, he made* ACIS *and* GALATEA, *the words Italian, and the Music different from ours.*[1] *It was composed at the request of* DONNA LAURA, *whether a Portuguese or a Spanish Princess, I will not be certain. But the pomp and magnificence of this lady should seem to speak her of Spanish extraction. For she lived, acted, and conversed with a state truly regal.*[2]

How Handel executed his task, we may guess from what he has since produced on the same and other subjects, under all the disadvantages of a language less soft and sonorous, and of Dramas constructed without art or judgment, order or consistency.

While he was at Naples he received invitations from most of the principal persons who lived within reach of that capital ; and lucky was he esteemed, who could engage him soonest, and detain him longest. . . . (Mainwaring, pp. 65-7.)

Handel finishes the serenata *Aci, Galatea e Polifemo* in Naples, 16th June 1708.

It is assumed that the serenata was written for and performed at the marriage of the Duca d'Alvito, whose name is added at the end of the manuscript, to Donna Beatrice Sanseverino, daughter of the late Prince di Monte-Miletto ; the wedding took place in Naples on 19th July 1708. (Flower, pp. 94 f.) Giuseppe Maria Boschi (see 26th December 1709) is said to have sung the part of Polifemo.

Handel composes the terzet *Se tu non lasci amore* in Naples, 12th July 1708.

Handel's elder sister, Dorothea Sophia, marries the lawyer, Dr. Michael Dietrich Michaelsen, at the home of her uncle, Georg Taust, jun., in Giebichenstein, 26th September 1708.

Cf. 23rd April 1683. The name Michaelsen was pronounced as if divided, Micha-elsen.

Back in Rome from Naples, Handel meets the composer Agostino Steffani, in Ottoboni's Rome palace, spring 1709.

Steffani had formerly been music director at the Hanover Court of the Elector Ernst August ; he was now in the service of Johann Wilhelm, Elector Palatine at Düsseldorf, the brother-in-law of Prince Gian Gastone de' Medici. The Elector Palatine invited Handel to his Court.

---

[1] This refers to the masque *Acis and Galatea*, c. 1719. (Ed.)
[2] The episode with *Donna Laura* is doubtful ; cf. next entry. (Ed.)

Handel's younger sister, Johanna Christiana, dies at Halle at the age of nineteen, 16th July 1709.

———

The nature of his design in travelling made it improper for him to stay long in any one place . . . It was his resolution to visit every part of Italy, which was any way famous for its musical performances. Venice was his next resort. He was first discovered there at a Masquerade, while he was playing on a harpsichord in his visor. [Domenico] SCARLATTI happened to be there, and affirmed that it could be no one but the famous Saxon, or the devil. Being thus detected, he was strongly importuned to compose an Opera. But there was so little prospect of either honour or advantage from such an undertaking, that he was very unwilling to engage in it. . . .

At last, however, he consented, and in three weeks he finished his AGRIPPINA [in 1709], which was performed twenty-seven nights successively ; and in a theatre which had been shut up for a long time, notwithstanding there were two other Opera-houses open at the same time ; at one of which GASPARINI presided, as LOTTI did at the other. The audience was so enchanted with this performance, that a stranger who should have seen the manner in which they were affected, would have imagined they had all been distracted.

The theatre, at almost every pause, resounded with shouts and acclamations of viva il caro Sassone ! *and other expressions of approbation too extravagant to be mentioned. They were thunderstruck with the grandeur and sublimity of his stile : for never had they known till then all the powers of harmony and modulation so closely arrayed, and so forcibly combined.*

This Opera drew over all the best singers from the other houses. Among the foremost of these was the famous VITTORIA, who a little before Handel's removal to Venice had obtained permission of the grand Duke to sing in one of the houses there. At AGRIPPINA her inclinations gave new lustre to her talents. Handel seemed almost as great and majestic as APOLLO, and it was far from the lady's intention to be so cruel and obstinate as DAPHNE. (Mainwaring, pp. 51-4.)

———

Handel's opera *Agrippina*, text by Cardinal Vincenzo Grimani (Viceroy of Naples), is produced at Venice, in the Teatro San Giovanni Crisostomo, 26th December 1709.

The cast was as follows :

 Claudio—Signor Antonio Francesco Carli, bass
 Agrippina—Signora Margherita Durastanti (alternating with Elena Croce), soprano
 Nerone—Signor Valeriano Pelegrini (called Valeriano), soprano
 Popea—Signora Diamante Maria Scarabelli, soprano
 Otone—Signora Francesca Vanini-Boschi, contralto
 Pallante—Signor Giuseppe Maria Boschi, bass
 Narciso—Signor Giuliano Albertini, alto
 Lesbo—Signor D. Nicola Pasini, bass
 Giunone—? (contralto)

According to the printed libretto Signor Boschi (cf. 16th June 1708) was also the " pittore di scena ". The opera was performed 27 times during that Carnival.

———

GIORGIO STELLA TO JOHANN WILHELM, ELECTOR PALATINE
AT DÜSSELDORF (Translated)

Venice, 10th January 1710.

As the opera at San Cassiano has commenced, I thought well to send you the opera [libretto] and six of the finest arias. They have instrumental accompaniments, but it was not possible for me to obtain the latter. I am not sending those [arias] from the San Giovanni Crisostomo theatre, which I believe will be sent by Valeriano [Pellegrini], who is much applauded, being a virtuoso singer.

(Einstein, 1907–8, p. 407. Translated by Streatfeild, 1909.) Stella was a singer in the service of the Elector Palatine. The opera at the San Giovanni Crisostomo was, of course, Handel's *Agrippina*.

———

Handel having now been long enough in Italy effectually to answer the purpose of his going thither, began to think of returning to his native country. Not that he intended this to be the end of his travels ; for his curiosity was not yet allay'd, nor likely to be so while there was any musical court which he had not seen. HANOVER *was the first he stopped at.* STEFFANI *was there, and had met with favour and encouragement equal, if possible, to his singular desert.* (Mainwaring, p. 69.)

———

On suggestions made to him in Venice by Prince Ernst of Hanover, the Elector's younger brother, and by Johann Adolf Baron Kielmansegg, his Master of the Horse, Handel goes to Hanover in spring 1710.

Since the death of Ernst August, in 1698, his son Georg Ludwig, later King George I, had been Elector of Hanover.

———

According to Hawkins (V. 267) Handel described his impressions at Hanover as follows : " When I first arrived at Hanover I was a young man. . . . I was acquainted with the merits of Steffani, and he had heard of me : I understood somewhat of music, and ", putting forth both his broad hands, and extending his fingers, " could play pretty well on the organ ; he received me with great kindness, and took an early opportunity to introduce me to the princess Sophia and the elector's son, giving them to understand, that I was what he was pleased to call a virtuoso in music ; he obliged me with instructions for my conduct and behaviour during my residence at Hanover ; and being called from the city to attend to matters of a public concern, he left me in possession of that favour and patronage which himself had enjoyed for a series of years."

The " princess Sophia " must have been the Elector's mother, the Dowager Electress Sophie, like Steffani a friend of G. W. Leibnitz, the philosopher. Her daughter, Sophie Charlotte (d. 1705), had been Queen to King Friedrich I of Prussia, and young Handel may have met her in Berlin ; her daughter-in-law, the unfortunate Sophie Dorothea, cannot be the Sophia referred to, and her grand-daughter, George's child, another

Sophie Dorothea, had been married, since 1706, to Friedrich Wilhelm I, King of Prussia.

———

At Hanover there was also a Nobleman who had taken great notice of Handel in Italy, and who did him great service (as will appear soon) when he came to ENGLAND *for the second time. This person was Baron* KILMANSECK [*Kielmansegg*]. *He introduced him at court, and so well recommended him to his Electoral Highness, that he immediately offered him a pension of* 1500 *Crowns per annum as an inducement to stay. Tho' such an offer from a Prince of his character was not to be neglected, Handel loved liberty too well to accept it hastily, and without reserve. He told the Baron how much he owed to his kind and effectual recommendation, as well as to his Highness's goodness and generosity. But he also expressed his apprehensions that the favour intended him would hardly be consistent either with the promise he had actually made to visit the court of the Elector Palatine, or with the resolution he had long taken to pass over into England, for the sake of seeing that of* LONDON.[1] *Upon this objection, the Baron consulted his Highness's pleasure, and Handel was then acquainted, that neither his promise nor his resolution should be superseded by his acceptance of the pension proposed. He had leave to be absent for a twelve-month or more, if he chose it ; and to go whithersoever he pleased. On these easy conditions he thankfully accepted it.* (Mainwaring, pp. 70-2.)

———

Handel is appointed *Kapellmeister* to the Elector of Hanover with a salary of one thousand thaler, 16th June 1710.

(Georg Fischer, 1899.)

———

Notwithstanding the new favour conferred upon him, he was still in possession of the privilege before allowed him, to perform his engagements, and pursue his travels. He considered it as his first and principal engagement to pay a visit to his Mother at Hall. Her extreme old-age . . . tho [*it*] *promised him but a melancholy interview, rendered this instance of his duty and regard the more necessary. When he had paid his respects to his relations and friends (among whom his old Master* ZACKAW *was by no means forgot) he set out for* DÜSSELDORF. *The Elector Palatine was much pleased with the punctual performance of his promise, but as much disappointed to find that he was engaged elsewhere. At parting he made him a present of a fine set of wrought plate for a desert, and in such a manner as added greatly to its value.*

From Düsseldorf he made the best of his way through HOLLAND *and embarqued for* ENGLAND. *It was in the winter of the year* 1710, *when he arrived at* LONDON, *one of the most memorable years of that longest, but most prosperous war . . . which England had ever waged with a foreign power.* (Mainwaring, pp. 72-4.)

———

Handel, receiving leave from Hanover, travels via Halle and Düsseldorf to London, in autumn 1710. He visits his mother and the Elector Palatine, arriving in London late in November or early in December.

———

[1] Mainwaring thought that Handel was invited to England by Charles, fourth Earl of Manchester, British Ambassador to the Venetian Republic. (Ed.)

N.B.—Prior to 2nd September 1752 [1] the British calendar differs from the Continental calendar in being eleven days behind. From the date of Handel's first arrival in London the British calendar is used in this book, the few Continental dates (given in brackets) being adjusted to unify the chronology. The "old style", however, of calculating the year from 25th March to 24th March, and of describing the first twelve weeks of a year as (e.g.) 1710–11 is disregarded : i.e. 22nd February 1711 is not recorded as of 1710–11.

—

Francesca Vanini-Boschi introduces a Handel aria in Alessandro Scarlatti's opera *Pirro e Demetrio* at the "Theatre in the Haymarket", London, 6th December 1710.

This opera, first performed there on 14th December 1708 and revived on 21st March 1716, was based on a libretto by Adriano Morselli, translated by the manager, Owen Swiney, with Italian lyrics by one Armstrong and English lyrics by Niccolò Francesco Haym, the music, augmented from Scarlatti's *Rosaura*, arranged by Haym. Signora Vanini, who sang the part of Ottone in *Agrippina* at Venice during the season 1709–10, introduced the aria "Hò un nun sò che nel cor" from that opera (the music of which was partly taken from *La Resurrezione*) but with English words : "'Tis not your wealth, my dear". The song was printed thus without, and later with, Handel's name, and also with words by Thomas D'Urfey : "In Kent so fam'd of old". Cf. May 1711. (Chrysander, I. 201 f. ; Smith, October 1935.)

—

FROM THE "BRITISH APOLLO", 18th December 1710
(On the pending improvements in the Haymarket Theatre, under
Aaron Hill's direction.)

> Groves in Nat'ral Forms appear,
> While their Inmates charm the Ear ;
>
> .   .   .
>
> Nay, Machines, they say, will move,
> Glorious Regions from above,
>
> .   .   .
>
> The Ruler of the Stage,[2] we find,
> A Youth of vast extended Mind ;
> No disappointments can controul,
> The Emanations of his Soul ;
> But through all Lets will boldly run,
> Uncurb'd, like th' Horses of the Sun.

(Brewster, pp. 91 f.) *Rinaldo* was thus heralded in a journal, though in one with which Hill, it is true, was closely connected.

---

[1] In 1752 the 3rd September "old style" became the 14th, as on the Continent. (Ed.)
[2] Aaron Hill, Esquire.

1711

At this time Operas were a sort of new acquaintance, but began to be established in the affections of the Nobility, many of whom had heard and admired performances of this kind in the country which gave them birth. But the conduct of them here, i.e. all that regards the drama, or plan, including also the machinery, scenes, and decorations, was foolish and absurd almost beyond imagination. . . . The arrival of Handel put an end to this reign of nonsense.

The report of his uncommon abilities had been conveyed to England before his arrival, and through various channels. Some persons here had seen him in Italy, and others during his residence at Hanover. He was soon introduced at Court, and honoured with marks of the Queen's favour. Many of the nobility were impatient for an Opera of his composing. To gratify this eagerness, RINALDO, *the first he made in England, was finished in a fortnight's time.* (Mainwaring, pp. 76-8.)

——

John Jacob Heidegger, a Swiss of German descent, was the assistant manager of the opera at the first Haymarket Theatre, opened in 1705. He introduced Handel into London society,[1] and Mary Granville, later, as Mrs. Pendarves and Mrs. Delany, a close friend of Handel's, but at the beginning of 1711 only ten years of age, recalled her first meeting with him in the following note : " In the year '10 I first saw Mr. Handel who was introduced to my uncle [Sir John Stanley, a commissioner of customs] by Mr. Heidegger, the . . . most ugly man that was ever formed. We had no better instrument in the house than a little spinet of mine, on which the great musician performed wonders. I was much struck with his playing, but struck as a child, not a judge, for the moment he was gone, I seated myself at my instrument and played the best lessons I had then learnt. My uncle archly asked me if I thought I should ever play as well as Mr. Handel. ' If I did not think I should,' cried I, ' I would burn my instrument ! ' Such was the innocent presumption of childish ignorance."

——

FROM THE " DAILY COURANT ", 13th February 1711

At the Queen's Theatre in the Hay-Market. . . . The new Sub-scription Opera, call'd Binaldo [*sic*], is just now printed, and to be sold at Rice's Coffee-house by the Playhouse in the Hay-Market.

The text was by Giacomo Rossi, after a sketch by Hill. The firstis sue of the libretto gives the name of the printer, Thomas Howlatt, and the place of sale as in the imprint above. The English translation, printed opposite the original Italian, is also by Hill. Under the cast is the note : " La Musica e del Signor

---

[1] Of Handel's alleged visits to the music club in the house of Thomas Britton, the " Small-Coal Man " (Hawkins, IV. 378 and V. 76), no contemporary records are known. (Ed.)

Georgio Frederico Hendel, Maestro di Capella di S.A.E. d'Hanover." Thus his
name was printed for the first time in England. The advertisement appeared six
times, its last appearance being on 20th February 1711.

———

FROM AARON HILL'S DEDICATION OF THE " RINALDO " WORD-BOOK
TO QUEEN ANNE, 24th February 1711

Madam,

Among the numerous Arts and Sciences which now distinguish the
Best of Nations under the Best of Queens ; Musick the most engaging of
the Train, appears in Charms we never saw her wear till lately ; when
the Universal Glory of your Majesty's Illustrious Name drew hither the
most celebrated Masters from every part of *Europe*.

In this Capacity for Flourishing, 'twere a publick Misfortune, shou'd
OPERA's for want of due Encouragement, grow faint and languish : My
little Fortune and my Application stand devoted to a Trial, whether such
a noble Entertainment, in its due Magnificence, can fail of living, in a
City, the most capable of *Europe*, both to relish and support it.

Madam,

This Opera is a Native of your Majesty's Dominions, and was consequently born your Subject : 'Tis thence that it presumes to come, a
dutiful Entreater of your Royal Favour and Protection ; a Blessing,
which having once obtain'd, it cannot miss the Clemency of every Air
it may hereafter breathe in. Nor shall I then be longer doubtful of
succeeding in my Endeavour, to see the *English* OPERA more splendid
than her MOTHER, the Italian.

———

HILL'S PREFACE TO THE WORD-BOOK of " RINALDO ",
24th February 1711

When I ventur'd on an Undertaking so hazardous as the Direction of
OPERA's in their present Establishment, I resolv'd to spare no Pains or
Cost, that might be requisite to make those Entertainments flourish in
their proper Grandeur, that so at least it might not be my Fault, if the
Town should hereafter miss so noble a Diversion.

The Deficiencies I found, or thought I found, in such ITALIAN OPERA's
as have hitherto been introduc'd among us, were, *First*, That they had
been compos'd for Tastes and Voices, different from those who were to
sing and hear them on the *English* Stage ; And *Secondly*, That wanting
the Machines and Decorations, which bestow so great a Beauty on their
Appearance, they have been heard and seen to very considerable
Disadvantage.

At once to remedy both these Misfortunes, I resolv'd to frame some
Dramma, that, by different Incidents and Passions, might afford the

II. HANDEL'S FATHER

After the engraving by J. Sandrart, designed by B. Block, *ca.* 1690 ; pencil
drawing by (?) William Nelson Gardiner.   (Gerald Coke, Esq.)

See pages 1-8

III. JOHN JAMES HEIDEGGER

Mezzotint after John Baptist Vanloo by John Faber, 1742. (H. R. Beard
Theatre Collection)

See page 31

Musick Scope to vary and display its Excellence, and fill the Eye with more delightful Prospects, so at once to give Two Senses equal Pleasure.

I could not chuse a finer Subject than the celebrated Story of *Rinaldo* and *Armida*, which has furnish'd OPERA's for every Stage and Tongue in *Europe*. I have, however, us'd a Poet's Privilege, and vary'd from the Scheme of Tasso, as was necessary for the better forming a Theatrical Representation.

It was a very particular Happiness, that I met with a Gentleman so excellently qualify'd as Signor *Rossi*, to fill up the Model I had drawn, with Words so sounding and so rich in Sense, that if my Translation is in many Places to deviate, 'tis for want of Power to reach the Force of his Original.

Mr. *Hendel*, whom the World so justly celebrates, has made his Musick speak so finely for its self, that I am purposely silent on that Subject ; and shall only add, That as when I undertook this Affair, I had no Gain in View, but That of the Acknowledgment and Approbation of the Gentlemen of my Country ; so No Loss, the Loss of That excepted, shall discourage me from a Pursuit of all Improvements, which can possibly be introduc'd upon our *English* Theatre.

(Smith, March 1935.) The operas based on Tasso's *Gerusalemme liberata* are indeed numerous, but are often entitled *Armida*. In the preface to his play *Elfrid*, 1710, Hill says he attempted a translation of Tasso's " Godfrey of Bulloign, and shall very suddenly publish a specimen . . .". The English text of *Rinaldo* was reprinted in Hill's *Dramatic Works*, 1760. Cf. 5th December 1732.

———

GIACOMO ROSSI'S ADDRESS TO THE READER OF THE " RINALDO "
LIBRETTO, 24th February 1711 (Translated)

The Poet to the Reader.

Here, kind reader, is the delivery of but a few evenings ; and though born at night, it nevertheless is not the abortive fruit of darkness but will show itself to be a true offspring of Apollo, lit by some few rays from *Parnassus*. The haste in bringing it to the light was due to my attempt to gratify the nobility with works of an uncommon note ; and I was prevailed upon in a worthy contest (not indeed with regard to the perfection of the Opera but only to the brevity of the time), for Mr. *Hendel*, the *Orpheus* of our century, while composing the music, scarcely gave me the time to write, and to my great wonder I saw an entire Opera put to music by that surprising genius, with the greatest degree of perfection, in only two weeks. I beg you, friendly reader, receive well this hasty work of mine, and if it does not merit your praises, at least do not keep from it your indulgence, which I should rather call a just consideration of such a limited time at my disposal. If someone is, after all, not satisfied, I am sorry ; but let these gentlemen reflect that their

H.–2

displeasure will stem from themselves and not from my writing, which, after all, was produced with that willing readiness which, showing due respect to all, can give satisfaction to everybody.

(Chrysander, I. 279.) Here follows the " Argument " in English, and not signed.—The words of Almirena's aria " Bel piacere " are not by Rossi, appearing originally in *Agrippina*.

———

FROM THE " DAILY COURANT ", 22nd February 1711

By Subscription.

At the Queen's Theatre in the Hay-Market, on Saturday next, being the 24th of February, will be perform'd a new Opera, call'd, Rinaldo. Tickets and Books will be delivered out at Mr. White's Chocolate-house in St. James's-Street, to Morrow and Saturday next.

This is the first London advertisement referring to a work by Handel, albeit, as usual, without the name of the composer. In subsequent cases such advertisements will only be quoted if they give interesting particulars. Otherwise, only the fact of a production, revival, or publication, will be noted, with reference to the newspaper. The above advertisement was repeated, as usual, on the two following days. There were only two performances in the opera house each week, on Wednesdays and Saturdays, when the playhouses were closed. *Rinaldo* was performed fifteen times before the season ended on 2nd June 1711. The dates were : 24th, 27th February ; 3rd, 6th, 10th, 13th, 17th, 20th, 24th March ; 11th, 25th April ; 5th, 9th, 26th May; and 2nd June. (Nicoll, 1925.)

———

CAST OF " RINALDO ", 24th February 1711

Goffredo—Signora Francesca Vanini-Boschi (called Boschi), contralto
Almirena—Mademoiselle Isabella Girardeau (called La Isabella), soprano
Rinaldo—Signor Niccolò Grimaldi (called Nicolini), soprano
Eustazio—Signor Valentino Urbani (called Valentini), alto
Argante—Signor Giuseppe Maria Boschi, bass
Armida—Signora Elisabetta Pilotti-Schiavonetti (called Pilotti), soprano
Mago—Signor Giuseppe Cassani, alto
Herald—Mr. Lawrence, tenor

The singers' names are given in the libretto and also in Walsh's edition of the songs from the opera. Signora Pilotti, who also sang Armida in the revivals of 1712–15 and 1717, was, like Handel, " in service of the Elector of Hanover ". Nicolini also sang Rinaldo at Dublin in March 1711, in the London revivals of 1712, 1715 and 1717, and at Naples in 1718. Handel directed from the harpsichord.

———

In this Opera the famous NICOLINI *sang. Its success was very great, and his [Handel's] engagements at Hanover the subject of much concern with the lovers of Music. For when he could return to England, or whether he could at all, was yet very uncertain. His Playing was thought as extraordinary as his Music. One of the principal performers here used to speak of it with astonishment, as far transcending that of any person he had ever known, and as quite peculiar to himself. Another, who had affected to disbelieve the reports of his abilities before he came, was heard to say, from a too great confidence in his own, " Let him come ! we'll Handle him, I warrant ye ! " There would be no excuse for recording so poor a pun, if any words could be found, capable of conveying the character of the speaker with equal force and clearness. But the moment he heard Handel on the organ, this great man in his own eye shrunk into nothing.* (Mainwaring, pp. 82–4.)

——

FROM THE " SPECTATOR ", 6th March 1711

An Opera may be allowed to be extravagantly lavish in its Decorations, as its only Design is to gratify the Senses, and keep up an indolent Attention in the Audience. Common Sense however requires, that there should be nothing in the Scenes and Machines which may appear Childish and Absurd. How would the Wits of King *Charles*'s Time have laughed to have seen *Nicolini* exposed to a Tempest in Robes of Ermin, and sailing in an open Boat upon a Sea of Paste-Board ?

. . . As I was walking in the Streets about a Fortnight ago, I saw an ordinary Fellow carrying a Cage full of little Birds upon his Shoulder ; and, as I was wondering with my self what Use he would put them to, he was met very luckily by an Acquaintance, who had the same Curiosity. Upon his asking him what he had upon his Shoulder, he told him, that he had been buying Sparrows for the Opera. Sparrows for the Opera, says his Friend, licking his Lips, what,? are they to be roasted ? No, no, says the other, they are to enter towards the end of the first Act, and to fly about the Stage.

This strange Dialogue awakened my Curiosity so far, that I immediately bought [the word-book of] the Opera, by which means I perceived that the Sparrows were to act the part of Singing Birds in a delightful Grove : though upon a nearer Enquiry I found the Sparrows put the same Trick upon the Audience, that Sir *Martin Mar-all* practised upon his Mistress ; for, though they flew in Sight, the Musick proceeded from a Consort of Flageletts and Birdcalls which was planted behind the Scenes. . . . The Opera of *Rinaldo* is filled with Thunder and Lightning, Illuminations, and Fireworks ; which the Audience may look upon without catching Cold, and indeed without much Danger of being burnt ; for there are several Engines filled with Water, and ready to play at a Minute's Warning, in case any such Accident should happen. However, as I have a very great Friendship for the Owner of this Theatre, I hope that he has been wise enough to *insure* his House before he would let this Opera be acted in it.

It is no wonder, that those Scenes should be very surprizing, which were contrived by two Poets of different Nations, and raised by two Magicians of different sexes. *Armida* (as we are told in the Argument) was an *Amazonian* Enchantress, and poor Signior *Cassani* (as we learn from the *Persons represented*) a Christian Conjurer (*Mago Christiano*). . . .

To consider the Poets after the Conjurers, I shall give you a Taste of the *Italian*, from the first Lines of his Preface. . . . *Behold, gentle Reader, the Birth of a few Evenings, which tho' it be the Night, is not the Abortive of Darkness, but will make itself known to be the Son of* Apollo, *with a certain Ray of Parnassus.* He afterwards proceeds to call Seignior *Hendel* the *Orpheus* of our Age, and to acquaint us, in the same Sublimity of Stile, that he Composed this Opera in a Fortnight. Such are the Wits, to whose Tastes we so ambitiously conform our selves. . . .

But to return to the Sparrows ; there have been so many Flights of them let loose in this Opera, that it is feared the House will never get rid of them ; and that in other Plays they may make their Entrance in very wrong and improper Scenes . . . besides the Inconveniences which the Heads of the Audience may sometimes suffer from them. I am credibly informed that there was once a design of casting into an opera the story of Whittington and his cat . . . but Mr. [Christopher] Rich, the proprietor of the playhouse [Drury Lane] . . . would not permit it to be acted in his house.

Before I dismiss this Paper, I must inform my Reader, that I hear there is a Treaty on foot with *London* and *Wise* (who will be appointed Gardeners of the Play-House) to furnish the Opera of *Rinaldo* and *Armida* with an Orange-Grove ; and that the next time it is Acted, the Singing Birds will be Personated by Tom-Tits : The Undertakers being resolved to spare neither Pains nor Money for the Gratification of the Audience.

C. [Joseph Addison]

The *Spectator* was a new magazine, this being its No. V. In the index of the book edition this article is listed as " Mynheer Hendel styled the Orpheus of the Age ". To make this article and the following documents clearer, some stage directions are quoted here in Hill's translation : Act I, Scene 5—" Armida in the Air, in a Chariot drawn by two huge Dragons, out of whose Mouths issue Fire and Smoke ". Act I, Scene 6—" A delightful Grove in which the Birds are heard to sing, and seen flying up and down among the Trees ". Act I, Scene 7— " A black Cloud descends, all fill'd with dreadful Monsters spitting Fire and Smoke on every side ". Act II, Scene 1—" Two Mermaids are seen Dancing up and down in the Water ". Act II, Scene 4—" The Mermaids Sing and Dance in the Water ". Act III, Scene 1—" Waterfalls ". Act III, Scene 2—" Thunder, Lightning, and amazing Noises ". Act III, Scene 4—" City of Jerusalem " (in the background).—Sir Martin Mar-all, in Dryden's play of 1666, lets his servant play and sing under Millicent's window ; she finds Sir Martin out when he goes on acting the serenade after the music's end. (Cf. Daponte-Mozart's *Don Giovanni*.)—George London & Henry Wise, a firm of gardeners, had the largest nursery in England.

———

FROM THE " SPECTATOR ", 16th March 1711

Sir,

The Opera at the *Hay-Market*, and that under the little *Piazza* in *Covent-Garden*, being at present the two leading Diversions of the Town, and Mr. *Powell* professing in his Advertisements to set up

Whittington and his Cat against *Rinaldo and Armida*, my Curiosity led me the Beginning of last Week to view both these Performances, and make my Observations upon them.

. . . the Undertakers of the *Hay-Market*, having raised too great an Expectation in their printed Opera, very much disappoint their Audience on the Stage.

The King of *Jerusalem* is obliged to come from the City on foot, instead of being drawn in a triumphant Chariot by white Horses, as my Opera-Book had promised me ; and thus while I expected *Armida*'s Dragons should rush forward towards *Argantes*, I found the Hero was obliged to go to *Armida*, and hand her out of her Coach. We had also but a very short Allowance of Thunder and Lightning ; th' I cannot in this Place omit doing Justice to the Boy who had the Direction of the Two painted Dragons, and made them spit Fire and Smoke : He flash'd out his Rasin in such just Proportions and in such due Time, that I could not forbear conceiving Hopes of his being one Day a most excellent Player. I saw indeed but Two things wanting to render his whole Action compleat, I mean the keeping his Head a little lower, and hiding his Candle.

. . . The Sparrows and Chaffinches at the Hay-Market fly as yet very irregularly over the Stage ; and instead of perching on the Trees and performing their Parts, these young Actors either get into the Galleries or put out the Candles ; whereas Mr. *Powell* has so well disciplin'd his Pig, that in the first Scene he and Punch dance a Minuet together. I am informed however, that Mr. *Powell* resolves to excell his Adversaries in their own Way ; and introduce Larks in his next Opera of *Susanna* or *Innocence betrayed*, which will be exhibited next Week with a Pair of new Elders.

As to the Mechanism and Scenary . . . at the *Hay-Market* the Undertakers forgetting to change their Side-Scenes, we were presented with a Prospect of the Ocean in the midst of a delightful Grove ; and th' the Gentlemen on the Stage had very much contributed to the Beauty of the Grove by walking up and down between the Trees, I must own I was not a little astonished to see a well-dressed young Fellow, in a full-bottom'd Wigg, appear in the midst of the Sea, and without any visible Concern taking Snuff.

I shall only observe one thing further, in which both Dramas agree ; which is, that by the Squeak of their Voices the Heroes of each are Eunuchs ; and as the Wit in both Pieces are equal, I must prefer the Performance of Mr. *Powell*, because it is in our own Language.

I am, &c.

R. [Sir Richard Steele]

Martin Powell produced puppet plays and operas, between 1710 and 1713, in " Punch's Theatre " at the Seven Stars in the Little Piazza, Covent Garden.

Steele wrote about him in the *Tatler* of 1709, and Sir Thomas Burnet in a pamphlet of 1715. He advertised several of his marionette operas in the *Spectator*, among them *Orpheus and Eurydice* (Lewis, pp. 254-6). *The History of Whittington, thrice Lord Mayor of London*, was advertised on 1st March 1711 in the *Daily Courant* : " With Variety of New Scenes in Imitation of the Italian Opera's ". See Addison's article of 6th March 1711. About 1739 an opera, *Whittington and his Cat*, was produced in Dublin, with text by Samuel Davey. (Nicoll, 1925, p. 317.)

———

FROM THE " DAILY COURANT ", 19th March 1711

At the Queen's Theatre in the Hay-Market, to Morrow being Tuesday, the 20th Day of March, will be perform'd an Opera, call'd, Rinaldo. With Dancing by Monsieur du Breil and Mademoiselle le Fevre just arriv'd from Bruxelles.

The Haymarket Theatre had a permanent group of dancers, with a ballet master, and the " Mermaids " (like the later Rhine maidens) certainly danced in Act II of all the performances of *Rinaldo*. Du Breil (Breuil ?) and Mlle Le Fevre, of whom nothing else is known, also danced in *Rinaldo* on 24th March 1711.

———

Rinaldo, the first Italian opera to be given in Ireland, is performed in Dublin by N. G. Nicolini's troupe, March 1711.

(Loewenberg, p. 65.) It is assumed that " N. G. Nicolini " was Niccolò Grimaldi, called Nicolini, the first Rinaldo. This was Handel's first contact with Dublin.

———

Rinaldo is given for the benefit of the castrato Valentini, the Eustazio of the opera, 11th April 1711.

The price of the tickets, half a guinea each, is mentioned here for the first time (*Daily Courant*). From later advertisements, however, it seems that the price mentioned referred only to pit and boxes, and to these only on benefit nights.

———

FROM THE " DAILY COURANT ", 24th April 1711

New Musick, just Publish'd. All the Songs set to Musick in the last new Opera call'd, Rinaldo : Together with their Symphonys and Riturnels in a Compleat Manner, as they are Performed at the Queen's Theatre. Compos'd and exactly corrected by Mr. George Friderick Hendell. Printed for J. Walsh . . . and J. Hare. . . .

This is the first advertisement of Handel's music, referring to his contact with the firm of John Walsh, at this time connected with John Hare. (Smith, August 1935.) The title of the first issue is : *Song's in the Opera of Rinaldo Compos'd by Mr Hendel*. That of the second and third issues (3rd May and 21st June 1711) reads : *Arie dell' Opera di Rinaldo Composta dal Signor Hendel Maestro di Capella di Sua Altezza Elettorale d'Hannover.* The title of the edition in three parts (see 5th June 1711) is : *The Symphonys or Instrumental Parts in the Opera Call'd Rinaldo As they are Perform'd at the Queens Theatre, Compos'd by Mʳ Hendel, Chapple Master to yᵉ Elector of Hanover.* (Smith, 1948, pp. 116-18.) These bibliographical details are given here to show how Handel was introduced in the music trade. It is remarkable, if Walsh's claim is true, that Handel himself corrected the song edition.

—

Rinaldo, " the last new Opera ", is performed " At the Desire of several Ladies of Quality ", 25th April 1711. (*Daily Courant.*)

—

FROM THE " POST-MAN ; AND THE HISTORICAL ACCOUNT, &c ",
3rd May 1711

New Musick, Just published,

All the Songs set to Musick in the last new Opera call'd Rinaldo : together with the Symphonys and Riturnels in a compleat manner, as they are perform'd at the Queen's Theatre, Compos'd and exactly Corrected by Mr. George Fridrick Hendell. . . . Printed for J. Walsh . . . and J. Hare. . . .

This advertisement refers to the second issue of the songs (cf. 24th April 1717).

—

NOTE WRITTEN BY OWEN SWINEY, 3rd May 1711

That Mʳ Collier pay back whatever he receiv'd out of ye Subscription money over and above what was due at ye end of ye subscription to Mr. Vanbrugh for Rent, and the receipt of ye gallery, &c., over and above the said Subscription money and Mr. Hill to clear all the charges of ye Six Nights Subscription.

Ye Receipts of ye Gallery, &c. :

	£	s.	d.
3rd night	18	9	9
4th night	27	2	6
6th night	19	8	3
	£65	0	6

(Cummings, 1914, p. 55.) This is one of the papers formerly in the possession of Sir Thomas Coke, Vice-Chamberlain (d. 1727), referring to the Theatres at Drury Lane and in the Haymarket. In 1917 these papers passed from Cummings's collection into that of Richard Northcott, whose collection was dispersed after 1931.—Sir John Vanbrugh, the architect of the Haymarket Theatre, and a playwright, still received the rent from the manager of the theatre. Owen Swiney was manager, with Colley Cibber, till 18th November 1710 when they went to Drury Lane ; in 1712 Swiney returned once more to the Haymarket.

William Colley, M.P. (" Mr. Collier "), was an influential shareholder in Christopher Rich's patent. Colley received from Hill payments for his share in the Haymarket Theatre. (Cf. 1747.) Whether the three nights quoted here refer to *Rinaldo* performances is not certain. The whole transaction is not quite clear.

—

NOTE WRITTEN BY HEIDEGGER, 5th May 1711

May the 5 1711, Mr. Collier agrees to pay Mr. Lunican for the copy of RINALDO this day the Sum of eight pounds, and three pounds every day RINALDO is play'd till Six and twenty pounds are pay'd, and he gives him leave to take the said Opera in his custody after every day of acting it, till the whole six and twenty pounds are pay'd.

(Cummings, 1914, p. 55.) According to other documents in Coke's papers' Lunican was a viola-player in the theatre orchestra, receiving 8d. payment for each performance. It may be assumed that he compiled a score out of the parts in use in the orchestra, perhaps because Handel gave up conducting from the harpsichord. It was certainly a private arrangement which had nothing to do with Handel's fees. The Whole would have been paid up on 29th January 1712.

—

Rinaldo, again " At the Desire of several Ladies of Quality ", is performed for the benefit of Signor Giuseppe and Signora Francesca Boschi, the Argante and Goffredo of the cast, 5th May 1711. (*Daily Courant*.)

—

The performance of *Rinaldo* on 9th May 1711, as usual desired by ladies, is advertised as the last of the season. (*Daily Courant*.)

There were, however, two more performances.

—

The advertisement of the *Rinaldo* performance on 26th May 1711 gives the full list of what were apparently the normal prices : Boxes, 8s. ; Pit, 5s. ; First Gallery, 2s. 6d. ; Upper Gallery, 1s. 6d.; Stage-Boxes, half a Guinea. (*Daily Courant*.)

—

THE FAMOUS MOCK SONG, TO HÒ UN NON SÒ CHE NEL COR, SUNG BY SIGNRA BOSCHI, IN THE OPERA OF " PYRRHUS ", CORECTLY ENGRAV'D (May 1711)

Good folks come here, I'll sing,
A song of th' Opera King,
Which is so much admir'd,
Let not your ears be tir'd.

Repeat.
Th' Italians boast
This Song's compos'd,
By some prevailing Ghost,
  The singer bears a name,
  Of most surprizing Fame,
No Master yet can tell,
If this voice came from Hell,
  It is suppos'd
  Th' infernal host,
Sent here this cunning Ghost,
The Britains to awake,
For some mischievous sake.
His shape was like a man,
The voice just like mad Grann,
Not any graces, tawny, ugly, brown,
Yet not withstanding won'drous pleas'd the towns
  And sung so brazen fac'd,
  That Monsters were amaz'd,
To hear a Porcupine,
  Cou'd charm great wits so fine.

—

Another King most stout,
Turn'd English Op'ras out,
Which Britains first admired,
But now alas are tired.
                    Repeat.
  It was suppos'd,
  They were compos'd,
By some poor harmless Ghost,
  Rinaldo had the name,
  Of most surprising Fame,
He and some other Spark,
Deceive all in the Dark.
  Home Hide the Carr,
  Swing Slanderer,
Cheat Bite Trick ev'ry where,
Say Op'ras have no need,
Of silly English Breed,
They cry th' Italian men,
Will show you what they can,
Come see this Hero big and Famous here,
Whose name is valiant Sign^r Cavalier,

H.–2 *a*

He kill'd so Brazen faced,
A Lion which amazed,
The mob for whom twas fit,
And scar'd them from their wit.

Printed in Walsh and Hare's periodical, *The Monthly Mask of Vocal Musick*, for May 1711, and apparently intended as a skit on Handel, *Rinaldo* and Nicolini. (Smith, October 1935.) Cf. 6th December 1710.

—

Rinaldo is performed, the very last time in the season, and on this occasion " at the Desire of several Persons of Quality ", apparently of both sexes, 2nd June 1711.

It was given in place of the advertised opera *Hydaspes* for the benefit of the box-keepers. (*Daily Courant.*) Francesco Mancini's opera *Hydaspes*, or rather *L' Idaspe fedele*, was produced in 1710, and its intended revival shows that *Rinaldo* was not the only opera performed at the Haymarket during this season. It was, in fact, revived on 2nd December 1711, with additional songs.

—

FROM THE " DAILY COURANT ", 5th June 1711

New Musick, just publish'd. All the Symphonys or Instrumental Musick in the last new Opera call'd Rinaldo, which together with their Songs makes that Opera Compleat as it was perform'd at the Queen's Theatre.

(Smith, August 1935.) Published by John Walsh, P. Randall and John Hare. Besides the short scores, which Walsh published as *Songs* (cf. 24th April 1711), he used to print an edition of the operas in three instrumental parts under the title of *Symphonys or Instrumental Musick*.

—

He had now been [about nine months] in England, and it was time for him to think of returning to Hanover. When he took leave of the Queen [Anne] at her court, and expressed his sense of the favours conferred on him, her Majesty was pleased to add to them by large presents, and to intimate her desire of seeing him again. Not a little flattered with such marks of approbation from so illustrious a personage, he promised to return, the moment he could obtain permission from the Prince, in whose service he was retained. (Mainwaring, p. 84.)

—

After the season Handel returns to Hanover, staying for a few days at Düsseldorf on his way back, June 1711.

—

JOHANN WILHELM, ELECTOR PALATINE, TO GEORG LUDWIG, ELECTOR OF HANOVER, DÜSSELDORF, 6th (17th) June 1711 (Translated)

Most Illustrious etc., Your Highness,

I have kept Capellmeister Händel, who will kindly hand over to you this note, for a few days here with me, in order to show him several *Instrumenta* and other things, and to learn his opinion of them. Therefore I entreat your Highness herewith, with cousinly cordiality and earnestly, that you may deign not to interpret amiss this delay, occurring against his will, and not to lay it to his charge, but to grant him your continuing grace and *protection*, even now as hitherto.

I am again, etc.,

Ddorff 17th June 1711.

(Einstein, 1906–7.) Original draft in Bayerisches Geheimes Staats-Archiv, Munich.

—

JOHANN WILHELM, ELECTOR PALATINE, TO THE DOWAGER ELECTRESS SOPHIE OF HANOVER, 6th (17th) June 1711 (Translated)

Most Illustrious etc., Your Highness,

The bearer of this note, Herr Händel, Capellmeister to your most beloved son, His Highness, Elector of Brunswick, will kindly communicate to you that I have kept him here with me for a few days, in order to show him several *instruments* and to learn his opinion of them. Now I place in Your Highness perfect confidence, as would a friend and a son, and herewith earnestly entreat you, at the same time, that you may deign to show me an acceptable favour, to my highest and everlasting *obligation* : straightway by your noble intercession, supreme above any other, persuade your son to this end, that he shall not interpret amiss the delay of the above-mentioned Händel, occuring against his will, and that consequently this man may be yet again established and *retained* in the grace and protection of his Prince Elector.

I am, Your etc.,

Ddorff 17 June 1711.

(Einstein, 1906–7.) Original draft in Bayerisches Geheimes Staats-Archiv, Munich. The Electors of Hanover were originally Dukes of Brunswick-Lüneburg.

—

Soon after his return to Hanover he made twelve chamber Duettos for the practice of the late Queen [Caroline], then electoral Princess. The character of these is well known to the judges in Music. The words for them were written by the Abbate MAURO HORTENSIO *[Ortensio Mauro], who had not disdained on other occasions to minister to the masters of harmony.*

Besides these Duettos (a species of composition of which the Princess and court were particularly fond) he composed variety of other things for voices and instruments. (Mainwaring, p. 85.)

———

The first daughter of Handel's sister, Dorothea Sophia Michaelsen, dies in the second year of her life, 13th (24th) June 1711.

(Chrysander, I. 310.)

———

FROM THE " POST-MAN ", 21st June 1711

New Musick published,

All the Songs set to Musick in the last new Opera call'd Rinaldo, together with its Pieces for the Harpsicord, as also the Symphonies and Returnels in a compleat manner, as they were performed at the Queens Theatre, and exactly corrected by Mr George Friderich Hendel . . . J: Walsh . . . and J. Hare. . . .

(Smith, August 1935.) This advertisement refers to the third issue of the *Songs* (cf. 24th April and 3rd May 1711) which, in fact, is another state : two pages are added to the aria *Vo' far guerra* for the " Harpsicord Peice Perform'd by Mr Hendel ". His performance in accompanying this aria was a special feature of *Rinaldo*. Cf. 31st January 1717.

———

HANDEL TO ANDREAS RONER

[Hanover, end of July, 1711.]

. . . Faites bien mes complimens à Mons. Hughes. Je prendrai la liberté de lui ecrire avec la premiere occasion. S'il me veut cependant honorer de ses ordres, et d'y ajouter une de ses charmantes poesies en Anglois, il me sera la plus sensible grace. J'ai fait, depuis que je suis parti de vous, quelque progrés dans cette langue. . . .

(Translation)

. . . Please convey my best compliments to Mr. Hughes. I shall take the liberty of writing to him at the earliest opportunity. If however he wishes to honour me with his commands and add thereto one of his charming poems in English, that will afford me the greatest possible pleasure. Since I left you, I have made some progress in that language. . . .

(John Hughes, 1772, I. 48 f. ; reprinted in *Gentleman's Magazine*, March 1785, pp. 165 f.) Andreas, later Andrew, Roner was a German musician residing in London ; he published, in 1721, *Melopeïa Sacra or a Collection of Psalms and Hymns*, translated by Mr. Addison and Sir John Denham. John Hughes's poems, printed posthumously in 1735, contain the cantata *Venus and Adonis* (cf. 1714), two arias from which, set by Handel, were published by William C. Smith in 1937 (Augener, London), after the manuscript copy in the British Museum. These were, presumably, Handel's first settings of English words. Among

Hughes's poems, set by various composers, is also to be found " Wou'd you gain the tender creature ", introduced in Gay's version of *Acis and Galatea*, as set by Handel in (?) 1720. Hughes, poet, painter and musician, died in 1720. It is strange that Roner corresponded with both friends in French. His letter to Hughes was published and reprinted together with Handel's letter to Roner.

———

RONER TO JOHN HUGHES (Translated)

Tuesday, July 31, 1711.

Having received this morning a letter from Mr. Hendel, I thought that I ought not to fail to communicate to you at once an extract that concerns you ; it is a reply to the compliments which you had been good enough to send through me. I shall be writing to him next Friday, so all you need do is to send me, if you please, what you wish to reach him ; and I can assure you, Sir, if the honour of your kind remembrance gives him true pleasure, I myself feel no less as the instrument for the furtherance of your correspondence, thereby affording you a proof of the extreme consideration with which I have the honour to remain. . . .

(John Hughes, 1772, I. 47 f. ; reprinted in *Gentleman's Magazine*, March 1785, p. 165.)

———

FROM THE " POST-MAN ", 6th September 1711

New Musick just published,

. . . The new Flute Master, the 7th Edit. . . . with the newest Aires both of Italian and English, particularly the Favourite Song Tunes in the Opera of Rinaldo, composed by Mr Hendell . . . pr. 1s. 6d. Printed for J. Walsh . . . and J. Hare. . . .

(Smith, August 1935.) It was the fashion to publish flute arrangements of opera airs.

———

FROM THE " DAILY COURANT ", 13th September 1711

Just Publish'd. The most Celebrated Aires and Duets in the Operas of Rinaldo, Hydaspes and Almahide, curiously contrived and fitted for two Flutes and a Bass with their Symphonies, introduced in a compleat manner in three Collections. As also the most celebrated Aires and Duets in the Opera of Rinaldo, for a single Flute. Price 1s. 6d. All fairly Engraven and Carefully Corrected. Printed for J. Walsh . . . and J. Hare. . . .

(Smith, August 1935.) *Almahide*, by (?) Giovanni Bononcini, was also produced in 1710. A similar advertisement appeared in the *Post-Man* of 9th October 1711.

———

FROM THE BAPTISMAL REGISTER OF THE CHURCH "ZU UNSER LIEBEN FRAUEN" AT HALLE, 12th (23rd) November 1711 (Translated)

☽ 23. Herr Michael Dietrich Michaelsen, *Doctor of Law*, one Daughter Johanna Friderica *nat. 20th inst.* Godparents : Frau Johanna Elisabeth, *née* von Alemann, wife of Herr Johann Friedrich von Hornig, Lord of the Manor at Zingst and Reinssdorff, Royal Prussian Finance Councillor in the Dukedom of Magdeburg,—Herr George Friedrich Händel, Court Capellmeister to the Elector of Hanover,—Frau Friderica Amalia, wife of Herr Schwartz von Oppin, Senior Bailiff. The child's grandmother, Frau Händel, stood proxy for Hornig's wife.

(Chrysander, I. 310.) Handel came from Hanover for the christening of his niece : she got one of her names from him, Friederika, and she became his favourite. He saw his mother again.

———

FROM THE "SPECTATOR", 26th December 1711

Mr. *Spectator*,

We whose Names are subscribed, think you the properest Person to signify what we have to offer the Town in Behalf of ourselves, and the Art which we profess, Musick. We conceive Hopes of your Favour from the Speculations on the Mistakes which the Town run into with Regard to their Pleasure of this Kind. . . . Musick . . . must always have some Passion or Sentiment to express, or else Violins, Voices, or any other Organs of Sound, afford an Entertainment very little above the Rattles of Children. It was from this Opinion of the Matter, that when Mr. *Clayton* had finished his studies in Italy, and brought over the Opera of *Arsinoe*, that Mr. *Haym* and Mr. *Dieupart*, who had the Honour to be well known and received among the Nobility and Gentry, were zealously inclined to assist, by their Solicitations, in introducing so elegant an Entertainment as the *Italian* Musick grafted upon *English* Poetry. For this End Mr. *Dieupart* and Mr. *Haym*, according to their several Opportunities, promoted the Introduction of *Arsinoe*, and did it to the best Advantage so great a Novelty would allow. It is not proper to trouble you with Particulars of the just Complaints we all of us have to make ; but so it is, that without Regard to our obliging Pains, we are all equally set aside in the present Opera. Our Application therefore to you is only to insert this Letter in your Papers that the Town may know we have all Three joined together to make Entertainments of Musick for the future at Mr. *Clayton*'s House in *York-Buildings*. . . . We aim at establishing some settled Notion of what is Musick, at recovering from Neglect and Want very many Families who depend upon it, at making all Foreigners who pretend to succeed in *England* to learn the Language of it as we ourselves have done, and not to be so insolent as

to expect a whole Nation, a refined and learned Nation, should submit
to learn them. . . .

We are,
Sir,
Your most humble Servants,
Thomas Clayton,
Nicolino Haym,
Charles Dieupart.

T.

Cf. 18th January 1712. This article and a second (see 18th January 1712)
appeared in nos. 258 and 278 of the *Spectator*. (Burney, IV. 225 ; Chrysander,
I. 298 f., 305.) The " T " at the end signifies that the letter was, if not written by,
at least forwarded by Steele. On 21st March 1711 Addison wrote about Italian
opera in England, with reference to *Arsinoe* and *Camilla*, and on 3rd April 1711
he wrote against Italian recitatives for English words, and about national music.
(Chrysander, I. 300.) Clayton, an English composer, set Addison's *Rosamond* in
1707 : a failure. The *Arsinoe*, produced in 1705, was a pasticcio of Italian songs.
While the music of *Camilla*, an Italian opera by (Marco Antonio) Bononcini
(1696), performed at Drury Lane in 1706, was adapted by Haym, neither he,
who played first 'cello in *Arsinoe*, nor Dieupart claimed collaboration when this
opera was successfully performed in 1705. Dieupart was a French musician and
composer ; Haym an Italian librettist and composer, later on good terms with
Handel. Steele asked Hughes to arrange Dryden's *Alexander's Feast* (later to be
set by Handel) for Clayton : it was performed, to Hughes's regret, on 29th
May 1711, in the same York Buildings in Villiers Street (Strand), which from
about 1680 till 1735 sometimes offered room to malcontent musicians. (Cf.
20th April 1732.) In 1710–12 Steele, who lived there from 1715 to 1724, himself
owned the concert-room, and suffered losses. It is clear that the three friends'
hopes in the " Opera ", *i.e.* the Haymarket Theatre, were disappointed mainly
by Handel's *Rinaldo*.

Here follows a chronological list of operas performed in London before
Rinaldo, all except four at the Haymarket Theatre, which from 1708 onwards
was the only and exclusive opera house in London : 1705—*Arsinoe*, Drury Lane
(the text translated from the Italian into English by Peter Anthony Motteux, a
Frenchman) ; 1706—*Camilla*, Drury Lane (text by Silvio Stampiglia, translated
by Swiney, music by (M. A.) Bononcini, adapted by Haym), and *The Temple of
Love* (text by Motteux, music by Gius. Fedele Saggione) ; 1707—*Rosamond*, Drury
Lane (the first original English opera), and *Thomyris*, Drury Lane (text by Motteux,
music by Aless. Scarlatti, Giov. Bononcini, and others, arranged by Pepusch,
and performed in two languages) ; 1708—*Love's Triumph* (text by Ottoboni,
translated by Motteux, music by Carlo Francesco Cesarini, Francesco Gasparini,
and others), and *Pyrrhus and Demetrius* (text by Adriano Morselli, translated by
Swiney, music by A. Scarlatti, arranged by Haym) ; 1709—*Clotilda* (text by
Giovanni Battista Neri, adapted by Heidegger, music by Francesco Conti,
A. Scarlatti and G. Bononcini, sung in two languages) ; 1710—*Almahide* (text
anonymous, music by ? G. Bononcini, sung in Italian with intermezzi in English),
and *L' Idaspe fedele* (text by ? Giovanni Pietro Candi, music by Francesco Mancini) ;
1711—*Etearco* (text by Silvio Stampiglia, music by G. Bononcini). An advertisement by Walsh and Hare in the *Daily Courant* of 6th March 1711, shortly after
the production of *Rinaldo*, starts with these words : " There being now 11
Opera's in Italian and English . . .". *Rinaldo* was no. 12.

1712

From the " Spectator ", 18th January 1712

Mr. *Spectator*,

You will forgive Us Professors of Musick if we make a second application to You, in Order to promote our Design of exhibiting Entertainments of Musick in *York-Buildings*. It is industriously insinuated that Our Intention is to destroy Operas in General ; but we beg of you to insert this plain Explanation of our selves in your Paper. Our Purpose is only to improve our Circumstances, by improving the Art which we profess. We see it utterly destroyed at present ; and as we were the Persons who introduced Operas, we think it a groundless Imputation that we should set up against the Opera it self. What we pretend to assert is, That the Songs of different Authors injudiciously put together and a foreign Tone and Manner which are expected in every Thing now performed amongst us, has put Musick it self to a stand ; insomuch that the Ears of the People cannot now be entertained with any Thing but what has an impertinent Gayety, without any just Spirit ; or a Languishment of Notes, without any Passion, or common Sense. We hope those Persons of Sense and Quality who have done us the Honour to subscribe, will not be ashamed of their Patronage towards us, and not receive Impressions that patronising us is being for or against the Opera, but truly promoting their own Diversions in a more just and elegant Manner than has been hitherto performed.

We are,
Sir,
Your most humble servants,
Thomas Clayton,
Nicolino Haym,
Charles Dieupart.

There will be no Performances in York-Buildings, *until after that of the Subscription.*   T.

Cf. 26th December 1711.

— — —

From the " Spectator ", 21st January 1712

At the Queen's Theatre in the Hay-Market, on Wednesday next, being the 23d of January, will be performed an Opera call'd Rinaldo. The Part of Argantes to be perform'd by Mr. [Salomon] Bendler, newly arrived, the Part of Godofredo [*sic*] by Signora Margarita de L'Espine, the Part of Eustacio by Mrs. Barbier.

Rinaldo was revived on 23rd January, with repeat performances on 26th, 29th January ; 7th, 9th, 13th, 23rd February, and 6th March 1712. Bendler did not appear in any later Handel opera. Francesca Margherita l'Épine (l'Éspine, or l'Espini), called La Margherita, sang for Handel in 1712 and 1713 ; she married the composer Pepusch in 1718. Mrs. Barbier, a contralto substituting for Signor Valentini, also sang for Handel in 1712 and 1713. Nicolini as Rinaldo and Signora Pilotti as Armida kept their parts, but Almirena was sung by Signora Manina. The performances were advertised as beginning at six o'clock, which was apparently the usual time. The prices vary now : at first pit and boxes are offered for half a guinea each, but later only the boxes on the stage cost as much, the other boxes costing 8s. and the pit 5s. ; the first gallery costs 4s., later 2s. 6d., but the upper gallery is always 1s. 6d. " No Person to stand on the Stage ", or " By her Majesty's Command no Persons are to be admitted behind the Scenes ".

Prior to the revival of *Rinaldo*, the opera *Antioco* (the libretto dedicated by Heidegger to the Dowager Countess Burlington) was produced at the Haymarket Theatre on 12th December 1711. On 27th February 1712 came *L' Ambleto* (text by Apostolo Zeno, music by Francesco Gasparini), on 3rd May *Hercules* (text by Giacomo Rossi, composer unknown), and on 5th June, the last novelty of the season and the last English grand opera for a long time, *Calypso and Telemachus* (text by John Hughes, music by John Ernest Galliard). On 15th March a concert was given for the benefit of Nicolini, with music first performed on the Queen's birthday (6th February) and with dancing by Mrs. Santlow and the young Mr. Camille.

Towards the end of the year 1712, he [Handel] obtained leave of the Elector to make a second visit to England, on condition that he engaged to return within a reasonable time. (Mainwaring, pp. 85 f.)

Handel returns to London in the late autumn, 1712.

He lived first with a Mr. Andrews, of Barn-Elms in Surrey, who also had a house in the City. Accepting another invitation, he moved to Burlington House in Piccadilly, where the Dowager Countess Juliana lived with Richard, Earl of Burlington (Hawkins). Whether Handel went to Burlington House in 1713 or 1714 is not certain. He stayed there for at least three years. Cf. 25th September 1717.

Handel finishes the opera *Pastor Fido*, or *The Faithful Shepherd*, 24th October 1712.

This information is given by Handel in his manuscript. Similar information, as to dates of starting and finishing works, is given in this book only when supplied by Handel himself in extant autographs.

Il Trionfo d' Amore, a collection of music, is performed at the opera house in the Haymarket on 12th and 15th November 1712, apparently to fill a gap before the production of Handel's new opera.

From the " Spectator ", 20th November 1712

Never Perform'd before.

At the Queen's Theatre in the Hay-Market, on Saturday next, being the 22d Day of November, will be presented a new Opera call'd The Faithful Shepherd. Compos'd by Mr. Hendel. The Parts to be performed by Signior Cavaliero Valeriano Pellegrini, Signor Valentino Urbani, Signiora Pilotti Schiavonetti, Signiora Margaretta de l'Epine, Mrs. Barbier and Mr. Leveridge.

Repeat performances on 26th, 29th November, 3rd, 6th, 27th December 1712, and 21st February 1713. The libretto was by Rossi (after Battista Guarini's pastoral play of 1585), who dedicated it to " Signora Anna Cartwright " on 12th November 1712. (Anne Cartwright, of Ossington, married her cousin, William Cartwright, of Marnham, and became the mother of John, the political reformer, and of Edmund, the inventor of the power-loom. The book is printed in Italian, with an English translation. Handel is again styled " Maestro di Capella di S.A.E. d'Hannover "

Cast of " Il Pastor fido ", 22nd November 1712

Mirtillo—Signor Valeriano, counter-tenor
Amarilli—Signora Pilotti, soprano
Eurilla—Signora Margherita, soprano
Silvio—Signor Valentini, alto
Dorinda—Mrs. Barbier, contralto
Tirenio—Mr. Leveridge, bass

Valeriano Pellegrini, " Cavaliere della Croce di San Marco ", who sang Nerone in *Agrippina* (Venice, 26th December 1709), remained in London till 1713. Valentini returned after a short absence. Richard Leveridge, born in 1670, also sang for Handel in 1712 and 1713.

From Francis Colman's " Opera Register ", 26th November 1712

The Stage & Scenes at ye Opera Theatre In ye Haymarket, having been altered & emended during ye vacant Season. They open'd ye House Novr ye 26th 1712. with a New Pastorall Opera called The Faithfull Shepherd. ye musick composed by Mr Hendel. ye parts performed by following Singers. Signor Cav. Valeriano Pellegrini. ye first time of his performing on this Stage. Signor Valentino Urbani returned again from Italy. Signora Pilotta Schiavonetti. Signora Margarita Del'Epine. Mrs Barbier. Mr Leveridge. all sung in Italian. This was not by Subscription but at ye usuall Opera Prices of Boxes 8s Pit 5s Gallery 2s. 6d. The Scene represented only ye Country of Arcadia. ye Habits were old.—ye Opera Short.

The opera diary in the British Museum, attributed to Francis Colman, playwright and later Envoy Extraordinary at Florence, begins with this entry. Entries which add nothing to other records are omitted here. The Handel entries were

printed in the *Mask*, July 1926 and January 1927 ; revised by Babcock in *Music &*
Letters, July 1943. The date of the first night was, in fact, the 22nd ; the 26th
was the second performance. The *Spectator* of the 24th announces the second night
as " Never Perform'd but once ".

———

FROM COLMAN'S " OPERA REGISTER ", 10th December 1712

Dec. 10th wensday. was performed a new Pastorall Opera called
Dorinda. The musick of this is taken out of Severall Italian opera's by
Nic° Haym. In this Sigra Margarita had no part. The other Singers
the Same as in the former, the Same Scene & Habits also & the same
prices. it was performed 4 times on the opera days successively.

(Eisenschmidt, II. 107.) The " former " opera was *Pastor Fido*.

———

Handel finishes the opera *Teseo*, 19th December 1712.

1713

The libretto, but not the production, of *Teseo* is advertised in the *Daily Courant*, 10th January 1713.

It was again printed in two languages, and dedicated by the author, Haym, to Richard Boyle, Earl of Burlington, Handel's (later ?) host (cf. 25th May 1715). Handel was styled, as usual, " Maestro di Capella di S. A. E. d'Hannover ". The opera was produced on 10th January with repeat performances on 14th, 17th, 21st, 24th, 28th January ; 4th, 11th, 14th, 17th February ; 17th March ; 18th April ; and 16th May. It has apparently never been revived.

———

CAST OF " TESEO ", 10th January 1713

Teseo—Signor Valeriano, soprano
Agilea—Signora Margherita, soprano
Medea—Signora Pilotti, soprano
Egeo—Signor Valentini, alto
Clizia—Signora Gallia, soprano
Arcane—Mrs. Barbier, contralto
Fedra—(?) Signora Manina, soprano
Minerva—Mr. Leveridge, bass

Signora Maria Gallia was the sister of Signora Margherita de l'Épine ; she had been married, since 1705, to the composer G. F. Saggione. John Ernest Galliard, the composer, born in Zell, Hanover, now played the oboe in the orchestra.

———

Handel finishes a Te Deum, later called the *Utrecht Te Deum*, 14th January 1713.

Cf. 7th July 1713.

———

FROM COLMAN'S " OPERA REGISTER ", *c.* 15th January 1713

neither of these two Opera's [Handel's *Faithful Shepherd* and *Dorinda*] produced full Houses. Mr O. Swiny ye Manager of ye Theatre was now setting out a New Opera, Heroick. all ye Habits new & richer than ye former with 4 New Scenes, & other Decorations & Machines. Ye Tragick Opera was called Theseus. Ye Musick composed by Mr Handel. Maestro di Capella di S. A. E. D'Hannover. The Singers. il Sig^r Valentino. la Sig^{ra} Margarita, ed la Sua Sorella. il Sig^r Valeriano. la Sig^{ra} Pilotta. Mrs Barbier. ye Opera being thus prepared Mr Swiny would have got a Subscription for Six times, but could not.—he then did give out Tickets at half a Guinea each, for two Nights ye Boxes lay'd open to ye Pit, ye House was very full these two Nights.

after these Two Nights [10th and 14th January] Mr Swiny Brakes &
runs away & leaves ye Singers unpaid ye Scenes & Habits also unpaid for.
The Singers were in Some confusion but at last concluded to go on with
ye operas on their own accounts, & divide ye Gain amongst them.

Swiney went to Italy. Heidegger succeeded him as manager.

———

From Colman's " Opera Register ", 17th January 1713

Janry 17th. Sat : They perform'd ye Opera Theseus at ye usuall
Opera prices.

According to the *Daily Courant* advertisement for 21st January, the prices
were once more as follows : " The Boxes on the Stage Half a Guinea, the other
Boxes 8s. the Pit 5s. the first Gallery 2s. 6d." ; the upper gallery was probably
1s. 6d., as usual.

———

From the " Daily Courant ", 24th January 1713

This present Saturday . . . the Opera of Theseus composed by Mr.
Hendel will be represented in its Perfection, that is to say with all the
Scenes, Decorations, Flights, and Machines. The Performers are much
concerned that they did not give the Nobility and Gentry all the Satisfaction they could have wished, when they represented it on Wednesday
last [the 21st], having been hindered by some unforseen Accidents at
that time insurmountable.

(Eisenschmidt, I. 20.)

———

From Colman's " Opera Register ", 31st January 1713

Janry ye 21th. 24th & 28th ye Same again. ye House was better filled
at this than at ye former Two Opera's. having perform'd it now Six
times Successively—for variety on Janry 31. Sat they perform'd Dorinda.

———

Handel's *Agrippina* is performed at Naples, with additional music
by Francesco Mancini, 4th (15th) February 1713.

(Loewenberg, p. 62.)

———

Handel's *Ode for the Birthday of Queen Anne*, written in January, is
performed at Court, 6th February 1713.

According to Handel's notes in the autograph, it was sung by Mrs.
Robinson (soprano), Mrs. Barbier (contralto), Mr. Elford and Mr. Hughes
(altos), Mr. Gates and Mr. Wheeley (basses). Messrs. Richard Elford,
Francis Hughes, Bernard Gates and Samuel Wheeley were professional
singers of sacred music, all except Elford connected with the Chapel Royal.
An earlier Ode for the same occasion was written by John Eccles in 1707.

The " Mrs. Robinson ", appearing in London in 1713 as a singer, was Anastasia Robinson, later Countess of Peterborough, who became famous in Handel parts between 1714 and 1724. It is said that Anastasia was born in, or about 1698, and that she was the daughter of a painter Robinson ; no marriage of hers, prior to that with the Earl of Peterborough, is known. She must have been very young when she started her career in 1713 (cf. 9th and 16th June). " Mrs. Barbier ", too, seems to have been unmarried. The style of " Mrs." was the equivalent of " Signora ", used for *signore* as well as *signorine*.

———

DIRECTIONS TO THE TREASURER OR TREASURERS OF THE OPERA
IN THE HAYMARKET

13 Febry 1712/3.

Whereas, there remains in your hands the Sume of One hundred Sixty two pounds Nineteen Shillings being the clear receipt of the Opera Since Mr Swiney left the House I do hereby direct you to pay the said Sume of One hundred Sixty two pounds Nineteen Shillings to the following psons in proportion to their Sev^{ll} contracts made wth Mr Swiney vizt Sin^r Valeriano, Sin^r Valentini Sini^{re} Pilotta and her husband, Sig^{re} Margerita, Mrs Barbier, Mrs Manio, Mr Hendell, Mr Heidegger, wch Method of paym^t You are to Observe in the clear receip^{ts} of the Opera which shall hereafter come into your hands But whereas Sign^r Valentini and Signr^a Pillotta have already receiv'd some Money from Mr Swiney in part of their contract, you are not to pay them out of these receipts till ye rest are paid their contracts in proportion to what they have been paid.

(?) T. Coke.

(Nicoll, 1925, p. 285.) Public Record Office, L.C. 7/3, No. 52. Nothing is known about Signora Pilotti's husband. " Mrs. Manio " is identical with Signora Manina. Heidegger seems to have been producer under Swiney's management. Leveridge and Signora Gallia, not mentioned here, probably had no regular contract. If the signature of these " Directions " is T. Coke, it refers to the Vice-Chamberlain mentioned before. Cf. Heidegger's Memoranda, mid 1713.

———

Pastor Fido, with the cast of 1712, is performed on 21st February 1713 : the last time in this version.

———

FROM THE " DAILY COURANT ", 25th February 1713

For the Benefit of Mr. Rogier.

At the Dancing-School, the Two Golden Balls, the upper End of Bow-street, Covent-Garden, . . . Wednesday, the 25th of February, will be Perform'd an extraordinary Consort of Vocal and Instrumental

Musick, by all the Masters belonging to the Opera. To begin at 7 of
the Clock. Tickets . . . 5s. . . .

Nothing is known about Mr. Rogier ; he may have been a distressed employee
of the Haymarket Theatre. Handel may have been one of the " Masters "
playing in the concert. Instead of Wednesday, Tuesday was the day for mid-
week opera performances during Lent (e.g., *Teseo* on Tuesday 17th February).

———

From Colman's " Opera Register ", 26th February 1713

Monr John James Heidegger, managed both this [*Ernelinda*] & ye
former Opera [*Pastor Fido* ?] for ye Singers.

Heidegger dedicated the libretto of the pasticcio opera *Ernelinda* to Richard,
Viscount Lonsdale, imploring his protection " at a time when we labour under
so many unhappy circumstances. . . . By these means, we may retrieve the
reputation of our affairs, and in a short time rival the stage of Italy " (Kelly,
II. 345).—Colman mentions Signora Vittoria Albergotti as a new singer in
Ernelinda. Thus she cannot have been identical with Signora Maria Gallia (see
10th January 1713) as Chrysander (I. 384) indicated.

———

From the " Daily Courant ", 3rd March 1713

For the Benefit of Signora Celotti.

An extraordinary Consort of Vocal and Instrumental Musick is to be
Performed at Stationer's-Hall, to Morrow being Wednesday, the 4th of
March, at 6 a Clock, by the best Hands of the Opera. Tickets . . . at
2s. 6d. each.

Again, Handel may have been one of the " Hands ". Nothing is known about
Signora Celotti. In the Stationers' Hall, at this time occasionally used for concerts,
Henry Purcell's music to Thomas Betterton's *Dioclesian* had been performed on
10th April 1712.

———

At a performance of *Dorinda* on 17th March 1713 an " Entertainment of Musick " is added, composed by (? Tommaso) Albinoni.

———

From Colman's " Opera Register ", 24th March 1713

March 24 they gave out in ye printed Bills that they would revive
ye Opera Rinaldo, but by some accident it was put off, & no Opera
perform'd this day.

The " printed Bills " refers to the advertisement in the *Daily Courant* of 23rd
and 24th March ; there were no hand-bills in use. *Rinaldo* was not revived until
6th May 1713. On 28th April *Ernelinda* was given for the benefit of Signora

Pilotti, with Signor Pietro Guacini in Valeriano's part: his illness might have been the reason for the postponement of *Rinaldo*.

—

From the " Guardian ", 4th April 1713

New Musick just Published for the Flute,

The fourth Book of the Flute-Master improved,

containing the most perfect Rules, and easiest Instructions for Learners, with . . . Mr. Hendle's choicest Arriets in the last new Opera's, pr. 1s. 6d. . . . Printed for L. Pippard at Orpheus next Door to Button's Coffee-house in Russel-street, Covent Garden.

A copy of the " Guardian " is in the Bodleian Library, Oxford.

—

From Colman's " Opera Register ", 15th April 1713

April 15th Wensday. Theseus, was design'd to be perform'd, but finding they could not get Company sufficient, it was put off untill the 18th.

The opera was advertised in the *Daily Courant*. Wednesday had been restored for mid-week opera evenings.

—

From Colman's " Opera Register ", 18th April 1713

April 18th Saty Theseus was perform'd tho a thin House.

—

For the benefit of Signora Margherita l'Épine a concert is held at the Haymarket Theatre on 25th April 1713, with arias from various operas sung by her, Signore Pilotti and Manina, Mrs. Barbier, and Signor Valentini.

Nothing from Handel's operas was included.

—

From the " Daily Courant ", 6th May 1713

At the Queen's Theatre in the Hay-Market . . . Wednesday, the 6th of May, will be Revived an Opera called, Rinaldo. With all the proper Scenes and Machines. The Part of Godofredo by Signora Margaretta, Argantes by Mr. Leveridge, Rinaldo by Mrs. Barbier, Eustacio by Signor Valentini, Armida by Signora Pilotti, Almirena by Signora Manina.

Of the 1711 cast only Signora Pilotti continued in her part up to 1717. Valentini, replaced by Mrs. Barbier in 1712, was back again, and Mrs. Barbier this time took Nicolini's part. Of the 1712 cast Signore Margherita and Manina retained their parts, but Leveridge, instead of Bendler, took Boschi's part. The singers of the Mago and the Herald are not known for the revivals between 1712 and 1717.

———

FROM COLMAN'S " OPERA REGISTER ", 9th May 1713

May 9 Rinaldo was revived for Mrs Barbier's Benefit. She perform'd ye part of Rinaldo.

The proceeds for Mrs. Barbier were only fifteen pounds (cf. Heidegger's Memoranda, mid 1713).

———

FROM THE " DAILY COURANT ", 11th May 1713

For the Benefit of Mr. Hendel.

At the Queen's Theatre in the Hay-Market, on Saturday next, being the 16th of May, will be Represented the Opera of Theseus. Not [sic] in all its former Perfection, viz. As Scenes, Flights and Decorations ; but with an Addition of several New Songs, and particularly an Entertainment for the Harpsichord, Compos'd by Mr. Hendel on purpose for that Day. The Boxes and Pit to be put together, and no Person to be admitted without Tickets, which will be deliver'd . . . at Half a Guinea each. Boxes upon the Stage 15s. Gallery 4s.

This advertisement was corrected the following day. The " Entertainment for the Harpsichord " was apparently an intermezzo, or a concerto, played by Handel.

———

FROM THE " DAILY COURANT ", 12th May 1713

For the Benefit of Mr. Hendel.

At the Queen's Theatre . . . the 16th of May . . . Theseus. Composed by Mr. Hendel. Not only in all its former Perfections, as Scenes, Flights, Machines, and Decorations. . . . N.B. In Yesterday's Courant, in the Advertisement of this Opera, by the Fault of the Writer of that Advertisement, it was said that this Opera would be Represented *Not in all its Perfection*, etc. whereas it should have been said, *Not only in all its Perfections*, etc. *but* etc.

———

FROM COLMAN'S " OPERA REGISTER ", 15th May 1713

May 15 Theseus for ye Benefit of Mr Hendel ye Composer.
Here ended ye Operas for this season.

Handel earned £73 10s. 11d. Cf. Heidegger's Memoranda, mid 1713.

———

A concert is given at the Haymarket Theatre on 9th June 1713, after the close of the season, for the benefit of Mrs. Robinson, at which she and Signor Valentini sing " several Opera Songs, Duetti's, and Cantata's, of the best Masters, never Sung before " (*Daily Courant*).

It is possible that Handel was represented in the evening's programme, which began at half-past eight " at the Desire of several Ladies of Quality ".

———

On 16th June 1713, Mrs. Robinson gives another late evening concert at the Haymarket Theatre, " With a new cantata and several Opera Songs, never Sung by her in Publick " (*Daily Courant*).

———

MEMORANDA, WRITTEN BY HEIDEGGER, PROBABLY MID 1713

	£	s.	d.
M. Long	150	0	0
M. Potter	72	0	0
Mr. Hendel	50	0	0
Sig. Nicolini	50	0	0
Pilotti	50	0	0
The Instruments	50	0	0
Sig. Valentini	38	0	0
	£460	0	0

	£	s.	d.
Mr. Hendel	761	0	0
	50	0	0
	£811	0	0

	£	s.	d.
Signora Margaritta in the first division	80	0	0
In the second	25	0	0
Her benefitt [25th April 1713]	76	5	8
Remains due to her	218	14	4
	£400	0	0

Mrs. Barbier has received :—

	£	s.	d.
In the first division	60	0	0
In the second	18	15	0
Her benefitt [9th May 1713]	15	0	0
Remains due to her	206	5	0
	£300	0	0

Mr. Hendel has received :—

	£	s.	d.
In the first division	86	0	0
In the second	26	17	0
His benefitt day [16th May 1713]	73	10	11
Remains due	243	12	1
	£430	0	0

Signr. Valeriano has received :—

	£	s.	d.
In the first division	129	0	0
In the second	40	6	0
His benefitt day [2nd May 1713]	73	19	0
Remains due to him	401	15	0
	£645	0	0

Signora Pilotti has received :—

	£	s.	d.
In the first division	89	5	0
In the second	27	14	0
From Mr. Swiney	53	15	0
Her benefitt day [28th April 1713]	75	7	3
Remains due to her	255	18	9
	£500	0	0 [sic]

Signr. Valentini has received :—

	£	s.	d.
Of Mr. Swiney	107	10	0
In the first division	86	0	0
In the second	26	17	0
His benefitt day [11th April 1713]	75	8	5
Remains due to him	241	14	7
	£537	10	0

Signora Manina received :—

	£	s.	d.
In the first division	20	0	0
In the second	6	5	0
Remains due to her	73	15	0
	£100	0	0

—

Cummings (1914, pp. 56 ff.) dated this document from the Coke papers as probably of 1711. The first section, up to the bill for Signora Margherita, may refer to the seasons of 1711 and 1712 because it includes the name of Nicolini. (Nothing is known of Messrs. Long and Potter.) The " Instruments " are apparently the instrumentalists in the orchestra. Handel's earnings of £811 (and £50 ?) seem to refer to 1711 and 1712. The other items certainly belong to the 1712–13 season (cf. Coke's Directions of 13th February 1713) : Mrs. Barbier and Signor Valentini did not join the company until 1712, and Signora Manina not until 1713. The date of the document cannot be before May 1713 because Handel's benefit night of 16th May is mentioned in it. The season closed on 16th May and it was probably written after that, perhaps in June. The meaning of the term " division " is not quite clear. Smith (1948, p. 37) thought that it meant " first and second payments " of " some agreed share-out of takings or profits ". In the light of Coke's Directions there seems, however, no doubt that these payments, or credits, were the salaries according to contracts, due probably in two terms. Swiney's rule at the Haymarket Theatre lasted, during Handel's time, from 17th April 1712 till 15th January 1713 only. It is noteworthy that Heidegger himself is not mentioned in these accounts.

———

It was not many months after his arrival at LONDON *that the peace of Utrecht was brought to a conclusion* [31st March 1713]. *Each year of this memorable reign had been so crowded with heroic achievements and grand events, that the poets and painters of our island seem to have sunk, as it were, under the load of matter, which had been heaped upon them. And had our musicians been thought equal to the task, a foreigner would hardly have been applied to for the song of triumph and thanksgiving, which was now wanted. The illustrious family which had taken Handel into its patronage, had not only been deeply concerned, but highly distinguished, in the course of the war. The military talents, and personal bravery of its members had contributed to its prosperous issue. And not only the august house of Hanover, but most of the protestant Princes of the country to which he was indebted for his birth and education, had concurred in the reduction of that overgrown power, which long had menaced their religion and liberty. These circumstances produced that particular sort of interest and attachment, which, when joined to the dignity and importance of a subject, dispose an artist to the utmost exertion of his powers. No performance can be thoroughly excellent, unless it is wrought* con amore, *as the Italians express it. Handel, it must be owned, had all these advantages. And it is not too much, perhaps it is too little to say, that the work was answerable to them. . . .*

The great character of the Operas which Handel had made in Italy and Germany, and the remembrance of RINALDO *joined with the poor proceedings at the Haymarket, made the nobility very desirous that he might again be employed in composing for that theatre. To their applications her Majesty was pleased to add the weight of her own authority ; and as a testimony of her regard to his merit, settled upon him a pension for life of 200l. per annum.*

This act of the royal bounty was the more extraordinary, as his foreign engagements were not unknown.

. . . The time had again elapsed to which the leave he had obtained, could in reason be extended. But whether he was afraid of repassing the sea, or whether he had contracted an affection for the diet of the land he was in ; so it was, that the promise he had given at his coming away, had somehow slipt out of his memory. (Mainwaring, pp. 86–9.)

———

FROM THE "FLYING POST; OR THE POST-MASTER", 7th July 1713

London, July 7.

Her Majesty has signified Her Pleasure, that She does not intend to go this Day to St. Paul's, but designs to return Thanks to God for the Peace in Her own Chappel.

———

Handel's *Utrecht Te Deum and Jubilate* are performed in St. Paul's Cathedral on 7th July 1713, with Messrs. Elford (alto), Hughes (tenor), Gates and Wheeley (basses).

(Pearce, 1928, pp. 234-6.) The Te Deum was finished on 14th January, but the Peace of Utrecht, between England and France, was not concluded until 31st March and proclaimed in London on 5th May. The Jubilate was written later. The same male singers who sang the *Ode for the Queen's Birthday* on 6th February performed the Te Deum, which was certainly approved, if not ordered, by the Queen who, however, was unable to attend the performance. Between 1694 and 1713 Henry Purcell's *Te Deum and Jubilate* had been performed on St. Cecilia's Day and on other occasions, in St. Paul's Cathedral, to which the members of Parliament used to go in procession. During the following years Purcell's and Handel's works were performed alternately until 1743, when Handel's *Dettingen Te Deum and Jubilate* superceded both. The only exception was in 1721 when, on 14th December, an unidentified *Te Deum* and an Anthem by Maurice Greene were performed in the Cathedral ; Greene was organist there from 1718 till 1755.

———

FROM MATTHESON'S "DAS NEU-ERÖFFNETE ORCHESTRE" ("THE NEWLY-INAUGURATED ORCHESTRA"), Hamburg, 1713 (Translated)

. . . Believe me, you masters of great *suffisance*, as many of you as are known to me, with a single exception, that one can set before you a [Thorough] Bass, which shall not be florid ; it shall go quite slowly ; consisting of minims, crotchets and quavers ; and these shall be *accurately* figured ; and if you, *sine haesitatione*, realise correctly the first 5, indeed the first 2, *chords*, then I will praise you.

(P. 65, ¶ 21 of *Caput Primus*, "Von den Tonis".) The exception was Handel, as is proved by Mattheson's *Das Beschützte Orchestre* ; cf. 19th July 1717. It is perhaps fitting to mention here a story recorded by Hawkins and retold by Kidson (pp. 76 f.). Mattheson published in 1714 his *Pièces de Clavecin* with I. D. Fletcher (not Richard Meares) in London. When Samuel Wheeley, the bass singer, told his friends about it at the Queen Ann Tavern, in St. Paul's Church Yard, Handel ordered a copy to be sent for, and played the lessons in the tavern (Hawkins).

1714

The opera season opens on 9th January 1714 with a revival of *Dorinda*, followed on 27th January by *Creso*.

New among the singers were Signora Catterina Galerati and Mrs. Robinson.

——

FROM THE " DAILY COURANT ", 22nd February 1714

To all Lovers of Musick.

This Day . . . at Stationer's Hall, for the Benefit of Mr. Wells and Mr. Kenny, will be an excellent Consort of Vocal and Instrumental Musick, performed by Eminent Masters, English and Foreign. Among other choice Compositions, a celebrated Song of Mr. Hendel's, by a Gentlewoman from Abroad, who hath never before exposed her Voice publickly in this Kingdom. To which will be added an uncommon piece of Musick by Bassoons only.

Nothing is known about these personages.

——

The new Italian opera *Arminio* (cf. 12th January 1737) is produced on 4th March 1714, a Thursday.

It was now forbidden to perform operas on Wednesdays and Fridays during Lent, and, since the Queen played Basset every Tuesday at Windsor, it was arranged to give the mid-week operas on Thursdays instead of Tuesdays as in 1713. According to Colman's *Opera Register*, the new opera was given " by subscription for six times at ye usuall rate of 10 Guin for 3 Tickets ", but on 10th April it was given for the benefit of Mrs. Robinson, and on 1st May for the benefit of Signora Margherita.

——

Five singers of the opera company : Mrs. Barbier, Signore Galerati and de l'Épine, Mrs. Robinson and Signor Valentini, sign a petition for the better regulation of their benefits, 16th March 1714.

This document was, about 1880, in the possession of Julian Marshall who, however, misunderstood the date of 16th March 1713–14 (Grove, *Dictionary of Music*, 1st and 2nd editions, I. 575).

——

Queen Anne dies, 1st August 1714. George, the Elector of Hanover, Handel's master, is proclaimed King on the same day.

——

On the death of the Queen in 1714, his . . . Majesty came over. Handel, conscious how ill he had deserved at the hands of his gracious patron, now invited to the throne of these kingdoms by all the friends of our happy and free constitution, did not dare to shew himself at court. To account for his delay in returning to his office, was no easy matter. To make an excuse for the non-performance of his promise, was impossible. From this ugly situation he was soon relieved by better luck than perhaps he deserved. It happened that his noble friend Baron Kilmanseck was here. He, with some others among the nobility, contrived a method for reinstating him in the favour of his Majesty. . . .

. . . As a token of it, the King was pleased to add a pension for life of 200l. a year to that which Queen ANNE had before given him. Some years after, when he was employed to teach the young Princesses, another pension of the same value was added to the former by her . . . Majesty. (Mainwaring, pp. 89-92.)

———

FROM THE " POST BOY ", 28th September 1714

On Sunday Morning last [the 26th], His Majesty went to His Royal Chappel at St. James's. . . . *Te Deum* was sung, composed by Mr. Handel, and a very fine Anthem was also sung. . . .

The King landed at Greenwich on 18th September, and arrived at St. James's Palace on the 20th. Although the *Te Deum* was apparently the *Utrecht* again, the circumstances seem to prove that Handel was not, as is usually assumed, out of George's favour. The Anthem was probably not of his composition. The note quoted above also appeared in the *Evening Post* of the same day (not available). Handel's name, in its English form, was printed correctly here for the first time.

———

The opera season at the King's Theatre in the Haymarket opens earlier than usual, on 23rd October 1714, three days after the Coronation, with a revival of *Arminio*, in the presence of the Prince and Princess of Wales, George and Caroline.

The prices on the first night were half a guinea for the best places, but were "common" on the second night, a Tuesday; no card-playing parties at St. James's Palace now interfered on those days. In October two new singers appeared: Signora Stradiotti for Mrs. Barbier, and Signor Filippo Balatti for Valentini. Colman calls Stradiotti "a very bad singer", but he also refers to de l'Épine as "a bad singer" at the same time. In November Signora Pilotti returned from abroad and Signora Diana Vico, a contralto, joined the company. On 16th November *Ernelinda* was revived, with the higher prices on the first night; the Royal visitors came on the second night and on subsequent occasions.

———

FROM THE " DAILY COURANT ", 30th December 1714

At the King's Theatre in the Hay-Market . . . Thursday, the 30th of December, will be perform'd an Opera call'd, Rinaldo. With all the proper Decorations as Originally. The Part of Rinaldo by Signora Diana Vico, Armida by Signora Pilotti, Almirena by Mrs. Robinson, Godofredo by Signora Galerati, Argantes by Signor Angelo Zanoni, lately arriv'd from Italy. . . . By Command, to begin at half an Hour after Five.

This revival was originally announced for Wednesday the 29th. Signora Vico, a contralto, and Signor Zanoni, a bass, were new in the company. Mrs. Robinson, who was indisposed in November, sang a Handel part for the first time, Signora Manina, the Almirena of 1713, having departed. Signora Vico succeeded Mrs. Barbier, Galerati succeeded Margherita, and Zanoni succeeded Leveridge. *Rinaldo* was also performed on 4th, 8th, 15th, 22nd, 27th, 29th January ; 5th, 12th, 19th February and 25th June 1715. The prices for the first night were again raised.

———

FROM COLMAN'S " OPERA REGISTER ", 30th December 1714

Dec. 30, Thursday. Rinaldo revived. Pit & Boxes open at 5 . . . no Dancing.

This remark refers to former performances with dancing (cf. 19th March 1711). Mr. Santlow (cf. 15th March 1712) danced in *Ernelinda* during November 1714. It is noteworthy that Colman, who twice before recorded the visits of the Prince of Wales to the opera house, does not mention a visit of the King to the *Rinaldo* revival until 15th January 1715. George I is said to have been at the first night, but this tradition is not tenable. Frederic Bonet, the Prussian Resident in London, does not refer to *Rinaldo* in his report of 24th December 1714 (4th January 1715), as indicated by Flower, p. 125. This report, telling of the festivities following the Coronation, is printed in the supplement (pp. 858-63) to the second edition of Wolfgang Michael's *Englische Geschichte im 18. Jahrhundert*, Vol. I, *Die Anfänge des Hauses Hannover*, Berlin, 1921, and is translated in the English edition of this volume, London, 1936 (pp. 372-8).

———

Silla, a new opera by Handel, and his shortest one, is said to have been performed in 1714 on the private stage of Burlington House.

The parts include : Silla—contralto ; Metella—soprano ; Lepido—soprano ; Flavia—soprano ; Claudio—contralto ; Celia—soprano ; Il Dio—bass ; Scabro—a mute part. Nothing is known of the singers, probably amateurs, if the opera was really performed. Handel used the music of *Silla* for his next opera, *Amadigi*. It is said the Earl of Burlington was in Italy from November 1714 till January 1715, and that, therefore, *Silla* was probably not performed before spring 1715. (Loewenberg in *Music & Letters*, October 1939, pp. 466 f.) It seems possible, however, that the performance took place in 1714, before November.

———

During the three first years . . . he was chiefly, if not constantly, at the Earl of BURLINGTON'S. *The character of this nobleman, as a scholar and virtuoso, is universally known. As* MR. POPE *was very intimate with his Lordship, it frequently happened that he and Handel were together at his table. After the latter had played some of the finest things he ever composed, Mr.* POPE [1] *declared, that they gave him no sort of pleasure ;*

[1] *The Poet one day asked his friend Dr.* ARBUTHNOT, *of whose knowledge in Music he had a high idea, what was his real opinion in regard to Handel as a Master of that Science? The Doctor immediately replied, "* Conceive the highest that you can of his abilities, and they are much beyond any thing that you can conceive." (Note by Mainwaring.)

IV. ANASTASIA ROBINSON, LATER COUNTESS OF
PETERBOROUGH

Mezzotint after John Vanderbank, 1723, by John Faber, 1727.
(H. R. Beard Theatre Collection)

See page 54

A P.r a Plasterer white washing&Bespattering
B. any Body that comes in his way
C. not a Dukes coach as appears by if Crescent at one Corner

D. Taste
E. a standing Proof
F. a Labourer
Price 6.d

V. "TASTE"

Engraving by William Hogarth, *ca.* 1732, showing the gateway of Burlington
House, Piccadilly.   Pope as "Plasterer" (A), the Duke of Chandos (B),
Lord Burlington (F) and a figure (E) of his architect, Kent (K-NT)

See pages 64 *and* 278-80

that his ears were of that untoward make, and reprobate cast, as to receive his Music,
which he was persuaded was the best that could be, with as much indifference as the airs
of a common ballad. A person of his excellent understanding, it is hard to suspect of
affectation. And yet it is as hard to conceive, how an ear so perfectly attentive to all the
delicacies of rhythm and poetical numbers, should be totally insensible to the charms of
musical sounds. An attentiveness too, which was as discernible in his manner of reading,
as it is in his method of writing. But perhaps the extravagant and injudicious praises,
which the passionate admirers of the Art are apt to bestow on such occasions, might provoke
one of his satyric turn to express himself more strongly than he would otherwise have done.
Perhaps too, a Genius so fond of exploring characters, and so eminently skilled in drawing
them, might think such an Artist as Handel a proper subject for experiments in this way.
The greatest talents are often accompanied with the greatest weaknesses. But the Bard
was much deceived if he imagined him weak enough to be mortified by a declaration,
which, whether real or pretended, deserved not the least regard. Handel minded it just
as much as Pope would have done a like assurance from him with respect to Poems,
which all the world besides have agreed to admire. (Mainwaring, pp. 93-5.)

———

Francesco Geminiani, violinist and composer, comes to London
in 1714, introduced by Baron Kielmansegg (cf. spring 1710), now
Master of the King's Horse,[1] to whom Geminiani in 1716
dedicated twelve trios. He plays at Court,[2] where he insists on
being accompanied by Handel (Hawkins, V. 239).

Geminiani later went to Dublin where he met Handel again in 1741/2.

———

Hughes's cantata *Venus and Adonis* (cf. end of July 1711) is printed
in *Poems and Translations. By Several Hands* in 1714, with the
note : " Set by Mr. Hendel ".

The book contains (pp. 123 ff.) " Four Cantata's after the Italian
Manner " by Hughes, Cantata III being that composed by Handel. In
Hughes's collected poems it was printed (II. 64 f.) with the note : " Set
by Mr. Handel ".

[1] It is not true that Sophie Charlotte, Baroness Kielmansegg, one of two German
mistresses of the King, and later Countess of Darlington, was the Baron's sister
(Chrysander, I. 426) ; she was, in fact, his wife. She was the daughter of Countess
Platen, the mistress of George I's father, Ernst August, Elector of Hanover. Her
daughter Marie married, in 1719, Emanuel Scrope, Viscount Howe. (Ed.)

[2] P. Robinson (*Music & Letters*, 1939) thinks that this joint performance at Court
took place in 1716, just after the publication of Geminiani's Opus 1. (Ed.)

H.–3

1715

NOTICE ISSUED BY THE MANAGERS OF THE HAYMARKET THEATRE
(1715 ?)

Whereas by the frequent calling for the songs again the Operas have been too tedious, therefore the singers are forbidden to sing any song above once ; and it is hoped nobody will call for 'em or take it ill when not obeyed.

(Cummings, 1914, p. 59.) This undated notice, preserved in the Coke papers, was apparently addressed to both sides of the curtain. It reminds one of the order given in Vienna by the Emperor Joseph II after the third performance of Mozart's opera *Le Nozze di Figaro* in 1786, forbidding da capo-calls after ensemble numbers.

———

Nicolini, the original Rinaldo of 1711–12, sings the part again in January 1715 ; Mrs. Barbier having sung it in 1713 and Signora Vico (once) in 1714.

———

FROM COLMAN'S "OPERA REGISTER", 15th January 1715

Jany 15th Satt. Do. [*Rinaldo*] ye King, Prince & Princesse [of Wales] present, & a full House.

Cf. 30th December 1714.

———

FROM COLMAN'S "OPERA REGISTER", 29th January 1715

Jany 29 Do [*Rinaldo*] Satt. a very thin house this night.

The fifth performance had been on Thursday the 27th.

———

A new Italian opera, *Lucio Vero* (text by Zeno) is produced at the Haymarket Theatre, "ye Musick managed by Nicᵒ Haym" (Colman), 26th February 1715.

There were four subscription nights in March, and two ordinary ones in April. In between *Arminio* was revived.

———

FROM THE "DAILY COURANT", 16th May 1715

By Subscription.

At the King's Theatre in the Hay-Market, on Saturday next, being the 21st of May, will be perform'd a New Opera call'd, Amadis. By Command, to begin at Six a Clock.

The production of Handel's new opera was postponed to the 25th, *L'Idaspe fedele* being revived on the 21st. This and the following advertisements are preserved only in the Rev. Charles Burney collection of cuttings, called *Theatrical Register*, in the British Museum, and in the Latreille collection of manuscript copies there.

—

FROM THE "DAILY COURANT", 25th May 1715

By Subscription.

At the King's Theatre in the Hay-Market, the present Wednesday, being the 25th of May, will be perform'd a New Opera call'd Amadis. All the Cloaths and Scenes entirely New. With variety of Dancing . . . the Tickets and Books will be deliver'd at Mrs. White's Chocolate-house in St. James's-street. . . . The Number of Tickets not to exceed 400. Boxes upon the Stage 15s. Gallery 5s. By Command to begin at Six a-clock. And whereas there is a great many Scenes and Machines to be mov'd in this Opera, which cannot be done if Persons should stand upon the Stage (where they could not be without Danger), it is therefore hop'd no Body, even the Subscribers, will take it Ill that they must be deny'd Entrance on the Stage.

Pit and other boxes were sold at half a guinea, as usual on first nights. Among the technical surprises there was a " fountain " on the stage.

—

FROM HEIDEGGER'S DEDICATION OF THE LIBRETTO OF "AMADIGI", 25th May 1715

To the Right Honourable *Richard* Earl of *Burlington* and *Corck*, Baron *Clifford* of *Landesbrough*, &c.

My Lord,

My Duty and Gratitude oblige me to give this Publick Testimony of that Generous Concern Your Lordship has always shown for the promoting of Theatrical Musick, but this Opera more immediately claims Your Protection, as it is compos'd in Your own Family. . . .

Cf. 10th January 1713 (Haym's dedication of *Teseo* to Burlington). Heidegger may possibly have been the author of the book. He refers, of course, to Burlington's hospitality to Handel.

—

CAST OF "AMADIGI DI GAULA", 25th May 1715

Amadigi—Signor Nicolini, alto
Oriana—Mrs. Robinson, soprano
Melissa—Signora Pilotti, soprano
Dardano—Signora Diana Vico, contralto
Orgando—?, soprano

—

FROM COLMAN'S " OPERA REGISTER ", 25th May 1715

May 25 Wensday Amadis of Gaul, a new Opera by Subscription with *Dancing*. Nic° Grimaldi   Mrs. Robinson   Pilotti   Sigra Diana Vico.

Repeat performances on 11th, 15th, 25th, 28th June, 2nd and 9th July 1715. Saturday 28th May was the King's birthday ; there was, therefore, no opera performance. One singer fell ill, and this caused further delay. Between 16th and 24th June it was very hot, and no performance was given. The subscription covered six evenings, and this number, excluding the benefit on 25th June, was reached on 9th July. Chrysander (I. 424) mentions two parodies of *Amadigi* ; but John Gay's " pastoral farce ", the *What d'ye Call it*, was produced at Drury Lane on 23rd February 1715, *i.e.* before the opera, and the burlesque *Amadis, or The Loves of Harlequin and Columbine* at Lincoln's Inn Fields was not produced until 24th January 1718.

———

FROM COLMAN'S " OPERA REGISTER ", 28th May till 11th June 1715

Satt. King George's Birth day ye 28th. *No Opera*. One of ye Singers being indisposed this opera was not perform'd again untill the 11th. Mrs. Robinson was sick, perform'd no more in this opera.

June 11. Satt. Amadis of Gaul ye 2[d] time by Subscription.

It is not known who substituted for Mrs. Robinson during the rest of the season. She sang her part again in 1716 and 1717.

———

FROM COLMAN'S " OPERA REGISTER ", 25th June 1715

June 25 Satt. Rinaldo for ye Benefit of Sigr Nic° Grimaldi.

This performance was not within the subscription.

———

The King attends the performances of *Rinaldo* on 2nd and 9th July 1715.

Cf. 15th January 1715.

———

FROM COLMAN'S " OPERA REGISTER ", July 1715

No Opera performed since ye 23 July, ye Rebellion of ye Tories and Paptists being ye cause—ye King and Court not liking to go into such Crowds these troublesome times.

(Nicoll, 1925, p. 230.) The opera season, having started prematurely, ended belatedly on 23rd July 1715. The Jacobite alarm, however, during the second half of the year kept the London theatres closed throughout the autumn and for part of the winter.

———

FROM MATTHESON'S HAMBURG OPERA LIST, November 1715 (Translated)

Rinaldo. Music by Herr *Händel.* Translation by Herr *Feind.*

(Chrysander, 1877.) It is not known how often the opera was performed this season. Cf. 18th August 1720 and 16th May 1723.

FROM BARTHOLD FEIND'S PREFACE TO HIS TRANSLATION OF THE " RINALDO " LIBRETTO, Hamburg, 1715 (Translated)

. . . That the world-famous Georg Friedrich Hendel, duly appointed Capellmeister to the Elector of Hanover, brought this lovely and acceptable child to birth within 14 days, without any squawking whatsoever, this is a matter for which so great a harmonic spirit as the Hendelian is fitted. The Italian author names him accordingly *l'Orfeo del nostro secolo* and an *Ingegno sublime* (*nella Musica* it is to be understood) ; suchlike honour is afforded to yet few, or indeed to no Germans by an Italian or Frenchman, which gentlemen themselves were accustomed otherwise to *scoff* at German songs. *Enfin,* no one, I suppose, would dispute with him the glorious musical title, except Envy itself. . . . Concerning the German verses, the translator of the Italian words has followed *metre* and meaning exactly according to the music of Capellmeister Hendel, almost slavishly where necessary, so that no single note of this admirable man might be lost. If one should observe that suchlike work should find some unexpected and acceptable approbation concerning the music, it may be possible in the future to avail oneself of it, and, if this is the case, all other operas of the incomparable composer will follow this one.

(Chrysander, I. 297.) Feind translated no other libretto of Handel's operas.

The Opera House in the Haymarket is not opened, as usual, in autumn 1715.

Cf. July 1715.

1716

FROM JOHN GAY'S " TRIVIA : OR, THE ART OF WALKING THE
STREETS OF LONDON ", January 1716

Yet *Burlington*'s fair Palace still remains ;
Beauty within, without Proportion reigns.
Beneath his Eye declining Art revives,
The Wall with animated Picture lives ;
There *Hendel* strikes the Strings, the melting Strain
Transports the Soul, and thrills through ev'ry Vein ;
There oft' I enter (but with cleaner Shoes)
For *Burlington*'s belov'd by ev'ry Muse.

(Chrysander, I. 415.)   These are lines 493-500 of Book II, " Walking by Day ",
of *Trivia*, published without date ; the second edition about 1721. It seems that
Gay met Handel at Burlington's.

———

FROM COLMAN'S " OPERA REGISTER ", 1st February 1716

Febry 1st 1715-16 began to open ye Theatre ye King pres with ye opera
of Lucius Verus.—[sung] by Nicº Grimaldi.

For the cause of the delay in opening the season, see July 1715 ; for the
opera revived here, see 26th February 1715. Colman says Nicolini is now " the
only good singer " in the company.

———

FROM COLMAN'S " OPERA REGISTER ", 16th February 1716

Febry the 16th Amadis. in this opera Mrs Robinson did sing also.

In 1715 Mrs. Robinson sang Oriana on the first night (25th May) only, falling
ill shortly afterwards   *Amadigi* was performed again this season on 21st February ;
3rd, 6th March ; 20th June and 12th July. There are no newspapers available
for this period, except some cuttings in the *Theatrical Register*. Burney's records
(IV. 257 f.) are not quite reliable.

———

FROM COLMAN'S " OPERA REGISTER ", 3rd March 1716

March 3 Amadis for ye Benefit of Mrs. Robinson.

On 10th March *Pirro e Demetrio* was revived, and on 18th April a new opera,
Clearte, was produced.

———

HANDEL to (?) THE SECRETARY OF THE SOUTH SEA COMPANY,
13th March (?) 1716

The 13 March 1715

Pray pay Mr Phillip Cooke my Dividend being Fifteen pounds on Five
hundred pounds, wch is all my Stock in the South Sea Company books &

for half a Year due at Christmas last & this shall be Your Sufficcient Warraant from

S�r

Your very humble Servᵗ

Georg Frideric Handel

(Coopersmith, 1943, p. 61.) Original in Gerald Coke's Handel Collection, Bentley, Hants. The signature only is in Handel's writing. Since the document was probably written by an expert hand, and since Handel's next communication to the Company is dated 29th June 1716, it is assumed that the date quoted above means 13th March 1716. It seems that by 1715 Handel had saved enough to invest £500 in this dubious enterprise.

———

FROM THE "DAILY COURANT", 20th June 1716

By Command.

For the Benefit of the Instrumental Musick.

At the King's Theatre in the Hay-Market, this present Wednesday, being the 20th of June, will be perform'd an Opera call'd, Amadis. With all the Scenes and Cloaths, belonging to this Opera : Particularly, the Fountain-Scene. To which will be added, Two New Symphonies.

This advertisement is preserved in a cutting only (*Theatrical Register*). It is assumed that Burney (IV. 25.7) gives the date 13th June in error ; Schoelcher (pp. 42, 44 and 365) corrects this to 20th June to agree with Colman's *Opera Register* and the *Daily Courant* advertisement as quoted by J. P. Malcolm. Chrysander (I. 424) follows Burney's dating. Burney, who describes this (IV. 291) correctly as the sixth performance of *Amadigi* during the season, knew of only one orchestral work written by Handel for the occasion : the (fourth) Oboe Concerto in F, called the *Orchestra Concerto*. Chrysander agreed with him. The identity of the other orchestral work is not known. The King is said to have attended this performance.

———

HANDEL TO (?) THE SECRETARY OF THE SOUTH SEA COMPANY, 29th June 1716

Sir,

What Ever my Dividend Is on five hundred punds South Sea Stock that The South Sea Company pays att the opening of their Books next August pray pay Itt To Mr. Thomas Carbonnel or order and you will oblidge.

Sir

Your H Servᵗ.

London this 29 June 1716   George Frideric Handel

British Museum, Add. MSS. 33,965, fol. 204. Facsimile : Flower, p. 331. Cf. 13th March 1716. This note is said to have been addressed to one " John G——" ; if so, it may have been either John Gore, in 1720, one of the directors, or John Grisby, accountant of the South Sea Company. Nothing is known of

Mr. Carbonnel. Handel, who only signed this document, probably needed the money for his impending journey to the Continent.

The King goes to Hanover on 7th July 1716, and Handel follows him one or two days later.

At the last performance of the season on 12th July 1716 Attilio Ariosti plays a solo on the viola d'amore between the acts of Handel's *Amadigi*.

According to Burney (IV. 257, 291), this fact was recorded in the *Daily Courant* of the same day. Ariosti, whom Handel had met in Berlin about 1700, was in England for the first time ; he stayed until 1728.

FROM A REPORT OF THE PRUSSIAN RESIDENT IN LONDON, FRIEDRICH BONET, TO BERLIN (Translated)

London, Tuesday 17th-28th July 1716.

. . . After dinner he [His Majesty] would take a walk alone in the gardens of St. James' or call on the Duchess of Munster ; in the evening he would be at the Princess [of Wales'] salon until midnight, or at the opera, to which he went *incognito* in a hired chaise and sat in a private box.

(Michael, 1921, pp. 864 f.) Original in the Geheimes Staats-Archiv, Berlin. The report is of 1716, not of 1717 as indicated by Flower (p. 126). Friedrich Wilhelm of Prussia, married to Sophie Dorothea, was the King's son-in-law. The title Duchess of Munster (in the peerage of Ireland) was the first bestowed by the King on his favourite mistress, Baroness Ermengard Melusina von der Schulenburg, who, in 1719, was raised to the British peerage as Duchess of Kendal. The princess mentioned in the report was, of course, Caroline, wife of the Prince of Wales, at this time in friendly intercourse with Sir Isaac Newton. It is related that the King used to sit, in the incognito box of the opera house, between Baroness von der Schulenburg and Petronilla, his daughter by her (cf. 25th November 1719).

Handel visits his family at Halle and his former university friend, Johann Christoph Schmidt, at Anspach during the summer and autumn of 1716. He persuades Schmidt to give up the wool trade and dedicate himself wholly to music.

Shortly after this, Schmidt and his small son followed Handel to London, where the two " John Christopher Smiths "—father and son having exactly the same names—became his closest friends. It is assumed that Handel returned to London from Hanover at the end of 1716, while the King did not come back until 18th January 1717.

The new season at the Haymarket Theatre opens on 8th December 1716 with a revival of *Clearte*.

1717

At the King's Theatre in the Hay-Market, this present Saturday . . . will be performed an Opera called Rinaldo ; the Part of Goffredo by Signor Antonio Bernacchi ; Almirena by Mrs. Robinson ; Rinaldo by Signor Cavaliero Nicolino Grimaldi ; Argantis by Signor Gaetano Berenstatt, lately arrived ; Armida by Signora Elizabeta Pilotti ; with all the original Scenes and Machines belonging to this Opera. . . . N.B. Servants will be allowed to keep Places in the Boxes. To begin exactly at Six a-Clock.

This advertisement is preserved in a cutting in the *Theatrical Register*. An earlier one, of 2nd January, has " Mr. Robinson " and " Nicholino Berenstaff ". In this, the last revival of *Rinaldo* until 10th February 1731, Signora Pilotti was the only singer surviving from 1711. Antonio Bernacchi sang the part of Goffredo, hitherto given to female singers. He was a newcomer, like Gaetano Berenstadt, an alto, for whom Handel altered Boschi's part of Argante and added some arias. No names are given for Eustazio and for the Mago. Repeat performances on 12th, 19th, 23rd, 26th January, 9th February, 9th March, 2nd, 18th May and 5th June 1717.—At Drury Lane Theatre *Camilla* was revived in January 1717, with Mrs. Barbier.

———

J. Walsh and J. Hare advertise in the *Post-Man* of 31st January 1717 for the following week (beginning on 4th February) William Babel(l)'s " Suits of the most Celebrated Lessons Collected and Fitted to the Harpsicord or Spinnet . . . with Variety of Passages by the Author ".

(Smith, August 1935, p. 695.) The collection contains four airs from *Rinaldo* and, according to Chrysander (*Collected Edition of Handel's Works*, Vol. 48), one of these (" Vo' far guerra ") gives some idea of " Handel's famous improvisation of Cembalo Solos ". The book was soon reprinted by Richard Meares and by John Young in London, and about 1745 by Veuve Boivin in Paris. (Cf. 21st June 1711.)

———

At the King's Theatre . . . this present Saturday . . . will be presented an Opera (not perform'd this Season) call'd, Amadis. The part of Amadis by Signor Cavaliero Nicolino Grimaldi, Dardanus by Signor Antonio Bernacchi, Oriana by Mrs. Robinson, Melisia by Signora Elizabetta Pilotti. Mrs. Robinson will perform all the Songs which was Originally Compos'd for this Opera. . . . To begin exactly at Six a-Clock.

This advertisement is preserved in the *Theatrical Register*. Only Bernacchi was new : he sang the part created by Signora Vico who had left the company.

H.–3 *a*

It seems that in 1716 Mrs. Robinson did not sing all the arias of her part, created in 1715. Repeat performances on 23rd February, 21st March, 11th April and 30th May 1717.

———

From the " Daily Courant ", 23rd February 1717

At the King's Theatre . . . this present Saturday . . . Amadis . . . N.B. This Opera will be performed without Scenes. The Stage being in the same magnificent Form as it was in the Ball [on the 21st].

Cutting in the *Theatrical Register*. Eisenschmidt (II. 102) finds it remarkable that *Amadigi* could have been performed without scenery. The " Ball " was apparently one of Heidegger's famous " Masquerades ".

———

Venceslao is produced at the Haymarket Theatre on 14th March 1717 and runs for three nights only.

———

From the " Daily Courant ", 21st March 1717

For the Benefit of Mrs. Robinson.

At the King's Theatre . . . this present Thursday . . . Amadis. With the Addition of a New Scene, the Musick compos'd by Mr. Hendel, and perform'd by Signor Cavaliero Nicolino Grimaldi and Mrs. Robinson. And Dancing by Monsieur de Mirail's Scholar, and Mademoiselle Crail, lately arriv'd from Paris.

Cutting in the *Theatrical Register* (British Museum). Originally planned for 23rd March. There is only one duet in the score of the opera : " Cangia al fine il tuo rigore ", sung by Amadigi and Oriana in Act III, Scene 3. The words of this duet, however, were already printed in the only edition known of the libretto (1715). The music of this additional scene was, in fact, based on a duet from *Silla* and was printed for the first time by Walsh in 1758, when introduced in the pasticcio *Solimano* (31st January 1758, Haymarket Theatre). Walsh never published songs from *Amadigi*.—The dancing scholar was apparently Mr. Glover (cf. 11th April 1717).

———

Tito Manlio is produced at the Haymarket Theatre, 4th April 1717.

———

From the " Daily Courant ", 11th April 1717

At the King's Theatre . . . this present Thursday . . . Amadis. With all the New Scenes belonging to the New Opera. To which will be added a New Scene, perform'd by . . . Grimaldi, and Mrs. Robinson. With several Entertainments of Dancing, by Mr. Glover, and Mademoiselle Crail ; particularly, a Spanish Dance.

Cutting in the *Theatrical Register*. The " New Opera " may have been *Tito Manlio*. The duet was, of course, that written for Mrs. Robinson's benefit (21st March 1717).

———

Rinaldo is given for the benefit of Signora Pilotti on 2nd May, and for Signor Berenstadt on 18th May 1717.

FROM THE " DAILY COURANT ", 30th May 1717

For the Benefit of the Instrumental Musick.

At the King's Theatre . . . this present Thursday . . . will be perform'd . . . Amadis. To which will be added Two Pieces of Musick between the Acts.

The " Two Pieces " may have been identical with the " Two New Symphonies " performed in *Amadigi* at the orchestra's benefit on 20th June 1716.

FROM THE " DAILY COURANT ", 5th June 1717

For the Benefit of the Box-Keepers.

At the King's Theatre . . . this present Wednesday . . . will be perform'd . . . Rinaldo. With Entertainments of Dancing by Mons. Salle, and Mademoiselle Salle, his Sister, the two Children, who never perform'd on this Stage before.

This was the first contact between Marie Sallé, then nine or ten years of age, and Handel. The famous dancer appeared in Handel operas in 1734 and 1735. She and her two years older brother were brought to England from France by their uncle, Francisque Moylin, and appeared for the first time at the Haymarket Theatre on 8th December 1716, in the opera *Clearte* (produced on 18th April 1716 and also performed on 1st June 1717).

The opera season ends with a performance of *Tito Manlio*, 29th June 1717.

FROM MATTHESON'S " DAS BESCHÜTZTE ORCHESTRE " (" THE ORCHESTRA DEFENDED "), Hamburg, [8th (19th) July] 1717 (Translated)

(Dedication.)

To . . . the *Capell-Meistern, Directoribus Musices*, world- and far-renowned German *Melothetis* . . . Herr Georg Friderich Hendel, Capell-Meister to the King of Great Britain and to the Elector of Brunswick-Lüneburg. . . . My especially esteemed gentlemen and chosen *Arbitris*.

(Text.)

. . . From the audacity, however, with which the *Opponens* speaks of it [the Thorough Bass], one could readily conclude that he fancies himself to be that single exception which I have mentioned on p. 65

of the [*Neu-Eröffnete*] *Orchestre*. But in that place I speak of such artists as are known to me ; since I have not at present the honour of knowing the organist gentleman and his power in *Accompagnement*, or Thorough Bass, he can be assured that I meant not him but the Capell-Meister Hendel.

The dedication is addressed to thirteen musicians, among them J. J. Fux, R. Keiser, J. Kuhnau and G. P. Telemann. The opponent was Johann Heinrich Buttstedt, organist in Erfurt, who, in 1714 and 1716, published two parts of a book called " Ut, Mi, Sol, Re, Fa, La, Tota Musica, *etc.*" The reference at the end is to p. 65 of the 1713 publication by Mattheson. The dedication is on p. v of the preliminaries and the text on p. 94 of his new book.

FROM THE " POLITICAL STATE OF GREAT-BRITAIN ", 1717

On *Wednesday* the 17th of *July*, in the Evening, the King, attended by their Royal Highnesses the Prince and Princess of *Wales*, and a numerous Train of Lords, Gentlemen, and Ladies, went up by Water to *Chelsea*, and was entertain'd with an excellent Consort of Musick by Count *Kilmanseck* ; after which, His Majesty and their Royal Highnesses supp'd at the Lady *Catherine Jones's*, at the House of the late Earl of *Ranelagh's* ; and about Three a Clock in the Morning, return'd by Water to *Whitehall*, and thence to St. *James's* Palace.

(Chrysander, III. 146.) Volume XIV of the *Political State* records events of the second half of 1717 ; the record quoted above is on p. 83. The entertainment, including Handel's *Water Music*, was arranged and paid for by Baron Kielmansegg, himself an amateur composer, who died on 15th November 1717. The following newspaper report is more explicit about the evening. Lady Catherine Jones was the widow of Arthur Jones, second Viscount of Ranelagh.

FROM THE " DAILY COURANT ", 19th July 1717

On Wednesday [the 17th] Evening, at about 8, the King took Water at Whitehall in an open Barge, wherein were also the Dutchess of Bolton, the Dutchess of Newcastle, the Countess of Godolphin, Madam Kilman-seck, and the Earl of Orkney. And went up the River towards Chelsea. Many other Barges with Persons of Quality attended, and so great a Number of Boats, that the whole River in a manner was cover'd ; a City Company's Barge was employ'd for the Musick, wherein were 50 Instruments of all sorts, who play'd all the Way from Lambeth (while the Barges drove with the Tide without Rowing, as far as Chelsea) the finest Symphonies, compos'd express for this Occasion, by Mr. Hendel ; which his Majesty liked so well, that he caus'd it to be plaid over three times in going and returning. At Eleven his Majesty went a-shore at Chelsea, where a Supper was prepar'd, and then there was another very fine Consort of Musick, which lasted till 2 ; after which, his Majesty came again into his Barge, and return'd the same Way, the Musick continuing to play till he landed.

(J. P. Malcolm, p. 145.)

___

REPORT WRITTEN BY BONET, THE PRUSSIAN RESIDENT, TO BERLIN
(Translated)

[London, 19th (30th) July 1717.]

A few weeks ago the King expressed to Baron Kilmanseck His desire to have a concert on the river, by subscription, similar to the masquerades this winter which the King never failed to attend. The Baron accordingly applied to Heidecker,—a Swiss by origin, but the cleverest purveyor of entertainments to the Nobility. The latter replied that, much as he would wish to comply with His Majesty's desires, he must reserve subscriptions for the great events, namely the masquerades, each of which brings him in three or 400 guineas net. Observing His Majesty's chagrin at these difficulties, M. de Kilmanseck undertook to provide the concert on the river at his own expense. The necessary orders were given and the entertainment took place the day before yesterday. About eight in the evening the King repaired to His barge, into which were admitted the Duchess of Bolton, Countess Godolphin, Mad. de Kilmanseck, Mrs. Were and the Earl of Orkney, the Gentleman of the Bedchamber in Waiting. Next to the King's barge was that of the musicians, about 50 in number, who played on all kinds of instruments, to wit trumpets, horns, hautboys, bassoons, German flutes, French flutes, violins and basses ; but there were no singers. The music had been composed specially by the famous Handel, a native of Halle, and His Majesty's principal Court Composer. His Majesty approved of it so greatly that he caused it to be repeated three times in all, although each performance lasted an hour—namely twice before and once after supper. The [weather in the] evening was all that could be desired for the festivity, the number of barges and above all of boats filled with people desirous of hearing was beyond counting. In order to make this entertainment the more exquisite, Mad. de Kilmanseck had arranged a choice supper in the late Lord Ranelagh's villa at Chelsea on the river, where the King went at one in the morning. He left at three o'clock and returned to St. James' about half past four. The concert cost Baron Kilmanseck £150 for the musicians alone. Neither the Prince nor the Princess [of Wales] took any part in this festivity.

(Michael, 1922, p. 585 ; extracts in English by William Barclay Squire in *Musical Times*, December 1922, p. 866.) Original in the Prussian State Archives, Berlin. Heidegger's " Masquerades " were held at the Haymarket Theatre during the carnival (cf. 23rd February 1717). " Mad. Were " is named by Bonet instead of the Duchess of Newcastle, mentioned in the newspaper ; she may have been Diana de Vere, the widowed Lady Oxford, or Baroness Margaret De La Warr. Madame Kielmansegg is given as the hostess, instead of Lady

Catherine Jones in the *Political State*. In its account of the presence of the Prince and Princess of Wales, the *Political State* seems to be wrong, since the newspaper does not mention them and Bonet declares them as absent. No information exists as to whether Handel himself conducted the *Water Music*, but it is probable that his musicians also played at supper. The " German flute " was the transverse flute, held horizontally, while the " French " one was the recorder, or *flûte à bec*. Squire stresses the fact that there was, of course, no cembalo in that orchestra. It is still not known how many movements Handel's *Water Music* contained in 1717, but it seems that two sets existed, one in F major and one in D major. Whether one of them was written before 1717, perhaps in 1715 as the legend of Handel's reconciliation with the King told us, is uncertain.

———

Handel's *Amadigi*, translated into German by Joachim Beccau, with the airs sung in Italian, is performed at Hamburg under the title *Oriana*, September 1717.

(Chrysander, 1877, column 246 ; Loewenberg, p. 68.) The printed libretto does not give the names of authors and composer. According to Percy Robinson (*Music & Letters*, 1939), there is a possibility that Handel went to Germany for a short visit in 1717 ; cf. Mattheson's *Ehrenpforte*, p. 97.

———

JAMES BRYDGES, EARL OF CARNARVON, TO JOHN ARBUTHNOT,
Cannons, 25th September 1717

Mr Handle has made me two new Anthems very noble ones & most think they far exceed the two first. He is at work for 2 more & some Overtures to be plaied before the first lesson. You had as good take Cannons in your way to London.

(Baker, p. 125.) Huntington Library, San Marino. This letter proves that Handel left his residence in Burlington House in the summer of 1717 at the latest. Lord Brydges, the later Duke of Chandos, built his famous summer palace at Cannons (Edgware) in 1713 and was a great patron of the arts. He had been Paymaster-General in Marlborough's Wars and augmented his fortunes in the " South-Sea Bubble ". For descriptions of Cannons cf. Macky (1722) and Defoe (1725) ; for the music establishment there, cf. 23rd August 1720. The chapel was not ready before 29th August 1720. The performances of Handel's first four *Chandos Anthems* probably took place in St. Lawrence's, Whitchurch, erected by Lord Brydges in 1714. Handel was invited to, and stayed at, Cannons not as conductor but as composer. In charge of the music there, not only before and after Handel's residence but also during it, was John Christopher Pepusch. It seems that among the first four of the eleven or twelve anthems written for Brydges, and later Chandos, the order of which is not ascertained, was " As pants the heart ", which became well known during the following years. Dr. John Arbuthnot, like Alexander Pope, met Handel at Burlington's.

———

FROM THE " POLITICAL STATE OF GREAT-BRITAIN ", 1717

On the 15th [November], in the Morning, dy'd the Baron de Kilman-seck, Master of the Horse to his Majesty, as Elector of Hanover ; a

Gentleman of Parts, who had a good Taste of Literature and Learning, and great Skill in Musick and Painting, and who was a great Encourager of Arts and Sciences.

(Chrysander, III. 146.)   Vol. XIV, p. 508.   Cf. 17th July 1717.

———

Two years he spent at CANNONS [1717–19], *a place which was then in all its glory, but remarkable for having much more of art than nature, and much more cost than art. . . . Whether Handel was provided as a mere implement of grandeur, or chosen from motives of a superior kind, it is not for us to determine. This one may venture to assert, that the having such a Composer, was an instance of real magnificence, such as no private person or subject ; nay, such as no prince or potentate on the earth could at that time pretend to.*
(Mainwaring, pp. 95 f.)

1718

There are no Handel records to be found in the London newspapers of 1718 and very few in 1719. Perhaps the fact that he stayed at Cannons was the reason for his disappearance from public attention, although it is quite possible that, during the winter, Handel moved with Lord Brydges to his town residence in Albemarle Street. The Haymarket Theatre was used in 1718 and 1719 for balls, masquerades, concerts, and (from November 1718 till April 1719) French comedies, while English operas were performed at the Theatre in Lincoln's Inn Fields.

——

FROM A LONDON NEWSPAPER, 15th February 1718

(On a Subscription Masquerade arranged by Heidegger in the Haymarket Theatre.)

The Room is exceedingly large, beautifully adorned, and illuminated with five hundred Wax Lights ; on the Sides are divers Beaufets, over which is written the several Wines therein contained, as Canary, Burgundy, Champagne, Rhenish, &c. each most excellent in its Kind ; of which all are at Liberty to drink what they please ; with large Services of all Sorts of Sweetmeats. There are also two Sets of Music, at due Distance from each other, performed by very good Hands. By the vast Variety of Dresses (many of them very rich) you would fancy it a Congress of the principal Persons of all Nations in the World, as Turks, Italians, Indians, Polanders, Spaniards, Venetians, &c. There is an absolute Freedom of Speech, without the least Offence given thereby ; while all appear better bred than to offer at any Thing profane, rude, or immodest, but Wit incessantly flashes about in Repartees, Honour, and good Humour, and all Kinds of Pleasantry. There was also the Groom Porter's Office, where all play that please ; while Heaps of Guineas pass about, with so little Concern in the Losers, that they are not to be distinguished from the Winners. Nor does it add a little to the Beauty of the Entertainment, to see the Generality of the Masqueraders behave themselves agreeable to their several Habits. The Number, when I was there on Tuesday, last week, was computed at 700, with some files of Musquetiers at Hand, for the preventing any Disturbance which might happen by Quarrels, &c. so frequent in Venice, Italy, and other Countries, on such Entertainments. At eleven o'Clock a person gives Notice that Supper is ready, when the Company pass into another large Room, where a noble cold Entertainment is prepared, suitable to all the Rest ; the whole Diversion continuing from nine o'Clock till seven next Morning. In short, the whole Ball was sufficiently illustrious, in every

Article of it, for the greatest Prince to give on the most extraordinary Occasion.

(Kelly, II. 347 f.) Kelly quotes the passage as from Mist's *Weekly Journal* ; it is not to be found there, nor in Applebee's *Weekly Journal*. This description is inserted here to show Heidegger's abilities and enterprise. Cf. Bonet's report of 19th July 1717. Heidegger enjoyed the favour of the King, but not that of the Bishop of London. Cf. spring 1724. According to Kelly (II. 351), a military guard was installed at the Haymarket Theatre for the balls in the season of 1725–6.

—

A concert for the benefit of Mrs. Robinson is given at the Haymarket Theatre, 15th March 1718.

(Kelly, II. 347 f.)

—

Handel's sister, Dorothea Sophia Michaelsen, dies at Halle, 28th July (8th August) 1718.

—

FROM JOHANN MICHAEL HEINECK'S FUNERAL SERMON FOR HANDEL'S SISTER, HALLE, 31st July (11th August) 1718 (Translated)

She confirmed by her example the truth of Solomon's words : The righteous hath hope in his death. Whence comes, however, this joyousness, since there is no joy at hand ? Why does hope flourish, even if the body, like a flower, withers away ? Why does faith not pine away, even if body and mind pine away ? No one can give us better answers to these questions than the blessed woman, whose voice is henceforth stilled. She uttered them oftentimes in life, in the words of Job : For I know that my Redeemer liveth, and that He shall stand at the latter day upon the earth. . . .

GOD had given her a devoted husband, a marriage fruitfully blessed, a goodly portion, many joys in her only brother, whose quite especially and exceptionally great *Vertues* even crowned heads and the greatest ones of the earth at the same time love and admire, and bestowed on her as well much contentment, yet everything must give place to her Redeemer. . . .

(Chrysander, I. 490 ff.) The sermon was printed, together with seven elegies written, or signed, by relatives of the deceased, in a booklet of 30 pages folio, and the printer's dedication mentions Handel. One copy was in W. H. Cummings's library (1917 sale, catalogue No. 823). It is noteworthy that the sister's favourite text was " I know that my Redeemer liveth ", from the Book of Job.

—

Rinaldo, with additional music by the conductor, Leonardo Leo, is performed in the Palazzo Reale at Naples, 20th September (1st October) 1718.

Nicolini, the first Rinaldo of 1711, sang his part again, having also sung it in 1712, 1715 and 1717. The occasion was the birthday of the Emperor,

Karl VI. Nicola Serina, who may have provided some comic scenes, signed the dedication of the libretto. Leo composed the prologue and several scenes.

———

FROM WILHELM WILLERS' THEATRICAL NOTES, HAMBURG, 23rd October (3rd November) 1718

Nov. 3. Opera Agrippina.

(Merbach, p. 355.) Willers was minister of Prussia (or Holland ?) in Hamburg. The opera, never performed in England, was produced on the Hamburg stage in Italian, on the occasion of reopening of the house under the new management of J. G. Gumprecht. The libretto, with a German translation added, does not mention the name of Handel or that of the author. The opera was performed again on 27th October (7th November) 1718.

———

FROM MATTHESON'S HAMBURG OPERA LIST, [23rd October] 1718 (Translated)

Agrippina. Music by Herr Händel. Performed in Italian.

(Chrysander, 1877, p. 246.)

———

FROM WILLERS' HAMBURG NOTES, 8th (19th) November 1718 (Translated)

Nov. 19. Gauffin has discourteously run away and threatened not to sing again, however he did sing in Agrippina and forthwith had his luggage removed.

The opera was performed again on 13th (24th) November, and the singer did not leave until 29th November (10th December) 1718.

———

FROM WILLERS' HAMBURG NOTES, 20th November (1st December) 1718

Dec. 1. Agrippina in Altona.

Altona is a town near Hamburg where the company, including the coarse Gauffin, was paying one of its regular visits.

———

FROM WILLERS' HAMBURG NOTES, 30th December 1718 (10th January 1719 (Translated)

Jan. 10. Agrippina, only 10 people.

Willers records further performances of *Agrippina* in Hamburg on 16th and 23rd February ; 27th April ; 1st, 4th, 8th, 10th, 25th May ; 15th, 22nd June ; 10th, 20th July ; 7th, 14th, 23rd August ; 7th, 27th September ; 25th October ; 1st, 27th November ; and 6th December 1719 ; 22nd January 1720 ; 5th and 23rd November 1722. All these dates are New Style, not changed to the British Calendar.

1719

During the last year of his residence at Cannons, a project was formed by the Nobility for erecting an academy at the Haymarket. The intention of this musical Society, was to secure to themselves a constant supply of Operas to be composed by Handel, and performed under his direction. For this end a subscription was set on foot : and as his . . . Majesty was pleased to let his name appear at the head of it, the Society was dignified with the title of the Royal Academy. The sum subscribed being very large, it was intended to continue for fourteen years certain. But as yet it was in its embrio-state, being not fully formed till a year or two after. (Mainwaring, pp. 96 f.)

FROM WILLERS' HAMBURG NOTES, 26th January (6th February) 1719

Feb. 6. Oriana.

Cf. September 1717. Repeat performances of *Amadigi* in German on 9th, 10th February ; 14th, 21st, 29th June ; 9th, 17th, 24th August ; and 2nd October 1719 ; 12th, 28th August ; and 12th September 1720 (New Style).

JONATHAN SWIFT TO (?) THE SECRETARY OF THE FIRST EARL
OF OXFORD

Dublin, Feb. 9, 1719.

. . . I have the honour to be Captain of a band of nineteen musicians (including boys), which are I hear about five less then my friend the D. of Chandos. . . .

(Historical MSS. Commission, 13th Report, Appendix, Part IV, Loder-Symonds Manuscripts, 1892, p. 404.) The letter refers to a singer, Lovelace, recommended by the Earl of Oxford to the Dean for the choir of St. Patrick's Cathedral ; he arranged for the Dublin organist, Daniel Roseingrave, then on a visit to London, to examine the singer there. It is possible that the poet met Handel at Chandos's home in 1718. According to Baker (p. xvii), who mentions this letter on p. 129, the " Concert " at Cannons consisted of about thirty performers, vocal and instrumental. Swift's information may have been inaccurate. Cf. 15th May 1721.

FROM THE " DAILY COURANT ", 16th February 1719

For the Benefit of Mr. Leneker, and Mrs. Smith.

At Mr. Hickford's Great Room in James-street near the Hay-market, on Wednesday next, being the 18th Day of February, will be perform'd, a Consort of Vocal and Instrumental Musick, by the best Hands. A new Concerto, Compos'd by Mr. Hendel, and perform'd by Mr. Mathew Dubourg. And a Piece for the Harpsicord by Mr. Cook. A Concerto and a Solo by Mr. Kytch. A Solo for the Bass-Viol, and German-Flute by Signor Pietro. Tickets . . . at 5s. each. To begin exactly at 7 a Clock.

(Chrysander, III. 148.) Handel's concerto has not been identified. This was the first public contact between Handel and Dubourg, a pupil of Geminiani. Dubourg was violinist, conductor and composer ; he went to Ireland in 1728, as Master of the State Music in Dublin, and joined the King's Band, as Festing's successor, in 1752. For Jean Christian Kytch, the oboist, see 15th May 1721. Signor Pietro was probably Pietro Castrucci, the violin player. Nothing is known about Cook, Leneker and Mrs. Smith.

———

HANDEL TO HIS BROTHER-IN-LAW, M. D. MICHAELSEN, 20th February
1719

Monsieur
mon tres Honoré Frere,

Ne jugez pas, je Vous supplie, de mon envie de Vous voir par le retardement de mon depart, c'est à mon grand regret que je me vois arreté icy par des affaires indispensables et d'ou, j'ose dire, mà fortune depend, et les quelles ont trainé plus longtems que je n'avois crû. Si Vous scaviez la peine que j'eprouve, de ce que je n'ai pas pu mettre en execution ce que je desire si ardement Vous auriez de l'indulgence pour moy. mais a la fin j'espere d'en venir à bout dans un mois d'icy, et Vous pouvez conter que je ne ferai aucun delay, et que je me mettrai incessamment en chemin, Je Vous supplie, Mon tres Cher Frere d'en assurer la Mama et de mon obeissance, et faites moy surtout part encore une fois de Vôtre Etat, de celuy de la Mama, et de Vôtre Chere Famille, pour diminuer l'inquietude et l'impatience dans la quelle je me trouve, Vous jugez bien, Mon tres Cher Frere, que je serois inconsolable, si je n'avois pas l'esperance de me dedommager bientôt de ce delay, en restant d'autant plus longtems avec Vous.

Je suis etonné de ce que le Marchand a Magdebourg n'a pas encore satisfait à la lettre de Change, je Vous prie de la garder seulement, et à mon arrivée elle sera ajustée. J'ay recus avis que l'Etain serà bientôt achemine pour Vos endroits, je suis honteux de ce retardement aussi bien que de ce que je n'ai pas pu m'acquitter plus tôt de ma promesse, je Vous supplie de l'excuser et de croire que malgré tous mes effors il m'a eté impossible de reussir, Vous en conviendrez Vous même lorsque j'aurai l'honneur de Vous le dire de bouche. Vous ne devez pas douter que je ne haterai mon voyage : je languis plus que Vous ne scauriez Vous imaginer de Vous voir. Je Vous remercie tres humblement des vœux que Vous m'avez adresses à l'occasion du nouvel'an. Je souhaite de mon côté, que le Toutpuissant veuille Vous combler et Vôtre Chere Famille de toutes sortes de Prosperites, et d'addoucir par ses pretieuses benedictions la playe sensible qu'il luy a plu de Vous faire essuyer, et qui m'a frappè egalement. Vous pouvez etre assuré que je conserverai toujours vivement le Souvenir des bontés que Vous avez eues par feue mà Soeur, et que les sentimens de mà reconnoissance dureront aussi longtems que mes jours. Ayez la bonté de faire bien mes Complimens à Mr. Rotth et a tous les bon Amis. Je Vous embrasse avec toute Votre Chere Famille, et je suis avec une passion inviolable toute ma vie

Monsieur

et tres Honoré Frere

à Londres   Vôtre

ce 20 de Fevrier   tres humble et tres obeissant

    1719.   Serviteur

George Frideric Handel.

A Monsieur,
Monsieur Michael Dietrich Michaëlsen,
Docteur en Droit
à Halle
en Saxe.

(Translation)

Honoured Brother,

I beg that you will not judge of my eagerness to see you by the lateness of my departure ; it is greatly to my regret that I find myself kept here by affairs of the greatest moment, on which (I venture to say) all my fortunes depend ; but they have continued much longer than I had anticipated. If you knew my distress at not having been able to perform what I so ardently desire, you would be indulgent towards me ; but I am hoping to conclude it all in a month from now, and you can rest assured that I shall then make no delay but set out forthwith. Pray, dearest brother, assure Mamma of this, as also of my duty ; and inform me once again of the state of health of yourself, Mamma and all your family, so as to relieve my present anxiety and impatience. You will realise, dearest brother, that I should be inconsolable, did I not expect very soon to make up for this delay by remaining all the longer with you.

I am astonished that the merchant at Magdeburg has not yet honoured the letter of exchange. Pray keep it and the matter will be put right when I come. I have been informed that the pewter will soon be despatched to your address ; I am as ashamed at this delay as at my own inability to carry out my promise earlier. I beg you to excuse it and to believe that it was impossible for me to succeed, in spite of all my efforts. You will yourself agree when I have the honour of telling you about it in person. You must not doubt that I shall hasten on my journey. I am longing to see you more than you can imagine. I thank you most humbly for the good wishes that you sent me for the New Year. On my part I trust that the Almighty will shower on you and your beloved family every kind of good fortune and will heal through His precious blessings the painful wound which it has pleased Him to make you suffer, and which has pained me no less. You can be assured that I shall always keep the most lively memory of your goodness

towards my late sister, and that my feelings of gratitude will endure all my days. Have the goodness to convey my compliments to Mr. Rotth and to all my good friends. I embrace you and all your dear family. I remain with steadfast devotion all my life,
Honoured Brother,
Your most humble and obedient servant,
George Frideric Handel.
London, February 20th, 1719.

To Mr. Michael Dietrich Michaëlsen,
Doctor of Law, Halle (Saxony).

(Chrysander, I. 493 f.) The original is in the Bibliothèque du Conservatoire, Paris, and has been kindly collated by Mad. Nanie Bridgman, of the Bibliothèque Nationale. The beginning of the letter indicates that Handel had been planning the journey to the Continent for some time before this date, and, therefore, that the " Academy " was already in preparation in 1718. On the other hand, it is possible that Handel was planning a private journey, and was just held up by the new designs of the " Academy ". The delay proved longer than the month he anticipated. Through the merchant of Magdeburg Handel apparently sent some money for his mother. Mueller von Asow, in his German edition of Handel's letters, treated " Etain " as a proper name instead of translating it as pewter. Christian August Roth (or Rotth), deacon of the Moritz Church in Halle, was Handel's cousin.

——

FROM THE " ORIGINAL WEEKLY JOURNAL ", 21st February 1719

Mr. Hendel, a famous Master of Musick, is gone beyond Sea, by Order of his Majesty, to Collect a Company of the choicest Singers in Europe, for the Opera in the Hay-Market.

(Chrysander, II. 16.) This news was premature (cf. 14th May 1719). It is, however, interesting to know that the preparations for the " Royal Academy of Music " were already in progress at the beginning of the year. The note also indicates that Handel had left Cannons by 21st February.

——

HANDEL TO JOHANN MATTHESON, AT HAMBURG

à Londres,
Fevr. 24, 1719.

Monsieur,
Par la Lettre que je viens de recevoir de votre part, datée du 21 du courant je me vois pressé si obligeamment de vous satisfaire plus particulierement, que je n'ai fait dans mes precedentes, sur les deux points en question, que je ne puis me dispenser de declarer, que mon opinion se trouve generalement conforme à ce que vous avez si bien deduit & prouvé dans votre livre touchant la Solmisation & les Modes Grecs. La question ce me semble reduit a ceci : Si l'on doit preferer une Methode aisée & des plus parfaites à une autre qui est accompagnée de grandes

difficultés, capables non seulement de degouter les eleves dans la Musique, mais aussi de leur faire consumer un tems pretieux, qu'on peut employer beaucoup mieux à approfondir cet art & à cultiver son genie ? Ce n'est pas que je veuille avancer, qu'on ne peut tirer aucune utilité de la Solmisation : mais comme on peut acquerir les mêmes connoissances en bien moins de tems par la methode dont on se sert à present avec tant de succes, je ne vois pas, pourquoi on ne doive opter le chemin qui conduit plus facilement & en moins de tems au but qu'on se propose ? Quant aux Modes Grecs, je trouve, Monsieur, que vous avez dit tout ce qui se peut dire là dessus. Leur connoissance est sans doute necessaire à ceux qui veulent pratiquer & executer la Musique ancienne, qui a été composée suivant ces Modes ; mais comme on s'est affranchi des bornes etroites de l'ancienne Musique, je ne vois pas de quelle utilité les Modes Grecs puissent être pour la Musique moderne. Ce cont là, Monsieur, mes sentimens, vous m'obligerez de me faire sçavoir s'ils repondent à ce que vous souhaitez de moi.

Pour ce qui est du second point, vous pouvez juger vous même, qu'il demande beaucoup de recueillement, dont je ne suis pas le maitre parmi les occupations pressantes, que j'ai par devers moi. Desque j'en serai un peu débarassé, je repasserai les Epoques principales que j'ai eues dans le cours de ma Profession, pour vous faire voir l'estime & la consideration particuliere avec laquelle j'ai l'honneur d'etre

Monsieur

votre tres humble & tres

obeissant serviteur

G. F. Handel.

(Translation)

London, February 24th, 1719.

Sir,

The letter that I have just received from you dated the 21st of this month obliges me with all haste to satisfy you more precisely than I had done in my previous letters on the two points in question. I must therefore declare that, in the matter of solmization and the Greek modes, my opinion conforms in general to what you have so ably deduced and proved in your book. The question, in my opinion, comes to this : whether one should [not] prefer a method at the same time simple and of the most perfect kind to another which is fraught with great difficulties, apt not only to give pupils a distaste for music but also to make them waste much precious time, which could be better employed in acquiring a profound knowledge of this art and in improving their natural gifts ? I do not mean to argue that solmization is of no practical use whatever, but as one can acquire the same knowledge in far less time by the method in use at present with such success, I see no point in not adopting the way which leads with greater ease and in less time to the proposed goal. Touching the Greek modes, I find, Sir, that you have said all that there is to be said on that score. Knowledge of them is no doubt necessary for those who wish to study and execute ancient music composed according to these modes ; but as we have [now] been liberated from the narrow limits of ancient music, I cannot see of what use the Greek modes can be to modern music. Such, Sir, are my views ; you will oblige me by informing me if they agree with what you wish from me.

As regards the second point, you can yourself judge that it demands more leisure than I can dispose of among the many pressing affairs that I have on hand. As soon as I am a little freer, I shall pass in review the main periods of my professional life, so that you may be assured of the particular esteem and consideration in which I have the honour to remain,

    Sir,

        Your most humble and

                obedient servant,

                      G. F. Handel.

This letter was published with a German translation by Mattheson in his periodical *Critica Musica* (II. 210-12) as early as 1725. Written on 24th February (7th March) in answer to Mattheson's letter of 10th (21st) February, it was received on 3rd (14th) March 1719 and answered again the same day ; which shows that the post between London and Hamburg was not too slow. Handel's letter refers to a previous one, since lost, and to Mattheson's book *Das Beschützte Orchestre* (cf. 19th July 1717). The second part of the letter is an answer to Mattheson's repeated request that Handel should write an autobiographical sketch for him (cf. 18th July 1735).

<hr>

A concert is given on 28th February 1719 for the benefit of Mrs. Ann Turner-Robinson, " who never sang but once in public " ; the concert being in three parts of which the second is " entirely new composed by Signr. Attilio Ariosti purposely on this occasion ". (Latreille's manuscript copy, probably from the *Daily Courant.*)

Ariosti's composition was a cantata ; see 21st March 1719. The concert was apparently given at the Haymarket Theatre.

<hr>

FROM THE PREFACE TO THE TEXT OF BARTHOLD HEINRICH BROCKES'
" PASSION ", Hamburg, spring 1719 (Translated)

It is not to be wondered at that the four great musicians, Herr *Keiser*, Herr *Händel*, Herr *Telemann* and Herr *Mattheson*, who, through their many and admirable masterpieces, given to the world of music, earned for themselves eternal honour, esteemed as their greatest pleasure the setting of such [a Text] to music, in which achievement they succeeded so uncommonly well that even the most prudent connoisseur of beautiful music must confess that he knows of no grace, art and natural expression of feeling which have been forgotten here, and that, without committing himself to a hazardous judgement, he does not know to whom the

highest rank is to be given. The music of Herr *Keiser* has been performed
at different times before now with the greatest approbation. The music
of Herr *Mattheson*, heard twice this year, has left with the hearer of it
an undying memory of his *Virtú*. Now, however, it is intended that
the music of Herr *Händel* shall be performed next Monday (in Passion
week) and that of Herr *Telemann* next Tuesday.

> (Mattheson, *Ehrenpforte*, 1740, p. 96 ; Chrysander, I. 449.) The text of
the Passion, written and published in 1712, is entitled : " Der für die Sünden der
Welt gemarterte und sterbende Jesus aus den vier Evangelisten in gebundener
Rede vorgestellet ". (The story of Jesus, suffering and dying for the sins of the
world, presented in verse according to the narrative as related by the four
Evangelists.) Reinhard Keiser (born in 1674) set the oratorio in the same year,
and it was performed in Passion week 1712 and later. Georg Philipp Telemann,
born like Mattheson in 1681, set the poem in 1716, Handel probably in 1717,
and Mattheson in 1718. The textbook of 1719 mentions only the coming performances of Handel's and Telemann's compositions, but Chrysander says that
all four settings were performed that year in the Cathedral. Handel sent one
manuscript from London to Hamburg, probably in 1717. (Cf. February 1723.)
Half of a manuscript copy preserved in Berlin was written by J. S. Bach and
inscribed : " Oratorium Passionale. Poesia di Brocks et Musica di Hendel ".
In 1795 Queen Charlotte presented Haydn with a manuscript of Handel's German
Passion to which he later considered adding a final chorus ; this manuscript
passed from Haydn to Breitkopf & Härtel who intended to publish the work.
The autograph is lost. Two other manuscript copies remain in the Royal Music
Library. In 1729 Handel composed nine arias from Brockes' *Irdisches Vergnügen
in Gott*. It is also noteworthy that Brockes translated James Thomson's *The
Seasons* into German, and that his text was set to music by one H. T. O. (Zurich,
1747).

———

A concert of vocal and instrumental music is given at the Haymarket Theatre on 21st March 1719, with Mrs. Turner-Robinson
and Signor Benedetto Baldassari. She sings Ariosti's cantata
again (cf. 28th February 1719). " The Concert will be performed
in a magnificent triumphant scene, exceeding 30 feet in length
any scene ever seen before. Painted by Signor Roberto Clerici."
(Latreille's manuscript copy, probably from the *Daily Courant*.)

> The two singers were to join the new opera company in 1720. Clerici
was to become the theatre painter of the opera, as " Ingegnero della
Reale Accademia " (Fassini, *Rivista musicale*, p. 38). Already in 1716
he had painted, for *Pirro e Demetrio*, an immense perspective view of a
royal palace, which was used again in 1717 for *Clearte*. (Latreille.)

———

Warrant and Instructions for Handel, issued by Thomas
Holles, Duke of Newcastle, the Lord Chamberlain, as
Governor of the Royal Academy of Music, 14th May 1719

Warrant to Mr Hendel to procure Singers for the English Stage,
    Whereas His Majesty has been graciously Pleas'd to Grant Letters
Patents to the Severall Lords and Gent. mention'd in the Annext List for

the Encouragement of Operas for and during the Space of Twenty one Years, and Likewise as a further encouragement has been graciously Pleas'd to Grant a Thousand Pounds p.A. for the Promotion of this design, And also that the Chamberlain of his Ma[ts] Household for the time being is to be always Governor of the said Company. I do by his Majestys Command Authorize and direct You forthwith to repair to Italy Germany or such other Place or Places as you shall think proper, there to make Contracts with such Singer or Singers as you shall judge fit to perform on the English Stage. And for so doing this shall be your Warrant Given under my hand and Seal this 14th day of May 1719 in the Fifth Year of his Ma[ts] Reign.

To M[r] Hendel Master
of Musick. . . .

Holles Newcastle.

Instructions to M[r] Hendel.

That M[r] Hendel either by himself or such Correspondenc[s] as he shall think fit procure proper Voices to Sing in the Opera.

The said M[r] Hendel is impower'd to contract in the Name of the Patentees with those Voices to Sing in the Opera for one Year and no more.

That M[r] Hendel engage Senezino as soon as possible to Serve the said Company and for as many Years as may be.

That in case M[r] Hendel meet with an excellent Voice of the first rate he is to Acquaint the Gov[r] and Company forthwith of it and upon what Terms he or She may be had.

That M[r] Hendel from time to time Acquaint the Governor and Company with his proceedings, Send Copys of the Agreem[ts] which he makes with these Singers and obey such further Instructions as the Governor and Company shall from time to time transmit unto him.

Holles Newcastle.

(Nicoll, pp. 285 f. ; the Instructions only, but not complete.) Public Record Office : L.C. 5/157, copybook, pp. 233-5. The Royal Letters Patent are of 8th May, the first list of subscribers, or patentees, later augmented, of 9th May 1719. The " space " of twentyone years was not achieved : the original Academy existed till 1728 only. The Royal subsidy of £1000 a year, called " Annuity or Yearly Bounty ", and granted at first for seven years only, seems to have been paid regularly from 1722 onwards, as long as the original Academy existed, and up to 1744, though not quite regularly, to the managers of the opera house. It is mentioned here whenever it appears in the Treasury books.—Handel did not go to Italy because he was able to complete his mission in Dresden. Nothing is known of his expenses and their repayment, nor are any of his reports to the Governor preserved. He is called in these documents " Master of Musick ", and later (30th November) " Master of the Orchestra ".

At the Theatre in Lincoln's Inn Fields a mock-opera is produced on 27th May 1719, under the title *Harlequin-Hydaspes* ; *or The Greshamite*, with arias from *Amadigi* and *Rinaldo*.

The text, by a Mrs. Aubert, was a parody of *L'Idaspe Fedele*, which, produced at the Haymarket Theatre on 23rd May 1710, ran until 1716 ; the music included some of Mancini's arias from that opera. (Loewenberg, p. 63.) " The part of Harlequin by the Author—who mimicks the famous Nicolini in his whole action " (*Daily Courant*, 19th May 1719 and later ; Chrysander, II. 30 f.). Originally planned for the 22nd, the first night was " unfortunately prevented . . . by the unexpected Arrest of the Person who was to have played the Doctor ". The theatre was managed by John Rich.

———

List of the 62 Original Subscribers to the Royal Academy of Music, probably from the second half of May 1719

(Each subscriber in the following list guaranteed £200 of the joint stock of £10,000, except where a different sum is indicated.)

Henry Duke of Kent, Thomas Holles Duke of Newcastle (1000), Charles Duke of Grafton, Henry Duke of Portland (600), Charles Duke of Manchester, James Duke of Chandois (1000), James Duke of Montrose, Charles Earl of Sunderland, Henry Earl of Rochester, James Earl of Berkeley, Richard Earl of Burlington (1000), George Henry Earl of Litchfield, Henry Earl of Lincoln, Henry Viscount Lonsdale, Thomas Earl of Strafford, William Earl Cadogan, Talbot Earl of Sussex, Henry Earl of Thomond, George Earl of Halifax, David Earl of Portmore, Count Bothmer, Allen Lord Bathurst, Robert Lord Bingley, George Lord Lansdowne, John Lord Gower, Henry Lord Carleton, Richard Lord Viscount Castlemayne (400), Charles Marquess of Winchester, James Lord Viscount Limerick, James Craggs, Esq ; Walter Lord Viscount Chetwynd, Sir John Jennings, Sir Hunger[d] Hoskins, Sir Matthew Decker, William Evans, Roger Jones, James Bruce, William Pult(e)ney, Thomas Coke, Richard Hampden, Sir John Guise, Thomas Harrison, Benjamin Mildmay, George Harrison, George Wade, Thomas Coke, Esq ; Vice Chamberlain, Francis Whitworth, William Chetwynd, Thomas Smith, Martin Bladen, Thomas Gage, Francis Negus, William Yonge, Bryan Fairfax, Kroynberg, Esq ; John Arbuthnot, Esq ; Sir George Coke, Sir Humphrey Howarth, Sir Wilfred Lawson, Henry Earl of Montroth [*recte* Mountrath], John Blith, William Lord North-Grey, Samuel Edwin.

Public Record Office : L.C. 7/3, No. 15. The following names are not to be found in the draft of the Academy bill, dated 9th May 1719 (L.C. 5/157, p. 229.) : the Earls of Litchfield and Lincoln, Count Bothmer (*recte* Baron Hans Caspar von Bothmer, Hanoverian Representative in London), Kroynberg (*recte* Kreyenberg, Hanoverian Resident in London), Blith, Lord North, and Edwin. According to this list, the intended stock of £10,000 was over-subscribed by £5600. Mainwaring (p. 97) gives £40,000 as the amount subscribed ; Hawkins (V. 273), Burney (IV. 258), Chrysander (II. 31) and others increased the sum to £50,000.

There is, however, no documentary evidence that anything like it was contemplated. The first signatory, the Duke of Kent, Lord Chamberlain until 1717, was originally intended to be Governor, but the second signatory, the Duke of Newcastle, his successor as Lord Chamberlain (1717–24), was, in fact, the first Governor ; he held the post until 1723. The Duke of Manchester was, it seems, Deputy Governor from November 1719 onwards. (He had been created Duke on 30th April 1719, and he died on 20th January 1722.) Since there were two subscribers named Thomas Coke, his title of Vice-Chamberlain was added to the second (cf. 3rd May 1711) ; the other one is later called " of Norfolk ". It will be noted that Handel's patrons, Burlington and Chandos, were, like the Lord Chamberlain, subscribers for five shares each. The subscription of £200 seems to have secured two permanent tickets.—Dr. Charles Burney was in possession of a document on vellum dated 1719, but apparently of a later date than the list preserved in the Public Record Office, and described as the " original deed of incorporation ", with the seals and signatures of 73 (instead of 62) subscribers to the Academy. Although still mentioned as " now before us " in Burney's article on Bononcini in Rees's *Cyclopaedia* of 1819 (vol. IV), it had, in fact, been sold on 15th August 1814 as lot 1048 of Burney's library (he had died four months earlier). On 20th February 1822 it appeared as lot 1409 in the sale of James Bartleman's Collection ; it was later in the collection of William Upcott, was sold again in 1846 and is now lost. Bartleman also acquired at the Burney sale " letters from the Academy to Signori Lotti and Pérez, and an Account of the Academy, &c.", the contents of which are not known. Hawkins (V. 273) gives a list of the Governors and Directors, apparently for 1719–20, which was reprinted by Burney (IV. 258). This list, however, was taken from the dedication of Alexander Malcolm's *Treatise of Musick*, published in 1721, and is quoted here under the date of February 1721. Other lists are to be found under 27th November 1719, 2nd April 1720 and 17th December 1726.

———

In May 1719 Handel goes to Düsseldorf, visiting the Court of the Elector Palatine, and to Halle where he stays with his family and where J. S. Bach, coming from Cöthen, is said to have just missed him (Chryander, II. 18 f.) ; finally, in summer 1719, he goes to Dresden, where he meets Antonio Lotti again and is able to fulfil his mission fairly well.

King George I went to Hanover on 11th May 1719, for the summer.

———

PAOLO ANTONIO ROLLI TO ABBATE GIUSEPPE RIVA (Translated)

Thistleworth, 13th July, 1719.

The Denys woman, alias Sciarpina, has already sung twice at the Princess's [of Wales]. She is certainly helping herself along ! The Man [Handel ?] loves and hides his feelings : but *quousque tandem* ?

La Zanzara Castratina [that shrill little pest of a human being] is staying with the Castrucci and Pippo, to serve that excellent lady the Princess twice a week through the whole season. Sandoni plays the harpsichord, is much appreciated and will once again be awarded a prize. I am glad of his successful introduction. He will do well for himself, so as to do well for his creature.

Attilio has returned to town. A lawsuit still pending has driven them from their Country house.

(Streatfeild, 1917, p. 432, in English.) Original in the Biblioteca Estense di Modena : Autografoteca Campori, as are all Rolli's letters to Riva, the Modenese Representative in London, at this time on holiday at home. Rolli's letters to his friends are full of allusions which are difficult to understand. He was a fertile Italian poet and librettist, and had been in London since 1716. He taught Italian to the daughters of Caroline, Princess of Wales, and himself courted the Princess, presenting to her his verses and his *Pastor Fido* (not Handel's text) in red morocco, and reading to her the first book of his translation of Milton's *Paradise Lost* which was published later.—" L' Uomo ", the man, or rather the monster, usually means Handel in Rolli's letters. Pippo was the nickname of Filippo Mattei, *recte* Amadei, violoncello player and composer. Pier Giuseppe Sandoni (*c.* 1680– *c.* 1750), later the husband of Signora Cuzzoni, played the harpsichord and the organ, and was also a composer. Attilio Ariosti, until 1715 in Berlin, came to London in time to be engaged as composer for the Royal Academy of Music, serving with Handel and Bononcini.

———

HANDEL TO THE EARL OF BURLINGTON, 15th July 1719

My Lord
    C'est toujours autant par un vive reconnoissance, que par devoir, que je me donne l'honneur de Vous dire le zele et l'attachement que j'ay pour Votre personne. Je Vous dois de plus un Conte exact de se que j'ay entrepris, et de la reussite du sujet de mon long voyage.
    Je suis icy à attendre que les engagements de Sinesino, Berselli, et Guizzardi, soyent finis, et que ces Messieurs d'ailleurs bien disposés, s'engagent avec moy pour la Grand Bretagne. tout sera decidé en quelques jours ; j'ay des bonnes esperances, et dés que j'auray conclû quelque chose de réel, je Vous l'ecrirai My Lord, comme a mon bienfaiteur, à mon Protecteur. Conservez moy, My Lord, Vos graces, elles me seront pretieuses, et ce sera toujours avec ardeur et fidelité que je suivray Vôtre service, et Vôs nobles volontés. C'est avec une soumission egalement sincere et profonde que je serai à jamais.
              My Lord

	Vôtre
à Dresde	tres humble tres obeissant, et tres devoue
ce 26/15 de Juillet	Serviteur
1719	George Frideric Handel

(Translation)

My Lord,
    It is always as much with deep gratitude as in duty bound that I have the honour to assure you of my zeal and devotion towards your person. I further owe you an exact account of what I have undertaken and of the successful outcome of my long voyage.
    I am waiting here for the engagements of Sinesino, Berselli and Guizzardi to be concluded and for these gentleman (who are, I may

add, favourably disposed) to sign contracts with me for Great Britain. Everything will be decided in a few days' time ; I have good hopes, and as soon as I have concluded something definite, I shall inform you of it, My Lord, as my benefactor and patron. Pray continue, My Lord, your favours ; they will be precious to me, and I shall always exert myself in your service to carry out your commands with zeal and fidelity. I remain always, My Lord, with sincere and profound submission,

Your

most humble, obedient and devoted

servant,

George Frideric Handel

Dresden, 26th/15th July 1719.

(Young, p. 36.)   Archives of the Duke of Devonshire, Chatsworth.   The letter has no addressee, but it is endorsed by the sixth Duke of Devonshire as " Mr. Handel to Ld Bn.", *i.e.* Lord Burlington, who was, as shown above, one of the main subscribers to the new opera scheme. The letter proves that Handel remained on good terms with him during his stay at Cannons, and it may even indicate that Burlington had again been his host in London from 1718 to 1719. Friedrich August I, Elector of Saxony, since 1697, as August II, King of Poland, kept a great Court at Dresden, and his Italian opera was famous on the Continent. This was apparently the reason why Handel travelled so far east in his search for singers. In September he played the harpsichord before the Elector and his son, later Friedrich August II (August III). (Cf. February 1720.) In August 1719 the Electoral Prince married the Archduchess Maria Josepha in Vienna, and on his return to Dresden the new opera house was opened there. Francesco Bernardi, called Senesino, the famous male soprano, came to London at the end of 1720 and Matteo Berselli, a tenor, a little earlier ; the singer Guizzardi, *recte* Guicciardi (see next entry), never came to England. Handel also engaged in Dresden the soprano, Margherita Durastanti, his first Agrippina (cf. 26th December 1709), whom Rolli in August 1719 called an elephant, and as second soprano, Maddalena Salvai. Senesino's salary was £2000 (later 1400 guineas), Signora Durastanti's £1600 for eighteen months, and Signora Salvai's, it is said, £700 per year.

———

ROLLI TO RIVA (Translated)

Richmond, I don't know which day of August 1719.

. . . Castrucci Senior is very ill with malarial fever. Mylord Burlington has left for Italy. It is said for certain that Durastanti will be coming for the Operas : Oh ! what a bad choice for England ! I shall not enter into her singing merits but she really is an Elephant ! They are still saying that Borosini is the tenor coming and not Guicciardi ! Big old Eiddegher has slept two nights in your bed : he sang Stefani's duets at the Princess's : he won 200 Guineas from Bannister in the evening and lost 240 to the same, in the morning. . . .

Yours

Rolli.

Original in Biblioteca Estense, Modena.   Rolli used to stay at Richmond during the summer months.   Francesco Borosini did not come to London until 1724 ;

Guicciardi never came (cf. 15th July 1719). The duets, in which Heidegger sang, were by Agostino Steffani.

———

FROM THE "LONDON GAZETTE", 6th October 1719

The Lord Chamberlain of His Majesty's household does hereby give Notice, that on Friday the 6th of November, at Ten in the Morning, there will be a General Court of the Patentees of the Royal Academy of Musick, held at the Opera-House in the Hay-Market, to consult about the Affairs of the said Company, at which every Subscriber is desired to take Notice.

(Chrysander, II. 32.) The notice was published repeatedly. Dent (1934, p. 60) thought Handel might have attended this meeting, but, in fact, he did not return until the end of the year.

———

FROM THE "LONDON GAZETTE", 7th November 1719

The Lord Chamberlain of His Majesty's Houshold does hereby give Notice, That on Wednesday the 18th Instant, at Twelve a-Clock, will be held a General Court of the Patentees of the Royal Academy of Musick, at the Opera-House in the Hay-Market, to chuse Directors ; which every Subscriber is desired to take Notice of ; and that Printed Lists of the Subscribers will be delivered at White's Chocolate-House on the 11th Instant.

No copy of the list seems to be preserved. The result of the election is not known, but at least eleven of the new directors are mentioned in the minutes of 27th November 1719.

———

FROM THE "LONDON GAZETTE", 21st November 1719

The Lord Chamberlain of His Majesty's Houshold, Governour of the Royal Academy of Musick, does hereby give Notice, That on Wednesday the 25th Instant, at Eleven a-Clock in the Forenoon, will be held a General Court at the Opera-House in the Hay Market, to chuse a Deputy-Governour, and to consult about the Affairs of the said Company.

It is assumed that the Duke of Manchester was elected then.

———

FIELD-MARSHAL COUNT JACOB HEINRICH FLEMMING TO FRÄULEIN PETRONILLA MELUSINA SCHULENBURG, 25th November (6th December) 1719 (Translated)

Dresden, December 6th, 1719.

. . . I hoped to see Mr. Hendel and intended to speak to him in laudatory terms of you, but there was no opportunity. I made use of your name to persuade him to call on me, but either he was not at his lodgings or else he was ill. It seems to me that he is a little mad ; however he should not behave to me in that way, as I am a musician [too]—that is, by inclination—and flatter myself on being, Mademoiselle, one of your most devoted servants, as you are the most charming of his pupils. I wished to tell you all this so that you in your turn may give your master a hint or two.

(Chrysander, II. 16 f. ; Opel, *Mitteilungen*, etc., 1885, p. 30 ; Rolland, 15th April 1910, p. 796.) Geheimes Staatsarchiv, Dresden. Chrysander wrongly dated this letter as of 6th October 1719. Dent (1934, p. 61) identified Handel's pupil as the subsequent Lady Chesterfield. The Baroness von der Schulenburg, newly created Duchess of Kendal, had two daughters, imported as nieces. The younger one, the King's child, was Petronilla Melusina, born 1693, created Countess of Walsingham in 1722, and married to Philip Dormer Stanhope, fourth Earl of Chesterfield, the statesman and famous letter-writer, in 1733. It is remarkable that Handel enjoyed Royal favours through the husband of one, and the daughter of the other of the King's mistresses. Flemming was general in the army and Prime Minister of Saxony (cf. Cannon, pp. 41 f.).

———

FROM THE MINUTES OF THE ROYAL ACADEMY OF MUSIC

27 Novr 1719

At a Court of the Royal Academy of Musick

Present : Governour, Deputy Governour, Directors : Duke of Montague, Duke of Portland, Lord Bingley, Mr. Bruce, Mr. Mildmay, Mr. Fairfax, Mr. Blathwayte, Mr. [George] Harrison, Mr. Smith, Mr. Whitworth, Doctor Arbuthnot, Mr. Heidegger.

Ordered

That a Letter be writ to Mr Hendell to make an Offer to Durastante of Five hundred pounds Sterling for three months to commence from the first day of March next or Sooner if possible, And that in Case she continues here the remainder of fifteen months, Eleven hundred pounds more, if not, One hundred pounds to bear her expences home.

That Mr Hendell be Ord'red to return to England & bring with him Grunswald the Bass upon the terms he proposes—And that he bring with him the proposalls of all the Singers he has treated with, particularly Cajetano Orsini.

(Public Record Office : L.C. 7/3.) The first season of the new opera was planned to begin on 1st March 1720 : it began, in fact, on 2nd April. It seems that the singers were to be engaged for eighteen months. Handel succeeded in bringing Signora " Durastante " (the corrupted form of Durastanti) to London. Nothing is known of Grunswald and Orsini, but Handel engaged Boschi again as bass, and Berselli as tenor. The meeting of the 27th November seems to have been the second held by the court of directors, the first having been on 6th November 1719. No names are added to the titles of the Governor, the Duke of Newcastle, and his Deputy, the Duke of Manchester. The Duke of Montague

VI. RICHARD LEVERIDGE

Mezzotint after T. Frye, by William Pether, 1727.   Frontispiece to
Leveridge's Collection of Songs, Vol. I.   (Fitzwilliam Museum)

See page 50

Paolo *Rolli*

VII. PAOLO ROLLI

Anonymous engraving, 1736.   Frontispiece to his translation of Milton's
Paradise Lost.   (Fitzwilliam Museum)

See page 93

was a new subscriber. It was John, the second Duke, whom we shall meet again in 1722 and 1749. Weinstock (p. 90) found out that the Colonel Blathwayt, or rather John Blaithwaite, had been a musical child prodigy and a pupil of Alessandro Scarlatti. His portrait is among the pictures of musicians in the Radcliffe Library, Oxford. Heidegger was the manager of the opera, Rolli its Italian secretary and librettist, and Roberto Clerici its decorator and machinist. (For the last-named cf. Eisenschmidt, II. 100 and 107.)

FROM THE MINUTES OF THE ROYAL ACADEMY OF MUSIC

30th November 1719

.   .   .   .   .

Ord'red

. . . That Mr Heidegger be also desir'd to speak to Seign^r Riva to write to Seign^r Senezino to engage him to be here in October next, to Stay till the End of May on the most reasonable terms he can get him, And in his Offer to mencon pounds Sterling & not Guineas, & to make his Offer for two Years in case he finds him more reasonable, proporconable for two Years, than One, And that Security shall be given him by any Merchant he desires.

It is the Opinion of the Board of Directors . . . that Mr Hendell be Ma^r of the Orchestra with a Sallary.

. . . that Seign^r Bona Cini be writ to, to know his Terms for composing & performing in the Orchestra.

(Public Record Office : L.C. 7/3.) Handel apparently did not succeed with Senesino. Riva was a personal friend of the latter, as was Rolli. Senesino arrived in London in the autumn of 1720, and stayed on. Handel's salary from the Royal Academy is not known, but is estimated as not more than £800 a year. Giovanni Bononcini also arrived in London in 1720 [1] ; his first opera to be performed there was *Astarto* on 19th November 1720. At the Court of 30th November 1719 were present, besides the directors mentioned on the 27th, the Earl of Burlington and Sir John Vanbrugh. Lord Percival was suggested as a subscriber ; he joined the Academy, and became one of the directors.

FROM THE MINUTES OF THE COURT OF DIRECTORS OF THE ROYAL ACADEMY OF MUSIC

2 December 1719

. . . That Mr Heidegger be desir'd to propose to Seign^r Portou the composing of an Opera.

. . . That Mr Pope be desir'd to propose a Seal with a Suitable Motto to it, for the Royal Academy of Musick,

And Doctor Arbuthnot be desir'd to acquaint him therewith.

(Public Record Office : L.C. 7/3, No. 15.) Giovanni Porta also came to England in 1720, but from Berlin. He composed the first opera produced by

---

[1] He came from Rome, as indicated in the dedication to the King of his *Cantate e Duetti* in 1721 : " Io sono uno di questi ultimi, che qui mi trovo, chiamato da Roma per servizio della Reale Accademia di Musica ". (Ed.)

H.–4

the Academy : *Numitore*, text by Rolli, performed 2nd April 1720.—Pope apparently did not comply with the directors' proposal forwarded to him by Arbuthnot.

___

FROM THE " LONDON GAZETTE ", 8th December 1719

The Directors of the Royal Academy of Musick, by virtue of a Power given them under the King's Letters Patents, having thought it necessary to make a Call of 5*l.* per Cent from each Subscriber, have authorized the Treasurer to the said Royal Academy, or his Deputy, to receive the same, and to give Receipts from each Sum so paid in ; this is therefore to desire the Subscribers to pay, or cause to be paid, the said fife per Cent according to the several Subscriptions, on the 18th or 19th Instant, at the Opera-House in the Hay-Market ; where Attendance will be given by the Deputy Treasurer from Nine till One in the Forenoon, who will give Receipts for every Sum so paid by each Subscriber as aforesaid.

(Chrysander, II. 32.) The time for the payment was extended. The Treasurer was James Bruce. The Deputy Treasurer was John Kipling (see 19th December 1734). Cf. 5th April 1720 and 27th February 1727.

___

FROM THE " LONDON GAZETTE ", 15th December 1719

The Governour and Court of Directors of the Royal Academy of Musick do hereby give Notice, that there will be a General Court held on Monday the 18th of January next, at Eleven in the Forenoon, at the Opera House in the Hay-Market ; of which every Subscriber to the said Royal Academy is desired to take Notice.

See 12th January 1720.

___

Prior to Handel's return to London, Heidegger, for the Court of Directors, negotiates with some more singers for the new opera company, December 1719.

Public Record Office : L.C. 7/3, No. 15. The singers were : Signor Benedetto Baldassari, called Benedetti (tenor), his wife (engaged ?), Signora Galerati (contralto, cf. 9th January 1714) and Mrs. Robinson (soprano). Ariosti negotiated with a Signora Mantilina, and Riva brought Senesino.

___

Agrippina is performed in the large Imperial ballroom on the Tummelplatz, Vienna, 1719.

This hall corresponds with the Grosse Redoutensaal on the Josefsplatz, and was used for the opera seria. The manuscript score of the performance is in the Nationalbibliothek, Vienna. The performance was formerly dated 1709, but Loewenberg (p. 62) corrected that date. Chrysander (II. 20 f.) suggested that the Vienna opera was the model for the new opera in the Haymarket. It may be mentioned here that, in Vienna in 1725–6, the celebrated Faustina had a salary of 12,500 florins, about £1250, but in London from 1726 onwards £2000.

—

FROM MATTHESON'S " EXEMPLARISCHE ORGANISTEN-PROBE "
(" EXEMPLARY TEST FOR ORGANISTS "), HAMBURG, 1719
(Translated)

. . . Well, what shall I say of F *minor* ? Even the well-known and everyday C *minor* modulates very often to A♭, as its *sixth*. As proof of this a *Cantata* by Msr. *Händel*, which lies just to hand, can serve. It is indeed not printed (incidentally, I do not know of anything by this most famous author, which has been printed or engraved,—and this surprises me) but is in many people's hands, and carries the title : *Lucretia.* The opening words are : O *Numi eterni &c.* and the following *Aria* has, at the very beginning of the second part, this sentence :

[Se il passo move, se il guardo gira.]

In this the whole *Ambitus* is contained in the key of G♯ *major*, or A♭, and anyone who does not know these as one and the same key is also *incapable* of playing these one and a half staves correctly.

(Part II, p. 167.) The book is dedicated to Gottfried von Wedderkop(p), Danish-Norwegian district president at Tremsbüttel, probably the son of Magnus von Wedderkopp, whose daughter Anne married Sir Cyril Wyche. (Cf. 17th August and 7th November 1703, 28th October–3rd November 1720.) The dedication is dated Easter 1719. The soprano cantata *Lucrezia* is one of many written by Handel in Italy. It was published about 1790 in Samuel Arnold's Handel edition, and printed in the Collected Edition, vol. LI, as no. 46 of the cantatas with basso continuo. The quotation corresponds to p. 37, stave 2, bar 5 –stave 3, bar 3. It was the first music by Handel printed in Germany ; as usual in books of that time, it was set in type. Cf. Mattheson's note to Niedt's *Handleitung*, beginning of 1721.

—

Handel's masque *Acis and Galatea*, written for Cannons, is performed there in (?) 1719.

Cf. 23rd August 1720.

1720

The Governour and Court of Directors of the Royal Academy of Musick, have appointed a General Court to be held on Monday the 18th Instant at 11 in the Forenoon, at their Office in the Hay-Market ; at which Time they design to proceed to the Choice of some new Directors ; as also to consult about other special Affairs relating to the Corporation : All Members of the said Corporation are desired to take Notice hereof.

Cf. 15th December 1719 and 30th January 1720. The altered list of directors may have corresponded with Hawkins' list, mentioned in the notes to May 1719 and February 1721.

———

FROM THE " LONDON GAZETTE ", 30th January 1720

The Governour and Court of Directors of the Royal Academy of Musick do hereby give Notice, That a General Court will be held on Wednesday the 3d of February next, pursuant to an Adjourment of the last General Court.

Cf. 12th January 1720.

———

FROM AN ACCOUNT OF THE COURT OF AUGUST II, KING OF POLAND, February 1720 (Translated)

(Hundred Ducats paid out to) Händel, Capellmeister to the King of England, who dutifully performed before His Majesty and His Royal Highness the Prince.

(Fürstenau, 1860 ; 1861–2, II. 152.) Cf. 15th July 1719. It seems that the payment for Handel's performance at the Dresden Court was arranged through the Saxon Resident in London ; hence the delay.

———

FROM " THE THEATRE ", 1st March 1720

Yesterday South Sea was 174. Opera Company 83, and a half. No Transfer.

(Chrysander, II. 30.) The Theatre had been edited by Sir Richard Steele since 2nd January 1720. This, like the two following notes in the same paper, were, of course, ironical remarks, comparing the " Academy of Music " with the doubtful South Sea Company, and their precarious shares with the dangerous ones of the latter.

———

FROM "THE THEATRE", 8th March 1720

At the Rehearsal on *Friday* last, Signior NIHILINI BENEDITTI rose half a Note above his Pitch formerly known. Opera Stock from 83 and a half, when he began ; at 90 when he ended.

(Chrysander, II. 30.) Cf. 1st March. The fictitious name of the singer combines those of Nicolini and Benedetto. The latter gave a concert on 11th March.

FROM "THE THEATRE", 12th March 1720

To Sir JOHN EDGAR, *Auditor-General of the World, and the Stage.*

Sir,

Your last Paper very rightly, and with great Justice, notify'd to the Town the Rise of the Opera-Stock, occasion'd by the Elevation of half a Note above the usual Pitch of Signior *Beneditti.* I hope, Sir, you will allow no one hereafter to call him no Man, when you shall have heard from me, how much he is a Man of Honour. It happen'd, Sir, in the casting the Parts for the new Opera, that he had been, as he conceiv'd greatly injur'd ; and, the other Day apply'd to the Board of Directors, of which I am an unworthy Member, for Redress. He set forth, in the recitative Tone, the nearest approaching ordinary Speech, that he had never acted any thing, in any other Opera, below the Character of a Sovereign ; or, at least, a Prince of the Blood ; and that now he was appointed to be a Captain of the Guard, and a Pimp . . . he found Friends, and was made a Prince. . . .

Hay-Market, March 9,   Musidorus.
    1719–20.

(Chrysander, II. 30.) Cf. 8th March. It seems that the remark about the exchange of parts for Benedetto Baldassari did not refer to Porta's opera *Numitore*, the first to be produced by the new opera company, but to Handel's *Radamisto*, the second new opera of the first season. The part of Tigrane was originally given to the tenor, who finally sang that of Fraarte.—The author of the letter may have been Dr. Arbuthnot.

FROM APPLEBEE'S "ORIGINAL WEEKLY JOURNAL", 12th March 1720

On Tuesday Night [the 8th] his Majesty went to the Opera in the Hay-Market, to see the Company of Comedians, lately arriv'd from France, performing their Tumbling, etc.

    .   .   .   .   .

A Legion of Italian Songsters, Comedians, &c. are coming hither from Italy, to perform at the Theatre's.

(Kelly, II. 348 f. ; Chrysander, II. 33.) The French comedians played at the Haymarket Theatre for nine nights, till 29th March ; after the opening of the opera season, they played on 26th April and from 29th April till 17th June, when each company had two nights every week. The Italians did not come to the Opera House.

The Academy of Music opens the new Opera with the production
of Giovanni Porta's *Numitore*, text by Rolli, 2nd April 1720.

Rolli's libretto contains, in the dedication, the new list of Governors
and twenty Directors : the Dukes of Newcastle (Governor), Manchester
(Deputy Governor), Grafton, Montague, Kent, Portland ; the Earls of
Burlington and Halifax, the Lords Bingley and Percival, Dr. Arbuthnot,
Colonel John Blaithwaite, James Bruce, Thomas Coke of Norfolk, Bryan
Fairfax, George Harrison, John Jacob Heidegger, Benjamin Mildmay,
William Pultney, Thomas Smith, Sir John Vanbrugh, and Francis
Whitworth.

———

FROM THE " LONDON GAZETTE ", 5th April 1720

The Directors of the Royal Academy of Musick, by Virtue of a Power
given them under the King's Letters Patents, finding it necessary to make
a further Call of 5*l.* per Cent from each Subscriber, have authorized the
Treasurer to the said Royal Academy or his Deputy, to receive the same,
and to give Receipts from each Sum paid in ; This is therefore to desire
the Subscribers to pay, or cause the said 5*l.* per Cent to be paid according
to the several Subscriptions on the 25th or 26th Instant, at the Opera-
House in the Hay-Market ; where Attendance will be given by the
Deputy Treasurer from Nine in the Morning till Two, who will give
Receipts for every Sum so paid by each Subscriber as aforesaid.

Cf. 8th December 1719.

———

FROM THE DIARY OF THE REV. WILLIAM STUKELEY, M.D.

Apr. 18 [1720]. At the Lincolnsh[r]. Feast, Ship Tavern, Temple barr.
pres[t.] Sir Is. Newton. Upon my mentioning to him the rehearsal of the
Opera to night (Rhadamisto) he said he never was at more than one
Opera. The first Act he heard with pleasure, the 2[d] stretch'd his patience,
at the 3[d] he ran away.

(Young, p. 37.) Stukeley, 1882, I. 59 ; quoted slightly differently in Stukeley,
1936, p. 14. The first rehearsal of the opera seems to have been held the day
before. Sir Isaac Newton, who did not attend the rehearsal with Stukeley, as
Young assumed, is said, on another occasion, to have remarked about Handel's
harpsichord playing that he found " nothing worthy to remark but the elasticity
of his fingers ". (The source, given by Young for this story, is incorrect ; the
right one could not be found.)

———

FROM THE " LONDON GAZETTE ", 26th April 1720

The Governour and Court of Directors of the Royal Academy of
Musick do hereby give Notice, that a General Court will be held on
Friday the 6th of May next, at Eleven of the Clock in the Forenoon,
whereof each Subscriber is desired to take Notice.

No minutes of the Court of Directors seem to be preserved after 1719.

———

Handel's new opera *Radamisto* is advertised in the *Daily Courant* of 25th April 1720 for the next day. On 26th April, without special cancellation, the first night is advertised for the 27th, while " At the particular desire of several Ladies of Quality " the French company plays on the 26th.

—

FROM THE " DAILY COURANT ", 27th April 1720

At the King's Theatre in the Hay Market, this present Wednesday . . . will be perform'd a New Opera call'd RADAMISTUS. . . . N.B. When the Tickets are dispos'd of, no Person will be admitted for Money. To begin at Half an Hour after Six.

The prices were half a guinea and five shillings.

—

HANDEL'S DEDICATION OF THE LIBRETTO OF " IL RADAMISTO ", [27th April] 1720

To the
KING'S
Most Excellent Majesty.

Sir,
The Protection which Your Majesty has been graciously pleased to allow both to the Art of *Musick* in general, and to one of the lowest, tho' not the least Dutiful of your Majesty's Servants, has embolden'd me to present to Your Majesty, with all due Humility and Respect, this my first Essay to that Design. I have been still the more encouraged to this, by the particular Approbation Your Majesty has been pleased to give to the Musick of this *Drama* : Which, may I be permitted to say, I value not so much as it is the Judgment of a Great Monarch, as of One of a most Refined Taste in the Art : My Endeavours to improve which, is the only Merit that can be pretended by me, except that of being with the utmost Humility.
SIR,
Your Majesty's
Most Devoted,
Most Obedient,
And most Faithful
Subject and Servant,
GEORGE-FREDERIC HANDEL.

(Chrysander, II. 46.) There are two issues of the libretto, both with the dedication, but distinguished by the different casts, the second belonging to the revival of 28th December 1720. It was unusual for a libretto to be dedicated by the composer, but Handel's dedication refers to the whole work. The text was by Haym. The " Argument " gives his source as the *Annals* of Tacitus, Book XII, chap. 51. It is, however, said to be based on Domenico Lalli's *L'amor tirannico o Zenobia* (first set by Francesco Gasparini in 1710). The libretto is printed, as usual, in Italian and English. The King's "Protection to the Art of Musick" was, of course, his patronage of the Royal Academy ; Handel's first contribution to the new scheme was the music of *Radamisto*, which earned him the King's "particular Approbation" and the grant of a copyright privilege, dated 14th June 1720. In signing himself the King's "subject", Handel anticipated an event of seven years later (see 20th February 1727). The text of the dedication may have been composed for Handel by Haym.

———

Cast of "Radamisto", 27th April 1720

Radamisto—Signora Margherita Durastini, called Durastanti, soprano
Zenobia—Mrs. Anastasia Robinson, contralto
Farasmane—Signor Lagarde, bass
Tiridate—Mr. Gordon, tenor
Polissena—Mrs. Ann Turner Robinson, soprano
Tigrane—Signora Catterina Galerati, soprano
Fraarte—Signor Benedetto Baldassari, tenor

In the revival of 28th December 1720, as will be seen, Durastanti took the part of Zenobia, and Galerati that of Fraarte. Mrs. Turner Robinson was married to John Robinson, organist and composer ; their daughter, a contralto, sang later in Handel oratorios, as Miss Robinson, as did also a Miss Turner, daughter of Dr. William Turner. Galerati, the Goffredo in *Rinaldo* of 1714, now returned to the Haymarket for two years. Baldassari had been in London before ; just arrived, he sang Darius in *L'Idaspe fidele* on 25th March 1712 (cf. advertisement in the *Spectator*). Pietro Castrucci is said to have played a violin solo in *Radamisto* (Burney). The opera was performed again on 30th April ; 4th, 7th, 11th, 14th, 18th, 21st May ; 8th and 22nd June ; the season closing on 25th June 1720.

———

From the Diary of Mary, Countess Cowper

Wednesday, April 27, 1720.
At Night, *Radamistus*, a fine opera of Handel's Making. The *King* there with his Ladies. The *Prince* in the Stage-box. Great Crowd.

Countess Cowper was Lady of the Bedchamber to the Princess of Wales. The King's ladies were apparently the Duchess of Kendal and her daughter, Fräulein Petronilla Melusina von Schulenburg, Handel's pupil. The crowd at the first night is described by Mainwaring (see next entry).

———

At this time Buononcini *and* Attilio *composed for the Opera, and had a strong party in their favour. Great reason they saw to be jealous of such a rival as Handel, and all the interest they had was employed to decry his Music, and hinder him from coming to the Haymarket : but these attempts were defeated by the powerful association above-mentioned, at whose desire he had just been to Dresden for Singers.*

In the year 1720, he obtained leave to perform his Opera of Radamisto. *If persons . . . who were present at that performance may be credited, the applause it received was almost as extravagant as his* Agrippina *had excited : the crowds and tumults of the house at Venice were hardly equal to those at* London. *In so splendid and fashionable an assembly of ladies (to the excellence of their taste we must impute it) there was no shadow of form, or ceremony, scarce indeed any appearance of order or regularity, politeness or decency. Many, who had forc'd their way into the house with an impetuosity but ill suited to their rank and sex, actually fainted through the excessive heat and closeness of it. Several gentlemen were turned back, who had offered forty shillings for a seat in the gallery, after having despaired of getting any in the pit or boxes.* (Mainwaring, pp. 98 f.)

—

Domenico Scarlatti's opera *Narciso* is produced at the Haymarket Theatre, 29th April 1720.

The original title of Scarlatti's opera, as produced in Rome in 1714, was *Amor d'un'ombra e gelosia d'un'aura.* (Frank Walker in *The Music Review*, August 1951, p. 194.) Apostolo Zeno's text was altered by Rolli, and four additional airs by Thomas Roseingrave were inserted. It is said that Scarlatti was in London at the time, but Burney (IV. 266) asserts that Roseingrave brought the score from Italy. Scarlatti's uncle, Francesco, came to London in 1719, and this may explain the mistake.

—

From the " Daily Courant ", 13th May 1720

. . . To-morrow . . . RADAMISTUS. Boxes 8s. Pit 5s. Gallery 2s. 6d. Boxes on the Stage Half a Guinea. NB. The Communication from the Stage to the Side Boxes on Market-Lane Side being taken off, the Admittance to them will be through the Passage that leads to the Pit on the Left Hand. To be admitted on the Stage One Guinea.

This was one of the Saturday performances. The prices were raised. Such admittance to the stage was extraordinary at the Haymarket Theatre.

—

The first Privilege of Copyright granted to Handel, 14th June 1720

George R.

George, by the Grace of GOD, king of *Great Britain*, *France* and *Ireland*, Defender of the Faith, &c. To all to whom these Presents shall come, Greeting : Whereas *George Frederick Handel*, of our City of *London*, Gent. hath humbly represented unto Us, That he hath with great Labour and Expence composed several Works, consisting of *Vocal* and *Instrumental* Musick, in order to be Printed and Published ; and hath therefore besought Us to grant him Our Royal Privilege and Licence for the sole Printing and Publishing thereof for the Term of Fourteen Years : We being willing to give all due Encouragement to Works of this Nature, are graciously pleased to condescend to his Request ; And we do therefore by these Presents, so far as may be agreeable to the Statute in that behalf made and provided, grant unto him the said *George Frederick Handel*, his Executors, Administrators and Assigns, Our Licence for the sole Printing and Publishing the said Works for the Term of Fourteen Years, to be

H.-4 *a*

computed from the Date hereof, strictly forbidding all our loving Subjects within our Kingdoms and Dominions, to Reprint or Abridge the same, either in the like, or any other Volume or Volumes whatsoever, or to Import, Buy, Vend, Utter or Distribute any Copies thereof Reprinted beyond the Seas, during the aforesaid Term of Fourteen Years, without the Consent or Approbation of the said *George Frederick Handel*, his Heirs, Executors and Assigns, under their Hands and Seals first had and obtain'd, as they will answer the contrary at their Perils : Whereof the Commissioners and other Officers of Our Customs, the Master, Wardens, and Company of Stationers, are to take Notice, that due Obedience may be rendred to our Pleasure herein declared. *Given at Our Court at* St. James's the 14*th Day of* June, 1720. *in the Sixth Year of Our Reign.*

> *By His Majesty's Command,*
> J. CRAGGS.

This privilege was printed and used for the first time for *Radamisto* in 1720 (published by Richard Meares), then for *Floridante* in 1722, *Ottone* and *Flavio* in 1723 (all published by Walsh), and for *Giulio Cesare* and *Tamerlano* in 1724 (John Cluer). It was not quoted, however, in the original edition of Handel's *Suites de Pièces de Clavecin* which appeared on 14th November 1720 (Smith and Meares). The privilege to print music had been granted to some English composers since the time of Queen Elizabeth, usually for twenty-one years, and licences were assigned by such composers to music publishers ; these privileges, however, came to an end under Charles I (1636). Since the time of Queen Anne it had become usual to grant, to composers or their publishers (cf. 31st October 1739), a privilege of publication, in the French manner, for fourteen years, which might be prolonged ; this was the Copyright Act of 1709. The prohibition of reprints was not always observed and the fact that Walsh was the most successful of the London music pirates seems to have been the reason why Handel finally went over to Walsh's camp for good.—James Craggs, the young Secretary of State, a friend of George I and Pope, was one of the first subscribers to the Royal Academy. Pope wrote his epitaph when he died in 1721, shortly before his father, one of the culprits of the South Sea Bubble.

―――

The first season of the Royal Academy of Music ends, 25th June 1720.

―――

FROM THE " POST-BOY ", 12th July 1720

This is to give Notice to all Gentlemen and Ladies, Lovers of Musick, that the most celebrated new Opera of Radamistus, compos'd by Mr. Handell, is now Engraving finely upon Copper Plates by Richard Meares, Musical Instrument-Maker and Musick-Printer. . . . NB. To make this Work the more acceptable, the Author has been prevailed with to correct the whole.

This notice, following soon after the granting of the privilege (14th June), may have been intended to deter other London music publishers from printing unauthorized editions of songs from *Radamisto*. Corrections by composers were not usual. It had recently become common practice to print music from stamped pewter plates, and therefore the printing from engraved copper plates was a point of recommendation for new music. Meares was opposed to the practices of Walsh and Hare. His book was not published until 30th December 1720.

FROM WILLERS' HAMBURG NOTES, 18th (29th) August 1720

Aug. 29. Rinaldo. 60 Rthl.

(Merbach, p. 356.) The sum of sixty Rheinthaler indicates the takings for the night ; the entries in Willers' diary are given in this form for the next six months. The opera was performed repeatedly in 1720 and 1721, but it was not Handel's. Handel's *Rinaldo* was produced in Hamburg in November 1715 and not revived until 16th May 1723.

EXTRACTS FROM MR. NOLAND'S CATALOGUE OF THE DUKE OF CHANDOS' MUSIC COLLECTION, SIGNED BY PEPUSCH, 23rd August 1720

(The figures in round brackets refer to volumes and pages of the *Collected Edition of Handel's Works*.)

[19 *Anthems in Score :*]

1. Handel   *Te Deum*, in score for 5 voices and 4 instruments [B flat] (XXXVII. 25)
2. ,,   ' O come let us sing unto the Lord ', for 5 voices and 4 instruments (XXXV. 41)
3. ,.   ' O praise the Lord with one consent ', for 5 voices and 4 instruments (XXXV. 98)
4. ,,   ' The Lord is my light ', for 5 voices and 4 instruments (XXXV. 151)
5. ,,   ' In the Lord put I my trust ', for 3 voices and 4 instruments (XXXIV. 37)
6. ,,   ' I will magnify thee O God my king ', for 5 voices and 4 instruments (XXXIV. 133)
7. ,,   ' As pants the hart '(XXXIV. 207) and
8. ,,   ' O sing unto the Lord ' (XXXIV. 109), both for 3 voices and 4 instruments
9. ,,   ' My song shall be alway ' (XXXV. 1) and
10. ,,   ' Let God arise '(XXXV. 211), both for 4 voices and 5 instruments
11. ,,   ' Have mercy on me O God ' (XXXIV. 79) and
12. ,,   ' Be joyful ' (XXXI. 46) [the *Utrecht Jubilate*, reduced from 4 voices], both for 3 voices and 5 instruments

.   .   .   .   .

Handel		*A score book with the following anthems :*
[19 a.]		' In thee O Lord I put my trust ' (XXXIV. 37)
	,,	' I will magnify thee ' (XXXIV. 133)

A book in score of 18 cantatas in Italian :

36.   ,,   ' Sento la che ristretto ', canto, p. 13 (LI. 56 or 57)

63.   [,,]   The songs in the opera *Rinaldo* with the symphonies
              [Walsh's 1711 edition]

73.   ,,   ' O the pleasure of the plain ', a masque for 5 voices and
              instruments in score [*Acis and Galatea*]

87.   ,,   *Amadis*, an opera, in score [1715, MS.]

[In Parts :]

104. ,,   A piece of music composed for Queen Anne's birthday,
              consisting of 1 treble, 1 contralto, 1 tenor, 1 bass, with
              instruments [1713]

117. ,,   Sonata for 2 violins, 1 hautboy, 1 bass (?)

121. ,,   *Te Deum* for 1 canto, 1 alto, 1 tenor, 1 bass ; 2 trumpets,
              2 hautboys, 2 violins, 1 tenor, 1 basso continuo [*Utrecht
              Te Deum*] (XXXI. 2)

122. ,,   *Jubilate*, for 1 canto, 1 alto, 1 tenor, 1 bass ; 2 trumpets,
              2 violins, 1 tenor, 1 bass (XXXI. 46)

All these [127] pieces of music I have in my care
            August 23   1720   J. C. Pepusch

(Baker, pp. 134-9.) Huntington Library, San Marino : Stow MS. no. 66.
James Brydges, since 1714 Earl of Carnarvon in succession to his father, had been
created Duke of Chandos on 29th April 1719. 1720 he called his " catastrophic
year " (Baker, p. 81) : it seems that even he suffered under the consequences of
the South Sea scandal. These events, however, may not have been the reason
why he asked for an inventory of his music and instruments in Cannons, and
probably in his town house too. Pepusch, still the Master of his Music, had the
music catalogued by one Mr. Noland, but checked the list himself before it was
forwarded to the Duke. There were two anthems by Pepusch himself in the
" score book ". The Handel items, extracted here from the modernized version
given by Baker, indicate which of his works were, or were intended to be,
performed at Cannons during and after his stay there, though they include some
works, like *Rinaldo* and *Amadis*, which were bought, or otherwise acquired, for
the library only. Besides the *Utrecht Te Deum and Jubilate* of 1713, there is, of
course, the *Chandos Te Deum* ; and besides the *Ode for Queen Anne's Birthday* in
1713, there are one of Handel's Italian cantatas, composed in Hanover about

1712, an unidentified trio sonata, and one of the two dramatic works supposed to have been written for Cannons : the masque of *Acis and Galatea* (text by John Gay, based on Ovid's *Metamorphoses*), but not *Haman and Mordecai*, later altered into the oratorio of *Esther*. The dates on which these two works were produced have not yet been established for certain. While the former might have been produced in 1719, the latter is supposed to have been performed on 29th August 1720 on the occasion of the opening of the chapel in Cannons, six days after Pepusch signed the list quoted above. The text of *Haman and Mordecai*, based on Racine, was written by an unidentified author, probably, like Gay, assisted by Pope.—The main section of the Handel items in Chandos's music collection, however, is occupied by the so-called Chandos Anthems (cf. 25th September 1717). Of the twelve anthems, no. 10, " O praise the Lord ye Angels of his ", is missing : it may have been of a later date (cf. 11th January 1724), or it may be spurious. The number of voices for which the anthems were written is not always given correctly in the catalogue : nos. 2 and 3 are, in fact, for four voices and no. 6 for three.—When Chandos's library was sold by auction in 1747 (12th March till April, 4000 numbers, thirty nights) no music was included. One volume, however, with the Handel items nos. 1 and 5 to 12 of Noland's list, later came into the possession of Cummings, and was sold by Sotheby on 21st May 1917 (no. 816), and then offered by Quaritch in October 1919 (no. 355) ; see Cummings, 1915, pp. 11 f., and Smith, 1948, pp. 199 f. The description of Cummings's score does not quite conform with that of Noland, but the differences are again in the numbers of voices employed.

PEPUSCH'S CATALOGUE OF THE MUSIC INSTRUMENTS BELONGING TO THE DUKE OF CHANDOS, 23rd August 1720

1. A chamber organ, 3 rows of keys, 18 stops — made by Jordan

2. A four-square harpsichord 3 rows of keys at one end, a spinet on the side; painted on the lid, Minerva and the nine Muses, by A. Tilens, 1625 — made by J. Ruckers, Antwerp

3. Harpsichord : 2 rows of keys — made by Hermanus Table, London

4. Spinet — made by Thomas Hitchcock
5. Double Bass, with case — made by Mr. Barrett
6. Violoncello or bass violin — made by Mr. Mears
7. Tenor violin — made by Mr. Mears
8. Violin ; and case : an inscription— ' In Absam proper Oeni Pontium 1660 ' — made by Jacobus Stainer

9. Violin similar inscription, date 1676 — made by Jacobus Stainer
10. Violin similar inscription, date 1665 — made by Jacobus Stainer
11. Violin similar inscription, date 1678 — made by Jacobus Stainer

besides these mention, 2 more made in London.
The following are in Albemarle Street

12. **Bass viol** — made by Henry Jay, Southwark, 1613

13. Harpsichord, 2 rows of keys
14. Spinet
15. Harpsichord with gut strings. This   made by Mr. Longfellow,
    stands at my house in Boswell   of Pembroke Hall, Cam-
    Court.   bridge

    The 2 following were found at Cannons since I made my first
    catalogue
16. Bass viol   made by Barrack Norman,
                                         1702
17. A basson   made by H. Wietzfell
18. 2 French hunting horns   made by Johann Licham
                                         Schneider, Vienna 1711
    Trumpet   made by John Harry, London
          All these instruments are under my care
              Aug. 23, 1720.   J. C. Pepusch.

(Baker, pp. 139 f.) Huntington Library, San Marino : Stow MS., no. 66. Signed on the same day as Noland's music catalogue. The present list certainly refers to objects in Cannons as well as in the Duke's town residence, since 1710 in Albemarle Street. The note added to no. 15, probably by the Duke himself, refers to the " Lake property " in Boswell Court ; Mary Lake was the maiden name of the Duke's first wife. Following her death in 1712, he married Cassandra Willoughby in 1713 ; Cassandra died in 1735, and in 1736 he married Lydia Lady Davall. Two of his wives are grouped below him on his tombstone in St. Lawrence, Whitchurch.

The following notes refer to the numbers in the list of instruments. (1) Abraham Jordan, senior (and junior ?), built, in 1720, the organ for the chapel at Cannons, supposed to have been played on by Handel ; it was sold by auction in 1747, after which it was repaired and taken to Trinity Church, Gosport, Hants (Victor de Pontigny, in Grove's *Dictionary*), where it still stands. The chamber organ, mentioned in the list, probably stood in the music room, on the ground floor next to the dining-room, at Cannons. (2) Lord Wilton, later James, 3rd Duke of Chandos, in his manuscript description of Cannons (about 1745), calls this instrument " a very curious peace of musick a harpsicord and virginall both in one ". It was probably made by Joannes Ruckers, junior ; the painting probably by Justus Tilens, a Fleming. (3) Hermanus Tabel transferred Ruckers' school to England (A. J. Hipkins, in Grove). (4) Hitchcock used to number his instruments, instead of dating them. (5) Thomas Barrett tried his hand at free imitations of Stradivarius (E. J. Payne, in Grove). (6) and (7) Richard Mears, as he used to spell his name in contrast to that of his father, Richard Meares, was also a music publisher (see 12th July and 2nd November 1720). (8) to (11) The famous Stainer (d. 1683) worked in Absam, near Innsbruck, the capital of the Austrian Tyrol. (12) Jay was one of the popular London viol makers. (13) This might have been the harpsichord bought by Chandos in June 1720 for £572 from Johann Christoph Bach (Baker, p. 131), probably the one who is supposed to have died in London in 1740, a cousin of Johann Sebastian's first wife and a music teacher in England. (15) Nothing is known of Mr. Longfellow. (16) Barak Norman lived from 1688 till 1740. (17) Hermann Wietfelt came from Burgdorf in Silesia. (18) Johannes Leichamschneider belonged to a Viennese family of instrument makers. (Some of this information was kindly supplied by Mr. Adam Carse, and by Dr. Victor Luithlen, Vienna.)

It is, perhaps, fitting to add here some details about the music personnel at Cannons, as known to Handel since 1717 and in service up to 1720 and later. The " Concert " consisted of about thirty singers and players. Baker (pp. 132 f.) gives an alphabetical list, collected from various documents. There were three treble voices, one alto, one tenor, two counter-tenors, and one bass. The names were : Thomas Bell and Thomas Gethin (Getting), counter-tenors, Morphew—alto, Peirson—treble voice, William Perry—(?) bass, Rigg(s)—treble, Amos Rogers— tenor, and the Duchess's page, Solway (Salway ?)—treble, George Vanbrugh(e)— bass (?) and song composer. Among the players were : Alexander Bitti—first violin, Pietro Chabout—flute and oboe, composer for these instruments ; Giraldo —second violin, Nicolino Hayme (Nicola Francesco Haym, or his son)—violon- cello, Jean Christian Kytch—oboe, George Monroe—harpsichord and organ, Thomas Rawling—second violin, Scarpettini—first violin, and John Tetlow— (first ?) violin, and valet. Francesco Scarlatti, Alexander's brother, who arrived in London (with his nephew Domenico ?), was recommended as violinist to the Duke by Dr. Arbuthnot, but apparently he never entered service at Cannons. Pepusch, Master of the Music until 1732, drew a salary of £100 a year (first mentioned at Michaelmas 1719). Nothing is known about Handel's fees. That he received £1000 for the masque of *Haman and Mordecai* was first related by Miss E. I. Spence in *How to be rid of a Wife* (1823) ; it is not plausible. Neither John Beard, nor Richard Elford, Francis Hughes, Bernard Gates or Samuel Weeley were among the singers at Cannons (cf. Chrysander, I. 460).

———

Rolli to Riva (Translated)

London, 29th August 1720.

. . . Portolongone fishes in deep waters and in order to scare the Music- lover (" Filarmonico "), I sent him a warning to keep his mouth shut under pain of the ban. No answer came ; no wonder ! Consider the size of the pill. Do not breathe a word, because it is a secret. Golden- square, who is truly golden, refuses any longer to wear the Operatic buskin just like the Venetian Minerva.

The honourable Earl of Burlington is in York and the good Bruce and Mr. Kent are with him.

Cuzzona has been engaged for this year ; as for next year she refuses to come for less money than at Siena. Mrs. Margherita is pregnant and the Directors [of the Academy] are very much annoyed about it. Some of them have complained with me of it, especially now that she was expected to be the leading lady in the Opera. Honest Avelloni is dis- tressed about it, and she flew into a rage, and you will see the result : she will return to Italy, regardless of her salary here of a thousand pounds and more per year. The half of this if saved means a lot of money in Italy, especially for someone like her who germinates yearly. . . .

No news yet from Bononcini. I had rather he came through Germany, since the Marseilles epidemic is said to be spreading. But I should not like it to end by putting us in quarantine, although it is damned silly to worry about an evil for which there is no remedy. "Go on there", Balaam kept saying to his ass. . . .

Original in Biblioteca Modense, Bologna. Margherita Durastanti was married to Casimiro Avelloni.

———

FROM THE " WEEKLY JOURNAL, OR BRITISH GAZETTEER ", 3rd September 1720

His Grace the Duke Chandois's Domestick Chappel at his Seat at Cannons near Edgworth, is Curiously adorned with Painting on the Windows and Ceiling, had divine Worship perform'd in it with an Anthem on Monday last [29 August], it being the first time of its being opened.

(Clark, p. 11.) There seems to be no doubt that this notice refers to the new chapel in Cannons itself. The anthem mentioned was, most probably, one or Handel's Chandos Anthems. In a letter written by Cassandra, Duchess of Chandos to Lady Buck in 1720 she enclosed two tickets for a " Masquerade ", " hoping that the entertainment would be as fine " as expected. Miss Winifred Myers, who found this letter in Cassandra's copy-books, preserved in the North London Collegiate School at Cannons, believes that the " Masquerade " was Handel's masque, *Haman and Mordecai*, later altered to the oratorio *Esther* ; she also believes that the opening celebrated on that day was the reopening of St. Lawrence, Whitchurch, near Cannons.

———

ROLLI TO RIVA (Translated)

London, 23rd September 1720.

On Monday last Senesino arrived in company with Berselli and Salvai. I heard the news while dining in Richmond on Tuesday and at once came up to town with our dear Casimiro. I am delighted to find this famous artist a man well-mannered, well-read, extremely kind and endowed with the noblest sentiments. Dear Riva, if it is ever true that one recognises a fine day from a fine morning, believe me it is the great exception to the rule. He and Salvai are not on good terms with each other. About her I have nothing to tell you, because I have seen her only once ; but of him I can say that you will find out at the first glance that the man is a noisy busybody and certainly not the soul of discretion.

I have found lodgings for Senesino and Berselli in Leicester Street near Leicester Fields [?], where they pay a yearly rent of 120 pounds for the whole house, because my invincible dislike for landladies causes them to dart off at the first condition of a contract. They are three groups to pay the rent : one half of it is paid by Senesino and his brother, the other half by Berselli and a certain Abbé, whose name I don't remember. . . .

The Alpine Proteus [Handel] has spoken of me in terms of great esteem to Casimiro, who has proved clearly to him on several occasions that I deserve some consideration. Dear Riva, I submit myself to all shows of humility towards him within the limits of decorum, and we shall see whether that bristly nature of his will soften. Yesterday I was called by the Board of the Royal Academy and commissioned to examine and shorten *Il Dramma dell' Amore e Maestà* (The Drama of Love and Majesty). I should make no progress without our Senesino and both of us would be at a loss without Heydeger : now you see if we can do more ! How I rejoice that Senesino has such a clever mind and understands the Cabal to perfection ! We are expecting you to come and make up the Triumvirate.

My dear Riva, what ruination has the Southsea crash caused ! The whole nobility is at its last gasp ; only gloomy faces are to be seen. Great bankers are going bankrupt, great shareholders just disappear and there is not an acquaintance or friend who has escaped total ruin. These rogues of Company Directors have betrayed everybody and I assure you the tragic worst is feared. You will have to return soon with the dearly beloved King George and you will witness it all for yourself. Our good Casimiro has only you for security and without your consent the stock of 1000 pounds cannot be transferred.

(Streatfeild, 1917, pp. 434 f.) Original in Biblioteca Estense, Modena. Cf. 30th November 1719. Francesco Bernardi, called Senesino, born in Siena about 1680, was a male soprano. He became an important figure in Handel's operas. Matteo Berselli was the new tenor, Signora Maddalena Salvai the second soprano of the company. Casimir was Signor Avelloni, Durastanti's husband. " Il Proteus alpino " was another nickname bestowed by Rolli on Handel. *Amore e Maestà* was a libretto by Antonio Salvi, set to music in 1715 for Florence by Giuseppe Maria Orlandini, and now arranged by Rolli and, with additional music by Filippo Mattei, performed at the Haymarket on 1st February 1721.—The South Sea Company, founded in 1711 to raise the credit of the State and to discharge its debts, purported to aim at monopolizing the trade with the Spanish Americas. In summer 1720 the " Bubble " collapsed and many people of " quality ", but still more ordinary people, came to grief. It is assumed that Handel also lost money in the crash. Cf. 13th March and 29th June 1716. For Handel's " South-Sea Annuities, 1751 ", bought from 4th June 1728 onwards, see that date and the balance of the dealing on 22nd June 1732.

—

ROLLI TO RIVA (Translated)

London, 29th September 1720.

We did not come to any final decision about the house which I spoke of in my last letter. Avelloni offered 110 pounds but the landlord refused to let it at less than 120 pounds. Perhaps if I had not said it was too dear, the bargain would have been struck. . . .

The stocks today have begun to rise. After their headlong fall, our subscription could not fetch 30% cash value. I hope there will soon be a tendency to rise and by God I intend to take advantage of it.

I am waiting anxiously for Senesino, whom I shall try to ingratiate with every art known to me and I shall explain everything to him in all honesty.

No other news from Bononcini, since I heard that he had received the money sent to him and had obtained credit of a hundred pistoles [at 18/- each] in Leghorn from a correspondent of Mr. Como's.

Original in Biblioteca Estense, Modena.

—

ROLLI TO RIVA (Translated)

London, 18th October 1720.

You must know that Madame Salvai has brought Polani with her from Holland ; you must know further that the name of Sanda [Sandoni ?] may not even be mentioned in the Board of Directors, because Amicone is there declared to be his host, at the suggestion, I suppose, of the Beneficiaries whom we shall soon see strut about, high-crested and puffed-up. I must tell you that Margherita, in conjunction with our Senesino, proposed the opera of " Amore e Maestà ". Which opera cannot be performed as at Florence, because it would then have so much endless recitative and so few arias, that Senesino would have only four in all. I was therefore instructed to polish it up and in accord with them both I removed and added and changed as was necessary. The Alpine Faun [Handel], according to the ancient system which he always proposes, in order to show that what has been done is the same as it was before, proposed Polani to rearrange and direct the opera. Our Senesino, naturally enough, was furious : the opera had been proposed by him, new music was necessary for the additional part and for that he wanted it to be varied ; he was opposed to making a pastiche of old arias and wanted to have a man at the harpsichord ; at his first outburst he [Handel] called him a damned Fool ; these were all motives for his resentment. The Faun obliged me to tell him not to oppose him and I was bearer of the Faun's embassy. But I could not restrain him [Senesino] and I advised him to go himself to speak to him [Handel] with gentle firmness and say to him that he wished to show all due deference to his advice, but that as regarded his personal estimation he begged him to take into consideration all the above-mentioned arguments ; that he entertained no personal animosity against anyone except Polani, but that he would have sung under him in any other opera which the esteemed Directors themselves might wish to choose ; not, however, in an opera which he himself had proposed and for the success of which the Board of Directors had made him responsible ; in short that it not being possible to perform this opera as it then was, there was no occasion for performing it in such a manner ; that he did not propose anyone else, while the Academy had at its disposal excellent musicians. The Man [Handel] was taken aback and asked him if this was a trick of mine . . . [unreadable word], but he obtained a non-committal reply and was informed that I had already given a copy of the opera to Polani and had only explained to him the Board's opinions so as to guide Polani, adding furthermore that he had not come to direct operas but to be a musician. Believe me, he [Senesino] spoke with remarkable eloquence, if he worded the reply as he repeated it to me. Rest assured also that the very first opera would fail utterly if directed by that stupid man—and all to the delight of the Savage [Handel]. Tomorrow Senesino must go before the Board of Directors ; he is this evening at Richmond at the repeated request of the royal Prince [of Wales] who is quite carried away by him, and I think that Margherita will go with him, if Casimiro is not so ill, as I am told he has been in the last days. Those Directors, who have already come to know of the facts, such as Arbuthnot and the most estimable Blaithwaite, have declared that they will be at the Board tomorrow of set purpose to do all that Signor Senesino shall desire because he is in the right ; and as the whole affair is proceeding with the utmost smoothness and restraint, so we hope that the Man [Handel] will set a good face on a bad game. But I am amused that he should suspect me and not trust my most polite manners in his majestic Faunlike presence.

They ought to be gibbeted these South Sea Directors, who have ruined all my friends—and I very much fear that they will in consequence have ruined the Academy. God damn'em. . . .

Bononcino is here already. Mylord Burlington had only just arrived in town when he went into the country for a fortnight and he told me that on his return he will have the house ready prepared for him. I am gradually instructing him and telling him the remuneration [due to me]. I find him well disposed to do his duty and my principal advice to him is to keep himself united to Senesino. He has already conceived a high opinion of him because he is very able.

(Streatfeild, 1917, pp. 435 f.; incomplete.) Original in Biblioteca Estense, Modena. *L'Alpestre Fauno* was a variant of *Il Proteus alpino* (see 23rd September 1720), and *Il Selvaggio* yet another of Rolli's nicknames for Handel.—Girolamo Polani was a Venetian singer and composer, recently arrived in England. Nothing, however, is known of his connection with the Haymarket Opera.—When the Houses of Parliament came to deal with the directors and other officers of the South Sea Company, from January 1721 onwards, their cashier, Robert Knight, fled to the Continent.—Rolli seems to have taught the Earl of Burlington Italian.

———

FROM MIST'S " WEEKLY JOURNAL ", 22nd October 1720

Next Saturday [the 23rd] the Cathedral at St. Paul's, which has been shut some time, will be opened, when a new Anthem will be sung ; there has been such Improvements made to the Organ, that it is now reckoned the best in Europe.

It is related that the organ in St. Paul's Cathedral, built by Bernard Schmidt, known as Father Smith, and opened in 1697, had a special attraction for Handel.

Maurice Greene, organist there since 1718, assisted him by acting as organ-blower whenever he liked to play it. Handel is said to have spent long evenings with the gentlemen of the choir of St. Paul's at the Queen Anne Tavern nearby. Cf. 24th (29th) August 1724.

———

FROM MATTHESON'S RECORDS, 28th October to 3rd November
(8th to 14th November) 1720 (Translated)

Lord Carteret . . . from the Swedish Legation, arrived in Hamburg on 8th November 1720, and found in the music of our Mattheson such delight, that at one time he sat by him and listened for two whole hours without leaving his place ; finally, in the presence of the illustrious company he passed this judgement : Händel indeed played the harp-sichord in a beautiful and finished manner ; but he did not sing with such taste and vigour. This great man [Carteret], who subsequently became Secretary of State, Lord Lieutenant of Ireland, &c., journeyed to England on 14th November in the company of Herr von Wich, his nearest kinsman.

(Mattheson, *Ehrenpforte*, p. 207 ; Chrysander, I. 247.) John Carteret, afterwards Earl Granville, had been Ambassador to Sweden since 1719, and became Lord Lieutenant of Ireland in 1724 (Smith, 1948, p. 18). He seems to have been connected with the family of Granville, to which Handel's friends Mary and Bernard belonged ; the latter were relatives of Cyril Wyche, once Handel's pupil in Hamburg (see 7th November 1703) and now his father's successor as " Envoy Extraordinary " (Smith, p. 17).

———

FROM THE " DAILY COURANT ", 2nd November 1720

This is to give Notice, That Mr. Handel's Harpsichord Lessons neatly Engraven on Copper Plates, will be published on Monday the 14th Instant, and may be had at Christopher Smith's the Sign of the Hand and Musick-Book in Coventry-street the Upper-End of the Hay-Market, and at Mr. Richard Mear's Musick-Shop in St. Paul's Church-Yard.

Cf. 9th November 1720. Christopher Smith was identical with Handel's friend, Johann Christoph Schmidt (cf. summer 1716, 3rd December 1720 and 28th January 1741 ; see also Smith, 1953, pp. 12 f.).

———

FROM THE " DAILY COURANT ", 7th November 1720

The Directors of the Royal Academy of Musick, by virtue of a Power given them under the King's Letters Patents, having thought it necessary to make a Call of 5l. per Cent from each Subscriber, have authorized the Treasurer to the said Royal Academy or his Deputy to receive the same, and to give Receipts for each Sum so paid in. This is therefore to desire the Subscribers to pay, or cause to be paid, the said 5l. per Cent, according to the several Subscriptions, on the 19th, 21st, and 22d of this

Instant November at the Opera House in the Hay-market, where Attendance will be given by the Deputy Treasurer, from Nine in the Morning till One in the Afternoon, who will give Receipts for every Sum so paid by each Subscriber as aforesaid.

A shorter notice appeared in the *London Gazette* of 8th November.

———

FROM THE " DAILY COURANT ", 9th November 1720

(Second advertisement of Handel's harpsichord lessons.)

. . . Note, The Author has been obliged to publish these Pieces to prevent the Publick being imposed upon by some Surreptitious and incorrect Copies of some of them that has got abroad.

(Chrysander, III. 186.) Cf. 2nd November 1720. It seems that this note, as well as Handel's own in the original edition of the *Suites de Pièces pour le Clavecin* (cf. 14th November 1720) refers to the Amsterdam edition of *Pièces à un & deux clavesins* by " Hendel ", published about 1719 by Jeanne Roger (no. 490), an incomplete copy of which is in the Bodleian Library, Oxford ; a later issue, published by her brother-in-law, Michel Charles Le Cène, is preserved in D. F. Scheurleer's Collection at the Hague. The contents of the Amsterdam edition are not the same as those of the London one, but some pieces in both are identical. The Amsterdam edition was probably based on a manuscript copy of harpsichord pieces by Handel, sold surreptitiously.

———

FROM THE " DAILY COURANT ", 14th November 1720

This Day is published.

Mr. Handel's Harpsichord Lessons. . . . Price One Guinea.

This was the first instrumental music to be published by Handel himself (cf. 31st January 1717). The book, 94 pages oblong folio, was engraved and printed, probably by John Cluer, " for the Author ". The first issue is without ornaments on the title-page (engraved by James Cole) and is not described there as " Premier Volume " ; the Privilege of 14th June 1720 follows the title-page. There are eight suites, and the fifth ends with variations on the air known, since the nineteenth century, as " The Harmonious Blacksmith ". The story that Handel was inspired by hearing the blacksmith William Powell, of Whitchurch, at work is, however, legendary.

———

HANDEL'S PRELIMINARY NOTE TO HIS " SUITES DE PIÈCES POUR LE CLAVECIN ", 14th November 1720

I have been obliged to publish some of the following Lessons, because surrepticious and incorrect Copies of them had got Abroad. I have added several new ones to make the Work more usefull, which if it meets with a favourable Reception ; I will still proceed to publish more, reckoning it my duty, with my Small Talent, to serve a Nation from which I have receiv'd so Generous a protection.

G F. Handel

This note indicates that Handel published the first volume of his "lessons" as a test. Although there were at least four issues printed, the success did not satisfy Handel enough to publish a second volume until 1733 ; he then did so with Walsh who, at the same time, reprinted the first volume with Handel's authority.

The second season of the Royal Academy of Music, at the Haymarket Theatre, opens with Bononcini's opera, *Astarto*, text by Rolli, altered from an earlier libretto by Apostolo Zeno and Pietro Pariati, 19th November 1720.

Rolli dedicated the libretto to the Earl of Burlington (cf. 10th January 1713). From the wording of the dedication it seems that Burlington saw Luca Antonio Predieri's setting of the original text in Rome (Teatro Capranica) during the season 1714–15 (Loewenberg, p. 74).—This was the first opera of Handel's rival to be produced in London.

MRS. MARY PENDARVES TO HER SISTER, MISS ANN GRANVILLE

London, 29th Nov. 1720.

The stage was never so well served as it is now, there is not one indifferent voice, they are all Italians. There is one man called Serosini who is beyond Nicolini both in person and voice.

(Delany, I. 57 f.) Mrs. Pendarves, later Mrs. Delany, born Granville, had known Handel since the beginning of 1711, and soon became his true friend. She misspells the name of the new singer, Senesino, *i.e.* the Sienese. He first appeared on the London stage in *Astarto*.

Walsh and Hare publish the third book of a harpsichord collection entitled *The Lady's Banquet*, 1st December 1720 (*Post-Boy*).

Nos. 1 and 2 of the "lessons" are minuets by Handel, printed later as part of his *Water Music*. The first is entitled *A Trumpet Minuet by Mr Hendell*, the second *A Minuet for the French Horn by Mr Hendell*. (Smith, 1948, pp. 274 f.)

FROM THE "POST BOY", 3rd December 1720

On Thursday the 15th instant, will be publish'd, (with his Majesty's Royal Privilege and Licence)

The Opera of Rhadamistus, composed by Mr. Handel ; the Elegancies of which, and the Abilities of its Author, are too well known by the Musical Part of the World, to need a Recommendation, unless it be by informing them, that there hath been such due Care taken in the Printing of it, (which consists of 124 large Folio Copper-Plates, all corrected by the Author) that the Printer presumes to assert that there hath not been in Europe a Piece of Musick so well printed, and upon so good Paper. Publish'd by the Author, and printed by Richard Meares, Musick-Printer in S Paul's Church-yard. Sold also by Christopher Smith . . . At both which Places Mr. Handel's Harpsichord Lessons are likewise sold.

The volume really is beautifully produced. Each copy, of which there were more than 100, bears a number of sale control, written in ink, but probably not by Handel himself, although the book was " Publisht by the Author ". The number of plates was, in fact, 123 ; they were engraved by Thomas Cross (see 30th December 1712). The production, not finished until 30th December, delayed the publication by Meares of Arcangelo Corelli's Opp. 1-4.

———

From the (?) " Daily Courant ", 28th December 1720

At the King's Theatre . . . this present Wednesday . . . will be perform'd an Opera, call'd, RADAMISTUS. . . . N.B. Four Hundred Tickets will be deliver'd out, and after they are disposed of, no Person whatsoever will be admitted for Money. A proper Officer will attend at each Door, to deliver every Subscriber his Ticket, without which he will not be admitted. No Persons are to be admitted behind the Scenes. . . . To begin exactly at Six.

Cutting in the *Theatrical Register*. The opera was given in a revised and augmented version. Repeat performances during the season on 31st December 1720 ; 4th, 21st, 25th January ; 21st and 25th March 1721.

Cast of the Revival of " Radamisto ", 28th December 1720

Radamisto—Signor Senesino, alto
Zenobia—Signora Durastanti, soprano
Farasmane—Signor Lagarde, bass
Tiridate—Signor Boschi, bass
Polissena—Signora Maddalena Salvai, soprano
Tigrane—Signor Matteo Berselli, tenor
Fraarte—Signora Galerati, (?) soprano

From the original cast of 27th April 1720 only Lagarde kept his part. Durastanti exchanged Radamisto for Zenobia, Galerati Tigrane for Fraarte. Senesino sang his first Handel part. Boschi returned to the Haymarket ; Salvai and Berselli were newcomers there.

———

The Little, or French, Theatre in the Haymarket, situated opposite the Opera House, opens, 29th December 1720.

The Little Theatre belonged to a carpenter, named Potter, who built it, and the French comedians played there, without licence, under the patronage of the Duke of Montague. The first season ran till 4th May 1721. Cf. 9th September 1721.

It should be mentioned here that the " Little Theatre in the Haymarket " corresponds with the present " Haymarket Theatre ", although the latter, built in 1820, stands just to the south of the old house. The Opera House of Handel's day, officially the " Theatre in the Haymarket ", stood on the other side of the street on the site now occupied by the Carlton Hotel, though the block in which it was situated, pulled down in 1893, extended as far north as the present " Her Majesty's Theatre ".

———

FROM THE " DAILY POST ", 30th December 1720

This Day publish'd . . . The most celebrated Opera of RADAMISTUS, composed by Mr. Handell, curiously engraved upon 123 Copper Plates, and printed upon fine Dutch Paper, the whole Work being corrected by the Author. Printed and Sold by Richard Meares, Musical Instrument Maker and Musick Printer, at the Golden Viol and Hautboy in St. Paul's Church-Yard. And whereas Mr. Handell has composed several more compleat, they will

The rest of the advertisement is missing in the copy in the British Museum ; it may have referred to Handel's harpsichord lessons.

———

FROM APPLEBEE'S " ORIGINAL WEEKLY JOURNAL ", 31st December 1720

On Wednesday Night [the 28th] the Royal Family with a great Number of the Nobility, etc. were to see the New Opera, call'd Rhadamistus, but Isabella did not Sing as was expected. . . .

Signior Nicoleni, the famous Italian Eunuch, is newly arriv'd here from Venice, and Sang last Wednesday Night at the New Opera with great Applause, 'tis said the Company allows him 2000 Guineas for the Season.

While Mary Granville-Pendarves compared the new star with the old one (see 29th November), this paper identifies him with Nicolini (cf. the following item). La Isabella too, Mlle Isabella Girardeau, was a star of the past.

———

FROM MIST'S " WEEKLY JOURNAL ", 31st December 1720

On Wednesday Night his Majesty and the rest of the Royal Family went to see the new Opera, called Rhadamistus, where the famous Nicolini performed with his wonted Applause.

(Chrysander, II. 56.) Senesino's name is again mixed up with that of Nicolini.

———

It may be thought, that the great excellence of SENESINO, *both as to voice and action, might have a considerable share in the wonderful impressions made upon the audience. . . . To the ladies especially, the merits of* SENESINO *would be much more obvious, than those of Handel.—Perhaps they would. That all depended on the Composer, I am as far from asserting, as I am from believing that any other person could have shewn such a singer to* **equal advantage.** *Let any impartial and competent judge consider, whether it is likely* *that the whole musical world could have afforded a composer besides himself, capable of furnishing* SENESINO *with such a song, as that of Ombra Cara in the very Opera before us.*

The great success of it matur'd the project before concerted for establishing an academy. For it could not be effected at once, as a considerable number of great persons had been instrumental in bringing over BUONONCINI *and* ATTILIO [*Ariosti*]. *And these foreigners they were the more unwilling to abandon, because they really had abilities in their profession. Perhaps the contests ran as high on both sides, as if the object of them had been much more important. Yet I cannot agree with some, who think them of no importance, and treat them as ridiculous. Those who thought their honour engaged to support the old Composers; who really preferred them to Handel; or fancied that it was a defect of humanity, or an act of injustice to discard them, not because they were unfit for their office, but because another foreigner was come, who was thought to be fitter;—had surely a right to interest themselves warmly in their defence, at a time when they were so much in want of assistance.*

And those, on the other hand, might as reasonably join in opposing them, who were firmly convinced of Handel's great superiority; and who thought it for the honour of the nation to inlist in its service the most eminent artists. (Mainwaring, pp. 100-102.)

———

" Mr. Handel " is among the subscribers for John Gay's " Poems on Several Occasions ", 1720.

Among the other subscribers were Burlington and Chandos, each for fifty copies, James Craggs junior, Heidegger, Anastasia Robinson and Pope.

———

The academy being now firmly established, and Handel appointed Composer to it, all things went on prosperously for a course of . . . years. And this may justly be called the period of musical glory, whether we consider the performances or the performers, most certainly not to be surpassed, if equalled, in any age or country. . . .

The perfect authority which Handel maintained over the singers and the band, or rather the total subjection in which he held them, was of more consequence than can well be imagined. It was the chief means of preserving that order and decorum, that union and tranquillity, which seldom are found to subsist for any long continuance in musical Societies. (Mainwaring, pp. 106 f.)

1721

From Mattheson's Notes to the Second Edition of Friederich Erhard Niedt's "Musikalische Handleitung zur Variation des General-Basses" ("A musical guide-book for varying the Thorough Bass"), Hamburg 1721 (Translated)

. . . The renowned Capellmeister Hendel has combined both styles of *Overtures* and *Symphonies* with each other in his *Rinaldo*. (I have said in the *Organisten-Probe*, p. 167, that nothing by the famous author is available in printed form ; such has happened *ex incuria*, and I did not remember the opera *Rinaldo*, which has been engraved.) He calls it also : The Symphony or Overture in Rinaldo. . . . I hope . . . the great man in England will take it in good part that mention was made of him here again. As always, this is done, according to my *Intention*, with fitting *Respect*, and I know in many pieces no better model to propose.

(Chrysander, I. 280-82.) Niedt, p. 107. The first edition was published in 1706. The preface to the second edition is dated by Mattheson, Michaelmas 1720. For the " Exemplarische Organisten-Probe ", see 1719. Walsh's edition of the *Songs in* . . . *Rinaldo* starts with the " Overture " ; the term " Symphonies " was used by Walsh for his editions of *Instrumental Parts* of Operas. His scores were " short scores ", and so the overture to *Rinaldo* was given on four staves.

———

Orlandini's *Amore e Maestà*, text by Salvi, altered by Rolli, with additional music by Filippo Amadei, is produced at the Haymarket Theatre, under the title *Arsace*, 1st February 1721.

Cf. 18th October 1720 and 23rd March 1721.

———

A General Court of the Royal Academy of Music, originally arranged for 20th February, is adjourned to 28th February 1721.
London Gazette, 14th and 21st February.

———

From Joseph Mitchell's " Ode on the Power of Musick ", February 1721

Musick religious Thoughts inspires,
And kindles bright Poetick Fires ;
Fires ! such as great [1] *Hillarius* raise
Triumphant, in their blaze ! . . .

[1] Aaron Hill, *Esq.*

> Others may *that* Distraction call,
> Which Musick raises in the Breast,
> To *me*, 'tis Ecstasy and Triumph all,
> The foretastes of the raptures of the blest.
> Who knows not this, when *Handell* plays,
> And *Senesino* Sings ?
> Our Souls learn Rapture from their Lays,
> While rival'd Angels show amaze,
> And drop their Golden Wings.

Copy in Gerald Coke's Handel Collection. 12 pp. fol. Stanza x, p. 8. The preface is dated London, 19th December 1720. The poem is dedicated to Alexander Malcolm, teacher of Mathematics in Edinburgh, who had just published his *Treatise of Musick*, under the date of 1721, in which Mitchell's poem is also to be found. Mitchell himself came to London in 1720 from Edinburgh.

———

List of the Academy's Governors and (twenty) Directors, 1720–21, as given in the Dedication of Malcolm's "Treatise of Musick", Edinburgh 1721

Thomas, Duke of Newcastle, Governor ; Lord Bingley, Deputy Governor ; Dukes of Portland and Queensbury ; Earls of Burlington, Stair(s), and Waldeck (Waldegrave) ; Lords Chetwind (Chetwynd) and Stanhope ; James Bruce ; Colonel Blathwayt (John Blaithwaite) ; Thomas Coke of Norfolk ; Conyers Darcey (d'Arcy) ; Brigadier-General Dormer ; Bryan Fairfax ; Colonel O'Hara ; George Harrison ; Brigadier-General Hunter ; William Poultney (Pulteney) ; Sir John Vanbrugh ; Major-General Wade ; and Francis Whitworth.

It was this list which Hawkins (V. 273) and Burney (IV. 258) reprinted without giving either the source or its date. This collection of high-ranking names impressed Mattheson (*Critica Musica*, vol. II, 1725, p. 147), and through him Johann Gottfried Walther (*Musicalisches Lexikon*, 1732, under Malcolm). The list apparently shows the result of the autumn election of 1720, the book having been prepared at that time. (The frontispiece was engraved in 1720.)

———

From the "Evening Post", 7th March 1721

Last Thursday [the 2nd] his Majesty was pleased to stand Godfather, and the Princess and the Lady Bruce, Godmothers, to a Daughter of Mrs. Darastanti, chief Singer in the Opera-House. The Marquis Visconti [appeared] for the King, and the Lady Litchfield for the Princess.

(Burney, IV. 280.) It was an exceptional favour, shown by the King and the Princess Royal, to Signora Durastanti and her husband, Casimiro Avelloni. She sang her new part, as Zenobia in *Radamisto*, for the last time on 25th February. Rolli and Senesino probably attended the christening, perhaps Handel too.

———

FROM THE "LONDON GAZETTE", 11th March 1721

The Court of Directors of the Royal Academy of Musick do hereby give Notice that they have ordered a Call of 5*l.* per Cent. from each Subscriber, and that the Deputy-Treasurer will attend at the Office, at the Opera-House in the Haymarket, on the 25th, 27th, and 28th Instant, from Nine in the Morning till Two in the Afternoon, in order to receive the same ; and all Parties concerned are desired to give Orders for the Payment thereof, at such Time and Place as aforesaid.

FROM THE "DAILY POST", 14th March 1721

The celebrated Opera of Radamistus . . . the best and most correct Piece of Musick extant. . . . And whereas Mr. Handel has composed several Additional Songs to make the said Work more obliging, they are now finish'd, the Edition containing 41 Copper Plates, engraven by the same Hand, which renders this Work cheaper than any Thing of this Nature yet publish'd ; which will be sold at the same Price as before, and such Gentlemen and Ladies as have already purchased it, may have the Additions Gratis, at the Place above-mentioned : Where also Mr. Handel's Lessons for the Harpsicord are sold.

The supplement is entitled *Arie Aggiunte di Radamisto.* . . . The additions comprise 10 songs and 1 duet. Cf. 28th December 1720 and 21st March 1721.

£500 are paid to Mr. Heidegger, the manager of the opera, " as a Present from His Majesty ", 18th March 1721.

Public Record Office : L.C.5/157, p. 401.

FROM THE "POST-BOY", 21st March 1721

The . . . Opera of Radamistus . . . several Additional Songs . . . they are now finish'd, and will be publish'd this Day. . . .

Cf. 14th March.

Such then was the state of things in the year 1720, at the time RADAMISTO *was performed. The succeeding winter brought this musical disorder to its crisis. In order to terminate all matters in controversy, it was agreed to put them on this fair issue. The several parties concerned were to be jointly employed in making an Opera, in which each of them was to take a distinct act. And he, who by the general suffrage, should be allowed to have given the best proofs of his abilities, was to be put into possession of the house. The proposal was accepted, whether from choice, or necessity, I cannot say. The event was answerable to the expectations of Handel's friends. His act was the last, and the superiority of it so very manifest, that there was not the least pretence for any further doubts or disputes. I should have mentioned, that as each made an overture, as well as an act, the affair seemed to be decided even by the overture with which Handel's began. The name of the Opera was* MUZIO SCAEVOLA. (Mainwaring, pp. 104 f.)

Handel finishes Act III of the opera *Muzio Scevola*, 23rd March 1721.

The Directors of the Royal Academy of Music invited three composers to set Rolli's libretto act-meal, a not unusual arrangement during the eighteenth and nineteenth centuries. It was formerly assumed that Ariosti, Bononcini and Handel, the Academy's own three composers, were chosen to satisfy the different claims of their followers by competition. In fact, it was not Ariosti, but Filippo Amadei, sometimes called Pippo and at other times Mattei, who set the first act. (Chrysander, II. 57 ; Loewenberg, p. 74.) Bononcini wrote the second act and Handel the third. Pippo, the distinguished violoncellist of the opera, had appeared as composer on 13th February 1719 at a London concert, which he gave with the violinist Stefano Carbonelli ; he appeared in this role again on 28th February of that year, and on 14th March 1722. (Chrysander, II. 56.) For his playing at Court cf. 13th July 1719. Rolli signed the libretto as Italian secretary of the Academy, and dedicated it to the King. In Handel's own copy of the bilingual libretto, the last blank leaf shows a washing-bill written by one of his domestics : " 12 shirts, 3 aprons, 1 hood, 7 combing clothes, 5 pairs coats 2 have buttons and 2 strings. Mr Handl ". (Cummings, January 1911, p. 19 ; no. 773 of Cummings sale, 17th–24th May 1917, bound together with 23 other Handel librettos.)

———

FROM THE " DAILY COURANT ", 28th March 1721

At the King's Theatre . . . this present Tuesday . . . will be perform'd A Serenata. Compos'd by Sig. Cavalliero Allessandro Scarlatti, perform'd by Sig. Francisco Bernardi Senesino, Signora Durastanti, Mrs. Anastasia Robinson, Signora Salvai, Sig. Boschi. . . . The Stage will be illuminated, and put in the same Form as it was in the Balls.

(Frank Walker, in *The Music Review*, August 1951, p. 197.) It is assumed that this concert was given by, or for the benefit of, Francesco Scarlatti, Alessandro's brother, who was in London from 1719 till about 1724, and usually had his benefit concerts in Hickford's Room, St. James's Street.

———

FROM THE " DAILY COURANT ", 12th April 1721

At the King's Theatre in the Hay-Market, on Saturday next, being the 15th Day of April, will be perform'd a new Opera, call'd, MUTIUS SCAEVOLA. The Pit and Boxes to be put together. . . . Tickets . . . will be deliver'd on Friday, at Mr. White's Chocolate-House in St. James's-street, at Half a Guinea each. N.B. No more than Four Hundred Tickets will be deliver'd out, and are to be had . . . at no other Place whatsoever. . . . Gallery 5s. To begin exactly at Six.

The same advertisement appeared in the *Daily Post*.

———

CAST OF " MUZIO SCEVOLA ", 15th April 1721

Larte Porsenna—Signor Boschi, bass
Muzio Scaevola—Signor Senesino, alto
Clelia—Signora Durastanti, soprano
Orazio—Signor Berselli, tenor
Irene—Mrs. Robinson, contralto
Fidalma—Signora Salvai, soprano
Lucio Tarquinio—Signora Galerati, contralto

The part of Lucio Tarquinio is not in Handel's preserved score of his Act III. Repeat performances on 19th, 22nd, 26th, 29th April ; 3rd, 6th, 13th, 17th May ; and 7th June 1720. Weinstock (p. 112) states that Mrs. Robinson's voice changed this year from soprano to contralto, through illness.

———

A MOTTO FOR THE OPERA OF MUTIUS SCAEVOLA

By Mr. [John] Gay.

Who here blames words, or verses, songs, or singers,
Like Mutius Scaevola will burn his fingers.

Printed in the *Additions to the Works of Alexander Pope, etc.*, 1776, I. 104.

———

A General Court of the Royal Academy of Music is held " on very special Affairs ", 18th April 1721. (*London Gazette*, 11th April.)

———

MONSIEUR DE FABRICE TO COUNT FLEMMING (Translated)

London, April 21, 1721.

. . . No doubt you will know that the Princess of Wales was safely delivered of a son last Saturday [the 15th]. The news was taken to the King by Lord Herbert during an opera called Mutius Scevola, where there was a particularly large audience on account of its being the first performance. The audience celebrated the event with loud applause and huzzas. Each act of this opera is by a different composer,—the first by a certain Pipo, the second by Bononcini, and the third by Hendell, who easily triumphed over the others.

(Fürstenau, 1860 ; Chrysander, II. 63 ; Opel, *Mitteilungen*, p. 31.) Sächsisches Geheimes Staatsarchiv, Dresden. One of the brothers de Fabrice was Hanoverian minister, the other Gentleman of the Bedchamber to the Prince of Wales, whom he had accompanied, as Prince George, to Italy in 1709–10. Cf. 15th January 1723 and 17th December 1726. Henry Herbert, ninth Earl of Pembroke, was Lord of the Bedchamber to the Prince. Flemming was the Saxon general and Prime Minister ; cf. 25th November 1719.

———

FROM HUMPHREY WANLEY'S NOTEBOOK, 15th May 1721

Mr. Kaeyscht (at the Duke of Chandos') has kindly promised to lend me the score of Mr. Handel's *Te Deum*, being his second, which he composed for the Duke of Chandos, who can likewise procure scores of all his services and anthems.

(J. R. Robinson, p. 84.) Strawberry Hill Collection. Wanley was librarian to the Earl of Oxford (cf. 9th February 1719). For the Te Deum and the Anthems, see 23rd August 1720 ; there were no " services " by Handel. Handel's first Te Deum (and Jubilate) was, of course, the *Utrecht*. Jean Christian Kytch (Kytsch, Keitch, Keutsch, Kaeyscht), the oboist in the Cannons " concert ", came from Holland ; he also played the German flute and gave a concert in Hickford's Room, February 1720. (Cf. 16th February 1719.) Cummings (1915) states that he played a bassoon obligato in *Rinaldo*, 1711. His nephew, a boy, was also in the Duke's orchestra. Kytch died before 1738, and it was the sight of his two destitute children, driving milk asses through the Haymarket, which led to the " Fund for the Support of Decay'd Musicians ", later called the Royal Society of Musicians, in which Handel took a lively interest.

———

Bononcini's *Ciro, or Odio ed Amore,* is produced at the Haymarket Theatre, 20th May 1721.

(Chrysander, II. 63.) Burney attributes the opera to Ariosti.

———

COUNT FLEMMING TO MONSIEUR DE FABRICE (Translated)

[Dresden, (? May) 1721.]

I am very glad also that the German has been victorious in composition over all the other musicians.

(Fürstenau, 1860 ; 1861–2, II. 152 f.; Chrysander, II. 63.) This is the reply to Fabrice's letter of 21st April.

———

FROM THE " DAILY COURANT ", 14th June 1721

At the King's Theatre in the Hay-Market, this present Wednesday . . . will be an Entertainment of MUSICK : Consisting of above 30 Songs, chosen out of former Opera's, perform'd by Signior Francisco Bernardi Senesino, Signior Boschi, Signora Darastanti, Mrs. Anastasia Robinson, Signora Salvai. . . . The Stage will be illuminated, and put in the same Form as it was in the Balls. . . .

Cutting in the *Theatrical Register* (British Museum). Among the " former Opera's " was certainly *Rinaldo*, and probably others by Handel. The same group of singers, in a similarly decorated house, performed an unidentified serenata by Alessandro Scarlatti on 28th March 1721 (Chrysander, II. 64).

———

FROM THE " DAILY COURANT ", 5th July 1721

For the Benefit of Signora Durastanti.

At the King's Theatre . . . this present Wednesday . . . will be perform'd a CONCERT of Vocal and Instrumental MUSICK, Compos'd by the best Masters : Particularly, Two new Cantata's by Mr. Hendel, and Sig. Sandoni ; Four Songs and Six Duetto's by the famous Signor Stefan, performed by Signora Durastanti, and Signor Senesino. . . . The Concert will not begin till Seven o'Clock.

(Chrysander, II. 64.) Of the two cantatas, apparently only one was by Handel, but it cannot be identified. About Sandoni see 13th July 1719. Stefan is Agostino Steffani, Handel's father-like friend at Düsseldorf.—The opera season ended on 1st July 1721 with *Ciro*.

FROM THE " LONDON GAZETTE ", 8th July 1721

The Court of Directors of the Royal Academy of Musick finding several Subscribers in Arrear on the Calls made on them this year, do hereby desire them to pay in the same before Thursday the 20th Instant, otherwise they shall be obliged to return them as Defaulters, at a General Court to be held that Day, for their Instructions how to proceed : And it appearing to the said Court of Directors on examining the Accounts, that when the Calls already made are fully answered, there will still remain such a Deficiency to render it absolutely necessary to make a further Call to clear this Year's Expence ; the said Court of Directors have therefore ordered another Call of 4*l*. per Cent. (which is the 6th Call) to be made on the several Subscribers, payable on or before the 27th Instant. Attendance will be given on that and the two preceeding Days, at the Office in the Hay-Market, in order to receive the same.

The notice also appeared in the *Daily Courant* on 10th July. Cf. 31st October 1721. The fact that the Directors of the Academy had called for only 25 per cent by the end of the 1720–21 season makes it impossible to believe that the opera had at that time spent all the £15,000 subscribed in 1719 (Schoelcher, p. 84). Only four previous calls of 5 per cent each could be traced in the newspapers (8th December 1719, 5th April and 8th November 1720, and 11th March 1721).

HILL TO JOHN RICH, 9TH SEPTEMBER 1721

I suppose you know, that the *duke of Montague*, and I, have agreed, and that I am to have that house [Little Haymarket Theatre] half the week, and his *french vermin*, the other half : but I would forbear acting at all there, this season, if you will let me your house [Lincoln's-Inn-Fields Theatre] for *two* nights a week, in *Lent*, and *three* a week, after.

Hill's Works, II. 46 f. Schoelcher, p. 55, thought the first of the two theatres was the Opera House. Brewster, pp. 101 f. Cf. 29th December 1720. Rich had opened the new Theatre in Lincoln's Inn Fields in 1714. Hill had a new company of players. During Lent, acting was permitted on four week-days only, Wednesdays and Fridays being excluded. Cf. Hill's letters to Montague, 21st–24th January 1722.

VIII. FRANCESCO BERNARDI, CALLED "SENESINO"

Mezzotint after Thomas Hudson, by Alexander Van Haecken, 1735. With
the open score of Handel's *Giulio Cesare*. (Gerald Coke, Esq.)

See pages 113 *and* 157

IX. SCENE FROM A HANDEL OPERA

Etched caricature by John Vanderbank, *ca.* 1723. Probably from *Flavio* (1723), Act III, Scene 4, with

FROM THE " LONDON GAZETTE ", 31st October 1721

By Order of a General Court of the Royal
Academy of Musick, held Oct. 25, 1721.

Whereas some few of the Subscribers to the Operas have neglected (notwithstanding repeated Notice has been given them) to pay the Calls which have been regularly made by the Court of Directors, and according to the Condition of the said Subscription, signed by each of the said Subscribers : These are to give further Notice to every such Defaulter, That unless he pays the said Calls on or before the 22d of November next, his Name shall be printed, and he shall be proceeded against with the utmost Rigour of the Law.

This notice also appeared in the *Daily Courant* of 2nd November. Burney (IV. 281) reckons this as the seventh call. The threats seem never to have been carried out. Cf. 8th July 1721 and 10th November 1722.

——

The opera season opens with a revival of *Arsace* on 1st November 1721 (cf. 1st February 1721), *Muzio Scevola* being revived on 7th, 10th and 13th November. For 20th November 1721 a General Court of the Academy is appointed to be held, " on particular Bussiness " (*London Gazette*, 16th November).

Chrysander, II. 85, states that the Duke of Manchester was elected Deputy-Governor this autumn. If so, it was a re-election ; he died in January 1722. Cf. May 1719, and 2nd December 1724.

——

FROM THE " LONDON GAZETTE ", 25th November 1721

Applications having been made to the Royal Academy of Musick, for Tickets intitling the Bearers to the Liberty of the House for this Season : The Academy agree to give out Tickets to such as shall subscribe on the Conditions following, viz. That each Subscriber, on the Delivery of the Ticket, pay 10 Guineas : That on the 1st of February next ensuing the Date of these presents, each Subscriber pay the further Sum of 5 Guineas : And likewise the Sum of 5 Guineas upon the 1st Day of May following. And whereas the Academy propose the Acting of 50 Operas this Season, they do oblige themselves to allow a Deduction proportionably, in case fewer Operas be performed than that Number. N.B. The Instrument lies open at White's Chocolate House for Subscribers to Sign on the foregoing Terms ; as also another at the Opera Office every Opera Night.

(North, 1846, p. 133 ; Schoelcher, p. 54 ; Chrysander, II. 85 f.) This was a new attempt to save the Academy. It was also the origin of the annual subscription system.

——

H.–5

Radamisto is performed again, 25th November 1721.

Repeat performances on 29th November; 2nd, 6th, 28th and 31st December.

—

Handel finishes the opera *Floridante*, 28th November 1721.

—

FROM THE "DAILY COURANT", 9th December 1721

At the King's Theatre . . . this present Saturday . . . will be perform'd a New Opera call'd FLORIDANTE. . . . And in Regard to the increase of the Number of Subscribers, no more than Three Hundred and Fifty Tickets will be delivered out . . . at Half a Guinea each. NB. No Tickets will be disposed of at the Theatre, nor any Money taken there but for the Gallery. . . . Gallery 5s.

—

FROM ROLLI'S DEDICATION, TO THE PRINCE OF WALES, OF THE WORD-BOOK OF "FLORIDANTE", 9th December 1721 (Translated)

I humbly dedicate to you this work of mine, because in it those two most noble qualities, so difficult to express—the Heroic Lover and the loving Hero—have been, I make bold to say, most vividly and feelingly celebrated in excellent music.

(Chrysander, II. 73.) According to Eisenschmidt (II. 12), the libretto is based on a drama entitled *La Costanza in Trionfo*. J. R. Clemens, of Mayfield in California, wrote in the *Sackbut* of 1931 that at the production of *Floridante* great offence was given to the Court, because in the plot a rightful heir is imprisoned and afterwards triumphs over the oppressor; at the "last circumstance there happened to be very great and unreasonable clapping in the presence of the great ones". No documentary evidence for this statement could be found.

—

CAST OF "FLORIDANTE", 9th December 1721

Floridante—Signor Senesino, soprano
Oronte—Signor Boschi, bass
Timante—Signor Baldassari, tenor
Coralbo—?, bass
Rossane—Signora Salvai, soprano
Elmira—Mrs. Robinson, soprano

The singer's name for the part of Coralbo is not given in the libretto; it may have been undecided when the book was printed. Repeat performances on 13th, 16th, 20th, 23rd, 27th, and 30th December 1721; 3rd, 5th January; 13th, 20th February; 25th, 28th April; 23rd and 26th May 1722.

—

FROM WALSH'S CASH-BOOK, 1721

1721 Opera Floridan—£72 0 0

(Macfarren, p. 22.) If this cash-book ever existed, the entry quoted above would be the first referring to Handel. Walsh, in company with John and Joseph Hare, printed the music of *Floridante*, " Publish'd by the Author ", with his privilege, in March of 1722. Meares, who reprinted a selection of airs, added in January 1723 the airs supplied by Handel in December 1722. As usual, Walsh also published, in May 1722, a selection of airs arranged for the flute. He was very generous in this first regular deal with Handel if he paid him £72. In 1722 he is said to have kept the same standard, but from 1723 to 1738 he paid Handel, according to the same cash-book, £26 5s. for each score. The exception of *Alexander's Feast* in 1737, when Handel received £105, would be understandable as it was published by a special subscription.

1722

Bononcini's *Crispo*, text by Rolli (adapted from Gaetano Lemer)
is produced at the Haymarket Theatre, 10th January 1722.

—

FROM MATTHESON'S HAMBURG OPERA LIST, [17th (28th)
January 1722] (Translated)

Zenobia. Composed by Herr *Händel*, translated by *Mattheson*. Scenery
painted by *Querfeld* and *Rabe*. Ballet Master, *Thiboust*.

(Chrysander, 1877, col. 247.) *Radamisto* was produced under the title *Zenobia,
oder Das Muster rechtschaffener ehelichen Liebe*, with German recitatives by Mattheson ; the airs being sung in Italian. (Loewenberg, p. 73.) According to Willers'
Hamburg Notes (Merbach, p. 358), the opera was performed seventeen times in
1722, six times in 1723, once each in 1724 and 1726, and three times in 1736 ;
twenty-eight performances in all. The painters mentioned were, probably,
Tobias Querfurt senior and, certainly, Johann Jürgen Rabe. The name of the
ballet master, too, is probably corrupt.

—

HILL TO THE DUKE OF MONTAGUE

1721–2, Jan. 20, Westminster.
. . . And the English company being now ready for opening [their
intended season at the Little Haymarket Theatre], I have warned them
[the French Actors] that they can have liberty to act at that House no
longer than Tuesday next. But they may certainly get permission to
act two or three times a week at the Opera House ; and if the rent must
be greater, the House will hold more company in proportion.
. . . and a word of yours to recommend 'em to the Opera House will
undoubtedly procure 'em admission in a Theatre where they may be
every way more advantageously posted.

(Buccleuch Manuscripts, I. 369. Brewster, p. 102.) Cf. 29th December 1720
and 9th September 1721. The French comedians, who acted in the new house
in 1720–21, played there again from November 1721 till April 1722 ; only five
of their performances were on Saturdays. It is remarkable that Hill could suggest
the Opera House as an alternative for the French Company, even on the days
when no operas were performed. The Duke had been one of the Academy's
directors (cf. 27th November 1719).

—

HILL TO THE DUKE OF MONTAGUE

1721–2, Jan. 21.
. . . Let the French Players agree for the Opera House, and if their
rent is too heavy, I will pay part for them, to make it easier.

(Buccleuch Manuscripts, I. 370.) This was apparently a postscript to Hill's letter of the 20th.

HILL TO THE DUKE OF MONTAGUE

1721–2, Jan. 24.

I will try, in respect of your Grace's hint, what I can do as to the Opera House for my company, though their voices will be no small sufferers by the exchange. But it will take up time, and we were ready for opening. And besides, my scenes for the first Play being made for your Grace's House, will not fit the other ; and they are all new, and very expensive, and done after a model perfectly out of the general road of scenery.

Your Grace will be so good to think of these things, and permit at least that my company should act twice a week (during Lent and after-wards) if I fail to get permission in the other House. This can be no disadvantage to the French Players, for they cannot play on Opera nights, and those will be the only nights my company will play on.

(Buccleuch Manuscripts, I. 370 f.) Hill was not successful, either at the other Theatre in the Haymarket, or at the new one. He finally produced his tragedy *King Henry the Fifth*, founded on Shakespeare's play, at Drury Lane Theatre on 5th December 1723. The Opera nights on which he hoped to play at the Little Theatre were apparently Wednesdays and Saturdays.

FROM THE "DAILY COURANT", 15th February 1722

At the King's Theatre . . . this present Thursday . . . will be a RIDOTTO. To begin with an Entertainment of Musick, consisting of 24 Songs chosen out of the late Operas, perform'd by Signor Francisco Bernardi Senesino, Signor Benedetto Baldassari, Mrs. Anastasia Robinson, and Signora Salvai. The Remaining Tickets will be deliver'd . . . at a Guinea each. N.B. There can be no Admittance in the Galleries, they being cover'd as formerly in the Balls. The Doors to be opened at Half an Hour after Seven a Clock at Night. . . .

Cf. 6th March. According to Burney, IV. 647, the *Ridottos* were a novelty of 1722 ; the performance went on for two hours, and then the ball started on the stage.

FROM THE TREASURY PAPERS, 16th February 1722

Memorial of the Royal Academy of Music to the Lords of the Treasury. The King having ordered 1,000*l*. per ann. for seven years, to be paid out of the Bounty Office, to the Royal Academy, they pray for a warrant for payment of 500*l*. Opera House in the Hay Market. 16 Feb. 1721–22.

(Calendar of Treasury Books and Papers, 1720–28, p. 121.) Cf. 14th May 1719 and 26th June 1722. It seems that this was the first payment out of the King's subsidy, this year issued in two parts.

———

Bononcini's *Griselda*, text by Rolli (adapted from Apostolo Zeno) is produced at the Haymarket Theatre, 22nd February 1722.

———

FROM THE "DAILY COURANT", 6th March 1722

At the King's Theatre . . . this present Tuesday . . . will be a RIDOTTO. To begin with an Entertainment of Musick, consisting of several Songs chosen out of the last new Opera's, and some new Cantato's, composed by Signor Bononcini, performed by Signor Francisco Bernardi Senesino, Signor Benedetto Baldassari, Mrs. Anastasia Robinson, and Signora Salvai. Tickets will be delivered . . . at One Guinea each. N.B. The Pit will be cover'd, and there will be Instruments in two Places. To begin at Half an Hour after Seven a-Clock. . . .

Cf. 15th February and 12th November 1722.

———

Walsh and the Hares advertise " The Overture and Song-Tunes, with their Symphonies, for a single Flute ; and the Duets for two Flutes, of the Opera of *Floridante* : Compos'd by Mr. Handell ", *Post-Boy*, 19th May 1722.

They also printed the score of this opera, as " Publish'd by the Author ", with Handel's privilege. Cf. 2nd August 1722.

———

The Academy's third season ends on 16th June 1722 with Bononcini's *Crispo*.

He was very successful during the year. When John, Duke of Marlborough died on this same 16th June, Bononcini was invited to write the Funeral Anthem.

———

FROM THE TREASURY PAPERS, 26th June 1722

1722

16 June Memorial Royal Academy of Music [to the] Lords of the Treasury For a warrant for 500*l*. for six months bounty due to them. *Minutes* :—" 26th June 1722. Orderd."

(Calendar, 1720–28, p. 189.) This may have been the payment asked for on 16th February 1722 ; but since the next recorded payment is of June 1723 and for £1000, that for the second half of 1722 must have been paid during that year.

———

FROM MATTHESON'S " CRITICA MUSICA ", HAMBURG, July 1722
(Translated)

In the *opera Porsenna*, of my composition, as it was performed here 20 years ago, and *accompanied* by Haendel under my *Direction*, is found an *Aria* whose opening words run : *Diese Wangen will ich küssen* (*These cheeks I would kiss*). It can well be that the melody may have seemed not unacceptable to *Haendel* : for he has not only in his *Agrippina*, which appeared in Italy, but also in another, new *opera*, recently performed in England and treating of *Mutio Scaevola*, chosen just this same melody, almost note for note. In *Agrippina* he has even remained in the same key, namely B♭. And there the words run so : *Sotto il lauro, che hai s'ul crine &c.* In the other, however, the key is changed and the words run : *A chi vive di speranza &c.* I will set out a fragment here ; not indeed as if I were accusing the man of *plagii* : far be that from me ; but because it demonstrates the priority and *prerogative* of *Semidiapentes*.

(Vol. I, part 1, no. 3, pp. 71 f.) *Critica Musica* was the first music periodical published in German. This passage, in which, for the first time, the suggestion is made that Handel borrowed from other composers, is very characteristic of Matteson's pettiness and jealousy. He returned to the point in 1740 (*Ehrenpforte*, p. 96). Chrysander (I. 191 f.), who does not quote the *Critica Musica* in this connection, refers to Matteson's *Vollkommener Capellmeister* (1739, p. 443) to show how the subject of a fugue in Matteson's *Cleopatra* (5th December 1704) compares with a similar fugue in Handel's *Agrippina*. *Porsenna*, the opera quoted here, was produced in Hamburg, among ten novelties of the season, in 1702, *i.e.* before Handel's arrival there, and it seems doubtful whether Matteson's opera remained in the repertoire till 1703-4. The manuscript of *Porsenna*, thought by Chrysander to be lost, is preserved (cf. Cannon, pp. 147 f.). *Muzio Scevola* is mentioned again by Matteson in January 1723. Nerone's aria in *Agrippina* is preserved in two versions, one in E minor and one, in fact, in B flat major (*Collected Edition*, LVII, 77 f.). The aria quoted from *Muzio Scevola* is Fidalma's in Act III, Scene 8, omitted in the *Collected Edition of Handel's Works*, but preserved among the Handel manuscripts in the Royal Music Collection (British Museum) : R.M. 20.b., fol. 38. *Semidiapente* (Latin) means diminished fifth.—The passage was not quoted either by S. Taylor or by P. Robinson (1906 and 1908).

—

Walsh and the Hares announce, as shortly forthcoming, " all the Favourite Songs in the three Acts of *Muzio Scevola*, with the most celebrated Overture in the said Opera ", *Post-Boy*, 2nd August 1722.

The edition contains the overture to Act II and four songs by Bononcini, three songs by Handel, and one by Pippo, but without the composers' names. Meares arranged another edition which may have been published before that of Walsh. In Walsh's advertisement the "Favourite Songs" from *Floridante* are mentioned as published, but the "Additional Songs" were not printed before 1723.

———

Handel finishes the opera *Ottone*, 10th August 1722.

———

Walsh and the Hares advertise "The Opera of Radamistus for a Flute; containing the Overture, Songs, Symphonies, and additional Airs . . .", *Post-Boy*, 2nd October 1722.

At about the same late time Meares, the original publisher of the opera, also printed such an arrangement, made by Mr. (J.?) Bolton. Cf. 20th May 1727.

———

Walsh and the Hares advertise "Favourite Songs in the Opera . . . of . . . Acis and Galatea ", *Post-Boy*, 18th October 1722.

(Smith, 1948, p. 204.) Walsh used a passepartout-title, and, inside, described the work correctly as a "Mask ". This, though anonymous, is the first edition of it. Similar advertisements appeared in the *Daily Courant* of 3rd, and in the *Post-Boy* of 6th December 1722.

———

FROM THE "LONDON JOURNAL ", 27th October 1722

There is a new Opera now in Rehearsal at the Theatre in the Hay-Market, a Part of which is reserv'd for one Mrs. *Cotsona*, an extraordinary Italian Lady, who is expected daily from Italy. It is said, she has a much finer Voice and more accurate Judgment, than any of her Country Women who have performed on the English Stage.

'Tis reported that the Managers of the Fund subscrib'd to the Opera will make a Dividend of their Profits some Time this Winter.

(Chrysander, pp. 88 and 86.) Cf. 22nd December 1722. According to Rolli's letter of 25th August 1720, the Academy had tried to engage Francesca Cuzzoni as early as 1720. If the opera in rehearsal was really *Ottone* (see 12th January 1723), as Chrysander assumes, then the time of preparation, three months, was quite unusually long. For the "dividend " cf. 16th February 1723. The news seems surprising in view of all the calls and reminders issued by the Courts of the Academy. The *London Journal* was, however, a gossip paper, as will be seen in the course of the following months.

———

The fourth season of the Academy opens on 27th October 1722 with a revival of *Muzio Scevola*.

There is some doubt about this date. The *Daily Courant* announces it, but has not the usual advertisement on the day of the supposed performance. The advertisement for the 31st does not mention a postponement from the 27th. Burney (IV. 286) thought the revival was on 10th November; Kelly (III. 350) on 31st October; Chrysander (II. 87) on 27th October; and Nicoll, otherwise very reliable, does not mention either of the two dates in his list of the performances of *Muzio Scevola*. The opera was probably revived on 27th October and was certainly performed on the 31st. An intended performance on 3rd November was postponed to the 10th, "for reason of the Indisposition of Sig. Senesino", and the last performance was on 13th November 1722; it was never revived again.—Haym succeeded Rolli in 1722 as Italian secretary and librettist to the Academy (cf. 27th November 1719 and 7th September 1725).

—

FROM THE "LONDON GAZETTE", 4th November 1722

The General Court of the Royal Academy of Musick held the 22d of November last, having ordered a further Call of 5l. per Cent, which is the 9th Call, to be made payable on all the Subscribers to the said Royal Academy on or before the 13th Instant. . . .

It seems that the notices of reminder were counted as calls too. Cf. 9th November 1723.

—

FROM THE "LONDON GAZETTE", 10th November 1722

At a General Court of the Royal Academy of Musick held the 8th Instant, it is resolved, that Notice be given to the several Defaulters in the Payment of their Calls, that they pay the same on or before the 22d Instant, when another General Court is to be held and new Directors chosen for the Year ensuing. And in case any Person shall not make their Payment in that Time, that they be proceeded against in Law, and their Names made publick.

Cf. 31st October 1721. The result of the election is not known; nor are the results for the following three years (see 17th December 1726).

—

FROM THE (?) "DAILY COURANT", 12th November 1722

By the Order of several Persons of Quality,

At the Long-Room at the Opera-House in the Hay-Market, will be an ASSEMBLY every Thursday during the Season, with a very good Set of Musick. The Day being changed from Friday to Thursday. To begin at Six a Clock. Tickets to be had at the said Long-Room, at 2s. 6d. each.

Cutting in the *Theatrical Register*. Thursday was one of the week-days when no opera was performed. It is not known where these "Assemblies" were

H.–5 *a*

instrumental concerts, given by members of the orchestra, nor for how long they went on. Cf. 15th February and 6th March 1722, and 31st January 1723.

———

Floridante is revived on 4th December, and performed again on 8th, 11th, 15th, 18th, 22nd and 26th December 1722.

Meares, who in 1722 published the *Celebrated Aires in the Opera of Floridante*, issued in January 1723 *All the Additional Celebrated Aires*. (*Daily Post*, 26th January 1723.)

———

FROM THE PARISH RECORDS OF ST. DIONIS BACKCHURCH, 15th December 1722

[The Church-wardens agree that Mr. Renatus Harris of Bristol should build an organ under certain conditions, *e.g.* . . . the touch to be] entirely to the satisfaction and good liking of Mr. Philip Hart . . . [and upon completion the organ] to be submitted to the judgment and determination of the following persons : John Loeillet, William Babel, George Frederick Handel, Dr. William Croft, and Mr. R. Courteville, all of them Professors and Masters of Music, or the majority of them.

(*Musical Times*, July 1904, p. 437 f.; probably published by the editor, F. G. Edwards.) The original not available in 1948. The exact words of the passages in square brackets are not known. The church was in the Whitechapel district. Renatus Harris, the most celebrated member of a family of English organ builders, was a serious competitor of Father Smith about 1690. Hart was organist at St. Andrew Undershaft, Leadenhall Street. Jean-Baptiste Loeillet, a Flemish flautist, oboist and composer, previously in the Haymarket orchestra, had returned to London about 1720. Babel (cf. 31st January 1717), a well-known harpsichord player, was, for a time, organist at All Hallows Church, Barking. Croft was organist at Westminster Abbey, and Ralph, or Raphael, Courteville at St. James's Church, Westminster. The organ was opened at the beginning of June 1724, and the certificate, dated 25th June, was signed by Croft, Courteville and Loeillet only.

———

FROM THE " LONDON JOURNAL ", 22nd December 1722

Mrs. Cotsona, the Italian Lady, whom we mentioned some time since to be coming over to England, to sing at the Opera, is married on her journey : She had Two Hundred and Fifty Pounds advanced by Heidecker, Master of the Opera House, before she set out, which if she should refund, and not come at all, would prove a double Disappointment to that Gentleman, not only in losing a Person so well qualified ; but he has taken a Sum of Money some Days since of a Person of Quality to pay Half a Guinea per Diem till she comes.

(Smith, 1950, p. 130.) It is supposed that Sandoni, the harpsichord master, was sent by Heidegger and Handel to bring Cuzzoni, and it was he who married her secretly. Cf. 27th October 1722 ; 11th January and 22nd August 1725.

———

From Mattheson's Hamburg Opera List, 27th December
1722 (7th January 1723) (Translated)

Muzio Scevola, done entirely in Italian, composed by Herr *Händel*.
Others say it is by one *Giovanni*.

(Chrysander, 1877, col. 248.) Cf. Mattheson's notes in *Critica Musica* of
January 1723. Giovanni indicates Bononcini. Apparently Mattheson learned the
truth after recording the first night.

—

From the " British Journal ", 29th December 1722

Seigniora *Cutzoni* is expected here with much Impatience for the
Improvement of our Opera Performances ; and as 'tis said, she far
excells Seigniora *Duristante*, already with us, and all those she leaves in
Italy behind her, much Satisfaction may be expected by those who of
later Years have contributed largely to Performances in this Kind, for
the great Advantage of the Publick, and softening the Manners of a rude
British People. The terms (this Lady does us this extraordinary Favour
upon) are reported with such Uncertainty, and it is so difficult to get
at the Truth, that we shall only say what is controverted by no one, That
she is to receive more Advantage than any one yet has on the like occasion;
tho' 1,500*l.* a Season in such cases is frequent.

(Smith, 1950, p. 130.) The salary is related as £2000, and a benefit. Signora
Cuzzoni arrived during the last week of 1722 (*London Journal*, 5th January 1723).

—

An Ode to Mr Handel,
On his Playing on the Organ (1722).
By Daniel Prat, M.A. Rector of Harrietsham, Kent.
Formerly Chaplain to His Majesty's Household at Kensington.

I.

How shall the MUSE attempt to teach,
Artist Divine ! in fitting Lays,
What Voice with equal Thought can reach
Thine and the sacred ORGAN's Praise ?
Oh ! might the Numbers flow with Ease,
As Thou our Spirits do'st command,
Which rise and fall by just Degrees,
Each Soul obsequious to thy Hand.

II.

With Joy and Wonder fill'd, we seem
Born on the swelling Sounds on high,
Like JACOB in his blissful Dream,
All Heav'n approaching to descry !

Now in more lengthen'd Notes and slow
We hear, inspiring sacred Dread,
The deep majestic Organ blow,
Symbol of Sounds that rowse the dead !

III.

A pleasing Horror fills the Dome !
The Statues o'er each antique Tomb
Attentive look ! while we like them become !
See ! All, resembling Statues stand,
Enchanted by thy Magic Hand !

A solemn Pause ensues − − − − − −
All Things are hush'd, and ev'ry Breath
Seems stop'd as in the Arms of Death !
Each restless Passion's softly lull'd to Peace,
And silent Thought seems only not to cease !
How dreadful is this Place ! What holy Fear
Thrills thro' our shudd'ring Veins ! Hail Heav'nly Choir
That round th' ETERNAL sing ! for surely here
JEHOVAH is ! far ye Profane retire.

Again we hear ! And Silence now is drown'd
In rapt'rous Notes, and Ecstasie of Sound !

I.

Fix'd in one solemn stedfast Gaze,
The rustic Hind, a human Brute,
Devours the Sounds, in deep Amaze,
Entranc'd, immoveable, and mute.
His wakening Soul begins to guess
Some God within that Frame must dwell,
Now full convinc'd that nothing less
Cou'd speak so sweet, so wond'rous well.

II.

What sacred Rage their Breast alarms,
Whose more than barb'rous ZEAL exclaims
Against the soft persuasive Charms
Of Musick, which the Savage tames ?
Such they that tore the THRACIAN Bard,
And with their frantic Clamour drown'd,
What Woods and Rocks with Rapture heard,
Both Voice and Harp's melodious Sound !

III.

Ev'n me, untaught my Voice to raise,
Wont still to haunt the silent Bow'r,
Thy Notes provoke to sing their Praise,
And oh ! that they inspir'd the Pow'r !
    But as th' unheeded Numbers flow,
Thy Skill no sooner they rehearse,
Than (as too groveling all and low)
My heighten'd Fancy scorns the Verse.

Thus the fond Bird whom Shade and Silence cheers,
Some great Musician's vary'd SOLO hears :
Her little Soul alarm'd his Notes essays,
She sings alternate as the Artist plays :
Warbling she strives, each Modulation tries,
Till tir'd, her weak Wings droop, and griev'd, she dies !

In *Roman* Strains this [1] STRADA sweetly sung,
But sweeter [2] PHILIPS in our ruder Tongue.

I.

While blest with thy Celestial Airs,
How vain we count the Views of Life,
The Miser's Hopes, the Lover's Cares,
Domestic Feuds, and Public Strife !
    No more amus'd with gaudy Sights,
The World seems now to disappear,
While Sound alone the Soul delights,
Which ravish'd wou'd for ever hear !

II.

Thy Music, like the sacred Page,
Tempers the Fierce, uplifts the Faint,
Composes Youth, enlivens Age,
Th' obdurate melts, inflames the Saint !
    Each now refin'd from low Desires,
Rais'd high by Thee, and nobler grown,
His elevated Thought admires,
And feels a Spirit not his own !

III.

But who can paint the Poet's Fires ?
How are Life's feeble Springs oppress'd
With the strong Rage thy Touch inspires,
While glowing Transports swell his Breast ?

[1] Fidicinis & Philomelae Certamen.   [2] Pastoral 5.

Rising with thy exalted Strain
His lab'ring Soul now fain wou'd fly,
Fain wou'd shake off this mortal Chain,
And reascend its Native Sky !
Thus led by MARO's Muse to CUMA's Cave,
We hear the inspir'd Maid divinely rave ;
Her changing Colour and disordered Hair
Raptures too great to be sustain'd, declare :
With heighten'd Features and wild glaring Eyes,
Panting for Breath, *The God, The God*, She cries :
The Voice not hers, and more than Mortal Sound,
From Vault to Vault like Thunder echo's round !

I.

Hark ! CORNET and CREMONA join,
Deep DIAPASON and BASSOON,
With FLUTE and VOICE HUMANE, divine !
A Choir of Instruments in One !
    Now loud all Stops in Consort blow !
By the harmonious Whirlwind driv'n,
Our Souls are ravish'd into Heav'n,
And seem to spurn the World below !

II.

Blest Emblem of Seraphic Joys !
Where various Forms and Pow'rs combine
In Harmony of Thought and Voice,
While All to hymn their SOV'RAIGN join !
    But Man, unhappy Man, whose Mind
In the same Heav'n was fram'd for Peace,
Varies discordant (like the Wind)
Whom GOD nor SOV'RAIGN long can please.

III.

Swol'n Thoughts in his tumultuous Soul
Now like the troubled Billows rowl ;
Becalm'd, they now to Spleen subside,
Low, languid, as the ebbing Tide !
    Yet as thy volant Touch pursues
Thro' all Proportions low and high
The wond'rous Fugue, it Peace renews
Serene as the unsully'd Sky,
Gladsome, as when AURORA's cheerful Beams
Dispell vain Phantoms and delusive Dreams.

Th' attending Graces with thy Fingers move,
And as they interweave the various Notes,
CONCORD and EASE, DELIGHT and purest LOVE
Flow where the undulating Music floats !
Base Spirits fly ; and All is Holy Ground
Within the Circle of the Sacred Sound !

I.

See ! DISCORD of her Rage disarm'd,
Relenting, calm, and bland as PEACE ;
Ev'n restless noisy FACTION charm'd,
And ENVY forc'd Thy Skill to bless !
    Here PHRENZY and distracted CARE
Pleas'd and compos'd wou'd ever dwell ;
While Joys unknown, till now, they share,
And feel a *Heav'n* possess'd for *Hell* !

II.

Shou'd HATE with FURIES leagu'd combine,
'Till All be into Ruin hurl'd,
Say, wou'd not HARMONY like Thine
Quell the wild Uproar of the World ?
    As when a raging Tempest roars,
Some secret Pow'r the storm restrains
Hush'd are the Waves, gay smile the Shores,
And Peace o'er all the Ocean reigns.

III.

Oh then that they whose Rage and Hate
A Brood of deadly Mischiefs nurse,
Who secret All our Ills create,
And then their own dire Off-spring curse,
    That All in one Assembly join'd,
Cou'd hear thy healing soothing Strain !
Soon shou'dst thou calm their troubled Mind,
And Reason shou'd her Seat regain :
Then in sweet Sounds like Thine, so soft a Style,
HOADLY or FLEETWOOD Silver-tongu'd shou'd shew
How Rage wou'd ravish from our frighted ISLE,
The dear-bought Blessings to the *Laws* we owe :
How from just *Laws* the WORLD derives Repose,
And HARMONY thro' all the glad CREATION flows !

Their Voice th' enlighten'd Crowd to Peace shou'd move,
And fix for ever firm in LOYALTY and LOVE.

This is the first of several poems dedicated to Handel during his lifetime. It was printed by Jacob Tonson in 1722, 9 pp. folio. Copy in Gerald Coke's Handel Collection. The poem was reprinted in 1781, in vol. 7, pp. 150-56, of *A Select Collection of Poems*, edited, in eight volumes by John Bowyer Nichols, 1780-82, and, separately, at Cambridge in 1791 under the title : "An Ode on the late celebrated Handel, on his playing the organ". The place indicated is probably St. Paul's Cathedral. Famianus Strada (1572-1649) was a Jesuit rhetorician and author in Rome ; Ambrose Philips' *Pastorals* 5 and 6 were published in 1709.

—

From Walsh's Cash-Book, 1722

1722   Opera Otho—£42 0 0

Although the opera was not performed until 12th January 1723, it seems that Walsh bought the rights to publish the music at the end of 1722. Cf. 19th March 1723.

—

From " A Journey Through England, In Familiar Letters from A Gentleman Here [*i.e.* John Macky] to His Friend Abroad ", London, 1722

(Cannons)

The Disposition of the Avenues, Gardens, Statues, Paintings, and the House of *Cannons*, suits the Genius and Grandeur of its great Master. The Chapel, which is already finished, hath a Choir of Vocal and Instrumental Musick, as the Royal Chapel ; and when his Grace goes to Church, he is attended by his *Swiss* Guards, ranged as the Yeomen of the Guards : his Musick also play when he is at Table, he is served by Gentlemen in the best Order ; and I must say, that few German Sovereign Princes, live with that Magnificence, Grandeur and good Order. . . .

The Chapel is incomparably neat and pretty, all finely plaistered and gilt by *Pargotti*, and the Cielings and Niches painted by *Paulucci* ; there is a handsome Altar Piece, and in an Alcove above the Altar a neat Organ ; fronting the Altar above the Gate, is a fine Gallery for the Duke and Dutchess, with a Door that comes from the Appartments above, and a Staircase that also descends into the Body of the Chapel, in case of taking the Sacrament, or other Occasion. In the Windows of this Chapel, are also finely painted some Parts of the History of the New Testament.

In that Court, which opens into the *Area*, is the dining room, very spacious . . . and at the End of it, a Room for his Musick, which performs both Vocal and Instrumental, during the Time he is at Table ; and he spares no Expense to have the best. . . .

. . . at the end of each of his chief Avenues, he hath neat Lodgings for Eight old Serjeants of the Army, whom he took out of *Chelsea-College*,

who guard the whole ; and go their Rounds at Night, and call the
Hours, as the Watchmen do at *London*, to prevent Disorders ; and wait
upon the Duke to Chapel on *Sundays* . . . and his Gentleman told me,
they are above a Hundred Servants in Family of one Degree or another.

Vol. II, pp. 5-10, Letter I, London. (Cummings, 1885, p. 7 ; 1904, pp. 57-9 ;
1915, pp. 12-14 ; Streatfeild, 1916, pp. 7 f.) Macky calls Edgware " the town of
Edger ". " Pargotti " is (Pietro Martine ?) Bagutti, stuccoer or plasterer ;
" Paulucci " is Antonio Bellucci. Cf. Defoe's *Tour*, 1725.

———

Jeanne Roger, of Amsterdam, publishes, about 1722, Handel's
twelve *Sonates pour un Traversiere, un Violon ou Hautbois Con
Basso Continuo* (publisher's number 534), later known as opus 1,
and his opus 2, *VI Sonates à deux Violons, deux haubois ou deux
Flutes traversieres & Basse Continue* (p. no. 535).

Cf. 9th November 1720. As in the case of the Amsterdam edition of
Handel's lessons, nothing is known about his connections either with the
publisher Jeanne Roger, or with her brother-in-law Michel le Cene.
Chrysander (III. 147-50, and volume 27 of the *Collected Edition*, pp. III f.)
thought it possible that opus 2, at any rate, was published by G. F. Witvogel
in Amsterdam (cf. 19th January 1733), and he believed that opus 1 and
opus 2 were written between 1724 and 1733. Walsh reprinted these
works in 1733 from Roger's plates, with some alterations (publisher's
numbers 407 and 408) and added : " This is more Correct than the former
Edition ". Walsh's deal with Roger indicates a legitimate connection
between Handel and the Amsterdam publishers.

1723

When a certain world-famous man came here to Hamburg for the first time, he knew how to compose practically nothing but regular fugues, and if *Imitationes* were as strange to him as a foreign tongue, they were also just as troublesome. What I can remember best is how he brought me his very first opera, scene by scene, and every evening would ask my thoughts about it, and what pains it cost him to conceal the pedant [in him]. . . .[1]

On the 7th of this month [27th December 1722] again a new opera was presented here, which bore the title : *Muzio Scevola*. It was sung, 'tis true, entirely in Italian ; yet [its dialogue] is translated into a fine *prosam*, and it is also adorned with a German prologue. As many *Actus* as are found therein, just so many composers have distinguished themselves with them. Namely, three. *Buononcini* has composed the first act ; the second, *Mattei* (who under the name of *Pipo*, i.e. *Filippo*, plays the *violoncello* in London) and Händel has shown his art in the third act. All these masterpieces have been sent here to us from England ; except the *Prologo* which is by Kaiser. If such-like musical aristocracy should now become supreme in opera writing, then, first of all, a monarch might arise with difficulty among the composers. Much less might one of them arise here, therefore great care should be taken to invest wisely the capital thrown out [*sic*].

Vol. I, part 4, no. 1, pp. 243 and 256. (The latter quoted by Chrysander, II. 62 f.) The world-famous man of the first passage is, of course, Handel. He wrote *Almira* in Hamburg in 1704 ; it was produced on 8th January 1705.—The libretto of the Hamburg *Muzio Scevola* has Keiser's prologue but does not give the name of the translator, nor of any of the authors (librettist, three composers, and writer of the prologue). A manuscript copy of the full score must have been sent from London to Hamburg. Mattheson mixes up the names of the composers of the first two acts ; he was, however, right in attributing one of these acts to Pippo and not to Ariosti. When he speaks of aristocracy he apparently means oligarchy, and the end of the quotation is quite incomprehensible.

———

At the King's Theatre . . . this present Saturday . . . will be presented, A New Opera call'd OTHO, King of Germany. Pit and Boxes

---

[1] No one need wonder over this. I learnt from him as well as he from me. *Docendo enim discimus.*

to be put together and in Regard to the Increase of the Numbers of the Subscribers, no more than Three Hundred and Fifty Tickets will be deliver'd out this Day, at Mrs. White's Chocolate-House in St. James's-street, at Half a Guinea each. N.B. No Tickets will be given out at the Door, nor any Persons whatever admitted for Money. Gallery 5s. By Command, no Directors, Subscribers, or any other Persons will be admitted behind the Scenes. To begin exactly at Six a-Clock.

The increasing number of subscribers is to be understood as relating to the Opera House, not the Academy ; cf. 25th November 1721. Kelly (II. 350) records that during the season of 1722-23 admission to practices of the operas was permitted, at one guinea each.—*Ottone, Re di Germania*, text by Haym, altered from Stefano Benedetto Pallavicino's *Teofane* was performed during this season on 12th, 15th, 19th, 22nd, 26th, 29th January ; 2nd, 5th, 9th, 12th, 16th February, on successive opera nights, and on 26th March, and 4th and 8th June 1723.

———

Cast of " Ottone ", 12th January 1723

Ottone—Signor Senesino, alto
Teofane—Signora Cuzzoni, soprano
Emireno—Signor Boschi, bass
Gismonda—Signora Durastanti, soprano
Adelberto—Signor Berenstadt, bass
Matilda—Mrs. Robinson, soprano

Cuzzoni was now the prima donna in Handel's operas, and was worthy of her partner Senesino. Berenstadt sang his second Handel part, his first having been Argante in the *Rinaldo* of 1717.

———

From Colman's " Opera Register ", January 1723

Anno 1722 Decr Sigra Faustina Cuzzoni first sung at ye Theatre above sd [in the Haymarket] towards ye end of this year in the Opera called Ottone—& was extreemly admired & often performed Sigra Durastanti Sigr Senesino Mrs An^a Robinson sung also in ye said Opera & pleased much.

Colman dated Cuzzoni's début too early, entering these notes some time after the first night. He also mixed the names of Cuzzoni and Faustina (Bordoni) who did not appear in London before 1726.

———

Monsieur de Fabrice to Count Flemming (Translated)

London, January 15th, 1722-23.
. . . In the end the famous Cozzuna not merely arrived but even sang in a new opera by Hendell, called Othon—the same subject as the one at Dresden—with enormous success ; the house was full to over-flowing. Today is the second performance and there is such a run on it that tickets are already being sold at 2 and 3 guineas which are ordinarily half a guinea, so that it is like another Mississippi or South Sea Bubble.

Over and above that, there exist two factions, the one supporting Hendell, the other Bononcini, the one for Cenesino and the other for Cossuna. They are as much at loggerheads as the Whigs and Tories, and even on occasion sow dissension among the Directors.

(Opel, *Mitteilungen*, p. 32 : dated 1722). Geheimes Staatsarchiv, Dresden. Fabrice alludes to Lotti's opera *Teofane*, produced at Dresden on the occasion of the marriage of the Electoral Prince (cf. 15th July 1719) on 2nd September 1719.— The Whigs were, in fact, Bononcini's patrons, while the Tories favoured Handel.

FROM THE "LONDON JOURNAL", 19th January 1723

His Majesty was at the Theatre in the Hay-Market, when Seigniora Cotzani performed, for the first Time, to the Surprize and Admiration of a numerous Audience, who are ever too fond of Foreign Performers. She is already jump'd into a handsome Chariot, and an Equipage accordingly. The Gentry seem to have so high a Taste of her fine Parts, that she is likely to be a great Gainer by them.

(Chrysander, II. 95 ; Smith, 1950, p. 131.) The King was present at the first night of *Ottone*. The Royal Family, it seems, attended the performance on the 22nd.

FROM THE "DAILY COURANT", 22nd January 1723

(" Ottone " repeated.)

. . . Whereas it has been usual to deliver out the Opera Tickets at White's Chocolate-House, the Royal Academy have judged it more Convenient that they for the future be delivered out at their Office in the Hay-Market. . . . Upon Complaint to the Royal Academy of Musick, that Disorders have been of late committed in the Footmen's Gallery, to the Interruption of the Performance ; This is to give Notice, That the next Time any Disorder is made there, that Gallery will be shut up.

The behaviour of the footmen in the galleries of the London theatres in general was frequently complained of in the papers. In 1742, Henry Fielding let his "Joseph Andrews" lead the opinion of all the other footmen at an opera, "and they never condemned or applauded a single song contrary to his approbation or dislike " (Brewster, p. 133).

A General Court of the Academy is held, 23rd January 1723. (*London Gazette*, 15th January.)

FROM A LONDON NEWSPAPER, 31st January 1723

UN PASSO TEMPO,

At the Long-Room, at the Opera-House in the Hay-Market, this present Thursday . . . with agreeable Entertainments for Ladies and

Gentlemen. Tickets to be had at the said Long-Room, at 5s. each. To begin at Eight a Clock in the Evening.

Cutting in the *Theatrical Register*. Kelly, II. 350, quotes the advertisement slightly differently, without giving the source. Cf. 12th November 1722.

———

JOHN GAY TO JONATHAN SWIFT IN DUBLIN

London, February 3, 1722–23.

. . . As for the reigning amusements of the town, it is entirely music ; real fiddles, base-viols, and hautboys, not poetical harps, lyres and reeds. There is nobody allowed to say, " I sing ", but an eunuch, or an Italian woman. Everybody is grown now as great a judge of music, as they were in your time of poetry, and folks, that could not distinguish one tune from another, now daily dispute about the different styles of Handel, Bononcini, and Attilio. People have now forgot Homer, and Virgil, and Caesar, or at least, they have lost their ranks ; for, in London and Westminster, in all polite conversations, Senesino is daily voted to be the greatest man that ever lived.

(Swift, Correspondence, vol. III, 1912, pp. 154 f. ; Chrysander, II. pp. 97 f.).

———

PETITION BY THE GRAND JURY FOR THE COUNTY OF MIDDLESEX TO THE HOUSE OF COMMONS, 12th February 1723

Whereas there has been lately publish'd a Proposal for Six Ridotto's, or Balls, to be managed by Subscription at the King's Theatre in the Hay-Market, &c. We the Grand Jury of the County of Middlesex, sworn to enquire for our Sovereign Lord the King, and the Body of this County, conceiving the same to be a Wicked and unlawfull Design, for carrying on Gaming, Chances by Way of Lottery, and other Impious and Illegal Practices, and which (if not timely suppressed) may promote Debauchery, Lewdness, and ill Conversation : From a just Abhorrence, therefore, of such Sort of Assemblies, which we apprehend are contrary to Law and good Manners, and give great Offence to his Majesty's good and virtuous Subjects, We do present the same and recommend them to be prosecuted and suppressed as common Nuisances to the Publick, as Nurseries of Lewdness, Extravagance, and Immorality, and also a Reproach and Scandal to Civil Government.

(J. P. Malcolm, II. 157 ; Chrysander, II. 103.) British Museum : Burney Collection, 1728, vol. II. This petition was printed as a broad-sheet, and presented by James Bertie, foreman of the Jury and Member of Parliament (*St. James's Journal*, 16th February 1723). The last three Ridottos were cancelled, but in 1724 they were held again under the name of Balls. Cf. February 1718 and spring 1724.

———

FROM THE " LONDON JOURNAL ", 16th February 1723

The Court of Directors of the Royal Academy of Musick in the Hay-market, have lately made a Dividend of Seven per Cent, on their

Capital ; and, it is thought, that if this Company goes on with the same Success as they have done for some Time past, of which there is no doubt, it will become considerable enough to be engrafted on some of our Corporations in the City, the Taste of the Publick for Musick being so much improv'd lately.

(Chrysander, II. 86.) Cf. 27th October 1722.

———

Ariosti's *Cajo Marzio Coriolano*, text by Haym, is produced at the Haymarket Theatre, 19th February 1723.

This was probably the first opera Ariosti wrote for London. (Loewenberg, p. 76.) The *British Journal* of 23rd February reports that this opera was "said to exceed any thing of the kind ever seen upon the stage" (Chrysander, II. 95).

———

From Mattheson's " Critica Musica ", Hamburg, February 1723 (Translated)

Lüneburg. Our Cantor *Dreyer* will perform on the coming Good Friday the ' Passion ' by Capellmeister *Händel*, and is now earnestly occupied with copying out the same. It is the famous *Oratorium* which was set to music first by Herr *Keiser*, then by Herr *Händel*, Herr *Telemann*, and the *Autore Criticae*, consequently by 4 Capellmeister.

Vol. 1, part 4, no. 2, p. 288. This was the *Brockes Passion* ; cf. spring 1719. Lüneburg is south of Hamburg. The performance was probably in the old *Johanniskirche*.

———

From the " London Journal ", 2nd March 1723

The new Opera Tickets are very high, and like to continue so as long as Mrs. Cotzani is so much admired. They are traded in at the other End of the Town, as much as Lottery Tickets are in Exchange-Alley.

(Chrysander, II. 95.) Cf. 15th and 19th January 1723. The official price of the tickets was not raised.

———

Walsh and the Hares advertise " the Masque of *Acis* and *Galatea*, and six Overtures for Violins in 4 Parts, for Concert, composed by Mr. Handel, Mr. Bononcini, and other eminent Authors ", *Post-Boy*, 2nd March 1723.

Handel's name is not mentioned for the " Masque ", and the edition of it has not been identified (Smith, 1948, p. 207). The overtures were apparently the first set of a long series, or rather of several series, started in 1723 by Walsh ; at first the overtures were by various composers, but soon, with Walsh specializing in the publication of his works, by Handel alone. There are collections for harpsichord, for four parts (two violins or oboes, tenor and bass), for seven or eight parts (' all the parts '), and, finally, of scores. The set advertised above was probably the collection of the overtures to *Astarto* (Bononcini), *Creso* (pasticcio), *Camilla* (Bononcini), *L'Idaspe fedele* (Mancini), *Thomyris* (pasticcio), and *Rinaldo*. The plates of the "four parts" edition were, of course, used for the "all the parts" edition.

Walsh and the Hares advertise their edition of *Ottone*, *Post-Boy*, 19th March 1723.

This time it is not a selection of Favourite Songs, but something like a short score of the whole opera, called *Otho, an Opera*, containing the overture and 28 vocal numbers, 92 pp. fol. The privilege of 1720 is inserted, the score being "Publish'd by the Author". In April 1723 Walsh started to issue "favourite songs" from plates of the "opera", probably to counteract Meares' publication of "favourite airs".

FROM THE "DAILY COURANT", 26th March 1723

For the Benefit of Signora Francesca Cuzzoni.

At the King's Theatre . . . this present Tuesday . . . will be perform'd . . . OTHO, King of Germany. With an Addition of Three new Songs, and an entire new Scene. . . . And particular Care will be taken to place Benches on the Stage for the Accommodation of the Company. . . . NB. Whereas this Benefit for Signora Cuzzoni is part of her Contract, the Directors of the Royal Academy of Musick resolve not to make use of the Liberty of the House for this Night.

(Burney, IV. 288 ; Chrysander, II. 95.) Handel's additions may be found in a 1723 issue of Walsh and Hares' *The Monthly Mask of Vocal Musick or the Newest Songs Made for the Theatre's & other Occasions*, probably published in April, with the four additional songs from *Ottone* : "Gode l' alma", "Spera, si mi dice", "Tra queste care ombre", all three sung by Signora Cuzzoni, and "Cara tu nel mio petto", sung by Berenstadt. (Copies in National Library of Scotland, Edinburgh, and in University Library, Cambridge.) In the Collected Edition of Handel's works, the first of these arias is printed in the main score (vol. LVI, p. 110), the three others, however, in the appendix (pp. 138, 142 and 132).

FROM THE "LONDON JOURNAL", 30th March 1723

On Tuesday last [the 26th] was perform'd the Opera of Otho, King of Germany, for the Benefit of Mrs. Cuzzoni ; and a considerable Benefit it was to her indeed, for we hear that some of the Nobility gave her 50 Guineas a Ticket. . . . As we delight so much in Italian Songs, we are likely to have enough of them, for as soon as Cuzzoni's Time is out, we are to have another over ; for we are well assured *Faustina*, the fine Songstress at Venice, is invited, whose Voice, they say, exceeds that we have already here ; and as the Encouragement is so great, no doubt but she will visit us, and, like others, when she makes her Exit, may carry off Money enough to build some stately Edifice in her own Country, and there perpetuate our Folly.

(Chrysander, II. 95 ; Smith, 1950, p. 131.) Faustina did not arrive until spring 1726.

FROM REED'S "WEEKLEY JOURNAL", 6th April 1723

We are told that the Italian Singers at our Opera, to the Number of five, of whom two are Eunuchs, have obtain'd a Permission from the King of France sign'd by his Majesty, the Duke of Orleans, and one of the Secretaries of State, to go over thither in July next, to perform twelve times, for which 'tis said the King will give them new Habits for the Theatre, and a Gratuity of 35,000 Livres, and that His Majesty intends to give the old Opera 23,000 Livres to make amends for the loss which they may suffer by the new one.

The same notice appeared in Appleby's *Original Weekly Journal* of the same day. Cf. *Le Mercure*, April 1723, quoted below.

———

FROM THE "LONDON JOURNAL", 8th April 1723

[The Court of Directors threatens defaulters that] proper measures will be taken to oblige them to pay what is due.

Cf. 31st October 1721.

———

FROM MATTHESON'S HAMBURG OPERA LIST, 17th (28th) April 1723
(Translated)

Floridantes. Music by Herr Kapellmeister *Händel.* Herr *Beckau* made the translation.

(Chrysander, 1877, col. 248.) The title was : *Der Thrazische Printz Floridantes.* Neither the names of the original authors nor that of Joachim Beccau are mentioned in the printed libretto. The 27 airs were sung in Italian ; " Dopo l'ombre " (I. 4) is missing in the score. According to Willers' Hamburg Notes (Merbach, p. 360), the opera was performed 11 times in 1723.

———

Walsh and the Hares advertise, from *Ottone*, " the Overture, Songs and Symphonies for a single Flute, and the Duets for two Flutes ", *Daily Courant*, 24th April 1723.

Similar arrangements were already published, in oblong octavo, from Handel's operas *Rinaldo, Radamisto* and *Floridante* ; others were to follow.

———

FROM "LE MERCURE", PARIS, April 1723
(Translated)

Several Italian members of the London Opera are due to come to Paris and give twelve performances during the month of July next, for which they will receive a considerable proportion of the receipts. Any surplus will be profit to the Academy, which will cease to function all that month. It will provide everything required for the Italians' per-formances—dresses, sets, choruses, ballets, orchestra, etc. Those who are to share the promised sum number five persons, viz. two women, two altos, and one bass. It is said that the price of the seats will be raised by a third and that there will be no free tickets.

(Loewenberg, p. xviii.) Cf. 6th April. This plan came to nothing. There exist librettos of *Ottone* and of *Giulio Cesare*, printed in Paris 1724, with Italian texts and French stage directions, which indicate a similar plan for the following summer, again without realization. Of the first of these, a copy is now in the Library of Congress, Washington ; for the other one, see *Catalogo della Libraria Floncel*, Paris, 1774, p. 106 (no. 2717) and p. 215 (no. 7326), to be found in the British Museum.

—

FROM MATTHESON'S " CRITICA MUSICA ", HAMBURG, April 1723
(Translated)

I know none of the old, worthy *Maitres* who surpasses *Johann Krieger* of Zittau in it [double fugue]. And among the younger men I have not yet come across anyone who would be so dexterous in it as Capellmeister *Händel* : not only in composing ; but in *extemporising* too, as I have listened to such a hundred times with the greatest astonishment.

Vol. 1, part 4, no. 4, p. 326. Johann Krieger, the younger of two brothers, was born in 1651, and lived in Zittau, Saxony, as organist and music director of the town.

—

Handel finishes his opera *Flavio*, 7th May 1723.

—

FROM THE " DAILY COURANT ", 14th May 1723

At the King's Theatre . . . this present Tuesday . . . will be performed a New Opera call'd, FLAVIUS. . . . By reason of the shortness of the Opera, to begin exactly at Eight a-Clock.

Flavio, Re de'Longobardi, text by Haym, partly founded on Pierre Corneille's *Le Cid* and altered from a libretto by Stefano Ghigi (Loewenberg, p. 76), was performed again on 18th, 21st, 25th, 27th, 30th May ; 11th and 15th June, but was not revived in the autumn.

—

CAST OF " FLAVIO ", 14th May 1723
Flavio—Signor Berenstadt, bass
Guido—Signor Senesino, alto
Emilia—Signora Cuzzoni, soprano
Teodata—Mrs. Robinson, soprano
Vitige—Signora Durastanti, soprano
Ugone—Mr. Gordon, tenor
Lotario—Signor Boschi, bass

Following Tiridate in *Radamisto*, Ugone was Mr. Gordon's second and last Handel part.

—

Rinaldo, first performed at Hamburg in November 1715 (cf. 18th August 1720), is revived there, 16th (27th) May 1723.

According to Willers's Hamburg Notes (Merbach, p. 360), where the performance is listed as " zum erstenmahl ", the opera was repeated ten times in 1723, twice in 1724, and once each in 1727 and 1730. Some airs were sung in Italian (Loewenberg, p. 65).

———

Walsh and the Hares announce the publication of *Flavio*, and that *Ottone, Floridante* " and other curious Pieces, by the same Author " are to be had from them, *Daily Courant*, 22nd May 1723.

Cf. 21st June 1723.

———

The fourth season of the Academy ends on 15th June 1723 with *Flavio*.

During the summer the Haymarket Theatre was redecorated (cf. 21st September 1723).

———

Walsh and the Hares advertise the " Celebrated Opera call'd Flavius ; containing all the Overture, Songs and Symphonies, as they were perform'd at the King's Theatre for the Royal Academy ; compos'd by Mr. Handell ", *Daily Courant*, 21st June 1723.

There are 64 pages folio, and Handel's privilege, the music being " Publish'd by the Author ".

———

FROM THE TREASURY PAPERS, ABOUT 26th June 1723

| 1723 | Memorial | Royal Academy of Music | Lords of the Treasury | For a warrant to pay 1000*l.* out of the Bounty Office and for 200*l.* to defray the taxes and other expenses attending the receipt of the 1000*l.* which his Majesty allowed. |

Minuted :—" 26th June 1723 1,000 *li.* order'd."

(Calendar, 1720–28, p. 247.) The taxes and other expenses, which the Academy apparently had to pay from the subsidy of 1722, were not granted.

———

Walsh and the Hares advertise their flute arrangement of *Flavio*, *Daily Courant*, 15th July 1723.

———

Ottone is produced in Italian at Brunswick, with additional airs by
Antonio Lotti, August 1723.

(Chrysander, II. 95 ; Loewenberg, p. 75.)   Karl Heinrich Graun, later
a well-known composer, sang the part of Adelberto.   Revived in August
1725.

—

FROM THE " BRITISH JOURNAL ", 21st September 1723

The House in which the Opera's, &c. are kept in the *Hay-Market*, is
beautifying and new painting by some of the best Masters ; Mr. *Heidiger*
the Master having ordered 1000*l.* to be expended on that Account, for
the better Entertainment of his Audiences in the Winter.

It seems that the Academy was able to spend the whole amount of the King's
subsidy (*cf.* 26th June 1723) on the redecoration of the Theatre.

—

FROM THE " LONDON GAZETTE ", 9th November 1723

The Court of Directors of the Royal Academy of Musick have ordered
a Call of 5*l.* per Cent, which is the 10th Call, to be made payable on all
the Subscribers to the said Royal Academy on or before the 23d Instant.
These are to give Notice, That the Deputy-Treasurer will attend at the
Office at the Opera House in the Hay-Market on the several Days following, viz. the 21st, 22d, and 23d Instant, from Nine in the Morning till
Two in the Afternoon, to receive the same.   And these are further to
give Notice, That a General Court, which is the Annual Court by
Charter, for chusing Deputy-Governour and Directors for the Year
ensuing, will be held on Friday the 22d Instant, at the Office aforesaid, at
Eleven in the Morning. . . .

The last call had been published on 4th November 1722.   The result of the
election is not known.

—

The fifth season of the Academy opens on 27th November 1723
with Bononcini's new opera, *Farnace*.

The libretto was dedicated, by the composer, to the Earl of Peterborough,
Anastasia Robinson's husband.   They were married secretly in 1722 ;
their marriage was made public in 1724, but not formally until 1735.

—

Ottone is revived, 11th December 1723.

Repeat performances on 14th, 18th, 21st, 28th December 1723 ; and
1st January 1724.

—

FROM WALSH'S CASH-BOOK, 1723

1723   Opera Flavio . . . £26 5 0

Cf. 21st June 1723.

1724

FROM THE "LONDON JOURNAL", 11th January 1724

Sunday last [the 5th], being the first Sunday since his Majesty's Arrival, *Te Deum* and a new Anthem were performed both Vocally and Instrumentally, at the Royal Chappel at St. James's, his Majesty and their Royal Highnesses being present.

George I had returned from a long sojourn in Hanover. The music was probably Handel's *Utrecht Te Deum and Jubilate*, often performed in London and at the newly founded Three Choirs Festival (September) until his *Dettingen Te Deum* became popular in 1743. The anthem may have been " O praise the Lord ye Angels of his " (cf. 23rd August 1720) or one of the eleven Chandos Anthems, arranged by Handel for the Chapels Royal. The names of the singers are indicated in Handel's manuscripts : Francis Hughes, alto, Thomas Bell, counter-tenor, Bernard Gates and Samuel Weeley, bass. In 1724, and again in 1736, appeared *A Collection of Anthems, performed in his Majesty's Chapels Royal, etc.* " Published by the Direction of the Reverend the Sub-Dean of his Majesty's said Chapels Royal ", *i.e.* George Carleton. This collection of the texts, without music, includes on p. 81 (p. 102 in 1736 edition), Psalm XLII, " As pants the hart ", " By Mr. George Frederick Handell, Composer to his Majesty ". Nothing is known of such an appointment in 1724. Cf. 1st April 1724.

FROM THE SAME

The Lord Bishop of London preached the 6th Instant, the annual Sermon before the Society for the Reformation of Manners at Bow-Church ; where was present the Right Honourable the Lord Mayor, Eight or Nine Bishops, and many other Persons of Distinction, who afterwards dined with the Lord Mayor.

On this occasion, Edmund Gibson preached against Heidegger's Masquerades, held this year at the Haymarket Theatre under the name of Balls. Of the balls subscribed, therefore, only six were given this winter. The sermon was not printed until July (*Daily Journal*, 7th July), but a letter in verse, addressed to the Bishop, was published under Heidegger's name in April (*Monthly Catalogue*, no. 13). The real authors, Macey, Cox and Povey, as well as the printer and publisher, were arrested shortly afterwards (*London Journal*, 2nd May). Macey may have been identical with John Macky (see his *Journey*, quoted at the end of 1722) ; Charles Povey was one of the others, but Cox has not been identified. Cf. February 1718 and 12th February 1723. (Chrysander, II. 104.)

Ariosti's opera *Vespasiano* (text by Haym) is produced at the Haymarket Theatre, 14th January 1724.

FROM MIST's "WEEKLY JOURNAL", 18th January 1724

We hear there have been strange Commotions in the State of Musick in the Opera-House in the Hay-Market, and that a civil Broil arose among the Subscribers at the Practice of the new Opera of *Vespasian*, which turn'd all the Harmony into Discord ; and if these Dissentions do not cease, it is thought *Opera* Stock will fall.

(Chrysander, II. 105.) For the newly granted admission to opera rehearsals, see 12th January 1723.

———

FROM THE "DAILY COURANT", 20th February 1724

At the King's Theatre . . . this present Thursday . . . will be performed, A New Opera, call'd, JULIUS CAESAR . . . at Six a-Clock.

Giulio Cesare in Egitto, text by Haym, was the most successful Handel opera until 1725 when *Rodelinda* was produced (Loewenberg, p. 77). It was repeated on 22nd, 25th, 27th, 29th February ; 3rd, 7th, 10th, 14th, 21st, 24th, 28th March ; 7th and 11th April, during 1724. It was revived at the beginning of 1725, 1730 and 1732, and went to 38 performances during these years.

———

FROM NICOLA FRANCESCO HAYM's DEDICATION OF THE LIBRETTO OF "GIULIO CESARE" TO CAROLINE, PRINCESS OF WALES, 20th February 1724 (Translated)

. . . In it are represented the famous deeds of Julius Caesar in Egypt, adorned with the music of Mr. George Frederic Handel ; and if he has the fortune to meet with Your Royal Highness's approval he will have nothing else to wish for.

Haym also reminds the Princess that the first musical sounds she heard were those produced by the voice of "Pistocio", *i.e.* Francesco Pistocchi, when this singer and composer was musical director to the Margrave of Ansbach, from 1687 to 1694.

———

CAST OF "GIULIO CESARE", 20th February 1724

Interlocutori Romani :
Giulio Cesare—Signor Senesino, alto
Curio—Signor Lagarde, bass
Cornelia—Mrs. Robinson, soprano
Sesto Pompeo—Signora Durastanti, soprano

Interlocutori Egizi :
Cleopatra—Signora Cuzzoni, soprano
Tolomeo—Signor Berenstadt, bass
Achilla—Signor Boschi, bass
Noreno—Signor Bigonsi, alto

In a mezzotint engraving of 1735 Senesino is represented with the score of *Giulio Cesare*. The score, published by Cluer (cf. 2nd May 1724), was the most complete of any Handel opera printed during his life-time.—Bigonsi, or Bigonzi, only sang this season at the Haymarket Theatre.—There exists an etched cartoon, sometimes ascribed to Hogarth and supposed to show a scene from *Giulio Cesare*, printed about 1725. From left to right, Senesino, Cuzzoni and probably Berenstadt can be recognized, but these three singers had no common scene in the opera. Eisenschmidt, II. 95, stresses the point that Signora Cuzzoni wears a kind of crinoline ; not, of course, true to the period of the plot, but in advance of the fashion of the day. Harry R. Beard, in 1950, suggested that the scene is from *Flavio*, III. 4, and the caricature from about 1723. Both representations are reproduced in this book.

JOHN BYROM TO HIS WIFE ELIZABETH, 3rd March 1724

I was engaged to dine at Mrs. de Vlieger's on Saturday [29th February], whence they all went to the opera of Julius Caesar, and I for one. Mr. Leycester sat by me in the front row of the gallery, for we both were there to get good places betimes ; it was the first entertainment of this nature that I ever saw, and will I hope be the last, for of all the diversions of the town I least of all enter into this.

Byrom, *Journal, etc.*, I. 69 f. The Lancaster poet and inventor of a shorthand system had been a contributor to the *Spectator*. He became a Jacobite, and was the author of the hymn " Christians, awake ", set to music by John Wainwright. Cf. May 1725. His friend was Ralph Leycester.

FROM THE " POST BOY " OF 7th March 1723 (1724)

This day is published

⁺₊⁺ An Epistle to Mr. Handel, upon his Opera's of FLAVIUS and JULIUS CAESAR. . . .

Printed for J. Roberts near the Oxford Arms in Warwick Lane. Pr. 4 d.

AN EPISTEL TO MR. HANDEL, UPON HIS OPERAS OF FLAVIUS AND JULIUS CAESAR [7th March 1724]

Orpheus in Sylvis, inter Delphinas Arion.
                                        VIRG. Ecl. 8.
Hear how Timotheus' various Lays surprize,
And bid alternate Passions fall and rise.
                                        POPE.

Crown'd by the gen'ral Voice, at last you shew
The utmost Length that *Musick*'s Force can go :
What Pow'r on Earth, but Harmony like Thine,
Cou'd *Britain*'s jarring Sons e'er hope to join ?
Like *Musick*'s diff'ring Sounds we all agree,
Form'd by thy skilful Hand to *Harmony* :
Our Souls so tun'd, that *Discord* grieves to find
A whole fantastick Audience of a Mind :
The Deaf have found their Ears,—their Eyes the Blind.

Some little *Rebels* to thy mighty Name,
Deny the Crown due justly to your Fame ;
No Sons of *Phœbus*, but a spurious Breed,
Who suck bad Air, and on thin Diet feed ;
Each puny Stomach loaths, and ill digests
The labour'd Greatness of thy finish'd Feasts :
Notes that the Passions move they can't admire,
But love,—and rage,—and rave,—with sober Fire ;
Supine in downy Indolence they doze,
Whilst *Poppy-Strains* their drowsy Eye-lids close,
And soothing whispers lull 'em to repose.
Since this lethargick Tribe you've overcome,
Let them beware the stupid *Midas'* Doom ;
Who *Pan*'s shrill Pipe t' *Apollo*'s Lyre prefers,
For Judgment justly wears the Ass's Ears.

To please this vitious Taste, what Arts were try'd ?
Our *Beaus* have scolded, and our *Belles* have cry'd,
And famous *Op'ras* reign'd their Day,—and dy'd :
Tho' crowded Theatres your Numbers grac'd,
To sooth the tastless Fews, you were displac'd ;
Pleasure too exquisite 'cause we enjoy'd,
Some eminent old Women they imploy'd ;
Whose fine-spun Notes, like *Musick* of the Spheres,
Quite out of reach, were lost to mortal Ears.

Amusements less polite the Town will charm,
We want some Crowd,—and Sounds,—to keep us warm ;
In Place of promis'd Heaps of glitt'ring Gold,
The good *Academy* got nought—but Cold.
Where cou'd they fly for Succour, but to You ?
Whose Musick's ever Good, and ever New.
All were o'er-joy'd to see Thee thus restor'd,
And Musick's Empire own its lawful *Lord* ;
In Extacies divine we all were wrapt,
And Foes to Musick wonder'd why they *clapt* ;
Spite of themselves th' *Insensibles* were charm'd,
And Sounds victorious, *Envy*'s Rage disarm'd.

Thus when the *Sun* withdraws his golden Rays,
Nor longer o'er the World his Light displays ;
The pale-fac'd *Moon* triumphant rules the Night,
Proud of her Silver Beams, and borrow'd Light ;
Pleas'd with her Throne, she faintly mimicks Day,
Whilst each small star darts forth its twinkling Ray :

But when the ruddy *Morn* reflects the *Sun*,
Bright in his glorious Blaze his Course to run ;
Then *Moon* and *Stars* superior Lustre fly,
And dimm'd by brighter Beams, inglorious lie.

Gerald Coke's Handel Collection, 4 pp. fol. Published anonymously.

———

MONSIEUR DE FABRICE TO COUNT FLEMMING (Translated)

London, March 10th, 1724.

. . . The opera is in full swing also, since Hendell's new one, called Jules César—in which Cenesino and Cozzuna shine beyond all criticism—has been put on. The house was just as full at the seventh performance as at the first. In addition to that the squabbles, between the Directors and the sides that everyone is taking between the singers and the composers, often provide the public with the most diverting scenes.

(Opel, *Mitteilungen*, p. 33.) Geheimes Staatsarchiv, Dresden. The seventh performance was on 7th March. The beginning of the letter deals with Heidegger.

———

MR. LECOQ TO GRAF ERNST CHRISTOPH MANTEUFFEL IN DRESDEN, 31st March 1724 (Translated)

. . . The passion for the opera here is getting beyond all belief. It is true that the music is beautiful and varied. There are three composers, including the famous Handel, each of whom writes two operas every winter. The orchestra, by and large, is of high quality and good care is taken to produce new voices at the theatre from time to time. Durastante, whom you know, retired on the day of her benefit with a cantata in praise of the English nation. She said that she was making way for younger enchantresses. That one day brought her more than a thousand pounds sterling. Her benefit last year brought in nearly as much, not to mention her salary of 1200 guineas a year. Have you ever heard, Monseigneur, of prodigality and favour to equal this towards a woman [already] old, whose voice is both mediocre and worn out ? That is what the English are like. . . .
London, March 31, 1724.

(Opel, *Mitteilungen*, pp. 33 f.) Geheimes Staatsarchiv, Dresden. Manteuffel was a Saxon Minister.

———

The new Lord Chamberlain, Charles, Duke of Grafton, becomes Governor of the Academy of Music, 1724.

Grafton was the third subscriber on the list of May 1719, the first two having, successively, held the office of Lord Chamberlain before him.

———

From the Records of the Royal Household, 1st April 1724

These are &c. to Mr George Fredericc Handle the sum of Three Pounds Eighteen Shillings and Six pence for Writing the Anthem which was perform'd at St James before His Ma^ty. And &c^a. Given &c^a. this 1st day of April 1724 in the Tenth Year of His Ma^ty's Reign.
To Charles Stanhope Esqr &c^a.

Holles Newcastle.

Public Record Office : L.C.5/158 (copybook), p. 248. The payment refers to the performance in St. James's Chapel on 5th January 1724. It is noteworthy that John Eccles, the salaried Master of the King's Music since 1700, received £11 for each of his musical manuscripts, "pricking and copying"; he wrote the annual music for New Year and for the King's Birthday. Newcastle was Lord Chamberlain and Stanhope was Treasurer to his Majesty's Chamber.

———

The Duke of Chandos to the Bishop of London

April. 7th 1724 Cannons.

My Lord. The young man who will have the Hon^r to deliver y^r Lordship this hath lived with me near ten years during which time he hath behaved himself with an uncommon sobriety & Diligence : He was at first my Page but finding in him an extraordinary Genius for Musick I made him apply himself to the Study & Practice of it & he hath been so successful in his Improvement under Mr Handell & Dr Pepusch, that he is become tho Young a perfect Master both for Composition & performance on the Organ & Harpsichord.

He hears there is a Vacancy of an Organist to the Chappel in the Banquetting House & hath desired me to recommend him to your Ldship's Favour for it, in whose Disposal he understands the Gift of it is.

As I realy take him to be a deserving Young Man & that he is of a very good Family (the Monroes) in Scotland I should be glad to do him so good an Office & entreat Your Ldp will permit me to ask your Favour in his Behalf that if you have not designed already this Employment for any other Y.L. will have the Goodness to bestow it upon him.
I am with great Respect
My Lord
Your L. &c.

Copybook in Huntington Library, San Marino. (Partly published in Baker, p. 130.) Gibson was Bishop of London from 1720 till 1748. He had some influence with George I who converted the Banqueting Hall, Whitehall, into a Royal Chapel. George Monroe (Monro, Munro), born about 1700, whom the Duke had recommended in January 1723 as organist to another chapel, did not succeed in either case, and was also unsuccessful against Thomas Roseingrave in November 1725, when they both applied for the post of organist at St. George's Church, Hanover Square, in the district of Handel's new and permanent residence (cf. 11th June 1724). Shortly afterwards Monroe became organist at St. Peter's Church, Cornhill, and in 1729 harpsichord player in the orchestra of the Theatre in Goodman Fields. He wrote some vocal music, and died about 1731. His musical education shows Handel and Pepusch in collaboration, probably at Cannons. An alleged pupil of Handel's, at about the same time, was Johan Helmich Roman, a Swedish violinist and composer, born in 1694, who, between 1714 and 1720, studied in London under Pepusch and Ariosti. (See Patrik Vretblad's biography, Stockholm, 1914, pp. 14-20.)

Bononcini's *Calfurnia* is produced at the Haymarket Theatre, 18th April 1724.

FROM THE " LONDON JOURNAL ", 2nd May 1724

(In an advertisement of " The Fine Book of Musick ", later called " A Pocket Companion for Gentlemen and Ladies ")

. . . The Proprietors of this Book are now Engraving, and will Publish in a Month's time (in a neat large Octavo Pocket Size) that Celebrated Opera of Julius Caesar, they having a Grant for the sole printing and Publishing the same. To which will be added the Overtures to all Mr. Handel's Opera's ; therefore beware of Spurious Editions, stampt on large Folio Pewter Plates.

John Cluer, music printer, had recently associated himself, as music publisher, with the bookseller B. Creake. The first volume of the *Pocket Companion*, edited by the organist Richard Neale and dedicated to the Duke of Chandos' elder son, John, Marquess of Carnarvon, contained 81 songs, arias, and minuets by various composers, among them twenty arias from Handel's operas : *Radamisto*, *Floridante*, *Flavio*, *Ottone*, and even two from *Teseo* (1712), the music of which had not then been printed. In this volume Cluer introduced pocket-size music, and he said in the preface that so far music had " appeared in the world . . . generally of a size more adapted to a library than to accompany one abroad ". The list of subscribers for the first *Pocket Companion*, in two editions, is the first survey of music lovers in Britain in Handel's time. (Cf. 20th March and 22nd December 1725.)—The warning at the end of the advertisement refers, of course, to Walsh, who used to print his music from folio plates of pewter, stamped instead of engraved. Handel seems to have had his first disagreements with Walsh. (Cf. 21st June 1723.) Cluer's edition of *Giulio Cesare* became the most beautifully printed of Handel's scores, when published, with his privilege, in July, after further advertisements on 6th and 11th June 1724. Nothing came of Cluer's plan to publish Handel's overtures : in 1727 Richard Meares published twelve overtures in four parts, and Walsh successively printed 65 overtures in parts and 33 in score. During the summer of 1724 Cluer published a flute arrangement of *Giulio Cesare*.

FROM THE " DAILY COURANT ", 8th May 1724

For the Benefit of J. Clegg (from Ireland), a Youth of Ten Years of Age, who play'd at Mrs. Barbier's Benefit. At the New Theatre, over-against the Opera-House in the Hay-Market, this present Friday . . . will be perform'd a Consort of Musick, several choice Concerto's by the Youth, never perform'd in Publick ; particularly, a Concerto of Vivaldi's, called La Temista di Mare, a Solo by Mr. Kitch, a Solo Song out of the Opera of Julius Caesar, the Song Part by Mr. Kitch, the Violin by the Youth, as done by Sig. Castruzzi in the Opera, a Solo of Sig. Geminiani's by the Youth.

John Clegg was a pupil of Dubourg and Bononcini, and first appeared in London in 1723. He later became leader of the orchestra at (?) Covent Garden, and died in Bedlam Hospital 1746. Mrs. Barbier's last appearance had been at Drury Lane in 1717. Vivaldi's concerto was, of course, called *La Tempesta di Mare* ; it is no. 5 of his op. 8, *Il Cimento dell' Armonia*, in E flat. Kitch was probably another spelling of the name of Kytch, the oboist, although nothing is known of his singing. Castrucci was the leader in the (old) Haymarket orchestra. The New Theatre is that founded in December 1720.

—

Aquilio Consolo, a pasticcio opera, is produced at the Haymarket Theatre, 21st May 1724.

Chrysander (II. 110) attributes the music to Ariosti.

—

From Mist's " Weekly Journal ", 23rd May 1724

It is said, that Bononcini not being engaged for the Year ensuing, by the Royal Academy of Musick, was about to return to his own Country ; but that a great Duchess hath settled 500*l*. per annum, upon him, to oblige him to continue here.

Bononcini's patron was Henrietta, Duchess of Marlborough (cf. 16th June 1722). There was no condition attached to her grant, as Mattheson relates (*Critica Musica*, II. 96), that Bononcini should not write operas any more (cf. 7th September 1725). His last opera written in London was *Astianatte*, produced at the Haymarket Theatre on 6th May 1727.

—

Ambrose Philips writes a farewell poem " To Signora Cuzzoni ", supposed to be returning to Italy, 25th May 1724.

The poem, of twelve lines only, was set to music, probably in 1728, by Henry Holcombe and published as a song in *The Musical Miscellany*, vol. V, 1731, pp. 116 f.

—

The Royal Academy of Music holds a General Court, 27th May 1724.

Cf. 28th November 1727.

—

" The Session of Musicians. In Imitation of the Sessions of the Poets ", [May] 1724

Apollo (the God both of Musick and Wit)
To summon a Court did lately think fit ;
No Poets were call'd, the God found, in vain
He hop'd, that a Bard should the Laurel obtain ;

Since what was his Right he could not dispose
To one noted for Sense, in Metre or Prose ;
The Laureat's Place to the Court he resign'd,
And the Bays for the best Musician design'd ;
As o'er these Twin-Arts he's known to preside,
To Sounds he'd allow, what to Wit was deny'd.

The long-expected Day's at last declar'd,
And th' *Op'ra House* for such a Crowd prepar'd ;
Just as when *H[eide]gg[e]r* with pious View,
(Careful of Innocence, to Virtue true)
All Sexes, Ranks, and Int'rests slyly joins,
Whilst the gay Hall with Lights the Day outshines :
Bright in his glorious Rays *Apollo* came,
And first his Officers of State did name ;
Th' Academy-Directors all appear'd,
And equal to their Skill in Sound's preferr'd ;
One waits his Nod, his Will another writes,
Some give him Tea, and some do snuff the Lights,
Soon as the God the lovely *Swiss* survey'd,
Master of Ceremonies he was made ;
B[ere]nst[at]t and *B[o]sc[h]i* (who peep'd in for sport)
Were pitch'd upon for Criers to the Court ;
In *Recitative* they roar the God's Commands,
Whilst Count *V-n-a* as the Porter stands.
No sooner was the God's dread Will made known,
The Time and Place proclaim'd, and fix'd his Throne,
Composers and Performers all prepar'd
To shew their Skill, and claim the great Reward ;
Like Bodies to their Centre swift they ran,
And each, by Merit, hop'd to be the Man.
But e'er my Muse proceeds, let's view the Race,
Whose various Tribes did round the spacious Place,
Like Brother *Homer*, tell each Hero's name,
Where his Abode, or whence his Parents came,
And what his Rank in the Records of Fame :
Masters of various Instruments flock here,
The *Scottish* Pipe and *British* Harp appear ;
Lutes and Guitars do form a beauteous Line,
Whilst Dulcimers with Pipe and Tabor join ;
From gay *Moorfields* sweet Singers did attend ;
Wapping and *Redriff* did their Fiddlers send ;
Of my Lord Mayor's choice Band there came the Chief,
Who whet his Lordship's Stomach to his Beef ;

The Parish Clerks and Waits form one large Group,
And Organists swell up that bright, psalm-singing Troop ;
Each Dancing-Master held it wond'rous Fit
To flourish thither with his little *Kit* ;
The *Play-house* Bands in decent Order come,
Conducted thither by a tragick Drum ;
Th' *Op'ra Orchest* them o'erlook'd with Pride,
And shew'd superior Skill in a superior Stride ;
Composers next march'd with an Air and Grace,
Some in a light, some in a solemn Pace ;
Various they seem to the Beholder's Eye,
These *Largo* walk—and others—*Presto* fly.
Above the Clouds they raise their Heads sublime,
They tread on Air, and step in Tune and Time !
None fail'd that e'er set Note, or grave or airy,
From Doctor *P[e]p[us]ch* down to Master *C[a]ry* ;
From this promiscuous Race such Clamour rise
As stun the God and rend the vaulted Skies ;
In Storms tempestuous some did loudly roar,
In sporting Waves some wanton'd to the Shore ;
With vast Cascades these thunder'd from on high,
In creeping Murmurs others glided by ;
Here blushing *Boreas* with his train did sound,
There milder Gales did gently sweep the Ground.
Thus Voices, Treble, Bass, and Tenor, join
In glorious Discord ! Harmony divine !
With Noise tumultuous into Court they rush,
Scarce could the God himself their Fury hush ;
In vain tall *B[eren]s[tat]t*, gaping o'er the Crowd,
With hideous Jaws, bawl'd Silence out aloud !
Till from his Throne the anger'd God arose,
Whose awful Nod the Tempest did compose ;
Then the Swiss Count proceeds, with comely Grace,
To rank each Candidate in 's proper Place.

    First *P[e]p[us]ch* enter'd with majestick Gait,
Preceded by a Cart in solemn State ;
With Pride he view'd the Offspring of his Art,
Songs, Solos, and Sonatas load the Cart ;
Whose Wheels and Axletree, with Care dispos'd,
Did prelude to the Musick he compos'd.
The God's soon own'd that if a num'rous Race
Could claim in any Art the highest Place,
His Quantity would never be despis'd,
But Quality alone in Sounds was priz'd,

He should be satisfy'd with his Degrees,
For new Preferment would produce new Fees.

His Fate, soft G[a]ll[ia]rd with Care attends,
In Sounds and Praise they still prov'd equal Friends.
Shewing his Hautboy and an *Op'ra* Air,
He gently whisper'd in his Godship's Ear :
So oft he was distinguish'd by the Town,
That, without Vanity, he claim'd the Crown.
The God replied—your Musick's not to blame,
But far beneath the daring Height of Fame ;
Who wins the Prize must all the Rest out-strip,
Indeed you may a Conjurer equip ;
I think your Airs are sometimes very pretty,
And give you leave to sing 'em in the City.

Amidst the Crowd gay L[eve]r[i]dge did stand,
Smiles in his Face, and—Claret in his Hand ;
The God suppos'd he did not come to ask
The Bays, but rather recommend his Flask ;
Old friend, says he, if that your Wine is right,
Let's talk—d'ye hear ? I'll sup with you to-night :
The Laurel, if you hope—to do you Justice,
You made—a charming Fiend in *Doctor Faustus*.

Pleas'd with their Doom, and hopeful of Success,
At[ti]l[i]o forward to the Bar did press :
The God perceiv'd the Don the Crowd divide,
And, e'er he spoke, stopp'd short his tow'ring Pride,
Saying—the Bays for him I ne'er design,
Who, 'stead of mounting, always does decline ;
Of Ti[tu]s Ma[nli]us you may justly boast,
But dull Ves[pasi]an all that Honour lost.

C[o]rb[et]t next him succeeded to the Bar,
And hop'd to fix his Fame by something rare ;
Up to the God, with Confidence he made,
And 's Instrument *De Venere* display'd.
How ! cries the God (and frowning told his Doom),
Am I for such poor Trifles hither come ?
Pray tickle off your *Venery* at home,
Or else to cleanly Edinburgh repair,
And from ten Stories high breathe Northern Air ;
With tuneful G[o]rd[o]n join, and thus unite,
Rough *Italy* with *Scotland* the polite.

Apollo's piercing Eye just then espy'd
Merry L[oe]i[l]l[e]t stand laughing at one side ;
He gently wav'd him to him with his Hand,
Wond'ring he at that Distance chose to stand.
Smiling, he said, I come not here for Fame,
Nor do I to the Bays pretend a Claim ;
Few here deserve so well, the God reply'd,
But modestly does always Merit hide ;
A supper for some Friends I've just bespoke,
Pray come—and drink your Glass—and crack your Joke.

Ill-fated R[osei]ng[ra]ve approach'd the Bar,
With meagre Looks, and thrumming a Guitar.
Quite out of Tune *Apollo* found his Head,
And, if he gain'd the Bays, he'd run stark mad ;
So call'd his Friends, and said—a little Rest,
A darken'd Room and Straw, would fit him best ;
Where, to employ him as he lay *perdu*,
He might new set *Roland le Furieux*.

Next him Ge[mi]n[ia]ni did appear,
With Bow in Hand and much a sob'rer Air ;
He simper'd at the God, as who would say,
You can't deny me, if you hear me play.
Quickly his meaning *Phœbus* understood,
Allowing what he did was very good ;
And since his Fame all Fiddlers else surpasses,
He set him down first Treble at *Parnassus*.

Gr[ee]n, C[ro]fts, and some of the Cathedral Taste,
Their Compliments in Form to *Phœbus* past ;
Whilst the whole Choir sung Anthems in their Praise,
Thinking to chant the God out of the Bays ;
Who, far from being pleas'd, stamp'd, fum'd, and swore,
Such Musick he had never heard before ;
Vowing he'd leave the Laurel in the lurch,
Rather than place it in an *English* Church.

D[ieu]p[a]rt, well powder'd, gave himself an Air,
As if he could not fail of Fortune there,
Who always prov'd successful with the Fair.
The God his Passion hardly could contain,
For spoiling Opera-Songs in *Drury Lane* :
But hop'd his Skill he'd in it's Sphere confine,
His Fire betwixt the Acts would brilliant shine.

As he walk'd off, who stepp'd into his Place,
But Signor P[ip]po with his four-string'd Bass :
How far his Merit reach'd, the God did know,
And bow'd to him and 's Bass prodigious low ;
Vowing to him alone the Bays he'd grant,
Could the *Orchestre* but his Presence want ;
Since that was Time and Reputation losing,
Keep to your playing, and leave off composing.

The God turn'd round and found, just seated by him,
His old Acquaintance, *Nicolino H[a]ym* ;
With a kind Smile he whisper'd in his Ear,
But what—no living Creature then could hear ;
Since that we're told, the God of 's special Grace
Confirm'd him in his Secretary's Place.

Had I a thousand Tongues, or equal Hands,
I could not speak, nor write the half of their Demands ;
A Blockhead's indignation it would raise,
When C[a]ry, by his Ballads, sought the Bays ;
Claude Jean Jillier, to his immortal glory,
Danc'd thither with his *Chansonettes a Boire* ;
Big with his Hopes small T[hom]p[so]n too repairs,
To claim the Crown by thin *North British Airs* ;
A title King *Latinus* strongly grounds
Upon his nice Anatomy of Sounds ;
E'en W[a]lsh perks up, and crys—the Laurel's mine,
What are your Notes, unless you wisely join
My brighter Name, in Print, to make 'em shine ?
Nay, Signor R[o]lli's Confidence affords
Some Plea—for finding scoundrel *Op'ra* Words.

The weary'd God the wretched Crowd surveys,
And met with nothing equal to the Bays ;
His radiant Eyes, eclips'd by sullen Care,
In vain look'd round, but H[A]N[DE]L was not there.
How could he hope to fill the vacant Throne,
In Absence of his fam'd, his darling Son ?

Just then grim B[ono]nc[in]i in the Rear,
Most fearless of Success, came to the Bar ;
Two *Philharmonick Damsels* grac'd his Train,
Whilst his strong Features redden'd with Disdain ;
Dear A[nasta]s[i]a hung upon his Arm,
Each Lisp and side-long Glance produc'd its Charm ;

Black P[e]g[g]y he was forced to hawl along,
Humming a Thorough-Base—and he a Song :
Silent, his rolling Eyes the God survey'd.
Then one Hand soothing Cr[is]po's Airs display'd,
The other held a decent *Roman* Maid.
But had you seen the vast and suddain Change !
Incredible ! to easy *Faith* most strange !
As Calms succeed a raging wint'ry Flood,
The restless Throng like senseless Statues stood ;
From the dull Cell of Sloth such Vapours rise,
As clap their Padlocks on all Ears and Eyes ;
Divinity itself could not withstand
Those peaceful Potions from a mortal Hand ;
O'er active Life Stupidity did creep,
The wakeful God of Day fell fast asleep.—

Not long they slept—*Fame*'s Trumpet, loud and vast,
Fill'd the large Dome with one amazing Blast ;
Straight were they freed from Sleep's lethargick Chains,
And captiv'd Life its Liberty regains ;
The Goddess, ent'ring, shook the trembling Ground,
Her breathing Brass from Earth to Heav'n did sound ;
One hand her Trumpet held with beauteous Grace,
The other led a Hero to his Place ;
Whose art, more sure than *Cupid*'s bow gives Wounds,
And makes the World submit to conqu'ring Sounds.
When he appeared,—not one but quits his claim,
And owns the Power of his superior Fame :
Since but one *Phœnix* we can boast, he needs no Name.
The God he view'd with a becoming Pride,
Determin'd not to beg, and easy if deny'd.
Him *Phœbus* saw with Joy, and did allow,
The Laurel only ought t' adorn his Brow ;
For who so fit for universal Rule,
As he who best all Passions can controul ?
So spoke the God—and all approv'd the Choice,
E'en Ignorance and Envy gave their Voice ;
Who wisely judg'd, the Sentence did applaud,
And conscious Shame the poor Pretenders aw'd.

Thus when the World in Nature's Lap first lay,
In all the Charms of Youth and Beauty gay ;
The joyous Parent o'er her Infant smil'd.
Whilst Satan view'd with Spite the faultless Child ;

H.–6 *a*

With hellish Malice frought, he wond'ring stood,
And tho' he curs'd it,—own'd that it was good.

(Chrysander, II. 113-16, 465-72.) A pamphlet of six leaves in folio ; copy in British Museum : 841.m.26. Recorded in *Monthly Catalogue*, no. 14, May 1724, p. 9. First reprinted by Chrysander, Leipzig 1859, under the title : *Händel Receiving the Laurel from Apollo*, 11 pp. 8vo (without the last six lines). The model for the anonymous poem was Sir John Suckling's " The Session of the Poets " (1637), another paraphrase of which appeared in 1725, after Godfrey Kneller's death, under the title " The Session of Painters ".—The names of the musicians are indicated in skeleton form, but in most cases have long since been identified and completed. Heidegger, the manager of the Academy, is also alluded to as promoting the Masquerades, and is later called by his nick-name, the Swiss Count. Count V–n–a, on the other hand, has not been identified. Henry Carey's name is misspelt as Cary. Pepusch's doctor's degree had to be paid for in Oxford in 1713. Some of Leveridge's songs were very convivial. His brandy nose shone in the Drury Lane farce of 1723-4, *The Necromancer, or Harlequin Doctor Faustus*. Attilio Ariosti's success and failure are duly listed. Three Scots follow : William Corbett, orchestra leader at the Haymarket before Handel's time ; the tenor Gordon ; and William Thomson (called Thompson), the collector of Scottish songs. Loeillet's name is badly abbreviated into L–i–lt. Roseingrave's fate is forecast : he died insane. William Croft shares the judgment on English church music with Maurice Green(e). Pippo (Filippo Amadei) is praised as violoncello player, Haym as Italian secretary to the Academy. Anastasia is, of course, Mrs. Robinson, and Peggy is Margherita Durastanti. William Thomson was the compiler of *Orpheus Caledonicus*, first published in 1725. Chrysander (who thought that Peggy was Margherita de l'Epine) had no hesitation in recognizing Handel as the victor, though it seems reasonable to suggest that Senesino may have been meant. Chrysander rightly stressed the fact that of all the composers assembled here, only Carey acknowledged Handel's genius. Cf. 15th August 1724.

———

FROM THE RECORDS OF THE PARISH OF ST. MARTIN-IN-THE-FIELDS

Highway Ratings, 20 December 1723 to 11 June 1724
George Frederick Hendell, Rent £20. Rate 3s. 4d.

Westminster Public Libraries, Historical Department. (Smith, 1950, p. 125.) The rate-book for July-December 1723 is missing. Handel apparently moved into his new house in Lower Brook Street, near Hanover Square, during this period. At this time the house, which Handel either built or bought when new, was in the parish of St. Martin-in-the-Fields ; after the completion of the Church of St. George, Hanover Square, in 1724, however, the house was included in the parish of the new church. The number, 57 Brook Street, was introduced about 1766 ; one hundred years later it became no. 25. The upper floor of the house, still standing between Hanover Square and Grosvenor Square, was added after Handel's time. Cf. April 1725 and 1st May 1759.

———

The fifth season of the Academy ends on 13th June 1724 with *Aquilio*.

Signora Durastanti, suffering under Signora Cuzzoni's success, now left England (cf. 26th January 1734) and Berenstadt, too, went abroad. Mrs.

Robinson abandoned the stage for good (see 27th November 1723). Of these three singers, Anastasia Robinson, now a patron of Bononcini, sang longest in Handel operas : from 1714 to 1724.—There is a reference in Winifred Smith's *The Commedia Dell' Arte*, New York, 1912, p. 227, to Italian comedians playing at the Haymarket Theatre in 1724, according to the title-page of a libretto : this was, of course, at the Little Theatre in the Haymarket.

———

FROM THE "DAILY POST", 3rd July 1724

This Day is publish'd,

A Collection of Original Poems, viz. . . . Epistle from S——o to A——a R——n. Epistle to Mr. Handel on his Opera's. The Session of the Musicians. . . . Printed for J. Roberts . . . 1724. Price 1s. 6d.

(Chrysander, II. 115 f.) Senesino's letter to Anastasia Robinson, spurious of course, seems not to be preserved. The "Session" was originally printed for M. Smith, and its single price was 6d.; that of the letter to Handel, 4d. Cf. March and May 1724.

———

Handel begins his new opera, *Tamerlano*, on 3rd July 1724 and finishes it on the 23rd.

———

According to librettos printed in Paris in 1724 a visit of the Haymarket Company is contemplated (for July ?), to perform *Ottone* and *Giulio Cesare* there.

Again it came to nothing ; cf. April 1723.

———

FROM MIST'S "WEEKLY JOURNAL", 15th August 1724

An ODE, on receiving a Wreath of Bays from a Lady.

I.

Let him, who, favour'd by the Fair
With Glove, or Ring, or Lock of Hair,
　　Think he's the happy man.—
The Crown, I wear upon my Head,
Has Energy to wake the dead,
　　And make a *Goose* a *Swan.*

2.

See ! how like *Horace*, I aspire !
I mount ! I soar sublimely higher !
　　And, as I soar, I sing !
Behold, ye Earth-born Mortals all,
I leave you in your kindred Ball,
　　And Heav'nward sweetly spring.

3.

To humble *Trophies* dully creep,
And, in your Urns inglorious sleep,
    Ye Roman *Caesars* now.—
Your Eagle's Flight was all in vain,
Since I've more Triumph in my Brain,
    And greater on my Brow !

4.

My Laurel, Rival of the Oak,
Malignant Planets, and the Stroke
    Of Thunder, cannot shake !
My Thoughts, inspired by Love and Bays,
O'er all your boasted Lands and Seas
    Despotic Empire take.

5.

Why did great *Alexander* grieve ?
Because no more he could atchieve !
    Had I been living then,
I could have taught the Hero how
He might have *made*, and *conquer'd* too,
    By *Fancy*, not with Men.

6.

Encircled with my sacred Wreath,
I ride triumphant over Death,
    And, as poetic Wheels,
I draw the Seasons of the Year,
I charm all Heav'n into my Sphere,
    And Hell my Fury feels !

7.

Avaunt low Flights—let us create
New Systems, and a new Estate,
    For Bards and Lovers fit.
No higher, than *Elysium*,
Have *Homer*, *Horace*, *Ovid* come,
    With all their towring Wit.

8.

To a new World, my Fair, let's fly,
A *Venus* Thou ! *Apollo* I !
   To raise a Race of Gods !—
Attend us, Poets, if you'd have
A Subject, Proof against the Grave,
   To eternize your Odes.

9.

Astrologers, your Stars despise,—
All Fate lyes in *Ophelia*'s Eyes !
   From them derive your Skill ;
Their Influence only can undo,
Amend, restore, confound, renew,
   Reanimate, and kill.

(Chrysander, II. 116 f., 472-4.) There is no doubt that this ode, purporting to be addressed by Handel himself to an admiring lady, refers to the May poem of the " Session ". Chrysander suggested that the unknown lady sent that poem to Handel with a " wreath of bays ", and that the ode, written by Handel's adversaries, was his pretended answer. Mist's *Weekly Journal* returned to the matter when it published, on 29th August, " Midas, a Fable " (see the note to the following entry).

———

FROM APPLEBEE'S " ORIGINAL WEEKLY JOURNAL ", 29th August 1724

On Monday last [the 24th] the Royal Highnesses, the Princess Anne and Princess Caroline, came to St. Paul's Cathedral, and heard the famous Mr. Hendel, (their Musick Master) perform upon the Organ ; the Reverend Dr. Hare Dean of Worcester attending on their Royal Highnesses during their Stay there.

(Chrysander, II. 121.) Copy in Bodleian Library, Oxford. A similar notice appeared in the *British Journal* of the same day. This is the first record of Handel's appointment as music teacher to the Princesses. For the organ at St. Paul's, cf. 22nd October 1720. The Dean of Worcester, the Rev. Dr. Francis Hare, was one of the Residentiaries of St. Paul's. He became Dean of St. Paul's in 1726 and Bishop of Chichester in 1731. On the same day, 29th August, appeared in Mist's *Weekly Journal* an anonymous poem : " Midas, a Fable", apparently inspired by Bononcini's friends and perhaps written by Rolli ; in it Handel is supposed to be impersonated, but the allusions, if any, are mysterious. (Chrysander, II. 117 f.)

———

FROM MIST'S " WEEKLY JOURNAL ", 17th October 1724

We hear that there is a new Opera now in Practice at the Theatre in the Hay-Market, called *Tamerlane*, the Musick composed by Mynheer

Hendel, and that Signior Borseni, newly arrived from Italy, is to sing the Part of the Tyrant Bajazet. *N.B.* It is commonly reported this Gentleman was never *cut out for a Singer.*

Handel was called Mynheer in the *Spectator* of 6th March 1711 ; it apparently meant a Dutchman, confusing Dutch for Deutsch. The new tenor was, in fact, Francesco Borosini, a remarkable singer, whom the Academy considered engaging as early as 1720 (cf. Rolli's letter of August 1720). He now came from the Prague Opera with his wife, Leonora d'Ambreville, a contralto of French origin. She never sang Handel parts, and both left London again in 1725.

———

FROM THE " DAILY COURANT ", 31st October 1724

At the King's Theatre . . . this present Saturday . . . will be per-form'd, a New Opera, call'd TAMERLANE. . . . And in Regard to the Number of Subscribers no more than Three Hundred and Forty Tickets will be deliver'd out. . . . To begin at Six a-Clock.

Thus opened the sixth season of the Academy. The libretto by Agostino Piovene, adapted by Haym, was dedicated to the Duke of Rutland, one of the Academy's directors and an amateur violinist. His Italian dedication contains the following details : " I, in obedience to the orders of my most noble patrons the directors of the Royal Academy of Music, having arranged for their theatre the present opera of ' Tamerlane ' . . ." Haym did not claim to be the author, although neither Handel nor Piovene are mentioned in the libretto. The opera was performed again on 3rd, 7th, 10th, 14th, 17th, 21st, 24th and 28th November 1724, and was revived on 1st May 1725 and 13th November 1731.

———

CAST OF " TAMERLANO ", 31st October 1724

Tamerlano—Signor Pacini, alto
Bajazete—Signor Borosini, tenor
Asteria—Signora Cuzzoni, soprano
Andronico—Signor Senesino, alto
Irene—Signora Dotti, contralto
Leone—Signor Boschi, bass
Zaide—(a silent part)

In addition to Borosini, Andrea Pacini and Anna Dotti were new singers in the company. Charles Frederick Weideman, originally Carl Friedrich Weidemann, an excellent flautist and oboist in the orchestra of the Haymarket Theatre, made a note in his copy of the first oboe part of Handel's Trio Sonatas, written about 1695 (Royal Music Library, in the British Museum) : " Tamerlan 1725. which was the first Opera I play'd in &cc : C : W : ". He probably started to play there in October 1724, not in May 1725.

———

LADY BRISTOL TO LORD BRISTOL

London, Oct. 31, 1724.
You know my ear too well for me to pretend to give you any account of the Opera farther than that the new man takes extremely, but the

woman is so great a joke that there was more laughing at her than at a farce, but her opinion of her self gets the better of that. The Royal family were all there, and a greater crowd than ever I saw, which has tired me to death, so that I am come home to go to bed as soon as I have finished this.

Bristol, *Letter-Books*, II. 371. (Eisenschmidt, I. 37.) The "new man" was apparently Pacini, the "woman" Signora Dotti.

———

FROM THE "LONDON JOURNAL", 14th November 1724

This Day is published,

The whole Opera of TAMERLANE in Score. Compos'd by Mr. Handel, Corrected and Figur'd by his own Hand. Engrav'd on Copper Plates. And to render the Work more acceptable to Gentlemen and Ladies, every Song is truly translated into English Verse, and the Words engrav'd to the Musick under the Italian, which was never before attempted in any Opera. Price 16s. (for the Flute 2s. 6d.) Engrav'd, Printed and Sold by J. Cluer. . . .

This time Cluer was very quick to forestall Walsh's edition of two sets of "Favourite Songs", published without his imprint. ("Printed and Sold at the Musick Shops" was Walsh's formula in such cases; he did not respect Handel's privilege, used in 1723 by his own firm.) Usually the figuring of the bass was done by the publishers. Cluer was able to use the translation of the airs from the bilingual libretto. The printing of single sheet songs with Italian and English texts became common for Italian airs. In Cluer's arrangement of this opera for the flute, the following note is to be found : "If J. Cluer's Name is not in the Title Pages of those Works, they are spurious Editions, and not those Corrected and Figur'd by Mr. Handel". In another advertisement of this opera (*London Journal*, 9th January 1725), Cluer adds : "also the whole Opera of JULIUS CAESAR in Score, and for the Flute".

———

Ariosti's *Artaserse* is produced at the Haymarket Theatre, 1st December 1724.

Haym dedicated the libretto, by Apostolo Zeno and Pietro Pariati, to the Duke of Richmond.

———

In the election of the new Deputy Governor of the Academy on 2nd December 1724, the second Duke of Manchester succeeds in competition with the Duke of Queensbury.

(Mattheson, *Critica Musica*, 1725, II. 96 ; Chrysander, II. 124 ; Eisenschmidt, I. 31 : the name of Queensbury transmuted to Queensberry and Queensborough.) The first Duke of Manchester, a previous Deputy-Governor, died in January 1722. Cf. May 1719 and 1st (20th) November 1721. William, the second Duke, was Charles's elder son.

———

Mrs. Mary Pendarves to Her Sister, Miss Ann Granville

December 12th, 1724.
Enclosed is a song out of Tamerlane, which is a *favourite*.

Delany, I. 101. Mary Granville's first marriage was to Mr. Pendarves (cf. beginning of 1711). This is her first letter mentioning a work by Handel, though she does not mention him by name. She probably speaks of a single sheet song from the opera, perhaps Senesino's *Bella Asteria*, which was printed in that form.

———

From George Vertue's Note Books, 1724

Mr P. Tillemans & Mr Jos. Goupee both joyntly imploy'd to paint a Sett of Sceenes for the Opera house in the Haymarkett. which were *much* approv'd of.

(Vertue, Note Books, III. 21.) British Museum : Add. MS. 23, 076. Peter Tillemans was a landscape and animal painter ; Joseph Goupy the well-known cartoonist, for some time a friend of Handel's. From Walpole's edition of *Anecdotes of Painting in England*, II. 675, by the painter Vertue, it is known that Goupy and Tillemans painted the decorations for Handel's *Admeto* and *Riccardo I* in 1727. Here, it seems, are testified decorations by the two painters for his *Rodelinda* on 13th February 1725. If, however, Vertue's remarks are retrospective, the " scenes " might have been those for *Tamerlano*, or even for *Giulio Cesare*.

1725

FROM COLMAN'S " OPERA REGISTER ", November 1724–January 1725

in Nov. 1724 begins Tamerlano Opera New Sigra Cuzzoni & Sigr
Senosino still remain here & are much esteemed Artaxerxes a New Opera
Julius Cesare in Egypt revived Opera

These cumulative notes refer to 31st October and 1st December 1724, and
2nd January 1725.

—

Giulio Cesare is revived, 2nd January 1725.

Repeat performances on 5th, 9th, 16th, 19th, 23rd, 26th January ;
2nd, 6th and 9th February. There were three new singers : Signora
Dotti sang the part of Cornelia (formerly sung by Mrs. Robinson),
Signor Borosini sang Sesto Pompeo (Signora Durastanti), and Signor
Pacini sang Tolomeo (Signor Berenstadt). It should be noticed that
here, as in other cases, parts were transferred from one voice to another :
a soprano part changed into a contralto, another soprano part into a tenor
part, and a bass into an alto ; the sex of the singers did not matter very
much in the time of the castrati.—It was probably at this revival that some
additional songs were inserted, two of which were printed by Cluer
(cf. 17th December 1725). Handel often added arias in later performances,
and it became a habit of his when he confined himself to oratorios.

—

FROM THE " DAILY JOURNAL ", 11th January 1725

ToMorrow Signiora Cuzzoni the famous Chauntress, is to be married
to San-Antonio Ferre, a very rich Italian, at the Chapel of Count Starem-
berg, the Imperial Ambassador.

(Smith, 1950, p. 131.) Cf. 22nd December 1722 and 22nd August 1725.
The mystery of Cuzzoni's marriages has not been cleared up. Conrad Sigmund
Anton Graf Starhemberg had been Ambassador in London since 1720, and, since
1722, had lived in Hanover Square. Cf. 7th September 1741.

—

Handel finishes the opera *Rodelinda*, 20th January 1725.

—

FROM THE " DAILY COURANT ", 13th February 1725

At the King's Theatre . . . this present Saturday . . . will be perform'd, A New Opera call'd, RODELINDA. . . . To begin at Six a-Clock.

The libretto by Antonio Salvi was arranged by Haym, who dedicated it to the
Earl of Essex. In the English version of *Dramatis Personae* " Mr. Hendal " is
given as the composer of the music. The opera was performed on 13th, 16th,

20th, 25th, 27th February ; 2nd, 6th, 9th, 13th, 16th, 20th, 30th March ; 3rd and 6th April ; it was revived in the following season on 18th December, and again in May 1731.

———

CAST OF " RODELINDA ", 13th February 1725

Rodelinda—Signora Cuzzoni, soprano
Bertarido—Signor Senesino, alto
Grimoaldo—Signor Borosini, tenor
Eduige—Signora Dotti, contralto
Unulfo—Signor Pacini, alto
Garibaldo—Signor Boschi, bass

———

FROM BYROM'S " LETTER TO R. L., ESQ;", 20th February 1725

If Senesino *do but rift,*
" O caro, caro ! " that flat fifth :
I'd hang if e'er an Opera Whitling,
Could tell Cuzzoni *from a Kitling.*

Dear Peter, if thou can'st descend
From *Rodelind* to hear a Friend,
And if those Ravished Ears of thine
Can quit the shrill celestial Whine
Of gentle Eunuchs, and sustain
Thy native English without pain,
I would, if t'aint too great a Burden,
Thy ravished Ears intrude a Word in.

(Streatfeild, p. 96.) Byrom, *Miscellaneous Poems*, I. 346 ; *Poems*, I. 30-34. The letter is addressed to Ralph Leycester, but is without date. The date is determined by Byrom's dated diary entry (*Remains*, I. 87) : " Wrote some verses to Leycester about the Opera ". Kitling is a very small fiddle.

———

FROM THE " DAILY COURANT ", 23rd February 1725

Mr. Senesino who was taken ill last Saturday Night [the 20th] during the Time of the Opera & not so well recovered to be certain whether he can be able to perform this Night, therefore the Opera that was then intended will not be performed 'till Thursday next.

The performance, advertised for the 23rd, could not take place.

———

Ottone is revived at Brunswick, February 1725.
Cf. August 1723.

———

FROM THE " LONDON JOURNAL ", 20th March 1725

Proposals for Engraving and Printing by Subscription, A Second Pocket Volume of Opera Songs and Airs, Collected out of all the Opera's

Compos'd by Mr. Handel, Bononcini, Attilio, and other Great Masters ; many of them never before printed ; all of which will be carefully Corrected & Figur'd for the Harpsichord, and Transpos'd for the Flute, with the Symphonies to them. N.B. The Musick in this Volume will be much more legible than the former, the Pages somewhat larger, but may be bound in the same size ; and since we have the Assistance of all the Great Masters, and shall be favour'd with Mr. Handel's Songs that were never before printed (which cannot be obtain'd by others), our Subscribers may assure themselves that this will be a far Better Collection than 'tis possible for any other Person to make.

The Undertakers are J. Cluer . . . and B. Creake . . . where Specimens of Work may be seen, and Proposals at Large had gratis, as also at the Musick Shops : Where likewise Subscriptions are taken for Printing The whole Opera of Rodelinda, in Score with all the Parts. In above 100 Copper Plates. Compos'd by Mr. Handel. The Quality, &c. who design to Subscribe to this Celebrated Opera, are desired to send their Names in 20 Days at farthest, otherwise they can't be Engrav'd in the Book.

For the *Pocket Companion*, see 2nd May 1724 and 22nd December 1725 ; the second volume was in large octavo. For the *Rodelinda* score, see 6th May 1725.

———

Ariosti's *Dario* is produced at the Haymarket Theatre, 10th April 1725.

This was the last opera by Ariosti written for the Academy.

———

At a revival of John Gay's farce *The What d'ye Call it*, at Drury Lane Theatre on 30th April 1725, the ballad " 'Twas when the seas were roaring ", generally attributed to Handel, is sung.

This " comick, tragick, pastorall Farce " was produced in 1715 at Drury Lane. The 1725 libretto does not mention Handel as the composer of the new ballad. It appeared, with the music, in single sheet folio editions, and in song collections. After it had been inserted into the *Beggar's Opera* (cf. 29th January 1728), Handel's name was added in 1729 in vol. II of the *Musical Miscellany*, published by John Watts, under the title *The Faithful Maid* (Squire, 1913, pp. 107-11).

———

FROM THE RATE-BOOKS OF THE PARISH OF ST. GEORGE, HANOVER SQUARE, April 1725

George Frederick Handell, Rent £35. First Rate 17s. 6d.

(Streatfeild, 1909, p. 88 ; Smith, 1950, p. 124.) Cf. 11th June 1724 : rent and rate for six months only. This is the first entry for a full year, and it is to be found for all the remaining years of Handel's life. Cf. 1st May 1759.

———

JOHN BYROM'S "EPIGRAM ON THE FEUDS BETWEEN HANDEL AND
BONONCINI", May 1725

Some say, compar'd to Bononcini,
That Mynheer Handel's but a Ninny ;
Others aver, that he to Handel
Is scarcely fit to hold a Candle :
Strange all this Difference should be
'Twixt Tweedle-dum and Tweedle-dee !

Byrom, *Miscellaneous Poems*, I. 343 f.; *Poems*, I. 35-7. Often attributed to
Swift. Cf. 3rd March 1724 ; 18th May, 5th June and 19th July 1725. In
Byrom's circle the epigram soon became known as his "Tweedle". For "Mynheer Handel" see 6th March 1711 and 17th October 1724. The epigram was
later set as a glee by Pieter Hellendaal, the elder (about 1780).

About one hundred years after Byrom's epigram was written, Charles Lamb
wrote in Vincent Novello's album :

> *Free Thoughts on some eminent Composers.*
>
> Some cry up Haydn, some Mozart,
> Just as the whim bites. For my part,
> I do not care a farthing candle
> For either of them, nor for Handel.
>
> .   .   .   .   .
>
> No more I would for Bononcini—
> As for Novello, and Rossini . . .

(*Musical Times*, March 1951, pp. 106 f.)

———

Tamerlano is revived at the Haymarket Theatre, 1st May 1725.
Repeat performances on 4th and 8th May.

———

FROM THE "DAILY POST", 6th May 1725

This Day is publish'd, and deliver'd to the Subscribers,

The whole Opera of Rodelinda in Score : Compos'd by Mr. Handel,
and engrav'd on 110 Copper Plates in 4to. Sold by J. Cluer . . . and
B. Creake. . . . Where the Opera for the Flute may be speedily had.
N.B. They are now going on with the utmost Diligence with their second
pocket Volume of Opera Songs in 8vo. in which there will be several of
Mr. Handel's Songs that were never before printed, which cannot be
obtain'd by others. Proposals may be had Gratis.

Cf. 20th March 1725. From now on Handel did not use his privilege of 1720
any more, probably being aware of its worthlessness against Walsh and his consorts.
Cluer decided not to use the octavo size as he did for *Giulio Cesare*, but a quarto,
in contrast to the usual folio. In Sir Newman Flower's Handel collection is a copy
of the score, dated in manuscript "Jan. 20, 1725" ; this means, of course, 1726.
Cf. 15th May 1725.

———

EXTRACTS FROM THE LIST OF SUBSCRIBERS FOR THE SCORE OF
" RODELINDA ", 6th May 1725

Dr. [John] Arbuthnot ; Theophil Cole ; [Henry] Carey, Master of Musick, 6 Books ; William Freeman, of Hamels, Hertfordshire ; [John Ernest] Galliard ; J. G. Gumprecht [of Hamburg] ; James Graves, Master of Musick ; Henry Holcombe ; Henry Harrington [senior] ; Newburgh Hamilton ; John Hare [junior], 12 Books ; [Charles] Jennens ; [Jean-Baptist] Loillet ; James Miller ; Richard Neale, Organist ; Philarmonica Club, 3 Books ; John Rich ; John Robinson ; Mr. Rawlins ; John Philip Smith ; [George ?] Vanbrugh, Master of Musick, 6 Books.

This is the first of ten lists of Handel subscribers (1725–40). Eight operas by Handel were published on subscription, one Ode (*Alexander's Feast*) and one set of concertos (opus 6) ; furthermore, two operas were printed on such a basis but were published without subscribers' lists : *Radamisto* on 15th February 1721 and *Serse* on 5th June 1738, the *Radamisto* copies being numbered. Of the *Rodelinda* score 120 subscribers ordered 162 copies. Chrysander, II. 129 f., suggests that the Italian competitors of Handel collected more subscriptions than he did, by being less scrupulous in doing it. William Freeman was the only subscriber whose name is to be found in all the lists (cf. 23rd March 1748 and 30th September 1749). Hamilton and Jennens became Handel's librettists. Miller and Rawlins were Gentlemen of the Chapel Royal. Neale was the editor of the first *Pocket Companion* (cf. 2nd May 1724). Rich was the manager of the Theatre in Lincoln's Inn Fields. Robinson, first a chorister of the Chapel Royal and later a well-known organist, was the husband of Ann Turner-Robinson. Vanbrugh was a singer at Cannons, about 1720. The Philarmonica Club met at the Castle Tavern in Paternoster Row (Chrysander, II, 123).

———

FROM BYROM'S DIARY, LONDON, 9th May 1725

Mr. Leycester left my epigram upon Handel and Bononcini in shorthand for Jemmy Ord.

(Streatfeild, p. 94.) Byrom, *Journal*, I. 130. Cf. May 1725. Ralph Leycester, Byrom's friend, was one of the subscribers to the first *Pocket Companion*. James Ord, a shorthand pupil of Byrom, was a brother of Robert Ord, another of Byrom's friends.

———

The pasticcio opera *Elpidia, or Li Rivali generosi* is produced at the Haymarket Theatre, 11th May 1725. Text by Apostolo Zeno, music by Leonardo Vinci and others, with recitatives provided by Handel.

This was probably the first of several cases where Handel, as music director of the opera, wrote recitatives for works by other composers. The tenor part in *Elpidia* was sung by Borosini (later by Luigi Antinori) and the contralto part by his wife, Leonora d'Ambreville.

———

FROM THE "LONDON JOURNAL", 15th May 1725

. . . The Engraving of this Opera [*Rodelinda*] hath retarded the Publication [by Cluer and Creake] of their Second Pocket Volume of Opera Songs and Airs. . . . The whole to be done in the same Character as the Specimen, which may be seen at the Places abovesaid [Cluer's and Creake's addresses] and at the Musick Shops. Subscribers to pay 5s. down and 5s. 6d. on Delivery of the Book. Note, In this Volume there will be several of Mr. Handel's Songs that were never before printed, which cannot be obtained by any other Persons ; which Songs alone are worth double the Money the whole Book is sold for.

Cf. 6th May and 22nd December 1725. A similar advertisement appeared in the *London Journal* of 12th June 1725.

———

FROM BYROM'S DIARY, LONDON, 18th May 1725

Mr. Leycester came there [to George's coffee-house] and Bob Ord, who was come home from Cambridge, where he said he had made the whole Hall laugh at Trinity College and got himself honour by my epigram upon Handel and Bononcini.

(Chrysander, II. 135.) Byrom, *Journal*, I. 136. Cf. 9th May 1725. Byrom was a fellow of Trinity College, Cambridge.

———

FROM BYROM'S DIARY, LONDON, 5th June 1725

Mr. Hooper . . . came over to us to Mill's coffeehouse, 2d., told us of my epigram upon Handel and Bononcini being in the papers.

(Chrysander, II. 135.) Byrom, *Journal*, I. 150. The Rev. Francis Hooper was another friend of Byrom's. Two pence was the price for a cup of coffee. Cf. 18th May.

———

HANDEL TO MICHAELSEN AT HALLE

A Londres ce $\frac{22}{11}$ de Juin

1725.

Monsieur
    et tres Honoré Frere,
Encore que je me trouve tres coupable de n'avoir pas satisfait depuis si longtems a mon devoir envers Vôus par mes lettres, neantmoins je ne desespere pas d'en obtenir Vôtre genereux pardon lorsque je Vous assurerai que cela n'est pas provenu de quelque oubli, et que mon Estime et Amitié pour Vous sont inviolables, comme Vous en aurez trouvé des marques, mon tres Honoré Frere, dans les lettres que j'ai ecrit a ma Mere.

Mon Silence donc, a ete plustôt un effêt de crainte de Vous accabler par une correspondence qui Vous pourroit causez de l'ennuy, Mais ce qui me fait passer par dessus ces reflexions, en Vous donnant l'incommodité par la presente, est, que je ne scaurois pas être si ingrat que de passer avec silence les bontés que Vous voulez bien temoigner a ma Mere par Vôtre assistance et Consolation dans son Age avancé, sans Vous en marquer au moins mes treshumble remercimens. Vous n'ignorez pas combien me doit toucher ce qui la regarde, ainsi Vous jugerez bien des Obligations que je Vous en dois avoir.

Je me conterois heureux, mon tres Cher Frere, si je pouvois Vous engager a me donner de tems en tems de Vous nouvelles, et Vous pourriez etre sur de la part sincere que j'en prenderois, et du retour fidel que Vous trouveriez toujours en moy. J'avois crû de pouvoir Vous renouveller mon Amitié de bouche, et de faire un tour en Vôs quartiers a l'occasion que le Roy s'en va a Hannover, mais mes souhaits ne peuventpas avoir leur effet encore, pour cette fois, et la situation de mes affaires me prive de ce bonheur là malgré que j'en aye. je ne desespere pas pourtant de pouvoir etre un jour si heureux, cependent, il me seroit une consolation bien grande, si j'oserois me flatter, que Vous me vouliez bien accorder quelque place dans Votre Souvenir, et de m'honorer de Vôtre amitié, puisque je ne finiray jamais d'etre avec une passion et attachement inviolable

Monsieur
et tres Honoré Frere
Vôtre
treshumble et tresobeissant
Serviteur
George Frideric Handel.

je fais bien mes treshumbles respects a
Madame Votre Epouse. et j'embrasse
tendrement ma Chere Fileule et le reste
de Votre Chere Famillie.
mes Complimens s'il vous plait a tous
les Amis et Amies.
    A Monsieur,
Monsieur Michael Dietrich
Michaelsen Docteur en Droit

à
Halle
en Saxe.

(Translation)

London, $\frac{22\text{nd}}{11\text{th}}$ June 1725.

Honoured Brother,
    Although I am much to blame for not having for so long done my duty towards you in the matter of letters, yet I do not despair of receiving

your generous pardon for this, when I assure you that it did not come about through forgetfulness, and that my esteem and friendship for you are unchanged, as you will have observed, dearest brother, from the letters that I have written to my mother.

My silence, therefore, has come rather from fear of imposing on you a correspondence that might cause you inconvenience. But I am emboldened to set aside these considerations and to incommode you with the present letter, since I could not be so ungrateful as to remain silent over the kindnesses which you are good enough to show my mother in her old age through your support and consolation, and not at least tender you my humble thanks therefore. You are well aware how much anything that concerns her must affect me, so you will easily judge how greatly I feel myself in your debt.

I should count myself happy, most dear brother, if I could prevail on you to send me your news from time to time, and you may rest assured of the sincere interest that I would take therein and of the faithful response that you would always find in me. I had hoped to be able to renew our friendship in person by a visit to your parts when the King departs for Hanover, but my hopes cannot be fulfilled this time, and the state of my affairs deprives me of that happiness despite all my expectations. However I do not despair of being so fortunate one day. Meanwhile it would be a very great consolation to me if I might dare flatter myself that you are good enough to accord me a place in your thoughts and to honour me with your friendship, since I shall never cease to be, with steadfast love and devotion,

Most honoured brother,

Your

most humble and obedient

servant,

George Frideric Handel.

I send my most humble respects to your wife and I tenderly embrace my beloved god-daughter and the rest of your dear family. My compliments please to all friends.

(Chrysander, II. 137 f.) Original lost. No letter written by Handel to his mother is known. Michaelsen's second wife was Christiane Sophia, *née* Dreissig (cf. 13th September 1725). Handel's favourite niece was Johanna Friederika.

———

Cluer and Creake advertise *Rodelinda* for the flute, *London Journal*, 12th June 1725.

———

The sixth season of the Academy ends on 19th June 1725 with *Elpidia*.

———

FROM BYROM'S DIARY, LONDON, 19th July 1725

Nourse asked me if I had seen the verses upon Handel and Bononcini, not knowing that they were mine ; but Sculler said I was charged with them, and so I said they were mine ; they both said that they had been mightily liked.

(Chrysander, II. 136.) Byrom, *Journal*, I. 173. Cf. 5th June. Nourse and Sculler were London acquaintances of Byrom's.

MRS. PENDARVES TO HER SISTER, MISS ANNE GRANVILLE, 22nd August 1725

Mrs. Sandoni (who was Cuzzoni) is brought to bed of a daughter : it is a mighty mortification it was not a son. Sons and heirs ought to be out of fashion when such scrubs shall pretend to be dissatisfied at having a daughter : 'tis pity indeed, that the noble name and family of the Sandoni's should be extinct. The minute she was brought to bed, she sang " La Speranza ", a song in Otho. . . .

(Smith, 1950, p. 130.) Delany, Autobiography, I. 117. Cf. 22nd December 1722 and 11th January 1725.

FROM THE " DAILY JOURNAL ", 31st August 1725

We hear that the Royal Academy [of] Musick, in the Hay Market, have contracted with famous Chauntess for 2500 *l.* who is coming over from Italy against the Winter.

This refers to Faustina, who did not appear in London until 6th May 1726, and received £2000 a year. She came from Vienna. Cf. 4th September.

Giulio Cesare is produced at Brunswick, in Italian, but under the title *Giuliò Cesar e Cleopatra*, August 1725.

(Loewenberg, p. 77.) Cf. August 1733.

FROM THE " LONDON JOURNAL ", 4th September 1725

Signiora *Faustina*, a famous Italian Lady, is coming over this Winter to rival Signiora Cuzzoni ; the Royal Academy of Musick has contracted with her for Two Thousand Five Hundred Pound.

Cf. 31st August.

RIVA TO LUDOVICO ANTONIO MURATORI (Translated)

Hanover, 7th September 1725.

The operas performed in England, fine though they are as regards the music and the voices, are so much hackwork as regards the verses.

Our friend Rolli, who was commissioned to compose them when the Royal Academy was first formed, wrote really good operas, but having become embroiled with the Directors, the latter took into their service one Haym, a Roman and a violoncellist, who is a complete idiot as far as Letters are concerned. Boldly passing from the orchestra to the heights of Parnassus, he has, for the last three years, been adapting—or rather making worse—the old librettos which are already bad enough in their original form. The *Capellmeisters*, who compose the operas, make use of these, with the exception of our compatriot Bononcino, who has sent for his [librettos] from Rome, they being composed by certain pupils of Gravina. If your friend wishes to send some, he must know that in England they want few recitatives, but thirty arias and one duet at least, distributed over the three acts. The subject-matter must be straightforward, tender, heroic, Roman, Greek, or even Persian, and never Gothic or Longobard. For this year and for the two following there must be two equal parts in the operas for Cuzzoni and Faustina ; Senesino is the chief male character, and his part must be heroic ; the other three male parts must proceed by degrees with three arias each, one in each Act. The duet should be at the end of the second Act, and between the two ladies. If the subject has in it three ladies, it can serve because there is a third singer here. If the Duchess of Marlborough, who gives 500 pounds a year to Bononcino, will consent to his presenting one of his operas at the Academy, this will be the *Andromache*, which is almost a translation of Racine's but without the death of Pyrrhus. It is excellently adapted as an opera. From this, your friend will be able to obtain an idea of the sort of operas which can serve in England. In the meanwhile, if he wishes to send an opera, I shall do my best to be of service to him and, if he has good taste, as I do not doubt will be the case, to have him commissioned for a pair of them. The packet might well be recommended to our Jewish friends who have a correspondence in Amsterdam. They might be asked to place it in some bale of silk and have it delivered to me as I pass through. . . .

(Streatfeild, 1917, p. 433.) Original in Biblioteca Estense, Modena : Archivio Soli Muratori. The great historian had asked Riva, now at the Hanoverian Court, whether he could help a young friend of his to get a commission for a libretto for the Haymarket Opera. Cf. 3rd October 1726.—One of the librettos, set by Bononcini before he came to London and altered for him by Rolli, was Apostolo Zeno's *Griselda*, produced in Milan in 1718 and in London in 1722. The subject of *Andromaca* was realized in Bononcini's opera *Astianatte*, text by N. Haym, based on an earlier libretto by A. Salvi (composed by Bononcini's brother Marc' Antonio in 1701) ; it was performed at the Haymarket Theatre between 6th May and 6th June 1727, with Senesino as Pirro, Cuzzoni as Andromaca, and Faustina as Ermione. Haym dedicated his libretto to the Duchess of Marlborough.—Gian Vincenzo Gravina, a famous playwright, died in 1718 ; his best pupil was Metastasio.

From " Parker's Penny Post ", 8th September 1725

The famous Italian Singer, who is hired to come over hither to enter-tain his Majesty and the Nobility in the Operas, is call'd Signiora Faustina ; whose Voice (as it is pretended) has not been yet equall'd in the World. Cf. 4th September.

———

Michaelsen's second wife, Christiane Sophia, dies at Halle, 11th (24th) September 1725.

Cf. 11th June 1725. In Cummings's collection (sold on 21st May 1917, catalogue no. 823, item 3) were Pastor Johann Georg Francke's funeral sermon and many elegies for the deceased, printed in a booklet of 40 pp. fol. For Michaelsen's first wife, Handel's sister, see 11th August 1718 ; for Francke see 22nd December 1730.

———

From Mattheson's Hamburg Opera List [16th (27th) September] 1725 (Translated)

Tamerlan. Music by Herr *Händel.* Translation by Herr *Praetorius.* On the occasion of the marriage of the King of France, a *Prologue* was performed before the opera : the music was by Herr *Telemann,* the poem by Herr *Praetorius.*

(Chrysander, 1877, col. 249.) The Hamburg libretto gives the names of " Hendel ", Haym and Johann Philipp Praetorius. The airs were sung in Italian ". The part of Bajazeth was provided with seven arias, set by the British Resident, Cyril Wyche (see 7th November 1703 and 28th October 1720). Telemann seems to have added the recitatives and two choruses in German (Schulze, p. 49). He is mentioned in the libretto as the composer of an " intermezzo " ; Loewenberg (p. 78) suggested it was *Die ungleiche Heyrath,* text by Praetorius after Pietro Pariati. The occasion of the prologue was the wedding of Louis XV with Maria Leszcynska.—Willers' Hamburg Notes (Merbach, p. 361) conform with Mattheson's List.

———

From Mattheson's Hamburg Opera List, [10th (21st) November] 1725 (Translated)

Julius Caesar in Egypt. Music by Herr *Händel.* Translation by Herr Secretär *Lediard.*

(Chrysander, II. 109 f.; and 1877, col. 249.) Thomas Lediard's translation was augmented by additions from the hand of Johann Georg Linike, leader of the Duke of Weissenfels's orchestra, who also provided the German recitatives ; the arias were sung in Italian (Loewenberg, p. 77). Freund and Reinking (p. 124) state that the music was by " Händel, Linke [*sic*] and Baptide " (Baptiste Anet ?). The frontispiece of the libretto shows the harbour of Alexandria, as painted by Signor Fabris for Act III, Scene 13. According to Willers' Hamburg Notes (Merbach, p. 361) the opera was performed 36 times, up to the end of the Hamburg opera in 1738 ; the performance on 29th May (9th June) 1727, in honour of George I, was given with prologue, illumination and fireworks. The production in 1725 led to an ugly controversy between Lediard, a Frenchman who was not quite master of the German language, and one Sivers (Chrysander, II. 109 f.). A pamphlet was printed in Hamburg under the pseudonym of Hans Sachs, the sixteenth century German poet, attacking the translator. A friend of Lediard, or he himself, replied under the pseudonym of Democritos in a pamphlet printed in Hamburg or Altona. Each of these 1725 pamphlets consists of four leaves only, in quarto, and contains a poem in old-style verses and a more outspoken prose section. Both refer to *Tamerlan* (cf. 16th September) and speak of the beautiful decor in *Julius Caesar*, but only Democritos mentions " die schöne Music " of the latter opera. The only copy known of these pamphlets, photostats of which are in Gerald Coke's Handel Collection, is in the Thüringische Landesbibliothek, Weimar.

—

FROM REED'S " WEEKLY JOURNAL ", 20th November 1725

Friday [the 19th] 7—Night came on the Election of an Organist of St. George's, Hanover-Square ; and the Salary being settled at 45*l.* per Annum, there were seven Candidates. . . . The Vestry, which consists of above thirty Lords and seventy Gentlemen, having appointed Dr. Crofts, Dr. Pepush, Mr. Bononcini, and Mr. Giminiani, to be Judges which of the Candidates perform'd best ; each of them composed a Subject to be carry'd on by the said Candidates in the Way of Fugeing, and one Hour was allowed for every one to play upon the four Subjects so appointed, one not to hear another, unless himself had done before : Only the four first perform'd, and all of them very masterly : In the Conclusion the Judges gave it for the famous Mr. Rosengrave, who made that Way of Performance his Study a great Part of his Life, and he was accordingly chosen.

(Hawkins, V. 264 ; Chrysander, II. 139.) Among the candidates were George Monroe (cf. p. 161) and the blind John Stanley, then thirteen years of age. Although the new church was near Handel's house (see 11th June 1724), he was not one of the judges, as Hawkins and Burney related ; Burney (IV. 264 f.) even adds that Handel sent his subject, without attending the competition. He probably declined to join his four colleagues in committee.

—

The Academy's seventh season starts on 30th November 1725 with a revival of *Elpidia* (Kelly, II. 351).

According to Chrysander (II. 31), who gives no source for this statement, the number of subscribers for the Academy during the season was 133.

—

Gabriel Odingsell's comedy *The Capricious Lovers* is produced at the Theatre in Lincoln's Inn Fields on 8th December 1725, with a duet, " Whine not, pine not ", sung by Mr. Leveridge and Mrs.

Chambers to the tune of a minuet from no. 4 of Handel's *Concerti grossi*.

The song was printed as a single sheet folio. The set of six oboe concertos, called *Concerti grossi*, was published in 1734 as op. 3, but no. 4 had already been performed on 20th June 1716, as "second overture" in *Amadigi*.

———

FROM THE "SUFFOLK MERCURY: OR, ST. EDMUNDS-BURY POST", 13th December 1725

Notice is hereby given, That on Friday the 17th of this Instant December, Cluer and Creake's Second Pocket Volume of Opera Songs, will be published and delivered to Subscribers. It is in a larger Size than the first, the Musick is legible as any Half-sheet Song, and the Collection is the best that ever was made, for there is not one Song in the Book but what is approved of by Mr. Handel.

Cf. 20th March and 17th December 1725. According to the London advertisement of 18th December the publication was further delayed till 22nd December. It would be strange that Handel should have been responsible for that third of the book which was not his contribution. It seems that the publishers styled him as editor of the volume. A "half-sheet" was what is now called a "single-sheet-folio".

———

FROM THE LIST OF MUSIC BOOKS GIVEN TO THE PHILO MUSICAE ET ARCHITECTURAE SOCIETAS BY THEIR PRESIDENT, WILLIAM GULSTON, 17th December 1725

One Large Book bound in red Calves Leather and Gilt Containing The Opera's of Rinaldo Etearco Hydaspes et Almahide.

Three Books bound in Sky Marbled Paper Containing the Symphony to S^d Opera's.

The Opera's of Camilla Thomyris—Clotilda Stiched.

The Symphonys to Said Opera's also Stiched.

(Rylands, p. 90.) British Museum: Add. MS. 23,202. This society was masonic and Geminiani was their "Dictator", *i.e.* musical director. They met at the Queen's Head Tavern, near Temple Bar, from 1724 till 1727 (the meeting room being called "Apollo"). The Philarmonica Club (see 6th May 1725) met at the same tavern before they moved to the Castle Tavern. No programme is preserved of the concerts performed by the Philo Musicae Societas. The music listed was in the editions printed by Walsh, in score and parts. The operas are all from the period 1706 to 1711 (cf. 26th December 1711), and it seems that the president disposed of the music.

———

Rodelinda is revived at the Haymarket Theatre, 18th December 1725. Repeat performances on 21st, 23rd, 28th December 1725; 1st, 4th, 8th and 11th January 1726.

Advertisements in *Daily Courant*. Colman's "Opera Register" does not list the performance of 23rd December. The five additional songs, printed by Walsh (cf. 15th January 1726), were probably inserted for this revival.

———

The second volume of Cluer and Creake's *Pocket Companion* is finally published, 22nd December 1725.

While the *London Journal* of 18th December announced delivery for the 22nd, the *Daily Post* of 23rd December advertised the book as published " This Day ", Mist's *Weekly Journal* of 25th December as " delivered ", and the *Suffolk Mercury* of 27th December (cf. 13th December) insisted that it had been out since the 17th. The first date seems to be the most likely.

Cf. 2nd May 1724. This second volume of the *Pocket Companion* contains 36 songs, 27 of which are from Handel's operas : *Flavio* again, *Muzio Scevola* (Act III), *Giulio Cesare* (10 arias, among them 2 additional ones), *Tamerlano, Rodelinda*, and 4 more arias from the unpublished *Teseo* ; also 1 each from *Pastor Fido* and *Amadigi*, neither previously published, even in spurious editions. The 2 additional arias from *Giulio Cesare*, probably inserted at the revival on 2nd January 1725, were : Cornelia's " La speranza all' alma mia " and Nireno's " Chi perde un momento ", both of which are printed in the appendix to vol. 68 of the Collected Edition. The aria from *Pastor Fido* (1712) was Eurilla's " Secondaste al fine ", that from *Amadigi* (1715) Amadigi's " Non sà temere ". Henry Carey wrote the English translations added to some of the arias. The volume is dedicated to Alexander Chocke, of the Exchequer, who subscribed for 28 copies of vol. 1, and for 48 of vol. 2.

Since this volume is mainly a Handel collection, an extract from the list of subscribers is given here. There were about 400 names for approximately 600 copies, among them : Dr. Arbuthnot ; Johann Sigismund Cousser of Dublin (an ardent, if distant, admirer of Handel's) ; Henry Carey ; William Freeman ; John Ernest Galliard ; Henry Harrington, senior ; John Hare, junior ; Charles Jennens ; Mrs. Elizabeth Legh, of Adlington Hall, Cheshire ; James Miller ; the Music Club in Cambridge ; Walter Powell, of Oxford ; John Rich ; and the Duke and Duchess of Richmond. The list is headed : " Persons of Quality, Gentry and others, who are Subscribers to and Encouragers of this New Method of Engraving and Printing Musick in Pocket Volumes ".

———

FROM " A JOURNEY THRO' THE WHOLE ISLAND OF GREAT BRITAIN. . . . BY A GENTLEMAN " [*i.e.* DANIEL DEFOE], Vol. II,
1725

. . . Near this Town [of Edgworth] . . . the present Duke of *Chandos* has built a most Magnificent Palace or Mansion House, I might say, the most Magnificent in *England*. . . .

This Palace is so Beautiful in its Situation, so Lofty, so Majestick the Appearance of it, that a Pen can but ill describe it, the Pencil not much better. . . .

. . . The Plaistering and Guilding is done by the Famous *Pargotti* an *Italian*. . . . The great *Salon* or *Hall*, is painted by *Paolucci*. . . .

Nor is the Splendor which the present Duke lives in at this Place, at all beneath what such a Building calls for. . . .

It is vain to attempt to describe the Beauties of this Building at *Cannons.* . . .

. . . *Cannons* had not been three Years in the Duke's Possession, before we saw this Prodigy rise out of the Ground. . . .

The inside of this House is as Glorious, as the outside is Fine . . . the Chapel is a Singularity, not only in its Building, and the Beauty of its Workmanship, but in this also, that the Duke maintains there a full Choir, and has the Worship perform'd there with the Best Musick, after the manner of the Chappel Royal, which is not done in any other Noble Man's Chappel in *Britain* ; no not the Prince of *Wales's*, though Heir Apparent to the Crown.

Nor is the Chapel only Furnish'd with such excellent Musick, but the Duke has a Set of them to entertain him every Day at Dinner. . . .

Two things extreamly add to the Beauty of this House, namely, the Chapel, and the Library. . . .

Here are continually maintained . . . not less than One Hundred and Twenty in Family . . . every Servant in the House is made easy, and his Life comfortable. . . .

Vol. II, Letter III, pp. 8-12. (1927 edition, I. 385-8.) Cf. Macky's *Journey*, 1722, which Defoe used for his book. The third edition, 1742, speaks of choir and music as past glories of Cannons. Defoe visited it at the time of the marriage of the eldest son, the Marquess of Carnarvon (1703–27), which was celebrated on 1st September 1724.

———

FROM MATTHESON'S " CRITICA MUSICA ", HAMBURG, 1725
(Translated)

Pourcel is a French name. An Englishman cannot pronounce it so, unless he says Paurcel, hence they have made Purcel out of it, just as Handel out of Hendel.

Vol. II, p. 149. Mattheson was wrong in his statement about Purcell's origin. The name Händel, in German, is pronounced Hendel.

———

FROM THE SAME

The final intention of Herr Fux [for a contribution to Mattheson's *Ehrenpforte* (" Roll of Honour ")] is seen in the former section, since nothing further has followed. The Capellmeister Händel, however, sings on quite another note, in the following courteous letter :

[Here follows Handel's letter to Mattheson, 24th February 1719.]

I received this estimable note, in which is to be found as much truth as discernment, on 14th March 1719, and answered it with the greatest pleasure by return of post. We see from it the spontaneous approval of one of the greatest Capellmeister in the world, who, besides his un-common musical learning, has other elegant *Studia*, has a perfect command of different languages, knows the world, and particularly the musical world of Italy, excellently, and hence knows very well how dross is to be discerned from gold. Furthermore we see from it that he offers so graciously to contribute his share to the *Ehrenpforte*, and promises to work at the description of his life (which must be full of honour and reward, and one of the most praiseworthy) as soon as he can gain a little time from the work, which he gave in those days, of establishing the Academy of Music ; although this hope has already flattered us in vain for over 6 years, the supposition remains that the admirable man, in seeing this essay, will perhaps remember his promise, and through the fulfilment of it revive the memory of others.

Vol. II, part 7, no. 2, pp. 209-13. In no. 1, pp. 185-7, Johann Joseph Fux's letter from Vienna of 4th December 1717 was printed, containing his refusal to write an autobiography for the *Ehrenpforte* (1740). Handel, who did not decline to do so, nevertheless never wrote it.—In the same Vol. II of his periodical, Mattheson wrote some critical remarks about Handel's St. John Passion of 1704 (pp. 1-29, and 33-56 ; Chrysander, I. 90-101).

1726

FROM THE " LONDON GAZETTE ", 3rd January 1726

The Court of Directors of the Royal Academy of Musick have appointed a Call of 5*l.* per Cent. which is the 16th Call, to be made payable on all the Subscribers to the said Royal Academy on or before the 18th Instant : Notice is hereby given, that the Deputy-Treasurer will attend on Monday, Tuesday, and Wednesday, the 16th, 17th, and 18th Instant, at the Office in the Hay-Market, from Nine a-Clock in the Morning till Two in the Afternoon, in order to receive the same.

Burney (IV. 314 and 337) states that this call was made in 1727, probably because, in the copy in the Burney Collection (now in the British Museum), this number of the *Gazette* is bound with the year 1727. Burney also relates that annual tickets were offered, at the same time, for the coming season. Cf. 18th March.

Elisa, text by Haym, music by (?) Niccola Porpora, is produced at the Haymarket Theatre, 15th January 1726.

There were two arias by Handel in the score : " Ti consola " and " Sedi Roma " (Chrysander, II. 140). Shortly afterwards Walsh and Joseph Hare—John, his father, having died in 1725—published a selection of six songs from *Elisa* (none by Handel), together with five additional songs from *Rodelinda*, two of which, " D'ogni crudel martir " (Rodelinda) and " Si rivedro " (Bertarido) are not in the Collected Edition of Handel's Works ; they were, however, reprinted about 1730 in Walsh's Handel Collection, *Apollo's Feast*, vol. III. *Elisa* was performed six times.

Ottone is revived, 5th February 1726.

Repeat performances on 8th, 12th, 15th, 19th, 22nd, 26th, 28th February ; 5th and 8th March. The performance due on 29th February (!), " His Royal Highness' Birthday ", was advanced to the 28th. There were three new singers for the parts of Gismonda, Adelberto and Matilda—originally sung by Signora Durastanti, Signor Berenstadt and Mrs. Robinson respectively—but it is not known whether and how Signor Baldi, a counter-tenor, Signora Dotti, a contralto, and Signora Costantini, a mezzo-soprano, were occupied.

Handel finishes the opera *Scipione*, 2nd March 1726.

H.–7

Handel's *Scipione* is produced at the Haymarket Theatre on Saturday, 12th March 1726.

There is no advertisement in the *Daily Post* or in the *Daily Journal.* Rolli's text was founded on Apostolo Zeno's *Scipione nelle Spagne* (Loewenberg, p. 79). The copy of the libretto in the Library of Congress, Washington, is the one prepared for George I's personal use : it is bound in red morocco, with gold tooling, and with the British Royal coat of arms on the front and back covers.

———

CAST OF " SCIPIONE ", 12th March 1726

P. C. Scipione—Signor Baldi, counter-tenor
Lucejo—Signor Senesino, alto
C. Lelio—Signor Antinori, tenor
Ernando—Signor Boschi, bass
Berenice—Signor Cuzzoni, soprano
Armira—Signora Costantini, mezzo-soprano
Rosalba—(?) Signora Dotti, contralto

The three new singers in the cast were : Baldi, Luigi Antinori, and Costantini. Baldi only stayed till 1728. Repeat performances on 15th, 19th, 22nd, 26th, 29th March ; 2nd, 12th, 16th, 19th, 23rd, 26th and 30th April.

———

FROM THE " LONDON GAZETTE ", 18th March 1726

The Court of Directors of the Royal Academy of Musick having ordered a Call of Five per Cent. which is the 17th Call, to be made payable on all the Subscribers to the said Academy on or before the 30th Instant. These are to give Notice, that the Deputy-Treasurer will attend at the Opera-Office in the Hay-Market, on the several Days following, viz. the 28th, 29th, and 30th Instant, from Nine a-Clock in the Morning till Two in the Afternoon, in order to receive the same.

Burney (IV. 329) quotes this call as of March 1727. In the British Museum copy this number of the *London Gazette* is bound with the year 1727. Cf. 3rd January 1726. Schoelcher (p. 85) states that this call was made in May, and the 19th in July 1727. The date of the 18th call is not known, but the 19th was made on 23rd December 1726.

———

Handel finishes the opera *Alessandro*, 11th April 1726.

———

FROM WILLERS' HAMBURG NOTES, 18th (29th) April 1726
(Translated)

April 29. *Gumbrecht* began with the opera *Julius Caesar.*

(Merbach, p. 362.) Cf. 10th November 1725. J. G. Gumprecht was the new director of the Hamburg Opera.

———

FROM WILLERS' HAMBURG NOTES, 4th (15th) May 1726
(Translated)

May 15. Otto for the first time.

(Merbach, p. 362.) Haym's text was translated by Johann Georg Glauche, the music adapted by Telemann, and the airs sung in Italian. According to Mattheson's Hamburg Opera List (Chrysander, 1877, col. 250), the full title was *Otto, König in Teutschland* ; Schulze states that one-third of the arias were new, *i.e.* supplied by Telemann. The opera was performed four times in 1726, and once each in 1727 and 1729.

—

Handel's *Alessandro* is produced at the Haymarket Theatre, 5th May 1726.

Again there is no advertisement in the *Daily Post*. The text was an original by Rolli, who seems to have found favour again with the directors of the Academy. While the libretto of *Scipione* does not indicate the name of the composer, Handel is duly named in the book of *Alessandro*. Repeat performances on 7th, 10th, 12th, 14th, 17th, 19th, 21st, 24th, 26th, 31st May ; 4th and 7th June. Eleven performances of an opera within a month was certainly an unusual event ; the reason is to be found in the cast. Cf. 8th February 1753.

—

CAST OF " ALESSANDRO ", 5th May 1726

Alessandro—Signor Senesino, alto
Rossana—Signora Faustina, mezzo-soprano
Lisaura—Signora Cuzzoni, soprano
Tassile—Signor Baldi, counter-tenor
Clito—Signor Boschi, bass
Leonato—Signor Antinori, tenor
Cleone—Signora Dotti, contralto

For the first time, the three great singers were united on the London stage. Faustina Bordoni, called Faustina, about the same age as Cuzzoni but much more attractive, came from a splendid engagement in Vienna, and, like Cuzzoni and Senesino, received £2000 a year. Compared with Cuzzoni, she had the added attraction of not having been married even once. In 1730, after her London engagement, she became the wife of the Composer Johann Adolph Hasse. The Academy had been eager to engage her since 1723 (cf. 30th March 1723) and during the summer of 1725 they succeeded, but Faustina, who asked for £2500 a year, was in no hurry to come. (A satirical poem on " Faustina " and the whole Academy, published by Henry Carey and partly reprinted by Chrysander, II. 151, speaks of " hundreds twenty five a year ", which may indicate that she received an advance payment of £2500 for two years.)

—

Cluer, in company not only with Creake but this time also with Christopher Smith, publishes the score of *Scipione* on 27th May 1726, simultaneously inviting subscriptions for the score of *Alessandro*. (*Daily Post*.)

—

EXTRACTS FROM THE LIST OF SUBSCRIBERS FOR THE SCORE OF
" SCIPIONE ", 27th May 1726

Dr. Arbuthnot, Mr. Cook at New York, J. S. Cousser at Dublin,
Henry Carey, William Freeman of Hamels, J. G. Gumprecht at Hamburg [cf. 18th April], Henry Harrington, Nuburgh Hamilton, Mr. Hare
6 Books, Mr. Jennens, Mrs. Eliz. Legh of Adlington, James Miller,
Philarmonica Club, John Rich, Mr. Robinson (Organist), Sgr. Sandoni
6 Books, Mrs. Wiedeman, and Mr. Zollman of Stockholm.

Cf. 6th May 1725. There were 58 subscribers for 80 copies. Mrs. Wiedeman
was apparently the wife of Carl Friedrich Weidemann, the flautist, who himself
subscribed for six of the later Handel works.

———

FROM THE " DAILY COURANT ", 13th June 1726

The Indisposition of Signior Senessino having hindered the Performance of the Opera [*Alessandro*] last Saturday Night [the 11th], any
Person that had Tickets for that Night, will have their Money returned
at the Office on the Delivery of their Tickets.

(Cutting in *Theatrical Register*.) The season, planned to end on the 11th June,
thus came to a premature close on 7th June. " Senesino went abroad ", says a
note in Colman's *Opera Register*, and he did not return to the Haymarket Theatre
until 7th January 1727.

———

Cluer and Creake advertise the publication of the score of *Alessandro*, *London Journal*, 6th August 1726.

Following *Giulio Cesare*, *Tamerlano*, *Rodelinda* and *Scipione*, this was
the fifth Handel score engraved and sold by Cluer ; all, except the first,
being in quarto.

———

EXTRACTS FROM THE LIST OF SUBSCRIBERS FOR THE SCORE OF
" ALESSANDRO ", 6th August 1726

Dr. Arbuthnot, Francis Brerewood, Mr. Cousser at Dublin, Mr. Cook
at New York, Henry Carey, William Freeman, Mr. Gumprecht at
Hamburg, Henry Harrington, Mr. Hare 18 Books, Mr. Jennens, Mr.
Loeillet, Mrs. Elizabeth Legh of Adlington, James Miller, Philarmonica
Club, John Rich, Mr. Robinson (Organist), Mr. Sandoni, Mr. Wiedeman,
and Mr. Zollman (of Stockholm).

Cf. 27th May 1726. There were 80 subscribers for 106 copies. For Francis
Brerewood, see 15th March 1748. He was not related to Thomas Brerewood ;
cf. 24th June 1727.

———

The Haymarket Theatre opens on 28th September 1726 with a
stagione of a company of Italian comedians.

They played on twelve nights during September and October ; the
prices of admission were 4s. and 2s. The guests were under the patronage

of the Dukes of Montague (cf. 29th September 1720) and Richmond. Cf. Kelly, II. 351, and Chrysander, II. 149 f. It was the first time during the reign of the Royal Academy of Music that the house was let to another company. The Duke of Richmond became Deputy-Governor in the autumn of this year ; cf. 17th December 1726.

RIVA TO MURATORI (Translated)

Kensington, 3rd October 1726.

All my readiness to obey you in the matter of the Opera, which you say will be sent me by post, will be in vain, because the composers of Music have already chosen the librettos for the coming season and are already at work on them. It will also be difficult to have it accepted for the year after, because the Academy have their own poet, and operas that come from Italy cannot be of service in this theatre. It is necessary to revise or rather deform them in order to render them acceptable. Few verses of recitative and many arias is what they want over here, and that is the reason why it has never been possible to perform some of Signor Apostolo's best operas [librettos] and why Metastasio's two finest operas, that is to say his *Dido* and his *Siroe*, have met the same fate. Besides, there are more poets here than are required ; in addition to the Academy's poet, there is Rolli, and one Brillanti from Pistoia, who manages very well. All the others remain idle, so that for your friend to make the journey here, would be both expensive and useless. That is what I am able to tell you, Sir, on this matter.

(Streatfeild, 1917, p. 433-5.) Original in Modena, cf. letter of 7th September 1725. Apostolo is Zeno. Metastasio's *Didone abbandonata* was set by Domenico Sarro for Naples in 1724 and by Leonardo Vinci for Rome in 1726 ; his *Siroe, rè di Persia* was also set by Vinci in 1726, but for Venice. These were the first librettos by Metastasio. It may be mentioned here that a manuscript copy of the score of Vinci's *Didone* in the British Museum contains corrections in Handel's handwriting ; it was, however, never performed in London. For Handel's *Siroe* see 17th February 1728. "Brillanti" has not been identified ; it may have been a nickname.

Walsh and Joseph Hare advertise their arrangement of *Alessandro* for the flute, *Daily Post*, 21st October 1726.

This was, of course, an unauthorised edition.

FROM MATTHESON'S HAMBURG OPERA LIST, [7th (18th) November] 1726 (Translated)

Alexander, somewhat altered by Herr *Wend* from that listed as No. 64 and provided with new Italian arias composed by Herr *Händel*.

(Chrysander, 1877, col. 250 ; Handel, II. 148.) No. 64 in Mattheson's list is Agostino Steffani's opera, *La Superbia d'Alessandro*, first performed in Hamburg in 1695, translated by one Fideler as *Der hochmüthige Alexander*. The libretto of 1726 states : " Die Music ist von dem berühmten Hn. Capell-Meister Hendel ". Hugo Riemann (*Denkmäler deutscher Tonkunst in Bayern*, Leipzig, 1911, vol. 21, p. x), however, says that it was by Steffani, with arias by Handel ; Merbach (p. 362) follows him. Loewenberg (pp. 45 and 80) says the music was by Steffani only. There seems no doubt, however, that Mattheson's record is correct. We now know that Gumprecht, the opera manager, subscribed for the score of Handel's *Alessandro*, published on 6th August 1726. The old and the new *Alessandro* were combined, again under the title of 1695, the text being arranged by Christian Gottlieb Wendt. The performance was mixed, in German and Italian.

—

Cluer and Creake advertise their arrangements for the flute of *Scipione* and *Alessandro*, *London Journal*, 19th November 1726. Cf. 21st October 1726.

—

FROM WILLERS' HAMBURG NOTES, 22nd November (3rd December) 1726 (Translated)

Dec. 3. Julius Cesar. 3 people present ; last performance of the company.

Cf. 18th April 1726.

—

FROM THE " LONDON JOURNAL ", 26th November 1726

From the Prologue, spoken by Mrs. Younger, at the Revival of the Opera *Camilla* at Lincoln's Inn Fields Theatre, 19th November 1726

. . . Ye British Fair, vouchsafe us your Applause,
And smile, propitious, on our English Cause ;
While Senesino you expect in vain,
And see your Favours treated with Disdain :
While, 'twixt his Rival Queens, such mutual Hate
Threats hourly Ruin to yon tuneful State.
Permit your Country's Voices to repair,
In some Degree, your Disappointment there :
Here, may that charming Circle Nightly shine ;
'Tis Time, when That deserts us, to resign.

(Chrysander, II. 152.) Rich, the manager of the theatre, used the vacancy in the other house, forced on the Academy by Senesino's absence and the growing jealousy of the two *prime donne*, to revive Marc Antonio Bononcini's (Giovanni's brother's) opera *Il Trionfo di Camilla* in the English version originally produced at Drury Lane in 1706. Mrs. Barbier and Mr. Leveridge were in the cast of 1726. For the " Rival Queens ", see July 1727.

—

Mrs. Pendarves to Her Sister, Anne Granville

Somerset House, November 27th, 1726.
Last Saturday [the 26th] I was at Camilla. . . . That morning I was entertained with Cuzzoni. Oh how charming ! how did I wish for all I love and like to be with me at that instant of time ! my senses were ravished with harmony. They say we shall have operas in a fortnight, but I think Madam Sandoni and the Faustina are not perfectly agreed about their parts.

(Delany, I. 125.)   Madame Sandoni was, of course, Signora Cuzzoni.

———

From the "Daily Courant", 5th December 1726

The Governour and Court of Directors of the Royal Academy of Musick do hereby give Notice, That a General Court will be held this Day . . . in order to Elect a Deputy-Governour and Directors for the Year ensuing.

Cf. 17th December.

———

From a London Newspaper, 17th December 1726

List of the Deputy-Governour and Directors of the Royal Academy of Music, chosen last Week :
Duke of Richmond, Deputy-Governour.   Earl of Albermarle ; Earl of Burlington ; Hon. James Bruce, Esq. Hon. Patee Byng, Esq. Sir John Buckworth, Bart.   Hon. James Brudenell, Esq.   Marquis of Carnarvon ; Earl of Chesterfield ; Henry Davenant, Esq.   Charles Edwin, Esq. Monsieur Fabrice ; Sir John Eyles, Bart.   Lord Mayor of London ; Lord Viscount Limerick ; Duke of Manchester ; Earl of Mountrath ; Sir Thomas Pendergrass, Bart.   Sir John Rushout, Bart. James Sandys, Esq.   Major General Wade ; Sir William Yonge ; Directors.

(Burney, IV. 314.)   According to Burney, the list was published in the *Daily Courant* of 17th December, but it is not to be found there ; nor is it in the *Daily Post* or the *London Journal*.   There are seven names from the original list of subscribers of 1719 : Burlington, Bruce, Limerick, Manchester (the second Duke), Mountrath, Wade, and Yonge.   The names of Albemarle, Pattee Byng, and perhaps Duckworth, are misprinted.   The lists of directors from autumn 1721 till autumn 1725 are not known.

———

The Academy announce their eighteenth call of 5 per cent from the subscribers, 23rd December 1726.

Burney (IV. 329) dates this call 1727 ; but since he misdates the calls of January and March 1726, it may be assumed that the December date is also wrong.   Cf. 18th October 1727.

1727

The eighth season of the Academy opens on 7th January 1727 with Ariosti's new opera *Lucio Vero*.

The three rival composers of 1720 met in competition this year for the last time on the stage of the Haymarket Theatre ; cf. 4th February 1727.

Mrs. Pendarves to Her Sister, Ann Granville

January 26th, 1726–7.

Mrs. Legh is transported with joy at living once more in "dear London", and hearing Mr. Handel's opera performed by Faustina, Cuzzoni & Senesino (which was rehearsed yesterday for the first time) that she is *out of her senses*. . . . Miss Legh is fallen in love with the *Basilisk*, and says he is the most charming man of the world ; he happened to commend Handel, and won her heart at once.

(Delany, I. 129.) The opera in rehearsal was *Admeto*. "Basilisk" was the nickname of Lord Baltimore, the widowed Mrs. Pendarves' most ardent suitor. Elizabeth Legh, of Adlington Hall, near Macclesfield in Cheshire, was a very keen amateur musician, a subscriber for much music, and was apparently in love with the inaccessible master himself. She was the daughter of a widower, owner of the old Hall, and sister of Charles Legh who later was on friendly terms with Handel. She never married. Cf. 4th January 1740 and January 1747.

From the "Flying-Post", 31st January 1727

On Saturday last [the 21st], the Directors of the Royal Accademy of Musick had a Meeting, in which it was proposed to desire Signior Bonocini to compose an Opera, the Animosities against that Great Master being worn off ; the Minority is like to become the Majority, and at the next Meeting the Directors will resolve, whether they will entertain the Publick with the Compositions of only one, or of several Masters.

(Copy in Bodleian Library, Oxford.) Cf. 23rd May 1724 and 4th February 1727.

From the "Daily Courant", 31st January 1727

At the King's Theatre . . . this present Tuesday . . . will be perform'd a New Opera call'd, Admetus. . . . No Subscriber, or any other

Person with a Subscriber's Ticket, will be admitted without producing it at the first Bar. . . . To begin at Six a-Clock.

Admeto, Re di Tessaglia, text altered from Aurelio Aurelli's *L'Antigona delusa da Alceste*, probably by Haym, was repeated on 4th, 7th, 11th, 14th, 18th, 21st, 25th, 28th February ; 4th, 7th, 11th, 14th, 18th, 21st, 25th March ; 4th, 15th and 18th April, during its first season : an unusual success. The libretto, bilingual as usual, gives Handel's name, and adds : "Le Nuove Scene sone del Sigr. Giuseppe Goupy ". This painter, who became Handel's friend for a time, and who also painted the sets for his *Riccardo I* (11th November 1727), is better known as a cartoonist. According to Vertue, Peter Tillemans was his collaborator at the Haymarket Theatre. In 1726 Goupy made an etching, " Mutius Scaevola burning his hand, in the presence of Porsena ", which seems to have been inspired by Handel's opera of 1721 (C. Reginald Grundy in vol. IX, pp. 78 f., of the Walpole Society Series, London, 1921).

———

CAST OF " ADMETO ", 31st January 1727

Admeto—Signor Senesino, alto
Alceste—Signora Faustina, mezzo-soprano
Ercole—Signor Boschi, bass
Orindo—Signora Dotti, contralto
Trasimede—Signor Baldi, counter-tenor
Antigona—Signora Cuzzoni, soprano
Meraspe—Signor Palmerini, bass

Lady Cowper, like the Countess of Burlington and Sir Robert Walpole, a partisan of Faustina, wrote in her copy of the libretto, opposite her favourite's name : " she is the devil of a singer " (Julian Marshall in Grove's *Dictionary*, 1st edition, I. 696). Palmerini was a singer ; he stayed for two years only. Johann Joachim Quantz, the German flautist and composer, who knew Senesino in Dresden in 1719, came on a visit to London in March 1727, and saw the famous three : Cuzzoni, Faustina and Senesino (cf. Quantz's autobiographical sketch in Marpurg's *Beiträge*, I. 213 and 240 f., under August 1754).

———

FROM THE " FLYING POST ", 4th February 1727

The Directors of the Royal Academy of Musick have resolved, that after the Excellent Opera composed by Mr. Hendel, which is now performing ; Signior Attilia shall compose one : And Signior Bononcini is to compose the next after that. Thus, as this Theatre can boast of the three best Voices in Europe, and the best Instruments ; so the Town will have the Pleasure of having these three different Stiles of composing : And, as Musick is a part of Mathematicks, and was always both by the Ancient Jews, and the Heathens, in the most Polite Courts, &c. esteemed a very rational and noble Entertainment ; this Polite and Rich Nation will by Collecting what is perfect out of various Countries, become the

H.–7 a

Place where all Travellers will stay to be diverted and instructed in this Science, as well as in all others.

(J. P. Malcolm, p. 342.) Copy in Bodleian. Cf. 31st January 1727. Bononcini's *Astianatte* (6th May) was produced before Ariosti's *Teuzzone* (1st November) : they were the last operas which these composers wrote for London.

—

FROM THE SONG, " THE RAREE SHOW ", SUNG BY MR. SALWAY IN LEWIS THEOBALD'S PLAY, " THE RAPE OF PROSERPINE ", MUSIC BY JOHN ERNEST GALLIARD, AT LINCOLN'S INN FIELD THEATRE, 13th February 1727

And for de Diversions, dat make a de Pleasure,
For dis Great Town,
Dey be so many, so fine, so pleasant, so cheap
As never was known ;
Here be de Hay-Market, vere de Italien Opera
Do sweetly sound,
Dat cost a de brave Gentry no more as
Two hundred thousand Pound.

(Chorus)
A very pretty Fancy, a brave gallante Show ;
Juste come from France toute Noveau.

British Museum : G. 306. (10.) Single sheet folio, without publisher's name, printed in London, [1727]. The play was a mixture between opera and pantomine (Nicoll), the word-book was printed. This is the second stanza of the song, written in the style of a Savoyard peep-show man.

—

HANDEL APPLIES FOR NATURALIZATION, 13th February 1727

To the Right Honourable The Lords Spiritual and Temporal
in Parliament assembled,
The Humble Petition of George Frideric Handel
Sheweth,—
That your petitioner was born at Hall in Saxony, out of His Majestie's Allegiance, but hath constantly professed the Protestant Religion, and hath given Testimony of his Loyalty and Fidelity to His Majesty and the good of this Kingdom,
Therefore the Petitioner humbly prays, That he may be added to the Bill now pending, entituled ' An Act for Naturalisating LOUIS SECHEHAYE ' And your petitioner will ever pray, &c.,

George Frideric Handel.

(Cummings, 1914, p. 64 : without source.) The original is not preserved in the Record Office of the House of Lords, and was probably abstracted during the nineteenth century. The year of Handel's naturalization is usually given as 1726, owing to a misunderstanding of the English calendar : February 1726 meant 1727. Since the House of Lords did not deal very often with such petitions, it was usual for several petitions to be added to a bill originally introduced for an earlier petitioner. Handel remained Lutheran.

———

FROM THE " JOURNALS OF THE HOUSE OF LORDS ", 13th February 1727

Hodie 1ᵃ *vice lecta est Billa*, intituled, " An Act for naturalizing *Louis Sechehaye*.

A Petition of *George Frideric Handel*, was presented to the House, and read ; praying to be added to the Bill, intituled, ' An Act for naturalizing *Louis Sechehaye*."

It is ORDERED, That the said Petition do lie on the Table, till the said Bill be read a Second Time.

———

FROM THE " JOURNALS OF THE HOUSE OF LORDS ", 14th February 1727

George Frideric Handel took the Oath of Allegiance and Supremacy, in order to his Naturalization.

ORDERED, That the Petition of *George Frideric Handel*, praying to be added to the above-mentioned Bill, which was Yesterday ordered to lie on the Table till the Second Reading thereof, be referred to the said Committee.

(*Musical Times*, 1st May 1901, p. 313 : under the date of 1726.) A committee was, as usual, appointed to consider the Sechehaye Act.

———

FROM THE " JOURNALS OF THE HOUSE OF LORDS ", 17th February 1727

The Lord *Waldegrave* reported from the Lords Committee to whom the Bill, intituled, " An Act for naturalizing *Louis Sechehay*", was committed : " That they had considered the said Bill, and also the Petitions to them referred ; and had gone through the Bill, and made some Amendments thereunto."

Which, being read Twice by the Clerk, were agreed to by the House.

(*Musical Times*, as before.) Lord Waldegrave had been one of the Academy's Directors during the year 1720–21 ; cf. p. 123.

———

FROM THE " JOURNALS OF THE HOUSE OF LORDS ", 20th February 1727

Hodie 3ᵃ *vice lecta est Billa*, intituled, " An Act for naturalizing *Louis Sechehaye*."

The Question was put, " Whether this Bill, with the
Amendments, shall pass ? "
It was Resolved in the Affirmative.

A Message was sent to the House of Commons, by Mr. *Kinaston* and Mr. *Thomas Bennett* :

To carry down the said Bill ; and acquaint them, that the Lords have agreed, to the same, with some Amendments, whereunto their Lordships desire their Concurrence. . . .

(*Musical Times*, as above.)   The records were interrupted here, and were continued after the communication with the House of Commons.

———

FROM THE " JOURNAL OF THE HOUSE OF COMMONS ", 20th February 1727

A Message from the Lords, by Mr. *Kinaston* and Mr. *Thomas Bennett*.

Mr. Speaker,

The Lords have agreed to the Bill, intituled, An Act for naturalizing *Louis Sechehaye*, with some Amendments :   To which the Lords desire the Concurrence of this House.

And then the Messengers withdrew.

.   .   .   .   .

The House proceeded to take into Consideration the Amendments, made by the Lords, to the Bill, intituled, An Act for naturalizing *Louis Sechehaye* :

And the said Amendments were read ; and are as follows ; *viz.*

Press 1, Line . . . 6.   After " *Verdun* ", insert " *George Frideric Handel*, Son of *George Handel*, by *Dorothy* his Wife, born at *Hall*, in Saxony. . . .

L. 17.   After " *Sechehay*," insert " *George Frideric Handel, Anthony Fursteneau*, and *Michael Schlegel*. . . .

L. 28.   [ditto.]

Pr. 2 . . . L. 21.   [ditto.]

At the End of the Title, add " *George Frideric Handel*, and others."

The said Amendments, being severally read a Second time, were, upon the Question severally put thereupon, agreed unto the House.

Ordered, That Sir *George Caswell* do carry the Bill to the Lords, and acquaint them, That this House hath agreed to the Amendments made by their Lordships.

FROM THE " JOURNALS OF THE HOUSE OF LORDS ", 20th February 1727 (continued)

. . . A Message was brought from the House of Commons, by Sir *George Caswell* and others :

To return the Bill, intituled, " An Act for naturalizing Louis *Sechehaye* ; and to acquaint this House, that they have agreed to their Lordships Amendments made to the said Bill.

The House was adjourned during Pleasure, to robe.

The House was resumed.

His Majesty, being seated on His Royal Throne . . . commanded . . . to signify to the Commons, " It is His Majesty's Pleasure, they attend Him immediately, in this House."

. . . The Clerk of the Crown read the . . . Titles of the . . . Bills to be passed. . . . .

" 3. An Act for naturalizing *Louis Sechehaye, George Frideric Handel, and others.*"

To these Bills the Royal Assent was severally pronounced, in these Words ; (*videlicet,*)

" *Soit fait comme il est desire.*"

. . . Mr. Speaker reported, That the House had attended his Majesty in the House of Peers ; and that his Majesty had been pleased to give the Royal Assent to One publick and Two private Bills, following ; *viz.*

An Act for naturalizing *Louis Sechehaye, George Frideric Handel,* and others.

The Deputy Gentleman Usher of the Black Rod, Mr. Sanderson, brought the King's Command to the House of Commons. The Consent to this Bill was one of George I's last functions.

———

FROM THE " CRAFTSMAN ", 27th February 1727

[In an article on John Kipling, the Treasurer of the Academy of Music.]

He is, in short, a Man of undoubted *Integrity*, of consummate Wisdom, and of exemplary *Gravity*. He is compos'd and sedate in his Conduct, rigid in his Morals, and tall in his Person ; slow in his Speech, yet using many words ; and, to conclude all, a TREASURER *with* clean *and* empty Hands !

I am persuaded, that every Reader must, by this Time, perceive that I can mean no body, in my Description of the fore-going character, but that very worthy and excellent man Mr. KIPLIN, *Treasurer to that Honourable Corporation, the Royal Academy of* MUSICK.

Cf. 31st October-19th December 1734.

———

Admeto is performed for the benefit of Signora Faustina, 7th March 1727.

(Burney, IV. 314.)

———

FROM COLMAN'S " OPERA REGISTER ", 18th–25th March 1727

Mar. 18th [*Admeto*] perform'd 13 times more wth this day—21 Do 25 Do—Satt day—Settimana Santa

Between 25th March and 4th April no opera was given, because of Holy Week.

———

FROM THE " BRITISH JOURNAL ", 25th March 1727

To Mr. HANDEL, *on his* Admetus.

Hail unexhausted Source of Harmony !
Thou Chief of all *Apollo's* tuneful Sons,
In whom the Knowledge of all Magick Numbers,
Or Sound melodious, is concentred !
The Envy, or the Wonder, of Mankind
May terminate, but never can thy Lays :
For, when absorb'd in Elemental Flame,
This World shall vanish, Music will exist ;
Then Thine, first of the Rest, shall mount the Skies,
Where, with its Heav'n born Parent soon commixing,
It breaks through Trumps of Seraphims and Angels ;
And fills the Heav'n with endless Harmony.

This poem, first published anonymously, was printed, in a slightly different version in Henry Carey's *Poems*, third edition, 1729 (see end of 1729).

FROM THE SAME

The Discontented Virgin.

.   .   .   .

VII.

At *Leicester Fields* I give my Vote
For the fine-piped *Cuzzoni* ;
At *Burlington's* I change my Note.
Faustina for my Money.

VIII.

Attilio's Musick I despise,
For none can please but *Handel* ;
But the Disputes that hence arise,
I wish and hope may end well.

.   .   .   .

(Chrysander, II. 161.) These are two out of ten stanzas. Leicester Fields may have been the quarter where Mary, Countess of Pembroke, Cuzzoni's patron, resided; Dorothy, Countess of Burlington sided with Faustina. Attilio is Ariosti. —The poem is also preserved in the Manuscripts of R. W. Ketton, Esq. (Historical MSS. Commission, 12th Report, Appendix, Part 9, 1891, p. 188) : the anonymous and undated version was reprinted by Streatfeild, 1909, pp. 99 f., and by Clemens, p. 156, as *Doggerel Verses*, without reference to the *British Journal* and Chrysander.

———

FROM COLMAN'S " OPERA REGISTER ", 4th–8th April 1727

Apr. 4 Easter Tuesday, Admetus again, & was declared for Satturday, but Signa Faustina being taken very ill — no Opera was perform'd—

during all this time the House filled every night fuller than ever was known at any Opera for so long together—16 times.

4th April was the sixteenth repeat performance. The performance on the 8th was cancelled, and there was no performance on the 11th. It seems that Cuzzoni did not lag behind Faustina even in being taken ill.

—

Ottone is revived on 11th and 13th April, *Floridante* on 29th April and 2nd May 1727.

—

MARY, COUNTESS PEMBROKE TO MRS. CHARLOTTE CLAYTON,
Spring 1727

I hope you will forgive the trouble I am going to give you having always found you on every occasion most obliging. What I have to desire is, that if you find a convenient opportunity, I wish you would be so good as to tell her Royal Highness [the Princess of Wales], that every one who wishes well to Cuzzoni is in the utmost concern for what happened last Tuesday at the Opera, in the Princess Amelia's presence ; but to show their innocence of the disrespect which was shown to her Highness, I beg you will do them the justice to say, that the Cuzzoni had been publicly told, to complete her disgrace, she was to be hissed off the stage on Tuesday ; she was in such concern at this, that she had a great mind not to sing, but I, without knowing anything that the Princess Amelia would honour the Opera with her presence, positively ordered her not to quit the stage, but let them do what they would : though not heard, to sing on, and not to go off till it was proper ; and she owns now that if she had not that order she would have quitted the stage when they cat-called her to such a degree in one song, that she was not heard one note, which provoked the people that like her so much, that they were not able to get the better of their resentment, but would not suffer the Faustina to speak afterwards. I hope her Royal Highness would not disapprove of any one preventing the Cuzzoni's being hissed off the stage ; but I am in great concern they did not suffer anything to have happened to her, rather than to have failed in the high respect every one ought to pay to a Princess of her Royal Highness's family ; but as they were not the aggressors, I hope that may in some measure excuse them.

Another thing I beg you would say is, that I, having happened to say that the Directors would have a message from the King, and that her Royal Highness had told me that his Majesty had said to her, that if they dismissed Cuzzoni they should not have the honour of his presence, or what he was pleased to allow them, some of the Directors have thought fit to say that they neither should have a message from the King, and that he did not say what her Royal Highness did me the honour to tell me he did. I most humbly ask her Royal Highness's pardon for desiring the Duke of Rutland (who is one of the chief amongst them for Cuzzoni) to do himself the honour to speak of it to her Royal Highness, and hear what she would be so gracious to tell him. They have had also a message from the King, in a letter from Mr. Fabrice, which they have the insolence to dispute, except the Duke of Rutland, Lord Albemarle, and Sir Thomas Pendergrass. Lady Walsingham having desired me to let her know how this affair went, I have written to her this morning, and, at the Duke of Rutland's desire, have sent an account of what was done at the Board, for her to give his Majesty.

As I have interested myself for this poor woman, so I will not leave anything undone that may justify her ; and if you will have the goodness to state this affair to her Royal Highness, whom I hope will still continue her most gracious protection to her, I shall be most extremely obliged to you. . . .

(Chrysander, II. 158-60.) Sundon, I. 229-32. The letter is undated there ; Chrysander thought it was written in April or May 1727. Countess Pembroke was Cuzzoni's patron ; cf. 25th March 1727. She was Mary Howe, the third wife of Thomas, Earl of Pembroke. Mrs. Charlotte Clayton, later Viscountess Sundon, was Lady of the Bedchamber to Caroline, Princess of Wales, and became Mistress of the Robes to her as Queen-Consort of George II. The King and his illegitimate daughter, Petronella Melusina, Countess of Walsingham, were apparently in Hanover at the time, and he never returned. The Earl of Albemarle, Monsieur Fabrice, and Sir Thomas Pendergrass were among the twenty Directors of the Academy elected on 5th December 1726 ; the Duke of Rutland, a Lord of the Bedchamber, was not one of them. If the scandal occurred during a performance of Bononcini's *Astianatte*, in May 1727, this would make it an even more remarkable forerunner of what happened on 6th June in the presence of the Princess of Wales herself.

———

Bononcini's *Astianatte* is produced at the Haymarket Theatre, 6th May 1727.

The text was by Haym, altered from Antonio Salvi, the original having been set to music by Bononcini's brother, Marc' Antonio, in 1701. Faustina sang the part of Ermione, Cuzzoni that of Andromaca ; cf. 6th June 1727. (Loewenberg, p. 81.) The libretto of this, Bononcini's last London opera, was dedicated to his patroness, the Duchess of Marlborough. Cf. middle of 1725.

———

Handel finishes the opera *Riccardo Primo*, 16th May 1727.

———

FROM THE " DAILY POST ", 20th May 1727

NEW MUSIC.

Mr. Handel's Opera of Admetus,

transposed for the Flute ; the Songs, Symphonies and Overture connected and fitted for that Instrument in a proper Manner by the same Hand that transposed Radamistus. Also

Six Overtures, viz. in Otho, Rodelinda, Elpidia, Tamerlane, Scipio, and Alexander ; being Concerto's in 7 Parts for Bases, Violins and Hautboys ; the favourite Songs in those Operas. . . .
All printed for and sold by Benjamin Cooke. . . .

Cooke was a new music publisher, who also printed songs from Bononcini's *Astianatte* (10th June). He published the flute arrangement of *Admeto*, as the title says, " by Authority of the Patentee ", *i.e.* Cluer, who was not ready with the score until 24th June 1727, by which time Cooke had already printed a second edition of the flute arrangement (*Daily Post*, 10th June). The arranger of *Radamisto* for the flute was Mr. Bolton, for Meares's edition (cf. 2nd October 1722). Of Cooke's edition of five Handel overtures, and Vinci's overture (cf. 11th May 1725), in seven parts, no copy seems to have survived ; his *Most Celebrated Songs* from those operas were published, without imprint, as " Sold at the Music-Shops ", a formula used by Walsh for pirated editions.

———

FROM WILLERS' HAMBURG NOTES, 29th May (9th June) 1727
(Translated)

June 9. Julius Cesar with elaborate illumination, fireworks and prologue ; to be repeated on the 12th and 16th.

(Merbach, p. 362.) Cf. 10th November 1725. The occasion was George I's birthday on 28th May.

———

FROM THE " LONDON JOURNAL ", 3rd June 1727

New Musick just published,

Admetus for a Flute . . . compos'd by Mr. Handell ; 18 Overtures by the same Author, being Concertos for Violins in all their Parts, as they are performed at the King's Theatre in their respective Opera's ; also several of them curiously done for the Harpsicord. . . . Printed and sold by J. Walsh . . . and J. Hare. . . .

This was probably advertised as a counter to Cooke's announcement of 20th May. " Just published " refers to the *Admeto* arrangements only. Walsh, up to then, had published the following Handel overtures in parts : *Rinaldo ; Floridante, Flavio, Ottone, Radamisto, Muzio Scevola, Acis & Galatea ; Teseo, Amadigi, Pastor Fido, Admeto, The Water Music, Giulio Cesare ; Admeto* (second overture), *Alessandro, Scipione, Rodelinda, Tamerlano* and *Agrippina*. The *Rinaldo* overture was first printed in a collection by various composers ; the *Water Music* overture was, of course, not to an opera. From Walsh's collection of Handel overtures arranged for the harpsichord, one or two sets of six had been published up to then, but not in the same order as the first sets for seven parts. The latter were advertised again on 14th October 1727.

———

The eighth season of the Academy ends on 6th June 1727 with a performance of Bononcini's *Astianatte*, in the presence of the Princess of Wales.

It resulted in the great scandal between the party of Cuzzoni and that of Faustina and in a scuffle between the two singers themselves. The conflict had been prepared by a number of pamphlets, published from March onwards. Chrysander (II. 161-9) lists, and quotes from, the following : *An Epistle from Signor Senesino to Signora Faustina* (8th March) ; *Faustina's Answer to Senesino's Epistle,* " said to be written by Pope " (17th March) ; another answer (25th March) ; *A Letter from a Gentleman in the Town, to a Friend in the Country ; containing . . . a very imperfect Judgment on our most famous Performers in Musick . . .* (April) ; and *An Epistle from Signora Faustina to a Lady,* apparently the Duchess of Marlborough (10th June). The names are all indicated by single letters only. Cf. the pamphlets published in June and July, under those dates.

———

FROM THE " BRITISH JOURNAL ", 10th June 1727

On Tuesday-night last [the 6th], a great Disturbance happened at the Opera, occasioned by the Partisans of the Two Celebrated Rival Ladies, Cuzzoni and Faustina. The Contention at first was only carried on by Hissing on one Side, and Clapping on the other ; but proceeded at length to Catcalls, and other great Indecencies : And notwithstanding the Princess Caroline was present, no Regards were of Force to restrain the Rudenesses of the Opponents.

The *London Journal* of the same day carried the report with slight alterations : " The Contention . . . proceeded . . . by the delightful Exercise of Catcalls, and other Decencies, which demonstrated the inimitable Zeal and Politeness of that Illustrous Assembly . . . but no Regards were of Force to restrain the glorious Ardour of the fierce Opponents." Finally, the *Craftsman* of the same day published a letter by " Phil-Harmonicus ", addressed to " Caleb D'Anvers ", the editor (Nicholas Armhurst), referring to the Catcalls and proposing a court of arbitration between the two *prime donne*.

———

George I dies at Osnabrück on 11th (22nd) June 1727 during a visit to the Electorate. George II is proclaimed King on 15th June.

———

FROM THE " LONDON JOURNAL ", 24th June 1727

This Day is published,

The whole Opera of ADMETUS in Score. Composed by Mr. HANDELL. Engraved, Printed and Sold in Cluer's Printing Office . . . and by Christopher Smith. . . .

The score had been in preparation and the subscriptions collected since April. The title-page bears the name of J. Cluer, but the style " Cluer's Printing Office " in the advertisement indicated that Cluer died about May 1727 ; his widow, Elisabeth, married, in 1731, Thomas Cobb, his successor, who in turn was succeeded in 1736 by his brother-in-law, William Dicey.

———

Extracts from the List of Subscribers for " Admeto "
24th June 1727

Thomas Brerewood ; Mr. Cook, at Newyork ; J. S. Cousser ; Henry Carey ; William Freeman ; Michael Festing ; Henry Harrington ; Mr. Hare, 12 Books ; Mr. Jennens ; Mrs. Legh of Adlington in Cheshire ; William Neale, at Dublin, 6 Books ; Philarmonica Club ; Mr. Quantz ; Mr. Rich ; Mr. Robinson, Organist ; Sgr. Sandoni, 6 Books ; Mr. Zollman.

There were 57 subscribers for 93 copies. Quantz came on a visit to London in spring 1727 ; cf. 31st January. Neale was a music dealer and publisher. Thomas Brerewood (not related to Francis, see 6th August 1726) provided English words to two arias from *Poro* (Smith, 1948, p. 210).

—

From " The Devil to pay at St. James's : or, A full and true Account of a most horrible and bloody Battle between Madam Faustina and Madam Cuzzoni, etc.",
[June] 1727

. . . it is not now (as formerly), *i.e.* are you High Church or Low, Whig or Tory ; are you for Court or Country, King *George*, or the Pretender : but are you for *Faustina* or *Cuzzoni, Handel* or *Bononcini.* There's the Question. This engages all the Polite World in warm Disputes ; and but for the soft Strains of the Opera, which have in some Measure qualified and allay'd the native Ferocity of the *English*, Blood and Slaughter would consequently ensue.

(Chrysander, II. 165.) The pamphlet was listed in the *Monthly Catalogue* for June 1727, no. 50, p. 69, but not advertised in Mist's *Weekly Journal* until July. It was reprinted in Dr. Arbuthnot's posthumous *Miscellaneous Works*, Glasgow 1751, I. 213-23, but it was not written by him.

—

From the " Daily Courant ", 13th July 1727

Whereas several Persons stand indebted to the Royal Academy for Calls and otherwise, the Court of Directors do hereby order Notice to be given, That they will pay or cause to be paid, at the Office in Hay-Market, or to the Person attending them in that Behalf, such Sum or Sums as they are owing, on or before Wednesday the 19th Instant, otherwise they shall be obliged to cause Process to be made at Law against them, in order to recover the same.

(Burney, IV. 326.) Schoelcher (p. 85), states that there was a nineteenth call to the subscribers in July.

—

From " The Contre Temps ; or, Rival Queans : a small Farce. As it was lately Acted . . . at *H—d—r's* [Heidegger's] private *The—re* [Theatre], near the *H—M—* [Hay-Market] ", (July) 1727

DRAMATIS PERSONAE.

F—s—na, Queen of *Bologna*.
C—z—ni, Princess of *Modena*.
H—d—r, High-Priest to the Academy of Discord.
H—d—l, Professor of Harmony to the Academy.
S—s—no, Chief of the Choir.
M—u—o, Violino Primo to the Queen of *Bologna*, to
    keep her Majesty's Body in Tune.
S—d—ni, Basso Continuo, and Treasurer to the Prin-
    cess of *Modena*.
    A Chorus of P—rs and Tupees, with Cat-calls.
Scene the Temple of Discord, near the *H—y M—t*.
    Time equal to the Representation.

H—d—r.

Dread Queen and Princess, hail ! we thus are met,
To settle Matters of the greatest Weight : . . .
With bright *F—s—na*, we lose all our Beaus ;
And D—k—s must die, when sweet *C—z—ni* goes :

H—d—l.

—Nor shall the *Saxon* ever more compose.

      .   .   .   .   .

(C—z—ni *lays hold of* Fau—na's *Head-Cloaths*. . . . F—s—na *lays Hand on* C—z—ni's *Head Dress*.) . . .

H—d—l.

I think 'tis best—to let 'em fight it out :
Oil to the Flames you add, to stop their Rage ;
When tir'd, of Course, their Fury will asswage.

      .   .   .   .   .

(. . . H—l *desirous to see an End of the Battle, animates them with a Kettle-Drum*. . . .)

S—s—no.

So have I seen two surly Bull-Dogs tare
Firm Limb from Limb, and strip the Flesh of Hair. . . .

(Chrysander, II. 163 f.) Listed in the *Monthly Catalogue* for July 1727, no. 51, p. 81. Attributed to Colley Cibber, in whose *Dramatic Works*, 1777, IV. 370-81, the pamphlet was, in fact, reprinted ; it seems, however, to be spurious, although the term " canary birds ", for the Italian singers, appears both in this pamphlet and in Cibber's famous "Apology" of 1740 (pp. 343-5). M—u—o is not Monroe (cf. 23rd August 1720 and 7th April 1724), who was a harpsichord player, like Cuzzoni's husband, Sandoni. The Munro in question was apparently in charge of Faustina's *claque*. The "Saxon", of course, is Handel himself, *il Sassone* of Italian days. The members of the chorus are Peers and Dupes. The Duke might have been Francesco of Parma, who died in 1727 (cf. Mainwaring, p. 109), or the Duke of Rutland, Cuzzoni's protector.

———

FROM THE "NORWICH MERCURY", 16th September 1727

[London,] *September* 9. Mr. Hendel, the famous Composer to the Opera, is appointed by the King to compose the Anthem at the Coronation which is to be sung in Westminster-Abbey at the Grand Ceremony.

The news was certainly published in London before this, but no newspaper with it in has been traced. Cf. 4th to 11th October.

———

FROM THE TREASURY PAPERS, ABOUT 30th September 1727

State of what is due to the Countess of Portland for the expense of their Royal Highnesses officers and servants under her government from Mich. 1726 to Mich. 1727 when the new establishment commenced. . . . To Mr. Handell 195 [pounds].

(Calendar of Treasury Papers, 1720-28, p. 468.) This is the first official record of Handel teaching Princesses Anne, Amelia, and Caroline, the daughters of George II. He seems to have taught Princess Anne since about 1720. The three Princesses were granted their own household in 1728. Elisabeth, Countess of Portland, was Duke Henry's wife.

———

The ninth season of the Academy opens on 30th September with a revival of *Admeto*, also performed on 3rd, 7th, 14th, 17th October and 4th November.

The part of Orindo, originally sung by Signora Dotti (contralto) was sung, probably in autumn 1727 and certainly in spring (25th May till 1st June) 1728, by Mrs. Wright, a soprano. During autumn 1727 the advertisements of the operas in the *Daily Courant* ended with the words : "Vivant Rex, & Regina".

———

FROM THE "DAILY COURANT", 2nd October 1727

My Lord Chamberlain, at the Request of the Directors of the Royal Academy of Musick, has ordered a General Court of the said Academy on the 6th Inst. upon extraordinary Business.

(Burney, IV. 326.)

———

FROM " PARKER'S PENNY POST ", 4th October 1727

Mr. Hendle has composed the Musick for the Abbey at the Coronation, and the Italian Voices, with above a Hundred of the best Musicians will perform ; and the Whole is allowed by those Judges in Musick who have already heard it, to exceed any Thing heretofore of the same Kind : It will be rehearsed this Week, but the Time will be kept private, lest the Crowd of People should be an Obstruction to the Performers.

(*Musical Times*, 1st March 1902, edited by F. G. Edwards.) The notice was printed again in *Norris's Taunton Journal* of 6th October, the day of the rehearsal. The *Norwich Gazette* of 7th October, in a report from London of the 5th, prints a variant of this notice, calling the composer " Hendal ".

—

FROM READ'S " WEEKLY JOURNAL ", 7th October 1727

Yesterday there was a Rehearsal of the Musick that is to be perform'd at their Majesties Coronation in Westminster Abbey, where was present the greatest Concourse of People that has been known.

(*Musical Times*, 1st March 1902.) A similar note appeared in the *British Journal* of the same day, wrongly dated 7th September.

—

The Coronation of George II and Caroline is held at Westminster Abbey, 11th October 1727.

There are two descriptions of the ceremonial, one printed in London and reprinted in Dublin in 1727, and the other, a German one, printed in Hanover in 1728. Both are of a general character, describing Coronation proceedings, with some reference to the present one ; they were probably written before the event. From the English version it would seem as if only three of Handel's four Coronation Anthems were performed ; the German version, however, quotes all of them (Chrysander, II. 171 f.). Handel's autographs give the names of the solo singers ; (Thomas ?) Bell, John Church, John Freeman, Bernard Gates, Francis Hughes, Mr. Leigh (or Lee), and Samuel Weeley. There were at least two altos and two basses among the singers, none of whose Christian names are given by Handel. Chrysander deduces from the manuscripts that there were 12 boys and 35 men, altogether 47 singers, performing ; and since the Chapel Royal had 36 only (10 boys and 26 men) eleven or more voices must have been invited to supplement the choir ; perhaps these really came from the Italian opera, as indicated on 4th October, although it seems unlikely that the soloists would have consented to sing as choristers. (Heidegger was in charge of the illuminations in Westminster Hall.) The report of the rehearsal, published on the 14th, speaks of 40 singers, and of an orchestra of about 160. The musicians were staged in an amphitheatrical arrangement. The organ, behind the altar, was built by Schrider (see 10th February 1728), but a double-bassoon of sixteen feet, made by the flute-maker Stanesby junior in 1739, was not used on that occasion ; according to Burney, it was not used until the Handel Commemoration in 1784 (*Account*, p. 7), but Eric Halfpenny (*Music &*

Letters, January 1953) suggested that Handel might have used it for *L'Allegro* in 1740.

———

FROM THE " NORWICH GAZETTE ", 14th October 1727

[London,] *October* 7. Yesterday there was a Rehearsal of the Corona-tion Anthem in Westminster-Abbey, set to Musick by the famous Mr. Hendall : There being 40 Voices, and about 160 Violins, Trumpets, Hautboys, Kettle-Drums, and Bass's proportionable ; besides an Organ, which was erected behind the Altar : And both the Musick and the Performers, were the Admiration of all the Audience.

Although this report refers to the final rehearsal, the description of the orchestra applies equally, of course, to the event itself.

———

The Academy announce their nineteenth call for 5 per cent from the subscribers, 18th October 1727.

(Burney, IV. 326). According to Burney, the money was payable by 25th October.

———

Ariosti's opera *Teuzzone*, text by Apostolo Zeno, is produced at the Haymarket Theatre, 21st October 1727.

This was Ariosti's very last opera, not only for London. It was per-formed 3 times. The libretto is dedicated by the composer to Friedrich Wilhelm I, King of Prussia, in memory of Ariosti's sojourn in Berlin, 1697–1703, where he was court composer to Queen Sophie Charlotte, George II's aunt and Friedrich Wilhelm I's mother. He was succeeded by Bononcini.

———

FROM THE " DAILY COURANT ", 21st October 1727

(Advertisement of *Teuzzone*.)

Tickets will be delivered at the Office at the Hay-Market, this Day : And having no Annual Subscribers admitted this Season, Four Hundred Tickets and no more will be given out. At Half a Guinea each. No Persons whatsoever will be admitted for Money nor any Tickets sold at the Bar, but in the proper Offices. The Gallery 5s. By His Majesty's Command, no persons whatsoever to be admitted behind the scenes. To begin exactly at Six o'Clock. Vivant Rex, & Regina. N.B. The Directors have caused the Tickets and Method of receiving them to be altered for the future, the better to prevent Frauds,—therefore will be placed at the fore and back Door leading into the Stone Passage, a Box into which the Gentlemen & Ladies are desired to drop their Tickets as they go into the House. The Subscribers will be admitted on producing their Silver Tickets only & not otherwise. The Gentlemen and others going into the Gallery are likewise desired to deliver their Tickets into the Box, to be placed at the Gallery Door for that Purpose.

Latreille's manuscript excerpts. No printed copy in the British Museum. The subscribers with the silver tickets were, of course, the Academy's, not the annual, subscribers.

———

George II's first birthday as King, on 30th October 1727, is celebrated by a Court ball at which some minuets, written by Handel for the occasion, are performed.

Cf. 18th November.

———

MRS. PENDARVES TO HER SISTER, ANN GRANVILLE

Somerset House, 11th Novr. 1727.

I was yesterday at the rehearsal of Mr. Handel's new opera called King Richard the First—'tis delightful.

. . . Masquerades are not to be forbid, but there is to be another entertainment *barefaced*, which are balls. . . . There is to be a handsome collation, and they will hire Heidegger's rooms to perform in.

(Delany, I. 144-6.) For the carnival twelve gentlemen intended to subscribe ten guineas each for every one of the twelve balls planned, with twenty-four couples a night.

———

FROM THE " DAILY COURANT ", 11th November 1727

At the King's Theatre . . . this present Saturday . . . will be perform'd a new Opera called, RICHARD the FIRST, King of ENGLAND . . . exactly at 6.

Riccardo I, Re d' Inghilterra, text by Rolli, decorations by Goupy and Tillemans (cf. 31st January 1727), was performed on 11th, 14th, 18th, 21st, 25th, 28th November ; 2nd, 5th, 9th, 12th and 16th December, and perhaps also in January 1728 ; it was never again revived in London. The libretto, which gives the names of Rolli, Handel and Goupy, also contains an Italian sonnet by Rolli, addressed to George II.

———

CAST OF " RICCARDO PRIMO ", 11th November 1727

Riccardo Io—Signor Senesino, alto
Costanza—Signora Cuzzoni, soprano
Berardo—Signor Palmerini, bass
Isacio—Signor Boschi, bass
Pulcheria—Signora Faustina, mezzo-soprano
Oronte—Signor Baldi, counter-tenor

———

CESAR DE SAUSSURE TO HIS FAMILY IN LAUSANNE (Translated)

Throughout the ceremonies a band of the most expert musicians and the best voices in England executed an admirable concert. They were directed by the celebrated Mr. Haendel, who had composed the anthem sung at Divine Service.

London, November 17, 1727.

(Saussure, *Lettres*, p. 260; *Letters*, p. 259.) The passage, referring to the Coronation on 11th October, is from Letter X ; the book was prepared for publication in 1765, but not printed until 1902 (translated) and 1903.

—

FROM THE " LONDON JOURNAL ", 18th November 1727

New Musick just published.

Minueets for his Majesty King George II's Birth-day 1727, as they were performed at the Ball at Court. Composed by Mr. Handell. To which is added, variety of Minuets, Rigadoons, and French Dances, performed at Court and publick Entertainments. . . . The Tunes proper for a Violin or Hoboy, and several of them within the Compass of the Flute. price 6d. . . . Printed for, and sold by J. Walsh . . . and J. Hare. . . .

(Chrysander, II. 175.) Cf. 30th October. If a copy of this edition exists, it would be a rarity. Cf. 3rd May 1729.

—

FROM (FELIX) " FARLEY'S BRISTOL JOURNAL ", 18th November 1727

There is to be a fine Te Deum Jubilate, and an Anteam perform'd at our Cathedral on Wednesday next [the 22nd], being S. Cecilia, in the morning, compos'd by the great Mr. Handell, in which above 30 voices and instruments are to be concerned.

For the benefit of Mr. Preist . . . will be perform'd at the Theatre on St. Augustin's Back, a consort of vocal and instrumental musick. . . . Besides a great variety of overtures and concerto's, compos'd by the great Mr. Handell, and other judicious authors, several favorite songs in the opera's of Scipio, in the Pastorals of Acis and Galatea, and in an Oratoria of Mr. Handell's, will be perform'd. . . .

(Latimer, p. 161.) This is the first record of Handel performances in the provinces in Great Britain. The day's arrangements forestall the Three Choirs Meetings, and music festivals in other towns. The Te Deum and Jubilate was the " Utrecht ", and the Anthem probably one of the " Chandos ". Nathaniel Priest was the organist at Bristol. The evening concert, beginning at six (when the Music Society held another concert in Merchant's Hall), was performed by the same number (thirty) of musicians, guests from London, Bath, Wells, etc. To call *Acis and Galatea* a pastoral was usual, but *Haman and Mordecai*, the first version of the oratorio *Esther*, was usually called a masque.—The first paragraph quoted is an editorial note, the second an advertisement.

MRS PENDARVES TO HER SISTER, ANN GRANVILLE

[Somerset House,] 25th November 1727.

Last Wednesday [the 22nd] was performed the musick in honour of St. Cecilia at the Crown Tavern. Dubourg was the first fiddle, and everybody says he exceeds all the Italians, even his master Geminiani. Senesino, Cuzzoni and Faustina sang there some of the best songs out of several operas, and the whole performance was far beyond any opera. I was very unlucky in not speaking to Dubourg about it, for he told me this morning he could have got me in with all the ease in the world. . . .

I doubt operas will not survive longer than this winter, they are now at their last gasp ; the subscription is expired and nobody will renew it. The directors are always squabbling, and they have so many divisions among themselves that I wonder they have not broke up before ; Senesino goes away next winter, and I believe Faustina, so you see harmony is almost out of fashion.

(Delany, I. 148 f.) The Music Club at the " Crown and Anchor " Tavern in the Strand met on Mondays. It also met each year on St. Cecilia's Day, when ladies and professional musicians were admitted. Chrysander (II. 123) quotes from the London Journal of 16th and 30th November 1723 details about such a concert on 22nd November of that year, at which Senesino and the violinist Carbonelli performed in the presence of two hundred ladies. The St. Cecilia concert of 1727 was a special event. Matthew Dubourg was going to Ireland in 1728, as Master of the State Music there.

———

FROM THE " LONDON GAZETTE ", 28th November 1727

The Governour and Court of Directors of the Royal Academy of Musick do hereby give Notice, that a General Court will be held on Monday the 4th of December next, in order to elect a Deputy-Governour and Directors for the Year ensuing. NB. It was ordered at a General Court held the 27th of May, 1724, that no Member of this Corporation should have a Vote in the Choice of a Deputy Governour or Directors, who have not paid the several Calls made by the Royal Academy at the Time of such Election.

(Burney, IV. 329.) According to the Earl of Shaftesbury's recollections in 1760 (see Appendix), Faustina's party was successful at the election.

———

Alessandro is revived on 26th December and repeated once, on 30th December 1717.

In Colman's *Opera Register* the revival is dated 29th December 1727, and repeat performances are entered under 2nd and 6th January 1728, " &c.".

———

FROM JOHN CHAMBERLAYNE'S " MAGNA BRITANNIAE NOTITIA ", 1727

The King's Officers and Servants in ordinary above Stairs,
under the Lord Chamberlain :

Composer of Musick for the Chapel Royal,
     Mr. George Handel.

(Chrysander, II. 175.) Chamberlayne's *Notitia,* with the second title, *The
Present State of Great Britain,* was the *Whitaker's Almanack* of the time ; this extract
is taken from Part II, p. 59. Greene was still the Composer to the Chapel Royal.
Handel's temporary commission was apparently connected with the setting of
the Coronation Anthems. In 1728 (identical with 1729) no name is given for
the " Composer of the Musick for the Chapel Royal " on p. 63 of the *Notitia.*
Maurice Green(e)'s name appears under the heading " Royal Chapels " as organist
and as composer ; from 1735 onwards also as " Composer of the Musick of the
Chapel Royal ". (Smith, 1948, pp. 53 f.)

1728

No copy of the *Daily Courant*, then the only London paper for opera advertisements, is known for January and February 1728. It seems improbable, however, that *Radamisto* was revived again during this period, as related by Burney (IV. 259) and later writers. (Loewenberg, p. 73.)

—

MRS. PENDARVES TO HER SISTER, ANN GRANVILLE

Somerset House, 29th Jan. 1727–8.

Yesterday I was at the rehearsal of the new opera composed by Handel : I like it extremely, but the taste of the town is so depraved, that nothing will be approved of but the burlesque. The Beggars' Opera entirely triumphs over the Italian one. . . .

(Delany, I. 158.) The date of this letter, given by the editor as 19th January, is impossible : if *Siroe*, finished on 5th February, was really rehearsed in January, it would have been rather near the end of the month, on the 28th. But the *Beggar's Opera* was not produced until the 29th at Lincoln's Inn Fields Theatre, and it is improbable that Mrs. Pendarves attended its rehearsal too. This famous ballad-opera, if not the first, the most successful of its kind, was written by John Gay, the music arranged by Johann Christoph Pepusch, who also wrote the overture. Among the tunes, taken from the works of various composers, were Handel's march from *Rinaldo* (later known as the Royal Guards' March), supplied with the words "Let us take the road"; and "'Twas when the seas were roaring", attributed to Handel (see 30th April 1725), with the new words "How cruel are the traytors". The great success of the *Beggar's Opera* led to a continuation of the story, by the same authors, called *Polly*, which, however, was not licensed for performance until 1777, at the Haymarket Theatre. The libretto, containing the tunes, as did that of the *Beggar's Opera*, was printed in 1729 and shows three Handel airs : "Abroad after misses most husbands will roam", after the "Trumpet Minuet" from the *Water Music*; "Brave boys, prepare", after the March from *Scipione*; and "Cheer up, my lads", after another minuet from the *Water Music*.

—

Handel finishes the opera *Siroe*, 5th February 1728.

—

FROM A PAMPHLET ADDRESSED TO *Fa—na Bo—ni* [FAUSTINA BORDONI], LONDON, 1728 (Translated)

A few days ago I was at a well-known Cafe and, according to my custom, was ascending the stairs to enter one of the upper rooms which are frequented by persons of worth and ability, when the voice of a man who was reading aloud a pamphlet in Italian caused me to halt in

my steps, also because I realised that it was concerned with music. . . .
All that I could understand was that the pamphlet was a reply to that
recently published booklet entitled *Avviso ai compositori,* and [I was curious]
to examine this reply especially as I had with me another written in
English. . . .

Meanwhile, I must tell you, I was curious to know how the author
of the " Advice " judged your two pamphlets and whether he thought
of replying to them : also whether he would allow *me* to compose a
reply, to be couched in terms such as are used by gentlemen who publish
their views upon matters of Science and the Fine Arts. I discovered that
he held of no account what, with good reason, he described as satires
that were as insipid as they were impertinent. He begged me not to take
the trouble of answering, saying that his friends, whom your two authors
had intended to offend, are—thanks to their extraordinary abilities—so
much above all that you say and have had said about them and are
associates of such fame in the world that they do not need any apology.
Only one thing distressed him, somewhat, that having, out of malice,
decided to make common cause with Mr. *Händel* you should have
published the statement that the " Advice " had been directed equally
against both, and that this fact was made manifest in that article which
speaks of the bad practice of over-burdening compositions with instru-
mentation. He did not address the " Advice " to you, still less to a
man of so great excellence as he [Handel], so that whoever reads the
article without prejudice or with partiality for Mr. *Händel,* will find
that where he does explain himself he is in no doubt but that the inter-
weaving of the instruments in the composition creates an excellent
effect, particularly if the composer understands their true nature and if
he is a skilful contrapuntist. This quality can most aptly be applied to
him [Handel], and your authors have made the mistake of imagining
that others can think him deserving of correction in this matter. My
friend has too much real love for good music in general not to esteem
highly such an able composer as Mr. *Händel* in fact is ; he is a man who
prefers Tasso to Ariosto, Raphael to Rubens. . . .

       I am your most affectionate Servant,
London, 9th February 1728, A.C.   [No signature.]

(Högg, pp. 58 f. : without commentary.) Conservatorio di Musica G. B.
Martini, Bologna : F. 44. This anonymous pamphlet is probably a unique copy.
The booklet, referred to in the pamphlet, was attributed by Chrysander (II. 183)
to Bononcini : *Advice to the Composers and Performers of Vocal Musick. Translated
from the Italian,* London, 1727. The original appeared later : *Avviso ai compositori ed ai cantanti,* London 1728 ; both published by Thomas Edlin. While
these booklets are in the British Museum, no copy is known of the answer,
published, according to the *Monthly Catalogue* (no. 57, p. 7), in January 1728 :
*Remarks on a Pamphlet lately imported from Modena call'd . . . which is given
gratis up one pair of stairs in Suffolkstreet,* printed by J. Roberts. Chrysander, who
states that Bononcini's residence was in Suffolk Street, suggested that the original

booklet was, in fact, printed first in Modena ; but the title of the *Remarks* probably hinted only at the supposed author who came from Modena. The author, it can now be proved, was Giuseppe Riva, the Modenese Resident in London. His *Avviso* was translated into German by Lorenz Christoph Mizler as *Nachricht vor die Componisten und Sänger* and printed as an appendix to Mizler's *Musikalischer Starstecher*, Leipzig 1740, pp. 111-18. Edlin also published Rolli's *Canzonette e Cantate*, London 1727. Handel's name is not mentioned in the *Advice*, but allusions indicate his work.

———

FROM THE " BRITISH JOURNAL, OR : THE CENSOR ", 10th
February 1728

The fine Organ made by Mr. Schrieder, which was set up in West-minster Abbey, and used on the Day of the Coronation, has been pre-sented to the said Abbey by his Majesty. It is accounted one of the best Performances of that Maker.

(Chrysander, II. 174.) Cf. 11th October 1727 and 15th August 1730. Christo-pher Schrider (Schreider) was one of Father Smith's workmen and his son-in-law, and, since 1708, his successor as organ-builder to the Court. Cf. 17th December 1737.

———

FROM MIST'S " WEEKLY JOURNAL ", 17th February 1728
This Day is published,

King Richard I. An OPERA. Compos'd by Mr. Handel. Engrav'd, printed and sold at Cluer's Printing Office. . . . Sold also by Christopher Smith . . . ; at both Places may be had Mr. Handell's Operas of Julius Caesar, Tamerlane, Rodelinda, Scipio, Alexander, Admetus, &c. . . . The abovesaid J. Cluer hath also this Day published Handel's Opera of K. Richard I. . . .

The first issue shows the name of J. Cluer only in the imprint. The score, in quarto, was not published on subscription, as were the four previous Handel scores printed by Cluer.

———

Handel's opera *Siroe* is produced at the Haymarket Theatre, 17th February 1728.

Since the *Daily Courant* of February is not available, no advertisement can be traced before 1st March ; it corresponds to that of 21st October 1727. Haym's text was based on the second book of Pietro Metastasio, later the famous librettist, which was set by Leonardo Vinci for Venice in 1726. The London libretto of *Siroe, Re di Persia* was dedicated " Alli Eccellent^{ml} ed Illustr^{ml} Signori Direttori, e Sottoscritti della Accademia Reale di Musica " by Haym. The opera was performed on 17th, 20th, 24th, 27th February ; 2nd, 9th, 12th, 16th, 19th, 23rd, 26th, 30th March ; 2nd, 6th, 9th, 13th, 23rd and 27th April. The performance advertised for 5th March was cancelled. All the performances were on Saturdays and Tuesdays.

———

CAST OF " SIROE ", 17th February 1728
Cosroe—Signor Boschi, bass
Siroe—Signor Senesino, alto

Medarse—Signor Baldi, counter-tenor
Emira—Signora Faustina, mezzo-soprano
Laodice—Signora Cuzzoni, soprano
Arasse—Signor Palmerini, bass

———

FROM THE "DAILY JOURNAL", 19th February 1728

On Saturday last [the 17th] the King, Queen and Princess Royal, and the Princesses Amelia and Carolina, went to the Opera House in the Hay-Market, and saw perform'd the New Opera call'd Siroe.

(Schoelcher, p. 80.) George II followed his father in showing a lively interest in the opera, especially in those by Handel. Handel's royal pupils, Anne in particular, visited his house frequently.

———

Walsh and Hare advertise *Riccardo Primo*, arranged for flute; *County Journal: or, The Craftsman*, 9th March 1728.

This paper is quoted from now onwards as the *Craftsman*, its original name.

———

FROM THE "LONDON JOURNAL", 23rd March 1728

. . . As there is nothing which surprizes all true Lovers of Music more, than the Neglect into which the *Italian* Operas are at present fallen; so I cannot but think it a very extraordinary Instance of the fickle and inconstant Temper of the *English* Nation : A Failing which They have always been endeavouring to cast upon their Neighbours in *France*, but to which They themselves have at least a good Title to ; as any one may be satisfied of, who will take the pains to consult our Historians. . . .

(Burney, IV. 333 ; Schoelcher, p. 86 ; Chrysander, II. 219 f.) This anonymous letter against the *Beggar's Opera* is usually attributed to Dr. Arbuthnot, but there is no proof of his authorship (cf. Aitken, pp. 113 f.). Perhaps Haym was the real author ; cf. 29th April 1728. In January 1728, a pamphlet, also attributed to Arbuthnot, was published against Heidegger : *The Masquerade. A Poem, inscrib'd to C—t H—d—g—r. By Lemuel Gulliver, Poet Laureat to the King of Lilliput ;* reprinted in Arbuthnot's *Miscellaneous Works*, II. 5-18 (Chrysander, II. 222).

———

FROM THE "CRAFTSMAN", 13th April 1728

POLLY PEACHUM.

A new Ballad. To the Tune of, *Of all the Girls that are so smart.*

I.

Of all the Belles that tread the Stage,
There's none like pretty *Polly*,
And all the Musick of the Age,
Except her Voice, is Folly.

II.

Compar'd with her, how flat appears
Cuzzoni or Faustina?
And when she sings, I shut my Ears
To warbling Senesino.

.   .   .   .   .

V.

Some Prudes indeed, with envious Spight
Would blast her Reputation,
And tell us that to Ribands bright
She yields, upon Occasion.

VI.

But these are all invented Lies,
And vile outlandish Scandal,
Which from Italian Clubs arise,
And Partizans of Handel.

.   .   .   .   .

Polly Peachum is the heroine of the Beggar's Opera.

———

From the " London Gazette ", 16th April 1728

The Court of Directors of the Royal Academy of Musick, pursuant to the Resolution of a General court of the said Academy held the 3d Instant, do hereby give Notice, that they have ordered another Call of 2l. 1 half per Cent. which is the 21st Call, to be made payable by all the Subscribers to the said Academy, on or before the 24th Instant ; and the Deputy Treasurer will attend at the Office in the Hay-Market, on Monday, Tuesday and Wednesday, the 22d, 23d, and 24th Instant, from Nine a-Clock in the Morning till Two in the Afternoon, in order to receive the same.

Cf. 23rd December 1726 ; the date of the twentieth call is not known. Chrysander, II. 187 f., states that the original subscribers to the Academy paid 99½ per cent (Weinstock, p. 140, makes it 100½ per cent), but once received a dividend of 7 per cent, and therefore got their ticket for nine years for 92½ guineas. He assumes that 100 guineas was the subscription for one ticket. In fact most of the 62 first subscribers signed for £200, probably for two permanent tickets, and would therefore have paid in £185 each. Chrysander also attempted to count the performances between 2nd April 1720 and 1st June 1728 : there were 487, of which 245 were Handel evenings, 108 Bononcini, 55 Ariosti and 79 other composers. To the subscribers, therefore, each ticket cost 4 shillings, less than the normal price for the Gallery, which was 5 shillings. This was the last call on the subscribers. Originally it had been hoped that their money would be sufficient for fourteen years, and not merely for nine.

———

Handel finishes the opera *Tolomeo*, 19th April 1728.

FROM MATTHESON'S POEM ADDRESSED TO JOHANN HEINRICH HEINICHEN, CONGRATULATING THE AUTHOR OF " GENERALBASS IN DER COMPOSITION ", 20th April (1st May) 1728 (Translated)

Composing, Händel ? What's the news ?
Why send our envoys packing ?
In form, and not in florid hues,
Your lovely art is lacking.

(Chrysander, II. 233.) This is the sixth of eleven stanzas forming the *Ode auf des S. T. Herrn Capellmeister Heinichen schönes neues Werck von General-Bass*, the second edition of which was published in Dresden in 1728. (The first edition, of 1711, was entitled *Neu erfundene und gründliche Anweisung, etc.*) Mattheson's poem is dated "Hamburg, den 1. May 1728". He refers to Handel's reluctance to write the promised autobiography for the *Ehrenpforte*. The original version was :

Was machst du, Händel, schreibst du nichts ?
Schickt man umsonst dir Boten ?
An Form der schönen Kunst gebricht's,
Und nicht an bunten Noten.

FROM THE " DAILY COURANT ", 29th April 1728

At the King's Theatre . . . To-Morrow . . . will be perform'd A New Opera called, PTOLEMY. . . .

Tolomeo, Re di Egitto, text by Haym ; the libretto dedicated to the Earl of Albemarle, one of the Academy's directors. In his dedication, Haym laments over the fate of Italian opera in London : " May your example give new vigour to the support of Opera, now fast declining in England." *Tolomeo* was performed on 30th April ; 4th, 7th, 11th, 14th, 18th and 21st May; and revived in 1730 and 1733.

CAST OF " TOLOMEO ", 30th April 1728
Tolomeo—Signor Senesino, alto
Seleuce—Signora Cuzzoni, soprano
Elisa—Signora Faustina, mezzo-soprano
Alessandro—Signor Baldi, counter-tenor
Araspe—Signor Boschi, bass

The Academy holds a General Court, 15th May 1728.
(Burney, IV. 338.)

H.–8

FROM THE "DAILY COURANT", 16th May 1728

Notice is hereby given, that the General Court of the Royal Academy of Musick stands adjourned till Eleven a-Clock on Wednesday next, the 22d Instant, in order to receive any further Proposals that shall be offered for carrying on the Operas.

(Burney, IV. 338.) Cf. 28th May.

———

Admeto is revived on 25th May 1728, and repeated on 28th May and 1st June.

The new libretto gives the name of Mrs. Wright for the part of Orindo. Cf. 30th September 1727.

———

FROM THE "DAILY COURANT", 28th May 1728

The General Court of the Royal Academy of Musick stands adjourn'd till To morrow, at Eleven a-Clock in the Forenoon, at the usual Place in the Hay market, when all the Subscribers to the said Academy are desired to be present.

(Burney, IV. 338.)

———

FROM THE "DAILY COURANT", 31st May 1728

The General Court of the Royal Academy of Musick stands adjourn'd till 11 a-Clock on Wednesday the 5th of June next, in order to consider of proper Measures for recovering the Debts due to the Academy, and discharging what is due to Performers, Tradesmen, and others ; and also to determine how the Scenes, Cloaths, etc. are to be disposed of, if the Operas cannot be continued.

N.B. All the Subscribers are desired to be present, since the whole will be then decided by Majority of the Votes.

(Burney, IV. 338 ; Chrysander, II. 220 f.) The same notice appeared in the *London Gazette* of 1st June 1728. Cf. 14th January 1729.

———

The last season of the Academy of Music ends on 1st June 1728.

———

Handel buys £700 South Sea Annuities (1751), 4th June 1728.

It seems that the Academy's financial difficulties did not affect Handel. This is the first of numerous entries from Handel's Stock and Drawing Accounts with the Bank of England, first used by Percy M. Young in 1947 (pp. 228-31) and printed in full in the *Supplement* to this book. There can be no doubt that, both prior to this and during the rest of his life, Handel had other accounts with private bankers for minor transactions.

———

FROM THE "BRITISH JOURNAL", 15th June 1728

The fine Opera of Admetus, that was to have been performed last
Tuesday-Night [the 11th] at the King's Theatre in the Hay-Market, was
put off on Account of Signora Faustina's being taken ill.

(Chrysander, II. 186.) The crucial season thus ended prematurely, on 1st June,
but it is not known why no performances were planned between 2nd and 10th
June. Shortly afterwards the three "canary-birds" went back to Italy, not to
return in the autumn, and the Haymarket Theatre remained deserted for a year.

—

SENESINO, *who, from his first appearance, had taken deep root, and had long been
growing in the affections of those, whose right to dominion the most civilized nations have
ever acknowledged, began to feel his strength and importance. He felt them so much,
that what he had hitherto regarded as legal government, now appeared to him in the light
of downright tyranny. Handel, perceiving that he was grown less tractable and obsequious,
resolved to subdue these Italian humours, not by lenitives, but sharp corrosives. To
manage him he disdained; to control him with a high-hand, he in vain attempted. The
one was perfectly refractory; the other was equally outrageous. In short, matters had
proceeded so far, that there were no hopes of an accommodation. . . . Whatever they
were, the Nobility would not consent to his design of parting with* SENESINO, *and Handel
was determined to have no farther concerns with him.* FAUSTINA *and* CUZZONI, *as if
seized with the contagion of discord, started questions of superiority, and urged their
respective claims to it with an eagerness and acrimony, which occasioned a total dis-union
betwixt them.*

*And thus the Academy, after it had continued in the most flourishing state for upwards
of nine years, was at once dissolved.*

The late Laureat [Colley Cibber, *cf.* July 1727], *who, now and then, has some strokes
of humour (for dulness too hath its lucid intervals), diverts himself much on the subject of
these musical frays. The unlucky effects of them at the marriage of the late Duke of
Parma, he describes with that pert kind of pleasantry, that native* gaillardise *which
attended him through life.*

*The fondness for Italian Singers, he thinks unaccountable: the expense and trouble
they occasion, exorbitant and ridiculous. He calls them costly Canary-birds; and on their
behaviour at the marriage solemnity just mentioned above, laments as follows, " What a
pity it is, that these froward Misses and Masters of Music, had not been engaged to entertain
the court of some King of* MOROCCO, *that could have known a good Opera from a bad
one! With how much ease would such a Director have brought them to better order? "—
But, had he known any thing of the true* [1] *spirit of Handel, he would not have wished
them under better government. It is true they mutinied, and rebelled at last. But the
slaves of Asiatic and of African Monarchs, have often done as much.*

He remained inflexible in his resolution to punish SENESINO *for refusing him that
submission, which he had been used to receive, and which he thought he had a right to
demand: but a little pliability would have saved him abundance of trouble. The vacancy*

[1] *Having one day some words with* CUZZONI *on her refusing to sing* Falsa imagine *in*
OTTONE; *Oh! Madame, (said he), je sçais bien que Vous êtes une veritable Diablesse:
mais je Vous ferai sçavoir, moi, que je suis Beelzebub le Chéf des Diables. With this he
took her up by the waist, and, if she made any more words, swore that he would fling her out
of the window. . . .*

*made by the removal of such a Singer was not easily supplied. The umbrage which he
had given to many of the Nobility, by his implacable resentments against a person whose
talents they so much admired, was likely to create him a dangerous opposition. For, tho'
he continued at the Hay-market, yet, in the heat of these animosities, a great part of his
audience would melt away. New Singers must be sought, and could not be had any
nearer than Italy. The business of choosing, and engaging them, could not be dispatched
by a deputy. And the party offended might improve the opportunity of his absence to his
disadvantage.* (Mainwaring, pp. 107-12.)

—

Handel buys £250 South Sea Annuities (1751), 2nd July 1728.

—

Handel buys £150 South Sea Annuities (1751), 11th July 1728.

—

J. Cluer advertises the score of *Siroe*, Mist's *Weekly Journal*, 13th
July 1728.

It seems that this score was already on sale in June.

—

Walsh and Hare advertise the flute arrangement of *Siroe*, *Craftsman*,
3rd August 1728.

—

Alessandro is performed at Brunswick, 6th (17th) August 1728.

(Loewenberg, p. 80.) The performance was in German, but the airs
and the final chorus were sung in Italian. The translation may have been
by Wendt ; cf. 7th November 1726.

—

Handel sells £50 South Sea Annuities (1751), 31st August 1728.

—

" At Lee's and Harper's great theatrical booth in the Bartholomew
Fair ", *The Quaker's Opera* is produced in September 1728, with
music by various composers, including Handel's march from
Scipione.

This ballad-opera, with text by Thomas Walker, was printed with the
airs. It was revived at the Little Haymarket Theatre on 31st October 1728.
The march from *Scipione* was used again in *Polly* (cf. 19th January 1728).

—

Walsh and Hare advertise " Favourite Songs " from *Tolomeo*,
Siroe and *Admeto*, in *The Craftsman*, 14th September 1728.

The selection from *Admeto* seems to have been published about two
months earlier.

—

Walsh and Hare advertise their flute arrangement of *Tolomeo* and a complete set of Handel's operas similarly arranged, *Daily Post*, 26th November 1728 (*Craftsman*, 30th November).

—

FROM THE "LONDON GAZETTE", 3rd December 1728

The Time appointed by the Charter of the Royal Academy of Musick for chusing a Deputy Governour and Directors of the said Academy, being on the 22d of November in each Year, or within Fourteen Days after ; Notice is hereby given, That a General Court, by Order of the Governour of the said Academy, will be held at Twelve o'Clock on Friday next, being the 6th Instant, at the usual Place in the Hay-Market.

The result of the election is not known. For the first time, St. Cecilia's Day is indicated as the proper time for elections.

—

Handel sells £1050 South Sea Annuities (1751), 10th December 1728.

—

FROM THE "LONDON JOURNAL", 21st December 1728

New Musick lately published,

I. The New Country Dancing-Master. Vol. III. Being a choice Collection of Country Dances. Performed at the Theatre, at Schools and publick Balls, with Directions to each Dance. The Tunes airy and pleasant for the Violin or Hoboy, and several of them within Compass of the Flute. Price 2s 6d. . . .

(Smith, 1948, p. 275.) This volume contains the "Trumpet Minuet" from Handel's *Water Music*. The title of the collection was chosen in imitation of the famous *Dancing Master*, founded by John Playford in 1650 and last published by John Young in 1728.

—

ROLLI TO SENESINO IN VENICE (Translated)

L. [London], 21st December [1728 ?].

I am replying to yours of the 28th October. I hope I have reciprocated your friendly action with regard to the Academy ; greatly astonished, I have sent an ode. . . .

The Man [Handel] returned from his travels very full of Farinello and extremely loud in his praises. The parties of the two prima donnas here are still green-eyed and watchful (*in viridi observantia*) ; and each side wants to have its way, so much so that to put the Opera again on its feet, they have finally decided to have both ladies back. The Man, my good friend, did not want this, but as the ladies have two parties and my friend Senesino has only one, so on that matter there was no other answer but that Senesino must be the first singer. Cuzzona is in his favour, Faustina is for herself and for him besides, Senesino is for everybody. They were wondering about the Impresario but it appears that the Man refuses to undertake the task and I am of the opinion that the Academy will, because that Body is not yet dissolved. Cuzzona's arrival in Vienna is known but so far there is silence as to the rest of the matter. I have heard it whispered that there, as elsewhere, she will obtain a gift and what follows. Can it be that the Laurenzana supporters have not been idle ? Those people, as you are well aware, know each other, without anyone else's warning.

On your return here you will be in no need of a protector : you will find two Brothers who will be no less friendly to you and who do not lack good behaviour and courage. If Faustina thought so also, she would meet with fewer expenses and less inconvenience, indeed also fewer complaints. But I do not want to expatiate on this subject. I know perfectly well that she has been false to me, and that I shall trim my sails according to the wind. What will she say if the dishonest Barbarian turns the tables on her ? That is what I prophesy he will do.

Riva is more than ever the same in every way : he puffs and snorts with anger, backbiting and raging over this same return. He used to delight in Farinello, presenting him as a novelty. I was laughing at him, and still do, and I laughed yesterday when he agreed with me on your inevitable return. He told me that Mr. Heydeger had already written to you about it. What a wicked race ! A wicked King gets a worse Counsellor. . . .

(Cellesi, 1930, pp. 321-3 : dating the letter 1729 ; Eisenschmidt, I. 40 : altering the date to 1728.) Biblioteca Comunale, Siena : *Lettere d'uomini illustri*, D.vi.22.c.302. The reference to Handel's continental journey indicates the year 1729, but he also might have been on the continent in autumn 1728. Handel did not succeed in engaging Farinelli, and when the latter came to London in 1734, it was to Handel's opponents. Nor could Handel ever bring back the two rival queens, or even one of them, to his company. Cuzzoni had no success in Vienna, because she demanded too high a salary. The rivalry between Cuzzoni and Laurenzana in Vienna in 1728 is also referred to in a letter by Riva to Muratori, 27th September 1730 (Sola, p. 298) ; Laurenzana, however, has not been identified. The " due Fratelli " are Rolli and his brother. Handel is called here *l'Uomo*, as usual, and also, it seems, *il Malonesta Barbaro*.

———

Handel subscribes for John Ernest Galliard's " Hymn of Adam and Eve ", from the Fifth Book of Milton's *Paradise Lost*, published privately in 1728.

A later issue bears Walsh's imprint.

———

From Chamberlayne's " Magna Britanniae Notitia ", 1728

The Establishment of their Royal Highnesses the Princess Royal, the Princess Amelia *and the Princess* Carolina :

	Per Ann.	l.	s.	d.
Dancing-Master, Mr. *Anthony L'abbé*		240	0	0
Musick-Master, Mr. *George-Frederic Handell*		200	0	0

(Chrysander, II. 175 ; the same, 1892, p. 525.) Cf. *c.* 30th September 1727 (Treasury Papers), 1727 (Chamberlayne) and 1735 (Chamberlayne). From 1735 onwards the appointment was for the two younger princesses only, the Princess Royal having married. In 1741 L'Abbé was followed as dancing-master by Mr. Glover. From 1748 the name of the " Musick-Master " is given first. Maurice Greene, Master of Music, and Composer to the Chapel Royal, had the same salary as Handel : £200 a year. The 1729 edition of the supplement, *A General List . . . of all the . . . Officers*, was only a reissue of that of 1728 ; the entry, in fact, remained unaltered until 1735.

From [James Ralph's] Pamphlet, " The Touch-Stone : or, Historical, Critical, Political, Philosophical and Theological Essays on the Reigning Diversions of the Town. . . . By a Person of Some Taste and Some Quality", 1728

I. Of Musick, Operas and Plays. Their Original, Progress, and Improvement, and the Stage-Entertainment fully vindicated from the Exception of Old *Pryn*, the Reverend Mr. *Collier*, Mr. *Bedford* and Mr. *Law*.

Of Musick : Particularly Dramatick.

. . . Not that I would entirely banish from the *Opera-Stage* Heroick Deeds, or Characters of the first Rank : Nor would I confine the *Dramma* to such alone : Our *English* History is prolifick of Ground-work for all Theatrical Entertainments. As our Nation can boast of Persons and Actions equal in Fame to any Part of the Antiquity ; so can we vie with their Golden Age, in *Sylvan* Scenes, and rural Innocence.

This amusing Variety in the Choice of Subjects for our Operas, will allow a greater Latitude in Composition than we have yet known : It will employ all our Masters in their different Talents, and in course destroy that Schism which at present divide our Lovers of Musick, and turns even Harmony into Discord : The Dispute will not then be, who is the justest, or brightest Composer, or which the finest Operas ; those of our own Growth, or those imported from *Italy* ? Every Man would be set to Work, and strive to excel in his own Way. *H—l* would furnish us with Airs expressive of the Rage of Tyrants, the Passions of Heroes, and the Distresses of Lovers in the Heroick Stile. *B—ni* sooth us with sighing Shepherds, bleating Flocks, chirping Birds, and purling Streams in the *Pastoral* : And *A—o* give us good Dungeon Scenes, Marches for a Battel, or Minuets for a Ball, in the *Miserere.* *H—l* would warm us in Frost or Snow, by rousing every Passion with Notes proper to the Subject : Whilst *B—ni* would fan us, in the *Dog-Days*, with an *Italian* Breeze, and lull us asleep with gentle Whispers : Nay, the pretty Operas from t'other Side the Water, might serve to tickle us in the Time of *Christmas-Gambols*, or mortify us in the Time of *Lent* ; so make us very merry, or very sad.

The pamphlet was reissued with a new title-page in 1731 as *The Taste of the Town : or, a Guide to all Publick Diversions.* Both are anonymous. Copies in Bodleian. The abbreviations of the names Handel, Attilio (Ariosti) and Bononcini are obvious.

FROM MATTHESON'S "DER MUSICALISCHE PATRIOT", HAMBURG, 1728
(Translation)

. . . It [*The Musical Patriot*] extols the Lord, Who . . . in these days has aroused much more splendid *ingenia musica* than in previous times, and has so richly endowed His people, that nothing can surpass them, as long as Germany, particularly, can still sparkle with *Bach, Händel, Heinichen, Keiser, Stölzel, Telemann* and others. . . .

Händel, at the recent Coronation in London, has conducted a choir of people, even more select. That shows style ! . . .
[Hamburg Opera List]
Anno 1704.
Almira. Music by Capellmeister *Händel.* Book by Herr *Feustking.* Attached to it was an *Epilogus*, called the *Genius* von *Europa*, composed by Herr *Keiser.*
Anno 1705.
Nero. Music by Herr *Händel.* Book by Herr *Feustking.*
Anno 1708.
Florindo. Herr *Händel* composed the music to verse compiled by Herr *Hinsch.*
Daphne. By the previous authors.

This was, it seems, the first time that the names of J. S. Bach and Handel appeared together in print, but the leading place was determined by the alphabet only.— *Almira* was produced, not in 1704, but on 8th January 1705.

FROM ROGER NORTH'S "MUSICALL GRAMARIAN", *c.* 1728

. . . As all things from low beginnings grow up to their full magnitude so our operas were performed by English voices, nay the Itallian of forrein operas were translated and fitted to ye musick, nay more some scenes were sung in English & others in Italian or Dutch rather then fail, wch made such a crowd of Absuritys as was not to be borne. But now the subscriptions with a Royall encouragement hath brought the operas to be performed in their native idiom and up to such a sufficiency that many have sayd, Rome & venice, where they heard them, have not exceeded.

Now having brought our English opera music to this pass It will scarce be manners to thro any censures at them but be they very great & good, there is no such perfection upon earth to or from wch somewhat may not a buon cento be added, or substracted, and perhaps alltered for the better. One thing I dislike is the laying too much stress upon some one voice, wch is purchased at a dear rate. Were it not as well If somewhat of that was abated & added to the rest to bring ye orchestre to neerer equality ? Many persons come to hear that single voice, who care not for all the rest, especially If it be a fair Lady ; And observing ye discours of the Quallity crittiques, I found it runs most upon ye point, who sings best ? and not whither ye musick be good, and wherein ? . . . And it is a fault in ye composition to overcalculate for ye prime voice, as If no other part were worth Regarding, whereupon the whole enterteinment consists of solos, and very little or no consorts of voices. . . . And now at last, from what I can perceiv, the Operas made In England of ye latter date, are more substantially musicall, than those wch are used notati out of Itally, wch latter have of late diverted from the Lofty style downe to the Ballad, fitt for the streets that receiv them, whereby it appears that the Itallian vein is much degenerated.

1729

FROM THE " LONDON GAZETTE ", 14th January 1729

The Governour of the Royal Academy of Musick, doth hereby order Notice to be given to the several Subscribers, That a General Court of the said Academy will be held at Eleven a Clock on Saturday next, the 18th Instant, at the usual Place in the Hay-Market, in order to consider some Proposals that will then be offered for carrying on Operas ; as also for disposing of the Effects belonging to the said Academy.

(Chrysander, II. 221.)   Cf. 1st June 1728 and 18th January 1729.   No other General Court seems to have been called after this date, to deal with the operas. The Academy became the landlord only of the Haymarket Theatre.

—

FROM THE DIARY OF VISCOUNT PERCIVAL, 18th January 1729

I went to a meeting of the members of the Royal Academy of Musick : where we agreed to prosecute the subscribers who have not yet paid ; also to permit Hydeger and Hendle to carry on operas without disturbance for 5 years and to lend them for that time our scenes, machines, clothes, instruments, furniture, etc.   It all past off in a great hurry, and there was not above 20 there.

(Egmont MSS., III. 329, supplementary matter.)   The first Viscount Percival, who in August 1733 became the first Earl of Egmont, had belonged to the Academy since 1719 (cf. 30th November 1719). He was an amateur musician, and became a member of the " Academy of Ancient Music ", a club which met at the " Crown and Anchor " Tavern.

—

Handel buys £700 South Sea Annuities (1751), 23rd January 1729.

—

Riccardo Primo is produced at Hamburg, 23rd January (3rd February) 1729.

(Merbach, p. 363.)   The title of the German version was *Der misslungene Braut-Wechsel oder Richardus I, König von England.*   Handel's Italian arias were augmented by recitatives and 14 arias in German, written by Telemann.   The opera was performed repeatedly during 1729, and was also given in Brunswick in February 1729 and February 1734 (Chrysander, II. 179 ; Loewenberg, p. 81).   The translator of Rolli's text was again Wendt.

—

Rolli to Senesino in Venice (Translated)

London, 25th [January] 1729.

Heydeger returned and said that he had not found any singers in Italy ; he protested that he did not wish to undertake anything without the two ladies ; he spoke only of them and proposed Farinello. In the end, hearing that your friends desired you back, he gave way, and you are once more on good terms with him. He was thinking more of a lucrative subscription than of anything else and he was calculating well, for in this way the two parties and your friends in each would be helping to fill up the annual subscription with 20 pounds per head. This was the scheme, on the basis of which, already known to you, I wrote you the first letter. But Handel was not to be duped by such a paltry stratagem. He revealed his rival's rascally deceit : the only aim of his useless and ridiculous voyage was to profit himself alone. So he [Handel] declared that there was need of a change and has renewed the old system of changing the singers in order to have the opportunity of composing new works for new performers. His new plans find favour at Court and he is satisfied. Faustina is not required, but they have lent quite a favourable ear to you. They want Farinello and Cuzzona, if she does not remain in Vienna, and the promoters are such as can pay. Mylord Bingley is at the head of the project, but the theatre has still to be found. So they called in Heydeger and they have granted him 2200 pounds with which to provide the theatre, the scenery and the costumes.

Handel will have 1000 pounds for the composition, whether it will be by himself or by whomsoever else he may choose. The subscription will be 15 guineas per person, and so far it is thought sufficient. A total of 4000 pounds is proposed for the singers—two at a 1000 pounds each with a benefit performance, and the rest, etc. Handel will shortly depart for Italy, where he will select the cast. Three representatives of the subscribers will go with him, in order to examine them, etc. That is the new system. Riva is already suffering from it, for you can well see what a very ill wind is blowing for Bononcino. So do tell Faustina that her dear little Handel will be coming to Italy, but not for her. Have I not already written you that she would after all have found him quite contrary to her opinions ?

Poor dear ! I am *so* sorry ! This treatment—and I say it for all to hear—is well deserved by all who sacrifice their friends, in order to make the most base advances to their enemies. Expenses must, as I fear, now exclude you ; otherwise I would not doubt that sooner or later I should find you here once more, in despite of the Man whose aim it has been to prevent your return. Farinello will come, attracted perhaps by the bait of a benefit performance, for no one—except you—has ever refused him [Handel], so brazen is his begging for charity.

I hear that Cuzzona has surmounted all difficulties in Vienna and it is quite probable that she will remain there in regular service. Without a doubt she made a good impression on the Emperor himself and on the Empress ; and over there the company of one's own husband makes a better impression than that of someone else's. . . .

(Fassini, 1914, pp. 84 f.; Streatfeild, 1917, pp. 438 f.; Cellesi, 1933, pp. 11 f.) Original in Biblioteca comunale, Siena. Cf. 4th to 7th February 1729. It appears from this letter that Heidegger had been to Italy before Handel went. Both were present at the meeting on 18th January 1729. All agreed to approach the famous soprano Carlo Broschi, called Farinelli, who, however, never came to Handel's opera. The " due donne " are, of course, Cuzzoni and Faustina, and the " due partiti " their respective followers. Only Senesino returned to Handel, but not until 1731. Cuzzoni, invited to Vienna by the Imperial Ambassador in London, Philipp Josef Graf Kinsky, sang at the Austrian Court but was not engaged for the Vienna Opera. Faustina married the composer Johann Adolph Hasse in 1729 in Venice, and sang there again with Senesino. Cuzzoni also went to Venice from Vienna, but sang on another stage. She met Senesino again in London in 1734. Handel's " emulo " was apparently Heidegger himself. Lord Bingley had been Deputy-Governor of the Academy in 1720–21. The salary of £1000 provided for Handel is given in figures here for the first time. It is to be assumed that his earlier salary from the Academy, from 1719 onwards, was less (cf. *Music & Letters*, July 1949, p. 260). The subscription in question was, of course, an annual one, for permanent tickets only, not for shares.

———

In spite of all . . . discouragements, to Italy he went, as soon as he had settled an agreement with HEIDEGGER *to carry on Operas in conjunction with him. The agreement was for the short term of three years, and so settled as to subsist only from year to year.*

On his arrival at Rome, he received a very friendly and obliging letter from Cardinal COLONNA, *with a promise of a very fine picture of his Eminence. But, hearing that the Pretender was then at the Cardinal's, he prudently declined accepting both the invitation and the picture.* (Mainwaring, pp. 112-13.)

———

FROM THE " DAILY POST ", 27th January 1729

Yesterday Morning Mr. Handell, the famous Composer of the Italian Musick, took his Leave of their Majesties, he being to set out this Day for Italy, with a Commission from the Royal Academy of Musick.

A similar notice appeared in the *Norwich Gazette* and the *Norwich Mercury* of 1st February 1729. Handel went to the Palace on Sunday morning, but he did not set out on Monday. His journey was postponed for about a week, as shown by Rolli's letter of 4th February. Chrysander (II. 224) assumed that Handel's journey started in late summer 1728 ; Burney, (IV. 339) in autumn 1728. Cf. 14th May 1719.

———

ROLLI TO SENESINO IN VENICE (Translated)

L. [London], 4th February 1729.

. . . The new Handeleidegriano [Handel-Heidegger] system is gaining ground. A general meeting was held and it was discussed. There were few present and only six or seven of these subscribed ; others did not refuse to do so, and others made request that they should first be notified who were the singers. The Royal wishes on this matter were made known and it was announced that Handel would soon leave for Italy in search of singers. By unanimous consent the two managers were granted the use of the Academy's dresses and scenery for five years. Handel is in fact departing today, and ten days ago Haym despatched circular letters to Italy to announce this new project and Handel's arrival to the professional singers. Farinello comes first in estimation, and all the more so as news has recently arrived from Venice, and particularly to the Resident Minister here, Vignola, that all throng to the theatre at which Farinello is singing, and that the theatre where you and Faustina are is nearly empty. The declared opinion of this R. [Rè, the King] on the two singers is for certain as follows : that he would contribute the sum promised, if both Cuzzona and Faustina returned here, that he would contribute the same amount if Cuzzona alone returned, but that if only Faustina returned, he would contribute nothing at all. It is very uncertain whether Cuzzona is returning or not. We are without letters from Vienna because of an interruption in the post, but the latest information was of gifts, not regular service. Nevertheless, since that lady's aim is to be in regular service, it is possible that she may succeed ; she has already made a good impression and is disposed to be content with a *mediocre* but certain and stable post, in preference to more lucrative but uncertain work. But Faustina will have more recent news from Vienna and from her beloved Empress who used to be so very fond of her. The purpose of this new scheme is to have everything new. Dear little Hendel, as a result of personal experience and from a desire to give everyone his due, detests that lady, the promoter of *Siroe*. I have always been and will always be most reserved towards him, nor did I wish him well on his departure ; but a few days ago Goupy came to pay a visit to my brother and questioned him about Handel's journey and the new system, in order to discover my sentiments. The replies which he received expressed approval. He [Goupy] added that Faustina had been the cause of the differences that had arisen between me and the friend [Handel]. To which my brother replied with scorn and resentment. He [Goupy] said that he detested the lady and repeated that everything will be new, insisting that the friend still hated Cuzzona.

Riva is furious, because he sees Bononcino excluded by his own pride and by that of the Chief Composer, on whom everyone else will have to depend.

7th.

They say that Farinello has already been engaged for next year here, and you also but elsewhere. If he has been engaged, we shall have to call upon you. . . . They are still talking of Carestini as second singer. It will not be difficult to obtain subscriptions, because cheap prices are popular with the majority. However, good sponsors never did any harm. I hear for certain that neither of the two ladies will be engaged—and both parties agree as to this. Thus, unless Cuzzona returns of her own accord, she will certainly not be invited to come. You will without doubt see Händel before the end of the Carnival, because, for sure, he is going directly to Venice for Farinello. I shall be curious to know how he will behave with you and with the celebrated prima donna ; who, I fear, in her anger against the unfaithful man, may have him *thrown into the Canal*.

(Fassini, 1914, p. 85 ; Streatfeild, 1917, pp. 439 f.; Cellesi, 1933, pp. 13 f.) Original in Biblioteca comunale, Siena. Cf. 25th January 1729. Haym was apparently still the Italian secretary of the Academy. The Emperor Karl VI's consort was Elisabeth Christine of Brunswick, who knew Faustina from her engagement in Vienna in 1724. While Faustina had a salary of 12,500 florins (£1250) a year in Vienna about 1725, Cuzzoni now asked for 24,000 florins a year there ; but she never appeared on the Vienna stage. Goupy, the painter, tried to mediate between Handel and Rolli, whose friend Riva sided with Bononcini. Giovanni Carestini, another castrato, did not join the London Opera until 1733.

———

At Drury Lane Theatre, on 6th February 1729, *The Village Opera* is produced, text by Charles Johnson, music by various composers ; the latter includes a Handel minuet, attributed to Monsieur Denoyer (a ballet master), sung as " Deluded by her mate's dear voice ".

The libretto of this ballad-opera was printed, as usual, with the tunes. After six performances at Drury Lane in 1729, and three at the Little Haymarket Theatre in January 1730, the opera was shortened and re-appeared at Drury Lane on 10th February 1730 (*q.v.*) as *The Chamber-Maid*.

———

MRS. PENDARVES TO HER SISTER, ANN GRANVILLE

Somerset House, 16th February, 1728–9
The subscription for the Opera next winter goes on very well, to the great satisfaction of all musical folks.

Delany, I. 188.

———

THE SAME TO THE SAME

From our fireside, 28 February, 1728–9.
On Wednesday [the 26th] I went in the afternoon to a concert of musick for the benefit of Mr. Holcomb. . . . Holcomb sang six songs ; we had two overtures of Mr. Handel's and two concertos of Corella

by the best hands. I was very well pleased ; the house was exceeding full and some very good company.

Henry Holcombe was a singer and composer ; he sang as chorister in Salisbury Cathedral, and later at Drury Lane. He subscribed for the scores of three Handel operas. It seems his concert was held on an afternoon at the Haymarket Theatre.

—

HANDEL TO MICHAELSEN, 28th February (11th March) 1729

a Venise ce 11 de Mars 1729.

Monsieur
    et tres Hoñoré Frere

Vous trouverez par la lettre que j'envoye icy a ma Mere que j'aye bien obtenu l'hoñeur de la Votre du 18 du passé.

Permettez moy que je Vous en fasse particulierement mes remerciments par ces lignes, et que je Vous supplie a vouloir bien continuer de me donner de tems en tems Vos cheres nouvelles pendant que je me trouve en voyage par ce pais cy, puisque Vous ne pouvez pas ignorer l'interest et la satisfaction que j'en prens. Vous n'avez qu'a les adresser toujours à Mr Joseph Smith Banquier à Venise (come j'ay deja mentioñé) qui me les enverrà aux divers endroits ou je me trouverai en Italie. Vous juge bien, mon tres Hoñoré Frere, du Contentement que j'ay eu d'apprendre que Vous Vous trouviez avec Votre Chere Famille en parfaite santé, et je Vous en souhaite du meilleur de mon Coeur la Continuation. la pensée de Vous embrasser bientôt me donne une vraye joye, Vous me ferez la justice de le croire. je Vous assure que c'a eté un des motifs principales qui m'a fait entre prendre avec d'autant plus de plaisir ce Voyage. J'espère que mes desirs seront accomplis vers le mois de Juillet prochain. En attendant je Vous souhaite toujours comble de toute prosperité, et faisant bien mes Complimens a Madame Votre Epouse et embrassant Votre Chere Famille je suis avec une passion inviolable
Monsieur,
       et tres Hoñoré Frere
         Votre
            tres humble et tresobeissant
              Serviteur
              Georg Frideric Handel.

A Monsieur
Monsieur Michaelsen
    Conseiller de Guerre de Sa Majeste Prussieñe.

(Translation)

Venice, 11th March 1729.

Honoured Brother,
    You will see from the letter that I am sending to my mother from here that I have indeed had the honour of receiving yours dated the 18th of last month.

Allow me to thank you most heartily for it by these lines. I beg you to continue to send me your news from time to time while I am travelling in this country, since you cannot but know the interest and satisfaction that I take in them. All you have to do is to address letters each time to Mr. Joseph Smith, Banker, at Venice (as I have already mentioned), who will send them on to me at the various places in Italy where I shall be. You can well judge, dear brother, of the pleasure it has given me to learn that you and your dear family are in perfect health, and I wish you continuation therein from the bottom of my heart. The thought of embracing you soon [in person] affords me a real joy ; pray do me the honour of believing this. I assure you that this was one of the main reasons why I undertook the present journey with all the more pleasure. I trust that my hopes will be fulfilled about next July. In prospect I wish you always every kind of prosperity. With my compliments to your wife and embraces for your dear family, I am with steadfast devotion,

Honoured brother,
Your most humble and obedient servant,

Georg Frideric Handel.

(Chrysander, II. 225 f.) Some of the originals of Handel's letters to his brother-in-law, Michaelsen, which Chrysander saw, are now lost. No letter written by Handel to his mother is known. Michaelsen married, on 7th (18th) September 1726, the sister of his late second wife, Sophia Elisabeth Dreissig. Handel intended to visit his relatives in Halle in July, but it seems he went there in June. Joseph Smith, banker, and later British Consul at Venice, the husband of the once famous London soprano, Catherine Tofts, was a great art collector. Handel, apparently, was introduced to Smith in the hope that the latter might serve him as an intermediary in Venice. He certainly found Senesino and Faustina there, while he may have met Farinelli in Rome. It is said that Handel also visited Florence and Milan. It is assumed that Handel dated his continental letters in the English style, which he normally used.

———

At the Smock Alley Theatre in Dublin, on 24th March 1729, another ballad-opera, *The Beggar's Wedding*, is produced, text by Charles Coffey, music by various composers ; among the arias is one from Handel's *Floridante*, the English words " Talk no more to me of glory ", originally supplied for " *Se risolvi abbondarmi* ", being altered to " Talk no more of Whig and Tory ".

The opera was performed at the Little Haymarket Theatre on 29th May and, in a shortened version, under the title *Phebe, or the Beggar's Wedding* at Drury Lane on 13th June 1729.

———

From the " Daily Journal ", 7th April 1729

At the King's Theatre in the Hay-Market, on Thursday next, being the 10th Day of April, will be An Assembly, *To begin with the Instrumental Opera of Radamistus*. . . . N.B. Every Ticket will admit either one Gentleman or two Ladies.

(Burney, IV. 339.) The Handel piece performed was apparently the overture to *Radamisto*. Heidegger seems to have used the house for concerts during the dead season of 1728-9 ; cf. 28th February.

—

From Byrom's " Epilogue to Hurlothrumbo, or : The Super-Natural ", a Play by Samuel Johnson, performed at the Little Theatre in the Haymarket, 7th April 1729

—Something hangs on my prophetic Tongue,
I'll give it Utterance—be it right or wrong :
Handel himself shall yield to *Hurlothrumbo*,
And *Bononcini* too shall cry—*Succumbo*.
That's if the Ladies condescend to smile ;
Their Looks make Sense, or Nonsense, in our Isle.

(Chrysander, II. 214.) Byrom, *Miscellaneous Poems*, I. 215-18 ; *Poems*, I. 138-47. The play, with music by the author, was produced on 29th March, and had such a success that it was given 15 times within a month. Byrom wrote to his wife on 2nd April : " For my part, who think all stage entertainments stuff and nonsense, I consider this a joke upon 'em all ". Johnson, a dancing master, came, like Byrom, from Cheshire. The text, and even some of the music, was printed. The epilogue was spoken at the second performance, on 7th April. The play was still well-known five years later (cf. 12th February 1734). It should be remembered that Byrom's epigram of May 1725 also dealt with Handel and Bononcini.

—

Walsh and Hare advertise seven collections of Handel's " most celebrated Songs, curiously fitted for a German Flute and Bass, with a complete Index to the Whole ", *Craftsman*, 19th April 1729.

According to Smith (1948, p. 275), the publishers advertised on the same day the collection of Handel minuets and marches, listed here under 3rd May 1729.

—

Walsh and Hare advertise " a general Collection of Minuets made for the Balls at Court, the Opera's and Masquerades, consisting of 60 in Number. Compos'd by Mr. HANDEL. To which is added, Twelve celebrated Marches made on several Occasions, by the same Author : All curiously fitted for a German Flute or Violin ", *Craftsman*, 3rd May 1729.

Three of the minuets are from the *Water Music* (Smith, 1948, p. 275 f.). Handel, of course, never wrote minuets, or other dances, for Heidegger's Masquerades, held at the Haymarket Theatre in carnival.

—

SIR LYONELL PILKINGTON TO HIS BROTHER-IN-LAW, GODFREY
WENTWORTH, AT BURTHWAIT

Paris, 4th (15th) May 1729.
You seem to despair of any more operas in England, but I fancy there
are some hopes yet of their returning. Handel is doing his endeavour
in Italy to procure singers, and I fancy his journey will be of more effect
than Heidegger's, but I'm told Senesino is playing an ungrateful part to
his friends in England, by abusing 'em behind their backs, and saying
he'll come no more among 'em. A Frenchwoman, whom I never will
forgive for supposing we English can have a fault, told me the other day,
that Senesino had built a fine house with an inscription over the door
to let the world know 'twas the folly of the English had laid the foundation
of it. Is this pardonable ?

(Streatfeild, 1909, p. 109.) Historical MSS. Commission, *Reports on MSS. in
Various Collections*, II. 411 f. It is assumed that this letter is dated in the English
style. Of Senesino, and later of Farinelli, it was said that they carried sacks of gold
with them when leaving England.

———

At the Theatre in Lincoln's Inn Fields, a ballad-opera, *The Wedding*,
is produced on 6th May 1729 ; text by Essex Hawker, overture
by Pepusch and, among the tunes by various composers, marches
from *Floridante* and *Scipione*, as well as two minuets, probably by
Handel, sung as " Si cara " (no. 12) and " Cloe proves false "
(no. 22).

The printed libretto contains the tunes.

———

ROLLI TO SENESINO IN (?) SIENA (Translated)

London, 16th May 1729.
I reply to your April letter. The news that reached Riva concerning
Händel's arrival in Venice was that you gave him a cold reception and
that he was complaining and protesting about it, adding that Princes
have a long reach, so that in the end you were reconciled to him and he
promised you to come to Siena on his return from Naples. Riva by
now is already in Vienna, so that I shall not see any letter of his until
next winter. *Gneo* is Faustina's name in that place [?] and yours is
Pallone [the Balloon]. Your declaration in favour of Cuzzona is taken
to mean that you are courting her. It is not necessary to say any truth,
just as it is well never to tell a lie. What does it matter to say which of
two women sings less badly or is less bad as an actress ? Hendel's new
company is composed as follows : the ladies Stradina and Somis,
Carestini, Balino Fabbri with his wife (to serve on occasion as Third
Lady) and an Italo-German bass. Handel has written that Carestini was
emulating Bernacchi. We shall see what comes of it and I shall give you

exact information. You have tried me and found that I have been able to inform you and tell you what has really happened better than the others ; after the first performances I shall write you some more forecasts. I hope you will have occasion to want Senesino, but not the two BB. . . .

(Cellesi, 1933, pp. 14-16.) Original in Biblioteca comunale, Siena. Nothing is known about Handel visiting Naples during this journey, and it is doubtful whether he went to Siena to see Senesino on his holiday. The opera budget for the singers was £4000 ; of this sum Handel had agreed for £3850, and perhaps for the full amount, because there was one lady engaged in the new company who never sang a Handel part. The company finally consisted of the following singers : Antonio Bernacchi, the male soprano, now returned to London (see 5th January 1717), for £1200 ; Antonia Margherita Merighi, a contralto profundo, for £800 ; Anna Strada (Signora del Pò), a soprano, for £600 ; Annibale Pio Fabri, called Balino, a tenor, for £500 ; Francesca Bertolli, mezzo-soprano, for £450 ; Johann Gottfried (now called Giovanni Goffredo) Riemschneider, bass, for £300 ; the remaining £150 might have been granted to Signora Fabri, who was, in fact, of little or no use for the opera. At least two singers also had a benefit granted : Signora Strada and Signor Fabri. Riemschneider had been Handel's school-fellow in Halle, and was engaged by him at Hamburg, where the bass returned after one year only ; his father, Gebhard Riemschneider, had been Cantor at Halle. " La Somis " may have been a daughter of the famous violinist, Giovanni Battista Somis.

———

FROM THE " LONDON GAZETTE ", 24th June 1729

Hanover, June [16th] 27, N.S.

Mr. Hendel passed through this Place some Days ago, coming from Italy, and returning to England.

(Chrysander, II. 232.) It seems that Handel had previously been in Hamburg, to engage Riemschneider, but without communicating with Mattheson. Then, after visiting the King's Electorate residence, he probably went to Halle, to see his mother and brother-in-law. During his stay in Halle, still in June 1729, Wilhelm Friedemann Bach visited Handel, bringing him Johann Sebastian's invitation to Leipzig, which he could not follow up.

———

FROM THE " DAILY JOURNAL ", 2nd July 1729

Mr. Handel, who is just returned from Italy, has contracted with the following Persons to perform in the Italian Opera's, vz.

Signor Bernachi, who is esteem'd the best Singer in Italy.

Signora Merighi, a Woman of a very fine Presence, an excellent Actress, and a very good Singer—A Counter Tenor.

Signora Strada, who hath a very fine Treble Voice, a Person of singular Merit.

Signor Annibal Pio Fabri, a most excellent Tenor, and a fine Voice.

His Wife, who performs a Man's Part exceeding well.

Signora Bartoldi, who has a very fine Treble Voice ; she is also a very genteel Actress, both in Men and Womens Parts.

A Bass Voice from Hamburgh, there being none worth engaging in Italy.

(Schoelcher, pp. 88 f.) The same report was printed in the *London Evening Post* of 3rd July and in the *London Journal* of 5th July (copy in the Bodleian Library, Oxford). If this information was given by Handel himself, then it was somehow corrupted by the papers : Signora Bertolli was a mezzo-soprano, and Signora Merighi was really a contralto profundo, although a counter-tenor is a deep contralto.

———

From " Brice's Weekly Journal ", Exeter, 4th July 1729

London, July 1. Mr. Handel, the famous Composer of the Musick for the Italian Opera's, arrived here last Sunday Night [29th June] from Italy, having contracted with 3 Men and 4 Women to come over hither in the Winter, to sing in the Opera's, for four thousand Pounds.

———

Handel sells £200 South Sea Annuities (1751), 8th July 1729.

———

Jean Jaques Zamboni to Count Manteuffel (Translated)

London, 8th/19th July 1729.

Mr. Handel, who has lately arrived from Italy, has made contracts with the best artists to put on good Italian opera, viz. Signor Bernachi, who is considered the best singer in Italy ; Signora Mirighi, who is a very handsome woman, an excellent actress and a fine singer ; Signora Trada, who has an excellent voice of great beauty and is a person of outstanding merit ; Signor Annibal Pio Fabri, who keeps excellent time and has a very fine voice ; and his wife, who excels at acting male parts ; Signora Bartoldi has a very beautiful voice and is also a very good actress both in male and female parts. Also he has engaged a bass in Hamburg, not having been able to find one in Italy.

(Opel, *Mitteilungen*, pp. 35 f.) Original in Geheimes Staatsarchiv, Dresden. Zamboni was an agent of the Saxon court ; for Manteuffel see 31st March 1724. The report quotes, in fact, the communication given by the Academy to the newspapers.

———

Handel sells £500 South Sea Annuities (1751), 10th July 1729.

———

Handel buys £400 South Sea Annuities (1751), 5th August 1729.

———

At the Little Theatre in the Haymarket a ballad-opera, *Damon and Philida*, is produced on 16th August 1729; text by Colley Cibber, the tunes by various composers, and among them a minuet by Handel.

This was the second version of Cibber's *Love in a Riddle*, produced at Drury Lane on 7th January 1729. The libretto of 1729 does not contain the reference to Handel, but the libretto of 1765, printed for a revival of *Love in a Riddle* at Drury Lane, has on page 5 : " Handel's Minuet ".

———

Admeto is produced in German at Brunswick, during the summer fair, August 1729.

(Chrysander, II. 157 ; Loewenberg, p. 81.) The translation was probably by G. C. Schürmann. This version was performed again at Brunswick in February 1732 and August 1739. Cf. 12th January 1730 (Hamburg).

———

ROLLI TO RIVA IN VIENNA (Translated)

London, 3rd September 1729.

You knew before that Attilio and Haym died. Now learn that the famous Rossi, Italian author and poet, is Handel's accredited bard. Nothing is known yet of the *virtuoso* C[uzzoni].

(Fassini, 1912, *Rivista musicale*, p. 580 ; Streatfeild, 1917, p. 440.) Original in Biblioteca Estense, Modena. Riva seems to have been transferred, about 1728, from London to Vienna. Haym, Rolli's successor as the Academy's Italian secretary and regular librettist, wrote the book of *Cajo Marzio Coriolano* for Ariosti in 1723, and he may also have arranged Zeno's text of *Teuzzone* for him in 1727. He died on 11th August 1729. Giacomo Rossi wrote the books of *Rinaldo* and *Il Pastor fido*, in 1711 and 1712, but he wrote nothing else for Handel.

———

Handel sells £50 South Sea Annuities (1750), 15th September 1729.

———

FROM THE " NORWICH GAZETTE ", 18th October 1729

[London] *October* 14. On Friday last [the 10th] several of the Italian Singers lately arrived from Italy, who are to perform in the Opera's, had the Honour of a private Performance before their Majesties at Kensington ; when the Harpsichord was played on by Mr. Handell, and their Performances were much approved. It is said, that at every opera Mr. Heydegger, who is master of the House, receives above £1000.

(Manuscript copy by Dr. Arthur Henry Mann in the Library of King's College, Cambridge. No copy of the issue preserved in the Central Library, Norwich.) The *Norwich Mercury* of the same day contains a similar notice from London, dated 16th October, but without the last sentence. This was, of course, a mistake, and probably refers to the King's continued subsidy of £1000 per annum.

———

FROM SWIFT'S " DIRECTIONS FOR A BIRTH-DAY SONG ", October 1729

> . . . Supposing now your Song is done,
> To Minheer Hendel next you run,
> Who artfully will pare and prune
> Your words to some Italian Tune.
> Then print it in the largest letter,
> With Capitals, the more the better.
> Present it boldly on your knee,
> And take a Guinea for your Fee.

The poem, referring to George II's birthday on 30th October, was a satire on Laurence Eusden, the Poet Laureate, who supplied New Year and Birthday Odes from 1719 till 1730. It was, however, addressed to the Rev. Matthew Pilkington who was also writing an ode for this occasion. (The same year he married Laetitia, the author of Memoirs quoted in 1748.) The lines referring to Handel are 275-82 of the poem, which was first published in 1765, in Swift's works. To style Handel *Mynheer* was a joke nearly twenty years old (see 6th March 1711, 17th October 1724 and May 1725).

———

ROLLI TO RIVA, IN VIENNA (Translated)

London, 6th November 1729.
Do you really want me to give you musical news ? If everyone were as well satisfied with the company as is the Royal Family, we should have to admit that there never had been such an Opera since Adam and Eve sang Milton's hymns in the Garden of Eden. They say that Signora Stradina has all the rapid execution of Faustina and all the sweetness of Cuzzona, and so on with all the others. We shall see how it turns out. The proof of the pudding is in the eating, as the English proverb says. The truth is that the said singer is simply a copy of Faustina with a better voice and better intonation, but without her charm and brio. Signora Merighi sings intelligently, Bernacchi is quite exceptional ; I have not heard any others. The parts have not yet been cast. There is a little Roman girl, coming for 450 Lire in all—pretty, they say, but I have not yet seen her. Poor thing, what with travelling and living expenses, she will not take ten guineas back home. You ought to come and protect her and help her and be pleasant to her without flattery. If you do not come quickly, I shall send you exact news without partiality. For I shall speak only of Results, that is whether the theatre was full or empty, on which all depends, be it good or bad. Bernacchi has 1200 guineas, Merighi 1000 or 900 with a benefit performance, Stradina 600 with a benefit performance, Fabri—they say—500, the bass 300 guineas —oh I am so weary of this news but one has to adapt oneself to circumstances. . . .

By the way I forgot to write you that Mr. Tom has succeeded you, because he is always with the lady singers.

(Fassini, 1912, *Rivista musicale*, p. 580 ; Streatfeild, 1917, p. 440.) Original in Biblioteca Estense, Modena. Cf. 16th May 1729. Rolli translated Milton's *Paradise Lost*. " La Romanetta " was Signora Bertolli. Mr. Tom cannot be identified.

———

Handel finishes the opera *Lotario*, 16th November 1729.

———

FROM THE " NORWICH GAZETTE ", 22nd November 1729

[London] *November* 18. We hear the Operas will be brought on the Stage the Beginning of December, with great Magnificence, the Cloaths for the Singers, Attendants and Soldiers, being all imbroidered with Silver, and seven Sets of Scenes entirely new. And 'tis said that they will begin with a new Opera call'd Lotharius.

(Dr. A. H. Mann's manuscript copy in King's College, Cambridge. No copy of the issue in Central Library, Norwich.)

———

MRS. PENDARVES TO HER SISTER, ANN GRANVILLE, (? 29th) November 1729

Bernachi has a vast compass, his voice mellow and clear, but not so sweet as Senesino, his manner better ; his person not so good, for he is as big as a Spanish friar. Fabri has a tenor voice, sweet, clear and firm, but not strong enough, I doubt, for the stage : he sings like a gentleman, without making faces, and his manner is particularly agreeable ; he is the greatest master of musick that ever sang upon the stage. The third is the bass, a very good distinct voice, without any harshness. La Strada is the first woman ; her voice is without exception fine, her manner perfection, but her person *very bad*, and she makes *frightful mouths*. La Merighi is the next to her ; her voice is not extraordinarily good or bad, she is tall and has a very graceful person, with a tolerable face ; she seems to be a woman about forty, she sings easily and agreeably. The last is Bertoli, she has neither voice, ear, nor manner to recommend her ; but she is a perfect beauty, quite a Cleopatra, that sort of complexion with regular features, fine teeth, and when she sings has a smile about her mouth which is extreme pretty, and I believe has practised to sing before a glass, for she has never any distortion in her face.

The first opera is Tuesday next, I have promised Mrs. Clayton to go with her.

(Delany, I. 184 f.) The letter was dated, by the editor, 5th December 1728. The year is obviously 1729, and since Mrs. Pendarves apparently wrote after the experience of the final rehearsal of *Lotario*, the day of writing may have been Saturday the 29th or Sunday the 30th of November. It is improbable that the rehearsal, to which patrons of the Academy had access, was held on the day before the production. And, of course, the letter was not written on the 5th December.

when Mrs. Pendarves had already attended, with Mrs. Clayton (cf. spring 1727), the first night of the new company. See her next letter (6th December 1729). Bertolli, who stayed on for several years, was courted in 1733 by the Prince of Wales. *The Spanish Friar* was a play by John Dryden, often revived in the first half of the eighteenth century.

———

FROM THE "DAILY JOURNAL", 2nd December 1729

At the King's Theatre . . . this present Tuesday . . . will be perform'd, A New Opera, call'd, LOTHARIUS. . . . To begin exactly at Six o'Clock. Note, The Subscribers Tickets will be deliver'd this Day to such as have not received the same, at the Office in the Hay-Market, on Payment of the Money due on the Subscription.

The book of *Lotario* was an arrangement (by Giacomo Rossi?) of Antonio Salvi's *Adelaide*, set by Giuseppe Maria Orlandini and performed in Venice earlier the same year. (Loewenberg, p. 84, correcting Burney, IV. 344, who states that it was altered from Matteo Noris's *Berengario, rè d'Italia*.) The opera was the first given by the second Academy of Music, which lasted from 1729 till 1733. It was performed on 2nd, 6th, 9th, 13th, 16th, 20th, 23rd December 1729; 3rd, 10th and 13th January 1730.

———

CAST OF "LOTARIO", 2nd December 1729

Adelaide—Signora Strada, soprano
Lotario—Signor Bernacchi, soprano
Berengario—Signor Fabri, tenor
Matilde—Signora Merighi, contralto
Idelberto—Signora Bertolli, mezzo-soprano
Clodomiro—Signor Riemschneider, bass

———

JOHN, LORD HERVEY TO STEPHEN FOX

December 2, 1729.

. . . I differ from you extremely in your opinion of Swift's pamphlet . . . for so far from neither liking nor disliking it, I do both in a great degree. We are to have an Opera tonight, the royal interpositions having found means to mediate between the incensed heroines, and compose the differences which arose on Stradina's name having the pas [place] of Merighi's in the libretto. The latter, in the first flush of her resentment on the sight of this indignity, swore nothing but that Parliament should make her submit to it. You think this perhaps a joke of mine ; but 'tis literal truth, and I think too absurd to be imputed to anything but Nature, whose productions infinitely surpass all human invention, and whose characters have so indisputably the first place in comedy. . . .

(*Lord Hervey and His Friends*, p. 41.) The pamphlet by Swift was probably the poem quoted under October 1729, circulating privately. Stephen Fox, later Lord Ilchester, was a close friend of Hervey, the chronicler of George II's reign. The copy of the libretto in the National Library of Scotland, Edinburgh, gives the names of the two ladies against their correct parts, but Strada's part and name are given first.

—

MRS. PENDARVES TO HER SISTER, ANN GRANVILLE

Saturday Morning, 6 Dec. 1729.

I think I have not said one word of the opera yet, and that is an impardonable omission ; but when you know the salutation I had upon my entrance into the Opera-house, you will not be surprized that I forgot all things I heard there . . . whether it was owing to that [bad news confirmed about a friend], or that the opera really is not so meritorious as Mr. Handel's generally are, but I never was so little pleased with one in my life. Bernachi, the most famous of the men, is not approved of ; he is certainly a good singer, but does not suit the English ears. La Strada and the rest are very well liked.

(Delany, I. 228 f.) It seems that the audience referred to was that of the first night.

—

Handel buys £300 South Sea Annuities (1751), 11th December 1729.

—

ROLLI TO RIVA IN VIENNA (Translated)

London, 20th [or rather, 11th ?] December 1729.

Nine days ago the opera *Lotario* was produced. I went only last Tuesday [the 9th], that is to the third performance. Everyone considers it a very bad opera. Bernacchi failed to please on the first night, but at the second performance he changed his method and scored a success. In person and voice he does not please as much as Senesino, but his great reputation as an artist silences those who cannot find it in them to applaud him. The truth is that he has only one aria in which he can shine, because . . . he has blundered in the opera as a whole. The libretto was performed last year by Faustina and Senesino at Venice under the title of *Adelaide*. The faithless wretch ! Strada pleases mightily, and *Alto* [the Great Man] says that she sings better than the two who have left us, because one of them never pleased him at all and he would like to forget the other. The truth is that she has a penetrating thread of a soprano voice which delights the ear, but oh how far removed from Cuzzona ! Bononcini, who was with me at the opera, agrees with me as to this. Fabri is a great success. He really sings very well. Would you have believed that a tenor could have such a triumph here in England ? Merighi is really a perfect actress and that is the general opinion. There is a certain Bertolli, a Roman girl, who plays men's parts. Oh ! my dear Riva, if you could only see her perspiring under her helmet—I am sure you would fall in love with her in your most Modenese fashion ! She is a pretty one ! There is also a bass from Hamburg [Riemschneider], whose voice is more of a natural contralto than a bass. He sings sweetly in his throat and nose, pronounces Italian in the Teutonic manner, acts like a sucking-pig, and looks more like a *valet* than anything. Oh, he is fine, I can tell you ! They are putting on *Giulio Cesare* because the audiences are falling away fast. I think the storm is about to break on the head of our proud *Orso* [Bear]. Not all beans are for market, especially beans so badly cooked as this first basketful. Aeydeger has won great praise for his dresses and not a little for his scenery in which at least he never sinks below *mediocrity*. And yet the great public failed to appear on the first night. We shall see what we shall see.

(Fassini, 1912, *Rivista musicale*, p. 529 ; Streatfeild, 1917, pp. 440 f.) Original in Biblioteca Estense, Modena. Some words are illegible, as often happens in Rolli's letters. The date of the letter is doubtful. It reads like 20th December, but Streatfeild altered it to 12th, correcting the first word into ten (*dieci*). Even reference to the Continental calendar cannot reconcile the dates. Rolli, however, was very uncertain about the date of the day on which he wrote a letter. *Alto* and *Orso* are two other nicknames for Handel. His *Giulio Cesare* was revived on 17th January 1730.

—

MRS. PENDARVES TO HER SISTER, ANN GRANVILLE

Pall Mall, 20 Dec. 1729.

The opera is too good for the vile taste of the town : it is condemned never more to appear on the stage after this night. I long to hear its dying song, poor dear swan. We are to have some old opera revived, which I am sorry for, it will put people upon making comparisons between these singers and those that performed before, which will be a disadvantage among the ill-judging multitude. The present opera is disliked because it is too much studied, and they love nothing but minuets and ballads, in short the *Beggars' Opera* and *Hurlothrumbo* are only worthy of applause.

(Delany, I. 229.) Cf. 6th December 1729. *Lotario* was, in fact, performed four more times after 20th December. The "old opera" was *Giulio Cesare*. For *Hurlothrumbo*, see 7th April 1729.

—

FROM COLMAN'S "OPERA REGISTER", November [recte December] 1729

In November 1729 Opera's began again with an entire new company of singers—La Sigra Strada del Pio was ye Cheife & best the rest little esteem'd an Eunuch called Bernacchi.

—

FROM HENRY CAREY'S " POEMS ON SEVERAL OCCASIONS ", 1729

The Laurel-Grove ;
or
The Poet's Tribute to Music and Merit.
And first,
To Mr. George-Frederick Handel.

Hail unexhausted Source of Harmony,
Thou glorious Chief of *Phoebus'* tuneful Sons !
In whom the Knowledge of all Magick Number,
Or Sound melodious does concentred dwell.
The Envy and the Wonder of Mankind
Must terminate, but never can thy Lays :
For when, absorb'd in Elemental Flame,
This World shall vanish, Music will exist :
Then thy sweet Strains, to native Skies returning,
Shall breathe in Songs of Seraphims and Angels,
Commixt and lost in Harmony Eternal,
That fills all Heaven ! – – – – – –

(Schoelcher, p. 69.) Carey, pp. 108 f. This is the first of eleven poems addressed
to musicians, in the third, much enlarged, edition of Carey's poems. (Cf. 25th
March 1727.)

———

FROM WALSH'S CASH-BOOK, 1729–30

1729 Opera Parthenope . . . £26   5   0

The opera, not finished until 6th February, was produced on 24th February and
published on 4th April 1730. This was the first Handel entry in Walsh's Cash-
Book since 1723 (*Flavio*), Cluer having been Handel's publisher in the meantime.

1730

Admeto is produced at Hamburg, 12th (23rd) January 1730.

(Chrysander, II. 157 ; Merbach, p. 363.) *Admetus, König in Thessalien*, translated into German by Christian Gottlieb Wendt, was also performed in Hamburg between 1731 and 1736. Willers' diary records five performances only, those between 1731 and 1733 being listed by his editor, Merbach, as performances of an opera by Telemann. The libretto of 1731 proves that the *Admetus* performed on 23rd December 1730 (3rd January 1731) was still Handel's opera ; it was repeated at the beginning of 1732, the end of 1733 and again in May 1734.

Giulio Cesare is revived at the Haymarket Theatre, 17th January 1730. Repeat performances on 24th, 27th, 31st January ; 3rd, 7th, 14th, 17th, 21st February ; 21st and 31st March.

The exact cast is not known, but Strada sang Cleopatra, the part created by Cuzzoni.

Handel sells £50 South Sea Annuities (1751), 26th January 1730.

Handel finishes the opera *Partenope*, 6th February 1730.

The ballad-opera, *The Chamber-Maid*, is produced at Drury Lane Theatre on 10th February 1730, with a Handel minuet sung as " Deluded by her mate's dear voice ".

Cf. 6th February 1729. This was a shortened version, by Edward Phillips, of Charles Johnson's *Village Opera*. The printed libretto avoids the mistake of the previous one, which attributed Handel's air to one " Denoyer ".

" Cluer's Printing-Office " advertise the score of *Lotario*, together with eight other Handel operas published by that firm ; " sold also at C. Smith's ", *Daily Post*, 13th February 1730.

It was unfortunate that the score appeared one month after the last performance of *Lotario*. This was the last opera printed by Cluer's widow. From now onwards Walsh was Handel's sole publisher. On 3rd March 1730 he brought out a flute arrangement of *Lotario*, which probably had no success. The widow Cluer let him have the unsold copies of the score.

X. HANDEL'S HOUSE IN BROOK STREET, now No. 25

From a water-colour signed L. M., nineteenth century. (Gerald Coke, Esq.)

See page 170

Thou tunefull Scarecrow, & thou warbling Bird,
No shelter for your Notes, these lands afford
This Town protects no more the Sing Song Strain
Whilst Balls & Masquerades Triumphant Reign
Sooner than midnight revels ere shoud fail
And ore Ridottos Harmony prevail.
That Cap (a refuge once) my Head shall Grace
And save from ruin this Harmonious face

XI. CUZZONI, FARINELLI AND HEIDEGGER

Engraving by Joseph Goupy, 1729–30, after a sketch by Marco Ricci,
1728–9. (Fitzwilliam Museum)

See page 255

FROM THE " DAILY COURANT ", 24th February 1730

At the King's Theatre . . . this present Tuesday . . . will be performed a new Opera, call'd, PARTHENOPE. . . . The Scenes and Dresses are all entirely new. . . . To begin exactly at 6.

Partenope, text by Silvio Stampiglia, was performed on 24th, 28th February ; 3rd, 7th, 10th, 14th and 17th March ; it was revived for the first time on 12th December 1730. Cf. 29th January 1737.

———

CAST OF " PARTENOPE ", 24th February 1730

Partenope—Signora Strada, soprano
Rosmira—Signora Merighi, contralto
Arsace—Signor Bernacchi, soprano
Armindo—Signora Bertolli, mezzo-soprano
Emilio—Signor Fabri, tenor
Ormonte—Signor Riemschneider, bass

———

FROM THE " DAILY JOURNAL ", 21st March 1730

For the Benefit of Signora *Strada del Po.*

At the King's Theatre . . . this Day . . . JULIUS CAESAR. With some *New Songs.* NB. This Night's Benefit, being Part of Signora *Strada's* Salary, it is not to be deem'd in the Number of Operas that the Proprietors are obliged to have perform'd this Season. . . .

The cast of the 1730 revival of this opera is not known, but Strada, apparently, sang Cleopatra, Cuzzoni's original part. It is not known which additional songs were used at this revival. According to Burney (IV. 348), the King attended the performance on 31st March, the last of this revival.

———

At Goodman's Field Theatre, on 2nd April 1730, a ballad-opera is produced, entitled *The Fashionable Lady, or Harlequin's Opera; in the Manner of a Rehearsal*, text by James Ralph ; among the 68 songs is " O cruel tyrant love ", attributed to Handel.

For James Ralph, see 1728 with reference to his pamphlet *The Touch-Stone.*

———

Walsh and Hare advertise " The Whole Opera of Parthenope. . . . Fairly engraven, and carefully corrected ", *Daily Journal*, 4th April 1730.

This was the first publication by Walsh of a Handel work within the new agreement, and he tried to improve his style of production, after Cluer's model. In December 1730 Walsh printed the overture of *Partenope* in parts, as one of the six overtures forming the fourth collection of such sets (Smith, 1948, p. 279).

———

FROM THE "DAILY COURANT", 4th April 1730

At the King's Theatre . . . this present Saturday . . . will be performed a New Opera, call'd ORMISDA. . . .

The text was by Apostolo Zeno, the music probably by Bartholomeo Cordans (Chrysander, II. 239) and others. There were 13 performances up to 9th June, and 5 more in November-December 1730. The revival during the autumn is listed, wrongly, in Colman's *Opera Register* under 1st February 1731.

—

MRS. PENDARVES TO HER SISTER, ANN GRANVILLE

Pall Mall, 4th April 1730.
Operas are dying, to my great mortification. Yesterday I was at the rehearsal of a new one ; it is composed of several songs out of Italian operas ; but it is very heavy to Mr. Handel's.

(Delany I. 253.) From 1730 onwards Handel, as the musical director of the Opera, provided recitatives to several pasticcios, compiled from works by various composers. The work in question was *Ormisda*.

—

The Female Parson, or The Beau in the Sudds, a ballad-opera with text by Charles Coffey, is produced at the Little Theatre in the Haymarket, on 27th April 1730 ; among the tunes by various composers are the gavotte from *Ottone* and a hornpipe in G major by Handel (British Museum, Add. MS. 29,371, folio 76 verso).

—

Tolomeo is revived at the Haymarket Theatre, 19th May 1730 ; repeat performances on 23rd, 26th, 30th May ; 2nd, 6th and 13th June.

The cast (compared with that of 1728) was as follows :

> Tolomeo—Signor Bernacchi (Senesino)
> Seleuce—Signora Strada (Cuzzoni)
> Elisa—Signora Merighi (Faustina)
> Alessandro—Signora Bertolli (Signor Baldi)
> Araspe—Signor Fabri (Boschi)

Cf. 30th April 1728 and 2nd January 1733. The *Daily Journal* of May 1730 is missing in the British Museum. From the issue of 2nd June, however, it can be seen that *Tolomeo* was advertised for this revival " With several Alterations. The Opera being short, it will not begin till Seven o'Clock." Handel's first season ended on 13th June (Burney, IV. 349).

—

ROLLI TO RIVA IN VIENNA (Translated)

London, 12th June, 1730.
I shall barely answer you on the matter of that *Coppia Eidegrendeliana* [Heidegger-Handel pair] and their worthless operas. Because in truth

they succeed no better than they deserve. The musicians will be paid, and that is all that can be done. I perceive besides that either there will be no operas in the new season or there will be the same Company, which is most certainly going from bad to worse. Strada is liked by the very few who wish to forget Cuzzona—as the rest of the rhyme goes they are after all most similar : *I ask your pardon, Sir*. With respect to my ears you were a thousand times right, but as far as my eyes are concerned, my dear *Signor Giuseppe*, you were a thousand times wrong. . . .

Marchetto Rizzi, a few days before his death, sent this man Goupy a caricature of Cuzzona and Farinello singing a duet. Goupy added Eideger in a sitting posture with his face turned up, and it was printed in honour and glory of that great band of rogues—the singers.

(Streatfeild, 1917, p. 441.) Original in Biblioteca Estense, Modena. This letter solves the mystery of a famous print, sometimes attributed to Hogarth and usually dated 1734. Marco, called Marchetto, Ricci, the well-known Italian painter and engraver, died on 10th (21st) January 1729 at Venice. He drew caricatures of actors, and he was last in London in 1727, when he might have seen Cuzzoni, but not Farinelli who did not go there until 1734. Ricci might have seen the two in Italy, but not together. They met in London in 1734 when they sang together in Hasse's *Artaserse*. There exist three states of the etching, suggested by Ricci in 1729, but made by Goupy in 1730, when the original designer had died. The first is without names, but already bearing the following verse :

> Thou tunefull Scarecrow, & thou warbling Bird,
> No shelter for your Notes, these lands afford
> This Town protects no more the Sing-Song Strain
> Whilst Balls & Masquerades Triumphant Reign
> Sooner than midnight revels ere shoud fail
> And ore Ridotto's Harmony prevail :
> That Cap (a refuge once) my Head shall Grace
> And save from ruin this Harmonious face

The second state bears, under the picture, the name of the Countess of Burlington, Faustina's patron, on the left, and that of Goupy as engraver on the right ; in the middle the names of Cuzzoni, Farinelli, and Heidegger, under their respective portraits. A third state has " Senesino " added below the name of Farinelli. The latter was unknown to the public in 1730, and the print could not have been sold then. This may have been the reason for adding Senesino's name. If, however, the order of the three states is as indicated above, the name of Senesino might have been added in 1734, when he and Farinelli were singing together on the same stage as Cuzzona. The verses would have been understood better in 1730 than in 1734. There remains the riddle of the Countess's name, placed as if she had been the designer : perhaps she added Heidegger's figure to Ricci's duet, or perhaps she wrote the verses. According to Henry Angelo's *Reminiscences*, published in 1828, I. 406 f., she " had a hand in fabricating " Goupy's cartoon of Handel (see 21st March 1754) as well as " the reputation of designing " the caricature of the trio. The grenadier's cap on the wall alludes to the fact that Heidegger served, for a short time, with the Guards in Queen Anne's days, the initials " A R " on the cap indicating *Anna Regina*.

HANDEL TO FRANCIS COLMAN, AT FLORENCE

a Londres ce $\frac{19}{30}$ de Juin, 1730.

Monsieur,

Depuis que j'ay eu l'honneur de Vous ecrire, on a trouvé moyen d'engager de nouveau la Sig^{ra} Merighi, et cõme c'est une voix de Contr'Alto, il nous conviendroit presentement que la Fem̃e qu'on doit engager en Italie fût un Soprano. J'ecris aussi avec cet ordinaire a Mr. Swinny pour cet effet, en luy recõmandant en meme tems que la Femme qu'il pourra Vous proposer fasse le Role d'home aussi bien que celuy de Fem̃e. Il y a lieu de croire que Vous n'avez pas encore pris d'engagement pour une Femme Contr'Alto, mais en cas que cela soit fait, il faudrait s'y en tenir. Je prens la Liberté de Vous prier de nouveau qu'il ne soit pas fait mention dans les Contracts du premier, second ou troisieme Rolle, puisque cela nous gêne dans le choix du Drama, et est d'ailleurs sujet a de grands inconveniens. Nous esperons ainsi d'avoir par Votre assistance un hom̃e et une Fem̃e pour la Saison prochaine, qui com̃ence avec le mois d'Octobr de l'añee Courante et finit avec le mois de Juillet 1731, et nous attendons avec impatience d'en apprendre des nouvelles pour en informer la Cour.

Il ne me reste qu'a Vous reiterer mes assurances de l'obligation particuliere que je Vous aurai de Votre Bonté envers moi a cet egard, qui ai l'hoñeur d'etre avec une affection respectueuse

> Monsieur
>> Vôtre
>>> tres humble et obeissant
>>>> Serviteur
>>>> George Frideric Handel.

A Monsieur Monsieur Colman
Envoyé extraord^{are} de S.M. Britanique,
aupres de S.A.R. le Duc de Toscane.
Firence

(Translation)

London, 19th-30th June, 1730.

Sir,

Since I had the honour to write to you last, a way has been found to re-engage Signora Merighi, and as she is a contralto, it would be convenient for us now if the woman to be engaged in Italy were a soprano. I am also writing by this ordinary post to Mr. Swinny in the same sense, at the same time recommending that any woman that he shall propose to you should be equally good at male and female parts. The supposition is that you have not yet entered into any contract for a female contralto, but should this have been done, then it would have to stand. I take the liberty of asking you once again that no specific mention be made in the contracts of *prima, seconda* or *terza donna*, since that embarrasses us in the choice of the opera and in any case is a source of great inconvenience. We hope thus to have with your assistance one man and one woman for the coming season (which begins in October this year and ends in July 1731) and we are awaiting with impatience to learn your news in order to inform the Court.

It remains only for me to reiterate to you my assurances of the peculiar obligation under which I shall be to you for your kindness in this matter, and I have the honour to be, Sir, with respectful affection,

> Your
> most humble and obedient
> > > servant,
> > > George Frideric Handel.

To Mr. Colman,
His Britannic Majesty's Envoy Extraordinary
at the Court of H.R.H. the Duke of Tuscany,
> > Florence.

(Colman, *Posthumous Letters*, pp. 19 f.) Original in the autograph collection of the late Karl Geigy-Hagenbach, Basel. Facsimile in Mueller von Asow, 1949, after p. 120. The last two lines of the address are written by another hand. Handel's first letter to Colman is lost. For Colman see 26th November 1712 ; for Swiney 15th January 1713 and 18th July 1730.

CAST OF " ADELAIDE ", AN OPERA PLANNED IN 1730

> Adelaide—Signora Merighi
> Adalberto—non parla
> Brunechilde—Signora Strada
> Berengario—Signor Bernacchi
> Ermanno—Signor Giuseppe Picini
> Luitolfo—Signora Margherita Bertoldi
> Atone—Signor Fabri

(Franz Michael Rudhart, *Geschichte der Oper am Hofe zu München*, Freising, 1865, I. 120 f.) The only known copy of the libretto is in the Bayerische Staatsbibliothek, Munich, and it was probably printed there. The opera was to be produced at the Haymarket Theatre, in honour of the Elector, Karl Albert von Bayern. The text is by Boccardi, of Turin, who calls himself " Pastor Arcade in Roma e nuovamente Compagno della Reale Società di Londra ", and adds : " La Musica e del Signor Hendell, maestro di Capella della Loro Maestá Reale delle Grande Bretagna et Academico Filharmonico ". (Cf. the cast of *Lotario*, 2nd December 1729.) The dedication to the Elector is dated 1st June 1730 ; in it Boccardi claims to be the author of an opera *Farnace* (not Porta's). He seems to have had the text published in the hope of Handel's setting it and in expectation of the Elector's gratitude. The singers Picini and Bertoldi were not in Handel's company ; perhaps the author intended to introduce them there.

Handel buys, from Joseph Goupy, £100 South Sea Annuities (1751), 4th July 1730.

—

OWEN SWINEY TO COLMAN, AT FLORENCE

Bologna [7th] 18 July 1730.

I am favoured wth y^{rs} of ye 15th instant, & shall Endeav^{r} to observe punctually w^{t} you write about. I find y^{t} *Senesino* or *Carestini* are desired at 1200 G^{s} each, if they are to be had ; Im'e sure that *Carestini* is Engaged at Milan, & has been so, for many Months past : and I hear y^{t} *Senesino*, is Engaged for ye ensuing Carnival at Rome.

If *Senesino* is at liberty (& will accept ye offer) then the affair is adjusted if Sig^{ra} Barbara Pisani accepts the offer I made her, which I really believe she will.

If we can neither get *Senesino*, nor *Carestini*, then Mr Handel desires to have a man (Soprano) & a woman contrealt, & y^{t} the price (for both) must not exceed *one Thousand* or *Eleven hundred* Guineas, & that the persons must sett out for London ye latter end of Augt or beginning of Septemb^{r}, and y^{t} no Engagem^{t} must be Made wth one with^{t} a certainty of getting the other.

Several of the persons recomended to Mr Handel (whose names he repeats in ye letter I received from him this Morning) are I think exceedingly indifferent, & Im'e persuaded wou'd never doe in England : & I think shou'd never be pitch'd on, till nobody else can be had.

I have heard a *Lad* here, of a^{bt} 19 years old, wth a *very good soprano voice* (& of whom there are vast hopes) who Im'e persuaded, would do very well in London, and much better than any of those mentioned in Mr Handel's letter who are not already engaged in case you cannot get *Senesino*. . . .

Having no time to answer Mr. Handel's Letter, this day, I hope you will be so good as to let him know y^{t} I shall Endeav^{r} to serve him to the utmost of my power, & y^{t} I shall do nothing but w^{t} shall be concerted by you.

(Colman, *Posthumous Letters*, pp. 21-5.) Cf. 19th June 1730. Swiney, who had left London in 1713, lived in Italy ; he returned to England about 1735, after which he assumed the name MacSwiney. Senesino joined Handel's company again at a salary of 1400 guineas a year, and Carestini was engaged in 1733. Signora Pisani never came to London. Handel's letter to Swiney is not preserved. See 29th July 1730.

—

Maria Augusta Flörke, the sister of Dr. Johann Ernst Flörke (see p. 415), dies at Halle, 17th (28th) July 1730.

In the Cummings sale, 17th-24th May 1917, there was a copy of the printed funeral oration, with many elegies, 50 pp. fol. (catalogue no. 823, item 4).

—

SWINEY TO COLMAN, AT FLORENCE

Rome, July [18th] 29, 1730.

I was in hopes of ye Hon^r of a Letter from you, to let me know whether *Senesino* had accepted the offer of 1200 G^s. If he does not, *then*, we must provide a *Soprano Man* & a *Contrealt Woman* (tho the *Merighi* stays) at ab^t 1000 G^s (both) or, Therab^{ts}—wth an absolute condition of their being in London by ye end of Septem^{br}.

I told you I had a young Fellow in View wth a good Voice & other requisites, in case *Senesino* (or some other fit person) cou'd not be Engaged—I have rec^d no answer, as yet, From the Sig^{ra} Barbara Pisani, but hope to have one by ye next week's ordinary—as soon as I receive it, I shall not fail to give you the purport of it.

(Colman, *Posthumous Letters*, pp. 25 f.)   Cf. 7th July and 16th October 1730.

———

FROM THE TREASURY MINUTE BOOK, 27th July 1730

The King allows 1,000*l.* to be paid the undertakers for the opera towards the discharging their debt, so prepare a sign manual, in the name of John James Heidegger, for that purpose.

(Calendar of Treasury Papers, 1729–30, p. 416).   The other undertaker was Handel.

———

FROM THE KING'S WARRANT BOOK, 27th July 1730

Royal sign manual directed to the Lords of Treasury for the issue of 1,000*l.* to John James Heidegger to be applied as royal bounty towards enabling the undertakers of the opera to discharge their debts.

Memorandum :—Warrant signed by the Lords of the Treasury, July 28.

(Calendar of Treasury Papers, 1729–30, p. 418.)

———

FROM THE ORDER BOOK OF THE TREASURY, 29th July 1730

1730
July 29.   John James Heidegger   1,000   0   0   Royal bounty to the
                                                  undertakers of the Opera

(Calendar of Treasury Papers, 1729–30, p. 580.)

———

FROM THE " NORWICH MERCURY ", 15th August 1730

[London,] *August* 8. This Day Mr. Handel, the famous Master of Musick, made Trial of the new Organ in Westminster-Abbey, upon which he play'd several fine Pieces of Musick, and gave his Opinion, that it is a very curious Instrument.

Cf. 11th October 1727 and 10th February 1728. Schrider's organ was enlarged by the Jordans (see 23rd August 1720) and opened by John Robinson, the Abbey's organist, on 1st August 1730, with Henry Purcell's anthem " O give thanks ". It was probably at this time that the organ was removed to the screen. " Curious " means remarkable.

Handel buys £150 South Sea Annuities (1751), 15th August 1730.

FROM THE " DAILY POST ", 28th August 1730

Signor Senesino, the famous Italian Singer, hath contracted to come over hither against the Winter, to perform under Mr. Heydegger in the Italian Operas.

(Burney, IV. 348 f.)

Siroe is performed at Brunswick, August 1730.
(Loewenberg, p. 83.) Cf. 17th February 1728 and 29th January 1735.

Ernelinda, an opera by Telemann, is produced at Hamburg on 16th (27th) September 1730, with some music by Handel added to the score.

Merbach does not mention the additional music ; the information was given privately by the late Dr. Loewenberg. At a revival in autumn 1731, the opera was called *Ermelinda*.

FROM THE " DAILY JOURNAL ", 9th October 1730

There are Grand Preparations making at the Opera-House in the Hay-Market, by New Cloaths, Scenes, &c. And, Senesino being arrived, they will begin to perform as soon as the Court comes to St. James's.

(Burney, IV. 348 f.)

HANDEL TO COLMAN, AT FLORENCE

à Londres $\frac{27}{16}$ d'Octobr 1730.

Monsieur

Je viens de recevoir l'honneur de Votre Lettre du 22 du passée N.S. par la quelle je vois les Raisons qui Vous ont determiné d'engager Sr Senesino sur le pied de quatorze Cent ghinees, a quoy nous acquiesçons, et je Vous fais mes tres humbles Remerciments des peines que Vous avez bien voulu prendre dans cette affaire. Le dit Sr Senesino est arrivé icy il y a 12 jours et je n'ai pas manqué sur la presentation de Votre Lettre de Luy payer a compte de son Salaire les cent ghinées que Vous

Luy aviez promis. Pour ce qui est de la Sig^{ra} Pisani nous ne l'avons pas
eüe, et comme la Saison est fort avancée, et qu'on comencera bientôt les
Opéras nous nous passerons cette année cy d'une autre Feme d'Italie
ayant deja disposé les Operas pour la Compagnie que nous avons presentement. Je Vous suis pourtant tres obligé d'avoir songé a la Sig^{ra}
Madalena Pieri en cas que nous eussions eu absolument besoin d'une
autre Femme qui acte en homme, mais nous nous contenterons des cinq
Personnages ayant actuellement trouvé de quoy suppléer au reste.

C'est a Votre genereuse assistance que la Cour et la Noblesse devront
en partie la satisfaction d'avoir presentement une Compagnie a leur gré,
en sorte qu'il ne me reste qu'a Vous en marquer mes sentiments particuliers
de gratitude et a Vous assurer de l'attention tres respectueuse avec la
quelle j'ay l'honneur d'etre
> Monsieur
> > Votre
> > > tres humble et tres obeissant
> > > Servietur
> > > George Frideric Handel

A Monsieur
Monsieur Colman
Envoyé Extraord^{inaire} de Sa Majesté Britañique
aupres de Son Altesse Royale le Grand Duc de Toscane
> > à
> > Florence

(Translation)
> > London, 27th/16th October 1730.

Sir,
     I have just had the honour of receiving your letter of the 22nd past
(N.S.), from which I see the reasons which determined you to engage
Signor Senesino at a salary of 1400 guineas, which we agree to ; and I
most humbly thank you for all the trouble which you have been kind
enough to take in this matter. Signor Senesino arrived here twelve days
ago and I have not omitted to pay him on the presentation of your
letter the hundred guineas of his salary on account, as you had promised
him. As regards Signora Pisani, we have not had her [here], and as the
season is well advanced and the opera will be opening soon, we shall
do without another Italian this year, having already chosen the operas
to fit our present company. However I am greatly obliged to you for
thinking of Signora Mad[d]alena Pieri in case we should find ourselves
quite unable to do without another woman able to take male parts. But
we shall content ourselves with the five, a way having now been found
for making up the rest.

     It is to your generous assistance that the Court and the Nobility will
in part owe the satisfaction of having in due course a company to their
taste, so that it remains for me only to convey to you my own feelings

of deep gratitude and to assure you of the great respect with which I
have the honour to be,

Sir,

Your

most humble and obedient

servant,

George Frideric Handel

To Mr. Colman,
His Britannic Majesty's Envoy Extraordinary
at the Court of H.R.H. the Duke of Tuscany,

Florence.

(Colman, *Posthumous Letters*, pp. 28 f.)   Original among the manuscripts of the
Royal College of Music, deposited in the British Museum.   For Pisani, see 7th and
18th July 1730.   Maria Maddalena Pieri, who was in Venice in 1730, also did
not come to London.   The only newcomer, besides the returned Senesino,
was Giovanni Commano, a bass, in place of Riemschneider who went back to
Hamburg.

———

The second season of the new Academy opens with a revival of
Scipione on 3rd November 1730 ; repeat performances on 7th,
10th, 14th, 17th and 21st.

The cast (compared with that of 1726) was as follows :

P. C. Scipione—Signor Fabri (Baldi)
Lucejo—Signor Senesino (Senesino)
C. Lelio—Signora Bertolli (Signor Antinori)
Ernando—Signor Commano (Boschi)
Berenice—Signora Strada (Cuzzoni)
Armira—Signora Merighi (Costantini)

The new version of the opera was slightly different from the original.

———

FROM COLMAN'S " OPERA REGISTER ", 3rd November 1730

Nov. 3 Tuesday Opera's began wth Scipio Senesino being return'd
charm'd much :   the rest as last year—Scipio 4 times to Saturday *ye
14 Nov* :   the King, Queen &c there each night.

The entry shows that the *Register* cannot have been written by Francis Colman,
who was in Florence at this time.

———

Silvia, or The Country Burial, a ballad-opera with text by George
Lillo, is produced at Lincoln's Inn Fields Theatre on 10th Novem-
ber 1730 ; among the tunes are one or two unidentified arias by
Handel.

The opera was revived, in a shortened version, on 18th March 1736 at
Covent Garden Theatre.

———

Handel buys £350 South Sea Annuities (1751), 26th November 1730.

—

Partenope is revived, 12th December 1730. Repeat performances on 15th, 19th, 29th December 1730 ; 2nd, 5th and 9th January 1731.

Cf. 24th February 1730. According to the heading of the additional song, " Seguaci di Cupido ", which Walsh published, in January 1731, in the second issue of his edition (cf. 4th April 1730), Bernacchi's part of Armindo was taken over by Senesino. Riemschneider's original part of Ormonte was apparently sung by the new bass, Commano.

—

Handel's mother dies at Halle, 16th (27th) December 1730.

—

From Johann Georg Francke's Funeral Sermon for Dorothea Händel, delivered in Halle on 22nd December 1730 (2nd January 1731), and Printed on Handel's Account (Translated)

She saw the light of this world for the first time in the year of Our Lord, 1651, on 8th February [according to the old calendar] at Diesskau. Her father was Herr Georg Taust, well-merited Pastor at the afore-mentioned Diesskau, who, however, was later duly appointed a servant of God's Word at the Parish of Giebichenstein and Crölwitz by the Principality of those days. Her mother was Dorothea, née Cuno, legiti-mate daughter of Johann Christoph Cuno, *Not. Publ.* and administrator of the Beesen Office, and also, after that, duly appointed supervisor of the saline springs in Halle. Her paternal grandfather was Johann Taust, who, because of the religious troubles of that time, and the severe per-secution of those who sympathised with the *Confession of Augsburg* [about 1625], and for love of the pure evangelical truth, left the Kingdom of Bohemia, freely renouncing all his estate, according to the Scripture, Matthew XIX, 29, and chose rather to live as a private person here in Halle, than in good esteem and with great fortune, in his Fatherland : for which staunch loyalty Almighty God richly repaid him. Her maternal grandmother was Catherina, née Olearius, legitimate daughter of the beloved Johann *Olearius*, *S.S. Theol. Doctor*, *Superintendent*, Rector and Incumbent at the Church of Our Lady.

Amongst the especial benefits which God showed her, she esteemed this : that she sprang from a priestly family, and had a pious father, who, through a sincere ardour for true religion, trod in the footsteps of his beloved father. On her mother's side, she could boast of a close relation-ship with the blessed family of *Olearius*, well-merited of the Church of

Christ, especially in this spot. That she earnestly applied herself to copy the virtues of her parents and grandparents redounded yet more to her fame.

The aforementioned pious parents, inasmuch as they were able, denied her nothing which could give her the agreeable upbringing pleasing to God and man : therefore her father, when he perceived in his child an alert mind and a good memory, wherewith God had endowed her above many others of her sex, did not content himself with the instructions by private teachers, but, as far as the duties of his office would permit, himself trained her, and took pains that she be firmly grounded in Christian principles as well as acquainted with the Holy Scriptures ; which work the Lord blessed in such a manner that, within a few years, indeed for the whole of her life, she could draw forth supply after supply from this treasure of goodliest texts, gathered in her youth, for her own and for other people's edification. This Christian conduct, and her additional pleasant gifts of mind and body, together with her perfect knowledge of household superintendence, moved many people, when she came of age, to solicit her parents for a marriage contract with her. Although her parents were at no time against such a happy change, but rather wished for her settlement, yet for love of them she could not be brought to do it, in no way whatsoever ; to forsake them when they were old (especially her father when he became a widower after her mother's death in 1681) she held to be against filial obligation ; indeed, love for her old father, who was suffering in consequence of a severe fall, was so great, that in the *Contagion* raging in those days she did not spare her own life (for which her father cared in sending his daughter away elsewhere) ; she would not leave him unvisited when the Parsonage at Giebichenstein was already greatly infected, nor considered that death, which had already torn away her young sister, her eldest brother, *Adjunctum* of his father, and his wife, through this epidemic, might also lay in wait for her in that place. She remained rather, in the execution of her filial duties, dauntless and confident, realising that God would uphold her in those dismal times, and could deliver her also from death ; indeed our blessed one often used to relate, to the Glory of God, how his Almighty protection came to be known to her in those days. When, however, the plague quite passed away again, and her old father, through a second *Adjunctum*, in the person of her youngest brother, was relieved in the duties of his office, which had become by then somewhat troublesome to him : the blessed woman was no longer able to resist the wise guidance of the Almighty, and the many persuasions of her father and other good friends, and resolved, after previous diligent prayer, in the name of God, to enter into Christian matrimony with him who had proposed to her, Herr Georg Händel, duly appointed Valet to H.R.H. August, Duke of Saxony, and *Administrator* Presumptive of the *Primate* Archbishopric of Magdeburg ; this marriage was shortly afterwards

solemnised on St. George's Day, 23rd April in the year 1683, at Giebichenstein, in a holy marriage service, which her father, to his greatest pleasure,
could himself conduct.

As marriages, which are not based upon passing *Interesse*, but rather
upon compatibility of soul and true virtue cannot be other than well-
prospered ; so this blessed woman lived with her husband until the day
of his death, all the time calmly, contentedly and peacefully in Christ ;
she bore also to him four children : two sons, of whom, however, the
first died in the same hour as he was born in the year 1684 ; whose loss
the good God retrieved, to the joy of his parents and his grandfather, by
the gift of another son, namely Georg Friederich, born 23rd February, in
the year 1685, who stands in especial grace, by reason of his exceptional
knowledge of music, as Director of Music to the reigning Majesty in
England and Elector of Hanover, George II, as also to the late King of
Great Britain, His Majesty George I, of glorious memory. And two
daughters, namely

I. Dorothea Sophia, born on 6th October, in the year 1687.

II. Johanna Christiana, born on 10th January, in the year 1690.

(Chrysander, I. 6-9, II. 227 f., 250.) 28 pp. fol. in all, of which pp. 20-28
contain the *Memoria Defunctae*. A copy of the sermon is preserved at Stolberg
in the Harz, and it was reprinted in 1939 at Halle. Another copy was in the
Cummings sale, 17th-24th May 1917, no. 823, item 1 ; in 1881 he thought this
was the only copy in existence (*Proceedings of the Royal Musical Association*, VII. 30).
For the inscription on the tomb of Handel's mother, see 11th February 1697. For
Olearius, cf. 18th February 1697.

———

*Christian August Rotth's Poem of Condolence Addressed to Handel,
Halle (1730).*

See *Addenda*.

———

In his collection " Les Parodies nouvelles et les Vaudevilles in-
connues ", 1730, Jean Baptiste Christophe Ballard, the Paris
publisher, prints the aria " Se risolvi abbandormi", from Handel's
Floridante, as "Daphnis, profitons du temps, Je vois déja l'Aurore".

(Philipp Spitta, *Musikgeschichtliche Aufsätze*, Berlin 1894, pp. 236 f.) Cf.
1734 and 1737.

———

From Giovanni Carlo Bonlini's " Le Glorie della Poesia,
e della Musica " (contained in the detailed Notices on
the Theatres of the City of Venice and in the most carefully Revised List of the Operas, etc.), Venice (1730)
(Translated)

1710. Winter. *Agrippina* 441. Theatre at S. Gio. Crisostomo 56.
Text by unknown author, music by George Frederic Hendel. This
Opera, like *Elmiro*, *Rè di Corinto*, and *Orazio*, which were performed

H.-9 a

at the same theatre more than twenty years ago, boasts a common origin from the same divine source.

(Chrysander, I. 189 f.) Page 158 of the book, published anonymously, with reference numbers corresponding to lists of operas, theatres and composers. *Agrippina* was, in fact, performed 27 times in Venice during the season of 1709–10. Cf. Quadrio, under 1744.

———

FROM WALSH'S CASH-BOOK, 1730–31

1730   Opera Porus . . . £26   5   0

The opera was not finished until 16th January ; it was produced on 2nd February and published on 2nd March 1731.

1731

Venceslao, a pasticcio-opera with text by Apostolo Zeno and recitatives by Handel, is produced at the Haymarket Theatre, 12th January 1731.

———

Handel finishes the opera *Poro*, 16th January 1731.

———

New Musick,

. . . . . .

Printed for and sold by *John Walsh*. . . .

. . . . . .

The whole Opera of Parthenope, with the Additional Song compos'd by Mr. Handel.

. . . . .

Seventeen of Mr. Handel's Opera's transposed for the Flute, neatly bound in 2 Vols. 4to.

Cf. 4th April and 12th December 1730. This second issue of the *Parthenope* score has the words "for the Royal Academy", referring to the performances at the King's Theatre, omitted from the title. Walsh was no longer associated with Joseph Hare. No copy is known of the bound collection of Walsh's flute editions of Handel's operas.

———

At the King's Theatre . . . on Tuesday next, being the 2d Day of February, will be perform'd, *a new opera*, call'd PORUS. . . . N.B. The Scenes and Habits are all intirely new.

Similar advertisements appeared in the *Daily Courant*; in these the word " Habits " was changed to " Cloaths ".

———

Poro is produced, 2nd February 1731.

Poro, re dell'Indie, text altered from Pietro Metastasio's *Alessandro nel-l'Indie*, was performed on 2nd, 6th, 9th, 13th, 16th, 20th, 23rd, 27th February ; 2nd, 6th, 9th, 13th, 16th, 20th, 23rd and 27th March ; and was revived in November 1731. The libretto has, as usual, an English trans-lation added, this time by Samuel Humphreys, the only author named in it. Humphreys, who in 1728 published a poem on Cannons, was now a kind of English secretary to the Opera.

———

CAST OF "PORO", 2nd February 1731

Poro—Signor Senesino, alto
Cleofide—Signora Strada, soprano
Erissena—Signora Merighi, contralto
Gandarte—Signora Bertolli, mezzo-soprano
Alessandro—Signor Fabri, tenor
Timagene—Signor Commano, bass

—

FROM THE "DAILY JOURNAL", 2nd February 1731

For the Benefit of a Gentlewoman lately arriv'd.

At Mr. Hickford's Great Room in Panton-Street, on Thursday the 4th of February, will be perform'd, *A Concert of* MUSICK. In which she'll perform on several Instruments, particularly on the Violin, she having been approv'd by Mr. *Handell*, and will play (besides Corelli's Vivaldi's, &c.) some Pieces of her own Composing. Tickets at 5 sh.

(Chrysander, III. 167.) The name of the performer is not known. Hickford's concert room was near the Haymarket.

—

HANDEL TO HIS BROTHER-IN-LAW, MICHAELSEN, AT HALLE

London den $\frac{23}{12}$ February 1731

Monsieur

et tres Honore Frere.

Deroselben geEhrtestes vom 6 January habe zurecht erhalten, woraus mit mehreren ersehen die Sorgfalt die Derselbe genoṁen meine Seelige Fr. Mutter geziemend und Ihrem lezten Willen gemäss zur Erden zu bestatten. Ich kan nicht umhin allhier meine Thränen fliessen zu lassen. Doch es hat dem Höchsten also gefallen, Dessen heyligen Willen mit Christlicher Gelassenheit mich unterwerffe. Ihr Gedächtniss wird indessen niṁer bey mir erlöschen, biss wier nach diesen Leben wieder vereiniget werden, welches der Grundgütige Gott in Genaden verleyhen wolle.

Die vielfältige *Obligationes* so ich meinem HochgeEhrten HEn Bruder habe vor die beständige Treüe und Sorgfalt womit Derselbe meiner lieben Seeligen Frau Mutter allezeit *assist*iret werde nicht mit Worten allein sondern mit schuldiger Erkäntlichkeit zu bezeügen mir vorbehalten.

Ich verhoffe dass Mhhhl Bruder mein letzteres so in Antwort auff dessen vom 28 *Decembris a.p.* geschrieben, mit den Inlagen an den HEn *Consistorial* Rath Frank und HEn Vetter *Diaconus* Taust wird zu recht erhalten haben. Erwarte also mit Verlangen Dessen HochgeEhrteste Antwort, mit angeschlossener *Notice* wegen der auffgewandten Unkosten, wie auch die gedruckte *Parentation* und Leichen *Carmina*.

Indessen bin sehr verbunden vor das lezt überschickte herrliche *Carmen* welches als ein hochgeschäztes Andenken verwahren werde.

Übrigens *Condolire* von Herzen Mhhhl Bruder und Dessen Hochge-Ehrteste Fr. Liebste wegen des *sensiblen* Verlustes so Sie gehabt durch das Absterben dessen Herrn Schwagers und bin sonderlich durch dessen Christmässige Gelassenheit erbauet. Der Höchste erfülle an uns allen dessen trostreichen Wunsch, in dessen allgewaltigen Schutz meinen HochgeEhrten HEn Bruder mit Dero gesamten liebwehrtesten *Familie* empfehle, und mit aller ersinlicher Ergebenheit verharre

Ew^r HochEdl.

Meines HochgeEhrtesten Herrn Bruders

tres humble et tres obeissant

Serviteur

George Friedrich Händel.

A Monsieur
Monsieur Michael Dietrich Michaëlsen
Conseiller de Guerre de Sa Majesté Prussienne

    a
        Halle
           en Saxe.

(Translation)

London, $\frac{23\text{rd}}{12\text{th}}$ February 1731

Honoured Brother,

I have received your most honoured letter of 6 January in good order, whence in several ways I perceive the carefulness which you took to inter my blessed mother with propriety, and in compliance with her last wishes. Here I cannot restrain my tears. Yet it has pleased the Almighty, to whose Holy Will I submit myself with Christian resignation. Her memory will, however, never become obliterated for me, until, after this life, we are again united, which may the beneficent God grant, in his grace.

The manifold obligations which I owe to my highly respected brother for the continual loyalty and care with which at all times he assisted my dear, blessed mother, I will not declare with words alone but reserve to myself the opportunity of showing my due gratitude.

I hope that my beloved brother will have received in good order my last letter, written in answer to his of 28th December of last year, with the enclosures for Consistorial Councillor Frank and my cousin, *Diaconus* Taust. I await therefore with longing your esteemed answer, with an enclosed *Notice* setting out the defrayed expenses, and also the printed *Parentation* and the Funeral Verses.

Meanwhile I am very obliged for the magnificent poem, lately transmitted, which I shall preserve as a highly treasured memorial.

For the rest I express my heart-felt sympathy to my beloved brother, and to his highly honoured wife, on account of the appreciable loss which you have had through the passing away of your brother-in-law, and I am particularly edified by his Christian composure. May the Almighty fulfil for us all his wishes full of consolation and to His omnipotent care I commend my highly honoured brother and all his beloved family, and with all imaginable devotion I remain,

My highly honoured brother's

tres humble et tres obeissant

Serviteur

George Friedrich Händel.

(Chrysander, II. 229 f.) Original in the autograph collection of Frau Marie Floersheim, Wildegg im Aargau, Switzerland. The paper has black edges and is sealed in black. Reproduced in facsimile in Antoine-E. Cherbuliez, *Georg Friedrich Händel*, Olten (1949), after p. 224. This is one of two letters written to Michaelsen in German. Handel uses his mother-tongue very uncertainly and mixes it with English, French and Latin words. He refers to the funeral of his mother, which he could not attend in time, to certain advance payments for the costs of this, and requests an account for the remainder. Johann Georg Franck was the priest who delivered the funeral sermon ; Johann Georg Taust, probably a grandson of Pastor Georg Taust (see 23rd April 1683), was deacon at the Church of St. Laurence, Halle. The " *Carmen* " might have been Roth's poem addressed to Handel (p. 265). The brother-in-law, referred to at the end, was probably a brother of Michaelsen's third wife. Handel even signs his name in mixed languages. The abbreviation " Mhhhl ", according to Mueller von Asow, means " Mein hochedler, hochgelahrter Herr " (my highly esteemed and learned sir). The letter referred to as previously written by Handel is lost. The promise of gratitude may refer to Handel's intention of making his niece, Michaelsen's daughter by his first wife, heir to his fortune.

———

FROM THE " DAILY COURANT ", 17th February 1731

Last Night their Majesties, together with the Prince of Wales, attended by the Earl of Grantham, the Lords Herbert and Hervey, &c. went to the Theatre in the Haymarket, to see acted the Opera of Porus.

(Harris Collection of cuttings.)

———

FROM THE " DAILY COURANT ", 24th February 1731

Yesterday there was a Rehearsal at St. Paul's, of the Musick that will be performed on Thursday [the 25th] before the Sons of the Clergy, at their annual Meeting, at which there was a great Appearance of Persons of the first Rank and Figure ; and their Collection on that Occasion amounted to above 200*l.*

(Chrysander, II. 271.) Cf. 27th February. This was one of many occasions on which Handel's music was performed for the benefit of charity ; the " Sons of the Clergy ", at St. Paul's Cathedral, were the first to enjoy his help, he being always ready to assist charitable institutions. The " Sons of the Clergy " was an old institution for the education of the sons of needy ministers. In 1709, music was added to the annual sermon at St. Paul's Cathedral, and this was followed by a dinner in Merchant Taylors' Hall. Since 1713 Handel's *Utrecht Te Deum and*

Jubilate had been the regular music for the Feast ; from 1743 onwards it was replaced by the *Dettingen Te Deum* (Schoelcher, p. 59, and Pearce, pp. 234-6). Cf. 17th February 1732. It is said that, from about 1720 to 1743, the overture to *Esther* was performed at St. Paul's on St. Cecilia's Day. It was certainly played as a prelude at the Feast of the " Sons of the Clergy".

FROM THE " CRAFTSMAN ", 27th February 1731

Tuesday [the 23rd] were rehearsed at St. Paul's, for the Festival of the Sons of the Clergy, which was celebrated on Thursday [the 25th], the great Te Deum and Jubilate, composed by Mr. Handel for the publick Thanksgiving upon the Peace of Utrecht, together with the two Anthems made by him for the Coronation of his present Majesty : As they are esteemed by all good Judges some of the grandest Compositions in Church Musick, and were perform'd by a much greater Number of Voices and Instruments than usual upon the like Occasion ; so there was a nobler Audience, and a more generous Contribution to the Charity, than has been known, the Collection amounting to 203*l.* 9s. 6d. which is very near double what has been given in any other Year.

On Thursday at the Feast, at Merchant Taylors Hall, the Collection amounted to 476*l.*

(Chrysander, II. 270 f.) It is not indicated which two of the four Coronation Anthems were performed. " Zadok the Priest " and " My heart is inditing " became very popular. *Read's Weekly Journal* of the same day, 27th February, states that the collection at the rehearsal was £700, instead of *c.* £200. The final figures were given, incorrectly, in the *Gentleman's Magazine* (see next entry).

FROM THE " GENTLEMAN'S MAGAZINE ", February 1731

Thursday, Feb. 25.

. . . . .

An account of the money collected on occasion of the feast of the sons of the clergy held this day.

Collected at the rehearsal	203	9	7
At the choir on feast day	341	6	6
At the hall	480	5	3
	718	11	4

(Chrysander, II. 271.) The *Gentleman's Magazine* was founded in 1731 and edited, until 1754, by Edward Cave. The pound figures should, probably, have read : 203, 134 and 380 ; the shilling figure of the sum 1 instead of 11.

Partenope is performed at Brunswick, February 1731.

This production, in Italian, was frequently revived there. (Chrysander, II. 239 ; Loewenberg, p. 84.) Cf. 1st September 1731.

The " Printing-Office in Bow-Church-Yard ", *i.e.* Cluer's widow, advertises a flute arrangement of the " Favourite Songs in the Opera of Porus ", 1st March 1731. (*Daily Journal* and *Daily Post.*)

———

Walsh advertises " The whole Opera of Porus in Score. . . . Engraven in a fair Character, and carefully corrected ", 2nd March 1731. (*Daily Journal* of 2nd and *Daily Post* of 3rd March.)

The time between the production of a new opera and the publication of the short score was now about a month.

———

FROM THE " DAILY ADVERTISER ", 8th March 1731

We are credibly inform'd, that the celebrated Signiora Cuzzoni, with another famous female Voice from Italy, are daily expected here, in order to perform in a new Opera which will be soon acted, and 'tis to be the last this Season.

(Chrysander, II. 324.) This was a rumour only.

———

FROM THE " DAILY JOURNAL ", 13th March 1731

At the Desire of several Persons of Quality.
For the Benefit of Mr. Rochetti.

At the Theatre-Royal in Lincoln's Inn-Fields, on Friday, being the 26th Day of March, will be presented, A Pastoral, call'd ACIS *and* GALATEA. *Compos'd by Mr. Handel.* Acis by Mr. Rochetti ; Galatea, Mrs. Wright ; Polypheme, Mr. Leveridge ; and the other Parts by Mr. Legar, Mr. Salway, Mrs. Carter, and Mr. Papillion.

(Schoelcher, p. 115 ; Chrysander, II. 264.) This was the first public performance of the work, originally written for Cannons, with an additional poem by John Hughes, and with adaptations from Pope's " Pastorals ", from his translation of Homer's *Iliad*, as well as from Dryden's translation of Ovid's *Metamorphoses* (Streatfeild, 1916, pp. 22 f.). It was planned for the 17th March, but postponed for unknown reasons. The advertisement of 15th March adds : " Coridon, Mr. Legar ; Damon, Mr. Salway ". That of 24th March : "With additional Performances, as will be expressed in the Great Bills ". And finally, on 26th March : " Likewise Mr. Rochetti will sing the Song, Son Confusa Pastorella, being the Favourite Hornpipe in the Opera of Porus ", ending with the words : *Multa Pauca faciunt Unum satis.* It is assumed that the performance had the consent of Handel. While Loewenberg (p. 87) thought that the performance was of sections only, Smith (1948, p. 209) says the work was given complete.

———

CAST OF " ACIS AND GALATEA ", 26th March 1731

Acis—Mr. Philip Rochetti, tenor
Galatea—Mrs. Wright, soprano

Polifemo—Mr. Richard Leveridge, bass
Coridon—Mr. Legar, ?
Damon—Mr. Thomas Salway, tenor

Of the cast of the serenata *Aci, Galatea e Polifemo*, performed in Naples on 16th June 1708, it is known only that Boschi sang the part of Polifemo. Of the masque *Acis and Galatea*, performed at Cannons about 1720, no details of the cast are known, although Boschi was then in London. The English version was now called a pastoral. Later descriptions were : Pastoral Opera, Serenata, Masque, Pastoral Entertainment, Pastoral Oratorio, or Oratorio. Rochetti and Salway sang their parts again at Oxford on 11th July 1733, but Mrs. Wright had to be content on that occasion with a minor part. Nothing is known about Mrs. Carter and Mr. Papillion, who may have sung in the chorus of the 1731 performance. All the singers seem to have been members of the company of Lincoln's Inn Fields Theatre. The part of Coridon was an innovation. This was a solitary performance. See 17th May 1732.

———

FROM COLMAN'S " OPERA REGISTER ", March 1731

March 1731 Porus K. of the Indies—New by Mr. Hendel : it took much son confusa Pastorella &c
Rinaldo—revived, with some alterations
Rodelinda, revived & took much

Although this survey is entered under March, it refers to 2nd February as well as to 6th April and 4th May. For the favourite aria from *Poro*, see 13th March 1731 ; it was provided by Thomas Brerewood junior with English words, " When the fearful Pastorella . . .", and was printed thus as " the bagpipe song in Porus ".

———

FROM THE " DAILY JOURNAL ", 2nd April 1731

At the King's Theatre . . . on Tuesday next, being the 6th Day of April, will be Reviv'd, An Opera, call'd, RINALDO. With New Scenes and Cloaths. . . . Great Preparations being required to bring this Opera on the Stage, is the Reason that no Opera can be perform'd till Tuesday next.

(Schoelcher, p. 103.) Copy in Bodleian Library, Oxford.

———

Rinaldo is revived at the Haymarket Theatre, 6th April 1731.
Produced on 24th February 1711, it was performed until 1714 and revived in 1717. The cast (compared with that of 1711) was as follows :

Goffredo—Signor Fabri, tenor (Signora Boschi)
Almirena—Signora Strada, soprano (Girardeau)
Rinaldo—Signor Senesino, alto (Nicolini)
Eustazio—? (Signor Valentini, alto)
Argante—Signora Bertolli, mezzo-soprano (Signor Boschi)
Armida—Signora Merighi, contralto (Pilotti)
Mago—Signor Commano (Cassani)

The libretto of 1731 was " Revised, with many Additions by the Author [G. Rossi], and newly done into English by Mr. [Samuel] Humphreys ". Repeat performances on 10th, 20th, 24th, 27th April and 1st May 1731.

—

Walsh advertises " The additional Favourite Songs in the Opera call'd Rinaldo ", together with " The whole Opera " ; and three volumes of *Apollo's Feast*, " Containing the most celebrated Songs out of Mr. Handel's, Bononcini's, and Attilio's [Ariosti's] Operas ", *Daily Post*, 21st April 1731.

Among the " additional " songs from *Rinaldo* was " Parolette, vezzi e sguardi ", sung by Signora Strada.

—

FROM THE " DAILY COURANT ", 4th May 1731

At the King's Theatre . . . this present Tuesday . . . will be revived an Opera, call'd RODELINDA. . . .

Repeat performances on 8th, 11th, 15th, 18th, 22nd, 25th and 29th May. The cast of this revival is not recorded, but Signora Bertolli sang the part of Eduigi, created by Signora Dotti in 1725, and Senesino again sang Bertarido. Strada apparently sang Rodelinda (Cuzzoni), Fabri Grimoaldo (Borosini), Signora Merighi Unolfo (Signor Pacini), and Commano Garibaldo (Boschi). Thus the cast can be reconstructed as follows (compared with that of 13th February 1725) :

> Rodelinda—Signora Strada (Cuzzoni)
> Bertarido—Signor Senesino (Senesino)
> Grimoaldo—Signor Fabri (Borosini)
> Eduigi—Signora Bertolli (Dotti)
> Unulfo—Signora Merighi (Signor Pacini)
> Garibaldo—Signor Commano (Boschi)

—

FROM THE " DAILY COURANT ", 22nd May 1731

[Under an advertisement of *Rodelinda*, to be performed on the same day :]

The Undertakers for the Opera have this Day finished the 50 Representations for which they were engaged this Year, but not having been able to compleat the like Number for the last Year, have therefore appointed two more Representations to be performed on Tuesday the 25th and Saturday the 29th Instant, on which Days the several Subscribers for this and the last Year will have Tickets delivered them at the Office gratis, or at the Door.

The two additional performances were of *Rodelinda*. The season ended on 29th May.

—

Handel buys £200 South Sea Annuities (1751), 5th June 1731.

—

HANDEL TO MICHAELSEN, AT HALLE

$$A \text{ Londres ce } \frac{10 \text{ d' Aoust}}{30 \text{ de Juillet}} \; 1731$$

Monsieur
    et tres Hoñoré Frere
    Je vois par la Lettre que Vous m'avez fait l'honneur d'ecrire du 12 Juillet. n.st. en Reponse a ma precedente, et par la specification que Vous y avez jointe, combien de peines Vous avez prises a l'occasion de l'Enterrement de ma tres Chere Mere.
    Je Vous suis d'ailleurs tres obligé des Exemplaires de l'Oraison Funebre que Vous m'avez envoyés et aux quels Vous avez voulu joindre un fait pour feu mon Cher Pere ; Je les attens de Mr Sbüelen.
    Je scaurai apres m'acquitter an partie des obligations que je vous ai.
    En attendant je Vous supplie de fair bien mes Respects et Compliments a Madame Votre Chere Epouse, a ma Chere Filleule, et au reste de Votre chere Famille, et d'etre tres persuadé Vous meme, que je suis avec une passion inviolable
        Monsieur
            et tres Honoré Frere
               Votre
                  tres humble et tres obeissant
                        Serviteur
                      George Frideric Handel.

A Monsieur
Monsieur Michael Michaëlsen
Conseiller de Guerre de Sà Majesté Prussienne
    à
        Halle
en Saxe.

(Translation)

$$\text{London, } \frac{\text{10th August}}{\text{30th July}} \; 1731$$

Honoured Brother,
    From the letter which you did me the honour of writing to me on July 12th (N.S.), in reply to my previous letter, and from the list which you enclosed, I am aware of all that you did on the occasion of the burial of my dear mother.
    Furthermore I am much obliged to you for the copies of the funeral oration which you sent me, and with which you were good enough to include one composed for my late father. I am expecting them from Mr. Sbüelen.

I shall have occasion later to repay in part the obligations under which I stand towards you.

Meanwhile I beg you to convey my respects and compliments to your dear wife, to my beloved god-daughter, and to the rest of your dear family.   Believe me, I am with steadfast devotion,

> Honoured Brother,
> Your
> most humble and obedient
> > servant,
> > George Frideric Handel.

(Chrysander, II. 230 f.)   Sibley Music Library, University of Rochester, N.Y. The words " Je les attens " at the end of the second paragraph were cut out with Handel's signature on the other side of the paper, when a former owner of the letter gave this autograph to the singer, Henriette Hendel-Schütz.   It has recently been possible to restore the letter and it was printed in full by Coopersmith, 1943, pp. 62 f.   Cf. 12th February 1731.   The merchant, Johann Wilhelm Sbüelen, to whose daughter Handel probably referred on 18th March 1704 and whom he mentioned again on 17th August 1736, was apparently his friend and agent in Hamburg. Handel alludes again, it seems, to his niece's expectations.

—

The Devil to pay, or, The Wifes metamorphos'd, a ballad-opera with a Handel Minuet sung as " Bacchus one day gaily striding " (words by Thomas Philips), is produced at Drury Lane Theatre, 6th August 1731.

The text was adapted by Charles Coffey and John Mottley from Thomas Jevon's play *A Devil of a Wife*.   It was later shortened from three acts to one, and was revived first on 19th December 1731 at Goodman's Fields Theatre, and then on 13th April 1733 at Covent Garden.   The Handel song was printed separately.

—

Handel sells £200 South Sea Annuities (1751), 14th August 1731.

—

From the Treasury Minute Book, 17th August 1731

Order for the preparation of a sign manual for issuing to Mr. Haidegger the King's allowance for the benefit of the opera as usual.

Calendar of Treasury Papers, 1731-4, p. 85.

—

From the Order Book of the Treasury, 30th August 1731

	£	s.	d.	
James Heidegger	1,000	0	0	Royal bounty to the
				undertakers of the Opera.

Calendar of Treasury Papers, 1731-4, p. 185.

—

FROM THE DIARY OF VISCOUNT PERCIVAL, 31st August 1731

Mr. Botmor came with Martini, the famous 'hautboy', and dined with me. We talked of the brutality and insolence of certain persons to their superiors, and Botmar told us three instances of it. Bononcini . . . came in the late Queen's time for England, where for a while he reigned supreme over the commonwealth of music, and with justice for he is a very great man in all kinds of composition. At length came the more famous Hendel from Hanover, a man of the vastest genius and skill in music that perhaps has lived since Orpheus. The great variety of manner in his compositions, whether serious or brisk, whether for the Church or the stage or the chamber, and that agreeable mixture of styles that are in his works, that fire and spirit far surpassing his brother musicians, soon gave him the preference over Bononcini with the English. So that after some years' struggle to maintain his throne, Bononcini abdicated. . . .

Egmont MSS., I. 201. Hans Caspar Freiherr von Bothmer was Hanoverian Representative in London (cf. May 1719) and an amateur oboist. Giuseppe San Martini was oboist of the Haymarket orchestra, and a composer. Bononcini left England in June 1731, after a disgraceful affair in the "Academy of Ancient Music", a society which met weekly in the "Crown and Anchor" Tavern ; cf. Schoelcher, pp. 148-55, who quotes extensively from a pamphlet of 1732, *Letters from the Academy of Ancient Music*, etc. Bononcini, however, returned to London in 1732 ; cf. 9th June 1732.

———

Partenope is performed at the Court theatre of Salzthal, the summer residence of Elisabeth Sophie Marie of Brunswick, for the birthday of the Dowager Duchess, 1st (12th) September 1731.

(Chrysander, II. 239.) According to the bilingual libretto, preserved in the Library of Congress, Washington, the performance was in Italian, probably by the Brunswick company who produced the opera in February 1731. Salzthal, or Salzdahlum, was built by Duke Anton Ulrich in 1696 and demolished in 1812. It was situated between Brunswick and Wolfen-büttel. In 1733 Friedrich, Crown Prince of Prussia, married a Brunswick princess there.

———

Handel sells £72 South Sea Annuities (1751), 29th September 1731.

———

FROM THE "DAILY COURANT", 13th November 1731

At the King's Theatre . . . this present Saturday . . . will be per-form'd, An Opera, call'd TAMERLANE. . . . N.B. The Silver Tickets are ready to be deliver'd to Subscribers, or their Orders, on Payment of the Subscription-money, at the Office in the Hay-Market.

This was the beginning of the season. *Tamerlano* was revived for three nights only : 13th, 16th and 20th November. Of the cast of 31st October 1724, only

Senesino, as Andronico, was included. Three singers had left the company :
Signora Merighi, Signori Commano and Fabri.

—

Poro is revived, 23rd November 1731.

Repeat performances on 27th, 30th November and 4th December. The
new libretto, a copy of which is preserved in the Schoelcher collection at
the Conservatoire, Paris, shows " many additions ". Of the original cast
of 2nd February 1731, Senesino as Poro and Strada as Cleofide remained.
Merighi's Erissena was sung by Bertolli, the latter's Gandarte by Campioli,
Fabri's Alessandro by Pinacci, and Commano's Timagene by Montagnana.
The three new singers were : Signor Antonio Gualandi, called Campioli,
contralto ; Signor Giovanni Battista Pinacci, tenor ; and Antonio
Montagnana, bass. Pinacci's wife, Signora Bagnolesi, another contralto,
appeared on 7th December.

—

Handel buys £472 South Sea Annuities (1751), 25th November
1731.

—

Walsh advertises the second edition of his score of the Mask, *Acis
and Galatea*, *Daily Journal*, 27th November 1731.

(Smith, 1948, pp. 211 f.) Cf. 2nd March 1723.

—

Admeto is revived with alterations, 7th December 1731.

The advertisement in the *Daily Courant* says : " Wherein Signora
Bagnoleti [*recte* Bagnolesi], lately arrived from Italy, is to perform ".
Senesino was again Admeto, with Strada, instead of Faustina, as Alceste.
Boschi's part as Ercole must have been sung by Montagnana ; the rest of
the cast is uncertain. Repeat performances on 11th, 14th, 18th December
1731 ; 4th, 8th and 11th January 1732.

—

FROM POPE'S " EPISTLE TO THE RIGHT HONOURABLE RICHARD, EARL
OF BURLINGTON ", PUBLISHED 13th December 1731

. . . And now the Chappel's silver bell you hear,
That summons you to all the Pride of Pray'r :
Light Quirks of Musick, broken and uneven,
Make the Soul dance upon a Jig to Heaven. . . .

(Chrysander, I. 488.) The first edition of this famous Epistle appeared in folio.
The second edition, in octavo, is entitled " Of Taste ", while the third edition has
the subtitle " Of False Taste ", suggested by Hill. It was generally assumed that
" Timon's Villa ", described in the Epistle, meant Cannons ; though the Duke of
Chandos allowed himself to be persuaded by Pope that it was not he who was
depicted as Timon. As for the music in Timon's Chapel, Mainwaring (pp. 188-
190) thought that the lines above alluded to music written for Cannons after

Handel's stay there, while Sherburn suggests that Bononcini's anthems for Blenheim may have been intended. Pope was not musical, but, however improbable it may be that he meant Chandos and Cannons, it seems quite impossible that he could have referred to Handel's Chandos Anthems in this way.

———

FROM THE "DAILY COURANT", 20th December 1731

. . . The same Evening [the 18th] the King and Queen, his Royal Highness the Prince of Wales, and the Three Eldest Princesses, went to the Opera House in the Hay-Market, and saw an Opera called Admetus.

———

The *Daily Post-Boy* of 22nd December 1731 publishes two anonymous letters in defence of Pope, but in a distorted form, printing the second one as a postscript to the first.

Copy in Bodleian Library. Only the second letter refers to Handel. It is reproduced here in the second, corrected, version published the next day, although this differs from the first only in spelling and in the addition of the date.

———

FROM THE "DAILY JOURNAL", 23rd December 1731

The following Letters having been incorrectly printed in a Daily Paper Yesterday, and the one being subjoined to the other as a Postscript from the same Hand, it was thought necessary to reprint them in this Paper correctly and separately, as they should be.

To J. G. Esq ;

.   .   .   .   .

Dec. 19

SIR,

I Really cannot help smiling at the Stupidity, while I lament the slanderous Temper, of the Town. I thought no Mortal singly could claim that Character of *Timon*, any more than any Man pretend to be Sir *John Falstaff*.

But the Application of it to the D. of Ch. is monstrous ; to a Person who in *every Particular* differs from it. . . . Is the *Musick* of his Chapel bad, or *whimsical*, or *jiggish* ? On the contrary, was it not the best composed in the Nation, and most suited to grave Subjects ; witness *Nicol. Haym*'s and Mr. *Handel*'s Noble *Oratories* ? Has it the Pictures of naked Women in it ? And did ever Dean Ch—w—d preach his Courtly Sermons there ? I am sick of such Fool-Applications.

(Sherburn, p. 134.) The first letter, often reprinted, was written by Pope to John Gay. The second letter, first reprinted by Sherburn, may also have been by Pope. "Noble Oratories", apparently, mean Anthems. Haym, better known now as one of Handel's librettists, wrote a Latin oratorio and at least one anthem, but not for Cannons ; he died in 1729. The Dean mentioned at the end may have been the " Knightly Chetwood ", Chaplain to James II, who died in 1720 (Sherburn).

—

AARON HILL TO POPE

Dec. 23, 1731.

Concerning your Epistle. . . . Two or three other likenesses concurred in the character ; such as . . . the pomp of the chapel, and its music ; for whether jiggish or solemn never struck the inquiry of a thousand, who remembers the duke's magnificence chiefly by that circumstance.

(Hill, Works, I. 106 f.) This was in answer to a letter written by Pope to Hill on 22nd December, in which he tried to convince Hill of his real intentions. Pope answered Hill on 5th February 1732, and told him that the Duke of Chandos was satisfied with his explanation.

—

FROM JAMES MILLER'S " HARLEQUIN-HORACE : OR, THE ART OF MODERN POETRY ", 1731

In Days of Old when *Englishmen* were *Men*,
Their Musick like themselves, was grave, and plain . . .
But now, since *Brittains* are become polite,
Since some have learnt to *read*, and some to write . . .
Since *Masquerades* and *Opera*'s made their Entry,
And *Heydegger* and *Handell* rul'd our Gentry ;
A hundred different Instruments combine,
And foreign *Songsters* in the Concert join . . .
In unknown Tongues mysterious Dullness chant,
Make Love in *Tune*, or *thro' the Gamut rant*.

. . . . .

Who'd seek to run such *rugged* Roads as these ?
When *smooth Stupidity*'s the Way to please ;
When gentle *H*—'s Singsongs more delight,
Than all a *Dryden* or a *Pope* can write.

(Chrysander, II. 223 f.) Pp. 28-32 and 36 of the first edition. The pamphlet was published anonymously. In its 1735 edition the " Singsongs " are attributed to " Cary " (Henry Carey), and in the 1741 edition the Heidegger line is altered into : " And Heydegger reign'd Guardian of our Gentry ".

—

Giulio Cesare in Egitto, in Italian but with the text reduced and altered, is performed at the Theatre near the Kärntnertor in Vienna, 1731.

(Loewenberg, p. 77.) The printed libretto does not mention Handel's name ; this, however, was a quite usual omission. There may have been some additional music by other composers.

1732

The opera *Ezio* is produced at the Haymarket Theatre, 15th January 1732.

The text by Pietro Metastasio was translated, for the bilingual libretto, by Samuel Humphreys. There were five performances only : on 15th, 18th, 22nd, 25th and 29th January (Nicoll). The King seems to have attended four of them, the second and the last in company with the Royal family. The newspapers of that month are missing in the Bodleian Library as well as in the British Museum (*Daily Courant, Daily Journal* and *Daily Post*). The overture used for *Ezio* was originally written for *Titus, l'Empereur*, an opera planned by Handel.

CAST OF " EZIO ", 15th January 1732

Valentiniano III—Signora Bagnolesi, contralto
Fulvia—Signora Strada, soprano
Ezio—Signor Senesino, alto
Onoria—Signora Bertolli, mezzo-soprano
Massimo—Signor Pinacci, tenor
Varo—Signor Montagnana, bass

Anna Bagnolesi, Pinacci's wife, sang for the first time in London.

Handel buys £150 South Sea Annuities (1751), 22nd January 1732.

Almira is revived at Hamburg, 27th January (7th February) 1732.

Cf. 8th January 1705. Willers writes in his Hamburg Notes : " zum erstenmahle Almira ", without giving Handel's name (Merbach, p. 364). There were alterations and the score was probably revised by Telemann (Loewenberg, p. 57). Only one repeat performance is recorded by Willers.

FROM THE " DAILY JOURNAL ", 31st January 1732

The Annual Feast of the *Sons* of the *Clergy* will be held at Merchant-Taylors-Hall in Threadneedle-Street on Thursday the 17th of February next.

.   .   .   .   .

Mr. *Handell's* Great Te Deum and Jubilate, with Two of his Anthems, will be vocally and instrumentally perform'd at the Divine Service ; and those Persons who bring Feast Tickets will be admitted into the Choir.

N.B. The Rehearsal of the Great Te Deum, and Jubilate, and Anthems, will be at.St. Paul's Cathedral on Monday the 14th of February next. (Chrysander, II. 271.) Cf. 24th February 1731, and 18th February 1732.

———

FROM COLMAN'S " OPERA REGISTER ", January 1732

In Janry Ezia—a New Opera, Clothes & all ye Scenes New—but did not draw much Company

———

Giulio Cesare is revived on 1st February 1732 ; repeat performances on 5th, 8th and 12th February.

Cf. 17th January 1730. Again, the cast is not known exactly. Senesino sang his original part of Giulio Cesare, and Strada, as in 1730, that of Cleopatra.

———

Handel finishes the opera *Sosarme*, 4th February 1732.

———

The " Printing Office in Bow-Church-Yard " advertises a selected score of *Ezio*, together with the arrangement for the flute, for 2s. 6d., 7th February 1732 (*Daily Courant, Journal* and *Post*).

In 1731 Cluer's widow married Thomas Cobb, who was now the owner of the firm. This unauthorized edition, as well as that published by Walsh shortly after, came too late, since the opera had been buried in its first month.

———

Walsh answers Cobb's advertisement of the 7th in the *Daily Post* of 8th February 1732, promising the " whole " *Ezio* (*Ætius*) for the following week, and adding : " N.B. There is publish'd a spurious Copy of those call'd the Favourite Songs in *Ætius*, with many Faults ; This is to give Notice that all who would have the Favourite Songs in *Ætius*, may have the Originals, finely printed and correct, where the whole Opera is sold."

Walsh did, in fact, issue a selection of songs in addition to the score. What he complained of now was exactly what he had done to Cluer in former years.

———

FROM THE " DAILY JOURNAL " AND THE " DAILY POST ",
14th February 1732

This Day publish'd,
The Whole Opera of Ætius in Score.

.   .   .   .   .   .

Printed for, and sold by John Walsh. . . .
Where may be had the following Pieces of Musick compos'd by Mr. Handel.

1. The whole Operas of Porus, Parthenope, Flavius, Otho, Floridante, and Rinaldo, in Score.
2. The Mask of Acis and Galatea.
3. Apollo's Feast, 3 Vol. containing the most celebrated Songs out of all the late Operas.
4. Twenty-four Overtures for Violins, &c. in eight Parts ; also the same Overtures curiously set for the Harpsichord.
5. Six celebrated Songs for French Horns, &c. in seven Parts.
6. The most celebrated Airs in the Operas of Porus and Parthenope for the German Flute, Vol. 2. Part 1 and 2. Also seven Collections of Opera Airs for a German Flute, Violin or Harpsichord, Vol. 1.
7. Seventy-two Minuets and Marches for a German Flute and a Bass.
8. A compleat Set of all the Operas transpos'd for the Flute, in 2 Vol. 4to.

(Chrysander, II. 250.)   It can be seen from this first collective advertisement of Handel works printed by Walsh that he now specialized as Handel's publisher.

———

Poro is performed at Hamburg, 14th (25th) February 1732.

(Chrysander, II. 247 ; Loewenberg, p. 85.)   The text was translated into German, the arias were sung in Italian, with German recitatives by Telemann.   The translation by Wend(t) was entitled *Triumph der Grossmuth und Treue, oder Cleofida, Königin von Indien.*   According to Willers' Hamburg Notes (Merbach, p. 364) the opera was performed from 1731 to 1736, twenty-seven times in all.   If his entries are correct, the title *Porus* was used for one or two performances before the name of *Cleofida* was introduced.   The librettos of 1731 as well as of 1736 have the full title as quoted above.   On 29th June (10th July) 1736, the second performance of that year and a special occasion, it was intended to add a prologue, but its recitation was prohibited.

———

FROM CHRISTIAN GOTTLIEB WENDT'S PREFACE TO HIS TRANS-
LATION OF THE TEXT OF " PORO ", PERFORMED AT HAMBURG,
14th (25th) February 1732 (Translated)

To demonstrate how worth seeing and hearing this same [opera] is, I hope it will be sufficient merely for me to recall that last year it was performed not only in London, with quite uncommonly large audiences, to the music of Hendel (which composition will also be heard in this town, and which is one of the most powerful even of this famous virtuoso's excellent works) under the name of ' Porus ' ; but also at Dresden on the express command of His Royal Majesty of Poland, set to music by the Capellmeister Hasse (altered somewhat in the literal and circumstantial, but not essential, structure, and more diffuse) under the name ' Cleofida ' : This latter *Rubric* has, however, been deliberately retained, so that prematurely scornful people might not, immediately on catching sight of the title-page, hastily rush out, with the reproach that one was presenting them with something old and warmed up ; for already, a good many years ago, a piece also called ' Porus ' has been seen here, but which bears not the slightest relationship to the present one. . . . I need not announce that our Herr Telemann has set to music the German recitatives.

(Chrysander, II. 247.) Johann Adolph Hasse, who married Faustina in Venice in 1730, went with her in 1731 to the Court of August II in Dresden.

———

FROM THE " DAILY COURANT ", 15th February 1732

At the King's Theatre . . . this present Tuesday . . . will be perform'd, A New Opera, call'd, SOSARMES. . . .

Sosarme, rè di Media, the text altered from Matteo Noris's *Alfonso Primo* (Loewenberg, p. 87). Handel's original title was *Fernando, rè di Castiglia*, but after finishing Acts I and II, he altered the cast and the title (Squire, 1927, p. 83). Repeat performances on 19th, 22nd, 26th, 29th February ; 4th 7th, 11th, 14th, 18th and 21st March ; revived in spring 1734. Burney, IV. 356, wrongly lists a performance on 19th February 1732. The English version of the bilingual libretto is again by Samuel Humphreys.

———

CAST OF " SOSARME ", 15th February 1732

Sosarme—Signor Senesino, alto
Haliate—Signor Pinacci, tenor
Erenice—Signora Bagnolesi, contralto
Elmira—Signora Strada, soprano
Argone—Signor Campioli, alto
Melo—Signora Bertolli, mezzo-soprano
Altomaro—Signor Montagnana, bass

———

Handel sells £50 South Sea Annuities (1751), 17th February 1732.

———

FROM THE " DAILY COURANT ", 18th February 1732

Yesterday was held the Annual Feast of the Sons of the Clergy, when Mr. Handell's *Te Deum* and *Jubilate*, compos'd for the Publick Thanksgiving for the Peace of Utrecht, together with the two Anthems made by him, one for his late Majesty, and the other for his present Majesty on his Coronation, were perform'd before a numerous and splendid Audience at St. Paul's Cathedral ; and the Rev. Dr. [Richard] Warren preached an excellent Sermon. The Collection at the Church Doors on that Occasion amounted to 76*l*. Afterwards they returned to

Merchant Taylors Hall to Dinner ; after which a very handsome Collection was made at the Basons [*i.e.* Basins].

For the Anthem written for George I, see 11th January 1724 ; the other was one of the four Coronation Anthems of 1727. For the collections, see *Gentleman's Magazine*, February 1732.

———

From Viscount Percival's Diary, 22nd February 1732

I went to the Opera Sosarmis, made by Hendel, which takes with the town, and that justly, for it is one of the best I ever heard.

(Flower, p. 212.) Egmont MSS., I. 224. Benjamin Rand, in his [*George*] *Berkeley and Percival*, Cambridge, 1914, p. 280, quotes the opera wrongly as *Susanna*.

———

Esther is performed privately at the " Crown and Anchor " Tavern in the Strand, 23rd February 1732.

This was the new title of the masque *Haman and Mordecai*, originally written for Cannons (cf. 29th August 1720). Since the chorus was provided by the Children and Gentlemen of the Chapel Royal, it was assumed that the production on the 23rd was just a rehearsal at the house (St. James's Street, Westminster) of their master, Bernard Gates. This is disproved by Viscount Percival's diary note of the same day. A manuscript copy of the score, sold by Messrs. Ellis about 1940 and quoted by Smith (1948, p. 126), gives the following details, which are almost identical with a note in the printed libretto : " Mr. Bernard Yates, Master of the Children of the Chapel Royal, together with a number of voices from the Choirs of the Chapel Royal and Westminster, join'd in Chorus's after the manner of the Ancients, being placed between the stage and the Orchestra ; and the Instrumental parts (two or three particular instruments, necessary on the Occasion Excepted) were perform'd by the members of the Philarmonic Society consisting only of Gentlemen ; at the ' Crown and Anchor ' Tavern in the Strand

    on Wednesday 23d of February 1731 ⎱ for the Philarmonic
    and Wednesday 1 of March 1731   ⎰ Society.
    and on Friday 3d of March 1731 for the Academy."

(At this time of the year, 1731 means 1732.) The Philarmonic Society, sometimes called Club, subscribed for Handel scores in 1725-7 and 1738-1740 : they met on Wednesdays. It was also called the " Society of the Gentlemen Performers of Musick ". In addition to Percival and Bothmer, Chandos had recently been admitted to the club, and he suggested that William Defesch's new oratorio *Judith* be performed there (Baker, p. 91). The Academy of Ancient Music, which met on other days at the same place, was a club of professionals. It is related that Handel attended one of these performances of *Esther* ; this was probably on the first night, his forty-seventh birthday. Cf. 20th April 1732.

———

Presumed Cast of " Esther ", 23rd February 1732
        Esther—Master John Randall
        Ahasuerus—Mr. James Butler

Haman—Mr. John Moore
Habdonah—Mr. Price Clevely
Persian Officer—Mr. James Allen
Israelites and Officers—Mr. Samuel Howard, Masters Thomas Barrow and
Robert Denham

Burney (1785, part 1, p. 22) gives the names of Randall, Beard and Barrow among the child performers ; they were all alive at the time of his writing. He also mentions Moore and Denham. Randall became organist of King's College and Professor of Music in Cambridge ; Howard was an organist and composer ; Barrow, leader of the altos in Handel's oratorios, was one of the singers in the *Messiah* performances at the Foundling Hospital in 1754 and 1759 ; Denham sang in 1755 at the Three Choirs Meeting in Worcester.

———

FROM VISCOUNT PERCIVAL'S DIARY, 23rd February 1732

From dinner I went to the Music Club, where the King's Chapel boys acted the *History of Hester*, writ by Pope, and composed by Hendel. This oratoria or religious opera is exceeding fine, and the company were highly pleased, some of the parts being well performed.

Egmont MSS., I. 225. (Flower, pp. 213 f., thought that this entry referred to the second performance, and that the music club met in St. James's Street, Westminster, *i.e.* at Gates's house.) Although Percival misspelt the word, the oratorio produced on that day was the beginning of a new and decisive period in Handel's artistic life.

———

FROM COLMAN'S " OPERA REGISTER ", February 1732

In Febry Sosarmes—a New Opera—took much by Hendell—& was for many Nights much crowded to some peoples admiration—

———

FROM THE " GENTLEMAN'S MAGAZINE ", February 1732

Thursday, Feb. 17.

.   .   .   .   .

Was held at *Merchant Taylor's Hall* the annual Feast of the Sons of the Clergy ; after a Sermon and the usual Musick at St. *Paul*'s. The Collections on this Occasion amounted to 1080*l.* 5s. Last Year but to 718*l.* 11s. 4d.

Cf. February 1731 and 18th February 1732.

———

Admeto is revived at Brunswick, February 1732.
(Chrysander, II. 157 ; Loewenberg, p. 81.) Cf. August 1729.

———

At Drury Lane Theatre Ben Jonson's comedy *The Alchemist* is revived, with music by Handel and other composers, 7th March 1732.

(Schoelcher, p. 119.) There may be some doubt whether the music in question was used for this revival, or for the next, on 20th December 1733, at the Little, then called the New, Theatre in the Haymarket. The advertisement in the *Daily Journal* for this later revival speaks of " select Pieces of Musick, compos'd by Sig. Corelli, Sig. Vivaldi, Sig. Geminiani and Mr. Handel, and Entertainments of Dancing ". And of yet another revival, at Drury Lane on 26th March 1739, the *London Daily Post* announces " Select Pieces of Musick. With Entertainments of Singing and Dancing ". There were, however, two publications by Walsh of the *Alchemist* music which can be dated as of 1732 and 1733, *i.e.* before the two later revivals. The one is *Tunes in the Alchemist for two Violins and a Bass*, advertised in various Walsh publications, a copy of which is in Mr. Gilbert S. Inglefield's collection (see 31st October 1734). The other is an edition of six songs in seven parts from *The Alchemist*, with Walsh's publisher's number 385, which indicates the year 1733. While these songs were identified by Julian Marshall as from *Giulio Cesare, Poro, Partenope, Admeto, Rinaldo* and *Riccardo Primo*, the dances were disclosed by Rolphino Lacy as being mainly from *Rodrigo*, composed in 1707 or 1708 for Florence. This proves that the arrangement was made with Handel's knowledge, because at that time nothing from *Rodrigo* had been printed. Handel's incidental music to *The Alchemist* was first printed in score by Samuel Arnold, in his Handel edition, vol. 17 (*c.* 1790), and then by Chrysander, in the Collected Edition, vol. 56.

————

Walsh advertises the " Favourite Songs ", with the " Overture in Score ", of *Sosarme* for 2s. 6d., *Daily Journal*, 11th March 1732.

Cf. 29th April 1732. This time, Walsh succeeded in forestalling competition from Cluer-Cobb ; the Printing Office did not publish anything from *Sosarme*.

————

After the successful run of Handel's *Sosarme*, Ariosti's *Coriolano* (1723) is revived at the Haymarket Theatre, 25th March 1732.

————

FROM JOHANN GOTTFRIED WALTHER'S " MUSICALISCHES LEXICON ", LEIPZIG, 1732 (Translated)

Hendel (Georg Friedrich) or Händel, a now highly renowned Capellmeister, residing in England, a native of Halle in Magdeburg, and *scholar* of the late Zachau about the year 1694, was born on 23rd February 1685. Of his compositions the following operas have been performed at the Hamburg *Theatrum* : 1704, *Almira* ; 1705, *Nero* ; 1708, *Florindo* and *Daphne* ; 1715, *Rinaldo* ; 1717, *Oriana* ; 1718, *Agrippina* ; 1722, *Zenobia* ; 1723, *Muzio Scevola* and *Floridantes* ; 1725, *Tamerlan* and *Julius Caesar* in Egypt ; and 1726, *Otto*, King of Germany. See the ' Musicalische Patriot ' of Capellmeister *Mattheson*, in the 23rd and 24th accounts. In the year 1720, 8 *Suites de Pièces pour le Clavecin* of his composition were engraved in London in 4to *oblongo.* See *Matthesonii Crit. Mus.* Part I, p. 45. More about him is to be expected in Herr Mattheson's musical ' Ehren-Pforte '.

P. 309. Walther's book was the first German dictionary of music, and the first of all such dictionaries with biographies of musicians. The preface is dated 16th February 1732. Mattheson's *Grundlage einer Ehren-Pforte* did not appear until 1740.

————

FROM VISCOUNT PERCIVAL'S DIARY, 17th April 1732

I carried him [my son] and my daughters to the rehearsal of the Opera of *Flavius.*

Egmont MSS., I. 257. From the entry in the diary, it seems that the final rehearsal of *Flavio* was held at midday.

————

Flavio is revived at the Haymarket Theatre, 18th April 1732.

Cf. 14th May 1723. Of the original cast, only Senesino sang, in the part of Guido. Strada sang Emila and Montagnana sang Lotario, the parts originally taken by Cuzzoni and Boschi, while Signora Bertolli and Signor Pinacci probably sang Durastanti's and Gordon's original parts of Vitige and Ugone. How the two contraltos, Signorine Bagnolesi and Campioli were employed in the parts of Flavio (Signor Berenstadt) and Teodata (Mrs. Robinson) is uncertain. *Flavio* was performed on 18th, 22nd, 25th and 29th April.

————

FROM THE " DAILY JOURNAL ", 19th April 1732

Never Perform'd in Publick before,

At the Great Room in Villars-street York Buildings, To-morrow, being Thursday the 20th of this Instant April, will be perform'd, ESTHER an ORATORIO *or, Sacred Drama.* As it was compos'd originally for the most noble James Duke of Chandos, the Words by Mr. *Pope,* and the Musick by Mr. *Handel.* Tickets to be had at the Place of Performance at 5s. each. To begin exactly at 7 o'Clock.

The earlier advertisements give the name of George Frederick Handel only, without distinguishing between words and music. The advertisement was repeated on the 20th. For the concert-room, cf. 26th December 1711 ; this, however, was not the end of this concert-room, as Hill's nephew hired it for an amateur performance in June 1735 (Brewster, p. 141). Cf. 23rd February 1732. The cast of this unauthorized performance is not known.

————

FROM THE SAME

By His MAJESTY'S *Command.*

At the King's Theatre in the Hay-Market, on Tuesday the 2d Day of May, will be performed, *The Sacred Story* of ESTHER : an *Oratorio* in

English. Formerly composed by Mr. *Handel,* and now revised by him, with several Additions, and to be performed by a great Number of the best Voices and Instruments.

N.B. There will be no Action on the Stage, but the House will be fitted up in a decent Manner, for the Audience. The Musick to be disposed after the Manner of the Coronation Service.

Tickets to be delivered at the Office of the Opera house, at the usual Prices.

This advertisement was inserted in answer to several which announced the performance for 20th April. It was Handel's own performance, carefully designed to meet competition. It is usually assumed that Handel confined the performance to the concert style under compulsion : according to Burney, the Bishop of London, still Gibson, opposed the idea of a " sacred story " performed on the stage. There is no proof for this tradition. For the Coronation Service see 11th October 1727.

———

T. Wood announces the libretto of *Esther* for 2nd May 1732 (*Daily Journal*, 25th April).

The libretto calls the work " an Oratorio : or, Sacred Drama ", as did the advertisements of the unauthorized performance on 20th April, but it follows the wording of the official production on 2nd May in the description : " The Musick formerly Composed by Mr. Handel, and now Revised by him, with severall Additions ", supplementing it with the note : " The Additional Words by Mr. [Samuel] Humphreys ".

———

Walsh advertises " A Second Collection of the most Favourite Songs in . . . Sosarmes ", *Daily Post*, 29th April 1732.

Cf. 11th March 1732.

———

From the " Daily Courant ", 2nd May 1732

By His Majesty's Command.

At the King's Theatre . . . this present Tuesday . . . will be perform'd Esther, an Oratorio, In English. Formerly composed by Mr. *Handel,* and now revised by him, with several Additions, and to be performed by a great Number of the best Voices and Instruments.

To begin at Seven o'Clock.

The advertisement in the *Daily Journal* speaks of " The Sacred Story of Esther : an Oratorio in English ". Repeat performances on 6th, 9th, 13th, 16th and 20th May. Spring revivals in 1733, 1735, 1736, 1737 and 1740.

———

H.–10

CAST OF " ESTHER ", 2nd May 1732

Ahasuerus—Signor Senesino, alto
Haman—Signor Montagnana, bass
Habdonah—Mr. Lowe, tenor
Esther—Signora Strada, soprano
Mordecai—Signora Bertolli, mezzo-soprano
Israelite Woman—Mrs. Davis (soprano)
Three Israelites—Mrs. Turner Robinson (soprano),
Signora Bertolli, and Mr. Lowe (tenor)

The three English singers were co-opted into the Italian company. Thomas Lowe became a regular singer in Handel's oratorios. Mrs. Ann Turner was married to John Robinson, now organist at Westminster Abbey ; their daughter became a contralto singer. Mrs. Davis sang in Handel oratorios in 1732 only ; cf. 10th June 1732, 13th November 1742 and 10th May 1745.

———

FROM THE " DAILY POST ", 2nd May 1732

We hear that the Proprietors of the English Opera will very shortly perform a celebrated Pastoral Opera call'd Acis and Galatea, compos'd by Mr. Handel, with all the Grand Chorus's and other Decorations, as it was perform'd before his Grace the Duke of Chandos at Cannons, and that it is now in Rehearsal.

A similar note appeared in the *Daily Journal* of 3rd May. It refers to a perform-ance at the New (formerly the Little) Theatre in the Haymarket, planned for the 11th but postponed until the 17th May. The words " Scenes, Machines " after " Chorus's " were omitted from this advertisement by mistake. Since 13th March 1732, a company led by Thomas Arne senior had been producing " English Operas " at the New Theatre. They opened with J. F. Lampe's *Amelia* ; this was followed in the autumn of 1732 by the same composer's *Britannia* (see 15th November) and in the spring of 1733 by Thomas Augustine Arne's *Opera of Operas*, a burlesque. Arne junior was the conductor ; Lampe and Henry Carey were associates of the Arnes. (Smith, 1948, pp. 212-14.) This production of *Acis and Galatea* was not sanctioned by Handel.

———

FROM VISCOUNT PERCIVAL'S DIARY, 2nd May 1732

I went to the Opera House to hear Hendel's " oratory ", composed in the Church style.

Egmont MSS., I. 266.

———

FROM THE " DAILY COURANT ", 3rd May 1732

Last Night their Majesties, his Royal Highness the Prince of Wales and the Three Eldest Princesses went to the Opera House in the Hay Market and saw a Performance called, (*Esther, an Oratorio*).

The Court also attended the performances on 6th, 13th and 20th May.

———

From the " Daily Courant ", 4th May 1732

.   .   .   .   .

Notice is hereby given, that if there are any Tickets which could not
be made Use of on Tuesday last [the 2nd], the Money will either be
returned for the same on sending them to the Office in the Haymarket
next Saturday [the 6th], or they will be exchanged for other Tickets for
that Day.

There were apparently too many tickets sold for the first performance of *Esther*.

———

From the " Daily Post ", 6th May 1732

At the New Theatre in the Hay-market, on Thursday next, being the
11th day of May, will be perform'd in English, a Pastoral Opera, call'd
Acis and Galatea. Composed by Mr. Handel. With all the Grand
Chorus's, Scenes, Machines, and other Decorations ; being the first Time
it ever was performed in a Theatrical Way.

The Part of Acis by Mr. Mountier, being the first Time of his appearing
in Character on any Stage ; Galatea, Miss Arne.

(Smith, 1948, p. 214.) The same advertisement, repeated during the following
days, was printed in the *Daily Journal*. Mountier, who in 1733 sang the part of
Adelberto in *Ottone*, transposed from bass to tenor, and whom Burney called " the
Chichester Boy " (from the Cathedral), was probably Thomas Mountier, who in
1740 was admitted to the Society of Musicians. Susanna Maria Arne, sister of
Thomas Augustine Arne, was a mezzo-soprano ; she was later married to Theophilus Cibber and became better known as Mrs. Cibber.

———

From Viscount Percival's Diary, 6th May 1732

In the evening [I] went to Hendel's oratorio. The Royal Family was
there, and the house crowded.

Egmont MSS., I. 271. This entry refers to *Esther* in the opera house. It should
be noted that Percival had learned to spell the uncommon term, oratorio.

———

From the " Daily Post ", 11th May 1732

At the New Theatre in the Hay-market, on Wednesday next, being
the 17th May . . . Acis and Galatea.

N.B. The Opera is obliged to be put off to Wednesday the 17th following, it being impossible to get ready the Decorations before that Time.

———

Handel buys £700 South Sea Annuities (1751), 11th May 1732.

———

FROM THE " DAILY COURANT ", 15th May 1732

The same Evening [Saturday, the 13th] their Majesties, his Royal Highness the Prince of Wales, and the Three Eldest Princesses, went to the Opera-House in the Hay-Market, and saw an Entertainment call'd ESTHER, an *Oratorio*, in English.

———

FROM THE " DAILY POST ", 17th May 1732

At the New Theatre in the Hay-market, this present Wednesday . . . will be perform'd in English, a Pastoral Opera, call'd ACIS and GALATEA. Composed by Mr. HANDEL. . . . Pit and Boxes to be laid together at 5s. Gallery 2s 6d. . . . To begin exactly at Seven o'Clock. . . .

(Smith, 1948, p. 213.) Cf. 13th and 26th March 1731. There was one other performance, on the 19th. A word-book (without Gay's name) was printed for this short-lived production, which was conducted by the younger Arne. The cast was : Mountier as Acis, Miss Arne as Galatea, Mr. Gustavus Waltz (supposed to have been Handel's cook) as Polifemo and Mrs. Susanna Mason as Damon ; there was also a " Chorus of Shepherds and Shepherdesses ". Other singers in the English Opera Company were Miss Cecilia Young, later married to T. A. Arne, Mr. Kelly and Mr. Snider.

———

FROM THE " DAILY COURANT ", 22nd May 1732

On Saturday [the 20th] in the Evening their Majesties, his Royal Highness the Prince of Wales, and the Three Eldest Princesses, went to the Opera-House in the Hay-Market, and saw an Entertainment of Musick call'd ESTHER, an *Oratorio*.

———

FROM COLMAN'S " OPERA REGISTER ", 23rd May 1732

May ye 23 Lucius Papirius a New Opera Handell it did not take

(Chrysander, II. 252.) *Lucio Papirio Dittatore*, text by Apostolo Zeno, the music probably that by Antonio Caldara, produced at Vienna in 1719. The name of Handel was inserted in the diary later, perhaps because he wrote the recitatives. The opera was performed four times only.

———

FROM COLMAN'S " OPERA REGISTER ", 29th May 1732

May 29 Hester Oratorio or sacred Drama, english all ye Opera singers in a sort Gallery no acting was performed six times & very full

This entry refers to the performances of *Esther* between 2nd and 20th May. The description of the oratorio is taken from the word-book. The placing of the singers and musicians corresponded to that in the Coronation Service of 1727.

———

Walsh advertises *Sosarme* for a German Flute and Bass ; also for a single Flute, *Daily Post*, 31st May 1732.

In the *Craftsman* of 10th June : " for a common Flute ".

FROM THE " LONDON MAGAZINE : OR, GENTLEMAN'S MONTHLY INTELLIGENCER ", May 1732

ESTHER : An ORATORIO ; or SACRED DRAMA. As it is now acted at the Theatre-Royal in the *Hay-Market* with vast Applause. The Musick being composed by the Great Mr. *Handel.*

[Here follows the full text, anonymously and not in its latest version.]

. . . . .

Monthly Catalogue of Books.

. . . . .

Acis and Galatea : An English Pastoral Opera. In three Acts. Set to Musick by Mr. Handel. Sold by J. Roberts. Price 6d.

Pp. 85 f. and 107. To style the King's Theatre as the Theatre-Royal was wrong. The text of *Esther* was that used on 20th April, without Handel's additions for his own performance on 2nd May 1732. The *Acis* word-book was that published by J. Watts on 11th May for the production on 17th May 1732.

FROM THE " DAILY COURANT ", 5th June 1732

At the King's Theatre . . . on Saturday next [the 10th] will be performed a Serenata call'd, ACIS and GALATEA. Formerly composed by Mr. *Handell*, and now revised by him, with several Additions ; and to be performed by a great Number of the best Voices and Instruments.

There will be no Action on the Stage, but the Scene will represent, in a Picturesque Manner, a rural Prospect, with Rocks, Groves, Fountains and Grotto's ; amongst which will be disposed a Chorus of Nymphs and Shepherds, Habits, and every other Decoration suited to the Subject.

The same advertisement appeared in the *Daily Journal.* Cf. 26th March 1731 and 17th May 1732. Handel's new version was a mixture of the Italian and the English ones. Several airs from the Neapolitan serenata (1708) and the Cannons masque (1719 ?), as well as three choruses, were interpolated in this bilingual version. (Cf. Smith, 1948, p. 217.)

Jonathan Tyers opens Vauxhall Gardens, 7th June 1732.

Cf. 15th April till 2nd May 1738.

FROM THE " DAILY POST ", 9th June 1732

Whereas Signor Bononcini intends after the Serenata composed by Mr. Handel has been performed, to have one of his own at the Opera-house, and has desired Signora Strada to sing in that Entertainment.

Aurelio del Po, Husband of the said Signora Strada, thinks it incumbent on him to acquaint the Nobility and Gentry, that he shall ever think himself happy in every opportunity wherein he can have the Honour to contribute to their Satisfaction ; but with respect to this particular Request of Signor Bononcini, he hopes he shall be permitted to decline complying with it, for Reasons best known to the said Aurelio del Po and his Wife ; and therefore the said Aurelio del Po flatters himself that the Nobility and Gentry will esteem this a sufficient Cause for his Noncompliance with Signor Bononcini's Desire ; and likewise judge it to be a proper Answer to whatever the Enemies of the said Aurelio del Po may object against him or his Wife upon this Occasion.

This public notice was reprinted in the *Gentleman's Magazine* of August 1732, together with the anonymous letter published in the *Craftsman* of 12th August 1732 (Schoelcher, p. 118). Bononcini's concert was, in fact, given, as " a pastoral entertainment " not as a " serenata ", at the end of the season, on 24th June, " by command of . . . Queen Caroline ", who was Regent in the King's absence ; she and three of the Princesses attended the evening (Burney, IV. 362 ; Kelly, II. 354). Nothing is known of Strada's husband ; Burney (IV. 426) states that in 1737-8 Aurelio del Po threatened Handel with arrest " for the arrears of her salary ". While this cannot be checked, the fact that Strada, alone of all his singers, stayed with Handel during his financial difficulties, is proved by events.

———

FROM THE " DAILY COURANT ", 10th June 1732

At the *King's Theatre* . . . this present Saturday . . . will be perform'd, A Serenata, call'd Acis and GALATEA. . . . To begin at 7 o'Clock. N.B. The full Number of Opera's agreed for in the Subscription being completed, the Silver Tickets will not be admitted, but only the Subscribers themselves in Person.

The same advertisement appeared in the *Daily Journal*. The wording is otherwise identical with that of 5th June. Repeat performances on 13th, 17th and 20th June. Cf. 5th December 1732. T. Wood published the word-book, again without Gay's name. See 17th May 1732.

———

CAST OF " ACIS AND GALATEA ", 10th June 1732

Acis—Signor Senesino, alto
Galatea—Signora Strada, soprano
Clori—Mrs. Robinson, soprano
Polifemo—Signor Montagnana, bass
Silvio—Signor Pinacci, tenor
Filli—Signora Bagnolesi, contralto
Dorinda—Signora Bertolli, mezzo-soprano
Eurilla—Mrs. Davis, soprano
Damon—Signor Campioli, alto

———

FROM VISCOUNT PERCIVAL'S DIARY, 20th June 1732

I went in the evening to the Opera House to hear the fine masque of *Acis and Galatea*, composed by Hendel.

Egmont MSS., I. 281. The Court was present at this, the last, performance of the season ; it was followed only by Bononcini's entertainment on the 24th.

———

Handel sells £1400 and £1000 South Sea Annuities (1751), 22nd June 1732.

———

Handel deposits £2300, 2nd August 1732.

———

FROM THE " CRAFTSMAN ", 12th August 1732

[Anonymous letter to the editor.]

. . . This brought me up, last Week, upon a Friend's having written me Word that some Musick of *Bononcini* was to be perform'd at the *Opera House*, of which He knew I was a great Admirer ; but being very much disappointed at the Performance, I went afterwards to pass the Evening with some of my Acquaintance, who were Lovers of *Musick* as well as my self, in order to get some Information about it . . . several Stories were told for and against the *two late famous Antagonists*. . . . At last, one of the Company had the Curiosity to ask what might have been the Occasion that the *Serenata* was not continued ; to which another made Answer that it fell out chiefly by the Means of *Strada's Husband*, who would not suffer his Wife to sing in it ; upon which He took out of his Pocket the *Daily Post* of *June* 9, and read an *Advertisement*, which *that Gentleman* had caus'd to be inserted there, in the following remarkable Style : [Here follows the advertisement quoted under that date.]

(Schoelcher, p. 118.) The rest of the letter, quoted by Schoelcher, is political farce.

———

FROM THE TREASURY MINUTE BOOK, 15th August 1732

Order for a sign manual for the issue of 1,000*l.* to the Music Academy as His Majesty's bounty for the opera the last season.

Calendar of Treasury Papers, 1731–4, p. 249. It is noteworthy that the enter-prise at the Haymarket Theatre was still called the Royal Academy of Music (see next entry).

———

FROM THE KING'S WARRANT BOOK, 15th August 1732

	£	s.	d.	
Royal Academy of Music	1,000	0	0	Royal bounty to the undertakers of the Opera.

Calendar of Treasury Papers, 1731–4, p. 340.

———

Poro is performed, in Italian, at the summer fair in Brunswick, August 1732.

(Chrysander, II. 247.) Copies of the libretto in the Hanover library and archives.

———

Partenope is performed at Wolfenbüttel on Emperor Karl VI's birthday, 20th September (1st October) 1732.

(Chrysander, II. 239.) Cf. 1st September 1731.

———

LORD HERVEY TO CHARLES, DUKE OF RICHMOND

St. James's, Oct. 31 : 1732.

I am going to Lady Pembroke's to hear the new Opera-Woman, Celestina ; the Operas begin on Saturday [4th November].

(March, p. 222 ; *Hervey and His Friends*, p. 145.) For Mary, Countess Pembroke, see Spring 1727. Signora Celeste Gismondi, otherwise Mrs. Hempson, called Celestina, was a mezzo-soprano, newly engaged by Handel. She sang for him in 1732 and 1733, remained in London till 1734, and died there in 1735.

———

The opera season opens on 4th November 1732 with *Catone in Utica*, text by Pietro Metastasio, the music probably by Leonardo Leo.

(Kelly, II. 354 ; Chrysander, II. 252.) Handel is supposed to have heard Leo's opera in Venice in 1729.

———

LORD HERVEY TO STEPHEN FOX

St. James's, November 4th, 1732.

I am just come from a long, dull, and consequently tiresome Opera of Handel's, whose genius seems quite exhausted. The bride's recommendation of being the first night, could not make this supportable. The only thing I liked in it was our Naples acquaintance, Celestina ; who is not so pretty as she was, but sings better than she did. She seemed to take mightily, which I was glad of. I have a sort of friendship for her, without knowing why. Tout chose que me fait resouvenir ce temps m'attendrit ; et je suis sur que ce soir à l'Opera j'ai soupiré cent fois.

(*Hervey and His Friends*, pp. 145 f.) If the date, 4th November, is correct, Hervey was wrong in assuming that the new opera was by Handel. Since he speaks of a first night and Kelly (II. 354) testifies that Celeste Gismondi appeared first in *Catone* on 4th November, it seems that Hervey made a mistake. (Cf. 15th November 1732.) He and Fox had been in Italy at the beginning of 1729, and might have met Handel there.

———

FROM THE "DAILY POST", 15th November 1732

We hear that yesterday there was a Rehearsal of the English Opera, "Britannia", at the New Theatre in the Haymarket. The Musick (set by Mr. Lampe) gave great Satisfaction to the Audience. . . . Miss Caecilia Young was particularly admired, which gave Occasion to the following Lines, alluding to the famous St. Caecilia :

"No more shall Italy its Warblers send
    To charm our Ears with Handel's heav'nly Strains ;
For dumb his rapt'rous [1] Lyre, their Fame must end.
    And hark ! Caecilia ! from the Ætherial Plains,
Her Sounds once call'd a Seraph from the Skies ;
    To sing like Accents see ! she hither flies."

(Smith, 1948, p. 174.) *Britannia*, text by Thomas Lediard, was produced on 16th November. There seems to have been a rumour that *Catone*, produced anonymously, was Handel's work ; see 4th November.

Judith, a pasticcio-opera, is produced at Hamburg, 16th (27th) November 1732.

(Loewenberg, pp. 64 and 84.) *Judith, Gemahlin Kayser Ludewigs des Frommen ; oder Die siegende Unschuld*, text translated by Johann Georg Hamann from Francesco Silvani's *L'Innocenza giustificata*, music by Fortunato Chelleri (1711), augmented by three Italian airs from Handel's *Lotario* and three new German airs by Georg Philipp Telemann, with German recitatives by Telemann. It was revived at Hamburg twice in 1733, three times in 1734, twice each in 1735 and 1736 and once in 1737 (Merbach, p. 364).

Handel finishes the opera *Orlando*, 20th November 1732.

John Christopher Smith's *Teraminta*, text by Henry Carey, is produced at Lincoln's Inn Fields Theatre, 20th November 1732 (*Daily Journal*).

The English opera company was now split into two : Lampe remained at the New Theatre in the Haymarket, and Arne went to the deserted Theatre in Lincoln's Inn Fields, where regular operas were performed during the winter. See 7th December. The younger Smith, son of Handel's old friend Schmidt, was now twenty years of age ; he was Handel's pupil and later his treasurer and copyist. The opera was repeated on 23rd and 30th November, and not again.

---

[1] The opera of "Cato" is not Mr. Handel's.

From Viscount Percival's Diary, 22nd November 1732

I . . . heard the practice of Alexander at the Opera House.

(Egmont MSS., I. 297.) This, apparently was not the final rehearsal of the revived *Alessandro*. Percival attended the "practice" before dinner and before going to the music club at the "Crown and Anchor" Tavern, it being St. Cecilia's Day.

Walsh advertises "Books of Solo's for a German Flute" (and continuo) by Handel and other "eminent Authors", *Daily Post*, 23rd November 1732.

Handel's book was his Opus I, reprinted from Jeanne Roger's plates (Amsterdam, *c.* 1722).

—

From the "Daily Journal", 25th November 1732

At the King's Theatre . . . this present Saturday . . . will be reviv'd, An Opera, call'd, ALEXANDER. . . . Tickets . . . at Half a Guinea each. Gallery five Shillings. . . . N.B. The Silver Tickets are ready to be deliver'd to Subscribers, or their Order, on paying the Subscription-Money, at the Office in the Hay-Market.

The cast of this revival (compared with that of the production on 5th May 1726) was as follows :

Alessandro—Signor Senesino (Senesino)
Rossane—Signora Strada (Faustina)
Lisaura—Signora Gismondi (Cuzzoni)
Tassile—Signora Bertolli (Signor Baldi)
Clito—Signor Montagnana (Boschi)
Leonato—(?) Signor Pinacci (Antinori)
Cleone— (?) Signora Bagnolesi (Dotti)

Like Signor Campioli, Pinacci and Signora Bagnolesi may already have left the company ; they never appeared at the King's Theatre again. Repeat performances on 28th November ; 2nd, 19th, 26th and 30th December.

—

Walsh advertises "The Favourite Songs in Esther, an Oratorio. To which is prefix'd, the Overture in Score. . . . Price 4s.," *Daily Journal*, 25th November 1732.

—

From Colman's "Opera Register", 25th November 1732

Nov. 25 Alexander reviv'd—The King &c all at ye Opera a full House

—

From Colman's "Opera Register", 28th November 1732

Nov. 28 Do [Alexander] a thin House

—

AARON HILL TO HANDEL

Dec. 5, 1732.

SIR,

I ought sooner, to have return'd you my hearty thanks, for the silver ticket, which has carried the obligation farther, than to myself ; for my daughters are, both such lovers of musick, that it is hard to say, which of them is most capable of being charm'd by the compositions of Mr *Handel*.

Having this occasion of troubling you with a letter, I cannot forbear to tell you the earnestness of my wishes, that, as you have made such considerable steps towards it, already, you would let us owe to your inimitable genius, the establishment of *musick*, upon a foundation of good poetry ; where the excellence of the *sound* should be no longer dishonour'd, by the poorness of the *sense* it is chain'd to.

My meaning is, that you would be resolute enough, to deliver us from our *Italian bondage* ; and demonstrate, that *English* is soft enough for Opera, when compos'd by poets, who know how to distinguish the *sweetness* of our tongue, from the *strength* of it, where the last is less necessary.

I am of opinion, that male and female voices may be found in this kingdom, capable of every thing, that is requisite ; and, I am sure, a species of dramatic Opera might be invented, that, by reconciling reason and dignity, with musick and fine machinery, would charm the *ear*, and hold fast the *heart*, together.

Such an improvement must, at once, be lasting, and profitable, to a very great degree ; and would, infallibly, attract an universal regard, and encouragement.

I am so much a stranger to the nature of your present engagements, that, if what I have said, should not happen to be so practicable, as I conceive it, you will have the goodness to impute it only to the zeal, with which I wish you at the head of a design, as solid, and unperishable, as your musick and memory. I am,

> Sir,
> *Your most obliged,*
> *And most humble Servant,*

A. HILL.

Hill, Works (1753, published after Hill's death, with Handel among the subscribers), I. 115 f. The appeal for English operas by Handel came just at the time when Handel was about to abandon opera for oratorio. Hill, who in his dedication of the *Rinaldo* libretto to Queen Anne, had already stressed the case for English operas (24th February 1711), did not offer himself to Handel as librettist in 1732. Cf. 10th February 1733. Hill had nine children ; three of his daughters were named Urania, Astræa and Minerva. The permanent tickets for theatres and other entertainments, like those for the pleasure gardens, were made from metal or ivory.

Acis and Galatea is revived, 5th December 1732 (*Daily Journal*).

See 10th June 1732. Repeat performances on 9th, 12th and 16th December. Cf. 7th May 1734.

The Theatre in Covent Garden, under the management of John Rich, opens, 7th December 1732.

Rich, with his company, moved to the new house from Lincoln's Inn Fields Theatre (1714–32). The old house was later used for various purposes. The first night at Covent Garden was a revival of Congreve's comedy *The Way of the World* (produced in 1700 at the old Theatre in Lincoln's Inn Fields), with the music by John Eccles. (Cf. 1738, last entry.)

Handel subscribes for John Christopher Smith's *Suites de Pièces pour le Clavecin*, volume 1, published for the Author by Thomas Cobb in 1732.

Cobb, who married Cluer's widow, was his successor. In 1733 Walsh reissued this volume, with the title-page ornamented like that of Handel's *Suites* ; he also published the second volume about 1735.

FROM THE PREFACE, "TO THE POETS OF FUTURE AGES", OF SAMUEL JOHNSON'S PLAY, "THE BLAZING COMET", 1732

. . . In these days, lives in *London*, without encouragement, the famous Mr. *Bononcini*, whose Musick for Celestialness of Stile, I am apt to think, will demand remembrance in the Soul after Fire has destroy'd all things in this World ; and I that have translated his Sounds into our own *English* Language, cannot say enough of this great Man, who is rival'd by Mr. *Handel*, a very big Man, who writes his Musick in the *High-Dutch* Taste, with very great success : so when you peruse these two Masters, you'll guess at the Men, and blush for the Taste of England. . . .

The preface is not signed but was apparently written by the author of the play ; cf. 7th April 1729. The sub-title of his play was : " The Mad Lovers ; or, The Beauties of the Poets ".

FROM " SEE AND SEEM BLIND : OR A CRITICAL DISSERTATION ON THE PUBLICK DVERSIONS, &C. . . . IN A LETTER FROM . . . LORD B – – – – – TO A – – – H – – –. ESQ ; " [1732]

. . . I left the *Italian* Opera, the House was so thin, and cross'd over the way to the *English* one, which was so full I was forc'd to croud in upon the Stage. . . .

This alarm'd *H—l*, and out he brings an *Oratorio*, or Religious *Farce*, for the duce take me if I can make any other Construction of the Word, but he has made a very good *Farce* of it, and put near 4000*l*. in his Pocket, of which I am very glad, for I love the Man for his Musick's sake.

This being a new Thing set the whole World a Madding ; Han't you be at the *Oratorio*, says one ? Oh ! If you don't see the *Oratorio* you see nothing, says t'other ; so away goes I to the *Oratorio*, where I saw indeed the finest Assembly of People I ever beheld in my Life, but, to my great Surprize, found this Sacred *Drama* a mere Consort, no Scenary, Dress or Action, so necessary to a *Drama* ; but H—l, was plac'd in Pulpit, (I suppose they call that their Oratory), by him sate *Senesino, Strada, Bertolli,* and *Turner Robinson,* in their own Habits ; before him stood sundry sweet Singers of this poor *Israel,* and *Strada* gave us a *Halleluiah* of Half an Hour long ; *Senesino* and *Bertolli* made rare work with the *English* Tongue you would have sworn it had been *Welch* ; I would have wish'd it *Italian,* that they might have sung with more ease to themselves, since, but for the Name of *English,* it might as well have been *Hebrew*. . . .

We have likewise had two Operas, *Etius* and *Sosarmes,* the first most Masterly, the last most pleasing, and in my mind exceeding pretty : There are two *Duetto*'s which Ravish me, and indeed the whole is vastly Genteel ; (I am sorry I am so wicked) but I like one good Opera better than Twenty *Oratorio*'s : Were they indeed to make a regular *Drama* of a good Scripture Story, and perform'd it with proper Decorations, which may be done with as much Preverence in proper Habits, as in their own common Apparel ; (I am sure with more Grandeur and Solemnity, and at least equal Decency) then should I change my Mind, then would the Stage appear in its full Lustre, and Musick Answer its original Design. . . .

(Flower, p. 219.) Pp. 10, 14-16, 19 f., 23 and 26 of the pamphlet. The fictitious addressee may have been Aaron Hill. The Italian Opera was, of course, the (old) Haymarket Theatre, the English Opera the New one. The oratorios were *Esther* and *Acis and Galatea.*

———

FROM WALSH'S CASH-BOOK, 1732

1732   Opera Ætius £26   5   0
        Opera Orlando . . .   26   5   0

The score of *Ezio* was published on 14th February 1732, that of *Orlando* not until 6th February 1733.

1733

Tolomeo is revived, 2nd January 1733.

Cf. 30th April 1728 and 19th May 1730. Repeat performances on 9th, 13th and 16th January. The cast (compared with those of 1728 and 1730) was as follows :

> Tolomeo—Signor Senesino (Senesino, Bernacchi)
> Seleuce—Signora Strada (Cuzzoni, Strada)
> Elisa—Signora Gismondi (Faustina, Merighi)
> Alessandro—Signora Bertolli (Signor Baldi ; Bertolli)
> Araspe—Signor Montagnana (Boschi, Fabri)

The libretto of 1730 was adapted, with additions and alterations, for the second revival.

———

FROM THE " DAILY JOURNAL ", 19th January 1733

We hear that most of the Musical Societies in Town have generously agreed to join their Asistance with the Gentlemen of the Chapel Royal, the Choirs of St. Paul's and Westminster, in the Performance of Mr. Handel's Great Te Deum, Jubilate, and Anthems, at St. Paul's, both in the Rehearsal and Feast of the Corporation of the Sons of the Clergy, in order to promote so great a Charity.

Cf. 1st February.

———

FROM THE SAME

NEW MUSICK.
This Day are Publish'd,
Neatly printed in Amsterdam,

· · · · ·

Five Sets of Lessons for the Harpsichord, Four by G. F. Handel, the other by Joseph Hector Fioco.

· · · · ·

Sold by Benj. Cooke. . . .

(Chrysander, III. 197 f.) There were ten items offered in this advertisement, of which the one quoted is no. 9. The publisher was Gérard Frédérik Witvogel in Amsterdam, Cooke being the importer. Fiocco was choirmaster at Antwerp. The music is printed on map paper in broadside oblong folios. A copy of the set is in the Fitzwilliam Museum, Cambridge. The five pieces are inscribed as Opp. 1-5, of which the Handel items are Opp. 2-4, with the publisher's numbers 4, 5, 10 and 11 (1732) : Sonata, Capriccio, Preludio ed Allegro and Fantasia. The four pieces were reprinted by Walsh in 1734, in Book 5 of *The Lady's Banquet*, then in Arnold's Handel edition, and finally in the Collected Edition. They are sometimes called the Third Collection of Handel's Suites. How Witvogel came to publish them is not known. Jacob Wilhelm Lustig, who may have been the mediator between Handel and Witvogel, did not come to London until 1734. He testified that the four pieces were written in Handel's youth (cf. 1763).

FROM THE " DAILY JOURNAL ", 27th January 1733

At the King's Theatre . . . this present Saturday . . . will be perform'd, a new Opera, call'd, ORLANDO. Wherein the Cloaths and Scenes are all entirely New. . . .

The text of *Orlando* is said to be by Grazio Braccioli (Loewenberg, p. 88), but Eisenschmidt, II. 15, denies this, without being able to give another source. The English version of the libretto is again by Humphreys. The libretto is dated 1732 ; since, however, January 1733 might have been styled 1732, the date does not prove, as Chrysander (II. 257) thought, that the production was intended for 1732. The first night was, in fact, planned for 23rd January 1733 (*Daily Journal*, 19th February), and Burney, IV. 366, gives this as the date of production, in which Nicoll follows him. The production was, however, postponed until 27th January. There were repeat performances on 3rd, 6th, 10th, 17th, 20th February ; 21st, 24th, 28th April ; 1st and 5th May. Burney also gives 10 performances for January and February, with 6 more in April and May ; both figures are wrong.

CAST OF " ORLANDO ", 27th January 1733

Orlando—Signor Senesino, alto
Angelica—Signora Strada, soprano
Medoro—Signora Bertolli, mezzo-soprano
Dorinda—Signora Gismondi, mezzo-soprano
Zoroastro—Signor Montagnana, bass

According to Handel's manuscript, Senesino's aria, " Già l' ebro mio ciglio " was accompanied by two " Violette marine con Violoncelli pizzicati per gli Signori Castrucci ". Pietro Castrucci, the leader of the opera orchestra, produced the new instrument on 28th February and 14th April 1732 (Chrysander, II. 256). His younger brother, Prospero, was for some years leader of the Music Society at the Castle Tavern, Paternoster Row.

The Boarding-School, or The Sham Captain, a ballad-opera with text arranged by Charles Coffey from Thomas D'Urfey's *Love for Money, or The Boarding-School* (1691), is produced at Drury Lane Theatre on 29th January 1733 ; with twenty-three songs by various composers, including a Handel minuet sung as " Come, boys, fill around ".

The tune has not been identified.

JOHN WEST, EARL OF DELAWARR TO CHARLES, DUKE OF RICHMOND, January 1733

There is a Spirit got up against the Dominion of Mr. Handel, a subscription carry'd on, and Directors chosen, who have contracted with

Senesino, and have sent for Cuzzoni, and Farinelli, it is hoped he will come as soon as the Carneval of Venice is over, if not sooner. The General Court gave power to contract with any Singer Except Strada, so that it is Thought Handel must fling up, which the Poor Count will not be sorry for, There being no one but what declares as much for him, as against the Other, so that we have a Chance of seeing Operas once more on a good foot. Porpora is also sent for. We doubt not but we shall have your Graces Name in our Subscription List. The Directrs. chosen are as follows. D. of Bedford, Lds. Bathurst, Burlington, Cowper, Limmerick, Stair, Lovel, Cadogan, DeLawarr, & D. of Rutland, Sir John Buckworth, Henry Furnese Esq., Sr. Micl. Newton ; There seems great Unanimity, and Resolution to carry on the Undertaking comme il faut.

(March, p. 234.) The name of the writer's title is spelt variously as Delaware, De La Warr, etc. He was Treasurer of the Household. The other noblemen were : John Russell, Duke of Bedford ; Allen Bathurst, Baron Bathurst ; Richard Boyle, Earl of Burlington (Handel's old protector) ; William, Earl of Cowper (the principal manager of the new Opera) ; James Hamilton, Viscount Limerick ; John Dalrymple, Earl of Stair ; Thomas Coke, Lord Lovel ; Charles, Baron Cadogan ; John Manners, Duke of Rutland ; the last three names have not been identified. The " Poor Count " is, of course, Heidegger, the " Swiss Count ", Handel's associate at the Haymarket Opera. Richmond joined the new Court of Directors, the anti-Handel, or Nobility Opera, at Lincoln's Inn Fields Theatre. Their first meeting was on 15th June 1733 at Hickford's Room in Panton Street, Haymarket ; it was called by Frederick, Prince of Wales, in opposition to the King, Handel's permanent protector. It seems from this letter, which was probably duplicated several times, that Strada was not wanted by the " Opera of the Nobility ", perhaps because her fidelity to Handel was known ; or perhaps the fidelity resulted from the fact that she was not wanted by the other side. This is the first documentary record of the growing opposition to Handel's opera, and of his new disagreement with Senesino, his *primo uomo*. At the very time Handel was taking his first steps away from opera to oratorio, he was forsaken by many friends in London society, and by nearly all his singers. At least five of these noblemen had been Directors of the original Royal Academy of Music : Richmond (Deputy-Governor in 1726–7), Bathurst, Burlington, Limerick and Stair. Chandos, however, was not among the new Directors.

———

Handel's *Utrecht Te Deum and Jubilate*, with two Anthems, are performed in St. Paul's Cathedral, 1st February 1733.

Cf. 10th February (Hooker's *Weekly Miscellany*).

———

FROM COLMAN'S " OPERA REGISTER ", 3rd February 1733

Febr 3 Do [*Orlando*] extraordinary fine & magnificent—perform'd several times until Satturday March 3d

When *Floridante* was revived in March, the performances of *Orlando* were interrupted.

———

Walsh advertises *Orlando*, " Engraven in a fair Character, and carefully corrected ", *Daily Journal*, 6th February 1733.

(Schoelcher, p. 122.) On 13th February Walsh advertised " The whole Opera of Orlando, in Score ".

From Fog's " Weekly Journal ", 10th February 1733

. . . There happen'd an Accident when I was last at the Opera of *Julius Caesar*, which will serve to explain this Part of *Vasconcellos* Character, and from which indeed I took the Hint of writing this Paper. A Piece of the Machinery tumbled down from the Roof of the Theatre upon the Stage just as *Senesino* had chanted forth these Words ;

> *Cesare non seppe mai, che sia timore.*
> *Cesar* does not know what Fear is.

The poor Hero was so frightened, that he trembled, lost his Voice, and fell a-crying.—Every Tyrant or Tyranical Minister is just such a *Cesar* as *Senesino*.

From a leading article in Fog's *Weekly Journal*, quoting Abbé Vertot's *Revolution of Portugal*. Vasconcellos was Premier of Portugal in 1640. The last revival of *Giulio Cesare* was in February 1732. The article was reprinted in the *London Magazine* of February 1733.

From the Same

On Saturday Night last [the 3rd], as her Majesty was coming from the Opera House in the Hay-market, the Fore Chairman had the Misfortune to slip, going down the Step by Ozinda's Coffee-house near St. James's House, by which Accident the Chair fell, and broke the Glasses ; but her Majesty happily got no Harm.

That night *Orlando* had been performed.

From Hooker's " Weekly Miscellany ", 10th February 1733

On Thursday last Week [the 1st] the Sons of the Clergy met at St. Paul's Cathedral, where Mr. Handel's *Te Deum and Jubilate*, and Two Anthems were performed by a great Number of Voices and Instruments, and the Rev. Dr. Stebbing preached an excellent Sermon suitable to the Occasion ; after which, they proceeded in their usual Order to dine at Merchant-Taylor's-Hall. At the Rehearsal, and on the Feast Day, at the Church and Hall, the Collections amounted to 945*l.* 10s. 3d.

The following excellent piece, written on this occasion, will, we doubt not, be highly obliging to all our Readers of Taste and Judgment.

AN ODE, ON OCCASION OF MR. HANDEL'S GREAT TE DEUM, AT
THE FEAST OF THE SONS OF THE CLERGY

So *David*, to the GOD, who touch'd his Lyre,
   The God, who did at once inspire
The *Poet*'s Numbers, and the *Prophet*'s fire,
   Taught the wing'd Anthem to aspire !
The Thoughts of Men, in Godlike Sounds he sung,
And *voic'd* Devotion, for an Angel's Tongue.
At once, with pow'rful *Works*, and skilful *Air*,
The Priestly King, who knew the weight of Prayer,
   To his high Purpose, match'd his Care ;
To deathless Concords, tun'd his mortal Lays,
And with a Sound, like Heav'ns, gave Heav'n its Praise.

Where has thy Soul, O Musick ! *slept*, since then ?
Or through what Lengths of deep Creation led,
Has Heav'n indulg'd th' all-daring Pow'r to tread ?
   On other Globes, to other Forms of Men,
Hast thou been sent, their maker's name to spread ?
Or, o'er some dying Orb, in tuneful dread,
Proclaiming *Judgment*, wak'd th' unwilling Dead ?
Or, have *new* Worlds, from wand'ring Comets, rais'd,
Heard, and leapt forth, and into *Being* blaz'd ?

     Say, sacred Origin of Song !
     Where hast thou hid thyself so long ?
Thou Soul of HANDEL !—through what shining Way,
Lost to our Earth, since *David*'s long past Day,
Didst thou, for all this length of Ages stray !
What wond'ring angels hast thou breath'd among,
By none, of all th' immortal Choirs out-sung ?

But, 'tis enough, since thou art here *again* ;
   Where thou hast wander'd gives no Pain :
We *hear*,—we *feel*, thou art return'd once more,
   With Musick, *mightier* than before ;
     As if in ev'ry Orb,
From every *Note*, of *God*'s, which thou wert shown,
   Thy Spirit did th' Harmonious Pow'r absorb,
And made the moving Airs of Heav'n thy *own* !

Ah ! give thy *Passport* to the Nation's Prayer,
   Ne'er did Religion's languid Fire
   Burn fainter—never more require
The Aid of such a fam'd Enliv'ner's Care :
Thy Pow'r can *force* the stubborn Heart to feel,
And rouze the Lucke-warm Doubter into *Zeal*.

> Teach us to pray, as *David* pray'd before ;
> Lift our Thanksgiving to th' Almighty's Throne,
> In Numbers like his own :
>   Teach us yet more,
> Teach us, undying Charmer, to compose
> Our inbred Storms, and 'scape impending Woes :
> Lull our wanton Hearts to Ease,
> Teach Happiness to *please* ;
> And, since thy Notes, can ne'er, in vain implore !
> Bid 'em becalm unresting Faction o'er :
> Inspire Content, and Peace, in each proud Breast,
> Bid th' unwilling Land be blest.
> If Aught we wish for seems too long to stay,
> Bid us believe, that Heav'n best knows its Day :
> Bid us, securely, reap the Good we may,
> Not, Tools to other's *haughty Hopes*, throw our own Peace away.

For the performance, see 19th January 1733 : it was again the *Utrecht Te Deum and Jubilate*, with two of the Coronation Anthems. The poem was reprinted in the *Gentleman's Magazine* of February 1733 (vol. III, p. 94) ; it was without signature. Chrysander (II. 474–6) added the pseudonym " Eusebius ". The author was Aaron Hill, as Schoelcher (p. 59) and Chrysander (II. 280 f.) indicate ; the poem is to be found in Hill's Works of 1753 (III. 167–9), but dated erroneously as of 1st February 1732. Cf. 5th December 1732.

———

Achilles, a ballad opera with text by John Gay, is produced at Covent Garden, 10th February 1733.

———

Handel finishes the oratorio *Deborah*, 21st February 1733.

———

From the " Gentleman's Magazine ", February 1733

Thursday, Feb. 1.

Mr. *Handel*'s *Te Deum* and *Jubilate*, with two Anthems, were perform'd before the Corporation of Clergy's Sons, at St. *Paul*'s Cathedral, by a much greater Number of Voices and Instruments than usual, about 50 Gentlemen performing *gratis*. . . .

(Chrysander, II. 271 f.)

———

Floridante is revived, 3rd March 1733.

Repeat performances on 6th, 10th, 13th March ; 8th, 15th and 19th May. The cast is not known, but apparently Senesino sang his original part of Floridante, as he did on 9th December 1721.

———

Rosamond, text by Addison, newly set to music by T. A. Arne, is produced at Lincoln's Inn Fields Theatre, 7th March 1733.

First composed by Clayton in 1707 (Drury Lane) and again by Henry Carey in 1729, it was set once more in 1767, by Samuel Arnold. Arne's setting was the most successful.

—

From the " Daily Journal ", 12th March 1733

By his Majesty's Command.

At the *King's Theatre* . . . on Saturday the 17th of March, will be performed, Deborah, an *Oratorio*, or *Sacred Drama*, In *English* Composed by Mr. *Handel*. And to be performed by a great Number of the best Voices and Instruments.

N.B. This is the last Dramatick Performance that will be exhibited at the King's Theatre till after Easter.

The House to be fitted up and illuminated in a new and particular Manner.

Tickets . . . at One Guinea each, Gallery Half a Guinea.

(Burney, IV. 366 ; Schoelcher, p. 127 ; Chrysander, II. 284 f.) This is the first time an oratorio was performed on a Saturday, the night of Italian operas. The prices were raised for the first night, which, both at this time and later, was outside the regular subscription. From the second performance onwards, the advertisements say : " N.B. Subscribers' silver tickets will be admitted "; the prices were normal again. The advertisement also appeared in the *Daily Post*, and was repeated in both papers until the day of the production. Cf. 14th April 1731.

—

Deborah is produced, 17th March 1733.

The word-book is by Samuel Humphreys, who dedicated it to Queen Caroline. Repeat performances on 27th, 31st March ; 3rd, 7th and 10th April. Revivals in April 1734, March 1735 (Covent Garden), November 1744 (Haymarket), March 1754 and March 1756 (Covent Garden).

—

Cast of " Deborah ", 17th March 1733

Deborah—Signora Strada, soprano
Barak—Signora Bertolli, mezzo-soprano
Abinoam—Signor Montagnana, bass
Sisera—Signor Senesino, alto
Jael—?, soprano
Israel Woman—Signora Gismondi, mezzo-soprano
Chief Priest of Baal—?, bass
Chief Priest of the Israelites—?, bass

—

FROM THE " BEE : OR, UNIVERSAL WEEKLY PAMPHLET ",
24th March 1733

The following Epigram, which has run about in Manuscript for two or three Days past, does not want epigrammatick wit. It needs no Explanation to People who know what is done in the World.

A Dialogue between two *Projectors.*

Quoth W— to H—l shall we two agree,
And Join in a Scheme of *Excise.* H. *Caro si.*
Of what Use is your Sheep if your Shepherd can't sheer him ?
At the Hay-Market *I, you at* We—er ? W. Hear him.
Call'd to Order the Seconds appear'd in their Place,
One fam'd for his Morals, and one for his Face ;
In half they succeeded, in half they were crost ;
The Tobacco *was sav'd, but poor* Deborah *lost.*

(Chrysander, II. 286 f., 479.) The epigram is anonymous ; it is sometimes attributed to Lord Chesterfield (who later in the year married Melusina, Countess of Walsingham). The abbreviations are : W— for Sir Robert Walpole, H—l for Handel, and We—er for Westminster, *i.e.* Parliament. The one famed for his morals may have been Lord Hervey, and the other, famed for his face, was, of course, Heidegger. On 14th March, three days before the production of *Deborah,* Walpole introduced in Parliament a Tobacco Excise Bill which was ardently opposed, and finally defeated by a majority, without a second reading. To draw a comparison between Handel and Walpole, as to their character, unpopularity, and courtly favour, seems to be a mistake ; it is, however, a greater one to assume that Walpole was Handel's protector. It was quite usual, at the time, to dress a political satire as an artistic dispute. The fact that the first night prices of *Deborah* were unpleasantly high was sufficient to bracket Handel's and Walpole's greediness as one attack against the public interest. Although Schoelcher (pp. 131 and 404) already recognized these circumstances, Joseph E. Cecci recently used this epigram, in a very ingenious article (*Musical Times,* January 1951) " Handel and Walpole in Caricature ", as an explanation of a well-known and a less-known etching by an anonymous London artist. The so-called " Handel Oratorio ", however, is no cartoon, and the other print certainly has nothing to do with Handel. Cf. 7th April 1733.

———

FROM VISCOUNT PERCIVAL'S DIARY, 27th March 1733

Went in the evening to see " Deborah ", an oratorio, made by Hendel. It was very magnificent, near a hundred performers, among whom about twenty-five singers.

Egmont MSS., I. 345.

———

LADY A. IRWIN TO LORD CARLISLE

London, 31 March [1733].

Last week we had an Oratorio, composed by Hendel out of the story of Barak and Deborah, the latter of which name[s] it bears. Hendel thought, encouraged by the Princess Royal, it had merit enough to deserve a guinea, and the first time it was performed at that price, exclusive of subscribers' tickets, there was but a 120 people in the House. The subscribers being refused unless they would pay a guinea, they, insisting upon the right of their silver tickets, forced into the House, and carried their point. This gave occasion to the eight lines I send you, in which they have done Hendel the honour to join him in a dialogue with Sir Robert Walpole. I was at this entertainment on Tuesday [the 27th] ; 'tis excessive noisy, a vast number of instruments and voices, who all perform at a time, and is in music what I fancy a French ordinary in conversation.

(*Musical Times*, 1st November 1899, p. 736.) Carlisle MSS., p. 106. The Princess Royal was Anne, a friend of Handel's, who is said to have encouraged the staging of *Esther* and of *Acis and Galatea* at the Haymarket Theatre in 1732. The poem in question is, of course, the epigram printed on 24th March.

———

FROM THE " DAILY JOURNAL ", 2nd April 1733

On Saturday Night last [31st March] the King, Queen, Prince, and the three eldest Princesses were at the King's Theatre in the Hay-market, and saw the Opera called Deborah.

———

Henry Fielding adds to *The Miser* an afterpiece : · *Deborah ; or, A Wife for You All*, 6th April 1733.

(Myers, 1948, pp. 43 f.) This trifle was never published, and is known only from a playbill ; it may have been a burlesque of Humphreys' word-book.

———

FROM THE " CRAFTSMAN ", 7th April 1733

SIR,

I am always rejoiced, when I see a *Spirit of Liberty* exert itself among any Sett, or Denomination of my Countrymen. I please myself with the Hopes that it will grow more diffusive ; some time or other become fashionable ; and at last useful to the Publick. As I know your Zeal for *Liberty*, I thought I could not address better than to you the following exact Account of the noble Stand, lately made by the polite Part of the World, in Defense of their Liberties and Properties, against the open Attacks and bold Attempts of Mr. H—l upon both. I shall singly relate the Fact, and leave you, who are better able than I am, to make what Inferences, or Applications may be proper.

The Rise and Progress of Mr. H—l's Power and Fortune are too well known for me now to relate. Let it suffice to say that He was grown so insolent upon the sudden and undeserved Increase of both, that He thought nothing ought to oppose his imperious and extravagant Will.

He had, for some Time, govern'd the *Opera's*, and modell'd the *Orchestre*, without the least Controul. No Voices, no *Instruments* were admitted, but such as flatter'd his Ears, though they shock'd those of the Audience. *Wretched Scrapers* were put above the *best Hands* in the *Orchestre*. No Musick but *his own* was to be allowed, though every Body was weary of it ; and he had the Impudence to assert, *that there was no Composer in* England *but Himself.* Even *Kings* and *Queens* were to be content with whatever low Characters he was pleased to assign them, as it was evident in the case of Signior *Montagnana* ; who, though a *King*, is always obliged to act (except an angry, rumbling Song, or two) the most insignificant Part of the whole Drama. This Excess and Abuse of Power soon disgusted the Town ; his Government grew odious ; and his *Opera's* grew empty. However this Degree of Unpopularity and general Hatred, instead of humbling him, only made him more furious and desperate. He resolved to make one last Effort to establish his Power and Fortune by Force, since He found it now impossible to hope for it from the good Will of Mankind. In order to This, he form'd a *Plan*, without consulting any of his *Friends*, (if he has any) and declared that at a proper Season he wou'd communicate it to the Publick ; assuring us, at the same Time, that it would be very much for the Advantage of the Publick in general, and his *Opera's* in particular. Some People suspect that he had settled it previously with the Signora *Strada del Po*, who is much in his Favour ; but all, that I can advance with certainty, is, that He had concerted it with a *Brother of his own*, in whom he places a most undeserved Confidence. In this Brother of his, *Heat* and *Dullness* are miraculously united. The *former* prompts him to any Thing new and violent ; while the *latter* hinders him from seeing any of the Inconveniences of it. As Mr. *H—l's Brother*, he thought it was necessary he should be a *Musician* too, but all he could arrive at, after a very laborious Application for many Years, was a moderate Performance upon the *Jew's Trump*. He had, for some Time, play'd a *parte buffa abroad*, and had entangled his *Brother* in several troublesome and dangerous Engagements, in the Commissions he had given him to contract with *foreign Performers* ; and from which (by the way) Mr. *H—l* did not disengage Himself with much Honour. Notwithstanding all these and many more Objections, Mr. *H—l*, by and with the Advice of *his Brother*, at last produces his *Project* ; resolves to cram it down the Throats of the Town ; prostitutes *great* and *aweful Names*, as the Patrons of it ; and even does not scruple to insinuate that they are to be Sharers of the Profit. His *Scheme* set forth in Substance, that the late Decay of *Opera's* was owing to their *Cheapness*, and to the great *Frauds* committed by the *Doorkeepers* ; that the *annual Subscribers* were a Parcel of *Rogues*, and made an ill Use of their Tickets, by often *running* two into the Gallery, that to obviate these Abuses he had contrived a Thing, that was better than an *Opera*, call'd an *Oratorio* ; to which none should be admitted, but by *printed*

Permits, or Tickets of one Guinea each, which should be distributed out of *Warehouses of his own*, and by *Officers of his own naming*; which *Officers* would not so reasonably be supposed to cheat in the Collection of *Guineas*, as the *Doorkeepers* in the collection of *half Guineas* ; and lastly, that as the very being of *Opera's* depended upon *Him singly*, it was just that the Profit arising from hence should be for his *own Benefit*. He added, indeed, one Condition, to varnish the whole a little ; which was, that if any Person should think himself aggriev'd, and that the *Oratorio* was not worth the Price of the *Permit*, he should be at Liberty to appeal to *three Judges of Musick*, who should be oblig'd, within the Space of seven Years at farthest, finally to determine the same ; provided always that the said *Judges* should be of his Nomination, and known to like no other Musick but his.

The Absurdity, Extravagancy, and Opposition of this *Scheme* disgusted the whole Town. Many of the most constant Attenders of the *Opera's* resolved absolutely to renounce them, rather than go to them under such Exortion and Vexation. They exclaim'd against the *insolent and rapacious Projector of this Plan*. The King's old and sworn Servants of the two Theatres of *Drury-Lane* and *Covent-Garden* reap'd the Benefit of this general Discontent, and were resorted to in Crowds, by way of Opposition to the *Oratorio*. Even the fairest Breasts were fir'd with Indignation against this *new Imposition*. Assemblies, Cards, Tea, Coffee, and all other Female Batteries were vigorously employ'd to defeat the *Project*, and destroy the *Projector*. These joint Endeavours of all Ranks and Sexes succeeded so well, that the *Projector* had the Mortification to see but a very thin Audience in his *Oratorio* ; and of about two hundred and sixty odd, that it consisted of, it was notorious that not ten paid for their *Permits*, but, on the contrary, had them given them, and Money into the Bargain, for coming to keep him in Countenance.

This Accident, they say, has thrown Him into a *deep Melancholy*, interrupted sometimes by *raving Fits* ; in which he fancies he sees ten thousand *Opera* Devils coming to tear Him to Pieces ; then He breaks out into frantick, incoherent Speeches ; muttering *sturdy Beggars*, *Assassination*, &c. In these delirious Moments, he discovers a particular Aversion to the City. He calls them all a Parcel of *Rogues*, and asserts that the *honestest Trader among them deserves to be hang'd*—It is much question'd whether he will recover ; at least, if he does, it is not doubted but He will seek for a Retreat in his *own Country* from the general Resentment of the Town.

> I am, *Sir*, *Sir*,
> Your very humble Servant,
> P—LO R—LI.

P.S. Having seen a little Epigram, lately handed about Town, which seems to allude to the same Subject, I believe it will not be unwelcome to your Readers.

EPIGRAM

Quoth *W—e* to *H—l*, shall We Two agree,
And exise the whole Nation ?
                                        H. si, Caro, si.
Of what Use are *Sheep*, if the *Shepherd* can't shear them ?
At the *Hay-Market* I, you at *Westminster.*
                                        W. Hear Him !
Call'd to Order, their *Seconds* appear in their Place ;
One fam'd for his *Morals*, and one for his *Face.*
In half They succeeded, in half They were crost :
The EXISE was obtain'd, but poor DEBORAH lost.

(Chrysander, II. 476-9.) The *Country Journal ; or the Craftsman* was a revolutionary paper, edited by " Caleb D'Anvers ", *i.e.* Nicholas Armhurst, assisted by Lord Bolingbroke, William Pulteney and Thomas Coke. Pulteney and Coke, of Norfolk, were two of the original subscribers to the Academy of Music in 1719. The *Craftsman* was in opposition to Robert Walpole. Although it seems incredible that the signature " P—lo R—li " could have been used without Paolo Rolli's consent, its veil was too thin to hide him if he wished to conceal his authorship ; and although he was very critical of Handel, Rolli never opposed him in public. The signature, therefore, may have been a fake, used to stress the opposition to Handel, even on the part of his former associates. At the beginning and at the end, there are indications that the writer was a born Englishman, and rather nationalistic. Again, as in the epigram, a variant of which is printed at the end, the letter seems to aim at Walpole in attacking Handel. This, also, is out of keeping with Rolli's character ; he would have been more likely to do the opposite. According to Schoelcher's (p. 404) and Chrysander's (II. 287-91) exegesis, Handel means Walpole ; the Opera : the state ; the orchestra : civil servants and Parliament ; composer : statesman ; Montagnana : the King ; his songs : a threatening proclamation and Parliamentary speech ; again, the Opera : the state's finances ; Strada : the Queen ; Handel's brother, supposed to be Heidegger : Horace Walpole ; a musician : again, a statesman ; a " parte buffa abroad ": Horace as ambassador in Paris ; the foreign Performers : foreign powers ; the late decay of operas : customs ; the doorkeepers : tax collectors ; the annual subscribers, as well as the " sturdy Beggars " (Horace Walpole's word) : the merchants of the City of London ; the oratorio : the excise ; the constant Attenders of the operas : the Government's supporters ; and so on. (The " Jew's Trump " is better known as the Jew's Harp.)—It was a nasty piece of journalism and must have hurt Handel deeply, even if he knew that the attack was directed primarily against Walpole, and that Rolli was not its real author. The letter was reprinted in the *London Magazine* of April 1732, under the heading : " A new Opera Scheme. One who signs himself Paolo Rolli, in a Letter to Mr. D'Anvers, says . . .". Cf. 24th May 1733.

———

MRS. PENDARVES TO HER SISTER, ANN GRANVILLE

Dangan, 11th April, 1733.
I am sorry the *Act* of Oxford happens this year ; I fear it will incommode me in my journey to Gloucester—the town will be so cramm'd :

and I have so much a higher pleasure in view than any entertainment they can give, that I have no thoughts of stopping there.

(Delany, I. 410.) Mrs. Pendarves wrote from Ireland, her future home. She had no idea what kind of entertainment was intended at Oxford. The Oxford " Act ", held again this year after a long interval and, as it turned out, for the last time, was the solemn assembly which met early in July for the purpose of conferring degrees : the graduates discussed their theses on the Saturday and the following Monday, while two of the new Doctors of Divinity preached sermons on the Sunday.

———

Esther is revived at the Haymarket Theatre, 14th April 1733.

Repeat performance on 17th April. According to Burney (1785, p. 23), Handel started to play organ concertos in the intervals in 1733 : on 17th March (*Deborah*) and 14th April (*Esther*).

———

KARL LUDWIG FREIHERR VON PÖLLNITZ TO A FRIEND

London, May 4, 1733.

. . . They have an *Italian* Opera, which is the best and most magnificent in *Europe*. . . . The Music of these Operas is generally composed by one *Hendel*, who is esteemed by a great many People beyond all Expression, but others reckon him no extraordinary Man ; and for my own Part, I think his Music not so affecting as 'tis elegant.

(Pöllnitz, *The Memoirs*, London 1737, II. 466.) The original edition, in French, first appeared in Liège in 1734 ; in it, III. 420, the passages referring to Handel run as follows : " La Musique de ces Opera est ordinairement de la composition d'un nommé *Hendel*, que beaucoup de gens estiment au-delà, de toute expression, & que d'autres regardent comme un homme ordinaire. Quant a moi, je trouve sa Musique plus savante que touchante."

———

FROM THE " CRAFTSMAN ", 12th May 1733

New Musick, this Day Published.

A choice Sett of Aires, call'd Handel's Water-Piece, composed in Parts for Variety of Instruments. Neatly engraven and carefully corrected, and never before printed. Price 1s 6d.

London : Printed for and sold by Daniel Wright. . . .

(Smith, 1948, pp. 281, 283.) The advertisement was also printed in Fog's *Weekly Journal* of the same day. No complete copy of Wright's edition is known, but there exists a set of five parts printed from Wright's plates by his successor, John Johnson, about 1740. (See *Music & Letters*, July 1949, pp. 262 f.) Nothing is known about the elder Wright's connection with Handel : his edition was unauthorized and there is even doubt whether the music was, in fact, by Handel. (See Smith, 1953, pp. 18 f.) Walsh's authorized selection from the *Water Music*, in seven parts, appeared later in the same year, 1733.

———

FROM THE "GRUBSTREET JOURNAL", 17th May 1733

Lately published,

OPERA'S, with the MUSICK, as perform'd at the Theatres-Royal, &c.
. . . Printed for J. Watts. . . .

DEBORAH. An Oratorio ; or, Sacred Drama. As it is perform'd at the
King's Theatre in the Hay-Market. The Musick compos'd by Mr.
HANDEL. The Words by Mr. Humphreys.

John Watts offered the librettos of the operas, listed in this advertisement, "on
the same Paper, for the Conveniency of Gentlemen binding them up in Volumes".
Among them were several ballad-operas, with the tunes, beginning with the
Beggar's Opera and *Acis and Galatea* (probably the word-book of May 1732).

———

Bononcini's *Griselda* is revived, 22nd May 1733.
Cf. 22nd February 1722.

———

FROM THE "FREE BRITON", 24th May 1733

A Letter to the Author of the last Craftsman . . .

A while ago you talked about Signor Montagnana, and of a *King* who
made *the lowest character in the whole drama.* Indeed, it is a fine way of
proving that you did *not affront the King*, when you told him *he had
astonished his people.* . . . This passage, to be sure, was meant as the finest
stroke of humour in this pious and loyal performance. . . .

Fra. Walsingham.

(Schoelcher, p. 403.) Cf. 7th April 1733. Walsingham was probably the
pseudonym of the editor, William Arnall.

———

Walsh advertises *Orlando* "transposed for a Common Flute",
Daily Journal, 25th May 1733.

———

FROM THE "BEE", 2nd June 1733

We are credibly informed, that one Day last Week Mr. *H—d—l,*
Director-General of the Opera-House, sent a Message to Signior *Senesino,*
the famous *Italian* Singer, acquainting Him, that He had no farther
Occasion for his Service : and that *Senesino* replied, the next Day, by a
Letter, containing a full Resignation of all his Parts in the *Opera,* which
He had performed for many Years with great Applause—We hope the
polite Mr. *Walsingham* will give us Leave to observe, upon this Occasion,
that the World *seems greatly* ASTONISH'D *at so unexpected an Event* ; *and*

that all true Lovers of Musick GRIEVE *to see so* fine a Singer *dismissed, in so critical a Conjuncture.*

The notice also appeared in the *Craftsman* of the same day. (Chrysander, II. 323.) Since January 1733, or even earlier, Senesino had been in contact with the proposer of the Nobility Opera.

———

Handel finishes the oratorio *Athalia*, 7th June 1733.

———

The season at the Opera House closes on 9th June 1733 with *Griselda*.

This was the fourth season of the Handel-Heidegger regime. With the exception of Signora Strada, the Italian singers now left Handel to join the Nobility Opera.

———

Walsh advertises Book II of *Forest Harmony*, a collection of airs, minuets and marches for two French horns, among them three pieces from Handel's *Water Music*, *Daily Post*, 12th June 1733.

(Smith, 1948, p. 282.) The several publications from the *Water Music* seem to indicate a performance in 1733 of the original, or another, set ; nothing, however, is known of such a performance. For the original performance see 17th July 1717.

———

FROM THE " DAILY POST ", 13th June 1733

The Subscribers to the Opera in which Signor Senesino and Signora Cuzzoni are to perform, are desired to meet at Mr. Hickford's Great Room in Panton-street, on Friday next [the 15th] by Eleven o'Clock, in order to settle proper Methods for carrying on the Subscription.

Such Persons who cannot be present are desired to send their Proxies. (Burney, IV. 367 f. ; Cummings, 1914, p. 69.) Cf. January 1733.

———

FROM THE " BEE ", 23rd June 1733

London, June 20.

Great Preparations are making for Mr. Handel's Journey to Oxford, in order to take his Degree of Musick ; a Favour that University intends to compliment him with, at the ensuing Publick Act. The Theatre there is fitting up for the Performance of his Musical Entertainments, the first [of] which begins on Friday Fortnight the 6th of July. We hear that the Oratorio's of Esther and Deborah, and also a new one never performed before, called Athaliah, are to be represented two Nights each ; and the Serenata of Acis and Galatea as often. That Gentleman's Great *Te Deum*, *Jubilate*, and *Anthems*, are to be vocally and instrumentally performed by the celebrated Mr. Powell, and others, at a solemn Entertainment for the Sunday. The Musick from the Opera is to attend Mr. Handel ; and we are informed, that the principal Parts in his Oratorio's, &c. are to be [sung] by Signora Strada, Mrs. Wright, Mr. Salway, Mr. Rochetti, and Mr. Wartzs.

(Chrysander, II. 306.) The *Bee*, on other occasions following the *Craftsman*, accepted this news without hesitation. Handel, invited by the Vice-Chancellor of Oxford, did not accept the honorary degree offered to him. With the exception of Signora Strada, who stayed with him when the other Italians left, his singers now were all English. Mrs. Wright, soprano, sang in Handel operas in 1727 and 1728. Thomas Salway and Philip Rochetti, tenors, sang in the performance of *Acis and Galatea* on 26th March 1731, as did Mrs. Wright. Gustavus Waltz, bass, whose name, here and elsewhere, is corrupted, sang Polyphemus on 17th May 1732. Walter Powell, tenor, was of local fame, formerly a chorister and now clerk of Magdalen College, Oxford, since 1732 Esquire Bedell of Divinity and member of the choirs of Christ Church and St. John's Colleges. (He never became a gentleman of the Chapel Royal, as sometimes stated, but he did sing in Handel oratorios at the Three Choirs Meetings.) The Sheldonian Theatre was the main place for the Act. For a full account of the proceedings, see the *Oxford Act*, published in June 1734 and quoted under that date. Flower (p. 230) quotes, in this connection, an Italian sketch of Handel's life, but the manuscript, preserved at the Conservatorio di Musica " G.B. Martini " in Bologna, was written after Handel's death and contains nothing which cannot be found in the contemporary records of Handel's visit to Oxford.

—

FROM THE KING'S WARRANT BOOK, 26th June 1733

£   s.   d.

Royal Academy of Music 1,000   0   0 Royal bounty to the undertakers
of the Opera.

Calendar of Treasury Papers, 1731-4, p. 493. There is no corresponding entry in the Treasury Minute Book.

—

FROM " THE MANNERS OF THE AGE : IN THIRTEEN MORAL SATIRS ",
[June] 1733

. . . The realm in doubt, till sages shall ordain,
If *Paul* henceforth, or *H—deg—r*, shall reign. . . .
If sacred opera's shall instruct us still,
And churches empty, as *ridotto's* fill ;
The *Hebrew* or the *German* leave the field,
And *David*'s lyre to *Handel*'s spinnet yield. . . .
'Twas once fair *Britain*'s glory and her praise
To bind her heroes brows with foreign bayes ;
Victorious wreaths from vanquish'd realms to bring,
She cannot conquer now—but she can sing ;
And while her warriors at the stage look gay,
Gentle or eager, just as fiddlers play ;

Made soft or fierce by *Handel*'s potent lyre ;
Their rage and love both modell'd by the wire ;
Of *Latin* eunuchs, and sweet tunes possest,
The opera is safe—and *England* blest.

. . . Tho' not a writer, yet a friend to wit,
Boyet is constant to his fav'rite pit ;
To want a darling bliss who never fears,
While *Italy* has tunes and *Britain* ears ;
His crown each week to pay, no mortal wrong,
For the two joys—a fiddle and a song . . .
Entring the stage, he knows not his design,
If *Porus* is that act to die, or dine ;
A stranger, as he sings, to what he wants,
If for his night-gown, or his sword he pants ;
Nor knows, when first he enters in the ring,
If [1] *Handel*'s lion is to fight, or sing. . . .

(R. M. Myers, 1948, pp. 19 and 27.) According to the *Gentleman's Magazine*, the book was published in June 1733. The quotations are from pp. 90, 116 and 540 ; from Satire IV, dedicated to Robert Walpole, and Satire XII, dedicated to Lord Onslow. The opera *L'Idaspe fedele* (1710) was by Mancini, not by Handel. For *Poro* see 2nd February 1731. H—deg—r is, of course, Heidegger.

———

THE DUKE OF CHANDOS TO HIS NEPHEW, HENRY PERROT, IN OXFORD, [July] 1733

Music, ladies & learning are each entertainments which cannot fail to gratify the passions of one who has so good a taste.

(Baker, p. 131.) In this letter the Duke introduced to his nephew, who was an undergraduate at Oxford, a harpist from the " Concert at Cannons ", probably Thomas Jones, " to try his fortune at the Act ". He suspects that the first two entertainments, ennumerated by him, will ride triumphant. Chandos seems not to have known at this time what role Handel was to play in the Act, although *Esther* has a harp part.

———

THE VICE-CHANCELLOR OF THE UNIVERSITY OF OXFORD TO THE HEADS OF THE COLLEGES AND HALLS, 4th July 1733

Gentlemen,
    You are desired to signify to your Societies, that during the approaching Solemnity which begins on the 6th Day of July, All Doctors wear their Scarlet Gowns.
    The Musick usually perform'd on Saturday Morning between the hours

———

[1] Opera of *Hydaspes*.

of 6 and 8, is remov'd from the Musick School to the Theater by Act of Convocation. . . .

Vice-Can. Oxon.

(Eland, p. 9.) Bodleian Library : B 3. 15. ART. A printed sheet of paper. The Vice-Chancellor, the Rev. Dr. William Holmes, President of St. John's College, was the initiator of Handel's visit to Oxford. The Music School of the University had its own Music Room ; the one still in existence, the oldest in Europe (Mee), was not opened till 1748. Convocation is the great legislative assembly of the University.

———

FROM DR. THOMAS HEARNE's DIARY, OXFORD, 5th July 1733

One Handel, a forreigner (who, they say, was born in Hanover) being desired to come to Oxford, to perform in Musick this Act, in which he has great skill, is come down, the Vice-Chancellour (Dr Holmes) having requested him to do so, and as an encouragement, to allow him the Benefit of the Theater both before the Act begins and after it. Accordingly he hath published Papers for a performance today at 5s. a Ticket. This performance began a little after 5 clock in the evening. This is an innovation. The Players might as well be permitted to come and act. The Vice-Chancellour is much blamed for it. In this, however, he is to be commended for reviving our Acts, which ought to be annual, which might easily be brought about, provided the Statutes were strictly followed, and all such innovations (which exhaust Gentlemen's pockets and are incentives to Lewdness) were hindered.

(Hearne, *Remarks*, XI. 224.) Hearne was a " staunch Jacobite ". The arrangement with Handel was such that he was allowed to give concerts within the University, partly to meet his expenses for the official performances. No printed bill of either is known. Handel's first performance at Oxford was *Esther*. The cast is not known, but Strada sang Esther and Powell Mordecai.

———

FROM THE " REGISTER OF WARRANTS FOR PAYMENT OF TRADESMEN &c." OF FREDERICK, PRINCE OF WALES, 5th July 1733

	£	s	d
To Mr In^o Kipling for the last Season of Operas' . . .	250	–	–

(British Museum : Add MS. 24, 403, fol. 43 a.) Kipling was the cashier of Handel's Opera House. Cf. 28th June 1734 and 5th July 1737.

———

FROM HEARNE's DIARY, 6th July 1733

The Players being denied coming to Oxford by the Vice-Chancellour and that very rightly, tho' they might as well have been here as Handel and (his lowsy Crew) a great number of forreign fidlers, they went to

Abbington, and yesterday began to act there, at which were present many Gownsmen from Oxford.

This being the Encoenia of the Theater of Oxford, Speeches, Declamations and Verses were spoke in the Theater, but I hear of nothing extraordinary in the performance.

Many years ago was printed with wooden cutts Brant's Ship of Fools, translated into English by Alex. Barclay. A Supplement should be put to it, containing an account of all those that encouraged Handel & his company last night at our Theater, and that intend to encourage him when our Act is over. The Vice-Chancellour is very right to have an Act, but then it should have been done in a statutable way, so as to begin today (the Encoenia being now reckoned part of the Act) being Friday & to end next Tuesday morning.

(Hearne, *Remarks*, XI. 225.) Abingdon is south of Oxford. The " players " were comedians, probably from London. *Encaenia* is the annual commemoration of founders and benefactors at Oxford University, usually held in June. Among the numerous young noblemen who recited, from 1 o'clock P.M. onwards, was Henege Finch, Lord Guernsey, a relative of Charles Jennens ; he read an oration " In Praise of True Magnificence " (Eland, pp. 10 f.). Cf. Handel's letter of 9th September 1742. Guernsey became the third Earl of Aylesford, and later owned Jennens' Handel scores, copied by the Smiths, and now in Sir Newman Flower's Handel Collection. One of the other papers was the Oratorium poem addressed to Handel, who was probably present. Sebastian Brant's famous *Narrenschiff* was translated as *The Shyp of Folys*, in 1509.

———

MUSICA SACRA DRAMATICA, SIVE ORATORIUM (CARMINE LYRICO)
Read by Henry Baynbrigg Buckeridge in the Theatre
at Oxford, on 7th July 1733

Satis superque audivimus *Orphea*
Pronos morantem fluminis impetus :
　　Saltus et auritos ferasque
　　Ducere carminibus peritum.

Pellaee Princeps, omnipotens lyra
Te vicit, Hosti cedere nefeium :
　　Iras amoresque excitavit
　　Timotheus variente dextra.

Procul profani cedite Musici,
Non ficta rerum, non steriles soni,
　　At sancta castas mulcet aures
　　Materies sociata chordis.

O Suada, sacro digna silentio,
Seu blanda saevi pectoris impetum
　　Delinit, aut victrix triumphos
　　Ingeminat graviore plectro.

Auditis ? O qui consonus intonat
Vocum tumultus ! Tollitur altius
   Iucundus horror, proripitque
   Ad superos animam *sequacem.*

Vicissitudo lenior ånxiam
Suspendit aurem, dum sociabilis
   Sermo sonorus praeparabit
   Grande melos vice gratiori.

Iam segniori Musica murmufat
Profunda pulsu : praescia dum canit
   Debora venturum triumphum, et
   Fausta Deo praeeunte bella.

Ad arma circum classica provocant,
Ad arma valles pulsaque littora :
   Iam refluo *Baracus* ingens
   Mergit equos equitesque fluxu.

Audin minaci murmure cornua
Laesa ? En ! tremendis fata tonitribus
   Remugit aurą, et militaris
   Harmoniae fremit omnis horror.

O surge victrix, surge potens Lyra.
Debora, Tu, Barace, minacium
   Victor Tyrannorum per urbes
   I celebres agita triumphos.

Sed praeparatam iam ferit artifex
Handelus aurem. *Musa* procax, tace.
   Victorias, pompas, triumphos
   Ille canet melior Poeta.

(Translation)

Musica Sacra Dramatica, Sive Oratorium (Carmine Lyrico)

Too often have we heard how *Orpheus'* Art
Would halt th' impetuous Motion of the Stream :
   The list'ning Glades and Beasts
   Skilful to lead in Song.

Great *Pella's* Prince, the Lyre omnipotent
Hath conquer'd thee, whom never Foe might quell :
   Timotheus varied Touch
   Bade Love and Anger flow.

Hence ye profane Musicians, be ye gone !
No fancied Tales, no unavailing Sounds,
   But join'd to Strings, a Theme
   Holy doth woo pure Ears :

H.–11

Persuasion, fittest heard in holy Calm,
Or mildly when the Rage of savage Breast
   She soothes, or conqu'ring, hymns
   Triumph with ampler Sweep :

But hark, the Voices how they thunder forth
Harmonious Tumult ! Higher yet is borne
   Glad Horror, and the Soul
   Obedient rapt to Heav'n.

And now a softer Variance doth suspend
The troubled Ear, till Speech in Unison
   Sonorous shall lead on
   The grand Song gratefully.

Then doth the Musick Murm'rings make profound
With Pulse more idle ; and prophetick sings
   Deborah sure Triumph, and
   Blest Wars when GOD doth guide.

To Arms around the Trumpets loud invoke,
To Arms the Valleys and the echoing Coasts ;
   Great *Barak*'s refluent Wave
   Rider and Steed doth whelm.

Hark, how with threat'ning Murmur are the Horns
Bruised ! The Fates with dreadful Thunderings
   Now th' Air resounds, and War
   Harmonious rolls around.

Arise victorious, thou whose Lyre prevail'd
Deborah ! Whom threat'ning Tyrants own'd their Lord,
   Barak, thro' all our Towns
   Thy populous Triumphs drive.

But *Handel*'s Master Touch now comes to play
On Ears expectant. Forward *Muse*, be still !
   For Vict'ries, Triumphs, Pomps
   No Bard can sing so well.

(Eland, p. 24.) Manuscript copy in Bodleian Library : Rawl. MS. C. 155, fol.
367, p. 4. Buckeridge was a gentleman commoner of St. John's College. Barak
is one of the personages in *Deborah*. The poem was translated into English by Mr.
Henry Gifford, of the Department of English, University of Bristol, for Cyril A.
Eland's paper on Handel in Oxford in 1733, and revised for this book : both authors
were good enough to consent to its publication here.

———

FROM APPLEBEE'S " ORIGINAL WEEKLY JOURNAL ", 7th July 1733

We hear from Oxford, that there is a curious Instrument lately
invented, and made by Mr. Munday an Organist, that has been blind
ever since he was five Years of Age. He plays upon the Harpsichord

and two Organs, either single or all together, with one set of Keys, wherein he makes 30 Varieties, without taking his Hands off.

(Eland, pp. 7 f.) This was a " claviorganum ", an earlier and simpler type of which is to be found in the Victoria and Albert Museum. It seems likely that Mr. Munday (Mundy ?) showed his invention to Handel.

—

FROM READ's " WEEKLY JOURNAL ", 7th July 1733

Oxford, July 2. Our Publick Act opens next Thursday [the 5th] Afternoon about Five o'Clock : Almost all our Houses not only within the City, but without the Gates, are taken up for Nobility, Gentry, and others : Many of the Heads of Houses and other Gentlemen of the University of Cambridge will be here on Wednesday Night ; and we are so hurry'd about Lodging, that almost all the Villages within three or four Miles of this City, make a good Hand of disposing of their little neat Tenements on this great Occasion.

(Eland, pp. 7 f.) Reprinted in the *Suffolk Mercury* of 9th July.

—

FROM HEARNE's DIARY, 8th July 1733

The Professor of Musick (who is Mr Richard Goodson) is on the Vespers, by virtue of the Statute, to read an English Lecture between 9 and 10 Clock in the morning in the Musick School, with a Consort of Musick also. But yesterday morning there was nothing done of that, only a little after six clock or about 7 was a sham consort by Goodson in the Theater, at which some Ladies were present, but not a soul was pleased, there being nothing of a Lecture. . . .

Half an hour after 5 Clock yesterday in the afternoon was another Performance, at 5*s*. a ticket, in the Theater by Mr Handel for his own benefit, continuing till about 8 clock. NB. his book (not worth 1*d*.) he sells for 1*s*.

(Hearne, *Remarks*, XI. 227.) The Oxford *Vespers*, was the Eve of the Act. Goodson, the younger, had been Professor of Music since 1718 ; he was a composer and organist of Christ Church and New College. The word-book of *Esther* was printed by John Watts in London, for Oxford, at the usual price of one shilling. It was probably on that day, when *Esther* was performed a second time, that Michael Christian Festing and Thomas Augustine Arne were present and heard Handel play his second organ concerto as an interlude in the oratorio ; they later told Burney they never heard such extempore or such " premeditated " playing (cf. p. 314).

—

On Sunday, 8th July 1733, Handel's *Utrecht Te Deum and Jubilate,* and two Coronation Anthems, are performed in St. Mary's Church under the direction of Powell.

The *Te Deum* was performed in the morning, and the *Jubilate* in the afternoon, sung by Powell, Roe and Waltz.

———

Handel's oratorio *Athalia* is produced at Oxford, 10th July 1733. The word-book, printed by John Watts for Oxford, was written by Humphreys, after Racine. The cast was as follows :

Athalia—Mrs. Wright, soprano
Josabeth—Signora Strada, soprano
Joas—the Boy (Goodwill), alto
Joad—(?) Mr. Powell, tenor
Mathan—Signor Rochetti, tenor
Abner—Mr. Waltz, bass

The production was at the Theatre, at half-past five. It was originally arranged for the 9th. A second performance was given on the 11th. Cf. 1st April 1735. " The Boy " was the usual name for an unbroken soprano or alto solo whose name was not to be given. The part of Abner was originally written for Montagnana (Smith, 1948, p. 176) ; this may indicate that *Athalia* was not especially composed for Oxford, or that Montagnana was expected to go there with Handel. (Chrysander, II. 317, states that the part of Joad was allotted to Montagnana.)

———

FROM HEARNE'S DIARY, 11th July 1733

Yesterday. . . . In the evening half hour after five a Clock, Handel & his Company performed again at the Theater, being the 3ʳᵈ time, at five shillings a Ticket.

(Hearne, *Remarks*, XI. 229.) This refers to the production of *Athalia* ; it seems that Hearne never attended Handel's performances.

———

FROM VISCOUNT PERCIVAL'S DIARY, 11th July 1733

I heard this day that the Prince [of Wales] . . . attempted to gain the favours of Mrs. Bartholdi, the Italian singer, and likewise of the Duchess of Ancaster's daughter, but both in vain.

(Egmont MSS., I. 390.) This refers to Signora Bertolli, formerly in Handel's opera company.

———

Acis and Galatea is performed at Christ Church Hall, Oxford, on 11th July, at 9 o'clock in the morning.

The cast was as follows :

Acis—Signor Rochetti, tenor
Galatea—Signora Strada, soprano

Polifemo—Mr. Waltz, bass
Coridon—Mr. Roe
Clori—Mrs. Wright, soprano
Sylvio—Mr. Powell, tenor
Damon—Mr. Salway, tenor

The version performed in Oxford was the bilingual one, of June 1732, with some alterations (information kindly supplied by Mr. Winton Dean). The libretto, of which no copy is available, was printed, like that of *Esther* and *Athalia*, by John Watts for Oxford (see *Gentleman's Magazine*, July 1733, p. 387), and according to Chrysander (preface to Vol. III of the Collected Edition) the title describes the work as " a Serenata : or Pastoral Entertainment ". Nothing is known about Mr. Roe, perhaps a local singer. It is said that this performance was for the benefit of some of Handel's musicians ; probably for Strada, Rochetti and Waltz.

———

FROM HEARNE'S DIARY, 12th July 1733

Yesterday morning from 9 clock in the morning till eleven, Handel & his Company performed their Musick in Christ Church Hall, at 3s a ticket. . . .

In the evening of the same day, at half hour after 5, Handel & his Crew performed again in the Theater at 5s per Ticket. This was the fourth time of his performing there.

(Hearne, *Remarks*, XI. 230.) The evening performance was a repeat of *Athalia*.

———

Deborah is performed at the Theatre in Oxford on the evening of 12th July 1733.

There is no word-book known ; otherwise the librettos for the Oxford Act were all printed in London by John Watts. Nothing is known of the cast. It is certain, however, that Strada sang Deborah, and it is probable that Waltz sang Abinoam, and Powell (see Hearne's entry of 13th July) Sisera, a part usually sung by an alto, but with an alternative for a tenor ; Mrs. Wright possibly sang Jael.

———

FROM HEARNE'S DIARY, 13th July 1733

Last night, being the 12th, Handel and his Company performed again in the Theater, being the 5th time of his performing there, at 5s. per Ticket, Mr Walter Powel (the Superior Beadle of Divinity) singing, as he hath done all along with them.

(Hearne, *Remarks*, XI. 230.) On 26th January 1732, Hearne noted in his diary : " Mr. Powell is a good natured man, & a good Singer, being Clarke of Magd. Coll. & singing man of St. John's ".

———

From Read's " Weekly Journal ", 14th July 1733

Oxford, July 8. On Friday last [the 6th] our Publick Act began, which was opened by a fine Concert of Musick by Mr. Handel and several of the best Performers (Vocal and Instrumental) in the Italian Opera's, and was graced with the Presence of a most noble and polite Audience, who were pleased to express their general Satisfaction. . . .

Mr. Handel has perform'd two of his Oratorio's by a Subscription of five Shillings with great Applause, which encourages him to continue them till the Conclusion of the Act.

———

From the " Craftsman ", 14th July 1733

Oxford, July 8. On Friday last [the 6th] began our publick Act with great Solemnity. . . . The Evening concluded with Mr. Handel's Oratorio, call'd *Esther*. On Saturday about Seven in the Morning there was a Piece of Musick performed in the Musick School . . . ; in the Afternoon there were Disputations in the Theatre, and afterwards an Oratorio.

This Day Mr. Handel's Te Deum and Anthems were perform'd in St. Mary's Church, before a numerous Assembly ; and To-morrow the Exercises in the Theatre are to be renew'd, and a new Oratorio perform'd, call'd *Athalia*. The University have been pleased to confer the Degree of Laws on the Right Hon. the Lord Sidney Beauclerck ; but Mr. Handel has not accepted his Degree of Doctor of Musick, as was reported, that Gentleman having declin'd the like Honour when tender'd him at Cambridge. There is a very great Appearance of Ladies at all the publick Entertainments, and the Town very full of Company.

The Act began, in fact, on Thursday the 5th. The music in the Theatre on Saturday morning was by Prof. Goodson. *Esther* was performed on the 5th and 7th. The production of *Athalia* was postponed from the 9th till the 10th. Handel was not really offered an honorary degree by Cambridge ; he is said to have refused such a suggestion because Greene, his " bellows-blower " at St. Paul's Cathedral about 1715, had received a Cambridge Doctor's degree, for setting Pope's " Ode for St. Cecilia's Day " to music, and since 1730 had been Professor of Music there. Modesty and the fee (of one hundred Pounds ?) asked for the honorary degree at Oxford are two other reasons given for Handel's refusal. Nothing is known for certain, however. The sentence referring to Handel's degree was reprinted in the *Suffolk Mercury* of 16th July, and quoted in Hearne's Diary on 18th July.

———

From the " Bee ", 14th July 1733

Oxford, July 10.

. . . As the Solemnity in conferring the Degrees on the Gentlemen before-mentioned engaged the Theatre to a very late Hour of that [yesterday's] Afternoon, Mr. Handel's new Oratorio, called Athalia, was deferred 'till this Day, when it was performed with the utmost Applause, and is esteemed equal to the most celebrated of that Gentleman's Performances : there were 3700 Persons present.

This paragraph also appeared in Read's *Weekly Journal* and in the *Universal Spectator* of that Day.

—

FROM THE "NORWICH GAZETTE", 14th July 1733

By the post today [the 10th] from Oxford it is advised, that the Publick Act opened there last Friday [the 6th] . . . towards Evening an oratorio of Mr. Handell's called Arthur [*sic*] was performed by about 70 Voices and Instruments of Musick, and was the grandest ever heard at Oxford. It is computed that the Tickets which were only 5s each amounted to £700.

From Dr. Mann's manuscript copy : no printed copy available. The last sentence appeared in the *Universal Spectator*, of the same day, in this version : " Oxford, July 8. . . . It is imputed Mr. Handel has got about 700l. already ".

—

FROM THE "WEEKLY REGISTER", 14th July 1733

Oxford. The Persons of Quality and Distinction who are come hither on this Occasion make a very grand Appearance, and are greater in Number than ever was known heretofore : the little Hutts of the neighbouring Villages are mostly filled with the Gentlemen of Cambridge and Eton, there being no Place empty in this or the Towns within five and six Miles about us.

(Eland, p. 8.) Copy in Bodleian Library, Oxford.

—

FROM HEARNE'S DIARY, 18th July 1733

The Prints speak of our late Act at Oxford after the following manner. They observe ' that our Public Act begun on Friday July 6 with great solemnity. . . . The evening concluded with Mr Handel's Oratorio called *Esther*. On Saturday July 7, after seven in the morning, there was a piece of musick [1] performed in the Musick School, and about nine the Lectures in the several other sciences ; in the afternoon there were disputations in the [Divinity School, Physick School, Law School and] Theatre, and afterwards an Oratorio. The next day, being Sunday July 8th, Mr Handel's *Te Deum* and Anthems were performed in St Mary's Church before a numerous Assembly, and the day after, being Monday, the Exercises in the Theatre were renew'd, and a new Oratorio performed called Athalia. (This is false, for 'twas not performed till

[1] But 'twas a very poor one, & there was no Musick Speech as used formerly to to be th' none hath been since 1693.

next evening, being Tuesday.) The University has been pleased to confer the Degree of Doctor of Laws, on the Right Hon. the Lord Sidney Beauclerck, but Mr Handel has not accepted his Degree of Doctor of Musick, as was reported, that Gentleman having declined the Honour, when tendered him at Cambridge. . . .' This is the Substance of the Prints of Monday July 16, as the Publishers received their Account from Oxford.

(Hearne, *Remarks*, XI. 232 f.) This is a digest from the newspapers quoted, with some remarks by the writer in brackets and in a footnote. The *Music Speech* had formerly been part of the *Encaenia* at Oxford.

—

FROM HEARNE'S DIARY, 19th July 1733

The Prints also, dated from London the 12th inst., say farther, that they write from Oxford, that on Monday, July 9th, the Theatre was again crowded . . . to hear the Disputations continued . . . ; and the next night (being Tuesday) another *Oratorio* of Mr Handel's, called Athalia, was performed in the Theatre, where 3700 Persons were present. . . .

And moreover from London of the 14th being Saturday 'tis noted that 'twas computed, that Mr Handel cleared by his Musick at Oxford upwards of 2000*l*.

(Hearne, *Remarks*, XI. 233.) The last note is known only from the *Norwich Gazette* of 21st July, but apparently appeared in a London paper before that date. What Hearne quotes from London papers of the 12th, was published, in fact, on the 14th.

—

FROM THE " NORWICH GAZETTE ", 21st July 1733

It is computed that the famous Mr. Handell cleared by his Musick at Oxford upwards of £2000.

From Dr. Mann's manuscript copy : no printed copy available. If it was true that Handel earned £700 up to the 8th of July, for the two *Esther* performances, it seems possible that the two *Athalia* performances and the single one of *Deborah* brought an additional sum of about £1300 (*Acis and Galatea* having been performed for the benefit of singers). Unfortunately, there is no entry in Handel's accounts with the Bank of England for the whole of 1733, and only one, on 26th June, in 1734. His expenses for the company's visit to Oxford, however, must have been considerable.

—

FROM THE " GENTLEMAN'S MAGAZINE ", July 1733

Friday, 6. . . . Begun the Publick Act at *Oxford*. . . . On *Sunday*, Mr *Handel's Te Deum* and Anthems were perform'd in St. *Mary's Church*.

. . . On *Tuesday* Mr *Handel's* new Oratorio, call'd *Athalia*, was perform'd with vast Applause, before an Audience of 3700 Persons. . . .
The Order of the Philological Performances at the *Oxford* Act.

CONCERT. I.

. . . 13. *Henry Baynbrigg Buckeridge*, of St John Baptist Coll. Gentleman-Commoner. *On the sacred Dramatic Music, or Oratorio.* In Lyric Verse.

CONCERT. II.

1. Ld. *Guernsey*, Son of the E. of *Aylesford*, of Univ. Coll. *The Praise of true Magnificence.* In Lyric Verse. . . .

"*Concert.*" stands for *concertatio, i.e.* disputation.

———

FROM THE "LONDON MAGAZINE", July 1733

WEDNESDAY, 11. Advice from *Oxford*. . . .
The Verses and Orations spoken by young Noblemen and others, were on the following Subjects, *viz. On the Oxford Act.* . . . *On the sacred Dramatic Music, or Oratorio. The Praise of true Magnificence.* . . .
. . . On the *Saturday* Mr. *Handel's* Oratorio of *Esther* was done a second Time.
On *Sunday* . . . at St. *Mary's* . . . Mr. *Handel's* *Te ·Deum, Jubilate,* and *Anthems,* were performed by a great Number of the best Instruments, the Vocal Parts by Mr. *Powel,* Mr. *Wartz,* and Mr. *Roe.* The Galleries both Morning and Afternoon were reserved for the Ladies, who made a most beautiful and grand Appearance to near 800.
On the *Monday.* . . . As the Solemnity in conferring the Degrees . . . engag'd the Theatre to a very late Hour of that Afternoon, Mr. *Handel's* new Oratorio, call'd *Athalia,* was deferr'd to the next Day, when it was performed with the utmost Applause, to an Audience of near 4,000.

———

Giulio Cesare is revived at Hamburg, 6th (17th) August 1733.
(Loewenberg, p. 77.) Cf. 10th November 1725.

———

FROM HEARNE'S DIARY, 8th August 1733

An old man of Oxford . . . observed to me, that our late Oxford Act was the very worst that ever was . . ., and I think his observation was just, tho' it must be said, that the Vice-Chancellor is to be commended for having an Act (tho' not for bringing Handel & his Company from London). . . .

(Hearne, *Remarks*, XI. 239.)

———

H.–11 *a*

HANDEL TO MICHAELSEN, AT HALLE

London, den $\frac{21}{10}$ August 1733.

Monsieur et tres Hoñoré Frere

Ich empfing dessen HochgeEhrtes vom verwichenen Monath mit der Innlage von unsern liebwehrtesten Anverwandten in Gotha, worauf mit dieser Post geantwortet. Ich freue mich von Herzen desselben und sämptlichen Wehrtesten Famille gutes Wohlseyn zu vernehmen, als dessen beharrliche Continuation ich allstets anerwünsche. Sonsten sehe die grosse Mühewaltung so sich mein HochgeEhrtester Herr Bruder abermahl genoṁen wegen der Einnahme und Ausgabe vom vergangenen Jahre vom ersten July 1732 bis dreysigsten July 1733, wegen meiner Seeligen Fr. Mutter hinterlassenen Hauses, und muss mier meine schuldige Dankbarkeit dessfalls vorbehalten.

Es erwehnet mein HochgeEhrter Herr Bruder dass es wohl nöthig wäre dass ich solches selbsten in Augenschein nähmen möchte, aber, wie sehr ich auch verlange denenselbigen Ihriges Orths eine Visite zu machen so wollen deñoch der mier bevorstehende unvermeidliche Verrichtungen, so mich gewiss sehr überhäuffen solches Vergnügen mier nicht vergönnen, will aber bedacht sein meine Sentiments dessfalls schrifftlich zu senden.

Es hat mein HochgeEhrter Herr Bruder sehr wohl gethan sich zu erinnern meiner lieben Seeligen Fr. Mutter letzten Willen wegen Ihres Leichensteines zu beobachten, und hoffe dass derselbe wird selbigen vollfüllen.

Ich ersehe aus der überschickten Rechnung dass de Fr. Händelin so im Hause wohnet sechs reichsthaler des Jahres Stubenzins gibet, ich könte wünschen dass solcher ins künfftige Ihr erlassen werden möcht so lange als Sie beliebet darinnen zu wohnen.

Ich übersende hierbey verlangter maassen die überschickte Rechnung von mier unterschrieben, meine obligation desfals werde gewiss nicht in vergessenheit stellen. Ich mache meine ergebenste Empfehlung an dero HochgeEhrteste Fr. Liebste. grüsse zum schönsten die wehrte Täustische Famille und alle gute Freunde. Ich werde bald wiederum meinem HochgeEhrtesten Herrn Bruder beschwehrlich fallen, hoffe aber, da ich desselben Gutheit kenne, dessfalls dessen pardon zu erhalten, ich bitte zu glauben dass ich lebenslang mit aller auffrichtigen Ergebenheit verbleiben werde

Meines Insonders HochgeEhrtesten Herrn Bruder
bereitwilligst gehorsamster Diener
George Friederich Händel.

A Monsieur
Monsieur Michael Dietrich Michaelsen
Conseiller de Guerre de Sa Majesté Prussienne
a Halle en Saxe

(Translation)

London, $\frac{21\text{st}}{10\text{th}}$ August 1733.

Honoured Brother,

I received your highly honoured letter of last month, with the enclosure from our beloved relatives in Gotha, which is answered by this post. I heartily enjoyed hearing of yours and of all your worthy family's well-being, and I desire always that this may continue. I see besides the great pains which my honoured brother has again taken on account of the receipts and expenditures of the past year, from the first of July 1732 to the thirtieth of July 1733 as regards the house left by my blessed mother, and I must keep in reserve my due gratitude in this connection.

My honoured brother mentions that it might well be necessary that I personally should inspect such, but however much I long to pay a visit to the people of your place, nevertheless the imminent and inevitable matters of business, which indeed quite overwhelm me, do not allow me such a pleasure ; I will, however, bear in mind to send in writing what I feel about it.

My honoured brother has done well in remembering to take heed of my dear, blessed mother's last wishes with regard to her tombstone, and I hope that he himself will fulfil those same wishes.

I perceive from the transmitted account that Frau Händel, who resides in the house, pays six Reichsthaler for a year's rent, I could wish that in the future she might be absolved from paying such, as long as she likes to remain in occupation.

I consign herewith, as desired, the transmitted account signed by me, and will surely not forget my obligation in the case. I pay my respectful regards to your honoured wife, graciously greet the worthy Taust family and all good friends. I shall soon be an inconvenience again to my honoured brother, but hope, as I know the goodness of the same, to receive his pardon in the matter ; I pray he will believe that I shall with all sincere devotion lifelong remain

My especially honoured brother's
willingly obedient servant,
George Friederich Händel.

(Mueller von Asow, pp. 128 f.) Original formerly in the collection of Dr. Ernst Foss, Berlin. The house in question was that called " Zum gelben Hirschen ", bought by Handel's father in 1665, and long supposed to be Handel's birthplace ; he was, in fact, born next door, in the house on the corner. For the tombstone of Handel's parents, see 11th February 1697. The Frau Händel mentioned at the end of the letter may have been the daughter-in-law of Handel's half-brother Karl, widow of the valet de chambre Georg Christian Händel. Handel did not go to the Continent in the summer of 1733, as assumed by Hawkins (V. 318) and Chrysander (II. 332).

FROM THE WORD-BOOK OF THE BALLAD-OPERA, "THE OXFORD ACT",
PUBLISHED August 1733

Act I.

Thoughtless. I am sure there were as many Books as cost me Twenty
Pounds all gone for Five. In the next Place, there's the Furniture of
my Room procur'd me some Tickets to hear that bewitching Musick,
that cursed HANDEL, with his confounded ORATIO's ; I wish him and
his Company had been yelling in the infernal Shades below. . . .

Act II.

Haughty. Our Cases run in a Parallel ; nay, 'tis worse with me, for I
question whether my gaping Herd of Creditors won't be for sequestring
my Fellowship or not. I don't see what Occasion we had for this Act,
unless it was to ruin us all : It would have been much more prudent, I
think, had it pass'd in the Negative ; for I am sure it has done more
Harm than Good amongst us ; no one has gain'd any thing by it but Mr.
HANDEL and his Crew.

Pendant. Very true ; we had Fiddlers enough here before, and by
squandering away the Profits of our Fellowships, we not only endanger
our Reputation, but our own dear Persons too, Brother : for this Act
has run me so far into Debt, that if a catchpole should clap me on the
Shoulder, I know of no other remedy to satisfy my Creditors but to go
to Jail.

Haughty. God forbid, Brother ; I dont doubt but what the Publick
Stock of the University is very much diminished too by these extravagant
expenses. And as for the younger Sort, nothing could have done them a
greater Piece of Disservice. There's my pupil DICK THOUGHTLESS says,
this last Fortnight has stood him in above an Hundred Pounds, and I
question whether it may not be true, for DICK's a generous young
Fellow. . . .

Act III.

Vice Chancellor. I dare say, if the Truth was known, most of your
money was spent in tickets to hear the ORATORIO's ; I must confess a
Crown each was rather too much ; but had you been contented with a
single one, without treating all your Acquaintance, that could never have
hurt you.

Haughty. Lord, Sir, you must excuse me ; so many years can never
have rolled over your head and find you ignorant that MUSICK has
Charms to sooth the savage Soul, and much more rational Men ; . . .
so you would not suppose US to be such Brutes as to engross all the
Pleasure to ourselves, without complimenting our Friends with a Par-
ticipation of it. . . .

(Schoelcher, p. 158 ; Chrysander, II. 309 ; Mee, p. XV ; Eland, pp. 20-22.)
Bodleian Library : Gough Oxf 59. pp. 7, 13 and 28. This is a scurrilous report of

the Act, in the form of a ballad-opera, the word-book printed in London, " As it was performed by a Company of Students at Oxford ". (1s.) The opera, probably never performed, contains on p. 18 a parody of Henry Carey's *Sally in our Alley*. The scene of the plot is Merton Walks, and the cast contains " Thoughless, a Scholar : Haughty and Pendant, Dons ". The pamphlet, printed by " L. Gulliver ", was listed as published in the *Gentleman's Magazine* of August 1733. Cf. the other " **Oxford Act** ", June 1734.

———

FROM ANTOINE FRANÇOIS PRÉVOST'S " LE POUR ET CONTRE ", PARIS, [August ?] 1733 (Translated)

. . . I have singular and curious facts to impart on England, whose literary history is little known outside its own frontiers. But I have to announce something even more pleasant for this first sheet—namely, the most remarkable ceremony which has just taken place in the University of Oxford for the reception of the famous musician *Handel* into the degree of *Doctor of Music*. It is the first of its kind. The English are persuaded that the best means of encouraging the Arts is to accord those who excel in them the most honourable distinctions. In this country whoever rises above his fellows, in whatever province [of art] it may be, passes for a great man. Father Courayer was seen in his place at this ceremony in his Doctor's robes. ⸳ . . .

Although I had only undertaken to describe what took place at Oxford on July 20th, on the understanding given to me that I would be sent a detailed account of it, which I have not yet received, yet I do not consider myself excused from carrying out that intention in part this very day, in order that my readers may learn to have confidence in my promises. . . .

The University of Oxford has this advantage that, being endowed with [so many] favours and riches by the kings of England and the liberalities of countless private persons, its happy members need not have any other cares but for honour and the advancement of knowledge. . . .

In accordance with these principles, which have led the University on numerous occasions of its own accord to single out merit and virtue for the receipt of its honours, it considers itself obliged to recognise the extraordinary talents of Mr. Handel in music. This ingenious man was born in Germany. He has lived in London a long time now ; few winters pass without seeing some admirable work appear from his pen. Never has perfection in any art been combined in the same man with such fertility of production. Every *opera* (a), every *concerto*, and so on, is a masterpiece. Recently he has introduced to London a new kind of composition which goes under the name of *Oratorio* (b). Although the subject is taken from Scripture, the audiences are no smaller than at the Opera. He is master of all the styles : the sublime, the tender, the gay, the graceful. Some critics however accuse him of having borrowed the matter of many beautiful things from Lully, especially from our French Cantatas, which he has the skill, so they say, to disguise in the

Italian style. But the crime would be venial, were it even certain ; and besides it will be agreed that, [considering] the multitude of works that Mr. Handel has composed, it is extremely difficult for there not to be occasionally coincidences with other composers' works (c).

Conscious of his eminent merit, the University of Oxford offered its highest honours to Mr. Handel, with the glorious title of *Doctor of Music*. The day of the ceremony was to be July 20 (d), for which date had been arranged the reception of a great number of other doctors and *Masters of Arts*. Mr. Handel went to Oxford, but they were surprised to see him refuse the marks of distinction which were proposed for him. Such modesty alone could bear comparison with his talents. He did not fail to express his lively gratitude to the University, and to contribute to making the ceremony for the other [recipients] the more brilliant. . . . It was so late when he [the Vice-Chancellor] concluded, that they were obliged to put off till the morrow the expression of Mr. Handel's gratitude. This took the form of an *Oratorio* of his composition, called *Athalie*, which is claimed to be the equal of all his best works hitherto. The audience numbered 3700 persons, almost all ladies and gentlemen of the highest rank. Never has there been such applause and marks of admiration.

(a) Competent musicians have informed me that *Julius Caesar*, *Scipione*, and *Rodelinda* are his best works.

(b) This is a kind of sacred cantata, divided into scenes, but without dramatic form and stage action.

(c) This does honour to our musicians without harming Mr. Handel.

(d) The 10th [or rather 11th] according to the English mode of reckoning.

Prévost d'Exiles, the author of the famous novel *Manon Lescaut*, lived in England from 1728 to 1730 and again from 1733 to 1734. From 1733 to 1740 he edited a weekly " d'un goût nouveau ", " par l'auteur des Memoirs d'un homme de Qualité ", *i.e.* anonymously. The numbers are not dated exactly, but the re-issue in book-form contains the dates on which publication of each of the ten octavo volumes was approved. The extracts quoted above are from vol. I, nos. VIII, p. 188, and IX, pp. 204-9, probably published in August 1733. Of Pierre François Courayer, since 1727 honorary D.D. Oxford, Prévost says on p. 209 : " Le Pere Corayer, ajoûte l'Auteur de cette Relation, qui est en Angleterre depuis sept ans, pour avoir défendu l'Eglise Anglicanne, se fit voir sur le Theatre pendant toute la cerémonie en robe de Docteur . . .". He held an Oxford degree.

———

Giulio Cesare is revived at Brunswick during the Summer fair, August 1733.

(Chrysander, II. 109 ; Loewenberg, p. 77.) Cf. August 1725. The libretto of *Giulio Cesare e Cleopatra* . . ., " da representarsi nel famosissimo teatro di Brounsviga nella fiera d'Estate l'anno 1733 ", was printed at Wolfenbüttel.

———

Handel finishes the opera *Arianna in Creta* (" Ariadne in Crete "), 5th October 1733.

———

Partenope is performed at Hamburg, 17th (28th) October 1733.

(Chrysander, II. 239 ; Merbach, p. 364 ; Loewenberg, p. 84.) The text was translated by Christian Gottlieb Wendt, with German recitatives by Reinhard Keiser, Handel's arias being sung in Italian. The opera was performed seven times in the season of 1733–4, five times in 1735, and nine times in 1736.

———

The opera season at the Haymarket Theatre opens on 30th October 1733, the King's Birthday, with a pasticcio-opera, *Semiramide riconosciuta*, text by Pietro Metastasio, with recitatives provided by Handel.

(Chrysander, II. 333 f.) Handel opened his house two months before the Nobility Opera was able to start, and, in spite of the fact that it was usual to give a ball at St. James's Palace on the King's birthday, he succeeded in having the Court, including the Prince of Wales, in the audience (*Daily Courant*, 31st October). For the new singers in Handel's company, see 13th November. The opera was repeated on 3rd, 6th and 9th November According to Colman, the King, Queen and Prince of Wales also attended the last performance. The music of *Semiramide* is said to have been probably mainly by Antonio Vivaldi (Smith, 1948, p. 178).

———

FROM COLMAN'S " OPERA REGISTER ", 30th October 1733

Haymarket. Handells House Sigra Margarita Durastanti return'd to England.

Oct. 30. Tuesday K. G. Birthday. Semeramis. a new Opera

———

FROM PRÉVOST'S " LE POUR ET CONTRE ", PARIS [October ?] 1733 (Translated)

The opera theatre [in London], built by Mr. Hydegger and owing its great reputation to the works of Mr. Handel, had maintained itself for several years with incredible success. It was there that was witnessed the spectacle of *Signora Faustina* making 1800 pounds sterling on one single benefit evening,—that is, about 40,000 French livres. *Signor Senesino, Signora Cuzzeni* and a number of other excellent singers have in their turn drawn benefits in proportion to their merits. The musicians were paid on a no less liberal scale, and the hope of gain attracted them from all quarters of Europe. . . . Winter is [now] coming on. You already know how there was an irreconcilable rupture between Senesino and Handel, and how the former produced a schism in the company and hired a separate theatre for himself and his partisans. His enemies sent for the best voices in Italy ; they pride themselves on keeping going despite his machinations and those of his clique. So far the English nobility has been divided ; victory will remain in the balance a long time if they have enough determination not to change their minds. But it is expected that the first few performances will put an end to the quarrel, since the better of the two theatres cannot fail to attract very soon the support of them all.

Vol. II., no. XVI., pp. 21-3. Probably published in October 1733, the book edition approved on 21st February 1734. No reference could be found, in previous issues of this magazine, to the quarrel between Handel and Senesino.

———

LADY BRISTOL TO HER HUSBAND, JOHN HERVEY, EARL OF BRISTOL

[London,] Nov. 3, 1733.

I am just come home from a dull empty opera, tho' the second time ; the first was full to hear the new man, who I can find out to be an extream good singer ; the rest are all scrubs except old Durastante, that sings as well as ever she did.

(*Letter-Books*, III. 108 ; Streatfeild, p. 130, quoting the letter without exact date, refers it to the second performance of *Cajo Fabricio*, which was on 8th December 1733 ; Flower, p. 284, quotes the letter as of 1741.) The Earl was the father of Lord John Hervey. The new opera was *Semiramide*, the new man Carestini ; see 13th November.

———

FROM THE " DAILY JOURNAL ", 13th November 1733

At the King's Theatre . . . this present Tuesday . . . will be reviv'd an Opera, call'd OTHO. . . .

N.B. The Princess Royal's Marriage being put off, the Opera will be perform'd this Day as usual.

Princess Anne was to have been married on the 12th to Prince William of Orange, but since he fell ill, the wedding was postponed (14th March 1734). The King, the Queen and the Prince of Wales attended the Opera. It was repeated on 17th, 20th and 24th November. The cast (compared with that of 12th January 1723) was as follows :

> Ottone—Signor Carestini (Senesino)
> Teofane—Signora Strada (Cuzzoni)
> Emireno—Mr. Waltz (Boschi)
> Gismonda—Signora Durastanti (Durastanti)
> Adelberto—Signor Scalzi (Berenstadt)
> Matilda—Signora Maria Caterina Negri (Robinson)

For an earlier revival, which did not materialize, Senesino, Strada, Montagnana, Gismondi, Mountier and Bertolli were chosen by Handel (Smith, 1948, p. 178). Of his new singers, Giovanni Carestini, whom Handel had tried to engage long before, had been a soprano, but changed his voice to an alto ; Signora Margherita Durastanti, called Durastini, who returned after nine years' absence, was a mezzo-soprano ; Carlo Scalzi, a second soprano ; Maria Caterina Negri a contralto (her sister Rosa, a soprano, came with her). For other revivals of *Ottone* see 5th February 1726 and 11th April 1727.

———

The orator John Henley mentions Handel in his speech on St. Cecilia's Day, 19th November 1733.

(Chrysander, III. 21.) No copy of Henley's advertisement in the *Daily Journal* of 17th November is available. Chrysander, who saw it, gives a German translation which may be re-translated : " The Harmony of Heaven, or the constituent parts and true Nature of Divine Music, with a clue, to review, to understand and to compose such Music on all occasions ; mistakes therein, and in the work of several organists, criticized ; the characters of Dr. Pepusch, Corelli, Bononcini, Handel, Purcell ; the great problem—Why are there only seven notes in Music?—resolved, etc. At the same time seasonable advice to the B. [Bishop of London] regarding an imminent opportunity [the marriage of Princess Anne] for not committing six mistakes."

———

Title of a Pamphlet as Advertised in the " Gentleman's Magazine ", November 1733

Do you know what you are about ? Or, a Protestant Alarm to Great Britain ; Proving our late Theatric Squabble to be a Type of the present Contest for the Crown of Poland ; and that the Division between Handel and Senesino has more in it than we imagine. Also that the latter is no Eunuch, but a Jesuit in Disguise. Printed for J. Roberts, price 6d.

(Chrysander, II. 338.) No copy of the pamphlet is known. The struggle between August III and Stanislaus Leszcynski for the throne of Poland led to the war of 1733–5.

———

Another pasticcio-opera, *Cajo Fabricio*, text by Apostolo Zeno, with recitatives by Handel, is produced at the Haymarket Theatre, 4th December 1733.

(Chrysander, II. 333.) Repeat performances on 8th, 15th and 22nd December ; the last attended by the King. Chrysander thought that Carestini made his first appearance in this opera. It seems that Johann Adolf Hasse's music of 1732 was used for the production (Smith, 1948, p. 183).

———

The Alchemist is performed at the New Theatre in the Haymarket, 20th December 1733 (with Handel's music ?).

Cf. 7th March 1732.

———

From the " Daily Post ", 25th December 1733

Last Night there was a Rehearsal of a new Opera at the Prince of Wales' House in the Royal Gardens in Pall Mall, where was present a great Concourse of the Nobility and Quality of both Sexes : some of the choicest Voices and Hands assisted in the Performance.

(Chrysander, II. 326.) See the following advertisement, printed in the same issue. The Prince resided, since 1732, in Carlton House.

FROM THE SAME

At the Theatre Royal in Lincoln's-Inn-Fields, on Saturday next, being the 29th Day of December, will be perform'd a new Opera, call'd ARIADNE. . . .

Ariadne in Naxus (*Arianna in Nasso*) was a new opera by Nicola Porpora, with text by Rolli (see Frank Walker in *Italian Studies*, VI. 48, 1950) ; the libretto was dedicated to the wife of the Spanish Ambassador, but the music to the British Nobility (cf. 28th March 1734). (It is noteworthy that Handel was about to produce his *Ariadne in Crete*.) The house of the Nobility Opera was that left by Rich when he moved to Covent Garden, and was used by Handel's antagonists for one season only, until he went to Covent Garden, and they to the Haymarket. The new company consisted of Handel's former singers : Senesino, Montagnana, Cuzzoni, Gismondi and Bertolli. Signora Cuzzoni, however, did not arrive until the spring of 1734 and, in the meantime, Maria Segatti was a useful addition to the company, which did not include Strada. Porpora was engaged as composer and conductor. Rolli was the poet of the company.

FROM JAMES BRAMSTON'S "THE MAN OF TASTE. OCCASION'D BY AN EPISTLE OF MR. POPE'S ON THAT SUBJECT. BY THE AUTHOR OF THE ART OF POLITICKS ", 1733

Without *Italian*, or without an ear,
To *Bononcini*'s musick I adhere. . . .
Bagpipes for men, shrill *German-flutes* for boys,
I'm *English* born, and love a grumbling noise.
The Stage should yield the solemn Organ's note,
And Scripture tremble in the Eunuch's throat.
Let *Senesino* sing, what *David* writ,
And *Hallelujahs* charm the pious pit.
Eager in throngs the town to *Hester* came,
And *Oratorio* was a lucky name.
Thou, *Heideggre* ! the English taste has found,
And rul'st the mob of quality with sound.
In *Lent*, if Masquerades displease the town,
Call 'em *Ridotto*'s, and they still go down :
Go on, Prime *Phyz* ! to please the British nation,
Call thy next *Masquerade* a *Convocation*.

The poem appeared anonymously in octavo and folio editions. The quotation is from pp. 13 f. For Pope's poem, see 13th December 1731. For the answer, cf. the next entry, *The Woman of Taste*.

FROM "THE WOMAN OF TASTE. OCCASIONED BY A LATE
POEM, ENTITLED, 'THE MAN OF TASTE'. BY A FRIEND OF THE
AUTHOR'S", 1733

... Wou'd you then grace the box, or ball adorn,
Let none perceive you were in Britain born ;
From *Paris* take your step, from *Rome* your song,
And breathe *Italian* musically wrong. . . .
  The joy of young and old, of maid and wife,
Ne'er miss the *Oratorio* for your life. . . .
  To make her triumphs and his art the greater,
Here *Handell* kills fair *Hester's* foes in metre ;
Flutes keep due measure with the victim's pangs,
Faustina quav'ring just as *Haman* hangs
Now warbling baudry – – – in a holier post,
Now chanting anthems to *the Lord of Host.*
To make the service to each master even,
By *Satan* now employ'd, and now by *heaven* ;
And either to displease exceeding loath,
Receives two honest fees to serve 'em both :
The beauteous *Hebrew* pensive for a time,
Marry'd by *Humphreys* to the king of rhime.
Each pulpit scorn'd, the good reforming age
More fond of morals taught 'em by the stage ;
(Which though they may some prelates hearts perplex,
Hit you and I, and all our modish sex.)
A vicious town and court, not half so soon
Made vertuous by a sermon as a tune ;
Whose melting notes the souls of sinners sooth,
Who fly from *Gibs* – – *n* to be sav'd by *Booth* ;
In pit or box perform their Maker's will,
Made saints by maxims taught 'em at quadrille :
From *Rich's* hands who absolution take,
Pardon'd by *Cibber*, though condemn'd by *W* – – – *ke.*

There were at least two editions of this poem, both printed in 1733. The
quotation is from pp. 7, 8-9. Cf. the previous entry, *The Man of Taste.* Edmund
Gibson was the Bishop of London and William Wake the Archbishop of Canterbury ; Barton Booth was an actor who died on 10th May 1733 ; Humphreys
wrote the word-book of *Esther* ; Rich was the manager of Covent Garden ;
Colley Cibber was the Poet Laureate.

———

FROM "POLYMNIA ; OR, THE CHARMS OF MUSICK", 1733

An Hymn or Ode, Sacred to Harmony ; Occasion'd by Mr. Handel's
Oratorio, and the Harmonia Sacra, Perform'd at Whitehall, by the
Gentlemen of the Chappel-Royal. By a Gentleman of Cambridge.

To Mr. Handel.

I raise my Voice, but you can raise it high'r,
And to bold Notes, can bolder string my Lyre :
Tun'd by thy Art, my artless Muse may live,
And from the pleasing Strains may Pleasure give.
Deep hid in Thought may buried Raptures roll,
Light up the Bard, and fire his kind'ling Soul.
If genial Beams, on Earth, th' Almighty spreads,
To ripen Metals, sleeping in their Beds.
Hence lively Brilliants into Being strive,
From waking Seeds, yet doubtful if alive.
Hence, may your Song, my rougher Song, refine ;
To pierce, like Diamonds, and like Diamonds, shine.
When melting Solo's steal th' attentive Ear,
Dead is my Sorrow, and extinct my Fear.
But when the full-mouth'd Chorus wounds the Sky,
The Dead with Fear awake, the Living die.
So with the rising Musick, Passions rise,
As with the dying Musick Passion dies.

(Myers, 1948, pp. 49 f.) There were three editions printed in 1733, but no copy is known in Britain. A copy of the third edition is in the Library of Columbia University, New York City. George I converted the Banqueting-House, Whitehall, into a Royal Chapel ; it was dismantled in 1890. " Harmonia Sacra " probably means nothing more than sacred music.

———

" Mr. Hendel, Docteur en Musique, London " subscribes for Georg Philipp Telemann's *Musique de Table* (Hamburg 1733).

Handel was the only subscriber in Britain. Between 1735 and 1746 he made good use of the book, taking sixteen movements by Telemann into his own works. Cf. Max Seiffert in " Bulletin de la Société ' Union musicologique ' ", IV. 1, La Haye 1924, and in " Beihefte zu den Denkmälern deutscher Tonkunst ", no. 11, Leipzig 1927 ; also Stanley Godman in " The Listener ", London, 6th September 1951.

———

1734

ROLLI'S SATIRICAL VERSES ON CARESTINI, (?) 1734

Che Scalzi e Carestin, que due Campioni
vengan per Handel, non è già una favola :
chè quel grand' Uom mai non si pone a tavola
senza un piatto di due grossi Capponi.

Ma il mandar via questo Cappone è un fallo,
fallo cagionator di sue ruine,
perchè il mio Senesin estimato è un Gallo
di tutte le Brittaniche Galline.

[Those two champions, Scalzi and Carestini, have come to Handel because that great man does not sit down to table without a dish of two fat capons. But to send away this capon would be a mistake that would undo him, for my Senesino is reckoned the cock of all the British chickens.]

(Cellesi, 1930, p. 320.) Manuscript in Biblioteca Comunale, Siena. Not in Rolli's *Rime*, printed at Verona in 1733, nor among the epigrams in volume 2 of his *De' Poetici componimenti*, Venice, 1753. *Il grand' Uom* is Handel.

DISPATCH ADDRESSED BY CASPAR WILHELM VON BROCKE, PRUSSIAN MINISTER IN LONDON, TO KING FRIEDRICH WILHELM OF PRUSSIA, 1st (12th) January 1734
(Translated)

Last Saturday [29th December 1733] the opening of the new *Opera-house* took place, which the *Noblesse* has undertaken since they were not satisfied with the *Conduite* of the *Directeur* of the old *Opera, Händel*, and, to abase him, planned a new one, to which over two hundred people *subscribed*, and each one contributed 20 *guineas*. The premier singer, *Senesino*, is stamped on the *Piquet* of the subscribers, and has the super-scription : *Nec pluribus impar*. It was this *Opera-house* which was first called the *Opera-house* of the rebels. Since the whole Court, however, was present at the first *Ouverture* it has become thereby *legalised* and *loyal*. In this the *genius* of the nation has shown itself, namely, how very inclined it is to *novelties* and *factions*. In the *preliminary treaties* which were drawn up for this *foundation*, the first article runs : Point d'accom-modement à jamais avec le Sr Händel.

(Friedlaender, pp. 103 f.) Geheimes Staatsarchiv, Berlin. Brocke was the first German to translate a Shakespeare play : *Julius Caesar* ; he was in London from 1733 to 1737. Friedrich Wilhelm I, first cousin to George II, liked Handel's music. It is assumed that the dispatch was written on 1st January 1734 old style, which was the 12th in the new one.

———

Arbace, with recitatives by Handel, is produced at the Haymarket Theatre, 5th January 1734.

(Schoelcher, p. 161 ; Chrysander, II. 334.) The word-book by Pietro Metastasio was set in 1730 as *Artaserse* by Leonardo Vinci for Rome and by Johann Adolf Hasse for Venice. Carestini sang in the Venice version, but according to Mrs. Pendarves (28th March 1734) it was Vinci's version which was used in London. There were eight performances of *Arbace* ; on the first night the Court was present without the Prince of Wales, but on 8th January the Prince also attended. Cf. 29th October 1734.

———

From the " Grub-street Journal ", 10th January 1734

Preliminary articles of peace between the Patentees and the Revel company of Comedians.

I. There shall instantly commence an entire Suspension of Arms on both Sides.

·   ·   ·   ·   ·

XIII. The most high and puissant John Frederick Handell, prince Palatine of the Hay-market, the most sublime John James Heidegger, Count of the most sacred and holy Roman Empire, and the most noble and illustrious Signior Senesino, little duke of Tuscany, do engage for themselves, their heirs and successors, to become guarantees for the due performance and execution of all, every, and singular the articles of this present treaty.

Done in the camp in New-palace-yard before Westminster-hall, this 28th day of November, in the year of our Lord 1733.

Copy in Bodleian Library, Oxford : N. 22863, c. 3. These are the first and last of the thirteen articles of an imaginary peace treaty. The satire was reprinted in the *London Magazine* of January 1734.

———

The King and the Prince of Wales attend a Ball at the Haymarket Theatre, 24th January 1734.

(Smith, 1948, p. 180.)

———

From the " Daily Journal ", 26th January 1734

At the King's Theatre . . . this present Saturday . . . will be perform'd a new Opera, call'd Ariadne. . . .

Arianna in Creta, text by Pietro Pariati (*Arianna e Teseo*), arranged by (?) Francis Colman, who died in Pisa on 9th (20th) April 1733, was performed on 26th, 29th January ; 2nd, 5th, 9th, 12th, 16th, 19th, 23rd, 26th February; 2nd, 5th, 9th, 12th,

16th March ; 16th and 20th April ; to be revived in November and December 1734. The libretto is bilingual, as usual ; the English version perhaps by Samuel Humphreys. (For the authorship of the text, see Frank Walker in *Italian Studies*, VI. 48, 1950.) The Court, including the Prince of Wales, attended the performances on 12th February and 5th March. For Porpora's *Arianna* see 29th December 1733.

———

CAST OF " ARIANNA IN CRETA ", 26th January 1734
Arianna—Signora Strada, soprano
Teseo—Signor Carestini, alto
Carilda—Signora Maria Caterina Negri, contralto
Alceste—Signor Scalzi, soprano
Minos—Mr. Waltz, bass
Tauride—Signora Durastanti, mezzo-soprano
Il Sonno—?, bass

Eisenschmidt (II. 93 f.) stresses the fact that the sleeping Teseo dreams of scenes which were apparently produced as a ballet (but not that of Covent Garden, as indicated by Eisenschmidt).

———

FROM THE DIARY OF THE EARL OF EGMONT, 29th January 1734

Went to Hendel's opera, called " Ariadne ".

(Egmont MSS., II. 18.) In August 1733, Viscount Percival became the first Earl of Egmont.

———

FROM COLMAN'S " OPERA REGISTER ", January 1734

Janry pmo Ariadne in Crete a new Opera & very good & perform'd very often—Sigr Carestino sung surprisingly well : a new Eunuch— many times perform'd

Loewenberg (p. 93) points out that this entry was written after the supposed author of the *Opera Register* and the assumed translator of Handel's *Arianna* died in Italy. While this entry is dated 1st January, the following is entered after one of 18th April : " Opera Lincolns Inn Fields. Senesino's House a new Opera open'd in January 1733–4 Ariadne in Naxus, Sig Senesino Sigra Cuzzoni return'd from Italy Sigra Celeste Sigra Bertolli Sigr Montagna Base & Sigra Sagatti ". Porpora is not mentioned. J. P. Malcolm (p. 351) quotes an unidentified source : " Senesino . . . is said to have hired the Theatre in Lincoln's-Inn-Fields for the Winter of 1733–4 as an Opera-House ". (Chrysander, II. 324.)

———

LADY BETTY GERMAIN TO LIONEL, FIRST DUKE OF DORSET, LONDON, January or February 1734

. . . The report goes that Dodington has made up all differences with the King and Prince [of Wales]. . . . Even about operas 'tis outrageous, and the delight of everybody's heart seems to be set upon the King's sitting by himself at the Haymarket House ; . . . and t'other day at

Dodington's the Prince was as eager and pressed me as earnestly to go to Lincoln's Inn Fields opera as if it had been a thing of great moment to the nation, but by good luck I had company at home.

Report on the MSS. of Mrs. Stopford-Sackville, London 1904, I. 157. George Bubb Dodington afterwards became Lord Melcombe.

—

Cupid and Psyche, or, Columbine Courtezan, a pantomime entertainment, is produced at Drury Lane on 4th February 1734 ; with music by John Frederick Lampe, who quotes some Handel tunes in the medley overture.

The author is unknown. Walsh printed the overture and selected airs. Waltz sang the parts of Bacchus and of Mynheer Bassoon. (Smith, 1948, p. 184.)

—

" Harmony in an Uproar : A Letter to F—d—k H—d—l, *Esq. ; M—r of the O—a H—e in the* Hay-Market, from Hurlothrumbo Johnson, *Esq.* ; *Composer Extraordinary to all the Theatres in* G—t-B—t—n, *Excepting that of the* Hay-Market, in which the Rights and Merits of both O—s are properly consider'd ." London, 12th February 1734

Wonderful SIR !

The mounting Flames of my Ambition having long aspir'd to the Honour of holding a small Conversation with you ; but being sensible of the almost insuperable Difficulty of getting at you, I bethought me, a Paper Kite might best reach you, and soar to your Apartment, though seated in the highest Clouds ; for all the World knows, I can top you, fly as high as you will.

But all preliminary Compliments, and introductory Paragraphs laid aside, let us fall to Business—You must know then, Sir that I have been told, and made to understand by your Betters, Sir, that of late you have been damn'd *Insolent, Audacious, Impudent* and *Saucy*, and a thousand things else, Sir (that don't become you) worse than all that—

Do you see, Sir,—as to Particulars, we scorn to descend to Particulars ; —for they are look'd upon as great Secrets ;—for your Enemies are very wise, damn'd cunning, and close ; confounded close some of them, and terrible Haidpieces, i' faith ; as you'll find to your Costs, before this Season is expir'd, though at the Expence of half their Estates.

Now, Sir,—you must know I make a formal Demand to you in the Name of all the Muses and Mortals devoted to those divine Sublimities ; Why this Discord ? Why these stupendous Alarms in the Affairs of Harmony ? Why, has Musick made so confounded a Noise, that the Great Guns upon the *Rhine*, and in *Italy*, affect not our Ears, deafned with an eternal Squawl or chatter about Operas ? . . .

And first for thee, thou delightful musical Machine. Why hast thou dar'd to rouse the roaring Lions, and wily Foxes of the *British* Nation ; who, but for Pity, could tear thy very Being to Atoms in the hundreth Part of an Allegro Minnum ; make Crotchets of thy Body, and Semiquavers of thy Soul ; and with the powerful Breath of their Nostrils, blow thy Existence beneath the lowest Hell.

Go then, thou mistaken Mortal, prostrate thy self before these *Grand Signiors* ; yield to their most unreasonable Demands ; let them spurn and buffet thee : Talk not foolishly of Merit, Justice or Honour, and they may prove so gracious, as to let thee live and starve ; else thy Destruction's sworn ; thy Foes are as merciful as wise, and will not leave thee worth a Groth ; the Mightiness and Wisdom of Man have vow'd it. . . .

. . . I am humbly of the Opinion, before I hear you, that you are certainly in the wrong : But to shew my Impartiality, since I am declared Umpire in this weighty Cause, I solemnly cite you before my Tribunal. . . .

But since you are called upon this solemn manner . . . I hope you'll behave like a Gentleman ; own yourself guilty at once, and save us a great deal of Time and Trouble. But before you proceed to your Defence, consider who you have to do with ; think of that, Sir, and tremble. Know, Mortal, that there are leagu'd against you as many *bl—e, g—n and r—d R—ns*, as would serve to hang up you, your Singers, and your whole *Orchestre*, like so many dead Moles upon a Hedge-Row : mighty Men, and wise Men ; some of them wise enough to be Justices of the Peace. Will not all this frighten you ?—Are you in your right Wits ? Rat me, if I don't think you in as bad a Situation, as if a Whirlwind, and a Earthquake, and a fiery Torrent from Mount *Ætna*, and as if—but I must defer my Similes 'till next Page.—

Well, Sir !—you need not give your self much pains about your Defence, I know all your Arguments, before I hear them.—I am sensible you wou'd have it believ'd in your Favour, *that you are no way to blame in the whole of this Affair ; but that when S—no had declared he would leave England, you thought yourself oblig'd in Honour, to proceed with your Contract, and provide for yourself elsewhere ; that as for C—oni, you had no Thoughts of her, no Hopes of her, nor no want of her, S—da being in all respects infinitely superior, in any Excellency requir'd for a Stage ; as for Singers in the under Parts, you had provided the best Set we ever had yet ; tho' basely deserted by Mon—na, after having sign'd a formal Contract to serve you the whole of this Season ; which you might still force him to do, where you not more afraid of W—r-H—ll, than ten thousand D—rs, or ten thousand D—ls.—I know,* you'll say, *that as you were oblig'd to carry on Operas this Winter, you imagin'd you might be at Liberty to proceed in the Affair, in that Manner which wou'd prove most to the Satisfaction of the unprejudic'd Part of the Nobility and Gentry and your own interest and Honour.*

I know you say, *it was impossible for you to comply with the unreasonable and savage Proposals made to you ; by which you were to give up all Contracts, Promises, nay risque your Fortune, to gratify fantastical Whims and unjust Picques.* I know *you'll say, that if you were misled, or have judged wrong at any Time in raising the Price of your Tickets, that ye were sufficiently punish'd, without carrying the Resentment, arising thereupon, to such a length.* I know you'll say, *considering that Entertainment in any light, it better merited so extravagant a Price, than any other Entertainment ever yet exhibited to this Nation, not excepting the most celebrated* Bear-Garden.—I know, you'll say, *that if*—

. . . Therefore I do here solemnly declare upon the Honour of an Esquire, and the Word of a Gentleman, that all you assert, is false,— utterly false, damnably false ; and that you're an impudent Liar, and a Scoundrel, and a Rascal ; and so G—d conf—nd you, and rot you and yours to all Eternity, and ten times worse than all that ; and if this Answer is not sufficient to convince you, and all the reasonable Part of this Town that you're positively in the Wrong, I have no more to say ; for nothing can be more plain on my side.

In the same Manner, argue your Partizans at the Chocolate and Coffee Houses.—Says a very fine Gentleman to me t'other Day (whom *Car—ino* I suppose has catch'd by the Ears)—*So Mr.* Hurlothrumbo, *I hear you're a great Stickler for the Opera at* L—n's-I— F—ds ; *a pretty Set of Singers, truly ! and for Composers, you out-do the World !*—*Don't you think*, says he, *at this Time of Life,* S—no *could twang a Prayer finely thro' th' Nose in Petticoats at a Conventicle ? Hah !*—*or what think you*, says he, *of* Si—ra Ce—sti *snuffling a Hymn there in Concert ; or Madam* B—lli, *with her unmeaning Voice, with as little Force in it as a Pair of Smith's Bellows with twenty Holes in the Sides : Your Base, indeed, makes a humming Noise, and could roar to some Purpose, if he had Songs proper for him ; as for your* S—ra Fag—tto, *she indeed may with her Master be sent home to School again ; and by the Time she is Fourscore, she'll prove a vast Addition to a Bonefire ; or make a fine* Duenna *in a* Spanish Opera.

Humph ! says he, *your Composers too have behav'd notably truly ;*—*your* Porpoise, says he, *may roul and rumble about as he pleases, and prelude to a Storm of his own raising ; but you should let him know, that a bad Imitation always wants the Air and Spirit of an Original, and that there is a wide Difference betwixt full Harmony, and making a Noise.*—*I know*, says he, *your Expectations are very high, from the Performance of the King of* Aragon ; *but that* Trolly Colly *Composer*, says he, *a stupid* Cantata-Thrummer, *must make a mighty poor Figure in an Opera ; tho' he was so nice last Winter, that he would not allow that* Han—l *could Compose, or* Sen—no *Sing : What Art he has us'd, to produce him now as the first Voice in* Europe, *I can't imagine, but you must not depend upon his Majesty too far*, says he ; *for to my Knowledge, he has been engag'd by a formal Deputation from the* General Assembly *of* N—th Br—n, *to new-set their* Sc—ch *Psalms, and be*

Clerk to the High Kirk in Edinburgh, *with a Salary of one hundred Pound* Scots, *per* Ann. . . .

. . . Therefore proceed we now without more delay to your Trial.— *Cryer—O yes ?—O yes ?—*&c.

This is to give Notice, to all Directors of Operas, Masters of Play-houses, Patentees with Patents or without, Composers, Performers, or other Masters that neither Compose nor Perform, all Dancing-Masters, Exhibiters of Poppet-Shews, Presidents of Bear-Gardens, Rope-Dancers, but particularly all Judges of Musick and others—That they now appear and produce their several Complaints against the Prisoner at the Bar, in order to bring him to speedy Justice.

Court. Frederick Handel, Hold up your Hand. Know you are here brought to answer to the several following high Crimes and Mis-demeanors, committed upon the Wills and Understandings, and against the Peace of our Sovereign Lord the Mobility of *Great-Britain,* par-ticularly this Metropolis : To which you shall make true and faithful Answer—So help you Musick—Swear him upon the two Operas of *Ariadne, alias* the *Cuckoo* and the *Nightingale.*

Imprimis, You are charg'd with having bewitch'd us for the Space of twenty Years past ; nor do we know where your Inchantments will end, if a timely Stop is not put to them ; they threatning us with an entire Destruction of Liberty, and an absolute Tyranny in your Person over the whole Territories of the *Hay-Market.*

Secondly, You have most insolently dar'd to give us good Musick and sound Harmony, when we wanted and desir'd bad ; to the great Encouragement of your Opera's, and the Ruin of our good Allies and Confederates, the Professors of bad Musick.

Thirdly,—You have most feloniously and arrogantly assum'd to your-self an uncontroul'd Property of pleasing us, whether we would or no ; and have often been so bold as to charm us, when we were positively resolv'd to be out of Humour.

Besides these, we can, at convenient Time or Times, produce and prove five hundred and fifteen Articles of lesser Consequence, which may in the whole, at least, amount to accumulative Treason—How say you, Sir, are you guilty of the said Charge or no ?

Prisoner.—Guilty of the whole Charge.

Court.—We knew it must be so ; Pshaw, pshaw, it could not be otherways—But to shew our Indulgence for your so readily complying, and saving us the Trouble of producing our several Evidences, and to demonstrate to the World our Impartiality in the whole Progress of this Affair, before we proceed to pass Sentence upon so old and notorious an Offender, we give you Leave to make a Speech, in which, if you behave prudently, it may occasion a Mitigation of the Rigour of the intended Sentence ; but be sure your Speech be a wise one, or it will not pass Muster with us *Aca—cians.*

Now set yourself in Order, look mighty Grave and wise ; as Wise as an Emperor in an Elbow-Chair ; screw your Muscles into Form ; so, now balance your Hands, and see-saw them up and down like an Orator —tolerably well.

Clerk of the Court—Frederick Handel, look full at the Court, and make Three Bows.

Court.—Sirrah—Demme, we say—Sirrah ! what has your Stupidity to offer in your Defence, that Sentence of Annihilation should not be immediately pronounc'd against you and your *Tramontani* of the *Hay-Market,* for daring to oppose our mighty Wills and Pleasures—well said Us !

Pris.—*Most Noble, Right Honourable, and superlatively excellent—*

Court.—Go on—Scoundrel—

Pris.—*I am almost confounded at being thus arraign'd before so August an Assembly of the wisest Heads of the Nation ; and to appear as a Criminal, where, tho' I am guilty of the Charge, I am as innocent of any Crime, as ignorant of any real Accusation. Wherein have I offended ?*

Court.—Why, you saucy Son of a B – – ch, do you pretend to impeach the Honour, Sense, or Power of the Court ? Wherein have you offended ? Unparallell'd Audaciousness ! when we have said you have offended. Scoundrel ! You're as impudent as a red hot Poker, which is enough to put any Face out of Countenance. But, Sirrah if you are not guilty by Law, we'll prove it logically—No Man is brought to this Bar, but who is guilty—You are brought to this Bar—

Ergo—Do you understand a Syllogism, Rascal ? It is plain as a *Dutchman's* Backside by Day-light ; no Man at the *Old Bailey* ever had a fairer Trial for his Life ; away with him, Gaoler, to the Condemn'd Hold,—till the Warrant is sign'd for his Execution.

[End of the Trial.]

Now, Sir, you may think this Usage very severe—But to shew you upon what a weak Foundation you build your Pretences to support an Opera, I'll prove by Twenty-five substantial Reasons, that you are no Composer, nor know no more of Musick than you do of Algebra. You may look grave at this Assertion, but hear me, and confute me.

First then, Sir,—Have you taken your Degrees ? Boh !—ha, ha, ha ! Are you a Doctor, Sir ? ah, ah ! A fine Composer indeed, and not a Graduate ; fie, fie, you might as well pretend to be a Judge, without having been ever call'd to the Bar ; or pretend to be a Bishop, and not a Christian. Why Doctor *Pushpin* and Doctor *Blue* laugh at you, and scorn to keep you Company ; and they have vow'd to me, that it is scarcely possible to imagine how much better they compos'd after the Commencement Gown was thrown over their Shoulders than before ; it was as if a musical—had laid Hands upon them, and inspired them with the Enthusiasm of Harmony.

Secondly, Sir,—I understand you have never read *Euclid*, are a declar'd Foe to all proper Modes, and Forms, and Tones of Musick, and scorn to be subservient to, or ty'd up by Rules, or have your Genius cramp'd : Thou *God* and *Vandal* to just Sounds ! we may as well place Nightingales and Canary-birds behind the Scenes, and take the wild Operas of Nature from them, as allow you to be a Composer : An ingenious Carpenter, with a Rule and Compass, will succeed better in Composition, thou finish'd Irregularity.

Thirdly, Sir—I have heard it own'd by some of your best Friends, that, being one *Sunday* in a Country Church, you made a terrible Blunder in singing the Psalms, put out the Clerk and the whole Congregation, to the great Disturbance of the Parson and his Flock ; nor did they recover the Confusion you threw them into, in a month after ; therefore I submit it to the proper Judges, if an Ignorant in a Country Psalm can be allow'd a Composer of Oratorio's.

Fourthly, Sir—It has been objected to you, I believe with some Truth (for I never knew one Man take your Part in it) that you can no more Dance a *Cheshire* Horn Pipe, than you can fly down a Rope from *Paul's* Church ; a Composer, and not Dance a *Cheshire* Round ! Incredible ! I have made it apparent to some Audiences, as Numerous as Polite, that the Beauty of Composition, and the Force of a fine Genius, lay in Singing, Dancing, and Fiddling at the same Time ; nor will it now be contested, that Footing it well is as necessary to shew a Man's brightest Parts, as any Productions of his Head-piece.

But as for my fifth Reason, Sir—That indeed wou'd be sufficient to convince the most Bigotted in your Favour of your Incapacity in this Art ; nor will it scarcely be believed, when I can demonstrate to the blind Understandings of your Admirers, that by G—d, you have made such Musick, as never Man did before you, nor, I believe, never will be thought of again, when you're gone.

My other twenty Reasons are full as strong as these, but my Printer says he can afford no more Reasons for Twelve-pence ; but surely these may be allow'd sufficient to the Reasonable ; and tho' you and your Friends have Fronts of a Metal some Degrees harder than *Corinthian* Brass ; yet how will them same metallick Countenances stare, when I shall assert, that to exhibit your Performances in the Perfection of your Art, it must be, not as a *Composer*, but a *Conjurer* ; yes, Sir, a *Conjurer*, look as grim as you please ; and the Whole of your Merit shall, in proper Colours, be shewn not to proceed from the Arts of Musick, but the *Black-Art*.

It has in many Particulars been made manifest to the religious Part of your Audiences, that for these twenty Years past (as was well observed in your Trial) you have practis'd Sorcery in this Kingdom upon his Majesty's Liege Subjects, and often bewitched every Sense we have ; there was not a Letter in one of your publick Bills, but had Magick in it ;

and if at any Time a Squeak of one of your Fiddles, or the Tooting of a Pipe was heard, Hey bounce ! we prick'd up our Ears like so many wild Colts ; away danced the whole Town, Helter skelter, like a Rabble-Rout after a mad Bull ; squeezing and pressing, and shoving, and happy were they that could be squeez'd to Death. You have rais'd the Dead, and engaged all the Heroes, antique or modern, from *Theseus* to *Orlando Furioso*, to fight your Battles for you ; you can call up Devils, and bring down Spirits to enchant us ; as if at any Time another Composer civilly introduc'd a Patient, Strolling, Pastoral Princess to instruct us, up starts one of your damn'd Knight-Errant *Alexanders* or *Julius Caesars*, and most inhumanly frighted the poor Lady out of her Wits, and laid, at one Stroke, the Composer flat on his Back. There is no bearing such Usage in a Christian Country ! nay, what is worse, and what I think should be taken Notice of by our pious reverend B—ch of B—ps [Bench of Bishops], whenever you gave us a Christian Hero, as *Rinaldo* or *Amadis*, you took Care to bring in some damn'd heathenish Wizard to play Pranks for them, and shew that you wholly worked by Witch-craft ; nay, such an Ascendant had you got over us, that we cried up every where other Composers for the first Masters in the World, and would not allow you to produce one Bar of tolerable Musick ; yet we never went near their Performances, and *nolens volens* were hurri'd away by some of your infernal Agents, to crowd your Houses ; and when we would have lock'd up our Wives and Daughters from your Power, *Presto* pass, they whipp'd through Key-holes, or Chimney-Tops, to you : If this is not being carried away by Inchantment, I can't tell what it is. If at any Time the Magick of your Opera lost its Force, by being too often us'd, away went the D—l [Devil] and you to work in a Vizard, to hide your evil Designs, and then out comes an Oratorio, or a Serenata ; and just as we had begun to recover our Senses, all of a sudden we run as mad as ever ; and hoity toity, away went we, like so many Witches on Broomsticks and Hobby-Horses, to the Prince of Darkness's Midnight Revels. If this is not downright Witchcraft, I never knew a Conjurer in my Life. But to put the Matter beyond all Dispute ; have you not this very Season imported from *Italy* an Arch Friend, one *Care—no*, that will play the Devil with us before he quits us, and leagu'd yourself to a notorious Witch, one *Str—da*, that never lets us be quiet Night or Day ; and as if these were not sufficient to play Tricks with the whole Kingdom, you have brought over the whole Family of the *Negri's*, to make Magicians, Sirens, Devils, and other Ministers of Darkness, to carry on your infernal Designs. But that ignorant, well-meaning Persons may no longer be seduc'd by you, or think that Musick is but a harmless Amusement, let them consider that nothing was ever looked upon more proper to carry on Inchantments by than Harmony ; it was always made use of by Antients and Moderns upon such Occasions, at all solemn Sacrifices, Invocations of Ghosts or Devils, calling up Spirits

from the Earth, or down from the Air, Musick was held the only Lure
to entice them ; nay, *Belzebub* himself has a great Command that Way,
and constantly entertains his Votaries at their Installations, Festivals, and
Nocturnal Meetings, with Operas, Symphonies, Voluntaries, and Madrigals in the Air, and I fear, Sir, has but too often lent a helping Hand to
you. But I hope this prudent Subscription at L— I-n-F—ds will put
an End to your Charms, and knock off the Fetters we have so long
wore ; nor are we without Hopes, that thro' you, Musick may receive
such a home Thrust, as she may never recover (at least in *England*) again :
And if the Statute for burning Witches and Wizards was in full Force, I
know who should soon be whipp'd into the Middle of a Bonefire of his
own Works, and like a Swan die to some Tune.

But to come a little nearer to the Merits of the Cause, and give you a
Wound where you think yourself most secure : *Your Party very con-
fidently, and with an Air of Wisdom, give out, that you are all very much
surpriz'd, that so weighty a Part of the Grand Leg—ture should employ both
their Time and Money so ill, as in setting up one O—ra H—se to ruin another,
without ever giving the Appearance of a formal Reason for acting so ; when
their precious Hours and vast Parts might, at this critical Juncture, be of infinite
Service to their Country ; when we are almost at a Loss how to behave.*

Mighty pretty, truly—how charmingly wise and sententious !
Notable Speech-makers indeed !—How Murder will out ! Does not
this Objection alone make good all that we have been disputing about
these three Hours ? Is it not obvious that so many great M—, mighty
great M— (who are so over loaded with the Burthen of publick Affairs,
that all common Necessaries of Life are neglected to attend that Service)
would ever have taken all this Trouble about so lousy and paltry a
Fellow as you ? Had not your Insolence arriv'd to such an unparelell'd
Pitch of Audaciousness, that it quite threaten'd the utter Ruin of the
Nation, had they not timely stood in the Gap made in our Liberties
and Properties by your Musick, the Torrent in another Year or two
might have swept away—God knows what—But, like true Patriots, they
interpos'd, and ventur'd Lives and Fortunes to save us.

You may, if you please, very pertly ask, *Pray how could all this be
effected by so innocent an Entertainment as an O—ra ?* How, you D—g ?
How could it be sooner effected than by an O—ra ? That Source of
Expence, Luxury, Idleness, Sloth, and Effeminacy, and all that ; a
damn'd Set of *Italian* Squeakers and Fiddlers : Nor indeed was there
any other Method left to ruin your Opera, and demolish the Ascendant
you had gain'd over us, but by setting up another Source of Expense,
Luxury, Idleness, Sloth, and Effeminacy, and all that ; and wisely
contriv'd too, Sirrah, that you might not have the whole Plunder of a
rich Nation to yourself, but that some of our most noted Spirits for
Sense and Patriotism might come in for a Share with you. For if one
O—ra was thought so very burthensome, and gave such Room for just

Complaints ; no Way so proper to make us sensible of its Weight, and our Mistake, as setting up two.

Nor is it these mighty Men alone that would devour you ; the whole musical World is united against you ; the King of *Arragon* swears you want Softness ; Signior *Porpoise* finds you deficient in Roughness ; Mr. *Honeycomb* protests, that he cannot adapt one Air of your Composition either to his Eyes or Nose ; and they are such Stuff as is only fit for the Throat of a *Care—ni* or a *Stra—a* ; Mr. *Gaynote* vows you produce no pretty Thing, that is to say, pleasingly pretty, to tickle the Ladies ; Dr. *Pushpin* affirms, you are no Mathematician ; and Dr. *Blue* roundly asserts in all Companies, that you are quite void of Spirit and Invention ; Nay, I can produce an *Italian* Nobleman, whose musical Judgment is universally allow'd of (especially if his Spectacles are on) who has assured me, that you know no more of Harmony, than he does of the Tricks of a *Faro-Table*, or a *Bowling-Green*. It is true, from his Dress and Situation of late, he may be look'd upon to puff a little of our Side ; but that is only by way of Amusement ; for to shew his Impartiality, he has often condescended to give you Hints for your Improvement ; and went so far as to invite you to eat a Tripe-soup and Fricassee of Sheep's Trottern, at *Little Pontack's* near St. *Martin's* Church, with him ; when he had a Scheme to propose of infinite Advantage to you, without any Prospect to himself, but the Payment of his Dinners, and the Liberty of your Gallery, which your Ignorance and Obstinacy refused. As for that indefatigable Society, the Gropers into Antique Musick, and Hummers of Madrigals, they swoon at the Sight of any Piece modern, particularly of your Composition, excepting the Performances of their venerable President, whose Works bear such vast Resemblance to the regular Gravity of the Antients, that when dress'd up in Cobwebs, and powdered with Dust, the Philharmonick Spiders could dwell on them, and in them, to Eternity.

But if my concise Method of reasoning, or happy Talent of convincing by Demonstration, have not been able to satisfy you, in order to make a compleat Conquest, I must attack you in your own Way, and draw a —— Cantata upon you; which is adapted to the Musick of an Ancestor of the King of *Arragon's*, who had the Honour to be Madrigal-Composer to the Children of Queen *Elizabeth's* Scullery : The Words I translated in the modern Taste, from the original *Italian* of that incomparable Dramatick Poet, Seignior *Rowley-Powley*.

·   ·   ·   ·   ·

L—I—F— TRIUMPHANT.

A CANTATA.

To the Tune of, Welcome Joan Saunderson, *&c.*

RECITATIVE.

Welcome sweet P—ra *to* Britain's *Shore,*
A—ne *now adds to our Musical Store.*

XII. HANDEL, 1738

Engraving by Jacob Houbraken. This is the first state, before lettering, of the
frontispiece to Handel's *Alexander's Feast*, published by John Walsh in 1738
and issued separately to subscribers to the score. The scene below is from
Alexander's Feast, designed by Hubert François Gravelot. (Fitzwilliam
Museum)

See pages 456 f.

XIII. A MUSICAL PARTY IN THE GARDEN OF KEW PALACE

Oil painting by Philip Mercier, 1733. The Royal Children : Frederick Lewis, Prince of Wales (violoncello) ; Anne, later Princess of Orange (harpsichord) ; Amalia Sophia (reading) ; and

AIR.

O my sweet P—ra !
  'Tis a fine Opera ;
We will play it then o'er and o'er,
  And over again, Nights full Threescore,
'Till the whole World comes near us no more.

Da Capo.

DUET.

This Opera will no farther go,
Hark ye, Sir Treasurer !—why say you so ?
It will not do ;—it ne'er can do,
Without you get in Don F—di—do [Ferdinando].

CHORUS.

He must come to, and he shall come to,
And he must come to, whether he will or no.

RECITATIVE.

Welcome sweet Arragon over the Main,
Is Don F—di—do safe landed from Spain ?

AIR.

O my Dear Arragon,
  This is a Paragon ;
We will play it over again,
  And over again, to free us from Pain ;
All in the Tweedeldum, deedeldum Strain.

Da Capo.

DUET.

Alas ! the poor Don no longer can go,
Then there is an End of all our fine Shew :
If this won't do, how shall we get Money ?
Why !—wait the Arrival of Madam Cuz—ni.

CHORUS.

She must come to, and she shall come to :
If she'll not come to, this will never do.

By this little Sketch, Sir, you find we are not at a Loss for Words, Sir,
nor Musick, Sir, to equal any Thing of yours ; and before this Season
is out, we shall firk you up with an Or—rio shall make your Hair stand
an end ; and I am determin'd (if nothing else will do) to be at the
Expence of Books and Masters to get a Smattering of the Black Art,

H.–12

that we may be able to play Conjurer against Conjurer, and Devil against Devil with you, to the End of the Chapter.

But now, Sir, that I have sung you a Song, give me Leave to tell you a Tale ; and perhaps before I have done with you, like my Betters, to shew my Breeding, I may chance to let a F— A— But to my Story— You must know then, Sir, I once went to the World in the Moon. . . . My Profession and Merit were soon known, it not being possible to hide any extraordinary Genius from the penetrating Capacities of that Country, particularly in the Art of Musick, of which they affect, to the greatest Degree, to appear very fond and very knowing ; but betwixt you and I, Sir, (but be sure you keep it secret) the Majority of its Inhabitants have their Ears placed so near their Backsides, that they frequently sit upon them.

However, the brilliant Rays of my Talents in that Art quickly enlighten'd that opaque Globe so far, that I was immediately admitted into the good Graces of the Court, and principal Grandees ; who were all ravished with the Novelty and Exquisiteness of my Compositions : In consequence of which I was declar'd principal Composer to their O—as ; and should have enjoy'd the same Station in the Court Chapels and Publick Temples, only that Place could not be conferr'd upon a Foreigner : Yet upon all solemn Occasions, they were obliged to have Recourse to me for their religious Musick, tho' their ordinary Services were all compos'd and performed by Blockheads that were Natives ; they claiming from several Laws a Right hereditary, to have the Places in their Temples supply'd with Fools of their own Country. But People of Taste in general being more nice in the Affairs of any Amusement than those of Religion, cou'd not bear that the Musick in their Operas should be so trifled with, and slabber'd over by unskilful Composers, or Performers ; therefore were at a prodigious Expence for Voices and Instruments from the Kingdom of the Sun, or other Countries of the fixed Stars.

No Merit can secure a Man from Envy, when eminent in any Profession ; of Course my Success raised me many Rivals ; the Moon-Calves (who have a mortal Aversion to being too long pleas'd with any Thing, and are only noted for Inconstancy) gave into their Projects, and formed strong Parties against me ; which always appear'd done more in Pique to me, than Love to them : But their Compositions proved so contemptible, and in all Respects so inferior to mine, that whenever we contended, I carry'd the Day, my Enemies still decreeing me the Prize, yet continuing my Enemies.

In this state for several Years I triumph'd almost absolute in the Empire of Musick, nor ever disturb'd, but from some small Malcontents without Doors, who either wish'd the total Ruin of Harmony, or were quite eat up with Spleen and Vapours, and did not know what they would be at : I was prodigiously caress'd at Court, the Royal Family (as in all other polite Arts and Sciences) being not only Lovers, but perfect Judges of Musick ; but more particularly the divine Princess *Urania*, who condescended to be my Scholar, and made that Proficiency, as seemed almost miraculous to me her Master ; nay to that exquisite Degree, that the Amusement only carried it to as great a Height in her, as in the most Ingenious, who made it their Profession : This Favour so far from diminishing, created me fresh Foes, who generally sprouted up from Stocks and Stones, like the new Race after *Ovid's* Deluge : Upon which the splenetick Tribe of fine Gentlemen and very fine Ladies, (quite out of Patience that I gave them no Musick to find Fault with) determin'd to oppose my Scheme, and have an O—a of their own, where they were sure to have as much bad Musick as their Hearts could desire : They listed Composers, who never dared to shew their Heads in *Moon-land* as such, but under their Banners ; and then taking into Pay some cast-off Performers, who had appeared in under Parts in my O—as, and some Strollers, who sung Ballads about the Streets, with an old noted Gelderino at their Head (who was almost past his Business, and had besides a great Hole quite through his Lungs, so that more of his Breath broke out downwards than upwards) with this Ragamuffin Troop they pretended to set up against me, having hired a large Booth for that Purpose, where there had been formerly Puppet-shows and Rope-dancing ; they made a vast Subscription to carry on this grand Design, drawing in most of the young Fellows of their Acquaintance, by great Promises and notorious Fal—ds [Falsehoods], but who soon became sick of the Project, and would have parted with their Billets at a very great Discount : The most violent (and who headed their Party) were the D—c [Duc] *de Buffalo*, the D—c *de Trincolo*, the M—qui [Marquis] *Sansterre*, C—te [Comte] *Spend-All*, C—te *Fat-head*, B—n [Baron] *Sad-dog*, and the Ch—r [Chevalier] *Squatt* : Nay, they went so far as to give out, that they received some Encouragement from Monseigneur, the K—g's [King's] eldest Son, who only laugh'd at them in his Sleeve.

I had then in Pay a perfect Set of Performers, particularly *Angelo Carrioli*, and *Coeleste Vocale* ; the Unprejudic'd were amaz'd at the Vastness of their Judgment and Justice as well as Beauty of their Execution. My opponents were obliged to make use of all their Interest and Industry, not only to get Company to their House, but to keep those who could not suffer their low Entertainments from coming to mine ; nor did they spare entering into the most indirect Means to ruin me ; having not only decoy'd a noted Performer from me, after having for a Term formally bound himself to serve me, but by some underhand Slight, they spirited away two very remarkable Monsters, the first Night of a new O—a, who had for a considerable Time been trained up, to the Stage ; but by good Luck, I had some more Monsters in another Den, tho' not so expert at their Business.

They open'd their Musicall Droll the first Night to a crouded Audience, Numbers being drawn thither by Curiosity, and by the Boldness and Stupidity of the Attempt ; their Success consisted in a full House that Night, but Applause no Night ; their Company dropped off at once, and then they had recourse to the most unfair and ungentlemanlike Behaviour that ever was known upon such an Occasion, to make an Audience ; even using F—ce [Force] rudely, to such as would not comply ; and b—ing [bribing] or hiring others, to visit their House.

For some time I played gently with these charming Gudgeons, and maugre all their pitiful Efforts kept my Head above Water ; but at last I came slap-dash upon them with a new O—a of my own Composition ; which answer'd to my Profit, and the Pleasure of the Town ; their Weakness was made manifest, they were defeated, and I triumphed. Indeed they made another small Push, in bringing upon the Stage one of the most execrable, low Entertainments that ever was heard ; it was receiv'd according to its Merit, which enhanc'd the Value of mine the more.

I might now have ruled, undisturb'd, the whole Empire of Harmony in the Moon, it being reckoned the highest Presumption or Rashness to oppose me in a Dominion so lawfully gain'd, and so equitably supported.

But being fir'd with a just Indignation at the unworthy Treatment I met with from a People I so long honour'd and charm'd with my Performances, and for whom I had incessantly laboured for above twenty Years, I resolved to quit the Country : Accordingly, as soon as my Contract for that Season was expir'd, I hired a large Palanquin, and carried off the Principal of my Voices and Performers instrumental to the Kingdom of the Sun ; where I was caress'd to the highest Degree, not oppress'd by the Great, nor chagrin'd by the impotent Attempts of any jealous Rival in the Art. There I remain'd several Years, honour'd and beloved, loaded with Riches and Reputation ; yet my kind Reception could never stifle my innate Love for my own Country ; where being happily arrived, I hope to spend the Remainder of my Days in that Quiet of Mind and reasonable Enjoyment of Fortune, which none of my mean-spirited Opposers ever can taste.

Now, Sir,—What think you of my Tale ?—Or how like you my Jaunt to the World in the Moon ?—If in this small Sketch of some Part of my Life, you find any Rules for your future Conduct, in observing them you may make me your Friend, and shew yourself a wise Man.

But to return to the Subject of the former Part of my Letter ; I think I have made it very plainly appear, that you or somebody else is damnably in the Wrong ; and I believe most People will allow (even the most warm Partisans of both Sides of the Question) that it is absolutely necessary, for the better Entertainment of the Court, Nobility, and Gentry, so contrive some Method of gently blowing into the Air one O—a H—e, and all concerned in it.

As you have some Reason to dread this Proposal, yet you cannot plead Ignorance, or not having timely Warning given you by,

     Wonderful SIR,

        Yours, as you merit it,

              Hurlothrumbo Johnson.

From my Apartments
in Moor-field-Pa-
lace, February 12,
1733.

(Schoelcher, pp. 169-72 ; Chrysander, II. 339-58.) This pamphlet was advertised in the *Daily Journal* of 18th March 1734. The printer was R. Smith, in the Strand. For the pseudonym of the author, " Hurlothrumbo Johnson ", see 7th April 1729 : *Hurlothrumbo* by Samuel Johnson, of Cheshire, was produced at the Little Theatre in the Haymarket on 29th March 1729. The text of the pamphlet was reprinted in the *Miscellaneous Works of the late Dr. Arbuthnot,* Glasgow, 1751, II. 18-42 ; and again in the London edition of 1770, II. 24-46, although Arbuthnot's son, George, protested publicly in 1751 against the inclusion of spurious pieces in the Glasgow edition. George A. Aitken, in *Life and Works of John Arbuthnot,* Oxford, 1892, p. 145, declares the pamphlet as spurious, and the *Cambridge Bibliography of English Literature* follows his judgment. The author of the pamphlet is not known. It was undoubtedly written by an adherent of Handel's, but probably without his knowledge. Some notes of explanation, including the completion of abbreviated names and the equivalents of pseudonyms, are possible : (Title) Frederick Handel, Esq ; Master of the Opera House . . . Great-Britain. (Paragraph 5) " musical Machine "—Handel. (P. 8) blue, green and red Ribbons. (P. 9) Senesino, Cuzzoni, Strada, Montagnana ; Westminster-Hall, Doctors, Devils ; " misled "—by Heidegger ? (P. 10) God confound. (P. 11) Carestino, Lincoln's Inn Fields, Senesino, Signora Celesti, Bertolli ; Signora " Fagotto "— Segatti ; " her Master "—Porpora ? (P. 12) " Porpoise "—Porpora ; " King of Aragon "—Carlo Aragoni, lute player in Porpora's orchestra (according to Burney's *Account*) ; (?) North Brethren ; Scotch Psalms. (P. 15) " Mobility "— pun, on mob and nobility ; " the two Operas of *Ariadne* "—by Porpora (" the Cuckoo ") and by Handel (" the Nightingale "). (P. 21) Academicians. (P. 24) " Sirrah "—Sir, " Demme "—Damned. (P. 28) Bitch. (P. 31) " Pushpin "— Pepusch (Doctor of Oxford, 1713), " Blue "—Greene (Doctor of Cambridge, 1730). (P. 32) To Euclid, the author of the *Sectio canonis,* another tract was also ascribed : the *Introductio harmonica,* which is, however, by Cleonides. (P. 34) " I "—Samuel Johnson, of Cheshire, as Lord Flame in his *Hurlothrumbo.* (P. 36) The price of the pamphlet was 1s. (P. 37) " another Composer "—Bononcini ; his *Pastoral Princess—Griselda* (see 22nd May 1733) ; Carestino, Strada, the sisters Negri, Lincoln's Inn Fields. (P. 41) " Honeycomb "—Henry Holcombe, singer, harpsichord player, and composer, who subscribed to some of Handel's scores ; " Gaynote "—? (John Gay died in 1732) ; " an Italian Nobleman "—? ; the " Society " for " Antique Musick "—the Academy of Ancient Music ; their " President "—since 1734 Pepusch. (P. 42) " Rowley-Powley "—Paolo Rolli, secretary of the Nobility Opera. (P. 43, the " Cantata ") Lincoln's Inn Fields Triumphant ; " Joan Saunderson "—? ; Porpora, his *Ariadne* ; " Don Ferdinando " (referring to his *Ferdinando,* see below)—Farinelli ? ; Cuzzoni did not return until spring 1734. (P. 44) Or-rio—Porpora's oratorio *Davide e Bersabea,* to be produced on 12th March 1734. (P. 45) Fart ; " the World in the Moon "— England. (P. 46) " Kingdom of the Sun "—Italy. (P. 48) " Princess Urania "—

Princess Anne ; " Gelderino "—Senesino ; " a large Booth "—Lincoln's Inn Fields Theatre ; the " Party "—the directors of the Nobility Opera (see January 1733) ; " the Duc de Buffalo "—Earl Delawarr ; " Monseigneur "—the Prince of Wales, the King's eldest son. (P. 49) " Angelo Carrioli "—Carestini, " Coeleste Vocale "—Strada ; " a noted Performer "—Montagnana ; the " new Opera "— *Ottone* recast (see 13th November 1733). (P. 51) " a new Opera of my own Composition"—Handel's *Ariadne* ; the " low Entertainment"—(?) *Apollo and Daphne*, an anonymous opera performed in 1734, or Porpora's *Ferdinando*, produced on 5th February 1734. (P. 53) The pamphlet suggests that Handel should go, for a time, to Italy ; " my own Country "—Germany. (P. 56) Opera House. (End) The date of the letter was the 12th February 1733-4.

FROM THE EARL OF EGMONT'S DIARY, 16th February 1734

Went to the Crown Tavern to hear the practice of Hendel's Te Deum, and other music to be performed at St. Paul's on Tuesday next [the 19th] at the Festival of the Sons of the Clergy.

Egmont MSS., II. 31. It was the *Utrecht Te Deum*. Cf. 23rd February. The rehearsal seems to have been held at the Academy of Ancient Music, which usually met on Friday, not on Saturday.

Circe, a pasticcio-opera with one or two arias by Handel, is produced at Hamburg, 18th February (1st March) 1734.

(Loewenberg, p. 93.) The text was by Johann Philipp Praetorius, after Jan Jacob van Mauricius, Dutch Minister at Hamburg. The music consisted of 21 German songs, mostly by Reinhard Keiser, and 23 Italian arias, four of which were by Handel, Hasse, and Vinci.

FROM THE " LONDON EVENING POST ", 23rd February 1734

New Musick.

This Day Published,

The Favourite Songs in the Opera, call'd Ariadne ; also the Favourite Songs in Arbaces ; with their Symphonies in Score.
Printed for *John Walsh*. . . .

Where may be had,

The celebrated Te Deum and Jubilate for Voices and Instruments ; as it was perform'd at St. Paul's. Composed by Mr. Handel.

The same advertisement appeared in the *Daily Journal* of 26th February. For *Ariadne* see 6th April. On 15th May, Walsh advertised both Handel's and Porpora's *Ariadne* in the *Daily Journal*. For *Arbaces* see 5th January. The *Utrecht Te Deum and Jubilate* was performed again on 19th February. Walsh's edition has the publisher's number 212, which indicates the middle of 1732 as the date of publication of the *Te Deum and Jubilate*.

Riccardo Primo is revived at Brunswick, February 1734.
Cf. 23rd January 1729.

———

FROM PRÉVOST'S " LE POUR ET CONTRE ", PARIS [February ?] 1734
(Translated)

There are at the present time six regular theatres in London, two for
opera and four playhouses. . . . Mr. Handel, enjoying the continued
patronage of the King and the Royal Family, is exploiting to the utmost
Signor *Carastini*'s charming voice ; and all the gentlemen of the Court
who idolize Signor *Senesino* are prodigal of their guineas in order to
raise him above his rival. . . . Nevertheless there are now some fears
for Mr. Handel's faction, since Signora Cuzzoni has made a move to
reinforce that of Senesino. . . .

Vol. III, no. XLI, pp. 257 f. For the London theatres cf. 2nd November 1734.

———

FROM THE " DAILY JOURNAL ", 11th March 1734

We hear, amongst other publick Diversions that are prepared for the
Solemnity of the approaching Nuptials, there is to be perform'd at the
Opera House in the Hay-Market, on Wednesday next [the 13th], a
Serenata, call'd, Parnasso in Festa. The Fable is, Apollo and the Muses,
celebrating the Marriage of Thetis and Peleus. There is one standing
Scene which is Mount Parnassus, on which sit Apollo and the Muses,
assisted with other proper Characters, emblematically dress'd, the whole
Appearance being extreamly magnificent. The Musick is no less entertaining, being contrived with so great a Variety, that all Sorts of Musick
are properly introduc'd in single Songs, Duetto's, &c. intermix'd with
Chorus's, some what in the Style of Oratorio's. People have been
waiting with Impatience for this Piece, the celebrated Mr. Handel having
exerted his utmost Skill in it.

(Schoelcher, pp. 163 f.)

———

FROM THE SAME

At the *King's Theatre* . . . on Wednesday the 13th Instant, will be
perform'd PARNASSO in FESTA : or, *Apollo and the Muses celebrating the
Nuptials of Thetis and Peleus*. A SERENATA. Being an Essay of several
different Sorts of Harmony. . . . To begin at Six o'Clock.

The author of the text is unknown. The music is, for the greater part, taken
from *Athalia*, still not performed in London, but most carefully selected and
adapted. (Chrysander, II. 319-21.) The Court attended the first night, on the
eve of the wedding of Princess Anne and the Prince of Orange on the 14th.
Repeat performances on 16th, 19th, 23rd and 26th March ; revivals in March 1737
(twice), November 1740 and March 1741 (once each). The libretto was printed
by Thomas Wood, in Italian and English, under the title : *The Feast of Parnassus*,

for the Nuptial of Thetis and Peleus. A Serenade . . . Done into English by Mr. George Oldmixon.

CAST OF " IL PARNASSO IN FESTA ", 13th March 1734

Apollo—Signor Carestini, alto
Orfeo—Signor Scalzi, soprano
Clio—Signora Strada, soprano
Calliope—Signora Durastanti, mezzo-soprano
Cloride—Signora Maria Caterina Negri, contralto
Eurilla—?, contralto
Euterpe—Signora Rosa Negri, soprano
Proteo—Mr. Waltz, bass

FROM THE " DAILY COURANT ", 14th March 1734

The same Evening [the 13th] their Majesties, his Royal Highness the Prince of Wales, with the rest of the Royal Family, and his Serene Highness the Prince of Orange, went to the Theatre in the Hay-Market, and saw a Serenata called *Parnasso in Festa*, or *Apollo and the Muses celebrating the Nuptials of* Thetis *and* Peleus.

(Schoelcher, p. 164.)

The Wedding of the Princess Royal and the Prince of Orange is held at the French Chapel in St. James's Palace on 14th March 1734 ; Handel performs his Wedding Anthem ("This is the day . . .") written for his pupil, Princess Anne.

Cf. 21st March. It is noteworthy that, when the wedding was originally planned, in October 1733, Maurice Greene was to write the anthem. The *Bee* of 23rd October, quoted by Chrysander (II. 321) relates : " Seats will be made round the Chapel for the Nobility as at the Coronation [in 1727], and a fine Anthem, composed by Dr. Green, will be performed by Mr. Abbot, Mr. Hughes, Mr. Chelsam, and the other Gentlemen of the Chapel Royal." They now sang in Handel's Anthem. The text is based on Psalms 45 and 118. The music is arranged from the Chandos Anthems, *Athalia*, and *Parnasso in Festa* (Weinstock, p. 189). Jacob Wilhelm Lustig, in the second edition of his book, *Inleiding tot de Muziekkunde*, Groningen 1771, p. 172, relates that Handel said to him in 1734 in London : " Since I left your native Hamburg . . . nothing on earth could induce me to teach music, with one exception—Anne, the flower of princesses." (Chrysander, II. 364 f.) It might be added that Lustig himself dedicated to her his Opus 1, six sonatas for the harpsichord, Amsterdam, *c.* 1736. He was born in Hamburg and became organist in Groningen, Holland. His music magazine is quoted in 1756.

FROM THE " BEE ", 16th March 1734

London, March 14.

Last Night [the 13th] Mr. Handell's new Serenata, in Honour of the Princess Royal's Nuptial's with the Prince of Orange, was perform'd . . .

and was received with the greatest Applause ; the Piece containing the most exquisite Harmony ever furnish'd from the Stage, and the Disposition of the Performers being contriv'd in a very grand and magnificent Manner.

(Chrysander, II. 320 f.)

———

MISS ANN GRANVILLE TO HER SISTER, MRS. PENDARVES

Gloster, 20 March, 1734.

. . . Oh the Serenata ! could I have heard it, or the Anthem Mr. Handel composed for the Princess ! 'tis a horrid thing to be removed from all harmony.

(Delany, I. 444.) The letter refers to *Parnasso in Festa* and the Wedding Anthem.

———

FROM THE " GRUB-STREET JOURNAL ", 21st March 1734

The nuptials of her royal highness the princess royal with the prince of Orange, was perform'd on thursday last [the 14th] . . . after the organ had play'd some time, his highness the prince of Orange led the princess royal to the rails of the altar, and kneel'd down, and then the Lord bishop of London perform'd the service ; after which the bride and bridegroom arose, and retir'd to their places, whilst a fine anthem compos'd by Mr. Handell, was perform'd by a great number of voices and instruments.

(Chrysander, II. 321.) Similar reports appeared in Read's *Weekly Journal* of 23rd March and in the *London Magazine* of March 1734.

———

FROM THE EARL OF EGMONT'S DIARY, 23rd March 1734

I went to the Opera House in the Haymarket to hear Hendel's *Serenata* composed in honour of the marriage, called " Apollo and Daphnis ". The Royal family was all there, the Prince of Wales excepted.

(Egmont MSS., II. 68.) The title of the serenata was, of course, *Il Parnasso in Festa*, and there was no Daphnis in the cast. The Prince might have been at the first night of the pasticcio *Belmira* in the Nobility Opera house.

———

MRS. PENDARVES TO HER SISTER, ANN GRANVILLE

L.B. St., 28th March, 1734.

I went [to the opera] with Lady Chesterfield in her box. . . . 'Twas Arbaces, an opera of Vinci's, pretty enough, but not to compare to Handel's compositions. . . . I went to the oratorio at Lincoln's Inn, composed by Porpora . . . some of the choruses and recitatives are

H.–12 a

extremely fine and touching, but they say it is not equal to Mr. Handel's oratorio of Esther or Deborah.

(Delany, I. 446, 450.) L.B.St. means Lower Brook Street, where Mrs. Pendarves had a house after her return from Ireland, in Handel's neighbourhood. Lady Chesterfield was Handel's former pupil, Melusina von der Schulenburg, Countess of Walsingham, the King's half-sister. For *Arbace* see 5th January. Porpora's oratorio was *Davide e Bersabea*, text by Rolli, composed " for the British Nobility " and produced on 12th March (Egmont, MSS. II. 54) ; performed again on 27th March, it was given seven times in all and was revived, with additions, in Lent 1735 (two performances).

———

Deborah is revived at the Haymarket Theatre, 2nd April 1734. The cast, compared with that of 17th March 1733, was as follows :

Deborah—Signora Strada (Strada)
Barak—(?) Signora Maria Caterina Negri (Bertolli)
Abinoam—(?) Mr. Reinhold (Montagnana)
Sisera—Signor Carestini (Senesino)
Jael—Signora Rosa Negri (unknown)
Israelite Woman—Signora Durastanti (Gismondi)
Chief Priest of Baal—Mr. Waltz (unknown)
Chief Priest of the Israelites—(?) Mr. Reinhold (unknown)

Thomas Reinhold, a bass of German descent, seems to have been in London for some time ; he sang for Handel from 1736 to 1750, and died in 1751. *Deborah* was performed on 2nd, 6th and 9th April ; the King attended the second and the third nights. Mr. Winton Dean discovered that the 1734 or 1735 performance of *Deborah*, or both, was sung half in English and half in Italian.

———

MRS. PENDARVES TO HER SISTER, ANN GRANVILLE

L.B. Str., 2nd April 1734.
[and] 4th April.

In the afternoon [of the 2nd] went with Lady Rich to the oratorio, Deborah by name, which I love (besides its own merit which is a great deal) for " sister Deborah's " sake. . . .

Next week I shall have a very pretty party. Oh that you were to be here ! The Percivals, Sir John Stanley, Bunny, Lady Rich and her daughter, Mr. Hanmer, Lady Catherine, Mr. Handel, and Strada, and if my Lady S. will lend me her harpsichord, she shall be of the party.

(Delany, I. 452, 454.) Lady Elizabeth Rich was the wife of Sir Robert, later Field-Marshal ; their daughter's name was also Elizabeth. Deborah was the nickname of Mrs. Sarah Chapon, an early friend of the writer. The Earl of Egmont also attended that performance (Egmont MSS., II. 75). For the musical party, see 12th April. Mr. Percival was Philip, a brother of the Earl of Egmont. Sir John Stanley was the sisters' uncle, who had introduced young Mary Granville to Handel at the beginning of 1711. " Bunny " was their brother, Bernard Granville, who became a close friend of Handel's. Lady Catherine, wife of Sir Thomas

Hanmer, M.P., was the eldest daughter of the Earl of Egmont. (Hanmer is known as the editor of a Shakespeare edition, 1743–4.) Lady S., usually called Lady Sun, was Judith Countess of Sunderland.

___

FROM THE "DAILY COURANT", 3rd April 1734

The same Evening [of the 2nd] the Prince and Princess of Orange, and her Royal Highness the Princess Caroline, went to the King's Theatre in the Hay Market, and saw an Oratorio, call'd, Deborah.

___

FROM THE "LONDON EVENING POST", 6th April 1734
MUSICK.
This Day is publish'd,

.   .   .   .   .

Printed for John Walsh . . .
Where may be had, just publish'd,

.   .   .   .   .

A second Collection of Favourite Songs in the Opera call'd Ariadne. To which is prefix'd, the Overture in Score. Composed by Mr. Handel. Cf. 23rd February.

___

MRS. PENDARVES TO HER SISTER, ANN GRANVILLE

L.B. Str^t, 12 April, 1734.

I must tell you of a little entertainment of music I had last week ; I never wished more heartily for you and my mother than on that occasion. I had Lady Rich and her daughter, Lady Cath. Hanmer and her husband, Mr. and Mrs. Percival, Sir John Stanley and my brother, Mrs. Donellan, Strada and Mr. Coot. Lord Shaftesbury begged of Mr. Percival to bring him, and being a *profess'd friend* of Mr. Handel (who was here also) *was admitted* ; I never was so *well* entertained at *an opera* ! Mr. Handel was in the best humour in the world, and played lessons and accompanied Strada and all the ladies that sang from seven o'the clock till eleven. I gave them tea and coffee, and about half an hour after nine had a salver brought in of chocolate, mulled white wine and biscuits. Everybody was easy and seemed pleased, Bunny staid with me after the company was gone, eat a cold chick with me, and we chatted till one o'the clock.

(Delany, I. 454.) This is a very touching description of an evening where Handel appeared at his ease. He went to his neighbour, the attractive widow of 35, he himself being 49 now, to meet a company of old, new and future friends, most of them amateur musicians, and all of them his followers. Philip Percival was a many-sided amateur of the arts, a viola-player, and even a composer in the favour of the Prince of Wales. Lady Catherine sang and played the harpsichord and Sir Thomas Hanmer, formerly Speaker of the House of Commons, and chief of the Hanoverian Tories, played the violin. Anthony, Earl of Shaftesbury was to become an ardent Handelian, as was his cousin, James Harris. Miss Anne Donellan, a relative of the Percivals, was a friend of Mrs. Pendarves, and Handel left her fifty guineas in his will. The Honourable Thomas Coote, of Coote Hill in Ireland, was another friend of the writer. Lady S. (Sunderland) seems to have lent her harpsichord for the party, and Handel played one or more of his " Suites de Pièces ", or exercises. The fare was very modest, and Mrs. Mary's description reminds one, in this respect too, of some diary entries about *Schubertiaden* in Vienna, ninety years later. Only her dates are not reliable : she speaks of next week on the 4th, and of last week on the 12th ; the party must have been on Sunday the 7th, or thereabouts.

———

MRS PENDARVES TO HER SISTER, ANN GRANVILLE

L.B. Str^t., 27 April, 1734.
Yesterday morning at the rehearsal of a most delightful opera at Mr. Handel's called Sosarme, which is acted to-night, and I doubt as I am to go out of town next week, I shall not be able to resist the temptation of it. (Delany, I. 463.)

———

Sosarme is revived at the Haymarket Theatre, 27th April 1734.
Repeat performances on 30th April and 4th May. The cast, compared with the original one of 15th February 1732, was as follows :

Sosarme—Signor Carestini (Senesino)
Haliate—Signora Durastanti (Pinacci)
Erenice—Signora Maria Caterina Negri (Bagnolesi)
Elmira—Signora Strada (Strada)
Argone—Signor Scalzi (Signor Campioli)
Melo—Signora Rosa Negri (Bertolli)
Altomaro—Mr. Waltz (Montagnana)

———

MRS. PENDARVES TO HER SISTER, ANN GRANVILLE

L.B. Str., 30 April [1734].
I go to-night to the opera with Lady Rich and Mrs. Donellan, to Sosarmes, an opera of Mr. Handel's, a charming one, and yet I dare say it will be almost empty ! 'Tis vexatious to have *such music* neglected.
(Delany, I. 466.) Both opera companies were doing badly. The Earl of Egmont wrote in his diary on 6th May : " In the evening I went to the opera called *Iphigenia*, composed by Porpora, and I think the town does not justice in condemning it." The fact was, two opera houses were too much for London.

———

Acis and Galatea is performed at Crow Street Music Hall, Dublin, 1st May 1734, for the benefit of Mrs. Raffa.
(*Musical Opinion*, April 1921, p. 609.) This performance is recorded only in a libretto which cannot be traced ; *Acis* was certainly performed in Dublin in 1734 and/or 1735.

———

FROM THE " DAILY JOURNAL ", 7th May 1734

At the King's Theatre . . . this present Tuesday . . . will be reviv'd a Serenata, call'd, ACIS and GALATEA. . . . Tickets . . . at Half a Guinea each. Gallery Five Shillings. . . . To begin at Half an Hour after Six o'Clock.

Formerly it seemed uncertain whether this revival took place on the 6th or the 7th. The reason was that the *Daily Journal* of 4th May was wrongly dated 6th May, and furthermore it advertised the revival for " Saturday, the 6th Day of May ", instead of Tuesday the 7th. This was, presumably, the mixed English-Italian version (Winton Dean). See 5th December 1732 and 24th March 1736.

FROM THE " DAILY JOURNAL ", 18th May 1734

At the King's Theatre . . . this present Saturday . . . will be perform'd, An Opera, call'd PASTOR FIDO. Composed by Mr. HANDEL. Intermixed with Chorus's. The Scenery after a particular Manner. . . . To begin at Half an Hour after Six o'Clock.

Cf. 22nd November 1712. Repeat performances on 21st, 25th, 28th May; 4th, 8th, 11th, 15th, 18th, 22nd, 25th, 29th June; 3rd, 6th and 15th July. (The performance on 15th June is doubtful : it is advertised on 13th June, for Saturday the 15th, but on 14th June the next performance is advertised for the 18th.) While the libretto of 1712 was printed by J. Gardyner, the " second edition ", with " large Additions ", was published by Thomas Wood. The cast, compared with that of 1712, seems to have been as follows :

Mirtillo—Signor Carestini (Valeriano)
Amarilli—Signora Strada (Pilotti)
Eurilla—Signora Durastanti (Margherita)
Silvio—Signor Scalzi (Valentini)
Dorinda—Signora Maria Caterina Negri (Barbier)
Tirenio—Mr. Waltz (Leveridge)

Cf. 9th November 1734.

MRS. PENDARVES TO HER SISTER, ANN GRANVILLE

L.B. Street, May 28th, 1734.
Donellan and I are to dine to-day with Sir John Stanley, and afterwards go with him to Pastor Fido.
(Delany, I. 472.)

The performance of *Pastor Fido* on 4th June is advertised as " Being the last Time of performing till after the Holidays ", *Daily Journal*, 1st June 1734.

Cf. 29th June. The Nobility Opera closed its first season on 15th June, having revived Bononcini's *Astarte* (adapted by Rolli, 19th November

1720) on 26th February, produced the pasticcio *Belmira* on 23rd March, and Porpora's *Enea nel Lazio*, text by Rolli, on 11th May.

—

Walsh advertises " Six Overtures for Violins, etc. in seven Parts, as they are performed at the King's Theatre in the Haymarket in the Opera's of Ariadne, Sosarmes, Orlando, Aethus, Porus, Esther. Compos'd by Mr. Handel, fifth Collection.—N.B. The same Overtures are also curiously set for the Harpsicord. The most celebrated Opera Aires in Ariadne, etc. by Mr. Handel, curiously fitted for a German Flute and Bass . . .", *Craftsman*, 22nd June 1734.

—

Handel withdraws £1300, 26th June 1734.

—

FROM THE PRINCE OF WALES'S " REGISTER OF WARRANTS ",
28th June 1734

To Mr Handel for the Season of Operas in the Haymarket ending this Year 1734   £   s   d
                                                           250 – –

(British Museum : Add. MS. 24, 403 f. 98 a.) Cf. 5th July 1734 and 5th July 1737.

—

The performance of *Pastor Fido* on 29th June is advertised as " Being the last Time of performing ", *Daily Journal*, 29th June 1734.

Cf. 1st (4th) June. It is said (Chrysander, II. 363) that the return to London from Holland, on 2nd July, of Princess Anne of Orange for a summer holiday caused Handel to prolong the opera season until 15th July, repeating *Pastor Fido* three more times. Lord Hervey, in his *Memoirs of the Reign of George the Second*, and Jacob Wilhelm Lustig, the Dutch organist who met Handel in London in 1734, in his *Inleiding tot de Muziekkunde*, tell of the Princess's tender care for her distressed teacher. Cf. end of 1734 and end of 1751.

—

FROM THE " OXFORD ACT " ACCOUNT, PUBLISHED June 1734

Thursday, July the 5th [1733]. About 5 o'Clock, the great Mr HANDEL shew'd away with his ESTHER, an Oratorio, or sacred Drama, to a very numerous audience, at 5 shillings a ticket. . . .

The next Morning, Saturday, July the 7th, there was a fine Performance of Instrumental Musick in the Theater, between 6 and 8 o'clock, under the care and inspection of Richard GOODSON, B.Mus., our Musick

Professor, who made it his sole business to perform everything very exactly, that could well be expected of him, during the whole time. . . .

The Chevalier HANDEL very judiciously, forsooth, ordered out Tickets for his ESTHER this Evening again.

Some of the Company, that had found themselves but very scramblingly entertained at our dry Disputations, took it into their Heads, to try how a little Fiddling would sit upon them.

Such as cou'dn't attend before, squeezed in with as much Alacrity as others strove to get out ; so that e're his [Handel's] Myrmidons cou'd gain their Posts, he found that he had little likelyhood to be at such a Loss for a House, as once upon a time, Folks say, he was.

However, in this Confusion, one of the good-natured Cantab's, cou'dn't help suggesting to him, that his only Way now wou'd be, to carry it off with an Air, and e'en be contented with what he cou'dn't help.

So that notwithstanding the barbarous and inhuman Combination of such a Parcel of unconscionable Chaps, he disposed, it seems, of most of his Tickets, and had, as you may guess, a pretty mottley Appearance into the Bargain. . . .

The Vice Chancellor, whose Province it was to take care of the Preachers for the next Day [the 8th], provided the Rev. Dr. THOMAS COCKMAN, Master of UNIVERSITY College, for the Forenoon.

After the Performance of Sieur HANDEL's TE DEUM with Instruments, The Doctor took his Text from ROM. XII. 2. . . .

There was then an Anthem very finely performed with Instruments.

The Person that the Vice-Chancellor pitched upon for the Afternoon, was the Rev. DR. THOMAS SECKER, Prebendary of DURHAM, and Rector of S. JAMES'S WESTMINSTER.

After a grand JUBILATE to the TE DEUM, he preached from DEUT. XXXII. 46.47. . . .

The Galleries here were reserved for the Ladies, where they made a very sparkling gaudy Shew ; and after another Anthem with Instruments was over, they were most of them carried away to NEW-COLLEGE Chapel, where they heard an Evening Service of the late famous Dr. BLOW, and another Anthem with Instruments, from whence they divided their Favours, and took to different Walks, as lay most convenient for the remaining Part of their Evening.

The next Morning, Tuesday, July the 10th at Eight o'Clock, there was an excellent LATIN Sermon. . . .

The Company in the Evening were entertained with a spick and span new Oratorio called ATHALIA.

One of the Royal and Ample had been saying, that truely, 'twas his Opinion, that the Theater was erected for other-guise Purposes, than to be prostituted to a Company of squeeking, bawling, out-landish Singsters, let the Agreement be what it would.

This Morning, Wednesday, July the 11th there was luckily enough, for the Benefit of some of HANDEL's People, a SERENATA in their [Christ Church's] Grand Hall.

After 'twas over, the Person was soon met with, and immediately 'twas down to the very Ground.

Oh !—Your Servant—Mr.— ! Sir, your very humble Servant ! Your Servant Sir !—

Well—but after all—your College Hall isn't half so bad a Room for Musick, it seems, as People fancied—didn't it sound excellently well ? —They say there was a deal of good Company. . . .

In the Evening, ATHALIA was served up again.

But the next Night he concluded with his ORATORIO of DEBORAH.

(Schoelcher, pp. 157 f. ; Chrysander, II. 308 f. ; Mee, pp. XIV f. ; Eland, pp. 12-19.) Bodleian Library, Oxford : GOUGH Oxf. 113 ; ADDS Oxf. 8⁰ 61. (Two copies.) The full title of the pamphlet is : " The Oxford Act. *A.D.* 1733. Being a particular and exact Account of that Solemnity. . . . In a letter to a friend in town." Listed in the *Gentleman's Magazine*, June 1734. The quotations are from pp. 3, 21, 31, 33, 43, 44-5 and 47. On Friday, 6th July 1733, at one o'clock, there was the celebration of the annual festival in honour of the new Sheldonian Theatre, called " Theatri Encaenia ". Dr. Cookman's sermon had been printed in the meantime. The " Cantab's ", *i.e.* the Cambridge gentlemen, dined on 10th July with the Proctors at University College Hall. The " Royal and Ample " are supposed to have been the members of Christ Church. Mee stresses the fact that, according to pp. 6, 10 and 13 of the pamphlet, the exercises of those taking their degrees were interspersed with music.

———

FROM LORD OXFORD'S " VISITORS " LIST, 12th July 1734, etc.

Mr. Handel, Brook Street.

Portland MSS., vol. VI (Harley Papers, vol. IV), p. 56. For Robert Harley, first Earl of Oxford, see 9th February 1719. The list probably refers to callers in Dover Street, after Lady Margaret Cavendish Harley's wedding to William, second Duke of Portland, on 20th June 1734.

———

Handel's fourteenth and, for the time, last season at the Haymarket Theatre ends on 15th July 1734.

Handel's contract with Heidegger ended on 6th July, and Heidegger let the house to the Opera of the Nobility. Handel agreed with John Rich to perform operas at the Theatre in Covent Garden, alternating with Rich's plays.

———

FROM PRÉVOST'S " LE POUR ET CONTRE ", PARIS [July ?] 1734
(Translation)

Mr. Handel, director of one of the two London operas, had undertaken to keep his theatre going in face of the opposition of all the English nobility. He flattered himself—unjustifiably—that his reputation would always bring him a sufficient audience ; but deprived of this support, he has incurred so much ruinous expense and [written] so many beautiful operas that were a total loss, that he finds himself obliged to leave London and return to his native land.

Vol. IV, no. LIV, p. 216. This was, of course, a false rumour.

—

Handel begins the opera *Ariodante*, 12th August 1734.
Cf. 24th October. This opera was written for Covent Garden.

—

HANDEL TO SIR WYNDHAM KNATCHBULL, AT ASHFORD

London, August 27, 1734

Sir

At my arrival in Town from the Country, I found my self honored of your kind invitation.

I am sorry that by the situation of my affairs I see my self deprived of receiving that pleasure being engaged with Mr. Rich to carry on the Operas at Covent Garden.

I hope at your return to Town, Sir, I shall make up this loss.

Meanwhile I beg you to be persuaded of the sincere respect with which
     I am
         Sir
            your
         most obedient and most humble
                     Servant
                  George Frideric Handel.

To Sir Wyndham Knatchbull, Bart.,
of Mersham le Hatch near
Ashford, Kent.

(Chrysander, II. 366 f.) Original formerly in the possession of the pianist Charles Salaman, and later in Mr. W. Westley Manning's collection, London. Mueller, in the English edition of Handel's letters (pp. 32 f.), printed this letter twice by mistake. Apart from the South Sea notes of 1716 and the application to the House of Lords in 1727, all of which were apparently written, or drafted, by another hand, this is the first Handel letter in English which has been preserved. Knatchbull seems to have been a new acquaintance of Handel's : he subscribed for Handel's works from 1736 onwards. Since 1730 he had been married to Catherine, the daughter of James Harris the elder, of the Close at Salisbury, and sister of James Harris the younger (cf. 12th April 1734 and 19th April 1737). It is not certain whether this invitation was to Knatchbull's country seat. From the end of July till the end of August Handel was in Tunbridge Wells for the cure, probably for the first time ; Tunbridge Wells is not far from Ashford.

—

FROM THE TREASURY MINUTE BOOK, 15th October 1734

Order for a sign manual for 1,000l. for the Opera undertakers.

(Calendar of Treasury Papers, 1731-4, p. 579.)   See next entry.

———

FROM THE TREASURY MINUTE BOOK, 23rd October 1734

Mr. Chancellor says the King intends that the 1,000l. for the undertakers of the Opera shall be paid to Mr. Hendell and not to the Academy
of Music, as the last 1,000l. was. So prepare a sign manual accordingly.

(*Monthly Musical Record*, June 1902.) Calendar of Treasury Papers, 1731-4,
p. 580. This was the first, and last, time that the Royal bounty, the annual subvention of the King to the opera, was paid not to the Academy, nor to Heidegger,
but to Handel. Whether this was due to the fact that Handel had left the Haymarket Theatre and was the most needy of the undertakers, or to the influence of
Princess Anne, or both, cannot be decided. During the following years the
subvention went to the Haymarket Theatre, even in Handel's absence. The
Chancellor of the Exchequer was Sir Robert Walpole. See 29th October.

———

Handel finishes the opera *Ariodante*, 24th October 1734.

Cf. 12th August.

———

FROM THE KING'S WARRANT BOOK, 29th October 1734

	£	s.	d.	
George Frederick	1,000	0	0	Same [Royal bounty] towards
Handel, Esq.				enabling the undertakers of the Opera
				to discharge their debts.

Calendar of Treasury Papers, 1731-4, p. 670. Cf. 31st October.

———

The Opera of the Nobility opens at the Haymarket Theatre on
29th October 1734 with *Artaserse*, music by Hasse and Riccardo
Broschi.

(Loewenberg, p. 84.) Cf. 1st December 1724 (Ariosti's *Artaserse*) and
5th January 1734 (Vinci's *Arbace*). The new version of Hasse's *Artaserse*
was performed 28 times during the season, and 8 times more in the first
half of 1736. It was in that opera that Carlo Broschi, called Farinelli,
Riccardo's brother, first appeared on the London stage. The famous
soprano, who had arrived a month before, outshone Carestini as well as
Senesino, the latter now advanced in age. He never sang a Handel part,
but when, following the usual etiquette, he presented himself at Court to
display his abilities, Princess Anne accompanied him and insisted on his
singing two Handel arias at sight, which he did with some difficulty.

(Burney, 1771, p. 216.)   The Royal family attended his first night (*The Suffolk Mercury*, 4th November 1734).

ORDER OF PAYMENT FOR £1000 TO HANDEL AND HIS RECEIPT,
31st October till 19th December 1734

George Frederick   Order is taken this 31st Day of October 1734
Handel Esqr By virtue of his Ma^{ts} General Letters of Privy
                   Seal bearing dato the 26th day of June 1727
                   and in pursuance of a Warrant under his
                   Ma^{ts} Royal Sign Manual dated the 28th
                   instant That you deliver and pay of such
                   his Ma^{ts} Treasure as remains in your
                   charge unto George Frederick Handel Esqr
                   or to his assigns the Sum of One thousand
                   pounds without account to be applyed
                   as Our Royal Bounty towards enabling
                   the Undertaker of the Opera to discharge   R. Walpole
                   their Debts and these together with his or
                   his assigns acquittance shall be your
                   Discharge herein
                                                       Wm Clayton
My Ld Onslow I pray pay this Order out of . . . & . . . Excise
                   14th Decr 1734   Will: Yonge
   Ex. Record. 14° Dec. 1734 . . . Onslow
                   Exam :   : Halifax
[On the back :]
                          19 December 1734
   Reced. the full Contents of the within written Order
                          George Frideric Handel
Witness
      John Kipling

Original in the possession of Mr. Gilbert S. Inglefield, Eggington House, Leighton Buzzard, Bedfordshire. The signatures on the order are those of Sir Robert Walpole, the Chancellor of the Exchequer; William Clayton and Sir William Yonge, Lords of the Treasury; Arthur Onslow, Treasurer of the Navy; George Montague, fourth Earl of Halifax, Auditor of the Receipt of the Exchequer; and John Kipling, Handel's witness, Deputy Treasurer of the Academy of Music, who probably took the money with him. Handel made no corresponding deposit into his account at the Bank of England. The " General Letters of Privy Seal ", referred to at the beginning, are entered in " Entry Books of King's Warrants " (T. 52), vol. 35, p. 34; they are, according to information kindly given by the Public Record Office, an authority to the Commissioners of the Treasury etc. to " Issue and pay or Cause to be Issued and paid all such Sum and Sums of mony for any publick or particular Uses or Services as we by any Warrant or Warrants under our Royal Sign Manual Shall Direct and Appoint ".

He now removed to Conventgarden, and entered into a partnership with RICH, *the master of that house.* HASSE *and* PORPORA *were the Composers at the Hay-market. When the former was invited over, it is remarkable, that the first question he asked, was, whether Handel was dead. Being answered in the negative, he refused to come, from a persuasion, that where his countryman was (for they were both Saxons by birth) no other person of the same profession was likely to make any figure. He could not believe that in a nation which had always been famous for sense and discernment, the credit of such an artist as Handel could ever be impaired. However, this mystery was explained to him in such a manner, and this explanation accompanied by such offers, that at length he got the better of his scruples, and consented to be engaged. He is remarkable for his fine elevated air, with hardly so much as the shew of harmony to support it. And this may serve not only for a character of* HASSE *in particular, but of the Italians in general, at the time we are speaking of. The opposition in which they were engaged against Handel, made him look upon that merit in his antagonists with much indifference, and upon this defect with still more contempt. He carried his contempt so far, as to endeavour to be as unlike them as possible. He could have vanquished his opponents at their own weapons; but he had the sense to discover, that the offended and prejudiced side would never have acknowledged his victory however decisive ; and that his new friends, for want of understanding the nature and use of such weapons, would not have discerned it however obvious.* (Mainwaring, pp. 116-18.)

————

LORD HERVEY TO HENRY FOX

St. James's, November 2, 1734

No place is full but the Opera. . . . By way of public spectacles this winter, there are no less than two Italian Operas, one French play house, and three English ones. Heidegger has computed the expense of these shows, and proves in black & white that the undertakers must receive seventy-six thousand odd hundred pounds to bear their charges, before they begin to become gainers.

Hervey and his friends, p. 211. Since Covent Garden now had operas as well as plays, the number of theatres was, in fact, five : Haymarket, Drury Lane, Covent Garden, Goodman's-Fields and, for French plays, the New (or Little) Theatre in the Haymarket. It is sometimes related (Burney, IV. 374 ; Schoelcher, p. 172) that Handel went, with his company, to the deserted Lincoln's Inn Fields Theatre, or to the New Haymarket Theatre, in autumn 1734 ; this is not true.

————

FROM THE "LONDON DAILY POST, AND GENERAL ADVERTISER", 4th November 1734

We are informed, that when Mr. Handel waited on their Majesties with his New Opera of *Ariodante*, his Majesty express'd great Satisfaction with the Composition, and was graciously pleased to Subscribe 1000*l.* towards carrying on the Operas this Season at Covent-Garden.

(Burney, IV. 382.) This notice appeared on page 1 of number 1 of a new paper. It seems quite possible that Handel played some extracts from his coming opera on the harpsichord at St. James's Palace. (Weinstock, p. 193, thought that Handel presented the King with the score.) Nothing is known for certain, however, of a Royal subvention to the operas at Covent Garden. Perhaps the payment to Handel for the season 1733–4 at the Haymarket was mistakenly thought to be for this new season. A more plausible statement is to be found under 9th November in the *Ipswich Gazette*.

FROM THE " BEE ", 9th November 1734

London, Novemb. 8.

Mr. Handel opens Tomorrow, at Covent-Garden Theatre, with the Opera of Pastor Fido, preceded by a new Dramatic Entertainment of Musick ; and we hear there was a Rehearsal this Day at Twelve o'Clock.

FROM THE " LONDON DAILY POST ", 9th November 1734

Covent-Garden.

.   .   .   .   .

At the Theatre-Royal in Covent-Garden, this present Saturday . . . will be perform'd PASTOR FIDO. An *Opera* ; With several Additions, Intermix'd with Chorus's. Which will be preceded by a new Dramatic Entertainment (in Musick) call'd, TERPSICHORE. . . . Tickets . . . at Half a Guinea each. First Gallery 4s. Upper Gallery 2s. 6d.

Cutting in the *Theatrical Register*. The new paper secured the advertisements of Handel's operas for itself. Cf. 18th May 1734. The prologue, " Terpsicore ", was acted in the " Temple of Erato, President of Musick ". The third edition of the libretto, bilingual as before, was again printed by Thomas Wood. Repeat performances on 13th, 16th, 20th and 23rd November. Wednesdays and Saturdays were the opera nights at Covent Garden. The tickets for the galleries were cheaper than at the Haymarket (5s.). This advertisement, like the following ones, was introduced by the words : " By his Majesty's Command ". This formula, however, does not indicate that the King had anything to do with the production. It simply means that the Theatres Royal at Covent Garden and in Drury Lane, as well as the King's Theatre in the Haymarket, were entitled to use such styles by appointment.

CAST OF " IL PASTOR FIDO ", 9th November 1734

Prologue :
Apollo—Signor Carestini
Erato—Signora Strada
Terpsicore—Mlle Marie Sallé

Drama :
Mirtillo—Signor Carestini
Amarillis—Signora Strada
Silvio—Mr. Beard
Dorinda—Signora Maria Caterina Negri
Eurilla—Signora Rosa Negri
Tirenius—Mr. Waltz

Signora Durastanti (Eurilla of 18th May) and Signor Scalzi (Silvio) seem to have left the company before they went to Covent Garden. Handel now engaged the tenor, John Beard, who for the rest of Handel's life, with only short interruptions, became his most valuable oratorio singer. Beard, still a young man in 1734, was a chorister at the Chapel Royal, but he was not in the Cannons Concert, as stated in the *Dictionary of National Biography*. For Sallé the dancer, who was back in London, see 5th June 1717 and 8th January 1735 ; she was engaged by Rich.

FROM THE " IPSWICH GAZETTE ", 9th November 1734

London, November 5.

We hear that his Majesty, who has already been graciously pleas'd to give his 1,000*l.* subscription to the Operas in the Haymarket, has likewise ordered 500*l.* to be given as his subscription to Mr. Handell, who is allow'd by all good Judges to be the finest Composer of Musick in the whole World. And

That Mr. Handell had got an extreme fine English Voice, who will speedily sing at the Theatre in Covent Garden, and who never sang on any stage.

We hear that both Operas (occasion'd by their dividing) are at a vast expence to entertain the Nobility and Gentry for the ensuing Season ; the Opera House in the Haymarket are reckon'd to stand near 12000*l.* and Mr. Handell at near 9000*l.* for the Season.

(J. P. Malcolm, p. 354.) Cf. 4th November. No entry about a new subscription for Handel's operas is to be found in the Calendars of Treasury Papers. The English singer was Mr. Beard.

ROLLI TO RIVA IN VIENNA (Translated)

London, 9th November 1734.

I know that you would have liked me to give you the latest theatre news, but although I did take some part therein last year, and may do so this year, I am so disgusted by it all that I do not care to talk about it, let alone write about it. However, I must have you know—for it deserves to be known—that Farinello was a revelation to me, for I realised that till then I had heard only a small part of what human song can achieve, whereas I now conceive I have heard all there is to hear. He has, besides, the most agreeable and clever manners, hence I take the greatest pleasure in his company and acquaintance. He has made me a present which I much desired and which will help me pass many pleasant hours, directing my thoughts to our country's and our common master's fame, which perhaps we two alone have further increased in poetical honour ; the present I mean is the Works and Verses of the *Abate* Metastasio, to whom, please, remember me.

(Fassini, 1912, *Rivista musicale*, p. 626 ; Streatfeild, 1917, p. 443.) Original in Biblioteca Estense, Modena. It means something for Rolli, Senesino's friend, to

speak in such terms of Farinelli.   Cf. his characterisation of Senesino, 23rd
September 1720.

———

FROM MATTHESON'S HAMBURG OPERA NOTES, 18th (29th) November
1734 (Translated)

Rodelinda, Queen of Lombardy.   The composition of the Italian arias
by Herr Händel.   [The dialogue] translated into prose by Herr Fischer,
done into rhyme by Herr Wendt : the recitatives that is to say.   Performed in Hamburg for the first time on 29th Nov. but indeed to little
applause. . . . See No. 225, where a *Flavius Bertaridus* was performed
[on 12th (23rd) November 1729, composed by Telemann] which
comprises this same story.

(Chrysander, II. 129 ; Merbach, p. 365.)   C. G. Wendt not only provided the
German recitatives, but also the translation of the arias in verse.   The arias were
sung in Italian.   It was performed twice only, but was repeated once in summer
1735, and twice in autumn 1736.

———

LADY ELIZABETH COMPTON TO ELIZABETH SHIRLEY, COUNTESS OF
NORTHAMPTON, 21st November 1734

A Scholar of Mr Gates, Beard, (who left the Chappell last Easter)
shines in the Opera of Covent Garden & Mr Hendell is so full of his
Praises that he says he will surprise the Town with his performances
before the Winter is over.

(Streatfeild, 1909, p. 136.)   Townshend MSS., p. 242.   Written from Golden
Square to Castle Ashby, but without address.

———

FROM THE " LONDON DAILY POST ", 27th November 1734

At the Theatre-Royal in Covent-Garden, [this present] Wednesday . . .
will be perform'd an OPERA, call'd, ARIADNE. . . . No Persons whatever
to be admitted behind the Scenes.

Cutting in *Theatrical Register*.   Repeat performances on 30th November, 4th,
7th and 11th December.   (Burney, IV. 374, speaks of six performances.)   The
parts of Signora Durastanti (Tauride) and Signor Scalzi (Alceste) in the original
cast, cf. 26th January 1734, were probably sung by Signora Rosa Negri and Mr.
Beard.

———

Walsh advertises " Two Collections of Favourite Songs in the
Opera's of Pastor Fido, and Ariadne with their Overtures in
Score.   By Mr. Handel ", *Craftsman*, 30th November 1734.

(Chrysander, II. 363.)   The two *Arianna* selections were published in
February and April 1734, but this was the first advertisement of those from
Pastor Fido.

———

FROM THE " CRAFTSMAN ", 7th December 1734

MUSICK,
This Day Published,
Compos'd by Mr. *Handel,*

I. A fourth Volume of Apollo's Feast : Or, the Harmony of the Opera Stage. Being a well chosen Collection of all the favourite and most celebrated Songs out of his late Opera's, with their Symphonies for Voices and Instruments. Engraven in a fair Character.—N.B. In this and the 1st, 2d and 3d Volumes are contain'd the most favourite Songs out of all the Opera's.

Also by the same Author,

II. Six Concerto's for Violins, &c. in seven Parts. Opera terza.

III. Six Sonata's or Trio's for two German Flutes or Violins, and a Bass. Opera seconda.

IV. Twelve Solo's for a Violin, German Flute or Harpsichord. Opera Prima.

V. Thirty Overtures for Violins, &c. in seven Parts.—N.B. The same Overtures are set for the Harpsichord.

VI. The Water Musick and six French Horn Songs. In seven Parts.

VII. The most celebrated Airs out of all the Opera's fitted for a German Flute, Violin and Harpsichord. In 12 Collections.

VIII. Nineteen Operas compleat. Printed in Score.

IX. Esther, an Oratorio, and the Mask of Acis and Galatea.

X. The Te Deum and Jubilate, as performed at St. Paul's.

XI. Two Books of celebrated Lessons for the Harpsichord.

All compos'd by Mr. *Handel,* and
Printed for John Walsh, at the Harp and Hoboy in Catherine-street in the Strand.

This was the longest Handel list, so far, to be advertised in a newspaper. It shows that Walsh really had become Handel's own publisher. The collection called *Apollo's Feast,* finally comprising six volumes, started about 1725 with a volume of arias by Handel, Bononcini and Ariosti, but later became a purely Handel collection. Opus 1 and Opus 2 were published in 1733, Opus 3 in 1734. The number of overtures in parts came to sixty ; that of the arrangements for harpsichord to the same figure. The *Water Music,* in parts, was published in 1733. (Smith, 1948, p. 283.) The *French Horn Songs,* in parts, were published in 1733 ; they are arrangements, for orchestra, of one aria each from *Giulio Cesare, Poro, Partenope, Admeto, Rinaldo,* and *Richard the First.* The opera scores, printed by Walsh, were never completed. The *Utrecht Te Deum and Jubilate* was issued in 1732. Of the *Lessons,* or rather *Suites de Pièces pour Clavecin,* Walsh had reprinted volume I in 1732, and published volume II in 1733.

———

Ottone is revived at the Haymarket Theatre, 10th December 1734.

The newspapers preserved from this period are very scanty. In a new one, *The Weekly Oracle : or, Universal Library* of 7th December, there is a rehearsal recorded, on the 5th, " before a numerous Audience of the first Quality ". Some cuttings from the *London Daily Post* are to be found in the *Theatrical Register*. A libretto, published by Charles Bennet, is lost. The composer's name is, as usual, not mentioned in the newspaper advertisements, but Burney (IV. 381) thought it probable that it was Handel's *Ottone*, performed by the rival company ; cf. 27th December (*The Prompter*). Repeat performances on 14th, 17th, 21st and 23rd December.

———

Oreste, a pasticcio-opera with an overture and three arias newly written by Handel, is produced at Covent Garden, 18th December 1734.

(Burney, IV. 378 ; Chrysander, II. 368.) The music was adapted from earlier works of Handel's ; he wrote the whole score himself. Mlle Sallé danced in this opera, but the tunes were from *Terpsicore*. One of her dances was called " The Grecian Sailor " (see 17th April 1735). The overture is printed in vol. 48, the three arias in vol. 49 of the Collected Edition. Nothing is known about the author, but a copy of the libretto is in the Schoelcher Collection, Conservatoire, Paris. Repeat performances on 21st and 28th December.

———

Handel signs the receipt for the £1000 Royal bounty, 19th December 1734.

Cf. 31st October. The payment was for the season 1733–4 at the Haymarket Theatre.

———

FROM THE " BEE ", 21st December 1734

London, December 19

Last Night their Majesties were at the Theatre Royal in Covent-Garden, to see the Opera of Orestes, which was perform'd with great Applause.

———

FROM " THE PROMPTER ", 24th December 1734

. . . Are not our *English* Singers shut out, with our *Mother-Tongue* ? So engrossing are *Italians*, and so prejudic'd the *English* against their own Country, that our Singers are excluded from our very Concerts ; *Bertolli* singing at the *Castle*, and *Senesino* at the *Swan*, to both their Shames be it spoken ; who, not content with monstrous Salaries at the Opera's, stoop so low as to be hired to sing at Clubs ! thereby eating some *English* Singers Bread. . . .

(Chrysander, II. 378.) At the " Castle Tavern ", in Paternoster Row, several music clubs held their meetings ; another one met at the " Swan Tavern ", later called the " King's Arms ", in Exchange Alley. It was nothing new for singers from the Italian Opera to visit such clubs on special occasions as guest performers :

Senesino sang, and Carbonelli played the violin, on St. Cecilia's Day, 1723, at the
" Crown Tavern " (Chrysander, II. 123). For *The Prompter*, see next entry.

—

FROM " THE PROMPTER ", 27th December 1734

Since . . . the WORDS, in our *Opera's*, are not only *silly*, but *un-
necessary*, and an Incumbrance upon the *Scale* of the Composer . . . I
wou'd recommend . . . that it shou'd be Lawful to use but ONE SINGLE
WORD, throughout the whole three Acts of an *Opera*. . . . If any Good
Christian can give Notice of a Word, more *properly adapted*, than
Quadrille, let him translate it into *Italian*, and convey it to the Lord
Chamberlain's Office, and He shall receive its *full Value*, out of the
Overplus of *Mr. Handel's Subscription* ; it being peculiar to the *Good
Fortune* of this Gentleman, that He is to contribute, his Assistance, toward
Entertainments, which his *Enemies* are *paid for*.

There are other references to operas in *The Prompter* of 28th January, 14th March
and 14th November 1735, and 30th April 1736, most of them signed P. Please.
The editors of this paper were Aaron Hill and William Popple. The last sentence
quoted apparently refers to *Ottone*, performed at the Haymarket Theatre.

—

FROM A LETTER, PROBABLY WRITTEN TO CATHERINE COLLINGWOOD

Bullstrode [Street], Dec. 27, 1734.
I don't pity Handell in the least, for I hope this mortification will
make him a human creature ; for I am sure before he was no better than
a brute, when he could treat civilized people with so much brutality as
I know he has done.

(Streatfeild, 1909, p. 135.) Throckmorton MSS., p. 257. No signature, nor
address. Apparently written to Catherine, daughter of George Collingwood, of
Elrington, Northumberland, who became the second wife of Sir Robert Throckmorton. Cf. 19th February 1737.

—

Walsh advertises *Pastor Fido*, arranged for a single flute, *Craftsman*,
28th December 1734.

—

FROM JEAN DE SERRÉ DE RIEUX' " LES DONS DES ENFANS DE LATONE :
LA MUSIQUE, ETC.", PARIS, 1734

. . . Mais pourquoi parcourir Naples, Venise, ou Rome ?
L'Angleterre empruntant l'Italique idiome,
N'a-t-elle pas cent fois fait retentir les airs
Du Dramatique éclat de ses doctes Concerts ?
D'un genie étranger la source inépuisable
Enfante chaque année un œuvre mémorable,

Qui d'une nation où fleurissent les Arts,
Charme, étonne & ravit l'oreille & les regards.
Dans l'Harmonique fond d'une Orgue foudroyante
HENDEL [1] puisa les traits d'une grace sçavante :
FLAVIUS, TAMERLAN, OTHON, RENAUD, CAESAR,
ADMETE, SIROÉ, RODELINDE, & RICHARD,
Eternels monumens dressés à sa mémoire,
Des OPERA Romains surpasserent la gloire.
Venise lui peut-elle opposer un rival ?
Son caractere fort, nouveau, brillant, égal,
Du sens judicieux suit la constante trace,
Et ne s'arme jamais d'une insolente audace. . . .

Pp. 102 f. The section containing these verses is entitled : " La Musique,
epitre en vers divisée en quatre chants. Troisième Édition, revûe, corrigée &
augmentée ". The number of the edition refers to the main part only, not to this
section, which was new. The verses are from " Chant Troisième ". " Renaud "
is " Rinaldo ". Handel was never organist of St. Paul's Cathedral. The next
section is a catalogue of all the French operas from 1645 till 1733. The last section
of the book, dedicated to the King (Louis XV), is " Nouvelle Chasse du Cerf ",
a Handel pasticcio ; see next entry.

———

FROM THE " ADVERTISSEMENT " OF " NOUVELLE CHASSE DU
CERF, DIVERTIMENT EN MUSIQUE ; COMPOSE DE PLUSIEURS AIRS
PARODIÉS SUR LES OPERA D'ANGLETERRE : AVEC DIFFÉRENTES
SYMPHONIES ÉTRANGERES ", Paris, 1734 (Translated)

. . . All the songs are parodies of a number of airs chosen from operas
of Mr. Hendel's composition, performed in England.

The merits of this ingenious composer are recognised all over Europe
and the crown which he received last year from the most illustrious
Englishmen puts him beyond all praise. As his infinitely correct and
graceful style seems to agree with our taste more closely than any other,
on the principle now accepted that everything essentially good in music
must appear so to all civilised nations, some have wished to try and see
whether French words, [if] exactly fitted, could gain new and added
graces under a foreign mask. . . .

(Chrysander, II. 183 f.) P. 300. There are nine airs by Handel, one by Nicola
Fago, and one from a sonata for violin with bass from Jean-Marie Leclair's Opus 2,
printed in the music appendix. The Handel airs are printed with the following
first lines : " L'Ombre fuit ", " Courons, volons ", " De Bacchus à l'envi ",
" Bacchus, tu charmes mon âme ", " Non, non, sans le vin ", " À jamais chantons
la gloire ", " Triomphez, Puissant Dieu " (Duo), " L'éclat de votre présence ", and
" L'Amour livre aux mortels ". The piece is called " Nouvelle " because in 1708
" La Chasse au Cerf ", a divertissement by Jean-Baptiste Morin, was performed ;

[1] Organiste de S. Paul de Londres né en Allemagne, & qui compose avec un
grand succès tous les Opéra d'Angleterre depuis plus de vingt ans, en langue
Italienne.

it was published in 1709 by Christophe Ballard. The "crown" mentioned in the foreword apparently refers to the honours Handel was offered at Oxford in 1733.

—

FROM LORD HERVEY'S MEMOIRS, 1734

. . . Another judicious subject of his [the Prince of Wales'] enmity was her [the Princess Royal's] supporting Handel, a German musician and composer (who had been her singing master, and was now undertaker of one of the operas), against several of the nobility who had a pique to Handel, and had set up another person to ruin him ; or, to speak more properly and exactly, the Prince, in the beginning of his enmity to his sister, set himself at the head of the other opera to irritate her, whose pride and passions were as strong as her brother's (though his understanding was so much weaker), and could brook contradiction, where she dared to resist it, as little as her father.

What I had related may seem a trifle, but though the cause was indeed such, the effects of it were no trifles. The King and Queen were as much in earnest upon this subject as their son and daughter, though they had the prudence to disguise it, or to endeavour to disguise it, a little more. They were both Handelists, and sat freezing constantly at his empty Haymarket Opera, whilst the Prince with all the chief of the nobility went as constantly to that of Lincoln's Inn Fields. The affair grew as serious as that of the Greens and the Blues under Justinian at Constantinople. An anti-Handelist was looked upon as an anti-courtier, and voting against the Court in Parliament was hardly a less remissible or more venial sin than speaking against Handel or going to Lincoln's Inn Fields Opera. The Princess Royal said she expected in a little while to see half the House of Lords playing in the orchestra in their robes and coronets ; and the King (though he declared he took no other part in this affair than subscribing £1,000 a year to Handel) often added at the same time he did not think setting oneself at the head of a faction of fiddlers a very honourable occupation for people of quality ; or the ruin of one poor fellow so generous or so good-natured a scheme as to do much honour to the undertakers, whether they succeeded or not ; but the better they succeeded in it, the more he thought they would have reason to be ashamed of it. The Princess Royal quarelled with the Lord Chamberlain for affecting his usual neutrality on this occasion, and spoke of Lord Delaware, who was one of the chief managers against Handel, with as much spleen as if he had been at the head of the Dutch faction who opposed the making her husband Stadtholder.

. . . She had Handel and his opera so much at heart that even in these distressful moments [of her departure] she spoke as much upon his chapter as any other, and begged Lord Hervey to assist him with the utmost attention.

(Chrysander, II. 364.)   Hervey, *Memoirs*, I. 313 f. and 411 ;   *Materials towards Memoirs*, pp. 273 f. and 371.   The *Memoirs*, begun in 1733, are based on Hervey's Journals of 1732–7, since lost.   He was a very close friend of Queen Caroline and Princess Anne, now married to William Prince of Orange.   Charles Fitzroy, second Duke of Grafton, had been Lord Chamberlain since 1724, and in this capacity was Governor of the Academy of Music.   For John West, first Earl Delaware (De La Warr) see January 1733.   On 21st October, after a summer visit to England, the Princess went back to the Hague, " to lie-in " ; the last paragraph quoted refers to her farewell from Hervey.

———

In vol. IV of Ballard's Paris collection, *Les Parodies nouvelles et les Vaudevilles inconnus*, 1734, the introductory march from *Scipione* is reprinted with the words :   " À toi Catin, Il faut que je t'en verse ".   Cf. 1730 and 1737.

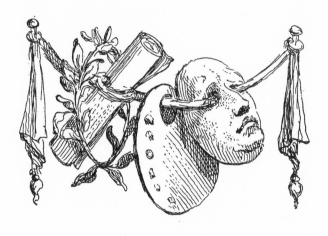

1735

FROM THE "LONDON DAILY POST", 8th January 1735

At the Theatre-Royal in Covent-Garden, this present Wednesday . . . will be perform'd a New OPERA, Calld ARIODANTE. . . .

The *London Daily Post* of 1735 is only partly preserved in the British Museum, but cuttings are to be found there in the *Theatrical Register*. The text of the opera, originally called " Ginevra Principessa di Scozia " and first composed by Jacopo Antonio Perti in 1708, is by Antonio Salvi. (Loewenberg, p. 94.) Repeat performances on 15th, 18th, 22nd, 29th January ; 5th, 12th, 20th, 24th February; and 3rd March ; revived in May 1736.

———

CAST OF " ARIODANTE ", 8th January 1735
Il Rè di Scozia—Mr. Waltz, bass
Ginevra—Signora Strada, soprano
Ariodante—Signor Carestini, alto
Lurcanio—Mr. Beard, tenor
Dalinda—Miss Young, soprano
Polinesso—Signora Maria Caterina Negri, contralto
Odoardo—Mr. Stopelaer, tenor

As in *Terpsicore* (9th November 1734) and *Alcina* (16th April 1735), there was dance music in *Ariodante*, especially designed for Mlle Sallé, who appeared at the end of the opera (Burney, IV. 388). The three works are sometimes called danceoperas. Miss Young, who appeared for the first time in a Handel cast, is apparently Cecilia, the later Mrs. Arne (cf. 17th May 1732). The second tenor, whose name was given as Mr. Stelaer, was Mr. Stop(p)elaer (A. Burgh, *Anecdotes of Music*, 1814, III. 101) ; in 1739 he sang the Amalekite in Handel's *Saul*.

———

Siroe is revived at Brunswick, 29th January (9th February) 1735. (Loewenberg, p. 83.) Cf. August 1730.

———

The Nobility Opera at the Haymarket Theatre produces *Polifemo*, text by Rolli, music by Porpora, 1st February 1735.

There exists a satirical engraving, entitled " Harmony " and published shortly after this performance (*The British Museum Catalogue of Satires in Prints and Drawings*. Division I. *Political Satires*, Vol. III, Part I, 1734-50, no. 2258). It shows Porpora playing on an organ, on the top of which is an owl hooting, and on the floor are three scrolls : " Poly—o an Opera ", " A—x—s an Opera", and " D——d an Oratorio ". They refer to Porpora's *Polifemo ; Artaserse* (29th October 1734, and still running) ; and *Davide e Bersabea*, sung seven times in March and April 1734, and revived on

28th February with two more performances in April 1735 (cf. 28th March 1734). Below the print is to be read :

> With Notes Harmonick, Solemn grave and Easy
> See Sirs, what Pains our Segnior takes to please ye :
> Since Airs thus Sweet proceed from Windy Bum,
> H——l avant, the Oratorio's Dumb.

The last line refers, of course, to Handel.

———

Walsh advertises *Pastor Fido* for a German flute and bass, as well as *Pastor Fido* and *Ariadne* for a common flute, *Craftsman*, 15th February 1735.

———

FROM THE " LONDON DAILY POST ", 5th March 1735

At the Theatre-Royal in Covent-Garden, this present Wednesday . . . will be perform'd an Oratorio, call'd AESTHER. With several New Additional Songs ; likewise two new Concerto's on the Organ.

The issue is wrongly dated 4th March. Earlier advertisements have : " With several New Additions both Vocal and Instrumental ". The announcement of the concertos, played by Handel on the organ in the intervals, was a novelty. It is not known when Handel's own organ was installed at Covent Garden ; he left it in his will to Rich, the manager of the house, where it was destroyed in the fire of 1808. Repeat performances on 7th, 12th, 14th, 19th and 21st March, all during Lent, on Wednesdays and Fridays. (The usual opera nights were Wednesday and Saturday.) The cast is not known, but Signora Strada certainly sang the part of Esther, as on 5th July 1733 at Oxford ; it seems probable that Carestini sang Ahasuerus, Waltz—Haman, Beard—Habdonah and Maria Caterina Negri—Mordecai.

———

FROM THE " BEE ", 15th March 1735

London, March 13

Signora Celeste Gismundi, a famous Singer, Wife to Mr. Hempson an English Gentleman, died on Tuesday [the 11th], after a lingering illness. She performed in Mr. Handel's Operas for several Winters with great Applause, but did not sing this Season on any Stage, on Account of her Indisposition.

(Chrysander, II. 325 : wrongly dated 19th March.) In fact Signora Celeste only sang for Handel during one season, that of 1732-3. When Durastanti returned in autumn 1733, Gismondi became superfluous. She sang in the Nobility Opera during 1734.

———

MRS. PENDARVES TO HER MOTHER, MRS. MARY GRANVILLE

15 March, 1734-5.

We [my sister Ann and I] were together at Mr. Handel's oratorio Esther. . . . My sister gave you an account of Mr. Handel's playing here for three hours together : I did wish for you, for no entertainment in music *could exceed it*, except his playing on the organ in Esther, where he performs a part in two concertos, that are the finest things I ever heard in my life.

(Delany, I. 530, 532.) Unfortunately, Ann's description of Handel playing the harpsichord in Mrs. Pendarves house (cf. 2nd-4th and 12th April 1734) is not known.

——

FROM THE " OLD WHIG : OR, THE CONSISTENT PROTESTANT ",
20th March 1735

A Letter to a Friend in the Country.

. . . The late Squabble at the Opera is pretty well adjusted. It had rose very high ; Parties were formed, and Protests were just ready to be enter'd, to which many fair Hands had threaten'd to subscribe ; when by accommodating Matters with *Senesino*, all the ruffled Passions were calmed, as it had been by the Melody of his Voice. *Farinello* surpasses every thing we have hitherto heard. Nor are we wanting in our Acknowledgments : For, besides the numerous Presents of considerable Sums made him by the Nobility, Foreign Ministers, and Others, (which amounted to some Thousand Pounds,) he had an Audience at his Benefit larger than was ever seen in an *English* Theatre ; and there was an Attention, that shew'd how much every one was charmed.—In the flourishing State of this Opera, 'tis no Wonder that the other Theatres decline. *Handel*, whose excellent Compositions have often pleased our Ears, and touched our Hearts, has this Winter sometimes performed to an almost empty Pitt. He has lately reviv'd his fine *Oratorio* of *Esther*, in which he has introduced two Concerto's on the Organ that are inimitable. But so strong is the Disgust taken against him, that even this has been far from bringing him crowded Audiences ; tho' there were no other publick Entertainments on those Evenings. His Loss is computed for these two Seasons at a great Sum. . . .

(Chrysander II. 381.) The two seasons were 1733–4 at the Haymarket and 1734–5 at Covent Garden.

——

Handel finishes the organ concerto in F, later printed as Opus 4, no. 4, 25th March 1735.

——

FROM THE " LONDON DAILY POST ", 26th March 1735

At the Theatre-Royal in Covent-Garden, this present Wednesday . . . will be perform'd an Oratorio, call'd DEBORAH. With a new Concerto on the Organ ; Also the First Concerto in the Oratorio of Esther. . . .

Cutting in the *Theatrical Register*. Repeat performances on 28th and 31st March. The new Concerto, apparently, was that finished the day before. For the repeat

Tha: Jennens Esq.
f Gopful unck to
Mr. Either Curzon.

XIV. CHARLES JENNENS

Oil painting by Thomas Hudson, *ca.* 1750.   (Mary, Countess Howe)

See page 394

XV. GIOACCHINO CONTI, CALLED "GIZZIELLO"

Mezzotint after Charles Lucy by Alexander Van Haecken, 1736.
(H. R. Beard Theatre Collection)

See page 404

performance on 31st March, the advertisement runs : " Also the two Concerto's in the Oratorio of Esther ". The cast of this revival of *Deborah* was probably identical with that of 2nd April 1734, except for Durastanti whose part may have been sung by Miss Young.

—

FROM THE " LONDON DAILY POST ", 1st April 1735

At the Theatre-Royal in Covent-Garden, this present Tuesday . . . will be perform'd an Oratorio, call'd ATHALIA. With a new Concerto on the Organ ; Also the first Concerto in the Oratorio of Esther, and the last in Deborah.

Cutting in the *Theatrical Register*. The " last " concerto in *Deborah* probably meant the one lately played in that oratorio. Repeat performances on 2nd, 3rd, 9th and 12th April. The cast, compared with that of 10th July 1733 in Oxford, was as follows :

> Athalia—Miss Young (Wright)
> Josabeth—Signora Strada (Strada)
> Joas—the Boy (Goodwill)
> Joad—Signor Carestini (Salvai)
> Mathan—Mr. Beard (Rochetti)
> Abner—Mr. Waltz (Waltz)

It is noteworthy that a company of French comedians at the New Haymarket Theatre intended to produce Racine's *Athalie* at the end of April ; this would have been the first performance of the tragedy in England.

—

FROM THE " LONDON DAILY POST ", 3rd April 1735

We hear that the Youth, (a new Voice) who was introduced in the Oratorio of Athalia, last Night, at the Theatre Royal in Covent Garden, met with universal Applause.

Cutting in the *Theatrical Register*. Chrysander, II. 374, wrongly quotes the *Daily Journal*. Probably written on 2nd April. It seems that " the Boy " was William Savage (see 16th April).

—

Handel finishes the opera *Alcina*, 8th April 1735.

—

MRS. PENDARVES TO HER MOTHER, MRS. MARY GRANVILLE

Lower Brook Street, April 12, 1735.
Yesterday morning my sister [Ann Granville] and I went with Mrs. Donellan to Mr. Handel's house to hear the first rehearsal of the new opera Alcina. I think it the best he ever made, but I *have thought so* of *so many*, that I will not say positively '*tis the finest*, but 'tis *so fine* I have not words to describe it. Strada has a whole scene of charming recitative —there are a thousand beauties. Whilst Mr. Handel was playing his

H.–13

part, I could not help thinking him a necromancer in the midst of his own enchantments.

(Delany, I. 533 f.) For Mrs. Donellan, see 12th April 1734. It is curious that Covent Garden should now be called " Handel's house " ; in the season of 1733-4, there was good reason to name the Haymarket Theatre thus, while Lincoln's Inn Fields Theatre was called either Senesino's or the Prince of Wales's, never Porpora's, house. The Strada scene referred to is probably the end of Act two ; " Ah ! Ruggiero crudel " with the aria " Ombre pallide ". Handel accompanied on the harpsichord.

———

From the " London Daily Post ", 16th April 1735

Their Majesties intend being at the Opera in Covent-Garden To-night ; and we hear the new Opera will exceed any Composition of Mr. Handel's hitherto performed.

(Burney, IV. 364.) No copy in the British Museum, or in the Bodleian Library.

———

From the Same

At the Theatre-Royal in Covent-Garden, this present Wednesday . . . will be perform'd a New Opera, call'd ALCINA. . . .

Cutting in the *Theatrical Register* from the issue of 19th April only. Text, according to Sonneck (1914) and Loewenberg (p. 94) by Antonio Marchi, and originally entitled *Alcina delusa da Ruggiero ;* Eisenschmidt (II. 15) denies this, without giving another source. (Cf. 5th July 1735.) Repeat performances on 19th, 23rd, 26th, 30th April ; 3rd, 7th, 10th, 14th, 17th, 21st, 28th May ; 4th, 12th, 18th, 25th, 28th June ; and 2nd July ; revived in November 1736 and June 1737.

———

Cast of " Alcina ", 16th April 1735

Alcina—Signora Strada, soprano
Ruggiero—Signor Carestini, alto
Morgana—Miss Young, soprano
Bradamante—Signora Maria Caterina Negri, contralto
Oronte—Mr. Beard, tenor
Melisso—Mr. Waltz, bass
Oberto—the Boy (Savage), (?) alto

Miss Young is called Mrs. in the libretto. If William Savage, who later became a famous alto, did not sing in *Athalia* on 1st April, this was his first appearance ; he even seems to have sung sections of Mr. Beard's part, although it was not usual to divide a part in an opera. Mlle Sallé danced again, her last part in London. Burney (1785, p. 24) tells of Carestini returning to Handel the aria " Verdi prati ", later so successful, and of Handel going to him and saying : " You toc ! don't I know better as your seluf, vaat is pest for you to sing ? If you vill not sing all de song vaat I give you, I vill not pay you ein stiver." Chrysander (II. 385) rightly objects that Handel would not have spoken in English to his Italian singers.

———

FROM THE "DAILY JOURNAL", 17th April 1735

At Covent Garden . . . the Play of Henry 4th, with Entertainments of Dancing. The Grecian Sailor, as it was performed in the Opera of Orestes ; and a Grand Ballet, called the Faithful Shepherd, as performed in the Opera of Pastor Fido.
(Schoelcher, p. 176 ; Wyndham, I. 46.) No copy known. Mlle Sallé, therefore, also danced in Shakespeare. For *Orestes*, see 18th December 1734 ; for *Pastor Fido*, 9th November 1734.

———

FROM PRÉVOST'S "LE POUR ET CONTRE", PARIS, [April ?] 1735 (Translated)

. . . And this is how the divine Sallé is treated today, to whom a year ago everyone talked of building altars, or at least monuments of eternal memory in Westminster Abbey. Let no one ask me for a translation of this satire : my tongue and my pen both refuse the task.

> The French us English oft deride
> And for our unpoliteness chide :
> Mam Sallé too (late come from France)
> Says we can neither dress nor dance.
> Yet she, as t'is agreed by most,
> Dresses and dances at our cost.
> She from experience draws her rules
> And Justly Calls the English fools.
> For such they are, since none but such
> For foreign Tilts would pay so much.

(Vol. VI, no. LXXVI, pp. 22 f.) As a companion piece to the English poem on Mlle Sallé, to whom Voltaire had dedicated some verses, a French poem is preserved, written by " an ingenious Gentleman of Paris " and printed in London papers after the close of the season (2nd July 1735) :

> Mistress Sallé toujours errante
> Et qui partout vit mécontente,
> Sourde encore du bruit des sifflets,
> Le cœur gros, la bourse légère,
> Revient, maudissant les Anglois,
> Comme en partant pour l'Angleterre,
> Elle maudissait les François.

The version printed by Dacier (1909, p. 171) is slightly different from the one preserved in Latreille's copies in the British Museum. For Sallé, see also Lynham, pp. 46-60 ; and Eisenschmidt, II. 90-95. About her costume, the London correspondent of the *Mercure de France*, possibly Charles Montesquieu, published the following description on 15th March 1734, quoted by H. Sutherland Edwards in Grove's *Dictionary* (first edition, I. 131) : " She ventured to appear without skirt, without a dress, in her natural hair, and with no ornament on her head. She wore nothing in addition to her bodice and under petticoat but a simple robe of muslin arranged in drapery after the model of a Greek statue."

———

FROM THE " GRUB-STREET JOURNAL ", 8th May 1735

On Mr. Handel's *performance on the Organ, and his* Opera *of* Alcina.
By a Philharmonick.

1.

Gently, ye winds, your pinions move
On the soft bosom of the air ;
Be all serene and calm above,
Let not ev'n Zephyrs whisper there.

2.

And oh ! Ye active springs of life,
Whose chearful course the blood conveys,
Compose a while your wonted strife ;
Attend—'tis matchless HANDEL plays.

3.

Hush'd by such strains, the soft delight
Recalls each absent wish, and thought ;
Our senses from their airy flight,
Are all to this sweet period brought :

4.

And here they fix, and here they rest,
As if 'twas now consistent grown,
To sacrifice the pleasing taste
Of ev'ry blessing to this one.

5.

And who would not with transport seek
All other objects to remove ;
And when an angel designs to speak,
By silence, admiration prove ?

6.

When lo ! the mighty man essay'd
The organ's heavenly breathing sound,
Things that inanimate [1] were made,
Strait mov'd, and as inform'd were found.

7.

Thus ORPHEUS, when the numbers flow'd,
Sweetly descanting from his lyre,
Mountains and hills confess'd the God,
Nature look'd up, and did admire.

[1] The disaffected.

8.

HANDEL, to wax the charm as strong,
    Temper'd ALCINA's [1] with his own :
And now asserted by their song,
    They rule the tunefull world alone.

9.

Or she improves his wonderous lay ;
    Or he by a superior spell
Does greater melody convey,
    That she may her bright self excel.

10.

Then cease, your fruitless flights forbear,
    Ye infants [2] in great HANDEL's art :
To imitate you must not dare,
    Much less such excellence impart.

11.

When HANDEL deigns to strike the sense,
    'Tis as when heaven, with hands divine,
Struck out the globe (a work immense !)
    Where harmony meets with design.

12.

When you attempt the mighty strain,[3]
    Consistency is quite destroy'd ;
Great order is dissolv'd again,
    Chaos returns, and all is void.

(Chrysander, II. 375 f. and 480 f.)   The three great composers might have been
Ariosti, Bononcini and Porpora.   For the pseudonym " Philharmonick ", cf. 10th
June 1727 (" Phil-Harmonicus ").   The poem was set to music by John Alcock,
organist from 1735 till 1736 at All Hallows Church, Bread Street, as successor
to John Stanley ; words and music were issued as a single sheet folio (copies
in the British Museum, and in Gerald Coke's Handel Collection).

—

FROM THE " LONDON DAILY POST ", 15th May 1735

Last Night their Majesties and the Princess Amelia were at the Opera
of Alcina, which meets with great Applause.

(Burney, IV. 384.)   No copy known.   The date is not given accurately by
Burney.

—

[1] An enchantress, *Strada*.   [2] Three great composers.   [3] The Opera.

MRS. PENDARVES TO SWIFT

May 16, 1735.

Our Operas have given much cause of dissension ; men and women have been deeply engaged ; and no debate in the House of Commons has been urged with more warmth ; the dispute of the merits of the composers and singers is carried to so great a height, that it is much feared, by all true lovers of music, that operas will be quite overturned. I own I think we make a very silly figure about it.

(Delany, I. 540.)

___

FROM THE " GENERAL EVENING POST ", 20th May 1735

Mr. Handel goes to spend the Summer in Germany, but comes back against Winter, and is to have Concerts of Musick next Season, but no Opera's.

(Chrysander, II. 388.) The notice was reprinted in the *Old Whig* on 22nd May. Handel did not go to Germany that summer. Hawkins (V. 353 and 356, but not 326) and Husk (p. 66) thought that Handel went to Aachen (Aix-la-Chapelle) for the waters ; he did not go until 1737. The losses of the two opera houses in two seasons were estimated as £9000 for Handel and £10,000 for the Nobility Opera (Chrysander, II. 382). Cf. 9th November 1734 (*Ipswich Gazette*) and 16th October 1735.

___

FROM PRÉVOST'S " LE POUR ET CONTRE ", PARIS [May ?] 1735
(Translated)

Signor Farinelli, who came to England with the highest expectations, has the satisfaction of seeing them fulfilled by generosity and favour as extraordinary as his own talents. The others were loved : this man is idolized, adored ; it is a consuming passion. Indeed, it is impossible to sing better [than he does]. Mr. Handel has not omitted to produce a new *Oratorio*, which is given on Wednesdays and Fridays, with chorus and orchestral accompaniments of great beauty. Everyone agrees that he is the Orpheus of his age and that this new work is a masterpiece. He plays the organ himself in it, with consummate skill. He is admired, but from a distance, for he is often alone ; a spell draws the crowd to Farinelli's. Imagine all Senesino's and Carastino's art combined, with a voice more beautiful than those two taken together. . . .

Vol. VI, no. LXXXX, pp. 103 f.

___

Handel withdraws £300, 30th June 1735.

___

FROM PRÉVOST'S " LE POUR ET CONTRE ", PARIS, [June ?] 1735
(Translated)

Mademoiselle Sallé, who had at first been as favourably received by the English as Farinelli (however, in due proportion to her talents), found herself afterwards bitterly attacked both in verse and in prose, without anyone knowing the reasons which might justify this change. . . . The opera *Alcine* was given, the story of which is taken from *Ariosto*. Mlle Sallé had composed a ballet, in which she cast herself for the role of Cupid and took upon herself to dance it in male attire. This, it is said, suits her very ill and was apparently the cause of her disgrace. Her admirers in France will be less chagrined than herself over an incident which may hasten her return to the Parisian theatre, especially since the poor success of her *benefit*, which did not bring her even half as much as last year's.

Prévost refers to Lodovico Ariosto's *L'Orlando furioso*. Mlle Sallé was hissed at one of the last performances of *Alcina*.

———

TITLE OF MATTHESON'S FUGUE COLLECTION, "DIE WOL-KLINGENDE FINGER-SPRACHE", HAMBURG, 1735 (Translated)

The Harmonious Language of the Fingers, in twelve fugues, designed on two to three subjects ; and dedicated to the nobly-born, deeply learned, and world-famous gentleman, Georg Friedrich Händel, Capellmeister to the King of Great Britain and to the Elector of Brunswick-Lüneburg, as a token of singular homage, by Mattheson.

This dedication appeared on the title-page of part one of Mattheson's fugues for the organ. The first part, containing twelve such fugues, was published by the author. The second part, without dedication, was published in 1737. A second issue of both parts was printed, from the original plates, under the title *Les Droit Parlans*, and issued by Johann Ulrich Haffner of Nuremberg in 1749, but without the dedication to Handel. Cf. Handel's letter to Mattheson, 29th July 1735.

———

Handel's season at Covent Garden ends on 2nd July 1735 with *Alcina*.

The Haymarket Opera closed on 7th June.

———

FROM THE "UNIVERSAL SPECTATOR", 5th July 1735

. . . If . . . an Opera, or a Poem, set to good Musick, gives us in some pleasing Allegory, a Lesson of Morality, I can't but think it preferable to either the Comick Vein or the Tragick Stile. . . . What put me on these Reflections was a young Gentleman, where I was in Company lately, being as he thought, very witty upon Opera's in general, and on that of *Alcina* in particular ; he cou'd find no Allegory in the whole Piece (perhaps he was only acquainted with the Sound of the Word) and nothing of a Moral ; I happen'd to differ from him in Opinion and had like to have drawn the Satyr of his Wit upon me. This Poem, which is said to be finely set to Musick by the inimitable Mr. Handell, is taken from *Orlando Furioso*, and is an Abstract of the 6th and 7th Book ; Rogero is the Hero in the Opera, who by a Hypo-griffin, is hurry'd away to the Island where Alcina keeps her Court. . . . The Opera goes no farther than the breaking of Alcina's Enchantment, and contains an agreeable Allegory ; Rogero is carry'd thro' the Air on a Hypo-griffin, by which is figur'd to us the Violence of youthful Passions. . . . Astolfo's . . . Advice to Rogero . . . proves that neither the Counsel of Friends, nor the Example of others suffering by the Corses we are ourselves pursuing, can stop the giddy head-strong Youth from the Chase of imaginary or fleeting Pleasures, which infallibly lead them to cruel Reflections and to too late Repentence. The Character of Alcina's Beauty, and Inconstancy proves the short Duration of all sublunary Enjoyments, which are lost as soon as attain'd. . . .

I think from what is said, that the Opera of Alcina affords us a beautiful and instructive Allegory ; but I fear the young Gentleman never gave himself the Trouble to crack the Nut that he might have the Pleasure of tasting the Kernel.

(Chrysander, II. 371 f.) The *Gentleman's Magazine* of July 1735 reprinted the article under the heading " Defence of Operas " ; the *London Magazine* of the same month printed an extract under the title " Of Tragedies, Comedies, and Opera's ". The original was printed as a leader. The editor of the paper was Henry Stonecastle, a pseudonym for Henry Baker, F.R.S., whom Prévost, in his magazine, called " the London Oracle ". Cf. 19th March 1743.

FROM THE " LONDON DAILY POST ", 10th July 1735

Yesterday Signor Caristina, a celebrated Singer in the late Opera's in Covent Garden Theatre, embarqued on Board a Ship for Venice.

Cutting in the *Theatrical Register*. On the same day, the *London Daily Post* seems to have published a report on Mlle Sallé's unfortunate farewell in *Alcina*, which may have occurred on 2nd July. Carestini sang again in London in 1740, in the pasticcio-opera *Meride e Selinunte* and in Hasse's *Olimpia in Ebuda*, both at the New Theatre in the Haymarket ; he never sang again for Handel.

At the Theatre in Lincoln's Inn Fields, *The Honest Yorkshire-Man*, a ballad-opera with words by Henry Carey, is produced on 11th July 1735 ; among the music by various composers is the duet, " Joys in gentle trains ", from *Athalia*, sung as " Love's a gentle gen'rous passion " (entitled " Chaste Love ").

The opera was transferred on 1st August, after one performance, to the New Theatre in the Haymarket and was revived, on 12th November 1735, at the Theatre in Goodman's Fields. The libretto with the airs, published in 1736, bears the notice : " Refused to be acted at Drury Lane playhouse ".

The original title of the opera was *The Wonder ! An Honest Yorkshire-Man.*

———

HANDEL TO MATTHESON, IN HAMBURG, 18th (29th) July 1735

A Londres. ce $\frac{29}{18}$ de Juillet 1735.

Monsieur,

Il y a quelque tems, que j'ay reçu une de Vos obligeantes Lettres ; mais à present je viens de recevoir votre derniere, avec votre ouvrage. Je vous en remercie, Monsieur, & je vous assure que j'ay toute l'estime pour votre merite ; je souhaiterois seulement, que mes circonstances m'etoient plus favourables, pour vous donner des marques de mon inclination à vous servir. L'ouvrage est digne de l'attention des Connoisseurs, & quant à moi, je vous rends justice. . . .

Au reste, pour ramasser quelque Epoque (de ma vie) . . ., il m'est impossible, puisqu'une continuelle application au service de cette Cour & Noblesse me detourne de tout autre affaire.

Je suis avec une consideration tres parfaite,
Monsieur,
Votre tres-humble et tres-obeissant Serviteur
G. F. Handel.

Monsieur Mattheson, secrétaire de
l'Ambassade britannique a Hambourg.

(Translation)

London, $\frac{29th}{18th}$ July 1735.

Sir,

It is some time since I received one of your courteous letters ; but I have just received your last, with the work that you enclosed.

I am much obliged to you for it, and I assure you that I have every esteem for your great talents. I should only wish that my circumstances were more favourable, so that I could give you some tokens of my desire to be of service to you. Your work is worthy of the attention of men of taste, and I for my part appreciate it fully. . . .

To put together events of any period of my life . . . is, moreover, impossible for me, since my continual application to the service of this Court and the Nobility keeps me from any other business.

I am with every consideration, Sir,
Your most humble and obedient servant,
G. F. Handel.

(Mattheson, *Grundlage einer Ehren-Pforte*, p. 97 f.) Original formerly in the Pölchau collection, Hamburg. Mattheson's text, which seems not very reliable, was reprinted, with variants, by Burney (*Account*, part 1, p. 52), by Schoelcher (pp. 366 f.), by Chrysander (II. 383 f.) and others. La Mara (I. 169) printed, in German translation, one sentence and a few words more (see *Addenda*). The letter arrived at Hamburg on 25th July (5th August). The work which Mattheson

H.-13 *a*

sent to Handel was the fugue collection dedicated to him (see middle of 1735).
The autobiographical sketch, which Mattheson expected from Handel (see 24th
February 1719) for the *Ehren-Pforte*, was never written.

———

HANDEL TO CHARLES JENNENS, AT GOPSALL

London July 28/1735.

S^r

I received your very agreeable Letter with the inclosed Oratorio. I
am just going to Tunbridge, yet what I could read of it in haste, gave me
a great deal of Satisfaction. I shall have more leisure time there to read
it with all the Attention it deserves. There is no certainty of any Scheme
for next Season, but it is probable that some thing or other may be done,
of which I shall take the Liberty to give you notice, being extreamly
obliged to you for the generous Concern you show upon this account.
The Opera of Alcina is a writing out and shall be sent according to your
Direktion, it is allways a great Pleasure to me if I have an opportunity to
show the sincere Respect with which I have the Honour to be

Sir

Your

Most obedient humble

Servant

George Frideric Handel

To

Mr. Jennens Junior

at Gopsal near Atherstone

Coventry bag.

(William Horsley, in the preface of his vocal score of *Messiah*, 1842.) Original
in the possession of Lord Howe, who kindly allowed all his Handel letters to be
re-checked. Handel went to Tunbridge Wells, probably for four weeks, as in
1734. The association between Handel and Jennens was, apparently, of a recent
date. The first word-book Jennens wrote for Handel was *Saul*, but that referred
to in this letter may have been another one. An interesting point is that Jennens'
collection of manuscript copies of Handel's scores, now in the Royal Music
Library (British Museum), started as early as 1735 ; the copy ordered was
probably written by Smith the elder. Jennens lived on his father's estate, in
Gopsall, Leicestershire ; he rebuilt the house luxuriously on succeeding his father
in 1747. He was an amateur writer, interested in music, and he subscribed for
every score, published by Handel on subscription, from 1725 till 1740.

———

FROM THE KING'S WARRANT BOOK, 20th August 1735

£   s.   d.

Royal Academy of Music   1,000   0   0   Royal bounty to the undertakers of the Opera.

(Calendar of Treasury Papers, 1735–8, p. 126.) There is no corresponding entry
in the Treasury Minute Book. This subvention went to the Opera of the

Nobility at the Haymarket Theatre for their first season there, 1734–5. It is remarkable that the receiver was still called the Royal Academy of Music.

———

FROM WILLERS' HAMBURG NOTES, 25th August (5th September) 1735
(Translated)

Sept. 5. Julius Cesar. NB. no one came and there was no performance. (Merbach, p. 366.) Cf. 10th November 1725 and 6th August 1733.

———

FROM THE " CRAFTSMAN ", 30th August 1735
Musick this Day Published,

.   .   .   .   .

Printed for and sold by John Walsh. . . .
Where may be had, just Published, price 2s. 6d.
I. The favourite Songs in the last new Opera, called ALCINA in Score. by Mr. Handel.
II. Twelve Duets for two Voices, with a thorough Bass for the Harpsichord. Collected out of all the late Opera's. Compos'd by Mr. Handel. To which is added, the celebrated TRIO in the Opera of Alcina.

.   .   .   .   .

(Chrysander, II. 373.) " The favourite Songs " were the first of three selections from *Alcina* (see p. 417). The trio before the final chorus was a favourite piece in *Alcina.*

———

Walsh advertises the " favourite Songs in the Opera of Ariodante ", *Craftsman*, 13th September 1735.
(Chrysander, II. 373.)

———

Handel withdraws £100, 15th September 1735.

———

FROM THE " GENERAL EVENING POST ", 16th October 1735
We hear that Mr. Handell will perform Oratorios, and have Concerts of Musick, this Winter, at Covent-Garden Theatre.
(Chrysander, II. 388.) The notice was reprinted in the *Old Whig* of 23rd October. Cf. 20th May 1735. The idea of an oratorio season was still very strange to the public.

———

The opera season at the Haymarket opens on 28th October 1735 with *Polifemo.*

———

LORD HERVEY TO MRS. CHARLOTTE DIGBY
St. James's, November 25th, 1735.
. . . I am this moment returned with the King from yawning four hours at the longest and dullest Opera that ever the enobled ignorance

of our present musical Governors ever inflicted on the ignorance of an English audience ; who, generally speaking, are equally skilful in the language of the drama and the music it is set to, a degree of knowledge or ignorance (call it which you please) that on this occasion is no great misfortune to them, the drama being composed by an anonymous fool, and the music by one Veracini, a madman, who to show his consummate skill in this Opera has, among half a dozen very bad parts, given Cuzzoni and Farinelli the two worst. The least bad part is Senesino's, who like Echo reversed, has lost all his voice, and retains nothing of his former self but his flesh. . . . Handel sat in great eminence and great pride in the middle of the pit, and seemed in silent triumph to insult this poor dying Opera in its agonies, without finding out that he was as great a fool for refusing to compose, as Veracini had shown himself by composing, nobody feeling their own folly, though they never overlook other people's, and having the eyes of a mole for the one, with those of a lynx for the other. That fellow having more sense, more skill, more judgement, and more expression in music than anybody, and being a greater fool in common articulation and in every action than Mrs. P—t or Bishop H—s, is what has astonished me a thousand times. And what his understanding must be, you may easily imagine, to be undone by a profession of which he is certainly the ablest professor, though supported by the Court : and in a country where his profession is better paid than in any other country in the world. His fortune in music is not unlike my Lord Bolingbroke's in politics. The one has tried both theatres, as the other has tried both Courts. They have shone in both, and been ruined in both ; whilst everyone owns their genius and sees their faults, though nobody either pities their fortune or takes their part.

(*Lord Hervey and His Friends*, pp. 238 f.) The opera produced at the Haymarket on this night was *Adriano in Siria*, text by Pietro Metastasio, music by Francesco Maria Veracini, violinist and composer, recently returned to London. The dedication in the libretto is signed by Angelo Corri. The opera was performed seventeen times during this season. Metastasio, whose name (as usual) did not appear on the title-page of the libretto, became the most prolific librettist of the century, and shortly after Handel's death, on 24th November 1759, Oliver Goldsmith's *Bee*, speaking " Of the Opera in England ", stated : " I might venture to say, that ' written by Metastasio ', put up in the bills of the day, would alone be sufficient to fill a house ". Senesino retired from the stage shortly after November 1735, and a song by Henry Carey, " The Ladies' Lamentation for ye Loss of S——, Sung by Mr. Roberts ", as well as George Bickham's cartoon of 1737, celebrated the occasion. Unfortunately, Mrs. P—t and Bishop H—s have not been identified. (The only contemporary Bishop in Britain, whose name corresponds with Hervey's abbreviation, would have been John Harris, of Llandaff.) Henry St. John, Viscount Bolingbroke, intrigued with the Jacobites while serving Queen Anne as well as the Georges. The addressee of the letter was Charlotte, wife of the Hon. Edward Digby, sister to Hervey's friends, Stephen and Henry Fox, later Lord Ilchester and Lord Holland.

———

Handel withdraws £50, 8th December 1735.

Walsh advertises *Alcina* and *Ariodante* arranged for the common flute, " To which is added the Dance Tunes from the late Opera's ", *London Daily Post*, 10th December 1735.

It seems that the two operas were published in one book ; the only copy known was offered by Messrs. Ellis in 1905 (Catalogue VII/I). The addition was a reminder of Mlle Sallé's collaboration with Handel.

FROM CHAMBERLAYNE'S " MAGNAE BRITANNIAE NOTITIA ", 1735

The Establishment of their Royal Highnesses the Princess Amelia *and the Princess* Caroline

. . . . . .

Per Ann.

	l.	s.	d.
Musick-Master, Mr. *George-Frederic Handell*, —	200	0	0

Cf. 1728. After the marriage of Princess Anne, Handel remained Amelia's teacher till the end of his life ; at least he was paid for it. The volumes of Chamberlayne's year-book for 1736 till 1755, when it ceased, all contain the same entry. Princess Caroline died in 1757, before Handel. The establishment of the two Princesses started on 2nd July 1734, three and a half months after the wedding of the Princess Royal ; cf. 27th September 1736.

Acis and Galatea is performed at Aungier-Street Theatre, Dublin, 1735.

(Lawrence, 1922, p. 404.) Cf. 1st May 1734. Signora Maria Caterina Negri was in Dublin in 1735.

TWO NOTES WRITTEN BY HANDEL ON AN AUTOGRAPH MANUSCRIPT, CONTAINING FIGURED AND UNFIGURED BASSES, ABOUT 1735

12 Gallons Port.
12 Bottles French   Duke Street, Meels.

James . . .
      Banker in Lombard Street
      pour M. Wesselow en france.
(Mann, pp. 194 and 196.)   Original in Fitzwilliam Museum, Cambridge.

Michel Charles Le Cène, of Amsterdam, reprints, about 1735, the two volumes of Handel's *Suites de Pièces pour le Clavecin*, published in London in 1720 and 1733 respectively.

1736

Radamisto is revived at Hamburg, 9th (20th) January 1736.
Cf. 17th January 1722.

—

Partenope is revived at Hamburg, 14th (25th) January 1736.
Cf. 17th October 1733.

—

Handel finishes the Ode *Alexander's Feast*, 17th January 1736.

—

Handel finishes the Concerto Grosso in C called the Concerto in
Alexander's Feast, 25th January 1736.

—

FROM THE "OLD WHIG", 12th February 1736

Friday [the 6th]

We hear that the Feast of the Sons of the Clergy will be on Thursday
Se'nnight [the 19th], that a new *Te Deum*, composed by Dr. Green,
will be performed at St. Paul's on that Occasion, with Mr. Handel's
Jubilate and Coronation Anthem. The Rehearsal will be the Tuesday
preceding [the 17th].

(Chrysander, II. 426.) Copy in Bodleian Library, Oxford. The paper quotes
from another, dated 6th February. Cf. 26th February 1736. Maurice Greene was
organist of St. Paul's Cathedral. Handel may have been very angry to see his
Utrecht Te Deum replaced by a new one, and that by Greene.

—

FROM THE "LONDON DAILY POST", 19th February 1736

At the Theatre-Royal in Covent-Garden, this Day [Thursday] . . .
will be presented an *Ode*, (never perform'd before,) call'd *The* FEAST *of*
ALEXANDER. Written by the late Mr. Dryden. And Set to Musick by
Mr. *Handel*. . . . To begin exactly at Six o'Clock.

(Chrysander, II. 427.) The text was arranged by Newburgh Hamilton. The
word-book was printed by J. and R. Tonson. The original was set in 1697 by
Jeremiah Clarke, and John Hughes's arrangement was composed by Thomas
Clayton in 1711. Hamilton thought that Handel, with his modern style, might

finally accomplish the task of setting Dryden's Ode in a manner worthy of the poetry. Repeat performances on 25th February, 3rd, 12th and 17th March.

From Newburgh Hamilton's Preface to the Word-book of " Alexander's Feast ", adapted by Him from Dryden's Poem, [19th February] 1736

I confess my principal View was, not to lose this favourable Opportunity of its being set to Musick by that great Master, who has with Pleasure undertaken the Task, and who only is capable of doing it Justice ; whose Compositions have long shewn, that they can conquer even the most obstinate Partiality, and inspire Life into the most senseless Words.

If this Entertainment can, in the least degree, give Satisfaction to the real Judges of *Poetry* or *Musick*, I shall think myself happy in having promoted it ; being persuaded, that it is next to an Improbability, to offer the World any thing in those *Arts* more perfect, than the united Labours and utmost Efforts of a *Dryden* and a *Handel*.

(Chrysander, II. 418 f.) Hamilton stressed the fact that he confined himself " to a plain division . . . into Airs, Recitative, or Chorus's " ; but he added a new conclusion, generally cut. For the poem, addressed by the author to the composer, see 17th February 1739.

Cast of " Alexander's Feast ", 19th February 1736

Soprano—Signora Strada
Contralto—Mrs. Arne-Young
Tenor—Mr. Beard
Bass—Mr. Erard

According to a manuscript copy of the continuo parts, in the possession of the Royal College of Music (deposited in the British Museum), the violoncelli were played by Andrea Caporale and Pasqualino de Mareis, the harpsichord by a Mr. Walsh. Cf. 22nd November 1736.

From the Earl of Egmont's Diary, 19th February 1736

In the evening I went to Mr. Hendel's entertainment, who has set Dryden's famous Ode on the Cecilia Feast to very fine music.

(Egmont MSS., II. 235.) Although Dryden's other ode, set by Handel, is known as the Ode for St. Cecilia's Day, *Alexander's Feast* was the first poem written for that occasion by Dryden.

From the " London Daily Post ", 20th February 1736

Last Night his Royal Highness the Duke, and her Royal Highness the Princess Amelia were at the Theatre Royal in Covent Garden, to hear

Mr. Dryden's Ode, set to Musick by Mr. Handel. Never was upon the like Occasion so numerous and splendid an Audience at any Theatre in London, there being at least 1300 Persons present ; and it is judg'd that the Receipt of the House could not amount to less than 450*l.* It met with general Applause, tho attended with the Inconvenience of having the Performers placed at too great a distance from the Audience, which we hear will be rectified the next Time of Performance.

(Schoelcher, p. 181.) For Handel's expenses, see 19th June ; for the orchestra, see 25th February 1736.

———

FROM THE " LONDON DAILY POST ", 25th February 1736

Covent-Garden . . . this Day . . . *The Feast of Alexander.* . . . For the better Reception of the Ladies, the Pit will be floor'd over, and laid into the Boxes ; and the Orchestre plac'd in a Manner more commodious to the Audience.

(Chrysander, II. 427.) Cf. 20th February.

———

FROM THE " OLD WHIG ", 26th February 1736

Friday [the 20th]

Yesterday [the 19th] the Sons of the Clergy held their Annual Feast with great Solemnity : They met at St. Paul's, where an excellent Sermon was preach'd before them, and a new Te Deum compos'd by Dr. Green, as likewise Mr. Handel's celebrated Jubilate and Coronation-Anthem, were perform'd by a vast Number of the best Hands and Voices ; after which they proceeded to an elegant Entertainment at Merchant-Taylors Hall. The Money collected in the Choir amounted to 84*l.* 3s. 6d. and that in the Hall to 505*l.* 3s. 6d. besides which several Sums were expected from Annual Benefactors, though not present at the Feast.

Copy in Bodleian Library, Oxford. The paper quotes another, of 20th February. Cf. 12th February.

———

FROM THE " DAILY POST ", 15th March 1736

The same [Saturday] Morning [the 13th] died, at his House in Catharine-street in the Strand, Mr. John Walsh, late Musick Printer and Instrument-Maker to his Majesty, which Place he had resign'd some Time since to his Son, Mr. John Walsh, who succeeds him in his Business.

(Chrysander, II. 428.) Similar obituaries appeared in the *Daily Journal* and in the *London Daily Post* of the same day. (Smith, *Walsh*, p. viii.) The *Gentleman's*

Magazine of March 1736, as well as the *Chronological Diary* for 1736 (supplement to the *Historical Register*), record that he was " worth 30,000*l*.".

—

FROM THE " DUBLIN GAZETTE ", 20th March 1736

We hear that for the Benefit of Mercer's Charitable Hospital in Stephen-street, towards the Maintenance and Support of the distressed Sick Poor received therein, there will be a solemn grand Performance of Church Musick at St. Michan's Church, on the 31st of this Inst., at Eleven o'clock, with the Church Service, and a Charity Sermon. Beside the best publick Performers in this Kingdom, there will assist about forty Gentlemen, skilled in Musick on various Instruments. The Musick appointed is the celebrated *Te Deum* and *Jubilate* of the famous Mr. Handel, with his *Coronation Anthem*, made on the King's Accession to the Crown, never heard before. Tickets will be distributed at the said Hospital, at Half a Guinea each.

(Townsend, p. 35.) Mercer's Hospital was opened in 1734. This was the first of the annual music performances for the hospital, and the first sacred music by Handel performed in Dublin. The Coronation Anthem, performed after the *Utrecht Te Deum and Jubilate*, has not been identified. " The publick performers " were the choristers, or " vicars choral ", from the two Anglican cathedrals, Christ Church and St. Patrick's. The place of performance was altered ; see 27th March.

—

John Osborn advertises his word-book of *Acis and Galatea, an English Pastoral Opera*, to be performed on the 24th, *London Daily Post*, 23rd March 1736.

(Smith, 1948, p. 222 f.) No copy of this edition is known ; it may have been a reprint of John Watts's word-book of 1732. On 24th March, Osborn and Thomas Wood advertised their word-books in the same paper, Osborn for 6d. and Wood for 1s. Wood's is described as a *Serenata*, " with several Additions and Alterations " ; it was the official version, printed in Italian and English. Of Wood's libretto, too, no copy seems to survive.

—

FROM THE " LONDON DAILY POST ", 24th March 1736

At the Theatre-Royal in Covent-Garden, this Day . . . will be reviv'd a Serenata, call'd ACIS *and* GALATEA. There will be no Action on the Stage, but the Scene will represent a Rural Prospect of Rocks, Grotto's, &c. amongst which will be dispos'd a Chorus of Nymphs and Shepherds. The Habits and other Decorations suited to the Subject. . . .

(Smith, 1948, p. 222.) No fountains are mentioned among the decorations, as they were on 5th June 1732 for the performance on the 10th at the Haymarket Theatre. Cf. 7th May 1734. Repeat performance on 31st March 1736 ; another revival on 13th December 1739. Mr. Winton Dean found a London libretto of

Acis, dated 1736 but not belonging to this March performance ; it is the Cannons version, in English, but in two acts only.

—

FROM THE EARL OF EGMONT'S DIARY, 24th March 1736

In the evening went to hear Handel's mask of *Acis and Galatea*.

(Egmont MSS., II. 248.) It is noteworthy that Egmont called the work a mask, and that he spelled Handel's name correctly for the first time. When Egmont went to the second performance, he called the work simply " Handel's music, *Acis and Galatea* " (II. 253).

—

Ch. N. Le Clerc, of Paris, receives a Royal Privilege for printing " deux livres de pièces de clavecin et un livre solo de Hendel ", 26th March (6th April) 1736.

(Brenet, p. 436.) Le Clerc reprinted the two volumes of the *Suites*, published in London in 1720 and 1733, and the Trio Sonatas, Opus 2, published in 1733 ; later he reprinted twelve Grand Concertos, Opus 6, published in 1740.

—

FROM THE " LONDON DAILY POST ", 27th March 1736

For the Benefit of Mr. Walker.
By the Company of Comedians.

At the Theatre-Royal in Covent-Garden, this Day . . . will be presented a Tragedy (not acted this Season), call'd ABRAMULE, or, Love and Empire. . . . To which . . . will be reviv'd a Farce . . . call'd A CITY RAMBLE ; or, The Humours of the Compter. . . . The Whole concluding with Mr. Handell's Water-Musick.

(Wyndham, I. 57.) The tragedy, by Dr. Joseph Trapp, had been played since 1704, and the farce, by Charles Knipe, since 1715 on various London stages. For the *Water-Music* cf. 11th May 1736 (under 8th May).

—

FROM THE " DUBLIN GAZETTE ", 27th March 1736

Whereas the Parish of St. Michan's have refused the use of their Church for the Performance of Divine Service in the *Cathedral* way (and not of an *Oratorio*, as falsely advertised), for the Benefit of Mercer's Charitable Hospital ; This is to inform the Publick, that the same charitable intention will be pursued at St. Andrew's Church, and a Sermon preach'd suitable to the Occasion.

(Townsend, p. 35.) Cf. 20th and 30th March. The word oratorio had not been used in the printed advertisement, and a misunderstanding arising from this was, apparently, the reason for St. Michan's refusal. The term " in the Cathedral way " was repeatedly used in Dublin during the following years, to ensure that the church authorities would not expect a concert of sacred music, but church music. Originally it may have referred to St. Paul's Cathedral where the same works of Handel's were performed for charity.

—

FROM THE " DUBLIN GAZETTE ", 30th March 1736

The Performance of Handel's *Te Deum* and *Jubilate*, &c., for the Benefit of Mercer's Hospital, appointed for the 31st Instant, is put off for a few days.

(Townsend, p. 36.) Cf. 27th March and 6th April.

—

FROM THE " DUBLIN GAZETTE ", 6th April 1736

. . . Church Musick at St. Andrew's Church on Thursday next the 8th of this Instant. . . .

(Townsend, p. 36.) Cf. 30th March and 10th April.

—

Esther is revived at Covent Garden, 7th April 1736.

(Burney, IV. 392.) Repeat performance on 14th April. The cast is not known for certain, but Strada sang the part of Esther.

—

FROM " PUE'S OCCURRENCES ", DUBLIN, 10th April 1736

On Thursday last [the 8th] . . . was perform'd a Grand *Te Deum*, *Jubilate*, and an Anthem, composed by the famous Mr. Handel. Mr. Dubourg play'd the first Violin, Signor Pasqualini the first Bass.

The principal Voices were Mr. Church, Mr. Lamb, Mr. Baileys, and Mr. Mason.

The performers were upwards of 70 in number, among whom were several noblemen and gentlemen of distinction, besides the best publick Hands in this kingdom ; 'twas the grandest performance ever heard here ; the whole was conducted with the utmost Regularity and Decency.

There were present, their Graces the Duke and Duchess, and Lady Caroline, attended by a vast number of the Nobility and Gentry of the first rank.

(Townsend, p. 36 f.) Matthew Dubourg, Handel's friend, had been Master of the State Music in Ireland since 1728. For Pasqualino, see 19th February 1736. (Was he identical with Nicolò Pasquali, the composer ?) John Church, William Lamb(e), James Baileys, and John Mason were the vicars choral of the two Dublin cathedrals. Lionel Cranfield Sackville, first Duke of Dorset, was Lord Lieutenant of Ireland. The charity sermon was given by Dean Richard Madden.

—

FROM THE " LONDON DAILY POST ", 13th April 1736

We hear, that Signior Conti, who is esteemed the best Singer in Italy, being sent for by Mr. Handell, is expected here in a few days.

(Schoelcher, p. 182.) This appeared while Farinelli was still singing at the Opera of the Nobility in the Haymarket. Gioacchino Conti, called Gizziello, was a soprano ; he appeared for the first time on 5th May, and stayed for a year with Handel.

———

FROM THE " OLD WHIG ", 15th April 1736

Friday [the 9th].

We hear that Mr. Handel has engag'd several of the finest Singers in Italy, and that they are expected here next Week, in order to perform eight Operas, for the Entertainment of her Royal Highness the future Princess of Wales.

(Chrysander, II. 389.) Reprinted from another paper, dated 9th April. Cf. 13th April. If the Prince of Wales did in fact arrange an opera season of Handel's for his bride, Augusta Princess of Saxe-Gotha, then he was no longer the protector of the Opera of the Nobility.

———

William Boyce's setting of John Lockman's poem, " David's Lamentation over Saul and Jonathan ", is produced by the Apollo Society at the Devil Tavern, Temple Bar, 16th April 1736.

This music club was founded about 1731 by Maurice Greene and Michael Festing. Handel is said to have remarked at that time : " De toctor Creen is gone to the tefel ! " (Charles Knight, London, 1841-4, Vol. VI, pp. 184-6.) The large room at the " Devil Tavern " was called the " Apollo ". Lockman's text was printed by R. Dodsley in 1736, and reprinted in 1740 in " A Miscellany of Lyric Poems . . . performed in The Academy of Musick, held in the Apollo " ; it was set to music again by John Christopher Smith, Handel's friend, and produced at Hickford's Room on 22nd February 1740. The statement in Grove's Dictionary, that Boyce's oratorio was revived at Covent Garden in 1740, seems to be wrong.

———

Handel finishes the opera Atalanta, 22nd April 1736.

———

MRS. PENDARVES TO SWIFT

London, April 22, 1736.

When I went out of town last autumn, the reigning madness was Farinelli ; I find it now turned on Pasquin, a dramatic satire on the times. It has had almost as long a run as the Beggar's Opera ; but, in my opinion, not with equal merit, though it has humour.

(Delany, I. 554.) Pasquin, Henry Fielding's " dramatic satire on the times ", was produced at the New Theatre in the Haymarket on 5th March 1736, and performed

64 times before the end of the season on 2nd July. Mrs. Pendarves spent the winter in Bath.

___

FROM THE EARL OF EGMONT'S DIARY, 27th April 1736

She [the Princess of Saxe Gotha] landed on Sunday [the 25th] at Greenwich. . . . On Monday he [the Prince of Wales] went again to her, and they passed the evening on the water with music.

I was present at the wedding [to-day], which ended about nine at night. The Bishop of London, as Dean of the Chapel, performed it, assisted by the Bishop of Hereford. There was a prodigious crowd. . . . The chapel was finely adorned with tapestry, velvet, and gold lace. . . . Over the altar was placed the organ, and a gallery made for the musicians. An anthem composed by Hendel for the occasion was wretchedly sung by Abbot, Gates, Lee, Bird, and a boy.

(Egmont MSS., II. 264.) Since the Royal couple took a lively interest in Handel during the days following the bride's arrival, it seems possible that the music played on the river was his *Water Music* of 1717, or, more probably, another set of it : there are at least two sets in the *Water Music*. The wedding in the Chapel Royal at St. James's Palace was held between 8 and 9 P.M. This was Handel's second *Wedding Anthem* (" Sing unto God "), the first having been written for Princess Anne (cf. 14th March 1734). Abbot sang on both occasions. He and Mr. Leigh, here spelt Lee, were altos. " Bird " was probably John Beard, the tenor, who had been chorister at the Chapel Royal in his boyhood ; the " boy " this time may have been Master Savage (see 16th April 1735) ; the two last, perhaps, introduced by Handel.

___

FROM THE " DAILY JOURNAL ", 28th April 1736

. . . When the Dean had finished the Divine Service, the married Pair rose and retired back to their Stools upon the Hautpas ; where they remained while an Anthem composed by Mr. Handel was sung by his Majesty's Band of Musick, which was placed in a Gallery over the Communion-Table.

(Schoelcher, pp. 184, 384.)

___

FROM THE " LONDON DAILY POST ", 29th April 1736

We hear Mr. Handel has compos'd a new Opera, on the Occasion of his Royal Highness's Marriage to the Prince of Saxe Gotha, and as the Wedding was solemnized sooner than was expected, great Numbers of Artificers, as Carpenters, Painters, Engineers, &c. are employed to forward the same, in order to bring it on the Stage with the utmost Expedition, and that several Voices being sent for from Italy, for that purpose, are lately arrived, who as we are informed, will make their first Appearance, in the Opera of *Ariodante*.

(Burney, IV. 394.) Instead of Prince, it should, of course, have read Princess. Since the new opera, *Atalanta*, was not ready, *Ariodante* was revived. As a result of the delay, the Haymarket Opera celebrated first, on 4th May, with *The Feast of Hymen* (" Festa d' Imeneo "), text by Rolli, music by Porpora. This was repeated three times up till 15th May. T. A. Arne wrote a Serenata, to words by Thomas Phillips, which was performed at Drury Lane.

———

The short opera season at Covent Garden opens on 5th May 1736 with a revival of *Ariodante*.

(Burney, IV. 394.) Repeat performance on 7th May. The cast of 8th January 1735 was altered in one part only : Conti, instead of Carestini, sang Ariodante. In Mlle Sallé's absence, however, the dances were omitted.

———

FROM THE " LONDON DAILY POST ", 6th May 1736

Last Night the Opera of *Ariodante* was performed at the Theatre in Covent-Garden, in which Signior Gieacchino Conti Ghizziello made his first Appearance, and met with an uncommon Reception ; and in Justice both as to Voice and Judgment, he may truly be esteem'd one of the best Performers in this Kingdom.

(Burney, IV. 394.) Cutting in Sir August Harris's collection, British Museum. Burney, in Rees's *Cyclopaedia*, states that Gizziello was Handel's first real male soprano ; Nicolini, Senesino, Carestini, and later Annibali were, in fact, altos.

———

FROM THE " LONDON DAILY POST ", (8th ?) May 1736

For the Benefit of Mr. WOOD.

At the Theatre-Royal in Covent-Garden, Tuesday next, May 11, will be presented a Comedy, call'd The *Inconstant* ; or, the *Way* to win *Him*. . . . With the Overture to the Opera of Ariadne. . . . End of Act I. A Chancon a Boire, to Musick of Mr. Handel's, sung by Mr. Leveridge and Mr. Laguerre. . . . After the Play. Mr. Handel's Water-Musick, accompanied with French-Horns, Kettle-Drums, &c. And a Grand Ballet, call'd The Faithful Shepherd, by Mr. Glover and others.

Cutting in Sir Augustus Harris's collection. The comedy, by George Farquhar, was produced at Drury Lane in 1702, and revived at Covent Garden on 6th April 1736 ; this was the second performance there. The second of the four Handel pieces was, apparently, a drinking song, but the music has not been identified. For the *Water Music*, see 27th March and 26th April 1736 ; for Mr. Glover, see 21st March and 11th April 1717. Leveridge, too, reminds one of Handel's early London days (cf. 22nd November 1712, 10th January 1713, and 26th March 1731).

———

FROM THE " LONDON DAILY POST ", 12th May 1736

At the Theatre-Royal in Covent-Garden, this Day . . . will be perform'd a New Opera, call'd ATALANTA. In Honour of the Royal

Nuptials of their Royal Highnesses the Prince and Princess of Wales. . . .
N.B. The Gallery Doors will be open'd at Four o'Clock, and the Pit and
Boxes at Five. . . . To begin at Seven o'Clock.

The author of the text is unknown ; it may have been Newburgh Hamilton.
The libretto, printed by Wood, is bilingual, and the title says : " On Occasion of
an Illustrious Marriage ". After repeat performances on 15th, 19th, 22nd, 26th,
29th May, 2nd and 9th June, it was revived in November of the same year. The
King went to Germany on 22nd May ; the Queen commanded the performance
on 2nd June, attending with the Duke of Cumberland (15 years of age) and the
Princesses ; she also went to the last performance of the season on 9th June.

———

CAST OF " ATALANTA ", 12th May 1736

Atalanta—Signora Strada, soprano
Meleagro—Signor Conti, soprano
Irene—Signora Maria Caterina Negri, contralto
Aminta—Mr. Beard, tenor
Nicandro—Mr. Waltz, bass
Mercurio—Mr. Reinhold, bass

For Reinhold, who may have appeared here in his first Handel part, see 2nd
April 1734.

———

FROM THE " LONDON DAILY POST ", 13th May 1736

Last Night was perform'd at the Theatre Royal in Covent Garden, for
the first Time, the Opera of *Atalanta*, composed by Mr. Handel on the
joyous Occasion of the Nuptials of their Royal Highnesses the Prince
and Princess of Wales. In which was a new Set of Scenes painted in
Honour of the Happy Union, which took up the full length of the
Stage : The Fore-part of the Scene represented an Avenue to the Temple
of *Hymen*, adorn'd with Figures of several Heathen Deities. Next was
a Triumphal Arch on the Top of which were the Arms of their Royal
Highnesses, over which was placed a Princely Coronet. Under the Arch
was the Figure of *Fame*, on a Cloud, sounding the Praise of this Happy
Pair. The Names *Fredericus* and *Augusta* appear'd above in transparent
Characters.

Thro' the Arch was seen a Pediment, supported by four Columns, on
which stood two Cupids embracing, and supporting the Feathers, in a
Princely Coronet, the Royal Ensign of the Prince of Wales. At the
farther end was a View of *Hymen*'s Temple, and the Wings were adorn'd
with the Loves and Graces bearing Hymenaeal Torches, and putting Fire
to Incense in Urns, to be offer'd up upon this joyful Union.

The Opera concluded with a Grand Chorus, during which several
beautiful Illuminations were display'd, which gave an uncommon
Delight and Satisfaction.

There were present their Majesties, the Duke, and the Four Princesses, accompanied with a very splendid Audience, and the whole was received with unusual Acclamations.

(Burney, IV. 395.) The same report, without the last paragraph, appeared in the *London Evening Post* of the same day, and was reprinted in the *Old Whig* of 20th May. The Prince and Princess of Wales were at Drury Lane on that night, to see Joseph Addison's tragedy of *Cato* (1713) and a farce, *Taste A-la-mode* ; but they probably visited Covent Garden on the second night, the 15th of May. According to Wyndham, II. 309 ff., the six wings of the decoration were still in existence in 1741. The painter may have been Joseph Goupy, who in 1736 became Painter and Surveyor of his Cabinet to the Prince of Wales. The master of the " Illuminations ", later called " Fireworks ", was Mr. Worman ; cf. 18th July 1741. The Royal children present were : William, Duke of Cumberland, and the Princesses Amelia, Caroline, Mary and Louisa.

———

FROM THE " LONDON DAILY POST ", 14th May 1736

To all Lovers of MUSICK,
This Day is publish'd,

Proposals for Printing by *Subscription,* the Opera of *Aralanta,* in Score, compos'd in Honour of the Happy Nuptials of their Royal Highnesses the Prince and Princess of Wales. By Mr. *Handel.*

    1. The whole will be Printed on the best Dutch Paper.

    2. The Price to Subscribers will be Half a Guinea, to be paid at the Time of Subscribing, which will be One Third Cheaper than any Opera yet printed in Score.

    3. The whole will be Corrected by the Author, and none will be sold after the Publication under 16s.

Those Lovers of *Musick* who are willing to encourage this Under-taking, are desir'd to send their Names immediately ; the Work being in such Forwardness, that it will be ready to be deliver'd to Subscribers by the Middle of June.

Subscriptions are taken in by John Walsh . . . and at most Musick Shops in Town.

(Chrysander, II. 390 f.) John Walsh junior, the successor to his father, started a new series of Handel scores to be printed on subscription. Following the example of Cluer, who published four scores in such form between 1725 and 1727, Walsh printed six between 1736 and 1740. *Atalanta* was the greatest success among these ten subscription scores : it had 143 subscribers for 181 copies, more than any other.

———

BENJAMIN VICTOR TO MATTHEW DUBOURG, AT DUBLIN

[London, *c.* 15th May 1736.]

. . . The two opera houses are, neither of them, in a successful way ; and it is the confirmed opinion that this winter will compleat your friend *Handel's* destruction, as far as the loss of his money can destroy him ; I make no question but you have had a better description of his new singer than I can give you ; I hear he supplies the loss of *Senesino* better than was expected, but it is principally in his action—his voice and manner being on the *new model*—in which *Farinelli* excels every one, and yet, the second winter, exhibited here to empty benches. We are not without hopes of *Senesino's* return to England, and of once more seeing him in his most advantageous light, *singing Handel's composition.*

On Tuesday last, we had a new opera of Handel's ; and at the appearance of that great prince of harmony in the orchestre, there was so universal a clap from the audience that many were surprized, and some offended at it. As to the opera, the critics say, it is too like his former compositions, and wants variety—I heard his singer that night, and think him near equal in merit to the late *Carestini*, with this advantage, that he has acquired the happy knack of throwing out a sound, now and then, very like what we hear from a distressed young calf.

. . . As to the Operas, they must tumble, for the King's presence could hardly hold them up, and even that prop is denied them, for his majesty will not admit his royal ears to be tickled this season. As to music, it flourishes in this place more than ever, in subscription concerts and private parties, which must prejudice all operas and public entertainments.

(Victor, I. 14 f. : dated " Nov. 1738 " ; Macfarren, p. 24 : without date ; Chrysander, II. 396 f. : dated November 1736.) To ascertain the correct date of this letter the following points have to be observed : Senesino left London before 1736, Farinelli in June 1737. Handel's substitute for Senesino was, first, Carestini (1733–5) and then Conti, who arrived in spring 1736. The " second winter " is apparently Handel's second season at Covent Garden, 1735–6. Chrysander, who presumed a misprint of one figure only, altered the date given in Victor's *Original Letters* (1776) from November 1738 to November 1736. There was, however, no " new opera of Handel's " produced in autumn 1736. The most probable choice for this new opera seems to be *Atalanta*, produced with Conti, the new singer, on 12th May 1736. Unfortunately, this was a Wednesday, the day of the week on which all the Handel novelties between Spring 1736 and autumn 1737 were produced. Since Victor speaks of " Tuesday last " we must assume that he attended the dress rehearsal on 11th May, and we may now date his letter, with some certainty, as of about 15th May 1736.

———

Walsh advertises the score of *Atalanta* as ready, Fog's *Weekly Journal,* 5th June 1736.

Copy in Bodleian Library, Oxford. This advertisement was repeated in the *London Daily Post* of 9th June and in the *London Evening Post* of 10th June ; the *Gentleman's Magazine* of June listed the score among the books of the month. Shortly after publishing the score, Walsh issued an arrangement of *Atalanta* for flute.

———

EXTRACTS FROM THE LIST OF SUBSCRIBERS FOR " ATALANTA ",
published on 5th June 1736

Apollo Society at Windsor Castle
The Countess of Burlington
The Reverend [Thomas] Broughton
The Marchioness of Carnarvon
Miss Edwards [singer]
William Freeman
Mr. [Bernard] Granville, 2 Books
Mr. [Bernard] Gates
James Harris
Mr. [Henry] Holcombe
Mr. [James] Heseltine, Organist of Durham
Mr. [John] Harris, Organ Builder and Harpsicord maker
Mrs. [Elizabeth] Hare, 2 Books

Charles Jennens, 2 Books
Sir Windham Knatchbull, Bart.
Mr. [John] Keeble
Mr. [Thomas] Lowe
The Duchess of Marlborough
Mr. Joseph Mahoon, Harpsicord maker to his Majesty
The Musical Society of Oxford
Dr. [John Christopher] Pepusch, 7 Books
Mr. William Savage
Mr. [Charles Frederick] Weideman
Mr. John Webber, Organist of Boston
Mr. [Christian Frederick] Zincke

Zincke was an enameller ; he was born in Dresden, but had lived in London
since 1706. A golden ring, with a supposed Handel portrait by Zincke, is now in
the Henry Watson Music Library, Manchester. A second state of the subscribers'
list has the name of (Isaac) Ximenes added.

———

The short opera season at Covent Garden ends on 9th June 1736
with *Atalanta*.

———

THOMAS GRAY TO HORACE WALPOLE, AT CAMBRIDGE

June 11 [1736] London.
It was hardly worth while to trouble you with a letter till I had seen
somewhat in town ; not that I have seen anything now but what you
have heard of before, that is, *Atalanta*. There are only four men and two
women in it. The first is a common scene of a wood, and does not
change at all till the end of the last act, when there appears the Temple
of Hymen with illuminations ; there is a row of blue fires burning in
order along the ascent to the temple ; a fountain of fire spouts up out of
the ground to the ceiling, and two more cross each other obliquely from
the sides of the stage ; on the top is a wheel that whirls always about, and
throws out a shower of gold-colour, silver, and blue fiery rain.   Conti I
like excessively in everything but his mouth which is thus, ⊜ ; but
this is hardly minded, when Strada stands by him. . . . I have . . . a
commission for your man (with your leave), that is, to call at Crow's
for me, and bid him send me *Atalanta* with all the speed he possibly can,
which I must owe him for till I come down again. . . .

(Gray, *Correspondence*, II. 44 f. ; *Walpole's Correspondence with Thomas Gray*, etc.,
New Haven, 1948, I. 102 f.)   Original in Waller Collection. Gray " was not

partial to the music of Handel ", said John Mitford (Gray's *Works*, 1816, vol. I, p. lvii). About 1740 he collected, in Italy, manuscript copies of various Italian operas ; these volumes, containing nothing by Handel, are now in the Walpole Collection of Mr. Wilmarth S. Lewis, the chief editor of Walpole's correspondence. In Handel's *Jephtha*, produced in 1752, Gray found the chorus " No more to Ammon's God and King " enchanting, and " he used to speak with wonder of that chorus" (Sir Uvedale Price, " An Essay on the Pictoresque, etc.", new edition, 1796-8, II. 191). Walpole was at King's College, Cambridge, but Gray, a member of Pembroke College, was absent from 6th June till 23rd October 1736. He saw the opera on the 9th, when the season closed. The sketch of Conti's " square cavernous mouth, in outline like a knuckle-bone " corresponds with Gray's description in a letter to Chute and Mann of July 1742 : " his mouth, when open, made an exact square". Gray apparently subscribed for *Atalanta* from Crow senior, the Cambridge bookseller and binder, who ordered seven copies of the score.

———

FROM THE " LONDON DAILY POST ", 18th June 1736

We hear that several Persons have been sent to Italy from the two Theatres, to engage some additional Voices, for the carrying on of Operas for the ensuing Season, and that Sig. Dominichino, one of the best Singers now in Italy, is engaged by Mr. Handel, and is expected over in a short time.

(Burney, IV. 398 : without date.) Signor Domenico Annibali, an alto, arrived in autumn ; cf. 5th October. For the new singers at the Haymarket see 18th November 1736.

———

FROM THE ACCOUNTS OF THE TREASURER OF LINCOLN'S INN FIELDS AND COVENT GARDEN THEATRES, 19th February till 19th June 1736

Mr. Handel's Music.

Dr.	Charge					Nights paid for	Cr.		
1735/6					1735/6				
ᴵʳsday Feby. 19	Alexander's Feast	52	5	8	Received⎫	For Rent & Actors	90	0	0
ᵢ 25	Alexander's Feast	52	5	8	Feb. 27 ⎭	Servants pr. list	14	11	4
. 3	Alexander's Feast	52	5	8	Mar. 3	Received in full	52	5	8
ᴵay 12	Alexander's Feast	19	5	8	,, 12	Received in full	19	5	8
d. 17	Alexander's Feast	19	5	8	,, 17	Received in full	19	5	8
d. 24	Acis & Galatea	19	5	8	,, 24	Received in full	19	5	8
d. 31	Acis & Galatea	19	5	8	,, 31	Received in full	19	5	8
d. Apl. 7	Esther	19	5	8	Apl. 7	Received in full	19	5	8
d. 14	Esther	19	5	8	,, 14	Received in full	19	5	8
d. May 5th	Ariodante	52	5	8	May 5	Received in full	52	5	8
ᴵ. 7	Ariodante	52	5	8	,, 7	Received in full	52	5	8
d. 12	Atalanta	52	5	8	,, 12	Received in full	52	5	8
15	Atalanta	52	5	8	,, 15	Received in full	52	5	8
d. 19	Atalanta	52	5	8	,, 19	Received in full	52	5	8
22	Atalanta	52	5	8	,, 22	Received in full	52	5	8
d. 26	Atalanta	52	5	8	,, 26	Received in full	52	5	8
29	Atalanta	52	5	8	,, 29	Received in full	52	5	8
d. June 2	Atalanta	52	5	8	June 2	Received in full	52	5	8
d. June 9	Atalanta	33	13	8	,, 19	Recd.	33	13	8
In all 19.									

(Husk, p. 68.) Original unknown. It is assumed that Rich, the owner of both houses, performed plays at Lincoln's Inn Fields when Handel occupied Covent Garden for oratorios or operas, except in Lent (12th March till 14th April 1736) when no plays were allowed on the London stage. The oratorio season opened on the Thursday before Lent, and there was one Friday in the short opera season after Lent ; but otherwise Wednesday and Saturday were Handel's nights. Chrysander thought that Tuesday and Saturday were the days when plays were not permitted during the season, but Handel had no Tuesday night within the terms of the bill. Chrysander, II. 319 f., calculated that Handel paid Rich £1533 : 11 : 4 for these 19 nights covering a period of four months : this was composed of £12 per day for the house, £7 : 5 : 8 per day for the servants and £33 per day for the actors, which Rich had to pay whether he employed them or not. These daily expenses of £52 : 5 : 8 were reduced to £19 : 5 : 8 during Lent when the actors were apparently not paid by Rich. Chrysander compares this sum of £52 : 5 : 8 with the salaries and incidental charges, excluding costumes and scenery, at Drury Lane which, according to the *Grub Street Journal* of 14th June 1733, amounted to £49. The smaller account for 9th June 1736 may be due to the fact that the Covent Garden season had ended when the extra performance of *Atalanta* was given at the Queen's command.

———

FROM THE KING'S WARRANT BOOK, 22nd June 1736

	£	s.	d.	
Royal Academy of Music	1,000	0	0	Royal bounty to the under-takers of the Opera.

(Calendar of Treasury Papers, 1735–8, p. 257.) This refers, of course, to the Haymarket Opera. Cf. 24th August 1736.

———

HANDEL TO THE EARL OF SHAFTESBURY, AT ST. GILES'S, WIMBORNE

London June 29ᵗʰ 1736

My Lord.

At my return to Town from the Country (where I made a longer stay than I intended) I found my self honourd with Your Lordships Letter. I am extremly obliged to Your Lordship for sending me that Part of My Lord Your Fathers Letter relating to Musick. His notions are very just. I am highly delighted with them, and can not enough admire 'em. Your Lordships kind remembrance of me makes me sensible to the utmost degree, and it is with the profoundest respect that I am

My Lord
Your Lordships
Most obedient and most humble
Servant
George Frideric Handel.

To
the Right Honourable
the Earl of Shaftesbury
A. Giles's.

(Handel, *Letters*, p. 37.) Victoria and Albert Museum, London. The address on a separate cover. The family seat of the Earls of Shaftesbury is St. Giles's House, Wimborne, Dorsetshire. For Anthony, the fourth Earl of Shaftesbury, see 12th April 1734, and his Handel memoirs of autumn 1760. The letter probably refers to the book *Soliloquy, or Advice to an Author*, 1710, by his famous father, the third Earl ; music is discussed in Part II, section II. (John M. Robertson's edition of Shaftesbury's works, 1900, I. 152-4.) We do not know where Handel was between 10th and 29th June ; he may have accepted Knatchbull's invitation to Ashford (see 27th August 1734). It is improbable that he went to Tunbridge Wells at this time of the year.

———

Poro is performed at Hamburg, 29th June (10th July) 1736.
    Cf. 14th February 1732.

———

FROM HENRY COVENTRY'S " PHILEMON TO HYDASPES ", FIRST
    " CONVERSATION WITH HORTENSIUS ", 1736

Hortensius, who had once been a slight performer in music . . . inquired much after the State of the *Opera* this Season, which, he said, must now, he suppos'd, be advanc'd to its highest *Glory* by the Arrival of the so much celebrated new *Singer*.

There was nothing (I told him) now remaining to make the entertainment complete, but that Mr *Handel's Compositions* should go along with the *Haymarket Voices* : For want of *which*, there had been but one *Opera* at that House during the Season, which had been thoroughly approved by the Town. The opera I meant of *Artaxerxes* which was originally composed in *Italy*. . . .

Copy in Bodleian Library, Oxford. The book was published under the pseudonym of Talbot ; it contained the two first conversations, on false religion. A second edition was issued in 1738. The third edition, with all the five conversations but without the passage quoted above, appeared posthumously in 1753, under the author's own name. He died in 1752. The passage quoted is followed by a eulogy of Senesino, in *Artaserse* and in general. The opera referred to must have been the one produced at the Haymarket Theatre on 29th October 1734, when Handel went to Covent Garden. The season was that of 1734-5, and the new singer was Farinelli.

———

Handel begins the opera *Giustino*, 14th August 1736.

———

HANDEL TO HIS BROTHER-IN-LAW, MICHAELSEN, AT HALLE

à Londres le $\frac{28}{17}$ d'Aoust 1736.

Monsieur et tres Honoré Frere
    Comme il ne me reste personne de plus proche que ma Chere Niece et que je l'ay toujours parfaitement aimée Vous ne pouviez pas

m'apprendre une plus agreable nouvelle que celle qu'Elle doit epouser une Personne d'un Caractere et d'un merite si distingué. Vôtre seule determination auroit suffi pour la mettre au comble de son bonheur ainsi je prens pour un Effet de Vôtre Politesse la demande que Vous faitez de mon approbation la bonne Education dant Elle Vous est redevable assurerà non seulement sa félicité, mais tournerà aussi a Vôtre Consolation, a la quelle Vous ne dautes pas que je ne prenne autant de part qu'il se puisse.

J'ay pris la Liberté d'envoyer à Monsieur Son Epoux pour un petit present de Nopces une Montre d'Or de Delharmes avec une Chaine d'Or et deux Cachets un d'Amatiste et L'autre d'Onyx. Agreez que j'envoye dans cette même occasion pour un petit Present de Nopces a mà chere Niece l'Epouse, une Bague de Diamant d'une Pierre seule qui pese sept grains et demi et quelque peu de chose de plus, de la premiere Eau et de toute Perfection. J'adresserai l'une et l'autre a Monsieur Sbüelen a Hambourg pour Vous les faire tenir. Les obligations envers Vous Monsieur et Madame Vôtre Epouse, que je Vous prie d'assurer de mes Respects, sont un point apart, dont je tacherai de m'aquitter à la premiere occasion. Permettez qu'apres cela je Vous assure qu'on ne scauroit etre avec plus de sincerité et de passion invariable que j'ay l'honneur de l'être Monsieur et tres Hoñoré Frere

> Vôtre
>> tres humble et tres obeissant
>>> George Frideric Handel.

A Monsieur,
Monsieur Michael Dietrich Michaelsen
Conseiller de Guerre de Sa Majesté Prussienne
　　　a Halle en Saxe.

(Translation)

London, $\frac{28\text{th}}{17\text{th}}$ August 1736.

Honoured Brother,

As I now have no nearer relative than my dear niece and have always loved her particularly, you could not apprise me of more welcome news than that she is to marry a person of such distinguished character and attainments. Your agreement alone would have sufficed to place her on the pinnacle of happiness, so I take the request that you make for my approval as a further proof of your condescension. The sound upbringing which she owes to you will assure not only her own happiness, but also afford you some consolation ; and you will not doubt but that I shall add my voice thereto to the best of my ability.

I have taken the liberty of sending the bridegroom as a small wedding-present a gold watch by Delharmes, with a gold chain, and two seal-rings, one of amethyst and the other of onyx. I trust you will approve my sending on the same occasion as a small wedding-present to the bride, my dear niece, a solitaire diamond ring ; the stone weighs a little over $7\frac{1}{2}$ grains, is of the first water and quite perfect. I shall despatch both to Mr. Sbüelen in Hamburg for delivery to you. My obligations towards you, Sir, and your wife (to whom I beg you to convey my respects) are another matter, and I shall endeavour to acquit myself of them at the earliest opportunity   Pray let me now assure you that no one could be with more sincerity and steadfast devotion than I have the honour to be,

Honoured Brother,

Your most humble and obedient [servant],

George Frideric Handel.

(Handel, *Letters*, p. 38 f.) Original formerly in the possession of Dr. Ernst Foss, Berlin. Johanna Friederika Michaelsen, Handel's favourite niece, then 25 years of age, married Dr. Johann Ernst Flörcke, professor of law at Halle University ; they had eight children, four of whom died young. For Johann Wilhelm Sbüelen, the merchant in Hamburg, see 30th July 1731.

—

Handel withdraws £150, 20th August 1736.

—

FROM THE TREASURY MINUTE BOOK, 24th August 1736

Order for the issue out of Civil List Revenue of sums as follow :—

.   .   .   .   .

	£	s.	d.
To the Academy of Musick	1,000	0	0

(Calendar of Treasury Papers, 1735–8, p. 183.)   Cf. 22nd June 1736.

—

Handel begins the opera *Arminio*, 15th September 1736.

—

FROM THE KING'S WARRANT BOOK, 27th September 1736

Royal Warrant by the Queen, as Guardian of the Kingdom, counter-signed by three Lords of the Treasury, establishing a yearly payment of 200*l.* to George Frederick Handel as music master, and 73*l.* 10s. to Paolo Antonio Rolli as Italian master to the Princesses Amelia and Caroline, same to date from 1734, Lady day, the date from which the salaries payable under the establishment of 1734, July 2, for the said Princesses commenced ; the above two sums having been omitted to be inserted in said establishment. Dated at the Court at Kensington.

(Calendar of Treasury Papers, 1735–8, p. 188.)   The King was on the Continent. Cf. 1735 (Chamberlayne). It seems curious that Handel and Rolli were still colleagues at St. James's. Rolli dedicated his translation of Milton's *Paradise Lost* to the Prince of Wales in 1736.

—

Handel withdraws £200, 28th September 1736.

—

FROM THE " DAILY POST ", 5th October 1736

Last Night the famous Signora Strada arriv'd from Holland, who is come on purpose to sing next Thursday [the 7th] in a Concert of Musick at the Swan Tavern in Exchange-Alley.

Sig. Dominico Annibaly, a famous Singer, is also arriv'd from the Court of Saxony for Mr. Handel's Opera.

(Burney, IV. 398 : without date ; Chrysander, II. 395 : *London Daily Post.*) During the summer, Strada had been in Holland with Princess Anne of Orange. For the " Swan Tavern ", see 24th December 1734. For Annibali, cf. 18th June 1736.

—

FROM THE " OLD WHIG ", 14th October 1736

From THURSDAY's [the 7th] *Papers.* On Tuesday last [the 5th] Signor Dominico Annibali, the celebrated Italian Singer lately arriv'd from Dresden, to perform in Mr. Handel's Opera in Covent-Garden, was sent for to Kensington, and had the Honour to sing several Songs before her Majesty and the Princesses, who express'd the highest Satisfaction at his Performance.

(Burney, IV. 398 : without date and title.)   Reprinted from another paper, dated 7th October.

—

Handel finishes the opera *Arminio*, 14th October 1736.

Cf. 15th September.

—

Handel finishes the opera *Giustino*, 20th October 1736.

Cf. 14th August.

—

FROM THE " LONDON DAILY POST ", 1st November 1736

Their Royal Highnesses the Prince and Princess of Wales intend to honour Mr. Handel with their Presence on Saturday next [the 6th] at the Opera of *Alcina*, which is the Reason for performing Operas earlier in the Season than intended.

(Burney, IV. 399.)   No copy available.

—

Alcina is revived, 6th November 1736.

Repeat performances on 10th and 13th November.   The part of Ruggiero, created by Carestini, was sung by Conti.   The ballet at the end of Act II, danced in 1734 by Mlle Sallé, was omitted. Thomas Wood printed a new edition of the libretto.

———

FROM THE "DAILY GAZETTEER", 6th November 1736

This Day their Royal Highnesses the Prince and Princess of Wales, will dine at their House in Pall Mall, and in the Evening will be present at the Opera call'd, *Alcina*, at the Theatre Royal in Covent Garden.

The notice also appeared in the *Daily Journal* of the same day.

———

FROM THE "LONDON DAILY POST", 8th November 1736

On Saturday last [the 6th] their Royal Highnesses the Prince and Princess of Wales were at the Theatre-Royal in Covent-Garden, to see the Opera of *Alcina*, which was perform'd to a numerous and splendid Audience : The Box in which their Royal Highnesses sat, was of white Satin, beautifully Ornamented with Festons of Flowers in their proper Colours, and in Front was a flaming Heart, between two Hymeneal Torches, whose different Flames terminated in one Point, and were surmounted with a Label, on which were wrote, in Letters of Gold, these Words, MUTUUS ARDOR.

(Burney, IV. 399 : *Daily Post.*)

———

Walsh advertises "The celebrated Songs in the Opera call'd *Alcina*", *London Daily Post*, 11th November 1736.

The three selections of Favourite Songs were now complete (see p. 395).

———

FROM THE "LONDON DAILY POST", 18th November 1736

Signora *Merighi*, Signora *Chimenti*, and *The Francesina* (Three Singers lately come from Italy, for the Royal Academy of Musick) had the Honour to sing before her Majesty, the Duke, and Princesses, at Kensington, on Monday Night last [the 15th], and met with a most gracious Reception, and her Majesty was pleased to approve their several Performances ; after which, *The Francesina*, performed several Dances to the entire Satisfaction of the Court.

(Burney, IV. 399.) Antonia Margherita Merighi, contralto profondo, who sang in Handel's company from 1729 to 1731, had returned to London. Margherita Chimenti, called La Droghierina, soprano, sang for Handel in 1738 ; Elisabeth Duparc, called La Francesina, soprano, also came to Handel in 1738, and sang for him till 1749. She was not a professional dancer.

———

Atalanta is revived on 20th November 1736, the birthday of the Prince of Wales.

(Burney, IV. 399.) Repeat performance on 27th November.

———

H.–14

Handel finishes the cantata " Cecilia volgi " on 22nd November 1736, St. Cecilia's Day.
Cf. 16th March 1737.

———

The Haymarket Opera opens its season with Hasse's *Siroe*, 23rd November 1736.
(Burney, IV. 400.)

———

From the " London Daily Post ", 27th November 1736

We hear that Signor Domenico Anibali is to make his first Appearance in the Opera of *Porus* on Wednesday next [the 1st of December] at the Theatre Royal in Covent-Garden.
The revival was postponed till 8th December.

———

Mrs. Pendarves to Her Sister, Ann Granville

Nov. 27, 1736.

Bunny came [on Tuesday last, *i.e.* the 23rd] from the Haymarket Opera, and supped with me comfortably. They have Farinelli, Merighi, with *no sound* in her voice, but thundering action—a beauty with *no other merit* ; and one Chimenti, a tolerable good woman with a pretty voice and Montagnana, who *roars as usual* ! With this band of singers and dull Italian operas, such as you almost fall asleep at, *they presume* to rival Handel—who has Strada, that sings better than ever she did ; Gizziello, who is much improved since last year ; and Annibali who has the best part of Senesino's voice and Caristini's, with a prodigious fine taste and good action ! We have had Alcina, and Atalanta, which is acted to-night for the last night with the fireworks, and I go to it with Mrs. Wingfield. Next Wednesday is Porus, and Annibali sings Senesino's part. Mr. Handel has two new operas ready—Erminius and Justino. He was here two or three mornings ago and *played to me both the overtures*, which are charming.
My brother has tied me down at last to learn of Kellaway ; he has paid him the entrance-money, which is two guineas, and has made me a present of Handel's Book of Lessons.
(Delany, I. 578 f.) Bunny is Bernard Granville, the sisters' brother. The Haymarket Opera began the new season with Hasse's *Siroe* on 23rd November (Burney, IV. 400). At Cuper's Gardens, in July 1741, the " fireworks " from *Atalanta* (cf. 13th May) became the " Fire Music " ; Schoelcher, p. 184, confused by this, mistook this music for Handel's *Firework Music* for 1749. His new operas were, of course, *Arminio* and *Giustino*. Joseph Kelway, a pupil of Geminiani, was organist of St. Martin-in-the Fields and harpsichord teacher to Queen Charlotte. Handel liked his organ playing and he published some harpsichord sonatas. Handel's Lessons, his *Suites des Pièces pour le Clavecin*, consisted of two books.

———

Poro, due to be revived on 1st December 1736, has to be postponed. (Chrysander, II. 399). See next entry.

—

FROM THE "LONDON DAILY POST", 2nd December 1736

Yesterday Signora Strada was taken violently ill of a Fever and Sore Throat, so that the Opera of *Porus* could not be performed as was intended ; which sudden Indisposition put it out of the Power of the Directors, to give earlier Notice to the Town of their Disappointment : On which Account they are obliged to defer the Performance of any Opera till further Notice.

During the month of December an influenza epidemic spread through London.

—

Poro is revived, 8th December 1736.

Repeat performances on 15th, 22nd December 1736, and 5th January 1737. The cast (compared with those of 2nd February and 23rd November 1731) was as follows :

Poro—Signor Annibali (Senesino)
Cleofide—Signora Strada (Strada)
Erissena—Signor Maria Caterina Negri (Merighi, Bertolli)
Gandarte—Signor Conti (Signora Bertolli, Campioli)
Alessandro—Mr. Beard (Fabri, Pinacci)
Timagene—Mr. Reinhold (Commano, Montagnana)

The libretto, printed by Thomas Wood, is called " The Fourth Edition " ; it is a reissue of one printed in 1734, in which year, it seems, it was intended to stage a revival at the Haymarket with Bertolli still cast as Erissena. The title-page of the 1736 edition also speaks of " additions " : " The three Songs mark'd thus (") were not composed by Mr. Handel ". The three songs were : " Tiranna la sorte ", set by Giovanni Alberto Ristori as " Tiranna tu ridi allora che uccidi " and sung by Annibale, who knew it from Dresden ; " Mira virtù che troppo ", and " Per l'Africane arene ". The first lines of these three songs are written down by Handel on a leaf in the Fitzwilliam Museum, Cambridge. The libretto, however, marks a fourth song, Poro's " Se sull' Idaspe ", as not set by Handel. (Chrysander, II. 246 f.)

—

FROM THE "DAILY GAZETTEER", 9th December 1736

Last Night her Majesty, the Duke and Princesses, were at the Theatre Royal in Covent Garden, to see the Opera call'd *Porus*.

(Burney, IV. 399 : *Daily Post*.) The *London Daily Post*, of the same day, printed the notice with an addition : " the three eldest Princesses ", *i.e.* Amelia, Caroline and Louisa. At about this time, Handel wrote " Lessons Composed for the Princess Louisa ", born in 1724 ; this note is to be found on a manuscript copy of suites nos. 1 and 2 of Handel's third collection of harpsichord lessons, in the Royal Music Library (British Museum) ; cf. Chrysander, III. 198 f.

———

FROM THE " LONDON DAILY POST ", 13th December 1736

Saturday last [the 11th] . . . their Royal Highnesses . . . sent Notice to the Theatre Royal in Covent Garden, that they could not be present at the Opera of *Porus*, which they had commanded.

There was no performance of the opera on that Saturday : in the afternoon news had arrived in London of a miscarriage to Princess Anne at the Hague.

———

Handel begins the opera *Berenice*, 18th December 1736.

———

FROM LORD HERVEY'S MEMOIRS, 1736

The Queen . . . always agreeing with him [Lord Hervey] when he said he wished this new favourite [of the King : Amelia Sophia von Walmoden] brought over [from Hanover] . . . frequently, when he talked to her on this subject . . . would begin to sing or repeat these words : " Se mai più saro gelosa mi punisca il sacro nume ", etc., which was the beginning of a song in one of Handel's operas, called *Porus*.

Hervey, *Materials*, p. 600. George II brought Frau von Walmoden to London in 1739, after the Queen's death, and made her Lady Yarmouth. The aria quoted is Poro's, but repeated by Cleofide in the duet. The meaning of the first line quoted is : " If I am no longer jealous, God will punish me."

———

FROM WALSH'S CASH BOOK, 1736

1736 Opera Atalanta	.	.	.	£26	5	0
1736 Opera Armenius	.	.	.	£26	5	0

These entries show that Walsh the younger maintained the same rate of payment to Handel for each opera score, even for those published by subscription, *i.e.* without risk. The first sum was probably paid in spring 1736, but *Arminio*, finished in October, was not produced until January 1737, and was published one month later.

———

The word-book of the anthems sung in the Chapels Royal is printed anew in 1736, by J. Bettenham for B. Barker and W. Parker ; it contains Handel's Chandos Anthem, " As pants the hart ".

Cf. 11th January 1724.

———

Handel subscribes for Barnabas Gunn's *Two Cantata's and Six Songs*, printed at Gloucester in 1736.

Gunn was organist at Gloucester Cathedral from 1730 till 1740.

—

An Anonymous Song, about 1736

The Taste

A Dialogue [between Colombino and Punchinello]

C. O, my pretty Punchinello,
　O, my little Dapper Fellow,
　Have you heard ye Farinelli
　Is coming over?

P. No, my Colombino,
　I hear that Carestino,
　Ye famous Carestino,
　Who has pleas'd both King and Queen, O,
　Sets out for Dover.

C. But I hope my Senesino
　Is no such Rover.

P. O no, your Senesino
　Has lick'd himself quite clean, O,
　Has Thousands got fifteen, O,
　And lives in clover.

C. After Porpora and Handel
　Where d'ye think ye Town will dandle
　Or which must hold the Candle?

P. I dont care a Farthing.
　But Harlequin O Lun O
　Has Cook'd a deal of Fun O
　Of Pantomime and Pun O
　And expects a mighty Run O
　　　　　　At Covent Garden.

C. Shall we go and see the Fun O
　　　　　　At Covent Garden?

P. In Play-houses full Six O
　One knows not where to fix O
　Till they let us in for Nix O—
　　　　　　That's Punches bargain.

Both. We'll see 'em round all Six O
If they'll let us in for Nix O—
That's always our bargain.

The song is known only from Vol. II of the *Musical Entertainer*, second issue, published after 1740, where it appeared as nos. 66 and 67. The words may be by Henry Carey, the tune is " Scacciata dal duo nido " from Handel's *Rodelinda*. The song is engraved on two pages, each ornamented by a vignette engraved by George Bickham : the first page is entitled " The Taste, a Dialogue ", which refers to the whole song ; the second page is headed " The Masque at the Old House ", which is the title of the second vignette, showing two animal masques on the stage of (?) the Haymarket Theatre. At the end of page two is, as usual, an arrangement of the tune for flute. (For the *Musical Entertainer*, see p. 463.) John Rich, the owner of Covent Garden Theatre, appearing under the name of Lun, played the part of Harlequin in the mute Pantomimes. *The British Museum Catalogue of Satires in Prints and Drawings* (Vol. II, nos. 1846 and 1847) dates the song as from about 1730. Covent Garden Theatre was opened in 1732, Farinelli arrived in London in 1734, Carestini left in 1735, and Senesino shortly afterwards. The song, therefore, cannot have been written before 1734, but might have been printed first about 1736, as a single sheet folio.

1737

MRS. PENDARVES TO HER SISTER, ANN GRANVILLE

Jan. 4, 1736–7.

To-morrow I go to the opera with Lady Chesterfield.

(Delany, I. 586.) It was the last performance of *Poro*. Lady Chesterfield was Handel's former pupil, Petronilla Melusina, née von der Schulenburg.

———

MRS. PENDARVES TO HER SISTER, ANN GRANVILLE

Jan. 8, 1736–7.

I was this morning regaled with Mr. Handel's new opera called Arminius, it was rehearsed at Covent Garden ; I think it as fine a one as any he has made, as I hope you will, 'tis to be acted next Wednesday [the 12th]. From the rehearsal I came home with my *neighbour Granville* !

(Delany, I. 587.) Bernard Granville, the sisters' brother, had recently moved into his house in Park Street, Grosvenor Square, close to Mary and Handel.

———

LADY LUCY WENTWORTH TO HER FATHER, THE EARL OF STRAFFORD

London, January 8, 1737.

Lady Anne [her sister] was last wensday [the 5th] at Mr. Hendle's house and she likes the new man much better then Conte' who she does not at all aprove of.

(*Wentworth Papers*, p. 528.) On 5th January *Poro* was given for the last time, with Annibali and Conti.

———

FROM THE " DAILY POST ", 12th January 1737

This Evening will be perform'd. . . . At the Theatre Royal in Covent-Garden, The Opera of *Arminius*.

(Burney, IV. 401.) Burney relates that the Prince and Princess of Wales attended this first night. Repeat performances on 15th, 19th, 22nd, 26th January and 12th February. The librettist is not known. Burney states that the book, not identical with the *Arminio* of Antonio Salvi, was the same as that used in 1714 when an anonymous opera *Arminio* was produced, on 4th March, at the Haymarket Theatre. The librettos of both London productions were printed. Schoelcher's remark (p. 184) that Heidegger, as author of the 1737 libretto, dedicated it to Marlborough's daughter, Lady Godolphin, has no foundation whatever.

———

CAST OF " ARMINIO ", 12th January 1737

Arminio—Signor Annibali, alto
Tusnelda—Signora Strada, soprano
Sigismondo—Signor Conti, soprano
Ramise—Signora Bertolli, mezzo-soprano
Segeste—Mr. Reinhold, bass
Varo—Mr. Beard, tenor
Tullio—Signora Maria Caterina Negri, contralto

Signora Bertolli, who had been in Handel's company from 1729 till 1733, came back to him from the Nobility Opera, but only for a year.

——

LADY LUCY WENTWORTH TO HER FATHER, THE EARL OF STRAFFORD

London, January 18, 1737.

Last Sunday [the 16th] there was a vast deal of musick at Church, too much I think, for I doubt it spoilt every body's devotion, for there was drums and Trumpets as loud as an Oritoria . . . his majesty . . . was not at the Opera a saterday as most people thought he wou'd to show he was safely arived.

(Myers, 1948, p. 47.) *Wentworth Papers*, pp. 530 f. Saturday, 15th January, was the second performance of *Arminio*.

——

FROM THE " CRAFTSMAN ", 22nd January 1737

To all Lovers of MUSICK.

This Day is publish'd,

Proposals for Printing by *Subscription,*

The *Opera* of *Arminius* in Score, as it is perform'd at the Theatre-Royal in Covent-Garden. Composed by Mr. *Handel.*

. . . . .

Subscriptions are taken in by John Walsh . . . and at most Musick Shops in Town.

Except that the word " subscribe " replaces the words " encourage this Undertaking ", this advertisement is identical with that used for *Atalanta* on 14th May 1736. *Arminio* was to be ready " by the Middle of February ".

——

Handel finishes the opera *Berenice*, 27th January 1737.

——

Partenope is revived, 29th January 1737.

Repeat performances on 2nd, 5th and 9th February ; the first and the third of the four performances by command of the Prince and Princess of Wales. The cast (compared with the original one of 24th February 1730) was as follows :

Partenope—Signora Strada (Strada)
Rosmira—Signora Bertolli (Merighi)

Arsace—Signor Annibali (Bernacchi)
Armindo—Signor Conti (Signora Bertolli)
Emilio—Mr. Beard (Fabri)
Ormonte—Signora Maria Caterina Negri (Signor Riemschneider)

One would have expected the part of Ormonte to be sung by Mr. Rein-hold, but it seems that Handel had it sung by a contralto.

———

FROM THE EARL OF EGMONT'S DIARY, 7th February 1737

In the evening I visited [my] son Hanmer, and found him so well that he was in the morning at the rehearsal of Handel's new opera.

(Egmont MSS., II. 342.) For Hanmer, Egmont's son-in-law, see 2nd and 12th April 1734. The new opera was *Giustino*, produced on 16th February.

———

FROM THE " CRAFTSMAN ", 12th February 1737

NEW MUSICK,

This Day is publish'd,

The whole *Opera* of *Arminius* in Score . . . by Mr. Handel.
Also Twenty Operas in Score, compleat by the same Author.
Printed for and sold by John Walsh. . . .

(Chrysander, II. 398.) Cf. 22nd January.

———

EXTRACTS FROM THE LIST OF SUBSCRIBERS FOR THE OPERA " ARMINIO ", PUBLISHED ON 12th February 1737

Apollo Society at Windsor Castle
The Marchioness of Carnavon
Earl Cooper
William Freeman
M. C. Festing
Mr. Granville 2 [copies]
Mr. Gates, one of the Gentlemen & Master of the Children of ye Chapel Royal
James Harris
John Harris, Organ Builder
Charles Jennens 2 [copies]
Sir Windham Knatchbull
Mr. Keeble
Mr. Low

The Musical Society Oxen.
Dr. Pepusch
James Peasable, Organist at South-ampton
Mr. [John] Robinson
Earl of Shaftsbury
John Snow of Oxford
John Stanley
Mr. [William] Savage
I. Scott, organist
Iohn Simpson, Musick seller 14 [copies]
Mr. Wiedman
Mr. Zink[e]

There were 108 subscribers, for 143 copies. Mary (Bruce) Marchioness of Carnarvon, was the wife of Henry, second son of the Duke of Chandos ; she died

H.-14 *a*

in 1738, twenty-eight years of age. The Earl of Cowper, until now the head of the Nobility Opera, became a regular subscriber for Handel's scores.

—

FROM THE " DAILY POST ", 16th February 1737
This Evening will be perform'd,

. . . . .

At the Theatre Royal in Covent-Garden, a new Opera, call'd *Justin*.

(Burney, IV. 403.) The first night was a Wednesday. The text was an altered version of Nicolo Beregani's libretto, set by Giovanni Legrenzi in 1683. (Loewenberg, p. 96.) *Giustino* was performed on 16th, 19th, 22nd, 25th February, 2nd, 4th March, 4th, 11th May, and 8th June.

—

CAST OF " GIUSTINO ", 16th February 1737
Anastasio—Signor Conti, soprano
Arianna—Signora Strada, soprano
Leocasta—Signora Bertolli, mezzo-soprano
Amanzio—Signora Maria Caterina Negri, contralto
Giustino—Signor Annibali, alto
Vitaliano—Mr. Beard, tenor
Polidarte—Mr. Reinhold, bass
La Fortuna—Mr. Savage, counter-tenor
Voci di dentro—(?), bass

—

MR. PENNINGTON TO MISS CATHERINE COLLINGWOOD, AT BATH

19th Feb. 1736–7.

. . . Partys run high in musick, as when you shone among us. Mr. Handel has not due honour done him, and I am excessively angry about it, which you know is of vast consequence.

Throckmorton MSS., p. 257 ; first quoted in *Sackbut*, 1931, p. 157, but without date. For Catherine Collingwood, see 27th December 1734. Nothing is known of Mr. Pennington.

—

FROM A LONDON NEWSPAPER, 22nd February 1737

(In an advertisement of *Giustino* to be performed on Tuesday, 22nd February 1737.)

The Days of Performance during Lent will be on Wednesdays and Fridays.

Cutting in Sir Augustus Harris' Collection. The issues of the *London Daily Post* for 1737, as well as those of various other papers for that year, are no longer available. From 2nd March (*Giustino*) till 1st April (*Il Trionfo del Tempo e della Verita*) there was a Handel performance every Wednesday and Friday at Covent Garden. Handel's repertoire was as follows :

<pre>
25th February—Giustino (Friday)
2nd March —   ,,
 4th   ,,   —   ,,
 9th   ,, —Il Parnasso in Festa
11th   ,,   —   ,,
16th   ,, —Alexander's Feast
18th   ,,   —   ,,
23rd   ,, —Il Trionfo
25th   ,,   —   ,,
30th   ,, —Alexander's Feast
1st April —Il Trionfo (Friday)
 4th   ,,   —   ,,   (Monday)
 5th   ,, —Alexander's Feast (Tuesday)
 6th   ,, —Esther (Wednesday)
 7th   ,,   —   ,,   (Thursday)
</pre>

For the last four performances, in Passion Week, Handel got special licence.

———

At Drury Lane Theatre, on 28th February 1737, *The Universal Passion*, a comedy by James Miller, based on Shakespeare's *Much Ado about Nothing* and Molière's *Princesse d'Élide*, is produced ; in Act II is an aria by Handel : " I like the am'rous youth that's free ", sung by Mrs. Catherine Clive.

(Squire, 1913, p. 105.) Catherine, called Kitty, Clive, née Rafter, was an actress who, in 1743, sang in Handel oratorios ; she played the part of Liberia in this production, and also spoke the epilogue, Theophilus Cibber speaking the prologue. Handel wrote the song for her (Schoelcher, p. 235). Cf. 1738–9 and 14th March 1741. James Miller wrote the word-book of *Joseph* (2nd March 1744).

———

Maurice Greene's oratorio *Jephtha* is produced at the Haymarket Theatre, Lent 1737.

Greene, since 1735 John Eccles' successor as Master of the King's Band of Music, set a poem by one Burnet, printed in the *Gentleman's Magazine* of March 1737, pp. 144–7. Nicoll, following Robert Watt (*Bibliotheca Britannica*) and Gordon Goodwin (*Dictionary of National Biography*), attributes the poem to John Hoadly, and quotes a word-book of 1737 and a reprint in *A Miscellany of Lyric Poems*, 1740 ; this latter collection had the subtitle ' performed in the Academy of Music, held in the Apollo ', i.e. the Apollo Society in the Devil's Tavern. Handel's *Jephtha* of 1752 was set to different words, but Morell, his librettist, used one couplet from Greene's word-book (Winton Dean).

———

FROM A LONDON NEWSPAPER, 4th March 1737

(In an advertisement of *Giustino* to be performed on that day, a Friday.)

Being the last Opera that will be perform'd 'till Easter.

Cutting in Sir Augustus Harris's Collection.

———

MISS ANN GRANVILLE TO HER MOTHER, MRS. GRANVILLE

[London], 8th March 1737.

Music is certainly a pleasure that may be reckoned intellectual, and we shall *never again* have it in the perfection it is this year, because Mr. Handel will *not compose any more* ! Oratorios begin next week, to my great joy, for they are the highest entertainment to me.

(Delany, I. 594.) The date of this letter may be wrong : the 8th was a Tuesday, and Handel's oratorio season began on Wednesday, the 9th. Perhaps the fear of the Handelians was concerned with operas only ; cf. James Harris's letter of 5th May.

———

Il Parnasso in Festa is revived, 9th March 1737.

(Burney, IV. 407 : performed " as an oratorio ".) Repeat performance on 11th March. The cast is not known, but Signora Strada and Maria Caterina Negri certainly sang the parts created by them on 13th March 1734.

———

FROM THE " LONDON DAILY POST ", 11th March 1737

We hear, since Operas have been forbidden being performed at the Theatre in Covent Garden on the Wednesdays and Fridays in Lent, Mr. Handel is preparing Dryden's Ode of Alexander's Feast, the Oratorios of Esther and Deborah, with several new Concertos for the Organ and other Instruments ; also an Entertainment of Musick, called Il Trionfo del Tempo e della Verita, which Performances will be brought on the Stage and varied every Week.

(Burney, IV. 403 ; Schoelcher, p. 85.) No copy available. Cf. 22nd February. *Deborah* was not revived during this season.

———

Handel finishes the second version of *Il Trionfo del Tempo e della Verità*, after a fortnight's work, 14th March 1737.

The first version was written about 1708 (cf. p. 20).

———

FROM A LONDON NEWSPAPER, 15th March 1737

By Command of their Royal Highnesses the Prince and Princess of Wales. At the Theatre-Royal in Covent-Garden, To-morrow, March 16, will be perform'd an Ode, written by Dryden, call'd ALEXANDER'S FEAST. With Concerto's on the Organ, and other Instruments.

Cutting in Sir Augustus Harris's Collection. A short advertisement is to be found in the *Daily Post* of 16th March. Repeat performances on 18th, 30th March, " by Desire " on 5th April, and finally on 10th and 25th June. At the beginning of 1736 the title of Handel's Ode had been *The Feast of Alexander ;* in the printed libretto, however, and always subsequently it was *Alexander's Feast.* The cast is not known exactly, but Strada and Beard sang their original parts of 19th February 1736, Annibali the part of Mrs. Arne-Young and Reinhold, apparently, the part of Erard. The first libretto known bears the date of 1736, but it already contains the additional cantata " Cecilia volgi ", finished on 22nd November 1736 and assigned to Signor " Arigoni ", a misprint for Annibali, and Signora Strada : it was an Italian interlude within the English ode. Since the old style year ended on 24th March 1736–7, the date 1736 is not incompatible with the performance on 16th March 1737. (Schoelcher, p. 384 ; Chrysander, II. 430.)

———

FROM THE " DAILY JOURNAL ", 17th March 1737

Last Night their Royal Highnesses the Prince and Princess of Wales went to the Theatre Royal in Covent Garden, where Mr. Dreyden's celebrated Ode called *Alexander's Feast* was performed with great Applause, and to the Satisfaction of a numerous Audience.

———

FROM A LONDON NEWSPAPER, 17th March 1737

Last Night Mr. Dryden's Ode, call'd *Alexander's Feast*, was performed at the Theatre Royal in Covent-Garden, to a splendid Audience, where his Royal Highness the Prince and the Princess of Wales were present, and seem'd to be highly entertain'd, insomuch that his Royal Highness commanded Mr. Handel's Concerto on the Organ to be repeated, and intends to Honour the same with his Presence once again, as likewise the new Oratorio call'd *Il Trionfo del Tempo e della Verita*, which is to be perform'd on Wednesday next [the 23rd].

Cutting in Sir Augustus Harris's Collection.

———

FROM THE " DAILY POST ", 23rd March 1737

This Evening will be perform'd,

At the Theatre-Royal in Covent-Garden, An Oratorio call'd Il Trionfo del Tempo e della Verita.

In Sir Augustus Harris's Collection is a cutting from another London newspaper, with the additional note : " By Command of their Royal Highnesses the Prince and Princess of Wales ". Repeat performances on 25th March (Burney, IV. 407), 1st and 4th April. The cast is not known, but it may have been as follows :

Tempo—Mr. Reinhold, bass
Disinganno—Signora Maria Caterina Negri, contralto
Bellezza—Signora Strada, soprano
Piacere—Mr. Beard, tenor

The Italian version was revived on 3rd March 1739. Cf. the final version, in English, 11th March 1757.

———

At the Academy of Ancient Music, in the " Crown and Anchor " Tavern, Handel's *Chandos Te Deum* is performed, 23rd March 1737.

A word-book, containing " Motets, Madrigals and other pieces, performed by the Academy of Ancient Music on Thursday, March 23rd, 1737 " (1738 ?), called the work the " Te Deum composed by Mr. Handel for the Duke of Chandos ". This word-book was reprinted in 1746, 1751 and 1755.

———

FROM THE " CRAFTSMAN ", 26th March 1737

To all Lovers of MUSICK.

On Wednesday the 30th Instant will be publish'd,

The whole *Opera* of *Justin* in Score, as it is perform'd at the Theatre-Royal in Covent-Garden. Composed by Mr. Handel.

Printed for and sold by John Walsh. . . .

(Chrysander, II. 397 f.) The invitation to subscribe, probably issued a month before, has not been traced.

———

EXTRACTS FROM THE LIST OF SUBSCRIBERS FOR " GIUSTINO ", PUBLISHED ON 30th March 1737

Right Hon. Marchioness Carnarvon
Right Hon. Earl Cowper
Wm Freeman
Mr. Granville 2 Books
Mr. Bernard Gates
James Harris 2 Books
Mr. James Harris, Organ Builder
Mrs. Hare 2 Books
Charles Jennens 2 Books
St Windham Knatchbul
Mr. [James] Kent, Organist of Trin. Coll. Camb.

Mr. [John] Keeble 2 Books
Musical Society Oxford
Dr. Pepusch
Mr. I [James] Peasable, Organist at Southampton
Right Hon. Earl of Shaftsbury
Mr. [Charles John] Stanley
Mr. [William] Savage
Mr. [John] Simpson, Musick Seller
Mr. John Snow of Oxon
Mr. Wiedeman
Mr. Zincke

There are 104 subscribers for 110 copies.

———

FROM A LONDON NEWSPAPER, 31st March 1737

At the Theatre-Royal in Covent-Garden, To-morrow, April 1, will be perform'd the last New Oratorio, call'd IL TRIONFO DEL TEMPO E DELLA VERITA. With Concerto's on the Organ, and other Instruments. . . .

Cutting in Sir Augustus Harris's Collection. A similar advertisement was probably printed for the first performance, on 23rd March.

—

FROM MATTHESON'S " KERN MELODISCHER WISSENSCHAFT " (" ESSENCE OF MELODIC SCIENCE "), HAMBURG, 1737 (Translated)

. . . Not to mention other instrumentalists, the renowned Händel has often played [ex tempore] accompaniments in his stage performances, where the solo harpsichord especially excelled in this [curious] style, according to the player's skill and pleasure : it is a performance which requires its own virtuoso, and other men, who tried to imitate it, did not succeed.

P. 23 of this text-book of composition, the preface to which is dated 26th January 1737.

—

Handel has permission to give performances on the first four days of Passion Week : Monday the 4th till Thursday the 7th April 1737.

(Burney, IV. 404.) Cf. 22nd February 1737.

—

Esther is revived, 6th April 1737.

(Burney, IV. 404.) The cast is not known, but may have been as follows :

           Ahasuerus—Signor Annibali, alto
           Haman—Mr. Reinhold, bass
           Habdonah—Mr. Beard, tenor
           Esther—Signora Strada, soprano
           Mordecai—Signora Bertolli, mezzo-soprano

Repeat performance on 7th April.

—

FROM A LONDON NEWSPAPER, 13th April 1737

At the Theatre-Royal in Covent-Garden, this Day, April 13, will be perform'd a New Opera, call'd DIDO.

Cutting in Sir Augustus Harris's Collection. This was a pasticcio-opera, the text by Giovanni Alberto Ristori, entitled *Didone abbandonata*, the music by various composers, arranged by Handel, with alterations. Among the singers was Annibali. Handel was unable to direct the opera : it was on the 13th April that he had the stroke paralysing his right arm. The opera was repeated on 20th, 27th April, and 1st June. From 13th April till the end of the season, operas, *etc.*, were performed on Wednesdays only, with four exceptions: 21st May—Saturday, 10th June—Friday, 21st June—Tuesday, and 25th June—Saturday.

———

JAMES HARRIS TO THE EARL OF SHAFTESBURY

Sarum April 19—1737

. . . Y^r Lord^p Observations on the Ode is certainly very Just. People came with an Expectation that Music was to give Them a prospect of Persepolis on Fire. But this indeed was to expect Pomegranates from an Orange Tree. . . .

. . . The Great are certainly of right the Natural Patrons of Arts & Sciences. Next to a free Governm^t their Countenance is ye greatest happiness wch can befall them. . . . This Good Fortune has made Y^r Lord^p Happiness in ye Musical Way by Sending Us Handel. . . .

Public Record Office: G. D. 24, Bundle XXVIII, No. 26. James Harris, the younger (1707-80), inherited the Close of Salisbury (Sarum) after the death of his father. He was cousin to the fourth Earl of Shaftesbury, his mother, the second wife of James Harris, the elder, having been Lady Elizabeth Ashley Cooper, the sister of the third Earl of Shaftesbury. He was also the brother-in-law of Sir Windham Knatchbull, whose wife, Catharine, was Harris's sister. In 1745 he married Elizabeth Clarke, and his son James (the third) later became the first Earl of Malmesbury. Harris is best known as the author of *Hermes*, and is usually called the Hermes Harris. He also published, in 1744, *Three Treatises* on art, music, painting, poetry and happiness. It is less known that he contributed the list of Handel's works to Mainwaring's biography of 1760, and that he adapted the words for a selection from Italian and German composers, edited by Joseph Corfe (*Sacred Music*, two volumes, about 1800). In 1762 a pastoral, *The Spring*, was produced at Drury Lane with text by Harris and music by Handel and other composers ; the same pastoral was performed at Oxford in 1763, and several times afterwards, under the title *Daphnis and Amaryllis*. Harris's political career started after Handel's death.

———

FROM THE " DAILY ADVERTISER ", 29th April 1737

For the Benefit of Mr. W. SAVAGE.

At the Castle Tavern, Pater-noster-Row, on Monday the 2d of May, will be an Entertainment of Vocal and Instrumental MUSICK. . . . And at the end of each Part will be perform'd one of Mr. Handel's Coronation-Anthems, with Voices and Instruments. . . .

" The Castle Tavern " was the meeting-place of the Philarmonica Club, now called the Castle Society, which, about 1744, moved to the King's Arms in Cornhill. William Savage, born about 1720, started his Handel career as " the boy " in 1735. There is no indication into how many " parts " the concert was divided, but it seems that all the four Anthems were performed, perhaps for the first time since 11th October 1727.

———

FROM THE " LONDON DAILY POST ", 30th April 1737

Mr. Handel, who has been some time indisposed with the rheumatism, is in so fair a way of recovery, that it is hoped he will be able to accompany the opera of Justin on Wednesday next, the 4th of May ; at which time we hear their Majesties will honour that opera with their presence.

(Burney, IV. 408.) No copy available. Cf. 14th May. Handel did not direct *Dido* on 13th April, or *Berenice* on 18th May, but he may have directed *Giustino* on 4th and 11th May. Burney adds : " but it does not appear that their Majesties were there ".

—

Giustino is performed again, 4th May 1737.

(Burney, IV. 408.) Repeated on 11th May. The Court intended to attend at least one of these performances.

—

JAMES HARRIS TO THE EARL OF SHAFTESBURY

Sarum May 5 1737

Y^r Lord^p'^{s} information concerning Mr Handel's Disorder was ye first I received—I can assure Y^r Lord^p it gave me no Small Concern—when ye Fate of Harmony depends upon a Single Life, the Lovers of Harmony may be well allowed to be Sollicitous. I heartily regrett ye thought of losing any of ye executive part of his meritt, but this I can gladly compound for, when we are assured of the Inventive, for tis this which properly constitutes ye Artist, & Separates Him from ye Multitude. It is certainly an Evidence of great Strength of Constitution to be so Soon getting rid of So great a Shock. A weaker Body would perhaps have hardly born ye Violence of Medicines, wch operate So quickly.

I rejoice to hear from y^r Lord^p that the Author's Bill is like to Succeed, and I am Sure ye Lovers both of Letters & of Harmony ought to be thankfull to y^r Lord^p for ye Pain you have taken in Solliciting it. Tis a bad Proof w^t remains of Gothic Barbarity we have Still amongst us that ye Bill Should have been opposed on acc^t of Mr Pope & Handel. It may however for our comfort be remembered th^t even in ye Augustan Age when Virgil & Horace were alive, at ye Same time lived Bavius & Maevius. The Success of this Bill will I hope give us ye Ode, which I have a vast desire to be possessed of. If Mr Handel gives off his Opera, it will be the only Pleasure I shall have left in ye musicall way, to look over his Scores, and recollect past Events—Here Strada used to shine— there Annibale—This was an Excell^t Chorus, and that a Charming peice of Recitative—In that I shall amuse my Self much in the Same manner as Virgil tells of ye Trojans . . . the War y^r Lord^p knows was renewed with double Earnestness & Vigour. May my Pleasure find ye Same Fate, & be lost by ye Return of that Harmony wch I have given over, Supported & carried on by ye Same Spirit & Resolution.

Public Record Office : G. D. 24, Bundle XXVIII, No. 27. Cf. 19th April. Although it seems difficult to explain this letter in its details, Harris's reaction to Shaftesbury's report on Handel's health is very telling. It was not just rheumatism which overcame Handel (see 30th April) but a paralytic disorder, laming his right arm (see 14th May). The "executive part" of his abilities refers certainly to his organ and harpsichord playing, implying the management of the Opera. We also learn, from this letter, of some recovery after severe treatment. The second part of the letter refers to hopes for an Ode, written by Pope and set to music by Handel, which were not realized. It is related (Chrysander, II. 432 f.) that the surgeon John Belcher, a friend of Pope's and of Handel's, suggested the setting of Pope's early " Ode for Musick ", otherwise known as " Euridice " or as " Ode for St. Cecilia's Day ". Since, however, this ode, in a revised version, had already been set by Greene in 1730, Handel did not agree. According to Burney (1785, p. 33), Handel answered : " It is de very ding vat my *pellows-plower* has set already for ein tocktor's tecree at Cambridge ". The names of Pope and Handel are nowhere mentioned in the printed records of the " Author's Bill ", *i.e.* the Copyright Bill, now being dealt with again in both Houses of Parliament. (The " Journals " of the two Houses do not give the full proceedings.) To understand these matters, it is necessary to remember that the first " Bill for Encouragement of Learning ", based on a petition of booksellers and printers in London against surreptitious editions, was introduced under Queen Anne, 12th December 1709 till 5th April 1710 ; it granted protection of fourteen years for new publications (cf. 14th June 1720). From 1735 till 1749 a " Society for the Encouragment of Learning " tried to improve the copyright (cf. Clayton Atto in the *Library*, 1939, pp. 263-88). From 3rd March till 5th May 1735 a bill for "better Encouragement of Learning " was discussed, first in the House of Commons and then in the House of Lords, but was not carried. From 5th April 1737 onwards, another bill for " more effectual securing sole Right of printed Books to Authors, &c.", brought in by Henry, Viscount Cornbury, was discussed in the House of Lords, but again not carried. The scheme was quite revolutionary : copyright for life and eleven years, or for twenty-one years in all if the author died within ten years after publication ; and for twenty-one years for posthumous works. (Cf. A. S. Collins, in the *Library*, 1927, p. 72.) The name of Shaftesbury is not mentioned in connection with the 1737 bill in any printed record.—It may be added here that the Earl of Egmont was also interested in repealing the bill of Queen Anne's time. On 17th March 1735 he subscribed ten guineas to a scheme for rescuing authors from the tyranny of printers and booksellers ; the scheme was promulgated by a group of noblemen and gentlemen, the Society mentioned above, with John, Lord Carteret (cf. 28th October 1720) at the head (Egmont MSS. II. 161). On 19th March 1737 Egmont visited Lord Limerick to discuss the " Act for Encouragement of Learning ", and especially the point that Irish reprints should not be forbidden, but only their import into England (Egmont MSS. II. 374).—Bavius and M(a)evius were Roman would-be poets, trying to disparage Horace and Virgil.

FROM THE " LONDON EVENING POST ", 14th May 1737

The ingenious Mr. Handell is very much indispos'd, and it's thought with a Paraletick Disorder, he having at present no Use of his Right Hand, which, if he don't regain, the Publick will be depriv'd of his fine Compositions.

FROM THE " DAILY GAZETTEER ", 18th May 1737

Last Night the King, Queen, and Princesses, went to the Opera in the Haymarket.

And this Evening their Majesties will be at the Opera in Covent Garden. (Burney, IV. 408.) At the Haymarket *Sabrina*, an opera with text by Rolli, who also arranged the music, was produced on 26th April ; in addition to Farinelli, a new singer appeared there : Signora Maria Antonia Marchesini, called La Lucchesina (Chrysander, II. 403).

———

FROM THE " DAILY POST ", 18th May 1737

This Evening will be perform'd,

.   .   .   .   .

At the Theatre-Royal in Covent-Garden, A new Opera, call'd *Berenice*.

(Burney, IV. 408.) Text by Antonio Salvi, originally composed by Jacopo Antonio Perti, 1709. (Loewenberg, p. 96.) Repeat performances on 21st, 25th May and 15th June. The libretto of *Berenice, regina d'Egitto* was, as usual, printed in Italian and English. Handel did not direct these performances. Burney relates that the King, the Queen and all the Royal family attended the first night. Conti and Strada sang in *Berenice* for the last time for Handel, and for the last time in London.

———

CAST OF " BERENICE ", 18th May 1737

Berenice—Signora Strada, soprano
Selene—Signora Bertolli, mezzo-soprano
Alessandro—Signor Conti, soprano
Demetrio—Signor Annibali, alto
Arsace—Signora Maria Caterina Negri, contralto
Fabio—Mr. Beard, tenor
Aristobolo—Mr. Reinhold, bass

It is related that the part of Fabio was divided been Beard and tweSavage : a procedure suitable for an oratorio rather than for an opera.

———

FROM A LONDON NEWSPAPER, 21st May 1737

We hear that the Directors of his Majesty's Opera-house in the Haymarket, have engaged for the ensuing Season, the famous Caffariello, reputed to be the best singer in Italy.

(Burney, IV. 412 f.) No copy available. Farinelli left the Haymarket Opera in June. Gaetano Majorano, called Caffarelli, an alto, came to London on 1st November, and sang in Handel's Opera for some months in 1738.

———

FROM THE " CRAFTSMAN ", 28th May 1737

MUSICK.

.   .   .   .   .

Just publish'd,

Proposals for printing by Subscription, the new Opera of *Berenice*, and *Alexander's Feast* ; an Ode, as they are perform'd at the Theatre-Royal in Covent-Garden. Composed by Mr. Handel. Subscriptions are taken in by John Walsh. . . .

(Chrysander, II. 428.) The proposals for *Alexander's Feast* were advertised in the same paper on 11th, 18th, 25th June and 2nd July. (Smith, 1948, p. 126.)

—

FROM A LONDON NEWSPAPER, 31st May 1737

By HIS MAJESTY's *Command*, At the Theatre-Royal in Covent-Garden, To-morrow, June 1, will be perform'd an Opera, call'd DIDO. . . . To begin at Seven o'Clock.

Cutting in Sir Augustus Harris's Collection. This was, in fact, a Command Performance. The operas now began later than during the winter.

—

FROM THE " CRAFTSMAN ", 4th June 1737

. . . However, if *this Bill* [for restraining the Liberty of the Stage] must pass . . . I hope our *Italian Opera's* will fall the first Sacrifice, as they not only carry great Sums of Money out of the Kingdom, but soften and enervate the Minds of the People. It is observable of the *antient Romans*, that they did not admit of any *effeminate Musick, Singing or Dancing*, upon their Stage, till *Luxury* had corrupted their Morals, and the Loss of *Liberty* follow'd soon after. If therefore it should be thought necessary to lay any farther Restraint upon the *most useful Sort of dramatical Entertainments*, the *worst* ought certainly to receive no Encouragement.

This article, first quoted by Bredenförder, was reprinted in the *London Magazine* for June 1737. It refers to the " Play House Bill ", dealt with in Parliament from 20th May till 21st June ; the bill was occasioned by a libel on the Government contained in a farce, *The Golden Rump*, at the Lincoln's Inn Fields Theatre. The Earl of Chesterfield spoke against the bill, in the cause of liberty, but it passed.

—

FROM A LONDON NEWSPAPER, 7th June 1737

At the Theatre-Royal in Covent-Garden, To-morrow, June 8, will be perform'd an Opera, call'd JUSTIN. . . .

Cutting in Sir Augustus Harris's Collection.

—

FROM A LONDON NEWSPAPER, 10th June 1737

By Command of their Royal Highnesses the Prince and Princess of WALES. At the Theatre-Royal in Covent-Garden, this Day, June 10, will be perform'd an Opera, call'd ALCINA. . . .

Cutting in Sir Augustus Harris's Collection. Repeated on 21st June. The cast or this revival was probably the same as on 6th November 1736. Schoelcher

(p. 422) quotes two advertisements from the *London Daily Post* of 20th and 23rd June, which may have referred to the operas : " Pit and Boxes (or Front Boxes) to be put together ", and " The Pit will be floor'd over and laid to the Boxes ".

———

The Opera of the Nobility comes to a premature end on 11th June 1737.

On 24th May *Demofoonte*, an anonymous opera, was produced ; a repeat performance on 28th May was cancelled owing to the indisposition of Farinelli. Nicoll gives the dates of 7th and 11th June for *Demofoonte* (second and third performances) as well as for *Sabrina*. Burney (IV. 412) states that *Sabrina* was performed on those days. *Sabrina* was announced again for the 14th, but Farinelli fell ill, and the last night of the season was cancelled. Farinelli left for Italy, never to return. Porpora followed him.

———

THE REPERTOIRE OF THE OPERA OF THE NOBILITY, 1733–7

Lincoln's Inn Fields

1733,	29 December	' Ariadne ' (text by Rolli, music by Porpora)
1734,	5 February	' Ferdinando ' (Porpora)
	12 March	' Davide e Bersabea ', oratorio (Rolli–Porpora)
	23 March	' Belmira ', pasticcio
	11 May	' Enea nel Lazio ' (Rolli–Porpora)

Haymarket

	29 October	' Artaserse ' (music by Hasse and Riccardo Broschi)
	10 December	' Ottone ' (Handel)
1735,	1 February	' Polifemo ' (Rolli–Porpora)
	8 April	' Issipile ' (Metastasio–Sandoni)
	3 May	' Ifigenia in Aulide ' (Rolli–Porpora)
	25 November	' Adriano ' (Veracini)
1736,	24 January	' Mitridate ', pasticcio
	2 March	' Orfeo ', pasticcio (text by Rolli)
	13 April (once)	' Honorius ' (D. Lolli and G. Boldoni, music by F. Campi)
	4 May	' The Feast of Hymen ' (Porpora)
	23 November	' Siroe ' (Metastasio–Hasse)
1737,	8 January	' Merope ' (text by Zeno)
	12 February	' Demetrio ' (Metastasio–Pescetti)
	Lent	' Jephtha ', oratorio (Greene)
	12 April	' La Clemenza di Tito ' (A. Cori, music by F. Veracini)
	26 April	' Sabrina ' (text, founded on Milton's ' Comus ', by Rolli, who also arranged the music)
	24 May	' Demofoonte ' (A. Cori, music by E. Duni)

In 1737, Italian intermezzi, or interludes, were occasionally sung between the acts of the serious operas.

———

FROM THE " LONDON DAILY POST ", 15th June 1737

To all Lovers of Music.

This Day is publish'd,

The whole Opera of Berenice in Score.

Those Gentlemen who intend to subscribe are desired to send in their Names immediately.

Subscriptions are taken in by John Walsh. . . .

(Schoelcher, *Handel Catalogue.*) No copy available. Since the text of this advertisement is taken, third hand, from a translation of the French catalogue of Handel's works, it is not quite reliable. Something went wrong with the subscription for *Berenice* : there is no list of subscribers in the score.

FROM A LONDON NEWSPAPER, 15th June 1737

(From an advertisement of the score of *Alexander's Feast* :)

The Work is in a great Forwardness and will be carefully corrected and done with all Expedition. Subscriptions are taken in by the Author, in his House in Brook-street, Hanover Square ; also by John Walsh. . . . The Price to Subscribers to be two Guineas, one Guinea to be paid at the Time of Subscribing, and the other on Delivery of the Book in Sheets. A Print of the Author will be curiously engrav'd and given to the Subscribers and Encouragers of the Work.

(Chrysander, II. 429.) Probably also from the *London Daily Post*, which is not available. The advertisement, apparently corresponding with the " Proposals " advertised on 28th May, was copied by Schoelcher for Chrysander. The " Print " was an engraved portrait of Handel.

FROM THE " CRAFTSMAN ", 18th June 1737

NEW MUSICK,

This Day is publish'd,

The New *Opera* of *Berenice* in Score . . . by Mr. Handel. . . .

Printed for and sold by John Walsh. . . .

Where may be had,

Proposals for printing by Subscription, *Alexander's* Feast, an Ode, wrote in Honour of St. Cecilia. By Mr. Dryden. Set to Musick by Mr. Handel.

(Chrysander, II. 398.) *Arminio*, for the flute, was published at the same time.

FROM A LONDON NEWSPAPER, 25th June 1737

By Command of their Royal Highnesses the Prince and Princess of WALES. At the Theatre-Royal in Covent-Garden, this Day, June 25,

will be perform'd an Ode, call'd ALEXANDER's FEAST. Written by
Dryden. . . .

Cutting in Sir Augustus Harris's Collection. This was probably the end of the
season. It is not true that Handel went bankrupt after this season ; this was
proved by Squire (1909) and Young (p. 63).

———

FROM THE PRINCE OF WALES's " REGISTER OF WARRANTS ",
5th July 1737

To Mr John Kipling for the Season of Opera's at Covent Garden
Theatre 1737

£   s   d
250   0   0

(British Museum : Add. MS. 24,404, fol. 66 b.)   Cf. 5th July 1733 and 28th
June 1734. On the same day, 5th July 1737, a sum of £250 was also paid to Joseph
Haymes for the opera season at the Haymarket Theatre ; Haymes, apparently the
cashier of the " Nobility Opera ", received the same amount from the Prince on
27th June 1735 and on 27th July 1736. His subscriptions to the two Opera houses
run from 1733 till 1737, but Handel's undertaking was not subsidized in 1735 and
1736.

———

Frederick, Prince of Wales, with several distinguished ladies and
noblemen of his household, goes from Kew to Vauxhall Gardens
by water, with music attending, 6th July 1737.

(Wroth, p. 291.) This fact is recorded here as being one of the occasions
on which movements from Handel's *Water Music* may have been performed.

———

FROM THE KING's WARRANT BOOK, 25th August 1737

£   s.   d.
Royal Academy of Music 1,000   0   0   Royal bounty to the undertakers
of the Opera.

(Calendar of Treasury Books, 1735–8, p. 432.) There is no corresponding entry
in the Treasury Minute Book. The subvention went to the Haymarket Opera.

———

Arianna in Creta is performed at Brunswick, August 1737.

(Loewenberg, p. 93.) It is not certain whether this was Handel's opera.

———

Handel withdraws £150, 1st September 1737.

———

*The observation that misfortunes rarely come single, was verified in Handel. His
fortune was not more impaired, than his health and his understanding. His right-arm was*

become useless to him, from a stroke of the palsy ; and how greatly his senses were disordered at intervals, for a long time, appeared from an hundred instances, which are better forgotten than recorded. The most violent deviations from reason, are usually seen when the strongest faculties happen to be thrown out of course.

In this melancholic state, it was in vain for him to think of any fresh projects for retrieving his affairs. His first concern was how to repair his constitution. But tho' he had the best advice, and tho' the necessity of following it was urged to him in the most friendly manner, it was with the utmost difficulty that he was prevailed on to do what was proper, when it was any way disagreeable. For this reason it was thought best for him to have recourse to the vapor-baths of Aix la Chapelle, over which he sat near three times as long as hath ever been the practice. Whoever knows any thing of the nature of those baths, will, from this instance, form some idea of his surprising constitution. His sweats were profuse beyond what can well be imagined. His cure, from the manner as well as from the quickness, with which it was wrought, passed with the Nuns for a miracle. When, but a few hours from the time of his quitting the bath, they heard him at the organ in the principal church as well as convent, playing in a manner so much beyond any they had ever been used to, such a conclusion in such persons was natural enough.

Tho' his business was so soon dispatched, and his cure judged to be thoroughly effected, he thought it prudent to continue at Aix about six weeks, which is the shortest period usually allotted for bad cases. (Mainwaring, pp. 121-3.)

———

Handel goes to Aachen (Aix-la-Chapelle) for the waters, September 1737.

It is not known exactly when he went abroad, but he returned to England at the end of October or the beginning of November.

———

From Johann Adolph Scheibe's " Critischer Musikus " (" Critical Musician "), Leipzig, 17th September 1737 (Translated)

. . . In several types of harpsichord pieces the German musical style is very markedly differentiated from the rest. With foreigners we find neither so perfect a composition, nor ornamentation, nor development of these pieces as with Germans ; as they, indeed, of all nationalities, know how to play this instrument with the greatest power and according to its true nature. The two great men among the Germans, Herr *Bach* and Herr *Händel*, testify to such most emphatically.

Published in 1739 as no. 15 in the edition of 1737-40, and on p. 147 of the 1745 edition of this periodical in book form. This seems to have been the first time that Johann Sebastian Bach and Handel were united as representatives of keyboard music.

———

" Color fa la regina ", " Die Farbe macht die Königin ", *Singspiel* by Leonhard Fischer, with some music by Handel, Hasse and others is produced at Hamburg, 2nd (13th) October 1737.

(Merbach, p. 368.)   Repeated three times in autumn 1737 and at the beginning of 1738.

———

PRINCE FRIEDRICH OF PRUSSIA TO PRINCE WILLIAM OF ORANGE,
8th (19th) October 1737 (Translated)

Rheinsberg, October 19, 1737.

Pray convey every expression of my duty to your wife ; she does me too much honour to be thinking of me in the matter of Hendel's operas. I am infinitely obliged to her for her attentions, but I beg you will tell her that Hendel's great days are over, his inspiration is exhausted and his taste behind the fashion.   Pray inform me if you have any singer and what kind of voice he has, and I will send you some airs by my composer, which I trust will be to the taste of your wife.

(Leopold von Ranke, *Sämtliche Werke*, Leipzig 1872, V. 173 ff. ; Friedlaender, pp. 102 f.) From 1736 till 1740 Frederick the Great, when Crown Prince, resided at Rheinsberg, near Berlin. He was a cousin of Princess Anne of Orange, Handel's pupil. His composer was probably Karl Heinrich Graun.

———

The Dragon of Wantley, text by Henry Carey, music by John Frederick Lampe, is produced at Covent Garden Theatre, 26th October 1737.

(Loewenberg, p. 97.) Although this was a satire on Italian *opera seria*, and was directed especially against *Giustino*, Handel is said to have liked it. (Cf. 19th January 1738.)   It was a great success.

———

FROM THE "LONDON DAILY POST", 28th October 1737

Mr. Handel, the Composer of the Italian Music, is hourly expected from Aix-la-Chapelle.

(Burney, IV. 428.)   No copy available.

———

Heidegger, the remaining "undertaker" of the Haymarket Opera House, opens a new season on 29th October 1737 with the pasticcio-opera *Arsace* (text by Salvi, altered by Rolli).

The Nobility had abandoned their scheme, after the departure of Farinelli in June. His substitute, Gaetano Majorano, called Caffarelli, was already engaged and arrived in London on 1st November (Burney, IV. 418). Pescetti was intended to be the successor of Porpora as composer of the house. The death of Queen Caroline, on 20th November, brought the season to an early end, and the new year altered the whole aspect of the Haymarket Theatre : Heidegger came to a new understanding with Handel.   *Arsace* was repeated on 1st November, and revived on 9th May 1738 : three performances in all.

———

FROM THE " LONDON DAILY POST ", 7th November 1737

[Mr. Handel is back from Aix-la-Chapelle] greatly recovered in his Health.

(Burney, IV. 418.) No copy available. Burney quotes the last words only. There is no proof for the story that Strada's husband sued Handel after his return, or before his journey, for salary arrears due to the singer (cf. 9th June 1732). She was not, however, in Handel's new company of 1738.

———

Handel begins the opera *Faramondo*, 15th November 1737.

———

FROM WILLERS' HAMBURG NOTES, 16th (27th) November 1737
(Translated)

Nov. 27. J. Cesar. NB. could not be played.

(Merbach, p. 368.) Cf. 10th November 1725.

———

Queen Caroline dies, 20th November 1737.

———

Handel finishes the Funeral Anthem for Queen Caroline, 12th December 1737.

Hawkins, (V. 416) states that the Anthem was ordered by the King on 7th December.

———

FROM THE " OLD WHIG ", 15th December 1737

On Friday [the 16th] will be a Practice of a fine solemn Anthem, composed by Mr. Handel, at the Banquetting House, Whitehall, which will be performed on Saturday Night in King Henry VII's Chapel at her Majesty's Burial.

(Chrysander, II. 436 f.) As mentioned before, the Banqueting Hall had been converted by George I into a Royal Chapel. Cf. 7th April 1734 and 4th January 1738.

———

FROM READ'S " WEEKLY JOURNAL ", 17th December 1737

They have fix'd up a Gallery in the said Chapel where an Organ is erected by Mr. Schrider, his Majesty's Organ-Builder for the Performance of the solemn Anthem.

.   .   .   .   .

The following Anthem is to be perform'd at her Majesty's Funeral which is set to Musick by Mr. Handell.

The ceremony was held in King Henry VII's Chapel, Westminster Abbey. For Schrider see 10th February 1728. The *Funeral Anthem* begins : " The ways of Zion do mourn "; the text was by the Sub-Dean of Westminster Abbey (see Hare's letter of 18th December).

SINGERS IN THE PERFORMANCE OF THE FUNERAL ANTHEM FOR QUEEN CAROLINE, 17th December 1737

Altos : Messrs. Thomas Elford, Francis Hughes, Leigh
Tenor : James Baileys
Basses : Messrs. (Thomas?) Baker, Bernard Gates, Wass, Samuel Weeley

It is related that John Randall turned the music for Handel, who played the organ (cf. 23rd February 1732).

THE DUKE OF CHANDOS TO HIS NEPHEW, THE REVEREND DR. THEOPHILUS LEIGH

Lond^n 18 Decem^r 1737.

The Solemnity of the Queen's Funeral was very decent, and performed in more order than any thing I have seen of the like kind. . . . It began about a quarter before 7, & was over a little after ten ; the Anthem took up three quarter of an hour of the time, of which the composition was exceeding fine, and adapted very properly to the melancholly occasion of it ; but I can't say so much of the performance.

(Baker, p. 260.)   Original in the Henry E. Huntington Library, San Marino, California.

FRANCIS HARE, BISHOP OF CHICHESTER, TO HIS SON, FRANCIS NAYLOR

London, December 18, 1737.

. . . The funeral service was performed by the Bishop of Rochester as Dean of Westminster. After the service there was a long anthem, the words by the Sub-dean, the music set by Mr. Handel, and is reckoned to be as good a piece as he ever made : it was above fifty minutes in singing.

Hare MSS., p. 237 ; Clemens, p. 159. Naylor was travelling abroad. The Dean was Joseph Wilcocks, the Sub-Dean Edward Willes. It was Willes who arranged the text (Psalms 15 and 61) for Handel and not Dr. Alured Clarke, Prebendary of Westminster Abbey, as Chrysander (II. 437) assumed.

FROM THE " DAILY GAZETTEER ", 19th December 1737

On Saturday last [the 17th] her late Majesty was interr'd in a new Vault, in King Henry the Seventh' Chaple. . . . After the Burial Service was over, the fine Anthem, set to Musick by Mr. Handel, was performed by upwards of 140 Hands, from the Choirs of St. James's, Westminster, St. Paul's, and Windsor. . . .

Chrysander, II. 437, quotes another report as printed in the *Daily Advertiser* of the same day. No copy of this is available but the report was reprinted in the *Grub-street Journal* on 22nd December (see next entry).

———

FROM THE "GRUB-STREET JOURNAL", 22nd December 1737

The funeral of her late Majesty was perform'd between the hours of six and nine last saturday night [the 17th]. . . . The fine Anthem of Mr. Handel's was perform'd about nine. The vocal parts were perform'd by the several choirs of the Chapel royal, Westminster-abbey and Windsor, and the boys of the Chapel-royal and Westminster-abbey; and several musical Gentlemen of distinction attended in surplices, and sang in the burial service. There were near 80 vocal performers, and 100 instrumental from his Majesty's band, and from the Opera, &c. *DA.*

(Chrysander, II. 437.) The cipher at the end indicates that this report first appeared in the *Daily Advertiser*; but Schoelcher, p. 193, quotes the same text from the *Daily Post*.

———

Handel finishes the opera *Faramondo*, 24th December 1737. Cf. 15th November.

———

Handel begins the opera *Serse*, 26th December 1737.

Handel's note on the manuscript reads: "angefangen den 26 Decembr 1737 od Montag, den 2 X tag". The 26th was a Monday, the "2 X tag" apparently means the second day of Christmas, *i.e.* our Boxing Day.

———

FROM WALSH'S CASH-BOOK, 1737

1737	Opera Justin	.	.	.	.	.	£26	5	0
1737	Opera Berenice		.	.	.	.	£26	5	0
1737	Opera Faramondo	.		.	.	.	£26	5	0
1737	Opera Alexander's Feast		.	.	.	.	£105	0	0

Giustino was published in March, *Berenice* in June 1737. *Faramondo* was not performed and published until 1738, but the year ending March 1737–8 covers this opera too. *Alexander's Feast*, an ode, not an opera, was different in size and price; it, too, was published within the year 1737–8, in March 1738. *Berenice* was not printed on subscription.

———

In Vol. VII of Ballard's Paris collection, "Les Parodies nouvelles et les Vaudevilles inconnus", 1737, an unidentified dance by

Handel is reprinted as a song : " Par les charmes d'un doux mensonge ".

Cf. 1730 and 1734.

—

From Lorenz Mizler's " Neu eröffnete musikalische Bibliothek " (" Newly inaugurated Musical Library "), Leipzig, 1737 (Translated)

. . . The German nation has indeed already obtained, in part, the victory [in music]. . . . Does not the admirable *Händel* delight the ears of the discerning English above all other composers living in England ? And who is he ? A German. . . . Where can other nations evince such keyboard masters as *Händel*, and our *Bach* here ?

Vol. 1, part 3, pp. 9 f. Cf. Mattheson, spring 1737. For Mizler, see also 1746 and 1747.

—

From Stössel's " Kurzgefasstes Musikalisches Lexikon " (" Concise Musical Dictionary "), Chemnitz, 1737 (Translated)

Hendel (Georg Friedrich) or Händel, a now highly renowned Capellmeister, residing in England, a native of Halle in Magdeburg, and a *scholar* of the late Zachau about the year 1694, was born on 23rd February 1685, was created *Doctor* of Music in London in 1733.

P. 178 of this dictionary, published by Johann Christoph and Johann David Stössel, in Chemnitz, Silesia. Cf. Walther's *Lexikon*, spring of 1732. The " Doctor " refers to Oxford's intention of giving Handel a degree.

—

Hermann von Balcke, a pasticcio opera with words by Georg Daniel Seiler, is produced at Elbing in East Prussia, 1737 ; with Italian arias from Handel's operas (1720–30), German arias and recitatives by Johann Jeremias du Grain.

(Döring, p. 155 ; Leux, pp. 441–51.) This opera was arranged to celebrate the fifth centenary of the foundation of the town of Elbing, now Elblag in Poland, near Danzig and the Baltic coast. Handel had nothing to do with it. The arias were selected from *Admeto, Alessandro, Ottone, Partenope, Radamisto, Riccardo Primo* and *Scipione*. There are about 30 arias, duets and choruses. Text and score are preserved in the municipal library, and thus it was possible to revive the opera in the spring of 1933, in the studio of Radio Königsberg. Hermann Balke was *Landmeister* of the Teutonic Knights in Prussia. He founded Elbing in 1237. Alexander Nevsky's victory over the Knights was in 1242.

—

FROM HENRY CAREY'S SONG "THE BEAU'S LAMENTATIONS FOR THE
LOSS OF FARINELLI", 1737–8

Fly Heidegger, fly, and my idol restore ;
O, let me but hear the enchanter once more,
For Handel may study, and study in vain
While Strada's expell'd, and my Broschi's in Spain.

(Chrysander, 1863, p. 362.) *The Musical Century, in One Hundred English
Ballads . . . the Words and Musick . . . by Henry Carey,* 2 Volumes, 1737–40
(II. 5). This collection, reprinted in 1740 and enlarged about 1743, consists of
single-sheet songs published earlier. Farinelli's original name was Carlo Broschi.

1738

There is no entry for 1738 in Handel's accounts with the Bank of England.
There is one entry each for 1737 and 1739.

—

From a London Newspaper, 3rd January 1738
Hay-Market.

At the King's Theatre in the Hay-Market, this Day, January the 3d, will be perform'd a New Opera, call'd FARAMONDO. . . . To begin at Six o'Clock. N.B. The remaining Silver Tickets will be deliver'd to the Subscribers this Day, on paying the Subscription, at the Office in the Hay-Market, where Subscription will be taken.

Cutting in Sir Augustus Harris' Collection. (Flower, p. 262.) The newspaper was probably the *London Daily Post*. After the Queen's death, the theatres remained closed for about six weeks. Handel was now back at the Haymarket, and once more with Heidegger. He opened the season on a Tuesday. Burney (IV. 418) thought that the first night had to be postponed till 7th January. *Faramondo* was performed on 3rd, 7th, 10th, 14th, 17th, 21st, 24th January and 16th May. The libretto was by Apostolo Zeno, with some alterations. Mainwaring (p. 124) relates that Handel received £1000 for *Faramondo* and *Alessandro Severo* (see 25th February) from Lord Middlesex ; but Middlesex did not interest himself actively in the Haymarket Theatre until the autumn of 1741.

—

Cast of " Faramondo ", 3rd January 1738
Faramondo—Signor Caffarelli, alto
Clotilda—Signora Francesina, soprano
Rosimonda—Signora Lucchesina, mezzo-soprano
Gustavo—Signor Montagnana, bass
Adolfo—Signora Chimenti, soprano
Gernando—Signora Merighi, contralto profundo
Teobaldo—Signor Lottini, bass
Childerico—Mr. Savage, (?) counter-tenor

This was a fairly new company, collected partly by Heidegger. Montagnana and Merighi, two of the apostates of 1733, were back with Handel. Signora Margherita Chimenti, called La Droghierina, also came from the Nobility Opera ; only Mr. Savage was from Handel's Covent Garden Company. Gaetano Majorano, called Caffarelli ; Elisabeth Duparc, called La Francesina ; Maria Antonia Marchesini, called La Lucchesina ; and Antonio Lottini were the four singers new to the house, the gentlemen also to London. The soprano, Signora Francesina, following Strada, was a permanent acquisition for Handel.

—

LORD WENTWORTH TO HIS FATHER, THE EARL OF STRAFFORD

London, January 3, 1738.

Mr. Hamilton has been at the rehearsal of Pharamond the new opera, and goes to it to-night. To be sure it will be vastly full, since there has not been one so long a time and a new person to sing into the [bargain].

Wentworth Papers, pp. 536 f. The last word is illegible. The "new person" was apparently La Francesina.

———

FROM A LONDON NEWSPAPER, 4th January 1738

Last Night the new Opera of *Faramondo* was perform'd at the King's Theatre to a splendid Audience, and met with general Applause. It being the first Time of Mr Handel's Appearance this Season, he was honour'd with extraordinary and repeated Signs of Approbation.

Cutting in Sir Augustus Harris's Collection. (Flower, p. 263.)

———

FROM THE "OLD WHIG", 4th January 1738

Writ after the rehearsal (in the Banqueting-House, Whitehall) of the Anthem, composed by Mr. Handell for her late Majesty's Funeral [on 16th December 1737]

Struck with the Beauties form'd by magic Dyes, [1]
From Group to group, the Eye in Transport flies ;
Till Seraph-accents, solemn, deep, and slow,
Melt on the Ear, in soft, melodious Woe.

Such Charms the two contending Arts dispense ;
So sweetly captivate each ravish'd Sense,
We ne'er can fix ; but must by Turns admire
The mimic Pencil, and the speaking Lyre.

L. [John Lockman]

(Chrysander, II. 444 f.) Cf. 15th December 1737. The ceiling of the Banqueting Hall, or House, was painted by Rubens on the continent, and the canvasses were sent to London. For Lockman, see 16th April 1736 and August 1759.

———

FROM THE "CRAFTSMAN", 7th January 1738

MUSICK.

This Day is Publish'd,

Proposals for Printing by Subscription the Opera of *Faramondo* in Score, as it is perform'd at the King's Theatre in the Hay-Market. Composed by Mr. Handel.

.   .   .   .   .

Subscriptions are taken in by John Walsh. . . .

Cf. 23rd January and 4th February.

———

[1] The Painting on the Ceiling by Rubens.

XVI. JAMES HARRIS

Oil painting, artist unknown.   (National Portrait Gallery)

See page 432

XVII. ELISABETH DUPARC, CALLED "LA FRANCESINA"

Mezzotint after George Knapton, by John Faber, 1737. (H. R. Beard Theatre Collection)

See page 447

FROM THE "DAILY POST", *c.* 15th January 1738

(In an obituary note on Samuel Humphreys.)

The admired Mr. Handel had a due Esteem for the Harmony of his Numbers ; and the great Maecenas, the Duke of Chandos, showed the Regard he had for his Muse, by so generously rewarding him for celebrating his Grace's Seat at Cannons.

(Handel Society, *Esther*, edited by Lucas, 1845, p. v.) The *Daily Post*, as well as the *London Daily Post*, from January the 1st till the 19th is not available. Humphreys died on 11th January. He arranged the *Esther* word-book in 1732 and wrote the books of *Athalia* and *Deborah* for Handel ; he also translated several Italian texts for the printed librettos, among them *Ezio, Poro, Rinaldo* (second version) and *Sosarme* ; all in 1731 and 1732. In 1728 he published "Cannons, a poem". "Numbers" here means verses.

———

LORD WENTWORTH TO HIS FATHER, THE EARL OF STAFFORD

London, January 19, 1738.

We was at Covent Garden Play House last night, my mother was so good as to treat us with it, and the Dragon of Wantcliff was the farce. I like it vastly and the musick is excessive pretty, and th' it is a burlesque on the operas yet Mr. Handel owns he thinks the tunes very well composed . . . it has been acted 36 times already and they are always pretty full. The poor operas I doubt go on but badly, for tho' every body praises both Cafferielli and the opera yet it has never been full, and if it is not now at first it will be very empty towards the latter end of the winter.

(*Wentworth Papers*, p. 539.) The writer was not quite sixteen years of age. He meant, of course, *The Dragon of Wantley* (cf. 26th October 1737) and Caffarelli in *Faramondo*.

———

FROM THE "LONDON DAILY POST", 23rd January 1738

This Day are publish'd, Proposals for Printing by Subscription, The Opera of *Faramondo*, in Score. . . .

1. The Work will be printed on good Paper.
2. The Price to Subscribers is Half a Guinea to be paid at the Time of Subscribing.
3. The whole will be corrected by the Author.
4. The Lovers of Musick, who are willing to subscribe, are desired to send in their Names immediately, the Work being in such Forwardness, that it will be ready to be deliver'd to Subscribers by the 4th of February next.

Subscriptions are taken in by John Walsh . . . and by most Musick-Shops in Town.

(Schoelcher, p. 194.)

———

H.–15

FROM THE "LONDON DAILY POST", 27th January 1738

On the 4th of February will be published, The Opera of Faramondo, in Score. . . . In a short Time will be publish'd, Alexander's Feast, an Ode, set to Musick by Mr. Handel.

Subscriptions are taken in by the Author, and John Walsh. . . .

The first sentence had already appeared in the issue of 23rd January. The last one is significant, because it was the first time that Handel admitted the public to his house ; they were dealt with, we may be sure, by a servant. His address, however, was not given until the next advertisement, on 4th February. For *Alexander's Feast*, cf. 28th May and 15th June 1737, 4th February and 14th March 1738.

———

La Conquista del Vello d'Oro, an opera by Giovanni Battista Pescetti, is produced at the Haymarket, 28th January 1738.

(Chrysander, II. 450.)

———

FROM THE "DAILY POST", 4th February 1738

This Day will be publish'd, ready to deliver to the Subscribers. The whole Opera of *Faramondo*, in Score. . . . Printed for and sold by John Walsh. . . . In a short Time will be publish'd, Alexander's Feast. . . . Subscriptions are taken in by the Author, in Brooks-street Hanover Square ; and John Walsh. . . .

The same advertisement was printed in the *Craftsman* of that day.

———

EXTRACTS FROM THE LIST OF SUBSCRIBERS FOR "FARAMONDO", PUBLISHED ON 4th February 1738

Her Royal Highness Princess Mary
Right Hon. Lord Cowper
William Freeman
Mr. Granville 2 Books
Mr. Gates, one of the Gentlemen of the Chappel Royal
James Harris 2 Books
Mr. [James] Haseltine, Organist of Durham
Iohn Harris, Organ Builder
Char. Jennens 2 Books
Sir Windham Knatchbull, Bart.
Mr. [John] Keeble

Mr. Mantel, Organist
The Musical Society at Oxford
Mr. [James] Peasable, Organist
Dr. Pepusch
Master Pepusch
Mr. [John] Robinson
Right. Hon. Earl of Shaftsbury
Mr. Iohn Stanley
Mr. [John] Simpson 10 Books
Mr. Benj: Short
Mr. Weideman
Mr. Zincke

———

Handel finishes the opera *Serse*, 14th February 1738.

—

From the " London Daily Post ", 25th February 1738

At the King's Theatre . . . this Day . . . will be perform'd an Opera, call'd ALESSANDRO SEVERO. . . . Tickets . . . half a Guinea. Gallery Five Shillings. . . . The Gallery will be open'd at Four o'Clock. Pit and Boxes at Five. To begin at Six o'Clock.

This was a pasticcio, with text by (?) Apostolo Zeno ; but it was a Handel pasticcio, with arias from *Ariadne, Arminio, Atalanta, Berenice, Ezio, Giustino, Orlando, Siroe, Radamisto* and *Riccardo Primo*. Handel added an overture, the recitatives and five new arias. A copy of the libretto, printed by J. Chrichley, is in the Schoelcher Collection at the Conservatoire, Paris. The overture is to be found in Vol. 48 of the Collected Edition of Handel's Works ; the five arias seem not to be printed. The cast may have been as follows :

> Alessandro—Signora Merighi
> Claudio—Signor Caffarelli
> Sallustia—Signora Francesina
> Albina—Signor Lucchesina
> Guilia—Signora Chimenti
> Marziano—Signor Montagnana

A manuscript score was also in Schoelcher's Collection, and now is in the State Library of Hamburg. No copy of Walsh's *Favourite Songs* (see 8th March) is known. The pasticcio was performed on 25th, 28th February ; 4th, 7th, 11th March, and 30th May. Cf. the Handel pasticcio of " Hermann von Balcke ", Elbing, 1737.

—

Alcina is performed in Italian at Brunswick, February 1738. (Loewenberg, p. 94.)

—

From the " London Daily Post ", 2nd March 1738

Next Week will be publish'd,

And ready to be delivered to the Subscribers, by the Author at his House in Brook-street, Hanover-square ; and by John Walsh in Catherine-street, *Alexander's Feast. An Ode.* Wrote in Honour of St. Cecilia. By Mr. Dryden. Set to Musick by Mr. Handel.

Note, Whereas a Print of the Author is now engraving by an eminent Hand, and is very near finish'd ; those Noblemen, Gentlemen and Ladies, who have done the Author the Honour of Subscribing, may be assured, as soon as it is finish'd, it shall be sent to their Houses, by John Walsh, the Undertaker of this Work for the Author.

(Schoelcher, p. 198 f., corrected by Chrysander, II. 429.) Although it appears from Walsh's Cash-Book, under the date of 1737, that Handel received £105 for *Alexander's Feast* as a lump sum, this advertisement indicates a quite different arrangement, with Handel as publisher of his own work, and Walsh as his agent.

Any payment from Walsh to Handel should have been a transfer, less commission. The engraved portrait of Handel was a premium for the subscriber, and a surprise.

———

FROM THE " LONDON DAILY POST ", 3rd March 1738

For the Benefit of Master Fery, who performs the Punch and Burgo-master, Scholar to Mons. Livier. At the Royal Theatre in Drury-Lane, this Day . . . will be performed a Concert of Vocal and Instrumental Musick. By the best Hands. Consisting of several select Pieces composed by Mr. Handel and other eminent Masters, and taken from the favourite Operas. The vocal Parts by Mr. Beard and Mrs. Clive, being several favourite Songs in Italian and English. . . . Likewise a Preamble on the Kettle-Drums by Master Fery, Concluding with the Anthem, *God save the King* . . . with two new Minuets, and a Chorus out of Atalanta for French Horns and Trumpets, the two French Horns to be performed by two little Negro-Boys, Scholars to Mr. Charles, who never performed before.

(Chrysander, 1863, p. 291 f.) Fery apparently did not become a master, but Mr. Charles was very well known in London and Dublin about 1740. The Anthem, called here " God save the King " for the first time, is the third, and last, section of " Zadok the Priest ", one of Handel's four Coronation Anthems of 1727.

———

Comus, a mask, altered from Milton by John Dalton with music by Thomas Augustine Arne, is produced at Drury Lane Theatre, 4th March 1738.

Comus, played by James Quin, opens the third Act with a speech, in which four phrases from Milton's *L' Allegro ed Il Penseroso* are quoted : " Hence, loathed Melancholy ", " Come, thou Goddess ", " Haste thee, Nymph " and " Come, and trip it ". The speech is recited, not sung. This fact led later writers and musicians to assume that Arne's *Comus* had some music by Handel inserted, although he did not set *L' Allegro ed Il Penseroso* until 1740. Samuel Arnold inserted in a manuscript score the corresponding numbers from Handel's work, and Cummings (1912, pp. 13, 25) started the fable that all choruses in Arne's *Comus* were borrowed from Handel. The fact that the opening bars of Arne's chorus " Away, away " were identical with the hunting chorus in Handel's *Parnasso in Festa* impressed Cummings so much that his judgment went astray. (Based on information kindly given by Mr. Julian Herbage.) *Comus* remained in the repertoire of Drury Lane and Covent Garden during the rest of Handel's life. On the first night Mr. Beard, Mrs. Clive and Mrs. Arne sang the vocal parts.

———

FROM THE " LONDON DAILY POST ", 8th March 1738

This Day is published, Price 1s. 6d. The Favourite Songs in the Opera call'd *Alexander Severo*, in Score. By Mr. *Handel*. Printed for and sold by John Walsh. . . . Where may be had, . . . *Alexander's Feast*. . . .

(Chrysander, II. 448.) No copy of the selection from *Alessandro Severo* is known. *Alexander's Feast* was advertised as ready and published in the *Craftsman* of 11th March.

—

EXTRACTS FROM THE LIST OF SUBSCRIBERS FOR " ALEXANDER'S FEAST ", PUBLISHED ON 8th (11th ?) March 1738

His Royal Highness, the Prince of Wales
His Royal Highness, the Duke of Cumberland
Her Royal Highness, the Princess of Orange
Her Royal Highness, the Princess Amelia
Her Royal Highness, the Princess Caroline
Her Royal Highness, the Princess Mary
  and the Princess Louisa.
Apollo Society at Windsor
Accademy for Vocal Musick in Dublin
Rt. Hon. Lady Burlington
Rt. Hon. Earl Cowper
Rt. Hon. Thos Carter, Master of the Rolls in Ireland.
  Two Books.
Mr. [Richard] Church, Org. of New College, Oxon.
Mr. [John] Church, at Dublin
Wm. Freeman
M. C. Festing
B. Granville
Dr. Green(e)
Bernard Gates, Master of the Children, and one of y^e
  Gentlemen of his Majesty' Chappel-Royal
Iohn Harris, Organ Builder
James Harris
James Haseltine, Organist of Durham
Wm. Hayes, of Oxon
Charles Jennens. Six Books.
Sir Windham Knatchbull, Bart. Two Books.
Mr. [John] Keeble
Musical Society of Oxon.
Musical Society on Wednesday at the Crown and Anchor
Musical Society at Exeter
Philharmonic Society. Two Books.
Iohn Pigott, Organist of Windsor
Rt. Hon. Earl of Shaftesbury
Rt. Hon. Countess of Shaftesbury
Rt. Hon. Countess Dowager of Shaftesbury
Mr. [Benjamin] Short

Iohn Christopher Smith
Iohn Stanley
Charles Weideman
Wm. Wheeler, Organist of Newbury
Mr. [Christian Frederick] Zinck(e)

The names of the Royal children are printed in the middle of the page. There were 124 subscribers for 146 copies. The subscription had been open since 28th March 1737 : nearly one year. The title of the score is " Alexander's Feast or the Power of Musick . . . With the Recitativo's, Songs, Symphonys and Chorus's for Voices & Instruments, Together with the Cantata, Duet, and Songs, as Perform'd at the Theatre Royal, in Covent Garden. Publish'd by the Author. London. Printed for & Sold by J. Walsh . . .". The cantata is " Cecilia volgi ", the duet " Tra amplessi innocenti ", and the additional song, sung by Annibali, " Sei del ciel dono perfetto ". The score has 193 pp. large folio. The price was two guineas. The engraved portrait was delivered afterwards, and not as part of the score. Chrysander (II. 430) quotes Horace Walpole's *Memoirs* (III. 304 f) : " In truth, I believe King George would have preferred a guinea to a composition as perfect as Alexander's Feast ". It seems, however, it was not usual during the eighteenth century for a King to subscribe for a book or for music. To allow his children to subscribe was certainly a royal favour, and more lucrative to the author.

———

From the " London Daily Post ", 10th March 1738

For the Benefit of Mr. Adcock.

At the *Swan Tavern* in *Cornhill*, this Day, will be performed A Grand *Concert* of *Vocal* and *Instrumental* Musick. . . . The Concert to conclude with the Coronation Anthem, call'd *God save the King*, compos'd by Mr. Handell.

(Chrysander, 1863, p. 292.) There was a trumpet player, Abraham Adcock, at the Three Choirs meetings, about 1755.

———

From the " Craftsman ", 11th March 1738

Musick, this Day is Publish'd, And ready to be deliver'd to the Subscribers, by the Author, at his House in Brook-Street, Hanover-Square. Alexander's Feast. . . . Printed for and sold by John Walsh. . . .

(Smith, 1948, p. 127 f.) Chrysander, II. 429, quotes the advertisement in the *London Daily Post* of 14th March. Cf. 8th March.

———

Partenio, an opera by Francesco Veracini, is produced at the Haymarket, 14th March 1738.

(Chrysander, II. 450.)

———

FROM THE " LONDON DAILY POST ", 28th March 1738

Hay-Market.

For the Benefit of Mr. *Handel,*

At the King's Theatre in the Hay-Market, this Day . . . will be performed AN ORATORIO. With a Concert on the Organ. . . . To begin at Six o'Clock.

N.B. For the better Conveniency there will be Benches upon the Stage.

(Burney, IV. 426 ; Schoelcher, p. 195 ; Chrysander, II. 449 f.) The time was the Passion Week. The word-book, a copy of which is in King's College, Cambridge, and another in New York Public Library, shows that what Handel offered his guests was not an oratorio, but a selection of sacred and secular music, English and Italian. The concert consisted of three sections. In Part One there was the Chandos Anthem " As pants the hart ", in Part Two arias from *Deborah,* in Part Three the Coronation Anthem " My heart is inditing ", as well as several other songs and duets. According to Burney the net receipts were not less than £800 ; when Mainwaring (p. 125) spoke of £1500 it was an exaggeration. (See next entry.) In his sketch of Handel's life (1785, p. 24), Burney relates that there were five hundred people on the stage alone, the benches being arranged in the form of an amphitheatre.

———

FROM THE EARL OF EGMONT'S DIARY, 28th March 1738

In the evening I went to Hendel's Oratorio, where I counted near 1,300 persons besides the gallery and upper gallery. I suppose he got this night 1,000*l.*

(Egmont MSS., II. 474.) Jonathan Tyers, the owner of Vauxhall Gardens, paid for fifty tickets (see 18th April).

———

FROM WALSH'S CASH-BOOK, (SPRING) 1738

1738   Opera Xerxes   .   .   .   £26   5   0

The opera was finished in February, produced in April and published in May.

———

FROM THE " LONDON DAILY POST ", 15th April 1738

The Effigie of Mr. Handel the famous Composer of Musick, is going to be put in Vaux-Hall-Gardens, at the Expence of Mr. Jonathan Tyers.

(Burney, IV. 428.) Tyers was the owner of this establishment, which had been opened about six years earlier. To erect a monument to a living artist was, and is, quite extraordinary.

———

FROM THE SAME

At the King's Theatre . . . this Day . . . will be perform'd a New Opera, call'd XERXES. . . . To begin at Six o'clock.

(Burney, IV. 423, 425.) The text was an arrangement of Niccolò Minato's libretto, first composed by Francesco Cavalli in 1654 (Loewenberg, p. 98). This was the only opera of Handel's with a comic plot, although the famous " Largo ", sung to the words " Ombra mai fu ", occurs in it. Repeat performances on 18th, 22nd, 25th April and 2nd May.

———

CAST OF " SERSE ", 15th April 1738

Serse—Signor Caffarelli, soprano
Arsamene—Signora Lucchesina, mezzo-soprano
Amastre—Signora Merighi, contralto profundo
Romilda—Signora Francesina, soprano
Atalanta—Signora Chimenti, contralto
Ariodate—Signor Montagnana, bass
Elviro—Signor Lottini, bass

———

FROM THE " LONDON DAILY POST ", 18th April 1738

We are informed from very good Authority ; that there is now near finished a Statue of the justly celebrated Mr. Handel, exquisitely done by the ingenious Mr. Raubillac, of St. Martin's-Lane, Statuary, out of one entire Block of white Marble, which is to be placed in a grand Nich, erected on Purpose in the great Grove at Vaux-hall-Gardens, at the sole Expence of Mr. Tyers, Undertaker of the Entertainment there ; who in Consideration of the real Merit of that inimitable Master, thought it proper, that his Effigies should preside there, where his Harmony has so often charm'd even the greatest Crouds into the profoundest Calm and most decent Behaviour ; it is believed, that the Expence of the Statue and Nich cannot cost less than Three Hundred Pounds ; the said Gentleman likewise very generously took at Mr. Handel's Benefit Fifty of his Tickets.

(Burney, IV. 428.) Louis François Roubiliac, who later made Handel's monument in Westminster Abbey, was a young sculptor, and this statue was his first public success. Handel must have sat for him. The statue is still in existence, in Novello's publishing house. It was first removed, within Vauxhall, from the grove to a small temple in the centre of the Gardens. The orchestra in Vauxhall played an assortment of music and sometimes included pieces by Handel. A statue of Milton, in lead, ordered later for the Gardens, is lost.

———

FROM THE " CRAFTSMAN ", 22nd April 1738

This Day is publish'd (And are ready to be deliver'd to the Subscribers for Alexander's Feast) A Print of Mr. Handel. Engraved by the celebrated Mr. Houbraken of Amsterdam. The Ornaments design'd by Mr. Gravelot. Printed for John Walsh. . . .

(Smith, 1948, p. 128.) Jacob Houbraken, the Dutchman, worked for London, and Hubert François Gravelot, the Frenchman, lived there for a time. The portrait was the well-known, and often imitated, half-length, with the scene from *Alexander's Feast* under the oval of Handel's likeness. The only copy known of the original state, without the later inscription, is in the Fitzwilliam Museum, Cambridge. (Cf. *Music & Letters*, July 1949, p. 261.) Chrysander, II. 430, who was not able to identify the portrait, thought it might have been by Hogarth.

———

The first meeting of the subscribers for the Fund for the Support of Decayed Musicians and their Families is held, 23rd April 1738.

The immediate cause of the foundation was the death of the impoverished Jean Christian Kytch, the oboist (see 23rd August 1720), in St. James's Market, and the subsequent discovery, by Festing, Weideman and Vincent, of his two neglected boys in the Haymarket. Handel was a subscriber from the beginning.

The first meeting, as well as the next on 7th May, was held at the "Crown and Anchor" Tavern, a favourite haunt of musicians and music lovers. It is usually assumed that this first meeting was on 19th April (Chrysander, III. 15), but the present Secretary of the Royal Society of Musicians of Great Britain assured the compiler of these documents that the date was the 23rd (see 7th May 1738).

———

From the "London Daily Post", 24th April 1738

This Day are published, Proposals for Printing by Subscription, The Opera of *Xerxes*. Compos'd by Mr. Handel. Which will be ready to be deliver'd by the 20th of May. Printed for John Walsh. . . . Where may be had, To which is prefix'd a curious Print of the Author, Alexander's Feast. . . .

Serse was the last opera score by Handel which it was intended to print by subscription. The publication was delayed until 30th May. Only one copy is known of *Alexander's Feast* with the engraved portrait, apparently as originally delivered; it is in the Rowe Music Library, King's College. Cambridge. Chrysander (II. 429) quotes the last sentence from the issue of 18th May.

———

From the "London Daily Post", 26th April 1738

(Advertisement of revival of *Arsaces* on 2nd May.)

    .   .   .   .   .

N.B. Having been impossible to perform the whole Number of Opera's this Season, each Subscriber may have a Ticket extraordinary deliver'd to him each Night the Opera is perform'd, upon sending his Silver Ticket to the Office.

(Chrysander, II. 456.) Burney, II. 426, explains that the number of performances promised to the subscribers could not be achieved owing to the stoppage occasioned by the six weeks' mourning in autumn 1737; this happened, of course, in Heidegger's time before Handel joined him in January 1738. *Arsace* (see 29th October 1737) was not revived until 9th May, and was then performed once only.

———

FROM THE "LONDON DAILY POST", 27th April 1738

The same Day [the 26th] a Statue of Mr. Handel, in Marble, was carried over the Water, to be put up in Vaux-Hall Gardens.

(Chrysander, III. 9.)

———

FROM THE "LONDON MAGAZINE", April 1738

To Mr. HANDEL. *Occasion'd by hearing a late Piece of Musick compos'd by him. By Mr.* BLYTHE.

N.B. *This Gentleman is now printing* a Collection *of his* Poems *by* Subscription.

> When *Orpheus* warbled on his flute, 'tis said,
> All nature danc'd to the sweet tunes he play'd :
> Exulting hills, with sympathetick life,
> Mov'd to the measures of his quick'ning fife :
> The listening trees, enamour'd with his notes,
> Trail'd after him their pompous length of roots :
> The wond'ring fry leap'd from their native main,
> And sought the shore, attracted by his strain :
> The feather'd quires forsook their rural bounds,
> Drawn by the magick of his moving sounds :
> His musick wou'd the lion's fury 'swage ;
> Tame hungry wolves, and quell the tiger's rage.
> Thus fiction tells of him, what now we see
> Heighten'd, oh *Handel*, and made true in thee.
> What thing so lifeless but thy lyre can move ?
> What rage so fierce but thou can'st tune to love ?
> If he attentive nature drew, before ;
> Thou canst attract her with a sweeter power.
> Were he on earth again to stand the test,
> His sounds, compar'd with thine, were noise confess'd :
> And the green laurel, he now wears, the nine
> Would justly from his brow transfer to thine.

Mr. Blythe's subscription seems not to have been successful. In fact, nothing is known about him.

———

FROM THE "LONDON DAILY POST", 2nd May 1738

Last Night the Entertainment of the Spring-Gardens, *Vaux-Hall*, was opened, and there was a considerable Appearance of Persons of both Sexes. The several Pieces of Music play'd on that Occasion had never [been] heard before in the Gardens. The Company express'd great Satisfaction at the Marble Statue of Mr. *Handel*, who is represented in a loose Robe, striking the Lyre, and listening to the Sounds ; which a little Boy,

carv'd at his Feet, seems to be writing down on the back of the Violoncello. The whole Composition is in a very elegant Taste.

(Schoelcher, p. 198.) The little genius at Handel's feet is writing down what he
sings on a leaf of paper, which lies on the back of a violin.

———

FROM THE LIST OF SUBSCRIBERS, PRINTED IN THE RULES OF THE
FUND FOR THE SUPPORT OF DECAYED MUSICIANS AND THEIR
FAMILIES, 7th May 1738

G. F. Handel, Esq.

(Schoelcher, p. 364 f.) This refers to the second meeting of the Fund ; cf. 23rd
April 1738. The first subscribers were the composers : Arne, Boyce, Carey,
Greene, Galliard, Handel, Hayes, W. Jackson, Leveridge, Pepusch, Smith and
Worgan ; and the virtuosi : Caporale, Courteville, Festing, Kelway, Rosein-
grave, Reading, Stanley, Vincent and Weideman. (Schoelcher also mentions
Keeble and Cervetto, but apparently by mistake.) Festing and Greene were the
moving spirits. The name of the Fund was later altered into the Society for the
Relief of Distressed Musicians, and finally into the Royal Society of Musicians of
Great Britain.

———

ABSTRACT OF THE LAW AND RESOLUTIONS OF THE FUND FOR THE
SUPPORT OF DECAYED MUSICIANS AND THEIR FAMILIES

May 8, 1738.

Whereas a Subscription was set on foot the beginning of the last
month, for establishing a FUND *for the Support of Decayed Musicians, or
their Families* ; which Subscription having already met with uncommon
success, the Subscribers have had two General Meetings, in order to form
themselves into a regular Society, by the name of THE SOCIETY OF
MUSICIANS, and have elected Twelve Governors for the present year ;
and also agreed to the following resolutions. . . .

(Burney, 1785, part 3, pp. 129 f. ; Smith, 1948, p. 168.)

———

FROM THE " COMMON SENSE : OR THE ENGLISHMAN'S JOURNAL ",
13th May 1738

To the Author of Common Sense.

Sir,

. . . *Wednesdays* and *Fridays* in *Lent*, have, for several Ages, been
appropriated for Fasting and Divine Worship, in the Churches of *England*
and *Rome*, and the Clergy of both have always zealously recommended
the strict Observance of them by their *pious Examples* ; but those Days
were never totally engrossed for Sacred Purposes, for Men were always
allowed to pursue their proper Employments ; and in our Days the
celebrated *Handell* has often exhibited his Oratorio's to the Town without

any Prohibition ; but every Body knows his Entertainments are calculated for the Quality only, and that People of moderate Fortunes cannot
pretend to them, although, as Free *Britons*, they have as good a Right to
be entertained with what they do not understand as their Betters.

Whether Mr. *Handell* has a License from the Ecclesiastical Court, or
from the Licensers of the Stage, for playing on *Wednesdays* and *Fridays*, I
can not tell ; but if he has not, I must think the Restraint laid on the
facetious Mr. *Punch*, from acting on those Days, seems a little partial ;
for he has at least as good a Pretence to the same Liberty, especially
considering the submissive Remonstrance and candid Office made by him
in his Petition to the Licenser of the Stage. . . .

                                       I am,
Dick's Coffee house   *Yours*, etc.
Temple Bar, 10th April.   *A. D.*

To the Worshipful Licensers of the STAGE,
The humble PETITION *of* PUNCH, *Master of the artificial Company
of Comedians in the* Haymarket.

                .   .   .   .   .

As Oratorio's have a Sanction for being founded upon Scripture
History, and on that Account are suffered to be exhibited on *Wednesdays*
and *Fridays* in *Lent*, Mr. *Punch* intends to divert the Town the ensuing
Lent with several entertaining Pieces of the same Kind, particularly, *the
History of Bell and the Dragon*, and *the Life and Death of* Haman, *Prime
Minister to King* Ahasuerus ; and between the Acts, *Punch* will perform
several serious Dances to the Organ, in the Habit of a Cardinal or an
Archbishop.

(Chrysander, II. 407 f.) Reprinted in the *London Magazine* of May 1738, p. 228.
Cf. 27th May. Chrysander, who recognized Sir Robert Walpole in the Haman
of the second letter, suggested Henry Fielding as author of both letters.

———

Walsh announces that the score of *Serse* will " be ready to be
deliver'd by the latter End of May ", *London Daily Post*, 16th
May 1738.

On the same day, *Faramondo* was performed once more.

———

FROM THE " LONDON DAILY POST ", 24th May 1738

                                           May 23, 1738.
All Persons that have subscrib'd or are willing to subscribe twenty
Guineas for an Italian Opera to be perform'd next Season at the King's
Theatre in the Hay-Market, under my Direction, are desired to send ten
Guineas to Mr. Drummond the Banker who will give them a Receipt,
to return the Money in case the Opera should not go on, and whereas

I declared I would undertake the Opera's provided I can agree with the Performers, and that 200 Subscriptions are procured, and as the greatest Part of the Subscribers have already paid the 10 Guineas ; it is desired that the remaining Subscribers will be pleased to send the Money to Mr. Drummond, on or before the 5th of June next, that I may take my Measures, either to undertake the Opera if the Money is paid, or give them up in case the Money is not paid, it being impossible to make the necessary Preparations, or to Contract with the Singers after that Time.

J. J. Heidegger.

(Chrysander, II. 451.) It is noteworthy that Handel's name is not even mentioned here. He was not Heidegger's associate, but his music director. Cf. 26th July. The name of Drummond is mentioned, at about the same time, as collecting money for the Foundling Hospital (Chrysander, III. 15 f.).

———

From the " London Daily Post ", 24th May 1738

In a few Days will be published, The Opera of *Xerxes*. . . .
N.B. Those Gentlemen, &c. who intend to subscribe are desir'd to send in their Names immediately.
Printed for John Walsh. . . .

———

Prince George William Frederic (son of the Prince of Wales), later George III, born 24th May 1738.

———

From the " Common Sense ", 27th May 1738

I made a Visit the other Morning to a Friend, at his Chambers in the *Temple*, and found him engaged with an ingenious Mechanick, who is the Maker of a certain little Musical Instrument, which, of late, is carried in the Pockets of all your Men of Wit and Pleasure about the Town. . . . As Operas were going down, he [the Artist] did not doubt but *Myn Heer Handel* himself would compose for it. . . .

In the book edition, Vol. II, 1739, pp. 97 and 100. Although this passage was not intended to be taken seriously, Handel had, in fact, something to do with mechanical musical instruments ; cf. William Barclay Squire, " Handel's Clock Music ", in the *Musical Quarterly*, New York, October 1919. For Mynheer Handel, cf. 6th March 1711 ; 17th October 1724 ; May 1725, and October 1729.

———

Walsh advertises the score of *Serse* as published, *London Daily Post*, 30th May 1738.

(Chrysander, II. 449.) It appeared without list of subscribers (cf. 24th April and 24th May) ; the demand was apparently too small.

———

FROM THE " LONDON MAGAZINE ", May 1738

The four underwritten Copies of Verses are ascrib'd to
Mr. LOCKMAN.

Suppos'd to be written under the Statue, *representing*
Mr. HANDEL, *in* Vauxhall-Gardens.

Drawn by the fame of these imbower'd retreats,
Orpheus is come from the *Elysian* seats ;
Lost to th' admiring world three thousand years,
Beneath lov'd *Handel*'s form he re-appears.
Sweetly this miracle attracts the eye :
But hark ! for o'er the lyre his fingers fly.

ANOTHER.

Fam'd *Orpheus* drew the *Thracians* with his lyre ;
The *Britons Handel*'s sweeter power admire :
O hear his strains, and this bright circle view,
You'll think this tributary marble due !

Seeing the Marble Statue (*carv'd by Mr.* Roubillac)
representing Mr. Handel, *in* Spring Gardens, Vauxhall.

That *Orpheus* drew a grove, a rock, a stream
By musick's power, will not a fiction seem ;
For here as great a miracle is shown—
Fam'd *Handel* breathing, tho' transformed to stone.

.   .   .   .   .

To be written under the Effigies of Mr. Handel *in*
Vaux-Hall *Gardens.*

ACROSTICK.

*H*igh as thy *genius,* on the wings of *fame,*
*A*round the *world* spreads thy *all-tuneful name.*
*N*ature, who *form'd* thee with peculiar care,
*D*id *art* employ, to *draw* a *copy here,*
*E*mblem of *that great self* ! whilst yet you live
*L*ending such *helps,* your *better part* can give.
                                    J. A. Hesse.

Upon Handel'*s Statue being placed in* Spring-Garden
at Vaux-Hall.

As in debate the tuneful sisters stood,
In what sequester'd shade, or hallow'd wood,
Should *Handel*'s statue (musick's master !) stand,
In which fair art well mimicks nature's hand ;

Thus spoke the god, that with enliv'ning rays,
Glads the whole earth, and crowns the bard
" Here bid the marble rise, be this the place,
" The haunt of ev'ry muse, and ev'ry grace ;
" Where harmony resides, and beauties rove :
" Where should he stand but in *Apollo's* grove ? "

(Burney, IV. 429 ; Schoelcher, p. 198.) Of the four poems by John Lockman,
the fourth, not reprinted here, is addressed to Roubiliac, but refers to other works
of the sculptor. The author of the acrostic is otherwise unknown. The last poem
is anonymous. Lockman's first poem was reprinted, with some alterations, in his
" Sketch of the Spring Gardens, Vauxhall, in a Letter to a Noble Lord ", *i.e.* the
Earl of Baltimore, London, *c.* 1762 ; no copy of this sketch is known, but an
extract was reprinted in the catalogue of the sale of Handel's statue, 16th March
1833 (copy in Gerald Coke's Handel Collection ; the statue went to the Sacred
Harmonic Society, and only later to Novello's). Lockman's third poem was also
reprinted in the sale catalogue. His fourth poem was entitled " To my friend Mr.
Roubillac, the Sculptor, after viewing his Rape of Lucretia, and other Models ".
In the June issue of the *London Magazine* appeared another poem : " To the Master
of Vaux-hall Gardens, on his employing the ingenious Mr. Roubillac to carve the
Statue of Mr. Handel ", signed : I. W., who compares Tyers with Maecenas.

———

FROM GEORGE BICKHAM'S " MUSICAL ENTERTAINER ", 6th June 1738

Come, Mira, Idol of ye Swains,
(So green ye Sprays, the Sky so fine,)
To Bow'rs where heav'n-born Flora reigns
And Handel warbles Airs divine.

The first volume of the beautifully ornamented collection of songs called the
Musical Entertainer, edited by Richard Vincent and engraved by George Bickham,
appeared in 1738. This extract is from song No. 2 in Vol. II, the sheet dated
" According to ye late Act [of Parliament], 6 June 1738 ". The title of the song
is : " The Invitation to Mira, Requesting Her Company to Vaux Hall Garden ",
the words by John Lockman (see May), the music by Thomas Gladwin, with a
vignette showing Handel's statue, engraved by Bickham junior after Gravelot (see
22nd April). Another view of Handel's statue illustrates an anonymous song,
" The Pleasures of Life ", sung at new Sadler's Wells " and issued as No. 6 of Vol.
II in 1740.

———

The season at the Haymarket Theatre ends on 6th June 1738 with
Partenio.

(Burney, IV. 426.)

———

FROM THE " LONDON DAILY POST ", 21st June 1738

On Saturday last [the 17th] set out for Breda Signiora Strada del Po,
to which Place she goes in Obedience to the Command of her Royal
Highness the Princess of Orange, from whence she intends to go to Italy ;
but before her Departure desires that the British Nobility and Gentry

(from whom she has received so many signal Marks of Favour) might be acquainted that it is no ways owing to her, that the present Scheme for performing Opera's next Winter in the Haymarket, under the Direction of Mr. Heydegger, has miscarried, as has been maliciously reported : she having agreed with Mr. Heydegger above a Month ago, as the said Gentleman can testify.

(Chrysander, II. 451 f.) This farewell notice was apparently written by Aurelio del Po ; cf. 9th June 1732. It has to be remembered that Signora Strada did not sing for Handel after June 1737, but she remained in London and was willing to come to a new agreement. Whether Handel was really offended by the alleged persecutions, on the part of her husband, for arrears of her salary, or whether her voice did not satisfy him any more, we do not know. She still enjoyed the favour of Princesse Anne, whom she had visited two years before (see 5th October 1736). She never returned to England. For Heidegger's scheme, see 26th July 1738.

———

I. W.'s poem addressed to Jonathan Tyers, as the Maecenas who ordered Roubiliac's statue of Handel, appears in the *London Magazine*, June 1738.

Cf. May 1738.

———

From the " London Daily Post ", 4th July 1738

We hear from Oxford, that on Thursday the 13th Instant (being in the Act Week) will be perform'd in a grand Manner, at the Theatre, Alexander's Feast, for the Benefit of Mr. Church and Mr. Hayes.

(Chrysander, II. 429.) John Church was a chorister ; William Hayes was organist of Magdalen College, Oxford, later Professor of Music there.

———

From the King's Warrant Book, 5th July 1738

£   s.   d.

Royal Academy of Music   1,000   0   0   Same [*i.e.*, Royal bounty] for the undertakers of the Opera.

(Calendar of Treasury Papers, 1735–8, p. 597.) There is no corresponding entry in the Treasury Minute Book. Cf. 16th February 1722 and 30th August 1731. After an interval of four years Handel participated again in the Royal subsidy, if only through Heidegger, the sole undertaker. See 9th June 1742.

———

Handel begins the oratorio *Saul*, about 23rd July 1738.

———

From the " London Daily Post ", 26th July 1738

Hay-Market.

July 25, 1738.

Whereas the Opera's for the ensuing Season at the King's Theatre in the Hay-Market, cannot be carried on as was intended, by Reason of the Subscription not being full, and that I could not agree with the Singers th' I offer'd One Thousand Guineas to One of them : I therefore think myself oblig'd to declare, that I give up the Undertaking for next Year, and that Mr. Drummond will be ready to repay the Money paid in, upon the Delivery of his Receipt ; I also take this Opportunity to return my humble Thanks to all Persons, who were pleas'd to contribute towards my Endeavours of carrying on that Entertainment.

J. J. Heidegger.

(Chrysander, II. 452.) Cf. 23rd (24th) May. The thousand guineas were apparently not offered to Signora Strada, who had a smaller salary and would have come to an agreement with Heidegger, but probably to Caffarelli. Of Handel's singers some stayed on : Signore Francesina and Lucchesina, as well as Mr. Savage. Beard and Waltz returned to him ; so did Mrs. Arne-Young.

MISS ELIZABETH ROBINSON TO THE DUCHESS OF PORTLAND (July 1738)

I arrived at Mount Morris rather more fond of society than solitude. I thought it no very agreeable change of scene from Handel and Cafferelli.

(Montagu, Correspondence, p. 27.) Miss Robinson married, in 1742, Edward Montagu, grandson of the Earl of Sandwich. For the Duchess of Portland, cf. 12th July 1734. The letter was an answer to one from the Duchess, dated 30th June 1738. Mount Morris, near Hythe, was the home of the Robinsons. Both ladies had returned to their homes after the London season.

FROM THE " LONDON DAILY POST ", 21st August 1738

On Saturday last [the 19th] the Entertainment of the Spring-Gardens, Vaux-hall, ended for this Season ; great Numbers of People came to it, th' the Evening was cold, and seem'd to threaten Rain. The whole was conducted with the usual Decency, and concluded with the Coronation Anthem, by Mr. Handel. The Company seem'd greatly satisfied on that Occasion.

(Schoelcher, p. 196.) Cf. 2nd May. The " Coronation Anthem " was apparently " God save the King " from Zadok the Priest. In 1740 Handel wrote a hornpipe, " composed for the Concert at Vauxhall " (Schoelcher, p. 196).

Handel begins the opera Imeneo, 9th September 1738.

JENNENS TO LORD GUERNSEY, 19th September 1738

Queen's Square, London, 19 September 1738.

Mr. Handel's head is more full of maggots than ever. I found yesterday in his room a very queer instrument which he calls carillon (Anglice, a bell) and says some call it a Tubalcain, I suppose because it is both in the make and tone like a set of Hammers striking upon anvils. 'Tis played upon with keys like a Harpsichord and with this Cyclopean instrument he designs to make poor Saul stark mad. His second maggot is an organ of £500 price which (because he is overstocked with money) he has bespoke of one Moss of Barnet. This organ, he says, is so constructed that as he sits at it he has a better command of his performers than he used to have, and he is highly delighted to think with what exactness his Oratorio will be performed by the help of this organ ; so that for the future instead of beating time at his oratorios, he is to sit at the organ all the time with his back to the Audience. His third maggot is a Hallelujah which he has trump'd up at the end of his oratorio since I went into the Country, because he thought the conclusion of the oratorio not Grand enough ; tho' if that were the case 'twas his own fault, for the words would have bore as Grand Musick as he could have set 'em to : but this Hallelujah, Grand as it is, comes in very nonsensically, having no manner of relation to what goes before. And this is the more extraordinary, because he refused to set a Hallelujah at the end of the first Chorus in the Oratorio, where I had placed one and where it was to be introduced with the utmost propriety, upon a pretence that it would make the entertainment too long. I could tell you more of his maggots : but it grows late and I must defer the rest till I write next, by which time, I doubt not, more new ones will breed in his Brain.

(Flower, p. 271 f.) Original in the archives of the Aylesford family. Jennens was the cousin of the second Earl of Aylesford, and Lord Guernsey (see 6th July 1733) was his son. The oratorio referred to is *Saul*, text by Jennens, finished at the end of the month. Handel used the carillon for the chorus " Welcome, mighty King " and the Sinfonia in Act I of *Saul* ; his description of it as Tubalcain, the smith in the Old Testament, was probably a joke. The small chamber organ, which allowed the free sight above the instruments, was built by Dr. Jonathan Morse (cf. 18th April 1750). The reference to Handel's finances is, of course, ironical. As for the position of the " Hallelujah " in the oratorio, Handel seems to have yielded to Jennens's protestations.

———

From the " London Daily Post ", 20th September 1738

This Day is publish'd, The Lady's Entertainment, 5th Book. Being a Collection of the most favourite Airs from the late Opera's, set for the Harpsichord or Spinnet. To which is prefixed the celebrated Organ Concerto, Compos'd by Mr. Handel. Printed for and sold by John Walsh. . . .

The book contains six arias from *Serse* and two from *Faramondo*. The concerto is the second in the first set of organ concertos, published on 4th October. Copy in King's College, Cambridge. The first four books of the *Lady's Entertainment* appeared about 1710 and contain nothing by Handel.

———

FROM THE "LONDON DAILY POST", 25th September 1738

To all *Lovers* of *Musick*.

Whereas there is a spurious and incorrect Edition of Six Concerto's of Mr. Handel's for the Harpsicord and Organ, publish'd without the Knowledge or Consent of the Author,

This is to give *Notice*,

(That the Publick may not be imposed on with a mangled Edition) That there are now printing from Mr. Handel's original Manuscript, and corrected by himself, the same Six Concerto's, which will be published in a few Days. Price 3s.

Printed for John Walsh. . . .

(Schoelcher, p. 201 : text altered ; Chrysander, III. 159 : dated 25th November.) The pirated first edition was entitled : *Six Concertos for the Harpsichord or Organ by Mr. Handel. Sold at the Musick Shops*, exactly as Walsh senior used to imprint his pirated editions. The original edition of the harpsichord or organ part only appeared on 4th October, cheaper than usual, on account of the competition.

—

Handel finishes the oratorio *Saul*, about 27th September 1738.

—

FROM WALSH'S CASH-BOOK, 28th September 1738

1738, Sept. 28th, six organ concertos in p. . . £26 5 0

" In p." means in parts. Opus 4 was published on 4th October.

—

Handel begins the oratorio *Israel in Egypt*, 1st October 1738.

—

FROM THE "LONDON DAILY POST", 4th October 1738

NEW MUSICK.

This Day is published, Price 3s.

Six Concerto's for the Harpsichord, or Organ.

Compos'd by Mr. *Handel*.

*** These Six Concerto's were publish'd by Mr. Walsh from my own Copy corrected by my self, and to him only I have given my Right therein.

George Frideric Handel.

Printed for and sold by John Walsh. . . .

In a few Days will be published,

The Instrumental Parts to the above Six Organ Concerto's.

(Chrysander, III. 159.) This was the harpsichord part only, without opus number, but with Handel's note on the title-page. The orchestral parts followed on 2nd December, with the opus number 4. The price for the whole was then 10s. 6d. In the advertisements the work is not called Opus 4 until 18th January 1739.

———

FROM WALSH'S CASH-BOOK, 7th October 1738

1738, Oct. 7th, six new sonatas   .   . £26 5 0

These are the seven (not six) sonatas for two violins and bass, published on 3rd March 1739 as Opus 5.

———

A LEAF FROM THE CASH-BOOK OF THE PUBLISHERS, JOHN WALSH SENIOR AND JUNIOR, 1721–7, October 1738

1722	Opera	Otho .					£ 42	0	0
1721	,,	Floridan					,, 72	0	0
1723	,,	Flavio					,, 26	5	0
1729	,,	Parthenope					,, 26	5	0
1730	,,	Porus					,, 26	5	0
1736	,,	Armenius					,, 26	5	0
1736	,,	Atalanta					,, 26	5	0
1737	,,	Berenice					,, 26	5	0
1737	,,	Justin					,, 26	5	0
1732	,,	Orlando					,, 26	5	0
1732	,,	Aetius					,, 26	5	0
1737	,,	Faramondo					,, 26	5	0
1737	,,	Alexander's Feast					,, 105	0	0
1738	,,	Xerxes					,, 26	5	0
1738, Sept. 28th, six organ concertos in p.							,, 26	5	0
1738, Oct. 7th, six new sonatas				.	.		,, 26	5	0

(Macfarren, p. 22.) The original leaf, of which the single items have been quoted at their respective dates, has not been traced. Macfarren says, that it was forwarded to him, as Secretary of the Handel Society, by one Mr. Nottingham in 1844, and that he published a faithful transcript. The list is not quite in chronological order, and is probably incomplete. Of Handel's operas, *Alessandro Severo*, *Arianna*, *Ariodante* and *Tolomeo* are missing. According to Schoelcher (p. 273), Mr. John Caulfield, whose father had worked as engraver for Walsh, told him the firm would have usually paid 20 guineas for an oratorio of Handel's. This corresponds to the normal payment of £26 : 5 : 0 for an opera here. The payment seems to have been made usually in January or February, *i.e.* at the end of the old style year.

———

FROM THE " COMMON SENSE ", 14th October 1738

(A Discourse upon the Fall of the Operas.)

. . . *Don Chrysostimus* informs us, that the Musician *Timotheus*, playing one Day upon the Flute before *Alexander* the *Great*, in the Movement called *Ortios*, that Prince immediately laid hold of his *Great Sword*, and was with Difficulty hindered from doing Mischief,—restrain'd, no Doubt, by some prudent, and pacifick Minister.—And Mr. *Dryden*, in his celebrated *Ode* upon St. *Caecilia*'s Day, represents that Hero, alternately affected, in the highest Degree, by tender or martial Sounds, now *languishing* in the *Arms* of his *Courtesan, Thais*, and anon *furious*, snatching a *Flambeau*, and *setting Fire* to the *Town* of *Persepolis*. This we have lately heard, set to Musick by the Great Mr. *Handel*, who, for a Modern, certainly excels in the *Ortios* or *Warlike Measure* :—But we have some *Reason to think* that the Impressions which it was observed to make upon the *Audience* soon gave Way to the *Phrygian*, or *Lascivious Movement*.

. . . The *Swiss* . . . have at this Time a Tune, which, when play'd upon their Fifes, inspires them with such a Love of their Country, that they run Home as fast as they can. . . . Could such a Tune be composed here, it would then indeed be worth the Nation's While to pay the Piper. . . . I would therefore, most earnestly recommend it to the Learned Doctor Green, to turn his Thoughts that Way.—It is not from the least Distrust of Mr. *Handel*'s Ability that I address myself preferably to Doctor *Green* : But Mr. *Handel* having the Advantage to be by Birth a *German*, might probably, even without intending it, mix some Modulations, in his Composition, which might give a *German* Tendency to the Mind, and therefore greatly lessen the National Benefit, I propose by it.

In the book edition, Vol. II, 1739, pp. 213 f. The allusions are to Handel's *Alexander's Feast*, the " Ortios " being, of course, Oratorios. The Swiss tune is the " Ranz des Vaches ", or " Kuhreigen " ; their " Fife " the Alpine horn. The writer's idea was a national anthem ; when this materialized, however, it was neither by Handel, nor by Greene, but anonymous.

—

Handel finishes the oratorio *Israel in Egypt*, 1st November 1738.

—

From the " London Daily Post ", 18th November 1738
(Advertisement by Orator Henley.)

St. Cecilia's Day ; why Sounds please, or not ; Talents of Dr. Pepusch, Mr. Handel, Dr. Green, &c. two Ladies Queens ; the Oxford Almanack, Motion against the Recorder, and the Test, &c. will be Oratory Subjects Tomorrow.

(Chrysander, III. 21.) Cf. 19th November 1733.

—

Walsh advertises the " Instrumental Parts to the . . . Six Organ Concerto's ", *London Daily Post*, 2nd December 1738.

(Chrysander, III. 159.) Cf. 4th October.

—

From Vertue's Note Books, 1738

a Sculptor of some merrit has several years been in England. and labouring to gain reputation has lately, as mentioned in the news papers. made a Statue in Marble of Mr Handel the famous Master of Music and great composer of Operas &c. (sd. to be like him in the moddel.) this Statue was made to be Set up in Foxhall Gardens. by . . . Robullac a French man *Sculptor* born in Switzerland or some part of it, but. had been many years in France & there made his studies. I have seen a Model in Clay the portrait of Farranelli the famous singer very like him, and well done. a bust of Sr Isaac Newton one of Oliver Cromwell &c. this statue of Handell is well wrought and with much Art. when considerd.

(Vertue, III. 84.) British Museum, Add. MS. 23,076 : Note Book A. f.

———

From Johann Adolph Scheibe's " Der critische Musikus " (" The Critical Musician "), Leipzig, 1738 (Translated)

Impartial Observations : a reply.

. . . Besides, my correspondent has gone astray a little in his letter, as he sets only the Capellmeister Händel against the Capellmeister [Johann Sebastian] Bach. He who has looked around the world of music to a limited extent only will have found without doubt more than one who would stand comparison with this great man.

Scheibe attacked Bach in no. VI of his periodical. The extract quoted is from the supplement to the book edition, p. 17. Cf. 1745.

———

Handel sets, for Mrs. Catherine Clive, a song from William Congreve's comedy *The Way of the World*, 1738/39.

The famous comedy was produced in 1700 at Lincoln's Inn Fields Theatre, with music by John Eccles. It was revived repeatedly at Drury Lane and Covent Garden (see 7th December 1732). For Mrs. Clive's benefit at Drury Lane, probably during the season 1738-9 when it was performed once only, Handel made a new setting of the song " Love's but the frailty of the mind ". Manuscript copies of his song are in the Royal Music Library (British Museum) and in the Fitzwilliam Museum, Cambridge. Cf. Schoelcher, p. 235.

1739

FROM THE "LONDON DAILY POST", 3rd January 1739

We hear, that on Tuesday se'nnight [the 16th] the King's Theatre will be open'd with a new Oratorio, compos'd by Mr. Handel, Call'd SAUL : And that at the same Theatre there will be a Masquerade on Thursday the 25 Inst.

(Burney, IV. 418 : wrongly dated 1738 ; Chrysander, III. 58.) On the same day, Heidegger gave "Leave & Licence to Angelo Corri to perform an Opera there ", *i.e.* at the Haymarket Theatre (Public Record Office : L.C. 5/161, p. 51). Handel hired the house from Heidegger, the licensee, for his first oratorio season there. The season consisted of twelve performances, mostly on Tuesdays.

—

MRS. PENDARVES TO HER SISTER, ANN GRANVILLE

7th January, 1738–9.

To-morrow I go to hear Mr. Handel's oratorio rehearsed.

(Delany, II. 24 : dated 9th January.) Since the rehearsal, open to friends, was on 8th January, the correct date would seem to be 7th January.

—

FROM THE "LONDON DAILY POST", 9th January 1739

At the King's Theatre in the Hay-Market, on Tuesday next, being the 16th Instant, will be perform'd a new *Oratorio*, call'd SAUL. . . . To begin at Six o'Clock.

(Burney, IV. 429.)

—

LORD WENTWORTH TO THE EARL OF STRAFFORD

London, January 9, 1739.

Mr. Handel rehearsed yesterday a new Oratorio call'd Saul, and Mr. Hamilton thinks it a very good one ; and for a chief performer he has got one Rusell an Englishman that sings extreamly well. He has got Francisschina for his best woman, and I believe all the rest are but indifferent.

(*Wentworth Papers*, p. 542.) Hamilton seems to have been young Lord Went-worth's tutor. Russell sang in *Saul* but never again in a Handel oratorio. He seems to have been identical with the actor-singer whom Smollett mentions in his *Advice* ; see 1746 (end). For the cast, see 16th January.

—

FROM THE MINUTES OF THE MEETINGS OF THE GOVERNORS OF
MERCER'S HOSPITAL, DUBLIN, 10th January 1739

The Day of the Musical Service att St Andrews Church is alterd from
Thursday the 8th Day of Feb^{ry} to Tuesday the 13th Day of February. . . .
The Governors of Mercer's Charitable Hospital give this publick
notice that . . . Divine Service will be perform'd as formerly after the
Cathedral manner, with Te Deum Jubilate and two new Anthems
Compos'd by Mr Handel.

From now onwards, these records are quoted as "Minutes of Mercer's
Hospital ". The two sentences were intended for publication in the newspapers.

—

FROM THE EARL OF EGMONT'S DIARY, 13th January 1739

This week the Lady Henrietta Powis, a young widow of 22 years old,
married Birde [Beard] the singing man. She is daughter to the Earl of
Walgrave, now Ambassador in France, and her first husband was son to
the Marquis of Powis. Her brother [James], an Ensign in the Guards,
told her that her lover had the pox, and that she would be disappointed
of the only thing she married him for, which was her lust ; for that he
would continue to lie every night with the player that brought them
together, and give her no solace. But there is no prudence below the
girdle. Birde continues to sing upon the stage. This lady had 600*l.*
a year jointure, 200*l.* of which is encumbered by former debts, and
200*l.* she has lately sold to pay his debts. To-day it is said her goods
have been sold.

(Egmont MSS., III. 4.) Cf. Lady Mary Wortley Montagu's letter to the
Countess of Pomfret, dated 1738 and quoted by Schoelcher, p. 281 (Montagu,
Letters and Works, II. 218 f.). Lady Henrietta, widow of Lord Edward Herbert,
Marquis of Powis (d. 1734), was the only daughter of James, Earl of Waldegrave
(cf. page 123). She and Beard married on 8th January 1739, and lived happily
until she died in 1753. Beard afterwards married Rich's daughter, and became
his successor at Covent Garden.

—

LORD WENTWORTH TO THE EARL OF STRAFFORD

London, January 13, 1739

I hear Mr. Handell has borrow'd of the Duke of Argylle a pair of the
largest kettle-drums in the Tower, so to be sure it will be most excessive
noisy with a bad set off singers ; I doubt it will not retrieve his former
losses.

(Myers, 1948, p. 47 : ascribed to Lady Lucy Strafford.) *Wentworth Papers*,
p. 543. John, Duke of Argyll and Greenwich was Master General of the Ordnance. The kettle-drums (cf. 24th February 1750) were used for the Hallelujah
Chorus in Act I, the "Dead March " in Act III, and some Sinfonias. These were

the original "Tower Drums", said to have been taken by Marlborough at the battle of Malplaquet in 1709.

—

Saul is produced at the Haymarket Theatre, 16th January 1739 (*London Daily Post*).

The text, often attributed to Newburgh Hamilton, was by Charles Jennens (cf. 19th September 1738). Carillons, trombones and kettle-drums were used. Repeat performances on 23rd January; 3rd, 10th, February; 27th March and 19th April. Revivals in March 1740 and 1741 at Lincoln's Inn Fields, in 1744 at Covent Garden, in 1745 at the Hay-market, in 1750 and 1754 at Covent Garden.

—

CAST OF "SAUL", 16th January 1739

Saul—Mr. Waltz, bass
Jonathan—Mr. Beard, tenor
David—Mr. Russell, counter-tenor
Abner—(?), tenor
Merab—Miss Cecilia Young (Mrs. Arne), soprano
Michael—Signora Francesina, soprano
Doeg—Mr. Butler, bass
Witch of Endor—Signora Lucchesina or Mrs. Arne-Young, soprano
Apparition of Samuel—Mr. Hussey, bass
An Amalekite—Mr. Stoppelaer, tenor
Abiathar—(?), bass
High Priest—Mr. Kelly, tenor

This was a large cast. Signora Lucchesina's real name was Antonia Marchesina. Cecilia Arne-Young had two sisters : Isabella senior (Mrs. Lampe), a soprano, and Esther, a mezzo-soprano. The part of Abiathar was probably sung by one of the basses employed in other parts. The two Italian ladies sang, of course, in English. The whole cast is only recorded in manuscript notes in a libretto in the Royal Academy of Music.

—

FROM THE "LONDON DAILY POST", 17th January 1739

Last Night the King, his Royal Highness the Duke, and their Royal Highnesses the Princesses, were at the Oratorio in the Hay-market ; it met with general Applause by a numerous and splendid Audience.

(Schoelcher, p. 258.) The Earl of Egmont also attended "Hendle's new oratorio" (Egmont MSS., III. 5).

—

FROM THE "LONDON DAILY POST", 18th January 1739

This Day are publish'd,
Proposals for Printing by Subscription,
Seven Sonata's, or Trio's, for two Violins, or
German Flutes, and a Bass. Opera Quinta.
Compos'd by Mr. *Handel.*

1. The Price is Half a Guinea to be paid at the Time of Subscribing.

2. The whole will be engraven in a fair Character, corrected by the Author, and will be ready to deliver to Subscribers by the 28th of February next.

Subscriptions are taken in by John Walsh . . . and at most Musick-shops in Town.

There follows a list of four other Handel publications, among them the six Organ Concertos, called for the first time " Opera 4 " (the six Oboe Concertos being Opera 3). Opus 5 was announced as published on 28th February.

———

FROM THE EARL OF EGMONT'S DIARY, 18th January 1739

I went at night to a public meeting of the vocal music club at the Crown Tavern, where the famous oratorio of Hendel, called " The Feast of Alexander ", was performed by the gentlemen of our club.

(Egmont MSS., III. 5.) The " gentlemen " of the club were those from the King's Chapel. The private meetings of the club were on Fridays. This was a public one, on Thursday. The club was the Academy of Ancient Music. A copy of the word-book, in Schoelcher's collection at the Paris Conservatoire, gives the date as 18th January 1738 (old style).

———

FROM THE " LONDON DAILY POST ", 22nd January 1739

Hay-Market . . . To-morrow . . . SAUL. With several new Concerto's on the Organ.

(Schoelcher, p. 204.)

———

Handel finishes the first of his *Concerti Grossi*, 25th January 1739.

———

At a benefit concert for the trumpet player Valentine Snow, at Hickford's Room in February 1739, " several Chorus's out of Acis and Galatea, Alexander's Feast, and Coronation Anthems " are performed.

(*Musical Times*, 1st September 1906, p. 603.) No advertisement to be found in *Daily Post* or *London Daily Post*. Cf. 9th February 1744.

———

Thomas Wood advertises the word-book of *Saul*, *London Daily Post*, 3rd February 1739.

(Schoelcher, p. 204.) This was the day of the third performance of the oratorio, which the Earl of Egmont attended (Egmont MSS., III. 18). The word-book has devices in Greek and Latin ; it is dated 1738, *i.e.* old style.

———

Walsh advertises " The celebrated Airs in Score of the Oratorio of *Saul* . . .", price 2s. 6d., *London Daily Post*, 12th February 1739. (Chrysander, III. 57.) Cf. 11th April.

———

Walsh advertises the second edition of *Alexander's Feast*, revived on the same day, *London Daily Post*, 17th February 1739.

(Schoelcher, p. 204.) The cantata, duet and additional song of the first edition (see 8th March 1738) are omitted, and the new chorus at the end, " Your Voices tune ", is not included.

———

FROM THE " DUBLIN GAZETTE ", 17th February 1739

On Tuesday last [the 13th] the *Te Deum, Jubilate* and two *Coronation Anthems* composed by Mr. Handel, were performed at St. Andrew's Church with the greatest Decency and Exactness possible, for the Support of *Mercer's Hospital,* at which were present Their Excellencies the Lords Justices, and Eight Hundred Persons of the best Quality and Distinction ; on which Occasion a most excellent Sermon was preached by the Rt. Rev. the Ld. Bishop of Kildare [Dr. Charles Cobbe].

(*The Irish Builder,* 15th January 1897.) The Lord Lieutenant of Ireland was away from Dublin. This report was, as usual, prepared by the Secretary of the Board of Governors of Mercer's Hospital. The same notice appeared in Faulkner's *Dublin Journal* on 21st February.

———

MRS. PENDARVES TO HER SISTER, ANN GRANVILLE

Park Street, 17th Feb. 1738–9.

I go to-night to the oratorio—no I mean to Alexander's Feast—with Mrs. Carey.

(Delany, II. 38.) Mrs. Pendarves was staying with her brother, Bernard Granville. *Alexander's Feast* was called an ode, as distinct from an oratorio.

———

Alexander's Feast is revived at the Haymarket Theatre, 17th February 1739.

The new edition of the word-book, printed again by J. and R. Tonson, contains the dedicatory poem by the author, addressed to the composer, and some additional notes within the text. Among these are, after the recitativo, " Timotheus . . .", on top of page 13 : " (A Concerto here, for the Harp, Lute, Lyricord, and other Instruments.) " ; at the beginning of Part Two, page 20 : " Concerto for two Violins, Violoncello, &c." ; at the end of page 23 : " Concerto for the Organ, and other Instruments ".

The cantata, printed in the first edition, is omitted. (Copies in Royal College of Music, London, and University Library, Cambridge.) Repeat performances on 24th February and 20th March.

—

HAMILTON'S DEDICATION OF THE NEW WORD-BOOK OF
" ALEXANDER'S FEAST " (17th February) 1739

To

Mr. HANDEL,

On his Setting to MUSICK

Mr. *Dryden*'s " FEAST OF ALEXANDER ".

Let others charm the list'ning scaly Brood,
Or tame the savage Monsters of the Wood ;
With magick Notes enchant the leafy Grove,
Or force ev'n Things inanimate to move :
Be ever Your's (my Friend) the God-like Art,
To calm the Passions, and improve the Heart ;
The Tyrant's Rage, and Hell-born Pride controul,
Or sweetly sooth to Peace the mourning Soul ;
With martial Warmth the Hero's Breast inspire,
Or fan new-kindling Love to chaste Desire.
That Artist's Hand, (whose Skill alone cou'd move
To Glory, Grief, or Joy, the Son of *Jove* ;)
Not greater Raptures to the *Grecian* gave,
Than *British* Theatres from you receive ;
That Ignorance and Envy vanquish'd see,
Heav'n made you rule the World by *Harmony*.
Two glowing Sparks of that Celestial Flame,
Which warms by mystick Art this earthly Frame,
United in one Blaze of *Genial Heat*,
Produc'd this Piece in Sense and Sounds complete ;
The *Sister Arts* as breathing from one Soul,
With equal Spirit animate the *Whole*.
Has *Dryden* liv'd the welcome Day to bless,
Which cloath'd his Numbers in so fit a Dress ;
When his majestick *Poetry* was crown'd,
With all your bright Magnificence of *Sound* ;
How wou'd his Wonder and his Transport rise,
Whilst fam'd *Timotheus* yields to you the Prize.

(Schoelcher, p. 180 ; Chrysander, II. 423 f. ; both attributing the poem to the first edition of 1736.) " Timotheus, oder Die Gewalt der Musik " (T., or the Power of Music) was the German title of Handel's *Alexander's Feast* in the nineteenth century.

—

Walsh announces the publication of Handel's Opus 5, the seven Sonatas for two Violins or German Flutes and a Bass, *London Daily Post*, 28th February 1739.

(Smith, 1954, p. 301.) Cf. 18th January. The subscription was again unsuccessful ; there is no list of subscribers.

———

FROM THE " LONDON DAILY POST ", 3rd March 1739

At the King's Theatre . . . this Day . . . will be reviv'd an Oratorio, call'd IL TRIONFO DEL TEMPO & DELLA VERITA, with several Concerto's on the Organ and other Instruments.

(Chrysander, III. 59.) There was only one performance.

———

FROM THE " LONDON DAILY POST ", 6th March 1739

We hear that on Tuesday the 20th of this Month the Feast of Alexander will be performed, for the Benefit of a Fund establish'd for the Support of decay'd Musicians and their Families ; and that Mr. Handel has generously given the Use of the Opera-House, and intends to direct the Performance.

(Chrysander, III. 16.)

———

A pastoral opera, *Angelica e Medoro*, text altered from Metastasio's *L'Angelica*, music by Pescetti, is produced at Covent Garden Theatre, 10th March 1739.

(Burney, IV. 429 f.) In the *London Daily Post* of 26th February the work was advertised as " a new serenata ", to be acted in the manner of an opera, with Signora Muscovita, just arrived from Italy, and Signora Marchesini (called Lucchesina, see 16th January). Moser (pp. 88 f.) thought that La Muscovita was identical with Christina Maria Avoglio, soon to be singing in Handel parts ; but several contemporary letters prove that she was somebody else, besides being the mistress of Lord Middlesex (see 28th November). The late Mr. Alan Yorke-Long, who has written an essay on the Nobility Opera, not yet published, found from the libretto of Pescetti's *Angelica e Medoro* that La Muscovita was Signora Lucia Panichi. Mrs. Cecilia Arne was also in the cast.

———

FROM THE " LONDON DAILY POST ", 20th March 1739

For the Benefit and Increase of a Fund established for the Support of Decay'd Musicians or their Families. At the King's Theatre . . . this Day . . . will be reviv'd an Ode, call'd *Alexander's Feast*. Written by Mr. Dryden. With several Concerto's on the Organ, and other

Instruments, Particularly a new Concerto on the Organ by Mr. Handel, on purpose for this Occasion. . . . To begin at Seven o'Clock.

(Schoelcher, p. 365.) Handel's name, as the composer of the Ode, was omitted by mistake. This was the first of several concerts given by Handel for the Musicians Fund. The organ concerto has not been identified.

FROM THE " LONDON DAILY POST ", 22nd March 1739

On Tuesday Night last [the 20th] Alexander's Feast was perform'd at the Opera House in the Haymarket, to a numerous and polite Audience . . . and we hear, several of the Subscribers (tho' they had Tickets sent them Gratis for this Performance) were so generous as to pay at the Doors, and others have since sent Presents to the Fund ; Mr. Handel gave the House and his Performance, upon this Occasion, Gratis, and Mr. Heidegger made a Present of Twenty Pounds to defray the other incident Expences.

(Burney, IV. 660.)

The Alchemist is performed at Drury Lane, 26th March 1739 (with Handel's music ?).
Cf. 7th March 1732 and 20th December 1733.

Handel withdraws the balance of £50, 28th March 1739.

Handel finishes the Organ Concerto in F (no. 1 of the second set), 2nd April 1739.
Cf. 20th March.

FROM THE " LONDON DAILY POST ", 4th April 1739

At the King's Theatre . . . this Day . . . will be perform'd a New Oratorio, call'd ISRAEL IN EGYPT. With several Concerto's on the Organ, and particularly a new one. . . . To begin at Seven o'Clock.

(Chrysander, III. 89.) The text seems to have been compiled by Handel himself ; he used Psalms 78, 105 and 106 as well as Exodus 15. Repeat performances on 11th and 17th April. The new organ concerto was that in F.

CAST OF " ISRAEL IN EGYPT ", 4th April 1739
First soprano—Signora Francesina
Second soprano—Master Robinson
Alto—Mr. Savage

Tenor—Mr. Beard
First Bass—Mr. Waltz
Second Bass—Mr. Reinhold

Robinson, the " boy ", may have been the son of John Robinson, the organist, and his wife Ann, the singer, known as Mrs. Turner Robinson.

———

FROM THE EARL OF EGMONT'S DIARY, 4th April 1739

In the evening I went to Hendel's new Oratorio, " The Israelites' flight out of Egypt ".

(Egmont MSS., III. 49.)

———

FROM THE " LONDON EVENING-POST ", 5th April 1739

The Office of *Licenser* being grown almost as formidable to *Authors*, as that of Inquisitor to *Jews* and *Hereticks*, the Patrons and Lovers of Musick were in great Pain for the Fate of the *new Oratorio* at the *Hay-Market* ; some Persons apprehending, with a good deal of Reason, that the Title of *Israel in Egypt* was, to the full, as obnoxious as that of *The Deliverer of his Country* : But as a *Permit* was granted for its Exhibition, we may conclude that Mr. *Handel* has work'd a greater Miracle than any of those ascrib'd to *Orpheus*, tho' the Poets give us their Words, that *Savages, Stocks* and *Stones*, were sensible of his Harmony.

———

FROM THE " LONDON DAILY POST ", 7th April 1739

Hay-Market . . . Wednesday next, April 11 . . . *Israel in Egypt*. With Alterations and Additions, and the two last new Concerto's on the Organ. (Being the last Time of performing it.)

(Schoelcher, p. 208.)

———

FROM THE " LONDON DAILY POST ", 10th April 1739

Hay-Market . . . To-Morrow . . . *Israel in Egypt*. Which will be shortned and Intermix'd with Songs. . . .

(Schoelcher, pp. 208 f.) Chrysander, III. 91, mentions four insertions in Handel's manuscript : (1) " Through the land " instead of the cancelled chorus " Egypt was glad when they departed ". (2) " Angelico splendor " after the chorus " But the waters overwhelmed the enemies". (3) " Cor fedele" ex G, in place of the chorus " And in the greatness of thine excellency . . . Thou sentest forth thy wrath ". (4) " La speranza la costanza " after the duet " Thou in thy mercy ". These new numbers were taken from *Athalia, Ottone* and other works, and were sung by La Francesina. Nos. 2 and 3 had been used in *Esther* (1737 ?) ; no. 3 was to be sung in the key of G.

———

Walsh advertises " The celebrated Airs in the Oratorio of Saul, in two Books ", *London Daily Post*, 11th April 1739.

Cf. 12th February ; the second book was published on 17th March (Smith, 1954, p. 281).

FROM THE " LONDON DAILY POST ", 13th April 1739

To the Author of the LONDON DAILY POST.

Sir,

Upon my Arrival in Town three Days ago, I was not a little surpriz'd, to find that Mr. Handel's last Oratorio, (*Israel in Egypt*) which had been performed but once, was advertis'd to be for the last time on Wednesday. I was almost tempted to think that his Genius had fail'd him, but must own myself agreeably disappointed. I was not only pleas'd, but also affected by it, for I never yet met with any Musical Performance, in which the Words and Sentiments were so thoroughly studied, and so clearly understood ; and as the Words are taken from the Bible, they are perhaps some of the most sublime parts of it. I was indeed concern'd, that so excellent a Work of so great a Genius was neglected, for tho' it was a Polite and attentive Audience, it was not large enough I doubt to encourage him in any future Attempt. As I should be extreamely sorry to be depriv'd of hearing this again, and found many of the Auditors in the same Disposition ; yet being afraid Mr. Handel will not undertake it without some Publick Encouragement, because he may think himself precluded by his Advertisement, (that it was to be the last time) I must beg leave, by your means, to convey not only my own, but the Desires of several others, that he will perform this again some time next Week.

I am, Sir,

Your very humble Servant,

A. Z.

(Schoelcher, p. 210.)   The initials A. Z. have not been identified.

FROM THE " LONDON DAILY POST ", 14th April 1739

We are inform'd that Mr. Handel, at the Desire of several Persons of Distinction, intends to perform again his last new Oratorio of Israel in Egypt, on Tuesday next the 17th Instant.

(Schoelcher, p. 211.)

FROM THE " LONDON DAILY POST ", 17th April 1739

We hear the Prince and Princess [of Wales] will be at the King's Theatre in the Hay-Market this Evening, to see *Israel in Egypt*.

(Chrysander, III. 92.)

XVIII. HANDEL'S STATUE IN VAUXHALL GARDENS, 1738

Original terracotta model by Louis François Roubiliac.
(Fitzwilliam Museum)

See page 456

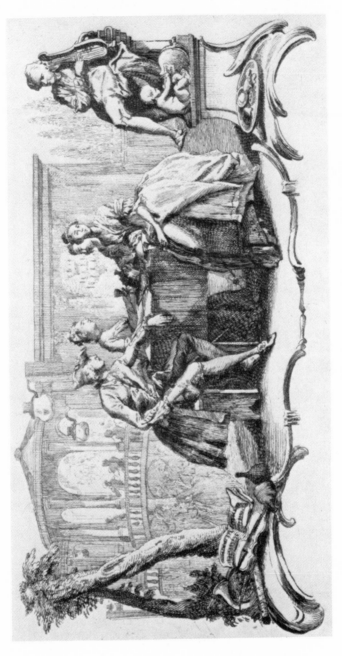

XIX. HANDEL'S STATUE IN VAUXHALL GARDENS

Engraving after Hubert François Gravelot by George Bickham, Jr., 1738. Vignette to the song "The Invitation to Mira", words by John Lockman, music by Thomas Gladwin, published in Bickham's *Musical Entertainer*, Vol. II, No. 1, plate 2. (Fitzwilliam Museum)

See page 463

FROM THE " LONDON DAILY POST ", 18th April 1739
Wednesday Morning, April 18, 1739.

SIR,

    I Beg Leave, by your Paper, to congratulate, not Mr. Handel, but the Town, upon the Appearance there was *last* Night at *Israel in Egypt.* The Glory of one Man, on this Occasion, is but of small Importance, in Comparison with that of so numerous an Assembly. The having a Disposition to encourage, and Faculties to be entertain'd by such a truly-spiritual Entertainment, being very little inferior to the unrivall'd Superiority of first selecting the noble Thoughts contained in the Drama, and giving to each its proper Expression in that most noble and angelic Science of Musick. This, Sir, the inimitable Author has done in such a manner as far to excel himself, if compar'd with any other of his masterly Compositions : As, indeed, he must have infinitely sunk beneath himself, and done himself great Injustice, had he fallen short of doing so.—But what a glorious Spectacle ! to see a crowded Audience of the first Quality of a Nation, headed by the Heir apparent of their Sovereign's Crown and Virtues, with his lovely and beloved Royal Consort by his Side, sitting enchanted (each receiving a superior Delight from the visible Satisfaction it gave the other) at Sounds, that at the same time express'd in so sublime a manner the Praises of the Deity itself, and did such Honour to the Faculties of humane Nature, in first *creating* those Sounds, if I may so speak ; and in the next Place, being able to be so highly delighted with them. Nothing shews the Worth of a People more, than their Taste for Publick Diversions : And could it be suppos'd, as I hope in Charity it may, or if this and such like Entertainments are often repeated, it will, that numerous and splendid Assemblies shall enter into the true Spirit of such an Entertainment, " Praising their Creator, for the Care he takes of the Righteous ", (see Oratorio, p. 6) and for the Delight he gives them:—*Did such a Taste prevail universally in a People, that People might expect on a like Occasion, if such Occasion should ever happen to them, the same Deliverance as those Praises celebrate ; and Protestant, free, virtuous, united, Christian England, need little fear, at any time hereafter, the whole Force of slavish, bigotted, united, unchristian Popery, risen up against her, should such a Conjuncture ever hereafter happen.*

    If the Town is ever to be bless'd with this Entertainment *again*, I would recommend to every one to take the Book of the Drama with them : For tho' the Harmony be so unspeakably great of itself, it is in an unmeasurable Proportion more so, when seen to what Words it is adapted ; especially, if every one who could take with them the Book, would do their best to carry a Heart for the Sense, as well as an Ear for the Sound.

    The narrow Limits of your Paper forbids entering into Particulars : But they know not what they fall short of in the Perfection of the Entertainment, who, when they hear the Musick, are not acquainted

H.–16

with the Words it expresses ; or, if they have the Book, have not the proper Spirit to relish them. The Whole of the *first* Part, is entirely Devotional ; and tho' the *second* Part be but *Historical*, yet as it relates the great Acts of the Power of God, the Sense and the Musick have a reciprocal Influence on each other.

"He gave them Hailstones for Rain, Fire mingled with Hail ran along the Ground " : And above all, " But the Waters overwhelm'd their Enemies, there was not one left."—The Sublimity of the great Musical Poet's Imagination here, will not admit of Expression to any one who considers the Sound and the Sense together.

The same of, " He is my God, I will prepare him an Habitation ; my Father's God." Page 13, in the third Part.

Again, " Thou didst blow with the Wind ; the Sea cover'd them, they sunk as Lead in the mighty Waters " ;—and, to name no more, " The Lord shall reign for ever and ever ", and Miriam's Song at the Conclusion.

'Tis a sort of separate Existence the Musick has in these Places apart from the Words ; 'tis Soul and Body join'd when heard and read together : And if People, before they went to hear it, would but retire a Moment, and read by themselves the Words of the Sacred Drama, it would tend very much to raise their Delight when at the Representation. The Theatre, on this occasion, ought to be enter'd with more Solemnity than a Church ; inasmuch, as the Entertainment you go to is really in itself the noblest Adoration and Homage paid to the Deity that ever was in one. So sublime an Act of Devotion as this *Representation* carries in it, to a Heart and Ear duly tuned for it, would consecrate even Hell itself.—It is the Action that is done in it, that hallows the Place, and not the Place the Action. And if any outward Circumstances foreign to me, can adulterate a good Action, I do not see *where* I can perform one, but in the most abstract Solitude.—If this be going out of the way, on this Occasion, the stupid, senseless *Exceptions* that have been taken to so truly religious Representations, as *this*, in particular, and the other *Oratorios* are, from the *Place* they are *exhibited in*, and to the attending, and assisting of them, by Persons of Piety and real Virtue, must be my *Apology*.

I have been told, the Words were selected out of the Sacred Writings by the Great Composer himself. If so, the Judiciousness of his Choice in this Respect, and his suiting so happily the Magnificence of the Sounds in so exalted a Manner to the Grandeur of the Subject, shew which Way his natural Genius, had he but Encouragment, would incline him ; and expresses, in a very lively Manner, the Harmony of his Heart to be as superlatively excellent, as the inimitable Sounds do the Beauty and Force of his Imagination and Skill in the noble Science itself.

I can't conclude, Sir, without great Concern at the Disadvantage so great a Master labours under, with respect to the many of his *Vocal Instruments*, which fall so vastly short in being able to do due Justice to what they are to perform ; and which, if executed in a manner worthy of it, would receive so great Advantage. This Consideration will make a human Mind serious, where a lighter Mind would be otherwise affected. I shall conclude with this Maxim, " That in Publick Entertainments every one should come with a reasonable Desire of being entertain'd themselves, or with the polite Resolution, no ways to interrupt the Entertainment of others. And that to have a Truce with Dissipation, and noisy Discourse, and to forbear that silly Affectation of beating Time aloud on such an Occasion, is, indeed, in Appearance, a great Compliment paid to the divine Author of so sacred an Entertainment, and to the rest of the Company near them ; but at the same time, in reality, a much greater Respect paid to themselves." I cannot but add this Word, since I am on the Subject, " That I think a profound Silence a much more proper Expression of Approbation to Musick, and to deep Distress in Tragedy, than all the noisy Applause so much in Vogue, however great the Authority of Custom may be for it." I am, Sir, &c.

R. W.

The original issue is not available, but fortunately the letter was reprinted in the same paper on 1st April 1740 : this is the source of the text above. From the introduction to the reprint (see 1st April 1740) it seems that the original was in great demand and soon sold out. Chrysander (III. 94-8), who intended to print the English version in an appendix never issued, suggested that the writer might have been Richard Wesley, one of the subscribers for the score of *Alexander's Feast*.

———

FROM THE " LONDON DAILY POST ", 19th April 1739

At the King's Theatre . . . this Day . . . will be perform'd the last New Oratorio, call'd SAUL. And not *Israel* in Egypt (as by Mistake was advertised in Yesterday's Bills and Papers). With a Concerto on the Organ, by Mr. Handel ; And another on the Violin, by the famous Sig. *Plantanida*, who is just arriv'd from Abroad.

(Schoelcher, p. 211 ; Moser, p. 140.) Giovanni Piantanida arrived with his wife, Constanza, called La Posterla, a singer. This was the twelfth night of Handel's season, including the charity performance on 20th March.

———

FROM THE SAME

We hear that Signiora Busterla, a famous Italian Singer arrived here last Tuesday [the 17th], and is to perform in the Opera's that are intended to be perform'd by Mr. Handel, after the Holydays.

(Chrysander, III. 453 ; Moser, p. 146.) For " La Posterla ", see 1st May, *i.e.* after Easter.

———

Handel finishes the opera *Jupiter in Argos*, 24th April 1739.

—

FROM THE " LONDON DAILY POST ", 1st May 1739

At the King's Theatre . . . this Day . . . will be acted a Dramatical Composition, call'd JUPITER IN ARGOS. Intermix'd with Chorus's, and two Concerto's on the Organ. . . . To begin at Seven o'Clock.

(Smith, 1950, p. 129.) Cutting in Sir Augustus Harris's Collection. The first six May issues of the paper itself are missing. The production was advertised during the last four week-days in April. Repeat performance on 5th May (cutting in the Harris Collection). The text is based on Antonio Maria Lucchini's libretto *Giove in Argo*, set to music in 1717 by Antonio Lotti and produced on 14th (25th) October 1717 in the Sala di Ridotto in Dresden ; it was revived on 23rd August (3rd September) 1719 for the opening of the new opera-house there, probably in Handel's presence. Handel's music for this " semi-pasticcio " was arranged from his earlier operas, with several new numbers : two recitatives, two arias, the final chorus, and perhaps more. Autographs are in the Royal Music Library (British Museum) and in the Fitzwilliam Museum, Cambridge. In 1935 Julian Herbage and R. Greaves, under the supervision of Sir Adrian Boult, arranged the music for *Perseus and Andromeda*, a masque ; broadcast performance in London, 8th October 1935 ; score published. Cf. Coopersmith, 1936 ; Loewenberg, p. 69. From Burney, IV. 430, to Young, p. 67, all the Handel biographers, with the exception of Chrysander, have doubted the production of *Jupiter in Argos* ; Chrysander, II. 453, even guessed the dates of performances.

—

DRAMATIS PERSONAE OF " JUPITER IN ARGOS ", 1st May 1739

Diana—soprano
Calisto—soprano
Iside—soprano
Arete—tenor
Ergasto—bass
Licaone—bass

It seems certain that Signora Posterla sang one of the three soprano parts, the others may have been sung by Francesina and Lucchesina. It is probable that the tenor part was sung by Beard ; the two bass parts were sung by Waltz and Reinhold. With the two performances on 1st and 5th May Handel's opera season (see 19th April) came to an early end.

—

The Academy of Ancient Music performs " The Song of Moses, and the Funeral Anthem for her late Majesty ", 10th May 1739.

Recorded in the printed word-book (Chrysander, III. 101). Handel used the " Funeral Anthem " of 1737 for *Israel in Egypt*, adding " Moses Song. Exodus. Chap. 15 " between 1st and 11th October 1738. The " Academy " arranged the parts differently, and Handel did not object. This was the old club at the " Crown and Anchor " Tavern, led by Dr. Pepusch ; since 1731 it had been without Dr. Greene, who had his Apollo Society at the "Devil's Tavern". While the " Apollo " published, in 1740, a "Miscellany of Lyric Poems", the "Academy" printed, in 1761 and again in 1768, "The Words of such Pieces as are most usually performed by the Academy of Ancient Music"; this contained, besides texts set by other composers, those of Handel's *Acis and Galatea, Alexander's Feast, Esther, Israel in Egypt* (in two acts, as above), *L'Allegro ed il Penseroso*, and the *Messiah*.

FROM JOHANN ADOLPH SCHEIBE'S "CRITISCHER MUSIKUS" ("CRITICAL MUSICIAN"), 23rd June 1739 (Translated)

. . . Possibly the greatest masters in these Cantatas [in chamber style] are, in particular, the renowned *Astorga, Marcello, Mancini* and *Conti*, and also *Händel, Heinichen* and *Bigaglia*. The first two show particularly penetrating industry in them and great understanding; but the last three such a natural, free and agreeable manner, that one cannot hear it without loving it, and which pleases, too, of its own accord, even without the aid of a painstaking singer.

To be found in No. 43 of the 1740 edition (1745, p. 401). The composers named are : Emanuele Astorga (born 1680), Benedetto Marcello (b. 1686), Francesco Mancini (b. 1679), Francesco Bartolomeo Conti (b. 1681); Johann David Heinichen (b. 1683) and Diogenio Bigaglia, another contemporary of Handel's.

FROM MATTHESON'S "DER VOLLKOMMENE CAPELLMEISTER" ("THE PERFECT CAPELLMEISTER"), HAMBURG, 1739 (Translated)

. . . Not to mention other [instrumental] artists, the renowned *Händel* has often played [extemporary] accompaniments in his stage performances, where the solo harpsichord excelled in this [fantastic] style, according to the player's skill and pleasure : it is a performance which requires its own virtuoso, and other men, who tried to imitate it, did not succeed ; even though, otherwise, they may have been firm in the saddle. . . .

A great fuss was made of the unique Tridentine organ. The organist himself, however, is said to have been astonished when he heard the Signor *Sassone* (so the Italians called *Händel*) play on it when he passed through there. . . . One may say that *Händel*, in particular, is not easily surpassed by anyone in organ playing ; unless it should be by *Bach* in Leipzig : therefore, these two, apart from alphabetical order, should stand in the forefront. I have heard them in their greatness, and played with the former several times in Hamburg as well as in Lübeck. He had a pupil in England, named *Babel*, of whom they said that he surpassed his master.

Pp. 88 and 479. The first passage, slightly altered, is repeated from Mattheson's *Kern Melodischer Wissenschaft*, spring of 1737.—Nothing is known of Handel visiting Trento in South Tirol, though it is possible he passed through it on his first journey to Italy. The organ referred to was, apparently, the one in the famous

church of S. Maria Maggiore, built in 1687 by Eugenio Gasparini. For William
Babell (died in 1723) see 31st January 1717 and 15th December 1722.

FROM THE "SCOTS MAGAZINE", EDINBURGH, July 1739

An Evening at Vaux-Hall.

London, May 28.

. . . after shewing tickets, or paying money, the Ladies and Gentlemen
walk in, survey the coop made to keep the footmen in, just at the door,
take a hasty circuit round the walks, the paintings not being yet let
down, take a view of *Handel*'s bust, curiously carved on a fine block of
marble, and plac'd on one side of the garden, striking his lyre :—but
before they have observed half of its beauties, the musick striking up,
the whole company crowd from every part of the gardens towards the
orchestra and organ. . . .

(W. Wroth, *The London Pleasure Gardens*, 1896, p. 293.)

MISS ANN GRANVILLE TO LADY THROCKMORTON, AT SCARBOROUGH,
YORKSHIRE

Northend, 22d August 1739.

Have you heard Mr. Kellaway upon the harpsichord ? he is at Scarborough and a most delightful player, very little inferior to Handel.

(Delany, II. 61.) For Kelway, see 27th November 1736. Burney, IV. 665,
describes his playing as of "masterly wildness . . . bold, rapid, and fanciful ".

The founder members of the Fund for the Support of Decayed
Musicians and their Families sign the Declaration of Trust, 28th
August 1739.

(Schoelcher, pp. 364 f. ; Smith, 1948, p. 168.) Cf. 23rd April and 7th
May 1738. There were 18 or 19 members present at the meeting, probably
held at the "Crown and Anchor" Tavern. A long list of founders is
given on pp. 9 f. of a pamphlet published about 1920 by the Royal
Society of Musicians of Great Britain ; the names of the others were
recorded in the Deed. Handel was among the signatories. According to
Burney (1785, part 3, p. 132) the Fund agreed with the corporation of the
Sons of the Clergy, in 1739, to perform twice a year at St. Paul's Cathedral,
the band being paid fifty pounds a year.

Admeto is revived at Brunswick, August 1739.

(Chrysander, II. 157 ; Loewenberg, p. 81.) Cf. August 1729 and
February 1732. According to Chrysander, II. 179, *Riccardo Primo* was also

revived at Brunswick in 1739 ; but Loewenberg, p. 81, does not confirm this.

—

At Booth Hall, Gloucester, one of two evening performances, on 5th and 6th September 1739, is dedicated to *Alexander's Feast*, with trumpets, French horns and kettle-drums.

The conductor was probably William Boyce ; the tickets were 2s. 6d. each. The *Gloucester Journal* reports : " We had the greatest appearance of Nobility and Gentry on this occasion ever known here ". Of the three towns which later formed the Three Choirs Meetings, Gloucester was the first to perform Handel odes and oratorios.

—

Walsh advertises *Acis and Galatea, a Masque*, and adds to his music list : "Where may be had, a Print of Mr. HANDEL ", *London Daily Post*, 6th September 1739.

(Smith, 1948, p. 224.) This was still the third edition. Cf. 7th December 1734 and 13th December 1739. The " Print " was Gravelot's engraving after Houbraken.

—

Handel begins the *Ode for St. Cæcilia's Day* on 15th September and finishes it on 24th September. He finishes his " Concerti Grossi " as follows : no. 1, in G, on 29th September ; no. 2, in F, on 4th October ; no. 3, in E minor, on 6th October ; no. 4, in A minor, on 8th October ; no. 5, in D, on 10th October ; no. 7, in B flat, on 12th October ; no. 6, in G minor, on 15th October ; no. 8, in C minor, on 18th October; no. 12, in B minor, on 20th October ; no. 10, in D minor, on 22nd October ; and no. 11, in A, on 30th October 1739. (No. 9, in F, is without date.)

—

The King, just returned from Kensington to St. James's Palace, visits Covent Garden Theatre, on 27th October 1739, where *The Rehearsal* by George Villiers, Duke of Buckingham, and the pantomime *Apollo and Daphne* are performed ; the tune of *Britons strike home*, played between the acts, is enthusiastically applauded by the crowd.

On 19th October George II declared war on Spain ; it was proclaimed publicly on the 23rd. In its early stages this was the " War of Jenkins' Ear ", so called after Robert Jenkins, Captain of an English trading ship, whose ear was torn off by the Spaniards. Later the war became part of the War of the Austrian Succession. The tune, " played for a Dance " (according to the *Gentleman's Magazine* of October 1739, p. 553), was by Henry Purcell, and was written in 1695 for the play *Bonduca ; or, The British Heroine*, founded on Beaumont and Fletcher's tragedy *Bonduca*. The text of the song is anonymous, but it was not by Sir John Vanbrugh, as the *Oxford Dictionary of Quotations* (1941, p. 447) suggests. At the Lord Mayor's Show " the Musick belonging to every Company had Orders to play *Britons strike home*" (*London Daily Post*, 30th October 1739). At Drury Lane Theatre, on the last day of 1739, a farce entitled *Britons Strike Home* ! *or, The Sailor's Rehearsal*, by Edward Philips, received its one and only performance. The word-book, printed, with the tunes, by J. Watts, quotes the words but not the music of the song. In volume II of George Bickham's *Musical Entertainer* (pp. 97 f.) words and music were reprinted in 1740.

———

FROM THE "LONDON DAILY POST", 29th October 1739

MUSICK.

This Day are Publish'd,

Proposals for Printing by Subscription,

With His Majesty's Royal Licence and Protection.

Twelve Grand Concerto's, in Seven Parts, for four Violins, a Tenor, a Violoncello, with a Thorough-Bass for the Harpsichord.

Compos'd by Mr. *Handel*.

1. The Price to Subscribers is Two Guineas, One Guinea to be paid at the Time of Subscribing, and the other on the Delivery of the Books.

2. The whole will be engraven in a neat Character, printed on good Paper, and ready to deliver to Subscribers by April next.

3. The Subscribers Names will be printed before the Work.

Subscriptions are taken by the Author, at his Home in Brook's-street, Hanover-square ; and John Walsh in Catherine-street in the Strand.

(Schoelcher, p. 227.)   For the Privilege see 31st October.   Cf. 21st April 1740.

———

Handel finishes the " Concerto Grosso " no. 11, in A, 30th October 1739.

———

Mattheson presses Handel, on 30th October (10th November) 1739 and again later, to write his autobiography for the *Ehrenpforte*. (Chrysander, III. 104.)   Cf. Autumn 1740.

———

THE SECOND PRIVILEGE OF COPYRIGHT FOR HANDEL'S WORKS, GRANTED TO JOHN WALSH, JUNIOR, on 31st October 1739

GEORGE R.

George the Second, by the Grace of God, King of *Great Britain, France*, and *Ireland*, Defender of the Faith, &c.   To all to whom these Presents shall come Greeting.   Whereas *George Frederick Handel*, of the Parish of *St. George the Martyr Hanover Square*, in Our County of *Middlesex*, Esq ; hath humbly represented unto Us, that he hath with great Labour and Expence composed several Works consisting of Vocal and Instrumental Musick, and hath authorised and appointed *John Walsh* of the Parish of *St. Mary le Strand*, in Our said County of Middlesex, to print and publish the same ; and hath therefore humbly besought us to grant Our Royal Privilege and Licence to the said *John Walsh* for the sole Engraving, Printing, and Publishing the said Works for the Term of Fourteen Years ; We being willing to give all due Encouragement to Works of this Nature, are graciously pleased to condescend to his Request ; and We do therefore by these Presents so far as may be agreeable to the Statute in that Behalf made and provided, grant unto him the said *John Walsh*, his Heirs, Executors, Administrators, and Assigns, Our Licence for the sole Printing and Publishing the said Works for the Term of Fourteen Years, to be computed from the Date hereof ; strictly forbidding all Our loving Subjects within our Kingdoms and Dominions to reprint or abridge the same, either in the like or in any other Size or Manner whatsoever ; or to import, buy, vend, utter, or distribute any Copy or Copies thereof, reprinted beyond the Seas, during the aforesaid Term of fourteen Years, without the Consent or Approbation of the said *John Walsh*, his Heirs, Executors, Administrators, and Assigns, under their Hands and Seals first had and obtained, as they will answer the contrary at their Perils ; whereof the Commissioners and Officers of Our Customs, the Master, Wardens, and Company of *Stationers* are to take Notice, that due Obedience may be rendered to our Pleasure herein declared.

Given at Our Court at *St. James's*, the Thirty-first Day of *October*, 1739, in the Thirteenth Year of Our Reign.

By His Majesty's Command,

HOLLES NEWCASTLE.

(Schoelcher, p. 92.) Cf. 14th June 1720. Handel's first privilege, granted to him personally and not to his publisher, expired in 1734. For five years he enjoyed no such protection. Since, however, Walsh senior, the most dangerous pirate printer of the 'twenties, had become satiated and was, moreover, by 1734 Handel's sole publisher, the latter did not suffer for lack of legal protection. Now, it was probably Walsh junior who insisted on applying for a new copyright, perhaps not so much for protection against pirated editions at home and abroad, as for the monopoly this privilege guaranteed him : he was now legally the sole publisher of Handel's works, and it is doubtful whether Handel could have published anything elsewhere, even had he renounced the Royal protection. This privilege was first used for the Twelve Grand Concertos, Opus 6, the tenth and last Handel work printed for subscribers (1740) ; then for *Samson* 1743, *Judas Maccabaeus* 1747, *Joshua* and *Alexander Balus* 1748, *Susanna* and *Solomon* 1749. After Handel's death, Walsh got a new privilege for his works, on 19th August 1760, which he used for the Six Organ Concertos, third series, Opus 7, in 1761. It is obvious that the privilege was not considered necessary for all Handel publications issued by Walsh.

———

FROM THE "LONDON DAILY POST", 17th November 1739

Lincoln's-Inn Fields.

At the Theatre-Royal in Lincoln's Inn Fields, on Thursday, November 22, (being St. Cecilia's Day) will be perform'd *An Ode of Mr. Dryden's,*

H.-16 *a*

With two new Concerto's for Instruments. Which will be preceded by *Alexander's Feast*. And a Concerto on the Organ . . .
∴ Particular Preparations are making to keep the House warm ; and the Passage from the Fields to the House will be cover'd for better Conveniency.
To begin at Six o'Clock.

(Schoelcher, pp. 225-7.) Handel hired the House from Rich for two seasons, using it for the first time on this occasion. The " Ode for St. Cecilia's Day " was produced there. The libretto (copy in Gerald Coke's Handel Collection) is entitled : " *Alexander's Feast ; or, the Power of Musick. An Ode. Wrote in Honour of St. Cecilia, And a Song for St. Cecilia's Day. Both written by Mr. Dryden. And Set to Musick by Mr. Handel.*" It was printed by J. and R. Tonson. The winter was very severe. The notice about the convenience of the audience was varied later (Chrysander, II. 111) : on 22nd November, " Particular Care will be taken to have the House well-aired . . ." ; on the 27th " Particular Care will be taken to have Guards plac'd to keep all the Passages clear from the Mob." Walsh advertised the score of *Alexander's Feast* in the same number of the *London Daily Post*, quoted above, and, referring to the Twelve Grand Concertos prepared on " 400 Plates ", he added " N.B. Two of the above Concerto's will be perform'd this Evening ". Repeat performance on 27th November.

———

PERFORMERS OF THE " ODE FOR ST. CECILIA'S DAY ",
22nd November 1739
Soprano—Signora Francesina
Tenor—Mr. Beard
The other singers have not been identified.

———

MRS. PENDARVES TO LADY THROCKMORTON, AT WESTON, NEAR
OULNEY, BUCKS.

Brook Street, 28 Novr. 1739.
The concerts begin next Saturday [1st December] at the Haymarket. Caristini sings, Peschetti composes ; the house is made up into little boxes, like the playhouses abroad ; Lord Middlesex is the chief under-taker, and I believe it will prove to his cost, *for concerts will not do.*

(Chrysander, III. 111.) Delany, II. 66 f. Mrs. Pendarves refers to the New Theatre in the Haymarket, then under the protection of Charles (Sackville) Earl of Middlesex, later second Duke of Dorset. He was an M.P., an intimate friend of Frederick Prince of Wales and, from 1743 till 1747, a Lord of the Treasury. Cf. January 1722, when the same theatre was under the protection of the Duke of Montague.

———

At the New Theatre in the Haymarket a serenata is produced under the title *Diana and Endimion*, 1st December 1739.

The music was by Giovanni Battista Pescetti. Carestini, returning to the London stage after four years, and La Muscovita (see 10th March) sang the leading parts. Repeat performances on 4th and 8th December. After this failure, concerts were given on 15th and 18th December, with Carestini singing Hasse's " Salve Regina " (Burney, IV. 430).

———

FROM THE " LONDON DAILY POST ", 13th December 1739

At the Theatre Royal in Lincoln's-Inn Fields, this Day, will be perform'd Acis and Galatea, A Serenata. With two new Concerto's for several Instruments, never perform'd before. To which will be added, The last New Ode of Mr. Dryden's, And a Concerto on the Organ. . . . Box Tickets will be sold this Day at the Stage-Door. Particular care will be taken to have Guards plac'd to keep all the Passages clear from the Mob. To begin at Six o'Clock.

(Chrysander, III. 111.) Repeat performances on 20th December 1739, 21st February and 28th March 1740 ; revived on 28th February 1741. For *Acis and Galatea*, see 24th March 1736. The work had been performed at Lincoln's Inn Fields on 26th March 1731.

———

FROM THE SAME

This Day is published,

Acis and Galatea. A Serenata, or Pastoral Entertainment. Written by Mr. Gay. To which is added, A Song for St. Caecilia's Day. Written by Mr. Dryden. Both set to Musick by Mr. *Handel*.

Printed for John Watts. . . .

*** The Price to Gentlemen and Ladies in the Theatre is One Shilling ; if more is ask'd, it is an Imposition.

(Chrysander, III. 111.) Copy of the libretto in Huntington Library, San Marino, California. This was the first time the word-book mentioned Gay as author of the English version. There is, of course, one inserted song by John Hughes (" Would you gain the tender creature "), and others were adapted from Dryden and Pope. See 13th March 1731.

———

FROM THE SAME

This Day is Published,

1. The Songs in the New Ode of Mr. Dryden's for St. Cecilia's Day, set to Musick by Mr. Handel. Price 3s.
2. Acis and Galatea, a Serenade (as it is now perform'd). Pr. 4s.
3. The Favourite Songs in Alexander's Feast. Price 5s.

Printed for John Walsh. . . .

At the same Place may be had the Original Score of Alexander's Feast, with the Chorus's, &c. Where may be had, Proposals for Printing by Subscription ; Twelve Grand Concerto's, in 7 Parts. Composed by Mr. Handel . . . the Delivery of . . . which will be in April next.

N.B. Two of the above Concerto's will be perform'd this Evening, at the Theatre-Royal in Lincoln's-Inn Fields. . . .

(Smith, 1948, pp. 225 f.) The advertised edition of *Acis and Galatea* was the fourth. The advertisement was repeated on 15th December and again later, with the Notabene altered to : "Four of the above Concerto's have been perform'd at . . ." (cf. 14th February 1740).

—

CAST OF "ACIS AND GALATEA", 13th December 1739

Acis—Mr. Beard, tenor
Galatea—Signora Francesina, soprano
Polyphemus—Mr. Reinhold, bass
Damon—the Boy (? Robinson), soprano

Master Robinson was a child of the organist John Robinson and the singer Mrs. Ann Turner Robinson.

—

RICHARD WEST TO HORACE WALPOLE

Temple, Dec. 13, 1739.

Plays we have none, or damned ones. Handel has had a concerto this winter. No opera, no nothing. All for war and Admiral Haddock.

(Chrysander, III. 110 f.) Horace Walpole's correspondence with Thomas Gray, Richard West, and Thomas Ashton (edited by W. S. Lewis, etc.), New Haven, 1948, I. 197. "A concerto" means a series of concert performances. Nicholas Haddock was Commander of the Fleet in the Mediterranean.

—

FROM GEORG PHILIPP TELEMANN'S AUTOBIOGRAPHY OF 1739 (Translated)

. . . An improvised test brought about the pronouncement that I should become a student of law and entirely forswear music. . . . I betook myself in 1701 to Leipzig ; on the way, in Halle, through my acquaintance with *Georg Fried. Händel*,[1] already in those days of consequence, I wellnigh imbibed again the poison of music. . . .

. . . The pen of the admirable *Johann Kuhnau* served me here [as organist and director of music at the new church in Leipzig] to emulate him in fugue and counterpoint ; in melodic movements, however, and their analysis, *Händel* and I were constantly occupied, with frequent visits on both sides, and also with correspondence.

(Mattheson, *Ehrenpforte*, 1740, pp. 358 f.) The sketch was written in 1739, but published the next year. The beginning of the quotation refers to Telemann's law studies in Leipzig.

[1] Who was then scarcely 16 years old.

1740

For the years 1740 till 1743 there are no entries in Handel's accounts with the Bank of England.

—

FROM THE AUTHOR'S TWO INTRODUCTORY ESSAYS TO THE WORD-BOOK OF JOHN LOCKMAN'S MUSICAL DRAMA, "ROSALINDA", SET TO MUSIC BY JOHN CHRISTOPHER SMITH AND PERFORMED ON 4th January 1740

Enquiry into the Rise and Progress of Operas and Oratorios

. . . Mr. *Addison*, Mr. *Gay*, &c. took up their Pens, and gave the Public Pieces which were thought no way injurious to their Reputation as Writers. But whether it was owing to the Inability of the Composers, the Defects of the Performers, or the too prevailing Influence of the *Italian* Opera, those *English* pieces had not the wish'd for Success, if we except *Acis* and *Galatea*, which in every Respect charms, to this Day, Persons of all Ranks and Capacities.

. . . However, some Attempts have been made, of late Years, to rescue the Drama in question from the Ignominy under which it had so long laboured ; by setting to Music Pieces which are excellent in themselves, as *Alexander's Feast*. . . .

Some Reflections concerning Operas, Lyric Poetry, Music, &c.

. . . Among the many Things I have been told [of the Effect which Harmony had upon some of the Brute Creation] I shall mention but one ; to which the Author of the Music of the following Drama, was, among other Persons, an Eye-witness.

It relates to a Pigeon in the Dove-house of Mr. *Lee* in *Cheshire*. That Gentleman had a Daughter who was extremely fond of Music, and a very fine performer on the Harpsicord. The Dove-house was built not far from the Parlour, where the musical Instrument stood. The Pigeon, whenever the young Lady play'd any Air, except *Spera si* in *Otho*,[1] never stirred ; but as soon as that Air was touched, it would fly from the Dove-house to the Window ; there discover the most pleasing Emotions ; and the Instant the Air was over, fly back again. The young Lady was so delighted with the Fancy, that she ever after called *Spera si* the *Pigeon's Air*, and wrote it under that Title in her Music-book. . . .

But notwithstanding the wonderful Sublimity of Mr. *Handel*'s Compositions, yet the Place in which Oratorios are commonly performed among us, and some other Circumstances, must necessarily lessen the

[1] By Mr. *Handel*.

Solemnity of this Entertainment, to which possibly, the Choice of the Subject of these Dramas may likewise sometimes contribute.

Rosalinda was performed six times between 4th January and 25th April at Hickford's Great Room, in Brewer Street. The first of the introductory essays refers to Addison's *Rosamond*, composed by Clayton (1707), and, probably, to Gay's *Beggar's Opera* (cf. 30th April 1724, 29th January 1728, and 10th February 1733). Gay was the author of *Acis and Galatea*, and Dryden of *Alexander's Feast*. The second essay tells of Elizabeth Legh (spelled Lee), of Adlington Hall, Maccles-field, Cheshire (see 26th January 1727). She died in 1734 (buried in Westminster Abbey) and her father, John, in 1739; her brother, Charles, became Handel's friend. If Handel's pupil, Smith, visited the place, it seems probable that the tradition there is true, that Handel himself stayed at Adlington Hall, either on his way to Dublin or on his way back (1741–2). While Lockman clearly quotes " Spera si mi " from *Ottone*, Hawkins (V. 415) as well as Schoelcher (p. 76 f.) speak of " Spera, si mio caro " from *Admeto*. Although Miss Legh was among the subscribers for *Admeto* in 1727, *Ottone* was not printed on subscription, and ownership of the original edition of the score proves nothing.

———

The Governors of Mercer's Hospital, Dublin, at their meeting on 8th January 1740, arrange a charity service to be held at St Andrew's Church on 14th February, with *Te Deum and Jubilate* and " two new Anthems ". (Minute Book.)

The service, with a sermon preached by the Bishop of Derry, was postponed, on 5th February, till 6th March, when the Lord Lieutenant of Ireland, the Primate and the Chancellor were present. One thousand copies of the anthems were printed for the congregation. The music was Handel's.

———

Handel sets to music the ode *L'Allegro, il Penseroso, ed il Moderato* between 19th January and 9th February 1740.

———

Acis and Galatea and the *Ode for St. Cecilia's Day* are advertised for Thursday the 7th, *London Daily Post*, 4th February 1740.

(Schoelcher, pp. 225 f.)

———

From the " London Daily Post ", 6th February 1740

In consideration of the Weather continuing so cold, the Serenata called Acis and Galatea, that was to be performed To-morrow Night at the Theatre-Royal in Lincoln's-Inn-Fields, will be put off for a few Nights further ; of which Notice will be given in the General and Daily Advertisers.

(Chrysander, III. 111.) The *London Daily Post* had the sub-title " General Advertiser " ; there was also a *Daily Advertiser*.

———

FROM THE " LONDON DAILY POST ", 11th February 1740

At the Theatre-Royal . . . Thursday next [the 14th], will be perform'd ACIS and GALATEA. . . .
Particular Care has been taken to have the House survey'd and secur'd against the Cold, by having Curtains plac'd before every Door, and constant Fires will be kept in the House 'till the Time of Performance.

———

FROM THE " LONDON DAILY POST ", 14th February 1740

Two chief Singers being taken ill, the Serenata call'd Acis and Galatea, that was to be perform'd this Day at the Theatre-Royal in Lincoln's-Inn Fields, must therefore be put off performing a few Days longer, whereof Notice will be given in the London Daily Post, and Daily Advertiser.
(Chrysander, III. 111.)

———

Walsh, in an advertisement in the *London Daily Post* of 14th February 1740, refers to the subscription for the " Twelve Grand Concerto's for Violins in seven Parts ", and adds : " Four of the above Concerto's have been perform'd at the Theatre-Royal in Lincoln's-Inn Fields ".

———

Handel finishes the Organ Concerto in B flat, Opus 7, no. 1, 17th February 1740.

———

FROM THE " LONDON DAILY POST ", 21st February 1740

At the Theatre-Royal . . . this Day . . ., will be perform'd ACIS and GALATEA, A Serenata. (*Being the last Time of performing in this Season.*) . . . To which will be added The last New ODE of Mr. DRYDEN'S. . . .
(Chrysander, III. 112.) Cf. 28th March.

———

John Christopher Smith's oratorio *David's Lamentation over Saul and Jonathan* is produced at Hickford's Great Room, Brewer Street, 22nd February 1740.
Lockman's text, first set by Boyce (cf. 16th April 1736), was more successful in the setting of Handel's pupil. It was performed six times between 22nd February and 2nd April.

———

FROM THE " LONDON DAILY POST ", 27th February 1740

Never perform'd before.
At the Theatre-Royal in Lincoln's-Inn Fields, this Day . . ., will be perform'd *L'Allegro il Penseroso ed il Moderato.* With two new *Concerto's*

for several Instruments, and a new *Concerto* on the Organ. . . . Pit and Galleries to be open'd at Four, and Boxes at Five. Particular Care is taken to have the House secur'd against the Cold, constant Fires being order'd to be kept in the House 'till the Time of Performance.

(Schoelcher, p. 229.) The text of the ode was Milton's, but augmented by a third part, called " Il Moderato ", written by Jennens. The last part was introduced by the Organ Concerto in B flat (see 17th February), each of the others by one of the new " Concerti Grossi ". For the double-bassoon, provided in the score, see 11th October 1727. The libretto was printed by J. and R. Tonson. Repeat performances on 6th, 10th, 14th March and 23rd April. Revived in January 1741 and March 1743.

———

CAST OF " L'ALLEGRO, IL PENSEROSO ED IL MODERATO ",
27th February 1740

Sopranos—Signora Francesina and the Boy (Robinson?)
Alto—Mr. Russell
Tenor—Mr. Beard
Bass—Mr. Reinhold

———

At the Music-Hall in Crow-street, Dublin, a benefit concert is given for Signor Dioniso Barbiatelli on 29th February 1740, with " Mr. Handel's favourite Songs in the Oratorio of Hester ".

(Faulkner's *Dublin Journal*, 26th February 1740.)

———

Walsh advertises " Songs in L'Allegro ed il Penseroso ", *London Daily Post*, 15th March 1740.

(Chrysander, III. 137.) The price, 4s., was added in the advertisement on 20th March. In his two selections Walsh called the ode after Milton's title. In the combined edition, however, he gave Handel's title in full. Cf. 7th and 13th May.

———

Saul is revived at Lincoln's Inn Fields on 21st March 1740, " With a Concerto for several Instruments, never perform'd before " (*London Daily Post*).

(Schoelcher, p. 226.) In addition to the new " Concerto Grosso " there was an organ concerto.

———

Esther is revived at Lincoln's Inn Fields on 26th March 1740, with the " Concerto Grosso " played on 21st March, and a concerto on the organ (*London Daily Post*).

(Schoelcher, p. 226.) The performance began at half-past six, while *Saul*, on the 21st, started at seven o'clock.

———

FROM THE " LONDON DAILY POST ", 28th March 1740

For the Benefit and Increase of a Fund established for the Support of
Decayed Musicians and their Families.

At the Theatre-Royal in Lincoln's-Inn Fields, this Day . . ., will be
performed ACIS and GALATEA, a Serenata. With the new Concertos,
performed in the same this Season, for several Instruments. To which
will be added, The last new Ode of Mr. Dryden's, and the Concerto
on the Organ, that was composed by Mr. Handel on the same Occasion
this Season. . . . To begin at Half an Hour after Six o'Clock. N.B.
Each Subscriber's Ticket will admit one into the Boxes or Pit, or two
into the Gallery.

(Burney, IV. 660.) For the concertos, cf. 22nd November and 13th December
1739, and 27th February 1740.

—

FROM THE " LONDON DAILY POST ", 1st April 1740

There having been a greater Demand for the Paper in which the
following Letter was printed the last Year, than there were Numbers to
supply, the *Writer* of it has been prevailed on to suffer it to be re-publish'd
at this Juncture. And as the *Entertainment* it refers to is to be represented
this Evening, 'tis humbly hoped it will not be thought an improper
Prelude to it ; having a Tendency to excite a due Solemnity of Mind
and Behaviour, with which such Pieces of *sacred Musick* ought to be
heard perform'd, either to do *Honour* to an *Audience*, or *Justice* to the
Performance.—And, if the *Effects* of our late *Humiliation* did not go off
with the *Weather*, it may be hoped, that what is therein said, on the
supposal of a *General Popish Alliance* against us, may, if attended to, help
us forward, in the right Way, to stand our Ground against *those* that
have already ; and as many more as shall hereafter, think fit to *declare*
against us.

Cf. 18th April 1739. " R. W." 's letter was reprinted on the occasion of the
revival of *Israel in Egypt*. The end of this introduction to the letter refers to the
Spaniards (see 27th October 1739).

—

Israel in Egypt is revived at Lincoln's Inn Fields on 1st April 1740,
" For that Day only in this Season ", " With a New Concerto for
several Instruments, And a Concerto on the Organ " (*London
Daily Post*).

(Schoelcher, p. 211.) The performance began at half-past six.

—

FROM THE " LONDON DAILY POST ", 2nd April 1740

The Fourteenth Night.

TWO ANTHEMS (*O Sing unto the Lord, and my Song shall be alway*) set
to Musick by Mr. HANDEL.

.   .   .   .   .

Will be perform'd (this Evening only) at Hickford's Great Room in Brewer street near Golden-Square, To-day.

The Vocal Parts by Mrs. ARNE, Mr. BEARD, Mr. RUSSEL, Mr. RHEIN-HOLD, and others. . . .

This was the fourteenth night in a series of concerts given at Hickford's. After the two Chandos Anthems, Smith's oratorio (see 22nd February) was repeated for the last time. Mrs. Robert Harrison, writing in the first edition of Grove's *Dictionary* (II. 396) on Hickford's Room, thought the Handel anthems were new, and performed there for the first time.

FROM THE " LONDON DAILY POST ", 21st April 1740

NEW MUSICK.
This Day is published,
(*With his* Majesty's Royal Licence and Protection,)
TWELVE GRAND CONCERTO'S FOR VIOLINS,
in Seven Parts.
Composed by Mr. HANDEL.

N.B. Those Gentlemen who are Subscribers are desired to send for their Books to the Author ; or J. Walsh. . . .

(Schoelcher, p. 227.) Cf. 29th October 1739. The work was called Opus 6 from the second edition (1746) onwards.

EXTRACTS FROM THE LIST OF SUBSCRIBERS FOR THE " TWELVE GRAND CONCERTOS IN SEVEN PARTS ", LATER CALLED OPUS 6, PUBLISHED ON 21st April 1740

His Royal Highness The Duke of Cumberland
Her Royal Highness The Princess of Orange
Her Royal Highness The Princess Amelia
Her Royal Highness The Princess Caroline
Her Royal Highness The Princess Mary
Her Royal Highness The Princess Louisa
Academy of Musick at Dublin, 2 Sets
Right Hon. Countess of Carlisle
Right Hon. Earl Cowper
Hon. Thos. Carter Esq. Master of the Rolls in Ireland
Crown and Anchor Society
Musical Society in Canterbury
Society of Musick at the Castle in Paternoster Row,
    3 Sets
Wm. Freeman
Mr. [William] De Fesch

Hon. B. Granville
James Harris
Charles Jennens, 2 Sets
Sir Windham Knatchbull Bart.
Ladies Concert in Lincoln
Monday Night Musical Society at yᵉ Globe Tavern
    Fleet St., 2 Sets
Musical Society at Oxford, 2 Sets
Philarmonic Society at the Crown and Anchor, 3 Sets
Iohn Rich, 3 Sets
Mr. [John] Robinson Organist
Right Hon. Countess Dowager of Shaftsbury
Right Hon. Countess of Shaftsbury
Right Hon. Earl of Shaftsbury, 2 Sets
Swan Society of Musick, 3 Sets
Salisbury Society of Musick
Benjamin Short
Jonathan Tyers, 4 Sets
Charles Weidman
Mr. [Christian Frederick] Zincke

This was the tenth, and last, list of subscribers for printed Handel scores. There were 100 subscribers for 122 copies. In the cases of three subscribers—Jennens, the Oxford Musical Society and the Earl of Shaftesbury—the numbers of sets are added by hand, probably because originally one copy only was ordered. The list is printed, on two pages of a leaf, in the part of the Violino Primo Concertino. This was the only instrumental work of Handel's printed by subscription. It seems that in this case Handel was his own publisher, with Walsh acting only as his agent.

———

From the " London Daily Post ", 23rd April 1740

At the Theatre-Royal . . . this Day . . . will be perform'd L'Allegro il Penseroso ed il Moderato. With Two New Concerto's on several Instruments, never perform'd before. And a Concerto on the Organ. . . . To begin at Half an Hour after Six o'Clock. (*Being the last Time of performing this Season.*)

———

Saul is performed at the Academy of Ancient Music, 24th April 1740.

(Schoelcher, p. 205.) The meetings of this club, under Pepusch, were at the " Crown and Anchor " Tavern. A copy of the printed libretto is in the British Museum.

———

MISS ANNE DONELLAN TO MISS ELIZABETH ROBINSON

London, April 1740

. . . My present delight is the fine lady who admires and hates to excess ; she doats on the dear little boy that dances, she detests Handel's Oratorios.

(Elizabeth Montagu, p. 44.) For Miss Donellan see 12th April 1734 ; for Miss Robinson see July 1738. The name of the " fine lady " is not indicated.

———

Walsh advertises the second collection of songs in *L'Allegro ed il Penseroso*, *London Daily Post*, 7th May 1740.

(Chrysander, III. 137.) Cf. 15th March.

———

FROM THE " LONDON DAILY POST ", 13th May 1740

MUSICK.

This Day is published,

L'ALLEGRO IL PENSEROSO ED IL MODERATO, the Words taken from MILTON. Set to Musick by Mr. HANDEL.

₊₊ Those Gentlemen who have already the first Collection of this Work, may have the second Part to compleat it. Price 3s.

(Chrysander, III. 137.) Cf. 15th March and 7th May. Walsh simply bound the two collections together when he gave the music its full title.

———

FROM THE " GENTLEMAN'S MAGAZINE ", May 1740

To Mr. HANDEL,

on hearing ' Alexander's feast,' ' L'Allegro, ed il Penseroso ', etc.

If e'er *Arion's* music calm'd the floods,
And *Orpheus* ever drew the dancing woods ;
Why do not *British* trees and forest throng
To hear the sweeter notes of *Handel's* song ?
This does the falsehood of the fable prove,
Or seas and woods, when *Handel* harps, would move.
If music was to touch the heart design'd,
To ease the pain'd, or charm the chearful mind ;
And has the ear in this no other part,
Than as it opes a passage to the heart ;
How comes it we those artless masters bear,
Who slight the heart, and only court the ear ?
And when they use a finer term, they cry
'Tis air, and into air they let it fly.
But *Handel's* harmony affects the soul,
To sooth by sweetness, or by force controul ;

And with like sounds as tune the rolling spheres,
So tunes the mind, that ev'ry sense has ears.
   When jaundice jealousy, and carking care,
Or tyrant pride, or homicide despair,
The soul as on a rack in torture keep,
Those monsters *Handel's* music lulls to sleep.
How, when he strikes the keys, do we rejoice !
Or when he fills a thousand tubes with voice,
Or gives his lessons to the speaking string,
And some to breathe the flute, and some to sing ;
To sound the trumpet, or the horn to swell,
Or brazen cylinder to speak compel ;
His art so modulates the sounds in all,
Our passions, as he pleases, rise and fall ;
Their hold of us, at his command they quit,
And to his pow'r with pride and joy submit.
   Thou, sovereign of the lyre, dost so excel,
Who against thee, against thy art rebel.
But uncontested is in song, thy sway ;
Thee all the nations where 'tis known obey :
E'en *Italy*, who long usurp'd the lyre,
Is proud to learn thy precepts and admire.
What harmony she had thou thence didst bring
And imp'd thy genius with a stronger wing ;
To form thee, talent, travel, art, combine,
And all the powers of music now are thine.

                                 G. O.

(Chrysander, III. 138 f.) The initials G.O. have not been identified.

———

Charles Corbett advertises the final state of Bickham's *Musical Entertainment* in two volumes, with figured bass by John Frederick Lampe ; the "Musick by *Purcell, Handell, Corelli, Green,* And other *Eminent Masters*", London Daily Post, 26th July 1740.

   Cf. 6th June 1738. Volume I in second edition.

———

Handel resumes work on the opera *Imeneo,* writing the overture on 9th September 1740.

   Cf. 9th September 1738. ———

FROM MATTHESON'S "GRUNDLAGE EINER EHREN-PFORTE" ("BASIS FOR A ROLL OF HONOUR"), HAMBURG (AUTUMN), 1740 (Translated)

   . . . Several great princes of art [have] been very dilatory in sending me their information. . . . Is it not a pity, for instance, that no detailed and well planned essay by *Keiser* and *Händel,* etc., from their own hand, can be imparted, as it can in the case of the praiseworthy *Telemann* ? They have both broken faith with me. One has died in the meantime ; and the other has put the matter aside. . . .

In the summer of 1703 he [Handel] came to Hamburg, rich in capability and goodwill. He made almost his first acquaintance with me, by means of which he had access to the organs and choirs of the town, to operas and concerts ; especially, however, was he led to a certain house, where everything was ardently devoted to music. At first he played second violin in the Opera orchestra, and behaved as though he did not know how many beans made five, for he was inclined by nature to dry jokes.[1] When, however, on one occasion, a harpsichord player was missing, he let himself be persuaded to stand in his stead, and did it manfully ; without anyone having suspected it possible, except me.

He composed at that time long, long arias, and almost endless cantatas, which still had not yet the right skill or the right taste, albeit a perfect harmony ; he was, however, soon fashioned in quite another form by the high school of the opera.

He was a skilful organist : more skilful than *Kuhnau* in fugue and counterpoint, particularly *ex tempore* ; but he knew very little about melodic writing before he got to the Hamburg Opera. . . .

Most of the time in those days my late father provided him with free board, and he repaid that by imparting to me several choice touches of counterpoint. However, I did no small service for him with regard to dramatic style, and one good turn deserved another.

We journeyed together on 17th Aug. of that same year, 1703, to Lübeck, and in the coach constructed many double fugues, *da mente, non da penna*. The President of the Privy Council, *Magnus von Wedderkopp*, had invited me there : in order to find for the admirable organist *Dieterich Buxtehude* a future successor. I took *Händel* with me. We played there almost every organ and harpsichord, and by reason of our playing made a particular decision, of which I have made mention elsewhere : namely, that he should play only the organ, and I the harpsichord. Besides, we listened to the above-mentioned artist, in his Marienkirche, with merited attention. Since, however, a marriage contract was proposed in connection with the affair, for which neither one of us showed the slightest desire, we left the place, after receiving many tokens of respect and enjoying entertainments. *Johann Christian Schieferdecker* thenceforth devoted himself more closely to his aim, and after the death of the father, *Buxtehude*, gained the lady and the fair employment, which today is laudably filled by *Johann Paul Kuntzen*.

[1] I know for certain, should he read this, he will laugh inwardly, for outwardly he laughs little. Especially if he remembers the pigeon-dealer, who travelled with us at that time on the mail-coach to Lübeck, likewise the pastry-cook's son, who had to work the bellows for us while we played in the Mary-Magdalene Church there. That was on 30th July 1703, as we had been out on the water on the preceding 15th. And hundreds of similar incidents hover still in my thoughts.

In the year 1704, when I was in Holland, intending to go to England,[1] I received on 21st March, in Amsterdam, such an obliging and emphatic letter from *Händel* in Hamburg, that it moved me, principally, to take the journey back home again. The said letter is dated 18th March 1704 and contains amongst other things these expressions. . . . [quoted pp. on 11 f.].

On 5th December of the above-mentioned year, when my third opera, *Cleopatra*, was performed, and *Händel* sat at the harpsichord, a misunderstanding arose : such a thing is nothing new with young people, who strive after honour with all their power and little consideration. I, as composer, conducted, and at the same time personated *Antonius*, who, about half-an-hour before the end of the play, commits suicide. Now until that occasion I had been accustomed, after this action, to go into the orchestra and accompany the rest myself : which unquestionably the author can do better than anyone else ; this time, however, it was denied to me. Instigated by several people, we thereupon, at the exit of the Opera House, on the public market place and with a multitude of onlookers, fought a duel, which might have passed off very unfortunately for both of us, had God's guidance not graciously ordained that my blade, thrusting against the broad, metallic coat-button of my opponent, should be shattered. No especial harm therefore came of the affair, and through the intervention of one of the most eminent councillors in Hamburg, as well as of the then lessees of the Opera House, we were soon reconciled again ; and I had the honour, on the same day, namely, 30th December, of entertaining *Händel*, whereupon we were both present in the evening at the rehearsal of his *Almira*, and became better friends than before. The words of Ecclesiasticus, ch. 22, fit the case here : *Though thou drawest a sword at thy friend, yet despair not : for there may be a returning to favour. If thou openest thy mouth against thy friend, fear not ; for there may be a reconciliation : except for upbraiding, or pride, or disclosing of secrets, or a treacherous wound : for, for these things, every friend will depart.*[2] I relate this event according to the true circumstances of it, because it is not yet so long since, that crooked people have wished to construe it crookedly.

Händel successfully performed his aforesaid opera, *Almira*, on 8th January 1705.[3] *Nero* followed on 25th Febr. In the last two beautiful operas I played the chief parts amid general applause, and after that I took a pleasant farewell of the theatre. . . . *Händel* remained for a farther 4 or 5 years with the Opera there, and had very many pupils besides.

He composed in 1708 *Florindo* as well as *Daphne* ; which, however, would not match *Almira*. In 1709 he composed nothing. After that the opportunity arose of setting out on a free journey to Italy with

[1] My inclination was always to England : and behold ! I gratified it in Hamburg, with more convenience.
[2] The German quotation, from " Syrach ", is shorter. (Ed.)
[3] Not 1704 as erroneously stated in the *Musikalischer Patriot*, which please alter.

Binitz. At Venice, in the winter of 1710, he produced his *Agrippina*, on the stage at *St. Gio. Crisostomo* : when, 8 years afterwards, it adorned the Hamburg theatre, people imagined, not unreasonably, that they could perceive in it various imitations from *Porsenna* etc., quite similar to the originals.

The remaining *Singspiele* from *Händel's* pen, as *Rinaldo*, 1715 ; *Oriana*, 1717 ; together with the just mentioned *Agrippina*, 1718 ; *Zenobia*, 1721 ; *Muzio Scevola* and *Floridante*, 1723 ; *Tamerlan, Julius Cäsar* and *Otto*, 1725 ; *Richardus I*, 1729 ; *Admetus*, 1730 ; *Cleofida* (also called by its correct name *Porus*) and *Judith*, 1732 ; lastly, *Rodelinda*, 1734, have been played here in Hamburg in his absence and [their scores] have been sent in from outside. Such was also the case with the music to Brockes' *Passion*, which he also composed in England, and had sent here by post in an uncommonly close-written score. . . .

While the Handelian operas are, most of them, composed to Italian words, yet they have been performed here partly in that language, but partly subjected to the greatest alterations through translation and interpolation. . . . In all 19 or 20 of his dramatic pieces are known here in Hamburg, although in London there are perhaps still more, from which arias have been engraved there, and are somewhat expensive.

In the year 1717 *Händel* was in Hanover, and was, if I am right, Capellmeister to the then Crown Prince and Elector, now King of England. I also received letters from him at the time, from the afore-mentioned Hanover, about the dedication to the second part of my *Orchestre*, which was entitled *Beschützte* (*Defended*), and dedicated to him amongst others. In consideration of this he sent to me from London, in 1719, and in still more detail, his thoughts about it, which have already found their place in the *Critica Musica*, Part II, pp. 210, 211. Just at that time he promised to send me the most memorable events of his life : I very much regret, however, that such has not yet happened ; but rather that, on my repeated solicitations, when I dedicated to him the *Fingersprache*, as all the world knows, the following answer came to hand on 5th August 1735 : [There follows Handel's letter of 18th/29th July 1735, in French, and in a German translation.]

Since that time, that is to say on 10 November 1739, when the Court and Nobility, indeed the whole nation, have been more intent on the harmful war than on plays and entertainments, and therefore no excuse could be made, a hint was again dropped, as polite as it was considerate, and accompanied by many reasons for compliance ; but it has proved to be as fruitless as the former ones. People have given me to understand, in confidence, that this famous man strives so industriously after the solution of a certain *Canon clausus*, which begins : *Frangit Deus omne superbum &c.*, that he puts everything else but that out of sight. But I will not, in the slightest degree, stand surety for the truth of such a statement.

I disclose therefore only what is known to me, and which I can recollect for certain from letters and diaries, and which I saw for myself. . . . The high price of these pieces [engraved in London] has prevented my ordering them all. Meanwhile, a man to whom I have rendered so much kindness in his first, somewhat feeble, excursion, to whom I have, besides showing him due honour in my writings, publicly dedicated not only the *Beschützte Orchestre*, but also just recently a considerable engraved work, and to whom, as a high prince of art, I have dispatched it, not without cost, might have communicated, if not to me, yet to the world of music that honours him, one proper specimen or other [of his life], or merely news of his praiseworthy professional activities. For we have been alike members of an Opera House, playfellows and accomplices, travelling companions and fellow boarders, *we took sweet counsel together, and walked into the House of God in company.*

Once the report had it that, on account of Italian spite and persecution, he was at the end of his tether. That was shortly before the time when, as mentioned before, he instanced in a letter to me *his unfortunate circumstances.*[1] I hear from a trustworthy source, that had the Royal Purse not taken care of him which occurred through the presentation of the score of a new opera, he would perchance have been a sorry sight. He has, moreover, as much as I could discover, no definite appointment or service at the Court, apart from his instruction of the princesses ; but maintains his state, and that indeed no mean one, from operas, concerts, and occasional music for the Coronation and the like.

The King of England retains, as King, no foreign so-called Capellmeister, but all offices in the music of the Church must, in the ordinary course, be filled by native composers. . . . Since English Church music must be so served, it is easy to understand why *Händel* has no established post there. . . .

People try to point out that now *Händel* has become a Licentiate, now a Doctor of Music : now again, that while he was at Oxford he declined the latter dignity with all courtesy, and so on. But without his confirming it, nothing of all this can be determined for certain. One has also not yet heard that he is married : albeit it were high time. . . .

Finally, the eulogies of our world-famous *Händel*, which could never be pitched too high, can be consulted and encountered in various places in my writings, as, for instance, in the *Critica*, in the *Musikalischer Patriot*, in the *Kern Melodischer Wissenschaft*, in the *Vollkommener Capellmeister*, and so on, so that it would only be superfluous to recapitulate the same here.

> *Dignum laude virum Musa vetat mori.*

(*Ehrenpforte*, p. xxiii (preface), pp. 93–101.) The book contains the lives of 148 " excellent " musicians. It had been planned since 1714. Johann Sebastian

---

[1] I believe he thought that I perhaps expected a gift from him.

Bach did not acknowledge Mattheson's request for information, and was therefore omitted (Cannon, p. 201). This alone would expose Mattheson's scholarship, but his story of Handel's life (the first attempt to write it) tells more of Mattheson, the man, colleague and friend, than of Handel. The dedication of the book is dated August 1740. For Telemann's contribution see (end of) 1739. The " certain house " in Hamburg was that of John Wyche (see 7th November 1703). For Wedderkopp, see 17th August 1703. Instead of going to England, Mattheson became secretary to the British Resident in Hamburg. Nothing is known of Herr von Binitz, the supposed patron of Handel on his journey to Italy. For the alleged plagiarisms from *Porsenna*, see July 1722. For Handel's *Brockes Passion*, see spring 1719 ; the autograph is lost. For Mattheson's book *Das beschützte Orchestre*, see 8th July 1717 ; for his *Fingersprache* (middle of) 1735. Handel's letter of 24th February 1719 was published in *Critica Musica*, 1725. The political situation in London. in the autumn of 1739 is referred to under 27th October 1739. The Enigma Canon, supposed to have been written by Handel, refers to his alleged haughtiness. Handel's letter of 18th (29th) July 1735 did not refer to any unfortunate circumstances of his. He never, to our knowledge, dedicated an opera in score to King George II, nor did he hand over to him the manuscript. Mattheson apparently did not know that Handel had been naturalized previously.

———

Handel finishes the opera *Imeneo*, 10th October 1740.

———

Handel begins the opera *Deidamia*, 27th October 1740.

———

FROM THE " GENTLEMAN'S MAGAZINE ", October 1740
On our late TASTE *in* MUSICK.
By a Gentleman of OXFORD.

.   .   .   .   .

See *Handel*, careless of a foreign fame,
Fix on our shore, and *boast* a *Briton*'s name :
While, plac'd marmoric in the vocal grove,[1]
He guides the measures listening throngs approve.

.   .   .   .   .

(Young, p. 64.) These verses are from a longer poem.

———

FROM THE " LONDON DAILY POST ", 8th November 1740
NEW MUSICK.
This Day is published,
A Second Set of
SIX CONCERTO'S FOR THE HARPSICHORD OR ORGAN.
Compos'd by Mr. HANDEL.
Printed for and Sold by J. Walsh. . . .

[1] *Vaux-hall.*

(Chrysander, III. 160.) For the first set see 4th October 1738. While the first set was called Opus 4, and the third, published posthumously, Opus 7, the second was given no opus number ; its contents were, in fact, mostly arrangements from the *Concerti grossi*, Opus 6.

———

FROM THE SAME

At the Theatre-Royal in Lincoln's-Inn Fields, this Day . . . will be perform'd a *Serenata*, PARNASSO IN FESTA. With *Concerto's* on the *Organ*, and several Instruments. . . . N.B. Perticular Care has been taken to air the House well, and keep it warm. To begin at Six o'Clock.

(Burney, IV. 432.) This was the beginning of Handel's second and last season at Lincoln's Inn Fields. Handel's evenings were now on Saturdays. Another performance of the serenata was on 14th March 1741 ; the last revival in Handel's lifetime.

———

MISS DONELLAN TO MISS ELIZABETH ROBINSON

[London,] 15 November [1740].
. . . Handel next week has a new opera, which those who have heard the rehearsal say is very pretty. Tell Pen the ' Lion Song ' is in it. . . .

(Montagu, p. 92 : dated 15th Nov. 1741.) The editor of the letter adds : " Does she mean ' The Messiah ', which he produced this year, but which at first was not appreciated ? " The date, as given above, is further proved by the writer mentioning the first appearance in London of Mrs. Woffington as Sir Harry Wildair in *The Constant Couple* on " next Monday ", *i.e.* on 21st November 1740 ; it was her third London part. The opera referred to was *Imeneo*. The " Lion Song " was Argento's aria " Su l'arena di barbara scena in campo feroce leone ", in Act II. " Pen " is Mrs. Pendarves.

———

Handel finishes the opera *Deidamia*, 20th November 1740.

———

FROM THE " LONDON DAILY POST ", 22nd November 1740

At the Theatre-Royal . . . this Day . . . will be perform'd an *Operetta*, call'd HYMEN. . . . To begin at Six o'Clock.

(Burney, IV. 432.) The issue of 22nd November is missing in the British Museum, but earlier advertisements of *Hymen* are preserved there. The author is not known. The word-book was printed by T. Wood ; the only known copy is in the National Library of Scotland, Edinburgh. There was only one repeat performance, originally planned for the 29th November, but owing to Signora Francesina's indisposition (Burney, IV. 432) postponed till 13th December. Handel, however, had the work sung at a concert in Dublin on 24th March 1742, under the title of a serenata.

———

CAST OF " IMENEO ", 22nd November 1740

Imeneo—Mr. Savage, counter-tenor
Tirinto—Signor Andreoni, soprano
Rosmene—Signora Francesina, soprano
Clomiri—Miss Edwards, soprano
Argeno—Mr. Reinhold, bass

Signor Andreoni and Miss Edwards were new singers in Handel's company.

—

FROM THE " LONDON DAILY POST ", 13th December 1740

*By Command of his Royal Highness the
Prince of Wales*

At the Theatre-Royal . . ., this Day . . ., will be perform'd a New *Operetta*, call'd HYMEN. . . .

_{*} Strict Orders have been given for Fires to be kept in the House to make it warm.

To begin at Half an Hour after Six o'Clock.

—

MRS. PENDARVES TO HER SISTER, MRS. DEWES, AT BRADLEY

Bullstrode, 21 Dec. 1740.

Mr. Handel has got a new singer from Italy. Her voice is between Cuzzoni's and Strada's—strong, but not harsh, her person *miserably bad*, being very low, and *excessively* crooked. Donellan approves of her : she is not to sing on the stage till after Xmas, so I shall not lose her first performance.

(Delany, II. 140.) Ann Granville married in 1740. The new singer, a soprano, was Signora Monza.

1741

FROM THE " LONDON DAILY POST ", 10th January 1741

At the Theatre-Royal in Lincoln's Inn Fields, this Day, will be per-form'd a New Opera, call'd DEIDAMIA. . . . To begin at Half an Hour after Six o'Clock.

(Burney, IV. 433, 436.) The text of Handel's last opera was again by Rolli ; it seems they were reconciled. There were three performances only : the repeats being on 17th January and (at six o'clock) on 10th February. The libretto, printed by J. Chrichley, is entitled : *Deidamia Melodrama di P.R. F.R.S.*

CAST OF " DEIDAMIA ", 10th January 1741

Deidamia—Signora Francesina, soprano
Nerea—Signora Monza, soprano
Achille—Miss Edwards, soprano
Ulisse—Signor Andreoni, soprano
Fenice—Mr. Savage, counter-tenor
Lycomede—Mr. Reinhold, bass

FROM THE " LONDON DAILY POST ", 14th January 1741

In a short Time will be publish'd,
The Opera of DEIDAMIA in Score.
Compos'd by Mr. *Handel.*
The Price to Subscribers is Half a Guinea, to be paid at the Time of Subscribing.
Subscriptions are taken in by J. Walsh. . . .

Once again Walsh tried a subscription, but without success. He published the first act on 29th January, as a specimen, and the score, fairly complete, was ready on 21st February. There is no list of subscribers. The price was 10s. 6d. to every-one.

FROM THE " LONDON DAILY POST ", 28th January 1741

For the Benefit of Mr. Christopher Smith, *Sen.*

. . . . .

At the New Theatre in the Hay-market, on Tuesday next [3rd February], will be perform'd A GRAND CONCERT of Vocal and Instru-mental MUSICK. . . . The Vocal Parts to consist of several of Mr. Handel's Chorus's. . . .

The benefit was for Johann Christoph Schmidt, the friend of Handel's youth (cf. summer 1716), probably arranged by his son, John Christopher Smith, Handel's pupil. According to Kidson (1900, p. 139), the father was identical with the Christopher Smith, " at ye Hand & Musick-Book in Coventry-street near ye Hay-market ", joint printer and seller of Handel's *Lessons* (2nd November 1720), *Radamisto* (3rd-15th December 1720), and *Riccardo Primo* (17th February 1728).

——

Walsh advertises the first collection of songs from *Deidamia*, price 4s., *London Daily Post*, 29th January 1741.

(Chrysander, II. 455.) Cf. 14th January and 21st February. The " First Collection " contained the overture and the first act.

——

FROM THE " LONDON DAILY POST ", 31st January 1741

At the Theatre-Royal . . . this Day, will be perform'd L'ALLEGRO, IL PENSEROSO ED IL MODERATO. *With several* New ADDITIONS *and* CONCERTOS *on the* ORGAN, *and several* INSTRUMENTS. . . . The Pit and Gallery Doors will be open'd at Four o'Clock. And the Boxes at Five. To begin at Half an Hour after Six o'Clock.

(Schoelcher, p. 233.) Chrysander, III. 128 f, enumerates the additions, eleven in all, one for (?) Mr. Beard, one for Signora Monza, and one taken from *Deidamia*. Three of the additional arias were published by Walsh in 1742. Repeat performances on 7th, 21st February and 8th April. It seems that Signora Monza sang in place of the Boy, while Signor Andreoni sang the part originally sung by an alto, and Miss Edwards may have sung another soprano part. Mr. Corfe (tenor) and Mr. Savage (counter-tenor) may also have been in the cast. Cf. 27th February 1740 and 18th March 1743.

——

Walsh again advertises the score of *L'Allegro*, *London Daily Post*, 2nd February 1741.

This was a new issue, with double pagination, and with the music in a different order. The price of 7s. was announced on 21st February.

——

FROM THE " LONDON DAILY POST ", 3rd February 1741

For the Benefit of Mr. Christopher Smith, sen. . . . At the New Theatre in the Hay-market, this Day will be perform'd a Grand Concert of Vocal and Instrumental Musick. . . . The Vocal Parts to consist of several of Mr. Handel's Chorus's.

(Smith, 1953, p. 13.)

——

A concert, which includes the Overture and the Dead March from *Saul*, is given for the Benefit of Mr. John Lyne at Hickford's Great Room, 5th February 1741. (*London Daily Post*.)

——

BARON BIELFELD TO BARON K * * * IN BERLIN

London, February 7, 1741

. . . During my first voyage to London, in the year 1736, I found two Italian opera companies there. The celebrated Mr. Hendel directed the one, and had as his leading singers Signor Conti-Giziello and Signora Strada, as well as an admirable bass. Apart from that his opera-house was noted for the quality of the music, which was perfectly written. This English Orpheus dictated the harmonies himself [presided at the harpsichord]. But he had a formidable rival, Mr. Heidegger, the manager of another opera company at the *Heymarket* Theatre. The latter offered the public the best productions of Messrs. Hasse and Porpora and had them performed by Messrs. Farinelli, Senesino and Madame Cuzzoni. The eminent skill of the composers, the extraordinary quality of the voices, the rivalry in performance—all this made London then the centre of. the musical world. But today it seems that Euterpe has abandoned the shores of Albion and we have nothing left but the *Oratorio*, that is, a kind of sacred concert, which Mr. Hendel occasionally puts on.

From Letter XXIX, written, perhaps, on 27th January (7th February). I. 266 f. of the original edition, IV. 63 f. of the English translation. Jakob Friedrich Freiherr von Bielfeld, author and diplomat, became, in 1740, secretary to the Prussian Legations at Hanover and London ; he stayed in London from the beginning of 1741 till May, and returned to Berlin the same year. Addressed probably to Baron Knobelsdorff ; see 10th March. In 1736 Handel's opera was at Covent Garden, the Nobility Opera at the Haymarket. The bass referred to may have been Waltz or Reinhold.

———

With the third, and last, performance of his opera *Deidamia*, Handel finally takes leave of the stage, 10th February 1741.

———

In St. Andrew's Church, Dublin, Handel's [Utrecht] *Te Deum and Jubilate* with two [Coronation] Anthems are performed, 14th February 1741.

There was a rehearsal on the 10th. The Governors issued a report on the 16th, published in the *Dublin Gazette* on the 17th : " perform'd . . . with the greatest Decency and Exactness, for the Support of Mercer's Hospital " ; " the Lord Justices and a great number of Persons of the First Quality and Distinction " attended, the Lord Bishop of Ferns (George Stone) preached the sermon.

———

FROM THE " LONDON DAILY POST ", 21st February 1741

This Day is published,

The whole Opera of DEIDAMIA in Score. *Compos'd by* Mr. HANDEL.

** Those Gentlemen, &c. who have the first Act of the above Work, may have the remaining Part separate to compleat their Opera.

Printed for J. Walsh. . . .

(Chrysander, II. 455.) Acts II and III were new. On 21st March the price,
10s. 6d., is added. Cf. 14th and 29th January.

———

The performance of *L'Allegro*, on 21st February 1741, is " By
Command of their Royal Highnesses the Prince and Princess of
Wales " (*London Daily Post*).

———

FROM THE " LONDON DAILY POST ", 26th February 1741

For the Benefit of Mr. Valentine Snow.

At the New Theatre in the Hay-market, this Day, will be perform'd
A GRAND CONCERT of Vocal and Instrumental MUSICK, By the best
Hands. Particularly . . . the Dead March in Saul to be perform'd with
the Sackbuts, To which will be added, set to Musick by Mr. Handel,
DRYDEN'S ODE ON ST. CECILIA'S DAY. The principal Voice-Part to be
perform'd by Mrs. Arne.

Snow was a well-known trumpet player. Sackbut was the old English name
for the trombone. Mrs. Arne was the former Miss Cecilia Young. For the
" Ode " cf. 28th February.

———

A concert is given at Hickford's Great Room on 27th February
1741, at which Mr. Parry plays a Handel concerto on the harp
(*London Daily Post*).

(Chrysander, III. 158.) Handel wrote a concerto for the harp to be
played by Mr. Powell junior in *Alexander's Feast* ; it appeared as no. 6 of
the six organ concertos, Opus 4, published in 1738. Chrysander suggests
that the concerto played by Parry was the same. Parry repeated his
performance on 13th March. The Powell in question is apparently
William Powell junior, one of the founder members of the Musicians
Fund in 1739. Parry, on the other hand, is plainly identical with John
Parry, of Rhuabon, North Wales, domestic harper to Sir Watkin Williams
Wynne, of Wynnstay, of whom William H. Husk, in the first edition of
Grove's *Dictionary*, relates that his playing is said to have been admired by
Handel.

———

FROM THE " LONDON DAILY POST ", 28th February 1741

At the Theatre-Royal . . . this Day, will be perform'd ACIS and
GALATEA, *A Serenata.* With *Concertos* on the *Organ*, and other *Instruments.*
And a *Concerto* by Signor *Veracini.* . . . To begin at Half an Hour after
Six o'Clock.

(Schoelcher, p. 233.) Cf. 21st February 1740. On 26th and 27th February, the
advertisement runs : ". . . To which will be added, MR. DRYDEN'S LAST NEW
ODE ". Instead, Francesco Veracini, the violinist, performed a concerto, probably

XX. CATHERINE (KITTY) CLIVE, *née* RAFTER

Mezzotint after Joseph Van Haecken, by Alexander Van Haecken.
(H. R. Beard Theatre Collection)

See page 427

XXI. THE MUSIC HALL, FISHAMBLE STREET, DUBLIN

Drawing, with facsimile from the autograph score of *Messiah*, by
F. W. Fairholt, *ca.* 1840. (Gerald Coke, Esq.)

See page 527

composed by himself. This alteration may have been caused by the performance of the *Ode for St. Cecilia's Day* at the New Theatre in the Haymarket on 26th February. When *Acis and Galatea* was repeated on 11th March, the " Ode " was performed afterwards.

—

FROM THE EARL OF EGMONT'S DIARY, 28th February 1741

Went . . . to hear Hendel's mask of *Acis and Galatea*, with Dryden's *Ode*.

(Egmont MSS., III. 196.) The Earl apparently expected the " Ode " to be performed, because it had been advertised twice for the 28th February.

—

Walsh advertises " Acis and Galatea a Serenade ; and the Songs in Dryden's New Ode ", *London Daily Post*, 28th February 1741. (Smith, 1948, p. 229.)

—

The Academy of Ancient Music performs Henry Purcell's *King Arthur* and Handel's Funeral Anthem for Queen Caroline, 4th March 1741.

This was a Thursday. The only record appears in the word-book (University Library, Cambridge ; Gerald Coke's Handel Collection).

—

BARON BIELFELD TO BARON KNOBELSDORFF IN BERLIN

London, March 10, 1741

. . . England has never produced any great painters, sculptors, engravers, musicians or other artists of outstanding merit. Sir Godfrey Kneller, who excelled in portrait-painting and who is buried in West-minster Abbey beside the Royal tombs, was a German ; so is Mr. Hendel, of whom I was speaking to you. . . .

From Letter XXXII. I. 306 in the original edition ; IV. 108–110 in the English translation. Cf. 7th February 1741. Hans Georg Wenceslaus Freiherr von Knobelsdorff was superintendent of the royal castles in Prussia, and director-general of building in the Prussian provinces. Earlier in this letter, Bielfeld gives him a lengthy description of Heidegger's *Ridottos*, still *en vogue*. The passage quoted here forestalls a poem by Klopstock, entitled " Wir und Sie ", set to music by Gluck, who visited London 1745-6. The stanzas referring to Kneller and Handel read :

Wen haben sie, der kühnen Flugs,
Wie Händel Zaubereyen tönt ?
Das hebt uns über sie !

Wer ist bei ihnen, dessen Hand
Die trunkne Seel' im Bilde täuscht ?
Selbst Kneller gaben wir !

H.-17

(Translation)
Whom have they, who, with gallant flight,
Like Handel, summons spirits up ?
We triumph over them !

Whose hand, among all theirs, deludes
With pictures the enraptured soul ?
We gave them Kneller too !

—

From the " London Daily Post ", 14th March 1741

Hay-Market.
For the Benefit and Increase of a Fund establish'd for the Support
of Decay'd Musicians *and their Families.*
At the King's Theatre in the Hay-market, this Day, will be perform'd
(with the Original Scenes and Habits) Parnasso in Festa. *Compos'd by*
Mr. Handel *for her Royal Highness the Princess of* Orange's *Wedding.* . . .
To begin at Half an Hour after Six o'Clock.

(Chrysander, III. 17.) While the benefit concert in 1740 (28th March) was
given at Handel's theatre, still Lincoln's Inn Fields, the performance on this
occasion was at Heidegger's theatre, probably because the decorations and the
costumes belonged to him ; Handel, however, had performed the work at the
Haymarket on its original production in 1734, at Covent Garden in 1737 and at
Lincoln's Inn Fields in 1740 (cf. 13th March 1734, 9th March 1737 and 8th
November 1740). This time, during the intervals, other members of the Fund
performed instrumental music, probably not by Handel : Weideman on the
German flute, Clegg on the violin, Caporale on the violoncello, Miller on the
bassoon and St. Martini (Sammartini) on the oboe.

—

From the Same

Drury-Lane.
By Command of their Royal Highnesses the Prince and Princess
of Wales.

.   .   .   .   .

For the Benefit of Mrs. Clive.
To-day, March 14. . . .
The Universal Passion.
Alter'd from Shakespeare.

.   .   .   .   .

With Entertainments of Singing and Dancing, particularly
The favourite Airs out of the L'Allegro il Penseroso compos'd by
Mr. Handel, to be sung by Miss Edwards.

.   .   .   .   .

(Schoelcher, p. 235.) The comedy had been played at Drury Lane since 1737
(see 28th February). This time it was performed twice only, probably with

Handel's song, written for Mrs. Clive. For Miss Edwards, see 31st January 1741.
"Il Moderato" was dropped from the title of Handel's Ode ; see 8th April.

FROM THE EARL OF EGMONT'S DIARY, 14th March 1741

Went to the Haymarket, to a music in favour of poor musicians' widows.

(Egmont MSS., III. 199.)

Saul is revived at Lincoln's Inn Fields on Wednesday, 18th March 1741, "With Concertos on the Organ, and several Instruments" (*London Daily Post*).

FROM THE "LONDON DAILY POST", 4th April 1741

To the Author, &c.

Sir,

At a Time when Party runs so high, and Politicks seem to have taken up not only all our publick Papers, but the Attention also of the Bulk of Mankind, it may seem strange to you to receive a Letter on the Subject of Musical Performances. . . .

I have been led into this Way of thinking [about the power of music] by one of Mr. *Handel's* Bills for *Wednesday* next [the 8th], when we are to have his last Oratorio at *Lincoln's-Inn-Fields*. He has charmed me from my Childhood to this Day, and as I have been so long his Debtor for one of the greatest Joys our Nature is capable of, I thought it a Duty incumbent upon me at this Time, when it is become a Fashion to neglect him, (unknown as his Person is to me) to recommend him to the public Love and Gratitude of this great City, who have, with me, so long enjoyed the Harmony of his Composition. *Cotsoni, Faustina, Cenosini,* and *Farinelli*, have charmed our Ears : We ran mad after them, and entered into Parties for the one or the other with as much Vehemence as if the State had been at Stake. Their Voice indeed was grateful to the Ear ; but it was *Handel* gave the Persuasion ; it was his Composition that touched the Soul, and hurried us into the mad Extremes of Party-Rage for the particular Performers. His Influence prevailed, tho' his Power was invisible ; and the Singer had the Praise and the Profit, whilst the Merit, unobserved, and almost unrewarded, was the poor, but the proud Lot of the forgotten Master.

Is there any Nation in the World, where the Power of Musick is known, in which *Handel* is not known ? Are we not, throughout the Earth, distinguished by the envied Title of Encouragers of Arts and Sciences ? and whilst they talk of the great Genius's which we have either produced or possessed, is *Handel* ever forgot amongst them ?

And shall we then, after so many Years Possession, upon a single Disgust, upon a *faux Pas* made, but not meant, so interely abandon him, as to let him Want in a Country he has so long served ? in a Country of publick Spirit, where the polite Arts are in so high Esteem, and where Gratitude and Rewards have so remarkably accompanied the Merit of those who have excelled in them, that the great Genius's of other Countries have often even regretted that Part of their Fate, which gave them Birth in any other Place. It cannot be ! if we are not careful for him, let us be for our own long-possessed Credit and Character in the polite World ; and if old Age or Infirmity ; if even a Pride so inseparable from great Men, a Pride which in *Horace* produced an *Exegi Monumentum*, in *Ovid* a *Jamque Opus Exegi* ; a Pride which placed the Sphere and Cylinder on the Monument of *Archimedes*, and one of *Corelli's* Tunes as an Epitaph upon his Tomb-Stone ; if even such a Pride has offended, let us take it as the natural Foible of the great Genius, and let us overlook them like Spots upon the Sun, which, Spots as they are, do not eclipse or obscure his great Talent.

You may, by this Time, Sir, easily see what I mean by this Letter ; I wish I could urge this Apology to its full Efficacy, and persuade the Gentlemen who have taken Offence at any Part of this great Man's Conduct (for a great Man he must be in the Musical World, whatever his Misfortunes may now too late say to the contrary :) I wish I could persuade them, I say, to take him back into Favour, and relieve him from the cruel Persecution of those little Vermin, who, taking Advantage of their Displeasure, pull down even his Bills as fast as he has them pasted up ; and use a thousand other little Arts to injure and distress him. I am sure when they weigh the Thing without Prejudice, they will take him back into Favour ; but in the mean time, let the Publick take Care that he wants not : That would be an unpardonable Ingratitude ; and as this Oratorio of *Wednesday* next is his last for this Season, and if Report be true, probably his last for ever in this Country, let them, with a generous and friendly Benevolence, fill this his last House, and shew him on his Departure, that *London*, the greatest and richest City in the World, is great and rich in Virtue, as well as in Money, and can pardon and forget the Failings, or even the Faults of a great Genius.

The Performance itself (the Musick as well as the Poetry) is noble and elevated, well devised, and of great Propriety. The Musician and the Poet walk Hand in Hand, and seem to vie which shall better express that beautiful Contrast of Mirth and Melancholy, which you have quite thro' the *Allegro* and *Il Penseroso*, and the happy Success which Mr. *Handel* has had in the Composition of this particular Piece, will appear, to any one, who listens with Attention to it, the strongest Argument for the Truth of what I have said, *That Musick is really a Language understood by the Soul, tho' only a pleasing Sound to the Ear.*

I heartily wish, that all the polite Part of his disgusted Friends, may do him the Honour of their Attendance ; in which Case, I doubt not but he will have the Fate of the Swan, who, just under the Knife of the Cook, was saved by the Sweetness of his last melancholy melodious Song. This, at least, I'm sure of, that they will generously consider how many the Misfortunes are, which the declared Displeasure of so many Gentlemen of Figure and Weight, must necessarily draw upon a Man in his publick Way of Life, and that they will reflect upon the Frog in the Fable, who, whilst the Boys wantonly pelted him with Stones, cry'd out to them in his *Hoarse Voice, Good Gentlemen forbear, it may be Sport to you, but it is Death to me.*

> I am, Sir,
> Your most humble Servant,
>
> J. B.

(Schoelcher, pp. 234 f. ; Chrysander, III. 140-3.) Cf. the open letter published on 18th April 1739, and reprinted on 1st April 1740, in the same paper. The unidentified writer of 1741, who speaks of Farinelli as one of Handel's singers, misunderstood him, although his enthusiasm seems genuine, and although Handel may really have been on the point of departure. There were no oratorios during the season of 1741-2, and Handel went to Ireland only. It is impossible to determine what people are referred to as offended by Handel, or how the offence was given. Probably the writer only alludes to the general estrangement between Handel and the London public. He had not written any new oratorio since 1738 (*Israel in Egypt*), and his latest operas were failures. There is one point in this open letter which is of historical interest : there were no hand-bills in Handel's day, but placards were in use and were called bills. No such placard, however, seems to have survived.

———

THOMAS DAMPIER TO COLONEL WILLIAM WINDHAM, AT GENEVA

Amsterdam, 4 April 1741

Mr. [Benjamin] Tate says he won't fail sending you next post an account of Locatelli. He plays with so much fury upon his fiddle that, in my humble opinion, he must wear out some dozen of them in a year ; for my part I look upon him to be as great a player as Handel, tho' this latter be so much bigger and taller.

(Clemens, p. 158.) Ketton MSS., p. 202. The Rev. Dr. Dampier was afterwards Sub-Master of Eton, and Dean of Durham. He and Tate were travelling with other British students. (Cf. Coxe, pp. 44, 46 and 63 f.) Pietro Locatelli, violinist and composer, settled down in Amsterdam, after years of travelling as a virtuoso. The letter may have been written on 24th March, but between Englishmen the old style calendar was probably usual. Tate, in fact, did write to his friends about Locatelli, but his letter has not been printed (Ketton MSS., p. 203).

———

FROM THE " LONDON DAILY POST ", 8th April 1741

At the Theatre-Royal . . . this Day, will be perform'd L'ALLEGRO, ED IL PENSEROSO. With Concertos on the Organ, and several Instruments. To which will be added, Mr. *Dryden*'s last New *Ode*.

☞ This being the last Time of performing, many Persons of Quality and others, are pleas'd to make great Demands for Box Tickets, which encourage me (and hope will give no Offence) to put the Pit and Boxes together, at Half a Guinea each. First Gallery 5s. Second Gallery 3s. To begin at Half an Hour after Six o'Clock.

(Schoelcher, pp. 233 f.) The third part of Handel's "Allegro" Ode, Jennens's addition, "Il Moderato", was abandoned when Handel performed another work with the Ode ; on such occasions the two Milton parts only were performed. The first person, in which the additional note is written, indicates that it was printed in Handel's name. The normal price for the Pit was 5s. This was the last concert of Handel's season, and was, in fact, a farewell.

———

FROM THE EARL OF EGMONT'S DIARY, 8th April 1741

I went to Lincolns Inn playhouse to hear Hendel's music for the last time, he intending to go to Spa in Germany.

(Egmont MSS., III. 210.) Although the Earl too speaks of " the last time " his remark about Handel going " to Spa " (Aix-la-Chapelle again ?) does not sound like a farewell. Handel did not go to Germany this year.

———

MISS DONELLAN TO MISS ELIZABETH ROBINSON, 11th April 1741

. . . The only show we have had since you left us was for Handel, his last night, all the fashionable people were there.

(Elizabeth Montagu, p. 70.) Miss Robinson had been in London, with Miss Donellan and the Duchess of Portland. Cf. April 1740.

———

Walsh advertises "The Favourite Songs in the Operetta call'd HYMEN in Score", for 4s., London Daily Post, 18th April 1741.

(Chrysander, II. 454.) This was, of course, a failure again, the opera having disappeared at the end of 1740 after two performances.

———

Handel finishes the duet " Quel fior ch'all' alba ride " on 1st July, and the duet " Nò di voi non vuò fidarmi " on 3rd July 1741.

The second duet was set again on 2nd November 1742.

———

FROM A LONDON NEWSPAPER, 4th July 1741

CUPER'S GARDENS.

By Desire of several Gentlemen and Ladies. This evening . . . will be perform'd the following Pieces of Musick, viz. : The Overture in Saul, with several grand Chorusses, Composed by Mr. Handel . . . the Fifth of Mr. Handel's new Grand Concertos ; . . . The whole to conclude with a new Grand Piece of Musick, an Original Composition by Mr. Handel, called Porto Bello.

(*Musical Times*, 1st February 1894, p. 88 ; Wroth, p. 250.) Not to be found in *London Daily Post*. Cuper's Gardens, founded by Boyder Cuper about 1690 on the south side of the Thames, opposite Somerset House, became a rival of Vauxhall and Marylebone when Ephraim Evans introduced concerts there from 1738 to 1740. Like Daniel Gough at Marylebone, he built a platform for an orchestra. While Jonathan Tyers boasted of Handel's statue, and Gough of a band " from the Opera and both Theatres ", Evans had an organ by Richard Bridge installed. He died in autumn 1740, and his widow became his successful heir. It was she who, during 1741 and 1759, introduced Handel, Corelli, Hasse, Arne and, her favourite composer, the organist Henry Burgess, junior, in the concerts at Cuper's Gardens, especially on Saturday evenings. She started on 16th June with a new grand concerto for the organ by Burgess, and the concert advertised above was probably the first with a Handel programme, although the blind harper Jones is said to have played Handel airs for Mr. Evans (Hawkins, V. 357). The song in question, text by Glover, begins " As near Portobello lying " and refers to Admiral Edward Vernon taking the defenceless Porto Bello " with six ships only ", in November 1739. He became popular in the days of the " War of Jenkins' Ear " (see 27th October 1739), and so did Richard Glover's ballad, " Admiral Hosier's Ghost ", published in 1740. Squire (1913, pp. 107-11) lists the song under the doubtful and spurious ones by Handel, published in contemporary song-books. The tune had been known since at least 1730 as " The Sailor's Complaint ", beginning " Come and listen to my ditty ". With Glover's words it was printed in single-sheet folios anonymously, but in 1754, in *The Muses' Delight* (p. 190), and in 1757, in *Apollo's Cabinet* (II. 190), it was printed with Handel's name. It became known as " Hosier's Ghost ", referring to Admiral Francis Hosier (d. 1727), and with different words, as " Saunders' Ghost ", referring to Admiral Sir George Saunders (d. 1734). For Cuper's Gardens, see also 18th July 1741, 25th August 1744, 23rd May 1748 and 4th September 1749.

FROM THE " LONDON DAILY POST ", 18th July 1741

CUPERS GARDENS.

This is to acquaint all Gentlemen and Ladies, that this Day will be perform'd

Several curious Pieces of Musick compos'd by Mr. Handel, Signor Hasse, Mr. Arne, Mr. Burgess, &c. in which will be introduced the celebrated Fire Musick, as originally compos'd by Mr. Handel, in the Opera of Atalanta, with great Applause ; the Fire-works consisting of Fire-wheels, Fountains, large Sky Rockets, with an Addition of the Fire-Pump, &c. made by the ingenious Mr. Worman, who projected the same at the above-mentioned Opera, and will be play'd off from the Top of the Orchestra by Mr. Worman himself.

N.B. Having added to the Band of Musick several curious Hands, the usual favourite Pieces will be likewise perform'd, *viz.* The Overture of Saul. . . .

⁎ The Widow Evans hopes as her Endeavours are to oblige the
Town, they will favour her Gardens with their Company. . . .

(Wroth, p. 250.) Performances on Saturdays, the 18th and 25th July. This
advertisement appeared every week-day between 17th and 28th July, but not on
11th July as Schoelcher (p. 184) indicates. On 27th July the following words were
added after " by Mr. Worman himself " : " who intends to make several beautiful
Alterations with the Sky Rockets ". This refers to a third performance, on 1st
August.

———

THOMAS DAMPIER TO HIS FRIENDS AT GENEVA

Mitcham [Surrey], 30 July 1741.
. . . Don't you think it odd in him [Benjamin Tate] to trust me with
talking of musick and Handel ? They have had several conferences
together, and I observed [Gasparo] Fritz's musick to lie before them,
and that the great man frequently cried Bravo and sometimes bravissimo.
He laughs very much at the opera which is preparing for next winter.
He has refused to have anything to do in the matter. There are eight
subscribers, each one 1,000 *l*. I can remember the names of some of
them : Lord Middlesex, Lord Brooke, Lord Conway, Lord Holderness,
Mr. Conway, Mr. Frederick, &c. Lord Middlesex it seems is the chief
manager in the affair : the men of penetration give hints that his Lordship's sole aim is to make his mistress, the Muscovita, appear to great
advantage upon the stage. With this intent, say they, he has taken care
to hire singers with voices inferior to hers ; and her's is not worth a
farthing. Lord Brooke is quite easy in the matter. I believe he would
pay a thousand pounds more rather than have anything to do in it in the
character of manager.

(Ketton MSS., p. 203.) Cf. 4th April, 5th November, 19th and 29th December
1741. The letter was addressed to William Windham, Benjamin Stillingfleet
(Windham's tutor), Thomas, Earl of Haddington, and others. Tate went (from
London ?) to Scarborough, and asked Dampier to write for both of them to
Geneva. Gasparo (Kaspar) Fritz, born in Geneva about 1716, and living at this
time in London, was a violinist and a composer of chamber music. The " great
man " (cf. Rolli's *L'uomo*) was, without doubt, Handel himself. In addition to
Tate and Dampier, Robert Price (see 19th December 1741) may have been present
at the " conference ". Lord Middlesex, who had managed the New Theatre in
the Haymarket since 1739 (cf. 28th November 1739), was now moving to the
" old " house opposite, for a kind of second Nobility Opera. Heidegger kept in
the background, but Rolli was still connected with the house. The Italian poet
Francesco Vanneschi became the assistant manager, and Baldassare Galuppi the
composer of the house. According to Burney (IV. 446) the singers were : Angelo
Maria Monticelli (male soprano), Signor Andreoni (male soprano, who sang for
Handel in 1740–41), Angelo Amorevoli (tenor), and Signora Visconti (soprano) as
prima donna ; the second and third women were Signore Panichi and Tedeschi.
As will be apparent from Dampier's, Price's and Walpole's letters, the " Muscovita " (cf. 10th March and 1st December 1739) was one of the two minor ladies,
namely Signora Panichi. Lord Middlesex's companions were : Francis (Greville)

Baron Brooke ; Francis Seymour, Baron Conway, and his brother, Henry Seymour Conway, captain-lieutenant (later field-marshal) ; Robert D'Arcy, fourth Earl of Holderness, Lord Lieutenant of the North Riding of Yorkshire ; and John Frederick, later Sir John, commissioner of customs. Walpole (see 5th November 1741) gives a few more names. Middlesex is said to have offered £3000 to Giuseppe Tartini, who, however, declined to come to London.

From the " Norwich Mercury ", 1st August 1741

[London,] *July* 28. We hear, that at Cuper's Gardens last Saturday Night [25th July], among several favourable Pieces of Musick, Mr. Handel's Fire-Musick, with the Fire-works, as originally perform'd in the Opera of Atalanta, were receiv'd with great Applause, by a numerous Audience.

Copy in Central Library, Norwich. Cf. 18th July.

Giustino is performed at Brunswick, with Italian airs and German recitatives and choruses, August 1741.

(Loewenberg, p. 96.) Translated into German by Christian Ernst Simonetti and Georg Caspar Schürmann. The latter, who probably wrote the recitatives, also contributed some additional music.

Handel writes the oratorio *Messiah* between 22nd August and 14th September 1741.

The autograph of the score is in the Royal Music Library, deposited in the British Museum, and has been reproduced twice in facsimile. A manuscript study for the air " He was despised ", preserved in the Fitzwilliam Museum, Cambridge, shows a piece of treble in A, inscribed " Der arme irische Junge " (The poor Irish boy), perhaps written in Dublin. (Mann's catalogue, p. 42.) Young (p. 101) calls it an Irish folksong.

From a London Newspaper, 7th September 1741

We hear from Italy that the famous singer, Mrs. C—z—ni is under sentence of death to be beheaded, for poisoning her husband !

(Schoelcher, p. 78.) This seems to have been pure gossip. Whether Signora Cuzzoni was married to Sandoni, who was still living, or to Signor Ferre (see 11th January 1725), to both or to neither, is not known. Cf. 18th May 1750 and 20th May 1751.

Horace Walpole to Sir Horace Mann in Florence

Downing Street, Oct. 8, 1741, O.S.

The Opera begins the day after the King's birthday : the singers are not permitted to sing till on the stage, so no one has heard them, nor

H.–17 *a*

have I seen Amorevoli to give him the letter. The Opera is to be on the French system of dancers, scenes, and dresses. The directors have already laid out great sums. They talk of a mob to silence the operas, as they did the French players ; but it will be more difficult, for here half the young noblemen in town are engaged, and they will not be so easily persuaded to humour the taste of the mobility : in short, they have already retained several eminent lawyers [boxers] from the Bear Garden to plead their defence.

(Walpole, *Letters*, 1891, I. 75.)   Cf. 30th July and 31st October.   The French players were at the New Theatre in the Haymarket in October 1738, soon after the passing of the Licensing Act.

———

Handel finishes the oratorio *Samson*, 29th October 1741.

He made, however, some important additions in October 1742.

———

Handel visits the Haymarket Theatre to attend the opening of a new season with the pasticcio opera *Alessandro in Persia*, 31st October 1741.

(Townsend, p. 51.)   Cf. 30th July, 2nd November and 29th December 1741.   The music was compiled, probably by Baldassare Galuppi, from works by Leonardo Leo, Johann Adolf Hasse, Giuseppe Arena, Giovanni Battista Pescetti, Giovanni Battista Lampugnani, and Giuseppe Scarlatti. The libretto was written by Francesco Vanneschi for Domenico Paradies (Lucca, 1738) ; Vanneschi was now the poet of the Haymarket Theatre and Lord Middlesex's assistant manager (Burney, IV. 446).   The two Scarlatti arias, formerly attributed to Domenico, were, in fact, by Giuseppe Scarlatti, as Frank Walker has proved (*The Music Review*, August 1951, p. 195).   Although Handel disliked it, the opera, which is highly praised by Burney (IV. 445 f.), was performed 21 times in 1741 and 1742.   Since the second performance was not until 10th November, it is assumed that Handel saw the first night, as he was on his way to Dublin before the repeat.

———

HORACE WALPOLE TO HORACE MANN

London, Nov. 2, 1741.

The opera will not tell so well as the two other shows [Balls at Sir Thomas Robinson's, the Lord Mayor's, and at Court on the King's birthday], for they were obliged to omit the part of Amorevoli, who has fever. The audience was excessive, without the least disturbance, and almost as little applause ; I cannot conceive why, for Monticelli . . . be able to sing to-morrow.

(Walpole, *Letters*, 1891, I. 84.)   In the last sentence quoted, the editor of Walpole's letters found some of the words illegible.   The description of the first night explains Handel's mirth (see 31st October and 29th December). Amorevoli did not appear on the stage until the middle of November.

—

Handel, on an invitation from the Lord Lieutenant of Ireland, William Cavendish, third Duke of Devonshire, goes on (?) 4th November 1741, via Chester and Holyhead, to Dublin, arriving there on the 18th.

    The date of Handel's departure is not certain ; but since the Lord Lieutenant of Ireland needed five days to travel from Dublin to London (*Gentleman's Magazine*, February 1742, quoted by Townsend), it may be assumed that Handel was two weeks on his journey, especially since he was detained in Chester, and may have visited Charles Legh at Adlington Hall, Cheshire. It is assumed that Handel went to Dublin intending to stay for the winter only, but he remained there until 13th August 1742. Whether he wrote *Messiah* for Dublin has not been decided, but people in Dublin thought so (see 10th April 1742 and 27th December 1752).

—

HORACE WALPOLE TO HORACE MANN

Downing Street, Nov. 5, 1741, O.S.

    Here is another letter . . . from poor Amorevoli ; he has a continued fever, though not a high one. Yesterday, Monticelli was taken ill, so there will be no opera on Saturday ; nor was on Tuesday. Monticelli is infinitely admired ; next to Farinelli. The Viscontina is admired more than liked. The music displeases everybody, and the dances. I am quite uneasy about the Opera, for Mr. Conway is one of the directors, and I fear they will lose considerably, which he cannot afford. There are eight, Lord Middlesex, Lord Holderness, Mr. Frederick, Lord Conway, Mr. Conway, Mr. Damer, Lord Brook, and Mr. Brand. The five last are directed by the three first ; they by the first, and he by the Abbé Vanneschi, who will make a pretty sum. I will give you some instances ; not to mention the improbability of eight young thoughtless men of fashion understanding economy : it is usual to give the poet fifty guineas for composing the books—Vanneschi and Rolli are allowed three hundred. Three hundred more Vanneschi had for his journey to Italy to pick up dancers and performers, which was always as well transacted by bankers there. He has additionally brought over an Italian tailor— because there are none here ! They have already given this *Taylorini* four hundred pounds, and he has already taken a house of thirty pounds a-year. Monticelli and the Visconti are to have a thousand guineas a-piece ; Amorevoli eight hundred and fifty : this at the rate of the great singers, is not so extravagant ; but to the Muscovita (though the second woman never had above four hundred) they give six ; that is for secret services. By this you may judge of their frugality ! I am quite uneasy for poor Harry [Conway], who will thus be to pay for Lord Middlesex's pleasures !

(Walpole, *Letters*, 1891, I. 87-9.) Cf. 30th July and 31st October. Henry Seymour Conway was Walpole's cousin and friend. Joseph Damer, later Baron Milton, became finally Earl of Dorchester. Thomas Brand was one of the original members of the Society of Dilettanti. Of La Muscovita Walpole wrote to Conway on 23rd April 1740 (*Letters*, I. 45) : " Sir, Muscovita is not a pretty woman, and she does sing ill ; that's all ". (She had appeared in London on 10th March and 1st December 1739.)

———

FROM THE " LONDON DAILY POST ", 11th November 1741

MUSICK.
This Day is published,
Compos'd by Mr. HANDEL,

·   ·   ·   ·   ·

3. Select Harmony, 4ᵗʰ Collection ; to which is prefix'd that celebrated Concerto in Alexander's Feast. . . .
All Compos'd by Mr. Handel. Printed for and sold by John Walsh. . . .

(Chrysander, III. 156.) Of the fifteen numbers advertised here the one quoted was the only new one. It contained three concertos by Handel, no. 4 being by Veracini, no. 5, and perhaps no. 6, by Tartini. Walsh added the names of the composers to nos. 1, 4 and 5 only.—It is at this point, at the end of 1741, that the students of Handel's life and work have to part from Chrysander, the great Handelian, who left his biography unfinished, though he nearly finished his complete edition of Handel's works.

———

FROM THE MINUTES OF MERCER'S HOSPITAL, DUBLIN,
14th November 1741

The Dean of Sᵗ Patricks consents to let the Gentlemen of Choir attend thereon.

St. Patrick's is one of the two cathedrals of Dublin, the other being Christ Church. The Dean of St. Patrick's was Jonathan Swift. The Gentlemen of the Choirs, called Vicar Chorals (Minor Canons), or at least most of them, sang in both cathedrals. The consent referred to the charitable music planned for 10th December in St. Andrew's Church. Cf. 28th January 1742.

———

FROM FAULKNER'S " DUBLIN JOURNAL ", 21st November 1741

Chester, Nov. 5. Yesterday arrived here, on his Way to Dublin, Mr. Maclaine, who was invited to play on our Cathedral Organ this Day, on which he performed so well, to the entire Satisfaction of the whole Congregation, that some of the best Judges in Musick said, They never heard that Organ truly plaid on before ; and his Performance was allowed to be very masterly, and in the finest Taste.

[Dublin, Nov. 21.] And last Wednesday [the 18th] the celebrated Dr. Handell arrived here in the Packet-boat from Holyhead, a Gentleman universally known by his excellent Compositions in all Kinds of Musick, and particularly for his *Te Deum, Jubilate, Anthems,* and other Compositions in Church Musick, (of which for some Years past have principally consisted the Entertainments in the Round Church, which have so greatly contributed to support the Charity of Mercer's-Hospital) to perform his Oratorio's, for which Purpose he hath engaged the above Mr. Maclaine, his Wife, and several others of the best Performers in the Musical Way.

(Townsend, p. 44 f.; his extracts were taken from the copy of the *Dublin Journal* in the Archbishop Marsh Library, Dublin.) George Faulkner, the printer of the *Journal,* was also a book publisher. Of Handel's involuntary stay in Chester, we know from Burney, then at the public school there. He " stayed on account of the wind being unfavourable for his embarking at Parkgate ". Handel wished to use the delay " in trying over some pieces of his new oratorio ". A house-painter named Janson was indicated to him as one of the best musicians attached to the Cathedral. Since the man could not sing at sight, or at least not " at first sight ", the rehearsal was soon over. The organist of Chester Cathedral was Edmund Baker, and he apparently introduced Maclaine, about whom nothing else is known, to Handel. It seems that Mrs. Maclaine was a soprano. The other singers who came from London were Signora Christina Maria Avoglio (spelled Avolio by Handel) and Mrs. Susanna Maria Cibber, née Arne.—The Round Church was another name for St. Andrew's Church, Dublin. There exists a collective word-book of sacred music, dated Dublin 1741, a copy of which is preserved at Trinity College there : " The Te Deum, Jubilate, Anthems, Odes, Oratorios and Serenatas, as they are performed by The Philharmonic Society in Dublin for the Improvement of Church Musick, and the Further Support of Mercer's Hospital ". It contains two Coronation Anthems, both Wedding Anthems, one Chandos Anthem (" O sing unto the Lord "), *Acis and Galatea, L'Allegro, ed Il Penseroso, Alexander's Feast,* the *Ode for St. Cecilia's Day, Deborah* and *Esther* by Handel ; but also one Cecilia Ode and the oratorio *Solomon* by William Boyce. (Schoelcher, p. 240.) It seems that at that time several of these works had not been performed in Dublin ; Boyce's *Solomon* was not produced at all until 1743.

—

The Governors of Mercer's Hospital announce, in Faulkner's *Dublin Journal* of 21st November 1741, that a divine service " After the Cathedral Manner " will be performed on 10th December in St. Andrew's Church, with a sermon to be preached by the Rev. Dr. [Patrick] Delany, and Handel's *Te Deum, Jubilate* and " two new Anthems " ; for the support of the hospital.

Dr. Delany, who later married Mrs. Mary Pendarves, née Granville, Handel's old friend, became indisposed, and the sermon was preached by Dean Owen. According to the Minutes of the Hospital, the music was to be borrowed from Mathew Dubourg, the violinist, who (as Johann Sigismund Cousser's successor) had been Conductor of the King's Band, or Master of the State Music, in Ireland since 1728 ; he was Handel's friend and soon became leader of the orchestra for the performances of Handel's oratorios in Dublin.

———

From "Pue's Occurrences", 21st November 1741

Wednesday last [the 18th] arrived from London, the celebrated Dr. Handell, Universally known by his excellent compositions in all kinds of Musick, he is to perform here this Winter, and has brought over several of the best performers in the Musical Way.

(Townsend, p. 45.) This notice was a shortened version of the one printed in Faulkner's *Journal*. Handel seems to have protested against being called Doctor, and the Dublin papers learned to call him Mister (Chrysander, II. 312).

———

From the Minutes of Mercer's Hospital, 21st November 1741

At a Meeting of the Governors . . . Novr 21. 1741

Present : John Putland Esqr Dean Owen. Dr Wynne. Ld Bpp of Cork Order'd That Mr Putland Dean Owen, & Doc^r Wynne be & are hereby desir'd to wait on Mr Handel & ask the favour of him to play on the Organ att the Musical Performance at St Andrew Church.

G. T. Maturin, Secretary.

(Townsend, p. 46.) At the same meeting it was decided to invite the Lord Lieutenant and Lady Devonshire, the Lord Primate (*i.e.* the Archbishop of Dublin), John Hoadly, and the Lord Chancellor, Thomas Wyndham. John Owen was Dean of Clonmacnois and a prebendary of Christ Church Cathedral. The Rev. John Wynne was precentor and sub-dean of St. Patrick's Cathedral. The Bishop of Cork was Robert Clayton. Gabriel Joseph Maturin, the secretary of Mercer's Hospital, was Dean of Kildare, and in 1745-6 Dean of St. Patrick's Cathedral. There was a rehearsal, a few days before the performance, but no audience was admitted.

———

From Faulkner's "Dublin Journal", 28th November 1741

Last Tuesday [the 21st] arrived in the Yatcht from Parkgate, Signiora Avolio, an excellent Singer, who is come to this Kingdom, to perform in Mr. Handel's Musical Entertainments.

(Townsend, p. 47.) Mrs. Cibber came to Dublin as guest actress, with Mr. John Rich, who (as Mr. Quin) acted with her at the Theatre Royal in Aungier Street. Her first appearance was as Indiana in Sir Richard Steele's comedy, *The Conscious Lovers*, on 12th December.

———

Heidegger gets a new leave and license to perform operas at the Haymarket Theatre, from 8th December 1741 till 30th October 1745.

(Public Record Office : L.C. 5/161, p. 97.) Cf. 3rd January 1739 and 23rd March 1749.

———

From Faulkner's " Dublin Journal ", 12th December 1741

Last Thursday [the 10th] was performed at the Round Church, for the Benefit of Mercer's Hospital, Divine Service after the Cathedral Manner, with the *Te Deum, Jubilate*, and one of the Coronation Anthems compos'd by Mr. Handel ; after which there was a most excellent Sermon, suited to the Occasion, preached by the Revd. Dean Owens, and after Sermon an Elegant and Grand Anthem composed on the Occasion, by Mr. Boyce, Composer to his Majesty, at the Request of several well-wishers to the Charity ; the Appearance was numerous, and it is hoped the Performance was so much to the Satisfaction of every Person who heard it, as to bespake the Favour of the Publick on the like Occasion.

Instead of " two new Anthems " by Handel (see 21st November), one of his Coronation Anthems and a new one by William Boyce were performed. Boyce had been composer to the Chapel Royal, and to the King, since 1736 ; on 2nd January 1742 the Governors' thanks were forwarded to him for composing the anthem (Minutes of Mercer's Hospital). He maintained friendly relations with Dublin, but did not live there. It is curious that Handel's performance on the organ, for which he was thanked afterwards, is not mentioned in the report.

—

From the Same

On Monday next being the 14th of December (and every Day following) Attendance will be given at Mr. Handel's House in Abby-street, near Lyffey-street, from 9 o'clock in the Morning till 2 in the Afternoon, in order to receive the Subscription Money for his Six Musical Entertainments in the New Musick-Hall in Fishamble street, at which Time each Subscriber will have a Ticket delivered to him, which entitles him to three Tickets each Night, either for Ladies or Gentlemen.—N.B. Subscriptions are likewise taken in at the same Place.

(Townsend, pp. 47 f.) No copy of this issue is available in Dublin, but copies of the advertisement, repeated on 15th and 19th December, are in the libraries there. The house in Abbey Street, which Handel rented in 1741–2, is still standing, but it was refaced in the nineteenth century. The new Music Hall was opened on 2nd October 1741, shortly before Handel's arrival. The " same Place " was the Music Hall.

—

From the Minutes of Mercer's Hospital, 12th December 1741

Order'd . . . that Dr Wynne be desir'd to thank Mr Handel for his attendance.

This refers, apparently, to Handel's organ playing on 10th December. Cf. 21st November, and Townsend's *History of Mercer's Hospital*, p. 35. The charitable concert was the sixth at St. Andrew's Church.

—

FROM FAULKNER'S " DUBLIN JOURNAL ", 19th December 1741

At the New Musick-hall in Fishamble-street, on Wednesday next, being the 23d Day of December, Mr. Handel's Musical Entertainment will be opened ; in which will be performed, *L'Allegro, il Penseroso, & il Moderato*, with two Concertos for several Instruments, and a Concerto on the Organ. To begin at 7 o'clock. Tickets for that Night will be delivered to the Subscribers (by sending their Subscription Ticket) on Tuesday and Wednesday next, at the Place of Performance, from 9 o'clock in the Morning till 3 in the Afternoon.—And Attendance will be given this Day and on Monday next, at Mr. Handel's House in Abbey-street, near Lyffey-street, from 9 o'clock in the Morning till 3 in the Afternoon, in order to receive the Subscription Money ; at which Time each Subscriber will have a Ticket delivered to him, which entitles him to three Tickets each Night, either for Ladies or Gentlemen.—NB. Subscriptions are likewise taken in at the same Place. Books will be sold at the said Place, Price a British Six-pence.

(Townsend, p. 48.) On 29th December, according to Townsend, the following words were added to this advertisement : " And no body can be admitted without a Subscriber's Ticket. The Subscribers that have not sent in their Subscription Money, are humbly desired to send it To-day or To-morrow morning, in order to receive their Subscription Ticket." The word-book, a copy of which is in the British Museum, shows that part 3, Jennens's " Il Moderato ", was, in fact, restored. During the following years, until Handel's death, the ode was performed alternatively with and without, part 3.

———

ROBERT PRICE TO THOMAS, EARL OF HADDINGTON, AT GENEVA

London, 19 December 1741.

I hope we may be able to get Fritz a little money by it [the publication, by subscription, of his trios], but they are such abominable Goths here that I can answer for nothing. They cannot bear anything but Handel, Courelli, and Geminiani, which they are eternally playing ever and ever again at all their concerts. I was at a concert at Lord Brooke's where Carbonelli played the first fiddle ; . . . Tate and I are of a concert of gentlemen performers where Festing plays the first fiddle. . . . We have had a good opera here, but a great many people have not liked it ; the singers are Monticelli, a soprano, the finest singer I ever heard, Amorevoli the famous tenor, Visconti the first woman a very good singer, the Muscovinta [or rather, Muscovita] an indifferent one, and two or three great scrubs. The first opera was made up of songs of different authors, among which were some exceeding fine ones ; the second opera is composed by Signor Galuppi ; I have heard it but once and therefore will not pretend to decide about it, but it seems to be pretty good.

(Clemens, p. 156.) Ketton MSS., pp. 205 f. Cf. 30th July. Gasparo Fritz's Opus 1, six string quartets, was published for the author, *i.e.* on his account, by

Walsh in 1742. Six string trios by Fritz were published in Paris about 1760 as his Opus 4. Robert Price and Benjamin Stillingfleet (cf. 30th July) were friends of John Christopher Smith, Handel's pupil, who communicated the principal facts of Handel's life to his first biographer, the Rev. John Mainwaring, shortly after Handel's death. It was Price, however, who contributed the critical part (pp. 165 ff.) to the anonymous book. Stillingfleet was the author of an anonymous treatise, sometimes attributed to Sir John Hawkins, *Principles and Power of Harmony* (1771), based on Giuseppe Tartini's *Trattato di Musica secondo la vera scienza dell'Armonia* (Padua, 1754) ; about Price's contribution to Mainwaring's Handel book (*Literary Life and Works*, II. 172) he wrote : " His comparison of the Italian and German music . . . was published in the Life of Handel, and drawn up at the request of the ingenious author ". (The catalogue of Handel's works was compiled for Mainwaring by James Harris.) Nothing else is known of Handel's connection with Fritz or Price. Giovanni Stefano Carbonelli was a well-known violin-player, the former leader in Handel's orchestra at the Haymarket Theatre, who in 1733 went, with Festing, to the rival opera house. The Society of the Gentlemen Performers was probably identical with the Apollo Society at the Devil Tavern, founded by Maurice Greene and Michael Christian Festing ; in 1742 Festing became music director of Ranelagh Gardens.

HORACE WALPOLE TO HORACE MANN

Christmas Eve, 1741.

We have got a new opera, not so good as the former ; and we have got the famous Bettina to dance, but she is a most indifferent performer. The house is excessively full every Saturday, never on Tuesday : here, you know, we make everything a fashion.

Walpole, *Letters*, 1891, I. 109. The new opera was Galuppi's *Penelope* (see 29th December).

FROM FAULKNER'S " DUBLIN JOURNAL ", 29th December 1741

Last Wednesday [the 23rd] Mr. Handell had his first Oratorio, at Mr. Neal's Musick Hall in Fishamble-Street, which was crowded with a more numerous and polite Audience than ever was seen upon the like Occasion. The Performance was superior to any Thing of the Kind in this Kingdom before ; and our Nobility and Gentry to show their Taste for all Kinds of Genius, expressed their great Satisfaction, and have already given all imaginable Encouragement to this grand Musick.

(Townsend, p. 49.) This was the first time that the New Music Hall was called " Neal's Musick Hall ", and it was not called so again for some time afterwards. There are two different versions of the ownership of John and William Neale, the music publishers in Dublin : one relates that they built the Music Hall, the other that they acquired it some time after Handel's visit. The notice quoted above seems to prove that the Neales had something to do with the house from the beginning. Townsend (p. 34) says that William Neale was the treasurer of the Charitable Musical Society and that he had " incurred some expense in the building of the Music Hall ".

HANDEL TO JENNENS

Dublin Decem^{br} 29. 1741.

S^r

it was with the greatest Pleasure I saw the Continuation of Your Kindness by the Lines You was pleased to send me, in Order to be prefix'd to Your Oratorio Messiah, which I set to Musick before I left England. I am emboldned, Sir, by the generous Concern You please to take in relation to my affairs, to give You an Account of the Success I have met here. The Nobility did me the Hoñour to make amongst themselves a Subscription for 6 Nights, which did fill a Room of 600 Persons, so that I needed not sell one single Ticket at the Door. and without Vanity the Performance was received with a general Approbation. Sig^{ra} Avolio, which I brought with me from London pleases extraordinary, I have form'd an other Tenor Voice which gives great Satisfaction, the Basses and Counter Tenors are very good, and the rest of the Chorus Singers (by my Direction) do exceeding well, as for the Instruments they are really excellent, Mr Dubourgh beeng at the Head of them, and the Musick sounds delightfully in this charming Room, which puts me in such Spirits (and my Health being so good) that I exert my self on my Organ with more than usual Success. I opened with the Allegro, Penseroso, & Moderato and I assure you that the Words of the Moderato are vastly admired. The Audience being composed (besides the Flower of Ladyes of Distinction and other People of the greatest Quality) of so many Bishops, Deans, Heads of the Colledge, the most eminents People in the Law as the Chancellor, Auditor General, &tc. all which are very much taken with the Poetry. So that I am desired to perform it again the next time. I cannot sufficiently express the kind treatment I receive here, but the Politeness of this generous Nation cannot be unknown to You, so I let You judge of the satisfaction I enjoy, passing my time with Honnour, profit, and pleasure. They propose already to have some more Performances, when the 6 Nights of the Subscription are over, and My Lord Duc the Lord Lieutenant (who is allways present with all His Family on those Nights) will easily obtain a longer Permission for me by His Majesty, so that I shall be obliged to make my stay here longer than I thought. One request I must make to You, which is that You would insinuate my most devoted Respects to My Lord and my Lady Shaftesbury, You know how much Their kind Protection is precious to me. Sir Windham Knatchbull will find here my respectfull Compliments. You will encrease my obligations if by occasion You will present my humble Service to some other Patrons and friends of mine. I expect with Impatience the Favour of Your News, concerning Your Health and wellfare, of which I take a real share, as for the News of Your Opera's, I need not trouble you for all this Town is full of their ill success, by a number of Letters from

Your quarters to the People of Quality here, and I can't help saying but that it furnishes great Diversion and laughter. The first Opera I heard my Self before I left London, and it made me very merry all along my journey, and of the second Opera, call'd Penelope, a certain noble man writes very jocosly, il faut que je dise avec Harlequin, nôtre Penelôpe n'est qu'une Sallôpe. but I think I have trespassed too much on Your Patience. I beg You to be persuaded of the sincere Veneration and Esteem with which I have the Honnour to be

S^r
            Your
                most obliged and most humble Servant
                                George Frideric Handel

(Milnes, pp. 13 f.) Original in the possession of Lord Howe. Facsimile in Mueller von Asow, pp. 145-7. Charles Jennens, the author of Saul and of " Il Moderato ", the third part added to Milton's L'Allegro ed Il Penseroso and now restored in Handel's work, was also the compiler of Messiah. The legend of his secretary " Pooley " being the real author of the text was first told in William Hone's The Every-Day Book : and Table Book, London, 1827, Vol. III, part 2, column 651 ; it was retold by Sir Newman Flower in the first edition of his Handel book, 1923, p. 269, but revoked by him in the revised edition of 1947, p. 288. (Another Handel legend, referring to his music played at Marylebone, is told in Hone's Year-Book, 1832, p. 501, and re-told by J. Thomas Smith, in his Topography and Historical Account of the Parish of St. Marylebone, 1833, pp. 34 f.; reproduced in Schoelcher, pp. 196 f., Chrysander, III. 182 f., and Williams-Blom, pp. 128 f.) For the text of Messiah and its author, cf. also : W. H. Husk in Notes and Queries, 26th February 1859, letter by the Rev. A. Bloxam to his brother, the Rev. Dr. Bloxam (British Museum, Add. MS. 39, 864), published by William C. Smith in Music & Letters, October 1950; see also Geoffrey Cuming in Music & Letters, July 1950. William Boyer, in a note on Jennens's will, suggested that Dr. Richard Bentley junior, his literary executor, " furnished the words to Jennens' idea of the oratorios ". The correct title of the oratorio was Messiah, without the definite article ; cf. Myers, 1948, p. 54, note 2. The " Lines " which Jennens sent to Handel were printed on the title-page of the first word-book, as well as the later ones : " Majora Canamus " from Virgil, Eclogue IV, words from I Timothy 3 : 16, and Colossians 2 : 3. The Dublin word-book, printed by George Faulkner in 1742, is preserved in the British Museum and in Gerald Coke's Handel Collection ; Trinity College, Dublin, has the title-page only. The tenor voice referred to was probably either James Baileys, or John Church, both of whom sang in Dublin in 1736 in the Utrecht Te Deum and Jubilate, and were to sing in Messiah. The counter-tenors were William Lamb(e) and Joseph Ward, the basses John Hill and John Mason. The orchestra was probably a mixed one, compiled from professional and amateur musicians. The " College " mentioned by Handel was, of course, Trinity College. The " Ode " was repeated in the second concert, on 13th January 1742. The " Nation " are the Irish people. The second series of Handel's concerts started on 17th February. Although Handel's royal appointment consisted only of his being music-master to the Princesses, he apparently needed the King's consent for absence from London, and for the prolongation of his stay in Dublin. Knatchbull's wife, Catherine, the daughter of James Harris senior, of Salisbury, died in 1741. " Your Opera's " are the operas in London, under Lord Middlesex's new management. The " first Opera " was the pasticcio Alessandro in

Persia produced on 31st October ; the second was Galuppi's *Penelope*, text by Rolli, produced on 12th December.—The letter has no address ; the envelope seems to have been lost.

—

FROM VERTUE'S NOTE-BOOKS, 1741

Mr Rubbilac Sculptor of Marble—besides several works in Marble—moddels in Clay. had Modelld from the Life several Busts or portraits extreamly like Mr Pope. more like than any other Sculptor has done I think Mr Hogarth very like.—Mr Isaac Ware Architect Mr Handel—&c and several others. being very exact Imitations of Nature—

(Vertue, III. 105.)   British Museum, Add. MS. 23,079 : Note Book B.4.

1742

A POEM BY ELIZABETH TOLLET, WRITTEN ABOUT 1742

To Mr. HANDELL.

The Sounds which vain unmeaning Accents bear,
May strike the Sense and play upon the Ear :
In youthful Breasts inspire a transient Flame ;
Then vanish in the Void from whence they came.
But when just Reason animates the Song,
With lofty Style, in Numbers smooth and strong,
Such as young *Ammon*'s Passions cou'd controul,
Or chear the Gloom of *Saul*'s distemper'd Soul ;
To these the Goddess Muse shall tune her Voice :
For then the Muse directs the Master's Choice.
Such Themes are suited to the Hero's Mind :
But rural Lays have Charms for all Mankind.
Whether the Poet paints the native Scene,
Or calls to trip it on the level Green :
Or leads the Wand'rer by the Moon along,
While the sweet Chauntress tunes her Even-Song :
The serious Mind with sudden Rapture glows ;
The Gazer sinks into sedate Repose :
And each in Silence doubts, if more to praise
The Pow'r of *Handell*'s Notes, or Milton's Lays.
One Labour yet, great Artist ! we require ;
And worthy thine, as worthy Milton's Lyre ;
In Sounds adapted to his Verse to tell
How, with his Foes, the *Hebrew* Champion fell :
To all invincible in Force and Mind,
But to the fatal Fraud of Womankind.
To others point his Error, and his Doom ;
And from the Temple's Ruins raise his Tomb.

(*Poems*, p. 136 f.) The authoress died in 1754, sixty years of age ; the poems were published in 1755. Three of her poems were set to music by Boyce, Samuel Howard and Thomas Roseingrave. W. T. Brooke, who reprinted the Handel poem in the *Musical Standard* of 29th June 1912, made the comment that *Alexander's Feast* and *Saul* were alluded to in the beginning, while *Samson* was suggested at the end. Mr. Winton Dean suggests that *L'Allegro* is alluded to in the middle of the poem (lines 12 to 20). Handel started to compose Milton's *Samson*, arranged for him by Newburgh Hamilton, on 29th October 1741. Miss Tollet may have given her poem to Handel in manuscript.

FROM THE MINUTES OF MERCER'S HOSPITAL, 4th January 1742

Order'd That John Rockfort John Ruthland, & Richd Baldwin Esq^{rs} be desir'd to apply in the name of the Governors of Mercer's Hospital to the Rev^d the Dean & Chapter of St Patricks Dublin for their leave that such of their Choir as shall be Willing may assist at the Phil-Harmonick Society Performances which are principally intended for the Benefit of the said Hospital and to notifie to them that the Dean & Chapter of Christ Church have been pleas'd to grant them the same request.

Cf. Minutes of 23rd January, and Swift's answer of 28th January. Ten of the Vicar Chorals of St. Patrick's Cathedral also sang at Christ Church. (Culwick pp. 6 f.) The Philharmonic Society in Dublin (see 21st November 1741) was especially dedicated to Mercer's Hospital ; its residence was in Fishamble Street, near Christ Church Cathedral, not in the New Music Hall, but opposite St. John's Church. The Charitable Music Society, for the relief of imprisoned debtors, which (according to Townsend and Flood) erected the Hall, transferred its meetings from the " Bear " in College Green to one of the smaller rooms there. The Academy of Music was housed in Crow Street. There were, however, more than these three charitable musical societies in Dublin (see Townsend, p. 33) : the city was not only very musical, but the gap between the life of the higher society and the mass of the people was appalling. Mercer's Hospital for distressed, sick poor was founded in 1734 by Mary Mercer, a spinster, who died in 1735.

———

FROM FAULKNER'S " DUBLIN JOURNAL ", 9th January 1742

By their Graces the Duke and Duchess of Devonshire's special Command, at the New Musick-hall in Fishamble-street, on Wednesday next, the 13th Day of January (being the second Night of Mr. Handel's Musical Entertainments by Subscription) will be performed, L'Allegro, il Penseroso, & il Moderato, with several Concertos on the Organ and other Instruments. . . . Printed Books are sold at the same Place, Price a British Six pence. To begin at 7 o'clock.

(Townsend, p. 52.)

———

FROM FAULKNER'S " DUBLIN JOURNAL ", 16th January 1742

By their Graces the Duke and Duchess of Devonshire's special Command, at the New Musick-hall . . . on Wednesday next, being the 20th . . . will be performed, Acis and Galatea ; to which will be added, an Ode for St. Cecilia's Day, written by Mr. Dryden, and newly set to Musick by Mr. Handel, with several concertos on the Organ and other Instruments. . . . To begin at 7 o'clock. N.B.—Gentlemen and Ladies are desired to order their Coaches and Chairs to come down Fishamble-street, which will prevent a great deal of Inconvenience that happened the Night before ; and as there is a good convenient Room hired as an Addition to a former Place for the Footmen, it is hoped the Ladies will order them to attend there till called for.—Printed Books are sold at the same Place, Price a British Six pence.

(Townsend, p. 53.) The advertisement also appeared in the *Dublin News-Letter* of the same day, but without the Notabene, which was added on 19th January in this form : " N.B. There is another convenient Passage for Chairs made since the last Night ". The " last Night " was apparently the 13th January. The word-book was printed by Faulkner ; a copy is in the British Museum.

—

FROM THE MINUTES OF MERCER'S HOSPITAL, 22nd January 1742

Agreed That the R^t Honble the Lords Mountjoy & Tullamore be desired to wait upon their Excellences the Lord Justices and request the favour of their Company at the Musical performance in St Andrews Church on Tuesday the 8th of February.

That the Honble Major Butler be desired to apply to the Government for a Captains Guard to attend at said Performance & dispose of the Guard to the best advantage.

The Governors of Mercer's Hospital give this publick Notice that there will be a Sermon preached at St Andrews Church, on Tuesday the 8th of February next when Divine Service will be performed as heretofore after the Cathedral manner with Te-Deum, Jubilate, & two new Anthems compos'd by Mr. Handel—Tickets to be had at the said Hospital at half a Guinea each.

N.B. Benefit arising hereby is the Chief Support of the Hospital.

(*Musical Times*, 1st October 1903, edited by F. G. Edwards.) Richard Wesley was in the chair at this meeting of the Governors. The two lords are William, Viscount Mountjoy and Charles, Baron Moore of Tullamore. The second half of the minutes was written for publication in the newspapers.

—

FROM THE " DUBLIN NEWS-LETTER ", 23rd January 1742

On Wednesday Evening [the 20th] the Masque of Acis and Galatea, with one of Mr. Dryden's Odes on St. Cecilia's Day, were performed at the New Musick-Hall . . ., before a very splendid Audience, so as to give infinite Satisfaction : Being both set to Musick and conducted by that great Master Mr. Handel, and accompanied all along on the Organ by his own inimitable Hand.

—

FROM FAULKNER'S " DUBLIN JOURNAL ", 23rd January 1742

By their Graces the Duke and Duchess of Devonshire's special Command, at the New Musick-hall . . . on Wednesday next [the 27th] will be performed, *Acis and Galatea* ; to which will be added an Ode for St. Cecilia's Day.

(Townsend, p. 58.)

—

FROM THE MINUTES OF MERCER'S HOSPITAL, 23rd January 1742

The Gentlemen deputed by this Board to the Chapter of St Patricks reported that they had applied to them according to the Order, Jan^{ry} 4 1741[–42], & receiv'd the following answer.

The Dean & Chapter of St Patricks are ready to concur with the Dean & Chapter of Christ Church in permitting the Choir to assist at the Musical Performance of the Philharmonick Society, if the Dean & Chapter of Christ Church will concur with them in permitting the Choir to assist at Mr. Handel's. They think that every argument in favour of the one, may be urged with equal strength at least in favour of the other, particularly that which with them is of greatest weight the advantage of Mercer's Hospital, Mr. Handel having offer'd & being still ready in return for such a favour to give the Governors some of his choisest Musick, & to direct & assist at the Performance of it for the benefit of the Hospital, which will in one night raise a considerable Sum for their use, without lessning the Anual Contribution of the Philharmonick Society or any of their other funds. & in order to prevent the permission to be brought into a precedent which some time or other may be of Evil consequence the Dean & Chapter of St Patricks will concur with the Dean & Chapter of Christ Church in any proper rule to hinder their Voices or other members of the Choir from performing at any publick Musical Performance excepting in Churches without the joint permission of both Deans & Chapters first had & obtained.

The above answer being read and a motion being made that application be made to the Chapter of Christ Church in persuance to the desire of the Chapter of St Patricks—is passed in the negative.

(Townsend, p. 32, 54.) Cf. 14th November 1741 and 28th January 1742. There was apparently rivalry between the two chapters. Swift, the Dean of St. Patrick's Cathedral, may have been prejudiced in favour of Handel, who was probably introduced to him by common friends, for instance Mrs. Pendarves. The Sub-Dean of that cathedral was Dr. John Wynne, one of the Governors of the Hospital and a member of the Charitable Musical Society. The Dean of Christ Church, Dr. Charles Cobbe, later Archbishop of Dublin, was one of the Trustees of the Hospital. According to the Minutes of that institution, under the date of 27th January, Swift granted his licence to six of St. Patrick's " Voices ", the Vicar Chorals, and two of the choristers. His letter of 28th January, however, denies this. The reason, it seems, was the state of Swift's mind ; later in 1742 he became insane.

—

DEAN SWIFT TO SUB-DEAN AND CHAPTER OF ST. PATRICK'S CATHEDRAL, 28th January 1742

[First Version]

. . . I do hereby require and request the Very Reverend Sub-Dean, not to permit any of the Vicar Chorals, choristers, or organists, to attende or assist at any public musical performances, without my consent, or his consent, with the consent of the Chapter first obtained.

And whereas it hath been reported, that I gave a licence to certain vicars to assist at a club of fiddlers in Fishamble Street, I do hereby declare that I remember no such licence to have been ever signed or sealed by me ; and that if ever such pretended licence should be produced, I do hereby annul and vacate the said licence ; intreating my said Sub-Dean and Chapter to punish such vicars as shall ever appear there, as songsters, fiddlers, pipers, trumpeters, drummers, drum-majors, or in any sonal quality, according to the flagitious aggravations of their respective disobedience, rebellion, perfidy, and ingratitude.

I require my said Sub-Dean to proceed to the extremity of expulsion, if the said vicars should be found ungovernable, impenitent, or self-sufficient, especially Taverner, Phipps, and Church, who, as I am informed, have, in violation of my Sub-Dean's and Chapter's order in December last, at the instance of some obscure persons unknown, presumed to sing and fiddle at the club above mentioned. . . .

[Second Version]

Whereas several of the Vicar Chorals have disobeyed and transgressed some rules and orders made by my Sub-Dean and Chapter for regulating their behaviour and conduct and pretend and give out that they have my licence under my hand to act contrary to the said orders made by my Sub-Dean and Chapter : Now I do hereby declare, that to the best of my remembrance I never did sign any licence to any of the said vicars to perform at any musical society contrary to the said orders nor did I ever design it.

And, if I have been so far imposed upon as to sign any deed or licence to the purposes aforesaid and it be produced to justify their behaviour, I do hereby annul and vacate the same. . . .

(Swift, *Correspondence*, VI, 220 f.) The organist of both cathedrals was Ralph Roseingrave. The Philharmonic Society was housed in Fishamble Street, opposite St. John's Church. John Phipps and John Church were Vicar Chorals of both cathedrals, the Rev. William Taverner of St. Patrick's only. The performance referred to was apparently the one of 10th December, at which Handel assisted (cf. 14th November 1741).

———

FROM FAULKNER'S " DUBLIN JOURNAL ", 30th JANUARY 1742

By their Graces the Duke and Duchess of Devonshire's special Command, at the New Musick-hall . . . on Wednesday next [3rd February] will be performed, an Oratorio called ESTHER, with Additions, and several Concertos on the Organ and other Instruments. . . . To begin at 7 o'clock. Printed Books are sold at the same Place, Price a British Six-pence.—N.B. It is humbly hoped that no Gentlemen or Ladies will take it ill, that none but Subscribers can be admitted, and that no Single Tickets will be delivered, or Money taken at the Door.

(Townsend, p. 58.) A copy of Faulkner's word-book is in the British Museum ; in it a concerto on the organ is indicated at the end of the second part of the oratorio.

———

FROM " PUE'S OCCURRENCES ", 3rd February 1742

(In the press, and shortly to be published :)

A Poem by Laurence Whyte on the General Effect and Excellency of Musick, particularly, on the famous Mr. Handel's performance, who has been lately invited into this Kingdom, by his Grace the Duke of Devonshire, Lord Lieutenant of Ireland, for the Entertainment of the Nobility and Gentry.

(Townsend, p. 29.) Cf. 20th April.

———

FROM FAULKNER'S " DUBLIN JOURNAL ", 6th February 1742

By the Desire of several Persons of Quality and Distinction there will be a new Subscription made for Mr. Handel's Musical Entertainments, for Six Nights more, on the same Footing as the last. No more than 150 Subscriptions will be taken in, and no Single Tickets sold, or any Money taken at the Door. Subscriptions will be taken in at Mr. Handel's House in Abby-street near Lyffee-street, on Monday next, being the 8th Day of February from 9 o'clock in the Morning till 3 in the Afternoon. The Performances are to continue once a Week, till the 6 Nights are over.

N.B. The Tickets for the last Night of the First Subscription, will be delivered to the Subscribers on Tuesday and Wednesday next, at the New Musick hall in Fishamble-street from 10 o'clock in the Morning till 3 in the Afternoon ; where Subscriptions are taken in likewise.

(Townsend, p. 59.) Since each subscriber received three tickets, 150 subscriptions covered 450 seats, out of the hall's capacity of 600.

———

Handel's *Utrecht Te Deum and Jubilate*, with two " new " Anthems, is performed at St. Andrew's Church for the benefit of Mercer's Hospital, 8th February 1742.

Cf. 22nd January. The performance is recorded in a word-book, a copy of which was in Dr. Mann's Handel collection at Cambridge. In Mann's essay on music in Dublin (manuscript in King's College, Cambridge) the word-book is described. The two anthems were the Coronation

Anthems : " My heart is inditing " and " Zadok the Priest ". Whether Handel again played the organ, as on 10th December 1741, is not known.

———

FROM FAULKNER'S " DUBLIN JOURNAL ", 9th February 1742

Whereas several of the Nobility and Gentry have been pleased to desire a second Subscription for Mr. Handel's Musical Entertainments, on the same Terms as the first ; Mr. Handel being a Stranger, and not knowing where to wait on every Gentleman, who was a Subscriber to his first, to pay his Compliments, hopes that those who have a Mind to subscribe again, will be pleased to send in their Names this Day (being Tuesday the 9th of February) and To-morrow, at the Musick-hall in Fishamble-street, where Attendance will be given from 10 o'clock in the Morning till 3 in the Afternoon, and every following Day at his House in Abby street near Liffey-street.

N.B. To-morrow being the last Night of Performance of his first Subscription, the Tickets will be delivered to the Subscribers this Day and To-morrow at the Musick-hall . . . where new Subscriptions taken in likewise.

(Townsend, p. 59.)   On 10th February *Esther* was repeated.

———

FROM THE SAME

It is humbly requested that the Ladies will order their Coaches to come down Fishamble-street every Saturday to the Assembly, as they do to Mr. Handel's Entertainment, which will prevent a great many Inconveniences.

(Townsend, p. 61.)   Starting on 24th October 1741, Mrs. Hamilton and Mrs. Walker gave an " Assembly" (ball) every Saturday at the New Music Hall.   As late as 20th December 1743, the *Dublin Journal* referred to " Mr. Handell's " nights, in advertising a benefit concert on the 21st.

———

FROM FAULKNER'S " DUBLIN JOURNAL ", 13th February 1742

By their Graces the Duke and Duchess of Devonshire's special Command, at the New Musick-hall . . . on Wednesday next [17th February] will be performed, *Alexander's Feast*, with Additions and several Concertos on the Organ.   Attendance will be given this Day at Mr. Handel's House in Abby-street, and on Monday, Tuesday, and Wednesday at the Musick-hall . . ., in order to deliver to Subscribers their new Subscription Tickets (by sending their Subscription Money) in which Places Subscriptions are taken in likewise.   None but Subscriber's Tickets can be admitted to the Publick Rehearsals.—N.B. For the conveniency of the ready emptying of the House, no Chairs will be admitted in waiting but hazard Chairs, at the new Passage in Copper Alley.

(Townsend, p. 60.) As in London, the subscribers were admitted to the final rehearsal. The Lord Lieutenant, with his family, left on 16th February for London.

—

FROM FAULKNER'S "DUBLIN JOURNAL", 20th February 1742

At the New Musick-hall . . . on Wednesday the 24 Inst. will be performed, *Alexander's Feast*, with Additions, and several Concerts on the Organ. . . .

(Townsend, p. 62.) The repeat performance of this Ode was postponed.

—

FROM FAULKNER'S "DUBLIN JOURNAL", 23rd February 1742

One of Mr. Handel's Principal Singers having fallen Sick, *Alexander's Feast*, that was to have been performed to Morrow is put off till Tuesday next being the second of March.

(Townsend, p. 62.) The singer may have been Mrs. Cibber (cf. 6th March). From March 1741 till February 1742, there was an epidemic of influenza in Britain ; more than 7500 people died (Baker, p. 425).

—

FROM FAULKNER'S "DUBLIN JOURNAL", 27th February 1742

At the New Musick-hall . . . on Tuesday next [2nd March] . . . *Alexander's Feast*. . . .

N.B. The Gentlemen of the Charitable Society on College-green, at the Request of Mr. Handel, have put off their weekly Concert until Tuesday the 9th of March.

For the Benefit of Monsieur de Rheiner, a distress'd foreign Gentleman, at the Theatre in Smock-Alley, on Thursday the fourth of March. . . . The Constant Couple [by George Farquhar]. . . . N.B. Monsieur de Rheiner has been oblig'd to put off his Day, which was to have been on Tuesday next, on account of all the best Musick being engaged to Mr. Handel's Concert. . . .

The second advertisement is quoted by Townsend, p. 62, under 2nd March.

—

HORACE WALPOLE TO HORACE MANN

[London, 4th March 1742.]
Thursday evening.

We have got another opera, which is liked. There was to have been a vast elephant, but the just directors, designing to give the audience the full weight of one for their money, made it so heavy, that at the *prova* it broke through the stage. It was to have carried twenty soldiers, with Monticelli on a throne in the middle. There is a new subscription begun for next year, thirty subscribers at two hundred pounds each. Would you believe that I am one ? You need not believe it quite, for I am but half an one ; Mr. Conway and I take a share between us. We keep Monticelli and Amorevoli, and to please Lord Middlesex, that odious Muscovita ; but shall discard Mr. Vanneschi. We are to have the Barberina and the two Fausans ; so, at least, the singers and dancers will be equal to anything in Europe.

(Walpole, *Letters*, 1891, I. 139 f.) The new opera was Galuppi's *Scipione in Carthagine*, produced on 2nd March ; the dedication of the word-book was signed by Vanneschi, who managed to stay on. Because Galuppi was sometimes called Il Buranello, after his birthplace, Burano near Venice, the authorship of the opera appeared doubtful to Nicoll. The prima ballerina of the following season was Sodi.

—

FROM THE MINUTES OF MERCER'S HOSPITAL, 4th March 1742

Whereas Mr Putland reported from a Committee appointed to consider of a Performance design'd for the Benefit of this Hospital the Infirmary & the Prisoner of the Marshalseas That it was the desire of the Gentlemen of that Committee that a deputation from the Trustees for those several Charities shou'd attend the Deans & Chapters of Christ Church & St Patricks to desire their leave that the Choir of both Cathedrals may assist at the said Performance.

Order'd That the Trustees of this Hospital do concur with the Committee provided that the whole benefit of the said Performance & of all Rehearsals previous to it shall be intirely applied to the support of the said Charities, & that Tickets be given out for whatever Rehearsals shall be necessary.

This refers to the first performance of Handel's *Messiah* on 13th April.

—

FROM FAULKNER'S "DUBLIN JOURNAL", 6th March 1742

The new Serenata called HYMEN, that was to have been performed on Wednesday next [the 10th], at Mr. Handel's Musical Entertainments at the New Musick-Hall in Fishamble-street, is by the sudden illness of Mrs. Cibber, put off to the Wednesday following ; and as many of Mr. Handel's Subscribers are obliged to go out of Town soon, it is humbly hoped that they will accept of the *Allegro ed il Penseroso* for the next Night's Performance, which will be on Wednesday the 10th of March....

(Townsend, pp. 67 f.) For the "operetta" *Imeneo*, in this English concert version called a "Serenata", see 22nd November 1740. The shortened title of the Ode indicates that part 3 was omitted at the last Dublin performance, which was, however, postponed till 17th March, and the Serenade till 24th March.

———

FROM FAULKNER'S "DUBLIN JOURNAL", 9th March 1742

Several Gentlemen and Ladies Subscribers to Mr. Handel's Musical Entertainments having desired that the Musical Performance should be put off till Wednesday se'night the 17th of March, Mrs. Cibber being in a fair Way of Recovery. The new Serenata called Hymen, will be certainly performed on that Day.

(Townsend, p. 68.)

———

FROM FAULKNER'S "DUBLIN JOURNAL", 13th March 1742

At the new Musick-hall . . . on Wednesday next [the 17th] . . . will be performed a new Serenata called HYMEN. With Concertos on the Organ and other Instruments. . . .

(Townsend, p. 69.) The performance was postponed for another week.

———

FROM FAULKNER'S "DUBLIN JOURNAL", 16th March 1742

At the new Musick-hall . . . To-morrow . . . will be performed *L'Allegro ed il Penseroso*, with Concertos on the Organ ; Mrs. Cibber continuing so ill that the new Serenata called HYMEN cannot be performed on that Day. . . .

(Townsend, p. 69.)

———

FROM FAULKNER'S "DUBLIN JOURNAL", 20th March 1742

At the new Musick-hall . . . on Wednesday next, being the 24th of March, will be performed . . . HYMEN. . . .

(Townsend, p. 69.) Repeat performance on 31st March. In the same issue of the *Journal*, the arrival in Dublin, on the 19th, of " Mr. Charles, an Hungarian, the famous French-Horn ", with his " second " (*sc.* horn) is reported. Cf. 3rd March 1738 and 1st May 1742.

———

FROM FAULKNER'S "DUBLIN JOURNAL", 27th March 1742

For Relief of the Prisoners in the several Gaols, and for the Support of Mercer's Hospital in Stephen's Street, and of the Charitable Infirmary on the Inns Quay, on Monday the 12th of April, will be performed at the Musick Hall in Fishamble Street, Mr. *Handel's new Grand Oratorio, call'd the* MESSIAH, in which the Gentlemen of the Choirs of both Cathedrals will assist, with some Concertoes on the Organ, by Mr. Handell. Tickets to be had at the Musick Hall, and at Mr. Neal's in

Christ-Church-Yard, at half a Guinea each. N.B. No Person will be admitted to the Rehearsal without a Rehearsal Ticket, which will be given gratis with the Ticket for the Performance when pay'd for.

(Townsend, pp. 69 f.) This advertisement was the first public announcement of Handel's *Messiah*. It was printed on the same day in the *Dublin News-Letter*, but with the variant " New Grand Sacred Oratorio " and the additional note : " Books are also to be had at a British sixpence each ". On 30th March, the *Dublin Journal* likewise gave the title as " Mr. Handel's New Grand Sacred Oratorio, called the MESSIAH ". The production was postponed till 13th April.

———

FROM FAULKNER'S " DUBLIN JOURNAL ", 30th March 1742

For the Benefit of Signora Avolio at the Musick-Hall . . . on Monday the 5th of April, will be a Concert of Vocal and Instrumental Musick. As Signora Avolio is a Stranger in this Country, she most humbly hopes, that the Nobility and Gentry, whom she hath had the Honour of performing before, will be pleased to honour her Benefit with their Presence, which she will acknowledge in the most grateful Manner. Tickets to be had at her Lodgings at Mr. Madden's in Strand-street, and the Printer's hereof, at a British Crown each.

The Printers were apparently Faulkner's.

———

FROM BOOK IV OF ALEXANDER POPE'S " DUNCIAD ", March 1742

. . . O Cara ! Cara ! silence all that train :
Joy to great Chaos ! let Division reign [1] : . . .
Strong in new Arms, lo ! Giant Handel stands,
Like bold Briareus, with a hundred hands ;
To stir, to rouze, to shake the Soul he comes,
And Jove's own Thunders follow Mars's Drums.
Arrest him, Empress ; or you sleep no more—
She heard, and drove him to th' Hibernian shore.

(Schoelcher, p. 241.) While Books 1-3 of the *Dunciad* were published in 1728, Book 4, written at the end of 1741, was issued in March 1742. The quotation is from the 1743 edition, pp. 160 ff., lines 53-4 and 65-70. Pope calls the empire of the philistines the " Kingdom of the Dull upon earth ". What he, and others afterwards, called Handel's " Cannon " were, of course, kettle-drums only. The " patch-work " mentioned in his footnote probably refers to the pasticcio *Alexander in Persia*, quoted as an example of Italian opera (see 31st October 1741).

———

[1] Allusion to the false taste of playing tricks in Music with numberless divisions, to the neglect of that harmony which conforms to the Sense, and applies to the Passions. Mr. *Handel* had introduced a great number of Hands, and more variety of Instruments into the Orchestra, and employed even Drums and Cannon to make a fuller Chorus ; which prov'd so much too manly for the fine Gentlemen of his age, that he was obliged to remove his Music into *Ireland*. After which they were reduced, for want of Composers, to practice the patch-work above mentioned.

FROM THE "GENTLEMAN'S MAGAZINE", March 1742

To Mrs. CIBBER, on her Acting at *Dublin*.

·   ·   ·   ·

Now tuneful as *Apollo's* lyre,
She stands amid the vocal choir ;
If solemn measures slowly move,
Or *Lydian* airs invite to love,
Her looks inform the trembling strings,
And raise each passion, that she sings ;
The wanton Graces hover round,
Perch on her lips, and tune the sound.

·   ·   ·   ·

O wondrous girl ! how small a space
Includes the gift of human race !

·   ·   ·   ·

Dublin, Mar. 11. 1742.

Susanna Maria Cibber, Arne's sister and second wife of Theophilus Cibber,
began as a singer in 1732, and made her first appearance as an actress in 1736 ; she
was soon accepted as the first tragedienne of her time (William H. Husk in Grove's
Dictionary). With her small mezzo-soprano voice, she was ideal for Handel's
oratorios. The Lydian Mode, the fifth of the Ecclesiastic Modes, was called the
Joyful because of its essentially jubilant character.

———

FROM FAULKNER'S "DUBLIN JOURNAL", 3rd April 1742

At the new Musick Hall . . . on Wednesday next, being the 7th of
April, will be performed an Oratorio call'd ESTHER, with Concertos on
the Organ, being the last Time of Mr. Handel's Subscription Performance. The Tickets will be delivered to the Subscribers on Tuesday next
at Mr. Handel's House in Abby-street, from Ten o'clock in the Morning
till Three in the Afternoon, and on Wednesday at the Musick Hall . . .
from Ten o'clock in the Morning till the Time of the Performance.

On Thursday next being the 8th Inst. at the Musick Hall . . . will
be the Rehearsal of Mr. Handel's new Grand Sacred Oratorio called
The MESSIAH, in which the Gentlemen of both Choirs will assist :
With some Concertos on the Organ by Mr. Handel. . . .

(Townsend, pp. 70 f.) The rehearsal seems to have been postponed till the 9th
(see next two entries).

———

FROM THE "DUBLIN NEWS-LETTER", 10th April 1742

Yesterday Morning, at the Musick Hall . . . there was a public
Rehearsal of the Messiah, Mr. Handel's new sacred Oratorio, which in
the opinion of the best Judges, far surpasses anything of that Nature,
which has been performed in this or any other Kingdom. The elegant

XXII. SUSANNA MARIA CIBBER

Mezzotint after Thomas Hudson, by John Faber.   (Gerald Coke, Esq.)

See page 544

XXIII. HANDEL'S HARPSICHORD

By Joannes Ruckers, Antwerp, 1612. This instrument was left by Handel to J. C. Smith, Sr., and given by his son to King George III, together with a marble bust of Handel by Roubiliac (1739). It was restored in 1885, and is now on loan in the Benton Fletcher Collection, Hampstead. (Crown copyright)

See page 691

Entertainment was conducted in the most regular Manner, and to the entire satisfaction of the most crowded and polite Assembly.

To the benefit of three very important public Charities, there will be a grand Performance of this Oratorio on Tuesday next [the 13th] in the forenoon. . . .

(Townsend, p. 87.)

FROM FAULKNER'S "DUBLIN JOURNAL", 10th April 1742

Yesterday Mr. Handell's new Grand Sacred Oratorio, called, The MESSIAH, was rehearsed . . . to a most Grand, Polite and crouded Audience ; and was performed so well, that it gave universal Satisfaction to all present ; and was allowed by the greatest Judges to be the finest Composition of Musick that ever was heard, and the sacred Words as properly adapted for the Occasion.

N.B. At the Desire of several Persons of Distinction, the above Performance is put off to Tuesday next [the 13th]. The Doors will be opened at Eleven, and the Performance begin at Twelve.

Many Ladies and Gentlemen who are well-wishers to this Noble and Grand Charity for which this Oratorio was composed, request it as a Favour, that the Ladies who honour this Performance with their Presence would be pleased to come without Hoops, as it will greatly encrease the Charity, by making Room for more company.

(Townsend, pp. 86 f.) This was the first, and perhaps the only, time that *Messiah* was said to have been composed for Dublin, and for the above charitable purpose. It seems quite plausible that this was, in fact, the case, and that Handel trained his singers and orchestra in other works, before producing this crowning one.

FROM FAULKNER'S "DUBLIN JOURNAL", 13th April 1742

The Stewards of the Charitable Musical Society request the Favour of the Ladies not to come with Hoops this Day to the Musick-Hall in Fishamble-Street : The Gentlemen are desired to come without their Swords.

This Day will be performed Mr. Handell's new Grand Sacred Oratorio, called The MESSIAH. . . .

(Townsend, pp. 87 f.) The same advertisement appeared in the *Dublin Gazette* and in the *Dublin News-Letter*.

CAST OF "MESSIAH", 13th April 1742

Sopranos—Signora Avoglio, Mrs. Maclaine
Contraltos (Mezzo-soprano and Altos)—Mrs. Cibber, Mr. William Lamb(e),
Mr. Joseph Ward

H.–18

Tenors—Mr. James Baileys, Mr. John Church
Basses—Mr. John Hill, Mr. John Mason

All the Gentlemen belonged to both cathedrals, except Mason, who belonged to Christ Church Cathedral only.

HORACE WALPOLE TO HORACE MANN

April 15, 1742.

Would you believe that our wise directors for next year will not keep the Visconti, and have sent for the Fumagalli ? She will not be heard to the first row of the pit.

(Walpole, *Letters*, 1891, I. 156.) The new singer, after getting one hundred ducats as advance payment, did not come to London in autumn 1742.

FROM FAULKNER'S " DUBLIN JOURNAL ", 17th April 1742

On Tuesday last [the 13th] Mr. Handel's Sacred Grand Oratorio, the MESSIAH, was performed at the New Musick-Hall in Fishamble-street ; the best Judges allowed it to be the most finished piece of Musick. Words are wanting to express the exquisite Delight it afforded to the admiring crouded Audience. The Sublime, the Grand, and the Tender, adapted to the most elevated, majestick and moving Words, conspired to transport and charm the ravished Heart and Ear. It is but Justice to Mr. Handel, that the World should know, he generously gave the Money arising from this Grand Performance, to be equally shared by the Society for relieving Prisoners, the Charitable Infirmary, and Mercer's Hospital, for which they will ever gratefully remember his Name ; and that the Gentlemen of the two Choirs, Mr. Dubourg, Mrs. Avolio, and Mrs. Cibber, who all performed their Parts to Admiration, acted also on the same disinterested Principle, satisfied with the deserved Applause of the Publick, and the conscious Pleasure of promoting such useful, and extensive Charity. There were about 700 People in the Room, and the Sum collected for that Noble and Pious Charity amounted to about 400*l*. out of which 127*l*. goes to each of the three great and pious Charities.

(Townsend, p. 88.) The same report, but without the last sentence, appeared in the *Dublin Gazette* and in the *Dublin News-Letter ;* it was probably composed by the secretary of Mercer's Hospital. Only *Pue's Occurences*, of the same day, carried a short individual report. It should be noticed that Mrs. Maclaine is not mentioned here : it is possible that she only sang in the second performance, on 3rd June, sharing Signora Avoglio's soprano part. The normal capacity of the Music Hall was 600 ; see Handel's letter of 29th December 1741.

FROM FAULKNER'S " DUBLIN JOURNAL ", 20th April 1742

On Mr. *Handel's* Performance of his *Oratorio*, call'd the *Messiah*, for the Support of Hospitals, and other pious Uses, at the Musick-hall in Fishamble-street, on Tuesday, April 13th, 1742, before the Lords Justices,

and a vast Assembly of the Nobility and Gentry of both Sexes.   By Mr.
L. Whyte.

> What can we offer more in *Handel*'s praise ?
> Since his *Messiah* gain'd him groves of Bays ;
> Groves that can never wither nor decay,
> Whose *Vistos* his Ability display :
> Here *Nature* smiles, when grac'd with *Handel*'s Art,
> Transports the Ear, and ravishes the Heart ;
> To all the nobler *Passions* we are mov'd,
> When various strains repeated and improv'd,
> Express each different Circumstance and State,
> As if each Sound became articulate.
>   None but the Great *Messiah* cou'd inflame,
> And raise his Soul to so sublime a *Theme*,
> Profound the Thoughts, the Subject all divine,
> Now like the Tales of *Pindus* and the *Nine* :
> Or Heathen Deities, those Sons of Fiction,
> Sprung from old *Fables*, stuff'd with Contradiction ;
> But our *Messiah*, blessed be his Name !
> Both Heaven and Earth his *Miracles* proclaim.
> His Birth, his Passion, and his Resurrection,
> With his Ascention, have a strong Connection ;
> What Prophets spoke, or Sybels could relate,
> In him were all their Prophecies compleat,
> The *Word* made Flesh, both God and Man became ;
> They let all Nations glorify his Name.
> Let Hallelujah's round the Globe be sung,
> To our *Messiah*, from a Virgin sprung.

(Townsend, pp. 89 f.)   The author was Laurence Whyte.   His first Handel
poem, advertised on 3rd February, was never published.   This may have been a
second version, written after the production of *Messiah*.   Line 6 resembles a passage
in the official report, printed on 17th April : " transport and charm the ravished
Heart and Ear ".

———

From Faulkner's " Dublin Journal ", 27th April 1742

We hear that Mrs. Cibber will perform next Friday [the 30th] at the
Musick-hall in Fishamble-street to the Charitable and Musical Society.

The Charitable Musical Society, founded at the beginning of the century,
transferred its meetings to the new Music Hall on completion of the latter in
autumn 1741, though, apparently, it kept its office in College Green (see 11th
May).

———

From Faulkner's " Dublin Journal ", 1st May 1742

At the Musick-hall . . . on Wednesday the 12th of May will be
performed a grand Concert of Musick, by Mr. *Charles* the Hungarian,

Master of the French Horn, with his Second, accompanied by all the best Hands in this City.—First Act, 1. An Overture with French Horns, called new Pastor Fido. . . . Second Act, 1. Handel's Water Musick, with the March in Scipio, and the grand Chorus in Atalanta. . . . Third Act, 1. The Overture in Saul, with the Dead March, composed by Mr. Handel, but never performed here before. . . . The Rehearsal for this grand Performance will be on Wednesday the 5th of May. . . .

(Townsend, p. 94.) Cf. 3rd March 1738 and 20th March 1742. Charles also performed on the clarinet, the " Hautbois de Amour ", and the shalambo, instruments never heard before in Ireland. The " new *Pastor Fido* " was from Handel's 1734 version. Cf. 11th and 15th May.

———

From Faulkner's " Dublin Journal ", 11th May 1742

As several of the Nobility and Gentry have desired to hear Mr. Handel's Grand Oratorio of Saul, it will be performed on the 25th Inst. at the New Musick-hall . . . with some Concertos on the Organ. Tickets will be delivered at Mr. Handel's House in Abbey-street, and at Mr. Neal's in Christ-church-yard, at Half a Guinea each. A Ticket for the Rehearsal (which will be on Friday the 21st) will be given gratis with the Ticket for the Performance. Both the Rehearsal and the Performance will begin at 12 at Noon.

(Townsend, pp. 94 f.: quoting an advertisement of 8th May.) The performance began, in fact, at 7 P.M.

———

From the Same

For the Benefit of Mr. Will. and Bar. Manwaring, at the Request of the Charitable Musical Society on College-green, on Monday the 17th Inst. will be acted, at the Theatre in Smock-alley, a Comedy. . . . At which Mr. Manwaring will play his own Medley Overture ; and Mr. Charles, with his Second, will perform the Water Musick, being the first time of his appearing on the Stage, in which he will be accompanied on the Kettle Drum by Mr. Kounty.

William Manwaring, or Mainwaring, was a music seller in College Green, in 1740–41 associated with the Neals. He was also Treasurer to the Charitable Musical Society. As far as is known he was not related to the Rev. John Mainwaring, Handel's first biographer. The other, Bartholomew (?), has not been identified. Charles played, from Walsh's parts, sections of Handel's *Water Music* on 12th and 17th May, and probably on 2nd June.

———

From Faulkner's " Dublin Journal ", 15th May 1742

Mr. Charles' late Concert [on the 12th] having given such general Satisfaction to the Audience, he has been desired to repeat his Performance once more before he leaves this Kingdom : Therefore, on Wednesday next [the 19th], at the Musick-hall . . . will be his second and last Grand Concert of Musick, wherein he will introduce . . . by particular Desire the Dead March in Saul. . . .

This concert was postponed from 19th May, at 1.30 P.M., until 2nd June, at 7.0 P.M.; some prices were also reduced. Charles either stayed on, or returned to Dublin ; at the beginning of 1742, he started to teach the French Horn, and also played in the orchestra of the Theatre Royal in Aungier Street. In November 1742 he took over Geminiani's " Concerts and Great Music Room " (*Dublin Journal*). In 1757, twelve Duettos for French Horns or German Flutes by Charles were printed in the second edition of *Apollo's Cabinet* by John Sadler in Liverpool.

———

FROM FAULKNER'S " DUBLIN JOURNAL ", 22nd May 1742

Yesterday there was a Rehearsal of the Oratorio of Saul at the Musick-Hall . . . at which there was a most grand, polite and numerous Audience, which gave such universal Satisfaction, that it was agreed by all the Judges present, to have been the finest Performance that hath been heard in this Kingdom.

[Performance on 25th May :] To begin at 7 o'clock. Books to be had at the Musick-hall, Price a British Sixpence.

(Townsend, p. 95.) No copy of the Dublin word-book seems to have been preserved.

———

HORACE WALPOLE TO HORACE MANN

Downing Street, May 26, 1742.
Our operas are almost over ; there were but three-and-forty people last night in the pit and boxes. There is a little simple farce at Drury Lane, called " Miss Lucy in Town ", in which Mrs. Clive mimics the Muscovita admirably, and Beard, Amorevoli tolerably. But all the run is now after Garrick, a wine-merchant, who is turned player, at Goodman's-fields. . . .

(Walpole, *Letters*, 1891, I. 168.) The last opera but one of the season at the Hay-market Theatre was Pergolesi's *Olimpiade*, on 20th April ; performed under the title of *Meraspe*, with Metastasio's text altered by Rolli, it was " more or less a pasticcio " (Loewenberg, p. 94). Thomas Gray wrote about it in a letter to John Chute, on 24th May ; he also mentioned the last opera of the season : *Cefalo e Procri*. After only three performances of this last opera, the season ended on 1st June. The farce, by Henry Fielding, had been played since 6th May, but was temporarily forbidden by order of the Lord Chamberlain. The reason was probably that people recognized in " Lord Bauble " the Earl of Middlesex. There even appeared a " Letter to a Noble Lord . . . occasioned by . . . a Farce, called Miss Lucy in Town ". There were songs in it.

———

FROM FAULKNER'S "DUBLIN JOURNAL", 29th May 1742

At the particular Desire of several of the Nobility and Gentry, on Thursday next, being the 3d Day of June, at the New Musick-Hall . . . will be performed, Mr. Handel's new grand sacred Oratorio, called MESSIAH, with Concertos on the Organ. Tickets will be delivered at Mr. Handel's House in Abby-street, and at Mr. Neal's in Christ-church-yard, at half a Guinea each. A Rehearsal Ticket will be given gratis with the Ticket for the Performance. The Rehearsal will be on Tuesday the 1st of June at 12, and the Performance at 7 in the Evening In order to keep the Room as cool as possible, a Pane of Glass will be removed from the Top of each of the Windows.—N.B. This will be the last Performance of Mr. Handel's during his Stay in this Kingdom.

(Townsend, pp. 95 f.)

———

SURVEY OF HANDEL'S PERFORMANCES IN DUBLIN

1741, 23 December—' L'Allegro, il Penseroso, ed il Moderato '
1742, 13 January   —ditto
      20 January   —' Acis and Galatea ' and ' Ode for St. Cecilia's Day '
      27 January   —ditto
      3 February   —' Esther '
      10 February   —ditto (end of the first subscription)
      17 February   —' Alexander's Feast '
      2 March   —ditto
      17 March   —' L'Allegro ed il Penseroso '
      24 March   —' Imeneo '
      31 March   —ditto
      7 April   —' Esther ' (end of the second subscription)
      13 April   —' Messiah ' (public rehearsal, 9 April)
      25 May   —' Saul ' (public rehearsal, 21 May)
      3 June   —' Messiah ' (public rehearsal, 1 June)
(Schoelcher, p. 246.)

———

FROM FAULKNER'S "DUBLIN JOURNAL", 8th June 1742

On Wednesday the 16th Instant, there will be a Concert of Vocal and Instrumental Musick, at the Musick-Hall . . . for the Benefit of Signora Avoglio. . . . N.B. As she is a Stranger in the Kingdom, she most humbly hopes, that our Nobility and Gentry, who are so remarkable for their great Humanity and Generosity to Strangers, will be pleased to countenance her in this Affair.

This was Signora Avoglio's second benefit concert (cf. 30th March). It was postponed till 23rd June.

———

FROM THE KING'S WARRANT BOOK, 9th June 1742

	£	s.	d.	
Royal Academy of Musick	1,000	0	0	Royal bounty towards enabling the undertakers of the Opera to defray expense thereof

(Calendar of Treasury Books and Papers, 1742–45, p. 182.) The Calendar for 1739–41 contains no entries referring to the Opera. Cf. 5th July 1738. This is not the last allowance for the Haymarket Opera (see 7th February and 2nd August 1744). It is remarkable that the name of the Royal Academy of Music still existed in the Treasury Papers, although nothing was left of that illustrious company, founded in 1719, except the licensee, Heidegger. This time Lord Middlesex and his noble friends were the recipients of the royal bounty. See also 22nd June.

FROM FAULKNER'S "DUBLIN JOURNAL", 15th June 1742

On Wednesday the 23d Instant, there will be a Concert of Vocal and Instrumental Musick . . . for the Benefit of Signora Avoglio. . . . Being the last time of her Performance in this Kingdom.

N.B. The above Concert is put off on account of the Players Arrival from England, who perform that Evening [the 16th], and have given up the Wednesday following [the 23rd] to Signora Avolio for her Performance.

The "Players" at the Theatre in Smock-Alley performed on the 16th, with Miss Margaret Woffington, in *The Constant Couple*. David Garrick came with the company.

FROM THE TREASURY MINUTE BOOK, 22nd June 1742

Order for the following issues out of the Civil List :—

.   .   .   .   .

	£	s.	d.
To the Academy of Music .	1,000	0	0

Calendar of Treasury Books and Papers, 1742–45, pp. 49.

FROM FAULKNER'S "DUBLIN JOURNAL", 3rd July 1742

Last Wednesday [30th June] the ingenious Mr. [Thomas Augustine] Arne, Brother to Mrs. Cibber, and Composer of the Musick of Comus, together with his Wife (the celebrated Singer) arrived here from London.

Arne's music to Dalton's arrangement of Milton's *Comus* was produced at Drury Lane in 1738. Neal and Mainwaring printed two collections of songs from *Comus* in 1741. Mrs. Cecilia Arne, *née* Young, sang in Handel parts both before and after 1742. The couple remained in Dublin until 1744. Mrs. Cibber sang Polly in the *Beggar's Opera* on 24th June at the Theatre Royal in Aungier Street.

FROM FAULKNER'S "DUBLIN JOURNAL", 13th July 1742

At the particular Desire of several Persons of Quality, for the Benefit of Mrs. Arne, at the Theatre-royal in Aungier-street, on Wednesday the 21st Inst. will be performed a Grand Entertainment of MUSICK, to be divided into three Interludes ; wherein several favourite Songs and Duettos will be performed by Mrs. Arne and Mrs. Cibber.—In the first Interlude (after an Overture of Mr. Handel's) . . . O beauteous Queen, from Mr. Handel's Oratorio of Esther, by Mrs. Cibber ; . . . O fairest of ten thousand Fair, a Duetto, from Mr. Handel's Oratorio of Saul, by Mrs. Arne and Mrs. Cibber.—In the second Interlude . . . Chi Scherza colle Rose, from Mr. Handel's Opera of Hymen, by Mrs. Cibber ; . . . Vado e Vivo, a Duetto of Mr. Handel's in Faramondo, by Mrs. Arne and Mrs. Cibber.—In the third Interlude . . . Un Guardo solo, from Mr. Handel's Opera of Hymen, by Mrs. Cibber ; (by particular Desire) Sweet Bird, from Mr. Handel's Allegro, by Mrs. Arne ; and Per le Porte del Tormento, a favourite Duetto from Mr. Handel's in Sosarmes, by Mrs. Arne and Mrs. Cibber. . . .

(Townsend, pp. 68, 100.) The same advertisement appeared in the *Dublin News-Letter*. In the end the concert was transferred to the "Great Room in Fishamble-Street", and repeated on 28th July. The programme, essentially a homage to Handel on the part of the sisters-in-law, is of interest not only because Handel certainly attended the concert, if he did not participate as accompanist of his arias and duets, but because it indicates which parts Mrs. Cibber sang in Handel's operas and oratorios in Dublin, although her *Imeneo* songs are from Tirinto's as well as from Imeneo's parts. Mrs. Arne apparently sang, at her concert, the parts of Signora Avoglio, who may already have departed. *Faramondo* and *Sosarme*, however, were not performed by Handel in Dublin. *Hymen*, or *Imeneo*, is here described as an opera, as in the original production.

___

FROM FAULKNER'S "DUBLIN JOURNAL", 24th July 1742

On Wednesday last [the 21st], at the Great Room in Fishamble-street was performed (for the Benefit of Mrs. Arne the celebrated Singer) a grand Entertainment of Musick, wherein she and Mrs. Cibber sang several favourite Songs and Duettos, with so great an Applause, that the whole Company desired it might be performed again next Wednesday [the 28th].

___

David Garrick plays *Hamlet* at the Smock-Alley Theatre, 12th August 1742. Handel is said to have attended this performance.

(Myers, 1948, p. 107.) Cf. February 1755. It would have been about this time that Handel took his leave of Swift, to whom he was probably introduced by some mutual friends, like Mrs. Pendarves. The anecdote told by Mrs. Letitia Pilkington (see end of 1754) refers to Handel's farewell. In a letter to Burney (IV. 662), dated 16th July 1788, Dr. W. C.

Quin, of Dublin, mentions a Mrs. Vernon (Dorothy Grahn) of Clontarf Castle, Cork, " a German Lady, who came over with King George I ", as being a friend of Handel's during his stay in Dublin. (Smith, 1954, p. 302.) There is some doubt about the *Forest Music*, for violin and harpsichord, composed by Handel for her. Townsend (p. 64) mentions it as unpublished ; but it had been edited by William Ware in Dublin, 1803 ; then arranged, *c.* 1815, in Smollet Holden's *Collection of Music* for military bands. In 1854, John Smith edited it for pianoforte alone, published in Dublin by Henry Bussell ; and in 1856 C. Lonsdale in London reprinted this arrangement, with a dedication to Schoelcher. Townsend suggests that Handel " interweaved the national music of Ireland with his own ", as a graceful compliment ; and Schoelcher (p. 257) that the first movement pictures the hunter going to the forest, while the second imitates Irish folk music. (The *Forest Music* has nothing to do with Walsh's collection, *Forest Harmony* ; see 12th June 1733.)

From the " Dublin News-Letter ", 14th August 1742

Yesterday the Right Hon. the Lady King, the celebrated Mr. Handel, and several other Persons of Distinction, embarked on board one of the Chester Traders, in order to go to Parkgate.

(Townsend, p. 100.) Handel returned by the same route by which he had travelled to Dublin ; probably without intermediate stops. (Cf. 9th September 1742.) He must have arrived in London near the end of August, having been away for ten months.

From Faulkner's " Dublin Journal ", 17th August 1742

Last Week Lady King, Widow of the late Rt. Hon. Sir Henry King, Bart. and the celebrated Mr. Handel so famous for his excellent Compositions and fine Performance with which he entertained this Town in the most agreeable Manner, embarked for England.

(Townsend, p. 101.) On 23rd August, according to the same journal, Mrs. Cibber and Mr. Arne followed Handel to London ; Arne, however, returned later to Dublin, to rejoin his wife.

From the " Gentleman's Magazine ", August 1742

GREEN-WOOD-HALL : *or* Colin's *Description (to his* Wife*) of the Pleasures of* SPRING GARDENS.

Made to a favourite Gavot *from an* Organ-Concerto *compos'd for* Vauxhall. By Mr. *Gladwin.*

· · · ·

As still, amaz'd, I'm straying
O'er this inchanted grove,
I spy a HARPER [1] playing
All in his proud alcove.

[1] *Mr* Handel's *statue.*

H.–18 *a*

> I doff my hat, desiring
>   He'd tune up BUXOM-JOAN :
> But what was I admiring !
>   Odzooks ! a man of stone.

.   .   .   .

The poem begins : " O Mary ! soft in feature, I've been at dear Vauxhall ".
There are six stanzas, the first being printed with the music ; this is the fourth.
The music is by Thomas Gladwin. The song was often reprinted in single sheet
folio. " Buxom Joan of Lymas's [Limehouse] Love to a Jolly Sailer ", a ballad,
the first three verses of which are from William Congreve's " Love for Love ",
sung " To an excellent new Play-house tune ", in fact a meaningless succession of
notes, was printed about 1693.

———

The Three Choirs Meeting is held at Gloucester, 8th and 9th
September 1742.

The *Gloucester Journal* remarked only that " The appearance of Persons
of Distinction was very extraordinary ". The works performed, in the
mornings at the Cathedral and in the evenings at the Booth Hall, are not
recorded. It is possible that Handel's *Dettingen Te Deum and Jubilate* was
performed on one morning, and it is probable that Dr. William Boyce was
the conductor of all the concerts.

———

HANDEL TO JENNENS, AT GOPSAL

London Septr 9.th 1742.

Dear S^r

It was indeed Your humble Servant which intended You a visit in
my way from Ireland to London, for I certainly could have given You
a better account by word of mouth, as by writing, how well Your
Messiah was received in that Country, yet as a Noble Lord, and no less
then the Bishop of Elphim (a Nobleman very learned in Musick) has
given his Observation in writing of this Oratorio, I send you here
annexed the Contents of it in his own words.—I shall send the printed
Book of the Messiah to Mr Sted for You. As for my Success in General
in that generous and polite Nation, I reserve the account of it till I have
the Hoñour to see you in London. The report that the Direction of the
Opera next winter is comitted to my Care, is groundless. The gentlemen
who have undertaken to middle with Harmony can not agree, and are
quite in a Confusion. Whether I shall do some thing in the Oratorio
way (as several of my friends desire) I can not determine as yet. Certain
it is that this time 12 month I shall continue my Oratorio's in Ireland,
where they are a going to make a large Subscription allready for that
Purpose.

If I had know'n that My Lord Guernsey was so near when I pass'd
Coventry, You may easily imagine, Sir, that I should not have neglected
of paying my Respects to him, since You know the particular Esteem I

have for His Lordship. I think it a very long time to the month of November next when I can have some hopes of seeing You here in Town. Pray let me hear meanwhile of Your Health and Wellfare, of which I take a real Share beeng with uncommon Sincerity and Respect

S^r

Your most obliged humble Servant

George Frideric Handel.

To

Charles Jennens Esqr Junior

at Gopsal near Atherstone

Coventry bag—

(Handel Society, *Messiah*, edited by Rimbault, 1850.) Original in the possession of Lord Howe. It seems that Handel tried to see Jennens at his father's estate, on the way back from Ireland. Gopsall, near Atherstone, lay north of Coventry, which means on the way to London. The Bishop of Elphin was Dr. Edward Synge. His critical observations, probably written in Dublin, are not preserved. Of Mr. Sted, if the name is written and read correctly, nothing is known. For Handel's praise of the Irish " Nation ", compare his letter of 29th December 1741. The word " middle " in reference to the Haymarket Opera may have been a pun on the name of Lord Middlesex. Handel's plan to visit Dublin again was never realized. For Lord Guernsey see 6th July 1733 and 19th September 1738 ; he inherited Jennens' collection of Handel scores, copied by Smith, now in the Handel Collection of Sir Newman Flower.

———

Handel writes the duet " Beato in ver chi può ", an Italian version of Horace's " Beatus ille ", 31st October 1742.

———

Handel writes the duet " Nò di voi non vuò fidarmi ", 2nd November 1742.

This is the second version ; cf. 3rd July 1741.

———

FROM FAULKNER'S " DUBLIN JOURNAL ", 13th November 1742

In the Beginning of December next, at Mr. Johnson's Hall in Crow-street, will be performed a Concert of Vocal and Instrumental Musick, for the Benefit of Miss Davis, a Child of 6 years old, who will perform a Concerto and some other Pieces upon the Harpsichord ; particularly she will accompany her Mother to a Song of Mr. Handel's, composed entirely to shew the Harpsichord ; the Vocal Parts to be performed by Mrs. Davis, and her Sister Miss Clegg, who never performed in publick before, some new Songs out of the last Operas, and three of the most favourite Duetts of Mr. Handel's to be performed by Mrs. Davis and her Sister. . . .

(Flood, pp. 442 ff.) The date of the concert was later altered to 11th December, and finally fixed for 5th February 1743. Miss Clegg and Mrs. Davis may have been the sisters of John Clegg, a distinguished violinist. Whether Mrs. Davis was identical with the one who sang in Handel oratorios in London in 1732 (cf. 2nd May and 10th June 1732) cannot be determined. The Davis family of Dublin probably had nothing to do with the sisters Davies in London, although Miss Davis played the harpsichord in London on 10th May 1745. Miss Marianne Davies did not appear in London as a harpsichord player until 30th April 1751 ; she appeared first when she was seven years of age. (Cf. also 19th March 1753.)

—

The *Utrecht Te Deum and Jubilate*, with two anthems, is performed in Salisbury Cathedral, 25th November 1742.

This may have been the first Handel music performed in Salisbury ; it was probably introduced by James Harris.

—

FROM FAULKNER'S "DUBLIN JOURNAL", 30th November 1742

The Musick for the Benefit of [Mercer's Hospital] at St. Andrew's Church, is put off, till some Time in February.

By Appointment of the Charitable Musical Society, for the Benefit and Enlargement of Prisoners confined for Debt, in the several Marshalseas of this City, on Friday the 17th of December next the Entertainment of Acis and Galatea, composed by Mr. Handel, will be performed at the Musick Hall in Fishamble Street. . . .

We hear that on Friday next [3rd December] (being particularly desir'd) at the great Room in Fishamble Street, Mrs. Arne will sing the Song Sweet Bird, accompanied on the Violin by Mr. Arne. . . .

(Townsend, p. 108.) The music in the church was given on 8th February 1743. *Acis and Galatea*, with Mrs. Arne, was rehearsed on 14th December, at Noon ; the Coronation Anthem " Zadok the Priest " was added to the bill, as well as a new solo by Mr. Dubourg. The singers were Mrs. Arne, Mrs. Storer, Mr. Colgan, and others. (*Journal*, 11th December.) " Many of the Ladies, of great Quality and Distinction, having come to a Resolution not to wear any Hoops" (*Journal*, 14th December). During 1742 the Charitable Musical Society released 142 languishing debtors at an expenditure of some £1225. The song which Mrs. Arne sang in the music club was from *L'Allegro*. It is not true, as stated by W. H. Grattan Flood (*A History of Irish Music*, Dublin, 1905, pp. 283 f.), and others after him, that Mr. and Mrs. Arne performed comic interludes between the acts of *Acis*.

1743

JOHN RICH AND HANDEL TO WILLIAM CHETWYND

Jany 10 1742–3

S^r

The following Oratorio of Samson is Intended to be perform'd at the Theatre Royal in Cov^t Garden with your permission I am

S^r

Y^r humble Servt
Jno Rich
George Frideric Handel

To
—— Chitwin Esqr
in Cork Street
Absent

(Coopersmith, 1943, p. 64.) Original in the Huntington Library, San Marino, California. The application, written by Rich, and signed by him as well as Handel, was addressed to William Richard Chetwynd, M.P., later Master of the Mint. He was, from 1737 onwards, inspector of stage-plays. The leaf on which this application is written was the first leaf of the manuscript word-book of *Samson* (cf. the inscription on the word-book of *Theodora*, February 1750). Handel returned to Covent Garden for his oratorio season. The last word of the address seems to have been written by another hand.

———

Handel finishes the Organ Concerto in A, later published as no. 2 of Opus 7, 5th February 1743.

———

A concert, in aid of Mercer's Hospital, is given in St. Andrew's Church, Dublin, with Handel's *Utrecht Te Deum and Jubilate* and the two " new " Anthems, performed " in the Cathedral manner ", 8th February 1743.

(Townsend, p. 108.) The concert, originally planned for the 15th, is advertised in Faulkner's *Dublin Journal* of 18th January, and mentioned in the Minutes of the Hospital on 22nd January.

———

FROM THE " DAILY ADVERTISER ", 12th February 1743

BY SUBSCRIPTION.

At the Theatre-Royal in Covent-Garden, on Friday the 18th inst. will be perform'd a new *Oratorio*, call'd SAMPSON.

Tickets will be deliver'd to Subscribers (on paying their Subscription-Money) this Day, and every Day following (Sunday excepted), at Mr. Handel's House in Brooke-Street, near Hanover-Square.

Attendance will be given from Nine o'Clock in the Morning till Three in the Afternoon.

. . . . .

Note, Each Subscriber is to pay Six Guineas upon taking out his Subscription Ticket, which entitles him to three Box-Tickets every Night of Mr. Handel's first six Performances in Lent. And if Mr. Handel should have any more Performances after the six first Nights, each Subscriber may continue on the same Conditions.

(Handel Society, *Samson*, edited by Rimbault, 1853, p. IV.) The same advertisement appeared in the *London Daily Post*. It was repeated, with variations, until the day of the production. The prices of single tickets were : Pit and Boxes, put together, half a Guinea, first gallery 5s., upper gallery 3s. 6d. It began at six o'clock. The whole arrangement of the subscription was after the model of Handel's Dublin concerts of 1741-2. From 23rd February onwards the title of the oratorio was spelt correctly (Samson) in the newspapers. This is the place to quote a memorandum, noted down by Handel on the sketch of a chorus (" For ever let his sacred praise ") and preserved in the Fitzwilliam Museum, Cambridge ; it is quoted by Schoelcher (p. 280), and more correctly by Mann (p. 184) :

Samson	140	. . . Recit.
Micah	97	
Manoah	76	
Dalilah	31	
Harapha	34	
Messenger	10	
	———	
	386	

(In fact, 388.) The figures refer, apparently, to pages of manuscript, and may be a copyist's bill, wrongly checked, or an estimate of the costs for the voice parts. The " Messenger " is a small tenor part, altered to " Officer " wherever it occurs in the manuscript word-book.

———

FROM FAULKNER'S " DUBLIN JOURNAL ", 12th February 1743

For the Benefit of Mr. Charles, French-horn Master, by his Majesty's Company of Comedians, at the Theatre Royal in Aungier-street, this Day, will be acted, a Comedy called Love for Love, with a grand Concert of vocal and instrumental Musick, viz. . . . At the End of the Play, a grand Concert, 1st. the Overture in Saul with the Dead March. 2d. a Song by Mr. [Joseph] Baildon. 3d. The Water Musick. 4th. The March in Scipio ; and 5th, the Grand Chorus in Atalantha, composed by the celebrated Mr. Handel. . . .

Congreve's comedy was a favourite play in Dublin.

———

FROM NEWBURGH HAMILTON'S PREFACE TO HIS WORD-BOOK OF
" SAMSON ", PRODUCED ON 18th FEBRUARY 1743

Several Pieces of *Milton* having been lately brought on the Stage with
Success, particularly his *Penseroso* and *Allegro*, I was of Opinion that
nothing of that Divine Poet's wou'd appear in the Theatre with greater
Propriety or Applause than his SAMSON AGONISTES. . . . But as Mr. *Handel*
had so happily introduc'd here *Oratorios*, a musical Drama, whose
Subject must be Scriptural, and in which the Solemnity of Church-
Musick is agreeably united with the most pleasing Airs of the Stage : It
would have been an irretrievable Loss to have neglected the Opportunity
of that great Master's doing Justice to this Work ; he having already
added new Life and Spirit to some of the finest Things in the *English*
Language, particularly that inimitable Ode of Dryden's, which no Age
nor Nation ever excell'd.

As we have so great a Genius among us, it is a pity that so many mean
Artifices have been lately us'd to blast all his Endeavours, and in him
ruin the ART itself ; but he has the Satisfaction of being encourag'd by
all true Lovers and real Judges of Musick ; in a more especial manner
by that illustrious Person, whose high Rank only serves to make his
Knowledge in all Arts and Sciences as conspicuous as his Power and
Inclination to patronize them. . . .

(Schoelcher, p. 280.) Hamilton, who dedicated this book to Frederick, Prince
of Wales (" that illustrious Person "), speaks of *Alexander's Feast* as Dryden's Ode,
which he arranged for Handel.

———

CAST OF " SAMSON ", 18th February 1743
Samson—Mr. Beard (tenor)
Manoa—Mr. Savage (counter-tenor)
Micah—Mrs. Cibber (mezzo-soprano)
Dalila—Mrs. Clive (soprano)
Harapha—Mr. Reinhold (bass)
An Israelite Officer—Mr. Lowe (tenor)
Israelite Women—Signora Avoglio and Miss Edwards (sopranos)
Philistine Women—Signora Avoglio, Miss Edwards (sopranos)
A Philistine—Mr. Lowe (tenor)

For Thomas Lowe, who now returned to Handel, see 2nd May 1732. *Samson*
was performed " with a new concerto on the organ " and, from the fourth performance onwards, with " a Solo on the Violin by Mr. Dubourg ", who had
returned temporarily to London. Repeat performances on 23rd, 25th February ;
2nd, 9th, 11th, 16th and 31st March. Revivals in 1744, 1745, 1749, 1752, 1753,
1754, 1755 and 1759.

———

LADY FRANCIS HERTFORD TO HER SON, LORD GEORGE SEYMOUR
BEAUCHAMP

[London,] Saturday, February 19, 1743.

Mr. Handel had a new oratorio called *Sampson* last night, but I have
seen nobody who was there, so can give you no account of it.

(Hertford, p. 242.) Lady Hertford, a friend of John Hughes, was Lady of the Bedchamber to Caroline both when Princess of Wales and when Queen Consort. Cf. 26th February.

———

HORACE WALPOLE TO HORACE MANN

Arlington Street, Feb. 24, 1743.

Handel has set up an Oratorio against the Operas, and succeeds. He has hired all the goddesses from farces and the singers of *Roast Beef* from between the acts at both theatres, with a man with one note in his voice, and a girl without ever an one ; and so they sing, and make brave hallelujahs ; and the good company encore the recitative, if it happens to have any cadence like what they call a tune.

(Schoelcher, p. 294. Walpole, *Letters*, 1891, I. 230.) The goddess from farces was apparently Mrs. Clive ; she and Mr. Lowe came from Drury Lane. Mrs. Cibber and Mr. Beard might also have been included in Walpole's reference. The galleries used to call for the ballad "The Roast Beef of Old England" between the acts, or before or after the play. (Cf. Hogarth's engraving of that name.)

———

Esther is performed by the Academy of Ancient Music, 24th February 1743.

Recorded in a printed word-book, a copy of which is in the National Library of Scotland, Edinburgh. The performance was probably at the " Crown and Anchor " Tavern, as usual.

———

FROM THE " LONDON DAILY POST ", 26th February 1743

MUSICK.

·   ·   ·   ·   ·

Handel's Water-Musick, set for the Harpsichord.

·   ·   ·   ·   ·

Handel's Cantata, with the Recitatives, Songs, and Duets.

·   ·   ·   ·   ·

Printed for J. Walsh. . . .

(Smith, 1948, p. 285.) The same advertisements appeared in the *Daily Advertiser* of 28th February. Walsh had published some numbers of the *Water Music* in parts in 1733. The arrangement of other numbers for harpsichord is complementary to the original edition. Added to these harpsichord pieces are two minuets with variations for the harpsichord by Geminiani. The " Cantata " was an off-print from *Alexander's Feast*, containing the cantata " Cecilia volgi ", the song " Carco sempre ", the duetto " Tra amplessi innocenti ", and the additional song " Sei del ciel ". Cf. 8th March 1738.

———

LADY HERTFORD TO HER SON, LORD BEAUCHAMP

[London,] Saturday, February 26, 1743.
They say the Ridotto was the worst that has been known. There was very little company of any kind, and not twenty people of distinction among them. The oratorio has answered much better, being filled with all the people of quality in town ; and they say Handel has exerted himself to make it the finest piece of music he ever composed, and say he has not failed in his attempt.

(Myers, 1948, p. 114.) Hertford, p. 244. Cf. 19th February. For the Ridottos, see 15th February 1722. This was still Heidegger's carnival entertainment at the Haymarket Theatre.

—

Berenice is performed at Brunswick, February 1743.

(Loewenberg, p. 96.) The performance was given with Italian airs and German recitatives and choruses ; the music was arranged by Georg Caspar Schürmann.

—

The Royal family attends the performance of *Samson*, 2nd March 1743.

Cf. 15th March (*Dublin Journal*).

—

HORACE WALPOLE TO HORACE MANN

[London,] March 3, 1743.
The Oratorios thrive abundantly—for my part, they give me an idea of heaven, where everybody is to sing whether they have voices or not.

(Walpole, *Letters*, 1891, I. 231.) Cf. 24th February.

—

FROM THE " DAILY ADVERTISER ", 12th March 1743

BY SUBSCRIPTION.
The Seventh Night.
At the Theatre-Royal in Covent-Garden, on Wednesday next [the 16th], will be perform'd . . . SAMSON. Being the last Time of performing in this Season. . . .
N.B. The Subscribers to Mr. Handel's Six former Performances, who intend to continue their Subscription on the same Conditions for six Entertainments more, are desir'd to send their Subscription-Money to Mr. Handel's House, in Brooke-Street ; where Attendance will be given

this Day, and on Monday and Tuesday next, in order to deliver out their Subscription-Tickets.

(Schoelcher, p. 279.) The advertisement also appeared in the *London Daily Post. Samson* was performed once more, on 31st March.

FROM FAULKNER'S "DUBLIN JOURNAL", 15th March 1743

Extract of a private Letter from London, March 8.

Our Friend Mr. Handell is very well, and Things have taken a quite different Turn here from what they did some Time past ; for the Publick will be no longer imposed on by Italian Singers, and some wrong Headed Undertakers of bad Opera's, but find out the Merit of Mr. Handell's Composition and English Performances : That Gentleman is more esteemed now than ever. The new Oratorio (called SAMSON) which he composed since he left Ireland, has been performed four Times to more crouded Audiences than ever were seen ; more People being turned away for Want of Room each Night than hath been at the Italian Opera. Mr. Dubourg (lately arrived from Dublin) performed at the last, and played a Solo between the Acts, and met with universal and uncommon Applause from the Royal Family and the whole Audience.

(Townsend, p. 109.) The "Undertakers" were Lord Middlesex and his friends. *Samson* was, in fact, written before Handel went to Dublin (see 29th October 1741). Dubourg first played his solo on 2nd March.

FROM THE "DAILY ADVERTISER", 17th March 1743

BY SUBSCRIPTION.

The Eighth Night.

At the Theatre-Royal in Covent-Garden, To-morrow, will be perform'd L'ALLEGRO ed il PENSEROSO. With *Additions.* And DRYDEN'S ODE on St. CAECILIA'S DAY. A *Concerto* on the *Organ.* And a Solo on the Violin by Mr. DUBOURG. . . . To begin at Six o'Clock.

Cf. 31st January 1741. "Il Moderato" was omitted again. Mr. Beard and Mr. Reinhold apparently sang their original parts ; Beard perhaps his additional air (cf. 31st January 1741). The first soprano part was probably sung by Signora Avoglio, the second by Miss Edwards, and the contralto part by Mrs. Cibber.

FROM THE "DAILY ADVERTISER", 19th March 1743

BY SUBSCRIPTION.

The Ninth Night.

At the Theatre-Royal in Covent-Garden, on Wednesday next [the 23rd], will be perform'd A NEW SACRED ORATORIO. With a *Concerto* on the *Organ.* And a Solo on the Violin by Mr. *Dubourg.*

Tickets will be deliver'd to Subscribers on Tuesday next, at Mr. Handel's House in Brooke-Street. . . . To begin at Six o'Clock.

(Schoelcher, p. 257.) The same advertisement appeared in the *London Daily Post*. It was repeated on 21st, 22nd and 23rd March. The galleries were opened at four o'clock. This was *Messiah*, the original title of which was avoided, at first, in London. Dubourg was probably also leader of the orchestra, as in Dublin. It may be mentioned here that the case of Handel's *Messiah* was parallel to that of Mozart's *Don Giovanni*, produced at Prague in 1787 and not performed at Vienna until 1788.

———

FROM THE SAME

NEW MUSICK.

This Day are publish'd, (Price 4s.)

Songs in the Oratorio call'd SAMSON, in Score. Compos'd by Mr. HANDEL.

Printed for J. Walsh. . . .

Of whom may be had, just publish'd,

1. L'Allegro il Penseroso. Compos'd by Mr. Handel. The Second Edition.

(Schoelcher, p. 279.) The same advertisement appeared in the *London Daily Post*. Of *Samson* this was the first selection ; see 31st March and 8th April. Walsh omitted the words " ed Il Moderato " in the advertisement only.

———

FROM THE " UNIVERSAL SPECTATOR ", 19th March 1743

The following Letter may to many of my Readers, especially those of a gay and polite Taste, seem too rigid a Censure on a Performance, which is so universally approv'd : However, I could not suppress it, as there is so well-intended a Design and pious Zeal runs through the whole, and nothing derogatory said of Mr. *Handel's* Merit. Of what good Consequences it will produce, I can only say—*Valeat Quantum valere potest.*

To the AUTHOR of the UNIVERSAL SPECTATOR.

SIR,

. . . My . . . Purpose . . . is to consider, and, if possible, induce others to consider, the Impropriety of *Oratorios*, as they are now perform'd.

Before I speak against them (that I may not be thought to do it out of Prejudice or Party) it may not be improper to declare, that I am a profess'd Lover of *Musick*, and in particular all Mr. *Handel's Performances*, being *one* of the *few* who never deserted him. I am also a great Admirer of *Church Musick*, and think no other equal to it, nor any Person so capable to compose it, as Mr. *Handel*. To return : An *Oratorio* either is an *Act* of *Religion*, or it is not ; if it is, I ask if the *Playhouse* is a fit *Temple* to perform it in, or a Company of *Players* fit *Ministers* of *God's Word*, for in that Case such they are made.

Under the *Jewish Dispensation*, the *Levites only* might come near to do the Service of the *Tabernacle*, and no common Person might so much as touch the *Ark* of *God* : Is *God's Service* less holy now ?

In the other Case, if it is not perform'd as an *Act* of *Religion*, but for *Diversion* and *Amusement* only (and indeed I believe few or none go to an *Oratorio* out of *Devotion*), what a *Prophanation* of *God's* Name and Word is this, to make so light Use of them ? I wish every one would consider, whether, at the same Time they are *diverting* themselves, they are not accessory to the breaking the *Third Commandment*. I am sure it is not following the Advice of the *Psalmist, Serve the Lord with Fear, and rejoice unto him with Reverence* : How must it offend a devout *Jew*, to hear the great *Jehovah*, the *proper* and most *sacred Name* of God (a Name a *Jew*, if not a *Priest*, hardly dare pronounce) sung, I won't say to a light Air (for as Mr. *Handel* compos'd it, I dare say it is not) but by a Set of People very *unfit* to *perform* so *solemn* a *Service*. *David* said, *How can we sing the Lord's Song in a strange Land* ; but sure he would have thought it much stranger to have heard it sung in a *Playhouse*.

But it seems the *Old Testament* is not to be prophan'd alone, nor *God* by the *Name* of *Jehovah* only, but the *New* must be join'd with it, and *God* by the most *sacred* the most *merciful Name* of *Messiah* ; for I'm inform'd that an Oratorio call'd by that Name has already been perform'd in *Ireland*, and is soon to be perform'd *here* : What the Piece itself is, I know not, and therefore shall say nothing about it ; but I must again ask, If the *Place* and *Performers* are fit ? As to the Pretence that there are many Persons who will say their *Prayers* there who will not go to *Church*, I believe I may venture to say, that the Assertion is *false*, without *Exception* ; for I can never believe that Persons who have so little regard for Religion, as to think it not worth their while to go to *Church* for it, will have any *Devotion* on hearing a *religious* Performance in a *Playhouse*. On the contrary, I'm more apt to *fear* it gives great Opportunity to *prophane* Persons to ridicule Religion at least, if not to blaspheme it ; and, indeed, every Degree of Ridicule on what is *sacred*, is a Degree of Blasphemy : But if the Assertion was true, are the most sacred Things, *Religion* and the *Holy Bible*, which is the *Word* of God, to be prostituted to the perverse Humour of a Set of obstinate People, on a Supposition that they may be forc'd thereby *once* in their Lives to attend to what is *serious* ?

How will this appear to After-Ages, when it shall be read in History, that in such an Age the People of England were arriv'd to such a Height of *Impiety* and *Prophaneness*, that most *sacred Things* were suffer'd to be us'd as *publick Diversions*, and that in a *Place*, and by *Persons* appropriated to the Performance not only of *light* and *vain*, but too often *prophane* and *dissolute* Pieces ? What would a *Mahometan* think of this, who with so much Care and Veneration keep their *Alcoran* ? What must they think of us and our *Religion* ? Will they not be *confirm'd* in their Errors ? Will not they be apt to say, that surely *we ourselves* believe it no better than a *Fable*, by the Use we make of it ; and may not the *Gospel*, by this Means (as well as by the wicked Lives of *Christians*) be hinder'd from spreading ? A Thing of no small Consequence, and which ought to be consider'd by us who have the lively Oracles committed to us, and are bound by all the Ties of *Gratitude* and *Humanity*, as well as *Honour* and *Conscience*, to endeavour to enlarge that *Kingdom* of *Christ*, which we pray *should come*.

PHILALETHES.

(Schoelcher, p. 258.) For the magazine and its editor, Henry Baker, cf. 5th July 1735. Under the pseudonym of Philalethes several contributions appeared in it, although the author of this letter, in the introduction not reprinted here, states that he is unknown to the editor. Among the regular contributors to the magazine was William Oldys, and perhaps also John Kelly and (Sir) John Hawkins. For actors as singers of oratorios, cf. Walpole's letter of 24th February. The tenor of this open letter makes it easier to understand why, at the beginning, Handel avoided the title *Messiah* for his oratorio in London. Cf. 31st March and 16th April.

—

CAST OF " MESSIAH ", 23rd March 1743

Sopranos—Signora Avoglio (or Miss Edwards), Mrs. Clive, the Boy
Contralto—Mrs. Cibber
Tenor—Mr. Beard
Bass—Mr. Reinhold

Other singers are not recorded. Repeat performances on 25th and 29th March. It is assumed that the King attended one of these performances, and that he then introduced the British tradition of standing during the Hallelujah Chorus, in Handel's time known as " For the Lord God Omnipotent reigneth " (cf. 25th May 1780). It is related that " All standing " became the rule first for the Dead March in *Saul*, and later, of course, for the National Anthem.

—

FROM THE " DAILY ADVERTISER ", 31st March 1743

Wrote extempore by a Gentleman, on reading the *Universal Spectator*.

On Mr. HANDEL's *new* ORATORIO,
perform'd at the Theatre Royal in Covent-Garden.

Cease, Zealots, cease to blame these Heav'nly Lays,
For Seraphs fit to sing Messiah's Praise !
Nor, for your trivial Argument, assign,
" The Theatre not fit for Praise Divine."

These hallow'd Lays to Musick give new Grace,
To Virtue Awe, and sanctify the Place ;

To Harmony, like his, Celestial Pow'r is giv'n,
T' exalt the Soul from Earth, and make, of Hell, a Heav'n.
(Schoelcher, p. 258.) Cf. 19th March and 16th April. Myers (1947, p. 30)
suggests the author may have been Jennens. The poem was printed below the
advertisement of the last performance of *Samson*, which marked the end of Handel's
oratorio season. Tickets for subscribers were given out at Handel's house on 30th,
and at the theatre on 31st March.

———

FROM THE SAME

MUSICK.

On Saturday next [2nd April] *will be publish'd,*

A Second Collection of Songs in the Oratorio of SAMSON ; to which
is prefix'd the Overture in Score.
Printed for J. Walsh. . . .

(Cf. 19th March and 8th April.) The same advertisement appeared in the *London
Daily Post.*

———

FROM THE " LONDON DAILY POST ", 8th April 1743

MUSICK.

This Day is publish'd, Price 2s 6d.

The Remaining Songs, which compleat the Oratorio of SAMSON, with
an Index to the whole.
N.B. The 1st and 2d Collection of Songs in the Oratorio, with the
Overture may be had separate.
Printed for J. Walsh. . . .

(Schoelcher, p. 279.) Cf. 19th and 31st March. The same advertisement
appeared in the *Daily Advertiser* of 9th April.

———

FROM FAULKNER'S " DUBLIN JOURNAL ", 9th April 1743

For the Benefit of the Charitable Infirmary on the Inns-quay, at the
Great Musick-hall in Fishamble-street, on Wednesday the 4th of May
next, at 6 in the Evening, will be performed, the Oratorio of Alexander's
Feast. Composed by Mr. Dryden, and set to Musick by Mr. Handel. In
which the Gentlemen of the Choirs of both Cathedrals, the celebrated
Mrs. Arne, and several other Voices, will assist. There will be a Grand
Rehearsal the Monday before, precisely at 12 o'clock.

The rehearsal on 2nd May started, in fact, at 11.30 A.M. Mr. Arne conducted.

———

HORACE WALPOLE TO HORACE MANN

Arlington Street, April 14, 1743.

I really don't know whether Vanneschi be dead ; he married some
low English woman, who is kept by Amorevoli ; so the Abbate turned

the opera every way to his profit. As to Bonducci I don't think I could serve him ; for I have no interest with the Lords Middlesex and Holderness, the two sole managers. Nor if I had, would I employ it, to bring over more ruin to the Operas. Gentlemen directors, with favourite abbés and favourite mistresses, have almost overturned the thing in England. . . . We are next Tuesday [the 19th] to have the Miserere of Rome. It must be curious ! the finest piece of vocal music in the world, to be performed by three good voices, and forty bad ones, from Oxford, Canterbury, and the farces ! There is a new subscription formed for an Opera next year, to be carried on by the *Dilettanti*, a club, for which the nominal qualification is having been in Italy, and the real one, being drunk : the two chiefs are Lord Middlesex and Sir Francis Dashwood, who were seldom sober the whole time they were in Italy.

(Walpole, *Letters*, 1891, I. 239 f.) Mann was in Italy. Vanneschi had not died, but remained the Haymarket poet and wrote, or arranged, the librettos of Gluck's two London operas in 1746. Amorevoli was the *primo uomo* of the Haymarket opera. Lord Holderness was one, now perhaps the only one, of Lord Middlesex's partners. Andrea Bonducci, an abbate like Vanneschi, lived in Florence and translated *The Rape of the Lock* and some other works of Pope into Italian ; he apparently hoped to follow Vanneschi as librettist in London. The mistress alluded to was La Muscovita. (Cf. 30th July 1741.) The " Miserere mei Deus ", as sung during Holy Week in the Sistine Chapel, was Gregorio Allegri's setting, of which three manuscript copies were known at that time, and, according to Hawkins, an incorrect one in the library of the Academy of Ancient Music, London ; it was first printed in Burney's *La Musica della Settimana Santa* in 1771. It was performed at the Haymarket Theatre, at the end of a concert consisting of various motets, choruses, concertos, etc., in three parts, " after the manner of an Oratorio ", and advertised (*Daily Advertiser*, 19th April 1743) as " *The celebrated Piece* of VOCAL MUSICK *from* Rome ". Francis Dashwood, Baron Le Despencer, had been a leading member of the " Dilettanti Society " since 1736 ; he was in the Prince of Wales's household, and later became Chancellor of the Exchequer. The Society confined its interests to the fine arts, and did not carry on the Haymarket Opera.

———

FROM THE " UNIVERSAL SPECTATOR ", 16th April 1743

As I inserted a Letter of my following Correspondent's, on Divine Subjects being exhibited in Theatres, under the Name of *Oratorios*, I think I am oblig'd, impartially, to give a Place to another Letter on this Subject.

To the AUTHOR *of the* UNIVERSAL SPECTATOR.

Mr. SPECTATOR,

Accidently taking up the *Daily Advertiser* of Thursday March 31, at the End of the Advertisement of Mr. *Handel's Oratorio*, I read the following Lines, said to be wrote Extempore by a Gentleman, on reading the *Universal Spectator* of March 19.

[Here follow the eight lines.]

As I could not forbear endeavouring to answer this, I send what I wrote for that Purpose, desiring you to dispose of it as you think proper, either to the *Flames*, or *publick Censure*.

> Mistake me not, I blam'd [1] no heav'nly Lays ;
> Nor *Handel*'s Art which strives a Zeal to raise,
> In every Soul to sing *Messiah*'s Praise :
> But if to *Seraphs* you the Task assign ;
> Are *Players* fit for *Ministry Divine* ?
> Or *Theatres* for *Seraphs* there to sing,
> The holy Praises of their Heav'nly King ?
> Ah no ! for *Theatres* let *Temples* rise,
> Thence *sacred Harmony* ascend the Skies ;
> Let *hallow'd Lays* to *Musick* give new Grace ;
> But when those *Lays* have *sanctify'd* the Place,
> To *Use Prophane*, oh ! let it ne'er be given,
> Nor make that Place a *Hell*, which Those had made a *Heav'n*.

I apprehend the Word *Theatre* to be of a great Latitude, and may be us'd in a figurative Sense for any Place, where an *Action*, or *Oration*, is made publick ; Or, if confin'd to a particular Form of Building, there might be a sacred Theatre for sacred Uses : And since so splendid a [2] Place has lately been erected for a mere trifling Entertainment, why can't the Lovers of *sacred Harmony* build one for theirs, then might they also have *fit Persons* to perform it as it ought (if it be perform'd at all), as an *Act* of *Religion*.

But since the *Poet* can here be understood to mean no other than those of *Drollery* and *ludicrous Mirth*, the Play-houses, I must again assert, that being such, they are for that Reason very *unfit* for *sacred Performances*. Nor can it be defended as *Decent*, to use the same Place one Week as a *Temple* to perform a *sacred Oratorio* in, and (when *sanctify'd* by those *hallow'd Lays*) the next as a Stage, to exhibit the *Bufoonries of Harlequin*. . . .

> I am, Sir,
>
> Yours, much oblig'd,
>
> PHILALETHES.

Cf. 19th and 31st March. The introduction is by the " author ", *i.e.* editor, Baker. John Rich, the manager of Covent Garden, under the name of Lun played the Harlequin in a special style.— It is, perhaps, fitting to insert here another reference to Handel printed in the *Universal Spectator*, which cannot be dated exactly. It has been found only in two selections from the magazine printed in book-form in 1736, 1747 and 1756. It is to be found in Vol. IV, p. 183, in the second and third editions. (Myers, June 1947, p. 409.) The letter to the editor, signed Phil-Harmonius, is listed in the index as " Letter on the Power of Musick ". The passage reads : " *Timotheus* could move *Alexander's* Passion as he pleas'd, and drive him into the greatest Fury ; but upon the Alteration of a Note could moderate it, and bring him to himself again. I am very glad, Mr. *Spectator*, for the Honour

[1] *Not the Poetry or Musick, the Place and Performers only, are found Fault with.   See* Universal Spectator, *March 19, 1743.*
[2] *The Amphitheatre in Ranelagh Gardens at Chelsea.*

of my Country, that I have Occasion here to mention Mr. *Dryden's* Ode upon that Subject, which I look upon to be the finest that ever was written in any Language ; and Mr. *Handel's* Composition has done Justice to the Poetry. I defy any one, who is attentive to the Performance of it, to fortify himself so well, as not to be mov'd with the same Passions, with which the *Hero* is transported." This refers, of course, to *Alexander's Feast*, performed (before 1747) between 1736 and 1742. The magazine ceased to appear in February 1746.

HORACE WALPOLE TO HORACE MANN

May 4, 1743.

We are likely at last to have no Opera next year : Handel has had a palsy, and can't compose ; and the Duke of Dorset has set himself strenuously to oppose it, as Lord Middlesex is the impressario, and must ruin the house of Sackville by a course of these follies. Besides what he will lose this year, he has not paid his share to the losses of the last ; and yet is singly undertaking another for next season, with the almost certainty of losing between four or five thousand pounds, to which the deficiencies of the Opera generally amount now. The Duke of Dorset has desired the King not to subscribe ; but Lord Middlesex is so obstinate, that this will probably only make him lose a thousand pounds more.

(Walpole, *Letters*, 1891, I. 244.) Mainwaring (p. 134) also speaks of " some return of his [Handel's] paralytic disorder " in 1743 (cf. 13th April 1737). Lionel Cranfield (Sackville), Duke of Dorset, Lord Steward of the Household, was Lord Middlesex's father. The King's subscription was the " bounty " of one thousand pounds paid to the " Royal Academy of Music ", in fact to the undertaker of the day at the Haymarket Opera (cf. 9th June 1742). It was paid once more to cover the season 1742-3, ending on 17th May 1743, and, for the last time, in 1744 to cover the season of 1743-4.

JOHN BRANSON, STEWARD, TO HIS MASTER, JOHN, DUKE OF BEDFORD

[London,] June 1743.

The Opera is a bankrupt. The Directors have run out £1,600, and called this General Meeting to get the consent of the subscribers to take this debt upon themselves. This I opposed, as they seemed to look upon it as a right, and by the great weight and interest I appeared with I reduced their motion, I think, to nothing, which, as it now stands, is that a letter should be wrote to every one of the two hundred pounds subscribing to desire them to pay their share of this deficiency if they think proper. Thus this important affair ended.

But the distress of the Directors is the most diverting thing I ever saw. The Duke of Rutland, whose name is signed to every contract, is as pale as death and trembles for his money. Lord M : importance is retired into the country to think of ways and means and Mr. Frederick is absconded. Lord Middlesex is only afraid that the credit of the English

Operas should be hurt, and, though his name is to no contract would be glad to pay a share with the other four.

(Thomson, pp. 289 f.) Gertrude, Duchess of Bedford and her daughter were regular opera goers. The Duke was a subscriber to the Middlesex Opera. Cf. 4th March 1742 and 14th August 1743.

Handel writes *Semele*, a " musical drama ", between 3rd June and 4th July 1743.

Handel just called it " The Story of Semele ".

Handel starts the *Dettingen Te Deum* on 17th July 1743, and finishes it the same month.

On 27th June, King George II led an army to victory against the French at Dettingen on the River Main. Britain was fighting, as the ally of Austria, for the recognition of Maria Theresa's succession.

FROM THE " DAILY ADVERTISER ", 19th July 1743

New Musick. This Day are publish'd, Handel's Six Overtures for Violins, &c. in eight Parts, from the Operas and Oratorios of Samson, the Sacred Oratorio, Saul, Deidamia, Hymen and Parnasso in Festa. The eighth Collection. . . . Printed for J. Walsh. . . .

(Smith, 1948, p. 83.) A similar advertisement appeared in the *London Evening Post* of 23rd July. *Messiah* is called The Sacred Oratorio. This was the first music printed from *Messiah*.

Handel writes the *Dettingen Anthem* between 30th July and 3rd August 1743.

HORACE WALPOLE TO HORACE MANN

Arlington Street, Aug. 14, 1743.

I am sorry you are engaged in the Opera. I have found it a most dear undertaking ! I was not in the management : Lord Middlesex was chief. We were thirty subscribers, at two hundred pounds each, which was to last four years, and no other demands ever to be made. Instead of that, we have been made to pay fifty-six pounds over and above the subscription in one winter. I told the secretary in a passion, that it was the last money I would ever pay for the follies of directors.

(Walpole, *Letters*, 1891, I. 264.) Cf. June 1743 (Branson).

From the " Daily Advertiser ", 24th August 1743

Musick.

This Day is publish'd, (Price 1s.)

Number I. of The entire Masque of Acis and Galatea, in Score, as it was originally compos'd, with the Overture, Recitativos, Songs, Duets, and Chorusses, for Voices and Instruments. Set to Musick by Mr. Handel.

I. This Work will be printed in a neat and correct Manner, and the Price to Subscribers is Half a Guinea.

II. A Number will be publish'd every Fortnight, at One Shilling, till the whole is finish'd.

N.B. This is the only Dramatick Work of Mr. Handel which has yet been publish'd entire.

Subscriptions are taken in by J. Walsh in Katherine Street in the Strand ; [John] Simpson, and [Elizabeth] Hare, in Cornhill ; [John] Johnson, in Cheapside ; [John] Barret, and Wamsley, in Piccadilly ; Mr. Cross, at Oxford ; and Mr. [Francis] Hopkins, at Cambridge.

Just publish'd, The Oratorio of Samson, in Score.

(Smith, 1948, p. 231 f.) A similar advertisement appeared in the *London Evening Post* of 3rd September. This was the fifth edition of *Acis and Galatea*. The issue in sections, not new in Walsh's publications, was completed in three months instead of the five allowed for in the scheme. The ten numbers were advertised singly until 19th November, the last number costing 1s. 6d., instead of the usual 1s. On 28th November the work was offered as a whole, in one volume. There is no list of subscribers. If Walsh intended an edition on subscription, it was not realized. Probably he used a new method, without providing such a list. It was quite unusual for Walsh to co-operate with other dealers in London, or in the provinces.

———

Handel writes the oratorio *Joseph* in August and September 1743. The end of part two is dated 12th September 1743.

———

From the " London Evening Post ", 27th September 1743

Yesterday a fine new Anthem and Te Deum, compos'd by Mr. Handel, to be perform'd on his Majesty's safe Arrival in his British Dominions, was rehears'd in the Chapel-Royal at St. James's before their Royal Highnesses the Princesses.

This was the Dettingen music. The notice was reprinted in the *Ipswich Journal* of 1st October (copy in Ipswich Public Libraries).

———

From the " London Daily Post ", 1st October 1743

For the Benefit of Mr. Clement.

At Ruckholt-House, near *Low-Layton* in *Essex*, on Monday next [the 7th] will be perform'd Mr. Dryden's Ode, call'd Alexander's Feast.

Compos'd by Mr. HANDEL. The Vocal Parts by Mr. Lowe, Mr. Baildon, Mr. Brett, and others. Tickets 3s. which entitles each Person to a Breakfast, as usual, and a Book of the Entertainment. To begin at Eleven o'Clock in the Morning. *In the* AFTERNOON will be Singing by the same Persons, and several Solo's and Concerto's on different Instruments. Admittance after Two o'Clock One Shilling. . . . This will be the last for this Season. The Marsh-Gate and Temple-Mills will be free for that Day.

(Smith, 1948, p. 189.) Ruckholt House, about a mile south of Low-Layton Church, was originally the residence of the Hickes family. In September 1743, and in May and June 1744, Boyce's oratorio *Solomon* was performed there. Cf. 11th June 1744. The tenor Thomas Lowe was a regular performer at Ruckholt House. Baildon, a brother of the composer Joseph Baildon, sang later in Handel oratorios in London. Nothing is known of Mr. Brett. No word-book of the performance has been traced.

—

FROM FAULKNER'S " DUBLIN JOURNAL ", 25th October 1743

Mr. Dubourg and Mr. Arne are to have six Oratorios of Mr. Handell's performed this Season, by Subscription, in which Mr. Lowe, Mrs. Arne, Mr. Colgan and Mrs. Storer will perform the vocal Parts.

(*Musical Antiquary*, July 1910, p. 220.) Dubourg was back in Dublin. Lowe (see 1st October) arrived there on 20th October. James Colgan was one of the Vicar Chorals of St. Patrick's Cathedral. For Mrs. Storer, see 25th January 1746. The plan seems to have been abandoned. Cf. 3rd December.

—

FROM THE " DAILY ADVERTISER ", 8th November 1743

At the King's Theatre in the Hay-Market, on Tuesday Se'nnight [the 15th], will be reviv'd an Opera, call'd ROXANA : or, ALEXANDER *in India.* Compos'd by Mr. HANDEL. With Dances and other Decorations entirely new. . . . To begin at Six o'Clock.

(Schoelcher, p. 308.) There seems to be some mystery about this opera. The advertisements give Handel's name, and call the performance a revival. It was probably performed without Handel's consent (cf. 10th December 1734). Schoelcher possessed the unique copy of the libretto : " Rossane. Melodramma per il Teatro S.M.B. di P.R. Londra, 1743." (S.M.B. means Suae Majestatis Britannicae ; P.R. stands for Paolo Rolli.) Burney (IV. 450), Nicoll (p. 398) and Loewenberg (p. 102) attribute the music to Giovanni Battista Lampugnani, Galuppi's successor at the Haymarket, and list other performances of the opera in 1746 and 1747, omitting the revival on 6th March 1744. Rolli was the author of Handel's *Alessandro* (5th May 1726, revived 26th December 1727 and 25th November 1732), and the text of that opera was reprinted in Rolli's *Componimenti poetici*, Verona, 1744, as *Alessandro*, without Handel's name. It is possible that Lampugnani arranged the original *Alessandro* by Handel for the performances of *Rossane* in 1743 and 1744, before he himself compiled the pasticcio *Alessandro nell' Indie*, music chiefly by himself and Gioacchino Cocchi, produced in 1746, and revived in 1747. Walsh printed the favourite songs from *Roxana* in 1743 or 1744, and a larger score about 1747, both under Handel's name ; arias from *Alessandro* were included as well as some from *Admeto* and *Siroe*. Walsh also printed a selection from the pasticcio, with Lampugnani's name added to the songs.

———

FROM THE " DAILY ADVERTISER ", 10th November 1743

Yesterday Mr. Handel's new Anthem and Te Deum, to be perform'd in the Chapel Royal at St. James's as soon as his Majesty arrives, was rehears'd at Whitehall Chapel.

For the Whitehall Chapel see 15th December 1737.

———

MRS. DELANY TO HER SISTER, MRS. DEWES

Charges Street, 10 Nov. 1743

That night [Tuesday last] Mrs. Percival came to invite us to dine with her yesterday, and to go in the morning to Whitehall Chapel to hear Mr. Handel's new Te Deum rehearsed, and an anthem. It is excessively fine, I was all rapture and so was your friend D.D. as you may imagine ; everybody says it is the finest of his compositions ; I am not well enough acquainted with it to pronounce that of it, but it is heavenly.

(Delany, II. 222.) For Mrs. Percival, cf. 2nd April 1734. Mary Pendarves, *née* Granville, married, on 9th June 1743, Patrick Delany, of Dublin. They lived for a time in London. She called him " D.D.", meaning Doctor of Divinity or/and Dr. Delany.

———

CAST OF " ROSSANE ", 15th November 1743
(Compared with the casts of *Alessandro* on 5th May 1726
and 25th November 1732)

Alessandro—Signor Monticelli (Senesino, Senesino)
Rossane—Signora Visconti (Faustina, Strada)
Lisaura—Signora Mancini (Cuzzoni, Gismondi)
Tassile—Signora Frasi (Signor Baldi, Signora Bertolli)
Clito—Signora Fratesanti (Signor Boschi, Signor Montagnana)
Leonato—? (Signor Antinori, ?)
Cleone—? (Signora Dotti, ?)

Signora Giulia Frasi, a soprano, was singing her first Handel part (Burney, IV. 449) ; five years later she became a great support for his oratorios. Repeat performances on 19th, 26th, 29th November ; 3rd, 6th, 10th, 13th, 17th, 20th, 27th and 31st December ; revived on 6th March 1744. (In the Haymarket Company were also Signora Galli, a mezzo-soprano who joined in January 1743, and, according to Burney, IV. 449, one Contini.)

———

HORACE WALPOLE TO HORACE MANN

London, Nov. 17, 1743.

The Opera is begun, but is not so well as last year. The Rosa Mancini, who is second woman, and whom I suppose you have heard, is now old.

In the room of Amorevoli, they have got a dreadful bass, who, the Duke of Montagu says he believes, was organist at Aschaffenburgh.

(Walpole, *Letters*, 1891, I. 278.) Clito, the bass part in *Rossane*, was sung by Signora Fratesanti. The bass singer of the season is not known.

MRS. DELANY TO MRS. DEWES

Charges Street, 18 Nov. 1743

I was at the opera of Alexander, which under the disguise it suffered, was infinitely better than any Italian opera ; but it vexed me to hear some favourite songs mangled.

(Delany, II. 227.)

FROM THE "DAILY ADVERTISER", 19th November 1743

Yesterday a Te Deum and Anthem, composed by Mr. Handel for his Majesty, were rehearsed before a splendid Assembly at Whitehall Chapel, and are said by the best Judges to be so truly masterly and sublime, as well as new in their kind, that they prove this great Genius not only inexhaustible, but likewise still rising to a higher Degree of Perfection.

(Schoelcher, p. 283.) Reprinted in Faulkner's *Dublin Journal*, 26th November. There were three, or perhaps four, rehearsals in all : on 26th September in the Chapel Royal at St. James's, on 9th and 18th November, and, according to Schoelcher, also on 25th November in Whitehall Chapel.

FROM FAULKNER'S "DUBLIN JOURNAL", 19th November 1743

By Appointment of the Charitable Musical Society, for the Benefit and Enlargement of Prisoners confined for Debt in the several Marshalseas of this City, at the Great Musick-Hall in Fishamble-street, on Friday the 16th Day of December next, in the Evening, will be performed, The MESSIAH, composed by Mr. Handell. And on Monday the 12th of December, at Noon, there will be a Rehearsal of the said Performance. . . .

Cf. 6th December.

PERFORMERS OF THE "DETTINGEN TE DEUM AND ANTHEM" 27th November 1743

Alto (?)—Mr. Abbot
Bass—Mr. Gates

The names of the other Gentlemen of the Chapel Royal, who sang on this occasion, are not recorded. For Abbot see 14th March 1734, and for Gates 17th

December 1737. Francis Hughes and Benjamin Mence, altos, and Wass, a bass, may have been among the singers.

———

From the " Daily Advertiser ", 28th November 1743

Yesterday his Majesty was at the Chapel Royal at St. James's, and heard a Sermon preach'd by the Rev. Dr. Thomas ; when the new Te Deum, and the following Anthem, both set to Musick by Mr. Handel, on his Majesty's safe Arrival, were perform'd before the Royal Family.

[Here follow the words of the Anthem : " The King shall rejoice . . .".]

Reprinted in Faulkner's *Dublin Journal* of 6th December. John Thomas was Chaplain to the King. With the appearance of the *Dettingen Te Deum* and *Anthem*, the popularity of the *Utrecht Te Deum and Jubilate*, in use since 1713, began to wane. Only the Corporation of the Sons of the Clergy, at their annual concerts in St. Paul's Cathedral, did not take to the new Te Deum ; they revived Henry Purcell's *Te Deum* when they abandoned the Utrecht one.

———

From the Same

Musick.
This Day are publish'd,

. . . . .

sold by J. Walsh . . .

Of whom may be had, just publish'd.

1. The entire Masque of Acis and Galatea, in Score, with the Songs, Recitativo, and Choruses, compos'd by Mr. Handel.

2. The Oratorio of Samson, in Score ; also set for a German Flute and Bass, in two Collections.

3. Apollo's Feast ; containing 500 choice Songs in Score from all the Operas compos'd by Mr. Handel, in five Volumes. . . .

(Smith, 1948, p. 233.) For *Acis and Galatea* see 24th August. *Apollo's Feast* was now complete (cf. 7th December 1734). Although a volume 5 had appeared at the beginning of 1741, the advertisement above probably refers to its second state.

———

From the " Daily Advertiser ", 2nd December 1743

Last Night there was a Meeting of the Prussian Garde du Corps Royal, at the Cardmakers Arms in Gray's Inn Passage, Red-Lyon-Square, and a grand Entertainment on that Occasion, when the Healths of the Kings of Great Britain and Prussia, the Prince and Princess of Wales, the Duke of Cumberland, and all the rest of the Royal Family, were drunk ; but in particular, Bumpers were drunk three times to his Majesty's King George, on account of the glorious Victory gain'd over the French at the Battle of Dettingen. The whole concluded with a grand Concert of Musick by the best Masters in England, and several fine Pieces of Mr. Handel's were perform'd, and finish'd with Britons strike home.

(Chrysander, 1863, p. 394.) Frederick the Great was a cousin of George II. The "best Masters" were the performing musicians. For the song *Britons strike home*, see 27th October 1739.

——

Walsh advertises the harpsichord arrangement of the six Handel overtures published in parts on 19th July, *Daily Advertiser*, 2nd December 1743.

(Smith, 1948, p. 83.) In this, the eighth book of the series, *Messiah* was again called "the Sacred Oratorio". On 12th December, however, in the *London Daily Post*, where the price of 3s. is added to the advertisement, the title is given as *Messia*. In the *Daily Advertiser* of 14th December it is still called "the Sacred Oratorio".

——

FROM FAULKNER'S "DUBLIN JOURNAL", 3rd December 1743

Mr. Arne proposes to exhibit, at the Theatre-Royal in Aungier-street, Four Performances in the Manner of the Oratorios in London. . . .

(Cummings, 1912, pp. 27 f.) Cf. 25th October 1743 and 14th February 1744.

——

FROM FAULKNER'S "DUBLIN JOURNAL", 6th December 1743

From the Charitable Musical Society.

The said Society having obtained from the celebrated Mr. Handell, a Copy of the Score of the Grand Musical Entertainment, called the MESSIAH, they intended to have it rehearsed on the 12th, and performed on the 16th of December Inst. for the Benefit and Enlargement of Prisoners confined for Debt, pursuant to their Advertisements ; and in order to have it executed in the best Manner, they had prevailed on Mr. Dubourg to give them his Assistance, and also applyed by a Deputation of the Society to the Members of the Choirs of the two Cathedrals to assist therein (the necessary Approbation of their so doing being first obtained on due Application) which several of them promised, and at a Meeting for that Purpose chose, and received their Parts ; but after Preparations had been made, at considerable Expense, to the Surprize of the Society, several of the Members of the said Choirs (some of whom had engaged as before mentioned) thought fit to decline performing, and returned their Parts, for Reasons that no way related to or concerned the said Society ; they are therefore obliged to postpone that Entertainment until Friday the 3rd Day of February next, to the great Detriment and Delay of their Charitable Intentions, the good Effects whereof have been manifested for several Years past. By that Time the Society will provide such Performers as will do Justice to that Sublime Composition, and for the future will take such Measures as shall effectually free them from Apprehensions of a second Disappointment to the Publick or themselves.

(Townsend, p. 114.) Cf. 19th November and 27th December 1743, and 14th January 1744. The disappointment may have been caused by Mr. John Church, against whom several gentlemen protested in the *Journal* on 17th December. He had been a Gentleman of the Chapel Royal, and was Vicar Choral of both cathedrals.

———

FROM FAULKNER'S " DUBLIN JOURNAL ", 27th December 1743

From the Charitable Musical Society.

Whereas it has been reported that the Messiah will not be performed on the 3d of February next, for the Enlargment of Prisoners confined for Debt, the said Society think it proper to assure the Publick, that there is no just Foundation for such said Report, and that particular Care will be taken by them, that the Performance shall be compleat, under the Direction of Mr. Dubourg, without the aid of those, who refused to assist therein, as mentioned in a former Advertisement. . . .

Cf. 6th December.

———

MISS CATHERINE TALBOT TO MRS. ELIZABETH CARTER

Cuddesdon, 27 December 1743.

. . . I will own the having been highly delighted with several songs in Sampson, and especially with the choruses. I heard that oratorio performed this winter in one of the College Halls, and I believe to the full as finely as it ever was in town : and having never heard any oratorio before, I was extremely struck with such a kind of harmony as seems the only language adapted to devotion. I really cannot help thinking this kind of entertainment must necessarily have some effect in correcting or moderating at least the levity of the age ; and let an audience be ever so thoughtless, they can scarcely come away, I should think, without being the better for an evening so spent. I heartily wish you had been with me when I heard it.

(Carter, *Letters*, p. 43 f.) Streatfeild (1909, pp. 176 f.) suggests the college was an Oxford one. Cuddesdon is south-east of Oxford.

———

Handel subscribes for William Boyce's " Solomon. A Serenata, in Score, taken from the Canticles " (text arranged by E. Moore), published by Walsh, for the Author, in 1743.

In the same year Handel did not subscribe for Maurice Greene's *Forty Select Anthems in Score*, also published by Walsh (Bumpus, I. 250).

1744

FROM THE " LONDON DAILY POST ", 9th January 1744

By *Particular* DESIRE,

Mr. HANDEL proposes to Perform, by *Subscription*, Twelve Times during next Lent, and engages to play two New Performances (and some of his former Oratorios, if Time will permit).

Each Subscriber is to pay Four Guineas at the Time he subscribes, which entitles him to one Box Ticket for each Performance.

Subscriptions are taken in at Mr. Handel's House in Brook-street, near Hanover square ; and at Mr. Walsh's, in Catherine-street in the Strand.

Those Gentlemen and Ladies who have already favour'd Mr. Handel in the Subscription are desired to send for their Tickets, at his House in Brook-street, where Attendance will be given every Day (Sunday excepted) from Nine o'Clock in the Morning untill Three in the Afternoon.

(Schoelcher, p. 286.) The number of concerts was increased from six to twelve. Cf. 20th October 1744. The new oratorio season was at Covent Garden.

FROM FAULKNER'S " DUBLIN JOURNAL ", 14th January 1744

From the Charitable Musical Society.

The said Society think themselves obliged to give the Publick an Account, that, in the Year 1742, they released out of the several Marshal-seas in and about this City, 142 Prisoners, whose principal Debts and Fees amounted to the Sum of 1225*l*. 17s. 1d. besides 33*l*. 16s. given to poor Creditors and out-going Prisoners : And they take this Occasion to return their humble Thanks to their kind Benefactors at their last Year's Entertainment of Acis and Galatea, and hope for the Continuance of their Favour for their ensuing Entertainment of the sacred Oratorio, call'd MESSIAH, and set by Mr. Handell, in the Performance whereof, at the usual Season, they were, by an Artifice (as is now well known to the Town) unhappily disappointed ; with this advantage however to the Audience, that the same will, upon the 1st and 3d of February next, be rehearsed, and executed to greater Perfection, under the Direction of Mr. Dubourg.

N.B. The Tickets given out for the 12th and 16th of December last, will be taken on the 1st and 3d of February next.

(Townsend, p. 115.) Cf. 30th November (17th December) 1742 and 6th December 1743.

From Faulkner's "Dublin Journal", 24th January 1744

The Rehearsal of Mr. Handell's sacred Oratorio, called the Messiah, will certainly be on Wednesday the 1st Day of Feb. next, at 12 o'Clock at Noon, at the Musick-hall in Fishamble-street ; and, if Lord Netterville's Trial should come on the Friday following, the Performance will be postponed to a further Day, of which Notice will be given at the Rehearsal. . . .

See 4th February. Nicholas, Viscount Netterville of Dowth was indicted for a murder, tried by the House of Lords on 3rd February, and honourably acquitted.

Mrs. Delany to Her Sister, Mrs. Dewes

Clarges Street, 24 Jan. 1743–4.
I was yesterday morning at Mr. Handel's to hear the rehearsal of Semele. It is a delightful piece of music, quite new and different from anything he has done : but I am afraid I shall hear no more music this year, and that will be a loss to me,—but the *harmony of friendship* must make up that loss. As we have a prospect of meeting soon I defer a particular account of it till we meet. Francesina is improved, and sings the principal part in it.

(Delany, II. 254.) Signora Elisabeth Duparc, called La Francesina, a soprano, who sang for Handel from 1738 till 1741, was back in his company.

From "Theatrical Properties and Scenery at Covent Garden in 1743", 30th January 1744

A list of Scenes . . . (*Back flats in Scene room*) . . . back Arch of Ariodante's pallace . . . (*Wings in the Scene Room*) 4 Ariodante's pallace . . . do. [12 ?] Atalanta's garden . . . (*Wings in Painters Room*) 2 of Ariodante's pallace, but are rubbed out and not painted . . . (*Painted pieces in the Scene Room*) . . . front of gallery in Ariodante, a small palace border in do., a frontispiece in do. (*Do. in Great room*) . . . a ground peice of Atalanta's garden. (*Do. in Yard*) . . . the falling rock in *Alcina*, four peices, the compass border to Atalanta's garden. (*Painted peices in Top Flies*) . . . a peice of a falling rock in the Operas . . . (*Do. in painting Room*) . . . 6 columns to Fame's temple [in *Justin*] (*Do. in Shop*) . . . a large border of Ariodante's pallace, and small transparent in *Atalanta* . . . two oxen in *Justin* . . . a border to frontispiece in *Ariodante*, four furrows in *Justin* . . . (*Properties on the Stage*) . . . a pyramid in Atlanti's garden. . . .

(Wyndham, II. 309-13.) British Museum : Add. MS. 12,201, f. 30. The scenery and set-pieces, preserved at Covent Garden in 1743, were from Handel productions of 1735-7 : *Ariodante*—8th January 1735, *Alcina*—16th April 1735, *Atalanta*—12th May 1736, and *Giustino*—16th February 1737. The décor of *Alcina* belongs to the last scene ; that of *Giustino* to I. 4 and III. 8 (Eisenschmidt,

II. 110). The decorations for the wedding-opera, *Atalanta*, may have been painted
by Goupy (cf. 13th May 1736).

FROM FAULKNER'S "DUBLIN JOURNAL", 31st January 1744

We hear that the Oratorio called the MESSIAH was privately rehearsed
last Night in the Presence of some of the best Judges, who expressed the
utmost Satisfaction on that Occasion. This fine Piece is to be publickly
rehearsed on Wednesday next [1st February] at Noon, for the Benefit
and Enlargement of Performers [or rather, Prisoners] confined for Debt ;
and as the Audience will be very numerous, we hear, the Ladies have
resolved to come without Hoops, as when the same was performed by
Mr. Handel.

(Townsend, pp. 115 f.) Cf. 4th February.

FROM FAULKNER'S "DUBLIN JOURNAL", 4th February 1744

From the Charitable Musical Society for the Relief
of poor Prisoners.

. . . On Account of Lord Netterville's Tryal, the Grand Performance
of the sacred Oratorio of the MESSIAH is put off to Tuesday the 7th Inst.
to begin at 6 o'Clock in the Evening precisely. . . .

We hear from all Hands of the great Satisfaction given last Wednesday
[the 1st] to a crowded Audience at the Rehearsal of the sacred Oratorio
of the Messiah ; nothing can come up to the choice of the Subject, the
Words are those of the sacred Text, the Musick extremely well adapted,
and the Execution, under Mr. Dubourg's Direction, by the most
celebrated Band of Vocal and Instrumental Musick, was carried on thro'
all the Parts, with universal Applause. . . .

(Townsend, pp. 115 f.) It was observed that at this rehearsal many ladies came
with hoops ; otherwise there would have been space for one hundred more seats.

FROM THE KING'S WARRANT BOOK, 7th February 1744

£   s.   d.

Royal Academy of Musick   1,000   0   0   Royal bounty to the undertakers of the Opera

(Calendar of Treasury Books, for 1742–5, p. 604.) Cf. 9th June 1742 and 4th
May 1743. See also 16th February 1744. This payment was apparently for the
season 1742–3, because in August 1744 another, the last, payment was ordered.

Mrs. Delany to Mrs. Dewes

Clarges Street, 7 Feb. 1743-4.

Semele is to be performed next Friday ; D.D. subscribes for me, and I hope not to miss one of the charming oratorios, except when I give up my ticket to him.

(Delany, II. 260.)

———

From the " London Daily Post ", 9th February 1744

For the Benefit of Mr. Edmund Larken. At Stationers-Hall, in Ludgate Street, to-day . . . will be perform'd the Masque of Acis and Galatea. With all the Chorus's composed by Mr. Handel. The Songs of *Galatea* to be perform'd by a celebrated *Young Lady*, being the first Time of her appearing in any Publick Concert. The other Parts, viz. *Acis, Polypheme,* &c. by the most eminent Performers. The First Violin by Mr. Brown. . . . The whole to conclude with the Coronation Anthem, God save the King. The Trumpet by Mr. Valentine Snow. . . . Printed Books of the Masque will be given Gratis at the Place of Performance.

(Smith, 1948, p. 234.) The advertisement appeared first on 4th February, but without the sentence referring to Handel's Coronation Anthem. Nothing is known of Mr. Larken, and of the lady only that she had a nine-year-old sister, singing an English and an Italian song. Abraham Browne, or Abram Brown, was leader of the King's Band and later music director of Ranelagh Gardens, both in succession to Michael Festing ; he also led the orchestra in the *Messiah* performances at the Foundling Hospital in 1754 and 1758, as well as the orchestra of the Three Choirs Meetings about 1755. Snow was a famous trumpeter. Stationers' Hall was an unusual concert room (cf. 3rd March 1713 and 22nd February 1714).

———

At the Music Hall in Crow-Street, Dublin, a concert is given for the benefit of Miss Davis (cf. 13th November 1742), with some music by Handel, 9th February 1744.

She performed " some of the most difficult and favourite Concerto's of Mr. Handell's and other Authors upon the Harpsichord, accompanyed with many other Instruments, and will accompany her Mother in a favourite Song of Mr. Handell's composed particularly for the Harpsichord ". (*Dublin Journal*, 4th February.)

———

From the " London Daily Post ", 10th February 1744

By Subscription.

At the Theatre-Royal in Covent-Garden, this Day . . ., will be perform'd Semele. After the Manner of an *Oratorio*, Set to Musick by Mr. Handel. . . .

(Schoelcher, p. 287.) William Congreve's text was published, under the title of " An Opera ", in 1710, having been set to music by John Eccles in 1707. Eccles's opera was advertised in *The Muses Mercury ; or the Monthly Miscellany* of January 1707 for production in the near future ; but the English edition of Pierre Beyle's *General Dictionary* (vol. IV. 1736) asserts that the opera was never performed. (See John C. Hodges, *William Congreve the Man*, New York, 1941, p. 73.) The original text was altered for Handel, perhaps by Newburgh Hamilton. Performed on 10th, 15th, 17th and 22nd February ; revived at the Haymarket in December 1744.

———

FROM THE SAME

This Day is published, Price 1s.
(*As it will this Evening be perform'd at the Theatre-Royal in Covent-Garden ;*)
   The Story of SEMELE ; Alter'd from the Semele by Mr. *Congreve.* Set to Musick by Mr. *Handel.*
      Printed for J. and R. Tonson, in the Strand.

   It is noteworthy that Tonson was the publisher of the original word-book in 1710.

———

CAST OF " SEMELE ", 10th February 1744

Jupiter—Mr. Beard, tenor
Cadmus—(?) Reinhold, bass
Athamas—Mr. Daniel Sullivan, alto
Somnus—Mr. Reinhold, bass
Apollo—?, tenor
Juno—Miss Young, mezzo-soprano
Iris—Signora Avoglio, soprano
Semele—Signora Francesina (Duparc), soprano
Ino—Miss Young, contralto
High Priest—(?) Reinhold, bass

   The Miss Young, who apparently sang two parts, was probably Esther Young, one of the two sisters of Mrs. Cecilia Arne, *née* Young.

———

MRS. DELANY TO MRS. DEWES

Feb. 11th, 1743–4.
   I was yesterday to hear Semele ; it is a delightful piece of music. Mrs. Donnellan desires her particular compliments to all *but* to my brother ; she bids me say " she loses half her pleasure in Handel's music by *his not being here* to talk over the particular passages ". There is a four-part song that is delightfully pretty ; Francesina is extremely improved, her notes are more distinct, and there is something in her running-divisions that is quite surprizing. She was much applauded, and the house full, though not crowded ; I believe I wrote my brother word that Mr. Handel and the Prince had quarelled, which I am sorry for. Handel says the *Prince* is quite out of *his* good graces ! there was no disturbance at the play-house and the Goths were not so very absurd as to declare, in a public manner, their disapprobation of such a composer.

(Delany, II. 262.) The sister's brother was Bernard Granville. The Prince is, of course, Frederick, Prince of Wales. The Earl of Egmont notes in his diary (III. 284) that he too was present at the first night. The vocal quartet, a rarity in Handel's operas and oratorios, is in the first scene of Act I.

———

FROM THE "LONDON DAILY POST", 13th February 1744

MUSICK.

This Day is publish'd,

Proposals for Printing by Subscription,

Semele, as it is performed at the Theatre-Royal in Covent-Garden, with the Overture, Symphonies, Songs, and Duet, Set to Musick by Mr. Handel.

1. The Price to Subscribers is Half a Guinea to be paid at the Time of Subscribing.

2. The Musick will be printed in a neat and correct Manner, and ready to deliver to the Subscribers by the 8th of March next.

Subscriptions are taken in by J. Walsh. . . .

This score also was published without subscribers' list. It was issued in three sections ; see 25th February, 2nd, 10th and 13th March.

———

FROM FAULKNER'S "DUBLIN JOURNAL", 14th February 1744

(In an advertisement of T. A. Arne's oratorio, "The Death of Abel" to be performed on 18th February at the Theatre Royal in Smock Alley.)

The Stage will be disposed in the same Manner as at Mr. Handel's Oratorios in London. . . . Ladies are required to sit in the Pit, as well as Boxes, as is the Custom at the Operas and Oratorios in London, for which purpose the Pit will be made thoroughly clean.

(Cummings, 1912, pp. 30 f.) Mrs. Arne and Mr. Lowe sang in the oratorio. The subject of Arne's oratorio was later composed by Nicola Piccinni (Haymarket, 24th February 1768) and by Johann Heinrich Rolle. For Arne's oratorio project, cf. 3rd December 1743.

———

Handel deposits £650, 14th February 1744.

———

FROM THE TREASURY MINUTE BOOK, 16th February 1744

Order for the following issues out of the Civil List revenues :—

.   .   .   .   .

	£	s.	d.
To the Opera . .	1,000	0	0

(Calendar of Treasury Books, 1742–5, p. 452.) Cf. 7th February.

———

Messiah is performed by the Academy of Ancient Music at the "Crown and Anchor" Tavern in the Strand, 16th February 1744. (Smith 1950, p. 132.) Cf. 30th April 1747 and 11th May 1758.

———

FROM FAULKNER'S "DUBLIN JOURNAL", 21st February 1744

For the Support of the Charitable Infirmary on the Inn's Quay at the Great Musick-hall in Fishamble-street on Monday the 27th of this Instant February, will be performed the sacred Oratorio called the MESSIAH, as it has been lately performed with general Applause, under the Direction of Mr. Dubourg. There will be a grand Rehearsal the Thursday before, precisely at Twelve o'Clock at Noon. . . . N.B. A Rehearsal Ticket will be delivered with the Performance Ticket, and a Book at the Rehearsal.

Messiah had been rehearsed on 1st and 2nd February, and performed on 7th February for the other charity.

———

Handel pays £650, from his accounts, to [Mr ?] Chambers, 21st February 1744.

———

MRS. DELANY TO MRS. DEWES

Clarges Street, 21 Feb. 1744.

Semele is charming ; the more I hear it the better I like it, and as I am a subscriber I shall not fail one night. But it being a profane story D.D. does not think it proper for him to go ; but when Joseph or Samson is performed I shall persuade him to go—you know *how much* he delights in music. They say Samson is to be next Friday, for Semele has a strong party against it, viz. the fine ladies, petit maîtres, and *ignoramus*'s. All the opera people are enraged at Handel, but Lady Cobham, Lady Westmoreland, and Lady Chesterfield never fail it.

(Young, p. 73.) Delany, II. 266 f. *Semele* was, in fact, a strange "oratorio" ; and for the friends of the Haymarket Opera, it was a strange opera. During Lent, Handel managed to perform an opera at the same low cost as an oratorio. His new oratorio *Joseph and his Brethren* was produced on 2nd March. Lady Chesterfield was, of course, his former pupil, Fräulein von Schulenburg. Lady Anne Cobham and Lady Mary Westmorland were married to generals.

———

FROM THE "LONDON DAILY POST", 24th February 1744

By SUBSCRIPTION.

The Fifth Night.

At the Theatre-Royal in Covent-Garden, this Day, will be perform'd an *Oratorio*, call'd SAMSON. With a *Concerto* on the *Organ*. . . . To begin at Six o'Clock.

Repeat performance on 29th February.

———

Walsh advertises " Songs in *Semele*. To which is prefix'd the Overture in Score ", *London Daily Post*, 25th February 1744.

Cf. 13th February. Walsh did not indicate that this was the first of three sections of the score offered to subscribers. The price was 4s. for part one.

———

MRS. DELANY TO MRS. DEWES

Clarges Street, Feby 25th, 1743–4.
I was last night to hear Samson. Francesina sings most of Mrs. Cibber's part and some of Mrs. Clive's : upon the whole it went off very well, but not better than last year. Joseph, I believe, will be next Friday, but Handel is mightily out of humour about it, for Sullivan, who is to sing Joseph, *is a block* with a very fine voice, and Beard has *no voice at all.*
The part which Francescina is to have (of Joseph's wife) will not admit of much variety ; but I hope it will be well received ; the houses have not been crowded, but pretty full every night.

(Delany, II. 271.) Mrs. Cibber sang Micah and Mrs. Clive Dalila in the production of *Samson* on 18th February 1743.

———

FROM THE " LONDON DAILY POST ", 29th February 1744

To-morrow will be publish'd, Price 1s.
JOSEPH and his BRETHREN. A Sacred Drama. By the Reverend Mr. *Miller*. Set to Musick by Mr. *Handel*. As it is perform'd at the Theatre-Royal in Covent-Garden.
Printed for and sold by J. Watts . . . and by B. Dodd. . . .

The author was James Miller. In the word-book some lines are marked with inverted commas, indicating that they were " omitted in the Representation, on account of the Length of the Piece ". On page 32, the duet Asenath-Joseph is converted into an air of Asenath, by an attached label. The libretto is dedicated by the author to John, Duke of Montague, Master General of the Ordnance (see 28th March 1749).

———

FROM JAMES MILLER'S DEDICATION OF THE WORD-BOOK OF " JOSEPH AND HIS BRETHREN " TO JOHN, DUKE OF MONTAGUE, PUBLISHED ON 1st March 1744

May it please your GRACE,
I have no other Apology to make for presuming to lay the following Performance at Your Grace's Feet, than the Countenance you are pleased to give to the Refined and Sublime Entertainments of this Kind, and the generous Patronage you manifest towards the Great Master, by whose Divine Harmony they are supported. A Master meritorious of such a Patron, as he may be said, without the least Adulation, to have shewn a
H.–19 a

higher degree of Excellence in each of the various kinds of Composition, than any one who has preceded him ever arrived at in a single Branch of it ; and to have so peculiar a Felicity in always making his Strain the Tongue of his Subject, that his Music is sure to talk to the Purpose, whether the Words it is set to do so, or not. 'Tis a pity however, My LORD, that such a Genius should be put to the Drudgery of hammering for Fire where there is no Flint, and of giving a Sentiment to the Poet's Metre before he can give one to his own Melody. . . .

(Schoelcher, pp. 286 f.) The dedication shows an arrogance even worse than that in Hamilton's preface to the book of *Samson* ; cf. 18th February 1743.

———

FROM THE " LONDON DAILY POST ", 1st March 1744

BY SUBSCRIPTION.
The Seventh Night.

At the Theatre-Royal in Covent-Garden, To-morrow will be perform'd a New *Oratorio*, call'd JOSEPH and his BRETHREN. With a *Concerto* on the *Organ*. . . . To begin at Six o'Clock.

Repeat performances on 7th, 9th and 14th March ; revived during Lent in 1745, 1747, 1755 and 1757.

———

FROM THE EARL OF EGMONT'S DIARY, 1st March 1744

In the evening, I went to Mr. Handel's Oratorio called " Joseph in Egypt ", an inimitable composition.

(Egmont MSS., III. 290.) It seems strange that the rehearsal should have been held on the evening before the first night. But the Earl wrote on 7th March of another performance of this oratorio he attended (III. 291).

———

Walsh advertises " A Second Set of *Songs* in Semele ", *London Daily Post*, 2nd March 1744.

Cf. 25th February.

———

CAST OF " JOSEPH AND HIS BRETHREN ", 2nd March 1744 (Friday)

Pharaoh—Mr. Reinhold, bass
Joseph—Mr. Sullivan, alto
Reuben—(?) Mr. Reinhold, bass
Simeon—(?) Mr. Beard, tenor
Judah—(?), tenor
Benjamin—" the Boy ", soprano
Potiphera—(?), contralto
Asenath—Signora Francesina, soprano
Phanor—Signora Galli, mezzo-soprano

Mr. Sullivan, who sang at Ranelagh in 1743 and at Bath in 1745 (" God save the King" on George II's birthday) as well as in April 1757 (*Acis and Galatea, Alexander's Feast*), had his second major part here ; see 10th February 1744. (Cf. Flood, p. 446, and Molly Sands in *Musical Times*, September 1948.) Beard may have sung either " Simeon " or " Judah ". Signora Galli, said to have been a pupil of Handel's, came from the rival house in the Haymarket.

—

FROM THE " LONDON DAILY POST ", 6th March 1744

For the Benefit of Signor MONTICELLI.

At the King's Theatre in the Hay-Market, this Day, will be perform'd an *Opera*, call'd ROXANA. The Musick compos'd by Mr. *Handel*. . . .

Cf. 8th (15th) November 1743. Repeat performances on 10th, 13th and 17th March. The sub-title of the performance in 1743, " Alexander in India ", is omitted. Revived on 20th February 1748.

—

Handel deposits £250, 6th March 1744.

—

Walsh advertises the " Third Set " of the " Songs in Semele ", with " an Index ", *London Daily Post*, 10th March 1744.

Cf. 25th February and 2nd March. The misprint " Re-publish'd ", contained in this advertisement, was corrected on the 12th, and the price, 2s. 6d., added. " Index " is the Table of Contents, listing the single songs. On 13th March Walsh advertises all the three " Acts " separately, and together for 10s. 6d.

—

MRS. DELANY TO MRS. DEWES

Clarges Street, March 10, 1743–4.

The oratorios fill very well, not withstanding the spite of the opera party : nine of the twelve are over. Joseph is to be performed (I hope) once more, then Saul, and the Messiah finishes ; as they have taken very well, I fancy Handel will have a second subscription ; and how do you think *I have lately been employed* ? Why, I have made a drama for an oratorio, out of Milton's Paradise Lost, to give Mr. Handel to compose to ; it has cost me a great deal of thought and contrivance ; D.D. approves of my performance, and that gives me some reason to think it not bad, though all I have had to do has been collecting and making the connection between the fine parts. I begin with Satan's threatenings to seduce the woman, her being seduced follows, and it ends with the man's yielding to the temptation ; I would not have a word or a thought of Milton's altered ; and I hope to prevail with Handel to set it without having *any of the lines put into verse*, for that will take from its dignity. This, and painting three pictures, have been my chief morning employment since I came to town.

(Young, p. 74.) Delany, II. 279 f. *Joseph* was repeated once on 14th March. *Saul* also was given twice, but *Messiah* was not performed in 1744. The next series of Handel's subscription oratorios began on 3rd November. " D.D." is Mrs. Delany's husband. She returned to London in the middle of January, just in time for the opening of Handel's Lent season. He did not accept her word-book of *Paradise Lost*, if it was ever finished. His pupil, John Christopher Smith, wrote an oratorio of that name in 1757-8 ; it was performed at Covent Garden on 29th February 1760, but his word-book was by Benjamin Stillingfleet, and had nothing to do with Milton. (Robert Price was the author of Smith's oratorio *Judith*.) Edward J. Dent suggested that the word-book written by Mrs. Delany might have been the same that is said to have been written by one Linley for Handel, later translated and arranged by Gottfried van Swieten for Haydn, and finally composed as *The Creation*. Dent, according to Young, added " that Linley was the nearest that German scholarship could approximate to Delany ". Haydn's word-book is based partly on the second part of Milton's epic, with recitatives from the Scriptures. Swieten, in the *Allgemeine Musikalische Zeitung* of 1799 (I. 254), calls the original anonymous ; Georg August Griesinger (no scholar) in the same magazine in 1809 (XI. 705) gives the name of Linley (not Lidley, nor Lindley) as having been told to him by Haydn. Donald Francis Tovey (*Essays in Musical Analysis*, V. 119) thought this could have been Thomas Linley, singing-master and concert-promoter (born 1733). At all events, Mrs. Delany's book opens with Satan, while Haydn's opens with God creating the world out of chaos.

———

FROM THE " GENERAL ADVERTISER ", 16th March 1744

By SUBSCRIPTION.

The Eleventh Night.

At the Theatre-Royal . . . this Day, will be perform'd an *Oratorio*, call'd SAUL. With a *Concerto* on the *Organ*. . . .

From 12th March onwards, the *London Daily Post and General Advertiser* was called the *General Advertiser*. *Saul*, produced in 1739, had last been performed in London in 1741. Repeat performance on 21st March.

———

MRS. DELANY TO MRS. DEWES

Clarges Street, March 22, 1743-4.

Last night, alas ! was the last night of the oratorio : it concluded with Saul : I was in hopes of the Messiah. I have been at ten oratorios, and wished you at every one most heartily . . . the oratorios took up two days in the week.

(Delany, II. 284.) Cf. 10th March. The Earl of Egmont also attended the twelfth night of Handel's subscription oratorios (MSS., III. 293).

———

MRS. DELANY TO MRS. DEWES

Clarges Street, April 3, 1744.
To-day I shall have a treat that I shall most ardently wish you and my mother your share of. Handel, my brother, and Donnellan *dine here*, and we are to be entertained with *Handel's playing over Joseph to us*. how often and how tenderly shall I think of *my Benjamin* !

(Delany, II. 290.) Cf. 12th April 1734. Benjamin was, of course, Ann Dewes, called after Joseph's youngest brother. The sisters' brother was Bernard Granville.

—

Handel pays, from his accounts, £226 : 5 : 6 to [Mr. ?] Chambers, 5th April 1744.

—

Handel buys, by certificates, £1300 3 per cent Annuities (1743), 10th April 1744.
These annuities existed from 1743 till 1760. " By certificates " means, probably, that Handel's account in these annuities was opened by original subscription.

—

FROM THE " GENERAL ADVERTISER ", 17th April 1744

For the Benefit of Mr. LEVERIDGE.
At the Theatre-Royal in Covent-Garden, this Day, will be perform'd a Comedy, call'd THE MISER. . . . With Entertainments of Singing and Dancing, particularly . . . [end of] Act III. The favourite Song in *Il Penseroso*, &c. beginning, *The Trumpets loud Clangor excites us to Arms*, compos'd by Mr. Handel, sung by Mr. Beard. . . .

(Chrysander, 1863, pp. 304 f.) The comedy was Henry Fielding's. Beard was one of the original cast in *L'Allegro ed il Penseroso* (1740).

—

Handel withdraws the balance of £23 : 14 : 6, 17th April 1744.

—

FROM THE " LONDON MAGAZINE ", April 1744

Hearing Mr. HANDEL'S SAMPSON, *at the Theatre in Covent-Garden.*
Rais'd by his subject, *Milton* nobly flew,
And all Parnassus open'd to our view :
By *Milton* fir'd, brave *Handel* strikes our ear,
And every power of harmony we hear.

When two such mighty artists blend their fire ;
Pour forth each charm that genius can inspire,
The man whose bosom does not raptures feel,
Must have no soul, or all his heart be steel.

On viewing Mr. HANDEL'S STATUE.
The stones obey'd when sweet *Amphion* sung,
And to his soft persuasion mov'd along.
Could his own statue hear his *Handel's* strain,
The life infus'd would beat in ev'ry vein,
And the dead stone appear the very man.

Samson was last performed on 29th March. The statue was, of course, that in
Vauxhall Gardens.

—

FROM THE " GENERAL ADVERTISER ", 4th May 1744
NEW MUSICK.
This Day is publish'd, Price 4s.
The FIRST ACT of
JOSEPH and his BRETHREN, an Oratorio. Compos'd by Mr. *Handel.*
The Remainder will be publish'd with all Expedition.

Walsh's name was omitted from the advertisement by mistake. See next entry.

—

FROM THE " GENERAL ADVERTISER ", 21st May 1744
This Day is published,
Which compleats the Whole, the Second *and* Third Act, *of* JOSEPH and
his BRETHREN, an Oratorio, in Score. Compos'd by Mr. Handel. Price
6s 6d.
Printed for J. Walsh. . . .

—

HANDEL TO MIZLER, 25th May 1744
See *Addenda.*

—

HANDEL TO JENNENS
London Juin 9ᵗʰ 1744
Dear Sir,
    It gave me great Pleasure to hear Your safe arrival in the Country,
and that Your Health was much improved. I hope it is by this time
firmly establichd, and I wish You with all my Heart the Continuation
of it, and all the Prosperity.
    As You do me the Hoñour to encourage my Musicall Undertakings,
and even to promote them with a particular Kindness, I take the Liberty
to trouble You with an account of what Engagement I have hitherto

concluded. I have taken the Opera House in the Haymarketh. engaged, as Singers, Sig^ra Francesina, Miss Robinson, Beard, Reinhold, Mr Gates with his Boyes's and several of the best Chorus Singers from the Choirs, and I have some hopes that Mrs Cibber will sing for me. She sent me word from Bath (where she is now) that she would perform for me next winter with great pleasure if it did not interfere with her playing, but I think I can obtain Mr Riches's permission (with whom she is engaged to play in Covent Garden House) since so obligingly he gave Leave to Mr Beard and Mr Reinhold.

Now should I be extreamly glad to receive the first Act, or what is ready of the new Oratorio with which you intend to favour me, that I might employ all my attention and time, in order to answer in some measure the great obligation I lay under. this new favour will greatly increase my Obligations. I remain with all possible Gratitude and Respect

S^r

Your

most obliged and most humble
Servant
George Frideric Handel

(Preface to William Horsley's vocal score of *Messiah*, London, 1842.) Original in the possession of Lord Howe. There is no address, but the letter apparently went to Gopsall. Among other mistakes in earlier publications of the letter, the tenth word in the second paragraph was read as "Messiah". Bernard Gates was Master of the Children in the Chapel Royal. Mrs. Cibber did not appear during that season until 12th January 1745. John Rich was the manager of Covent Garden Theatre. The new oratorio was *Belshazzar*.

—

FROM THE "GENERAL ADVERTISER", 11th June 1744

At RUCKHOLT-HOUSE, Low-Layton, in Essex, on this Day will be performed ALEXANDER'S FEAST ; the Vocal Parts by Mr. Brett, Signiora Avolio, Mr. Waltz, Mr. Barrow, &c. and several Concertos on the German Flute by Mr. Burk Thumoth. The Breakfasting to begin at 10 o'Clock, each Person to pay Two Shillings Admittance.—There will be Singing in the Afternoon, by the Persons above mentioned ; each Person to pay (after Two o'Clock) One Shilling Admittance. The Evening Entertainments to begin at Four o'Clock, and continue 'till Eight at Night.—Proper Cooks are provided every Day in the Week, and Plenty of Fish ; and the Doors free, except Monday. A Book of the Entertainment will be given to each Person at the Place of Performance. The Gates at Hummerton and Temple-Mills will be Toll-free.

(Smith, 1948, pp. 189 f.) Cf. 1st October 1743. The 1744 season began on 7th May, and concerts were given every Monday. Handel's ode was performed on

11th, 18th and 25th June. (The newspaper of 11th June is missing in the British Museum.) Thomas Barrow, an alto, sang as a boy in *Esther* (23rd February 1732) and was to sing in *Messiah* in 1754 and 1759. Thumoth, an Irish musician, gave a concert in London on 14th May. Mr. Lowe and Miss (Esther) Young sang at Ruckholt House in May and on 4th June.

———

LADY ETHELDREDA TOWNSHEND TO ISABELLA, COUNTESS OF DENBIGH, 22nd June 1744

Monticelli and all the singers and dancers of the opera go away next week, there being no more of these entertainments next winter, Mr. Hendell having taken the House at the Hay Market to perform his Oratorios in all the next season.

(Denbigh MSS., p. 250.) The season of the Haymarket Opera ended on 16th June (Schoelcher, p. 291). Handel opened his oratorio season there on 3rd November.

———

Handel begins the " musical drama ", called *Hercules*, 19th July 1744.

———

HANDEL TO JENNENS

July 19. 1744

Dear Sir

At my arrival in London, which was Yesterday, I immediately perused the Act of the Oratorio with which you favour'd me, and, the little time only I had it, gives me great Pleasure. Your reasons for the Length of the first act are intirely Satisfactory to me, and it is likewise my Opinion to have the following Acts short. I shall be very glad and much obliged to you, if you will soon favour me with the remaining Acts. Be pleased to point out these passages in the Messiah which You think require altering.—

I desire my humble Respects and thanks to My Lord Guernsey for his many Civility's to me—and believe me to be with the greatest Respect

Sr

Your

Most obedient and most humble

Servant

George Frideric Handel

To

Charles Jennens (junior) Esqr.

at

Gopsal

near Atherstone

Leicestershire

(Schoelcher, pp. 288 f.) Original in the possession of Lord Howe. Cf. 9th June. The relation between Jennens and Handel, in reference to *Messiah*, reminds one of the later behaviour of Gottfried van Swieten to Haydn, in advising him how to compose *The Creation* and *The Seasons*. The word-book was printed complete, with notes about omissions in the music. Lord Guernsey was Jennens's friend, and had been acquainted with Handel since the Oxford days. We do not know where Handel was between the middle of June and the middle of July, but he was certainly not on the Continent.

—

FROM THE KING'S WARRANT BOOK, 2nd August 1744

£   s.   d.

Royal Academy of Musick   1,000   0   0   Royal bounty to the under-
                                                 takers of the Opera

(Calendar of Treasury Books, 1742–5, p. 628.) There is no corresponding entry in the Treasury Minute Book. Cf. 7th February 1744. This is the last payment known for the Haymarket Opera ; but it should be observed that the Calendars for the period after 1746 have not been published yet.

—

The Duke of Chandos, Handel's former patron, dies 9th August 1744.

—

HORACE WALPOLE TO HORACE MANN

London, Aug. 16, 1744.

Lord Middlesex's match is determined, and the writings signed. She proves an immense fortune ; they pretend a hundred and thirty thousand pounds—what a fund for making operas !

(Walpole, *Letters*, 1891, I. 321.) The Earl of Middlesex married Grace Boyle, daughter and sole heiress of Richard, Viscount Shannon.

—

Handel finishes *Hercules*, about 20th August 1744.

The last date in the manuscript is 17th August, but a later date seems to have been cut off by the binder.

—

HANDEL TO JENNENS

Dear Sir
     The Second Act of the Oratorio I have received Safe, and own my self highly obliged to You for it. I am greatly pleased with it, and shall

use my best endeavours to do it Justice. I can only Say that I impatiently wait for the third Act and desire to believe me to be with great Respect

Sr

Your

London   most obliged and most humble
Agost y 21.   Servant
1744.   George Frideric Handel.

To
Charles Jennens (Junior) Esqr
at
    Gopshall
      near Atherstone
        Leicestershire
(Schoelcher, p. 289.) Original in the possession of Lord Howe. Cf. 19th July.

—

Handel begins the oratorio *Belshazzar*, 23rd August 1744.

—

FROM THE " DAILY ADVERTISER ", 25th August 1744
CUPER'S GARDENS.

The Widow Evans . . . is resolv'd to entertain [the Town]. . . . Her Band of Musick (which is by the best Judges allow'd to be inferior to none) will perform . . . Mr. Handel's grand Chorusses out of several of his Oratorios. . . .

    Cf. 4th and 18th July 1741.

—

FROM THE " DAILY ADVERTISER ", 28th August 1744
For the Benefit of Mr. BLOGG.

At Lord Cobham's Head, Cold-Bath-Fields, Tomorrow, the 29th instant, will be perform'd a CONCERT of Vocal and Instrumental MUSICK. The Vocal Parts by Mr. Blogg, Mr. Jenkin Williams, and others ; particularly several favourite Songs out of Saul and Samson, by Mr. Blogg. . . . To conclude with the Coronation Anthem, set by Mr. Handel. After the Concert a Ball. . . .

(Chrysander, 1863, p. 395.) Nothing is known about the two singers. The Anthem was the chorus from *Zadok the Priest* : " God save the King ". See 12th September.

—

FROM A LONDON NEWSPAPER 12th September 1744

At the Green House at Windsor, this Day, a Grand Concert, to conclude with the Coronation Anthem of " God save the King ".

(Chrysander, 1863, p. 395.) Dr. Mann, in his manuscript notes, quotes this from the *Daily Advertiser*. It is not, however, to be found there, or in the *General Advertiser* or in the *Daily Post*. For the anthem see 28th August.

—

HANDEL TO JENNENS

Dear S^r

    Your most excellent Oratorio has given me great Delight in setting it to Musick and still engages me warmly. It is indeed a Noble Piece, very grand and uncommon ; it has furnished me with Expressions, and has given me Opportunity to some very particular Ideas, besides so many great Choru's. I intreat you heartily to favour me Soon with the last Act, which I expect with anxiety, that I may regulate my Self the better as to the Length of it. I profess my Self highly obliged to You, for so generous a Present, and desire You to believe me to be with great Esteem and Respect

Sr

Your

London   Most obliged and most humble

Sept^{br} 13.   Servant

1744   George Frideric Handel

To
Charles Jennens (Junior) Esqr
at Gopsal near Atherstone
        Leicestershire

(Schoelcher, p. 289.) Original in the possession of Lord Howe. Cf. 21st August.

—

HANDEL TO JENNENS

Dear S^r

    I received the 3^d Act, with a great deal of pleasure, as you can imagine, and you may believe that I think it a very fine and sublime Oratorio, only it is realy too long, if I should extend the Musick, it would last 4 Hours and more.

    I retrench'd already a great deal of the Musick, that I might preserve the Poetry as much as I could, yet still it may be shortned. The Anthems come in very proprely. but would not the Words (tell it out among the Heathen that the Lord is King) Sufficient for one Chorus ? The Anthem (I will magnify thee O God my King, and I will praise thy name for ever and ever, vers). the Lord preserveth all them that love him, but scattreth abroad all the ungodly. (vers and chorus) my mouth shall speak the Praise of the Lord and let all flesh give thanks unto His holy name for ever and ever Amen.) concludes well the Oratorio. I hope you will make a visit to London next Winter. I have a good Set of Singers. S. Francesina performs Nitocris, Miss Robinson Cyrus, Mrs. Cibber Daniel, Mr. Beard (who is recoverd) Belshazzar, Mr Reinhold Gobrias, and a good Number of Choir Singers for the Chorus's. I propose 24 Nights to perform this Season, on Saturdays, but in Lent on Wednesday's or Fryday's. I shall open on 3ᵈ of Novembʳ next with [?] Deborah. I wish You heartily the Continuation of Your health, and professing my [?] grateful acknowledgments for your generous favours, and am with great Esteem and Respect

Sr

London   Your
Octoᵇʳ 2   most obliged and most humble Servant
1744.   George Frideric Handel

To Charles Jennens Esqr.
Gopsall
Leicestershire.

(Schoelcher, p. 289.) Original in the possession of Lord Howe. The two words preceded by a question mark are not fully legible. Cf. 13th September. The first chorus, mentioned by Handel, is adapted from the Chandos Anthem " O come let us sing " ; the final chorus of *Belshazzar* is based on the Chandos Anthem " I will magnify thee ". The oratorio seems to have been finished before the middle of October.

—

FROM THE " DAILY ADVERTISER ", 20th October 1744

By particular Desire.

Mr. HANDEL proposes to perform by Subscription, Twenty-Four Times, during the Winter Season, at the King's Theatre in the Hay-Market, and engages to exhibit two new Performances, and several of his former Oratorios. The first Performance will be on Saturday the 3d of November, and continue every Saturday till Lent, and then on Wednesdays and Fridays. Each Subscriber is to pay Eight Guineas at the Time he subscribes, which entitles him to one Box Ticket for each Performance.

Subscriptions are taken in at Mr. Handel's House in Brooke-Street, near Hanover-Square ; at Mr. Walsh's, in Katherine-Street in the Strand ; and at White's Chocolate-House in St. James's Street.

Those Gentlemen and Ladies who have already favoured Mr. Handel in the Subscription, are desired to send for their Tickets at his House in

Brooke-Street, where Attendance will be given every Day (Sunday excepted) from Nine o'Clock in the Morning till Three in the Afternoon.

(Schoelcher, p. 291.) The same advertisement appeared in the *General Advertiser*, and was repeated on 3rd November. *Hercules* and *Belshazzar* were the two new oratorios. Of the 24 nights planned only 16 were given, the last being on 23rd April. Cf. 9th January 1744 and 17th January 1745.

——

Between October 1744 and Spring 1745, the Philharmonic Society in Dublin perform five Handel oratorios at their Music Room in Fishamble Street : *Acis and Galatea, Alexander's Feast, Athalia, Esther, Israel in Egypt.*

(Townsend, p. 116, based on Faulkner's *Dublin Journal.*) These performances were private.

——

From the Records of the Manchester Subscription Concerts, 1st November 1744–20th August 1745

[In the music collection :]
Handel's Overtures, compleat.

(Harland, pp. 66 f.) Cf. 22nd January 1745.

——

From the Records of the Manchester Subscription Concerts, 2nd November 1744

[Performed :]
Overture to *Otho.* . . .

(Harland, pp. 66 f.) Handel was prominent in these Manchester concerts. Up to 20th August 1745, 24 overtures, the *Water Music*, 4 organ concertos (nos. 3–6) and 1 grand concerto (no. 5) were performed there, some of them repeatedly.

——

From the " Daily Advertiser ", 3rd November 1744

By Subscription.
The first Night,
At the King's Theatre in the Hay-Market, This Day . . . will be perform'd an Oratorio, call'd Deborah. With a Concerto on the Organ. Pit and Boxes to be put together . . . tickets will be delivered . . . at the Opera-Office . . . at Half a Guinea each. The Gallery Five Shillings. The Gallery to be opened at Four o'Clock, Pit and Boxes at Five. To begin at Six o'Clock. . . .

(Schoelcher, p. 291.) The advertisement also appeared in the *General Advertiser*. Repeat performance on 24th November.

——

Handel deposits £500, 3rd November 1744.

—

FROM THE " DAILY ADVERTISER ", 5th November 1744

As the greatest Part of Mr. HANDEL's Subscribers are not in Town, he is requested not to perform till Saturday the 24th Instant ; but the Subscription is continued to be taken in at Mr. Handel's House in Brooke-Street, near Hanover-Square ; at Mr. Walsh's . . . ; and at White's Chocolate-House. . . .

(Schoelcher, p. 291.) The same notice appeared in the *General Advertiser*.

—

Handel deposits £100, 9th November 1744.

—

FROM THE MINUTES OF MERCER's HOSPITAL, DUBLIN,
10th November 1744

Agreed that the Cathedral Service for the benefit of the Sd. Hospital at the Conclusion Hilary Term. . . .

N.B., Mr. Handel's Grand Te Deum Composed on the Victory att Dettingen and performed before His Majesty upon his arrival, is intended to be performed at the same time.

The performance was on 14th February 1745 at St. Michan's Church. This church had previously refused to allow such services to be held for Mercer's Hospital. The organ, built in 1724, is said to have been played by Handel during his stay in Dublin, 1741-2. The *Utrecht Te Deum and Jubilate* was replaced, as at St. Paul's Cathedral, by the new Dettingen Te Deum. Handel's name does not appear again in the Minutes until 5th April 1749.

—

FROM THE RECORDS OF THE MANCHESTER SUBSCRIPTION CONCERTS,
13th November 1744

Overture to *Samson*. . . .
2nd Act. Overture to *Alcina*. . . .
3rd Act . . . Overture to *Saul*.
(Harland, pp. 66 f.)

—

FROM THE RECORDS OF THE MANCHESTER SUBSCRIPTION CONCERTS,
27th November 1744

Overture to *Rodelinda*. . . .
(Harland, pp. 66 f.)

—

FROM THE " DAILY ADVERTISER ", 1st December 1744

By SUBSCRIPTION.

The Third Night.

At the King's Theatre . . . this Day . . . will be perform'd SEMELE. After the Manner of an Oratorio, set to Musick by Mr. *Handel.* . . . To begin at Six o'Clock.

(Schoelcher, p. 292.) A copy of the new word-book, showing additions and alterations, and indicating a concerto on the organ, is in the Bibliothèque de l'Arsenal, Paris. It contains the words of five Italian arias, printed next to the original English ones, four of which have been identified as taken from *Alcina, Arminio* and *Giustino* (1734–6). The same advertisement appeared in the *General Advertiser*. Repeat performance on 8th December, attended by the Earl of Egmont (MSS., III. 304). Then followed an interval, till 5th January 1745.

———

Handel deposits £50, 11th December 1744.

———

FROM THE RECORDS OF THE MANCHESTER SUBSCRIPTION CONCERTS, 11th December 1744

Overture to *Acis and Galatea.* . . .
2nd Act. Overture to *Radamistus.* . . .
Handel's water music.

(Harland, pp. 66 f.)

———

Handel subscribes in 1744 for Thomas Chilcot's " Twelve English Songs with their Symphonies. The Words by Shakespeare, and other Celebrated Poets ", and for William Felton's " Six Concerto's for the Organ or Harpsichord with Instrumental Parts ", both published by John Johnson.

Chilcot was organist of the Abbey Church in Bath. In the same year Handel is said to have declined to subscribe for Felton's *Opera Seconda* also containing six organ concertos and published about 1745 by the same publisher. (Burney, *Account*, pp. 32 f. ; Chrysander, III. 165 f.) Burney's reference was Abraham Browne (cf. 9th February 1744).

———

FROM JAMES HARRIS'S " THREE TREATISES . . . THE SECOND CON-CERNING MUSIC, PAINTING, AND POETRY . . .", 1744

. . . Such [a great Professor of Music], above all, is *George Frederick Handel* ; whose Genius, having been cultivated by continued Exercise ; and being itself far the sublimest and most universal now known, has justly placed him with out an Equal, or a Second. This transient Testimony could not be denied so excellent an Artist, from whom this

Treatise has borrowed such eminent Examples, to justify its Assertions in what it has offer'd concerning Music.

P. 99. There are no musical quotations in the book, but there are allusions to *Deborah* and the Coronation Anthems on page 67. Music is treated in it as an imitation of nature. The book was revised for a second edition, published in 1765, and was reprinted in 1792 in vol. 5 of Harris's *Miscellanies*. Cf. 19th April 1737.

———

FROM FRANCESCO SAVERIO QUADRIO'S BOOK, " DELLA STORIA, E
DELLA RAGIONE D'OGNI POESIA ", MILANO, 1744

GIORGIO FEDERICO HENDEL, Inglese, fioriva circa il 1710, nel qual anno pose in musica l'AGRIPPINA d' Incerto.

(Chrysander, I. 190.) Vol. 3, part 2, p. 519. *Agrippina*, text by Vincenzo Grimani, was produced in Venice on 26th December 1709 (N.S.). Cf. 1730 : Bonlini's *Le Glorie della Poesia*.

1745

FROM THE " GENERAL ADVERTISER ", 5th January 1745

By SUBSCRIPTION.

The Fifth Night.

At the King's Theatre . . . this Day, will be perform'd HERCULES,
A new Musical Drama. Compos'd by Mr. *Handel.* . . . To begin at
Half an Hour after Six o'Clock.

The word-book was by the Rev. Thomas Broughton. It was printed for J. and
R. Tonson and S. Draper, and advertised on the same day. The advertisements
also appeared in the *Daily Advertiser.* Repeat performance on 12th January.
Like *Semele* (10th February 1744), *Hercules* was performed without action.
When it was revived on 24th February 1749, it was called an oratorio.

—

CAST OF " HERCULES ", 5th January 1745

Hercules—Mr. Reinhold, bass

Dejanira—Miss Robinson, contralto

Hyllus—Mr. Beard, tenor

Iöle (Iole)—Signora Francesina, soprano

Lichas—Mrs. Cibber, mezzo-soprano

Priest of Jupiter—?, bass

Miss Robinson (see pp. 591 and 596) was the daughter of John Robinson,
organist of Westminster Abbey, and the soprano singer Mrs. Ann Turner (who
died in 1741). It seems that Mrs. Cibber was indisposed on the first night, and
her part was taken by another singer ; cf. 9th January.

—

Handel deposits £50, 5th January 1745.

—

Walsh advertises that " Hercules, in Score, will speedily be publish'd by Subscription, at Half a Guinea ", *Daily Advertiser,* 8th
January 1745.

The score was published, without subscribers' list, at the beginning of
February.

—

FROM THE RECORDS OF THE MANCHESTER SUBSCRIPTION CONCERTS,
8th January 1745

Overture to *Atalanta* . . . 2nd Act. Overture to *Ariodante.* . . .
(Harland, pp. 66 f.)

—

FROM THE " DAILY ADVERTISER ", 9th January 1745

[At the end of an advertisement of *Hercules* to be performed
again on 12th January.]

Mrs. CIBBER *being perfectly recover'd of her late Indisposition, will certainly
perform on Saturday next, in* Hercules.

(Smith, 1948, p. 152.)   The Earl of Egmont attended the performance on 12th
January (MSS., III. 306).

—

FROM THE " DAILY ADVERTISER ", 17th January 1745

Sir.

Having for a Series of Years received the greatest Obligations from
the Nobility and Gentry of this Nation, I have always retained a deep
Impression of their Goodness.   As I perceived, that joining good Sense
and significant Words to Musick, was the best Method of recommending
this to an English Audience ; I have directed my Studies that way, and
endeavour'd to shew, that the English Language, which is so expressive
of the sublimest Sentiments is the best adapted of any to the full and
solemn Kind of Musick.   I have the Mortification now to find, that my
Labours to please are become ineffectual, when my Expences are considerably greater.   To what Cause I must impute the loss of the publick
Favour I am ignorant, but the Loss itself I shall always lament.   In the
mean time, I am assur'd that a Nation, whose Characteristick is Good
Nature, would be affected with the Ruin of any Man, which was owing
to his Endeavours to entertain them.   I am likewise persuaded, that I
shall have the Forgiveness of those noble Persons, who have honour'd
me with their Patronage, and their Subscription this Winter, if I beg
their Permission to stop short, before my Losses are too great to support,
if I proceed no farther in my Undertaking ; and if I intreat them to
withdraw three Fourths of their Subscription, one Fourth Part only of
my Proposal having been perform'd.

I am, sir,

Your very humble Servant,

G. F. Handel.

Attendance will be given at Mr. Handel's House in Brook's Street,
near Hanover-Square, from Nine in the Morning till Two in the Afternoon, on Monday, Tuesday, and Wednesday next, in Order to pay back
the Subscription Money, on returning the Subscription Ticket.

(Smith, 1948, pp. 152 f.)   Cf. 20th October 1744 and 25th January 1745.

—

A concert, for the benefit of the widow Farmborough, given at
the Swan Tavern in Exchange Alley, Cornhill, on 17th January

1745, concludes with the Coronation Anthem of *God save the King*. (*Daily Advertiser*, 15th January.)

(Chrysander, 1863, p. 395.) Cf. 12th September 1744.

——

FROM THE " DAILY ADVERTISER ", 18th January 1745

To the Author.

Sir,

    Upon Reading Mr. Handel's Letter in your Paper this Morning I was sensibly touch'd with that great Master's Misfortunes, failing in his Endeavours to entertain the Publick ; whose Neglect in not attending his admirable Performances can no otherwise be made up with Justice to the Character of the Nation, and the Merit of the Man, than by the Subscribers generously declining to withdraw the Remainder of their Subscriptions.

    I would lament the Loss of the Publick in Mr. Handel, in Strains equal to his if I was able, but our Concern will be best express'd by our Generosity.

We are, Sir,

Your obedient Servants,

Subscribers.

St. James's,

Jan. 17, 1744–5.

(Smith, 1948, p. 153.)

——

Handel withdraws £200, 19th January 1745.

——

FROM THE " DAILY ADVERTISER ", 21st January 1745

To Mr. Handel.

' Tu ne cede malis, sed contra audentior ito.' [Virgil, *Æneid*, Book 6, line 95.]

While you, Great Master of the Lyre ;

Our Breasts with various Passions fire ;

The Youth to Martial Glory move,

Now melt to Pity, now to Love ;

While distant Realms Thy Pow'r confess,

Thy happy Compositions bless,

And Musical Omnipotence

In adding solemn Sounds to Sense ;

How hard thy Fate ! that here alone,

Where we can call thy Notes our own ;

Ingratitude shou'd be thy Lot,

And all thy Harmony forgot !

Cou'd Malice, or Revenge take Place,

Thou'dst feel, alas ! the like Disgrace
Thy Father *Orpheus* felt in *Thrace*.
There, as dear *Ovid* does rehearse,
(And who shall question *Ovid's* Verse ?)
The Bard's enchanting Harp and Voice
Made all the Savage Herd rejoice,
Grow tame, forget their Lust and Prey,
And dance obsequious to his Lay.
[1] The *Thracian* Women 'tis wellknown,
Despis'd all Music, but their own ;
[2] But chiefly ONE, of envious Kind,
[3] With Skin of Tyger *capuchin'd*,
Was more implacable than all,
And strait resolv'd poor *Orpheus* Fall ;
Whene'er he play'd, she'd make [4] a *Drum*,
Invite her Neighbours all to come ;
At other Times, wou'd send about,
And dreg 'em to a Revel-*Rout* :
Then she : [5] Behold, that Head and Hand
Have brought to scorn the Thracian Band ;
Nor ever can our Band revive,
While that Head, Hand, or Finger live.
She said : [6] The wild and frantic Crew
In Rage the sweet Musician slew :
[7] The Strains, which charm'd the fiercest Beasts,
Cou'd move no Pity in their Breasts.

Here *Ovid*, to the Sex most civil,
Says, in their Cups they did this Evil,
When nightly met to sacrifice
To *Bacchus*, as his Votaries :
The Deed the God so much provokes,
He turn'd the Wretches into Oaks.

But HANDEL, lo ! a happier Fate
On thee, and on thy Lyre, shall wait;
The Nation shall redress thy Wrong
And joy to hear thy *Even Song* :

[1] Ecce Nurus Ciconum.—
[2] E quibus una, levern jactato crine per auram.—
[3] —Tectae lymphata ferinis
  Pectora velleribus.—
[4] Tympanaque plaususque, et Bacchei ululatus
  Obstrepuere sono Citharae.—
[5] En, ait, en, hic est nostri Contemptor.—
[6] —Tum denique Saxa
  Non exauditi rubuerunt sanguine Vatis.—
[7] —Nec quicquam voce moventem
  Sacrilegae perimunt.—

The Royal Pair shall deign to smile ;
The Beauties of the British Isle,
The noble Youth, whom Virtue fires,
And Martial Harmony inspires,
Shall meet in crouded Audiences :
Thy Foes shall blush ; and HERCULES
Avenge this National Disgrace,
And vanquish ev'ry Fiend of *Thrace*.

Ov. Met. l. ii. [or rather, Book xi.]

(Smith, 1948, pp. 153-5.) The middle section of this poem refers to "female machinations", as H. C. Colles pointed out in *The Times* of 18th July 1936, after Wm. C. Smith had reprinted it in the *Musical Times* of that month. Apparently this section was aimed at Lady Brown, first mentioned as Handel's opponent by Burney (IV. 671) although Mainwaring (pp. 134 f.) had probably already implied it, without mentioning any name. She is, however, mentioned by Horace Walpole in his letter of 13th February 1743 to Horace Mann (1891 edition, I. 229) as being the wife of Sir Robert Brown, formerly merchant in Venice and British resident there, created Baronet in 1732, and till 1743 Paymaster of His Majesty's Works. She was Margaret Cecil, grand-daughter of the third Earl of Salisbury. Her private concerts were held on Sunday nights (not on the nights of Handel's oratorios, as Flower, p. 306, states), and such violation of the Sabbath was not without danger. These concerts, dedicated to "foreign musicians in general, of the new Italian style" (Burney), were under the direction of the mysterious "Count St. Germain" who lived in London about 1745 (cf. Johan Franco, in *The Musical Quarterly*, New York, October 1950). Burney, the witness for Lady Brown, settled in London in 1745, staying there till 1750 (Burney, IV. 666 f.; Chrysander, III. 217). He also testifies that Handel's rehearsals were held not only at his house, but sometimes also at Carlton House, the Prince of Wales's.

———

FROM THE "DAILY ADVERTISER", 21st January 1745

After reading Mr. Handel's Letter to the
Public in this Paper on Thursday last

An Epigram.
Romans, to shew they Genius's wou'd prize,
Gave rich Support ; and dead, did Bustos rise :
But wiser we, the kindred Arts to serve.
First carve the Busts ¹ ; then bid the Charmers starve.

(Smith, 1948, p. 156.)   "Bustos" for busts.

———

FROM THE RECORDS OF THE MANCHESTER SUBSCRIPTION CONCERTS,
21st January 1745

[Acquired for the music collection :]
48 Overtures of Handel, £2. 7s.

¹ Mr. Handel's elegant Marble Statue in Vaux-Hall Gardens.

[Performed in a concert on that day :]
. . . 2nd Act. Overture to *Ariadne*. . . .

(Harland, pp. 66 f.) For the first item cf. 1st November 1744 ; the 48 overtures were apparently Walsh's edition in parts.

FROM THE " DAILY ADVERTISER ", 25th January 1745

Sir,

The new Proofs which I have receiv'd of the Generosity of my Subscribers, in refusing upon their own Motives, to withdraw their Subscriptions call upon me for the earliest Return, and the warmest Expressions of my Gratitude ; but natural as it is to feel, proper as it is to have, I find this extremely difficult to express. Indeed, I ought not to content myself with bare expressions of it ; therefore, though I am not able to fulfil the whole of my Engagement, I shall think it my Duty to perform what Part of it I can, and shall in some Time proceed with the Oratorios, let the *Risque* which I may run be what it will.

I am, Sir,
Your very humble Servant,
G. F. Handel.

(Smith, 1948, p. 156.)

Handel deposits £150, 1st February 1745.

FROM THE RECORDS OF THE MANCHESTER SUBSCRIPTION CONCERTS, 5th February 1745

Overture to *Lothario* . . . 2nd Act. Overture to *Mutius Scaevola*. . . . (Harland, pp. 66 f.)

FROM THE " DAILY ADVERTISER ", 11th February 1745

By SUBSCRIPTION.
The seventh Night.

At the King's Theatre . . . on Saturday next, the 16th instant, will be perform'd a new Musical Drama, call'd HERCULES, Compos'd by Mr. *Handel*. . . .

This third performance was postponed till 1st March, perhaps owing to Mrs. Cibber's indisposition, but the oratorio was never performed again at the Haymarket Theatre ; it was revived in February-March 1749 and in February 1752 at Covent Garden. On 9th February 1745 a pasticcio opera, *L'Incostanza delusa*, was produced at the New Theatre in the Haymarket, now under the musical direction of Geminiani. The word-book was by Vanneschi, and some of the arias were by St. Germain (see 21st January). Pasquali was the leader of the orchestra, and the first singers were Signore Frasi and Galli. The opera, repeated on 16th February, was performed ten times, the last time being on 20th April. Burney (IV. 452) dates the first night, wrongly, as of 7th April ; he was also mistaken in saying that Prince Lobkowitz (the father of Beethoven's protector, cf. 7th January 1746) attended the rehearsals of that opera with St. Germain : he did not arrive in London until autumn 1745.

———

FROM THE " GENERAL ADVERTISER ", 11th February 1745

NEW MUSICK.

This Day is publish'd, Price 10s. 6d.

HERCULES in Score. Compos'd by *Mr. Handel.*

Printed for J. Walsh. . . .

Cf. 8th January.

———

FROM FAULKNER'S " DUBLIN JOURNAL ", 16th February 1745

Last Thursday [the 14th] Mr. Handel's New Te-Deum on the Victory at Dettingen, his Jubilate and two Anthems, were perform'd at St. Michan's Church, for the Support of Mercer's Hospital ; some Persons of Quality, and many Gentlemen, obliged the Governors with their Assistance in the Performance. . . . The whole Performance was conducted with the greatest Decency and Solemnity, and Five hundred Persons of the first Quality and Distinction were present thereat. . . .

Cf. 10th November 1744. It seems that the *Dettingen Te Deum* was supplemented by the *Utrecht Jubilate,* familiar in Dublin.

———

FROM THE RECORDS OF THE MANCHESTER SUBSCRIPTION CONCERTS, 19th February 1745

Overture to *Scipio* . . . 2nd Act. Overture to *Tamerlane.* . . .

Harland, pp. 66 f.

———

A concert for the benefit of the trumpeter Valentine Snow, given at the New Theatre in the Haymarket, concludes " with the Coronation Anthem, GOD SAVE THE KING ", 20th February 1745.

(Chrysander, 1863, p. 395.) Cf. 17th January.

———

FROM THE " DAILY ADVERTISER ", 1st March 1745

By SUBSCRIPTION.

The Seventh Night.

At the King's Theatre . . . this Day, will be perform'd an Oratorio, call'd SAMSON. . . . To begin at Half an Hour after Six o'Clock.

Proper Care will be taken to keep the House warm.

This was the first performance since 12th January, and the first since Handel's resolution to continue the series of oratorios. Repeat performance on 8th March, when the Earl of Egmont was present (MSS., III. 309).

———

FROM THE " DAILY ADVERTISER ", 4th March 1745

To Mr. Handel.

Sir,

It was with infinite Pleasure I read the Advertisement of your Intention to perform the Oratorio of Samson, and waited with Impatience till the Day came ; but how great was my Disappointment to see the most delightful Songs in the whole Oratorio took from one, who, by her Manner of singing them charm'd all the Hearers ; Was she once instated in the Part she always used to perform, your Samson would shine with the greatest Lustre, and be justly admir'd by all.

I am, Sir,

Your Friend and Well-Wisher,

A. Z.

(Smith, 1948, p. 157.) Cf. 25th February 1744. Smith suggests that the writer referred to Mrs. Cibber who was replaced by Signora Francesina, but was now back in Handel's company.

———

FROM THE " DAILY ADVERTISER ", 13th March 1745

By SUBSCRIPTION

The ninth Night.

At the King's Theatre . . . this Day, will be perform'd an *Oratorio*, call'd SAUL. . . . To begin at Half an Hour after Six o'Clock.

There was one performance only.

———

FROM THE " DAILY GAZETTEER ", 13th March 1745

After hearing (last Spring) Mr. HANDEL'S
Oratorio of SAUL.

The Doctrine taught Us by the SAMIAN [1] Sage,
That Spirits transmigrate from Age to Age ;
Successively thro' various Bodies glide,
(The Soul the same, the Frame diversify'd ;)
At last, tho' long exploded, Credit gains ;
For lo ! convinc'd by sweetly-magic Strains,
With Extasy th' Opinion We allow,
Since,—Proof that *Orpheus* was, is *Handel* now.

[1] *Pythagoras.*

Too faint's the Hint ; the Muse her Voice must raise,
And, from a nobler Source, our Lyrist praise.
Ye purer Minds, who glow with sacred Fire ;
Who, to th' eternal Throne, in Thought aspire ;
For Dissolution pant, and think each Day
An Age, till You th' Aetherial Climes survey ;
Who long to hear the Cherubs mingled Voice
Exult in Hymns, and bid the Stars rejoyce ;
Bid universal Nature raise the Theme
To Boundless Goodness, Majesty supreme :
O listen to the Warblings of his Shell,
Whose wondrous Power can fiercest Grief dispell !
O to his Sounds be due Attention given
Sweet Antepast of Harmony in Heaven !

(Chrysander, III. 57 f.) *Saul* was performed on 16th and 21st March 1744, and revived once on 13th March 1745.

———

FROM THE " DAILY ADVERTISER ", 15th March 1745

By SUBSCRIPTION.

The tenth Night.

At the King's Theatre . . . this Day, will be perform'd an *Oratorio*, call'd JOSEPH. . . . To begin at Half an Hour after Six o'Clock.

Repeat performance on 22nd March. On 20th March, Defesch's oratorio " Joseph " was produced (with cheap prices) at Covent Garden, with a repeat performance on 3rd April. Nicoll listed the two Covent Garden performances of 1745 under Handel's " Joseph ". (Hogarth's satirical engraving of oratorio singers, sometimes called " Handel's Chorus ", refers to Defesch's oratorio " Judith ".)

———

FROM THE " DAILY ADVERTISER ", 20th March 1745

For the benefit of Mrs. ARNE.

At the Theatre Royal in Drury-Lane, this Day . . . will be perform'd an Historical Musical Drama, call'd ALFRED *the Great, King of* ENGLAND. . . . The Musick by Mr. *Arne*. . . . This Day is fix'd on to avoid interfering with Mr. Handel.

(Smith, 1948, p. 157.) The same courtesy was observed for the repeat performance on 3rd April. *Alfred*, the masque by Thomson and Mallet, with Arne's music (including " Rule Britannia ") was first performed privately, for the Prince of Wales at Cliveden House, in 1740. The first advertisement of 1745 called it " The Distress of King Alfred the Great, with his Conquest over the Danes " (2nd March). Mr. and Mrs. Arne returned to Drury Lane from Dublin in 1744.

———

H.–20

FROM THE " GENERAL ADVERTISER ", 26th March 1745

This Day is published, Price 1s.

BELSHAZZAR, an Oratorio. As it is to be perform'd on Wednesday next [the 27th] at the King's Theatre in the Haymarket. The Musick by Mr. *Handel.*

—*Grave & immutabile Sanctis*
Pondus adest Verbis, & Vocem Fata sequuntur.
                                        Stat. Theb. Lib. I.
Printed by and for J. Watts, and sold by him . . . and B. Dod. . . .
The device quoted is from the title-page of the word-book.

———

FROM THE " DAILY ADVERTISER ", 27th March 1745

By SUBSCRIPTION.
The twelfth Night.
At the King's Theatre . . . this Day, will be perform'd a new Oratorio, call'd BELSHAZZAR. . . . To begin at Half an Hour after Six o'Clock.

(Schoelcher, p. 290.) The book was by Jennens. In the *General Advertiser* the oratorio was called " BELTESHAZZAR ", probably a misprint. Repeat performances on 29th March and 23rd April. Revived in February 1751.

———

CAST OF " BELSHAZZAR ", 27th March 1745
Belshazzar—Mr. Beard, tenor
Nitocris—Signora Francesina, soprano
Cyrus—Miss Robinson, contralto
Daniel—(?) Miss Robinson, contralto
Gobrias—Mr. Reinhold, bass
Arioch—?, tenor
Messenger—?, bass
The part of Daniel was to have been sung by Mrs. Cibber (see 2nd October 1744), but it seems that, in fact, she did not create it.

———

MRS. ELIZABETH CARTER TO MISS CATHERINE TALBOT

London, 2 March [or rather, April] 1745
Handel, once so crowded, plays to empty walls in that opera house, where there used to be a constant *audience* as long as there were any dancers to be *seen*. Unfashionable that I am, I was I own highly delighted the other night at his last oratorio. 'Tis called Belshazzar, the story the taking of Babylon by Cyrus ; and the music, in spite of all that very bad performers could do to spoil it, equal to any thing I ever heard. There is a chorus of Babylonians deriding Cyrus from their walls that has the best expression of scornful laughter imaginable. Another of the

Jews, where the name, Jehovah, is introduced first with a moment's silence, and then with a full swell of music so solemn, that I think it is the most striking lesson against common genteel swearing I ever met with.

(Carter, *Letters*, I. 89 f.) The date given there is a mistake on the part of the writer, or the editor. The letter refers to one of the two performances in March 1745.

FROM THE "DAILY ADVERTISER", 9th April 1745

By SUBSCRIPTION.

The fourteenth Night.

At the King's Theatre . . . this Day, will be perform'd A SACRED ORATORIO. With a *Concert* on the *Organ*. . . . To begin at Half an Hour after Six o'Clock.

In earlier advertisements *Messiah* is called "THE SACRED ORATORIO" (*Daily Advertiser*, 6th April) and "the SACRED ORATORIO" (*General Advertiser*, 8th April). Repeat performance on 11th April.

FROM THE "DAILY ADVERTISER", 10th April 1745

For the Benefit and Increase of a Fund establish'd for the Support of decay'd MUSICIANS *or their Families.*

At the Theatre Royal in Covent-Garden, this Day, will be perform'd an *Entertainment* of Vocal and Instrumental *Musick*, as follows.

FIRST PART.

The Overture of Samson.

Total Eclipse, in the Oratorio of Samson, by Mr. Beard.

. . . . .

Return, O God of Hosts, in Samson, by Miss Robinson.

Myself I shall adore, in Semele, by Signora Francesina.

Del Minacciar del Vento, in Otho, by Mr. Reinhold.

SECOND PART.

. . . . .

O ruddier than the Cherry, in Acis and Galatea, by Mr. Reinhold.

O Sleep, in Semele, by Signora Francesina.

. . . . .

. . . . .

THIRD PART.

. . . . .

Why does the God of Israel sleep, in Samson, by Mr. Beard.

. . . . .

Trio in Acis and Galatea, by Signora Francesina, Miss Robinson, and
Mr. Reinhold.
Mr. Handel's Grand Sonata.

.   .   .   .   .

To begin exactly at Six o'Clock.
The trio is " The flocks shall leave the mountains ".

—

FROM THE RECORDS OF THE MANCHESTER SUBSCRIPTION CONCERTS,
16th April 1745

Overture to *Flavius* . . . third organ concerto of Handel . . . 2nd
Act. Overture to *Richard the First.* . . .
(Harland, pp. 66 f.)

—

Handel's oratorio series, originally planned for twenty-four nights,
ends on 23rd April 1745, the sixteenth night, with the third
performance of *Belshazzar* (*Daily Advertiser*).
Cf. 20th October 1744.

—

FROM THE " DAILY ADVERTISER ", 29th April 1745
For the Benefit of Miss Robinson.
At the King's Theatre in the Hay-Market, this Day . . . will be
perform'd an Entertainment of Vocal and Instrumental Musick, as follows.

FIRST PART.
The Overture in Pharamond.

.   .   .   .   .

Del Minacciar del Vento, in the Opera of Otho, by Mr. Reinhold.

.   .   .   .   .

Mi Lucina, in Alcina, by Miss Robinson.

SECOND PART.
The Overture in Alcina.

.   .   .   .   .

Honour and Arms, in the Oratorio of Samson, by Mr. Reinhold.

.   .   .   .   .

A Concerto Grosso.

THIRD PART.
The new Overture of Pastor Fido.
Si l'Intendesti, in Pharamond, by Mr. Beard.

.   .   .   .   .

Trio in Acis and Galatea, by Miss Robinson, Mr. Beard ; and Mr. Reinhold.

. . . . .

To begin at half an Hour after Six.

Cf. 10th April. This concert was originally planned for 24th April. In addition to the three singers from Handel's oratorio company, who performed on 10th April, Signora Frasi, from the opera at the New Theatre in the Haymarket, appeared this time, but sang nothing by Handel. The aria from *Alcina* begins, in fact, " Mi lusinghe i dolce ". The " Concerto Grosso " was probably by Handel. The " new " overture of *Pastor Fido* was that of the 1734 version. Several arias were sung from Lampugnani's *Alceste*, produced at the Haymarket Theatre on 28th April 1744 (Burney, IV. 451).

———

Walsh announces that the " celebrated Oratorio, call'd BEL-SHAZZER will be published in a short Time ", *General Advertiser*, 29th April 1745.
Cf. 18th May.

———

FROM THE RECORDS OF THE MANCHESTER SUBSCRIPTION CONCERTS, 30th April 1745

Overture to *Esther* . . . fourth organ concerto of Handel . . . 2nd Act. Overture to *Atalanta*. . . .

(Harland, pp. 66 f.) Cf. 8th January.

———

FROM THE " DAILY GAZETTEER ", 2nd May 1745
This Day is Published,
(Price Sixpence)
AN ODE, to Mr. HANDEL.

. . . . .

Printed for R. Dodsley, at Tully's Head, in Pall-Mall ; and sold by M. Cooper, at the Globe in Pater-noster Row.

The same advertisement appeared in the *General Advertiser*. Only two copies of the Ode are known to exist : one in the Bodleian Library, Oxford, the other in the University of Texas, Austin (Texas). Photostat copies in Gerald Coke's Handel Collection, and in the Sterling Memorial Library, Yale University, New Haven (Connecticut). The pamphlet consists of half-title, title with ornamental device (Tully's Head), " Advertisement " (argument) on pp. (5) and (6), and the poem on pp. 7-16, octavo. (The numbering between lines 120 and 140 is incorrect.) In his Advertisement, the anonymous author claimed that the metre of this Ode has never been used since Milton. It was tempting to consider William Collins as the author, but the late E. H. W. Meyerstein, after very careful research, suggested that the Ode might have been written by Thomas (born 1728) or, more probably, by his brother Joseph Warton (born 1722). Cf. Joseph Warton's *Odes on Various Subjects*, published, as was his anonymous *The*

Enthusiast, by Dodsley in 1746 ; Ode XI, " To a Lady who hates the Country ", refers to Handel and Monticelli. Cf. also Joseph Warton's Essay on Pope, of 1756.

AN ODE, TO MR. HANDEL, LONDON, 1745

Τω γαρ οντι το πρωτον αυτης και καλλις-ον εργον ἡ εις τους Θεους ευχαρις-ος ες-ιν αμοιβη, επομενον δε τουτω και δευτερον το της ψυχης καθαρσιον και εμμελες, και εναρμονιον συς-ημα. PLUT. περι Μουσικης.

> O decus Phœbi & dapibus supremi
> Grata testudo Jovis : o laborum
> Dulce lenimen !   HOR.

Printed for R. DODSLEY at Tully's Head in Pall-mall.

While you, great Author of the sacred song,
With sounds seraphic join the seraph host,
    Who, wond'ring with delight,
    Hear numbers like their own,

And hail the kindred lay ; forgive the Muse,   5
That in unhallow'd, humble measure strives
    With them to praise, with them
    Too impotent to sing :

Yet her's the task to form the myrtle wreath,
And twine the vernal treasures of the grove,   10
    Whose mingling honours crown
    The fav'rites of the Nine.

For thee, most favour'd of the sacred train,
The choicest flow'rs shall breathe, for thee the bloom
    Whose beauty longest boasts   15
    The freshness of the spring :

Whether by thee the rural reed inspir'd,
And wak'd to blythe simplicity, beguiles
    The labour'd shepherd's toil,
    In soft Sicilian strain,   20

Sweet'ning the stillness of the grove, whose shades
Fond fancy paints enlivened by the lay ;
    Or whether taught the flow
    Of some smooth-gliding stream,

The melting flute in liquid warbles sooths,   25
And feigns to bubble, tuneful to the tale
    Of ACIS, injur'd boy,
    Chang'd to a murm'ring rill :

Or, kindling courage in the glowing breast,
The voice of Battle breathes the big alarm,　　　　30
　　The Trumpet's clangor fills,
　　And thunders in the Drum.

Or mid' the magic of successive sounds,
That rule alternate passions as they rise,
　　Again TIMOTHEUS lives,　　　　35
　　Again the victor yields

To sacred Melody : while those sweet gales
That breathe fresh odours o'er Elysian glades,
　　And amaranthine bow'rs
　　(Where now the golden harps　　　　40

Of blissful bards are strung) the numbers waft
To DRYDEN's laurel'd shade ; he yet more blest,
　　Smiles, conscious of the charms
　　Of heav'n-born Harmony,

That prove the pow'r he sings, and grace the song :　　45
Nigh whom, supreme amidst the tuneful train,
　　In lovely greatness shines
　　The Bard, who fearless sprung

Beyond the golden sphere that girts the world,
And sung embattled Angels : He too hears　　　　50
　　Enchanting accents, him
　　Delights the lovely lay,

Responsive to his own ; in pensive thought
Now lowly languid to the lulling lute,
　　That suits the Cypress Queen　　　　55
　　And makes deep sadness sweet ;

Or to the plaintive warbles of the wood,
Whose wanton measure, in the gentle flow
　　Of soft'ned notes, returns
　　Wild echoes to the strain.　　　　60

But hark ! the Dryad MIRTH with cheering horn
Invites her mountain-sister to the chace,
　　The jocund rebecks join
　　The merriment of MAY

Ver. 53. See *Il Penseroso* set to Music by Mr. *Handel.*
Ver. 57. Alluding to the Song, *Sweet Bird, &c.*
Ver. 61. See *L'Allegro.*

That to the tabor trips, and treads the round   65
Of rustic measures to the sprightly pipe,
    Mingled with merry peals
    That fill the festal joy.

But O ! great master of ten thousand sounds,
That rend the concave in exulting song,   70
    And round *anointed* Kings
    In shouting Pæans roll :

Master of high Hosannahs, that proclaim
In pomp of Martial Praise the GOD of HOSTS,
    Who treads to dust the foe,   75
    And conquers with the sling :

O ! taught the deep solemnity of grief,
That swells the sullen slowness of the trump,
    And gives the gentler woe
    Of soothing flutes to join   80

In sweet response the thunder of the field :
What breath divine first blending with thy soul,
    Infus'd this sacred force
    Of magic Melody,

Nor here confin'd ? for higher yet the strain,   85
That suits thy Lay, mellifluous AMBROSE, rais'd
    To mighty shouts return'd
    By hymning Hierarchies,

Who sound *thrice Holy !* round the saphire throne
In solemn jubily ; the strain that fills   90
    With force of pleasing dread
    The seraphs awful blast,

'Till fervent Faith and smiling Hope behold
The dawn of endless day : or speaks the GOD
    Whose Vengeance widely spreads   95
    The Darkness palpable,

Ver. 73. See the Epinicion in *Saul.*
Ver. 77. Alluding to the *Dead March* in *Saul.*
Ver. 86. St. *Ambrose*, stiled *Doctor Mellifluus.*
Ver. 92. Alluding to the symphony of the words *We believe that thou shalt come to be our Judge*, in the new *Te Deum.*

And kindles half the storm, with thunder hail,
Hail mixt with Fire ; divides the deep Abyss,
    And to the vast profound
    The horse and rider hurls ;   100

Tremendous theme of song ! the theme of love
And melting mercy HE, when sung to strains,
    Which from prophetic lips
    Touch'd with ethereal fire,

Breath'd balmy Peace, yet breathing in the charm   105
Of healing sounds ; fit prelude to the pomp
    Of choral energy,
    Whose lofty accents rise

To speak MESSIAH's names ; the God of Might,
The Wond'rous and the Wise—the Prince of Peace.   110
    Him, feeder of the flock
    And leader of the lambs,

The tuneful tenderness of trilling notes
Symphonious speaks : Him pious pity paints
    In mournful melody   115
    The man of sorrows ; grief

Sits heavy on his soul, and bitterness
Fills deep his deadly draught—He deigns to die—
    The God who conquers Death,
    When, bursting from the Grave,   120

Mighty he mounts, and wing'd with rapid winds,
Thro' Heav'ns wide portals opening to their Lord,   125
    To boundless realms return'd,
    The King of Glory reigns.

Pow'rs, dominations, thrones resound HE REIGNS,   130
High Hallelujah's of empyreal hosts,
    And pealing Praises join
    The thunder of the spheres.

But whither Fancy wafts thy wanton wing,
That trembles in the flight ? oh ! whither stretch'd
    Pursues the lofty lay,   135 .
    Worthy the Master's name,

Ver. 100. See the Oratorio of Israel in Egypt.
Ver. 102, to v. 114. See the sacred Oratorio of Messiah, Part I.
Ver. 106 to v. 120. See Messiah. Part II.

H.–20 a

Whose Music yet in airy murmurs plays
And vibrates on the ear ?—Preserve, ye gales,
　　Wrapt in the sweet'ned breeze,
　　Each dying note : Ye winds,   140

Be hush'd, while yet the sacred numbers live.
But hence ! with ideot leer, thou dim-ey'd form
　　Of Folly, taught to list
　　In shew of senseless glee

To empty trills, enervate languishment   145
And mimic'ry of sounds : hence ! blast of Hell,
　　That lov'st, with venom'd breath,
　　To taint the ripening bloom

That merit boasts ; thee, Envy, black Despair,
Thee kindred fiends to native realms recall,   150
　　There dart the livid glance,
　　And howling bite the chain.

——

Handel pays, from his accounts, £210 to [Miss] Robinson, 4th
May 1745.

This was the first time that one of Handel's singers was paid through the
Bank of England. Cf. 11th May.

——

Handel deposits £100, 9th May 1745.

——

FROM THE " DAILY ADVERTISER ", 10th May 1745

For the benefit of Miss Davis. A Child of eight Years of Age, lately
arriv'd from Ireland. At Mr. Hickford's Room in Brewer-Street, this
Day, the 10th instant, will be perform'd a Concert of Vocal and Instru-
mental Musick. Several favourite Organ Concertos and Overtures of
Mr. Handel's . . . with two remarkable Songs, Composed by Mr.
Handel, entirely for the Harpsichord, accompanied by Miss Davis, with
some select Songs to be perform'd by Mrs. Davis a Scholar of Bonon-
cini's. . . . Note, Miss Davis is to perform on a Harpsichord of Mr.
Rutgerus Plenius's making, Inventor of the new deserv'd famous
Lyrichord.

(Smith, 1948, p. 159.) For Miss Davis, see 13th November 1742 ; for Mrs.
Davis, 2nd May and 10th June 1732. Roger Plenius invented the Lyrichord,
patented in London in 1741 ; according to A. J. Hipkins in Grove's *Dictionary*

(first edition, III. 639), it was a "harpsichord strung with wire and catgut . . . actuated by moving wheels . . . the bow of the violin and organ . . . imitated".

———

Handel pays £400, from his accounts, to [Signora] Francesina, 11th May 1745.

Cf. 4th May.

———

Handel pays the balance of £140, from his accounts, to [Mr ?] Jordan, 13th May 1745.

This payment seems to refer to Abraham Jordan, the younger, the organ builder. Cf. 1st August.

———

FROM THE RECORDS OF THE MANCHESTER SUBSCRIPTION CONCERTS,
14th May 1745

Overture to *Alexander* . . . 2nd Act. First overture to *Admetus* . . . Handel's water music.

(Harland, pp. 66 f.) *Admeto* has a second overture for Act II.

———

Walsh advertises the score of *Belshazzar* for 10s. 6d., *General Evening Post*, 18th May 1745.

The advertisement appeared in the *General Advertiser* on 20th May.

———

HORACE WALPOLE TO GEORGE MONTAGUE

Arlington Street, May 25, 1745.
The Master of the House [Horace's brother, Edward Walpole, of Englefield Green] plays extremely well on the bass-viol, and has generally other musical people with him . . . he is perfectly master of all the quarrels that have been fashionably on foot about Handel.

(Walpole, *Letters*, 1891 edition, I. 363.)

———

FROM THE RECORDS OF THE MANCHESTER SUBSCRIPTION CONCERTS,
28th May 1745

Overture to *Parthenope* . . . fifth organ concerto, Handel . . . 2nd Act. Overture to *Julius Caesar*. . . .

(Harland, pp. 66 f.)

———

FROM THE SAME RECORDS, 25th June 1745

Overture to *Rodelinda* . . . sixth organ concerto, Handel . . . 2nd
Act. Overture to *Otho*. . . .

(Harland, pp. 66 f.) Cf. 2nd and 27th November 1744.

———

FROM SCHEIBE'S " CRITISCHER MUSIKUS ", SECOND EDITION,
LEIPZIG, 1745 (Translated)

. . . Bach, [Heinrich] Bokemeyer, Fux, [Johann Gottlieb] Graun,
[Karl Heinrich] Graun, [Christoph] Graupner, Hasse, Händel, [David]
Heinichen, Kayser [or rather, Keiser], [Balthasar] Schmidt, [Gottfried
Heinrich] Stölzel, Telemann. . . . All these names were recorded in the
Book [of Eternity] with golden letters.

. . . *Joh. Kuhnau, Reinhard Kaiser, Telemann*, and *Händel* especially, are
those men with whom our Fatherland can set foreigners at defiance. . . .

Kuhnau was above all a powerful composer of music for the Church,
and for keyboard. . . . *Kaiser's* movements are elegant, amorous and
show all the passions whose might has subjugated most completely the
human heart. . . . And yet, great as they were, they must yield to a
Telemann and a *Händel*. These two great men themselves take over,
therefore, what the other two had in part begun, but had not entirely
accomplished. And we can say of each of them that the characteristics
of a *Kuhnau*, and of a *Kaiser*, have been united in him. *Händel*, although
many times developing not his own thoughts but those of others,
especially the inventions of *Reinhard Kaiser*, has manifested all the time
a great understanding and a powerful deliberation, and assuredly has
shown in all his pieces how refined and delicate his taste in the arts must be.

. . . One may put all this forward in contrasting the characteristic
qualities of a *Telemann*, and of a *Händel* [with those of Kuhnau and
Keiser]. Who will not be obliged to concede to me that there is in the
works of both these famous men a far more refined and purified taste, and
that therefore they indeed deserve to be greatly preferred above those
other two ?

Händel seems . . . to possess a greater grace [than Telemann]. Italy
has long since admired his Italian vocal pieces and operas, and his
harpsichord pieces are incomparable, and to the connoisseur of the
harpsichord almost indispensable. Finally, we know what attention this
admirable artist has won for himself from a wise and profound nation,
even as *Telemann* has become the admiration of France.

Pp. 147 f., 340, 762-4, 765 f. The addition to the 1739 edition of Scheibe's
collected papers is not dated ; but the preface is dated 17th April 1745. Cf. 23rd
June and 17th September 1739. While Mattheson charged Handel with borrowing
from his own works (cf. July 1722, and autumn 1740), Scheibe suggests that

Handel plagiarized Keiser. (Mattheson is quoted from the *Ehrenpforte*, 1740, only, and Scheibe, first mentioned in Burney's sketch of 1785, p. 55, in Percy Robinson's book of 1908, p. 69.)

———

FROM THE RECORDS OF THE MANCHESTER SUBSCRIPTION CONCERTS,
9th July 1745

Overture to *Tamerlano* . . . water music.

(Harland, pp. 66 f.) Cf. 11th December 1744 and 19th February 1745.

———

Walsh advertises " A Grand Collection of English Songs " by Handel, for 5s., *Daily Advertiser*, 13th July 1745.
    On 8th August he added " from the late Oratorios ". (Smith, 1948, p. 159.)

———

During George II's absence in Hanover, Charles Stuart, the Young Pretender, lands in Scotland, mid July 1745.

———

FROM THE RECORDS OF THE MANCHESTER SUBSCRIPTION CONCERTS,
23rd July 1745

First overture to *Admetus* . . . 2nd Act. Fifth grand concerto, Handel. . . .

(Harland, pp. 66 f.) Cf. 14th May.

———

FROM THE " DAILY ADVERTISER ", 1st August 1745

To be Sold a Pennyworth, At the Opera-House, Two Second-hand Chamber Organs. Enquire of Mr. Jordan in Budge-Row, near London-Stone.

(Smith, 1948, p. 159.) " Pennyworth " means at bargain price ; perhaps, at any price. The entry of a payment to Jordan in Handel's bank account on 13th May makes it probable that these two organs belonged to him, and may have been forfeited through failure to make the full payment due to Jordan.

———

FROM THE RECORDS OF THE MANCHESTER SUBSCRIPTION CONCERTS,
20th August 1745

1st Act. Overture to *Esther* . . . fifth organ concerto, Handel . . .
2nd Act. Overture to ye sacred oratorio . . . overture to *Deidamia*.

(Harland, pp. 66 f.) Cf. 30th April and 28th May. In his edition of the overture, Walsh called *Messiah* the " sacred oratorio ".

———

THE REV. WILLIAM HARRIS TO HIS SISTER-IN-LAW, MRS. (?) THOMAS
HARRIS, AT SALISBURY

Grosvenor Square, August 29, 1745.
I met Handel a few days since in the street, and stopped and put him in
mind who I was, upon which I am sure it would have diverted you to
have seen his antic motions. He seemed highly pleased, and was full of
inquiry after you and the Councillor. I told him I was very confident
that you expected a visit from him this summer. He talked much of his
precarious state of health, yet he looks well enough. I believe you will
have him with you ere long.

(Streatfeild, 1909, p. 188.) Malmesbury, *Letters*, I. 3. William Harris was
chaplain and secretary to the Bishop of Salisbury, who lived in Grosvenor Square.
Thomas, another brother of Handel's friend James Harris, was a Master in
Chancery. The letter seems to have been written to Thomas's wife, not to
Elizabeth Harris, James's wife. It was to Thomas Harris, and about this time, that
Handel gave his portrait painted by Balthasar Denner in 1736. (In 1748 John
Faber's mezzotint portrait of Handel was published.) Handel may have visited
the Harris family at Salisbury repeatedly. That he went to Tunbridge Wells in
1746, or 1747, as stated in Henry Elwig's *Biographical Dictionary of Notable People
at Tunbridge Wells*, 1941, p. 8, is not proved. He visited the spa in 1734, 1735 and
1758.

———

JENNENS TO AN UNKNOWN FRIEND

Gops[all]. Aug. 30. 1745.
. . . I shall show you a collection I gave Handel, call'd Messiah, which
I value highly, & he has made a fine Entertainment of it, tho' not near so
good as he might & ought to have done. I have with great difficulty
made him correct some of the grossest faults in the composition, but he
retain'd his Overture obstinately, in which there are some passages far
unworthy of Handel, but much more unworthy of the Messiah.

(Townsend, pp. 118 f.) Original in the possession of Lord Howe. That this
letter is to be found among Jennens's papers, may indicate that he never posted it.
If, however, this was the draft, it would have been better for the honour of the
compiler of the *Messiah* word-book had it never been written.

———

Handel writes the duet " Ahi nelle sorti umane ", 31st August 1745.
This seems to have been the last of Handel's Italian duets.

———

FROM THE " DAILY ADVERTISER ", 9th September 1745

Last Saturday [the 7th] Evening the Entertainments of the Spring-
Gardens, Vaux-Hall, ended for this Season.
*After hearing Mr. Handel's God save the King, sung and play'd in
Vaux-Hall-Gardens during the Thunder and Lightening, last Saturday.*

Whilst grateful *Britons* hymn the sacred Lay,
And, for their Sovereign, every Blessing pray ;
Consenting Jove bids awful Light'nings rise,
And thunders his great *Fiat* from the Skies.

(Chrysander, 1863, pp. 395 f.)   The song is, again, from the Coronation Anthem, *Zadok the Priest*.   A week before, Arne's Ode on the King's safe arrival was produced in Vauxhall Gardens.   George II returned from Hanover earlier than intended, for political reasons.

———

FROM THE " GENERAL ADVERTISER ", 9th September 1745

They write from Gloucester, that they have had a great Resort of Gentry, at the Meeting of the Choirs of Worcester, Hereford, and Gloucester in that City : The Collection at the Church on Wednesday last [the 4th] amounted to 70*l*. and it was expected that on Thursday it would be very large, the Musical Performance being the best ever-known upon the like Occasion.

On the second evening, *Acis and Galatea* was performed in the Boothall.   The conductor of the Meeting was probably William Boyce.   The price of a ticket was 2s. 6d.

———

After a performance of Ben Jonson's comedy *The Alchymist*, at Drury Lane Theatre on 28th September 1745, Mrs. Cibber, Mr. Beard and Mr. Reinhold sing Arne's arrangement of " God save the King ".

The song, now to become the National Anthem, was published anonymously in 1744.   At Drury Lane, Mr. Lacy, " Master of his Majesty's Company of Comedians ", was just about to raise a company of Gentlemen Volunteers.   The demonstration on that Saturday was apparently their doing.   (Cf. Percy A. Scholes, " God Save the King ! " 1942, pp. 8-11.) There were no oratorios or operas in London that autumn.

———

GEORGE FAULKNER TO WILLIAM BOWYER IN LONDON

Dublin, October 1, 1745.

. . . I shall finish the volume [8 of Swift's Works] with a cantata of the Dean, set to music, which in my opinion, will have a greater run with the lovers of harmony than any of the Corelli's, Vivaldi's, Purcell's, or Handel's pieces.   When Arne, the famous composer, was last in Ireland, he made application to me for this cantata, which I could not then procure, to set it to music.   Perhaps he may do it now, and bring it on the stage, which, if he does, will run more than the Beggar's Opera, and therefore I would have you get it engraved in folio, with scores for bass, etc., which will make it sell very well.   I believe you might get something handsome for it from Rich, or the managers of Drury-lane, for which I shall send you the original manuscript. I am thus particular, that you may have the profit to yourself, as you will have the trouble.

(Swift, *Correspondence*, VI. 223 f.) The Dean had died shortly before. Faulkner was publisher in Dublin, Bowyer in London. The cantata is the satirical one, beginning, "In Harmony wou'd you Excel". It was composed, not by Arne, but by the Rev. Dr. John Echlin. Faulkner printed the music with the text in 1746, and it was reprinted in 1937 in Harold Williams's edition of Swift's poems. The cantata was probably never performed. (Rich was the manager of Covent Garden.)

———

THE EARL OF SHAFTESBURY TO HIS COUSIN, JAMES HARRIS

London, October 24, 1745.
Poor Handel looks something better. I hope he will entirely recover in due time, though he has been a good deal disordered in his head.

(Streatfeild, 1909, p. 188.) Malmesbury, *Letters*, I. 9.

———

FROM THE (?) "DAILY ADVERTISER", 26th October 1745

At the late Wells, the bottom of Lemon Street, Goodman's Fields, on Monday next [the 28th] will be performed a Concert of Vocal and Instrumental Musick. Divided into two Parts. The Concert to conclude with the Chorus of *Long live the King*.

(Chrysander, 1863, p. 406.) Chrysander quotes this advertisement of Goodman's Fields Theatre from the *General Advertiser* ; it is, however, not to be found there. The *Daily Advertiser* of this date is missing in the British Museum. The chorus was, of course, "God save the King" from the Coronation Anthem ; see 9th September. But in the meantime the National Anthem had been publicly sung on 28th September at Drury Lane Theatre, and to distinguish it from Handel's chorus, the latter was renamed. The 30th of October was George II's birthday. Like Covent Garden, the Theatre in Goodman's Fields played the National Anthem each night at the end of the performance.

———

FROM THE "GENERAL ADVERTISER", 14th November 1745

By His Majesty's Company of Comedians,
At the Theatre-Royal in Drury-Lane, this Day will be presented a Comedy, call'd The RELAPSE ; or, VIRTUE IN DANGER. . . . With Entertainments, viz. . . . End of the Play. A Chorus Song, set by Mr. *Handel*, for the *Gentlemen Volunteers* of the CITY of LONDON. . . . To begin exactly at Six o'Clock.

(Chrysander, 1863, p. 406.) It seems that Handel wrote this song, beginning " Stand round, my brave boys", words by John Lockman, for the company raised by Lacy, the manager of Drury Lane (cf. 28th September). It was sung by the tenor Thomas Lowe who, both before and after this time, was one of Handel's singers. The song was repeated " by particular Desire " the next day ;

on the 16th, after another play, it was sung " by Mr. Lowe and others ", and in this way it was performed again on the 18th, 19th and 20th. Lowe also sang the new National Anthem at Drury Lane in October. (The comedy was by Sir John Vanbrugh.)

———

FROM THE " GENERAL ADVERTISER ", 15th November 1745

NEW MUSICK.

This Day is published,

A SONG made for the Gentlemen Volunteers of the City of London, and sung by Mr. LOWE, at the Theatre-Royal in Drury-Lane. Set to Musick by Mr. HANDEL.

Printed for John Simpson. . . .

(Chrysander, 1863, p. 406.) Cf. 14th November. The sheet-song was reprinted in the *London Magazine* of November, p. 560 f. (Squire, 1909, pp. 423-33.)

———

FROM THE " GENERAL EVENING POST ", 26th November 1745

MUSICK.

[Proposals for Subscription for John Travers's " Eighteen Canzonets " for two and three voices, signed by (John) Walsh, (John) Johnson, (Benjamin) Cooke, JOHN SIMPSON, and Walmesley & Co.]

Of whom may be had, this Day publish'd,

A Song made for the Gentlemen Volunteers of the City of London, and sung by Mr. LOWE, at the Theatre Royal in Drury-lane, with universal Applause. Set to Musick by Mr. Handel.

(Chrysander, 1863, p. 406.)

———

FROM FAULKNER'S " DUBLIN JOURNAL ", 14th December 1745

On Thursday last [the 12th] Cathedral Service, with Mr. Handel's Te Deum Jubilate and Coronation Anthem, and Mr. Boyce's Anthem, were performed as usual at St. Michan's Church, for the Benefit of Mercer's Hospital. . . .

This seems to have been the *Dettingen Te Deum*, with the *Utrecht Jubilate*, and probably *Zadok the Priest*.

———

MRS. DELANY TO MRS. DEWES

Delville, 21 Dec., 1745.

Last Monday [the 16th] the Dean and I went to the rehearsal of the Messiah, for the relief of poor debtors ; it was very well performed, and I much delighted. You know how much I delight in music, and that piece is very charming ; but I had not courage to go to the performance at night, the weather was so excessively bad, and I thought it would be hazardous to come out of so great crowd so far, that is my kind guardian thought so for me.

(Delany, II. 408.) The Delanys now lived in Ireland, and Mrs. Mary cultivated her Handel worship in Dublin. Dr. Patrick Delany had been appointed Dean of Down in May 1744. His residence was Delville.

—

FROM RICHARD POWNEY'S "TEMPLUM HARMONIAE", LONDON, 1745

. . . Multa quidem documenta sibi vocisque lyraeque,
Harmoniae studiosa diu, dabit Itala tellus ;
Harmoniae genetrix tellus, magnique *Corelli*.
   Neve peregrinae solito novitatis amore
Percitus, interea patrium aspernabere morem
Cantandique modos ; si quid *Purcellius* olim
Lusit amabiliter ; vel si quid *Greenius* audet
Et templi super esse choris dignatus & aulae.
Handelium nostrâ merito miraberis urbe
Donatum, terris quo gratior advena nunquam
Appulit Angliacis, modulandi aut clarior arte :
Sive juvat scenae juveniles prodere curas
Virgineosque ignes ; majori aut pandere plectro
Heroas veteres & amico numine gentem
Dignatam, summique juga exsuperare Sionis.
Agminis ipse sui princeps, ac tempore certo
Sceptra manu vibrans, chordas centum, oraque centum
Dirigit ; aure avidâ excipiunt plebesque patresque
Concentum altisonum, ingeminantque sedilia plausus.
Qualis Parnassi aut Pindi de vertice sacro
Musarum exultat coetu stipatus Apollo,
Coelestesque choros attentaque sidera mulcet.

   Lib. II, pp. 20 f. The passage was kindly translated into English verse by Mr. Henry Gifford, of Bristol University. Line 9 (10) seems to refer to Handel's naturalization in 1727.

(Translation)

. . . Full many Proofs both of the Voice and Lyre,
Of Harmony long studious, will she give,
PHOEBUS ! to thee, the fam'd *Italian* land
Mother of Harmony and great *Corelli*.
   And yet despise not, in thy wonted Love
Of foreign Novelty, our native Fashion
And Modes of Song, if *Purcell* ever play'd
Aught of Delight, or *Greene* dare aught, esteem'd
Worthy to rule the Choirs of Temple and Court.
Handel, enroll'd our Son, thou shalt admire

Justly, for ne'er did Stranger land more welcome
On *Anglian* Shore, or one more fam'd in Musick :
Whether he please to bring upon the Stage
The Cares of Youth, or virgin Flame ; or show
With grander sweep old Heroes and a Race
Rightly of Heav'n belov'd, and scale the Peaks
Of topmost *Sion*. For himself he leads
A Host his own, and in due measur'd Time
Wielding the Sceptre in his Hand directs
A Hundred Strings, a Hundred Voices too.
With eager Ear Princes and Folk receive
The grand Accord, and the Rows ring Applause.
So from *Parnassus* or from *Pindus* height
APOLLO leaps, throng'd by the *Muses* Train,
And soothes the heav'nly Choirs and watchful Orbs.

———

Handel is elected the first honorary member of the Society of
Musical Science at Leipzig, 1745.

Lorenz Christoph Mizler founded the " Societät der musikalischen
Wissenschaften " in 1738 ; the members were expected to study the laws
of composition. Johann Sebastian Bach joined the Society after Handel's
appointment. The Society was dissolved in 1755. Cf. Mizler's report of
1746.

———

Mme Boivin of Paris reprints, about 1745, William Babell's
Suites of Lessons for the Harpsichord, including early opera arias
by Handel (published 1717), the solo sonatas with bass, Opus 1
(1733), and the organ fugues (1735).

1746

During 1746 there is no entry in Handel's accounts with the Bank of England.

From the " General Advertiser ", 7th January 1746

At the King's Theatre in the Hay-Market, this Day, will be perform'd a *Musical Drama*, in Two Parts, call'd LA CADUTA de GIGANTI, The FALL of the GIANTS. *With* DANCES *and other* DECORATIONS *Entirely New*. . . . To begin at Six o'Clock. . . .

This was the first of two Gluck operas produced in London (see 4th March). The music was partly new and partly taken from earlier works ; it was arranged by the composer specially for these productions. He is said to have come to London on the invitation of Lord Middlesex, who was managing the Haymarket Theatre again, after Handel's oratorio year. On the other hand it is related that Gluck came to London with his protector, Prince Ferdinand Philipp Josef Lobkowitz, who was also the protector of Count St. Germain (cf. 21st January 1745) ; on the way they are said to have attended the coronation of Franz I, on 28th September 1745, at Frankfurt am Main. While the Prince stayed for two years in London with the (first) Duke of Newcastle, the British representative at the coronation, Gluck went back to the Continent after the spring of 1746. His first London opera was produced " before the Duke of Cumberland, in compliment to whom the whole was written and composed " (Burney, IV. 453). Vanneschi's textbook alluded to the defeated Jacobites. A young dancer from Vienna, Eva Veigel, called La Violetta, and soon to become Mrs. Garrick, appeared in the dances of Gluck's opera. Horace Walpole, in a letter to Horace Mann of 12th August 1746 (1891 edition, II. 48), speaks of Lord Middlesex, just two years after his marriage, protecting his new mistress Nardi against her rival, Violetta. Burney, in his sketch of 1785, tells of Handel's remark to Mrs. Cibber about Gluck : " He knows no more of contrapunto as mein cock " ; " mein cock " [cook] is supposed to have been the bass singer Waltz, and the occasion the performance of Gluck's first opera. Walsh printed six favourite songs from *La Caduta de Giganti*. It should be observed that Gluck's opera, performed six times, was called in the bills " a Musical Drama ", as had been Handel's *Hercules* a year before at the same house (see 5th January 1745).

FROM FAULKNER'S " DUBLIN JOURNAL ", 14th January 1746

For the Benefit of the Hospital for poor distressed Lying in Women in George's-lane, on Thursday the 13th of February next, will be performed Mr. Handel's grand Oratorio of HESTER. The Rehearsal will be on Monday the 10th of February.

For the Support of the Charitable Infirmary on the Inns Key, on Thursday the 23th of January, will be performed Mr. Handel's Grand

Oratorio of DEBORAH, at the Musick-Hall, in Fishamble-Street. The Rehearsal will be on Monday the 20th of January.

The dates for *Esther* were postponed till 17th and 20th February ; the rehearsals of *Deborah* till 21st January. The rehearsals were, as usual in Dublin, at noon, the performances at 6.30. An undated word-book of *Esther*, printed in Dublin by James Hoey, wrongly attributes the text to Dr. Arbuthnot ; this, however, was probably the word-book for the 1757 Dublin performance. The same attribution is to be found in a Dublin word-book of 1764.

———

MRS. DELANY TO MRS. DEWES

Delville, 25 Jan. 1745–6.

On Tuesday last [the 21st] I went to hear Deborah performed, for the support of one of the infirmaries. It is a charming piece of music, and was extremely well performed ; we have a woman here, a Mrs. Storer, who has a very sweet and clear voice, and though she has no *judgment* in music, Dubourg manages her so well in his manner of accompanying her, as to make her singing very agreeable.

(Delany, II. 415 f.) For Mrs. Storer, see 25th October 1743.

———

FROM THE " GENERAL ADVERTISER ", 31st January 1746

We hear, that Mr. *Handel* proposes to exhibit some Musical Entertainments on Wednesdays or Fridays the ensuing Lent, with Intent to make good to the Subscribers (that favoured him last Season) the Number of Performances he was not then able to complete in order thereto he is preparing a New Occasional Oratorio, which is design'd to be perform'd at the Theatre-Royal in Covent-Garden.

(Schoelcher, p. 302.) Cf. 20th October 1744 and 23rd April 1745. There were eight " Nights " remaining from the subscription of 1744-5. Handel gave three performances of the new oratorio in February, and nothing else. He never again attempted a subscription for his performances.

———

THE REV. WILLIAM HARRIS TO MRS. THOMAS HARRIS, AT SALISBURY

Lincoln's Inn, February 8, 1746.

Yesterday morning I was at Handel's house to hear the rehearsal of his new occasional Oratorio. It is extremely worthy of him, which you will allow to be saying all one can in praise of it. He has but three voices for his songs—Francesina, Reinholt, and Beard ; his band of music is not very extraordinary—Du Feche is his first fiddle, and for the rest I really could not find out who they were, and I doubt his failure will be in this article. The words of his Oratorio are scriptural, but taken from various parts, and are expressive of the rebels' flight and our pursuit of them. Had not the Duke carried his point triumphantly, this Oratorio could not have been brought on. It is to be performed in public next Friday [the 14th].

(Streatfeild, 1909, p. 191.) Malmesbury, *Letters*, I. 33 f. Burney, who speaks of rehearsals in Handel's house, may have been one of the string players. Willem (William) De Fesch (Defesch), an organist and violinist of Flemish origin, was, in 1745, a competitor of Handel's as oratorio composer (see 15th March 1745). The "occasion" for which the oratorio was written was the retreat of the rebels, who threatened London itself. The homage to the Duke of Cumberland reminds one of Gluck's opera *La Caduta de Giganti* (7th January). The compiler of the word-book may have been the Rev. Dr. Thomas Morell, Handel's next librettist. It was printed for J. and R. Tonson and S. Draper, and entitled *The New Occasional Oratorio. . . . The Words taken from Milton, Spenser, &c.* (Copies in the British Museum, *etc.*) Milton's translation of the Psalms was used. In Act III, written, perhaps, against time, Handel introduced not only his "God save the King" from the Coronation Anthems, but four arias from *Israel in Egypt*. The famous aria "O Liberty" was originally written for the *Occasional Oratorio* and afterwards used in *Judas Maccabaeus* (see 1st April 1747). The address of the writer of this letter, Lincoln's Inn, would seem to indicate Thomas Harris, Master in Chancery ; but the editor of the Malmesbury letters attributes this one also to William Harris (cf. 29th August 1745 and 28th March 1747).

FROM THE "GENERAL ADVERTISER", 14th February 1746

At the Theatre-Royal in Covent-Garden, this Day, will be perform'd *A New Occasional* ORATORIO. With a New *Concerto* on the *Organ*. . . . To begin at Half an Hour after Six o'Clock.

** The Subscribers, who favour'd Mr. Handel last Season with their Subscription, are desired to send to the Office at Covent-Garden Theatre, on the Day of Performance, where Two Tickets shall be deliver'd to each Gratis, in Order to make good the Number of Performances subscrib'd to last Season.

(Schoelcher, p. 302.) Repeat performances on 19th and 26th February ; revived in March 1747.

CAST OF THE "OCCASIONAL ORATORIO", 14th February 1746

Soprano I—Signora Francesina
Soprano II—(?)
Tenor—Mr. Beard·
Bass—Mr. Reinhold

FROM FAULKNER'S "DUBLIN JOURNAL", 22nd February 1746

Last Thursday [the 20th] Evening the Oratorio of Hester was performed to a most polite and numerous Audience for the Benefit of the Lying-in Hospital in George's Lane, which his Excellency the Earl of

Chesterfield honoured with his Presence, as did many Persons of the greatest Nobility and Distinction ; the Numbers of which amounted to above five hundred. The whole Entertainment, both vocal and instrumental, was universally allowed to be as well performed, as ever was known, and to the entire Satisfaction of all the Audience. . . . N.B. The Gentleman, who gave a Messiah Ticket for this Performance, is desired to send a genuine Ticket or the Money, or else he will be called upon.

Cf. 14th January. Philip Dormer Stanhope, fourth Earl of Chesterfield, was Viceroy of Ireland 1745–6. The price for the best tickets was half a guinea.

Gluck's second London opera, *Artamene*, text by Bartolomeo Vitturi, arranged by Vanneschi, is produced at the Haymarket Theatre, " With Dances and other Decorations Entirely New ", *General Advertiser*, 4th March 1746.

Eight performances ; the last being on 12th April. Walsh again printed some " favourite Songs " from the opera.

From the " General Advertiser ", 25th March 1746

For the Benefit and Increase of a Fund *establish'd for the Support of* Decay'd Musicians, *or their* Families.

At the King's Theatre in the *Hay-Market*, this Day, will be performed an Entertainment of Vocal and Instrumental *Musick*, as follows.

Part I.

Overture. *Della Caduta de Giganti*, compos'd by Signor Gluck.
Air. *Care Pupille* in La Caduta de Giganti, sung by Signor Jozzi.
Air. *Men Fedele*, by Mr. Handel, sung by Signor Monticelli.

Part II.

Air. *Return, O God of Hosts*, in the Oratorio of Samson, sung by Signora Frasi.
Air. *Il Cormeo*, by Mr. Handel, sung by Signor Monticelli.
Air. Pensa che il Cielo trema, in *La Caduta*, sung by Signor Ciacchi.
Air. *Mai l'Amor mio verace*, in ditto, sung by Signora Imer.

Part III.

Air. *Volgo Dubbiosa*, in La Caduta, sung by Sign. Pompeati.
Air. *The Prince unable to conceal his Pain*, in Alexander's Feast, sung by Signora Frasi.

A Grand Concerto of Mr. Handel's.

To begin at Six o'Clock.

．　　　．　　　．　　　．　　　．

This was an occasion for Handel and Gluck to meet. It is noteworthy that, at a charity concert, the singers of Middlesex's opera company were allowed to sing Handel arias, though these were not in their repertoire. The arias from Gluck's first opera were, of course, sung by the original cast. The first of these arias was added to the programme in the second of four advertisements, on 22nd March. Of Handel's arias, " Men fedele " and " Il cor mio " (corrupted into " Il Cormeo ") were from the opera *Alessandro*. Monticelli, like Signora Frasi, had sung in the " Roxana " version of *Alessandro* on 15th November 1743. Frasi had not yet sung in a Handel oratorio.

———

HORACE WALPOLE TO HORACE MANN

Arlington-Street, March 28, 1746.

The operas flourish more than in any latter years ; the composer is Gluck, a German : he is to have a benefit, at which he is to play on a set of drinking-glasses, which he modulates with water : I think I have heard you speak of having seen some such thing.

(Walpole, *Letters*, 1891 edition, II. 14.) In John Simpson's edition of Gluck's *Six Sonatas for two Violins and a Thorough Bass*, published in November 1746, he is called " Composer of the Opera ". Gluck gave his " glass harmonica " concert on 23rd April at the New Theatre. He played " on 26 drinking glasses tuned with spring water, accompanied with the whole band, being a new instrument of his own invention ". In Dublin, however, an anonymous " Inventor " gave a concert " upon Glasses " as early as 3rd May 1743 in Smock Alley Theatre (Faulkner's *Dublin Journal*) ; it was Richard Pockrich who seems to have played Handel's *Water Music* in Dublin before 1759. Out of these " musical glasses " grew the glass harmonica (cf. 30th April 1751).

———

The Duke of Cumberland defeats the Pretender's forces at Culloden, 16th April 1746.
Cf. July 1746.

———

FROM THE " GENERAL ADVERTISER ", 26th April 1746

NEW MUSICK.

This Day is published,

THE OCCASIONAL ORATORIO IN SCORE, compos'd by Mr. Handel.

．　　　．　　　．　　　．　　　．

Next Week will be published,

Twelve Duets for two Voices from the late Oratorios. Compos'd by Mr. Handel.

The oratorio had been first advertised on 3rd April 1746 (Smith, 1954, p. 281). A second book of twelve duets was published shortly after April 1746.

———

MRS. DELANY TO MRS. DEWES

Delville, 26 April, 1746.
On Thursday [the 24th] I went to the music for the benefit of the Hospital of Incurables, which was crowded—the piece performed was Alexander's Feast ; and yesterday went to see the Beggar's Opera.

———

Handel begins the oratorio *Judas Maccabaeus*, 8th or 9th July 1746.

———

FROM THE " LONDON MAGAZINE ", July 1746

A SONG *on the* VICTORY *obtained over the* REBELS *by his Royal Highness the* DUKE *of* CUMBERLAND
The Words by Mr. Lockman. Set by Mr. Handel. Sung by Mr. Lowe, &c.
[Here follows the song, with five verses.]
The song refers to the battle of Culloden. Since the tune is similar to the aria " Volate amori " from *Ariodante*, it is possible that someone else arranged Handel's music to the English words of this topical song. Lowe sang it in Vauxhall Gardens. Lockman and Lowe were also engaged in Handel's Volunteer song (see 14th November 1745). Cf. Squire, 1909, p. 432 f. Beethoven's two patriotic songs for Vienna's plight in 1796-7, written before and after Haydn's Austrian Anthem, provide a parallel to Handel's songs.

———

FROM A LONDON NEWSPAPER, SUMMER 1746 (July or August)

We hear that at Cuper's Gardens last Night, among several Pieces of Musick, Mr. Handel's Fire Musick, with the Fireworks as originally performed in the Opera of Atalanta, was received with great Applause by a numerous Audience.
(Schoelcher, p. 184.) Cf. 18th July 1741.

———

Walsh advertises the second edition of Handel's *Twelve Grand Concertos* in seven parts, Opus 6, *General Advertiser*, 11th August 1746.
Cf. 21st April 1740 and 19th November 1746.

———

Handel finishes the oratorio *Judas Maccabaeus*, 11th August 1746.

———

MRS. ELIZABETH CARTER TO MISS CATHERINE TALBOT

Deal, Sept. 5, 1746.
I seldom hear an agreeable air but it recalls to my mind almost every pleasing occurrence of my life, and gives me a new enjoyment of it.

Every body I either love or admire, every conversation that struck me with peculiar pleasure, and every fine passage of a favourite author, the powerful magic of Mr. Handel conjures up to my thoughts.

(Myers, 1948, p. 144.)   Carter, *Letters*, I. 165.

John Frederick Lampe's *Musick on the Thanksgiving Day*, written to celebrate the suppression of the Stuart rebellion, is performed in the Savoy Chapel by the " Churchwardens and all the Gentlemen belonging to the German Lutheran Church . . . in their native language ", 9th October 1746.

(Smith, 1948, p. 191.)   In the grounds of the Savoy Hospital were also a palace and a chapel ; the latter, called the German (Lutheran) Chapel, existed from about 1730 until 1876.   (Cf. Rev. John Loftie, *Memorials of the Savoy*, London 1878.)

The *Dettingen Te Deum* is performed in Salisbury Cathedral, 17th October 1746.

John Stevens was the new organist at Salisbury. He and James Harris started a long series of Handel performances there.

Walsh advertises the third edition of Handel's Opus 6, for one guinea, *General Advertiser*, 19th November 1746.

Cf. 11th August. It seems improbable that the second edition was sold out within three months.

From Tobias Smollett's Satire, " Advice ", 1746

[A dialogue between Poet and Friend.]

Poet. . . . Again shall *Handel* raise his laurel'd brow,
Again shall harmony with rapture glow !
The spells disolve, the combination breaks,
And rival Punch no more in terror squeaks.
Lo, R—*ss*—*l* [1] falls a sacrifice to whim,
And starts amaz'd in *Newgate* from his dream :

[1] The person here meant, by the qualifications above described, had insinuated himself into the confidence of certain Ladies of Quality, who engaged him to set up a puppet-shew, in opposition to the oratorio's of *H—d—l*, against whom they were unreasonably prejudiced.   But the town not seconding the capricious undertaking, they deserted their manager whom they had promised to support, and let him sink under the expence they had entailed upon him :   He was accordingly thrown into prison, where his disappointment got the better of his reason, and he remain'd in all the ecstasy of despair ; till at last, his generous patronesses, after much solicitation, were prevailed upon, to collect five pounds, on the payment of which, he was admitted into Bedlam, where he continues still happily bereft of his understanding.

With trembling hands implores their promis'd aid ;
And sees their favour like a vision fade ! . . .

(*Musical Times*, 1st October 1895.) P. 13 of the anonymous pamphlet of 16 pages folio. Copy in Gerald Coke's Handel Collection. A tenor named Russell sang in *Saul* on 16th January 1739 ; the Russell referred to by Smollett was actor and singer ; the two may have been identical. The ladies in question may have been Lady Brown and her friends (cf. 21st January 1745).

———

From Joseph Warton's " Ode to a Lady who hates the Country ", 1746

Come wildly rove thro' desart dales,
To listen how lone nightingales
    In liquid lays complain ;
Adieu the tender, thrilling note,
That pants in Monticelli's throat,
    And Handel's stronger strain.

Odes on Various Subjects, published by R. Dodsley, anonymously, in 1746, and reprinted in 1747, p. 39. This is the fourth stanza of Ode XI. Cf. 2nd May 1745.

———

From Mizler's " Neu eröffnete Musikalische Bibliothek " (" Newly inaugurated Music Library "), Leipzig, 1746 (Translated)

Detailed information of the Society of Musical Science in Germany, from the year of its inauguration, 1738, till the end of the year 1745. All the members of the Society follow one another in this order.

.   .   .   .   .

11. *Georg Friedrich Händel* Capellmeister to His Majesty the King of Great Britain. Is elected by all the members of their own accord and the first award of honour was conceded to him in the year 1745.

(Bishop.) Vol. 3, part 2, p. 357 ; cf. also pp. 346 and 356. There were twelve members in all, among them Telemann. Mizler was their secretary. In 1746 the Society issued a medal in gold, silver and copper, inscribed : " Societ : Scientiar : Music. in Germ. Instavr.". Cf. 1745 and June 1756. Handel probably received a golden specimen as the first and only honorary member.

1747

Domenico Paradies' opera *Phaeton*, words by Vanneschi, is produced at the Haymarket Theatre, 17th January 1747.

(Burney, IV. 456.) The libretto, with an introductory "Discourse on Operas", is dedicated to Lord Middlesex.

—

Mrs. Delany to Mrs. Dewes

Pall Mall, 21 Jan. 1746–7.

. . . Just as I came to this place, in came Mr. Handel, and he has prevented my adding any more. . . . " The Allegro " is a *drawing*, I have imagined in imitation of Mr. Handel's *Let me wander, etc.*, and I have brought in all the images as well I could. " The Penseroso " is in embryo.

(Delany, II. 451.) The Delanys were in London on a visit. "This place" means at this point of the letter. Mrs. Delany was an amateur painter. The aria quoted is from *L'Allegro*.

—

From the " Gentleman's Magazine ", January 1747

A Hunting Song. *By* C.L. *Esq* ;

·   ·   ·   ·   ·

Hark the lively tun'd horn, how melodious it sounds,
To the musical notes of the merry mouth'd hounds.

·   ·   ·   ·   ·

See, see where she goes, and the hounds have a view,
Such harmony *Handel* himself never knew.

·   ·   ·   ·   ·

C. L. is Charles Legh, of Adlington Hall, Macclesfield, in Cheshire, the brother of the late Elisabeth Legh. His *Hunting Song* was first set to music by " a Gentleman of Wygan ", in fact by Mr. Ridley, organist of Prestbury, Cheshire. The amateurish poem was later set by Handel himself, and his autograph is still preserved at Adlington Hall (cf. *Musical Times*, December 1942). Handel gave the manuscript to Legh in 1751. His setting was used in John Stanley's " dramatic pastoral " : *Arcadia, or The Shepherd's Wedding*, produced at Drury Lane, for George III's marriage, on 26th October 1761 (text by Robert Lloyd).

—

A pasticcio opera, *Le triomphe de l'amour et de l'hymen*, words by M. de Séré, with arias by Handel and others, the orchestral music chiefly by Jean Baptist Morin, is produced in Paris, January 1747.

Manuscript in Bibliothèque nationale, Paris.

—

FROM FAULKNER'S "DUBLIN JOURNAL", 7th February 1747

On Thursday last [the 5th] Cathedral Service, with Mr. Handel's Te Deum, Jubilate, and Coronation Anthem, were performed (as usual) at St. Michan's Church, for the Benefit of Mercer's Hospital. . . .

Handel deposits £400, 28th February 1747.

FROM THE "GENERAL ADVERTISER", 6th March 1747

At the Theatre-Royal in Covent-Garden, this Day . . . will be perform'd The OCCASIONAL ORATORIO. . . . To begin at Half an Hour after Six o'Clock.

Cf. 14th February 1746. Repeat performances on 11th and 13th March. This was the opening of a Lent season of Handel oratorios, without subscription or special announcement, but without reduction of prices of admission either.

Handel deposits £100, 7th March 1747.

FROM THE "GENERAL ADVERTISER", 16th March 1747

At the Theatre-Royal . . . on Wednesday next [the 18th], will be perform'd an Oratorio, call'd JOSEPH, and His BRETHREN. . . . To begin at Half an Hour after Six o'Clock.

Produced in March 1744, revived in March 1745. This second revival was postponed till 20th March.

THE EARL OF SHAFTESBURY TO HIS COUSIN, JAMES HARRIS,
IN SALISBURY

London, March 17, 1747.

The trial [of Lord Lovat] interrupts our harmonious system extremely. To-morrow Handel has advertised ' Joseph ', though I hope he will not perform, for nothing can be expected whilst the trial lasts. The week after, we flatter ourselves that ' Judas ' will both give delight to the lovers of harmony and profits to the fountain whence it flows. However, I am not certain that ' Judas ' will be performed next week.

(Malmesbury, Letters, I. 58 f.) The trial of Simon Fraser, Baron Lovat, a Jacobite intriguer, immortalized by Hogarth, began on 16th March : he was beheaded for high treason. Judas Maccabaeus was not produced until 1st April.

FROM THE " GENERAL ADVERTISER ", 18th March 1747

The Oratorio of *Joseph and His Brethren*, which was to have been performed this Night, at the Theatre-Royal . . ., is *put off*, upon Account of the Trial of Lord Lovat.

Handel buys £1700 3 per cent Annuities (1743), 19th March 1747.

Joseph and His Brethren is revived at Covent Garden, 20th March 1747.
Repeat performance on 25th March. Further revivals in Lent 1755 and 1757.

Handel deposits £100, 21st March 1747.

Domenico Terradellas' opera *Bellerofonte*, text by Vanneschi, is produced at the Haymarket Theatre, 24th March 1747.
(Burney, IV. 456.)

THE REV. WILLIAM HARRIS TO HIS BROTHER JAMES, IN SALISBURY

Lincoln's Inn, March 28, 1747.
Handel's ' Judas Maccabaeus ' certainly comes on next Wednesday [1st April].
(Malmesbury, *Letters*, I. 63.) For the writer cf. 8th February 1746.

FROM THE " GENERAL ADVERTISER ", 1st April 1747

At the Theatre-Royal . . . this Day . . . will be perform'd a New Oratorio, call'd JUDAS MACCHABAEUS. *With a New* CONCERTO. . . . To begin at Half an Hour after Six o'Clock.

The text was by the Rev. Dr. Thomas Morell (cf. 8th February 1746). According to Morell's memoirs, written about 1764 and printed in the Hodgkin MSS., Handel asked Morell in 1746, on the recommendation of the Prince of Wales, to write an oratorio text for him. *Judas* was " designed as a compliment to the Duke of Cumberland, upon his returning victorious from Scotland ", the Duke being personified in the Jewish hero. Morell got a present from the Duke. (Cf. Appendix.) Repeat performances on 3rd, 8th, 10th, 13th and 15th April ; from 8th April onwards " *With* ADDITIONS ". Revived in February 1748.

CAST OF " JUDAS MACCABAEUS ", 1st April 1747

Judas Maccabaeus—Mr. Beard, tenor
Simon—Mr. Reinhold, bass
First Israelite Woman—Signora Gambarini, soprano
Second Israelite Woman—Signora Galli, mezzo-soprano
Israelite Man—Signora Galli
Messenger—?, contralto
Eupolemus—(?) Mr. Reinhold, bass

Signora Gambarini was in Handel's company for a short time only. Signora Galli, specializing in male parts, belonged to the Haymarket Opera ; it seems that Handel's relations with that house had become very friendly (cf. the Handel pasticcios of *Rossane* in 1743 and of *Lucio Vero* in 1747, both produced at the Haymarket).

—

J. Watts advertises the word-book of *Judas Maccabaeus*, General Advertiser, 2nd April 1747.

(Schoelcher, pp. 303 f.) The word-book of the " Sacred Drama " is dedicated, by Morell, to Prince William, Duke of Cumberland, as " This Faint Portraiture of a Truly Wise, Valiant, and Virtuous Commander ". On page 14 of the first edition, at the entrance of the Messenger in Act III, the following passage is to be found : " Several Incidents were introduced here by Way of Messenger and Chorus, in Order to make the Story more complete ; but it was thought they would make the Performance too long, and therefore were not set, and therefore not printed ; this being designed not as a finished poem, but merely as an Oratorio." (Schoelcher, p. 303.) There are several issues of the word-book of 1747, with additional songs on interleaves.

—

Handel deposits £250, 9th April 1747.

—

FROM THE " GENERAL ADVERTISER ", 14th April 1747

For the Benefit and Increase of a FUND *establish'd for the Support of Decay'd* MUSICIANS, *or their Families.*

At the King's Theatre in the Hay-Market, this Day . . . will be perform'd an Entertainment of Vocal and Instrumental MUSICK, as follows.

FIRST PART.

.   .   .   .   .

. . . . .
O *Placido il Mare*, in Siroe, sung by Signora Casarini.

SECOND PART.

.   .   .   .   .

O *Sleep*, in Semele, sung by Signora Frasi.
. . . . .

.   .   .   .   .

La Dove, in Admetus, sung by Signor Casarini.
.   .   .   .   .

THIRD PART.

.   .   .   .   .

To Song and Dance, in Samson, sung by Signora Frasi.
.   .   .   .   .

Dica il Falso, in Rossane, sung by Signora Casarini.

A Grand Concerto of Mr. Handel's.

.   .   .   .   .

To begin exactly at Six o'Clock.

As in 1746, the singers of the Haymarket Opera were allowed to perform, not only from their own repertoire, but from Handel's operas and oratorios as well. The aria from *Admeto* was also sung by Signora, not Signor, Casarini.

———

MISS CATHERINE TALBOT TO MRS. ELIZABETH CARTER, 18th April 1747

. . . This play [a farce by Garrick], and one oratorio, are the sum of the public places I have been at, unless you will add two very moderate drums, and one concert. Those oratorios of Handel's are certainly (next to the *hooting of owls*) the most solemnly striking music one can hear. I am sure you must be fond of them, even I am who have no ear for music, and no skill in it. In this last oratorio he has literally introduced guns, and they have a good effect.

(Streatfeild, 1909, p. 197.) Carter, *Letters*, I. 203. The concert was probably that for the Musicians' Fund, the oratorio *Judas Maccabaeus*. The "guns", like the previously mentioned "cannons", were kettle-drums. Thirty years later, Richard Brinsley Sheridan in *The Critic*, and even in its early sketch called *Jupiter*, explains off-stage gun-shots thus : "This hint I took from Handel".

———

Handel deposits £150, 24th April 1747.

———

Handel withdraws £1000, 29th April 1747.

———

FROM THE "GENERAL ADVERTISER", 30th April 1747

The Rehearsal of the Musick for the Feast of the Sons of the Clergy, will be at St. Paul's, on Tuesday the 5th of May, and the Feast on Thursday following. . . .

N.B. Mr. Handel's New Te Deum, Jubilate and Coronation Anthem,

XXIV. FIREWORKS IN THE GREEN PARK, 27TH APRIL 1749

An anonymous engraving. (Gerald Coke, Esq.)

See page 667

XXV. THOMAS CORAM

Mezzotint after William Hogarth, by James McArdell, 1749.
(Gerald Coke, Esq.)

See page 669

with a New Anthem by Dr. Green, will be Vocally and Instrumentally perform'd. . . .

The Feast of the Sons of the Clergy was still held annually; it seems that the *Dettingen Te Deum* was performed with the *Utrecht Jubilate*, as in Dublin.

———

Walsh advertises the score of *Judas Maccabaeus*, *General Advertiser*, 30th April 1747.

(Smith, 1954, p. 280.)

———

Extracts from *Messiah* are performed at the Academy of Ancient Music, 30th April 1747.

(Smith, 1950, p. 132.) Recorded in a printed libretto, of which the only copy known is in the Schoelcher Collection, Conservatoire, Paris. The word-book mentions neither *Messiah* nor Handel. Cf. 16th February 1744 and 11th May 1758.

———

At the Kongl. Svenska Skådeplatsen in Stockholm a pasticcio, called *Syrinx, or the Waternymph transformed into Reed*, is produced on 9th (20th) May 1747 ; the great bass arias by Handel, the great discant arias by Karl Heinrich Graun, and a few arias, duets and recitatives by Mr. Ohl.

Manuscript score in the Kungl. Musikaliska Akademiens bibliotek, Stockholm. The libretto was printed in 1747 and reprinted in 1748 and 1770. Details are given in F. A. Dahlgren's list of Swedish plays from 1737 till 1863, Stockholm, 1886, pp. 357 f. Ohl was organist at the Dutch Church in Stockholm ; he probably arranged the pasticcio.

———

Handel begins the oratorio *Alexander Balus*, 1st June 1747.

———

From the " Accounts of Covent Garden Theatre ", June 1747

Reced of Mr. Handell for Rent of his 10 Oratorio's   210   –   –

British Museum : Egerton MS. 2268, vol. II, fol. 167 (or rather, 169) verso. The opposite page is dated 1st June 1747. Handel, in fact, performed on twelve nights : *Occasional Oratorio* three times, then *Joseph and His Brethren* three times, and finally the new *Judas Maccabaeus* six times. Cf. 19th June 1736. In 1735 and 1736 Handel paid £19 5s. 8d. for the Wednesday and Friday nights in Lent at Covent Garden. £210 for ten nights in 1747 amounts to a little more per night.

———

Handel finishes the oratorio *Alexander Balus*, 4th July 1747.

———

H.-21

Handel begins the oratorio *Joshua*, 19th July 1747.

———

Handel finishes the oratorio *Joshua*, 19th August 1747.

———

FROM THE " GENERAL ADVERTISER ", 30th October 1747

Whereas a Subscription is begun for an Italian Opera this Season, at the King's Theatre in the Hay-Market, which will open November the 14th, Gentlemen and Ladies who please to subscribe, are desir'd to send to the Opera-Office of the said Theatre. Where Attention will be given to take in Subscriptions.

———

FROM THE " GENERAL ADVERTISER ", 13th November 1747

Yesterday was Rehears'd, at the King's Theatre in the Haymarket, the Opera of LUCIUS VERUS : This Drama Consists of Airs, borrow'd entirely from Mr. Handel's favourite Operas : and so may (probably) be justly styl'd the most exquisite Composition of Harmony, ever offer'd to the Publick. The Lovers of Musick among us, whose Ears have been charm'd with Farinello, Faustina, Senesino, Cuzzoni, and other great Performers will now have an Opportunity of Reviving their former Delight ; which, if not so transporting as then, may yet prove a very high Entertainment. Mr. Handel is acknowledged (universally) so great a Master of the Lyre ; that nothing urg'd in Favour of his Capital Performances, can reasonably be considered as a Puff.

The Haymarket Opera was still under the management of Lord Middlesex and his friends.

———

FROM THE " GENERAL ADVERTISER ", 4th November 1747

At the King's Theatre in the Hay-Market, this Day, will be perform'd an *Opera*, call'd LUCIUS VERUS. . . . To begin exactly at Six.

(Burney, IV. 456 f.; Schoelcher, p. 307.) This was a Handel pasticcio, consisting of arias from *Admeto, Radamisto, Riccardo Primo, Siroe*, and *Tamerlano*. The full title was *Lucio Vero, Imperatore di Roma*. The text seems to have been the old one by Apostolo Zeno, composed repeatedly since 1700, and used in 1727 (7th January) by Ariosti at the Haymarket Theatre. It was used there again, when in 1773 a pasticcio opera was produced, with music by Handel and other composers. The 1747 opera was performed every Saturday from 14th November till 26th December 1747, and also on 2nd and 9th January, and 19th March 1748. Cf. 5th December 1747. Walsh published favourite songs from *Lucius Verus*, " The Musick by Mr. Handel ". It is characteristic of Walsh's publishing habits that the book is printed from his plates of the scores of the Handel operas used for the pasticcio ; it has triple pagination, because some of the plates had been used for another purpose in the meantime. The title of the pasticcio and the names of the new singers are stamped on the top outside corner of page one of each song. Handel, of course, had nothing to do with the pasticcio or with its publication.

—

CAST OF " LUCIO VERO ", 14th November 1747

Lucius Verus—Signora Pirker, soprano
Berenice—Signora Casarini, soprano
Lucilla—Signora Frasi, soprano
Vologesus—Signora Galli, mezzo-soprano
Flavius—Signora Sibilla, soprano
Anicetus—Signor Ciacchi, (?) tenor

Signora Frasi sang Vologesus in 1748.

—

FROM THE " GENERAL ADVERTISER ", 5th December 1747

Several Airs in the Opera of Lucius Verus, now performing at the King's Theatre . . . will be chang'd for others ; all compos'd by Mr. Handel.

—

FROM FAULKNER'S " DUBLIN JOURNAL ", 5th December 1747

On Thursday last [the 3rd] Mr. Handel's Great Te Deum, Jubilate, and Anthems, were performed at St. Andrew's Church, for the Benefit of Mercer's Hospital. . . .

The " Cathedral Service " previously held at St. Michan's Church was now transferred back to St. Andrew's Church.

—

Handel subscribes for William Boyce's *Twelve Sonatas for two Violins with a Bass*, published by Walsh for the Author, 1747.

The list of subscribers is to be found in the second, the dated, issue.

—

Acis and Galatea is performed by the Musical Society at the Castle in Paternoster Row, 1747.

(Smith, 1948, p. 236.) Recorded in a word-book only. The same society performed *Acis* in 1755.

—

FROM " AN ACCOUNT OF THE PLAYS PRINTED IN THE ENGLISH LANGUAGE . . . TO THE YEAR 1747 "

Mr. *Hill's* Dramatic Pieces are, . . .

RINALDO ; an Opera, after the *Italian* Manner, performed at the Queen's Theatre in the *Hay-market*, in the Year 1714, of which Theatre Mr. *Hill*, was, for that Year, Master himself, having farmed it of Mr. *Collier*.

The Music was set by Mr. *Handel*, who then made his first Appearance in *England*, and accompanied the voices himself on the Harpsichord in the Orchestre, and performed his Part in the Overture, wherein his Execution seemed as astonishing as his Genius in the Composition.

P. 248 of the " Account ", printed as an appendix to Thomas Whincop's tragedy *Scanderbeg. Rinaldo* was, of course, produced in 1711. For Collier, see 3rd May 1711.

———

FROM MIZLER'S " NEU ERÖFFNETE MUSIKALISCHE BIBLIOTHEK ",
LEIPZIG, 1747 (Translated)

. . . At the end of this chapter [on theatrical style] the author [Mattheson, *Der Vollkommene Capellmeister*] mentions the greatest masters of the organ. The two greatest in the world, and without any dispute, are *Händel* in England, and *Bach* in Leipzig, whom no one approaches, unless he should be a pupil of *Händel's*, named *Babel*, of whom they say that he surpassed his master. . . .

. . . The author [Bellermann] . . . praises the custom, introduced in England, of making Bachelors, Masters and Doctors of Music, an honour which has befallen *Pepusch* and the prince of composition, the excellent *Händel*. As far as Herr *Händel* is concerned, I must contradict Herr Bellermann, because I know more of the facts. This admirable musician, from whom indeed six Doctors of Music could be fashioned, wrote the following words to me in a letter of 25th May 1744 : " *I neither could nor would accept the Doctor's degree, because I was overwhelmingly busy.*"

Vol. 3, part 3, pp. 531 and 567 f. For Mattheson's original passage, see middle of 1739. Babell died in 1723.—For Bellermann's original passage (1743) and Handel's letter to Mizler (1744), see *Addenda*.

1748

Walsh publishes a score of *Roxana* by Handel, about 1748.

Cf. 8th and 15th November 1743. Burney (IV. 450), assuming that the *Roxana* of 1743 was by Lampugnani, states that it was published about 1747 as *Alessandro nell' Indie*. From *Rossane*, the new version of Handel's *Alessandro*, favourite songs were printed in 1743 or 1744, including a song from *Admeto* and two from *Siroe* ; this larger score was published about 1748. (Cf. 20th February.) Of Lampugnani's pasticcio *Alessandro nel-l'Indie* a selection was published about 1747. All this music was printed by Walsh.

———

An overture by Handel is performed at a concert given in the Music Hall, Fishamble Street, Dublin, for the benefit of Signor Putti, 14th January 1748. (*Dublin Journal*, 12th January.)

Putti was singer, harpsichord player, and composer.

———

From Faulkner's " Dublin Journal ", 26th January 1748

Last Thursday [the 21st] Il Allegro, Il Penseroso, written by Mr. Milton, and set to Musick by Mr. Handell, was performed at the Musick-Hall in Fishamble-street, to a very numerous and polite Audience, for the Benefit of the Hospital for Incurables.

The Governors of the Lying-in-Hospital in George's-lane give Notice, that they have fixed on the 11th Day of February next, for the Perform-ance of Mr. Handel's last and grand Oratorio called Judas Maccabaeus, for the Support of the said Hospital.

———

From Faulkner's " Dublin Journal ", 2nd February 1748

We are informed that the Oratorio called Samson, which is to be performed on Thursday next [the 4th] at the Great Room in Fishamble-street, is the Masterpiece of that great Man Mr. Handel ; and as it is the first Time of its being performed in Ireland, will be honour'd by great Numbers of the first Rank, and all true Lovers of Musick.

———

From Faulkner's " Dublin Journal ", 13th February 1748

Last Thursday [the 11th] Evening the celebrated Oratorio of Judas Maccabaeus . . . was performed to a most grand and polite Audience . . .

under the Conduct of Mr. Dubourg, to the entire Satisfaction of all the Company. . . .

On 26th January the *Dublin Journal* called Handel's friend Matthew Dubourg " Chief Composer and Master of the Music attending his Majesty's State in Ireland ".

———

FROM THE " GENERAL ADVERTISER ", 20th February 1748

At the King's Theatre in the Hay-Market, this Day, will be perform'd an *Opera*, call'd ROXANA. *Compos'd by Mr.* HANDEL. . . . To begin at Six o'Clock.

Cf. 15th November 1743 and 6th March 1744. Repeat performances on 27th February, 8th and 12th March.

———

FROM FAULKNER'S " DUBLIN JOURNAL ", 23rd February 1748

By particular Desire of several Persons of Quality and Distinction.

For the Benefit of Mr. *Bar. Manwaring.*

At the great Musick-Hall in Fishamble-street, this Evening . . . will be performed Mr. Handell's most celebrated Masque of ACIS and GALATEA. Made for the Entertainment, and at the Request of the Duke of Chandos. With all the proper Chorus's, Recitatives, &c. and performed by the best Voices in the Kingdom. . . . Printed Books of this Entertainment will be delivered the above Night gratis. . . .

Cf. 18th and 25th November 1748. For Bartholomew Manwaring see 11th May 1742.

———

FROM THE " GENERAL ADVERTISER ", 26th February 1748

At the Theatre-Royal in Covent-Garden, this Day . . . will be perform'd an *Oratorio*, call'd JUDAS MACCABAEUS. With a *Concerto.* . . . To begin at Half an Hour after Six o'Clock.

(Schoelcher, p. 305.) This was the opening of a new Lent oratorio season. In the same issue Walsh advertised his score of the oratorio, and Watts his word-book. Repeat performances on 2nd and 4th March and, " With Additions ", on 1st, 4th and 7th April.

———

Handel deposits £300, 27th February 1748.

———

Handel deposits £200, 3rd March 1748.

———

Handel deposits £100, 5th March 1748.

———

FROM THE " GENERAL ADVERTISER ", 8th March 1748

For the Benefit of Signora GALLI.

At the King's Theatre in the Hay-Market, this Day . . . will be perform'd an *Opera*, call'd ROXANA. Compos'd by Mr. *Handel.*

Signora *Galli* will sing the Part of *Alexander*, with all the Original Songs of Signor *Senesino.* . . .

Here the fact is disclosed that *Rossane* was an arrangement of *Alessandro*. The part of Alessandro in *Rossane* was first sung by Signor Monticelli on 15th November 1743 ; Senesino had sung it in the original *Alessandro* in 1726 and 1732. Repeat performance on 12th March.

———

FROM THE " GENERAL ADVERTISER ", 9th March 1748

At the Theatre-Royal in Covent-Garden, this Day, will be perform'd a New Oratorio, call'd JOSHUA. And a New Concerto. . . . To begin at Half an Hour after Six o'Clock.

(Schoelcher, p. 305.) Schoelcher's statement, on page 308, that *Alexander Balus* was produced on this day, is a mistake. The word-book was again by Morell. Repeat performances on 11th, 16th, and 18th March.

———

CAST OF " JOSHUA ", 9th March 1748

Joshua—Mr. Lowe, tenor
Caleb—Mr. Reinhold, bass
Othniel—Signora Galli, contralto
Achsah—Signora Casarini, soprano
Angel—? Signora Galli, mezzo-soprano

The lady singers were again from the Haymarket Opera ; cf. 1st April 1747.

———

Handel deposits £250, 10th March 1748.

———

HANDEL TO MRS. FRANCIS BREREWOOD, 15th March 1748

Madame

I gave order that you and Mr Brerewood should be free of the House in my oratorios all this season. I am glad of this Opportunity to shew you the true Esteem and Regard with which I am

Madam
Your
very humble Servant

March. 15. 1748.   G. F. Handel

(Coopersmith, 1943, p. 64.) Original formerly in the collection of Dr. Edward Brooks Keffer, Philadelphia. Francis Brerewood was one of the subscribers for the *Alessandro* score (6th August 1726) ; he was not related to Thomas Brerewood junior who subscribed for the score of *Admeto* (24th June 1727). His father's name, however, was also Thomas Brerewood, of Harton. The Brerewoods were a Chester family, and another Francis was Treasurer of Christ Hospital, London, about 1710.

—

Handel deposits £140, 15th March 1748.

—

Handel withdraws £990, 19th March 1748.

—

The Merry Wives of Windsor, with Colley Cibber's " Masque of Music in two Interludes " called *Venus and Adonis*, is performed at Covent Garden for the benefit of Mr. Beard, 21st March 1748.

The advertisement in the *General Advertiser* adds that " the Stage (for the better Accommodation of the Ladies) will be form'd into an Amphitheatre, illuminated, and enclos'd, as at an Oratorio ".

—

FROM THE " GENERAL ADVERTISER ", 23rd March 1748

At the Theatre-Royal in Covent-Garden, this Day, will be perform'd a New *Oratorio*, call'd ALEXANDER BALUS. And a new *Concerto*. . . . To begin at Half an Hour after Six o'Clock.

The subject of this oratorio is a historic continuation of *Judas Maccabaeus*. The author of the word-book, advertised by Watts and Dod, was again Morell. He dedicated it to William Freeman for his " particular Affection for Music, and true Taste of Harmony ". Freeman was one of the most persistent of the subscribers for Handel's scores : his name is to be found in the list of subscribers for all ten published in this way between 1725 and 1740. Since about 1740 his family had resided at Hamels, near Braughing, Hertfordshire. Cf. Handel's letter of 30th September 1749. The new oratorio was repeated on 25th and 30th March 1748, and was revived in March 1754.

—

CAST OF " ALEXANDER BALUS ", 23rd March 1748

Alexander Balus—Signora Galli, mezzo-soprano
Ptolomee—Mr. Reinhold, bass
Jonathan—Mr. Lowe, tenor
Cleopatra—Signora Casarini, soprano
Aspasia—Signora Sibilla, soprano

Again, there were two ladies engaged from the Haymarket Opera. Signora Sibilla, who did not belong to that house, was the daughter of a German pastor, Gronamann, and became the first wife of Thomas Pinto, the violinist, whose second wife was Charlotte Brent (for her father, see 26th February 1752).

—

Handel deposits £300, 26th March 1748.

—

At a performance of Ben Jonson's comedy *The Silent Woman*, given at Covent Garden on 28th March 1748 for the benefit of Mr. [Colley] Cibber, Mrs. Storer sings " 'Tis Liberty " and Miss Falkner " Smiling Liberty " (" Come, ever smiling Liberty "), from *Judas Maccabaeus*, after Act II.

" Miss Falkner " may have been identical with the soprano, Faulkner, who sang in Handel oratorios in 1750 and 1751.

———

Handel deposits £100, 31st March 1748.

———

At a performance of George Farquhar's comedy *The Recruiting Officer*, given at Covent Garden on 31st March 1748 for the benefit of Mr. Leveridge, Miss Falkner sings " Liberty " in an interval.

This was probably the aria from *Judas Maccabaeus* : " Come, ever smiling Liberty ".

———

Walsh advertises the score of *Joshua*, *General Advertiser*, 2nd April 1748.

On 7th April Walsh adds : " With His Majesty's Royal Licence ". The Privilege of 31st October 1739 is reprinted in the score.

———

FROM THE " GENERAL ADVERTISER ", 5th April 1748

For the Benefit and Increase of a FUND *establish'd for the Support of* Decay'd Musicians *or their* Families.

At the King's Theatre in the Hay-Market, this Day . . . will be per-form'd an Entertainment of Vocal and Instrumental MUSICK.

.   .   .   .

SECOND PART.

.   .   .   .

Heart, thou Seat of soft Delight, in Acis and Galatea, by Signora Frasi.

.   .   .   .

.   .   .   .

THIRD PART.

.   .   .   .

.   .   .   .

The Prince unable to conceal his Pain, in Alexander's Feast, by Sig. Frasi. *Come, ever smiling Liberty*, in Judas Maccabeus, by Signora Casarini.

.   .   .   .

A Grand Concerto of Mr. Handel's.

.   .   .   .

To begin exactly at Six o'Clock.

.   .   .   .

———

H.-21 a

Handel deposits £200, 5th April 1748.

—

Handel's Lent season ends on 7th April 1748 with *Judas Maccabaeus*. (Schoelcher, p. 305.)

—

FROM THE " GENERAL ADVERTISER ", 8th April 1748

The MORNING CONCERT.

SIG. PASQUALI's *Bath Lyrick-Ode*, will be perform'd on Wednesday Morning, April 27,

At HICKFORD's ROOM *in* Brewer Street,

With the other following Songs, &c. sung by Signora GALLI.

1. *He was despised*, in the Messiah, by Mr. Handel. . . . 5. *Powerful Guardians*, &c. in Alexander Balus.

To begin at 12 o'Clock in the Morning.

☞ The Ladies are desired to come in their Capuchins.

The Words of the Ode, and of the other Songs will be printed together, and deliver'd in the Room. . . .

From 1748 till 1751 Niccolò Pasquali lived in Edinburgh.

—

At a performance of Charles Shadwell's comedy *The Fair Quaker of Deal*, given at Covent Garden on 13th April 1748, for the benefit of Mr. and Mrs. Dunstall, Mrs. Lampe and Miss Young, Mrs. Lampe sings " Myself I shall adore ", from *Semele*, after Act IV.

Mrs. Isabella Lampe was a sister of Miss Esther Young and Mrs. Cecilia Arne, *née* Young.

—

At a performance of Mrs. Susannah Centlivre's comedy *The Wonder*, given at Covent Garden on 15th April 1748 for the benefit of Mrs. Storer, she sings, in an interval, " *The Smiling Hours*, a Song of Mr. Handel's " (from *Hercules*).

—

FROM THE " GENERAL ADVERTISER ", 19th April 1748

NEW MUSICK.

This Day is Publish'd, Price 4s.

(With His Majesty's Licence,)

Songs in the Oratorio of ALEXANDER BALUS. In which is contain'd *Powerful Guardians*. The Remainder of the Oratorio will be publish'd next week.

Printed for J. Walsh. . . .

Contrary to Walsh's practice of not dating music, this selection is marked " April 19th, 1748 " ; the engraver probably copied it from a manuscript note made by the publisher for private use. Cf. 5th May. The aria quoted became very popular (see 8th April).

———

At a performance of Thomas Southerne's tragedy *Oroonoko*, given at Covent Garden on 20th April 1748 for the benefit of Mr. Lalanze, Mrs. Storer sings "Consider fond Shepherd", from *Acis and Galatea*, and " 'Tis Liberty alone ", from *Judas Maccabaeus*, in the intervals.

———

At a performance of Sir John Vanbrugh's comedy *The Pilgrim*, given at Covent Garden on 21st April 1748, for the benefit of Mr. James, Mr. Stoppelaer and Mrs. Bland, Miss Falkner sings two arias " Come. ever smiling Liberty " and " 'Tis Liberty ", from *Judas Maccabaeus*, in an interval.

Stoppelaer may have been the tenor who sang in *Saul* on 16th January 1739.

———

At a performance of *Hamlet*, given at Covent Garden on 27th April 1748 for the benefit of Mr. Marten and the treasurer Mr. White, Miss Falkner again sings the two arias from *Judas Maccabaeus* (see 21st April) in an interval.

At Covent Garden Theatre it was usual to give benefit performances in March and April not only for the principal actors, but also for the leading officials of the house.

———

LADY LUXBOROUGH TO WILLIAM SHENSTONE

Barrels, 28 April 1748.

Our friend Outing . . . went . . . to the Oratorio of Judas Maccabaeus, where he was highly entertained ; and he speaks with such ecstasy of the music, as I confess I cannot conceive any one can feel who understands no more of music than myself ; which I take to be his case. But I suppose he sets his judgment true to that of the multitude ; for if his ear is not nice enough to distinguish the harmony, it serves to hear what the multitude say of it.

(Streatfeild, 1909, pp. 194 f.) Luxborough, *Letters*, p. 20. Outing was Luxborough's steward. Henrietta, the friend of the poet Shenstone, was married to Robert Knight, of Barrels, since 1746 Baron Luxborough in the Irish Peerage.

———

Handel withdraws £600, 2nd May 1748.

———

From the " General Advertiser ", 5th May 1748

New Musick.

This Day is Publish'd, Price 10s. 6d.

Alexander Balus, an Oratorio in Score. Compos'd by Mr. *Handel.*
Those Gentlemen, &c. who have the first Part of the above Oratorio,
may have the second and third Act separate to compleat it. Price 6s. 6d.
Printed for J. Walsh. . . .

Cf. 19th April. Half a guinea was Walsh's ordinary price for an oratorio score
at this time.

———

Handel begins the oratorio *Solomon,* 5th May 1748.

———

Handel sells £3000 3 per cent Annuities (1743), and buys, by
subscription, £4500 4 per cent Annuities (1748), 6th May 1748.
Cf. 10th April 1744 and 22nd January 1749.

———

From the " General Advertiser ", 23rd May 1748

Cupers-Gardens.

Is Open'd for the Season, with a good Band of Vocal and Instrumental
Musick. Which will be Divided every Evening into two Acts. The
Vocal by Signora Sibilla. In the first set this Evening, She sings Powerful
Guardians in Alexander Balus, Mr. Handel . . . in the second Act
May Balmy Peace, Occasional Oratorio, Mr. Handel. . . . To conclude
with the Fireworks . . . the Company . . . own they never saw any
Thing in Fireworks so beautiful picturesque.

(*Musical Times,* 1st February 1894, p. 88 : dated 1743.) For Cuper's Gardens
see 4th July 1741 and 4th September 1749. For Signora Sibilla see 23rd March
1748 ; she sang there again, as Mrs. Pinto, in 1750. (The Haymarket Opera
closed on 14th May 1748.)

———

Handel finishes the oratorio *Solomon,* 13th June 1748.

———

From the " Accounts of Covent Garden Theatre ", [June] 1748

Reced by D⁰ [balance] Mʳ Handel for 10 Oratorio's   £111.   2.   8
                                            Rent   £200

(Wyndham, I. 60.) British Museum : Egerton MS. 2269. Cf. June 1747.
Handel performed 13 times during Lent 1748 ; 10 times before April. The
account may have been made out before June, or else the rent was settled by a
lump sum in June.

———

At the Oxford Act, the new Music Room in Holywell is opened with *Esther*, 9th July 1748.

(Mee, p. 8.) The only known copy of the word-book is in Yale University.

—

Handel writes the oratorio *Susanna* between 11th July and 24th August 1748.

—

At the Three Choirs Meeting in Gloucester, on 14th and 15th September 1748, the *Dettingen Te Deum* and *Utrecht Jubilate* are performed on the first morning, and one Coronation Anthem on the second morning, both in the Cathedral; in the evenings, in the Boothall, "Several grand pieces by Mr. Handel, particularly the Oratorio, *Samson*" (*Gloucester Journal*).

The same newspaper states : " The date of the Festival was altered to avoid clashing with Burford Races ".

—

The Peace of Aix-la-Chapelle ends the War of the Austrian Succession, 7th October 1748.

—

LADY LUXBOROUGH TO WILLIAM SHENSTONE

Barrels, Sunday, October 16th 1748.

The great Handel has told me that the hints of his very best songs have several of them been owing to the sounds in his ears of cries in the street.

(Chrysander, III. 189.) Luxborough, *Letters*, p. 58. In the Fitzwilliam Museum, Cambridge, is an autograph note in which Handel has written down the music and words of a cry heard by " John Shaw, near a brandy shop St. Giles's in Tyburn Road " who " sells matches about " : " buoy any matches, my matches buoy ". Young, p. 138, speaks of Elviro's " flower-selling song " from *Serse*.

—

Alexander's Feast and *Acis and Galatea* are performed at Salisbury, 19th and 20th October 1748.

—

FROM FAULKNER'S " DUBLIN JOURNAL ", 5th November 1748

Philharmonic Room, Fishamble-street.

For the Support of Incurables, on Thursday next, being the 10th Inst. November, will be performed ALEXANDER'S FEAST, in which Miss OLDMIXON (being requested) will perform.

On Friday next, at the Musick-hall in Fishamble-street, will be performed the celebrated Oratorio of ESTER, composed by Mr. Handel. Mrs. Arne being recovered from her late Illness will certainly perform in the above Oratorio.

For the Benefit of Miss OLDMIXON, at the Philharmonick Room in Fishamble-street, on Thursday the 17th of this Inst. November, will be performed Mr. Handel's celebrated Oratorio of SAMSON. The Whole will be conducted by Mr. Dubourg. Tickets . . . at an English Crown each. To begin at 7 o'Clock.

These three advertisements appeared one after the other in the same issue.

—

FROM FAULKNER'S " DUBLIN JOURNAL ", 22nd November 1748

Acis and Gallatea was performed last Friday [the 18th] Evening at the great Musick-Hall in Fishamble-street, to a most crowded Audience, in which Mrs. Arne (tho' but just recovered out of a violent Fever) gave entire Satisfaction, and it was at the same time unanimously requested to be performed again next Friday, the 25th Instant.

(Cummings, 1912, p. 38.) Mrs. Arne was temporarily back in Dublin. During this November Dublin had five evenings of Handel oratorios.

—

FROM THE " GENERAL ADVERTISER ", 9th December 1748

For the Benefit of Mr. WALTZ.

At the New Theatre in the Haymarket, this Day, will be perform'd a *Concert* of Vocal and Instrumental MUSICK. The Vocal Parts by Signora Sybilla, Miss Young, Mr. Waltz, Mr. Hague and Mr. Messing, jun. The first Violin by Mr. Freak. And the rest of the Instruments by the best Masters.

Act I. The Overture in Otho. . . . Two Songs by Signora Sybilla, viz. Powerful Guardians, and Come ever Smiling Liberty, compos'd by Mr. Handel. . . .

Act II.

     .   .   .   .

Concluding, with the Water-Musick of Mr. Handel's, accompanied with Four Kettle-Drummers.

(Smith, 1948, p. 191.) The kettle-drums were handled by John Mitcheal Axt and others. John George Freak(e) gave his own concert on 9th December 1748, and played in the *Messiah* performances of 1754 and 1758.

—

FROM FAULKNER'S " DUBLIN JOURNAL ", 13th December 1748

As it has been maliciously insinuated that the Musical Entertainment of ACIS and GALATEA, which is to be performed on Tuesday the 13th

Inst. at the Great Musick-hall in Fishamble-street, for the Benefit of a young Gentleman in Distress, who has taken his Master's Degree in Trinity College, Dublin, would be postponed. This is to give Notice that the said Entertainment will positively be performed as above mentioned, many of the Nobility and Gentry having according to their usual Benevolence, most generously contributed to the Relief of this unfortunate Gentleman, by taking a large Number of Tickets, and the best Musical Hands and Voices will perform on this generous Occasion.

After two performances in November, *Acis and Galatea* was repeated once more. The oratorio *Solomon*, performed on 16th December, was, however, not Handel's, as Cummings (1912, p. 38) states, but Boyce's.

Handel deposits £112 : 9 : 5, 23rd December 1748.

From John Henley's " Oratory Magazine ", Number III [1748]

A spiritual Excellency is greater than a sensitive one ; there was more Perfection in *Pythagoras's* finding his celebrated Proposition, than there was in *Faffy's* making a Mouse-trap, or an Oratorio on *Saul* from my Lecture proposing *Saul* as the best Theme of that Kind, in Honour of St. *Cecilia's* Day ; numerous other Hints and Pieces have been taken from this Plan and Performance, not only not own'd, but ungratefully us'd for it.

(Chrysander, III. 20.) Page 10 of Number III. Cf. 19th November 1733. The passage is from one of Henley's speeches. *Saul* was produced in 1739. It happens that Henley also wrote *The History of Queen Esther : A poem in four books*, before Handel wrote his oratorio.

From Mrs. M. Laetitia Pilkington's Memoirs, Dublin, 1748

Mr. *P—n* . . . the Husband of my Youth . . . took an invincible Aversion to Counsellor *Smith*, because he excelled him on the Harpsichord. It happened one Evening that this Gentleman sang and played to us the Oratorio of Queen *Esther* ; unfortunately for me I was so charmed with it, that at the Conclusion of the Music I wrote the following Lines. . . . I then was continually told with a contemptuous jibing Air, O my Dear ! a Lady of your Accomplishments ! why Mr. *Smith* says you write better than I. . . .

(Myers, 1947, pp. 10 f.) Pilkington, I. 116. The Rev. Matthew Pilkington (cf. p. 246) and his friend John Smith were living in Dublin about 1733, when this occurred. Her lines are a poem addressed to Smith.

1749

Handel deposits £50, 17th January 1749.

———

Handel sells, in seven shares, £7750 4 per cent Annuities (1748), 22nd January 1749.

Cf. 6th May 1748, 22nd February, 7th April, 7th September and 9th November 1749.

———

FROM FAULKNER'S "DUBLIN JOURNAL", 7th February 1749

For the Benefit of Mrs. ARNE, at the Great Musick-Hall in Fishamble-street, on Tuesday the 7th February 1748 will be performed the celebrated Masque of ACIS and GALATEA. In which will be introduced several favourite Songs and Duets by Mrs. ARNE and Mrs. LAMPE, never performed here. The whole will be attended by all the Voices of the Society, and conducted by Mr. LAMPE. Tickets . . . at an English Crown each.

N.B. Diana, a new Cantata (in the Hunting Style) composed by Mr. Lampe will be sung by Mrs. Lampe.

(*The Musical Antiquary*, July 1910, p. 225.)   Cf. 22nd November and 13th December 1748.

———

Handel deposits £75, 9th February 1749.

———

FROM THE "GENERAL ADVERTISER", 10th February 1749

At the Theatre-Royal in Covent-Garden, This Day . . . will be perform'd a New ORATORIO, call'd *SUSANNA*. *With a* CONCERTO. . . . To begin at Half an Hour after Six o'Clock.

The author of the word-book is not known. Repeat performances on 15th, 17th and 22nd February ; revived in March 1759.

———

CAST OF "SUSANNA", 10th February 1749

Susanna—Signora Frasi, soprano
An Attendant—Signora Sibilla, soprano
Daniel—the Boy, soprano
Joacim—Signora Galli, mezzo-soprano
First Elder—Mr. Lowe, tenor

Second Elder—Mr. Reinhold, bass
Chelsias—Mr. Reinhold
A Judge—?, bass

—

Handel deposits £235, 11th February 1749.

—

THE COUNTESS OF SHAFTESBURY TO JAMES HARRIS, IN SALISBURY

[London,] February 11, 1749

My sister went with me last night to hear the Oratorio, where we wished much for the agreeable company of our Salisbury friends.

I cannot pretend to give my poor judgment of it from once hearing, but believe it will insinuate itself so much into my approbation as most of Handel's performances do, as it is in the light *operatic* style ; but you will receive an opinion of it from much better judges than myself, as I saw both my cousins Harris peeping out of a little box, and very attentive to the music. I think I never saw a fuller house. Rich told me that he believed he would receive near 400*l.*

(Streatfeild, 1909, pp. 199 f.) Malmesbury, *Letters*, I. 74. James Harris was Lord Shaftesbury's cousin ; his brothers Thomas and William lived in London. Rich, the manager of Covent Garden, referred, apparently, to Handel's takings.

—

TOBIAS SMOLLETT TO ALEXANDER CARLYLE, 14th February 1749

I have wrote a sort of Tragedy on the Story of Alceste, which will (without fail) be acted at Covent Garden next Season and appear with such magnificence of Scenery as was never exhibited in Britain before.

The Times Literary Supplement, 24th July 1943 (edited by Henry W. Meikle). Smollett delivered his manuscript in autumn 1749, and Handel wrote the music in December 1749 and January 1750 ; Servadoni painted the scenery. The piece was never performed. Cf. 8th January 1750.

—

Handel deposits £227 : 10 : 7, 17th February 1749.

—

SIR EDWARD TURNER TO SANDERSON MILLER, AT RADWAY

[London,] February 21st, 1748 [1749].

Will not the sedate Raptures of Oratorical Harmony attract hither an Admirer of the sublime in music ? Why was not Susannah attended by the Elder of Radway ? Solomon is the next new piece (for so Guernsey informs us, and Handell always verifyes the Prophecys of Guernsey) that will be exhibited. Glorious Entertainment ! Divine Efficacy of Music !

(Sanderson Miller, pp. 131 f.) Miller's home was in Warwickshire. Lord Guernsey was Handel's and Jennens's friend. For *Susanna* see 10th February, for *Solomon* 17th March.

———

Handel deposits £115 in cash, and buys, by subscription, £7700 4 per cent Annuities (1748), 22nd February 1749.

Cf. 22nd January.

———

FROM THE " GENERAL ADVERTISER ", 24th February 1749

At the Theatre-Royal in Covent-Garden, This Day, will be perform'd an ORATORIO, call'd *HERCULES. With a* CONCERTO. . . . To begin at Half an Hour after Six o'Clock.

Cf. 5th January 1745. Repeat performance on 1st March. Signora Frasi probably sang the part of Dejanira, Galli—Lichas, Sibilla—Iole, Lowe—Hillus, and Reinhold certainly Hercules.

———

Handel deposits £185, 25th February 1749.

———

An anonymous masque, *The Temple of Peace*, is produced at the Theatre Royal in Smock Alley, Dublin, with music by Arne, Boyce, Galliard, Handel, Purcell, and the rest by Pasquali, February 1749.

Word-book in the British Museum. On page 12, the air VIII, sung by Bacchus, is " Let the deep bowl my praise confess " from *Belshazzar*, with the Chorus "See the God of Drinking comes ", probably a variant of the famous chorus from *Joshua*, " See the conquering hero comes ". The music was apparently arranged by Pasquali. The occasion was the Peace of Aix-la-Chapelle.

———

FROM THE " GENERAL ADVERTISER ", 3rd March 1749

At the Theatre-Royal in Covent-Garden, This Day, will be perform'd an Oratorio, call'd *SAMSON. With a* CONCERTO. . . . To begin at Half an Hour after Six o'Clock.

Cf. 18th February 1743, 24th February 1744 and 1st March 1745. The cast is not known, but Reinhold certainly kept his part of Harapha and Lowe probably his two smaller parts. Repeat performances on 8th, 10th and 15th March.

———

Handel deposits £190, 6th March 1749.

———

Walsh advertises the score of *Susanna, General Advertiser*, 8th March 1749.

———

WILLIAM DUNCOMBE TO MRS. ELIZABETH CARTER

Soho, 8th March, 1749.

. . . P.S. The following Epigram, addressed to Mr. Mason, of Cambridge, was writ by my son, who is now at his College.—

Soft harmony has Handel crown'd
Titian for painting is renown'd,
And Dryden for poetic ease :
These all with different beauty please.

But Mason can at once inspire
The pen, the pencil, and the lyre ;
And Dryden's ease the Nine impart,
With Titian's skill and Handel's art.

Pennington, p. 99. William Duncombe, later Vicar of Hearne, near Canterbury, translated Horace and probably provided Handel with the text of *The Choice of Hercules* (1st March 1751). His son, the Rev. John Duncombe, at Corpus Christi College in 1745-8, was also a miscellaneous writer. William Mason, Gray's friend, belonged to St. John's College ; he was an amateur of painting and music.

———

Handel deposits £400, 11th March 1749.

———

FROM THE " GENERAL ADVERTISER ", 13th March 1749

To Mr. H⁓

Sir,

A Number of your Friends have wished to see performed the Oratorio of JOSHUA, which, if you would direct to be performed this Season, would be much gratified, and in particular

Your Humble Servant,

A. VIRTUOSO.

Joshua, produced in 1748, was not revived until 1752. Virtuoso means professional musician.

———

FROM THE " GENERAL ADVERTISER ", 17th March 1749

At the Theatre-Royal in Covent-Garden, This Day, will be perform'd a New Oratorio, call'd *SOLOMON*. *With a* CONCERTO. . . . (To begin at Half an Hour after Six o'Clock.)

(Schoelcher, p. 312.) The author of the text is not known. Repeat performances on 20th and 22nd March ; revived in March 1759.

———

CAST OF " SOLOMON ", 17th March 1749

Solomon—Signora Galli, mezzo-soprano
Zadok—Mr. Lowe, tenor
A Levite—Mr. Reinhold, bass
Pharaoh's daughter (Queen to Solomon)
Nicaule (Queen of Sheba)   —Signora Frasi, soprano
First Harlot (First Woman)
Second Harlot (Second Woman)—Signora Sibilla, soprano

———

Handel deposits £300, 18th March 1749.

———

FROM THE " GENERAL ADVERTISER ", 21st March 1749

For the Benefit and Increase of a FUND, *established for the Support of*
DECAY'D MUSICIANS *or their Families.*

At the *King's Theatre* in the *Hay-Market.* This Day . . . will be
perform'd an *Entertainment* of *Vocal* and *Instrumental*

MUSICK.

·   ·   ·   ·   ·

PART II.

·   ·   ·   ·   ·

Prove Sono ; composed by Mr. Handel, sung by Signora Galli.

PART III.

·   ·   ·   ·   ·

Heroes, when with Glory burning ; compos'd by Mr. Handel, sung by
Signora Galli.
O Sleep ; compos'd by Mr. Handel, sung by Signora Frasi.

·   ·   ·   ·   ·

O Lovely Peace ; compos'd by Mr. Handel, sung by Signora Frasi and
Signora Galli.

A GRAND CONCERTO of Mr. HANDEL'S.

·   ·   ·   ·   ·

To begin at Six o'Clock.

·   ·   ·   ·   ·

" Prove sono " may be a corruption of " Priva son d'ogni " from *Giulio Cesare* ;
" Heroes, when with glory burning " is from *Joshua,* " O sleep " from *Semele,* and
" O lovely peace " from *Judas Maccabaeus.*

———

FROM THE " GENERAL ADVERTISER ", 23rd March 1749

At the Theatre-Royal in Covent-Garden, This Day, will be perform'd
an Oratorio, call'd *MESSIAH. With a* CONCERTO. . . . (To begin at Half
an Hour after Six o'Clock.)

(Schoelcher, pp. 258, 275 and 311.) There was no previous advertisement, as
was usual for the oratorios. There was one performance only, the first since the

three in March 1743. The title was now, as in Dublin, *Messiah*. (It may be of interest that Thomas Sherlock was at this time Bishop of London, having succeeded Gibson in 1748.) On 23rd March, Watts advertised the word-book of *Messiah* as to be published " To-morrow ", that is, too late.

—

Mr. Louis Monnet gets leave and license to perform French and Italian comedies and comic operas at the "Little Theatre in St. James's Haymarket", 23rd March 1749.

(Public Record Office : L.C.5/161, p. 301.) According to Burney (IV. 457 f.), the Italian company under Dr. Croza left the Hamyarket Theatre and went in November 1749 to the New Theatre, playing there until Croza ran away in April 1750.

—

THE DUKE OF MONTAGUE TO CHARLES FREDERICK, 28th March 1749

I don't see any kind of objection to the rehersal of the [fireworks] musick at Voxhall being advertised, and when that is done, if any questions are asked how it comes to be there, the true reason must be given.

I think Hendel now proposes to have but 12 trumpets and 12 French horns ; at first there was to have been sixteen of each, and I remember I told the King so, who, at that time, objected to their being any musick ; but, when I told him the quantity and nomber of martial musick there was to be, he was better satisfied, and said he hoped there would be no fidles. Now Hendel proposes to lessen the nomber of trumpets, &c. and to have violeens. I dont at all doubt but when the King hears it he will be very much displeased. If the thing war to be in such a manner as certainly to please the King, it ought to consist of no kind of instrument but martial instruments. Any other I am sure will put him out of humour, therefore I am shure it behoves Hendel to have as many trumpets, and other martial instruments, as possible, tho he dont retrench the violins, which I think he shoud, tho I beleeve he will never be per-suaded to do it. I mention this as I have very lately been told, from very good authority, that the King has, within this fortnight, expressed himself to this purpose.

Gentleman's Magazine, May 1856, pp. 477 f. Reprinted in *The Leisure Hour*, 11th August 1877 (from the notes of the late Edward Rimbault, not " from State Papers ", as indicated there). Although this and other letters referring to Handel's *Fireworks Music* had twice been printed, they remained unknown to Handel biographers, with two exceptions : Schoelcher, who in the French manuscript of his life of Handel quotes the 1856 publication, and Romain Rolland (1910, p. 127), who knew it from Schoelcher's manuscript in the Conservatoire, Paris. John, second Duke of Montague (cf. 29th February 1744), was Master General of the Ordnance—for the second time, in succession to the Duke of Argyll. Charles Frederick, afterwards Sir Charles, was " Comptrollor of his Majesty's Fireworks as well as for War as for Triumph ", and later Surveyor-General of the Ordnance.

Unfortunately, the editor of the *Gentleman's Magazine*, Sylvanus Urban, only published parts of their correspondence, now lost, but it is to be assumed that he selected all the essential passages. As for the Fireworks, they were already planned after the armistice agreed on in May 1748, and prepared in July 1748 for a performance in Lincoln's Inn Fields, in front of the Duke of Newcastle's house, at an estimate of £8000. The structure in St. James's Upper or Green Park was begun on 7th November, after the Peace of Aix-la-Chapelle in October 1748, and finished the day before the Fireworks, which were held on 26th April 1749. When Handel was asked to write the music, and when he wrote it, is not known. The rehearsal was on 21st April at Vauxhall Gardens, without Fireworks. There are 9 trumpets and 9 horns in Handel's score, as well as 24 hautboys, 12 bassoons, a double-bassoon, 3 pairs of kettle-drums (certainly lent by the Ordnance). The string parts were added later.

———

Handel deposits £280, 30th March 1749.

———

FROM THE " GENERAL ADVERTISER ", 5th April 1749

The Rehearsal of the Musick, composed by Mr. Handel for the Royal Fireworks, will be at the Spring Gardens, Vauxhall, on Monday se'night the 17th Instant.

Cf. 28th March. The rehearsal, first postponed till the 24th ; was finally held on 21st April.

———

FROM THE MINUTES OF MERCER'S HOSPITAL, DUBLIN, 5th April 1749

On Application of the Dean and Chapter of Christ Church to the Governors of this Hospital to lend them the Scores & Parts both Vocal & Instrumental of Mr Handels Te-Deum Jubilate, and one Coronation Anthem to be performed before the Government in their Cathedral on the 25th Instant April, being the Thanksgiving day for ye Peace.

The application was granted. The old manuscript music is still preserved at the Hospital.

———

Handel withdraws £2012 : 10 : 0, and buys £2000 4 per cent Annuities (1748), 7th April 1749.

———

THE DUKE OF MONTAGUE TO MR. FREDERICK, 9th April 1749

I think it would be proper if you woud write an other letter to Hendel, as from yourself, to know his absolute determination, and if he wont let us have his overture we must get an other, and I think it woud be proper to inclose my letter to you in your letter to him, that he may know my centiments ; but don't say I bid you send it to him.

Gentleman's Magazine, May 1856, p. 478. The correspondence between Handel and Frederick is not preserved. The letter to be enclosed is apparently the long one, written on the same day. The " overture " is the whole music, the introduction to the Fireworks.

———

THE DUKE OF MONTAGUE TO MR. FREDERICK

Sunday, 9 April, 1749.

Sir,—In answer to Mr. Hendel's letter to you (which by the stile of it I am shure is impossible to be of his inditing) I can say no more but this, that this morning at court the King did me the honor to talke to me conserning the fireworks, and in the course of the conversation his Majesty was pleased to aske me when Mr. Hendel's overture was to be rehersed ; I told his Majesty I really coud not say anything conserning it from the difficulty Mr. Hendel made about it, for that the master of Voxhall, having offered to lend us all his lanterns, lamps, &c. to the value of seven hundred pounds, whereby we woud save just so much money to the office of Ordnance, besides thirty of his servants to assist in the illuminations, upon condition that Mr. Hendel's overture shoud be rehersed at Voxhall, Mr. Hendel has hetherto refused to let it be at Foxhall, which his Majesty seemed to think he was in the wrong of ; and I am shure I think him extreamly so, and extreamly indifferent whether we have his overture or not, for it may very easily be suplyed by another, and I shall have the satisfaction that his Majesty will know the reason why we have it not ; therefore, as Mr. Hendel knows the reason, and the great benefit and saving it will be to the publick to have the rehersal at Voxhall, if he continues to express his zeal for his Majesty's service by doing what is so contrary to it, in not letting the rehersal be there, I shall intirely give over any further thoughts of his overture and shall take care to have an other.

I am, S^r

Your most humble
servant,
Montague.

Gentleman's Magazine, May 1856, p. 478. It seems that Frederick did not forward Montague's letter, with his own, to Handel. All the letters known remained in Frederick's private possession. The " master " of Vauxhall was Handel's friend, Tyers. The alternative place for the rehearsal was apparently the Green Park itself, and Handel might have preferred to have it there.

———

FROM THE " GENERAL ADVERTISER ", 10th April 1749

For the Benefit of Miss CASSANDRA FREDERICK, *a Child of Five Years and a Half old, and a Scholar of Mr. Paradies,*
At the New Theatre in the Hay-market, this Day . . . will be performed a Concert of Vocal and Instrumental *MUSICK*.

This Child will perform on the Harpsichord . . . a Concerto of Mr. *Handel's*. . . . To begin precisely at Seven o'Clock.

The child, apparently, was no relation to Mr. Charles Frederick ; she lived with her mother in Soho. Domenico Paradies (Paradisi), harpsichord player and composer, lived in London as a teacher.

From the " General Advertiser ", 13th April 1749

The Public are desired to take Notice, that the Rehearsal of the Music for the Royal Fireworks, which was to have been in the Spring-Gardens, Vauxhall, on Monday next [the 17th], is put off.

Cf. 15th, 18th and 19th April.

From the " General Advertiser ", 15th April 1749

We hear from Oxford, that on Wednesday [the 12th] Afternoon the Oratorio of Esther was performed there to a crouded Audience with great Applause, the Vocal Parts by the Gentlemen of the several Choirs in the University, and the Instrumental by near Fifty Hands from London, and other Places.

The opening of Dr. Radcliffe's Library in Oxford was celebrated by three Handel performances at the " Theatre " : *Esther* on 12th, *Samson* on 13th, and *The Sacred Oratorio* (*Messiah*) on 14th April.

From the " General Advertiser ", 17th April 1749

On Thursday last [the 13th] Dr. Radcliffe's Library at Oxford was opened. . . . [In the theatre] the Overture in the occasional Oratorio was play'd . . . [and finally] the following Anthem, compos'd by Mr. Handel, was vocally and instrumentally performed :

Let thy Hand be strengthened, and thy Right Hand be exalted.

Let Justice and Judgment be the Preparation of thy Seat ; Money and Truth shall go before thy Face.   Hallelujah.

. . . In the Afternoon the Oratorio of Sampson was perform'd in the Theatre, with great Applause, to a crowded Audience, by the same Persons who perform'd Esther the Day before. . . .

Friday [the 14th]. . . . In the Afternoon the Sacred Oratorio was perform'd in the Theatre to a full Audience. The Band of Musick was under the Direction of Dr. Hayes. . . .

The Anthem, the words of which were corrected on 18th April (*Mercy and Truth*), is one of the four Coronation Anthems. Another of these anthems was performed on Friday morning. William Hayes was Professor of Music, and received an honorary degree in music on this occasion.

Walsh advertises *Solomon*, composed by " Mr. Handell ", *General Advertiser*, 17th April 1749.

——

THE DUKE OF MONTAGUE TO MR. FREDERICK, 17th April 1749

The Duke [of Cumberland], as I told you, intends to hear the rehersal of Hendel's musick. You was saying you thought Munday woud be a good day for it. Munday is a drawing-room day and therefore, may be, woud not be agreable to the Duke. Woud Saturday be a good day ? Tuesday woud be too near the firework day, I believe. But I think it woud be quite right and well taken to know of the Duke what day he woud lyke best, and ill taken if you do not ; and I wish you coud contrive to see C. Napier to-morrow morning and talke to him about it, and get him to know of the Duke what day he woud lyke to have it. If there is but a day or two's notice in the news there will be people enough there ; but it shoud certainly not be advertised tyll you know what day the Duke woud lyke it on.

Gentleman's Magazine, May 1856, p. 478. (In the reprint of the letter in *The Leisure Hour*, 11th August 1877, it is wrongly dated 11th April 1749.) Mr. Napier was probably in the Duke of Cumberland's household. The Duke of Montague and his family are depicted in a drawing by Marcellus Laroon, of 1736, showing them with musicians in his house, where the British Museum now stands. (Reproduced from the original in the British Museum, in *The Chord*, London 1900, No. 4, opp. p. 68.)

——

FROM THE " GENERAL ADVERTISER ", 18th April 1749

The Publick may be assured, that the *Rehearsal* of the *Musick* composed by Mr. HANDEL, for the Royal Fireworks, is now fixed for Monday next the 24th Inst. at the Spring Garden, *Vauxhall*. To begin at 12 o'Clock at Noon.—No Persons to be admitted without Tickets, (at Half a Crown each, and to admit one Person only) which are ready to be delivered. . . —N.B. Tickets given out for the 17th Instant, will be taken the 24th.

Cf. 13th and 19th April.

——

FROM THE " GENERAL ADVERTISER ", 19th April 1749

By *Special Desire*, the *Rehearsal* (in the Spring Garden, VAUXHALL) of Mr. HANDEL'S *Musick* for the Royal-Fireworks, which was advertis'd for Monday the 24th Instant, is now appointed for Friday next the 21st, and to begin at 11 o'Clock in the Morning. . . . N.B. Any Persons who have already taken out Tickets for the abovesaid Rehearsal, and cannot conveniently come to it on Friday next, may have their Money return'd, any Time before that Day, at the several Places where they purchased their Tickets.

Cf. 18th April. Mr. Frederick seems finally to have got his answer from the Duke of Cumberland.

FROM THE " GENERAL ADVERTISER ", 21st April 1749

For the Benefit of Miss OLDMIXON

At Hickford's Room in Brewer street, this Day . . . will be perform'd ACIS and GALATEA. Compos'd by Mr. HANDEL. The Performance will be conducted by Mr. Dubourg who will Play a Solo. The Vocal Parts by the best Performers. To begin at Half an Hour after Seven o'Clock. Tickets . . . at Five Shillings each.

(*Musical Times*, 1st September 1906, p. 604.) Miss Oldmixon, like Dubourg, came from Dublin. The performers were : Miss Oldmixon, Signora Galli, Mr. Beard and Mr. Reinhold. About 1750, *Acis and Galatea* was performed several times at Hickford's Room. According to the *Musical Times* there was a perform-ance, at some unknown date about 1750, for the benefit of the sister of the late Robert Hiller, of Westminster Abbey ; the advertisement of this performance is quoted as follows : " The Public may be assured that Justice will be done to this excellent composition, as the capital Performers in England have generously engaged their Assistance on this Occasion."

FROM THE " GENERAL ADVERTISER ", 22nd April 1749

Yesterday there was the brightest and most numerous Assembly ever known at the Spring Garden, Vauxhall ; on Occasion of the Rehearsal of Mr. Handel's Music, for the Royal Fire Works.

Several Footmen who attended their Masters, &c. thither, behaved very sausily, and were justly corrected by the Gentlemen for their Insolence.

(Schoelcher, pp. 313 f.) There were 12,000 visitors. Cf. *Gentleman's Magazine*, April 1749.

FROM " A VIEW OF THE PUBLIC FIRE-WORKS, *etc.*", April 1749

. . . The Steps, which go up to a grand Area before the Middle Arch, where a Band of a hundred Musicians are to play before the Fire-Works begin ; the Musick for which is to be composed by Mr. Handel. . . .

This unofficial programme is printed on a single-sheet oblong-folio. Copy in the British Museum : 1889. b. 10.

FROM " A DESCRIPTION OF THE MACHINE FOR THE FIREWORKS . . .
EXHIBITED IN ST. JAMES'S PARK, THURSDAY, APRIL 27, 1749, ON
ACCOUNT OF THE GENERAL PEACE, SIGNED AT AIX LA CHAPELLE,
OCTOBER 7, 1748 "

After a grand Overture of Warlike Instruments, composed by Mr.
Handel, a Signal is given for the Commencement of the Firework, which
opens by a Royal Salute of 101 Brass Ordnance.

The manuscript and a copy of the *Description*, printed " by Order of his
Majesty's Board of Ordnance " are in Gerald Coke's Handel Collection. The
manuscript has an engraving added, published on 5th April. This official programme was edited by the performers of the fireworks, Gaetano Ruggieri (one of
two brothers famous in fireworks) and Giuseppe Sarti, of Bologna. It was printed
by W. Bowyer, and sold by R. Dodsley and M. Cooper, with a privilege dated
21st April. 16 pages quarto. The machine for the fireworks was invented and
signed by the Chevalier Servadoni, scene designer to the French court (cf. January
1750).

———

BYROM TO HIS WIFE, 27th April 1749

Green Park, 7 o'clock, Thursday night,
before Squib Castle.

Walking about here to see sights I have retired to a stump of a tree
to write a line to thee lest anything should happen to prevent me by
and by . . . they are all mad with thanksgivings, Venetian jubilees,
Italian fireworks, and German pageantry. I have before my eyes such a
concourse of people as to be sure I never have or shall see again, except
we should have a Peace without a vowel. The building erected on this
occasion is indeed extremely neat and pretty and grand to look at, and
a world of fireworks placed in an order that promises a most amazing
scene when it is to be in full display. His Majesty and other great folks
have been walking to see the machinery before the Queen's Library ;
it is all railed about there, where the lords, ladies, commons, &c. are
sat under scaffolding, and seem to be under confinement in comparison
of us mobility, who enjoy the free air and walks here.

It has been a very hot day, but there is a dark overcast of cloudiness
which may possibly turn to rain, which occasions some of better habits
to think of retiring ; and while I am now writing it spits a little and
grows into a menacing appearance of rain, which, if it pass not over, will
disappoint expectations. My intention, if it be fair, is to gain a post
under one of the trees in St. James's Park, where the fireworks are in
front, and where the tail of a rocket, if it should fall, cannot but be
hindered by the branches from doing any mischief to them who are
sheltered under them, so I shall now draw away to be ready for near
shelter from either watery or fiery rain.

11 o'clock : all over, and somewhat in a hurry, by an accidental fire
at one of the ends of the building, which, whether it be extinguished

I know not, for I left it in an ambiguous condition that I might finish my letter, which otherwise I could not have done. I saw every fine show in front, and I believe no mischief was done by the rockets, though some pieces of above one pound and a half fell here and there—some the next tree to my station, and being on the watch I perceived one fall, and after a tug with four or five competitors I carried it off.

My dear, I shall be too late if I don't conclude ; I am all of a sweat with a hasty walk for time to write ; and now I'll take some refreshment and drink all your healths.

(Byrom, *Selection*, p. 257 f.)   Cf. 3rd March 1724 and May-July 1725.   It is noteworthy that Byrom does not mention Handel's music.   Neither did Horace Walpole, in a letter to Horace Mann, on 3rd May 1749 (1891 edition, II. 151). The Queen's Library was built for Queen Charlotte, but was demolished in the nineteenth century.   According to Hawkins, V. 410 f., concerts were held there, under Handel's direction, at which the Princesses and their friends played.

From the " Daily Advertiser ", 29th April 1749

His Majesty and the Duke of Cumberland, attended by the Dukes of Montague, Richmond, and Bedford, and several others of the Nobility, were at the Library to see the Fireworks, from whence they walk'd about 7 o'Clock into the Machine, after visiting which his Majesty made a present of a Purse to the Officers employ'd in the different Branches. The whole Band of Musick (which began to play soon after 6 o'Clock) perform'd at his Majesty's coming and going, and during his Stay in the Machine.

The original is not in the British Museum.   Reprinted in the *Gentleman's Magazine* of April 1749, p. 186.   On the evening of the 29th April there was an anonymous " Serenade " at the Haymarket Theatre, entitled *Peace in Europe*.

From the " Gentleman's Magazine ", April 1749

Friday, 21.

Was performed, at *Vauxhall Gardens* the rehearsal of the music for the fireworks, by a band of 100 musicians, to an audience of above 12,000 persons (tickets 2s. 6d.).   So great a resort occasioned such a stoppage on *London Bridge*, that no carriage could pass for 3 hours.—The footmen were so numerous as to obstruct the passage, so that a scuffle happen'd, in which some gentlemen were wounded.

[About the performance.]

Tickets were delivered for places erected by the government for seeing the fireworks ; each member of the privy council had 12, every peer 4, every commoner 2, and a number was dispersed to the lord mayor, aldermen, and directors of the trading companies.

.   .   .   .   .

While the pavilion was on fire, the Chevalier *Servandoni*, who designed
the building, drawing his sword and affronting *Charles Frederick*, Esq ;
Comptrollor of the Ordnance and Fireworks, he was disarmed and taken
into custody, but discharg'd the next day on asking pardon before the
D. of *Cumberland*.

(Schoelcher, pp. 312-14.) The first passage was quoted by Scott Goddard in the
Radio Times of 15th November 1938. The second paragraph is part of a report
which uses the official programme. Mr. Frederick was not seriously hurt. (The
Duke of Montague died in the following July.) It may be added here that the
cannons fired at the beginning of the celebration were not part of Handel's music.
According to William McNaught (*Musical Times*, May 1950), the order and use
of Handel's *Fireworks Music* would have been as follows : 1. Overture, arranged
from two existing concertos and, probably, played before the fireworks began.
2. Bourrée, 3. " La Paix ", 4. " La Réjouissance " ; these three pieces being played
as accompaniments to allegorical fire-pictures; 5. two Minuets. There is no contemporary evidence, however, that any part of the music was played after the
fireworks began.

———

FROM THE MINUTES OF THE GENERAL COMMITTEE OF THE FOUNDLING
HOSPITAL

AT THE HOSPITAL, May 7, 1749

Mr. Handel being present and having generously and charitably offered
a performance of vocal and instrumental musick to be held at this
Hospital, and that the money arising therefrom should be applied to the
finishing the chapel of the Hospital.

Resolved—That the thanks of this Committee be returned to Mr.
Handel for this his generous and charitable offer.

Ordered—That the said performance be in the said Chapel on
Wednesday, the 24th inst., at eleven in the forenoon.

Resolved—That the gentlemen present and the rest of the members of
the General Committee, or any two of them be a Committee to carry into
execution this intention with the advice and direction of Mr. Handel.

Resolved—That George Frederick Handel Esq. in regard to this his
generous proposal be recommended to the next General Court to be
then elected a Governor of this Hospital.

(Bronslow, 1847 ; 1858, p. 72.) The meetings of the court were held every
quarter. This was the beginning of Handel's patronage of the " Hospital for the
Maintenance and Education of Exposed and Deserted Young Children ", founded
nine years earlier by Captain Thomas Coram, and favoured with equal zeal by
Hogarth. It was better known, and still is, as the Foundling Hospital.

———

FROM THE SAME, 10th May 1749

The Minutes of the last Meeting were Read and Approved. The
Secretary acquainted the Committee That Mr. Handell called upon him

last Saturday [the 6th], and returned his Thanks to the Committee for the Honour intended him of being a Governor of this Hospital ; But he desired to be excused therefrom, for that he should Serve the Charity with more Pleasure in his Way, than being a Member of the Corporation.

The Treasurer acquainted the Committee That the 24th instant being Prince George's Birth Day, Mr. Handel desires his intended Performance may be on Tuesday the 23rd instant, and that thereupon he had Stopped the Printing of the Tickets and the Advertizement.

ORDERED

That 1,300 Tickets be printed off for the said Performance on Tuesday the 23rd instant, and that the Advertizement ordered, the last Meeting be published for the first time in the Daily Advertizer tomorrow.

Handel, in spite of his protest, was elected a Governor on 9th May 1750. Prince George later became King George III.

———

FROM THE " GENERAL ADVERTISER ", 15th May 1749

This Day . . . will be exhibited the Entertainments of Musick at CUPER'S-GARDENS, and to continue the Summer Season ; to conclude every Evening with an exact Representation of the Magnificent Edifice, with its proper Ornaments, viz. Emblematic Figures, Transparencies, etc. and the Fireworks to imitate, as near as possible, the Royal ones, exhibited (on Account of the Peace) in the Green Park.—N.B. Great Care will be taken to keep out Persons of ill Repute.—The Fireworks have already given the greatest Satisfaction to a Number of Gentlemen and Ladies, who declared them exceeding beautiful, and nearly representing the Royal ones.

(Wroth, p. 251.) Cf. 23rd May 1748 and 4th September 1749. There is no doubt that, had Handel's Fireworks Music been available, Mrs. Evans would have had it performed, though probably on a reduced scale.

———

FROM THE " GENERAL ADVERTISER ", 19th May 1749

Hospital for the Maintenance and Education of Exposed and Deserted Young Children, May 10, 1749.

GEORGE-FREDERICK HANDELL,

Esq ; having generously offered his Assistance to promote this Charity, on Thursday the 25th Day of this Instant May, at Twelve o'Clock at Noon, there will be a Grand Performance of Vocal and Instrumental MUSICK. Under his Direction, consisting of several Pieces composed by him.

First. The Musick for the late *Royal Fireworks* and the *Anthem* on the *Peace.*

Second. Select Pieces from the Oratorio of *Solomon,* relating to the *Dedication of the Temple.*

Third. Several Pieces composed for the Occasion, the Words taken from Scripture, and applicable to this Charity and its Benefactors.

The Performance will be in the Chapel, which will be sash'd, and made commodious for the Purpose . . . printed Tickets . . . are . . . delivered at Half a Guinea each, at the Hospital.

N.B. There will be no Collection ; and Mr. *Tonson* having printed the Words of the Performance, for the Benefit of this Charity, Books may be had . . . at One Shilling each.

By Order of the General Court,

HARMAN VERELST, Sec.

The word-book, a copy of which is in King's College, Cambridge, bears the date of 25th May, although the performance was postponed till 27th. In it the three parts of the concert are described as follows : " I. The Musick as composed for the Royal Fire-Works. The Anthem composed on the Occasion of the Peace. II. Symphony. Chorus (Your Harps). Air, etc. III. A Concerto. The Anthem composed on this Occasion. Chorus (Blessed are they) and Verse." The title is " A Performance of Musick . . . The Musick compos'd by Mr. Handel." The strings to the Fireworks Music were probably added for this performance. The Peace Anthem is the Dettingen Anthem, with new words. Part II was a selection from *Solomon.* Part III was the so-called " Foundling Hospital Anthem ", sung by Signor Guadagni, Mr. Lowe, and others. This " Anthem ", performed again in the old picture gallery of the new house in June 1949, contains some original solos, a duet, and choruses from the Funeral Anthem (17th December 1737) and *Susanna,* ending with the Hallelujah Chorus from *Messiah.*

—

FROM THE " GENERAL ADVERTISER ", 23rd May 1749

Hospital for the Maintenance . . . of . . . Young Children, in Lamb's Conduit Fields, May 19, 1749.

Notice is hereby given that Alterations being necessary to be made for the Reception of some Persons of High Distinction, the MUSICK, which was advertised for *Thursday* the 25th, to be performed in the Chapel, is deferred till *Saturday* the 27th, at Twelve at Noon, and the Tickets for the 25th will be then received.

Lamb's Conduit Fields is now Brunswick Square. For the cause of the postponement see 31st May.

—

FROM THE " GENERAL ADVERTISER ", 26th May 1749

We are assured, that their Royal Highnesses the Prince and Princess of Wales, and the young Princes and Princesses will Honour the Foundling Hospital with their Presence To morrow, at the Grand Performance of Musick, composed by Mr. Handel, for the Benefit of that Charity ; and that above One Hundred Voices and Performers have engaged to assist upon that Laudable and Charitable Occasion.

(*Musical Times*, 1st May 1902.) Cf. 31st May.

———

FROM THE "LONDON EVENING POST", 30th May 1749

Last Saturday [the 27th] several curious Pieces of Musick, composed by Mr. Handel, were perform'd in the new Chapel at the Foundling-Hospital, at which were present their Royal Highnesses the Prince and Princess of Wales, some others of the Royal Family, and a prodigious Concourse of the Nobility and Gentry.

(*Musical Times*, 1st May 1902 ; also quoting an unidentified report, that " the performance was most complete and solemn ".)

———

FROM THE MINUTES OF THE GENERAL COMMITTEE OF THE FOUNDLING HOSPITAL, 31st May 1749

The Secretary acquainted the Committee That on the 19th instant he had seen a Letter from Mr. Schrader to Mr. Handel signifying the Desire of His Royal Highness the Prince of Wales for deferring Mr. Handel's Musical Performance to Saturday the 27th instant, which he had communicated to Mr. Waple and Mr. White, and by their Directions had wrote the following answer to Mr. Handel.

Sir,

I have communicated to the Governor's Mr. Schrader's Letter to you, who are extreamly sensible of His Royal Highnesses Goodness in promoting your Charitable Intentions, by Honouring your Performance with His Presence : And I am commanded to acquaint you That they have given orders for deferring the Performance until Saturday the 27th instant at Twelve at noon, and have given Directions for erecting a Seat in the Hospital for the Reception of their Highnesses and Family, which will be made commodious and private, and to which there is a private way through the garden without passing through the Body of the Chapel.

That the Secretary do write to the President, Vice Presidents and Noblemen of the General Committee and acquaint them That their Royal Highnesses the Prince and Princess of Wales do intend to Honour the Hospital with their Presence at Mr. Handel's Musical Performance on Saturday next, at which time the Committee hope They will favour the Corporation with their Company.

RESOLVED

That the Earl of Macclesfield, Lord Charles Cavendish, Sir William Heathcote, and the Treasurer, be desired to conduct Their Royal Highnesses to and from their Seat in the Chapel.

•   •   •   •   •

XXVI. THE FOUNDLING HOSPITAL : INTERIOR OF THE CHAPEL

Engraving by John Sanders, 1773.   The organ, presented by Handel, shown here after alteration.   (Gerald Coke, Esq.)

See page 687

XXVII. HANDEL'S WILL

First page, dated 1st June 1750. (Gerald Coke, Esq.)

See page 691

RESOLVED

That the Thanks of this Committee be returned to George Frederick Handel Esqr for the generous Assistance he gave to this Charity by his most excellent Performance of Musick on Saturday last [the 27th] ; and that Mr. Handel be desired to return the Thanks of this Committee to the Performers who voluntarily assisted him upon that occasion.

RESOLVED

That the Thanks of this Committee be returned to the Master of the Children of the King's Chapel for his and their Attendance at the said Performance.

ORDERED

That the Treasurer do Pay the Secretary Fifty Pounds for Mr. Handel to dispose of in such manner as he shall think fit.

(*Musical Times*, 1st May 1902, edited by F. G. Edwards.) Mr. Schrader was probably one of the Prince's household. Messrs. Wapple and T. White were Governors of the Hospital. The second paragraph only is a copy of the letter to Handel. The third paragraph should have been headed " Ordered ", not by the Committee but by the two Governors. This also applies to the fourth paragraph, referring to noble Governors and the Treasurer. The Master of the Children was still Bernard Gates. The fifty pounds intended to be distributed among the performers (cf. 4th May 1750) was probably a gift from an unknown friend of the Hospital : see next entry.

———

FROM THE " GENTLEMAN'S MAGAZINE ", May 1749

SATURDAY 27. The Pr. and Prss of *Wales*, with a great number of persons of quality and distinction were at the chapel of the *Foundling*'s hospital ; several pieces of vocal and instrumental musick, compos'd by *George Frederick Handel*, Esq ; for the benefit of the foundation. . . . There was no collection, but the tickets were at half a guinea, and the audience above a thousand, besides a gift of 2000*l.* from his majesty, and 50*l.* from an unknown.

(Clark, 1852.) See J. M. Coopersmith, in *Notes*, Washington, December 1950, p. 132, reviewing Hubert Langley's edition of the *Foundling Hospital Anthem*, 1949.

———

FROM THE " GENERAL ADVERTISER ", 2nd June 1749

NEW MUSICK.

.   .   .   .   .

Printed for J. Walsh. . . .

By whom will Speedily be published,

The Musick for the Royal Fireworks, composed by Mr. Handell, for Violins, Hoboys, French Horns, Trumpets, &c.

It is noteworthy that the string parts were already added ; cf. 19th May.

———

H.–22

FROM THE " GENERAL ADVERTISER ", 24th June 1749

NEW MUSICK.

.   .   .   .   .

Printed for J. Walsh. . . .
Of whom may be had just published
For CONCERTS

Eighty Songs selected from Mr. Handel's latest Oratorios, for Violins, &c. in 6 Parts ; the Song Part with the Words for a Voice, Hoboy, German Flute or Harpsichord, done in the Original Keys, to be performed either by Voice or Instruments ; being the most Capital Collection of Songs ever published, with an Index to the Whole.

☞ The Song Part may be had separate, without the Instrumental Parts, which is intended for the Improvement of young Ladies and Gentlemen in Singing on the Harpsichord.

(Chrysander, III. 170.)

———

Handel writes the oratorio *Theodora* between 28th June and 31st July 1749.

———

Handel makes a contract with Dr. Jonathan Morse, of Barnet, for building an organ to be given by Handel to the Chapel of the Foundling Hospital, July 1749.

Cf. 2nd May 1750.

———

FROM THE " GENERAL ADVERTISER ", 4th September 1749

At CUPERS-GARDENS, the Entertainments of Vocal and Instrumental Musick will, during the short Remainder of the Summer Season, begin at Five, and end at Nine, (with several favourite Songs by Signora Sybilla, particularly, *My Faith and Truth*, out of the Oratorio of Sampson) and to conclude with a Curious and Magnificent Firework . . . N.B. The Entertainments of this Place End on Thursday next, the 7th Instant.

Cf. 23rd May 1748. For the miniature temple in Cuper's Gardens see 15th May 1749.

———

FROM THE " GENERAL ADVERTISER ", 6th September 1749

Yesterday Morning, and not before, died at his House at Richmond, aged 85, John-James Heidegger, Esq ; whose well known Character wants no Encomium ; of him, it may be truly said, what one Hand received from the Rich, the other gave to the Poor.

Heidegger's house, with its beautiful interior decorations, still stands in Richmond.

———

Handel buys £1000 4 per cent Annuities (1748), 7th September 1749.

———

FROM WILLIAM HUGHES' SERMON, "THE EFFICACY AND IMPORTANCE OF MUSICK", PREACHED AT WORCESTER CATHEDRAL-CHURCH, 13th September 1749

. . . Far be it from me to cast the least injurious Reflection upon those, whom Nature has denied the Pleasure, of relishing the engaging Measures, either of *Handel*,[1] or of *Purcel*. . . .

Pp. 10 f. of the printed text of 1749, in which the footnote was added to the sermon given at the annual meeting of the Three Choirs. Hughes was a Minor Canon of the Cathedral Church of Worcester. See the following entry.

———

FROM THE "GENERAL ADVERTISER", 19th September 1749

Last Week was held at Worcester the Annual Meeting of the Three Choirs of Gloucester, Hereford and Worcester, at which were present a great Number of Nobility, Gentry, and Ladies. Mr. Purcell's Te Deum and Jubilate were Vocally and Instrumentally perform'd on Wednesday [the 13th] ; and Mr. Handell's on Thursday, at the Cathedral. . . .

———

At Salisbury, on 19th September 1749, one of Handel's two Te Deums and two of his (Coronation) Anthems are performed in the Cathedral in the morning, *Acis and Galatea* being given in the Assembly Room in the evening. On 20th September the other Te Deum is performed in the Cathedral in the morning, and his Fireworks Music and *Ode for St. Cecilia's Day* in the Assembly Room in the evening.

———

HANDEL TO JENNENS, 30th September 1749

Sir

Yesterday I received Your Letter, in answer to which I hereunder specify my Opinion of an Organ which I think will answer the Ends You propose, being every thing that is necessary for a good and grand Organ, without Reed Stops, which I have omitted, because they are continually wanting to be tuned, which in the Country is very inconvenient, and should it remain useless on that Account, it would still be very expensive althou' that may not be Your Consideration. I very well approve of Mr Bridge who without any Objection is a very good

[1] To do justice in all respects to the Character of Mr. *Handel*, who has open'd such uncommon Scenes of Delight, who in the greatest Variety of Instances has long since prov'd himself the most perfect Master of Harmony that any Age ever produc'd, would rather require a Volume, than this poor, and imperfect Sketch.

Organ Builder, and I shall willingly (when He has finished it) give You my Opinion of it. I have referr'd You to the Flute Stop in M$^{r.}$ Freemans Organ being excellent in its kind, but as I do not referr you in that Organ, The System of the Organ I advise is, (Vizt

The Compass to be up to D and down to Gamut,
full Octave,   Church Work.

One Row of Keys, whole Stops and none in halves.

Stops

An Open Diapason—of Metal throughout to be in Front.

A Stopt Diapason—the Treble Metal and the Bass Wood.

A Principal—of Metal throughout.

A Twelfth—of Metal throughout.

A Fifteenth—of Metal throughout.

A Great Tierce—of Metal throughout.

A Flute Stop—such a one is in Freemans Organ.

I am glad of the Opportunity to show you my attention, wishing you all Health and Happiness,

I remain with great Sincerity and Respect

Sir

Your

London, Sept. 30.   most obedient and must humble

1749.   Servant

George Frideric Handel.

(*Musical Times*, 1st August 1904.) Original, without envelope, in the possession of Lord Howe. Richard Bridge was a well-known organ builder who, in 1730, had built the organ in Christ Church, Spitalfields, then the largest in England. He probably also built the organ of William Freeman, Handel's admirer, at Hamels, near Braughing in Hertfordshire. Jennens intended to have the new organ in his residence at Gopsall, which was being restored in a princely manner.

———

From " Boddely's Bath Journal ", 6th November 1749

For the *Benefit* of Mr. *Andrews*, lately arriv'd from Ireland ; and Mr. *Leander*, from the Opera-House, London. At Mr. Wiltshire's *Room*, This present Monday . . . will be a *Grand Concert* of Vocal and Instrumental Musick.

.   .   .   .   .

To conclude with Mr. *Handell*'s celebrated Fire Musick.

The *Concert* to begin exactly at Seven o'Clock.

After the *Concert* there will be a *Ball*.

This seems to have been the first performance in Bath of any Handel music. Nothing is known about the two beneficiaries ; but Thomas Chilcot, the organist of the Abbey Church, who played a harpsichord concerto on this occasion, may have been the conductor of Handel's music. It seems that it was the music from *Atalanta*, not the *Fireworks Music*, which was given.

———

Handel withdraws the balance of £157 : 10 : 0, and buys £250 4 per cent Annuities (1748), 9th November 1749.

—

The Chaplet, William Boyce's successful " musical entertainment ", text by Moses Mendez, is produced at Drury Lane Theatre, 2nd December 1749.

(Loewenberg, p. 108.)

—

FROM FAULKNER'S " DUBLIN JOURNAL ", 9th December 1749

On Thursday last [the 7th], Dr. Purcell's Grand Te Deum, Mr. Handel's Jubilate and Anthems, were performed as usual, at St. Andrew's Church, for the Benefit of Mercer's Hospital. Several Gentlemen of Quality and Distinction assisted at the Performance, which was Conducted with the greatest Decency and Order. There was a numerous Audience of the Nobility and principal Persons of this Kingdom.

The " Cathedral Service " was back again in the Round Church, after some performances in St. Michan's Church.

—

Handel begins the incidental music for Smollett's *Alceste*, 27th December 1749.

Cf. 14th February 1749 and 8th January 1750.

—

FROM HENRY FIELDING'S " HISTORY OF TOM JONES ", DUBLIN, 1749

It was Mr. *Western*'s Custom every Afternoon, as soon as he was drunk, to hear his Daughter [Sophia] play on the Harpsichord : for he was a great Lover of Music, and perhaps, had he lived in Town, might have passed for a Connoisseur : for he always excepted against the finest Compositions of Mr. *Handel*. He never relished any Music but what was light and airy ; and indeed his most favourite Tunes, were *Old Sir* Simon *the King*, St. George, *he was for* England, *Bobbing* Joan, and some others.

His Daughter tho' she was a perfect Mistress of Music, and would never willingly have played any but *Handel*'s, was so devoted to her Father's Pleasure, that she learnt all those Tunes to oblige him.

The popular songs mentioned are : " Old Simon the King ", " St. George for England ", and " Bobbing Joe ", also called " Bobbing Joane " ; all were known before 1700.

—

FROM [ELIZA HAYWOOD'S] " EPISTLES FOR THE LADIES ", LONDON, 1749

From Eusebia *to the* Bishop of * * , *on the Power of Divine Music.*

It is a vulgar Aphorism, that those who are untouched with Music, have no Souls. . . .

I was led into these Reflections by being last Night at Mr. *Handel's* fine Oratorio of *Joshua*, where, though the Words were not quite so elegant, nor so well as I could have wished adapted to the Music, I was transported into the most divine Exstasy.—I closed my Eyes, and imagined myself amidst the angelic Choir in the bright Regions of everlasting Day, chanting the Praises of my great Creator, and his ineffable *Messiah.*—I seemed, methought, to have nothing of this gross Earth about me, but was all Soul !—all Spirit !

. . . I should be glad there were *Oratorios* established in every City and great Town throughout the Kingdom . . . to be given gratis. . . .

(Myers, 1948, pp. 125 f.)   The passage occurs on p. 79 f. of Vol. I.

—

FROM VERTUE'S NOTE BOOKS, 1749

a Model of Clay baked done by Mr Roubilliac of Mr Handel Musician . . . the Model in clay baked. of Mr Handel done by Mr Roubillac— the same from which the statue in Foxhall Gardens—was done as big as the life—in marble by Mr Rubillac an excellent statue—this modell near 2 foot high is in posses of Mr Hudson painter—

(Vertue, Note Books, III. 144.)   British Museum : Add. MS. 23,074.   This model of the Handel statue in Vauxhall Gardens is now in the Fitzwilliam Museum, Cambridge.   For Hudson, cf. 18th April 1750.

1750

Handel finishes the music to Smollett's tragedy *Alceste*, 8th January 1750.

The play was never performed, and Smollett's text (see 14th February 1749) is lost. Handel's music is preserved, and some of it, including one song with Smollett's verses, was used by him for *The Choice of Hercules*, " a musical interlude ", in the summer of 1750 ; two other songs were used for the revival of *Alexander Balus* in 1751 and one for the revival of *Hercules* in 1752. It is noteworthy that Hercules, under the name of Alcides, was one of the personages in the tragedy of *Alceste*. Rich commissioned this play from Smollett in 1748, and the incidental music, supposedly in settlement of a debt, from Handel in 1749. He also commissioned expensive decorations from Chevalier Servandoni, the artist of the Fireworks in Green Park. It is not known what finally frustrated the production, which was planned for the beginning of 1750. Handel's intended cast was as follows :

> Syren—Miss Young, contralto
> Charon—Mr. Waltz, bass
> Calliope—Mrs. Arne, (?) mezzo-soprano
> Apollo—Mr. Lowe, tenor
> a soprano—Miss Faulkner

Other parts, without songs, were Admetus, Alceste, and probably Pluto, Hercules, Thetis, her brother Lykomedes, and the other Muses (beside Calliope, the Muse of Epic). See " Poetry preserved in Music ", by O. E. Deutsch, in *Modern Language Notes*, Baltimore, February 1948. Cf. 1st March 1750. Two of Servandoni's decorations, " The Court of Pluto " and " The Drawing Room of Venus ", were used at Covent Garden, about 1770, for other plays with music produced there.

———

Handel deposits £8000, 22nd January 1750.

———

Handel finishes the Organ Concerto in G minor, Op. 7, no. 5, 31st January 1750.

———

FROM THE MINUTES OF THE GENERAL COMMITTEE OF THE FOUNDLING HOSPITAL, 7th February 1750

[Resolved] That it be referred to the Sub-committee to consider the manner of opening the Chapel, and having a performance of musick, and that they do consult Mr. Handel thereupon.

[Ordered] That the Secretary do wait upon Mr. Handel to propose a performance of musick and voices on Tuesday, the first of May next.

(*Musical Times*, 1st May and 1st June 1902, edited by Frederick George Edwards.) The sub-committee dealt with the chapel, which, although already in use, was not quite finished : the formal opening was postponed again and again between 3rd May 1750 and 16th April 1753, when it finally took place. The spring performance of *Messiah* became a regular event in the history of the Foundling Hospital.

TITLE OF AN ODE WRITTEN IN GERMAN FOR HANDEL'S BIRTHDAY ON
11th (22nd) February 1750 (Translated)

When Georg Friedrich Händel, Esq., happily experienced his joyous birthday in London on 22nd February 1750, Magister Christian Rotth, of Halle, wished to present the awakened Choir of Muses with the following Ode, by way of congratulation and from a sense of truest friendship. Halle, Johann Friedrich Grunert.

(*Händel-Jahrbuch*, 1933, p. 30 ; Richard Bräutigam, "Hallisches Schrifttum zur Biographie Händels ", in G. F. *Händel : Abstammung und Jugendwelt*, Halle, 1935, p. x.) The Ode, written by Rotth, Handel's cousin, and printed by Grunert, seems to be lost ; only the title of the four-page folio sheet is known. Cf. 265.

Handel pays £50 from his account to an unknown person, 13th February 1750.
The entry says " To Cash Receipt " ; the money was probably sent for.

THE EARL OF SHAFTESBURY TO HIS COUSIN, JAMES HARRIS, IN SALISBURY

London, February 13, 1750.
I have seen Handel several times since I came hither, and think I never saw him so cool and well. He is quite easy in his behaviour, and has been pleasing himself in the purchase of several fine pictures, particularly a large Rembrandt, which is indeed excellent. We have scarce talked at all about musical subjects, though enough to find his performances will go off incomparably.

(Streatfeild, 1909, p. 204.) Malmesbury, *Letters*, I. 77. We know that Handel owned two pictures by Balthasar Denner, left to Jennens, and two landscapes by Rembrandt, left to Bernard Granville. All trace of the Rembrandts has been lost ; they may now go under the name of Philips Koninck, Rembrandt's pupil. The large Rembrandt, which Handel bought in 1750, was a view of the Rhine ; the smaller one, the subject of which is unknown, was given to him by Granville, to whom it was returned after Handel's death. (Cf. the codicil of 4th August 1757.) It seems that Handel paid nearly £8000 for the " fine pictures ", if the movements in his bank accounts refer to this purchase. (Cf. 22nd January and 22nd February 1750.) The performances mentioned at the end of the letter are the oratorios which began on 2nd March.

Handel withdraws £7926, and the balance of £24, 22nd February 1750.

Judas Maccabaeus is performed in the Music Hall, Fishamble Street, Dublin, for the Benefit of the Hospital for poor distressed Lying-in Women, in George's Lane, 22nd February 1750.

This, the second Dublin performance of the oratorio, is recorded in a word-book, a copy of which is in Gerald Coke's Handel Collection.

HANDEL TO THE KEEPER OF THE ORDNANCE OFFICE, 24th February 1750

S^r

I having received the Permission of the Artillery Kettle Drums for my use in the Oratorio's in this Season ;

I beg you would consign them to the Bearer of this Mr. Frideric Smith

I am

Saturday   Your very humble Servant
Febr : 24   G. F. Handel
1750.

(Cummings, 1904, p. 37 : facsimile.) Original in the British Museum : Add. MS. 24, 182, f. 15. Cf. 13th January 1739. Handel borrowed the kettle-drums for the whole of his oratorio season in Lent ; he seems to have needed them more for the revivals of *Saul* and *Judas Maccabaeus* than for the new *Theodora*. Nothing is known of Mr. Smith, who signed a receipt, on 26th February, as Frederick Smith. The " Principal Storekeeper of the Ordnance " was Andrew Wilkinson.

HANDEL'S NOTE ON MORELL'S MANUSCRIPT OF THE WORD-BOOK OF
" THEODORA ", [February 1750]

I intend to perform this Oratorio at the Theatre Royal in Covent Garden.

George Frideric Handel.

(Cummings, 1904, p. 37 ; Flower, p. 329 : facsimile.) Original in the collection of Sir Newman Flower. Addressed to the Inspector of Stage-Plays. Cf. 10th January 1743 and 10th February 1752.

Theodore Jacobsen, the architect of the Chapel in the Foundling Hospital, and Hogarth are requested to consult with Mr. Wragg, his Majesty's Smith, concerning his gift of iron rails for the Altar, February 1750. (Minutes of the Governors of the Foundling Hospital.)

Nichols and Wray (p. 207) quote the minutes as referring to Jacobsen and Handel : a misprint.

FROM THE " ACCOUNTS OF COVENT GARDEN THEATRE ", 1st March 1750

Thursday 1 March Advanc'd to'wards purchasing Mr Smollet's copy of Alceste .   .   .   . 100 – –

British Museum : Egerton MS. 2269 (Vol. III), fol. 120, or rather 121, recto. One would have expected the date to be 1749. The fact that, on 14th February

H.-22 *a*

1749, Smollett spoke of the play as finished and that it was abandoned at the beginning of 1750 (cf. 8th January 1750) suggests an advance to the author in 1749 rather than in 1750. But the weekday, Thursday, added to the date proves that the date of the entry was, in fact, 1st March 1750.

MRS. DELANY TO MRS. DEWES

St. James's Place, 1 March, 1749–50.
To-morrow oratorios begin—Saul, one of my beloved pieces—I shall go.

(Chrysander III. 57.)   Delany, II. 541.

FROM THE " GENERAL ADVERTISER ", 2nd March 1750

At the Theatre Royal in Covent-Garden, this Day, will be performed an Oratorio, called SAUL. . . . To begin at half an Hour after Six o'Clock.

Cf. 13th March 1745. Repeat performance on 7th March ; revived in March 1754.

Handel deposits £200, 3rd March 1750.

FROM THE " GENERAL ADVERTISER ", 9th March 1750

At the Theatre Royal in Covent-Garden, this Day will be performed an Oratorio, called JUDAS MACCABEUS. . . . To begin at half an Hour after Six o'Clock.

Cf. 1st April 1747 and 26th February 1748. Repeat performances on 14th, 28th and 30th March.

Handel deposits £200, 9th March 1750.

On 10th March 1750 Mrs. Elizabeth Pappett, spinster, gets the licence to perform operas and other theatrical entertainments at the Haymarket Theatre until 10th March 1755.

Public Record Office : L.C. 5/161, p. 327. Heidegger had died on 5th September 1749. Miss Pappet was his natural daughter ; she later married Vice-Admiral Sir Peter Denis, Bt. Cf. 17th January 1751.

Handel deposits £100, 12th March 1750.

Handel deposits £200, 15th March 1750.

FROM THE " GENERAL ADVERTISER ", 16th March 1750

At the Theatre Royal in Covent-Garden, this Day will be performed a
New Oratorio, called THEODORA. *With a New Concerto on the Organ.* . . .
To begin at half an Hour after Six o'Clock.

The text was by Morell, probably based on Robert Boyle's *The Martyrdom of
Theodora and of Didymus*, 1687 (Winton Dean's suggestion). Repeat performances
on 21st and 23rd March ; revived 5th March 1755 (once).—It seems fitting to
insert here a reminiscence of Handel's organ concertos at Covent Garden, by the
Rev. William Mason (1724–94), who in 1782 published a *Critical and Historical
Essay on Cathedral Music*, as a preface to a book of words of anthems ; it was
reprinted in York in 1795 as *Essays, historical and critical on English Church Music*.
After quoting Rousseau he says, on page 45 : " This is Rousseau's idea of a good
Preluder, and if any of my Readers are old enough to recollect how the great
Handel executed that kind of Capriccio, which he usually introduced upon the
Organ between one of the Acts of his Oratorios in Covent-Garden Theatre, he
will, I believe, agree with me, that words cannot more perfectly express the
supreme excellency of that performance, than these which I have translated from
this Swiss Critic. For myself, I own that the superior manner, in point both of
Vocal and Instrumental Performers, by which his Oratorios have been since
executed in Westminster Abbey [1784 ff.] and elsewhere, cannot compensate for
the want of that Solo, now alas ! to be heard no more." Cf. 25th December 1755.

———

CAST OF " THEODORA ", 16th March 1750

Valens—Mr. Reinhold, bass
Didimus—Signor Guadagni, alto
Septimius—Mr. Lowe, tenor
Theodora—Signora Frasi, soprano
Irene—Signora Galli, mezzo-soprano
Messenger—?, tenor

———

Handel deposits £100, 17th March 1750.

———

A pasticcio opera, *L'Andromaca*, with music by Girolamo Abos,
Andrea Bernaschoni, Handel, Hasse, Niccolò Jomelli and Georg
Christoph Wagenseil, is produced at the Theater nächst der
Hofburg in Vienna, 19th (30th) March 1750.

The libretto was probably that by Apostolo Zeno, which had been set
by Antonio Caldara in 1724.

———

MRS. ELIZABETH MONTAGU TO HER SISTER, MISS SARAH ROBINSON,
(?) 20th March 1750

I was not under any apprehension about the earthquake, but went that
night to the Oratorio, then quietly to bed. . . . The Wednesday night

the Oratorio was very empty, though it was the most favourite performance of Handel's.

(Streatfeild, 1909, pp. 204 f.)   Montagu, *Correspondence*, p. 274.   The date of the letter, as given hitherto, namely 20th February 1750, is impossible : there were no oratorios in February 1750, and no earthquakes in London in 1751.   The disturbance began on 5th February 1750, according to a letter from Horace Walpole to Horace Mann ; the peak was on 19th February.   Probably because of this, Handel's oratorio season did not begin until 2nd March.   The only Wednesday performances before 21st March were on 7th March, *Saul*, and on 14th March, *Judas Maccabaeus*. A possible solution, therefore, is that the date of the letter was, in fact, 20th March 1750 ; the writer visiting *Judas* on the 14th.

———

Princess Amelia attends the second of the three performances of *Theodora*, but the audience is " very thin ", 21st March 1750.

(*Musical Times*, 1st June 1873.)   Morell, in Hodgkin MSS., testifies to the details, written from memory about 1764 (see *Appendix*).

———

From the " General Advertiser ", 29th March 1750

For the Benefit of Miss Cassandra Frederick, *a Child of Six and a Half Old, a Scholar of Mr.* Paradies.   At Hickford's Room in Brewer street, This Day . . . will be performed a Concert of Vocal and Instrumental Musick.   This Child will perform on the Harpsichord . . . two Concertos of Mr. *Handel*'s.

Cf. 10th April 1749.

———

Handel deposits £150, 29th March 1750.

———

At a performance of Beaumont and Fletcher's comedy, *Rule a Wife and have a Wife*, given at Covent Garden Theatre on 29th March 1750, for the benefit of Mr. Leveridge, Mr. Lowe and Miss Falkner sing the duet " O Lovely Peace ", from *Judas Maccabaeus*, at the end of Act I.

———

From the " Student or Oxford Monthly Miscellany ",
31st March 1750

Trin. Coll., Cambridge, 8 March 1750. . . . Must we not . . . with some concern see so many Students, who are equally destin'd to the common task of learning, debauch'd by Sound, neglecting Locke and Newton for Purcell and Handel, and instead of Philosophers commencing (O ridicule ! O shame to common sense !) downright Fiddlers. . . . In a word, . . . our books, I expect, will be changed into fiddles, our schools will be turned into musick-rooms, and Aristotle kick'd out for Corelli.

Cantab.

(*Cambridge Review*, 13th June 1942, reprinted by O. E. Deutsch.) Vol. I, no. 3, p. 72. The magazine was later called *The Student or Oxford and Cambridge Monthly Miscellany*, but did not last very long. The correspondence from Cambridge is entitled " Fiddling considered, as far as it regards an University ". Cf. Hearne's Oxford remarks of 1734, and 30th April 1750.

FROM THE " GENERAL ADVERTISER ", 4th April 1750

At the Theatre Royal in Covent-Garden, this Day, will be performed an Oratorio, called SAMPSON. . . . To begin at half an Hour after Six o'Clock.

Cf. 3rd March 1749. Repeat performance on 6th April. Signor Gaetano Guadagni, a male alto, who sang the part of Micah, had been engaged, like Signora Frasi, during the season of 1748–9 at the Haymarket Theatre as member of an Italian company of comic singers, under the direction of Dr. Croza. Burney (IV. 457 f.) relates that Guadagni " applied to me for assistance " when he studied Mrs. Cibber's parts in *Samson* and *Messiah*.

FROM THE " GENERAL ADVERTISER ", 12th April 1750

At the Theatre Royal in Covent-Garden, this Day, will be performed a sacred Oratorio, called MESSIAH. (*Being the Last* This Year.) . . . To begin at half an Hour after Six O'Clock.

" Being the Last " refers to the oratorios performed this season. Watts advertised his word-book of *Messiah* on 10th April, this year in time. He repeated the advertisement on 24th April for the performance on 1st May. Guadagni probably sang that spring for the first time in *Messiah*. Handel wrote a florid version of " Thou art gone up on high " for him (Tenbury manuscript of *Messiah*).

PHILIP DORMER STANHOPE, 4TH EARL OF CHESTERFIELD, TO SOLOMON DAYROLLES, AT THE HAGUE

London, 14 April O.S. 1750

I could not refuse this recommendation of a *virtuoso* to a *virtuoso*. The girl is a real prodigy. . . . The great point is to get the Princess of Orange to hear her, which she thinks will *make her fortune*. Even the great Handel has designed to recommend her there ; so that a word from your Honour will be sufficient.

Chesterfield, *Letters*, IV. 1524, no. 1698. Dayrolles, a diplomat, was a godson of Lord Chesterfield, then the King's Resident at the Hague. Anne, Princess of Orange, had, of course, as Princess Royal, been Handel's former pupil ; so had Lady Chesterfield as Fräulein von Schulenburg. The young lady may have been Miss Cassandra Frederick (see 29th March 1750).

MADAME ANNE-MARIE FIQUET DU BOCAGE TO HER SISTER, MADAME DU PERRON

London, April 15, 1750.

The Oratorio, or pious concert, pleases us highly. *English* words are sung by *Italian* performers, and accompanied by a variety of instruments. HANDEL is the soul of it : when he makes his appearance, two wax lights are carried before him, which are laid upon his organ. Amidst a loud clapping of hands he seats himself, and the whole band of music strikes up exactly at the same moment. At the interludes he plays concertos of his own composition, either alone or accompanied by the orchestra. These are equally admirable for the harmony and the execution. The *Italian* opera, in three acts, gives us much less pleasure. . . .

(Myers, 1948, p. 149.) Fiquet, I. 14 f. Madame Fiquet du Bocage, a French poetess, was on a visit to London with her husband. At the Haymarket Theatre, Legrenzio Vincenzo Ciampi's *Adriano in Siria* had been performed since 20th February ; it was followed on 27th April by Pergolesi's *La serva padrona*. After this season there was a longer period without operas in London.

———

FROM THE " GENERAL ADVERTISER ", 16th April 1750

The Rehearsal of the *Musick* for the *Feast* of the *Sons* of the *Clergy*, will be perform'd at St. Paul's on Tuesday the 24th of this Instant April, and the Feast the Thursday following. . . . Feast Tickets at Five Shillings each. . . . N.B. Mr. *Handel's* new *Te Deum, Jubilate* and *Coronation Anthem*, with a new Anthem by Dr. Green, will be vocally and instrumentally perform'd. . . .

In addition to the *Dettingen Te Deum*, it seems that the *Utrecht Jubilate*, and perhaps *Zadok the Priest*, were also performed.

———

FROM THE MINUTES OF THE GENERAL COMMITTEE OF THE FOUNDLING HOSPITAL, 18th April 1750

The Secretary acquainted the Committee that Mr. Handel had agreed to the following Advertizement to be published for his intended Performance.

Hospital for the Maintenance and Education of Exposed and Deserted Young Children in Lamb's Conduit Fields, April 18th, 1750.

George Frederick Handel, Esq. having presented this Hospital with a very fine Organ for the Chapel thereof, and repeated his offer of assistance to promote this Charity ; on Tuesday the First Day of May 1750 at Twelve o'Clock at noon Mr. Handel will open the said Organ ; and the sacred Oratorio called ' Messiah ' will be performed under his direction.

Tickets . . . at half a Guinea each.

Ordered—That the said Advertizement be published [daily in the *Daily Advertiser*, twice a week in the *General Advertiser*, the *Gazetteer* and some evening papers].

(*Musical Times*, 1st May 1902.) The advertisements appeared from 21st April onwards, with the note : " There will be no collection ". The organ was built by Dr. Jonathan Morse, of Barnet, called Moss in Jennens's letter of 19th September 1738. Edward John Hopkins, in his article on the organ in Grove's *Dictionary*, thought that the organ of the Foundling Hospital was built by Parker and opened in 1749. The organ was already in need of repair about 1765 and, in 1769, it was replaced by a new organ built by Thomas Parker.

—

From the Same

[The Treasurer reports] That Mr. Hudson had offered to present the Hospital with Mr. Handel's picture, and that Mr. Handel had consented to sit for it.

(*Musical Times*, 1st May 1902.) Although Thomas Hudson painted several oils of Handel, and probably one from life, he did not give one to the Foundling Hospital, whose thanks were forwarded to Hudson for his offer. Perhaps the Hudson portrait in the possession of the Royal Society of Musicians is the one intended for the Hospital. Another came from Jennens to Lord Howe.

—

Handel withdraws £950 in cash and buys £1100 4 per cent Annuities (1746), 19th April 1750.

—

At a performance of Congreve's comedy, *The Double Dealer*, given at Covent Garden Theatre on 19th April 1750 for the benefit of Miss Falkner, she sings " O Sleep ", from *Semele*, after Act II.

—

From the " Student ", Oxford, 30th April 1750

C.C.C. [Corpus Christi College], Cambridge, April 5, 1750. . . . I see no reason why our schools may not be frequented as well as our musick-meetings, and Newton and Locke still have their followers as well as Handel and Corelli. . . .

Granticola.

(*Cambridge Review*, 13th June 1942.) Vol. I, no. 4, p. 131. Cf. 31st March 1750. This answer by another Cambridge man was entitled " Musick no improper part of an University Education ". The discussion was concluded by a sonnet, " On the Power of Musick ", by " A.".

—

INVITATION TO THE " MESSIAH " PERFORMANCE IN THE FOUNDLING
HOSPITAL, 1st May 1750

At the Hospital
For the Maintenance and Education of exposed and deserted Children in
Lambs Conduit Fields,
On *Tuesday* y^e *first* day of *May 1750* at *12* o'Clock *at Noon* there will
be Performed in the Chapel of the said Hosiptal, a Sacred Oratorio called
" *The Messiah* "
Composed by George Frederick Handel Esqr
The Gentlemen are desired to come without Swords, and the Ladies
without Hoops.
NB. There will be no Collection. Tickets may be had of the Steward
of the Hospital, at Arthur's Chocolate House in St James's Street, at
Batson's Coffee House in Cornhill & at Tom's Coffee House in Devereux
Court at half a Guinea each.

(Rockstro, p. 298 ; facsimile in Nichols and Wray, opposite p. 203.) The
engraved plate used for this invitation was intended also for further performances
of sacred oratorios ; in fact it was used exclusively for *Messiah* ; the words and
figures in italics are inserted by hand. The plate is ornamented with Hogarth's
design of the Foundling Hospital's Coat of Arms ; by a coincidence this contains
part of the arms of Handel's birthplace, Halle.—It may be noticed that in the
original text of the advertisement White's Coffee House (later White's Club) in
St. James's Street is mentioned.

———

FROM DR. WILLIAM STUKELEY'S DIARY

1 May, 1750. An infinite croud of coaches at our end of the town to
hear Handel's music at the opening of the Chapel of the Foundlings.

(Myers, 1948, p. 138.) Stukeley, *Memoirs*, III. 9. The foundation-stone of the
chapel was laid on 1st May 1747.

———

FROM THE MINUTES OF THE GENERAL COMMITTEE OF THE FOUNDLING
HOSPITAL, 2nd May 1750

Resolved
That the Thanks of this Committee be given to George Frederick
Handel Esqr for his Performance in the Chapel Yesterday, of the Oratorio
called " Messiah ", to a very numerous Audience, who expressed the
greatest Satisfaction at the Excellency thereof, and of his great Benevol-
ence, in thus promoting this Charity ; which the Chairman accordingly
did.
Ordered
That a Copy of the said Minute be signed by the Secretary & given to
Mr. Handel.
Mr. Handel attending and having generously offered another Performance of ye Oratorio called Messiah on Tuesday the 15th instant,

Resolved

That the Thanks of this Committee be given to Mr. Handel for his said kind Offer, and the Committee do accept hereof.

Resolved

That the following Advertizement be published. . . .

(Nichols and Wray, pp. 203 f.) The net result of the performance on 1st May was £728 3s. 6d.

From the Same

Mr. Handel acquainting the Committee that Dr. Morse, of Barnet, had not finished the organ for the Chapel of this Hospital pursuant to the contract he made with him in July last for that purpose.

Ordered—That the Secretary do write to Dr. Morse to press his finishing the organ for immediate use, and that he may find able persons to have as many stops as he can, for chorus's, before Tuesday, the 15th inst.

(*Musical Times*, 1st May 1902.) Later minutes show that Dr. Morse attended a meeting on 30th May, and that twenty pounds were paid to him on 6th February 1751 " for the diapason stop " after having " delivered all the pipes ". He died on 20th October 1752, sixty-two years of age. The organ, apparently, was not ready on 15th May 1750.

From the " General Advertiser ", 4th May 1750

Hospital . . . in Lamb's Conduit Fields, May 2, 1750.

A Computation was made of what Number of Persons the Chapel of this Hospital would conveniently hold, and no greater Number of Tickets were delivered to hear the Performance there on the First Instant. But so many Persons of Distinction coming unprovided with Tickets and pressing to pay Tickets, caused a greater Number to be admitted than were expected ; and some that had Tickets not finding Room going a way. To prevent any Disappointment to such Persons, and for the further Promotion of this Charity, this is to give Notice, that *George-Frederick* Handel, Esq; has generously offered, that the Sacred Oratorio called MESSIAH, shall be performed again under his Direction, in the Chapel of this Hospital on Tuesday the 15th Instant, at Twelve of the Clock at Noon, and the Tickets delivered out, and not brought in on the 1st Inst. will be then received. . . .

HARMAN VERELST, Se.

(Schoelcher, p. 269.)

CHRISTOPHER SMITH'S RECEIPT FOR FEES DUE TO THE PERFORMANCE OF " MESSIAH" IN THE FOUNDLING HOSPITAL ON 1st May 1750

May 4, 1750.

Received of Taylor White, Esq., Treasurer to the Hospital for the Maintenance and Education of exposed and deserted young Children,

Thirtyfive pounds for the Performers in the Oratorio of Messiah on Tuesday the 1st instant in the Chapel of the said Hospital to be Distributed and paid over persuant to the Directions of my Master George Frederick Handel, Esq., by me.

£35 - -   Christopher Smith.

(*Musical Times*, 1st May 1902.) The signature is that of Christopher Smith the elder, Handel's amanuensis. " Peter [le Blond], Mr. Handel's servant " got one guinea, but Smith returned his guinea to the Funds, as did Mr. Beard, the tenor, his two guineas. The rest was probably distributed among the musicians; but see 13th June.

———

FROM THE COURT MINUTES OF THE GOVERNORS OF THE FOUNDLING
HOSPITAL, 9th May 1750

George Frederick Handel, Esq., having presented this Hospital with an Organ, for the Chapel thereof . . .

Resolved—That the thanks of this General Court be severally given to the said Mr. Handel . . . for the same, which the Vice-President accordingly did.

Resolved—That they [Handel and other benefactors] be now Balloted for, to be Elected Governors and Guardians of this Hospital, and the said George Frederick Handel [and others] were accordingly elected by Ballot.

(*Musical Times*, 1st May 1902.) The Court met quarterly. Cf. 7th May 1749. Handel seems to have been present, except at the ballot.

———

FROM THE " REGISTER OF GOVERNORS " OF THE FOUNDLING HOSPITAL,
9th May 1750

[Elected :] George Frederick Handel, Esq.—Great Brook Street

(Nichols and Wray, p. 363.)

———

FROM THE " ACCOUNTS OF COVENT GARDEN THEATRE ", 14th May 1750

Reced by D⁰ [balance] Mʳ Handell's Rent for 12 Oratorio's   76.   18.   2

(Wyndham, I. 60 and 117.) British Museum : Egerton MS. 2269, Vol. III, fol. 160 (or rather 161) verso. There were, in fact, twelve oratorios performed between 2nd March and 12th April 1750.

———

Repeat performance of *Messiah* in the Chapel of the Foundling Hospital, 15th May 1750.

———

A concert is given, at Hickford's in Brewer Street, for the benefit of Signora Cuzzoni, now returned to London, 18th May 1750. (*General Advertiser.*)

Cuzzoni was past her glory. She is said to have left London shortly after this concert, returning in her poverty to the Continent. She was certainly back in London, however, a year later ; if, in fact, she had ever left. Cf. 16th April and 20th May 1751. According to Burney (IV. 460), it was on this occasion, in 1750, that Felice de Giardini first appeared in London, playing a solo for the violin by Giov. Batt. Sammartini. In 1752 Giardini became the leader at the Italian Opera, and in 1756 manager there. (Flower's statement, p. 325, that Signora Cuzzoni sang in *Messiah* on 18th May 1750, has no foundation.) A curious fact is related in a letter which Horace Walpole wrote to Horace Mann on 2nd August 1750 : " Another celebrated Polly has been arrested for thirty pounds, even the old Cuzzoni. The Prince of Wales baled her—who will do as much for him ? " (1857 edition of Walpole's *Letters*, II. 219.)

—

HANDEL'S WILL, 1st June 1750

In the Name of God Amen.

I George Frideric Handel considering the Uncertainty of human Life doe make this my Will in manner following

viz.

I give and bequeath unto my Servant Peter le Blond, my Clothes and Linnen, and three hundred Pounds sterl: and to my other Servants a year Wages.

I give and bequeath to Mr Christopher Smith my large Harpsicord, my little House Organ, my Musick Books, and five hundred Pounds sterl:

Item I give and bequeath to Mr James Hunter five hundred Pounds sterl:

I give and bequeath to my Cousin Christian Gottlieb Handel of Coppenhagen one hundred Pounds sterl:

Item I give and bequeath to my Cousin Magister Christian August Rotth of Halle in Saxony one hundred Pounds sterl:

Item I give and bequeath to my Cousin the Widow of George Taust, Pastor of Giebichenstein near Halle in Saxony three hundred Pounds sterl: and to Her six Children each two hundred Pounds sterl:

All the next and residue of my Estate in Bank Annuity's or of what soever kind of Nature,

I give and bequeath unto my Dear Niece Johanna Friderica Flöerken of Gotha in Saxony (born Michäelsen in Halle) whom I make my Sole Exec^trix of this my last Will.

In witness Whereof I have hereunto set my hand this 1 day of June 1750.

George Frideric Handel

(Clark, 1836, p. 18 ; Cummings, 1904, pp. 66–72.) There are two copies of the will : the official one, published in German in 1827 (*Musikalischer Anzeiger*, Frankfurt am Main) and then in English by Clark, in the Registry of the Prerogative Court of Canterbury, at Doctor's Commons; and the private one, now in the Handel Collection of Gerald Coke, published by Cummings. In the official copy, paragraph two of the will proper has the word Senior added to Christopher Smith's name, but cancelled again. In the private copy, paragraph three, one line and one word are cancelled after the bequest to James Hunter ; they are illegible. The private copy also shows an alteration in the last paragraph but one : " Bank Annuity's " is substituted for " South Sea Annuity's ", the latter being crossed out. In an unauthorized copy of the will, the words are extended to " Bank Annuity's, 1746, sft. sub : ". The private copy, including the codicils of 1st August 1756, 22nd March 1757, 4th August 1757, and 11th April 1759 (written by other hands and only signed by Handel), has been reproduced in facsimile, and photographs are to be found in the Fitzwilliam Museum, Cambridge. There are no signatures of witnesses to the will of 1st June 1750 in either copy. Of the original legatees mentioned here, Christopher Smith was, of course, Handel's compatriot Johann Christoph Schmidt, now his amanuensis ; Hunter, who copied some of the Handel scores in the Granville collection (British Museum), was a " scarlet-dyer at Old Ford " (Hawkins, V, 410 f.) ; Christian Gottlieb Händel was a grandson of Handel's brother Karl, born in 1714 ; Georg Taust, the younger, had been Handel's uncle ; Johanna Friederika Flörke, *née* Michaelsen, was the second child of Handel's sister Dorothea Sophia who was married to Michael Dietrich Michaelsen. Handel's large harpsichord, made by Johannes Ruckers in 1612, came into the King's possession through John Christopher Smith ; the small one, made by Andreas Ruckers in 1651, is now in the Victoria and Albert Museum. A fuller description of the private will is to be found in *The Antique Collector*, February 1942, pp. 9–12, in an article by O. E. Deutsch ; of both copies in *Music & Letters*, January 1953, pp. 15-18, in an article by Wm. C. Smith.

———

FROM THE MINUTES OF THE GENERAL COMMITTEE OF THE FOUNDLING HOSPITAL, 13th June 1750

The Secretary acquainted the Committee, that Mr. Gates the Master of the Children of the King's Chapel, having received, by Mr. Handel's order, Seven Guineas for their Performance, in the Chapel of this Hospital on the 1st and 15th May last, had brought to the Secretary Five pounds Nineteen shillings thereof, chusing only to be reimbursed the One Pound Eight shillings he paid for the Two Days Coach hire for the said children to and from the Hospital, which the Secretary paid to the Treasurer as the Benefaction of the said Mr. Gates to this Hospital.

ORDERED

That the Secretary do return the Thanks of this Committee to Mr. Gates for the same, and sign a Copy of this Minute for that purpose.

(John Tobin, " ' Messiah ' Restored—An Apology ", *Musical Times*, April 1950, p. 133.) Cf. 4th May.

———

MRS. DELANY TO HER BROTHER, BERNARD GRANVILLE, AT LONDON
Delville, 17 June 1750.
I am glad the Foundling Hospital was so full, and carried on with such decency ; I am sure it pleased our friend Handel, and I love to have him pleased.
Delany, II. 556.

———

Handel writes the "musical interlude", called *The Choice of Hercules*, between 28th June and 5th July 1750.

———

Johann Sebastian Bach dies, blind, at Leipzig, 17th (28th) July 1750.
Although they never met, there seems to have been some communication between the two contemporaries. The autograph of Handel's cantata *Armida abbandonata*, written in Italy, was probably in Bach's possession : for perhaps as long as two hundred years, it has been kept with Bach's own manuscript copies of two orchestral parts of that cantata (Breitkopf & Härtel archives, Leipzig). In the possession of the Preussische Staatsbibliothek, Berlin, are two other copies of Handel music, made by Bach : the Brockes Passion (pp. 1-23 copied by Bach, the rest by Anna Magdalena Bach) and the parts of the "Concerto Grosso" in E minor. Carl Philipp Emanuel Bach refers to Handel in two letters : to J. J. Eschenburg, the translator of Burney's Handel sketch of 1785, on 21st January 1786, where he compares Handel unfavourably with Bach as an organ player (without having heard him !) ; and to Friedrich Nicolai on 22nd (27th ?) February 1788, where he refers to Handel's journeys from England to Germany. The first letter is printed in Ludwig Nohl's *Musikerbriefe*, second edition, 1873 ; the second letter in the *Allgemeine deutsche Bibliothek*, Vol. 81, part 1, pp. 295-303 (1788). The second is reprinted in *The Bach Reader* (New York, 1945, pp. 281-8) by Hans T. David and Arthur Mendel, where, however, August Friedrich Christoph Kollmann is suggested as writer of the letter, published anonymously.

———

Handel sells £300 4 per cent Annuities (1746), 2nd August 1750.

———

Handel buys £150 4 per cent Annuities (1746), 9th August 1750.
It seems that Handel kept three hundred pounds in cash for his journey to Germany.

———

FROM THE "GENERAL ADVERTISER", 21st August 1750
Mr. Handel, who went to Germany to visit his Friends some Time since, and between the Hague and Harlaem had the Misfortune to be overturned, by which he was terribly hurt, is now out of Danger.
Apparently Handel left shortly after the 9th August, and he seems to have visited his relatives in Halle, for the last time. No details are known of his accident near Haarlem.

———

The *Gentleman's Magazine* of August 1750 (p. 371) prints a song, " The Address to Sylvia ", with the tune of " Lascia la spina " from *Il Trionfo del Tempo e della Verità*.

———

Messiah is performed, under William Boyce, at the College Hall, in Hereford, mid-September 1750.

(Basil Williams, *The Whig Supremacy, 1714–1760* ; Oxford 1939, p. 392.) There was no newspaper in Hereford. In *Berrow's Worcester Journal* there is no reference to this performance. Boyce conducted the Three Choirs Meetings from about 1737 onwards.

———

At Salisbury, on 4th October 1750, one of Handel's two Te Deums and two of his Anthems are performed in the Cathedral in the morning, *Messiah* being given in the new Assembly Hall in the evening when a new organ is opened. On 5th October the other Te Deum and two other Anthems are performed in the morning and *L' Allegro, il Penseroso, ed il Moderato* (instead of the *Ode for St. Cecilia's Day*, as originally planned) in the evening.

———

FROM THE " GENERAL ADVERTISER ", 18th October 1750

For the Benefit of a Gentleman who has wrote for the STAGE.

At the New Theatre in the Hay-market, This Day . . . will be a Concert of MUSICK. Particularly, in the Concert will be performed the March in Judas Maccabaeus, the Side Drum by Mr. J. Woodbridge, late Kettle-Drummer to the Hon Admirable Boscawen.

And also, a Preamble on the Kettle-Drums, ending with Handel's Water-Musick. . . .

The " Admirable " was Admiral Edward Boscawen.

———

MRS. DELANY TO MRS. DEWES

Delville, Nov. 30, 1750.

Yesterday we were at a charitable music, performed in the round church of Dublin ; we had Corelli's 8th Concerto, Mr. Handel's Te Deum [and] Jubilate, and two anthems ; I cannot say there was so great a crowd as I wished to see on the occasion.

(Delany, II. 620.) The " round church " was St. Andrew's. The performance, in aid of Mercer's Hospital, was given " with the greatest Decency and Exactness " (Faulkner's *Dublin Journal*, 1st December).

———

MRS. DEWES TO HER BROTHER, BERNARD GRANVILLE, AT LONDON

Welsbourne, 3rd Decr 1750.

I hope you find Mr. Handel well. I beg my compliments to him : he has not a more real admirer of his great work than myself ; his wonderful Messiah will never be out of my head ; and I may say *my heart* was raised almost to heaven by it. It is only those people who have not felt the leisure of devotion that can make any objection to that performance, which is calculated to raise our devotion, and make us truly sensible of the power of the divine words he has chose beyond any human work that ever yet appeared, and I am sure I may venture to say ever will. If anything can give us an idea of the Last Day it must be that part— " The trumpet shall sound, the dead shall be raised ". It is [to] few people I can say so much as this, for they would call me an enthusiast ; but when I wish to raise my thoughts above this world and all its trifling concerns, I look over what oratorios I have, and even my poor way of fumbling gives me pleasing recollections, but I have nothing of the Messiah, but *He was despised*, &c. Does Mr. Handel do anything new against next Lent ? surely Theodora will have justice at last, if it was to be again performed, but the generality of the world have ears and *hear not*.

(Delany, II. 623 f.) This letter proves that Mrs. Dewes was a true sister of Mrs. Delany and their brother Bernard Granville ; all three ardent Handelians. (His house was in Park Street, near Grosvenor Square.) We do not know when Handel returned from Germany, but it seems possible that Granville visited him for the first time after his accident. The aria " He was despised " is not among the *Songs in Messiah*, published by Walsh, according to Smith (1948, p. 86 f.), about 1749 ; she must have had a manuscript copy. But her letter indicates that even those favourite songs may not have been on sale before 1751. *Theodora* was produced in March 1749 and received only three performances ; it was published in score by Walsh in 1751, but there was no revival until March 1755.

—

MRS. DELANY TO MRS. DEWES

Delville, 10 Dec. 1750.

On Tuesday morning next [the 11th], the rehearsal of the Messiah is to be for the benefit of debtors—on Thursday evening it will be per-formed. I hope to go to both ; our new, and *therefore* favourite performer Morella is to play the first fiddle, and conduct the whole. I am afraid *his French taste* will prevail ; I shall *not be able to endure* his introducing *froth and nonsense* in that sublime and awful piece of music. What makes me fear this will be the case, is, that in the closing of the eighth concerto of Corelli, instead of playing it *clear and distinct*, he filled it up with *frippery and graces which quite destroyed the effect* of the sweet notes, and solemn pauses that conclude it.

(Delany, II. 626.) The performance of *Messiah* was on Friday, the 14th. The new leader and conductor was Signor Giovanni Battista Marella (sometimes spelt Morella), who in 1753 published six sonatas for a violin and bass as his Opus 1 in

Dublin. Corelli's Concerto no. 8, performed in St. Andrew's Church on 29th November, was very popular at this time, and is still played as *Christmas Concerto*.

—

FROM FAULKNER'S "DUBLIN JOURNAL", 11th December 1750

The Rehearsal of the MESSIAH will begin this Morning at twelve o'Clock. The Performance will be on Friday next, and will begin at six o'Clock. Tickets . . . at Half a Guinea each.

Philharmonic Room, Fishamble-street, December 8, 1750.

To-morrow the 12th Inst. the Society for the Support of Incurables will have the following Pieces performed.—Act I. Overture in Esther . . . Act III. . . . Songs, Let me wander, in Penseroso. . . .

N.B. On Thursday the 31st of January next, the Grand Oratorio of JOSHUA will be performed, for the Support of the Hospital for Incurables.

—

HANDEL TO GEORG PHILIPP TELEMANN, AT HAMBURG

à Londres ce $\frac{25}{14}$ de December^{bre} 1750.

Monsieur

Jetois sur le point de partir de la Haye pour Londres, lorsque Votre tres agreeable Lettre me fut rendu par Mr Passerini. J'avois justement le tems de pouvoir entendre chanter son Epouse. Votre Appuy et recommandation suffisoit a exiter ma curiosité non seulement, mais aussi a Luy accorder toute l'approbation, cependant j'étoit bientôt convaincu moy meme de son rare merite. Ils s'en vont pour l'Ecosse, a remplir le devoir d'un Engagement qu'ils ont pour des Concerts, pendant une saison de six mois. Là Elle pourrà se perfectioner dans la Langue Angloise, et alors (comm'ils ont intention a sejourner pour quelque tems a Londres) je ne manquerai pas de Leur rendre toutes les services qui dependront de moy.

D'ailleurs j'etois fort touché de Vos expressions polies et toutes remplies d'Amitié, Vos manieres obligeantes et Votre Reputation m'ont fait trop d'impression sur mon Coeur et sur mon Esprit, pour ne pas Vous rendre le Reciproque due a Votre gentilesse. Soyez sûr que Vous trouverai toujours en moy un retour plein de sincerité et de veritable Estime.

Je Vous remercie du bel Ouvrage du Sisteme d'intervalles que Vous avez bien voulu me communiquer, il est digne de Vos Occupations et de Votre Scavoir.

Je Vous felicite de la parfaite Santé que Vous jouisse dans un Age assez avancé, et je Vous souhaite de bon Coeur la Continuation de toute sorte de prosperité pendant plusieurs Ans a l'avenir. Si la passion pour les Plantes exotiques & & pourroit prolonguer Vos jours, et soutenir la vivacité qui Vous est naturelle, Je m'offre avec un sensible plaisir a y contribuer en quelque maniere. Je Vous fais donc un Present, et je Vous envoye (*par l'adresse cy jointe*) une Caisse de Fleurs, que les Connoisseurs de ces Plantes m'assurent d'être choisies et d'une rareté charmante, s'il medisent le vray, Vous aurez des Plantes les meilleures de toute l'Angleterre, la saison est encore propre pour en avoir des Fleurs, Vous en serez le meilleur Juge, j'attens Vôtre decision la dessus. Cependant ne me faites pas languir longtems pour Votre agreable Reponse a celle cy, puisque je suis avec la plus sensible Amitie, et passion parfaite

Monsieur

Votre

tres humble et tres obeissant

Serviteur

George Frideric Handel.

(Translation)

London, 25th/14th December, 1750.

I was on the point of leaving the Hague for London when your most agreeable letter was delivered to me by Mr. Passerini. I had just enough time to be able to hear his wife sing. Your patronage and approval were enough not only to excite my curiosity but also to serve her as sufficient recommendation ; however I was soon convinced myself of her rare quality. They are leaving for Scotland to fulfil concert engagements there for a season of six months. There she will be able to perfect herself in the English language ; after that (as they intend to remain some time in London) I shall not fail to be of service to them in all ways that may depend on me.

Moreover I was greatly touched by your most friendly expressions of goodwill ; your kindness and your renown made too much impression on my heart and mind for me not to reciprocate them as you deserve. Pray be assured that you will always find in me a like sincerity and true regard.

I thank you for the splendid work on the system of intervals which you were good enough to send me ; it is worthy of your time and trouble and of your learning.

I congratulate you on the perfect health that you are enjoying at your somewhat advanced age, and I wish you from my heart every prosperity for many years to come. If your passion for exotic plants etc. could prolong your days and sustain the zest for life that is natural to you, I offer with very real pleasure to contribute to it in some sort. Consequently I am sending you as a present (*to the address enclosed*) a crate of flowers, which experts assure me are very choice and of admirable rarity. If they are not telling the truth, you will [at least] have the best plants in all England, and the season of the year is still right for their bearing flowers. You will be the best judge of this ; I await your decision on the matter. But do not let me have to wait for your agreeable reply about this for too long, since I am, with perfect friendship and devotion,

Sir,

Your most humble and most obedient

servant,

George Frideric Handel.

(Kitzig.)   Original in University Library Dorpat = Tartu.   Handel met Telemann in Halle in 1701, when the latter was on his way to Leipzig.   The beginning of the letter suggests that Handel did really return from Germany, again via the Hague, in late autumn (cf. 3rd December).   Giuseppe Passerini, a violinist, came (perhaps from Scotland) to London in 1752, with his wife Christina, and (according to Moser, pp. 200 f.) later conducted *Messiah* in Dublin ; he also played in Bath about 1755.   Signora Passerini, a soprano, sang in London in operas in 1753–54, and from 1754 onwards in Handel oratorios. (Cf. Chrysander, 1895, p. 14.)   Telemann's essay, mentioned by Handel as sent to him, was *Das neue musikalische System*, published in Mizler's *Neu-eröffneter musikalischer Bibliothek*, 1752, III. 713 ff.   The messenger for the plants was a Captain Jean Carsten (see 20th September 1754).

———

FROM FAULKNER'S " DUBLIN JOURNAL ", 15th December 1750

Last Night there was a most polite and very numerous Audience at the Musick Hall in Fishamble-street, at the Oratorio of the MESSIAH, the Performance of which gave universal Satisfaction to the whole Audience.

———

MRS. DELANY TO MRS. DEWES

Delville, 15 Dec. 1750.
This week I have had a feast of music.   At the rehearsal on Tuesday morning [the 11th], and last night at the performance, of the Messiah, very well performed indeed, and the pleasure of the music greatly heightened by considering how many poor prisoners would be released by it. . . .   We go this afternoon to the Bishop of Derry's, to hear Morella ; he conducted the Messiah very well—*surprizingly* so, considering he was *not before acquainted* with such sublime music.

(Delany, II. 628.)   The Bishop of Derry was William Barnard.

———

MRS. DELANY TO HER BROTHER, BERNARD GRANVILLE, IN LONDON

Delville, Dec. 18, 1750.
I was at the rehearsal and performance of The Messiah, and though *voices* and *hands* were wanting to do it justice, it was very tolerably performed, and gave me great pleasure—'tis heavenly.   Morella conducted it, and I expected would have *spoiled it*, but was agreeably surprized to find the contrary ; he came off with great applause.   I thought it would be impossible for his wild fancy and fingers to have kept within bounds ; but Handel's music inspired and *awed him*.   He says (*but I don't believe him*) that he *never* saw any music of Handel's or Corelli's till he came to Ireland.   I heard him play at the Bishop of Derry's a solo of Geminiani's which he had never seen ; he played it cleverly, as his execution is extraordinary, but his taste in the adagio part was *ill suited* to the music. He is young, modest, and well-behaved, as I am told, and were he to play

under Mr. Handel's direction two or three years, would make a surprizing player. We are so fond of him here, that were it known I gave this hint, I should be *expelled* all musical society, as they so much fear he should be tempted to leave us.

. . . Pray make my compliments to Handel. Is *Theodora* to appear next Lent ?

(Delany, II. 629-31.) Cf. 15th December ; for *Theodora*, 3rd December. Marella does not seem to have fulfilled Dublin's expectations.

—

FROM THE SATIRICAL POEM "THE SCANDALIZADE", 1750

Ho ! there, to whom none can forsooth hold a candle,
Called the lovely-faced Heidegger out to George Handel,
In arranging the poet's sweet lines to a tune,
Such as God save the King ! or the famed Tenth of June.

(Cummings, 1902, p. 42.) Copies in the Bodleian Library, Oxford, and in Yale University, New Haven, Connecticut. The pamphlet is attributed to Macnamara Morgan and William Kenrick. It was reprinted in the collection *Remarkable Satires*, also called *Satires on several Occasions*, London, 1760, a copy of which is in the Library of Congress, Washington. Heidegger, whose ugliness was notorious, died in 1749.

—

SONG ON A GOLDFINCH FLYING OUT AT THE WINDOW WHILE A LADY WAS PLAYING AND SINGING DEAR LIBERTY (about 1750)

To Handel's pleasing Notes as Chloe sang
The Charms of heaven'ly Liberty,
A gentle Bird, 'till then with Bondage pleas'd,
With Ardour panted to be free ;
His Prison broke, he seeks the distant Plain,
Yet e'er he flies tunes forth this parting Strain . . .
Liberty, dear Liberty,
Forgive me, Mistress, since by thee
I first was taught sweet Liberty.

Single-sheet folio. Copies in the British Museum (dated : 1730 ?) and Gerald Coke's Handel Collection. Reprinted 1756 in the *Literary Magazine* (I. 480), with slightly different title. The stanza printed here is the first of three. The music quotes Handel's tune from *Judas Maccabaeus*, " 'Tis Liberty, dear Liberty ", at the corresponding line. Author and composer are unknown.

—

FROM JOHANN CHRISTOPH VON DREYHAUPT'S " BESCHREIBUNG DES . . .
SAALE-KREISES, *etc.*, Halle, 1750

See page 768.

—

1751

Handel writes the Organ Concerto in B flat, Op. 7, no. 3, between 1st and 3rd January 1751.

———

MRS. DELANY TO MRS. DEWES

Delville, 12 Jan., 1750–51.
Next Tuesday [the 15th] we propose going to the rehearsal of Judas Maccabeus, for the Infirmary of Incurables.
(Delany, III. 5 f.) The performance was in the Music Hall on 17th January. A copy of the word-book is in the University Library, Cambridge.

———

Messrs. Domenico Paradies and Francesco Vanneschi get leave and license to perform Italian operas at the Haymarket Theatre, 17th January 1751.
Public Record Office : L.C.5/161, p. 343. There was no time limit. On 16th May 1757, the permit was granted to Vanneschi alone, for the period from 1st July 1757 till 1st July 1758. Cf. 10th March 1750.

———

Handel begins the oratorio *Jephtha*, 21st January 1751.

———

FROM FAULKNER'S " DUBLIN JOURNAL ", 22nd January 1751

[Extracts.]
23 January : ' Acis and Galatea ', Philharmonic Room, Fishamble Street, presented by the Society for the Support of Incurables.
25 January : ' Acis and Galatea ', same place, by the Charitable Musical Society.
31 January : ' Joshua ', Music Hall, Fishamble Street (Conductor B. Manwaring), for the Support of the Hospital of Incurables ; rehearsal 29 January, at noon ; book gratis.
14 February : ' Deborah ' (probably in the Music Hall), for the benefit of the Charitable Infirmary on the Inns Quay ; rehearsal 11th February.
18 February : ' Esther ', Philharmonic Room, Fishamble Street (Miss Oldmixon among the singers), for the benefit of Mr. B. Manwaring.
With *Messiah* on 14th December 1750 and *Judas Maccabaeus* on 17th January 1751, this was a good beginning to a Handel season in Dublin. On 12th March followed *Samson*, and on 22nd March *Acis and Galatea* again. Cf. the season 1751–2.

———

MRS. DELANY TO MRS. DEWES

Delville, 2 Feb. 1750–51.
We went to the rehearsal of Joshua last Tuesday [29th January] ; were charmed with it—never heard it before, but it was so cold on Thursday I had not courage to go to the night performance of it.

(Delany, III. 12 f.)

———

MRS. DELANY TO MRS DEWES

Delville, [c. 9th] Feb. 1751.
Next Monday [the 11th] we go to the rehearsal of Deborah ; it is to be performed on Thursday for the benefit of an hospital.

(Delany, III. 16.)

———

MRS. DELANY TO MRS. DEWES

Delville, [c. 13th] Feb^y, 1750–51.
Last Monday [the 11th] we went to the rehearsal of Deborah, which was delightful.

(Delany, III. 18.)

———

HANDEL'S FIRST PERSONAL NOTE IN THE SCORE OF "JEPHTHA", 13th February 1751

biss hierher koṁen den 13 Febr. ☿ 1751 verhindert worden wegen relaxation des gesichts meines linken auges (got as far as this on Wednesday 13th February 1751, unable to go on owing to weakening of the sight of my left eye).

(Engel. I. 182.) Original in the Royal Music Library (British Museum). Handel was working on the second part of the oratorio, when he had to stop. The word "relaxation" is crossed out and "so relaxt" added at the end. The astrological sign, one of those Handel had used in his manuscripts since 1739, means Wednesday. This was the beginning of Handel's eye troubles. It is interesting to observe that, in this state of mind, he writes German. Cf. 23rd February.

———

FROM THE "GENERAL ADVERTISER", 22nd February 1751

At the Theatre Royal in Covent-Garden, This Day . . . will be perform'd an Oratorio call'd BELSHAZZAR. With a Concerto on the Organ. . . . To begin at Half an Hour after Six o'Clock.

Cf. 27th March 1745. Repeat performance on 27th February. The word-book, a copy of which is in the British Museum, shows that this was a shortened version. The cast is not known. Cf. 22nd February 1758.

———

Handel deposits £445, 23rd February 1751.

———

HANDEL'S SECOND PERSONAL NOTE IN THE SCORE OF " JEPHTHA ",
23rd February 1751

den 23 ♄ dieses etwas besser worden wird angegangen (Saturday the
23rd of this month [February 1751] a little better, started work again).

(Engel, I. 183.) Cf. 13th February. This was Handel's birthday. The astrological sign means Saturday. The last word but one was read as " wieder " by
Wm. C. Smith (Catalogue of the Handel Exhibition, Edinburgh, 1948, p. 9).

———

FROM THE " GENERAL ADVERTISER ", 1st March 1751

At the Theatre Royal in Covent-Garden, This Day, will be perform'd
ALEXANDER'S FEAST.   And an Additional New Act, call'd The CHOICE
of HERCULES.   With a New Concerto on the Organ. . . . To begin at
Half an Hour after Six o'Clock.

The libretto, a copy of which is in the Bodleian Library, Oxford, shows that the
new organ concerto was played after the Ode, the " new act " counting as " Act
the Third " after the two of *Alexander's Feast*.   *The Choice of Hercules*, otherwise
called " a musical interlude ", was probably written for Handel by William
Duncombe (cf. 8th March 1749) ; it was founded on a poem by Robert Lowth.
This poem, based on Prodicus of Ceos's discourse of *Horai*, had been published in
Joseph Spence's *Polymetis* in 1747.   The air " Enjoy the sweet Elysian grove "
was taken from the Smollett-Handel *Alceste* (see 8th January 1750).   Repeat
performances on 6th, 8th and 13th March.

———

CAST OF " THE CHOICE OF HERCULES ", 1st March 1751

Pleasure—Miss Faulkner, soprano
Virtue—(?) Mrs. Arne, soprano
Hercules—Miss Young, mezzo-soprano
An Attendant on Pleasure—Mr. Lowe, tenor

———

Handel deposits £305 : 9 : 0, 2nd March 1751.

———

Handel deposits £300, 7th March 1751.

———

FROM THE " LONDON ADVERTISER, AND LITERARY GAZETTE ",
8th March 1751

We are credibly informed, that a Handkerchief was very unluckily
stained last Wednesday [the 6th] Night in one of the Side Boxes at the
Oratorio, from the Lady's not understanding the Difference between the

antiquated French fashion of Painting, and the modern English custom of Enamelling.

At the same Time a formidable Attack was made in an opposite Box, by a very dangerous Lover, on a very sensible and worthy Heart. The Hero seemed to conceive himself, through the whole Performance, the Alexander, to whom the Power of the Music was addressed ; and appeared particularly moved at the Expression,

> Lovely Thais sits beside thee,
> Take the Good the Gods provide thee.

.   .   .   .   .

On Wednesday Night several Coaches in waiting at the Oratorio, at Covent Garden, had their Coronets and other Ornaments at the Top, unscrewed and carried off.

By mistake, the same paper announced " *Sampson* " for performance on this day (8th March), whereas *Alexander's Feast* and *The Choice of Hercules* were repeated. By another mistake, the *General Advertiser* of the 9th printed an advertisement of these two works to be repeated on the 11th : they were repeated on the 13th.

———

Handel deposits £200, 9th March 1751.

———

COUNTESS OF SHAFTESBURY TO JAMES HARRIS, AT SALISBURY

[London,] March 13, [1751?]

My constancy to poor Handel got the better of . . . my indolence, and I went last Friday [the 8th] to ' Alexander's Feast ' ; but it was such a melancholy pleasure, as drew tears of sorrow to see the great though unhappy Handel, dejected, wan, and dark, sitting by, not playing on the harpsichord, and to think how his light had been spent by *being overplied in music's cause.* I was sorry to find the audience so insipid and tasteless (I may add unkind) not to give the poor man the comfort of applause ; but affectation and conceit cannot discern or attend to merit.

(Squire, 1909.) *Malmesbury Letters,* I. 3 : dated 1745. There was, however, no performance of *Alexander's Feast* in that year. The description of Handel's condition fits in with the year 1751.

———

Handel deposits £140, 14th March 1751.

———

SIR EDWARD TURNER TO SANDERSON MILLER

London, March 14th, 1750[-51].

Noble Handel hath lost an eye, but I have the Rapture to say that St. Cecilia makes no complaint of any Defect in his Fingers.

(Myers, 1948, p. 150.) Sanderson Miller, p. 165 : dated 1750, without explanation. Cf. 13th and 23rd February and 15th June.

———

FROM THE " GENERAL ADVERTISER ", 15th March 1751

At the Theatre Royal in Covent-Garden, This Day, will be perform'd an Oratorio, call'd ESTHER. With a Concert on the Organ. . . . To begin at Half an Hour after Six o'Clock.

Cf. 26th March 1740. There was one performance only.

Samson is performed by the Musical Society at the " Castle Tavern " in Pater-noster Row, 16th March 1751. (Word-book in the British Museum.)

MRS. DELANY TO MRS. DEWES

Delville, 16 March, 1750–51.

Tuesday [the 12th] . . . in the afternoon, went to hear " Samson " *murdered most* barbarously ; I never heard such a performance called music in my life ! what should be grave we turned to merriment.

(Delany, III. 28.)

FROM THE " CALEDONIAN MERCURY ", EDINBURGH, 18th March 1751

For the *Benefit* of Mr. *Macdougall.*

At the New Concert-Hall in the Canongate, on Tuesday the 26th of March, will be performed the celebrated *Mask* of ACIS and GALATEA, Set to Musick by Mr. Handel. The Vocal Parts by Mrs. *Lampe* and Mrs. *Storer*, and others, and the Instrumental Parts by the best *Masters.* To begin precisely at Six o'Clock. . . . Pit and Boxes 2s. 6d. Gallery 1s. 6d.

(David Fraser Harris, p. 267 ; Percy M. Young, in *Musical Times*, February 1950, p. 52.) The concert was conducted by John Frederick Lampe, who died in July of this same year. This is the only dated record, during his lifetime, of a Handel performance in Edinburgh. Hugo Arnot, in his History of Edinburgh, 1779, tells of overtures played at the Cross Keys Tavern (Steil's Tavern), before 1728, and, according to information kindly supplied by Dr. Henry G. Farmer, Handel was frequently performed at St. Mary's Chapel Concerts before 1762.

FROM THE " GENERAL ADVERTISER ", 20th March 1751

At the Theatre Royal in Covent-Garden, This Day, will be perform'd an Oratorio, call'd JUDAS MACCHABAEUS. With a Concerto on the Organ. . . . To begin an Half an Hour after Six o'Clock.

Cf. 9th March 1750. Next day a repeat performance was advertised for the 22nd, but it was cancelled because of the Prince of Wales's death on the 20th.

Handel deposits £400, 21st March 1751.

—

FROM THE "LONDON ADVERTISER", 22nd March 1751

Last Night an Order came to both Theatres to forbid their Performance on the Account of his Royal Highness the Prince of Wales's Death ; and we hear all public Diversions will be discontinued during his Majesty's Pleasure. There was no Music at Ranelagh Yesterday Morning, nor any Concert at the King's Arms in Cornhill last Night.

This order cancelled the second performance of *Judas Maccabaeus* on 22nd March, and closed Handel's Lent season prematurely. The concert for the Musicians' Fund, advertised for the 26th March at the Haymarket Theatre, was first postponed to 2nd, and finally to 16th April. The funeral of the Prince was on 13th April. It seems that Handel intended to revive *Alexander Balus* (see 23rd March 1748) in 1751 ; a word-book, dated 1751, was printed by J. Watts, and Chrysander, in his preface to Vol. XXXIII of the Collected Edition, mentions the performance as a fact. This oratorio, however, was not revived until 1754.

—

Acis and Galatea is performed again at the Philharmonic Room, Fishamble Street, Dublin, by the Charitable Musical Society, 22nd March 1751. (Faulkner's *Dublin Journal*, 19th March.)

—

Handel withdraws £1790 : 9 : 0, and buys £1350 4 per cent Annuities (1746), 28th March 1751.

—

Handel deposits £250, 4th April 1751.

—

FROM THE "LONDON ADVERTISER", 6th April 1751

The Rehearsal of the Music for the Feast of the Sons of the Clergy, will be performed at St. Paul's Cathedral, on Tuesday the 30th of this Month ; and the Feast will be held at Merchant-Taylors-Hall, on Friday, May 3, 1751. . . .

N.B. Mr. Handel's new Te Deum, Jubilate and Coronation Anthem, with a new Anthem by Dr. Boyce, will be Vocally and Instrumentally performed. . . .

(Schoelcher, p. 336.)

—

FROM THE "GENERAL ADVERTISER", 10th April 1751

NEW MUSICK.

This Day is published,

Handel's Second Set of eighty Songs selected from his Oratorios, for the Harpsichord, Voice, German Flute, or Hoboy.—

H.-23

☞ The Instrumental Parts to these celebrated [songs] may be had to complete them for Concerts.

Printed for J. Walsh. . . .

Now printing, and speedily will be published,
The Choice of Hercules, composed by Mr. Handel.

—

FROM THE " GENERAL ADVERTISER ", 15th April 1751

Hospital . . . in Lamb's Conduit Fields, April 11, 1751.

GEORGE FREDERICK HANDEL, Esq; having repeated his offer to promote this Charity, The Sacred Oratorio, call'd MESSIAH, will be perform'd under his *Direction,* on *Thursday* the 18th *Instant,* at *Twelve o'Clock* at *Noon* precisely, in the *Chapel* of this *Hospital* ; and he will perform on the *Fine Organ,* which he has given to the Corporation. . . .

By Order of the General Committee,

HARMAN VERELST, *Sec.*

Note. The Doors of the Chapel will be open at Ten o'Clock, and there will be no Collection.

Tickets were sold at half a guinea. Cf. (end of) April 1751. Watts advertised his word-book on 13th April.

—

FROM THE " GENERAL ADVERTISER ", 16th April 1751

For the Benefit and Increase of a FUND *established for the Support of Decay'd* MUSICIANS, *or their Families.*

At the King's Theatre in the Haymarket, This Day . . . will be perform'd an Entertainment of Vocal and Instrumental MUSICK. As follows,

PART I. ...

Air. *Why does the God of Israel sleep,* composed by Mr. Handel, sung by Mr. Beard. . . .

Air. *Falsa imagine,* composed by Mr. Handel, sung by Sig. Cuzzoni. . . .

PART II. ...

Air. *Father of Heaven,* composed by Mr. Handel, sung by S. Galli. . . .

Air. *Benche mi siu crudele,* composed by Mr. Handel, sung by Sig. Cuzzoni. . . .

PART III. ...

Air. *Return, O God of Hosts,* composed by Mr. Handel, sung by Sig. Frasi. . . .

Air. *Tune your Harps,* composed by Mr. Handel, sung by Mr. Beard.

Duetto. *Piu amabile belta,* composed by Mr. Handel, sung by Sig. Cuzzoni and Sig. Guadagni.

A Grand Concerto of Mr. Handel's.

.   .   .   .   .

To begin exactly at Six o'Clock.

The concert was postponed from 26th March till 2nd April, and then once again. For Signora Cuzzoni, cf. 18th May 1750 and 20th May 1751. The arias and the duet are from *Samson, Ottone, Judas Maccabaeus, Ottone, Samson, Esther,* and *Giulio Cesare.* The part of Teofane in *Ottone* was that in which Signora Cuzzoni made her London début, on 12th January 1723 ; cf. 23rd May 1751.

———

From the " General Advertiser ", 18th April 1751

We hear that the Ladies who have Tickets for the Oratorio of Messiah at the Foundling-Hospital, this Day the 18th Instant, intend to go in small Hoops, and the Gentlemen without Swords, to make their Seats more convenient to themselves.

(*Musical Times,* 1st May 1902 : dating the notice as of 1752.)

———

From the " London Daily Advertiser ", 19th April 1751

Yesterday there was a very numerous Appearance of Gentlemen and Ladies at the Oratorio of Messiah, for the Benefit of the Foundling Hospital.

On 18th April the *Daily Advertiser* changed its name to *London Daily Advertiser.*

———

From the " General Advertiser ", 23rd April 1751

For the Benefit of Master Jonathan Snow, *a Youth of Ten Years of Age.*

At the New-Theatre in the Haymarket, This Day . . . will be performed a Concert of Vocal Musick. Viz. Part I. A grand Concerto for Trumpets and French Horns. To which will be added, The Dead March in Saul. Air. The Song and Chorus of *Happy Pair* in Alexander's Feast compos'd by Mr. Handel . . . Trio. *The Flocks shall leave the Mountains,* compos'd by Mr. Handel. . . . The Whole to conclude with the Coronation Anthem, both Vocal and Instrumental, of *God save the King.*

The trio is from *Acis and Galatea,* the Coronation Anthem is *Zadok the Priest.* Jonathan Snow, probably the son of the trumpeter Valentine Snow, became an organist and composer. Cf. 2nd May 1757.

———

At a performance of Nicholas Rowe's tragedy, *Jane Shore,* given at Covent Garden on 23rd April 1751 for the benefit of Miss Falkner, she sings two arias, " Softly sweet in Lydian measures " and " The Prince unable to conceal his pain ", from *Alexander's Feast*, after Act III.

———

Marianne Davies, seven years of age, plays a concerto by Handel on the harpsichord, at her concert at Hickford's Rooms, 30th April 1751. (*General Advertiser.*)

> She also played on the German flute, and sang some songs. (Squire in Grove, first edition, IV. 608.) It is tempting to believe that the Davis family of Dublin (see 2nd May 1732, 13th Nov. 1742 and 10th May 1745) were the family of the two famous sisters Davies of London ; but there is no proof for it. Marianne Davies, like the girl from Ireland, played the harpsichord, and later became an accomplished player on the glass-harmonica, 1762, invented by Benjamin Franklin, supposedly her uncle. (Cf. Gluck's drinking glasses, 28th March 1746.) She travelled on the Continent with her younger sister, Cecilia, a singer, and met Dr. Anton Mesmer, the magnetist, and the Mozart family in Vienna in 1768 ; she met Mozart again in Milan in 1771. Cf. 19th March 1753 and 28th April 1756. Signora Frasi, Mr. Beard and Master Arne assisted Miss Davies, as singers, at her 1751 concert.

———

FROM THE " GENTLEMAN'S MAGAZINE ", April 1751

THURSDAY 18.

Was performed in the chapel of the *Foundling Hospital*, the sacred oratorio *Messiah*, under the direction of G. F. *Handel*, Esq; who himself play'd a voluntary on the organ ; the amount of the sum for the tickets delivered out was above 600*l*.

> (Clark, 1852.) Handel may have played his organ concerto in B flat, composed at the beginning of 1751, but more probably an improvisation. (Chrysander, III. 161.)

———

Walsh advertises the score of *The Choice of Hercules* for 5s., *General Advertiser*, 4th May 1751.

> In the score were printed Walsh's " Proposals for Printing by Subscription Theodora ", dated " London, May 4, 1751 ". The latter score appeared on 20th June, without list of subscribers.

———

FROM THE " GENERAL ADVERTISER ", 9th May 1751

Hospital . . . in Lamb's Conduit-Fields, May 8, 1751.

At the Request of several Persons of Distinction, GEORGE FREDERICK HANDEL, Esq; has been applied to for a Repetition of the Performance of the Sacred Oratorio, call'd MESSIAH, which he having very charitably agreed to, This is to give Notice, That the said Oratorio will be performed in the Chapel of this Hospital on Thursday the 16th Inst. (being *Ascension-Day*) at *Twelve o'Clock* at *Noon* precisely. . . .

HARMAN VERELST, *Sec.*

(Schoelcher, pp. 269 f.)

———

FROM THE "LONDON DAILY ADVERTISER", 17th May 1751

Yesterday the Oratorio of Messiah was performed at the Foundling Hospital, to a very numerous and splendid Audience ; and a Voluntary on the Organ played by Mr. Handel, which met with the greatest Applause.

A similar note appeared in the *General Advertiser* of the same day (Schoelcher, p. 270).

———

FROM THE "GENERAL ADVERTISER", 20th May 1751

For the Benefit of Signora CUZZONI.

At Mr. Hickford's in Brewer-street, on Wednesday next [the 22nd] will be a Concert of MUSICK. The Vocal Parts by Sig. Guadani, Sig. Palma, and Signora Cuzzoni, who, by particular Desire, will sing *Affenai del Pensier, Return O God of Hosts, Falsa Imagine,* and *Salve Regina* ; and the Instrumental Parts will consist of Mr. Handel's and Mr. Geminiani's Concertos. To begin exactly at Seven o'Clock.

See next entry.

———

FROM THE SAME

I am so extremely sensible of the many Obligations I have already received from the Nobility and Gentry of this Kingdom (for which I sincerely return my most humble Thanks) that nothing but extreme Necessity, and a Desire of doing Justice, could induce me to trouble them again, but being unhappily involved in a few Debts, am extremely desirous of attempting every Thing in my Power to pay them, before I quit England ; therefore take the Liberty, most humbly to intreat them, once more to repeat their well-known Generosity and Goodness, and to honour me with their Presence at this Benefit, which shall be the last I will ever trouble them with, and is made solely to pay my Creditors ; and to convince the World of my Sincerity herein, I have prevailed on Mr. Hickford to receive the Money, and to pay it to them.

I am, Ladies and Gentlemen,
Yours very much obliged, and most devoted humble Servant

F. CUZZONI.

As some of the performers were engaged for this day, the concert was postponed till 23rd May. Cuzzoni's letter was inserted again on 21st and 23rd May. The arias were from *Ottone*, except the second one which was from *Samson*. The *Salve*

Regina was probably Pergolesi's, not Hasse's. The Handel Concerto was No. 5 of his Grand Concertos, and Geminiani's was No. 6 of Opus 3. Angelo Morigi played a violin solo, Mr. Miller a bassoon solo, and Mr. Beneki a violoncello solo. Cf. 18th May 1750 and 16th April 1751. From her letter it seems that Cuzzoni continued to live in London during 1750–51 ; this concert, apparently, was her final farewell.

FROM THE MINUTES OF THE GENERAL COMMITTEE OF THE FOUNDLING HOSPITAL, 29th May 1751

The Secretary acquainted the Committee, That Mr. Bernard Gates the Master of the King's Singing Boys, brought to him Five pounds and Seven shillings, the Surplus of Six Guineas he had received, by Order of Mr. Handel, for the Boys Performances, Twice, in the Oratorio of Messiah in the Chapel of the Hospital, after deducting Nineteen Shillings for their Coach hire ; which he desired the Committee to accept of as his Benefaction to this Hospital ; which the Secretary paid to the Treasurer.
ORDERED
That the Secretary do return the Thanks of this Committee to Mr. Gates, for the same.
Cf. 13th June 1750.

FROM THE " GENTLEMAN'S MAGAZINE ", May 1751

THURSDAY 16.

The Oratorio of *Messiah* was again performed at the *Foundling* hospital, under the direction of George Frederick Handel, Esq; who himself play'd the organ for the benefit of the charity : there were above 500 coaches besides chairs, &c. and the tickets amounted to above 700 guineas.

(*Musical Times*, 1st May and 1st June 1902.)

Handel withdraws £250, 13th June 1751.

FROM THE " GENERAL ADVERTISER ", 15th June 1751

On Thursday last [the 13th] Mr. Handel arrived in Town from Cheltenham Wells, where he had been to make use of the Waters.

Handel may have been there three weeks, in any case not more than four. After his return he was treated for his eyesight by Samuel Sharp, surgeon to Guy's Hospital since 1733.

Walsh advertises the score of *Theodora*, *General Advertiser*, 20th June 1751.
Cf. 4th May.

Walsh offers complete sets of all Handel's oratorios, "neatly bound", in eleven volumes, *General Advertiser*, 29th June 1751.

There is no indication of the price. Cf. 8th February 1753.

—

Handel deposits £175, 8th August 1751.

—

At Gloucester, on 28th and 29th August 1751, one of the Coronation Anthems is performed on the first morning and one of the Te Deums on the second morning, both in the Cathedral; in the evenings *Alexander's Feast* and *L'Allegro ed il Penseroso* are performed in the Booth Hall. (*Gloucester Journal.*)

—

Handel withdraws £50, 29th August 1751.

—

Handel finishes the oratorio *Jephtha*, 30th August 1751.

—

Handel withdraws £25, 5th September 1751.

—

FROM THE " GENERAL ADVERTISER ", 3rd October 1751

Salisbury, Sept. 30. . . . The Anniversary Festival of Music was celebrated here on the 26th and 27th Instant. The Performance in the Church on the first Day consisted of Mr. Handel's Te Deum, compos'd for Duke Chandos, and two of his celebrated Coronation Anthems. On the second Day, his Te Deum, compos'd for his present Majesty, together with the remaining two Coronation Anthems. At the Assembly-Room on the first Evening was perform'd Alexander's Feast; on the Second the Oratorio of Samson, both set to Music by the same great Composer. The Performers were more than Forty in Number, among which were several, as well vocal as instrumental from Oxford, Bath, and London. The Performance itself was accurate and just (there being scarce an Error throughout the Whole) and met with general Applause from a very polite and numerous Audience.

(Schoelcher, p. 336.) The *spiritus rector* of this festival was, without doubt, James Harris.

—

Handel withdraws £60, 23rd October 1751.

—

FROM THE "LONDON DAILY ADVERTISER", 25th October 1751

Wednesday [the 23rd] Evening the Masque of Acis and Galatea, a celebrated Composition of Mr. Handel's, was performed at the Castle Tavern in Pater-noster Row, in which Mr. Beard and Signora Frasi met with universal Applause from a numerous and polite Audience.

The Musical Society at the "Castle Tavern" had performed the masque in 1747, and again in 1755. (About 1750 the St. Caecilia Concert at the "Crown Tavern" behind the Royal Exchange also performed the work, under the title of a Serenata; cf. Smith, 1948, p. 236.) According to a word-book in Schoelcher's collection, the Castle Society seems to have performed *Samson* the same year.

—

FROM FAULKNER'S "DUBLIN JOURNAL", 5th November 1751

[Extracts.]

8 November : 'Acis and Galatea' (instead of 'Athalia', as previously announced), to be performed by the Charitable Musical Society, (Philharmonic Room,) Fishamble Street.

21 November : 'Alexander's Feast' and Grand Coronation Anthem ("My heart is inditing"), to be conducted by Dubourg in the Music Hall, Fishamble Street, for the new Dublin Charity for Decayed Musicians and their Families.

Athalia was postponed till 15th November.

—

FROM THE SAME, 9th November 1751

[Extracts.]

15 November : 'Athalia', conducted by Marella for the Charitable Musical Society, (Philharmonic Room,) Fishamble Street.

16 November : 'Deborah' (probably in the Music Hall), for the Charitable Infirmary.

21 November : see advertisement of 5th November.

29 November : 'Messiah', Music Hall, conducted by Marella, for the 'Relief and Enlargement' of poor prisoners ; rehearsal 27th November ; book gratis.

5 February 1752 : 'Joshua', Music Hall, for the Hospital of Incurables.

—

MRS. DELANY TO MRS. DEWES

Delville, 14th Dec. [or rather, Nov.] 1751.

Yesterday we heard the rehearsal of "Deborah". What a charming oratorio it is !

(Delany, III. 67.)

—

MRS. DELANY TO MRS. DEWES

Delville, 16th Nov., 1751.

I have got Theodora, and have great pleasure in thrumming over the sweet songs with Don. [Mrs. Donellan], who sings every evening. . . .

Did you hear that poor Handel has lost the sight of one of his eyes ? I am sure you (who so truly taste his merit) will lament it : so much for England !

(Delany, III, 59 and 61.) Mrs. Donellan was, it seems, on a visit to Ireland, from London. Mrs. Delany got the score of *Theodora*, published by Walsh.

FROM FAULKNER'S "DUBLIN JOURNAL", 7th December 1751

On Thursday last [the 5th], Mr. Handel's grand Te Deum, Jubilate, and two Anthems were performed at St. Andrew's Church, with the greatest decency and exactness possible, for the support of Mercer's Hospital. His Grace the Duke of Dorset Lord Lieutenant, favour'd the Hospital with his Presence, and above four Hundred Persons of the first Quality and Distinction were at this Performance.

Lionel Cranfield Sackville, first Duke of Dorset, was Lord Lieutenant of Ireland from 1730 to 1737, and again from 1750 to 1755.

Handel withdraws £20, 20th December 1751.

FROM THE "GENERAL ADVERTISER", 27th December 1751

This Day . . . will be exhibited At the New Theatre in the Haymarket, a Grand Concert of Vocal and Instrumental MUSICK, by Gentlemen. . . . To be divided into Three Acts. Act I. will contain, 1. A grand Piece with Kettle-Drums and Trumpets. . . . 3. Overture by Mr. Handell. . . . Act the Second, . . . 2. Overture to Ariadne. . . . 5. March in Judas Macchabeus, with the Side-Drum. Act the Third, . . . 5. Handel's Water-piece. . . .

One movement of the *Water Music* was sometimes called the *Water Piece* (or Peice) ; it is the opening of the second half, in D major. The concert was repeated on 30th December ; the programme was slightly different and contained, by Handel, the march from *Judas Maccabaeus* and the *Water Music* " with a Preamble on the Kettle-Drums ". Cf. 21st January and 6th February 1752.

FROM THE "LONDON DAILY ADVERTISER", 28th December 1751

At the Great-Room in Dean-street, Soho, This Day . . . will be performed the *Third Night* of the SUBSCRIPTION CONCERTS. . . . *First Act.*

H.–23 *a*

Overture, Esther . . . *But oh sad Virgin*, Handel, Signora Francesina. . . .
Cutting in Harris Collection. No complete issue available. The aria is from
L'Allegro.

———

FROM THE " UNIVERSAL MAGAZINE ", December 1751

An Account of the FOUNDLING HOSPITAL.

. . . And the fine Organ, is the gift of the inimitable Mr. Handel,
whose admirable compositions and excellent performances of sacred
music have been of the greatest benefit to this charity, on which occasions,
not only the skill, but the charity of the Gentlemen of the King's chapel,
and of the Choirs of St. Paul's and Westminster have always been
remarkable.

———

FROM HENRY FIELDING'S " THE HISTORY OF AMELIA ", 1751
BOOK IV, CHAP. IX.

. . . Upon the evening . . . the two ladies went to the oratorio, and
were there time enough to get the first row in the gallery . . . Amelia
. . . being a great lover of music, and particularly of Mr. Handel's compositions. Mrs. Ellison was, I suppose, a great lover likewise of music. . . .
   Though our ladies arrived full two hours before they saw the back of
Mr. Handel ; yet this time of expectation did not hang extremely heavy
on their hands. . . .

BOOK X, CHAP. II.
What happened at the Masquerade.

. . . At this instant a great noise arose near that part where the two
ladies were. This was occasioned by a large assembly of young fellows,
whom they call bucks, who were got together, and were enjoying, as
the phrase is, a letter, which one of them had found in the room . . .
one of the bucks . . . performed the part of a publick orator, and read
out the following letter. . . .
   ' And so ends the dismal ditty.' . . .
   ' Tom,' says one of them, ' let us set the ditty to musick ; let us subscribe to have it set by Handel ; it will make an excellent oratorio.'
   ' D—n me, Jack,' says another, ' we'll have it set to a psalm tune, and
we'll sing it next Sunday at St. James's church, and I'll bear a bob,
d—n me.'
   The Masquerade is, of course, at the Haymarket Theatre. The letter is in prose.

———

FROM [WILLIAM HAYES'S] " THE ART OF COMPOSING MUSIC
BY A METHOD ENTIRELY NEW, SUITED TO THE MEANEST
CAPACITY, ETC.", 1751

As Music is become not only the Delight but the Practice also of most
People of Fashion, and as *Italian Music* in particular beyond all other is

countenanced and encouraged, I cannot but with the utmost Satisfaction, congratulate this my native Country thereupon.

Music, till of late, has been thought a very difficult, abstruse Kind of Study : But then, every one knows *Music* itself was not what it now is, nay, we ourselves are proportionably altered since then. And what is the Alteration owing to ? Truly, to this happy Relish of the pathetic Tenderness which breathes in every Strain of the modern *Italian Music*. It would formerly have sweated a Man in a frosty Morning, to have executed properly a Song or a Lesson : but the gentle Strains we now boast require no such Labour.

There are remaining still among us some indeed who contend for the more manly Strokes of Handel ; but alas ! I pity them. For why should it not be in this Particular as in all other polite Things, where nothing is so much required as Ease and Negligence ?

As for your manly Things (as these oldfashioned Folks are pleased to call them) I hate and detest them ! For what can be more disagreeable and impertinent, than when you are soothed and lulled into a pleasing *Reverie*, to be roused, to be awakened (if it be not too vulgar an Expression) by one of those manly Things ? In my Opinion nothing could be more impertinent and unpolite ; and therefore justly exploded by the modern Adepts.

There was a Time when the Man-Mountain, *Handel,* had got the Superiority, notwithstanding many Attempts had been made to keep him down ; and might have maintained it probably, had he been content to have pleased People in their own Way ; but his evil Genius would not suffer it : For he, imagining forsooth that nothing could obstruct him in his Career, whilst at the Zenith of his Greatness, broached another Kind of Music ; more full, more grand (as his Admirers are pleased to call it, because crouded with Parts) and, to make the Noise the greater, caused it to be performed, by at least double the Number of Voices and Instruments than ever were heard in a Theatre before : In this, he not only thought to rival our Patron God, but others also ; particularly *Aeolus, Neptune,* and *Jupiter* : For at one Time, I have expected the House to be blown down with his artificial Wind ; at another Time, that the Sea would have overflowed its Banks and swallowed us up : But beyond every thing, his Thunder was most intolerable—I shall never get the horrid Rumbling of it out of my Head—This was (literally you will say) taking us by Storm : hah ! hah ! but mark the Consequence— By this Attempt to personate *Apollo,* he shared the Fate of *Phaëton* ; *Heidegger* revolted, and with him most of the prime Nobility and Gentry. From this happy *Aera* we may date the Growth and Establishment of *Italian Music* in our Island : Then came the healing Palm of *Hasse* and *Vinci, Lampugnani, Piscetti* [Pescetti], *Gluck,* etc. etc.

(Myers, 1948, p. 48.) The passage quoted is the beginning of the satirical pamphlet, published anonymously. When Philip Hayes, William's son and successor at Oxford, edited the latter's *Cathedral Music* in 1759, he did not mention this pamphlet, but says, on page 1 of the introduction : " He was present at the memorable public Act in 1732 [or rather, 1733], and a Visitant at the Warden's of Merton College, highly gratified by the excellent Performances he heard under the Direction of the immortal Handel, from whose great Powers and Spirit he caught those Sparks of Fire that flew from this great Luminary, which proved a further Incitement to his musical Studies ". William Hayes, organist and composer, was at Worcester Cathedral from 1731 to 1734 and at Magdalen College, Oxford, from 1734 to 1737 ; he had been Professor of Music at Oxford University since 1741 and in 1749 received the degree of Doctor of Music there. The pamphlet in question was aimed at Barnabas Gunn (cf. end of 1736), the title-page and frontispiece of whose next publication (*Twelve English Songs, Serious and Humorous*) contained a very amusing allusion to the attack. (Cf. O. E. Deutsch in *Musical Times*, September 1952, and E. Croft-Murray, p. 14.)

1752

FROM THE " GENERAL ADVERTISER ", 11th January 1752

At the Great-Room in Dean-street, Soho, This day . . . will be performed the *Fifth Night* of the SUBSCRIPTION CONCERTS. Which will be continued every Saturday Night till the whole are compleated. FIRST ACT. Overture, Alexander. *To Song and Dance*, Handel, Miss Sheward. . . .

The aria is from *Samson*. Signore Francesina and Galli, Signori Giardini (violin) and Pasqualini (violoncello), Messrs. Vincent (harpsichord), Ogle (oboe) and Baumgarden (bassoon) also performed at this concert. Tickets for one night were half a guinea each, for the series three guineas single, or five guineas double. The double tickets were for two gentlemen, or one gentleman and two ladies.

A concert, beginning with " Samson's Overture, by Mr. Handel ", is given at Hickford's Great Room in Brewer Street for the benefit of Mr. Charles Barbandt, 14th January 1752. (*General Advertiser*, in Sir Augustus Harris's collection of cuttings.)

FROM THE " GENERAL ADVERTISER ", 21st January 1752

This Day . . . will be exhibited, At the Castle Tavern in Pater-noster Row, a Grand Concert of MUSICK. . . . Act I. . . . 5. Mr. Handel's Water-Piece, with a Preamble on the Kettle-Drums. . . . Act the Third, . . . 5. March in Judas Maccabeus, with the Side-Drum. . . .

Harris Collection. Cf. 27th December 1751.

MRS. DELANY TO MRS. DEWES

Delville, Jan. 26th, 1752.

Last Saturday [the 25th] we were invited to the Primate's to hear music. . . .

Our music was chiefly Italian—the *Stabat Mater*, sung by Guadagni (whom you heard sing in Mr. Handel's oratorios) and Mrs. Oldmixon ; Dubourg the principal violin. . . .

(Delany, III. 80 f.) The Primate of Ireland was George Stone, Archbishop of Armagh. Guadagni seems to have been on a visit to Dublin. The *Stabat Mater* was probably Pergolesi's.

FROM THE " GENERAL ADVERTISER ", 27th January 1752

By Desire,

For the Benefit of Miss THOMPSON,

At the King's Arms Tavern, Cornhill, this Day . . . will be perform'd a Concert of Vocal and Instrumental MUSICK. The principal Parts as follows, . . . two Songs of Mr. Handel's, by Mrs. Thompson in the first Act. In the Second Act will be the most favourite Songs and Chorusses in *Acis and Galatea* ; the Part of Galatea to be performed by Miss Thompson, and the Rest of the Parts by Performers of the first Class. Tickets to be had at Mr. Walsh's. . . .

Harris Collection.

———

FROM THE " GENERAL ADVERTISER ", 6th February 1752

The Tenth Day.

At the particular Desire of several Persons of Quality.

For the Benefit of BENJAMIN HALLET,

A Child of Nine Years of Age.

At the New Theatre in the Hay-market, This Day will be exhibited a Grand Concert of MUSICK. By Gentlemen mask'd after the Manner of the Grecian and Roman Comedy. . . . To be divided into Three Acts. Act the First, will contain . . . 5. Mr. Handel's Water-piece, with a Preamble on the Kettle Drums. Act the Second . . . 5. Overture in Otho. . . . Act the Third . . . 5. March in Judas Maccabeus, with the Side-Drum.

The New Theatre had a series of subscription nights. According to the advertisement, Master Hallet, three years previously, had played the flute for fifty nights at Drury Lane ; and the following year he had played the violoncello. At this concert he recited a prologue and an epilogue.

———

Judas Maccabaeus is performed (?) in Dublin, for the benefit of the Lying-in Hospital (Marella conducting), 7th February 1752.

According to Flood, this performance took place nine days after the 29th January.

———

Handel submits the manuscript of the word-book of *Jephtha* to the Inspector of Stage-Plays, with the following note at the end :

George Frederic Handel

London Covent Garden

February 10th 1752.

The manuscript is in the Huntington Library, San Marino, California. Cf. 10th January 1743 and February 1750.

———

FROM THE " GENERAL ADVERTISER ", 14th February 1752

At the Theatre-Royal in Covent-Garden, This Day will be performed an Oratorio, call'd JOSHUA. . . . To begin at Half an Hour after Six o'Clock.

Cf. 9th March 1748. Repeat performance on 19th February. This was the beginning of Handel's Lent season.

———

FROM THE " GENERAL ADVERTISER ", 21st February 1752

At the Theatre-Royal in Covent-Garden, This Day will be performed HERCULES. . . . To begin at Half an Hour after Six o'Clock.

In 1745 (5th January) *Hercules* had been called a musical drama and in 1749 (24th February) an oratorio ; this time Handel avoided any description. There was one performance only.

———

FROM THE " GENERAL ADVERTISER ", 22nd February 1752

At the Great-Room in Dean-street, Soho, This Day . . . will be performed the *Eleventh Night* of the SUBSCRIPTION CONCERTS. FIRST ACT. Overture, Handel. *Let me wander*, Handel, Miss Sheward. *Dimmi caro*, Handel, Signora Francesina. . . . *Dica il falso*, Handel, Signora Francesina. . . . SECOND ACT. *Si l' intendesti si*, Handel, Signora Francesina. . . .

The arias are from *L'Allegro, Scipio, Alessandro* and *Faramondo*.

———

FROM THE " GENERAL ADVERTISER ", 26th February 1752

At the Theatre-Royal in Covent-Garden, This Day, will be performed a new Oratorio,· call'd JEPTHA. . . . To begin at Half an Hour after Six o'Clock.

Jephtha was the correct title of Morell's word-book, advertised by Watts as *Sacred Drama*. Repeat performances on 28th February and 4th March; revived in March 1753. Uvedale Price, in *An Essay on the Picturesque, etc.* (London 1796–8, II. 191), refers to the chorus " No more to Ammon's God and King ", from *Jephtha*, as " a chorus, which Mr. [Thomas] Gray (by no means partial to Handel) used to speak of with wonder ". That Gray was not partial to Handel cannot be proved by his manuscript copies of Italian operas, collected in Italy about 1740, which, of course, contained nothing by Handel. Cf. 25th December 1755.

———

CAST OF " JEPHTHA ", 26th February 1752
Jephtha—Mr. Beard, tenor
Storge—Signora Galli, mezzo-soprano
Iphis—Signora Frasi, soprano
Hamor—Mr. Brent, alto
Zebul—Mr. Wass, bass
Angel—the Boy, (?) alto

———

Handel deposits £600, 27th February 1752.

FROM THE " GENERAL ADVERTISER ", 2nd March 1752

By particular Desire of several Persons of Quality.
For the Benefit of Miss ISABELLA YOUNG,
Scholar of Mr. WALTZ.

At the New Theatre in the Haymarket. This Day . . . will be performed a CONCERT of Vocal and Instrumental MUSICK. The Vocal
Part by Miss [Isabella jun.] Young. Add the Instrumental Parts by the
best Masters. And one of Mr. Handel's Organ Concertos will be also
performed by Miss Young. . . .

(Smith, 1948, p. 193.) This was one of the two nieces of Mrs. Cecilia Arne, *née*
Young ; the other being Mary. Both were singers, Isabella a soprano and Mary a
mezzo-soprano. (Cf. Molly Sands, in the *Monthly Musical Record*, October
1943.) There were two Misses Isabella Young, but the other, her aunt, had
married the composer Lampe, and was now his widow. All these ladies, however,
sometimes sang under their maiden names after they were married.

FROM THE MINUTES OF THE GENERAL COMMITTEE OF THE FOUNDLING
HOSPITAL, 4th March 1752

The Secretary acquainted the Committee, that George Frederick
Handel Esqr had, again, offered his generous Assistance to this Charity,
by the performance of " Messiah " in the Chapel of this Hospital, on
Thursday the Ninth of next Month.

Resolved

That the thanks of this Committed be returned to Mr. Handel for his
said Intention, and that the Secretary do acquaint him, that the Committee think themselves under great obligations for the same.

(Nichols and Wray, p. 204.)

FROM THE " GENERAL ADVERTISER ", 6th March 1752

At the Theatre-Royal in Covent-Garden, This Day will be perform'd
an Oratorio, call'd SAMSON. . . . To begin at Half an Hour after Six
o'Clock.

Cf. 4th April 1750. Repeat performances on 11th and 13th March.

FROM FAULKNER'S " DUBLIN JOURNAL ", 10th March 1752

Last Saturday [the 7th] Morning died, aged 84, the celebrated *Signor
Petro Castrucci*, last Scholar of Corelli, who was for 25 Years first Violin
to the Opera in London, and at five this Evening is to be interred at
St. Mary's ; and, on Account of his great Merit, will be attended by the

whole Band of Musick from the New Gardens in Great Britain Street, who will perform the Dead March in Saul, composed by Mr. Handel.

(W. H. Grattan Flood, in the *Musical Times*, 1st October 1904, p. 640.) In its report on the funeral, the *Dublin Journal* of 14th March added that Mr. Dubourg was the chief mourner. Castrucci came to England with Lord Burlington in 1715, when he was forty-seven years of age. For several years he was the first violin, or leader, in Handel's opera orchestra ; he retired to Dublin when he was dismissed from the Haymarket opera in 1737.

Handel deposits £430, 12th March 1752.

From the " General Advertiser ", 14th March 1752

London Hospital.

The Anniversary Feast of this Charity is appointed to be held at Merchant-Taylors Hall, on Thursday the 19th of March, 1752, after a Sermon preached before his Grace the Duke of *Devonshire*, President, and the rest of the Governors, by . . . the Lord Bishop of *Lichfield and Coventry*, at Christ-Church in Newgate-Street. Prayers will begin at Eleven o'Clock.

N.B. The Te Deum, and two Anthems composed by Mr. Handel, with the Jubilate, &c. will be Vocally and Instrumentally performed at Church. . . .

William Cavendish, third Duke of Devonshire, was Lord Lieutenant of Derby. The Bishop of Lichfield, Chester, and Coventry was Frederick Cornwallis.

At a concert for the benefit of Miss Sheward, given at the Great Room in Dean Street, she sings " L' Amor che per te sento " from *Alessandro*, 17th March 1752.

From the " General Advertiser ", 18th March 1752

At the Theatre-Royal in Covent-Garden, This Day will be performed an Oratorio, call'd Judas Macchabaeus. . . . To begin at Half an Hour after Six o'Clock.

Cf. 20th March 1751. Repeat performance on 20th March 1752.

Handel deposits £300, 19th March 1752.

FROM THE " GENERAL ADVERTISER ", 24th March 1752

For the Benefit and Increase of a FUND *established for the Support of Decay'd* MUSICIANS, *or their Families.*

At the King's Theatre in the Haymarket, This Day . . . will be performed an Entertainment of Vocal and Instrumental MUSICK. As follows,

PART I. . . .

Air. *Thro' the Land so lovely blooming* ; compos'd by Mr. Handel, sung by Mr. Beard.

. . . . .
Air. *Honour and Arms* ; . . ., sung by Mr. Wass.
. . . . .

PART II. . . .

Air. *Father of Heaven* ; . . ., sung by Sig. Galli.
Air. *Revenge,* Timotheus *cries* ; . . ., sung by Mr. Wass.
. . . . .

Air. *See,* Hercules, *how smiles you Myrtle Plain* ; . . ., sung by Signora Frasi.
Air. *The Trumpets loud Clangor* ; . . ., sung by Mr. Beard.

PART III. . . .

Air. *Love in her Eyes sits playing* ; . . ., sung by Mr. Beard.
Trio. *The Flocks shall leave the Mountains* ; . . ., sung by Signora Frasi, Mr. Beard, and Mr. Wass.

A Grand Concerto of Mr. Handel's.

. . . .

To begin exactly at Six o'Clock.

. . . .

The arias are from *Athalia, Samson, Judas Maccabaeus, Alexander's Feast, The Choice of Hercules, Ode for St. Cecilia's Day,* and *Acis and Galatea* ; the trio, also, is from the last work.

———

Handel deposits £640, 24th March 1752.

———

FROM THE " GENERAL ADVERTISER ", 25th March 1752

At the Theatre-Royal in Covent-Garden, This Day will be performed a sacred Oratorio, call'd MESSIAH. . . . To begin at Half an Hour after Six o'Clock.

Cf. 12th April 1750. Repeat performance on 26th March, " Being the Last [Oratorio] this Year ".

———

FROM THE " COVENT-GARDEN JOURNAL ", 31st March 1752

. . . When Mr. Handel first exhibited his Allegro and Penseroso, there were two ingenious Gentlemen who had bought a Book of the Words, and thought to divert themselves by reading it before the Performance begun. *Zounds* (cried one of them) *what damn'd Stuff it is ! Damn'd Stuff indeed*, replied his Friend. *God so !* (replied the other, who then first cast his Eyes on the Title-Page) *the Words are Milton's.* . . .

S.

The signature letter indicates the name of Henry Fielding, who from 4th January till 25th November 1752 edited this journal, under the pseudonym of " Sir Alexander Drawcansir, Knt. Censor of Great Britain ". (Cf. the new edition of the journal, by G. E. Jensen, New Haven, 1915, 2 vols., I. 289.)

From the " General Advertiser ", 1st April 1752

Hospital . . . in Lamb's Conduit-Fields, March 31, 1752.

George Fredrick Handel, Esq; having repeated his Offer to promote this Charity, the Sacred Oratorio, call'd *Messiah*, will be perform'd under his Direction, on Thursday the 9th of April, 1752, at Twelve o'Clock at Noon precisely, in the Chapel of the Hospital ; and he will perform on the fine Organ which he gave to the Corporation. . . .

By Order of the General Committee,

Harman Verelst, Sec.

N.B. There will be no Collection.

The tickets were again half a guinea each.

Handel deposits £320, 2nd April 1752.

From the " General Advertiser ", 4th April 1752

At the Great-Room in Dean-street, Soho, This Day, will be performed the *Seventeenth Night* of the Subscription Concerts. *First Act.* Overture of Rodelinda, Handel. . . . *Second Act* . . . *With ravish'd Ears,* Handel, Miss Sheward. . . .

The aria is from *Alexander's Feast.*

In the same issue of the journal, Walsh advertises the score of *Jeptha* (or rather, *Jephtha*).

From the " General Advertiser ", 7th April 1752

The Rehearsal of the Musick for the Feast of the *Sons* of the *Clergy*, will be performed at St. Paul's Cathedral, on Tuesday April 14, and the Feast will be held at Merchant-Taylors Hall, on Thursday April 16, 1752. . . .

N.B. Mr. Handel's new Te Deum, Jubilate and Coronation Anthems, with a new Anthem by Dr. Boyce, will be Vocally and Instrumentally performed. . . .

N.B. Two Rehearsal and two Choir Tickets will be given with each Feast Ticket.

The tickets were 5s. each.

———

FROM THE " GENERAL ADVERTISER ", 11th April 1752

At the Great-Room in Dean-street, Soho, This Day, will be performed the *Eighteenth Night* of the SUBSCRIPTION CONCERTS. *First Act.* Overture, Handel. . . . *Second Act.* . . . *Ye verdant Plains*, Handel, Miss Sheward. . . .

The recitative (with the aria, *Hush, ye pretty warbling choir*) is from *Acis and Galatea*.

———

FROM THE MINUTES OF THE GENERAL COMMITTEE OF THE FOUNDLING HOSPITAL, 15th April 1752

The Secretary acquainted the Committee, That he had paid Mr. Christopher Smith, Fifty One Pounds two shillings and Six pence, the amount of the distributions and Gratuities, for the Performance of Messiah on the 9th instant ; and that Mr. Beard agreeing to perform gratis, no Distribution was set against his Name.

RESOLVED

That the Thanks of this Committee, be given to George Frederick Handel Esqr for his excellent Performance in the Chapel of this Hospital, on the 9th instant, of the Sacred Oratorio called Messiah, to a most Noble and Grand Audience, who expressed the greatest satisfaction at the Exquisiteness of the Composition, the completeness of the Performance, and the great Benevolence of Mr. Handel, in thus promoting this Charity.

(*Musical Times*, 1st May 1902.)

———

FROM THE " GENERAL ADVERTISER ", 22nd April 1752

For the Benefit of a *Publick Charity*.

At the King's Theatre in the Haymarket, This Day . . . will be performed an Entertainment of Vocal and Instrumental MUSICK. As follows.

PART I. . . .

Air. *Thro' the Land so lovely blooming*, compos'd by Mr. Handel, sung by Mr. Beard.

. . . . .

Air. *Oh ! ruddier than the Cherry*, . . . sung by Mr. Wass.

. . . .

PART III. . . .

. . . . .

Trio. *The Flocks shall leave the Mountains*, . . . sung by Signora Frasi, Mr. Beard, and Mr. Wass.

A grand Concerto of Mr. Handel's.

.   .   .   .

To begin exactly at Half an Hour after Six.

The charity, which was kept nameless, was the Lock Hospital for women in distress, founded in 1746 and still in existence : a new and regular object of Handel's benevolence. (See 4th November 1752, 7th May 1753 and Spring 1759.) Performances in aid of this hospital were given annually : at the Haymarket Theatre, by Rich at Covent Garden, and by Garrick at Drury Lane. The first aria is from *Athalia*, the second aria and the Trio from *Acis and Galatea*.

———

MISS TALBOT TO MRS. CARTER

Cuddesden, April 22, 1752.

I had vast pleasure in carrying my mother this year for the first time to hear the Messiah at the Foundling. She was as much charmed as I expected.

(Carter, *Letters*, II. 75.)

———

FROM THE MINUTES OF THE GENERAL COMMITTEE OF THE FOUNDLING HOSPITAL, 29th April 1752

The Treasurer acquainted the Committee, That he had received Six hundred and forty Two Pounds one shilling and Six pence, for 1223 Tickets at the Oratorio the 9th instant ;—that he had paid Fifty four pounds five shillings and Six pence for the Charges thereof ; and that he had paid into the Bank of England the residue, being fivehund^d and Eighty Seven pounds Sixteen shillings.

———

FROM THE " GENTLEMAN'S MAGAZINE ", April 1752

THURSDAY 9.

Was perform'd at the *Foundling* chapel Mr *Handel's* oratorio of the *Messiah*, and the number of tickets given out was 1200, each 10s. 6d.

———

Handel withdraws £2140 : 2 : 0, and buys £2000 4 per cent Annuities (1746), 12th May 1752.

———

FROM THE " GENERAL ADVERTISER ", 17th August 1752

We hear that George-Frederick Handel, Esq; the celebrated Composer of Musick was seized a few Days ago with a Paralytick Disorder in his Head, which has deprived him of Sight.

———

The British Calendar (Old Style) changes to the continental calendar (new style) during the night of 2nd-3rd September 1752.

The 3rd September became the 14th, and the year ended on 31st December, instead of on 24th March.

———

FROM BERROW'S " WORCESTER JOURNAL ", 14th September 1752

On Wednesday [the 20th] will be perform'd, at the Cathedral, in the Morning, Purcel's Te Deum and Jubilate, an Anthem by Dr. Boyce, and Mr. Handel's celebrated Coronation Anthem ; and at the Town-Hall, in the Evening, A CONCERT of VOCAL AND INSTRUMENTAL MUSICK. On Thursday will be perform'd, at the Cathedral, in the Morning, Mr. Handel's Te Deum and Jubilate, a New Anthem by Dr. Boyce, and the same Coronation Anthem ; and at the Town-Hall, in the Evening, THE ORATORIO OF SAMSON.

———

At Salisbury, St. Cecilia celebrations are held on 27th and 28th September 1752 : in the mornings, in the Cathedral, one of Handel's Te Deums and the Coronation Anthem *Zadok the Priest* are performed as well as detached pieces from *Messiah* ; in the evenings, in the Assembly Hall, *Samson* is performed on the first day, and *Judas Maccabaeus* on the second day.

———

FROM THE MINUTES OF THE GENERAL COMMITTEE OF THE FOUNDLING HOSPITAL, 25th October 1752

ORDERED

That the Secretary do apply to Mr. Handel, Dr. Boyce, and Mr. Smith, for their Assistance, in a Musical Performance in the Chapel, on that Day [28th December].

(Nichols and Wray, p. 207.) " Mr. Smith " was Handel's pupil, John Christopher Smith. The formal opening of the Chapel in the Foundling Hospital, originally planned for 3rd May 1750, had to be postponed yet again, till 2nd February, and was finally held on 16th April 1753.

———

FROM THE " GENERAL ADVERTISER ", 4th November 1752

Yesterday George-Frederick Handel, Esq; was couch'd by William Bromfield, Esq; Surgeon to her Royal Highness the Princess of Wales, when it was thought there was all imaginable Hopes of Success by the Operation, which must give the greatest Pleasure to all Lovers of Musick.

The date of this notice has been given as 4th May 1752 since Schoelcher misdated it on p. 321. (See Rockstro, p. 351, who speaks of "Bramfield"; Cummings, 1904, p. 39, and Flower, p. 344; the date of the operation is given correctly in Rolland's Handel biography, 1910, p. 123.) Bromfield (1712–92) was surgeon to the Lock Hospital and St. George's Hospital as well as to the Prince of Wales. For Handel's blindness, see Coats (pp. 8 f.) and James (p. 168). According to James, Handel was probably couched for cataract; he became practically blind within nine months, possibly from glaucoma set up by the operation. Cf. also John Taylor's memoirs, quoted under 1761. See 27th January 1753.

———

FROM BODDELY'S " BATH JOURNAL ", 13th November 1752

The Lovers of Musick here have always wished for the Performance of an ORATORIO : This therefore is to inform them, that on Monday next, November the 20th, will be performed ALEXANDER'S FEAST, so justly admir'd for its Excellence in the Musical Way, set to Musick by our British Orpheus Mr. Handel, with all the Recitativos, Songs, Symphonies, and Chorus's, as performed at the Theatre-Royal in Covent-Garden.—As Nothing of this Kind was ever performed here, and as the Managers will be at a great Expence in getting such a Number of Voices and Instruments, 'tis hoped they will have Encouragement, as they flatter themselves the Performance will please.

(Wright, August 1935.)

———

FROM THE SAME, 20th November 1752

By Desire. At Mr. *Simpson's Theatre,* This present Monday . . . will be perform'd that Celebrated *Entertainment,* call'd ALEXANDER'S FEAST. In the Manner of an Oratorio, As Perform'd at the Theatre-Royal in Covent-Garden. . . . (To begin at Six o'Clock.)

As nothing of this kind was ever performed here, the Managers will spare no Expence in collecting a sufficient Number of proper Voices and Instruments, as they have Nothing more at Heart than the Desire of pleasing.

Tickets . . . [at 5s. and, for the gallery, 2s. 6d.] ; where *Books* of *Alexander's Feast* are sold.

The word-book was probably a London edition.

———

MRS. DELANY TO MRS. DEWES

Delville, 25th Nov., 1752.

Poor Handel ! how feelingly must he recollect the " *total eclipse* ". I hear he has now been couched, and found some benefit from it.

(Delany, III. 177.) Cf. 4th November. Handel, in fact, played in *Samson* on 4th April 1753, and the words " Total eclipse ! no sun, no moon ! . . ." were understood by the whole audience.

———

Handel's cousin, Christian August Rotth (Roth), dies at Halle, 5th December 1752.

Cf. 20th February 1719 and 11th February 1750. He was born six months after Handel.

———

FROM THE MINUTES OF THE GENERAL COMMITTEE OF THE FOUNDLING HOSPITAL, 6th December 1752

RESOLVED

That there be a Rehearsal of Sacred Music in the Chapel of this Hospital, on Thursday the 25th next Month, and That Twelve hundred Tickets be prepared for that Purpose, at half a Guinea each.

RESOLVED

That Twelve hundred Tickets for admitting Persons into the Chapel, at the Opening thereof the Second of Febr^y next, be prepared, to be delivered without Money ; and that there be a Note on the said Tickets, giving Notice, That there will be a Collection for this Charity, at the Chapel, on that Day.

RESOLVED

That it be referred to the Sub-Committee, to consider of the disposal of the Tickets for admittance at the Opening of the Chapel.

(Nichols and Wray, p. 207.) The Sub-Committee was dealing with the Chapel only. The opening was postponed till 16th April 1753.

———

FROM FAULKNER'S " DUBLIN JOURNAL ", 15th December 1752

[Extracts.]

19 December : ' Messiah ', Great Music Hall, Fishamble Street, conductor Marella ; tickets, half a guinea each, for rehearsal (15th December) and performance. Book gratis. Charitable Musical Society, for poor prisoners in the several Marshalseas of Dublin.

23 January 1753 : ' Deborah ', Music Hall, for the Charitable Infirmary on the Inn's Quay. Rehearsal on 19th January.

13 February 1753 : ' Joshua ', Music Hall, for the Hospital of Incurables.

———

MRS. DELANY TO MRS. DEWES

Delville, 15 [or rather, 16th] Dec., 1752.

Yesterday morning we went to the rehearsal of the " Messiah ", it was very tolerably performed. I was a little afraid of it, as I think the music *very affecting*, and I found it so—but am glad I went, as I felt great comfort from it, and I had the good fortune to have Mrs. Bernard sit by me, the Primate's sister, a most worthy sensible woman, of an exalted mind ; it adds greatly to the satisfaction of such an entertainment to be seated by those who have the same relish for it we have ourselves. *The babblers* of my acquaintance were at a distance, indeed I took care to place myself *as far from them as I could.* Do you remember *our* snug enjoyment of Theodora ? I could not help thinking with great concern of poor Handel, and lamenting his dark and melancholy circumstances ; but his mind I hope will still be enlightened for the benefit of all true lovers of harmony.

(Delany, III. 184.)

————

BENJAMIN VICTOR TO THE REV. WILLIAM ROTHERY, IN CHELSEA

[Dublin,] December 27, 1752.

. . . You must be a lover of music—If *Handel's Messiah* should be performed in London, as it undoubtedly will in the lent season, I beg it as a favour to me, that you will go early, and take your wife with you, your time and money cannot be so well employed ; take care to get a book of the oratorio some days before, that you may well digest the subject, there you will hear *glad tidings* and truly divine rejoicings at the birth of *Christ*, and feel real sorrows for his sufferings—but, oh ! when those sufferings are over, what a transporting full chorus ! where all the instruments, and three sets of voices are employed to express the following passage, which I must quote—

" Lift up your heads, O ye gates ! and be ye lift up ye
Everlasting doors, and the king of glory shall come in.
Who is the king of glory ? The Lord strong and mighty,
He is the king of glory !
And he shall reign for ever, King of Kings, Lord of Lords."

How truly poetical is the diction of the Oriental writers.

Mr. Handel, when he was here, composed this excellent oratorio, and gave it to a charitable musical society ; by whom it is annually performed, for the relief of poor debtors, and very well, as we have good cathedral singers, to whom this music is chiefly adapted—the performance is just over, and you will conclude I am never absent. As much as I detest fatigue and inconvenience, I would ride forty miles in the wind and rain to be present at a performance of the Messiah in London, under the conduct of Handel—I remember it there—He had an hundred instruments, and fifty voices ! O how magnificent the full chorusses.

(Myers, *Moral Criticism*, pp. 35 f.) Victor, I. 189 f. Although the writer errs in assuming that Handel wrote *Messiah* in Dublin, he certainly believed, with other Irishmen, that it was written for Dublin.

————

Esther is performed at the Castle Tavern in Paternoster Row, 1752.
The only record of this performance is the libretto, a copy of which is
in the Schoelcher Collection, Conservatoire, Paris.

———

Messiah is performed (?) at Oxford, 1752.
The only indication of this performance is a word-book, entitled *The
Sacred Oratorio, Set to Music by Mr. Handel* and dated 1752, a copy of which
is in the Bodleian Library.

———

FROM CHARLES AVISON'S " ESSAY ON MUSICAL EXPRESSION ", 1752

. . . To these [Corelli, Domenico Scarlatti, Caldara and Rameau] we
may justly add our illustrious HANDEL ; in whose manly Style we often
find the noblest Harmonies ; and these enlivened with such a Variety
of Modulation, as could hardly have been expected from one who hath
supplyed the Town with musical Entertainments of every Kind, for
thirty Years together.[1]

Pp. 53-5, 62-7 (74) of the first and the second editions ; the latter appeared in
1753, revised and enlarged. Avison, organist in Newcastle, was a pupil of
Geminiani, whom he describes as the great model for composition. Cf. William
Hayes's reply of January and Avison's riposte of February 1753.

[1] The celebrated LULLI of *France*, and the old [Alessandro] SCARLATTI at *Rome*, may
be considered in the same Light with HANDEL. They were both voluminous Composers, and were not always equally happy in commanding their Genius. Yet, upon
the whole, they have been of infinite Service in the Progress of Music : And if we
take away from their numerous Works, all that is indifferent, there will still enough
remain that is excellent, to give them a distinguished Rank.
    It is pretty remarkable, that the three Masters here mentioned, have, perhaps,
enjoyed the highest local Reputation, having all been the reigning Favourites among
the People, in the several Countries where they resided : and thence have been
regarded as standing Models of Perfection to many succeeding Composers.
    The *Italians* seem particularly indebted to the Variety and Invention of [Alessandro]
SCARLATTI ; and *France* has produced a RAMEAU, equal, if not superior to LULLI. The
English, as yet, indeed, have not been so successful : But whether this may be owing
to any Inferiority in the Original they have chose to imitate, or to a want of Genius,
in those that are his Imitators (in distinguishing, perhaps, not the most excellent of his
Works) it is not necessary here to determine. . . .
    I have chosen to give all my Illustrations on this Matter [Sounds and Motions]
from the Works of Mr. HANDEL, because no one has exercised this Talent more
universally, and because these Instances must also be most universally understood. . . .
    What shall we say to excuse this same great Composer, who, in his Oratorio of
Joshua, condescended to amuse the vulgar Part of his Audience, by letting them *hear
the Sun stand still.*

1753

Handel converts £12,000 4 per cent Annuities (1746) into £12,000 Reduced 3 per cent Annuities, 2nd January 1753.

The so-called Reduced 3 per cent Annuities existed from 1752 till 1889.

———

FROM THE " CAMBRIDGE CHRONICLE ", 13th January 1753

Mr. Handel has so much recovered his sight that he is able to go abroad.

(From a manuscript copy of Dr. Mann's.) This issue of the journal is not available in Cambridge. " Abroad " means out of doors.

———

The music for the opening of the Foundling Hospital Chapel is rehearsed, 25th January 1753.

Cf. 6th December 1752.

———

FROM THE " LONDON DAILY ADVERTISER ", 27th January 1753

At the Great Room in Dean-street, Soho . . . Saturday the 27th Instant, will be performed the second Night of the Subscription *Concerts*. . . . ACT I. . . . *My Faith and Truth*, Handell, Sig. FRASI . . . ACT II. . . . *Myself I shall adore*, Handell, Miss TURNER. . . .

The arias are from *Samson* and *Semele*. Miss Turner was the daughter of Dr. William Turner (1651–1740), chorister and composer ; she must not be mistaken for Mrs. Ann Turner-Robinson, who died in 1741. Miss Turner sang at the Castle and at the Swan and, in 1755, at the Three Choirs Meeting.

———

FROM A LONDON NEWSPAPER, 27th January 1753

Mr. Handel has at length, unhappily, quite lost his sight. Upon his being couch'd some time since, he saw so well, that his friends flattered themselves his sight was restored for a continuance ; but a few days have entirely put an end to their hope.

(Schoelcher, pp. 321 f.) The notice is not to be found in the collection called *Theatrical Register*, nor in the *London Daily Advertiser, Public Advertiser, London Evening Post*, etc. Cf. 4th November 1752.

———

FROM [WILLIAM HAYES'S] " REMARKS ON MR. AVISON'S ESSAY ON MUSICAL EXPRESSION ", 1753

. . . If these [*Duets* of STRADELLA and STEFFANI] are excelled by any, they are by Mr. HANDEL'S twelve *Chamber Duets*, composed for the late Queen : Who did him the Honour to perform a Part in them. . . .

. . . I can see no Business RAMEAU has in Company with Men whose Works have been thoroughly proved, and have stood the never-failing Test of Time [*i.e.*, CORELLI, D. SCARLATTI, and CALDARA], unless it be purely for the sake of mortifying his Contemporary Mr. HANDEL ; and if this be his Aim, he certainly will miss of it. But it manifestly appears to be his principal Design, by his ridiculous Fondness and Partiality to some Masters, to draw a Veil over, and eclipse his great and glorious Character : Poor Creature ! He might just as easily with the Palm of his Hand stop the Current of the most rapid River ; or persuade a Man with his Eyes wide open, that the Sun affordeth no Light, when shining in it's full meridian Lustre. To evince the Truth of this Assertion, let us consider what immediately follows : " To these we may justly add our illustrious HANDEL . . . who hath supplied the Town with musical Entertainments of every Kind, for thirty (he might have said forty) Years together." What an awkard Compliment is this ; (*as could hardly have been expected !* &c.) with what Reluctance it seemeth to come ; and at best amounts to little more than if he had said,—considering what a Quantity of Music of every Kind, he hath supplied the Town with for so many Years ; it is well it is no worse. . . . And all this [long Detail of RAMEAU's Excellencies], industriously placed directly under the *little* he says of Mr. Handel, or as it were in his very Face. . . . Were a thousand of these puny Performances [of RAMEAU's Opera Chorusses] opposed to one Oratorio Chorus of Mr. Handel, it would swallow them up, even as the Rod of AARON converted into a Serpent, devoured those of the Magicians.

In the next Paragraph of the Annotations, the celebrated LULLI and the old SCARLATTI are to be considered in the same Light with HANDEL : Why ? *because they were both voluminous Composers ; and were not always equally happy in commanding their Genius.* He does indeed acknowledge *they have been of infinite service in the Progress of Music.* . . . Likewise, *that they were the reigning Favourites among the People in the several Countries where they resided. . . .* This seems to be owning rather too much : For a stronger Proof there cannot be of real superior Merit, than a Man's being universally admired and esteemed, in the Country where he resides, and imitated by his successors as the standing Model of Perfection : But all this mighty yielding, is only for the sake of an Opportunity of sneering both HANDEL and his Brethren the Musicians of our own Country ; which will evidently appear by the subsequent Paragraph.

" The *Italians* seem indebted to . . . SCARLATTI ; and *France* has produced a RAMEAU, equal if not superior to LULLI. The *English*, as yet indeed, have not been so successful. . . ." What a saucy Piece of Insinuation is here !—If I have been any way severe in my Reflections, this surely, is sufficient for my Justification. . . .

I believe no reasonable Person, or Judge of Words and Music, will deny that the beautiful, *picturesque* Scenes, which MILTON describes [in

L'allegro il Penseroso], are greatly heightened and assisted, by the Music Mr. HANDEL has adapted to them : And yet it consisteth chiefly of the *mimetic* or *imitative* Kind ; not that it is defective, either in *Air* or *Harmony*. The characters of *Chearfulness* and *Melancholy* are nevertheless finely supported : And therefore I must insist upon it, there cannot be a more complete Model of true *musical Expression*, notwithstanding it abounds with *Imitation*. And this is the Method, which not only Mr. HANDEL, but all other sensible Composers, make their Study and Practice, although Mr. *Avison* insinuates to the contrary. . . .

. . . There is not a Scene which MILTON describes, were CLAUDE LORRAIN or POUSSIN to paint, could possibly appear in more lively Colours, or give a truer Idea of it, than our GREAT MUSICIAN has by his *pictoresque* Arrangement of musical *Sounds* ; with this Advantage, that his Pictures *speak*. Let it here be noted, I mention not this Work as the most capital of his Performances ; but, as I said before, on account of it's consisting chiefly of Imitation, and as a perfect Piece of it's Kind ; his *Symphonies* forming the most beautiful Scenery, copied from simple Nature. But if you are inclined to drink more copious Draughts of this divine Art, look into, or rather hear, if possible, his Oratorio of *Israel in Egypt* ; there you will find he has exerted every Power human Nature is capable of. In this truly sublime Composition, he has discovered an inexhaustible Fund of Invention, the greatest Depth of Learning, and the most comprehensive Talent in expressing even inarticulate Nature, as well as things which are obvious to our Sense of Hearing only, by articulate Sounds ; not to mention such an Assemblage of Vocal and Instrumental Parts, blended with such Purity and Propriety ; which alone would render this Work infinitely superior to any Thing the whole musical World hath hitherto produced. . . .

This brings me within sight of our Author's main Drift and Design, in depreciation and lowering the Characters of HANDEL and CORELLI ; which very clearly is to aggrandize two Masters, whom he boldly affirms to have *excelled all the Moderns ; one in Vocal the other in Instrumental Music.* But his Spleen is more particularly vented against HANDEL, for no other Reason, but his being universally admired, on account of both these Excellencies being united in HIM. We must not therefore be surprized, that his transcendent Merit, and the Applause he has met with as the natural Consequence of it, should create Envy, Jealousy, and Heart-burning in the Breasts of those who are less conspicuous ; however excellent in a particular Branch : Nor if, failing to meet with a Share of public Acknowledgment equal to their Expectations, they descend to the mean Practice, of puffing one another at the Expence of his Reputation. Perhaps Mr. AVISON may think himself in Duty, or upon the Principle of Gratitude, bound to compliment GEMINIANI :—But what can induce GEMINIANI to set AVISON in Competition with HANDEL ? Surely nothing but to gratify *Pique*, and to magnify his own Performances ;

and that this has frequently been the Case, is too notorious to need an Instance. . . .

But for the truly *Great* and *Heroic*, he must yield to HANDEL, even in the Application of the above Instruments [Violins and other Strings]. And as the Style of these two Masters is different, although each excellent in the Kind, so also is their Method of Study : The one slow, cautious, and elaborate ; the other, rapid, enterprizing, and expeditious. The one frequently revising, correcting, altering, and amending until his Piece be completely polished ; the other having once committed *his* to Writing, resteth satisfied, and transmitteth it to his Copyist ; who being accustomed to write after him, may perchance transcribe it in as little Time as he was making it ; but I would defy any other Man to accomplish it in less than double that Time. In short, GEMINIANI may be the *Titian* of Music, but HANDEL is undoubtedly the RUBENS. To conclude :

Perhaps, as I have been so particular in delivering my sentiments concerning the Hero of the Essay, You may expect me to give you a Detail of the various Excellencies, which still remain unmentioned in HANDEL ; and to point out wherein he excels *all others* of his Profession : The Man, who hath so bravely withstood the repeated Efforts of *Italian Forces* :—Who hath maintained his Ground against all Opposers :—Who at the Age of *Seventy*, with a broken Constitution, produced such a Composition,[1] which no Man mentioned in the Essay beside, either is, or ever was (so far as it hath appeared to us) equal to, in his highest Vigour ;—And, to the Astonishment of all Mankind, at the same Period of Life, performed Wonders on the Organ, both set Pieces and *extempore* ; —I say, perhaps you may expect me to enter into *Particulars*, to *defend* and *characterize* this Man :—but the first would be an endless Undertaking ;—his Works being almost out of Number.—The second, a needless one, the Works themselves being his best Defence :—And the third, I must acknowledge is above my Capacity ; and therefore once more refer you to his Works, where only his true character is to be found ; except in the Hearts of Thousands his Admirers. Thus far as a Musician only : As a moral, good, and charitable Man, let Infants, not only those who feel the Effects of his Bounty, but even such who are yet unborn, chaunt forth his Praise, whose annual Benefaction to an Hospital for the Maintenance of the *Forsaken, the Fatherless, and those who have none to help them*, will render HIM and his MESSIAH, truly Immortal and crowned with Glory, by the KING OF KINGS and LORD OF LORDS.

Hayes's *Remarks* on Avison's *Essay* of 1752 appeared anonymously, probably in January of 1753. The passages quoted are from pp. 57-62, 65-8, 110 f., and 128-30. Avison replied in another pamphlet on 22nd February 1753.

———

[1] The Oratorio of *Jephtha*.

FROM THE " WORLD ", 8th February 1753

TO MR. FITZ-ADAM.

Totum mundum agit histrio.

Sir,

   . . . I myself remember, how . . . the great Senesino, representing Alexander at the siege of Oxydracae, so far forgot himself in the heat of the conquest, as to stick his sword into one of the pasteboard stones of the wall of the town, and bore it in triumph before him as he entered the breach ; a puerility so renowned a General could never have committed, if the ramparts had been built, as in this enlightened age they would be, of actual brick and stone.

Will you forgive an elderly man, Mr. Fitz-Adam, if he cannot help recollecting another passage that happened in his youth, and to the same excellent performer ? He was stepping into Armida's enchanted bark ; but treading short, as he was more attentive to the accompanyment of the orchestra than to the breadth of the shore, he fell prostrate, and lay for some time in great pain, with the edge of a wave running in his side. In the present state of things, the worst that could have happened to him, would have been drowning ; a fate far more becoming Rinaldo, especially in the sight of a British audience !   [Horace Walpole.]

(Schoelcher, pp. 75 f.) Adam Fitz-Adam was the pseudonym of the editor, Edward Moore. The theatre *habitué*, who alludes to Colley Cibber's naturalism in stage décor, and congratulates Garrick on having introduced a cascade of real water on his stage, was Horace Walpole. Senesino first sang *Alessandro* on 7th May 1726 (it was revived with him in 1727, 1728 and 1733), and *Rinaldo* on 6th April 1731. Oxydracae is not a place, but one of the peoples in India conquered by Alexander.

———

Walsh advertises Handel's 22 oratorios in score, bound in 12 volumes, *Public Advertiser* of 8th February 1753.

(Smith, 1948, p. 85.) Cf. 27th June 1751. The *General Advertiser* had changed its name to *Public Advertiser* in December 1752.

———

FROM FAULKNER'S " DUBLIN JOURNAL ", 13th February 1753

[Extracts.]

13 February : ' Joshua ', Music Hall, conductor B. Manwaring. Rehearsal on 8th February at noon. Tickets half a guinea each. Book gratis. Arranged by the Charitable Musical Society, for the Hospital for Incurables on Lazer's Hill.

20 February : ' Judas Maccabaeus ', Music Hall, conductor Marella. Rehearsal on 16th February. Tickets half a guinea each. Book gratis. For the Lying-in Hospital in George's Lane.

26 February : ' Esther ', Music Hall, conductor Marella. Ticket a British crown each. For the benefit of Miss Oldmixon.

FROM AVISON'S " REPLY TO THE AUTHOR OF REMARKS ON THE ESSAY ON MUSICAL EXPRESSION [i.e. WILLIAM HAYES] ", 22nd February 1753

. . . The Heat of his Rage seems to be kindled at the Affront which he would insinuate I have put upon the *English* Composers. And to draw their severest Resentment upon me, he hath also as falsely insinuated that I have equally injured the great Original which they have imitated.

Then he produces the following Passage.—" The *Italians* seem particularly indebted to . . . SCARLATTI . . . it is not necessary here to determine."—This he calls a saucy Insinuation. But saucy to whom ? If to his Doctorship only, I am entirely unconcerned about it. But if to Mr HANDEL, I would be the first to condemn it, and erase it from my Essay : This, however, I believe, none but our Critic will suspect ; though every one will easily perceive his Reason for quoting and perverting it, *viz.* to take off the Odium from such meagre Composers as himself, and to throw it all upon the Character of Mr HANDEL.

I could wish to know whence this unnatural Conjunction comes, and what Mr HANDEL has done, that he deserves to be treated with that Air of Familiarity which our Author puts on, when he calls him his Brother. —*Poor Doctor* ! I know not what Tables of Affinity or Consanguinity can prove you even his Cousin-German. Is Mr HANDEL an *Englishman* ? Is his very Name *English* ? Was his Education *English* ? Was he not first educated in the *Italian* School ? Did he not compose and direct the *Italian* Operas here many Years ? It is true, he has since deigned to strengthen the Delicacy of the *Italian* Air, so as to bear the rougher Accent of our Language. But to call him, on that Account, Brother to such Composers as our *Doctor*, I am persuaded, is an Appellation, that he would reject with the Contempt it deserves. . . .

. . . I will beg Leave to deliver my Sentiments of Mr HANDEL, which, I am sure will contradict nothing I have said in my Essay ; and, I flatter myself, will be assented to by the *rational* Part of our musical Judges.

Mr HANDEL is in Music, what his own DRYDEN was in Poetry ; nervous, exalted, and harmonious ; but voluminous, and, consequently, not always correct. Their Abilities equal to every Thing ; their Execution frequently inferior. Born with Genius capable of *soaring the boldest Flights* ; they have sometimes, to suit the vitiated Taste of the Age they lived in, *descended to the lowest*. Yet, as both their Excellencies are infinitely more numerous than their Deficiencies, so both their Characters will devolve to latest Posterity, not as Models of Perfection, yet glorious Examples of those amazing Powers that actuate the human Soul.

XXVIII. ADMISSION TICKET TO THE PERFORMANCE OF
HANDEL'S *HERCULES* ON 21ST FEBRUARY 1752

Engraving after John Devoto, by J. Atkins. (British Museum)

See page 719

XXIX. JOHN STANLEY

An anonymous engraving. (H. R. Beard Theatre Collection)

See page 737

Avison published his answer to Hayes's *Remarks* (January 1753) in the form of an open letter to a friend in London, and included it as an appendix to the second edition of his *Essay* (1753). The date of the letter indicates a separate publication before that. The passages are from pp. (35), 43-51 of the book. Cf. M. Kingdon-Ward's article on Avison in the *Musical Times*, September 1951, p. 399.

———

Esther is performed by the Academy of Ancient Music, 22nd February 1753.

This performance is recorded in a word-book, a copy of which is in the National Library of Scotland, Edinburgh.

———

FROM THE " PUBLIC ADVERTISER ", 2nd March 1753

At the King's Theatre in the Haymarket, This Day will be performed ALEXANDER'S FEAST. By Mr. *Handel*. With a Concerto on the Organ, by Mr. *Stanley*, who is to conduct this Performance. Before the President, Vice-Presidents, and Governors of the *Small-Pox Hospital*.

☞ *This being a Morning's Entertainment, it is not expected that the Ladies should come Full-dressed.*

*** Books of the ODE will be delivered gratis at the Theatre. . . .

(Schoelcher, pp. 323-4.) This was the first time that John Stanley, the organist and composer, blind from the age of two, conducted a Handel oratorio. But he was not yet Handel's substitute : the oratorios at Covent Garden went on with the master. They even started, a week later, with the same *Alexander's Feast*. The earlier advertisements of the Haymarket performance do not speak of Stanley, but indicate that the music began at 12 o'clock noon, followed by an anniversary dinner in Merchant Taylors Hall at 3 o'clock ; the gentlemen attending both to " join the procession from the Theatre ". A copy of the word-book in the Schoelcher Collection, Conservatoire, Paris.

———

FROM THE " PUBLIC ADVERTISER ", 3rd March 1753

At the Great Room in Dean-street, Soho, This Day, will be perform'd the *Seventh Night* of the SUBSCRIPTIONS CONCERTS. Act I. . . . *Our Fruits*, Handel, Miss Turner ; . . . *O Sleep*, Handel, Sig. Frasi. . . . Act II. Overture in Saul, Handel ; *Return, O God of Hosts*, Handel, Sig. Guadagni. . . .

The arias are from *Joseph and His Brethren, Semele* and *Samson*.

———

A concert, with the Overture to *Samson* introducing the second part, is given at the Great Room in Dean Street, for the benefit of the violinist John George Freake, 5th March 1753.

Freake, who also composed, played in *Messiah* in 1754 and 1758.

———

H.-24

FROM THE " PUBLIC ADVERTISER ", 9th March 1753

At the Theatre Royal in Covent Garden, This Day will be performed
ALEXANDER'S FEAST. With an Interlude, call'd The CHOICE of HERCULES.
. . . To begin at Half an Hour after Six o'Clock.

(Schoelcher, p. 322.) This was the beginning of Handel's season, first advertised
on 3rd March, the day after the performance of *Alexander's Feast* at the Haymarket
Theatre. The Covent Garden performance was apparently conducted by Handel,
who, however, did not play an organ concerto. Repeated on 14th March. A copy
of the word-book is in the National Library of Scotland, Edinburgh.

———

FROM THE " PUBLIC ADVERTISER ", 16th March 1753

At the Theatre Royal in Covent Garden, This Day, will be performed
an Oratorio, call'd JEPHTHA. . . . To begin at Half an Hour after Six
o'Clock.

Repeat performance on 21st March.

———

FROM THE " PUBLIC ADVERTISER ", 19th March 1753

For the Benefit of Miss DAVIES,
(*A Child of Nine Years old*)

At the Great Room in Dean-street, Soho, This Day, will be a Concert
of Vocal and Instrumental MUSICK. The first Violin by Signor Chabran.
Act I. . . . Concerto Harpsichord, IV. Handel, Miss Davies. Act II.
. . . *Powerful Guardians*, Handel, Sig. Galli ; . . . by Desire, Song,
Return, O God of Hosts, Handel, Sig. Guadagni ; . . . Song, *The smiling
Dawn of happy Days*, Jeptha, Handel, Miss Bennet. . . .

Cf. 30th April 1751. Nothing is known about Signor Chabran and Miss
Bennet. The arias are from *Alexander Balus*, *Samson*, and *Jephtha*.

———

FROM THE " PUBLIC ADVERTISER ", 23rd March 1753

At the Theatre Royal in Covent Garden, This Day, will be performed
an Oratorio, call'd JUDAS MACCHABAEUS. . . . To begin at Half an Hour
after Six o'Clock.

Repeat performances on 28th and 30th March.

———

FROM THE MINUTES OF THE SUB-COMMITTEE FOR THE CHAPEL OF
THE FOUNDLING HOSPITAL, 31st March 1753

In pursuance of the Reference from the last General Court relating to
the Sermon to be preached on Monday the 16th of next month by the

Bishop of Worcester in the Chapel of this Hospital at the Opening thereof for Divine Service, and to the Performance at the same time of the Te Deum Jubilate and Anthem on this occasion composed by George Frederick Handel Esqr

Resolved

That 800 printed Tickets be made out and delivered at half a Guinea each . . . in the following Form, vizt

In the Chapel of the Hospital

. . . On Monday the 16th Day of April 1753 will be a Sermon . . . And the Te Deum Jubilate and an Anthem on this Occasion composed by George Frederick Handel Esqr will be performed under his Direction. Prayers to begin at Eleven o'clock in the Forenoon.

Resolved

That Notice be published in the Daily and Publick Advertisers alternating every day beginning on Tuesday the 3^d of next month. . . .

(Nichols and Wray, p. 208.) The sermon was preached by Isaac Maddox, Lord Bishop of Worcester. He was elected one of the Governors of the Hospital, and, at the same time, John Waring was chosen as Reader of the Chapel.

—

FROM THE " PUBLIC ADVERTISER ", 2nd April 1753

For the Benefit of Signora FRASI.

At the New Theatre in the Haymarket, this Day . . . will be performed ACIS and GALATEA. By Mr. *Handel*. With a Concerto on the Organ by Mr. Stanley. First Violin, with a Solo, by Sig. Giardini. . . .

(Loewenberg, p. 88.) The performance had been advertised since 3rd March, but the concerto and the solo were not mentioned until 27th March.

—

FROM THE " PUBLIC ADVERTISER ", 3rd April 1753

Yesterday was rehearsed at St. Margaret's Church, Westminster, to a numerous Audience, Mr. Handel's Grand Te Deum ; the Coronation Anthem, and an Anthem of Dr Boyce's, which met with great Applause, and it will be performed this Day at the same Church for the Benefit of the Westminster Infirmary.

—

FROM THE " PUBLIC ADVERTISER ", 4th April 1753

On Monday se'nnight [the 16th] the new Chapel at the Foundling Hospital will be preached in, for the first time, by the Lord Bishop of Worcester ; and at the same Time will be performed an Anthem, under the Direction of Mr. Handel, for the Benefit of the said Hospital.

—

FROM THE " PUBLIC ADVERTISER ", 4th April 1753

At the Theatre Royal in Covent Garden, This Day will be performed an Oratorio, call'd SAMSON. . . . To begin at Half an Hour after Six o'Clock.

Repeat performances on 6th and 11th April.

———

THE LORD CHAMBERLAIN TO THE MANAGER OF THE THEATRE IN COVENT GARDEN, 11th April 1753

These are strictly to charge and command you not to act any Plays, Oratorios or any other Theatrical Performance in Passion Week for the Future on any Pretence whatsoever. Given under my hand this 11th day of April 1753 in the Twenty-sixth year of his M$^{ty's}$ reign.

Grafton.

(Public Record Office : L.C.5/162, pp. 2 f.) On the same day orders were issued to four theatres in London : the Opera House in the Haymarket (" not to have any Oratorio, Concert, Masquerade or Assembly "), to the Theatre Royal in Drury Lane (" not to act any Plays, Oratorios or any other Theatrical Performances "), to the Theatre in Covent Garden (" A like Order ", see above), and to the Little (or rather, New) Theatre in the Haymarket (similar). Handel seems never to have performed an oratorio during Passion Week, except in 1737 when he got special permission for it (cf. 4th–7th April 1737). The manager of Covent Garden Theatre was still John Rich. Charles, Duke of Grafton was Lord Chamberlain of the Household.

———

FROM THE MINUTES OF THE GENERAL COMMITTEE OF THE FOUNDLING HOSPITAL, 11th April 1753

The Committee taking Notice of an extraordinary Paragraph, in three of the Daily Papers on Tuesday the 3rd Instant, relating to a Funeral Anthem preparing by Geo. Frederick Handel Esqr to be performed in the Chapel of this Hospital after his Death, and expressing their surprize thereat.

RESOLVED

That the Secretary do acquaint Mr. Handel, That the said Paragraph has given this Committee great Concern ; they being highly sensible, that all Well-wishers to this Charity must be desirous for the Continuance of his Life, who has been and is so great and generous a Benefactor thereto.

(Bronslow, 1847 ; 1858, p. 74.) None of the three newspapers has been traced. This gossip may have been caused by the fact that Handel provided an anthem for the opening of the Chapel of the Foundling Hospital, probably the so-called Foundling Anthem of 1749. The text of the lost London newspaper notice may be reconstructed from the German version : see page 742 (*Hallische Zeitung*). Cf. 14th (24th) May 1759.

———

FROM THE " PUBLIC ADVERTISER ", 13th April 1753

At the Theatre Royal in Covent Garden, This Day, will be performed a Sacred Oratorio, call'd MESSIAH. . . . To begin at Half an Hour after Six o'Clock.

There was one performance only.

———

The Chapel of the Foundling Hospital is finally opened for divine service on 16th April 1753 ; an anthem by Handel, probably his " Foundling Anthem ", is performed.

(Nichols and Wray, p. 207.)   Cf. 6th December 1752, 25th January and 31st March 1753.

———

FROM THE " LONDON DAILY ADVERTISER ", 19th April 1753

On Tuesday the 1st of next Month, the sacred Oratorio called Messiah, is to be performed in the Chapel of the Foundling Hospital, George Frederick Handel, Esq; the exquisite Composer thereof, having repeated his Offer of Assistance to promote that Charity, to which he has been so great an annual Benefactor. . . .

The same notice appeared in the *Public Advertiser.*

———

FROM THE " PUBLIC ADVERTISER ", 30th April 1753

For the Benefit and Increase of a FUND *establish'd for the Support of* DECAY'D MUSICIANS, *or their Families.*

At the King's Theatre in the Haymarket, This Day . . . will be performed an Entertainment of Vocal and Instrumental MUSICK. As follows :
Part I. . . . *Return, O God of Hosts*, composed by Mr. Handel, sung by Sig. Guadagni. . . .
Part III. . . .*Quella fiamma*, . . . sung by Sig. Frasi ; . . . Trio, *The Flocks shall leave the Mountains*, . . . sung by Sig. Frasi, Mr. Beard, Mr. Wass. Grand Concerto, composed by Mr. Handel. . . .

The arias are from *Samson* and *Arminio*, the trio from *Acis and Galatea.*

———

FROM THE SAME

For the Benefit of Miss ISABELLA YOUNG,
Scholar of Mr. WALTZ.

At the New Theatre in the Haymarket, This Day . . . will be performed a Concert of Vocal and Instrumental MUSICK. The Vocal Parts by Miss Young ; and the Instrumental Parts by several of the Best Masters ; (and by particular Desire) several of Mr. Handel's Organ Concertos will be performed by Miss Young. . . .

(Smith, 1948, p. 193.)   Cf. 2nd March 1752.

———

From the " Public Advertiser ", 30th April 1753

Hospital for the Maintenance and Education of exposed and deserted young Children.

This is to give Notice, That towards the Support of this Charity, the Sacred Oratorio called Messiah, will be performed in the Chapel of this Hospital, To morrow the First of May 1753, at Twelve o'Clock at Noon precisely. . . .

By Order of the Committee,

Harman Verelst, Sec.

———

From the " Hallische Zeitung ", Halle an der Saale, Spring 1753 (Translated)

London, 10th April.

Notwithstanding the fact that the noted Händel, this Lully of Great Britain, has had the misfortune to lose his sight, yet he, like Homer and Milton, does not allow his muse to remain idle. Perhaps the work which he now shapes will be, however, his last opus. It is to become his echo, and after his death is to be sung in the Foundling Hospital, and the profits which are earned by it he has made over to this House.

The passage, quoted by Adlung in 1758, is from no. 65 of the journal of Handel's birthplace, which did not use the date of the day. The gossip came from London newspapers : see 11th April 1753.

———

From the " Public Advertiser ", 2nd May 1753

Yesterday the Sacred Oratorio, call'd Messiah, was perform'd in the Chapel at the Foundling Hospital, under the Direction of the inimitable Composer thereof, George Frederick Handel Esq; who, in the Organ Concerto, play'd himself a Voluntary on the fine Organ he gave to that Chapel.

(Schoelcher, pp. 271 and 323.)

———

From the " Public Advertiser ", 3rd May 1753

The Rehearsal of the Musick for the Feast of the Sons of the Clergy, will be performed at St. Paul's Cathedral, on Tuesday May 8, and the Feast will be held at Merchant-Taylors Hall, on Thursday May 10, 1753.

. . . . .

☞ Mr. Handel's new Te Deum, Jubilate and Coronation Anthem, with an Anthem by Dr. Boyce, will be Vocally and Instrumentally performed.

. . . . .

☞ Two Rehearsal and Two Choir Tickets will be given with each Feast Ticket. . . .

The Feast, as usual, was at noon.

———

FROM THE "LONDON DAILY ADVERTISER", 4th May 1753

. . . We have in none of the polite Arts so conspicuous, and one is sorry to add, that there are in none so frequent Instances, of the Effect of this little Cunning, as in the modern Music. Whether we look upon the Composers, or the Performers, in this Light, those who are in the Secret will have Reason to lament, and those who are out of it to wonder, at the constant and unalterable Preference that is given to every foreign, against every English Name, in the Lists of Performances : Nay, if we look into the greater Part of them, we shall find, that even *Handel* is become so near an Englishman, by his having lived long among us, that his Pieces are given but very sparingly in the Entertainment ; and Compositions which of all others are most calculated for the English Ear are seldom allowed an Hearing. . . .

It would not be easy to persuade the Man of true Judgment that the Composers of any Nation at this Time are superior to our own ; suffering us to claim Mr. Handel as naturalis'd, and making it a Fashion to encourage but a little, those who have been born among us.

The *London Daily Advertiser* had a regular leader, entitled " The Inspector ". This one, dealing with " Modern Music " and filling two of the six columns, ends with a recommendation for a charity concert of English music, to be held at Hickford's Rooms the next day.

———

FROM THE "PUBLIC ADVERTISER", 7th May 1753

Towards the Increase of a FUND *for Extending the* BUILDING *of a* PUBLIC CHARITY.

At the King's Theatre in the Haymarket, This Day . . . will be performed an Oratorio, call'd JUDAS MACCHABAEUS. Composed by Mr. HANDEL. . . .

Cf. 22nd April 1752. The charity was the Lock Hospital. The takings at this performance were £84 : 2 : 6. Handel became a Governor of this Hospital too. (*A Short History of the London Lock Hospital and Rescue Home*, 1906, p. 5.) Bromfield, Handel's and the Hospital's surgeon, was an amateur of the arts, interested in literature as well as music, and may have suggested this concert.

———

FROM THE MINUTES OF THE GENERAL COMMITTEE OF THE FOUNDLING HOSPITAL, 8th May 1753

The Treasurer reported, that on the 16th of April, the Sum of £148.11.6. was received for Tickets at the Opening the Chapel, whereout was paid for Charges £45.4. and the Net Produce amounted to £103.7.6 ; and that on the 1st May, the Sum of £558.1.6. was recd. for Tickets at the

Oratorio of Messiah, whereout was paid for Charges £62.1.6, and the Net Produce amounted to £496, making together £599.7.6.

———

From the "London Magazine", May 1753

Tuesday, May 1. The sacred oratorio, called the Messiah, was performed at the chapel to the Foundling-hospital, under the direction of George Frederick Handel, Esq; the composer of that solemn piece of musick, for the benefit of that noble charity ; there were above 800 coaches and chairs, and the tickets amounted to 925 guineas.

Cf. the official account of 8th May.

———

From the "World", 28th June 1753

. . . Those who have studied the works of Corelli among the modern-ancients, and Handel in the present age, know that the most affecting passages of the former owe their excellence to *Simplicity* alone ; and that the latter understands it as well, and attends to it as much, though he knows when to introduce with propriety those niceties and refinements which, for want of propriety, we condemn in others. . . .

[Joseph Warton.]

This, number 26 of the magazine, contains the essay on Simplicity only. The book edition of the magazine, dedicated to Moore's co-editor, Lord Chesterfield, has a key to the names of contributors (1772, I. 162 f.). For Warton see 2nd May 1745.

———

From "Jackson's Oxford Journal", 7th July 1753

Oxford, July 7.

On Monday last [the 2nd] was celebrated here, the annual Solemnity of commemorating all the benefactors to the University, according to the Institution of Lord Crewe, Bishop of Durham . . . in the Evening Alexander's Feast was performed to a crowded Assembly.

———

The Three Choirs Meeting is held at Hereford on 12th and 13th September 1753. The Coronation Anthem (*Zadok the Priest*) and the *Dettingen Te Deum with Jubilate* are performed in the mornings in the Cathedral ; and *Samson* on the second evening in the College Hall. Boyce conducts.

The rehearsal was on 10th September, at 5 P.M. (Berrow's *Worcester Journal*).

———

At Salisbury, on 19th and 20th September 1753, one overture (*Esther* ?), one Te Deum and two Coronation Anthems are performed each morning in the Cathedral; in the evenings, *L' Allegro ed il Penseroso*, on 19th, and *Judas Maccabaeus*, on 20th, are performed in the Assembly Hall.

—

FROM FAULKNER'S "DUBLIN JOURNAL", 10th November 1753

The celebrated Oratorio of Sampson will be performed for the Benefit of Miss Oldmixon, at the Great Musick Hall in Fishamble Street, on Monday the 19th of November, Conducted by Mr. Dubourg ; and we hear that his Grace the Duke of Dorset, will Honour the Performance with his Presence.

—

FROM THE "GRAY'S INN JOURNAL", 24th November 1753

True Intelligence

.   .   .   .   .

Robin-Hood Society, Nov. 19.

.   .   .   .   .

I cannot help wondering, that, while we have *Handel, Arne, and Boyce,* the *English* will lavish Sums upon a false and depraved Taste, merely to be thought Judges of what they do not understand.

(Bredenförder.)

—

Handel subscribes for *The Works of the late Aaron Hill*, published in 1753 in four volumes.

Hill, Handel's first English librettist, had died in 1750. The edition was for the benefit of his family.

H.–24 *a*

1754

FROM " GRAY'S INN JOURNAL ", 9th February 1754

. . . We may also boast an equal Excellence [as in Painting] in Music ; for though Mr. *Handell* is not an *Englishman*, it is however a convincing Proof of our national Taste, that we have made it worth his while to fix his Residence among us. . . .

X.

(Myers, 1948, p. 231.) This was written as a protest against Voltaire's statement that the English are happy in philosophy, but not in the polite arts : the stage, painting and music.

FROM THE " PUBLIC ADVERTISER ", 13th February 1754

For the Benefit of Sig. GALLI.

At the New Theatre in the Haymarket, This Day . . . will be perform'd ACIS and GALATEA. Composed by Mr. Handel. . . .

Cf. 2nd April 1753. There was interval music consisting of a violoncello solo played by Salvadore Lanzetti, an Italian aria sung by Signora Galli and a violin solo played by Pieter Hellendaal (the elder) ; cf. Smith, 1948, pp. 237 f.

FROM " JACKSON'S OXFORD JOURNAL ", 23rd February 1754

Oxford, Feb. 23

On Monday Night next [the 25th] at the Musick Room in Holliwell will be performed L'Allegro & Il Penseroso, set to Musick by Mr. Handel.

A word-book in the Schoelcher Collection (Conservatoire, Paris) indicates that the *Ode for St. Cecilia's Day* was also performed on the same occasion.

FROM THE " PUBLIC ADVERTISER ", 25th February 1754

For the Benefit of Signora FRASI.

At the King's Theatre in the Haymarket, on Tuesday, April 2, will be performed, SAMSON, an Oratorio by Mr. HANDEL. With a Concerto on the Organ by Mr. Stanley. . . .

This performance was cancelled, and *Samson* was revived at Covent Garden on 29th March ; but it is noteworthy that, during February and March 1754, Handel's works appeared in the advertisements of three London theatres.

From the " Public Advertiser ", 28th February 1754

For the Benefit and Increase of a Fund *established for the Support of Decayed* Musicians, *or their Families.*

At the King's Theatre in the Haymarket, This Day . . . will be performed an Entertainment of Vocal and Instrumental Musick. *As follows* ; . . . Part II. . . . Song, *Endless Pleasure*, composed by Mr. Handel, sung by Mr. Beard. . . . Grand Concerto composed by Mr. Handel. . . .

The song is from *Semele*. Dubourg played a violin concerto on this evening.

—

From the " Public Advertiser ", 1st March 1754

At the Theatre-Royal in Covent Garden, This Day, will be perform'd an Oratorio, call'd Alexander Balus. . . . To begin at Half an Hour after Six.

Cf. 22nd March 1751. Repeat performance on 6th March.

—

From the " Public Advertiser ", 8th March 1754

At the Theatre-Royal in Covent-Garden, This Day, will be perform'd an Oratorio, call'd Deborah. . . . To begin at Half an Hour after Six.

Cf. 3rd November 1744. Repeat performance on 13th March.

—

From the " Public Advertiser ", 12th March 1754

At the King's Theatre in the Haymarket, This Day, will be presented an Opera, called Admeto. The Music composed by Mr. *Handel*. And New *Decorations*. . . . To begin at Half an Hour after Six precisely. . . .

(Burney, IV. 463 ; Loewenberg, p. 81.) This was the last revival, during his lifetime, of any Handel opera. Cf. 31st January and 3rd October 1727, 25th May 1728 and 7th December 1731. Repeat performances on 16th, 19th, 23rd March and 6th April 1754. This revival was, of course, not arranged by Handel himself ; the Haymarket Theatre was still under the management of Vanneschi. Walsh advertised his *Favourite Songs* again, published in 1727 or 1728.

—

From the " Public Advertiser ", 15th March 1754

At the Theatre-Royal in Covent Garden, This Day, will be perform'd an Oratorio, call'd Saul. . . . To begin at Half an Hour after Six.

Cf. 7th March 1750. Repeat performance on 20th March.

—

An engraving of Joseph Goupy's Handel cartoon is published, 21st March 1754.

(Schoelcher, p. 143.) There are two paintings of Goupy's cartoon, and two engravings, which are not identical with the paintings. Only one engraving is dated ; it bears the text :

The Charming Brute

The Figure's odd—yet who wou'd think ?
Within this Tunn' of Meat & Drink
There dwells the Soul of soft Desires
And all that HARMONY inspires.

Can contrast such as this be found ?
Upon the Globe's extensive Round :
There can—yon Hogshead is his Seat,
His sole Devotion is—to Eat.

In the lower part of the picture is a scroll on which are the words " I am myself alone". The undated engraving (*c.* 1745 ?), in which the organ-player looks to the right, is inscribed :

Strange Monsters have Adorn'd the Stage,
Not Afric's Coast produces more,
And yet no Land nor Clime nor Age,
Have equal'd this Harmonious Boar.

Lira e lodovole quando giuesta e la Cagione.

PLINIO.

The dated engraving is similar to the pastel preserved in the Fitzwilliam Museum, Cambridge. Whether one of the originals was painted in 1733, as Laetitia-Matilda Hawkins (*Anecdotes, Biographical Sketches and Memoirs*, 1822, I. 196 f.) related, is not known. She tells an anecdote explaining how Handel and Goupy were estranged at that time because of Handel's mean-ness as Goupy's host ; but Whitley's story (1. 72) seems more credible, namely that the published cartoon cost Goupy a legacy from Handel for having represented him as gluttonous.

——

FROM THE " PUBLIC ADVERTISER ", 22nd March 1754

At the Theatre-Royal in Covent-Garden, This Day, will be perform'd an Oratorio, call'd JOSHUA. . . . To begin at Half an Hour after Six.

Cf. 14th February 1752. There was one performance only.

——

FROM THE " PUBLIC ADVERTISER ", 27th March 1754

At the Theatre-Royal in Covent Garden, This Day, will be perform'd an Oratorio, call'd JUDAS MACCHABAEUS. . . . To begin at Half an Hour after Six.

Cf. 23rd March 1753. Repeat performance on 3rd April.

——

FROM THE " PUBLIC ADVERTISER ", 29th March 1754

At the Theatre-Royal in Covent Garden, This Day, will be perform'd an Oratorio, call'd SAMSON. . . . To begin at Half an Hour after Six.

Cf. 4th April 1753. There was one performance only.

—

FROM THE " PUBLIC ADVERTISER ", 5th April 1754

At the Theatre-Royal in Covent Garden, This Day, will be perform'd a Sacred Oratorio, call'd MESSIAH. Being the Last This Season. . . . To begin at Half an Hour after Six.

Cf. 13th April 1753. This single performance concluded the oratorio season ; but see 23rd May.

—

FROM THE " PUBLIC ADVERTISER ", 2nd May 1754

Hospital for the Maintenance and Education of exposed and deserted young Children.

.   .   .   .

Note, Mr. Handel's Sacred Oratorio of MESSIAH will be performed in the Chapel of the Hospital on Wednesday the 15th of May.

On 11th May Watts advertised his word-book of *Messiah* ; it was a new edition.

—

The Conscious Lover is given at Covent Garden Theatre on 3rd May 1754, for the benefit of Mr. Legg and Miss Young ; Mr. Legg sings "Honour and Arms", from *Samson*, at the end of Act III.

Mr. Legg also sang in the Foundling Hospital production of *Messiah* on 15th May.

—

Walsh advertises a tenth set of songs from Handel's oratorios, in vocal score, *Public Advertiser*, 8th May 1754.

—

FROM " JACKSON'S OXFORD JOURNAL ", 11th May 1754

Oxford, May 11.

On Monday next [the 13th], *Acis* and *Galatea*, an Oratorio, will be performed at the Musick Room in this City.

—

Handel conducts *Messiah* for the last time at its performance in the Foundling Hospital's Chapel, 15th May 1754. Cf. 25th June.

———

MRS. DELANY TO MRS. DEWES

Suffolk Street, 16th May, 1754.

D.D. [the Rev. Patrick Delany] gave Miss Mulso a ticket for the "Messiah", and I took her with me—my brother [Bernard Granville] called for us both ; the music was *too fine*, I never heard it so well performed. The chapel is fine, and the sight of so many poor children brought up (I hope to good purpose), was a pleasant sight.

(Delany, III. 272.) The Delanys were on a visit to London. Their friend was Miss Hester Mulso.

———

FROM "JACKSON'S OXFORD JOURNAL", 18th May 1754

Oxford, May 18.

We are assured, that on Monday next [the 20th] the Oratorio of *Esther* will be performed at the Musick Room in Holliwell.

———

FROM THE "PUBLIC ADVERTISER", 23rd May 1754

At the particular Desire of several Persons of Quality. At the Theatre Royal in Covent Garden, This Day . . . will be performed L' ALLEGRO IL PENSEROSO, of *Milton*. To which will be added An ODE on St. CECILIA'S DAY, by *Dryden*. The Music of both composed by Mr. *Handel*. The First Violin with a Concerto, by Sig. Giardini. . . .

Cf. 18th March 1743. The announcement of Giardini's performance was added to the later advertisements.

———

FROM THE MINUTES OF THE GENERAL COMMITTEE OF THE FOUNDLING HOSPITAL, 29th May 1754

The Treasurer reported, that the Net Money arising from the Performance of the Oratorio of the Messiah in the Chapel of this Hospital the 15th instant, amounted to the sum of £607.17.6. . . .

	£	s.	d.
To wit . . .			
For 1219 Tickets, and by Cash received	666.	15.	0
Paid for Musicians, Constables, etc., as by the following Account	58.	17.	6
	£607.	17.	6

		£ s. d.			£ s. d.
	Messrs. Brown . .	£1. 1. –		Brt. forwd.	19. 8. 6
	Collet	15. –			
	Freek	15. –		Christo. Smith	
	Claudio	10. –		Org. . . .	
	Scarpettini	10. –			
	Wood	10. –		Beard . . .	
	Wood Jnr.	10. –		Frasi	6. 6. –
Violins	Jackson	10. –		Galli	4. 14. 6
	Abbington	10. –		Passerini	4. 14. 6
	Dunn	10. –		Wass	1. 11. 6
	Stockton	10. –		Boys	3. 3. –
	Nicholson	10. –		Baildon	10. 6
	Neal	8. –		Barrow	10. 6
	Davis	8. –		Cheriton	10. 6
	Rash	8. –		Ladd	10. 6
	Smith	8. –	**Singers**	Baildon Junr.	10. 6
	Warner	8. –		Vandenon	10. 6
Tenors	Warner Jnr.	8. –		Champness	10. 6
	Rawlins	8. –		Courtney	10. 6
	Ebelin	8. –		Wilder	10. 6
	Gillier	10. 6		Dupee	10. 6
Violoncelli	Haron	10. 6		Walz	10. 6
	Hebden	10. 6		Cox	10. 6
				Legg	10. 6
Contra Bassi	Dietrich	15. –		Le Blanc	1. 1. –
	Thompson	15. –		Gundal	10. 6
	Baumgarden	10. –	**Servts**	Prince	10. 6
Bassoons	Jarvis	8. –		Lee	10. 6
	Goodman	8. –		Shepherd	10. 6
	Dyke	8. –			
	Eyford	10. –		Musick Porters	1. 1. –
Hautboys	Teede	10. –			£50. 18. 6
	Vincent	10. –		Presented Mr. Ch. Smith	5. 5. –
	Simpson	8. –			£56. 3. 6
	Adcock	10. 6			
	Willis	8. –		To the Constables	2. 2. –
	Fr. Smith	10. 6			
	Trova	10. 6		Organ Blowers 4/-	
	Miller	10. 6		Porterage of Tickets 8/-	12. –
	Carried up,	£19. 8. 6			£58. 17. 6

(John Tobin, *Musical Times*, April 1950.) This is the first list of *Messiah* performers preserved at the Foundling Hospital ; these lists give the names of numerous London musicians.   (Cf. 1st/2nd May 1758 and 10th May 1759.)   The violin players were Abram Brown, John Collet(t), John George Freek (Freake), Claudio, Gaetano Scarpettini, Thomas Wood, Wood junior, William Jackson, Joseph Abbington, Dunn, Thomas Stockton, Nicholson, Neal, Davis and Rash. Of

the " tenor " (viola) players only Thomas Rawlins can be identified. The violon-
cellists were probably Peter Gillier, Claudius Heron and John Hebden. Of the
two double bass players only (Christian ?) Dietrich is known. The bassoons were
played by Samuel Baumgarden, Jarvis, Adam Goodman and Dyke. The oboists
were Eyford, William Teede (Teide), (Richard ?) Vincent and Redmond Simpson
(Dubourg's son-in-law). Abraham Adcock and Justice Willis played the trumpet,
Fr. Smith the kettle-drums, Trowa and Miller the horn. (Mr. Adam Carse was
kind enough to help to identify the musicians named in the Foundling Hospital
lists.)—John Christopher Smith, who played the organ for Handel, and the tenor
Beard, did not accept payment : Smith seems, in fact, to have given to the charity
instead. The paid singers were : Giulia Frasi, Signora Galli, Christina Passerini,
Mr. Wass (bass), Mr. Gates's " boys " from the Chapel Royal, Baildon senior and
junior, Thomas Barrow (alto), David Cheriton, Thomas Vandernan (two of the
Gentlemen of the Chapel Royal), Samuel Champness (bass), Gustavus Waltz (bass,
not a soloist any more), Legg (presumably a bass), and some more, unidentified.
Of the servants, " Le Blanc " was apparently Peter Le Blond, Handel's valet (cf.
1st June 1750).

FROM THE MINUTES OF THE·GENERAL COMMITTEE OF THE FOUNDLING
HOSPITAL, 5th June 1754

This Committee having experienced the great Benefit which have
arose to this Corporation from Mr. Handel's charitable Performances of
Sacred Music ; and that it may be very proper to put such Performances
under proper Regulations

Resolved That Mr. Handel be consulted thereupon, and that the
Treasurer and Mr. Fauquier be desired to wait on Mr. Handel for that
Purpose.

Cf. 25th June. Taylor White was the Treasurer of the Hospital, Francis Fauquier
one of its Governors.

———

FROM " JACKSON'S OXFORD JOURNAL ", 15th June 1754

Oxford, June 15.

We can assure our Readers, from very good Authority, that at the
next Commemoration of Founders and Benefactors to the University,
viz. on the 2d of July, the Right Hon. the Earl of Westmorland, the
present High Steward, and Lady Westmorland, intend to honour that
Solemnity with their Presence. . . . And that in order to welcome the
High Steward on his first Appearance there since he accepted that Office,
several Oratorios will be perform'd in the Theatre ; a numerous Band
of Vocal and Instrumental Performers being already engaged for that
Purpose.

See next entry.

———

FROM THE SAME, 22nd June 1754

Oxford, June 22.

On Wednesday the 3d, Thursday the 4th, and Friday the 5th of July,
being the three Days following the Commemoration of Founders and

Benefactors to the University, *L'Allegro il Penseroso*, &c. *Judas Macchabaeus*, and MESSIAH will be performed in the Theatre. The principal Vocal Parts by Signora Frasi, Mr. Beard, Mr. Wass, and others ; and the Instrumental Parts by many of the most excellent Performers of every Kind from London. Further Particulars will be specified in the Bills of each Day's Performance.

Cf. 29th June and 6th July.

—

FROM THE MINUTES OF THE GENERAL COMMITTEE OF THE FOUNDLING HOSPITAL, 25th June 1754

Mr. Fauquier reported, that Mr. White being ill he had waited on Mr. Handel in pursuance of a Minute of the 5th instant ; and that Mr. Handel approved of the Committee's appointing Mr. Smith Organist to the Chapel, to conduct his Musical Compositions ; but that on Acco^t of his Health he excused himself from giving any further Instructions relating to the Performances.

(Nichols and Wray, p. 205.) Smith was organist there from 1754 till 1770. Cf. 29th May.

—

FROM "JACKSON'S OXFORD JOURNAL", 29th June 1754

On Wednesday the 3d, Thursday the 4th, and Friday the 5th of July, being the three Days following the Commemoration of Founders and Benefactors to the University.

L' Allegro il Penseroso, &c. *Judas Macchabaeus*, and *Messiah*, will be perform'd in the Theatre at Oxford. The principal Vocal Parts by Signora Frasi, Mr. Beard, Mr. Wass, and others ; and the Instrumental Parts by many of the most excellent Performers of every Kind from London.—The whole Number of Performers will amount to near an Hundred.—From so numerous and well-chosen a Band, it is not doubted but these Performers will, at least, equal in Grandeur and Elegance, any of the Kind that have been exhibited in this Kingdom : And it is hoped they will not fail of affording entire Satisfaction to the splendid and polite Audience which is expected on this Occasion.

—

FROM THE SAME, 6th July 1754

Oxford, July 6.

. . . On Wednesday [the 3rd] . . . in the Afternoon L' Allegro, il Penseroso, and il Moderato, were perform'd in the Theatre ; and on Thursday Afternoon Judas Macchabaeus.

Yesterday . . . in the Afternoon the Oratorio of Messiah was perform'd in the Theatre. These three Musical Entertainments have been attended with very crouded Audiences, and have done Honour to the Professor of Music, the Conductor of them.

The Professor was Dr. William Hayes.

—

Handel buys £1,500 Reduced 3 per cent Annuities, 19th July 1754.

—

FROM JOHANN JOACHIM QUANTZ'S AUTOBIOGRAPHY, POTSDAM,
August 1754 (Translation)

. . . On 10th March [1727] I left Paris ; and arrived safely in London via Calais on the 20th of the same month. . . . At that time Italian opera in London was in full flush. *Admetus*, composed by *Händel*, was the latest, and had magnificent music. *Faustina, Cuzzoni* and *Senesino*, all three virtuosos of the front rank, were the chief performers in it, the rest were middling. . . . The orchestra consisted for the greater part of Germans, several Italians, and a few Englishmen. *Castrucci*, an Italian violinist, was the leader. All together, under *Händel's* conducting, made an extremely good effect.

The second opera which I heard in London was by *Bononcini* ; it was not, however, so greatly acclaimed as the first. *Händel's* harmonic structure [Grundstimme] prevailed over *Bononcini's* melodic invention [Oberstimme]. . . .

Only few solo instrumentalists were there . . . *e.g.* Händel, as is well known, on the harpsichord and organ. . . .

Published in Marpurg's *Historisch-Kritische Beyträge zur Aufnahme der Musik*, Berlin, 1754, Vol. 1, part 3, pp. 239 f. and 241 f. The dates mentioned correspond to the English 27th February and 9th March 1727. The passage was reprinted, in Dutch, in Lustig's Amsterdam magazine, *Samenspraaken*, July 1756, no. 7, pp. 362-364.

—

The Three Choirs Meeting is held at Gloucester from 11th till 13th September 1754 ; the evening performances, in the Boothall, are: *L' Allegro ed il Penseroso* on the 11th, *Judas Maccabaeus* on the 12th and 13th.

—

HANDEL TO TELEMANN, AT HAMBURG, 20th September 1754

Monsieur

Il y a quelque temps que j'ay fis preparer une provision de plantes exotiques pour vous les envoyer, quand Jean Carsten le Capitain (a qui je fis parler pour vous les faire tenir) me fit dite qu'il avoit apri que vous etiez defunt ; vous ne doutez pas que ce rapport m'affligea extremement. Vous Jugeréz donc de la Joye que je dois avoir entendre que vous vous trouvez en perfaite Santé. Le même Capitain Jean Carsten qui vient d'arrive icy de retour de vos quartiers, me mandes par un amy cette bonne nouvelle, et que vous lui avoit Consignè une Liste de plantes exotiques, pour vous les procurer, j'ay embrassé cette occasion avec beaucoup de plaisir, et j'ay eû Soin de faire trouvér cettes plantes, et vous les aurez presque toutes ; Come le Capitain Ca[r]sten ne doit pas partir d'icy qu'au mois de Decembre prochain, il a bien voulû ce Charger de les envoyer par le premier vaisseau qui partira d'icy, dont vous trouverez dans cet Billet cy joint le nom du Capitain et du vaisseau. Je souhaite que ce petit present que j'ose vous offrir vous soit agreable ; Je vous supplié a me vouloir donner des nouvelle de vôtre Santé que je vous souhaite trè perfaite et toute Sorte de proscrité qui suis avec un estime inviolable,

Monsieur

vôtre tres humble et tres obeissant serviteur

G: F: Händel

a Londres ce 20 Sep^r.

    1754.

(Translation)

Sir,

    Some time ago I had a selection of exotic plants made ready to be sent to you, when Captain John Carsten (to whom I spoke about delivering them to you) informed me that he had learnt of your death. You will not doubt that this report caused me extreme sorrow. You will therefore judge of my joy on hearing that you are in perfect health. The same Captain John Carsten, who has just arrived here from your part of the world, sent me this good news by a friend, and also [informed me] that you had entrusted to him a list of exotic plants to be procured for you. I profited by this occasion with the greatest pleasure, and I have been at pains to have these plants found, and you shall have nearly all of them. As Captain Carsten is not due to leave till next December, he has been good enough to see to their despatch by the first vessel leaving here ; you will find the name of the captain and the vessel on the enclosed paper. I trust that this little present which I take the liberty of offering you, will be acceptable. I pray you to send me news of your health, which I trust is excellent. I wish you all prosperity and am, with steadfast devotion,

Sir,

Your most humble and obedient servant,

G. F. Handel

London, September 20th, 1754.

(Kitzig ; Arro.) Original in the University Library Dorpat = Tartu. Written by another hand, signed by Handel. Cf. 14th December 1750.

—

FROM "JACKSON'S OXFORD JOURNAL ", 21st September 1754

Gloucester, Sept. 14. On Wednesday [the 11th] and Thursday last [the 12th] the annual Meeting of the Three Choirs of Gloucester, Worcester, and Hereford, was held here : at which was a very numerous and splendid Appearance of Gentlemen and Ladies. On Wednesday Morning was preach'd a Sermon suitable to the Occasion ; the Musical Performances each Day met with a general Applause, and the Charity Collection amounted to 187*l*. And, to promote the laudable Undertaking of erecting a County Hospital here, the Oratorio of Judas Maccabeus, which was the Entertainment for Thursday Evening, was performed also Yesterday Morning [the 13th], when upwards of Fifty Pounds was collected.

—

At Lynn in Norfolk, a new organ by John Snetzler is opened in St. Margaret's Church and is played by Charles Burney ; the celebration ends with one of the Coronation Anthems (*Zadok the Priest* ?), 22nd October 1754.

Burney, who had left London in 1750, was organist in King's Lynn from 1751 till 1760.

—

From "Jackson's Oxford Journal" 9th November 1754

For the Benefit of Mr. Orthman, On Friday 15th Inst. November, 1754, Will be performed at the Music Room *Alexander's Feast*. In which Signor Passerini who was first Violin, and Signora Passerini a principal Singer at the Opera last Winter, will perform in each Capacity. To begin exactly at Seven o'Clock. . . .

E. C. Orthman was an Oxford singer : cf. 19th (24th) November 1757.

—

From Faulkner's " Dublin Journal ", 7th December 1754

On Thursday last [the 5th] Mr. Handel's Grand Te Deum Jubilate and two Anthems, were performed at St. Andrew's Church . . . for the Support of Mercer's Hospital. Their Excellencies the Lords Justices favoured the Hospital with their Presence.

—

Draft of Petition to Parliament by the Governors of the Foundling Hospital, 1754

. . . That in order to raise a further sum for the benefit of the said charity, George Frederick Handel, esq;, hath been charitably pleased to give to this Corporation a composition of musick, called ' The Oratorio of the Messiah ' composed by him the said George Frederick Handel, reserving to himself the liberty only of performing the same for his own benefit during his life : and whereas the said benefaction cannot be secured to the sole use of your petitioners except by the authority of

Parliament, your petitioners, therefore, humbly pray, that leave may be given to bring in a Bill for the purpose aforesaid.

(Bronslow, 1847, p. 143 ; 1858, pp. 73 f.) The idea behind this attempt to secure a private right of performance for *Messiah* may have arisen out of a misunderstanding between Handel and the Foundling Hospital. In any case, when the draft was shown to him, Handel protested against it or, as the Minutes say, " the same did not seem agreeable to Mr. Handel for the present ". He gave a copy of the score, in manuscript, to Mercer's Hospital, the first beneficiary, as well as to the Foundling Hospital, without, however, abandoning any of his rights, or envisaging a monopoly for any single charitable institution.

———

Deborah is performed at Edinburgh, 1754.

The only record of this performance was found in a word-book printed in Edinburgh by T. and W. Ruddimans.

———

John Sadler, a music publisher in Liverpool, uses the fictitious imprint, " Henry Purcell, at Handel's Head ", for a London issue of his collection *The Muses Delight*, 1754.

The original edition of " *The Muses Delight*. An Accurate Collection of English and Italian Songs, Cantatas and Duets, set to Music for the Harpsichord, Violin, German Flute, etc. With Instructions for the Voice, Violin, Harpsichord . . . also, a Compleat Musical Dictionary . . .", was published in Liverpool in 1754. It contains six songs by Handel. A later edition, printed in Liverpool in 1756, is called *Apollo's Cabinet: or the Muses Delight*.

———

FROM MRS. PILKINGTON'S MEMOIRS, 1754

[Swift] fell into a deep Melancholy, and knew no body ; I was told the last sensible Words he uttered, were on this Occasion : Mr. *Handel*, when about to quit *Ireland* went to take his leave of him : The Servant was a considerable Time, e'er he could make the Dean understand him ; which, when he did, he cry'd, " Oh ! a *German*, and a Genius ! A Prodigy ! admit him." The Servant did so, just to let Mr. *Handel* behold the Ruins of the greatest Wit that ever lived along the Tide of Time, where all at length are lost.

Vol. III, pp. 170 f. The author died in 1751 and the Memoirs were edited by her son in Dublin. The passage refers to August 1742. It was first quoted in the *Monthly Review, or Literary Journal* of December 1754 (XI. 409), then in *Jackson's Oxford Journal* of 29th January 1791, and finally in *Records of my Life* (I. 334) by John Taylor, the younger, in 1832.

1755

FROM BENJAMIN MARTIN'S "MISCELLANEOUS CORRESPONDENCE IN
PROSE AND VERSE", January 1755

To Mr. Handel. On the Loss of Sight

Homer and Milton might complain
They roll'd their sightless orbs in vain ;
Yet both have wing'd a daring flight,
Illumin'd by celestial light.
Then let not old Timotheus [1] yield,
Or, drooping, quit th' advent'rous field ;
But let his art and vet'ran fire
Call forth the magic of his lyre ;
Or make the pealing organ speak
In sounds that might the dead awake :
Or gently touch the springs of woe,
Teach sighs to heave, or tears to flow :
Then with a more exalted rage
Give raptures to the sacred page,
Our glowing hearts to heaven raise
In choral songs and hymns of praise.

(Bishop, p. viii.)   The *Miscellaneous Correspondence*, " containing a Variety of
Subjects, relative to Natural and Civil History ", was a monthly journal, edited by
Benjamin Martin.   The poem was reprinted in the book-edition, 1759, I, 5.   It is,
perhaps, fitting to insert here what Burney wrote about Handel's playing of the
organ during the last years of his life (1785, pp. 29 f.) : " To see him . . . led to
the organ . . . at upwards of seventy years of age, and then conducted towards
the audience to make his accustomed obeisance, was a sight so truly afflicting and
deplorable to persons of sensibility, as greatly diminished their pleasure in hearing
him perform."

———

John Christopher Smith's opera *The Fairies* is produced at Drury
Lane Theatre, 3rd February 1755.
G. C. D. Odell (*Shakespeare from Betterton to Irving*, I. 358) attributes the
text to David Garrick.   Loewenberg (p. 116) corrected this statement in
accordance with Garrick's letter to James Murphy French of December
1756 and Horace Walpole's letter to Richard Bentley of 23rd February
1755 : the text was written by Smith himself and was based on Shakespeare's *A Midsummer Night's Dream*.   Garrick produced the opera, an

[1] A musician, in the times of *Philip* of *Macedon*, banish'd by the *Spartans* for adding
a tenth string to the lyre.

English one, in opposition to the Italian Opera. See his prologue, quoted at the end of February 1755.

———

FROM THE " PUBLIC ADVERTISER ", 14th February 1755

At the Theatre-Royal in Covent-Garden, This Day will be presented ALEXANDER'S FEAST. With an Interlude call'd The CHOICE of HERCULES. . . . To begin exactly at Six o'Clock.

Cf. 9th March 1753. Repeat performance on 19th February. This was the beginning of a new oratorio season. In the *Public Advertiser* of 8th February 1755, and subsequently, were advertised the performances at the New Theatre in the Haymarket, of " Mrs. Midnight's Route. In which will be introduced a Burlesque *Ode*, after the Manner of Alexander's Feast. "

———

FROM THE " PUBLIC ADVERTISER ", 21st February 1755

At the Theatre-Royal in Covent-Garden, This Day will be performed L'ALLEGRO ED IL PENSEROSO. With Dryden's ODE on *St. Cecilia's Day*. . . . To begin exactly at Half an Hour after Six o'Clock.

Cf. 18th March 1743. There was one performance only.

———

FROM THE SAME

NEW MUSICK.

.   .   .   .

Printed for J. Walsh.
Of whom may be had,
Handel's Songs, selected from all his Oratorios, for the Harpsichord and Voice, bound in three Volumes, or in twelve Collections unbound, at 5s. each.
The Instrumental Parts may be had separately, to compleat them for Concerts. . . .

This collection now comprised 240 songs ; volume 3 was new.

———

FROM " JACKSON'S OXFORD JOURNAL ", 22nd February 1755

Oxford, Feb. 22. On Monday next [the 24th] at the Music Room *L'Allegro Il Penseroso* will be perform'd.

———

MRS. DELANY TO MRS. DEWES

Bolton Row, 22 Feb., 1755.
My brother and Mr. Thynne dined with us at Babess's and at six went to the Oratorio Penseroso, &c.—very well performed. I hope you will come time enough for an oratorio or two.

(Delany, III. 334.) Mrs. Delany was still on a visit to London. Their brother was Bernard Granville.

—

FROM THE " PUBLIC ADVERTISER ", 26th February 1755

At the Theatre-Royal in Covent-Garden, This Day will be performed an Oratorio, call'd SAMSON. . . . To begin exactly at Half an Hour after Six o'Clock.

Cf. 29th March 1754. Repeat performance on 7th March.

—

FROM THE " PUBLIC ADVERTISER ", 28th February 1755

At the Theatre-Royal in Covent-Garden, This Day will be performed an Oratorio, call'd JOSEPH and HIS BRETHREN. . . . To begin exactly Half an Hour after Six o'Clock.

Cf. 20th March 1747. There was one performance only.

—

FROM THE " GENTLEMAN'S MAGAZINE ", February 1755

PROLOGUE *to the* FAIRIES. *An* OPERA.
Written and spoken by Mr. GARRICK.

.   .   .   .

Three nights ago, I heard a *Tête a Tête*
Which fix'd, at once, our *English opera's* fate :
One was a youth born here, but flush from *Rome.*
The *other* born abroad, but here his home ;
And first the *English foreigner* began,
Who thus address'd the *foreign Englishman* :
An *English opera* ! 'tis not to be borne ;
I, both my country, and their music scorn,
Oh, damn their *Ally Croakers*, and their *Early-Horn.*
Signor si—bat sons—wors recitativo :
Il tutto, è bestiale e cativo,
This said, I made my *exit*, full of terrors !
And now ask mercy, for the following errors :
   Excuse us first, for foolishly supposing,
Your *countryman* could please you in composing ;
An *op'ra* too !—play'd by an *English* band,
Wrote in a language which you understand—
I dare not say, WHO wrote it—I could tell ye,
To soften matters—Signor Shakespearelli : . . .
But why would this rash fool, this *Englishman*,
Attempt an *op'ra* ?—'tis the strangest plan !

Struck with the wonders of his master's art,
Whose *sacred dramas* shake and melt the heart,
Whose heaven-born strains the coldest breast inspire,
Whose *chorus-thunder* sets the soul on fire !
Inflam'd, astonish'd ! at those magic airs,
When *Samson* groans, and frantic *Saul* despairs,
The pupil wrote—his work is now before ye,
And waits your stamp of infamy, or glory.
Yet, ere his errors and his faults are known,
He says, those faults, those errors, are his own ;
If thro' the clouds appear some glimm'ring rays,
They're sparks he caught from his great master's blaze !

(Schoelcher, p. 335.) Cf. 3rd February. The authorship of the text is revealed in Garrick's prologue. Smith was Handel's pupil in composition ; he was, of course, naturalized, like his master. According to Walpole, there were two Italians and a French girl in the cast, besides the chapel boys. For Garrick's acquaintance with Handel cf. 12th August 1742.

———

MRS. DELANY TO MRS. DEWES

Bulstrode, 3rd March, 1755.

I wrote you a letter last week with a full account of my travels to and in London. The oratorio was miserably thin ; the Italian opera is in high vogue, and always full, though one song of the least worthy of Mr. Handel's music is worth all their frothy compositions.

(Delany, III. 338 f.) Cf. 22nd February. Mrs. Delany seems to refer here to "Joseph and his Brethren" on 28th February. At the Haymarket Theatre, the Italian opera, under the management of Vanneschi, had a new star, Regina Mingotti.

———

FROM THE "PUBLIC ADVERTISER", 5th March 1755

At the Theatre-Royal in Covent-Garden, This Day will be performed an Oratorio, call'd THEODORA. . . . To begin exactly at Half an Hour after Six o'Clock.

Cf. 16th March 1750. There was one performance only.

———

FROM THE "PUBLIC ADVERTISER", 11th March 1755

For the Benefit of Miss TURNER.

At the Great Room in Dean-street, Soho, This Day . . . will be performed ESTHER. An ORATORIO. Composed by Mr. *Handel*. The Vocal Parts by Miss *Turners*, &c. . . .

———

From the " Public Advertiser ", 12th March 1755

At the Theatre-Royal in Covent-Garden, This Day will be performed an Oratorio, call'd Judas Macchabaeus. . . . To begin exactly at Half an Hour after Six o'Clock.

Cf. 27th March 1754. Repeat performance on 14th March.

———

From " Jackson's Oxford Journal ", 15th March 1755

On Monday, the 17th of March, will be perform'd at the Music-Room in Holywell, the Oratorio of *Judas Maccabeus*, being the Last Performance in the Old Subscription. The First Performance in the New Subscription, on the 31st of March, will be the two last Parts of The *Messiah*.

No. 98, p. 3.

———

From the " Public Advertiser ", 17th March 1755

For the Benefit and Increase of a Fund establish'd for the Support of Decay'd Musicians, or their Families.

At the King's Theatre in the Haymarket, This Day will be perform'd a Grand Entertainment of Vocal and Instrumental Musick . . . Part III. . . . Song, *Return, O God of Hosts*, compos'd by Mr. Handel, sung by Signora Frasi. . . . Grand Concerto, compos'd by Mr. Handel. . . .

The song is from *Samson*.

———

From the " Public Advertiser ", 19th March 1755

At the Theatre-Royal in Covent-Garden, This Day will be performed a Sacred Oratorio, call'd Messiah. . . . To begin exactly at Half an Hour after Six o'Clock.

Cf. 5th April 1754. Repeat performance on 21st March ; this was the end of the season.

———

William Shenstone to Lady Luxborough, 30th March 1755

The Leasowes, March the 29, 1755.

. . . 'Tis now Sunday March the thirtieth. . . .

I was shewn a Letter yesterday from Sr Harry Gough to Mr. Pixell, which said Sir H. laments that the Town at Present is much fonder of Arne than Handel. . . .

(Shenstone, *Letters*, Oxford edition, p. 438.) Sir Henry Gough, of Edgbaston, was a friend of the Rev. John Pixell, an amateur composer. On 12th March 1755

Thomas Augustine Arne produced his first oratorio, called *Abel*, from which the Hymn of Eve became very popular.

———

FROM THE " LONDON DAILY ADVERTISER ", 5th April 1755

From the INSPECTOR, April 5.

To the AUTHOR.

Sir,

A Pamphlet was delivered to me some few days since, containing the Plan of an Academy for the Encouragement of Genius, and the Establishment of Painting, Sculpture, and Architecture in Britain.

. . . In musick we have seen the composer of the Messiah, rewarded by the universal voice, with honourable advantages, continued to him many years ; and such as even caprice itself could never supersede more than for some short interval. As life declines in him, we see the master who has given examples of his abilities for succeeding him, distinguished much to his advantage, and yet more to his honour : The most warmly, by the most judicious. . . .

The paper is not in the British Museum, but the article was reprinted in the *London Magazine* of April 1755. " The Inspector " was the title of the regular leader of the paper, probably written by the " author ", or editor, himself. In March 1755 the *London Magazine* published a poem by Boyce on the same subject, an Academy of Fine Arts.

———

FROM THE " PUBLIC ADVERTISER ", 18th April 1755

Hospital for the Maintenance and Education of exposed and deserted young Children.

This is to give Notice, That towards the Support of this Charity, the Sacred Oratorio called MESSIAH, will be performed in the Chapel of this Hospital on Thursday the 1st of May 1755, at Twelve o'Clock at Noon precisely. . . .

By Order of the General Committee,

S. MORGAN, Sec.

The advertisements of the *Messiah* performances in the Foundling Hospital in 1755 and 1756 do not mention Handel's name. John Christopher Smith conducted in his place.

———

FROM " JACKSON'S OXFORD JOURNAL ", 26th April 1755

At the Musick-Room, in Oxford, On Monday, the fifth of May, will be performed The Oratorio of *Athalia*.

Athalia was produced at Oxford on 10th July 1733.

———

FROM BODDELY'S " BATH JOURNAL ", 28th April 1755

On Wednesday, the 30th of this Instant April, At the THEATRE in ORCHARD-STREET, Will be perform'd the ORATORIO of Judas Maccabeus.

The principal Vocal Parts by Signiora Passerini, Mr. Sullivan, and Mr. Champness, With several good Voices from LONDON, SALISBURY, GLOUCESTER, and other Cathedrals. The Instrumental Parts by Signior Passerini, and several additional Performers. The Whole conducted by Mr. CHILCOT, who will play a Concerto on the Organ. And on Saturday, the 3d of May, will be perform'd The ORATORIO of SAMPSON. . . .

Thomas Chilcot, composer and conductor, had been organist of the Abbey Church, Bath, since 1733.

———

FROM THE " PUBLIC ADVERTISER ", 2nd May 1755

Yesterday the Messiah, composed by Mr. Handel, was performed at the Foundling Hospital for the Benefit of that Charity to a very numerous and polite Audience.

———

FROM " JACKSON'S OXFORD JOURNAL ", 3rd May 1755

Notice is hereby given, That the Performance of the Oratorio of *Athalia*, which is intended on Monday the 5th Instant, will, for the Convenience of the Subscribers and others, begin soon after Six-o'Clock.

———

FROM BODDELY'S " BATH JOURNAL ", 12th May 1755

At Mr. WILTSHIRE'S ROOM, On Wednesday, the 14th of May, will be perform'd the ORATORIO of Alexander's Feast. And on Saturday, the 17th of May, will be perform'd The MESSIAH. . . . The principal Vocal Parts by Signiora PASSERINI, Mr. COAFF, Mr. NORRIS, Mr. OFIELD, and Mr. CHAMPNES or Mr. HAYS ; with some other Voices from several Cathedrals. Those Ladies and Gentlemen who intend to honour them with their Presence, are desired to send their Names to Sig. PASSERINI. . . . N.B. Those Ladies and Gentlemen . . . may have Books of the Oratorio. . . After the Performance will be a Ball.

(Myers, 1948, p. 161.) The conductor was Dr. William Hayes. The singers were : Christina Passerini (soprano), (?) Corf (tenor), (Charles ?) Norris (. . .), Samuel Champness (bass), and Dr. Hayes (bass). Giuseppe Passerini was the leader, and perhaps the promoter, of these early performances of Handel's oratorios in Bath.

———

Handel buys £500 Reduced 3 per cent Annuities, 14th May 1755.

———

FROM " JACKSON'S OXFORD JOURNAL ", 21st June 1755

On Monday the 23d Instant, will be performed the Masque of *Acis and Galatea* ; being instead of the Choral Music for May last.

Choral Music for Monday the 30th Instant, will be *Alexander's Feast*.

Likewise on Wednesday the 2d of July will be performed the Oratorio of *Judas Maccabaeus*; being instead of the Choral Music for August next.

To each of these Performances, the Annual Subscribers will be admitted, by Virtue of their Tickets : Gentlemen and Ladies, without Tickets, to pay two Shillings and Six-pence each.

Cf. 15th (17th) March.

———

FROM THE SAME, 28th June 1755

Oxford, June 28, 1755

The Subscribers to the Musical Performances are desired to take Notice, That the Choral Music for Monday the 30th Instant, is, *Alexander's Feast* ; and that on Wednesday the 2d of July, will be performed the Oratorio of *Judas Maccabaeus*, being instead of the Choral Music for August next. . . .

N.B. As these Performances come so near to each other, it is intended to improve them with the following additional Instruments ; viz. An Hautboy, Trumpet, and Bassoon.

———

FROM THE SAME, 2nd August 1755

On Monday the 4th Instant, at the Music Room, will be perform'd L'Allegro il Penseroso, &c.

N.B. There will be no other Choral Performance till October.

Cf. 23rd (25th) February 1754 and 22nd (24th) February 1755.

———

FROM BERROW'S " WORCESTER JOURNAL ", 28th August 1755

[Three Choirs Meeting on 10th and 11th September at Worcester.]

Mr. Handel's New Te Deum and Jubilate, Mr. Purcell's Te Deum and Jubilate with Dr. Boyce's Additions, with a New Anthem composed for the last Meeting of the Corporation of the Sons of the Clergy at St. Paul's by Dr. Boyce, and Mr. Handel's Coronation Anthem, will be performed in the Cathedral Church.

The Oratorio of Sampson by Mr. Handel, and Dr. Boyce's Solomon with several other Pieces of Musick, will, in the Evenings of the said Days, be performed in the Great Hall in the College of Worcester. . . . Care has been taken to engage the best Masters that could be procured.— The Vocal Parts (beside the Gentlemen of the Three Choirs) will be performed by Mr. Beard, Mr. Wasse, Mr. Denham, Mr. Baildon, Miss Turner and Others. The Instrumental Parts by Mr. Brown, Mr. Miller, Mr. Adcock, Mr. Messing, &c &c—the Musick to be conducted by Dr. Boyce.

Beard (tenor), Wass (bass), Mr. Baildon and Miss Turner are already known ; Robert Denham, who had sung as a boy chorister in *Esther* on 23rd February 1732, became a useful member of the Meetings. Abraham Browne was the leader of the orchestra, Miller played the bassoon, Abraham Adcock the trumpet, and Messing the French horn. The charity of the Three Choirs was similar to that of the St. Paul's corporation.

———

FROM " JACKSON'S OXFORD JOURNAL ", 30th August 1755

Worcester, April [or rather, *August*] 28. From the general Preparation already making, there is the greatest Likelihood of a very grand and numerous Appearance at our Musick-Meeting, which begins on Wednesday se'nnight, the 10th of September.

———

FROM THE SAME, 20th September 1755

Worcester, Sept. 11. At the Triennial Meeting here, last Week, of the Three Choirs (Worcester, Glocester, and Hereford) the two Days Collection at the Cathedral amounted as follow, viz.

	l.	s.	d.	
On Wednesday,———	192	5	0	Halfpenny
On Thursday,———	56	1	6	
Sent in afterwards,———	3	3	0	
Total	251	9	6	Halfpenny

Which is 67*l.* 17*s.* 6*d.* Halfpenny more than was collected here this Time three Years, and upwards of 64*l.* more than was collected last Year at Gloucester.—*So considerable an Increase in this charitable Collection, must needs be a very pleasing Reflection to every noble and compassionate Mind.*

———

FROM THE SAME, 22nd November 1755

On Monday next, the 24th Instant, At the Music Room, will be performed, *Dryden's Ode on St. Cecilia's Day,* And *Handell's Te Deum.*

It is related that *Alexander's Feast* was performed on that day, with the (Dettingen) *Te Deum* ; but this seems to be a mistake.

———

FROM FAULKNER'S " DUBLIN JOURNAL ", 6th December 1755

On Thursday last [the 4th] Mr. Handel's Grand Te Deum Jubilate and two Anthems, were performed at St. Andrew's Church . . . for the Support of Mercer's Hospital ; his Excellency the Lord Lieutenant honoured the Hospital with his Presence. . . .

———

MRS. DELANY TO MRS. DEWES

Spring Gardens, 11 Dec. 1755.

I had two musical entertainments offered me yesterday—a concert at Lady Cowper's, and Mr. Handel at Mrs. Donnellan's. She has got a new harpsichord of Mr. Kirkman's, but public calamities and private distress takes up too much of my thoughts to admit of amusement at present.

(Delany, III. 383.) " Spring Gardens ", the new London home of the Delanys, had been bought by Mrs. Delany in 1754. Countess Georgina Cowper arranged regular concerts at her house. Jacob Kirkman, of German origin, was a famous harpsichord builder. Apparently Handel was invited by Mrs. Donellan to try the instrument. Cf. 12th April 1734.

———

FROM FELIX FARLEY's " BRISTOL JOURNAL ", 20th December 1755

On Wednesday, the 14th of January, 1756, will be open'd the New Musick Room with the oratorio of the Messiah, the band will be composed of the principal performers, (vocal and instrumental) from London, Oxford, Salisbury, Gloucester, Wells, Bath, &c. Between the acts will be performed a concerto on the organ, by Mr. Broderip, and a solo on the violin, by Mr. Pinto. . . .

(Myers, 1948, p. 161.) Latimer, p. 308. The extracts from the Bristol papers, 1756–8, were contributed by Mr. G. E. Maby, of the University Library, Bristol. John Broderip had been organist at Wells since 1741. (He was the father of Robert Broderip, the music publisher ; cf. Chatterton's poems, and London Chronicle, 10th October 1758.) The New Music Room, erected in 1754/5, was in Prince's Street. Two letters by " Laicus Philalethes ", in the Bristol Journal of 10th and 17th January 1756, refer to " the elegance of the room " and the " brilliant and numerous company ".

———

WILLIAM MASON TO THOMAS GRAY, 25th December 1755

Chiswick Dec. 25th—55
. . . There is a sweet Song in Demofoonte called Ogni Amante sung by Riccarelli. Pray look at it. Tis almost $\dfrac{\text{Notatim}}{\text{verbatim}}$ the Air in Ariadne, but I think better. I am told tis a very old one of Scarlattis wch if true Handel is almost a musical Lauder.

Gray, Correspondence, I. 451. Mason was Gray's friend, and became his biographer. (He was staying at Chiswick, with Lord Holderness.) Demofoonte, text by Metastasio (1732), was a pasticcio opera, produced at the Haymarket Theatre on 9th December 1755. Walsh printed the Favourite Songs, including the one quoted, shortly afterwards. It was sung by Signor Ricciarelli (see Messiah performance of 3rd May 1759). There is a resemblance between the duet " Mira adesso " from Handel's Arianna and the trio " Ecco il ciel di luce " in Domenico Scarlatti's Narciso ; but they have no affinity with " Ogni amante " from Demofoonte. William Lauder was a literary forger, exposed in 1756 : he attempted to prove, by forgery, that Milton was a plagiarist. Handel had also been accused of plagiarism by Mattheson. For Mason, cf. 16th November 1750 ; for Gray, 26th February 1752. In 1778 Mason wrote to Horace Walpole deprecatingly about Handel (1891 edition of Walpole's Letters, VII. 26, note).

———

FROM JOHANN CHRISTOPH VON DREYHAUPT'S "BESCHREIBUNG DES . . . SAALE-KREISES . . . INSONDERHEIT DER STÄDTE HALLE, ETC." ("DESCRIPTION OF THE . . . SAALE DISTRICT . . . PARTICULARLY OF THE TOWNS OF HALLE, ETC."), HALLE, 1750 (Translated)

194. GEORG FRIEDRICH HAENDEL

A highly famous *musician* and Capellmeister, for some time resident in England. . . . He had from youth up a great urge towards *music* . . . On his journey in Italy, because of his great skill and technical device in playing the harpsichord, [he was] greatly admired even by the Italians, indeed, such playing was ascribed by several superstitious people to secret, diabolical art. He . . . is unmarried, and lives at present in London, where as *Director* of the *Opera* he enjoys a large *pension*. Of his *compositions* the following operas were performed at the Hamburg Theatre : *Almira*, 1704. *Nero*, 1705. *Florindo* and *Daphne*, 1708. *Rinaldo*, 1715. *Oriana*, 1717. *Agrippina*, 1718. *Zenobia*, 1721. *Muzio Scaevola*, and *Floridante*, 1723. *Tamerlan* and *Julius Caesar* in Egypt, 1725. *Otto*, King of Germany, 1726. . . .

Vol. II, p. 625. The heading of the list is : "Pagus Neletici et Nudzici". The no. 194 refers to the lives of famous Halle citizens ; no. 195 is Handel's half-brother, Gottfried Händel, Dr. med., who died of the plague in 1682. The preface to volume I is dated 1749 ; that to volume II, 30th September 1750, Halle. Handel's modest pensions, paid by the Court, had nothing to do with the Opera. *Oriana* was the Hamburg title for *Amadigi*, *Zenobia* that for *Radamisto*.—This item should have been inserted on page 699.

A NEW SONG

The Words by a Gentleman on hearing a little Miss perform on the Harpsicord and German Flute. Set to Musick by Mr. Richard Davies, ca. 1755.

> In *Handel*'s works she does rejoyce
> Tho' ass in *Chaplet* was by *Choice*
> Design'd to make us jolly.
> She said, A *Song* I never like
> But when both words and Musick strike
> So answer'd pritty *Polly*.

Single sheet folio ; copies in the British Museum and in Gerald Coke's Handel Collection. The stanza quoted is the third of four. The author of the text is not known. The poem probably refers to Marianne Davies, and Richard Davies may have been a relative of the two sisters. Cf. 30th April 1735, 19th March 1753 and 28th April 1756. The reference to William Boyce's musical entertainment, *The Chaplet*, text by Moses Mendez, produced at Drury Lane Theatre on 2nd December 1749, is not clear ; nor is the allusion to one of several "Pretty Polly" songs.

XXX. HANDEL : A CARTOON

Engraved by Joseph Goupy, 1754. (Fitzwilliam Museum)

See page 748

XXXI. MARY DELANY, *née* GRANVILLE

Engraving by Joseph Brown, 1861, after an enamel
portrait. (Fitzwilliam Museum)

See pages 31 and 825

1756

Messiah is performed at Bristol, 14th January 1756.
Cf. 20th December 1755.

———

FROM "JACKSON'S OXFORD JOURNAL", 24th January 1756

Oxford, January 24, 1756.
The Subscribers are desired to take Notice, that, on Monday, February 2, the Choral Music will be the Oratorio of *Esther*. This Performance is postponed a Week longer than was intended, with the Hopes of making the Boys tolerably perfect in their Parts ; being all very young and inexperienced, and upon that Account hope favourable Allowances will be made.

———

MRS. DELANY TO MRS. DEWES

New Street, Spring Gardens,
31st Jan., 1756.
My brother is very happy : he has made a purchase of *an organ that proves excellent*, I have not yet seen it.

(Delany, III. 405.) An anonymous note, quoted in the second series of Delany's Autobiography, I (IV). 568, and probably given by Handel to Bernard Granville, the owner of this organ, runs : " Father Smith's chamberorgans generally consist of a stop diapason of all wood. Sometimes there is an open diapason of wood. Down to Cesaut, an open flute of wood, a fifteenth of wood, a bass mixture of wood ; that is to the middle C. of two ranks, the cornet of wood of two ranks to meet the mixture in the middle. Sometimes the mixture is of mettle, as is the cornet. N.B.—If it is stil'd ' *a furniture* ' it is *not* one of his, that is, *if* the mixture is stil'd so *it is not*. Remark that the wooden pipes are all clean yallow deal." Mr. Granville, under Handel's supervision, bought an organ by Father Smith, *i.e.* Bernard Smith, who had built the organ in St. Paul's Cathedral, which had been an attraction for Handel in 1718-19.

———

John Christopher Smith's opera, *The Tempest*, is produced at Drury Lane Theatre, 11th February 1756.
Cf. 3rd February 1755. Like his *Fairies*, this opera was based on Shakespeare. (Odell, p. 362.)

———

FROM "JACKSON'S OXFORD JOURNAL", 21st February 1756

Notice is hereby given, That the next Choral Music will be on Monday, the First of March ; and that the Performance will be the First and Second Acts of the Oratorio of *Samson*.
Cf. 13th (22nd) March.

———

H.-25

FROM THE " NORWICH MERCURY ", 28th February 1756

CAMBRIDGE, *February 26.*

On Thursday [the 26th] Night the Mask of Acis and Galatea was perform'd at Trinity College Hall, before a very numerous Audience, and was conducted by Dr. Randall, Professor of Musick in this University.

(Deutsch, in *Cambridge Review*, 25th April 1942.) John Randall, who, as a boy, had sung Esther on 23rd February 1732, and, as a youth, had turned the pages for Handel at the production of the " Funeral Anthem " on 17th December 1737, became organist of King's College, Cambridge, in 1743, and succeeded Maurice Greene as Professor of Music at Cambridge University in 1755, taking his doctor's degree in 1756. He also became organist of Trinity, St. John's and Pembroke Colleges.

———

FROM THE " PUBLIC ADVERTISER ", 5th March 1756

At the Theatre Royal in Covent-Garden, This Day . . . will be presented an Oratorio call'd ATHALIA. . . . To begin exactly at Six o'Clock.

Cf. 1st April 1735. Repeat performances on 10th and 12th March. This was the beginning of the oratorio season. Watts advertised a new word-book (copy in the British Museum) on 1st March.

———

FROM THE " NEW YORK MERCURY ", 8th March 1756

On Thursday the 18th instant, will be open'd at the City Hall in the City of New York, a *New Organ*, made by Gilbert Ash, where will be performed, a *Concert* of Vocal and Instrumental Musick. In which, among a variety of other selected pieces, will be introduced a song, in praise of musick, particularly of an organ ; and another favourite song, called ' The Sword that's drawn in Virtue's cause ', both compos'd by Mr. Handel. . . .

(Sonneck, 1907, p. 162.) The second song is from the *Occasional Oratorio*. The first may have been the additional song to *Alexander's Feast* : " Your voices tune and raise them high ".

———

FROM " JACKSON'S OXFORD JOURNAL ", 13th March 1756

Oxon, March 10, 1756.

Those Gentlemen who are inclin'd to favour the Musical Society with their Subscriptions for the ensuing year, are desired to take Notice, That the Performances of that Society will be continued from Lady-Day next, to Lady-Day 1757, in the same Manner, and upon the same Conditions, as are contain'd in the printed Articles for this present Year.

H. B. Steward.

N.B. The next Choral Music will be on Monday the 22d Inst. and the Performance, *Mr. Handel's Te Deum compos'd for the Victory at Dettingen,* and the *last Act of Samson.*

Cf. 21st February (1st March).

———

FROM THE " PUBLIC ADVERTISER ", 17th March 1756

At the Theatre Royal in Covent-Garden, This Day will be performed an Oratorio call'd ISRAEL IN EGYPT. . . . To begin exactly at Half an Hour after Six o'Clock.

Cf. 1st April 1740. Repeat performance on 24th March.

———

FROM THE " PUBLIC ADVERTISER ", 19th March 1756

At the Theatre Royal in Covent-Garden, This Day, will be performed an Oratorio call'd DEBORAH. . . . To begin exactly at Half an Hour after Six o'Clock.

Cf. 8th March 1754. There was one performance only.

———

FROM THE " PUBLIC ADVERTISER ", 26th March 1756

At the Theatre Royal in Covent-Garden, This Day will be performed an Oratorio call'd JUDAS MACCHABAEUS. . . . To begin exactly at Half an Hour after Six o'Clock.

Cf. 12th March 1755. Repeat performance on 31st March.

———

MRS. DELANY TO MRS. DEWES

Spring Gardens, 27th March 1756.

Mary is now practising the clavichord, which I have got in the dining-room that I may hear her practise at my leisure moments. . . . Her uncle Granville has given her a guinea to go to the oratorio ; it is diverting to hear all her projects for laying it out. I think it will end in two plays *instead* of *one oratorio.*

We are both invited to go to Lady Cowper's next Wednesday [the 31st] to a concert ; I shall carry her there, and give up the oratorio. . . .

Wednesday, I spent with Mrs. Donnellan instead of going to Israel in Egypt ; and how provoking ! she had Mrs. Montagu, Mrs. Gosling, and two or three fiddle faddles, so that I might as well have been at the oratorio.

I was last night at " Judas Maccabeus ", it was charming and full. " Israel in Egypt " did not take, it is too solemn for common ears.

(Chrysander, III. 102.) Delany, III. 415, 417. Mary, Anne Dewes's daughter, then about ten years of age, was Mrs. Delany's and Bernard Granville's niece. The concert was at Countess Georgina Cowper's (cf. 11th December 1755). Mrs. Donellan's guests were Mrs. Elizabeth Montagu and Mrs. Gosling, a banker's wife. *Israel in Egypt* was performed on 17th March, *Judas Maccabaeus* on 26th and 31st March.

FROM THE " PUBLIC ADVERTISER ", 2nd April 1756

At the Theatre Royal in Covent-Garden, This Day will be performed an Oratorio call'd JEPHTHA. . . . To begin exactly at Half an Hour after Six o'Clock.

Cf. 16th March 1753. There was one performance only.

MRS. DELANY TO MRS. DEWES

Spring Gardens, 1st [or rather 3rd] April, 1756.

The oratorio last night was " Jephtha " ; I never heard it before ; I think it a very fine one, but very different from any of his others.

(Delany, III. 419.) The date, as given in the *Autobiography* must be wrong. Handel's name is not mentioned in the letter.

FROM THE " PUBLIC ADVERTISER ", 7th April 1756

At the Theatre Royal in Covent-Garden, This Day will be performed a Sacred Oratorio, call'd MESSIAH. . . . To begin exactly at Half an Hour after Six o'Clock.

Cf. 19th March 1755. Repeat performance on 9th April, " Being the *Last* this *Season* ", *i.e.* the end of the oratorio season.

FROM THE MINUTES OF THE GENERAL COMMITTEE OF THE FOUNDLING HOSPITAL, 7th April 1756

Mr. Handel having renewed his charitable offer of performing the Oratorio ' Messiah ' at the Chapel of this Hospital,

Resolved—That the said performance be on Wednesday, the 19th of next Month, and that the Secretary do write a letter to Mr. Handel to return him Thanks and acquaint him with the Day fix'd upon, and to desire that he will please to give people Directions to Mr. Smith the Organist of this Hospital, in relation thereto.

(*Musical Times*, 1st May 1902.) John Christopher Smith was now Handel's representative.

FROM THE " PUBLIC ADVERTISER ", 10th April 1756

The *Rehearsal* of the *Music* for the *Feast* of the *Sons* of the *Clergy*, will be at St. Paul's on Tuesday the 4th, and the Feast at Merchant Taylors-Hall, on Thursday the 6th Day of May next. . . .

☞ Mr. Handel's Overture in Esther, Grand Te Deum, Jubilate and Coronation Anthem, with a new Anthem by Dr. Boyce, will be Vocally and Instrumentally performed.

Note, In order that the Choir may be kept as warm as possible, the West Doors only will be opened. . . .

—

MISS CATHARINE TALBOT TO MRS. ELIZABETH CARTER

St. Paul's, April 13, 1756.

The only public place I have been to this winter, was last Friday [the 9th], to hear the Messiah, nor can there be a nobler entertainment. I think it is impossible for the most trifling not to be the better for it. I was wishing all the Jews, Heathens, and Infidels in the world (a pretty full house you'll say) to be present. The Morocco Ambassador was there, and if his interpreter could do justice to the divine words (the music any one that has a heart must feel) how must he be affected, when in the grand choruses the whole audience solemnly rose up in joint acknowledgment that He who for our sakes *had been despised and rejected of men*, was *their Creator, Redeemer, King of kings, Lord of lords* ! To be sure the playhouse is an unfit place for such a solemn performance, but I fear I shall be in Oxfordshire before it is to be heard at the Foundling Hospital, where the benevolent design and the attendance of the little boys and girls adds a peculiar beauty even unto this noblest composition. But Handel who could suit such music to such words deserves to be maintained, and these two nights [7th and 9th March], I am told, have made amends for the solitude of his other oratorios. How long even this may be fashionable I know not, for next winter there will be (if the French come) two operas ; and the opera and oratorio taste are, I believe, totally incompatible. Well they may !

(Carter, *Letters*, II. 226 f.) If another season of French comic opera was, in fact, planned at the New Theatre in the Haymarket, it seems to have come to nothing. At the Haymarket Theatre, Vanneschi went bankrupt, and Signora Mingotti and Giardini became the managers for one year (1756–7). See Burney, IV. 467.

—

FROM "JACKSON'S OXFORD JOURNAL", 24th April 1756

Oxford, April 23, 1756.

Choral Music To be perform'd on Monday next [the 26th] is, The Third Part of *Messiah*, and two *Coronation Anthems*, viz. *My Heart is inditing*, &c., *The King shall rejoice*, &c.

—

Marianne Davies gives a concert at the Great Room in Dean Street, Soho, 28th April 1756. (*Public Advertiser.*)

(Squire in Grove's *Dictionary*, first edition, IV. 608.) Cf. 30th April 1751 and 19th March 1753.

—

From Jacob Wilhelm Lustig's "Samenspraaken over muzikaale beginselen" (Discourses on the rudiments of music), Amsterdam, April 1756 (Translated)

Hendel always gives convincing proofs of great sense and profound deliberation ; in fact, all his compositions show clearly how pure and delicate his taste in the fine arts must be. He seems to surpass Telemann in grace ; it also seems that his Italian vocal music, long since admired in Italy, and his incomparable keyboard music are almost indispensable to connoisseurs. . . .

11. Georg Friedrich Hendel, Master of Music to His Royal British Majesty, etc. ; elected spontaneously by all the members [of the " Society of Music Sciences "] *honoris causa*.

No. 4, pp. 159 and 204. The first passage is taken from a comparison between Kuhnau, Kaiser, Telemann and Handel. The second paragraph is from a list of the members of Mizler's " Societät " (see 1745 and 1746). Lustig's periodical appeared monthly, but the numbers bear the date of the year only. His order of merit among the German composers is taken from Scheibe (cf. middle of 1745). See J. du Saar, *Het leven en de werken van Jacob Wilhelm Lustig*, Amsterdam 1948.

———

Mrs. Cecilia Arne advertises her benefit concert for 4th May 1756 at the Music Hall in Fishamble Street, Dublin, with selections from T. A. Arne's *Alfred* and Handel's *Samson* (Faulkner's *Dublin Journal*).

The concert was postponed till 15th May, and finally cancelled. (Faulkner's *Dublin Journal*, 20th April 1756, etc.) See *Musical Antiquary*, July 1910, p. 230.

———

From the " Public Advertiser ", 8th May 1756

Hospital *for the Maintenance and Education of exposed and deserted young Children.*

This is to give Notice, that towards the Support of this Charity, the Sacred Oratorio called Messiah, will be performed in the Chapel of this Hospital on Wednesday the 19th instant, at Twelve o'Clock at Noon precisely. . . .

By Order of the General Committee.

S. Morgan, Sec.

As in 1755, Handel's name is not mentioned ; Smith conducted. The tickets were half a Guinea each.

———

From " Jackson's Oxford Journal ", 22nd May 1756

On Monday the 24th Instant, Will be performed, The *Mask* of *Acis and Galatea* : being The Choral Musick for the present Month.

Oxford, May 21, 1756.

Cf. 21st (23rd) June 1755.

———

FROM LUSTIG'S " SAMENSPRAAKEN ", AMSTERDAM, May 1756
(Translated)

In our last issue I forgot to tell you that the judgment of the author of the *Critischer Musikus*, placing those masters of music, Hasse and Graun, above all other composers known to him (p. 160), is based only on their ability to handle vocal music of [a certain] kind. On pp. 776-794 of that book he gives irrefutable proofs of this taken from their operas *La clemenza di Tito*, *Rodelinda* and *Cleopatra* without, however, giving any musical examples to illustrate his argument ; but this, of course, does not mean one could not find similar examples in the works of Hendel and some other composers.

No. 5, p. 234. The author of *Der critische Musikus* was Scheibe. The operas mentioned are : *Tito Vespasiano* by Hasse, *Rodelinda* and *Cleopatra e Cesare* by Graun. (See mid 1745.)

———

FROM " JACKSON'S OXFORD JOURNAL ", 19th June 1756

Oxford, June 19.

On Tuesday the 6th of July (being the day appointed for commemorating the Benefactors to the University) will be performed in the Theatre, the Oratorio of Judas Maccabaeus ; on Wednesday the 7th, Joshua ; and on Thursday the 8th, the Messiah. The principal Parts to be sung by Signora Frasi, Miss Young, Mr. Beard, Mr. Thomas Hayes, and Others. The Choruses will be supported by a great Number of Voices and Instruments of every Kind requisite, and no Expense will be spared to make the whole as grand as possible.

Repeat performance on 3rd July.

———

Handel buys £1,000 Reduced 3 per cent Annuities, 23rd June 1756.

———

FROM LUSTIG'S " SAMENSPRAAKEN ", AMSTERDAM, June 1756
(Translated)

The Society of Music Science decided unanimously to commemorate its foundation by a medal in gold, silver and copper, to be engraved by the famous Andreas Vestner, senator and medallist at Nuremberg. For a Hasse in Italy, a Handel in England and a Telemann in France are sufficient proof that German composers are supreme even in the styles of their adopted countries.

No. 6, p. 287. The passage again refers to the Mizler " Societät ". Vestner died in 1754. Cf. Mizler, 1746.

———

FROM " JACKSON'S OXFORD JOURNAL ", 10th July 1756

Oxford, July 10. . . . During these three Days [6th till ·8th] the Oratorio's (conducted by Dr. Hayes) were attended with crowded

Audiences, viz. on Tuesday Evening, Judas Maccabaeus ; on Wednesday, Joshua ; on Thursday, the Messiah ; all composed by Mr. Handel.

According to pencil notes in the Bodleian copy of the word-book of "Joshua " the cast was as follows :

Joshua—Mr. Beard, tenor
Caleb—Mr. [Thomas] Hayes, bass
Othniel—Miss Young (Mrs. Scott ?), contralto
Achsah—Signora Frasi, soprano
Angel—Dr. [William] Hayes, bass

The part of the Angel was originally written for a soprano. Hayes was Professor of Music at Oxford University.

———

THE FIRST CODICIL TO HANDEL'S WILL, 6th August 1756

I George Frideric Handel make this Codicil to my Will.

I give unto my Servant Peter le Blond Two Hundred Pounds additional to the Legacy already given him in my Will.

I give to M⸓ Christopher Smith Fifteen Hundred Pounds additional to the Legacy already given him in my Will.

I give to my Cousin Christian Gottlieb Handel of Coppenhagen Two Hundred Pounds additional to the Legacy given him in my Will.

My Cousin Magister Christian August Rotth being dead I give to his Widow Two Hundred Pounds and if she shall die before me I give the said Two Hundred Pounds to her Children.

The Widow of George Taust and one of her Children being dead I give to her Five remaining children Three Hundred Pounds apiece instead of the Legacy given to them by my Will.

I give to Doctor Morell of Turnham Green Two Hundred Pounds.

I give to M⸓ Newburgh Hamilton of Old Bond Street who has assisted me in adjusting words for some of my Compositions One Hundred Pounds.

I make George Amyand Esquire of Lawrence Pountney Hill London Merchant Coexecutor with my Niece mention'd in my Will, and I give him Two Hundred Pounds which I desire him to accept for the Care and Trouble he shall take in my Affairs. In Witness whereof I Have hereunto set my hand this Sixth day of August One Thousand and Seven Hundred and Fifty Six.

George Frideric Handel.

On the day and year above written this Codicil was read over to the said George Frideric Handel and was by him Sign'd and Publish'd in our Presence.

Tho: Harris.
John Hetherington.

(Schoelcher, pp. 325 and 341.) Cf. 1st June 1750. Magister Rotth died in 1752. The Rev. Thomas Morell was one of Handel's librettists : several word-books of the oratorios were written by him. George Amyand, a Hamburg merchant, probably Jewish, later became M.P. for Barnstaple and was created baronet in 1764. (Young, p. 77.) Thomas Harris was one of the three brothers of Salisbury. John Hetherington belonged to the Middle Temple. Cf. 22nd March 1757.

———

The *London Magazine* prints " A new Song " by Handel, August 1756.
" Ye verdant hills, ye balmy vales," was, in fact, an aria from *Susanna*.

———

FROM LUSTIG'S " SAMENSPRAAKEN ", AMSTERDAM, August 1756
(Translated)

It is only fair that every piece of music should be judged according to the purpose for which it was composed ; *e.g.*, the keyboard fugues of Hendel, J. S. Bach and Hurlebusch will not, like opera arias, please every listener at once ; on the contrary, they are suited only to those amateurs who take the trouble to hear, to play, in ᴵᵉed to study them often.

No. 8, p. 392. The name of Handel also appears in the September issue of Lustig's magazine, where he quotes the anonymous letter addressed to the " Marquis de B.", published in Berlin in 1748. (See *Addenda*.)

———

FROM " JACKSON'S OXFORD JOURNAL ", 4th September 1756

The Meeting of the *Three Choirs of Worcester, Glocester*, and *Hereford*, For the *Benefit* of the *Widows* and *Orphans* of the *Poor Clergy* of the *Three Dioceses*, Will be held at *Hereford* On *Wednesday* and *Thursday* the 15th and 16th of *September*. . . . On *Wednesday* will be performed, at the Cathedral, in the Morning, Mr. *Purcel's Te Deum* and *Jubilate*, with Dr. *Boyce's* Additions ; an *Anthem* of Dr. *Boyce's*, and Mr. *Handel's* celebrated *Coronation-Anthem* ; and at the College-Hall, in the Evening, the *Oratorio* of *Samson*, in which will be introduced the *Dead March* in *Saul*. On *Thursday* will be performed, at the Cathedral, in the Morning, Mr. *Handel's* New *Te Deum* and *Jubilate*, a New *Anthem* of Dr. *Boyce's*, and the same *Coronation-Anthem* ; and at the College-Hall, in the Evening, Dr. *Boyce's Solomon*, with several *Instrumental Pieces* of *Musick*. And on Friday Evening, at the College-Hall will be performed *L'Allegro*, *Il Penseroso*, and *Dryden's Ode*, set to Musick by Mr. *Handel*. The *Vocal Parts* by the Gentlemen of the *Three Choirs*, Signora *Frasi*, Mr. *Wass*, and Others. The *Instrumental Parts* by Signor *Arrigoni*, Mr. *Thompson*, Mr. *Millar*, Mr. *Adcock*, Mr. *Messinge*. There will be a *Ball* each Night in the College-Hall, gratis, for the Gentlemen and Ladies who favour the Concerts with their Company ; to which no Person will be admitted without a Concert Ticket. Tickets . . . Price 5s. . . . The Performers are desired to meet on Monday, the 13th, in the Morning, in order to rehearse, and to dine with the Stewards the Day following. There will

H.–25 *a*

be an Ordinary for the Subscribers and Others, on Wednesday at the Green-Dragon, and on Thursday at the Swan and Falcon.

Carlo Arrigoni, lutenist and composer, died about 1743 ; the leader at Hereford was probably a violinist of the name Arrizoni. (Robert ?) Thompson was a double bass player. (John ?) Miller, or Millar, played the bassoon, Abraham Adcock the trumpet, and (Frederick ?) Messing the French horn. Boyce conducted. An " Ordinary " was a post coach.

———

FROM THE " SALISBURY AND WINCHESTER JOURNAL ", 11th October 1756

On Wednesday and Thursday [the 6th and 7th] was celebrated our Musical Festival of St. Cecilia. There was each Morning a grand Performance in our Cathedral Church, by a large Band of Instruments and voices : the musick opened the first Day with a Concerto of Geminiani, and the second with a Concerto of Corelli ; after each of which, were perform'd in the Proper Parts of the Service, a Te Deum of Mr. Handel, and two of his Anthems. On the same Days, in the Evening, were perform'd at the Assembly-Room, the Musical Drama of Hercules, and the Oratorio of Esther, both compos'd by the incomparable Genius Mr. Handel. The Musick went off with great Spirit and Exactness, and was attentively heard by a very brilliant and polite Audience.

In the word-book of Esther (copy in the British Museum) the Salisbury Assembly Room is called the " Theatre ".

———

FROM " JACKSON'S OXFORD JOURNAL ", 23rd October 1756

Musick Room, On Monday Evening, the 25th Instant, will be performed, Handel's Te Deum, and Dryden's Ode on St. Cecilia's Day ; with an additional Bass Song.

Mee stated that Alexander's Feast was performed on this day.

———

FROM BODDELY'S " BATH JOURNAL ", 15th November 1756

Signor and Signora PASSERINI
Will perform the Two ORATORIOS of
JUDAS MACCABEUS and MESSIAH.

With an able Band of Vocal and Instrumental Performers, from London, Salisbury, and other Cathedrals ; the first Performance being Judas Maccabeus, will be at Mr. Wiltshire's Great Room, on Saturday next, the 20th Instant ; And that of the Messiah, at Mr. Simpson's Great Room, on Wednesday the 24th.

The Subscription is One Guinea, for which every Subscriber is to receive four Tickets, and a Book of each Oratorio. Tickets to Non-Subscribers, at Half-a-Guinea each for the Front-Seats ; and Five Shillings for the Back Places. Signor and Signora Passerini having experienced that the ordinary Price will not defray the Expence, as, with all the Success which they had here before, they received little or no Profit thereby, is the Reason of raising the Price of the single Tickets. They hope the Honour of a general Encouragement, and they will endeavour to give all the Satisfaction in their Power. . . .

From the " Public Advertiser ", 25th November 1756

For the Benefit of the *City* of *London Lying-In Hospital,*
in Aldersgate Street.

The Oratorio of Sampson will be performed at Haberdashers Hall in Maiden Lane, on Thursday the 2d of December next, at Six o'Clock in the Evening. . . .

(Schoelcher, p. 337.) See 2nd December. The performance was on 9th December, but the word-book bears the original date ; copy in the Schoelcher Collection, Conservatoire, Paris. Chrysander, in the preface to Vol. 22 (pp. II and IV) of the Collected Edition discusses the alterations made for this performance.

From Lustig's " Samenspraaken ", Amsterdam, November 1756
(Translated)

If one would conclude from Marchand's defeat in Dresden that he was a bad musician, it would be absolutely wrong. Hen . . . himself always made a point of avoiding the company of and contact with Bach, that Phoenix in composition and improvisation ! . . .

[From a list of famous musicians in Paris.]

Février, organist of the Royal Jesuit College, published two books of Pièces de clavecin, with beautiful fugues in Hendel's manner.

No. 11, pp. 594 and 598. Louis Marchand, a well-known French organist, avoided competition with J. S. Bach when challenged by him to play on the organ in Dresden, in 1717.—Henry Louis Février was a minor organist.

From the " Public Advertiser ", 2nd December 1756

The Oratorio of Sampson, which was to have been performed This Day . . . is obliged to be postponed till Thursday the 9th, on Account of the Indisposition of Signora Frasi. . . .

See 25th November.

From " Jackson's Oxford Journal ", 4th December 1756

Oxford, Dec. 4th, 1756.

The Choral Music on Monday next, the 6th Instant, will be the Oratorio of *Esther* ; in which are included, Two of the Coronation Anthems, viz. *My Heart is inditing*, and, *God save the King*.

N.B. Mr. Price is expected from Glocester, and Mr. Bidlecomb from Salisbury.

Price was one of the singers ; Bidlecomb played the trumpet.

FROM FAULKNER'S " DUBLIN JOURNAL ", 11th December 1756

By Appointment of a Committee of the Charitable Musical Society, for the Relief and Enlargement of Poor Prisoners confined for Debt in the several Marshalseas in the City and Liberties of Dublin. At the Great Musick-Hall in Fishamble Street, on Thursday the 16th of December 1756, will be performed the Grand Sacred Oratorio called the MESSIAH : Composed by Mr. *Handel*. The Whole is Conducted by Mr. *Lee*. . . .

Rehearsal on 13th December. Samuel Lee, a pupil of Dubourg, was Master of the City Music and had a music shop on the Little Green. In 1742 he is said to have acted as Handel's copyist (Flood, p. 40).

FROM THOMAS SHERIDAN'S " BRITISH EDUCATION : OR, THE SOURCE OF THE DISORDERS IN GREAT BRITAIN ", 1756

. . . What then must it [the mighty force of oratorial expression] be, when conveyed to the heart with all the superadded powers and charms of musick ? No person of sensibility, who has had the good fortune to hear Mrs Cibber sing in the oratorio of the Messiah, will find it very difficult to give credit to accounts of the most wonderful effects produced from so powerful an union. And yet it was not to any extraordinary powers of voice (whereof she has but a very moderate share) nor to a greater degree of skill in musick (wherein many of the Italians must be allowed to exceed her) that she owed her excellence, but to expression only ; her acknowledged superiority in which could proceed from nothing but skill in her profession.

(Myers, 1948, p. 100.) P. 417. Cf. 13th April 1742.

FROM JOSEPH WARTON'S " ESSAY ON THE GENIUS AND WRITINGS OF POPE ", 1756

. . . I have dwelt chiefly on this ode [Milton's ' On the Morning of Christ's Nativity '] as much less celebrated than L'Allegro and Il Penseroso, which are now universally known ; but which by a strange fatality lay in a sort of obscurity, the private enjoyment of a few curious readers, till they were set to admirable music by Mr. Handel. . . .

It is to be regretted, that Mr. Handel has not set to music the former [Pope's ' Ode for Music '], as well as the latter [Dryden's ' Alexander's Feast '], of these celebrated odes, in which he has displayed the combined powers of verse and voice, to a wonderful degree. No poem indeed, affords so much various matter for a composer to work upon ; as Dryden has here introduced and expressed all the greater passions, and as the transitions from one to the other are sudden and impetuous. Of which we feel the effects, in the pathetic description of the fall of Darius, that immediately succeeds the joyous praises of Bacchus. The symphony, and air particularly, that accompanies the four words, " fallen, fallen, fallen, fallen ", is strangely moving, and consists of a few simple and touching notes, without any of those intricate variations, and affected divisions, into which, in compliance with a vicious and vulgar taste, this great master hath sometimes descended. Even this piece of Handel, so excellent on the whole, is not free from one or two blemishes of this sort, particularly in the air, " With ravished ears, &c ".

Quoted from the third edition, 1772, pp. 39, 61-3. All three editions were published anonymously. Pope's *Ode for Music*, another St. Cecilia poem, published in 1713, was abbreviated and altered for Maurice Greene's setting for his Cambridge Doctor's degree, in 1730. For Joseph Warton, and his brother Thomas, see 2nd May 1745. Thomas Warton, in his edition of Milton's *Poems upon several Occasions*, 1785, p. x, says : " L'ALLEGRO and IL PENSEROSO were set to music by Handel ; and his expressive harmonies here received the honour which they have so seldom found, but which they so justly deserve, of being *married to immortal verse*".

———

Handel subscribes for Elizabeth Turner's " Collection of Songs With Symphonies and a Thorough Bass, With Six Lessons for the Harpsichord ", printed for the author and sold in the College of Physicians, Warwick Lane, 1756.

The title-page has a vignette, engraved by A. Green after S. Wale, depicting Apollo in front of a lady at the harpsichord ; her music on the floor shows the names of Corelli, Purcell, Handel and Boyce.

———

L'Allegro, Il Penseroso, ed Il Moderato is performed by the Society at the Castle in Paternoster Row, 1756.

This performance is recorded in a printed word-book, a copy of which was on sale at B. F. Stevens & Brown, London, in October 1950 (Cat. 11, no. 292).

1757

FROM "FARLEY'S BRISTOL JOURNAL", 3rd February 1757

At the opening of the new organ in the great Musick-Room, on Wednesday, March 2d, will be perform'd the oratorio of Judas Macchabeus ; and on Thursday the 3d of March, the oratorio of Messiah. The Band will be composed of the principal performers (vocal and instrumental) from Oxford, Salisbury, Gloucester, Wells, Bath, etc. etc. Each night will be perform'd a concerto on the organ by Mr. Broderip, to begin at six o'clock precisely. Tickets . . . Price five shillings each. The rehearsal of Judas Macchabeus will be on Tuesday March 1st, at ten o'clock in the morning, and that of Messiah at six in the evening ; where gentlemen and ladies will be admitted paying five shillings (for each rehearsal) at the door.

(Myers, 1948, p. 161 ; Latimer, p. 308.) For Broderip, see 20th December 1755.

—

FROM "JACKSON'S OXFORD JOURNAL", 5th February 1757

Oxford, February 4, 1757.

On Monday next [the 7th] will be performed, at the Musick Room, the First Act and Part of the Second of the *Messiah*, beginning at " *Lift up your Heads, O ye Gates, &c.*".

Cf. 26th (28th) March.

—

FROM THE SAME, 19th February 1757

Oxford, 19th February, 1757.

On Monday next [the 21st] will be perform'd, at the Musick-Room, The Masque of *Acis and Galatea*.

—

FROM THE "PUBLIC ADVERTISER", 25th February 1757

At the Theatre Royal in Covent-Garden, This Day will be presented an Oratorio call'd ESTHER. With new *Additions* . . . to begin at Half an Hour after Six o'Clock.

Cf. 15th March 1751. Repeat performance on 2nd March. A new word-book was printed for this revival (copy in the British Museum). This was the beginning of the new oratorio season.

—

FROM THE " PUBLIC ADVERTISER ", 4th March 1757

At the Theatre Royal in Covent Garden, This Day will be presented an Oratorio call'd ISRAEL IN EGYPT . . . to begin at Half an Hour after Six o'Clock.

Cf. 24th March 1756. There was one performance only.

———

FROM THE " PUBLIC ADVERTISER ", 9th March 1757

At the Theatre Royal in Covent-Garden, This Day will be presented an Oratorio call'd JOSEPH and HIS BRETHREN . . . to begin at Half an Hour after Six o'Clock.

Cf. 28th March 1755. There was one performance only.

———

FROM THE " PUBLIC ADVERTISER ", 11th March 1757

At the Theatre Royal in Covent-Garden, This Day will be presented an Oratorio call'd The TRIUMPH of TIME and TRUTH. Altered from the Italian, with several new Additions. . . . To begin at Half an Hour after Six o'Clock.

The first version of *Il Trionfo del Tempo e della Verità* was that of *c.* 1708; the second Italian version was performed at Covent Garden on 23rd March 1737 and revived there on 3rd March 1739. Now an English version had been made, with words by Thomas Morell. Mrs. Delany referred to it in a letter of January 1757 which has been lost (Delany, III. 458). Repeat performances on 16th, 18th and 23rd March. Revived on 10th February 1758.

———

CAST OF " THE TRIUMPH OF TIME AND TRUTH ", 11th March 1757
Time—Mr. Champness, bass
Counsel (or Truth)—Miss Young (Mrs. Scott ?), mezzo-soprano
Beauty—Signora Frasi, soprano
Pleasure—Mr. Beard, tenor
Deceit—Signora Beralta, soprano
Signora Beralta sang this Handel part only ; nothing is known about her.

———

FROM " JACKSON'S OXFORD JOURNAL ", 12th March 1757
Oxford, March 11, 1757.
On Monday next [the 14th] will be performed, at the Musick Room, *Alexander's Feast.*
N.B. On the 22d Instant the new Subscription will be open'd.

———

FROM THE " PUBLIC ADVERTISER ", 14th March 1757

For the Benefit of Signora FRASI.

At the Great Room in Dean-street, Soho, This Day . . . will be performed an Oratorio called SAMSON. *By Mr. Handel*. With a Concerto on the Organ by Mr. Stanley. . . .

THE SECOND CODICIL TO HANDEL'S WILL, 22nd March 1757

I George Frideric Handel do make this farther Codicil to my Will.

My old Servant Peter Le Blond being lately dead I give to his Nephew John Duburk the sum of Five Hundred Pounds.

I give to my Servant Thomas Bramwell the Sum of Thirty Pounds in case He shall be living with me at the time of my Death and not otherways.

In Witness whereof I have hereunto set my hand this Twenty Second day of March one thousand Seven hundred and Fifty Seven.

George Frideric Handel.

On the day and year above written this Codicil was read over to the said George Frideric Handel and was by him Sign'd and Publish'd in our Presence.

Tho: Harris.

John Hetherington.

(Schoelcher, pp. 325, 342.) Cf. 1st June 1750. John Duburk, otherwise spelled Du Bourk, succeeded his uncle in Handel's service ; on the latter's death he was able to buy his furniture for £48 (cf. 27th August 1759).

FROM THE " PUBLIC ADVERTISER ", 24th March 1757

For the Benefit and Increase of a FUND establish'd for the Support of DECAY'd MUSICIANS, or their FAMILIES.

At the *King's Theatre* in the *Haymarket*, This Day . . . will be a Concert of Vocal and Instrumental *Music*.

. . . . . .

Part III. . . . Song, Sig. Ricciarelli, Verdi prati, del Sig. Handel. . . . Coronation Anthem, God save the King.

Ricciarelli, from the Haymarket Opera, sang in *Messiah* on 3rd May 1759. The aria is from *Alcina*. The closing anthem was from *Zadok the Priest*. On the same day, 24th March 1757, Hasse's oratorio *I Pellegrini al Sepolcro* was performed at Drury Lane Theatre.

FROM THE SAME, 25th March 1757

At the Theatre Royal in Covent-Garden, This Day will be presented an Oratorio call'd JUDAS MACCHABAEUS. . . . To begin at Half an Hour after Six o'Clock.

Cf. 26th March 1756. There was one performance only.

FROM "JACKSON'S OXFORD JOURNAL", 26th March 1757

Oxford, March 25.

At the Music-Room on Monday Evening the 28th Instant (being the first Night of the New Subscription) will be performed so much of the *Messiah* as was omitted in a former Performance.

N.B. Mr. Price is expected from Glocester, and the Trumpet from Salisbury.

Cf. 7th February. For Mr. Price and the trumpet player, see 4th (6th) December 1756.

———

FROM THE "PUBLIC ADVERTISER", 30th March 1757

At the Theatre Royal in Covent-Garden, This Day will be presented a Sacred Oratorio call'd MESSIAH. . . . To begin at Half an Hour after Six.

Cf. 7th April 1756. Repeat performance on 1st April, when the season ended.

———

FROM THE "BATH ADVERTISER", 9th April 1757

For the *Benefit* of Mr. *Linley*, Mr. *Richards*, and Mr. *Sullivan*. At the *Theatre* in Orchard-Street, On Monday, April 18, will be perform'd, in Manner of an *Oratorio*, ACIS and GALATEA. The Music composed by Mr. *Handel*. Between the Acts a Solo on the Violincello by Mr. *Richards*.

And on Wednesday, the 20th, ALEXANDER'S FEAST. Wrote by Mr. *Dryden*. And set to Music by Mr. *Handel*. Between the Acts, A Concerto on the Harpsichord by Mr. *Chilcot*.

An additional Band of Performers is engaged from Gloucester, Salisbury and Bristol. . . .

To begin each Night at half an Hour past Six o'Clock.

Thomas Linley, the elder, born at Bath in 1725, was a composer and conductor ; he was a pupil of Chilcot and Paradies. John Richards was band-leader at Drury Lane and played in *Messiah* performances at Gloucester, Hereford and Bath. Daniel Sullivan, a male alto, had sung in *Semele* and in *Joseph and his Brethren* in 1744. Thomas Chilcot was organist at Bath.

———

Walsh advertises the score of *The Triumph of Time and Truth*, *Public Advertiser*, 18th April 1757.

———

Handel deposits £1,200, 19th April 1757.

———

FROM THE "PUBLIC ADVERTISER", 22nd April 1757

For the Benefit of Mr. *Jonathan Snow*.

At the *New Theatre* in the *Haymarket*, Monday next [the 25th] will be performed a Masque, called ACIS and GALATEA. By Mr. *Handel*. . . .

Printed Books of the Masque may be had . . . at Sixpence each. . . .
(Smith, 1948, pp. 241 f.) On 23rd April, " By particular desire " is added to the
advertisement. The performance was postponed till 2nd May. For Master
Jonathan Snow, now 16 years of age, see 23rd April 1751.

———

FROM " JACKSON'S OXFORD JOURNAL ", 23rd April 1757

Oxford, April, 23.
On Monday next [the 25th] will be performed, at the Musick Room,
The two first Acts of *Judas Maccabaeus*.
Cf. 14th (16th) May.

———

FROM THE " PUBLIC ADVERTISER ", 28th April 1757

Hospital for the Maintenance and Education of exposed and
deserted young Children.
This is to give Notice, that under the Direction of G. F. *Handel*, Esq;
the sacred Oratorio, called MESSIAH, will be performed in the Chapel of
this Hospital, for the Benefit of this Charity, on Thursday May 5, 1757,
at Twelve at Noon precisely. To prevent the Chapel being crouded,
Gentlemen are desired to come without Swords, and Ladies without
Hoops. . . .
                    By Order of the General Committee,
                                        S. *Morgan*, Sec.

———

FROM THE " LONDON CHRONICLE : OR UNIVERSAL EVENING POST ",
7th May 1757

Yesterday was perform'd at the Foundling Hospital, under the Direction
of George Frederick Handel, Esq; the sacred Oratorio called the Messiah,
to a numerous and polite Audience, who expressed the greatest Satisfaction
on that Occasion.
This issue of the new paper, appearing three times a week, is dated 5th-7th May :
" Yesterday " means here 5th May. The part usually sung by Signora Frasi was
performed this time by " Mr. Savage's celebrated Boy " (see 2nd July). This boy
may have been the son of William Savage, who sang Handel parts from 1735
onwards.

———

Handel deposits £250, 12th May 1757.

———

FROM " JACKSON'S OXFORD JOURNAL ", 14th May 1757

Oxford, May, 14.
On Monday next [the 16th] will be performed, at the Musick Room,
The Choice of Hercules, and the last Act of *Judas Macabaeus*.
Cf. 23rd (25th) April.

———

The leave and license to perform Italian operas at the Haymarket Theatre, granted to Domenico Paradies and Francesco Vanneschi on 17th January 1751, is renewed on 16th May 1757, for Vanneschi alone, for the period from 1st July 1757 till 1st July 1758.

Public Record Office : L.C. 5/161, p. 343. According to Burney, IV. 467, Vanneschi went bankrupt in 1756 and, during 1756–7, the operas were managed by Signora Mingotti and Signor Giardini. On page 468, Burney relates that Signora Colomba Mattei and her husband, Signor Trombetta, were Mingotti and Giardini's successors for 1757–8, when Thomas Pinto followed Giardini as leader of the orchestra.

—

From the " Public Advertiser ", 9th June 1757

RANELAGH-HOUSE.

For the Benefit of the *Marine Society*, towards cloathing Men and Boys for the Sea to go on Board his Majesty's Ships, This Day will be performed Acis and Galatea. Compos'd by Mr. *Handel* ; the Performance to be conducted by Mr. *Stanley*, in which he will play a Concerto on the Organ. Each Person to pay 5s. at the Door. Tea, Coffee, &c. included, as usual. To begin at Seven o'Clock.

(Loewenberg, p. 88 ; Smith, 1948, p. 242.)

—

From " Jackson's Oxford Journal ", 25th June 1757

June 23d, 1757.

The Anniversary Commemoration of the Benefactors To the University of Oxford, will be held on Wednesday, the 6th of July next ; on which, and the following Evening, will be performed, at the Music Room, an Oratorio by a considerable Number of Hands and Voices from London, and other Places.

Oxford, June 25.

On Monday next [the 27th] will be performed, at the Music Room, The Epinicion, and third Act of *Saul*.

The " Epinicion ", or song of triumph, opens the oratorio.

—

From the Same, 2nd July 1757

Oxon, July 2, 1757.

On Wednesday, the 6th Instant, will be performed, in the Music-Room, *Messiah*, or the *Sacred Oratorio*; and on Thursday, the 7th, the Oratorio of *Esther* : By a considerable Number of Voices and Instruments, from London and other Places ; particularly Mr. Savage's celebrated Boy, who supplied the Place of Signora Frasi in the last Performance of

Messiah at the Foundling Hospital : Mr. Price, Mr. Miller, Mr Adcock, and several others.

———

FROM THE SAME, 9th July 1757

Oxford, July 9.

. . . In the Evening [of the 6th] the Oratorio of *Messiah* was performed, at the Music Room in Holiwell, to a very numerous Audience ; as was that of *Esther* on Thursday [the 7th] Evening.

———

FROM THE SAME, 16th July 1757

GLOCESTER *Music-Meeting.*

This is to give *Notice,* That the *Meeting* of the *Three Choirs* of *Glocester, Worcester,* and *Hereford,* will be held at *Glocester,* on *Tuesday* the 13th of *September* next. On *Wednesday* the 14th will be performed, in the Cathedral Church, Mr. *Henry Purcell's* TE DEUM, and two of Mr. *Handell's* CORONATION-ANTHEMS. On *Thursday* the 15th, Mr. *Handell's* TE DEUM, composed for the Victory of *Dettingen,* and [the] two other of his CORONATION ANTHEMS. The Evening Entertainments as follow : On *Wednesday* will be performed the *Oratorio* of JUDAS MACCHABEUS ; on *Thursday,* the *Mask* of ACIS and GALATEA ; and on *Friday,* the 16th, the MESSIAH, or *Sacred Oratorio* ; by a numerous Band of Vocal and Instrumental Performers from *London, Salisbury, Bath, Oxford,* and other Places ; particularly Signora *Frasi,* Mr. *Beard,* Mr. *Wass,* and Mr. *Hayes* ; Three Trumpets, a Pair of Kettle-drums, Four Hautboys, Four Bassoons, Two Double basses, Violins, Violincelloes, and Chorus Singers in Proportion. The Music to be conducted by Dr. *Hayes.* . . . The Steward Dinner will be at the Bell on Tuesday the 13th, and a Ball in the Evening. . . . The Musical Performance, and a Ball after each, will be at the *Booth-Hall,* properly fitted up for that Purpose. *NB.* The Performers are expected to be at *Glocester* on *Monday* the 12th, early enough to Rehearse One of the Pieces intended for the Evening Performance.

———

FROM THE SAME, 30th July 1757

Oxford, July, 30.

The Choral Music on Monday next [1st August] will be *L'Allegro Il Penseroso.*

———

Handel withdraws £350, 4th August 1757.

———

THE THIRD CODICIL TO HANDEL'S WILL

I George Frideric Handel do make this farther Codicil to my Will. My Cousin Christian Gottlieb Handel being dead, I give to his Sister

Christiana Susanna Handelin at Goslar Three hundred pounds. and to his Sister living at Pless near Teschen in Silesia Three hundred pounds.

I give to John Rich Esquire my Great Organ that stands at the Theatre Royal in Covent Garden.

I give to Charles Jennens Esquire two pictures the Old Man's head and the Old Woman's head done by Denner.

I give to   Granville Esquire of Holles Street the Landskip, a view of the Rhine, done by Rembrand, & another Landskip said to be done by the same hand, which he made me a Present of some time ago.

I give a fair copy of the Score and all Parts of my Oratorio called The Messiah to the Foundling Hospital.

In witness whereof I have hereunto Set my hand this fourth day of August One thousand seven hund$^{d.}$ & fifty seven.

George Frideric Handel.

On the day & year above written this Codicil was read over to the said George Frideric Handel and was by him signed and published in our presence.

Tho: Harris.
John Maxwell.

(Schoelcher, pp. 325, 342.) Cf. 1st June 1750. Christian Gottlieb Händel's younger sister was Rahel Sophia. Rich was the manager of Covent Garden Theatre ; when Handel's own organ was installed there is not known, but it stood there till 1808, when it was destroyed in the great fire of the house. Balthasar Denner's heads of old people were famous as " genre " pictures. Two Handel portraits by Denner were painted before 1740 ; one is in the National Portrait Gallery, the other was in the possession of Lord Sackville, Sevenoaks. The large Rembrandt was bought by Handel in 1750 ; like the doubtful small Rembrandt, it seems to have been lost. (The words " Landskip said to be done " are missing in earlier publications of the will.) The Christian name of Granville, which Handel could not remember, was Bernard. Handel had previously given another copy of *Messiah* to Mercer's Hospital in Dublin. Nothing is known of Mr. Maxwell, who probably substituted for Mr. Hetherington.

—

FROM " FARLEY'S BRISTOL JOURNAL ", 6th August 1757

For the benefit of clergymens' widows and children, on Wednesday the 7th of September next, will be perform'd in the Cathedral church of Bristol, Mr. Handel's Te Deum, Jubilate, and Coronation Anthem, together with other choice pieces of church musick. A large band of the best vocal and instrumental performers will attend on this occasion, under the conduct of Dr. Hayes, Professor of Musick, in Oxford.—The rehearsal will be on Tuesday the 6th, at eleven o'clock in the morning, during divine service, to which none will be admitted without tickets, at five shillings each ; and the same tickets will introduce the bearers

of them into the choir the next day without any further expense. The
oratorio of Sampson will be perform'd in the evening.

(Latimer, p. 327.)

From " Farley's Bristol Journal ", 13th August 1757

The oratorio of Sampson will be perform'd on the 7th in the evening ;
and there will be a rehearsal of the same on the evening of the 6th, to
which any person may be admitted paying five shillings at the door.

From the Same, 27th August 1757

The oratorio of Sampson will be perform'd at the New Assembly-
Room. . . . The publick may be assur'd that the undertaker has spared
no expense to render the performance compleat. . . .

A pasticcio opera *Les ensorcelés, ou Jeanott et Jeanette,* ' *Parodie des
Surprises de L'amour* ', words by Marie Justine Benoit Favart and
Jean Nicolas Guerin de Frémicourt, music—including the aria
" Verdi prati " from *Alcina* sung as " Etant jeunette "—selected
and arranged by Harny de Guerville, is produced in Paris by the
Comédiens italiens—1st September 1757.

In Jean Dubreuil's *Dictionnaire lyrique portatif,* published in Paris in 1758,
I. 235, the same tune is printed with the words :

> Le badinage,
> Les ris et les jeux
> Sont faits pour votre age
> Et vous pour eux.

From the Same, 3rd September 1757

The part of Dalilah [in *Samson*] to be perform'd by Signora Passerini,
from London.

From the Same, 10th September 1757

On Wednesday last [the 7th] the Clergy and Sons of the Clergy held
their annual feast at the Cooper's Hall in King-street, having first attended
divine service at the Cathedral ; where the solemn musical performances
gave general satisfaction, and served greatly to advance the collection at
the church door. In the evening was performed before a large genteel
audience, and with universal applause, the oratorio of Sampson ; and
tho' we cannot as yet ascertain the exact sum, we are assured that the
monies raised by these means for the benefit of widows and children,

vastly exceed any former contributions. As this method will be continued yearly 'tis presumed nothing will be omitted to render the scheme as truly useful and extensively beneficial as possible.

—

FROM " JACKSON'S OXFORD JOURNAL ", 10th September 1757

Glocester, Sept. 9. From the Number of Lodgings already taken, and still taking, a great Deal of Company is expected here next Week on Account of our Musick-Meeting and Races.

—

> The Three Choirs Meeting is held in Gloucester from 14th till 16th September 1757 ; the music is mostly by Handel.
> Cf. 16th July.

—

FROM " JACKSON'S OXFORD JOURNAL ", 17th September 1757

Glocester, Sept. 16. This Week was held here the annual Meeting of the Three Choirs of Glocester, Worcester, and Hereford, which was distinguished by the Presence of the Earl of Shrewsbury, the Lords Litchfield, Tracey, Moreton, and Chedworth, Sir Francis Dashwood, and many other Gentlemen and Ladies of Rank and Distinction. The Musical Performances were conducted by Dr. Hayes, and gave great satisfaction and Pleasure to every Body : And the Sermon was preached by the Right Reverend the Bishop of the Diocese, which seemed to have its proper Effect upon the Hearers, whose Contribution to the Charity amount to a much larger Sum than ever was given at either of the Choirs, 297*l.* being collected at the Church Doors ; to which, 'tis said, is intended to be added what may remain of the Money taken at the Booth-Hall, after defraying Expences ;—so amiable, so truly Christian, the Disposition of the Two Stewards.

> The Bishop of Gloucester was James Johnson.

—

FROM THE SAME, 29th October 1757

Oxford, October 28.

The Choral Music on Monday next [the 31st] will be *The Choice of Hercules*, and *Dryden's Ode for St. Cecilia's Day.*

N.B. A Trumpet from Salisbury.

> (Mee, p. 19.) The trumpet player was probably Mr. Bidlecomb ; see 4th (6th) December 1756.

—

FROM THE SAME, 19th November 1757

Oxford, Nov. 19, 1757.

For the Benefit of Mr. Orthman. On Thursday the 24th of November Inst. will be performed in the Music Room, A Miscellaneous Concert of

Vocal and Instrumental Music ; Particularly, several favourite Songs by Signiora Peralta, who performed last Winter in Mr. Handel's Oratorios, and at the Opera House. . . .

For Signora Beralta, see 11th March. She did not arrive, and Mr. E. C. Orthman (cf. 9th November 1754) apologized for this on 26th November.

FROM THE SAME, 26th November 1757

Oxon, November 25, 1757.
The Choral Music, On Monday next [the 28th], will be *Acis and Galatea*.

FROM FAULKNER'S " DUBLIN JOURNAL ", 3rd December 1757

Thursday [the 1st] Mr. Handel's grand Te Deum Jubilate and two Anthems, were performed at St. Andrew's Church . . . for the Support of Mercer's Hospital ; their Graces, the Duke and Duchess of Bedford honoured the Hospital with their Presence. . . .

John Russell, fourth Duke of Bedford, was Lord Lieutenant of Ireland in 1756–7. Nothing is known of a performance of *Acis and Galatea* in Dublin in December 1757, as suggested by Smith (1948, p. 235) ; nor is anything known of a performance of *Esther* there in 1757, although a word-book, dated Dublin 1757, is said to have been in the collection of Mr. Ponder.

FROM THE " BATH ADVERTISER ", 24th December 1757

The First Subscription Oratorio of Mr. and Mrs. Passerini, Will be at Mr. Wiltshire's Great-Room, And on Thursday next [the 29th] will be performed SAMPSON, Composed by Mr. *Handel*. The Vocal Parts by Mrs. *Passerini*, and the Singers of several Cathedrals in England. The Instrumental by Mr. *Passerini*, all the best Performers of Bath, and some additional Hands from other Places of England. Mr. and Mrs. *Passerini* have spared no Expence or Labour to get a sufficient Number of Singers able to perform the two Oratorio's in as much perfection as possible out of London. To begin exactly at *Six* o'Clock. . . . The Subscription is One Guinea, for which the Subscribers will receive six Tickets, three to be admitted in the first Performance, and three in the second. . . . extraordinary Tickets at 5s. each, for the Front Seats ; and Tickets at 2s. 6d. each for the second Seats : Also Books of the Oratorio's at 6d. each.

At some time after 15th November 1756 the Passerinis seem to have been naturalized (but see 3rd September 1757). The advertisement reads a little ambiguously as to the number of performances and oratorios. It may be assumed, however, that before *Samson* another oratorio was given. A copy of the *Samson* word-book is in Gerald Coke's Handel Collection.

1758

A pasticcio opera called *Solimano*, text by (?) Giovanni Ambrogio Migliavacca, music by Ferdinando Giuseppe Bertoni, Handel and Davide Pérez, is produced at the Haymarket Theatre, 31st January 1758.

(Burney, IV. 469.) The Handel numbers were : a duet from *Amadigi* ("Cangia al fine il tuo rigore", see Chrysander, I. 421), and one aria each from *Poro* and *Radamisto*. The duet was, in fact, printed for the first time in Walsh's edition of favourite songs from *Solimano*, and was reprinted in Vol. IX of his collection *Le Delizie dell' Opera*. Signor Potenza sang the two Handel arias and, with Signora Mattei, the Handel duet. Hasse's opera *Solimano*, text by Migliavacca, was produced in Dresden in 1753.

———

FROM "JACKSON'S OXFORD JOURNAL", 4th February 1758

Oxford, February 3, 1758.
On Monday the 6th Instant the Choral Music will be the first Part and the latter Half of the second Part of *Messiah*, beginning at, *Lift up your Heads*, &c.

N.B. Mr. Price is expected from Glocester, and Mr. Bidlecomb from Salisbury.

Cf. 25th February (13th March). Price was a singer, Bidlecomb a trumpet player ; cf. 4th December 1756.

———

FROM THE "PUBLIC ADVERTISER", 10th February 1758

At the Theatre Royal in Covent Garden, This Day will be presented an Oratorio called The TRIUMPH of TIME and TRUTH. With several New *Additions.* . . . To begin at Half an Hour after Six o'Clock.

This was the beginning of the oratorio season. Cf. 11th March 1757. Repeat performance on 15th February. A new edition of the word-book was issued for this revival. Mrs. Passerini sang the part of Deceit, created by Signora Beralta.

———

MRS. DELANY TO MRS. DEWES

Spring Gardens, 11th Feb., 1758.
D.D. [Dr. Delany] treated Sally [Miss Sarah Chapone] with the "Triumph of Time and Truth" last night, and we went together, but it did not please me as usual ; I believe the fault was in my own foolish spirits, that have been of late a good deal harrassed, for the performers

are the same as last year, only there is a new woman instead of Passarini, who was *so* frightened that I cannot say whether she sings well, or ill.

(Delany, III. 480 f.) Miss Chapone was Mrs. Delany's god-daughter. The writer seems to have mixed up Signore Beralta and Passerini, the former having sung in 1757, the latter in 1758.

———

Walsh advertises the fourth volume of Handel's oratorio songs, in vocal score, *Public Advertiser*, 18th February 1758.

———

FROM THE " PUBLIC ADVERTISER ", 22nd February 1758

At the Theatre Royal in Covent Garden, This Day will be presented an Oratorio called BELSHAZZAR. With new Additions and Alterations. . . . To begin at Half an Hour after Six o'Clock.

Cf. 22nd February 1751. There was one performance only. The cast was as follows : Belshazzar—Mr. Beard, Nitocris—Signora Frasi, Cyrus—Miss Young (Mrs. Scott), Daniel—Miss Frederick, and Gobrias—Mr. Champness. Samuel Champness, the new bass, took part in the Handel festival of 1784, and died in 1803.

———

FROM THE SAME, 24th February 1758

At the Theatre Royal in Covent Garden, This Day will be presented an Oratorio called ISRAEL IN EGYPT. With new Additions and Alterations. . . . To begin at Half an Hour after Six o'Clock.

Cf. 4th March 1757. There was one performance only.

———

FROM " JACKSON'S OXFORD JOURNAL ", 25th February 1758

Oxon, February 24, 1758.

The Subscribers to the Musical Society are desired to take Notice, that the Choral Music is deferred 'till Monday the 13th of March, when the remaining Part of *Messiah* will be perform'd.

Cf. 4th (6th) February.

———

FROM THE " PUBLIC ADVERTISER ", 1st March 1758

At the Theatre Royal in Covent Garden, This Day will be presented an Oratorio called JEPHTHA. With new Additions and Alterations. . . . To begin at Half an Hour after Six o'Clock.

Cf. 2nd April 1756. There was one performance only. In an undated word-book in King's College Library, Cambridge, there are manuscript notes, appar-

ently referring to this revival and indicating some changes in the cast : Storge—
Miss Frederick, Hamor—Miss Young (Mrs. Scott) and Zebul—Mr. Champness.

FROM JOHN BAKER's " DIARY ", 2nd March 1758

Mr. Banister and I in his chariot to Handel's, Lower Brook Street,
where heard rehearsed the Oratorio of ' Judas Maccabaeus ', by Frasi,
Miss Young als [alias] Miss Scott, Cassandra Frederica, Beard, Champness,
Baildon, etc.

(John Baker, Diary, p. 106.) Baker was a barrister, and John Banister had just
stood godfather to his daughter Mary, baptized on 27th February. From this
entry, a rare occasion, we learn who sang at the revival of this oratorio in 1758
(cf. 25th March 1757). Only Mr. Beard, as Judas Maccabaeus, was left of the
original cast (1st April 1747) ; Champness sang Reinhold's part as Simon, and
Baildon possibly the smaller part of Eupolemus. It is more difficult to distribute
the female parts among the ladies named by Baker : Signora Frasi—First Israelite
Woman (Gambarini), Mrs. Scott (formerly Miss Isabella Young, junior)—Second
Israelite Woman (Galli), and Miss Frederick—Israelite Man (Galli). This,
however, is conjectural. It is noteworthy that Handel had all these people to his
house for rehearsal the day before the performance.

FROM THE " PUBLIC ADVERTISER ", 3rd March 1758

At the Theatre Royal in Covent Garden, This Day will be presented
an Oratorio called JUDAS MACCABAEUS. With New Additions and
Alterations. . . . To begin at Half an Hour after Six o'Clock.

Cf. 25th March 1757. Repeat performance on 8th March. It must have been
to the performance on the 3rd that Morell, the author of the word-book, referred
in his recollections, about 1764 (see Appendix) : " The success of the Oratorio
was very great, and I have often wished, that at first I had ask'd in jest, for the
benefit of the 30th night, instead of the 3rd. I am sure he [Handel] would have
given it to me ; on which night there was about £400 in the House."

FROM THE SAME, 6th March 1758

For the Benefit of Signora FRASI.

At the King's Theatre in the Haymarket, This Day . . . will be performed an Oratorio call'd SAMSON. By Mr. Handel. With a Concerto
on the Organ by Mr. Stanley. . . .

☞ This is the only Opportunity the Public will have of hearing this
favourite Oratorio, Mr. Handel being determined not to perform it this
Season.

It seems that Handel consented to this performance. John Baker attended it
with his second wife, Mary, née Ryan (Diary, p. 106).

FROM THE " PUBLIC ADVERTISER ", 10th March 1758

At the Theatre Royal in Covent Garden, This Day will be presented a sacred Oratorio called MESSIAH. . . . To begin at Half an Hour after Six o'Clock.

Cf. 30th March 1747. Repeat performances on 15th and 17th March. This was the end of the oratorio season.

———

FROM BAKER'S " DIARY ", 10th March 1758

Went après midi con Uxor in chariot to ' Messiah ', could not get seat in Upper Gallery, sat in lower.

(Myers, 1948, p. 155.) *Diary*, p. 106.

———

FROM " JACKSON'S OXFORD JOURNAL ", 18th March 1758

The First Choral Performance in the New Subscription, will be Part of *Judas Maccabaeus*, On Monday the 27th Day of this Instant March.

———

Handel deposits £900, 21st March 1758.

———

FROM THE " PUBLIC ADVERTISER ", 31st March 1758

For the Benefit of MRS. ABEGG.

At the Great Room in Dean-street, Soho, This Day will be perform'd the Oratorio of ACIS and GALATEA. Compos'd by Mr. Handel. . . .

Originally advertised for 27th March, but postponed because of the illness of Mrs. Abegg, of whom nothing is known. (Fräulein Meta Abegg, famous through Schumann's Opus 1, came from Mannheim.) This performance was apparently repeated on the next day.

———

FROM THE SAME, 1st April 1758

For the *Benefit* of
A Widow Gentlewoman in great Distress.

At the Great Room in Dean-street, Soho, This Day . . . will be perform'd ACIS and GALATEA. A Serenata. Compos'd by Mr. *Handel*.

The Vocal Parts by Mr. Beard, Mr. Champness, Master Soaper, Miss Young, &c. First Violin by Mr. Brown ; Second Violin by Mr. Froud ; First Violoncello by Mr. Gordon ; Harpsichord by Mr. Cooke. . . .

Books of the Serenata will be sold at the Place of Performance.

Cf. 31st March. The tickets were 5s. each. Beard sang the part of Acis, as he had done since 13th December 1739 ; Champness sang Polyphemus, Master

Soaper, or Soper (cf. 16th-17th August 1758, Bristol) Damon, and Miss Young (Mrs. Scott) was Galatea. The leader of the orchestra was Abraham Browne.

———

FROM THE SAME, 4th April 1758

For the Benefit and Increase of a FUND establish'd for the Support of Decay'd Musicians, or their Families.

At the King's Theatre in the Hay-market, Thursday, April 6, will be a Concert of Vocal and Instrumental MUSICK.

PART I. . . . Song, Signor Pazzagli, Why does the God of Israel sleep, by Mr. Handel, in the Oratorio of Sampson. Song, Signora Frasi, Wise Mens Flattery, . . . in the Oratorio of Belshazzar. . . .

PART II. . . . Song, Signora Frasi, He shall feed his Flock, . . . in the Messiah. . . . Song, Signor Pazzagli, He was despised, . . . in the Messiah. . . .

PART III. . . . Song, Signora Frasi, Ye sacred Priests, . . . in Jephtha. . . . Coronation Anthem, God save the King, by Mr. Handel. . . .

———

FROM THE SAME

HOSPITAL FOR SMALLPOX AND INOCULATION,

March 18, 1758.

The Anniversary Feast of the Governors of this Charity will be held at Drapers Hall in Throgmorton-street, on Wednesday the 12th of April next, after a Sermon preached . . . at St. Andrew's Church, Holborn. . . .

There will be a full Band of Vocal and Instrumental Music to perform the Te Deum, and an Anthem composed by G. F. Handel, Esq; not used on any other Occasion but this, will be vocally and instrumentally performed, under the Direction of Mr. Stanley. . . .

The anthem was probably one of the Chandos Anthems.

———

FROM THE SAME, 5th April 1758

The Trustees of the *Westminster-Hospital* of Public Infirmary in James-street, Westminster, are desired to meet together at the said Hospital on Friday the 7th of April, at Ten o'Clock in the Forenoon in order to proceed to St. Margaret's Church, to hear the Anniversary Sermon. . . .

Mr Handel's New Te Deum ; a new Anthem by Dr. Boyce ; Grand Chorus from the Messiah, for the Lord God Omnipotent reigneth ; and the Coronation Anthen, God save the King, will be performed under the Direction of Dr. Boyce. . . .

———

FROM THE " PUBLIC ADVERTISER ", 11th April 1758

The *Rehearsal* of the *Music* for the *Feast* of the *Sons* of the *Clergy*, will be held at St. Paul's Cathedral, on Tuesday the 18th, and the Feast at Merchant-Taylors Hall on Thursday the 20th of April. . . .

The Overture of Esther, Mr. Handel's New Te Deum and Jubilate, the Grand Chorus from the Messiah, with an Anthem particularly composed for this Charity, by Dr. Boyce, will be vocally and instrumentally performed. To conclude with Mr. Handel's Coronation Anthem. . . .

Two Rehearsal and two Choir Tickets for the Music, are given with every Feast Ticket.

———

Inscription on a Token in the Foundling Hospital, Maria Augusta Handel, born April 15, 1758.

(*Musical Times*, 1st May 1902, p. 310.) This foundling was named after Handel, as Governor. The token is a large, coin-like, piece of metal. (It may be mentioned here that in 1825 one George Frederick Handel Cubitt joined the Royal Society of Musicians.)

———

FROM THE " PUBLIC ADVERTISER ", 19th April 1758

To the *Lovers of Music*, particularly those who admire the Compositions of GEO. FREDERICK HANDEL, Esq; F. BULL, at the White House on Ludgate Hill, London, having at a great Expence procured a fine Model of a Busto of Mr. Handel, proposes to sell by Subscription, thirty Casts in Plaister of Paris. The Subscription Money, which is to be paid at the Time of subscribing, and for which a Receipt will be given, is one Guinea ; and the Cast, in the Order in which they are finished, will be deliver'd in the Order in which the Subscriptions are made. The Busto, which will make a rich and elegant Piece of Furniture, is to be twenty-three Inches and a half high, and eighteen Inches broad. The Model may be viewed till Monday next [the 24th], at the Place abovementioned. . . .

(Schoelcher, pp. 354 f.) The rest of the advertisement offers a mezzotint portrait of Daniel Waterland, D.D., Master of Magdalene College, Cambridge, for 1s. 6d. It may be assumed that this bust was by Roubiliac ; one marble bust of Handel came to the Foundling Hospital, another to Windsor Castle. It is not known whether Mr. Bull's subscription had any success, or if any of his plaster copies are in existence.

———

FROM BODDELY'S " BATH JOURNAL ", 24th April 1758

For the Benefit of the GENERAL HOSPITAL, On Wednesday next, the 26th and 27th Inst. On the *Morning* of each Day, will be vocally and Instrumentally performed in the *Abbey Church*, A Grand Te Deum and

Two Anthems, of Mr. *Handel's*, A *Concerto* on the *Organ* by Mr. *Chilcot*, and a *Concerto* on the *Violin* by Signor *Passerini*. . . .

On Wednesday Evening, at Mr. Wiltshire's, will be performed The Oratorio of *Sampson*, And on Thursday, at Mr. Simpsons, *L'Allegro Il Penseroso*.

The principal Vocal Parts by Signora Passerini and Mr. Linley ; with the additional Assistance of the Singers from the several Cathedrals of Oxford, Salisbury, Gloucester, Bristol, &c.—The Instrumental by the best Hands. . . .

. . . Books of the Oratorio's are sold, and a Scheme of the Music for the Church, in which are printed the Words of the Anthems.—Oratoria Books 6d. each ; Books of the Church Performance 3d. each.

—

FROM THE " PUBLIC ADVERTISER ", 26th April 1758

MIDDLESEX-HOSPITAL

For Sick and Lame, and for Lying-in Married Women, in Marylebone-Fields, Oxford-Road.

The Anniversary Sermon of this Charity will be preached at the Parish Church of St. Ann, Westminster, on Wednesday May 10. . . .

Mr. Handel's Te Deum and Coronation Anthem, with an Anthem compos'd by Dr. Boyce, and the Chorus, *For the Lord God Omnipotent reigneth*, from the Messiah, will be performed by Mr. Beard, Mr. Baildon, Mr. Wass, and others. . . .

—

Messiah is performed in the Chapel of the Foundling Hospital, 27th April 1758.

During this April six performances of Handel's music were advertised in aid of London charities.

—

FROM BODDELY'S " BATH JOURNAL ", 1st May 1758

On Wednesday and Thursday last [26th and 27th April], Mr. Handel's Grand Te Deum and Two Coronation Anthems were performed at the Abbey Church ; and on the Evenings of the same Days the Oratorio's of Sampson, and the Allegro il Penseroso were performed at the Rooms, which gave general Satisfaction. There was a Collection each Day at the Church Door for the Benefit of the General Hospital, which amounted to 18*l*.—It is with great Pleasure we hear that these Entertainments are to be continued once every Season ; which at the same Time they contribute to the Amusement of the Company which resort to this Place, will greatly forward this noble and extensive Charity, which is highly deserving the Attention of the Public.

———

ORCHESTRA BILL FOR THE " MESSIAH " PERFORMANCE AT THE FOUNDLING HOSPITAL, COMPILED *c.* 1st May 1758

A List of the Performers and [. . .]
Messiah on Thursday April the 27th 1758.—

Messrs Brown . . £1   1   –

Violins
Collet . . ,, – 15 –
Freeks . . ,, – 15 –
Frowd . . ,, – 15 –
Claudio . . ,, – 10 –
Wood . . ,, – 10 –
Wood Junr . ,, – 10 –
Denner . . ,, – 10 –
Abbington . ,, – 10 –
Grosman . ,, – 10 –
Jackson . . ,, – 10 –
Nicholson . ,, – 10 –

Tenners
Rash . . ,, – 8 –
Warner . . ,, – 8 –
Stockton . ,, – 8 –

Hautbois
Eyferd . . ,, – 10 6
Teede . . ,, – 10 6
Vincent . . ,, – 10 –
Weichsel . ,, – 8 –

Bassoons
Miller . . ,, – 10 6
Baumgarden . ,, – 10 6
Goodman . ,, – 8 –
Owen . . ,, – 8 –
                £12   6   –

Violoncellos
Gillier . . £– 10 6
Haron . . ,, – 10 6
Hebden . . ,, – 10 6

Double Basses
Dietrich . ,, – 15 –
Sworms . ,, – 10 –

Horns, Drums
Adcock . . ,, – 10 6
Willis . . ,, – 10 6

Trumpets, & Kettle
Trowa . . ,, – 10 6
Miller . . ,, – 10 6
Fr: Smith . ,, – 10 6
                £ 5   9   –
brought over . ,, 12 6 –
in all . . £17 15 –

Cf. 2nd May. "Tenners" for tenors = tenor violins (violas). The musicians, as far as they can be identified, were : Abraham Brown(e), John Collet(t), John George Freake (spelled variously), Thomas Wood and Wood junior, Joseph Ab(b)ington, (John Joseph ?) Grosman, William Jackson, Thomas Stockton, Philip Eiffert (?), William Teide (Teede), Richard or Thomas Vincent, Carl Weichsel, (John ?) Miller, Samuel Baumgarden, Adam Goodman, John or Thomas Owen, Peter Gillier, Claudius Heron, John Hebden, Christian Dietrich, John Adam Schworm (?), Abraham Adcock (trumpet), Justice Willis (trumpet) and Joseph Troba (?). Cf. the lists of 29th May 1754 and 10th May 1759.

———

General Bill for the " Messiah " Performance on 27th April,
DATED 2nd May 1758

*Singers at the Performance of the Oratorio at the Foundling
Hospital*

Sig^{ra} Frasi	. . £6 6 –		

Sig^ra Frasi   . . £6 6 –   *Servants*
Miss Frederick .   . „ 4 4 –   John Duburg Mr Handels
Miss Young [Mrs. Scott] „ 3 3 –   Man .   . . £1 1 –
Mr Beard   . . „ – – –   Evens .   . . „ – 10 6
Mr Champness .   . „ 1 11 6   Condel   . . „ – 10 6
Mr Wass .   . . „ 1 1 –   Green .   . . „ – 10 6
6 Boy's .   . . „ 4 14 6   Mason .   . . „ – 10 6
Bailden   . . . „ 1 1 –   Musick porters .   . „ 1 11 6
Barrow .   . . „ 1 1 –   £ 4 14 6
Champness   . . „ – 10 6   Singers .   . „ 27 16 6
Bailden Junr   . . „ – 10 6   Orchestra   . „ 17 15 –
Ladd   . . . „ – 10 6   £50 6 –
Cox   . . . „ – 10 6   Mr Smith   . „ 5 5 6
Munck   . . . „ – 10 6
Reinhold .   . . „ – 10 6   May 2 1758   £55 11 6
Walz   . . . „ – 10 6
Courtney   . . „ – 10 6   Received of Lan' Wilkinson, the
Kurz   . . . „ – 10 6   sum of Fifty Five Pounds Eleven
                  £27 16 6   Shillings for the Performance of
                  the Oratorio 27 April 1758 in full
                  of all Demands
                        by me
                    Christopher Smith

                    £55 11 0
      For the Consta^ble for
        their Attendance   3 3 –
                    £58 14 –

It seems that there were two singers of the name of Champness as well as two
Baildons. Thomas Barrow (alto) and other Gentlemen of the Royal Chapel
had already sung in the 1754 production of the *Messiah*. Frederick Charles
Reinhold, son of Thomas Reinhold, and Waltz, bass soloist in earlier days, now
sang in the chorus too. Beard, as usual, took no payment. For John Duburk
see 22nd March 1757. The recipient of the money seems to have been Christopher
Smith, the Elder (Johann Christoph Schmidt). " Lan' " stands for Lancelot (see
10th May 1759). The bill for the orchestra is written on a separate sheet (see
previous entry).

———

Messiah is performed by the Academy of Ancient Music, 11th
May 1758.
H.–26

Recorded in a word-book (copy in the British Museum). Cf. 16th February 1744 and 30th April 1747.

—

FROM "JACKSON'S OXFORD JOURNAL", 13th May 1758

Music Room, May 12.

On Monday se'nnight, the 22d Inst. there will be an extraordinary Instrumental Concert :—The Gentlemen of the Musical Society being under a Necessity of postponing, on Account of the Absence of the Choristers, the Choral Musick, viz. *Acis and Galatea*, which was intended for this Month, till the 12th of June.

N.B. Mr. Eiffort, the Hautboy from London, and Mr. Price from Glocester are expected here on the 22d.

—

Handel withdraws the balance of £2169 : 18 : 0 and buys £2500 Reduced 3 per cent Annuities, 19th May 1758.

—

FROM "JACKSON'S OXFORD JOURNAL", 10th June 1758.

Oxford, June 10.

On Monday the 12th Instant, will be performed at the Music Room, *Acis and Galatea*.

The Part of Galatea by Miss Thomas.

—

THE REV. WILLIAM HANBURY'S PROPOSALS FOR THE CHARITABLE FOUNDATION OF CHURCH-LANGTON, MID 1758

. . . That on the day of their meeting [annually at the end of September], not only a sermon be preached, but, that God in all things may be glorified, Handel's or Purcel's *Te Deum* be performed.—This will give spirit to the congregation, and excite an holy emulation in all Christian duties. . . .

(Hanbury, p. 12.) The first general meeting of the Trustees was on 26th September 1758. When they met again, at the Hind in Lutterworth, on 11th June 1759, Hanbury extended his proposals. The first performances were given, under Dr. Hayes's direction, on 26th and 27th September 1759 : on the first day various church music by Handel, on the second day *Messiah*. The singers and players are named on p. 54 of Hanbury's book.

—

FROM "JACKSON'S OXFORD JOURNAL", 1st July 1758

Oxford, July 1, 1758.

On Tuesday the 4th of this Instant, will be performed at the Music Room A Concert of Vocal and Instrumental Music. In which will be introduced a Concerto on the Bassoon and Hautboy by Messrs. Miller and Eiffort from London. Each Act to conclude with a Coronation Anthem.

———

FROM " FARLEY'S BRISTOL JOURNAL ", 5th August 1758

On Thursday, the 17th instant August, will be held the annual meeting of the Clergy and Sons of the Clergy, on which day, and the preceeding one, in the morning will be performed at the Cathedral, Mr. Handel's Te Deum, and the Jubilate, with two Coronation anthems, And in the evening of the 17th, the Messiah, for the benefit of clergymen's widows and orphans. . . . The same band will perform, the Allegro and Penseroso, set to musick by Mr. Handel, on Wednesday evening the 16th at the Assembly Room, in Princess street, for the benefit of Mr. Combe, organist of the Cathedral.

(Latimer, p. 327.) The Assembly Room in " Princess Street " was identical with the Music Room in Prince's Street. George Coombes had been organist of Bristol Cathedral since 1756.

———

MRS. DELANY TO MRS. DEWES

Mount Panther, 8th August, 1758.

On Saturday we dined at Mr. Baily's. . . . I was surprised there at meeting Mrs. Arne (Miss Young that was) ; they have her in the house to teach Miss Bayly to sing . . . she sings well, and was well taught by Geminiani and Handel. . . .

(*Musical Antiquary*, July 1910, pp. 232 f.) Delany, III. 502. " Mr. Baily ", or " Bayly ", was later Dean Bailey. Mrs. Cecilia Arne, *née* Young, was badly treated by her husband, Thomas Augustine Arne, and her voice, like her face, had lost its bloom.

———

FROM " JACKSON'S OXFORD JOURNAL ", 12th August 1758

Glocester, Aug. 12. On Sunday last [the 6th] was held at Painswick, about six Miles from this City, a grand Meeting of the Parishes of Painswick, Stroud, and Chalford, where were performed Mr. Handel's Te Deum and the Jubilate, with two Anthems. The Parts, both Vocal and Instrumental, were executed in a masterly Manner, and gave great Satisfaction to, at a moderate Computation, near 5000 People.

The three places are south of Gloucester.

———

FROM " FARLEY'S BRISTOL JOURNAL ", 12th August 1758

For the benefit of clergymen's widows and children. On Wednesday and Thursday the 16th and 17th inst. August, will be perform'd in the Cathedral-Church of Bristol, in the morning, Mr. Handel's Te Deum, the Jubilate, and two Coronation anthems. With other select pieces of church-musick. . . . And in the evening of the 17th will be perform'd also in the Cathedral, The Sacred Oratorio : a large band of vocal and instrumental performers will attend on this occasion, viz.—Dr. Hayes from Oxford ; Signor Pinto, and Mr. Vincent, from London ; Mr. Wass, Master Soper, and another boy from the King's Chapel ; together with others from Wells, Gloucester, Worcester, and Salisbury, the same band will likewise perform on Wednesday the 16th in the evening, at the New Assembly-Room in Princess street, the Allegro, Il Penseroso, Ed Moderato . . . for the benefit of Mr. Combe, organist of the Cathedral. . . .

—

FROM JOHN WESLEY'S JOURNAL, BRISTOL, 17th August 1758

Thur. 17.—I went to the cathedral to hear Mr. Handel's *Messiah.* I doubt if that congregation was ever so serious at a sermon as they were during this performance. In many parts, especially several of the choruses, it exceeded my expectation.

(Myers, *Criticism*, pp. 36 f.) Wesley, *Journal*, IV. 282. Wesley preached in Bristol on the same day.

—

FROM " FARLEY'S BRISTOL JOURNAL ", 19th August 1758

On Thursday last [the 17th] was held the annual meeting of the Clergy and Sons of the Clergy : when a numerous company of gentlemen, viz. The Right Worshipful the Mayor . . . attended divine service at the Cathedral . . . and afterwards went in procession . . . to the Cooper's Hall to dinner.—The several collections amounted to 203*l*. 16*s*., a much larger sum than hath been collected in any preceeding year. This extraordinary advance of the Charity was greatly owing to the admirable performances of the compleatest band of musick, that ever was in Bristol ; as the best judges allow it to be, and the splendid appearance of company at the Oratorio on Thursday evening unanimously testify. . . .

A libretto of *Saul*, printed by Farley in 1758 (copy in the Schoelcher Collection, Conservatoire, Paris), indicates a performance of this oratorio. There is, however, no other reference to it and it seems that the performance was only projected.

—

FROM THE " LONDON CHRONICLE ", 24th August 1758

*On the Recovery of the Sight of the Celebrated Mr. Handel, by the
Chevalier Taylor*

From the hill of Parnassus adjourning in state,
On its rival, Mount Pleasant, the Muses were sate ;
When Euterpe, soft pity inciting her breast,
Ere the Concert begun, thus Apollo address'd :

" Great Father of Music and every Science,
In all our distresses, on thee our reliance ;
Know then in yon villa, from pleasures confin'd
Lies our favourite, Handel, afflicted and blind.

" For him who hath travers'd the cycle of sound,
And spread thy harmonious strains the world round,
Thy son Æsculapius' art we implore,
The blessing of sight with a touch to restore."

Strait Apollo replied : " He already is there ;
By mortal's call'd, Taylor, and dubb'd Chevalier :
Who to Handel (and thousands beside him) shall give
All the blessings that sight in old age can receive.

" By day the sweet landscape shall play in the eye,
And night her gay splendors reflect from the sky;
Or behold a more brilliant Galaxy near,
Where H—n, B—y, and P—t appear.

" But far greater transports their moments beguile,
Who now catch their infants reciprocal smile :
While S—pe, for sweetness of temper ador'd,
Partakes in the joy of each patient restor'd.

" Hence the barking of Envy shall now be soon o'er,
And Jealousy raise her false cavils no more ;
For the Wise will think facts, the most stubborn of things,
When testify'd too, by dukes, princes, and kings.

" And could he from one (far the best) meet regard,
To experience his art and his merit reward ;
He again my sons altars with incense would crown,
And to his own realms fix immortal renown."

This said : They their instruments tun'd ; and begun
A Cantata in praise of their president's son :
Then with Handel's Concerto concluding the day,
To Parnassus they took their aerial way.
                                        Tunbridge Wells, Aug. 15.

(Smith, 1950, pp. 128 f.)   That Handel went to Tunbridge Wells, which he knew
from 1734 and 1735, in the summer of 1758, is testified by Baker's *Diary* of 26th
August and 2nd September.   According to the poem, written more in praise of the
eye-specialist than of the composer, he must have been there from the beginning
of August, at the latest.   John Taylor, the elder, known as " the Chevalier ",

sometimes practised in Tunbridge Wells during the summer, and Handel may have gone there to be treated by him. Dr. William King wrote about his meeting Taylor there in 1748. (See Coats's essay on Taylor.) Another poem, "On Dr. Taylor, who came to Tunbridge Wells in the year 1758", is reprinted in Lewis Melville's "Society at Royal Tunbridge Wells, etc.", London 1912, pp. 106 f. Cf. Taylor, 1761, quoted in the *Appendix*. The names in cipher probably refer to other patients of Taylor's. Handel was not really cured.—"Mount Pleasant" is one of the hills on which Tunbridge Wells is situated; on it, in Handel's day, stood the best lodging-house in the town, originally the house of Lord Egmont.

———

Walsh advertises "A grand Collection of new English Songs, composed by Mr. Handel", *Public Advertiser*, 26th August 1758.

These were songs from oratorios.

———

FROM BERROW'S "WORCESTER JOURNAL", 26th August 1758

Upon Wednesday, August the 30th at the Cathedral . . . Purcell's Te Deum and Jubilate, with Dr. Boyce's Alterations : An Anthem of Dr. Boyce's, "O be joyful", &c.: and Mr. Handel's Coronation Anthem.

Upon Thursday, August the 31st, at the Cathedral . . . Mr. Handel's New Te Deum and Jubilate : An Anthem of Dr. Boyce's, "Lord, thou hast been our Refuge", &c. : And the Coronation Anthem.

Upon Wednesday, Thursday and Friday evenings, at the College-Hall —the Oratorios of Judas Maccabaeus, Alexander's Feast, and the Messiah.

Care has been taken to engage the best Performers from London, and other Places ; amongst whom are,—Signiora Frasi, Messrs. Beard, Wass, Pinto, Millar, Thompson, Adcock, Vincent, &c.

———

FROM BAKER'S DIARY, 26th August 1758

Left horse and took post chaise . . . to River Head 12 miles—thence fresh chaise 14 to Tunbridge Wells. . . . At Wells then and after Handel and his Dr. Murrell, Taylor the occulist. . . .

Diary, p. 114. "Dr. Murrell" was apparently the Rev. Dr. Thomas Morell, Handel's librettist.

———

FROM "JACKSON'S OXFORD JOURNAL", 2nd September 1758

Glocester, September 1. This Week was held at Worcester the Annual Meeting of the Three Choirs . . . at which were present the Right Rev. the Lord Bishop of Worcester, Lord Coventry and his Lady, and the Countess Dowager, Lord Sandys and his Lady, the Lords Littleton, Plymouth, and Archer, and a numerous Appearance of Gentlemen and Ladies of Rank and Distinction . . . the Charity Collection, 'tis said, exceeds any before at either of the Choirs. In regard to the Performances, they met with general Approbation, being skillfully conducted, and masterly executed. . . .

From Baker's Diary, Tunbridge Wells, 2nd September 1758

I walked up by Handel's lodging about 2 miles about (quarrel with hay makers as went along).

Diary, p. 116. It may be mentioned here that David and Eva Garrick came to Tunbridge Wells in September ; if Handel was still there they may have met him.

Walsh advertises an eleventh set of Handel's overtures in eight parts, including *Time and Truth,* with an index to the whole collection, *Public Advertiser,* 21st October 1758.

From "Jackson's Oxford Journal", 28th October 1758

Oxford, October 26th.

On Monday the 30th Instant, will be performed at the Music Room, *L' Allegro, il Penseroso.* Mr. Savage's Boy is expected from London, and Mr. Price from Glocester.

From the Minutes of Mercer's Hospital, Dublin, 18th November 1758

Agreed that the Oratorio of Esther be perform'd at Mr Neils great Room in Fishamble Street this year for the Benefit of this Hospital.

"Neil" stands for Neale, and "this year" means this season. See 2nd December.

William Shenstone to the Rev. Richard Graves

The Leasowes, Nov. 25, 1758.

. . . My principal *excursions* have been . . . and to the Worcester Music-meeting. I need not mention what an appearance there was of company at Worcester ; dazzling enough, you may suppose, to a person who, like me, has not seen a public place these ten years. Yet I made a shift to enjoy the splendor, as well as the music that was prepared for us. I presume, nothing in the way of harmony can possibly go further than the Oratorio of The Messiah. It seems the best composer's best com-position. Yet I fancied I could observe *some parts* in it, wherein Handel's judgment failed him ; where the music was not equal, or was even *opposite,* to what the words required. . . .

(Myers, 1948, pp. 166 f.) Original in the Assay Office Library, Birmingham. Shenstone, *Letters,* Oxford edition, p. 494 ; Minneapolis edition, p. 356. Cf. 29th

March 1755. For the Worcester meeting see 26th August and 2nd September 1758.

FROM FAULKNER'S "DUBLIN JOURNAL", 28th November 1758

At the Great Musick-Hall in Fishamble Street, on Thursday the 14th of December, 1758, will be performed the Grand Sacred Oratorio, called the MESSIAH ; composed by Mr. Handel, the whole to be conducted by Mr. Lee.

Cf. 11th December 1756 ; as then, the performance was given for poor debtor prisoners. The rehearsal was on 12th December, at Noon.

FROM THE MINUTES OF MERCER'S HOSPITAL, 2nd December 1758

Agreed . . . That instead of the oratorio Esther mentioned at the last board the masque of Acis & Galatea be performed at the great room in Fishamble Street this year for the benefit of this Hospital.

Agreed That Messrs Brownlow Hutchison & the Lord Mornington be requested to manage at the Performance of the Musick on Thursday the 6th of Feb^{ry} next.

Cf. 18th November. Garrett Colley Wellesley, Earl of Mornington, father of the Duke of Wellington, was a composer and later Professor of Music. Before he succeeded to the Earldom in 1758, he was, as Lord Mornington, leader of the band in Fishamble Street. The Right Hon. William Brownlow played the harpsichord in the same orchestra. Francis Hutcheson, from Glasgow, wrote music under the pseudonym Francis Ireland.

FROM THE "ABERDEEN JOURNAL", 18th December 1758

For the *Benefit* of Mr. *Rocke* A CONCERT To be held in the Concert-Hall, To-morrow the 20th, To begin precisely at 6 o'Clock. *Act I.* Overture in Ariadne. . . . *Act III.* The 5th of Handel's Grand Concertos. . . .

(Farmer, p. 61.) Rocke, a German, went to Aberdeen from London in August 1758 as leader of the Aberdeen Musical Society, founded in 1749. According to Farmer (p. 115 f.), the Society listed the following Handel works in its Music Inventory for 1749 : Overtures, Sonatas (in three parts), the new Music for the Royal Fireworks, the first collection of Oratorios (Songs), and Select Airs ; and in the inventories for 1752–5 : the parts of the Organ Concertos, and of the Twelve Grand Concertos.

Samson is performed by the Castle Society in Pater-Noster-Row, 1758.

Recorded in a printed word-book, a copy of which is in the Library of Congress, Washington.

Les Amans trompés, " pièce en un act mêlée d'ariettes par (Louis) Anseaume et (Pierre Augustine) de Marcouville ", containing the aria " Se risolvi abbandormi " from *Floridante* sung as " Lorsque deux cœurs d'un tendre feu ", is produced at The Hague, 1758.

Although the score, the parts and the printed libretto, preserved at The Hague, are dated 1758, the first recorded performance there, by the Théâtre français, was in May 1762. (According to information kindly supplied by D. F. Balfoort, Adj. director of the " Dienst voor Schone Kunsten der Gemeente ",'s Gravenhage.) The aria was printed in 1758 in Jean Dubreuil's *Dictionnaire lyrique portatif*, Paris, I. 267, with the same French words. The aria, with other French words, " Daphnis, profitons du temps . . .", had been printed in Paris in 1730 by Ballard in *Les Parodies nouvelles et les vaudevilles inconnus*, I. 68. The Hague libretto, printed by A. Constapel, was no. 1 of Vol. I of *Nouveau Théâtre de la Haye*.

———

FROM VINCENZIO MARTINELLI's " LETTERE FAMILIARI E CRITICHE ",
LONDRA 1758 (Translated)

. . . This truth was well understood by Bononcini, and equally well by Handel and Gemignani, to whom is due England's adoption of this most refined taste, which is the basis of all the sublime and beautiful in every one of the arts, especially in music. . . .

P. 371. The passage is from one of three letters on music, addressed to the " Conte di Buckinghamshire " ; this is no. 55 of 59 undated letters and, therefore, was probably written shortly before publication.

———

FROM [WILLIAM HUGHES's] " REMARKS UPON MUSICK, TO WHICH ARE ADDED SEVERAL OBSERVATIONS UPON SOME OF MR. HANDEL's ORATORIO's, AND OTHER PARTS OF HIS WORKS ", WORCESTER 1758

. . . What the great Master of Tragedy has said upon another Occasion, may with a little seasonable Alteration be said of many Composers (and that without any singular Reflection) when compar'd with Mr. *Handel* ;

> Why Man ! *He* does bestride the Musick World
> Like a *Colossus* ; and We poor, petty Composers,
> Walk under his huge Legs, and pick up a
> *Crotchet* to deck our humble Thoughts.

Quoted from the second edition, 1763, pp. 45 f. ; it forms the end of the pamphlet. The first edition was published anonymously, by " a lover of harmony ", probably after attending the Worcester Meeting of 1758 (30th August-1st September). The parody is based on *Julius Caesar*, I. 3.

H.-26 *a*

FROM JAKOB ADLUNG'S "ANLEITUNG ZU DER MUSIKALISCHEN
GELAHRTHEIT" ("PRIMER OF MUSICAL ERUDITION"), ERFURT
1758 (Translated)

Hendel or Händel, (Georg Fr.) of Halle in the district of Magdeburg,
at present in his 71st year, is said to have no definite appointment or
service at the Court in London ; but yet earns a great deal through
operas, concerts and occasional music. 1st May 1753 he performed in
the Chapel of the [Foundling] Hospital an oratorio, The Messiah, of two
hours' duration. They counted more than 800 coaches ; the tickets
brought in 995 guineas, which amount to nearly 9,000 Fl.[1]

. . . . .

Händel's harpsichord pieces are among the best ; see above, § 26 about
him. In 1720, 8 Pieces for the Clavecin, composed by him, were engraved
in London in oblong 4to.

The passages quoted are from Part I, chapter 1, § 26, and from Part II, chapter
16, § 360. The first part deals with theory, and its first chapter is dedicated to the
friends of music, in alphabetical order. The second part deals with the practice of
music, and its sixteenth chapter with some of the composers for the keyboard,
also in alphabetical order. Handel's age in 1758 was seventy-three. The takings
in 1753 were 925 guineas (see *London Magazine*, May 1753). Walther is quoted
under Spring 1732, Mattheson's *Ehrenpforte* under Autumn 1740, and the Halle
newspaper under Spring 1753. For the " Societät der musikalischen Wissenschaften ", see 1745.

[1] He is one of the greatest masters in composition and harpsichord playing.
Walther has his " Life ", and also the " Ehrenpforte ", although he himself did not
transmit it ; in the latter it was considered doubtful that he was a Doctor of Music.
The Halle newspaper, in no. 65 of 1753, reported from London that this Lully of
Great Britain, although he has lost his sight, does not allow his muse to remain idle.
They say that the work which he now shapes will perhaps be his last opus, which
after his death shall be sung as his echo in the Foundling Hospital, for which House
the profits from it were intended. That he is a member of the Society is mentioned
in § 2.

1759

FROM THE MINUTES OF MERCER'S HOSPITAL, DUBLIN, 6th January 1759

Ordered that the following Advertisement be printed in the usual newspapers, viz :—Faulkners [Dublin Journal], the [Dublin] Gazette, and the Universal Advertiser :—

The Governors of Mercer's Hospital give Notice that the Masque of Acis & Galatea will be performed by Gentlemen & others for the Benefit of said Hospital at the great Musick Hall in Fishamble Street on Tuesday the 6th of February at Seven O'Clock in the Evening. There will be a publick Rehearsal on Saturday the 3d of February at 12 O'Cl. at Noon. Tickets for said Performance to be had at said Hospital at Half-a-Guinea each, with the Tickets for the Rehearsal as usual.

Cf. 13th January.

———

Princess Anne, widow of William, Prince of Orange, dies, 12th January 1759.

Jakob Wilhelm Lustig (see 1751 and 1756), in Friedrich Wilhelm Marpurg's *Kritische Briefe über die Tonkunst*, Berlin, 1763, II. 463, calls Princess Anne the only music pupil of Handel's. She certainly was his favourite pupil, and remained his friend during her residence in Holland. According to Cardanus Rider's almanac, *British Merlin*, Handel was still (nominally) music teacher to Princess Amelia in 1759.

———

FROM THE MINUTES OF MERCER'S HOSPITAL, 13th January 1759

Ordered : That the following Words be added to the Advertisement etc.,

The Governors request that no Ladys will have any Drum that night, the Benefit arising from this Performance being a principal Support of the Hospital.

Cf. 6th January. A " Drum " was a fashionable evening assembly in a private home.

———

FROM FAULKNER'S " DUBLIN JOURNAL ", 10th February 1759

On Tuesday last [the 6th] the celebrated Masque of Acis and Galatea, was performed. . . .

———

FROM THE " PUBLIC ADVERTISER ", 1st March 1759

For the Benefit of Signora FRASI.

At the Great Room in Dean-street, Soho, This Day, will be performed L' ALLEGRO IL PENSEROSO ED IL MODERATO. By Mr. *Handel*. With a

Concerto on the Organ by Mr. *Stanley*. The principal Vocal Parts by Signora Frasi, Mr. Beard, Mr. Wass, &c. . . . To begin exactly at Half after Six.

———

FROM THE "PUBLIC ADVERTISER", 2nd March 1759

At the Theatre Royal in Covent-Garden, This Day will be perform'd an Oratorio call'd SOLOMON. With new Additions and Alterations . . . to begin at Half an Hour after Six.

Cf. 17th March 1749. Repeat performance on 7th March. This was the beginning of Handel's last oratorio season. In the same issue J. and R. Tonson advertised a new edition of the word-book.

———

FROM THE SAME, 9th March 1759

At the Theatre Royal in Covent-Garden, This Day will be perform'd an Oratorio call'd SUSANNA. With new Additions and Alterations . . . to begin exactly at Half an Hour after Six.

Cf. 10th February 1749. There was one performance only. On the same day the Tonsons advertised a new edition of the word-book.

———

FROM THE SAME, 14th March 1759

At the Theatre Royal in Covent-Garden, This Day will be perform'd an Oratorio call'd SAMSON . . . to begin exactly at Half an Hour after Six.

Cf. 26th February 1755. Repeat performances on 16th and 21st March. In the same issue the Tonsons advertised a new (and altered) edition of the word-book.

———

FROM "JACKSON'S OXFORD JOURNAL", 17th March 1759

Music Room, March 16th, 1759.
On Monday next [the 19th], being the last Choral Night upon the present Subscription, will be perform'd, *Alexander's Feast*. A Voice is expected from London, Mr. Price from Glocester, and Mr. Biddlecombe from Salisbury, with a Boy from that Choir.

Price was a singer, and Bidlecombe a trumpet player. The "Boy" was probably Master Norris, who sang at Oxford in July 1759.

———

FROM THE "PUBLIC ADVERTISER", 23rd March 1759

At the Theatre Royal in Covent-Garden, This Day will be presented an Oratorio call'd JUDAS MACCABAEUS . . . to begin at Half an Hour after Six.

Cf. 3rd March 1758. Repeat performance on 28th March. J. Watts advertised his 1757 word-book in the same issue.

———

FROM THE SAME, 30th March 1759

At the Theatre Royal in Covent-Garden, This Day will be presented a Sacred Oratorio call'd The MESSIAH . . . to begin at Half an Hour after Six.

Cf. 10th March 1758. Repeat performances on 4th and 6th April.

———

DIARY NOTE, OR LETTER, WRITTEN BY SELINA, COUNTESS OF HUNTINGTON (Spring 1759 ?)

I have had a most pleasing interview with Handel—an interview which I shall not soon forget. He is now old, and at the close of his long career ; yet he is not dismayed at the prospect before him. Blessed be God for the comforts and consolations which the Gospel affords in every situation, and in every time of our need ! Mr. Madan has been with him often, and he seems much attached to him.

Huntington, *Life*, I. 229. According to the editor of her papers, Lady Selina was born in 1707. The " Queen of the Methodists " had known Handel in her younger days but it was after a long break in their intercourse that she visited him, " at his particular request ", about the time of his death. The Rev. Martin Madan (1726–90), a friend of hers, was a hymn composer, and one of the founders of the Lock Hospital, where he acted as chaplain. Cf. 22nd April 1752.

———

The last performance of *Messiah*, on 6th April 1759, is announced in the *Public Advertiser* as " Being the last Time of performing IT this Season ".

The " IT " refers to *Messiah*, not, as usual, to the oratorios in general.

———

FROM THE " PUBLIC ADVERTISER ", 7th April 1759

HOSPITAL,

For the Maintenance and Education of Exposed and Deserted Young Children,

This is to give Notice, That towards the Support of this Charity the sacred Oratorio MESSIAH Will be performed in the Chapel of this Hospital, under the Direction of *George-Frederick Handel*, Esq; on Thursday the Third Day of May next, at Twelve o'Clock at Noon precisely. . . .

T. *Collingwood*, Secretary.

The performance had to be conducted by John Christopher Smith ; cf. 19th April.

———

FROM THE " WHITEHALL EVENING-POST ; OR, LONDON INTELLIGENCER ",
7th April 1759

Last Night ended the celebrated Mr. Handel's Oratorios for this
Season, and the great Encouragement they have received is a sufficient
Proof of their superior Merit. He began with Solomon, which was
exhibited twice ; Susanna once ; Sampson three Times ; Judas Maccabaeus twice ; and the Messiah three Times.

And this Day Mr. Handel proposed setting out for Bath, to try the
Benefit of the Waters, having been for some Time past in a bad State of
Health.

If Handel really intended going to Bath, he must have found he was no longer
able to make the journey. The first paragraph was reprinted in the *Norwich
Mercury* of 14th April. Cf. 12th April.

———

THE FOURTH, AND LAST, CODICIL TO HANDEL'S WILL, 11th April 1759

I George Frideric Handel make this farther Codicil.

I Give to the Governors or Trustees of the Society for the Support of
decayed Musicians and their Families one Thousand pounds to be disposed of in the most beneficiall manner for the objects of that Charity.

I Give to George Amyand Esquire one of my Executors Two Hundred
pounds aditional to what I have before given him.

I Give to Thomas Harris Esquire of Lincolns Inn Fields Three Hundred
Pounds.

I Give to Mʳ John Hetherington of the First Fruits Office in the Middle
Temple One Hundred pounds.

I Give to Mʳ James Smyth of Bond Street Perfumer Five Hundred
Pounds.

I Give to Mʳ Mathew Dubourg Musician One Hundred Pounds.

I Give to my Servant Thomas Bremwell Seventy Pounds aditional to
what I have before given him.

I Give to Benjamin Martyn Esquire of New Bond Street Fifty Guineas.

I Give to Mʳ John Belchar of Sun Court Threadneedle Street Surgeon
Fifty Guineas.

I Give all my wearing apparel to my servant John Le Bourk.

I Give to Mʳ John Cowland of New Bond Street Apothecary Fifty
Pounds.

I hope to have the permission of the Dean and Chapter of Westminster
to be buried in Westminster Abbey in a private manner at the discretion
of my Executor, Mʳ Amyand and I desire that my said Executor may
have leave to erect a monument for me there and that any sum not
Exceeding Six Hundred Pounds be expended for that purpose at the
discretion of my said Executor.

I Give to Mʳˢ Palmer of Chelsea widow of Mʳ Palmer formerly of
Chappel Street One Hundred Pounds.

I Give to my Maid Servants each one years wages over and above what shall be due to them at the time of my death.

I Give to M.ᵣˢ Mayne of Kensington Widow Sister of the late M.ᵣ Batt Fifty Guineas.

I Give to M.ᵣˢ Donnalan of Charles Street Berkley Square Fifty Guineas.

I Give to M.ᵣ Reiche Secretary for the affairs of Hanover Two Hundred Pounds.

In Witness whereof I have hereunto set my hand and Seal this Eleventh day of April 1759.

G. F. Handel.

This Codicil was read over to the said George Friderick Handel and by him Signed and Sealed in the Presence, on the day and year above written, of us

A. J. Rudd.
J. Christopher Smith.

Cf. 1st June 1750. The Society provided for in the first paragraph was that later known as the Royal Society of Musicians of Great Britain, at the foundation of which in 1739, Handel had participated. For Amyand, see 6th August 1756. Thomas Harris was a Master in Chancery. Hetherington signed the first and second codicils as a witness, with Harris. For Smyth, the perfumer, see 17th April 1759. Dubourg was a friend from Handel's early days in London, and was his assistant in Dublin in 1741–2. Bramwell is mentioned on 22nd March 1757. Martin was the would-be biographer of the third Lord Shaftesbury. Belchar had suggested to Handel that he should compose Pope's Cecilia Ode (see pp. 326, 434, 781). Duburk's name was sometimes spelled Du Bourk ; cf. 22nd March 1757. It was quite unusual for anyone to suggest that he be buried in Westminster Abbey and have a monument to himself erected there ; but the suggestion was accepted with grace. Miss Donellan, Mrs. Delany's friend, had been a friend of Handel's since about 1735 (see 12th April 1734). "Reiche" may have been Christian Reich, mentioned on 17th June 1759. Nothing is known of the other people mentioned in this codicil. While Christopher Smith, the father, is provided for in the will itself, his son, who signed as witness with the unidentified Mr. Rudd, is not mentioned ; he inherited indirectly only, from his father, all the Handel autographs, now in the Royal Music Library (deposited in the British Museum). Cf. *Anecdotes of . . . Handel and . . . Smith*, pp. 48 f.

———

FROM THE "PUBLIC ADVERTISER", 12th April 1759

The trustees of the Westminster Hospital or Infirmary in James-street, Westminster, are desired . . . on Thursday the 26th Day of April, at Ten in the Forenoon . . . to proceed to St. Margaret's Church to hear the Anniversary Sermon. . . .

Mr. Handell's New Te Deum, the Grand Chorus, for the Lord God Omnipotent reigneth, from the Messiah, a new Anthem composed by Dr. Boyce, and Mr. Handell's Coronation Anthem (God save the King) will be performed under the Direction of Dr. Boyce. . . .

The public Rehearsal will be at St. Margaret's Church on Monday the 23d instant, at Ten. . . .

Cf. 5th April 1758.

___

From the " Whitehall Evening Post ", 12th April 1759

Mr. Handel, who was in Hopes to have set out for Bath last Saturday [the 7th], has continued so ill, that he could not undertake the Journey.

Cf. 7th April. This second notice also was reprinted in the *Norwich Mercury*, on 14th April. According to Burney (1785, p. 31), a Dr. Warren attended Handel in his last illness.

___

From the " Gazetteer and London Daily Advertiser ". 13th April 1759

Yesterday morning died George-Frederick Handel, Esq.

(*Musical Times*, 1st April 1909, p. 242 ; reprinted by F. G. Edwards.) On the same day, the *Public Advertiser* printed an identical notice. On the 14th, the *London Chronicle* called Handel " the great musician ", the *London Evening Post* called him " the famous Musician ", and the *Universal Chronicle, or Weekly Gazette* said " greatly regretted ". All these five papers agreed that Handel died on Thursday the 12th. In fact, he was still alive when all these papers, except the *London Evening Post* of the 14th, were printed.

___

Handel dies on Saturday, 14th April 1759, at eight o'clock in the morning.

___

From the " Whitehall Evening Post ", 14th April 1759

This Morning, a little before Eight o'Clock, died (between 70 and 80 Years of Age) the deservedly celebrated George Frederick Handell, Esq; When he went home from the Messiah Yesterday Se'nnight [6th April], he took to his Bed, and has never rose from it since ; and it was with great Difficulty he attended his Oratorios at all, having been in a very bad State of Health for some Time before they began.

Handel died at seventy-four years of age. The notice was reprinted in the *Gazetteer* of 16th April, which altered the words " This morning " to " Saturday morning ", and " Yesterday " to " Friday ". It was also reprinted in the *Norwich Mercury* of 21st April, and in Faulkner's *Dublin Journal* of 24th April. John Baker entered in his *Diary* (p. 123) on the 14th : " Handel died ".

___

From the " Public Advertiser ", 16th April 1759

Last Saturday [the 14th] and not before died at his House in Brook street, Grosvenor square, that eminent Master of Musick George Frederick Handel, Esq;

Although this paper was one of the five which had reported Handel's death two days too early, the words " and not before " were not a correction of the statement on 13th April. This was just the usual formula. Handel's house in Brook Street had hitherto been called near Hanover Square ; the street runs between Grosvenor Square and Hanover Square.

———

FROM THE " LONDON CHRONICLE ", 17th April 1759

By the death of Mr. Handel, who died at his house in Brook-street, Grosvenor-square, on Saturday last (and not before) a considerable pension reverts to the crown. We hear he will be buried in the burial-ground at the Foundling Hospital near to Capt. Coram.

(Schoelcher, p. 346.) This, too, was one of the papers which had reported Handel's death prematurely. It is not known for certain whether, at the end of his life, Handel was still in possession of all three royal payments : £200 pension from Queen Anne's time, £200 from George I's time, and £200 as salary for teaching the Princesses ; or whether only the salary was left to him (Smith, 1948, p. 64). If he ever had the idea of being buried in the grounds of the Foundling Hospital, near its founder, Coram, the last codicil proves that, at the end, he wished to be buried in Westminster Abbey. A similar notice appeared on the same day in the *London Evening Post*, which, having said that Handel died on the 12th, omitted the words " and not before ". The *Whitehall Evening Post* printed the notice in a shorter version. But the *Universal Chronicle*, a weekly, reprinted it in full on 21st April, after the burial in Westminster Abbey. The first sentence was also reprinted in Boddely's *Bath Journal* of 23rd April, and probably in other provincial papers.

———

FROM THE " GAZETTEER ", 17th April 1759

On GEORGE FREDERICK HANDEL, *Esq.*
who performed in his celebrated Oratorio of
Messiah, *on the 6th, and dyed the 14th Instant.*

To melt the soul, to captivate the ear,
(Angels his melody might deign to hear)
T' anticipate on Earth the joys of Heaven,
Was Handel's task ; to him the pow'r was given !
Ah ! when he late attun'd Messiah's praise,
With sounds celestial, with melodious lays ;
A last farewel his languid looks exprest,
And thus methinks th' enraptur'd crowd addrest :
" Adieu, my dearest friends ! and also you,
" Joint sons of sacred harmony, adieu !
" Apollo, whisp'ring, prompts me to retire,
" And bids me join the bright seraphic choir !
" O for Elijah's car," great Handel cry'd ;
Messiah heard his voice—and Handel dy'd.

Lincoln's Inn, April 16, 1759.   H—y.

(*Musical Times*, 1st April 1909, edited by F. G. Edwards.) Printed, slightly differently, in the *London Evening Post* and in the *Whitehall Evening Post* of the same day, 17th April 1759. Reprinted in the *Universal Magazine* of April and, anonymously, in the *Scots Magazine* of May 1759. A manuscript copy of the poem is inscribed in a copy of Mainwaring's *Memoirs of the Life of the late G. F. Handel* (1760) in the University Library, Cambridge ; another is in the British Museum : Add. MS. 33,351, f. 24. The British Museum manuscript, copied from the *Scots Magazine*, adds : " Mr Handel Perform'd the Messiah at Covent G^d Ap^r 6th 1759 —Played a Concerto, upon the Harpsecord, and Dy'd, on the 14th of the said April, in the 75th Year of His Age—Quite sensible to the Last—". The *Whitehall Evening Post* of 14th April, and the *Gazetteer* of 16th April following it, state that Handel's last appearance was at the " Messiah " performance of 30th March ; the poem, however, in its various versions, assumes that Handel's last performance was on 6th April, when *Messiah* was given for the third, and last, time during the season. The documents quoted under 7th April make the second statement more plausible. Handel's presence on 6th April is further testified in *An Account of the Life of George Frederick Handel, Esq.*, printed in the *Annual Register for the Year 1760*, second section, pp. 9-19. The cipher " H—y " has not been explained.

FROM THE " PUBLIC ADVERTISER ", 17th April 1759

An ACROSTIC.

He 's gone, the Soul of Harmony is fled !
And warbling Angels hover round him dead.
Never, no, never since the Tide of Time,
Did Music know a Genius so sublime !
Each mighty Harmonist that's gone before,
Lessen'd to Mites when we his Works explore.

(Schoelcher, p. 334 : dated 17th May.)

JAMES SMYTH TO BERNARD GRANVILLE

London, April 17th, 1759.

Dear Sir,
        According to your request to me when you left London, that I would let you know when our good friend departed this life, *on Saturday last at 8 o'clock in the morn died the great and good Mr. Handel.* He was sensible to the last moment ; made a codicil to his will on Tuesday, ordered to be buried privately in Westminster Abbey, and a monument not to exceed £600 for him. I had the pleasure to reconcile him to his old friends ; he saw them and forgave them, and let all their legacies stand ! In the codicil he left many legacies to his friends, and among the rest he left me £500, and has left to you the two pictures *you formerly gave him.* He took leave of all his friends on Friday morning, and desired to see nobody but the Doctor and Apothecary and myself. At 7 o'clock in the evening he took leave of me, and told me we " should meet again " ; as soon as I was gone he told his servant " *not* to let me come to him any more, for that he had *now done with the world* ". He died as

he lived—a good *Christian*, with a true sense of his duty to God and man, and in perfect charity with all the world. If there is anything that I can be of further service to you please to let me know. I was to have set out for the Bath to-morrow, but must attend the funeral, and shall then go next week.

> I am, dear Sir,
> Your most obedient humble servant,
> James Smyth.

He has left the Messiah to the Foundling Hospital, and one thousand pounds to the decayed musicians and their children, and the residue of his fortune to his niece and relations in Germany. He has died worth £20,000, and left legacies with his charities to nearly £6000. He has got by his Oratorios this year £1952 12s. 8d.

(Delany, III. 549 f.) Smyth was the perfumer of Bond Street, apparently in Handel's special confidence, and his prospective companion to Bath. The 11th April, when the last codicil was signed, was a Wednesday. Among the " old friends " estranged from Handel, was Christopher Smith, the elder, whose name remained in the main part of the will ; Handel was finally reconciled to Smith. Of the two Rembrandts which Handel left to Granville, only the smaller one was a gift from him (see 4th August 1757). The Doctor was probably Dr. Warren, mentioned by Burney, and the Apothecary John Cowland, provided for in the last codicil. The servant was Duburk. Handel's final credit at the Bank of England was £17,500. All his legacies together amounted to more than £9,000. There were eleven oratorio performances during Handel's last season. It seems he kept proper books.

———

The Foundling Hospital announces that *Messiah* will be performed on 3rd May under the direction of Mr. (John Christopher) Smith, *Public Advertiser*, 19th April 1759.

Cf. 7th April.

———

From the " Whitehall Evening Post ", 19th April 1759

We hear that Mr. Handel is to be bury'd in Westminster-Abbey, by his own Direction, in as private a Manner as possible ; that he has left all his Music to Mr. Smith ; a Thousand Pounds to the Society of Decay'd Musicians ; and some other Legacies ; but the Bulk of his Fortune, which is about 20,000*l*. to a near Relation or two abroad.

Mr. Smith is Christopher the elder. The notice was reprinted in the *Norwich Mercury* and in *Jackson's Oxford Journal* of 21st April.

———

From the " Public Advertiser ", 20th April 1759

This Evening the Remains of Mr. Handel will be buried in Westminster Abbey. The Gentlemen of his Majesty's Chapels Royal, as well as the

Choirs of St. Paul's and St. Peter's, will attend the Solemnity, and sing Dr. Croft's Funeral Anthem.

(*Musical Times*, 1st April 1909, edited by F. G. Edwards.) St. Peter's is another name for the Abbey.

———

FROM THE BURIAL REGISTER OF WESTMINSTER ABBEY, 20th April 1759

George Frederick Handel Esqr was buried April 20th 1759 in the South Cross of the Abbey.

(*Musical Times*, 1st April 1909, p. 242 ; edited by F. G. Edwards.)

———

FROM THE FUNERAL BOOK OF WESTMINSTER ABBEY [20th April 1759]

No. 14. George Frederick Handal Esqr Died April 14. 1759 in the 76th year of his Age ; and was Buried by the Dean on ye 20 ; in the South Cross ; 8 feet from the Duke of Argyle's Iron Railes ; 7 feet from his Coffin ; which is Lead : N.B. There may be made very good graves on his Right and Left by Diging up a Foundation of an old Staircase ; Room at the feet : Mr. Gordin. U.T.

(*Musical Times*, 1st April 1909, pp. 242 f.; edited by F. G. Edwards.) The Funeral Book was kept by the Clerk of the Works. For the Duke of Argyll, see 13th January 1739 ; when he died in 1743, an elaborate monument in marble, made by Roubiliac, was erected in the Abbey. The " Room at the feet " was used 110 years later for the remains of Charles Dickens. When Handel's grave was dug up in 1870, the red velvet of his coffin became visible. His age was seventy-four, not seventy-five. " U.T." means undertaker.

———

FROM THE " UNIVERSAL CHRONICLE ", 21st April 1759

An Attempt towards an EPITAPH.

Beneath this Place
Are reposited the Remains of
GEORGE FREDERICK HANDEL.
The most excellent Musician
Any Age ever produced :
Whose Compositions were a
Sentimental Language
Rather than mere Sounds ;
And surpassed the Power of Words
In expressing the various Passions
Of the Human Heart.

He was born in Germany Anno 1685, and having, with universal Applause, spent upwards of fifty Years in England, he died on the 14th Day of April 1759.   H.

The author of this epitaph, which was not used, is unknown ; perhaps he was identical with " H—y ", who wrote the poem published on 17th April. The epitaph was printed, on the same day (21st April), in the *Norwich Mercury*, as "From Lloyd's Chron." (*Lloyd's Evening Post and British Chronicle*) of 19th April. No copy of this paper, however, is available. Cf. p. 834.

—

FROM THE "LONDON EVENING-POST", 24th April 1759

On Friday Night [the 20th] the Remains of the late Mr. Handel were deposited at the Foot of the Duke of Argyle's Monument in Westminster-Abbey ; the Bishop, Prebendaries, and the whole Choir attended, to pay the last Honours due to his Memory ; and it is computed there were not fewer than 3000 Persons present on this Occasion.

(*Musical Times*, 1st April 1909, edited by F. G. Edwards.) This note was reprinted in *Jackson's Oxford Journal* of 28th April, in Boddely's *Bath Journal* of 30th April, in the *Gentleman's Magazine* and in the *Scots Magazine* of April 1759. The Bishop of Rochester, Dr. Zachary Pearce, was also Dean of Westminster. Cf. the *Annual Register for the Year 1760*.

—

MEMORANDUM ON HANDEL'S WILL, 26th–30th April 1759
vide REGISTER OFFICE BOOK A-K 1348 :

MEMORANDUM that GEORGE FRIDERIC HANDEL of Brooke Street Hanover Square, Esq. in the Probate Late of the Parish of St. George Hanover Square In the County of Middx. Esq. died possessed of SEVENTEEN THOUSAND FIVE HUNDRED POUNDS Reduced Annuities at £3 per cent & by his last Will & Testament dated 1st. June 1750 appointed JOHANNA FRIDERICA FLOERKEN Sole Executrix with four Codicils respectively dated the 6th. Aug. 1756, 22nd. March 1757, 4th. Aug. 1757 & 11th. April 1759 wherein he appoints GEORGE AMYAND Esq. Co Executor making no mention of the said Anns. they are at the disposal of the said George Amyand Esq. he only having proved the Will.

Power reserved to make the like grant to Johanna Friderica Floerken Wife of   Floerken the Neice of the said decd. & Executrix named in the said Will when she shall apply for the same.

Probate dated at Doctrs. Comm. 26 April 1759
Regd. 30th. April 1759

(Young, p. 230.) Archives of the Bank of England. The full name of Johanna Friederika's husband was Prof. Dr. Johann Ernst Flörke ; the form Floerken (Flörken) is feminine. Cf. 11th October 1759.

—

FROM THE "UNIVERSAL CHRONICLE", 28th April 1759

Friday night, about eight o'clock, the remains of the late Mr. Handel were deposited . . . in Westminster Abbey ; and though he had mentioned being privately interred, yet, from the respect due to so celebrated a man, the Bishop, Prebends, and the whole Choir attended. . . . A monument is also to be erected for him, which there is no doubt but his works will even outlive. There was also a vast concourse of people of all ranks.

(Schoelcher, p. 347.) The words omitted here are identical with those in the *London Evening Post* of 24th April.

———

Acis and Galatea is performed in Mr. Simpson's Room at Bath, " after the Manner of an Oratorio ", for the benefit of John Richards, leader of the orchestra, 28th April 1759. (Boddely's *Bath Journal*, 23rd April.)

(Young in *Musical Times*, February 1950.) Acis was sung by Daniel Sullivan (alto), Damon by Mr. Offield, Polyphemus by Thomas Linley, and Galatea by Miss Rosco ; the choruses were sung by singers from the Cathedrals of Salisbury, Bristol, etc. The Handel performances are listed in these documents up to the end of 1759.

———

FROM BENJAMIN MARTIN'S " MISCELLANEOUS CORRESPONDENCE, IN PROSE AND VERSE ", April 1759

On the Death *of Mr.* HANDEL.

Nec tantum Phœbo gaudet Parnassia rupes :
Nec tantum Rhodope mirantur & Ismarus Orphea.

VIRGIL.

How frail is life ! how vain is human pride !
Judges, philosophers and kings have dy'd :
Ev'n they, who could by musick's magic art
To the rapt soul coelestial Joys impart.
The *Destinies* have cut the fatal thread,
And HANDEL now is number'd with the *dead*.
The weeping *Muses* round his sacred urn,
With heads reclin'd, in solemn silence mourn.
They wept not more, when the fierce *Thracian* crew,
At *Bacchus'* orgies, their lov'd *Orpheus* slew :
When o'er the plains his mangled limbs were strew'd,
And in his blood the *dames* their hands embru'd.
Who cou'd like *Handel* with such art controul
The various passions of the warring soul ?
With sounds each intellectual storm assuage,
Fire us with holy rapture, or with rage ?
Hark ! with what majesty the organs blow,
While numbers faithful to his fancy flow :
Triumphant fly in echoing fugues the notes,
And on the air the swelling music floats.
With mingl'd sounds harmoniously it roars,
And in the soul seraphic pleasures pours.
Sometimes soft strains and melting numbers rise,
And set calm, rural scenes before my eyes ;

I seem with joy to wander, not unseen,[1]
Thro' meadows, hedge-row elms, and hillocks green.
Where the industrious ploughman, near at hand,
Sings in rude measures o'er the furrow'd land :
Sometimes in brisker notes the bells ring round,
And *fancy* thinks the jocund *Rebecks* sound.
But when *Urania* does her *son* inspire,
And bids him to coelestial sounds aspire,
Then all the soul is seiz'd with holy love
Preludious to the rapt'rous joys above.
The pious *Saint* in bliss extatic dies,
And sees all *Heav'n* before his longing eyes.
When *Orpheus* (as the poets sing) was slain,
His *Harp* was wafted to th' aetherial plain,
Himself, chang'd to a *Swan*, sail'd down the stream,
Moving, majestic 'midst the wat'ry gleam.
But THOU, superior in th' harmonious art,
Thyself in *Heav'nly* songs must bear a part :
Thy *Soul* is now transported to the sky,
To join in *Choirs divine* to all ETERNITY.
           16th of *April*, 1759.

The *Miscellaneous Correspondence* (cf. January 1755) was a London monthly, edited by Benjamin Martin. The anonymous poem appeared in no. 4 of 1759. The magazine was reprinted in book-form in 1764, where this poem is to be found in volume III. The allusion to *L'Allegro ed Il Penseroso* refers to the aria " Let me wander, not unseen ".

———

FROM THE " SCOTS MAGAZINE ", EDINBURGH, April 1759

DEATHS. *April* 12. At London, George Frederic Handel. . . . " He was perhaps as great a genius in music, as Mr Pope was in poetry ; the musical composition of the one being as expressive of the passions, as the happy versification of the other excelled in harmony. *Gr. Mag.*"

The Edinburgh magazine, giving the wrong date of Handel's death twice in this issue, probably quotes from the *Grand Magazine of Universal Intelligence.*

———

FROM THE RATE-BOOK OF THE PARISH OF ST. GEORGE, HANOVER SQUARE, 1st May 1759

Geo. Frederick Handall, Rent £40. Three Ratings £2 10s 0d.

(Smith, 1950, p. 125.) Handel's servant, John Duburk, became owner of the house.

———

George Amyand, the co-executor of Handel's will, pays £2470 Reduced 3 per cent Annuities to Christopher Smith, of Dean

[1] *Alluding to the* Allegro *of* Milton, *set to music by* Mr. Handel.

Street, Soho, and £600 likewise to John Du Burk, of Hanover Square, 2nd May 1759.

Smith, the elder, was the friend of Handel's youth. His Legacy, under the will and the first codicil, was £2000 ; Duburk's, under the second codicil, £500. The apparent increase of the legacies may be explained by the documents of 16th May and 17th June : £1254 Annuities for £1000 cash.

———

When the news of Handel's death arrives in Halle, on 2nd May 1759, prayers are arranged at the church where he had been baptized.

(Schoelcher, p. 334.)

———

Messiah is performed in the Chapel of the Foundling Hospital, 3rd May 1759.

Cf. 10th May.

———

In Giardini's *Concerto spirituale* at Covent Garden Theatre, on 4th May 1759, the overture to *Saul* and the *Funeral Anthem* (for Queen Caroline) are performed, and Mr. Beard sings a Handel song.

(*Public Advertiser.*)

(Schoelcher, p. 337.)

———

MRS. DELANY TO MRS. DEWES

Delville, 5th May, 1759.

I was very much pleased with Court's lines on Mr. Handel ; they are very pretty and very just. D.D. [Doctor Delany] likes them extremely. I could not help feeling a damp on my spirits, when I heard that great master of music was no more, and I shall now be *less able* to bear any other music than I used to be. I hear he *has* shewed his *gratitude* and *his regard* to my brother by leaving him some of his pictures ; he had *very good ones.* I believe when my brother wrote last to me, which was from Calwich, he had not had an account of his legacy ; it was from Mrs. Donnellan I had it, to whom Handel has left 50 pounds. I want to know what the pictures are ? I am sure you were pleased with the honours done him by the Chapter at Westminster.

(Delany, III. 550 f.) Court, whoever he was, may have been the author of the poem published on 17th April. A touching picture of Mrs. Delany in old age is contained in the following extract from Mary Hamilton's diary on 15th March 1784 : " The Musick consisted of some of Handel's finest Songs wᶜʰ my Uncle [Sir William Hamilton] had got set in Italy by an Italian [Lorenz Moser], for Trios. . . . He brought an excellent Tenor player—one Broggio, an Italian, & Cervetto, yᵉ fine Violoncello performer. . . . My Uncle played the second Tenor. . . . I was so enchanted with the song of ' I know that my Redeemer liveth ', that I was going to desire Sir Wᵐ to play it again, but looking towards dear Mrs. Delany I forbore . . . the tears were trickling down her venerable cheeks. . . ." (Elizabeth and Florence Anson, *Mary Hamilton*, London, 1925, p. 172.) The occasion was a party at Mrs. Delany's house in London. She was then eighty-four years of age, and died in 1788. *Handel's Posthumous Trios for a Violin, Tenor & Violoncello*, " Sonatas " arranged from " Songs ", were printed by Robert Birchall about 1785, and reprinted by John Bland about 1790. Sir William Hamilton, who met Moser in Naples, was then on holiday in London. The 'cello player was James Cervetto, the younger.

———

The rehearsal of the music for the Feast of the Sons of the Clergy is held at St. Paul's Cathedral on 8th May, the Feast itself being held there on 10th May 1759 ; the overture to *Esther*, the (*Dettingen*) *Te Deum, Jubilate*, the grand chorus (" For the Lord God Omnipotent reigneth ") from *Messiah*, and the Coronation Anthem (" God save the King ") are performed.

(Schoelcher, p. 337.)

———

GENERAL BILL FOR THE " MESSIAH " PERFORMANCE AT THE FOUNDLING HOSPITAL (ON 3rd May), 10th May 1759

Singers.					Servants.			
Sig^ra Frasi	.	.	£6	6	–	Evens	.	.	£–	10	6
Sig^r Ricciarelli .	.	,, 5	5	–	Condell	.	.	,, –	10	6
Mrs Scott	.	.	,, 3	3	–	Mason	.	.	,, –	10	6
Mr Beard	.	.	,, –	–	–	Green	.	.	,, –	10	6
Mr Champness .	.	,, 1	11	6	Thomas M^r			
6 Boys	.	.	,, 4	14	6	Handels man	.	,, –	10	6
Bailden	.	.	,, 1	1	–	John Duburgh	.	,, 1	1	–
Barrow	.	.	,, 1	1	–	The Musick porters	,, 1	11	6

May 10th 1759 Rec^d of Mr Lancelet Wilkinson the Sum of Fifty Six pounds twelve Shill^s in full of all Demands.

by me
Christopher Smith.

(*Musical Times*, 1st May 1902, edited by F. G. Edwards.) The signature of the receiver is that of Smith the elder. His son, the organist of the Chapel, conducted, while Samuel Howard played the organ ; both were unpaid, as was Beard. Thomas Bramwell is mentioned twice but the first entry is crossed out. For the singers, cf. the bill of 2nd May 1758. The bill for the orchestra in 1759 is also preserved ; since, however, it is almost identical with that of 1758, and amounts to the same sum, it is not reproduced here. According to Clark, 1852, the benefit which the Foundling Hospital derived from the performances of *Messiah* in 1751–77 was £10,299. John Christopher Smith was the conductor from 1759 till 1768, and John Stanley from 1769 till 1777.

———

FROM THE " PUBLIC ADVERTISER ", 14th (17th) May 1759

Hospital for . . . deserted young Children, May 9, 1759.

In grateful Memory of GEORGE FREDERICK HANDELL, Esq. ;   On Thursday the 24th Day of May, at the Chapel of this Hospital, under the Direction of *John Christopher Smith*, will be a Performance of *Sacred Music*, which will begin exactly at Twelve o'Clock at Noon. . . . Mr. Stanley, for the Benefit of this Charity, will on this Occasion perform a Concerto on the Organ.

(Schoelcher, p. 334.) The last sentence was added to the advertisement on 17th May. A copy of the word-book is in the British Museum. It bears, on the title-page, the note : " In grateful memory of his many noble Benefactions to that Charity ". The *Whitehall Evening Post* of 17th May 1759 remarked, in announcing this concert : " but we don't apprehend it is the Dirge that has been so much talked of ". Cf. 11th April 1753. The programme consisted of the " Foundling Hospital Anthem " (cf. 25th May 1749) and the four Coronation Anthems.

———

Handel's co-executor, Mr. Amyand, distributes £1254 Reduced 3 per cent Annuities between Peter Gillier senior, Christian Reich, of Westminster, and Thomas Wood, of St. Giles in the Fields, 16th May 1759.

The payment is explained in the minutes of the Musicians Society of 17th June.

———

The Governors of the City of London Lying-In Hospital for Married Women, in Aldersgate Street, hold their anniversary feast at Drapers Hall on 16th May 1759 ; in St. Andrew's Church, Holborn, two choruses from *Messiah* are sung : " Worthy is the Lamb ", and " The Lord God Omnipotent reigneth ", as well as the " Grand Coronation Anthem ". (*Public Advertiser*, 12th May.)

Beard and the " Gentlemen of St. Paul's " sang, Stanley played the organ.

———

At Bath, on 16th and 17th May 1759, the *Grand Te Deum* and several anthems are performed in the Abbey-Church in the mornings, and *Judas Maccabaeus* and *Messiah* in the Assembly

Hall in the evenings. All are conducted by Dr. Hayes. (Boddely's *Bath Journal*, 14th and 21st May.)

(Myers, 1948, pp. 161 f.)

———

Messiah, conducted by Prof. John Randall, is performed in the Senate House of Cambridge University, 17th May 1759.

(Deutsch, in *Cambridge Review*, 25th April 1942, p. 261.) Cf. 26th (28th) February 1756.

———

Mr. Amyand, Handel's co-executor, pays £400 Reduced 3 per cent Annuities to William Delacreuze, of Castle Street, and £100 likewise to Henry Monk, of Dublin, 25th May 1759.

These, apparently, were creditors.

———

Two Coronation Anthems, " The King shall rejoice " and " Zadok the Priest ", are performed in the Music Room at Oxford, 28th May 1759.

———

Handel's co-executor, Mr. Amyand, pays £500 Reduced 3 per cent Annuities to William Prevost junior, of Shad[well on the] Thames, 8th June 1759.

This again was a payment to a creditor, not to a legatee.

———

John Christopher Smith, Handel's pupil and organist at the Chapel of the Foundling Hospital, delivers to its Governors " a copy of the Score of the Musick for the Oratorio *Messiah* left to this Hospital by George Frederick Handel " (Minutes of the Hospital), 13th June 1759.

(Clark, 1852.) The copy may have been made after Handel's death.

———

L'Allegro ed Il Penseroso is performed at Ranelagh House for Mr. Beard's benefit, 13th June 1759.

Mr. Stanley played an organ concerto.

———

FROM THE MINUTES OF THE SOCIETY FOR THE SUPPORT OF DECAYED MUSICIANS AND THEIR FAMILIES

June 17, 1759.

Dr. *Buswell*, late Gentleman of the Chapel-Royal, and one of the committee of the SOCIETY accounts, reported, that Twelve Hundred and Fifty-four pounds stock, of the reduced Bank Annuities, now standing in the names of Mr. *Thomas Wood*, Mr. *Peter Gillier*, and Mr. *Christian Reich*, in the books of the company of the Bank of England, had been transferred to them by *George Amyand*, esq. one of the executors of the last Will and Testament of GEORGE FREDERIC HANDEL, esq. deceased, in full satisfaction and discharge of the Legacy of One Thousand Pounds, given and bequeathed by the said GEORGE FREDERIC HANDEL, in and by one of the Codicils to his last Will, to the SOCIETY, by the name of *The* SOCIETY *for the Support of Decayed Musicians and their Families* ; to be disposed of in the most beneficial manner for the support of that Charity.

(Burney, 1785, pp. 133 f.) Cf. 16th May. John Buswell was a singer and composer ; Mus. Bac. Cambr. 1757, Mus. Doc. Oxon. 1759. Thomas Wood was a violinist and Peter Gillier a violoncellist ; both played in *Messiah* in 1754 and 1758. The bequest was the largest the Society had so far received.

———

George Amyand, as co-executor of Handel's will, pays £700 Reduced 3 per cent Annuities to Edward Shewell, goldsmith, of Lombard Street, on 27th June, and the same sum likewise to James Smyth, perfumer, of New Bond Street, on 28th June 1759.

For Shewell see 31st October, and for Smyth see 17th April ; the latter was left £500 in Handel's fourth codicil.

———

During Commemoration at Oxford, three Handel oratorios— *Samson, Esther* and *Messiah*—are performed in the Sheldonian Theatre, all conducted by Dr. Hayes, 3rd to 5th July 1759.

(Schoelcher, p. 337.) The *Public Advertiser* of 5th July reported from Oxford : " The University is quite full of Nobility and Gentry ; so much Company not having been seen here since the last Public Act in 1733." That was the summer of Handel's visit to Oxford. This time, T. A. Arne was made Doctor of Music.

———

CHARLES BURNEY TO PHILIP CASE

Lynn, July 23rd, 1759.

Sir,

I fear I shall not be able to propose any useful hints as to the Furniture of the Barrel Organ you mentioned to me, unless I was informed what Stops it contained, what is its Compass, together with the Size & Number of its Barrels. However I will suppose it capable of performing the following Pieces, wch in the serious Way w^d if well adapted to the Instrument afford great pleasure to the admirers of such Compositions.

1. Corelli's 8th Concerto (or the favourite movem^t of it).
2. He was despised & rejected—in Handel's Messiah.
3. Powerful Guardians—set by D^o
4. Return O God of Hosts—in Samson.
5. Tis Liberty alone—in Judas Maccabeus.
6. Handel's Second Organ Concerto, or Part of it.

7. Geminiani's 1st Concerto op 2da, or Do.
8. King of Prussia's March.
9. March of the 3^d Regiment of Guards.
10. Hasse's 1st Concerto.
11. Rende me il Figlio mio, del Sig^r Cocchi, nel Ciro riconosciuto.
12. The Simphony & last Movem^t of Handel's Coronation Anthem.

If these Compositions or any Part of them should be approved & practicable, it will be necessary to have them judiciously suited & adjusted to the Genius of the Organ & filled up with such Simphonies & accompanym^{ts} as will best compensate for the Want of a Voice in the Songs or a Number of Instruments in the other Pieces.

I am, Sir,
Your Most Obed^t & Most Humble Servant
Chas. Burney.

(Deutsch, in *Musical Times*, July 1949.) Townshend MSS., pp. 395 f. Burney was still organist at King's Lynn, Norfolk. Nothing is known of Mr. Case, or whether he had the barrel-organ fitted with Burney's programme. Corelli's 8th is one of the 12 *Concerti Grossi*, Op. 6. "Powerful Guardians" is from *Alexander Balus*. Handel's 2nd organ concerto is apparently that in B flat, from Op. 4. Geminiani's 1st is one of the *Concerti Grossi*, Op. 2. The King of Prussia (Frederick II)'s March is by Gualtero Nicolini. The March of the Third Regiment of Guards was apparently not the March from *Scipio*, although Burney (IV. 303) tells us that it was used from about 1750 by the Life Guards ; it was, in fact, the one also known as "Captain Reed's March". Hasse's 1st concerto seems to be one of his 6 concertos, Op. 4. Gioacchino Cocchi's opera was a novelty of 1759. The "Simphony", or overture, and the last movement of Handel's Coronation Anthem were probably the introduction to *Zadok the Priest* and "God save the King" from the same.

———

Acis and Galatea is performed as "Mr. Beard's Night", at the Long-Room, Hampstead ; with Signora Frasi, Miss Young, Mr. Champness, and Mr. Beard, 13th August 1759. (*Public Advertiser.*)

(Schoelcher, p. 337.) Beard had sung the part of Acis since 13th December 1739 ; Frasi was Galatea, Young (Mrs. Scott) probably Damon, and Champness certainly Polyphemus. Stanley played a concerto on the harpsichord, and there was a ball afterwards.

———

An Inventory of the Household Goods of George Frederick Handel Esqr: Deceased taken at his Late Dwelling House in Great Brook Street St Georges Hanover Square & By Order of the Executor Sold to M^r Jno Du Bourk this twenty Seventh of Augt 1759 by the Appraisement of us whose names are Underwritten.

In the Garretts

4 Old Chairs 3 Old Trunks a Wainscot Oval table a Bedsted wth Lincey Fun^e : a Feather bed bolster and 1 Pillow 3 blanketts & a

Quilt an Old Sadle a Window Curtain & an Old Grate—2 p^r Stairs Closset 2 Old Globes & Frames & Chimney board

2 p^r Stairs foreward

a Bed Stead wth whole teaster Crimson haritteen furniture a feather bed bolster & 2 pillows a White Mattress three blankets & a Quilt 3 p^r of Red Window Curtains & Rods a Stove tongs & Poker. 6 Old Matted Chairs a Round Close Stool & white pann a Wicker Fire Screen a Glass in Wall^e Frame—

2 p^r Stairs Backwards

An Old bedsted wth Red half teaster furniture a feather bed a Bolster 2 Blanketts & an Old Quilt an Oval Wains^t table & 3 Old Chairs — — —

Dineing Room

An Iron Hearth wth Dogs Brass Mounted tongs & Shovell, 2 Wall^e Round Card tables 7 Wall^e Matted Chairs & a Leather Stool, 2 Sconces in Gilt Frames a Chimney Glass in d^o & Broke — — —

In the one p^r of Stairs Backwards

A Stove Compleat bellows & Brush. 4 Matted Chairs a Wall^e Card table a p^r of Old Green Silk window Curtains & a Window Seat a Chimney Glass in a Gilt Frame & a Pier Glass in Ditto — — —

In the Closset a Lincey Curtain an Old Stove & a Small Cupboard

On the Stairs & in ye Passage

an Eight Day Clock in a Wall^e frame & a Sq^{re} Lanthorn —

In the Fore Parlor

A Sq^{re} Stove Poker Shovel Fender bellows & Brush a Wainscot Oval table a Square black table 6 Old Matted Chairs a Sconce in a Gilt frame a Chimney Glass in d^o an Old Wall^e Desk 2 p^r of Harritten Window Curtains Vallsents & Rods 5 Couler'd China Coffee Cups & 6 Saucers a Blue & white Spoon boat — — —

In the Back Parlor

an Easy Chair & Cushion an Old Stove Comp^t a Wallnuttren Desk a dressing Swing Glass in a black frame an Old Bason Stand a Wicker fire Screen a deal Chest & Bracketts & a Square deal box a Large Linnen Press a Small Deal bookcase 2 Wig block fixt — — —

In the Clossett a Large Nest of drawers & a Wind^w Curtain

In the Kitchin

A Large Rainge with Cheeks Keeper & Iron Back a Crain & Pott Hooks a Fender Shovel Tongs & Poker & Bellows a Salamander a Chaffing Dish 2 hanging Irons 3 flat Irons a Jack Compleat & Lead Weight 2 Standing Spitt racks and three Spitts a Gridiron & 2 Trivetts. a Flesh Fork & Iron Scure an Iron Plate warmer 8 Brass Candelsticks 2 Coffee Pots a Drudger & 2 Pepper Boxes a Slice a

Ladle & a Scimmer & a Basting Ladle   a Copper Grater   a Warming Pann   a Copper Drinking Pott   a tin driping Pann & Iron Stand   a boyling Pot & Cover   a Dish Kittle   a Fish Kittle Compleat   2 Stue panns & Covers   2 Frying Panns   5 Sausepanns & 3 Covers   a Copper watter Candlestick   12 Pewter Dishes & 26 Plates   a tea Kittle   a Coffee Mill   2 Wains^t tables   5 Old Chairs   an Arm Easy Cheir   a plate Rack   a Choping board   a Spice Drawer   a Pewter Shaveing basson   about 30 pss of Earthen & Stone Ware & a Towel Rowl   a box wth 12 Knives & 12 Forks   4 Glass Salts & Mustard Glass   2 Coal boxes   a Meat Screen & a Clever   a p^r of Stepts &c. —— ——

In Back Kitchin

An Old Stove & Shovell   a Copper Fixed & Iron work   2 Formes & 5 Washing tubbs   a Cloaths horse & a Horse to dust Cloaths on   2 Old Chears & a Wig block   a bedstead & Curtains   a feather bed   bolster & 1 Pillow   one blankett & a Rugg   an Old Chair —

In the Area & Vault

a Large Lead Cistern & Brass Cock & beer Stylion —

All the Before written Goods &c. is Appraised & Valued to the Sum of Forty Eight Pounds   the Day and Year beforementioned.

£48   0   0

By us $\begin{cases} \text{James Gordon} \\ \text{William Askew} \end{cases}$

(Schoelcher, pp. 344 f.) Original in the British Museum : Eg. 3009. E., ff. 1-18. Bound up with Chrysander's Pedigree of Handel. A few of the abbreviations and curiously spelled words may be explained here : Fun^e means Furniture, Compt— complete, Stue—Stew, Stepts—Steps, Vallsents—Valence. The "lead cistern", mentioned near the end, may have been the one W. H. Cummings saw in the house in 1893 : "a fine cast-lead cistern, on the front of which in bold relief I read ' 1721. G.F.H.' " Smith, 1948, pp. 49 f., suggested that Handel might have brought that cistern with him when he bought the house ; that was in 1724. It should be mentioned that Cummings was, after William Snoxell (sale 1879), the owner of the private copy of Handel's will and codicils as well as of this inventory (sale 1917). Gordon and Askew were valuers. John Duburk bought the household goods for the price asked for, £48, and apparently the house too. It is strange that the house was not mentioned in Handel's will.

———

FROM THE "LONDON MAGAZINE", August 1759

To the Manes of Mr. HANDEL.

By Mr. Lockman.

To mourn o'er thee, I call not on the nine,
Nor wait for influence at Apollo's shrine ;
Vain fictions ! O for David's sacred string !
Who but a muse divine of thee should sing ?—

Fall'n thy slow wasting tenement of clay,
Back to the stars thy spirit wing'd her way ;
For heav'n indulgent only lent thee here,
Our pangs to soften, and our griefs to chear ;
Our jarring passions sweetly to controul,
And lift to exstasy th' aspiring soul.

O wondrous sounds, thine from yon region came,
And hence, thus strongly, they each breast inflame !
Such strains thou heard'st at thy return to skies,
When the Messiah bless'd thy ravish'd eyes.
Cherubs, in his high praise, thy anthems sung,
And heav'n with thy great hallelujahs rung.

(Myers, 1948, pp. 158 f.) Reprinted in the *Scots Magazine* of September. For Lockman, see 16th April 1736, May 1738, 4th January and 22nd February 1740, 14th November 1745 and July 1746.

———

At Hereford, during the Three Choirs Meeting from 12th till 14th September 1759, the " celebrated Coronation Anthem " is performed on the first morning, the *New Te Deum and Jubilate* with the same Coronation Anthem on the second morning and *Messiah* on the third morning, all in the Cathedral ; *Joshua* is given in the College Hall on the first evening. (Berrow's *Worcester Journal*, 6th September.)

The concerts were conducted by the Rev. Richard Clack, vicar choral and organist at Hereford. Among the singers were Signora Frasi, Benjamin Mence (alto) and Mr. Wass ; among the players Adcock, Millar, Vincent senior and junior, Richards and Stefano Storace (double bass).

———

Samson is performed in Salisbury Cathedral, at the Annual Musical Festival, September 1759.

Recorded in a word-book, copies of which are in the Royal College of Music, and in Gerald Coke's Handel Collection.

———

Messiah, conducted by William Hayes, is performed at Church-Langton, Leicestershire, 26th September 1759.

(Myers, 1948, pp. 162-4.) In 1767 the Rev. William Harbury gave a description of this performance in his book on the Charitable Foundation at Church-Langton ; it was reprinted by Myers. For Hayes see 1751 and January 1753 ; in 1768 he published *Anecdotes of the Five Music Meetings at Church-Langton*. It seems remarkable that it was possible to perform *Messiah* in several places outside London, although nothing of it was printed except the scanty selection of Walsh's *Songs in Messiah* : there must have been several manuscript copies of Handel oratorios in full score to serve the provinces.

———

Benjamin Bonnet, Notary Public in London, issues a protest, on 10th October 1759, stating the refusal of George Amyand, Handel's co-executor, to accept a bill of exchange drawn upon him by Jean George Taust, Jean Geoffrey Taust, Jean Frederyck Taust, Christiana Dorothea Taust and Charles Auguste Fritze, " Curateur de la dite Demoiselle Tauste " [minor] for £1500, on the ground that the same should have been drawn for £1200 only.

Original in the possession of the Royal College of Music, deposited in the British Museum. Annexed are copies of the bill, signed at Halle on 19th September 1759, and the verification of the signatures. These documents, referring to the five remaining children of George Taust (see 6th August 1756), were formerly in the possession of Dr. Theodor Roehrig, in Halle, a descendant of the Taust family. From the same source the Royal College of Music acquired an office copy of Handel's will, with the four codicils, and a copy of the memorandum of grant of probate (see 26th-30th April 1759), which Roehrig got from his aunt, Auguste Kroll's widow. The manuscript catalogue of music autographs in the possession of the Royal College of Music lists these documents as nos. 2190-92. (Cf. Smith, 1953, p. 18.)

———

George Amyand, the co-executor of Handel's will, pays £9000 Reduced 3 per cent Annuities to Johanna Friderica Floerken, wife of Johann Ernst Floerken, Director of the University of Halle in Saxony, 10th October 1759.

Handel's niece was executrix of his will and his sole heir. Her husband was now *Rektor* of the University of Halle, besides being Professor of Law. Cf. 26th-30th April.

———

Acis and Galatea is performed in the Music Room at Oxford, 29th October 1759.

———

Handel's co-executor pays £500 Reduced 3 per cent Annuities to James Sinclair, mariner, of Shadwell, £876 likewise to Lewis Morel, goldsmith, of Fleet Street, and £600 likewise to Edward Shewell, goldsmith, of Lombard Street, 31st October 1759.

Sinclair later became senior master in the Navy (Young, p. 231). For Shewell, see 27th June. These payments to Handel's creditors were the last Amyand had to execute. A document, showing in detail how Handel's will was executed, seems to be lost, and its contents remain unknown. In *Notes and Queries*, 1857, Series II, no. 70, p. 348, appeared a letter, signed H., which says : " I was shown the other day a skin or parchment containing the original legal release of Handel's executor, with detailed statement of accounts . . . It came into the hands of the present possessor as packing

H.–27

with a parcel from London, and may be of no value beyond the ' vile use '. . .". Schoelcher was still in London at this time and it seems curious that he did not follow up this hint. It is true his life of Handel may already have been finished, but he was still working on the French version. Perhaps it was a hoax after all.

—

Alexander's Feast is performed at the " Half-Moon Concert " in Cheapside, 12th November 1759. (*Public Advertiser*, 10th November.)

(Schoelcher, p. 337.) These concerts were arranged for subscribers. According to Schoelcher, *Samson* should have been performed on 15th November " for the St. Cecilia Society " ; there is, however, no record of such a performance. The overture to *Samson* was usually played at the Society's commemoration concerts.

—

Walsh announces the issue of volume 5, containing 80 songs from Handel's oratorios in vocal score and in four instrumental parts, with an index to the 400 songs of the collection, *Public Advertiser*, 19th November 1759.

—

L'Allegro ed Il Penseroso is performed in the Music Room at Oxford, 10th December 1759.

—

Esther is performed by the Castle Society, at Haberdashers-Hall, 1759.

Recorded in a word-book, a copy of which is in the Library of Trinity College, Cambridge.

—

An undated manuscript, written by Mattheson, contains a German epigraph for Handel, entitled : " Grabschrift auff den berühmten Capell-meister Hendel, so in Hamburg auff ihn verferttiget worden " [1759]. (Music library, Dr. Werner Wolffheim, Berlin ; sale catalogue, 2nd volume, 1st and 2nd June 1929, no. 96.)

SUPPLEMENT

HANDEL'S ACCOUNTS AT THE BANK OF ENGLAND

First quoted by Young, pp. 228-32. Published here in full by kind
permission of the Bank of England.

HANDEL'S STOCK ACCOUNT AT THE BANK OF ENGLAND, 1728–59

fo. 7/124

George Frederick Handell.
later described George Frederic Handel.

South Sea Annuities 1751.

1728				1728			
31 Aug.	To Philip Hollingworth	50		4 June	By Maurice Birchfield	700
10 Dec.	,, John David	250		2 July	,. Leman Hutchins	200
	,, Elizabeth Hougham	800		,,	,, Abel Castelfrank	50
1729				11 July	,, Elizabeth Eliot	100
8 July	,, Thomas Bunting	200		,,	,, John Rodbard	50
10	,, Robert Harle	500				
15 Sep.	,, Christopher Whit-more	50		1729		
				23 Jany.	,, John Simpson	500
1730					,, John Rice	200
26 Jan.	,, do.	50		5 Aug.	,, Christopher Whit-more	400
1731				11 Dec.	,, John Hanbury	300
14 Aug.	,, Sʳ Philip Yorke	200				
29 Sep.	,, Joint Stock S.S.A.	72		1730		
				4 July	,, Joseph Goupy	100
1732				5 Aug.	,, Christopher Whit-more	150
17 Feb.	,, William Adams	50				
22 June	,, do.	1400		26 Nov.	,, William Whitmore	350
	,, Dʳ Melchior van Susteren	1000				
				1731		
				5 June	,, Edward Corbett &c. Exors.	200
				25 Nov.	,, Henry Carington	472
				1732		
				22 Jan.	,, William Adams	150
				11 May	,, Benjamin Webb	700
		£4622				£4622

fo. 877

George Frideric Handel. Esq.
of Brooke Street. Hanover Square.

4% Annuities 1748.

1749		
22 Jan.	To William Lateward. of Fenchurch St. Gent.	1000
	„ John Glessell. of Exchange Alley. Gent.	1500
	„ John Castell. London. Gent.	1500
	„ John Simons. Jermyn St. Vintner.	1600
	„ John Bolders. Lombard St. Goldsmith	1000
	„ John Lucey. of Rotherhithe. Gent.	950
	„ Edmund Jew. DD. of Boldon. Durham.	200
		£7750

1748			
6 May	By Subscrip.		4500
1749			
7 Apr.	„ John Hale London. Broker.	of	2000
7 Sep.	„ David Abarbanel London. Gent.	of	1000
9 Nov.	„ Joseph Jones jnr. London. Broker.	of	250
			£7750

No. 874

George Frideric Handel. Esq.
of Brooke Street Hanover Square.

4% *Annuities 1746.*

1750				**1749**		
2 Aug.	To John Fleming. of	200		22 Feb.	By Subs	7700
	Exchange Alley.					
	Broker.			**1750**		
	„ Thomas Barwick of	100		19 Apr.	„ David Abarbanal. of	1100
	Fryday St. Mercer.				Bevis Marks. Ald-	
1753					gate. Merchant.	
2 Jan.	„ Anns. Consd	12000		9 Aug.	do.	150

1751
28 Mar. „ Rt. Hon. Jacob　1350
Lord Visct Folke-
stone. Baron of
Longford.

1752
2 May „ Robert Chambers.　900
of Hackney. Gent.
„ RobertWright.DD.
of Hackney. and
Jonathan Cham-
bers of Bucklers-
bury. Merchant.　1100

£12300　　　　£12300

---

fo. D.1468

George Frederic Handel. Esq.
of St George. Westminster.

3% *Annuities 1743.*

1748
6 May To Gwyn Goldstone of 2500
Howard St. Mer-
chant.
„ „ Henry Carington of 500
Hoxton. Gent.

1744
10 Apr. By Certificates.　1300

1745
19 Mar. „ Catherine Delaplace
of St Mary le Bow.
Midsx. Widow.　200

1747
19 Mar. „ Thomas Holmes of
Wevill. Co. South-
ampton Esq. &
John Eames of
Portsmouth. Gent. 1500

£3000　　　　£3000

fo. D.2646
M.2583

George Frideric Handell. Esq.
of Brooke Street. Hanover Square.

Reduced 3% Anns.

1759				1753		
2 May	To	Christopher Smith of Dean Sᵗ Soho. Gent.	2470	2 Jan.	By Anns. 1746 Con'	12000
,,	,,	John Du Burk of Hanover Sq. Gent	600	1754 19 July	,, Benjamin Jones. of Bow. Gent.	1500
16 May	,,	Peter Gillier senior Christian Reich. of Westminster. Gents. Thomas Wood. Gent. of St. Giles in the Fields	1254	1755 14 May	,, Philip Hale. of Basing Lane. Sugar Refiner.	500
25 May	,,	William Delacreuze. of Castle Street. Esq.	400	1756 23 June	,, Stephen Gardes of Rathbone Place. Gent.	1000
,,	,,	Henry Monk. of Dublin. Esq.	100	1758 19 May	,, John Jones. of Sᵗ Anns. Soho. Gent.	2500
8 June	,,	William Prevost. jnr. of Shad. Thames. Gent.	500			
27 ,,	,,	Edward Shewell. of Lombard Sᵗ. Goldsmith	500			
28 ,,	,,	James Smith, of New Bond Sᵗ. Perfumer.	700			
11 Oct.	,,	Johanna Friderica Floerken. Wife of Johan Ernst Floerken. Director of the University of Halle in Saxony.	9000			
31 ,,	,,	James Sinclair of Shadwell. Mariner	500			
,,	,,	Lewis Morel. of Fleet Sᵗ. Goldsmith	876			
,,	,,	Edward Shewell of Lombard Sᵗ. Goldsmith	600			
			£17500			£17500

[The shading of the first christian name is a device, still known, meaning "Death in course of proof".]

HANDEL'S DRAWING ACCOUNT AT THE BANK OF ENGLAND, 1732-58

fo. 97/2674

George Fred^k Handel. Esq.

1734						1732			
June 26	To Cash Him	1300				Aug. 2	By Cash	2300	

1735			
June 30	,,	,,	300
Sep. 15	,,	,,	100
Dec. 8	,,	,,	50

1736			
Aug. 20	,,	,,	150
Sep. 28	,,	,,	200

1737			
Sep. 1	,,	,,	150

1739
Mar. 28 ,,   ,,   ye
         balance.   50
                     £2300   £2300

1743 [1744]						1743 [1744]			
Feb. 21	To Cash Cham-					Feb. 14	By Cash	650	
	bers	650				Mar. 6	,, ,,	250	
1744									
Apr. 5	,, do.	226	5	6		1744			
17	,, Him:	23	14	6		Nov. 3	,, ,,	500	
						9	,, ,,	100	
[1745]						Dec. 11		50	
Jan. 19	,, do.	200							
May 4	,, Robinson	210				[1745]			
11	,, Francesina	400				Jan. 5		50	
13	,, Jordan	140				Feb. 1		150	
						1745			
						May 9		100	
		£1850						£1850	

1747				1746 [1747]			
Apr. 29	To Cash Him	1000		Feb. 28	By Cash	400	
				Mar. 7	,, ,,	100	
				21	,, ,,	100	
				1747			
				Apr. 9	,, ,,	250	
				24	,, ,,	150	
		£1000				£1000	

1747 [1748]				1747 [1748]			
Mar. 19 To Cash Him	990			Feb. 27 By Cash	300		
				Mar. 3 ,, ,,	200		
1748				5 ,, ,,	100		
May 2 ,, ,,	600			10 ,, ,,	250		
				15 ,, ,,	140		
1749							
Apr. 7 ,, ,,	2012	10		1748			
Nov. 9 ,, ,,	157	10		Mar. 26 ,, ,,	300		
				31 ,, ,,	100		
				Apr. 5 ,, ,,	200		
				Dec. 23 ,, ,,	112	9	5
				[1749]			
				Jan. 17 ,, ,,	50		
				Feb. 9 ,, ,,	75		
				11 ,, ,,	235		
				17 ,, ,,	227	10	7
				22 ,, ,,	115		
				25 ,, ,,	185		
				Mar. 6 ,, ,,	190		
				11 ,, ,,	400		
				18 ,, ,,	300		
				1749			
				Mar. 30 ,, ,,	280		
	£3760				£3760		

[1750]		[1750]	
Feb. 13 To Cash Receipt.	50	Jan. 22 By Cash	8000
22 ,, ,, Him.	7926		
,, ,,	24		
	£8000		£8000

1750				[1750]			
Apr. 19	To Cash Him	950		Mar. 3	By Cash	200	
				9	,, ,,	200	
				12	,, ,,	100	
				15	,, ,,	200	
				17	,, ,,	100	
				1750			
				Mar. 29	,, ,,	150	
				[1751]			
				Feb. 23	,, ,,	445	
				Mar. 2	,, ,,	305	9
				7	,, ,,	300	
				9	,, ,,	200	
1751				1751			
Mar. 28	To Cash Him	1790	9	Mar. 14	By Cash	140	
June 13	,, ,,	250		21	,, ,,	400	
Aug. 29	,, ,,	50					
Sep. 5	,, ,,	25		1751			
Oct. 23	,, ,,	60		Apr. 4	,, ,,	200	
Dec. 20	,, ,,	20		,, ,,	,, ,,	50	
				Aug. 8	,, ,,	175	
1752							
May 12	,, ,,	2140	2	1752			
				Feb. 27	,, ,,	600	
1757				Mar. 12	,, ,,	430	
Aug. 4	,, ,,	350		19	,, ,,	300	
				24	,, ,,	640	
[1758]				Apr. 2	,, ,,	320	
May 19	,, ,, (Bal.)	2169	18				
				1757			
				Apr. 19	,, ,,	1200	
				May 12	,, ,,	250	
				1758			
				Mar. 21	,, ,,	900	
		£7805	9			£7805	9

(Sig. in Firm Book : " George Frideric Handel in Brooke Street
Hanover Square ".)

APPENDIX

1760–80

From Oliver Goldsmith's Essay "On the Different Schools of Music", first published in the "British Magazine", February 1760

. . . Musicians seem agreed in making only three principal schools in music ; namely, the schools of Pergolese in Italy, of Lully in France, and of Handel in England. . . .

The English school was first planned by Purcell . . . he might have continued as head of the English school, had not his merits been entirely eclipsed by Handel. Handel, though originally a German, yet adopted the English manner : he had long laboured to please by Italian composition, but without success ; and though his English oratorios are accounted inimitable, yet his Italian operas are fallen into oblivion. . . . Handel's true characteristic is sublimity ; he has employed all the variety of sounds and parts in all his pieces : the performances of the rest may be pleasing, though executed by few performers ; his require the full band. The attention is awakened, the soul is roused up at his pieces ; but distinct passion is seldom expressed. In this particular he has seldom found success ; he has been obliged, in order to express passion, to imitate words by sounds, which, though it gives the pleasure which imitation always produces, yet it fails of exciting those lasting affections which it is in the power of sounds to produce. In a word, no man understood harmony so well as he ; but in melody he has been exceeded by several.

(Myers, 1948, p. 38.) For the distinctions between national schools of music, cf. Avison in 1752. The " rest ", as opposed to Handel, are the other composers. Cf. April 1760.

———

Memoirs of the Life of the late G. F. Handel is published anonymously, spring 1760.

This was the first biography of a musician in any language. The author was John Mainwaring (1724–1807), a young theologian of St. John's College, Cambridge. He was rector of Church Stretton, Salop, and later Professor of Divinity at Cambridge. His biographical information came from John Christopher Smith ; the list of Handel's works was provided by James Harris, and some observations on the works by Richard Price. Identical extracts from the little book appeared in the *Gentleman's Magazine* of April and May, in the *London Chronicle* of 14th and 17th June and in the *Universal Magazine* of June 1760. Reviews appeared in the *Critical Review* of April, and in the *Monthly Review, or Literary Journal* of June 1760, the latter with some extracts from the book. It was translated into German by Johann Mattheson, with numerous remarks by the translator, Hamburg, 1761. While the original has never been reprinted, the German edition has been newly edited by Bernhard Paumgartner, Zürich, 1947, and by Hedwig and E. H. Mueller von Asow in their bi-lingual edition of Handel's letters, Lindau and Vienna, 1949. An abridged version in French was published in Paris in 1768 (see *Bibliography*).

OBJECTIONS TO GOLDSMITH'S ESSAY, BY A CORRESPONDENT, WITH GOLDSMITH'S REPLIES TO THEM, "BRITISH MAGAZINE", April 1760

To the Author of the British Magazine.

. . . The author of this article seems too hasty in degrading the harmonious Purcell, from the head of the English school, to erect in his room a foreigner (Handel), who has not yet formed any school.[1] The gentleman, when he comes to communicate his thoughts upon the different schools of painting, may as well place Rubens at the head of the English painters, because he left some monuments of his art in England.[2] He says, that Handel *originally* a German (as most certainly he was, and continued so to his last breath), yet adopted the English manner.[3] Yes, to be sure, just as much as Rubens the painter did. . . .

Feb. 18, 1760.   S. R.

(Myers, 1948, p. 38.) The cipher S. R. has not been explained. Tobias Smollett, the editor of the magazine, sent S. R.'s "Objections" to Goldsmith; he then published them, together with Goldsmith's riposte as below. The February

[1] Handel may be said as justly as any man, not Pergolese excepted, to have founded a new school of music. When he first came into England his music was entirely Italian : he composed for the opera ; and though even then his pieces were liked, yet did they not meet with universal approbation. In those he has too servilely imitated the modern vitiated Italian taste, by placing what foreigners call the *point d'orgue* too closely and injudiciously. But in his oratorios, he is perfectly an original genius. In these, by steering between the manners of Italy and England, he has struck out new harmonies, and formed a species of music different from all others. He has left some excellent and eminent scholars, particularly Worgan and Smith, who compose nearly in his manner,—a manner as different from Purcell's as from that of modern Italy. Consequently Handel may be placed at the head of the English school.

[2] The Objector will not have Handel's school to be called an English school, because he was a German. Handel, in a great measure, found in England those essential differences which characterize his music : we have already shown that he had them not upon his arrival. Had Rubens come over to England but moderately skilled in his art ; had he learned here all his excellency in colouring and correctness of designing ; had he left several scholars excellent in his manner behind him, I should not scruple to call the school erected by him the English school of painting. [It is] not the country in which a man is born, but his peculiar style either in painting or in music, that constitutes him of this or that school. . . . Kneller is placed in the German school, and Ostade in the Dutch, though both born in the same city. . . . There might several other instances be produced ; but these, it is hoped, will be sufficient to prove, that Handel, though a German, may be placed at the head of the English school.

[3] Handel was originally a German ; but by a long continuance in England, he might have been looked upon as naturalized to the country. I don't pretend to be a fine writer : however, if the gentleman dislikes the expression (although he must be convinced it is a common one), I wish it were mended.

[Oliver Goldsmith.]

quotation is from Vol. I, pp. 74-6, the April one from pp. 181-4. John Worgan, a pupil of Thomas Roseingrave, was an organist and composer ; he wrote several oratorios. Kneller was born in Lübeck, Ostade in Haarlem. Handel had, in fact, been naturalized.

—

Walsh is granted a new Royal privilege, for publishing the third series of Handel's Organ Concertos, 19th August 1760.

(Chrysander, III. 162.) Cf. 14th June 1720 and 31st October 1739. Walsh published the six organ concertos on 23rd February 1761 as Handel's opus 7. The privilege, again valid for 14 years, covered another Handel publication, which was not quite new. It is mentioned in the following passage of the document, signed by William Pitt, then Secretary of State : " Our Trusty and Wellbeloved *John Walsh*, Our Musical Instrument maker, hath by his Petition humbly represented unto Us, that he hath at a great Expence and Labour Purchased and Collected several Pieces of Vocal and Instrumental Musick, Composed by the late *George Frederick Handel* Esqr (Viz) Six Concertos for the Harpsicord and Organ with the Instrumental Parts for Concerts, Entitled A Third Set, and a Selected Collection of Songs from his Operas and Oratorios for the Harpsicord and Concerts, never before Collected & Published together."

—

THE EARL OF SHAFTESBURY'S MEMOIRS OF HANDEL [AUTUMN 1760]

[In April and May 1760 the *Gentleman's Magazine* printed some extracts from John Mainwaring's *Memoirs of the Life of the late G. F. Handel*, published anonymously shortly before. The *London Chronicle* reprinted the extracts on 14th and 17th June 1760. It is to the latter that Shaftesbury refers ; p. 579 of the *London Chronicle* corresponds to pp. 215 f. of the *Gentleman's Magazine* of May 1760 ; the whole quotation refers to pp. 98-113 of Mainwaring's book.]

(London Chronicle, Page 579, &c.)

The method of this Subscription [for the " Academy of Music "] was, for each Subscriber to sign a Bond for £200, which Sum was to answer, all calls that might be made, upon the Subscribers for Expences in carrying on the Opera's exceeding the Sums collected each night at the House. And a sett of Directors were Elected, for carrying on the Affairs of the Academy ; which was Incorporated by a Charter. The Directors were for the most part Persons of Distinction.

Quaere What is mean't by Handell's Association ? As he was only employed as a Composer, in the same way as Buononcini. " Was put in Possession of the House." Here is a mistake again, the House being in Possession of the Academy.

In this Opera of Muzio Scaevola, there were three Composers vizt Handell, Buononcini, and (Quaere) Peebo ? [Pippo.] " And Handell was chief Composer for almost nine years." " Handell and Senesino quarell'd " here is another great mistake.

In the year 1727, Violent Parties were formed, between the 2 famous Singers, Faustini & Cuzzoni ; and in the Election for Directors, Faustini's Party carried it. These Animosities were very prejudicial to the Interest of the Academy, and the Houses began to grow thinner upon it. The Beggar's Opera appearing soon after, gave such a Turn to the Town, that Opera's were generally neglected : And as their Expences were great, and their Receipt small, the Sums Subscribed for was determined in the Summer 1728. And tho' the Term of the Charter was then unexpired, yet the Fund for maintaining Opera's being exhausted, they ceased of course,—and the Singers left England. This is the real Cause of the discontinuance of Opera's at that time.

In the Spring 1729 a fresh Subscription was on foot for performing Opera's, under the Patronage of The Princess Royal. Fifty Opera's were engaged to be performed, for a Subscription of 15 Guineas a Ticket ; and they were to be under the Direction of Mr Heidegger, and Mr Handell, who were joint Partners in the Thing and their Partnership was for 5 Years. To Execute this Scheme, Mr Handell went to Italy, where he hired Strada, Bernachi &c^a. When at Rome Mr Handell waited on his old Friend, Cardinal Ottoboni, who received him with the greatest marks of Friendship and Esteem.

" Rais'd a Subscription against him." Here is another strange mistake in regard to the time. For in performing the Opera's in the Winter 1729, which began with that of Lotharius ; the Town received them very favourably, and in the Spring following (1730), a 2^d Annual Subscription, was set on foot upon the same Terms with the former ;—but the Town having expressed a Desire of having Senesino, Mr Handell hired him in the room of Bernachi. They open'd with the Opera of Scipio, and Senesino at his first appearing on the Stage, was received with the greatest Applause.

In this Spring (1732) a 4th Ann^l Subscrp^n was set on foot for the ensuing Season, upon the same terms, but the Subs^n for the 50 Opera's for this Season, having been all performed about the end of May, the Town being yet very full, M^r H: perform'd in the Hay Market the Masque of Acis & Galatea ; This was perf^d in Italian, & some additional Songs were thrown into it, & the Stage was disposed in a pretty Manner. It had happened that the preceding Season, only 49 Opera's had been perform'd instead of 50 Subscribed for, so that the Subscribers Tickets of last Year were admitted to this Performance, as were the Subs^{rs} themselves. This Entertainment was performed at least twice which in reality was to the Subscribers of this Year a present of 2 Performances gratis. And in the Spring it was that M^r H: perform'd the Oratorio of Esther in Publick, to which he made considerable Additions.

In the Spring 1733, Mr Handell finding that the Oratorio of Esther, had been well received, the Oratorio of Deborah, which he reckoned into the number of the 50 Opera's Subscribed for, and—as he had taken great Pains, and as this was a new kind of Musick attended with some Extraordinary Expence, and more over for his own Benefit, he took double Prices, vizt a Guinea for Pit & Box's. This Indiscreet Step disgusted the Town, and he had a very thin House ; however the great

Merit of the Piece prevail'd, so far, that it had a considerable run, and was received with great Applause.

About this time, a misunderstanding happen'd,—between Mr Handell and Senesino, and some of the other Singers ; whose Party being very numerous, taking advantage more over of the Disgust Mr Handell had given to the Town (in taking a Guinea for his Benefit Subscription) a Subscription was raised for carrying on Opera's in Lincoln's-Inn-Fields ; and where Senesino was to have the principal part ; and Porpora was the Composer. What help'd to disgust the Town was, Mr Handell's putting his Benefit upon an Opera Day. Mr Handell's Subscription in the Hay Market was a very small one ; and tho' he had hired the famous Carastini, Strada and some other good Singers ; his Houses were generally very thin, 'till the Opera of Ariadne was exhibited, which gained him several full Houses. He Perform'd his Oratorio of Deborah again a few times this Season. At the end of this Season (1733/4) the 5 Years Partnership with Mr Heidegger being determin'd, the Hay Market House was lett to the Gentlemen, who had carried on the Opera's in Lincoln's Inn Fields : And Mr Handell associated himself with Mr Rich to carry on Opera's in Covent Garden.

(N.B. 1733 Handel at Oxford. Athalia.)

His Performers were the same as at the Hay-Market the preceding Season, but his Antagonists, had not only the advantage in getting the Hay-Market House ; but had besides the benefit of the famous Farinelli, so that they carried away the Town, for they had immense Houses, when Mr Handell's were very empty. The Opera of Alcino which he performed, gave some turn in his favour, and a little recovered his losses ; however he desisted for that time, from Solliciting any further Subscription.

The Year after Viz^t (1735/6) Mr Handell performed his celebrated Composition of Alexander's Feast, and a few times afterwards his Opera of Attalanto. Encouraged by the Success he met with this Year, he, in Partnership with Mr Rich, set forward a fresh Subscription for Opera's for the ensuing Season ; and in that, tho' he had several Capital Singers, and Exhibited such a Variety of Excellent New Opera's, vizt Arminius, Justin, Berenice, and the Il Trionpho del Tempo, he met with no Success. Great fatigue and disappointment, affected him so much, that he was this Spring (1737) struck with the Palsy, which took entirely away, the use of 4 fingers of his right hand ; and totally disabled him from Playing : And when the heats of the Summer 1737 came on, the Disorder seemed at times to affect his Understanding. His Circumstances being in a manner ruined, he entered into an Agreement to Compose, for the Gentlemen at the Hay Market,[1] and by the advice of his Physicians went to the Baths of Aix-la-Chapelle.

[1] And from this time, there was never any Contest between M^r H: and any Sett of Gentlemen.

These Baths had an amazing effect upon him, for in a few times using them, the use of his fingers was restor'd to him ; his Spirits grew Calm, and he was able to perform upon the Harpsicord. His recovery was so compleat, that on his Return from thence to England, he was able to Play long Voluntaries upon the Organ. In one of the great Towns in Flanders, where he had asked Permission to Play, the Organist attended him, not knowing who he was ; and seem'd Struck with Mr Handell's Playing when he began : But when he heard Mr Handell lead off a Feuge, in Astonishment he ran up to him, & embracing him, said " You can be no other but the great Handell."

Very soon after Mr Handell's arrival in England, her late Majesty Queen Caroline Died. The King's Composer (or some one else) was directed to Compose an Anthem, but the thing requiring haste ; and The King being willing, this should be Executed in the best manner, an Intimation was given to Mr Handell that he should Compose it, and this he immediatly set to Work upon, and in 8 Days time finish'd that Inimitable Piece of Harmony. The King was so well satisfied with his Work, that, He, honour'd him with a gracious message expressing His Satisfaction.

This Winter (1737/8) Mr Handell Composed for the Gentlemen at the Hay Market, the Opera's of Faramondo and Xerxes ; and made up the Pasticio of Allessandro Severo. It was in this Season (1737/8) that Mr Handell had his great Benefit at the Hay Market, which enabled him to Discharge his Debts ; the Gentlemen having been so obliging to lend him the House.

No fresh Subscription for Opera's being set on foot at this time, the Opera Singers left England : And, Mr Handell, the ensuing Winter hired the Hay Market House for the Performance of his Oratorio's. He began (1738/9) with the Oratorio of Saul, and he afterwards performed that Majestic Composition of Israel in Egypt : But his Singers in general not being Capital, nor the Town come into a relies of this Species of Musick, he had but a disadvantageous Season.

The latter end of the Summer following, he Composed his 12 Instrumental Concertos ; and in the Winter after, hired Lincoln's Inn Fields Play House for his Performances, which he continued twice a Week, throwing in sometimes an Opera, and during the Winter, that of Hymen was Compos'd.

In Novem^r 1739, he performed his 2^d Ode of Dryden's, on St Cecilia's Day, then set to Musick.

Between this Year (1739/40), he met with but indifferent Success : However he was resolved to try once more, and again performed in the same manner as the preceding Winter at Lincoln's Inn Fields Play House.

It was in the Winter 1740/1, that he performed his Opera of Diedamar [Deidamia] : However finding that notwithstanding there was no Opera (nor had been any since the Year 1738 ;) he met with little encouragement, he gave over his Performances and in the Year 1741 went to Ireland.

In Lent 1743, at Covent Garden he performed his Oratorio of Sampson, and it was received with uncommon Applause. He afterwards performed The Messiah. But partly from the Scruples, some Persons had entertained, against carrying on such a Performance in a Play House, and partly for not entering into the genius of the Composition, this Capital Composition, was but indifferently relish'd.

The Lent following (1743/4), he again performed Oratorio's at Covent Garden, and met with Success. The New one this Year, was that of Joshua ; and he also set a Dramatic Piece of Mr Congreve's called Semele. This Season likewise proved a good one to him.

Opera's after having been revived for two Seasons, ceasing again. Mr Handell hired the Hay Market House, and began Performances in the Oratorio manner in the Winter 1744. The Drama of Hercules, and the Oratorio of Belshazzer were new this Winter, but this proved a very bad Season and he performed with considerable loss.

The Lent following (1745/6), he perform'd only a very few times, his Occasional Oratorio at Covent Garden. It was then new.

In 1746/7 he performed again, Wednesdays and Fridays in Lent ; and the Oratorio of Judas Maccabeus, went off with very great Applause. He continued his Performances in Lent to the time of his Death.

Public Record Office : Shaftesbury Papers, Sect. VI, Bundle XXVIII, no. 84. The manuscript is a fair copy, by another hand, with some corrections and additions, probably written by the author (" Quaere " means query). Streatfeild, 1909, quoted three sentences and a few separate words, only, of these memoirs, which had been mentioned as early as 1872, by Alfred J. Horwood, in the Third Report of the Historical Manuscripts Commission (pp. 216 f.). The Earl of Shaftesbury, James Harris's cousin and like him an ardent Handelian, started to write some marginal notes to Mainwaring (probably without knowing the author, or the book itself, which was quoted second-hand in the London Chronicle). But soon Shaftesbury, disregarding Mainwaring, whose memoirs were themselves second-hand, started writing his own memoirs of Handel. It seems a pity that Shaftesbury confined himself to Handel's performances, telling us nothing of the man, whom he must have known very well. (At St. Giles, the residence of the Shaftesburys, there is still a large collection of Handel scores.) In any case, his recollections, though not faultless, give a rough sketch of Handel's professional life in London, written by one in the know, and probably from Handel's own viewpoint. The remark in paragraph 7 about there being one performance short of the number promised to subscribers was one of the sentences published by Streatfeild. Smith, 1948, p. 216, refers to the advertisement of 10th June 1732, which shows that the season of 1731-2 was not short of one evening but, on the contrary, contained more performances than were promised. It seems, however, that Shaftesbury was referring to the previous season, 1730-31.

———

A New and General Biographical Dictionary, published in 1761, contains, in Vol. VI, pp. 307-14, an anonymous article on Handel, with critical remarks on Mainwaring's indulgence towards Handel's gluttony.

Cf. 21st March 1754.

———

FROM THE "HISTORY OF THE TRAVELS AND ADVENTURES OF THE CHEVALIER JOHN TAYLOR, OPHTHALMIATER", 1761

. . . I have seen a vast variety of singular animals . . . and particularly at *Leipsick*, where a celebrated master of music, who had already arriv'd to his 88th year, received his sight by my hands ; it is with this very man that the famous *Handel* was first educated, and with whom I once thought to have had the same success, having all circumstances in his favour, motions of the pupil, light, &c. but upon drawing the curtain, we found the bottom defective, from a paralytic disorder.

John Taylor, the elder, 1703–72, was an itinerant oculist. He dedicated this autobiography to his son, John the younger (1724–87), also an oculist. The passage quoted is from I. 25. The father was in Leipzig in 1748, or between 1750 and 1752. If he alludes to Johann Sebastian Bach, who was not educated with Handel, the dates are wrong : Bach died in 1750, sixty-five years of age. We cannot even guess whom Taylor meant ; he was very unreliable in his records. For Handel's eye troubles, cf. 13th and 23rd February, 14th March, 15th June and 16th November 1751, 17th August and 4th November 1752, 13th and 27th January 1753, January 1755, 24th and 26th August 1758 ; Coats, pp. 9 f., and James, p. 168.

———

FROM THE "LONDON CHRONICLE", 15th July 1762

Last Saturday [the 10th] was opened in Westminster-Abbey near the Poets Corner the monument in memory of the late George Frederick Handel, Esq. He is represented pointing to the back of the monument, where David is playing on the harp. In Mr. Handel's right hand is a pen, writing part of the Messiah, "I know that my Redeemer liveth, &c." and the following inscription,

GEORGE FREDERICK HANDEL,

Born February 23, 1684,

Died April 14, 1759.

This report was reprinted in the *Annual Register . . . of the Year 1762*, pp. 93 f. The year of Handel's birth on the Abbey monument has never been corrected to 1685. It is not true that the day of his death was altered into "April 13", as related by Burney and Schoelcher. (The figures are Roman.) The spelling of Handel's second Christian name was the usual one ; he himself liked to spell it Frideric, a compromise between the German Friedrich and the English Frederick. The monument was by Roubiliac, the sculptor of Handel's statue in Vauxhall Gardens (see 18th April 1738). The terracotta model for the marble statue in the Abbey is in the Ashmolean Museum, Oxford. There is no epitaph. The costs were covered by Handel's fourth codicil (11th April 1759). Roubiliac also made two busts of Handel : one is preserved at the Foundling Hospital, the other (formerly in the possession of the Smiths, father and son) is at Windsor Castle. All Roubiliac's portraits of Handel are without wig, and apparently very realistic. For the care he took in modelling Handel's ear, see John Thomas Smith, *Life of* [*Joseph*] *Nollekens and his Times*, 1829, II. 87. Roubiliac died before the Handel monument was unveiled, on 15th January 1762.

———

FROM TOBIAS SMOLLETT'S "CONTINUATION OF THE COMPLETE HISTORY OF ENGLAND", 1762

In the spring of this year [1759] the liberal arts sustained a lamented loss in the death of George Frederic Handel, the most celebrated master in music which this age produced. He was by birth a German ; but had studied in Italy, and afterwards settled in England, where he met with the most favourable reception, and resided above half a century, universally admired for his stupendous genius in the sublime parts of musical composition.[1]

(Myers, 1948, p. 158 : dating the book 1760.) III. 95 f. In the footnote there follows a list of five Scotsmen, all of them more than one hundred years of age, who died within a few months in 1759. For Smollett's connection with Handel, see 8th January 1750.

———

FROM FRIEDRICH WILHELM MARPURG'S "KRITISCHE BRIEFE ÜBER DIE TONKUNST" ("CRITICAL LETTERS ON MUSIC"), BERLIN, 1763 (Translated)

Anne, Crown Princess of Great Britain, consort of Wilh. Car. Heinr. Friso, late Prince of Orange, hereditary Stadholder of the United Netherlands, Hendel's only female pupil of music, was unusually accomplished in singing and, especially, in Thorough Bass ; used to hold in the evenings of fine days, when she was well, a public two-hour concert. Departed this life on 12th January 1759. . . .

Hendel, Witvogel has printed under his name 5 pieces for the clavecin in map-size. Hendel used to say he had written them in his early youth.

Quoted from Vol. II, part 4, pp. 463 and 467. This contribution was from "Conrad Wohlgemuth", a pseudonym of Lustig (see p. 360 and, *passim*, 1756). Willem IV, originally Johann Wilhelm Friso von Nassau-Diez, died in 1751, and his widow, Anne, became Stadholder of the Netherlands. (It may be mentioned here that young Mozart wrote K. 22-24 for Willem V, Anne's son, 1766.) For Witvogel, see 19th January 1753.

———

FROM THE "HISTORICAL ACCOUNT OF THE CURIOSITIES OF LONDON AND WESTMINSTER", 1764

[Of Westminster Abbey and its Curiosities.]

20. *George Frederick Handell.* This is the last Monument which that eminent Statuary *Rubiliac* lived to finish. 'Tis affirmed, that he first

[1] One would be apt to imagine that there was something in the constitution of the air at this period, which was particularly unfavourable to old age. . . .

became conspicuous, and afterwards finished the Exercise of his Art with a Figure of this extraordinary Man. . . .

The last sentence refers, of course, to Roubiliac's statue in Vauxhall Gardens.

—

FROM A LETTER OF THOMAS MORELL TO . . . (*c.* 1764)

. . . And now as to Oratorio's :—" There was a time (says Mr Addison), when it was laid down as a maxim, that nothing was capable of being well set to musick, that was not nonsense." And this I think, though it might be wrote before Oratorio's were in fashion, supplies an Oratorio-writer (if he may be called a writer) with some sort of apology ; especially if it be considered, what alterations he must submit to, if the Composer be of an haughty disposition, and has but an imperfect acquaintance with the English language. As to myself, great a lover as I am of music, I should never have thought of such an undertaking (in which for the reasons above, little or no credit is to be gained), had not Mr Handell applied to me, when at Kew, in 1746, and added to his request the honour of a recommendation from Prince Frederic. Upon this I thought I could do as well as some that had gone before me, and within 2 or 3 days carried him the first Act of *Judas Maccabaeus*, which he approved of. " Well," says he, " and how are you to go on ? " " Why, we are to suppose an engagement, and that the Israelites have conquered, and so begin with a chorus as

Fallen is the Foe

or, something like it." " No, I will have this," and began working it, as it is, upon the Harpsichord. " Well, go on ", " I will bring you more tomorrow." " No, something now,"

" So fall thy Foes, O Lord "

" that will do," and immediately carried on the composition as we have it in that most admirable chorus.

That incomparable Air, *Wise men flattering, may deceive us* (which was the last he composed, as *Sion now his head shall raise*, was his last chorus) was designed for *Belshazzar* but that not being perform'd he happily flung it into *Judas Maccabaeus*. N.B. The plan of *Judas Maccabaeus* was designed as a compliment to the Duke of Cumberland, upon his returning victorious from Scotland. I had introduced several incidents more apropos, but it was thought they would make it too long and were therefore omitted. The Duke however made me a handsome present by the hands of Mr Poyntz. The success of this Oratorio was very great. And I have often wished, that at first I had ask'd in jest, for the benefit of the 30th Night instead of a 3d. I am sure he would have given it me : on which night the[re] was above 400*l.* in the House. He left me a legacy however of 200*l.*

The next year he desired another and I gave him *Alexander Balus*, which follows the history of the foregoing in the *Maccabees*. In the first part there is a very pleasing Air, accompanied with the harp, *Hark, Hark he strikes the Golden Lyre*. In the 2d, two charming duets, *O what pleasure past expressing*, and *Hail, wedded Love, mysterious Law*. The 3d begins with an incomparable Air, in the affettuoso style, intermixed with the chorus Recitative that follows it. And as to the last Air, I cannot help telling you, that, when Mr Handell first read it, he cried out " *D—n* your Iambics ". " Dont put yourself in a passion, they are easily Trochees." " *Trochees, what are Trochees?* " " Why, the very reverse of Iambics, by leaving out a syllable in every line, as instead of

> *Convey me to some peaceful shore,*
> *Lead me to some peaceful shore.*"

" That is what I want." " I will step into the parlour, and alter them immediately." I went down and returned with them altered in about 3 minutes ; when he would have them as they were, and set them most delightfully accompanied with only a quaver, and a rest of 3 quavers.

The next I wrote was *Theodora* (in 1749), which Mr Handell himself valued more than any Performance of the kind ; and when I once ask'd him, whether he did not look upon the Grand Chorus in the Messiah as his Master Piece ? " *No* ", says he, " *I think the Chorus at the end of the 2d part in Theodora far beyond it*. He saw the lovely youth &c."

The 2d night of *Theodora* was very thin indeed, tho' the Princess Amelia was there. I guessed it a losing night, so did not go to Mr Handell as usual ; but seeing him smile, I ventured, when, " Will you be there next Friday night," says he, " and I will play it to you ? " I told him I had just seen Sir T. Hankey, " and he desired me to tell you, that if you would have it again, he would engage for all the Boxes." " *He is a fool ; the Jews will not come to it (as to Judas) because it is a Christian story ; and the Ladies will not come, because it [is] a virtuous one.*"

My own favourite is *Jeptha*, which I wrote in 1751, and in composing of which Mr Handell fell blind. I had the pleasure to hear it finely perform'd at Salisbury under Mr Harris ; and in much greater perfection, as to the vocal part, at the Concert in Tottenham Court Road.

The *Triumph of Time and Truth*—in 1757. The words were entirely adapted to the music of *Il Trionfo del Tempo*, composed at Rome in about 1707.

To oblige Mr Handell's successor, I wrote *Nabal* in 1764, and *Gideon*. The music of both are entirely taken from some old genuine pieces of Mr Handell. In the latter is an inimitable Chorus—*Gloria Patri, Gloria filio*, which at first sight I despaired of setting with proper words ; but at last struck out *Glorious Patron, glorious Hero* &c. which did mighty well. . . .

Hodgkin MSS., p. 91. The addressee of this letter is unknown ; it may have been written a few years later than 1764. The air " Wise men flattering " was, in fact, performed with *Belshazzar* in 1758. The words are, however, added to some librettos of *Judas Maccabaeus* dated 1756 and 1757, but these may not have been issued till 1758 or even 1759. (Information kindly supplied by Mr. Winton Dean.) The oratorio-pasticcios *Nabal* and *Gideon*, words by Morell, were performed at Covent Garden in 1764 and 1769 respectively ; the music was arranged by John Christopher Smith, " Handell's successor ". Cf. 1 April 1747.

———

The full score of *Messiah* is published by Walsh's successors, Randall & Abell, 4th July 1767 (*Public Advertiser*).

———

FROM [SIR JOHN HAWKIN'S] " AN ACCOUNT OF THE INSTITUTIONS AND PROGRESS OF THE ACADEMY OF ANCIENT MUSIC ", 1770

. . . In the Month of February 1731-2, the Academy had given a signal proof of the advantages arising from its institution : the Oratorio of Esther, originally composed for the duke of *Chandois*, was performed in character by the members of the Academy, and the children of the Chapel Royal, and the applause with which it was received, suggested to Mr. *Handel*, the thought of exhibiting that species of composition at Covent Garden theatre ; and to this event it may be said to be owing, that the public have not only been delighted with the hearing, but are now in possession of, some of the most valuable works of that great master.

Cf. 23rd February (3rd March) 1732. Handel produced *Esther* on 2nd May 1732 at the Haymarket Theatre.

———

FROM THE " PUBLIC ADVERTISER ", 14th February 1771

To the Printer of the Public Advertiser.

Jan. 27.

SIR,

As a Proof of your Impartiality, you are desired to insert the following Answer to a Letter dated from Gopsal, Leicestershire, which appeared in your Paper on Saturday last [26th January]. A Gentleman of great Probity and Worth has been there attacked in the most virulent and insulting Manner for having suffered an Author to dedicate to him " A Specimen for a projected Edition of Shakespeare ". . . . I assert that Mr. Jennens . . . understands Music, Poetry, and Painting. . . . His Taste in Music is still less disputable [than that in Painting] : The Compilation of the Messiah has been ever attributed to him. Handel generally consulted him ; and to the Time of his Death lived with him in the strictest Intimacy and Regard. . . . Were Handel and Holdsworth Men so mean or despicable as to offer Incense at the Shrine of Ignorance ?

If Adulation was the Idol of Mr. Jennens' Heart, is it likely that he would have sought for it from the Bluntness of the one, or the sober Dignity of the other ? Would he not (for the Ear of Flattery is seldom nice) have rather expected it from some languid Musician, or some adulterate Critic ? . . .

INDEPENDENT.

(Schoelcher, p. 231.) This letter was written by a friend, or servant, of Jennens, in answer to another, dated " Gopsal, Jan. 21 ", and signed PHILOVETULUS, who is said to have been George Steevens. The first letter, published on 26th January 1771 in the same paper, refers to Jennens's protest against a critical remark about the dedication to him of a new Shakespeare edition. Jennens himself, starting in 1770, edited six plays of Shakespeare ; he died in 1773, and the last volume did not appear until 1774. Edward Holdsworth, a classical scholar who, in 1742, published his letters to a friend, i.e. Jennens, and who died in 1746, left his notes on Virgil to Jennens, who ornamented his grave and erected in the wood of Gopsal a monument to his friend, with a figure by Roubiliac. Holdsworth's and Joseph Spence's translation of Virgil's works first appeared in 1753, and Holdsworth's remarks on Virgil were published by Spence in 1768.

———

Johanna Friederike Flörke, née Michaelsen, Handel's favourite niece and sole heir, dies, 24th February 1771.

As was the custom in that part of the Continent, obituary verses, signed by her daughter and her sons-in-law, were printed in her honour. A copy of the 12-page pamphlet containing them was in the sale of W. H. Cummings's collection in 1917 (catalogue no. 823, item 5).

———

A law student named Händel, of Fiddichow near Schwedt (on the Oder), tries, from 23rd June till 28th August 1772, to get some share of Handel's estate.

(" Mitteilungen für die Berliner Mozart-Gemeinde ", Berlin, 1902, pp. 105 f.) Original documents in Preussisches Geheimes Staatsarchiv, Berlin.

———

JAMES BEATTIE TO THE REV. DR. LAING

Aberdeen, 25th May 1780.

I lately heard two anecdotes, which deserve to be put in writing and which you will be glad to hear. When Handel's " Messiah " was first performed, the audience was exceedingly struck and affected by the music in general ; but when that chorus struck up, " For the Lord God Omnipotent reigneth ", they were so transported, that they all, together with the king (who happened to be present), started up, and remained standing till the chorus ended : and hence it became the fashion in England for the audience to stand while that part of the music is performing. Some days after the first exhibition of the same divine oratorio, Mr. Handel came to pay his respect to lord Kinnoull, with whom he was particularly acquainted. His lordship, as was natural, paid him some compliments on the noble entertainment which he had lately given the town. " My lord," said Handel, " I should be sorry if I only entertained them, I wish to make them better." These two anecdotes I had from lord Kinnoull himself. You will agree with me, that the first does great honour to Handel, to music, and to the English nation : the second tends to confirm my theory, and sir John Hawkins testimony, that Handel, in spite of all that has been said to the contrary, must have been a pious man.

(Myers, 1948, p. 79.) Beattie, *Letters*, II. 77 f. The performance mentioned was, of course, the first in London (not in Dublin) ; cf. 23rd March 1743. Thomas Hay, 8th Earl of Kinnoull, was a Commissioner of the Revenue. Sir John Hawkins (see 1770) published, in 1776, his *General History of the Science and Practice of Music*, with many references to Handel. The passage referred to is to be found on pp. 408 f. of Vol. V : " He was a man of blameless morals, and throughout his life manifested a deep sense of religion. In conversation he would frequently declare the pleasure he felt in setting the Scriptures to music : and how much the contemplating the many sublime passages in the Psalms had contributed to his edification ; and now that he found himself near his end, these sentiments were improved into solid and rational piety, attended with a calm and even temper of mind. For the last two or three years of his life he was used to attend divine service in his own parish church of St. George, Hanover-square, where, during the prayers, the eyes that at this instant are employed in a faint portrait of his excellencies, have seen him on his knees, expressing by his looks and gesticulations the utmost fervour of devotion." And Burney wrote in 1785 (pp. 33 f.) : " But though he was so rough in his language, and in the habit of swearing, a vice then much more in fashion than at present, he was truly pious, during the last years of his life, and constantly attended public prayers, twice a day, winter and summer, both in London and Tunbridge."

ADDENDA

Page 1 (23rd April 1683) : The Elector of Brandenburg was Friedrich III, as King of Prussia (1688–1713) Friedrich I.

Page 1 (23rd February 1685) : Since 1680 Halle belonged to Brandenburg, and thus to Prussia.

Page 2 (after 6th October 1687) : Handel's father is appointed surgeon to Johann Adolf I, Duke of Saxe-Weissenfels, 3rd February 1688. (Spitta, 1869.)

Page 47 (26th December 1711) : Dryden's *Alexander's Feast* was originally set by Jeremiah Clarke in 1697.

Page 49 (21st January 1712) : The text of *Antioco* was by Apostolo Zeno, the music by Francesco Gasparini.

Page 100 (after 30th January 1720) : Walsh and John Hare advertise "A Collection of Minuets . . . for the Year 1720 . . . by Mr. Hendell, etc. . . . for the Violin or Hautboy", 5th February 1720. (Smith, 1954, p. 302.)

Page 134 (after 6th March 1722) : Walsh and the Hares advertise the score of *Floridante*, 28th March 1722. (Smith, 1954, p. 289.)

Page 135 (2nd August 1722) : Meares advertises his " Most Favourite Songs " from *Muzio Scevola* on 23rd August, Walsh his selection on 25th August 1722. (Smith, 1954, p. 290.)

Page 151 (19th March 1723) : Walsh and the Hares advertise four "Additional Songs " from *Ottone* in April 1723. (Smith, 1954, p. 291.)

Page 162 (2nd May 1724) : Cluer's score of *Giulio Cesare* is published on 24th July 1724. (Smith, 1954, p. 289.)

Page 174 (17th and 31st October 1724) : Handel's autograph score of *Tamerlano* contains some numbers of " Il Bajazet ", another version of Agostino Piovene's book, produced, with music by Francesco Gasparini, at Reggio, in 1719, where Borosini sang the part of Bajazet. (Smith, 1954, p. 293.)

Page 193 (5th February 1726) : Walsh and Joseph Hare publish five new songs from the 1726 performances of *Ottone*. (Smith, 1954, p. 291.)

Page 209 (29th May 1727) : The devices by the translator of *Giulio Cesare*, Thomas Lediard, for the firework display in Hamburg are extant. (Croft-Murray, p. 5.)

Page 217 (18th November 1727, " London Journal ") : Walsh and Joseph Hare first advertise Handel's *Minuets* for the King's birthday, on 11th November 1727. (Smith, 1954, p. 302.)

Page 226 (4th June 1728) : Hawkins (V. 410 f.) mentions Mr. Gael Morris, " a broker of the first eminence ", as Handel's financial adviser.

Page 259 (after 18th July 1730) : Walsh and Joseph Hare advertise " Six Solos, Four [nos. 1–3 by Handel] for a German Flute and a Bass and two for a Violin with a Thorough Bass . . . Compos'd by Mr. Handel, etc.", 22nd July 1730. (Smith, 1954, p. 300.)

Page 265 (after 22nd December 1730) :

CHRISTIAN AUGUST ROT[T]H'S POEM OF CONSOLATION ADDRESSED TO HANDEL, HALLE (1730)

An Tit. Herrn *George Friedrich Händel* Seinem Hochgeehrten Herrn Vetter Wolte Bey dem schmerzlichen Verluste Dessen geliebtesten

Mutter Frauen Dorothea Händelin diese Trauer-Zeilen aus Halle in
Sachsen nach Engelland mitleydigst übersenden
M. *Christian August Roth*
s.s. Theol. Baccal. und Diaconus zu St. Moritz.

Herr Vetter,
Darf ich Ihn durch schwarze Littern grüssen,
Und bis nach Engelland mit diesen Zeilen gehn,
So wird dies Trauer-Blatt mein Beyleyd in sich schliessen
Und aus ergebner Pflicht zu Seinen Diensten stehn.
Mich deucht, ich sehe noch das freundliche Willkommen,
Womit er unverhofft mein Haus beglückt gemacht,
Als er vergangenes Jahr die Reise vorgenommen,
Und auch in Gegenwart au seinen Freund gedacht.
Die Freude mehrte sich bei denen Anverwandten,
Sobald der erste Tritt in diese Stadt geschehn.
Ja viele wünschten Ihn, die seinen Namen kannten,
In seiner Seltenheit dasselbemahl zu sehn.
Die treueste Mama vergoss viel Freuden-Thränen,
Da Sie bei Finsterniss die fremde Hand bekam.
So mag auch ich anitzt die Worte nicht erwehnen,
Mit welchen Sie zuletzt betrübten Abschied nahm.
Allein nun ist die Lust auf einen Tag verschwunden,
Nach dem die Todes-Pest Ihm Schmerz und Trauer bringt.
Die Hoffnung ist dahin von den vergnügten Stunden,
Was wunder, dass ein Schwert in seine Seele dringt?
Er, als der eintzige von denen nächsten Erben,
Erfährt durch rauhe Luft des Himmels strengen Schluss,
Dass die Getreueste nach zwey Geschwistern sterben,
Und ihn als Ueberrest zurücke lassen muss.
Gewiss, wer diesen Fall vernünftig überlegt,
Der kann, so hart er ist, nicht Stahl und Eisen sein,
Denn wer ein Mutter-Herz zu finstern Grabe trägt,
Der scharrt den grössten Schatz mit grösster Wehmuth ein.
Gesetzt, das Alter sey nicht mehr so stark an Kräften,
So liebt ein frommer Sohn doch was Ihn erst geliebt,
Weil das Gebet zu Gott bei den Berufs-Geschäften,
Ihm alles Wohlergehn Zeit ihres Lebens giebt.
Dergleichen hat er auch beständig sehen lassen,
Davon Sein letzter Brief der Wahrheit Zeuge bleibt,
Denn er bemühet sich beweglich abzufassen,
Was Ihm die Zärtlichkeit in seine Seele schreibt.
Der Inhalt ging dahin, das Leben zu vermehren,
Und der Entkräfteten durch Mittel beizustehn,
Den kalten Todes-Gift noch länger abzuwehren,

Und auch mit Rath und That Ihr an die Hand zu gehn.
Jedoch die Zeit war aus von Ihrem Tugend-Leben,
Das Sie bis achtzig Jahr in dieser Welt gebracht.
Drum hat Sie gute Nacht durch Ihren Tod gegeben,
Und Ihren Jahres-Schluss noch dieses Jahr gemacht.
O selig ! wer sich hier dergleichen Lob erwirbt,
Als die Wohlselige bey Jedermann erlangt,
O selig ! wer wie Sie so wohl und glücklich stirbet,
Der findet, dass der Geist mit Ehren-Kronen prangt.
Dies Hochgeehrtester, wird Er bei sich bedenken,
Und der Wohlseligen geliebtesten Mama
Zwar noch den Thränen-Zoll bei stillen Seufzern schenken,
Weil er das letzte mal Ihr holdes Auge sah ;
Allein, Er wird sich auch durch wahre Grossmuth fassen,
Indem Ihr Segens-Wunsch auf Seinem Haupte ruht,
Und vor die Seinigen den Trost zurücke lassen,
Dass alles heilig sey, was Gottes Wille thut.
Derselbe lasse nun Denselben lange leben,
Und lege seiner Zahl so viele Jahre bey,
Als er der Seligsten auf dieser Welt gegeben,
Damit das Neue Jahr Ihm höchst erspriesslich sey.
Ich aber will hiermit die Trauer-Zeilen schliessen,
Zu welchen ich sofort mich höchst verbunden fand :
Doch lass Er nun darauf nichts mehr von Thränen fliessen,
Denn Seine Seligste lebt itzt in Engelland.

(Précis)

Magister Christian August Roth, Bachelor of Theology and Deacon of the Church of St. Moritz, would like, with sympathy, to transmit from Halle in Saxony to George Friedrich Händel, his cousin in England [Engelland = the land of angels], the following verses of condolence on the painful loss of his beloved mother.

Cousin, if I greet you in black letters, and approach you in England [see supra] with these lines, it is that this poem of condolence may attest to you my sympathy, and also show that I am conscious of my duty as your humble servant. It seems to me as though I could still see the kind welcome, when you so surprisingly brought happiness to my house last year, and remembered me, as you used to do [in letters], in person. The joy of your relatives began when you entered the town. Everybody wanted to see you, even if they knew you only by name. Your faithful mother wept tears of joy when she felt in the darkness the hand of the stranger. And even today I would not like to mention the words with which she then bade you farewell. But now all that pleasure has suddenly vanished, for Death has flung you into pain and grieving. Hope for such pleasant hours is gone, and so your soul must bleed.

Through Heaven's destiny you, the last of her nearest and dearest, have lost a most faithful mother, and this, after the loss of two sisters, leaves you alone. No one can be so without feeling as not to understand that to bury one's mother is the richest of woes. Even though she was so well advanced in years, yet a pious son could never forget her who first loved him ; in the midst of his daily occupations he could not forget those prayers which brought to him her life's blessing. This son has ever shown such piety—the last time in a letter which clearly revealed his tenderness. In it he bade us shelter her in life, by all means to succour her, to hold off death as long as possible, and to help her by word and deed. But the appointed span of her virtuous life expired at eighty years. She bade the world farewell, and her tally of years ended before the year ended. Blessed be she who has earned for herself so much praise from all in this world ; who died in such blessedness and whose spirit has conquered with such honour. You will realise all that if you remember your mother with tears and sighs, since you could not see her once more. But your great heart also knows that her blessing rests on your head, and that it behoves us, who remain behind, to do God's Will. May God give you long life, many years, as many as those with which he favoured her, and may the New Year be gracious to you. With that I end this poem of condolence which I have felt compelled to write. Do not shed upon it further tears—like you, your mother is now in the land of angels [Engelland].

("Euterpe", Leipzig, [March ?] 1870, no, 3, pp. 44 f. ; edited by F. K.) Printed copy of the original in the archives of the Church of St. Moritz, Halle (not available in 1953). For Handel's reaction to the poem cf. his letter to Michaelsen, 12th February 1731. Handel's letter alluded to in the poem is apparently lost. For another poem by Rotth, addressed to Handel, cf. p. 680. For various reasons a précis was preferred here to a translation.

Page 270 (after 17th February 1731) : The " Printing Office " of Cluer's widow advertises " Favourite Songs in . . . Porus ", a pirated edition, 17th February 1731. (Smith, 1954, p. 291.)

Page 272 (after 2nd March 1731) : Walsh advertises his edition of " Favourite Songs in . . . Porus ", 3rd March 1731. (Ditto.)

Page 276 (after 17th August 1731) : Walsh advertises "A Choice Collection of [24] English Songs. Set to Musick by Mr. Handel ", 28th August 1731. (Smith, 1954, p. 298.)

Page 344 (after 4th February 1734) : Walsh advertises " The Favourite Songs in . . . Arbaces ", 5th February 1734. (Smith, 1954, p. 287.)

Page 358 (23rd February 1734) : " Favourite Songs in Arbaces ", see preceding note.

Page 393 (18th July 1735) : The missing words, indicated by dots, were translated from French into German, and now from German into English as follows : " I should like the profits to come up to your expectation, and I regret being unable myself to provide, according to your wishes, the market, as this is not my province "; ". . . and to send it to you as you want . . .".

Page 395 (after 20th August 1735) : Walsh advertises Handel's Opus 3, " Six Fugues or Voluntarys for the Organ or Harpsicord ", 23rd August 1735. (Smith, 1954, p. 306.)

Page 445 (1737) : The history of *Hermann von Balcke* has been told differently by Wm. C. Smith (1954, p. 289).

Page 470 (1738/39) : According to Wm. C. Smith (1954, p. 299) Handel's song was written for the performance on 17th March 1740 of *The Way of the World*, and the Fitzwilliam manuscript is autograph.

Page 475 (12th February 1739) : This was the first selection of "Airs" from *Saul*, the second being advertised on 17th March 1739. (Smith, 1954, p. 281.)

Page 480 (11th April 1739) : Walsh advertises both selections of "Airs" from *Saul* in one volume on 19th March 1739. (Smith, 1954, p. 281.)

Page 486, 1st line : The organ in Trent Cathedral was built between 1532 and 1536 by Caspar Zimmermann, called *Meister Caspar* in German, and *maestro Gaspar* in Italian sources. There have been several renovations, the most important of which was undertaken in 1686/7 by Eugen Kaspar, called *Casparini* in German and *Gasparini* in Italian. This organ existed until the beginning of the nineteenth century. (Information kindly supplied by Dr. Walter Senn, Innsbruck.)

Page 505 (1740) : At the end of the last but one paragraph insert : " ; it was, however, frequently reported in English Court Journals [Hof-Zeitungen] that a marble statue in his honour was erected in Vauxhall Gardens by a few private individuals : which is at least of some importance . . .".

Page 508 (after 22nd November 1740) : Walsh advertises the fourth collection of his " Select Harmony ", containing Handel's Oboe Concertos in C, B flat and B flat, on 11th December 1740 ; no copy known. (Smith, 1954, p. 304.)

Page 577 (end) :

From Constantin Bellermann's " Programma in quo Parnassus Musarum . . . enarrantur ", Erfurt, 1743 (Translated)

It is a good and excellent custom of the English University in Oxford to grant the honours of Bachelor, Master, and Doctor in this subject [music] with the usual academic solemnities. As I know, this honour was bestowed upon Pepusch as well as upon Händel, the great composer to the court of His Majesty, the King of Great Britain ; this very miracle in the art of music, both in England and, perhaps, in Germany, favourably obtained it a few years ago. . . .

Like Händel among the English, Bach deserves to be called the miracle of Leipzig, as far as music is concerned.

Pp. 19 and 39. Copy belonging to the Öffentliche Wissenschaftliche Bibliothek, Berlin, now in Westdeutsche Bibliothek, Marburg an der Lahn. The second passage quoted by Spitta (1873, I. 801 f.). It is known that Handel did not accept the degree of Doctor of Music in Oxford 1734.

Page 590 (4th May 1744) : Walsh advertises Act II of *Joseph and his Brethren*, 19th May 1744. (Smith, 1954, p. 280.)

Page 590 (after 21st May 1744) :

Handel to Mizler

[London,] 25. May 1744.

. . . Ich habe das Doctorat wegen überhäufter Geschäfte nicht annehmen können oder wollen.

(Translation)

[London,] May 25th, 1744.

. . . I neither could nor would accept the Doctor's degree, because I was overwhelmingly busy.

Mizler, vol. 3, part 3, pp. 567 f. Cf. p. 644. Handel's letter was probably written in French. The translation of the one sentence, related by Mizler, made it a little obscure. The further translation, into English, might have obscured it even more. The meaning, however, seems fairly clear.

Page 655 (end) :

FROM [CHRISTIAN GOTTFRIED KRAUSE'S] " LETTRE A MONS. LE MARQUIS DE B. SUR LA DIFFERENCE ENTRE LA MUSIQUE ITALIENNE ET FRANÇAISE ", BERLIN, 1748 (Translated)

German music has no flavour peculiarly its own. But our Händel and Telemann are at least a match for the French, and Hasse and Graun for the Italians.

No copy of the original pamphlet could be traced. Marpurg, however, in his " Beyträge " (vol. I, no. 1, pp. 1-46) of 1754 gives a German translation where the passage quoted above is to be found on p. 22.

Page 659 (17th March 1749) : Smith (1954, p. 281) attributes the text of *Solomon* to Thomas Morell.

Page 673 (2nd June 1749) : Walsh advertises the *Fireworks Music*, in parts, as published, 24th June ; an arrangement for the German flute, violin, or harpsichord, 22nd July 1749. (Smith, 1954, p. 305.)

Page 730 (end) :

FROM JOHANN CARL CONRAD OELRICH's " HISTORISCHE NACHRICHT VON DEN AKADEMISCHEN WÜRDEN IN DER MUSIK " (HISTORICAL REPORT ON THE ACADEMIC DEGREES IN MUSIC), BERLIN, 1752 (Translated)

Finally I must make brief mention of the admirable musician, *Herrn Georg Friederich Händel* in London, of whom, it is true, report says that he has received a Doctor's degree of music.[1] But although he earned such honour long since, and although it was even offered to him, yet he has always declined it : at least he was still not a Doctor in the year 1744, as it becomes evident from a letter he sent to Herr *Lorentz Christoph Mizler* on 25th May 1744.[2] Meanwhile many other tokens

[1] See *Constantin Bellermann's* Progr. in quo parnassus musarum, voce, fidibus, tibiisque resonans, sive musices, divinae artis, laudes, diversae species, singulares effectus atque primarii auctores succincta, praestantissimique melpoetae cum laude enarrantur. Erford. 1743. 4to.

[2] He expressly states in it : *I neither could nor would accept the Doctor's degree, because I was overwhelmingly busy.* See Mizler's *Musikalische Bibliothek*, vol. 3, part 3, p. 568. Consequently, a sentence such as this : " In the year 1733 he was made Doctor of music in London ", which can be read of *Händel* in the *kurzgefasstes musikalisches Lexikon*, issued in *Chemnitz* in 1737 and 1749, in 8vo, may be entirely disregarded.

of esteem have come the way of the well-deserving *Herr Händel* ; among
other things a marble statue in his honour has been erected in Vauxhall
Gardens by some individuals.[1]

Page 771 (17th March 1756) : For this revival of *Israel in Egypt* (cf. 11th April
1739) Handel substituted the "Lamentation" by a part of Act I of *Solomon.*
(Abraham, p. 92.)
Page 781 (end) :

FROM FRIEDRICH WILHELM ZACHARIAE'S POEM "DIE TAGESZEITEN"
(THE TIMES OF THE DAY), ROSTOCK, 1756 (Translated)

O that *Orpheus* of the *British,* in *Vauxhall*[2] and *Ranelagh*[2] commended,
Who in *St. Paul's* enchants, and in the Theatres bewitches,
Why, he belongs to us ; the marble which celebrates him,
Also for Germany serves as memorial stone,
Nor has his fatherland lost him . . .

P. 93. The preface is dated : 1st May 1755. The poem consists of four
books, corresponding to the four times of the day. The lines quoted above
are from book 3, "Der Abend" (The Evening). A second, improved
edition of the poem appeared in 1757, and a new, completely revised one in
1767. In this, the third edition, the lines are altered and Handel spoken of
as deceased. This version has been quoted in Ernst Otto Lindner's "Geschichte des deutschen Liedes im 18. Jahrhundert" (Leipzig, 1871, p. 88) and
the "marble" taken as the monument in Westminster Abbey. Zachariae,
a musician as well as a poet, who translated Milton's *Paradise Lost* (Altona,
1760), referred, of course, originally to the statue in Vauxhall Gardens only.

Page 785 (18th April 1757) : According to Wm. C. Smith (1954, p. 282) Walsh
advertised *The Triumph of Time and Truth* first on 16th April 1757.
Page 806 (26th August 1758) : According to Wm. C. Smith (1954, p. 282)
Walsh advertised "A Grand Collection of Celebrated English Songs Introduced
in the late Oratorios" first on 13th July 1758.

[1] This was reported in English Court Journals [Engländischen Hofzeitungen], as
Herr Mattheson states in the . . . *Grundlage einer musikalischen Ehrenpfort,* p. 101.
[2] Where the two most famous concerts in England are held.

BIBLIOGRAPHY

I. MANUSCRIPT SOURCES

Bank of England : Handel's Accounts.

Bodleian (Oxford) : B.3.15.Art.

British Museum : Accounts of Covent Garden Theatre, 1746/7 and 1749/50. (Egerton MS., 2269, vol. III.)

— List of "Dramas of Italian Opera, acted in England", 1705-76. (Add. MS., Burn. 521.b.)

— Poem addressed to Handel, 1759. (Add. MS. 33,351, f. 24.)

— Register of performances at London Theatres, 1710-29. (Egerton MSS., 2321-2.)

— Theatrical Properties and Scenery at Covent Garden Theatre in 1743. (Add. MS. 12,201, f. 30.)

BURNEY, CHARLES, *D.D.* : Theatrical Register. (A collection of notebooks, containing MS. material and cuttings from books and newspapers, dealing with the history of the stage in England, 1660-1801.) British Museum : 938. a.-d. 84 vols.

COLMAN, FRANCIS (?) : Opera-Register from 1712 to 1734. (A brief account of operas performed at the Haymarket Theatre.) British Museum, Add. MS. 11,258, ff. 19-32. (First used in Michael Kelly's "Reminiscences", London, 1826, vol. II, Appendix. *See also* Bibliography of Books and Articles, *under* Colman, Francis.)

ELAND, CYRIL A.: Handel's Visit to Oxford, A.D. 1733. Compiled from the authorities with additional notes. [Oxford, 1935.] Manuscript. Copy in Gerald Coke's Handel Collection.

Foundling Hospital (London) : Records.

GERALD COKE'S Handel Collection, Bentley (Hants.) : Handel's Will, with four Codicils. Private copy. (The official copy is in the Registry of the Prerogative Court of Canterbury, at Doctor's Commons. Both of these copies are signed, five times, by Handel. An official copy, unsigned, is in the MS. collection of the Royal College of Music, no. 2190, deposited in the British Museum.)

— A Description of the Machine for the Fireworks . . . 1749.

GORDON, JAMES, and WILLIAM ASKEW : An Inventory of the Household Goods of G. F. Handel. British Museum, Egerton MS., 3009.E.

HUNTINGTON (HENRY E.) Library and Art Gallery, San Marino, California : The Duke of Chandos Manuscripts.

LATREILLE, FREDERICK : Play-Bills of London Theatres, copied and compiled . . . together with copies of documents and extracts relating to theatrical affairs ; 1702-1752. [London, 19th Century.] British Museum, Add. MSS. 32,249-32,252 and 47,612-47,617.

MANN, ARTHUR HENRY : A chronological Life of Handel. Consisting entirely of dates. Eight books of loose leaves. Mann Music Library, Mn. 21. 30-37 (King's College), Cambridge.

863

MANN, ARTHUR HENRY : Early Music in Dublin and Musical Performances for the Benefit of Mercer's Hospital in Dublin, 1737–51. Being extracts from the Hospital Governors' Minutes. Ditto, Mn. 24.

— Extracts from *Faulkner's Journal*, Dublin, March 1741–44. Ditto, Mn. 24.

MARSHALL, JULIAN : Catalogue of the printed editions (excluding the Collected Edition of the *Deutsche Händel-Gesellschaft*) of Handel's works, in the National Library of Scotland, Edinburgh (together with Marshall's, later Lord Balfour's Handel Collection). Another copy, in the Royal Music Library, R.M. 18.b.1 (British Museum).

Mercer's Hospital (Dublin) : Records.

Public Record Office : G.D. 24, Bundle XXVIII, nos. 26, 27. L.C. 5/157, 158. L.C. 7/3. Shaftesbury Papers, Sect. VI, Bundle XXVIII, no. 84.

SCHOELCHER, VICTOR : An Account of the Performances of Oratorios by Handel from 1732 to 1759. Translated by Julian Marshall (Royal Music Library, R.M. 18.b.2, ff. 15–22, British Museum).

— An Account of the Performances of Operas given by Handel from 1711 to 1714. Translated by Julian Marshall. Copied by A. H. Mann. Fragment. Mann Music Library (King's College), Cambridge.

— " Catalogue chronological et raisonné " of Handel's works. French original in the Library of the Conservatoire, Paris. Copy in the Royal Music Library, R.M. 18.b.2, ff. 33–370 (British Museum). English translation, by Miss S. A. A. P. Mann, with additional notes from Julian Marshall's catalogue of printed editions and by A. H. Mann. Mann Music Library, Mn. 24 (King's College), Cambridge.

— " Catalogue méthodique " of the dates of composition and first performances of Handel's works. Translated by Julian Marshall. Royal Music Library, R.M. 18.b.2, ff. 1–14 (British Museum).

— List of Handel manuscripts in the British Museum, Buckingham Palace [Royal Music Library, now in the British Museum], Fitzwilliam Museum and Lennard Collection [now in the Fitzwilliam Museum]. Translated by Julian Marshall. Royal Music Library, R.M. 18.b.2, ff. 23–32 (British Museum).

VERTUE, GEORGE : Note Books Af (1722–39), B.4 (1741) and (1749). British Museum, Add. MSS. 23,076 ; 23,079 ; and 23,074.

WALES, FREDERICK PRINCE OF : Register of Warrants for Payment of Tradesmen &c., July 1736–Sept. 1738. British Museum, Add. MSS. 24,403–24,404.

Westminster Public Libraries, Historical Department : Rate books of the Parish of St. George, 1724–60.

YORKE-LANG, ALAN : " The Opera of the Nobility ". A Dissertation, presented for the Osgood Memorial Prize 1951. Oxford (1951).

2. EIGHTEENTH CENTURY PERIODICALS

Aberdeen Journal (Aberdeen) : 1758.
Appleby's Original Weekly Journal : 1719, 20, 23, 24, 33.
Bath Advertiser (Bath) : 1757.
The Bee ; or, *Universal Weekly Pamphlet* : 1733, 34, 35.
Berrow's Worcester Journal (Worcester) : 1750, 53, 56, 59.

Boddely's *Bath Journal* (Bath) : 1749, 52, 55, 56, 58, 59.
Brice's *Weekly Journal* (Exeter) : 1729.
The British Apollo : 1710.
The British Journal [from 1728 onwards] : or, *The Censor* : 1722–24, 27, 28.
The British Magazine (Smollett) : 1760.
The Caledonian Mercury (Edinburgh) : 1751.
Cambridge Journal (Cambridge) : 1753.
Common Sense : or, *The Englishman's Journal* : 1738.
The Country Journal ; or, *The Craftsman* (1726–27 : *The Craftsman*) : 1728, 29, 31–38.
The Covent-Garden Journal (Fielding) : 1752.
The Craftsman : see *The Country Journal*.
Critica Musica (Mattheson, Hamburg) : 1722, 23.
The Critical Review (Smollett) : 1760.
Der critische Musikus (Scheibe, Leipzig) : 1738.
The Daily Advertiser : 1737, 43–45.
The Daily Courant : 1711, 13–17, 20–26, 28–32, 34.
The Daily Gazetteer : 1736, 37, 45.
The Daily Journal : 1725, 28–36.
The Daily Post : 1720, 21, 23–27, 29–33, 35–38.
The Daily Post-Boy : see *The Post Boy*.
The Dublin Gazette (Dublin) : 1736, 39, 41.
The Dublin Journal (Dublin) : 1739–59.
The Dublin News-Letter (Dublin) : 1742.
The Evening Post : see (from 12 December 1727 onwards) *The London Evening Post*.
Faulkner's Journal : see *The Dublin Journal*.
Felix Farley's Bristol Journal (Bristol) : 1727, 56, 57, 58.
The Flying Post ; or, *The Post-Master* : 1713, 27.
Fog's Weekly Journal : see *Mist's Weekly Journal*.
The Free Briton : 1733.
The Gazetteer and London Daily Advertiser : 1759.
The General Advertiser : see *The London Daily Post*.
The General Evening Post : 1735, 45.
The Gentleman's Magazine : or, *Monthly Intelligencer* (from 1736 onwards : *The Gentleman's Magazine and Historical Chronicle*) : 1731–33, 35, 36, 40, 42, 47, 49, 51, 52, 55, 59, 60.
Gloucester Journal (Gloucester) : 1739, 42, 45, 48, 51, 54, 57.
The Gray's Inn Journal : 1753, 54.
The Grub-street Journal : 1733–35, 37, 38.
The Guardian : 1713.
Hallische Zeitung (Halle an der Saale) : 1753.
Historisch-Kritische Beiträge zur Aufnahme der Musik (Marpurg, Berlin) : 1754.
Hooker's Weekly Miscellany : 1733.
The Ipswich Journal (Ipswich) : 1734, 43.
Jackson's Oxford Journal (Oxford) : 1753–59.
Journals of the House of Commons : 1727.
Journals of the House of Lords : 1727.

Kritische Briefe über die Tonkunst (Marpurg, Berlin) : 1763.

Lloyd's Evening Post and British Chronicle : 1759.

The London (Daily) Advertiser (and Literary Gazette) : 1751–53, 55. From 18 April 1751 onwards the word *Daily* was added to the title, from 25 November 1751 to 21 July 1753 the alternative title was omitted.

The London (from 18 April 1751 onwards, Daily) Advertiser (until 24 November 1751 and from 22 July 1753 onwards) and Literary Gazette : 1751–53, 55.

The London Chronicle : or, *Universal Evening Post* : 1757–60, 62.

The London Daily Post, and General Advertiser (from 12 March 1744 onwards, *The General Advertiser* ; from December 1752 onwards, *The Public Advertiser*) : 1734–41, 43, 44–52.

The (London) Evening Post : 1721, 34, 36, 37, 39, 43, 49, 59.

The London Gazette : 1719–21, 1726–29.

The London Journal : 1722–29.

The London Magazine ; or, *Gentleman's Monthly Intelligencer* (from 1736 onwards : *The London Magazine And Monthly Chronologer*) : 1732–34, 36, 37, 38, 44–46, 53, 59, 60.

Le Mercure (Paris) : 1723.

Miscellaneous Correspondence, in Prose and Verse (Editor, Benjamin Martin) : 1755, 59.

Mist's [from 1729 onwards : *Fog's*] *Weekly Journal* ; or, *Saturday's Post* : 1718, 20, 24, 28, 33.

The Monthly Review, or *Literary Journal* : 1754, 60.

The Muses Mercury : or, *The Monthly Miscellany* : 1707.

Der musicalische Patriot (Mattheson, Hamburg) : 1728.

Musikalische Bibliothek, Neu eröffnete (Mizler, Leipzig) : 1737, 46, 47.

Neu eröffnete Musikalische Bibliothek : see *Musikalische Bibliothek*.

The New York Mercury (New York) : 1756.

Norris's Taunton Journal (Taunton) : 1727.

The Norwich Gazette (Norwich) : 1727, 29, 33.

The Norwich Mercury (Norwich) : 1727, 29, 30, 41, 56, 59.

The Old Whig : or, *The Consistent Protestant* : 1735–38.

The Oratory Magazine : 1748.

The Original Weekly Journal : see (from July 1720 onwards) *Applebee's Original Weekly Journal*.

Parker's Penny Post : 1727.

The Post Boy (from 1728 onwards, *The Daily Post-boy*) : 1714, 20–24, 31.

The Post-Man, and the Historical Account : 1711, 17.

Le Pour et Contre, Ouvrage périodique d'un goût nouveau ; *etc.*: Par l'Auteur des Mémoires d'un homme de qualité [*i.e.* Prévost] (Paris) : 1733–35.

The Prompter : 1734.

The Public Advertiser (see *The London Daily Post*) : 1753–59, 71.

The Publick Register ; or, *Weekly Magazine* : 1741.

Pue's Occurances (Dublin) : 1736, 41, 42.

Read's Weekly Journal, or, *British-Gazetteer* : 1720, 23, 25, 27, 31, 33, 37.

St. James's Journal : 1723.

The Salisbury and Winchester Journal (Salisbury) : 1756.

Samenspraaken over muzikaale beginselen (Lustig, Antwerp) : 1756.

The Scots Magazine (Edinburgh) : 1739, 59.
The Spectator : 1711, 12.
The Student : or, *Oxford Monthly Miscellany* (Oxford) : 1750.
The Suffolk Mercury : or, *St. Edmunds-Bury Post* (Bury St. Edmunds) : 1725, 33, 34.
The Theatre (Steele) : 1720.
The Universal Chronicle ; or, *Weekly Gazette* : 1759.
The Universal Magazine of Knowledge and Pleasure : 1751, 59, 60.
The Universal Spectator, and Weekly Journal (Baker) : 1733, 35, 43.
The Weekly Journal : *see* Applebee, Brice, Fog, Mist, Read, and *Universal Spectator*.
The Weekly Journal : or, *British Gazetteer* : see (from 1731 onwards) *Read's Weekly Journal*.
— or, *Saturday's Post* : see *Mist's Weekly Journal*.
The Weekly Miscellany : see *Hooker's Weekly Miscellany*.
The Weekly Oracle : or, *Universal Library* : 1734.
The Weekly Register : or, *Universal Journal* : 1733.
The Whitehall Evening Post : or, *London Intelligencer* : 1759.
The World : 1753.
Unidentified London Newspapers : 1734, 35, 37–39, 41, 45, 52, 53.

★

Burney, Charles, *D.D.*: Collection of newspapers. (Mainly 18th century London papers.) British Museum.
— Theatrical Register. (Cuttings from London newspapers.) *See* Manuscript Sources.
Harris, Sir Augustus : Collection of Newspaper Cuttings on London Theatres. (British Museum, State Papers Room.)

3. BOOKS AND ARTICLES

ABRAHAM, GERALD (editor) : *Handel : A Symposium*. London, 1954.
ADEMOLLO, ALESSANDRO : G. F. Haendel in Italia. (*Gazetta musicale di Milano*, vol. 44.) Milano, 1889.
ADLUNG, JAKOB : *Anleitung zu der musikalischen Gelahrtheit*. Erfurt, 1758.
AITKEN, GEORGE A. : *Life and Works of John Arbuthnot*. Oxford, 1892.
ALCOCK, JOHN : see Anonymous : *On Mr. Handel*.
ANONYMOUS : *An Account of All the Plays printed in the English Language . . . to the Year 1747*. (Appendix to Thomas Whincop's tragedy, ' Scanderbeg '.) London, 1747.
— [ascribed to William Coxe] : *Anecdotes of George Frederick Handel and John Christopher Smith*, etc. London, 1799.
— *Annual Register . . . Of the Year 1762*. London.
— *Calendar of Treasury Papers*. Edited by J. Redington. Vol. VI (1720–28). London, 1889. *Calendar of Treasury Books and Papers*. Edited by W. A. Shaw. Vol. I (1729–30). London, 1897. Vol. II (1731–34). London, 1898. Vol. III (1735–38). London, 1900. Vol. V (1742–45). London, 1903.
— *Catalogue of Prints & Drawings in the British Museum*. Division I. Political and Personal Satires. Vol. II. 1689–1733. London, 1873. Vol. III. Part I. 1734–1750. Part II. 1751–*c*. 1760. London, 1877.

ANONYMOUS [ascribed to Colley Cibber] : *The Contre Temps*; or, *Rival Queans*: a small Farce. As it was lately Acted . . . at H—d—r's private The—re, near the H—M—. London, 1727.

— [ascribed to John Arbuthnot] : *The Devil to pay at St. James's* : or, *A full and true Account of a most horrible and bloody Battle between Madam Faustina and Madam Cuzzoni*, etc. London, 1727.

— *Do you know what you are about ?*, etc. London, 1733. (No copy known.)

— *An Epistle to Mr. Handel, upon his Operas of Flavius and Julius Caesar.* London, 1724.

— Fireworks in the Green Park at the Peace of Aix La Chapelle. (*The Gentleman's Magazine*, New Series, vol. XLV.) London, May 1856.

— *Fitzwilliam Museum.* Commemorative Exhibition of the two hundred and fiftieth anniversary of the births of George Frederick Handel and Johann Sebastian Bach, 1685–1750. (Catalogue.) [Cambridge,] 1935.

— *Georg Friedrich Händel. Abstammung und Jugendwelt. Festschrift zur 250. Wiederkehr des Geburtstages*, etc. Halle, 1935.

— George Frederick Handel. (Special number of *Musical Times*, 14 December 1893.) London. (With contributions by Joseph Bennett, W. H. Cummings, A. J. Hipkins, A. H. Mann, and Sir Walter Parratt.)

— The Handel Portrait at Gopsal. (*Musical Times*, 1 December 1902.) London.

— [ascribed to John Arbuthnot] : *Harmony in an Uproar: A Letter to F—d—k H — — — d — — — l, Esq ; . . . from Hurlothrumbo Johnson, Esq. ;* etc. London, 1734.

— *An Historical Account of the Curiosities of London and Westminster.* London, 1764.

— *The History and Topography of Ashbourn.* Ashbourn, 1839.

— [Christian Gottfried Krause] : *Lettre à Mons. le Marquis de B. sur la différence entre la musique italienne et française.* Berlin, 1748. (Translated, with notes, into German in F. W. Marpurg's *Historisch-Kritische Beyträge zur Aufnahme der Musik*, I. 1–46, Berlin, 1754.)

— *The Manners of the Age* : In Thirteen Moral Satires. London, 1733.

— *National Library of Scotland.* George Frederic Handel, 1685–1759. Catalogue of an Exhibition held during the Edinburgh Musical Festival . . . (With Introduction by Wm. C. Smith.) [Edinburgh,] 1948.

— *An Ode to Mr. Handel.* London, 1722.

— *On Mr. Handel.* Set to music by John Alcock. [London, c. 1735.]

— *The Oxford Act, a new Ballad Opera*, etc. London, 1733.

— *The Oxford Act. A.D. 1733* ; Being a particular and exact account of that Solemnity . . . In a Letter to a Friend in Town. London, 1734.

— *Poems and Translations.* By Several Hands. London, 1714.

— *The Political State of Great-Britain.* Vol. XIV. London, 1717.

— *Polymnia ; or, The Charms of Musick. An Hymn or Ode . . . Occasion'd by Mr. Handel's Oratorio . . . Perform'd at Whitehall . . .* By a Gentleman of Cambridge. London, 1733.

— *Report on Manuscripts in Various Collections.* Vol. II. (Historical Manuscripts Commission.) London, 1903.

ANONYMOUS : Roubiliac's Statues of Handel. (*Musical Times*, 1 September 1905.) London.

— *The Royal Society of Musicians of Great Britain*. London, [*c*. 1920].

— *The Scandalizade*. London, 1750.

— *See and Seem Blind* : or, *A Critical Dissertation on the Publick Diversions, &c. . . . In a Letter from . . . Lord B — — — — — to A — — — H — — —, Esq.* ; London, [1732].

— *The Session of Musicians*. In Imitation of the Session of the Poets. London, 1724.

— *Song on a Goldfinch flying out at the Window while a Lady was playing & singing* [*Handel's*] *Dear Liberty*. London, *c*. 1730.

— *To the Poets of Future Ages*. Preface of Samuel Johnson's play, *The Blazing Comet*. London, 1732.

— An unknown Portrait of Handel. [Relief cast in Sir John Soane Museum.] (*Musical Times*, 1 December 1905.) London.

— *A View of the Public Fire-Works*, etc. London, 1749.

— Where the *Messiah* was first performed. (*Musical Times*, 1 December 1903.) London.

— *The Woman of Taste : Occasioned by a late Poem, entitled The Man of Taste*, by a Friend of the Author's [*i.e.* of John Bramston's]. London, 1733.

ANSON, ELIZABETH and FLORENCE : *Mary Hamilton*. London 1925.

ARBUTHNOT, JOHN : *The Miscellaneous Works of the late Dr. Arbuthnot*. 2 vols. Glasgow, 1751 ; London, 1770.

— *See* Anonymous : *The Devil to pay*, etc., 1727.

— *See* Anonymous : *Harmony in an Uproar*, etc., 1734.

— *See* also Aitken, G. A.

ARMSTRONG, BENJAMIN JOHN : *Some Account of the Parish of Little Stanmore, alias Whitchurch, Middlesex . . .* with a Supplement by Edward Cutler [on Handel's relation with Whitchurch]. Edgware, 1895.

ARNOT, HUGO : *The History of Edinburgh*. Edinburgh, 1779.

ARRO, ELMAR : Kaks tundmatut Händel kirja. [Handel's two letters to Telemann, with facsimile of the second letter.] (*Eesti Muusika Kunkiri*, I. 2, pp. 48-50. February, 1929.) Tartu.

AVISON, CHARLES : *An Essay on Musical Expression*. London, 1752.

— *A Reply to the Author of Remarks on the Essay on Musical Expression* [*i.e.* William Hayes]. London, 1753.

BAKER, C. H. COLLINS and MURIEL I. : *The Life and Circumstances of James Brydges, First Duke of Chandos, Patron of the Liberal Arts*. Oxford, 1949.

BAKER, JOHN : *Diary*, etc. Edited by Philip C. Yorke. London, (1931).

BEARD, HARRY R.: An etched caricature of a Handelian opera (*The Burlington Magazine*, September 1950). London.

BEATTIE, JAMES : *The Letters . . . from Sir William Forbes's Collection*. 2 vols. London, 1820 [or rather, 1819-21].

BELLERMANN, CONSTANTIN : Programma in quo Parnassus musarum, voce, fidibus, tibiisque resonans ; siue musices, diuinae artis, laudes, diuersae species, singulares effectus, atque primarii auctores succincte, praestantissimique melopoetae cum laude enarrantur. Erfordiae, 1743.

BICKHAM, GEORGE, junior (engraver) : *The Musical Entertainer*. [Edited by Richard Vincent.] 2 vols. London, [1738-40].

BIELFELD, JAKOB FRIEDRICH FREIHERR VON : *Lettres familières et autres.* 2 vols. La Haye, 1763.
— *Freundschaftliche Briefe.* 2 vols. Danzig, 1765.
— *Letters,* etc. Translated, from the German, by W. Hooper. 4 vols. London, 1768–70.
BISHOP, JOHN : *Brief Memoir of Handel.* London, 1856. (Offprint of the preface of Bishop's vocal score of *Messiah.*)
BLAINVILLE, MONSIEUR DE : *Travels through Holland, Germany, Switzerland and other parts of Europe ; but especially Italy.* Translated by George Thurnbull, William Guthie, and others. 3 vols. London 1743–5. (1757. 1767.)
BONLINI, GIOVANNI CARLO : *Le Glorie della Poesia, e della Musica. Contenute Nell'esatta Notitia De Teatri della Città di Venezia, e nel Catalogo Purgatissimo De Drami Musicali,* etc. Venezia, [1730].
BOULTON, WILLIAM BIGGS : *The Amusements of London.* 2 vols. London, 1901.
BRAMSTON, JOHN : *The Man of Taste.* Occasion'd by an epistle of Mr. Pope's on that subject. London, 1733.
BREDENFÖRDER, ELISABETH : *Die Texte der Händel-Oratorien.* Leipzig, 1934.
BRENET, MICHEL (pseudonym for Marie Bobillier) : *La librairie musicale en France de 1653 à 1790.* (*Sammelbände der Internationalen Musik-Gesellschaft,* vol. VIII.) Leipzig, 1906/7.
BREWSTER, DOROTHY : *Aaron Hill. Poet, Dramatist, Projector.* New York, 1913.
BRIDGE, JOSEPH COX : The Organists of Chester Cathedral. (*Journal of the Architectural, Archaeological, and Historic Society,* vol. XIX.) Chester, 1913.
BRISTOL, JOHN HERVEY, EARL OF : *Letter-Books of John Hervey, First [or rather Fourth] Earl of Bristol.* 3 vols. Wells, 1894.
B. (BROOKE), W. T.: Elizabeth Tollet and Handel. (*Musical Standard,* 29 June and 13 July 1912.) London.
BROWNLOW, JOHN : *Memoranda : or, Chronicles of the Foundling Hospital.* London, 1847.
— *The History and Design of the Foundling Hospital.* London, 1858.
BUCCLEUCH AND QUEENSBERRY, DUKE OF : *The Manuscripts of the ——.* Preserved at Montague House, Whitehall. (Historical Manuscripts Commission.) 2 vols. London, 1899–1903. [Vol. I contains the Montague Papers.]
BUCKERIDGE, HENRY BAYNBRIGG : *Musica Sacra Dramatica, sive Oratorium.* (*Carmine Lyrico.*) Oxford, 1733.
BUMPUS, JOHN S.: *A History of English Cathedral Music 1549–1889.* 2 vols. London, [1917].
BURNEY, CHARLES : *A General History of Music.* 4 vols. London, 1776–89.
— *An Account of the Musical Performances in Westminster Abbey and the Pantheon, May 26th, 27th, 29th ; and June the 3rd, and 5th, 1784, in Commemoration of Handel.* London, 1785. (With a sketch of the life of Handel, pp. 1–56.) Translated into German by Johann Joachim Eschenburg. Berlin and Stettin, 1785.
— Handel. (In Abraham Rees : *The Cyclopaedia,* vol. 17.) London, 1819. (A variant only of Handel's life in Burney's *Account* of 1785.)
— *The Present State of Music in France and Italy.* London, 1771.
BYROM, JOHN : *Epilogue to Samuel Johnson's play,* ' *Hurlothrumbo : or, The Super-Natural* '. London, 1729.

Byrom, John: *Miscellaneous Poems*. 2 vols. Manchester, 1773.
— *The Private Journal and Literary Remains*. Edited by Richard Parkinson. 4 vols. (Chetham Society, vols. 32, 34, 40 and 44.) Manchester, 1854–57.
— *The Poems*. Edited by Adolphus William Ward. 4 vols. (Chetham Society, New Series, vols. 29, 30, 34 and 35.) Manchester, 1894–95.
— *Selections from the Journals & Papers*. Edited by Henri Talon. London, 1950.
Cannon, Beekman C.: *Johann Mattheson, Spectator in Music*. New Haven, 1947.
Carey, Henry : *Poems on Several Occasions*. Third edition. London, 1729.
Carlisle, Lord : *Carlisle Manuscripts*. (Historical Manuscripts Commission, 15th Report, Appendix, Part VI.) London, 1897.
Carse, Adam : *The Orchestra in the XVIIIth Century*. Cambridge, 1940.
Carter, Elizabeth, and Catherine Talbot : *A Series of Letters between Mrs. Elizabeth Carter and Miss Catherine Talbot, from the Year 1741 to 1770*. 4 vols. London, 1809.
— *see also* Pennington, M.
Ceci, Joseph E. : Handel and Walpole in Caricature. (*Musical Times*, January 1951.) London.
Cellesi, Luigia : Un poeta romano [Rolli] e un sopranista senese [Senesino]. (*Bulletino Senese di Storia Patria*, Nuova Serie, Anno I, fasc. II.) Siena, 1930.
— Attorno a Haendel. Lettere inedite del poeta Paolo Rolli [to Senesino]. (*Musica d' Oggi*, January 1933.) Milano.
Chamberlayne, John : *Magnae Britanniae Notitia* ; or, *the present State of Great-Britain*. London, 1727–55.
Cherbuliez, Antoine-E. : *Georg Friedrich Händel. Leben und Werk*. Olten, 1949.
Chesterfield, Philip Dormer Stanhope, 4th Earl of : *Letters*. Edited by Bonamy Dobrée. 6 vols. [London,] 1932.
Chrysander, Friedrich : *G. F. Händel*. Vols. 1, 2, and first half of 3. Leipzig, 1858–67. Reprint, 1919.
— Prefaces (in German or English) to : *Georg Friedrich Händels Werke*. Leipzig, 1858–1902. 93 vols.
— Henry Carey und der Ursprung des Königsgesanges " God save the King ". (*Jahrbücher für musikalische Wissenschaft*, vol. I.) Leipzig, 1863.
— Mattheson's Verzeichniss Hamburgischer Opern von 1678 bis 1728, gedruckt im *Musikalischen Patrioten*, mit seinen handschriftlichen Zusätzen und Berichtigungen. (*Allgemeine Musikalische Zeitung*, 28 March–2 May 1877.) Leipzig.
— Georg Friedrich Händel. (*Allgemeine Deutsche Biographie*, XII. 777–93.) Leipzig, 1880.
— *Handel's Pedigree*. Drawn up from authentic Documents. London, [*c*. 1890. Broad-sheet].
— Der Bestand der Königlichen Privatmusik und Kirchenkapelle in London von 1710 bis 1755. (*Vierteljahrsschrift für Musikwissenschaft*, vol. VIII.) Leipzig, 1892.
— Die Originalstimmen zu Händel's Messias. (*Jahrbuch der Musikbibliothek Peters*, vol. II.) Leipzig, 1895.
Cibber, Colley : *The Dramatic Works*. 5 vols. London, 1777.

CIBBER, COLLEY : see also Anonymous : *The Contre Temps*, etc. 1727.

CLARK, RICHARD : *Reminiscences of Handel, His Grace the Duke of Chandos, Powells the Harpers, the Harmonious Blacksmith*, etc. London, 1836.

— On the Sacred Oratorio of " The Messiah ", previous to the Death of G. F. Handel. London, 1852.

CLEMENS, J. R.: Handel and Carey. (*The Sackbut*, vol. XI.) London, 1931.

CLERC, JEAN-LOUIS : *L'enchanteur Carabosse* : Le Zuricois J.-J. Heidegger. Lausanne, 1942.

COATS, GEORGE : The Chevalier Taylor. (*Royal London Ophthalmic Hospital Reports*, vol. XX.) London, May 1917.

COLMAN, FRANCIS (?) : Opera-Register from 1712–34, *etc.* A brief account of operas performed at the Haymarket. Handel entries, edited by E. R. Page. (*The Mask*, July 1926 and January 1927.) London. Revised by Robert W. Babcock. (*Music & Letters*, July 1943.) London.

COLMAN, GEORGE : *Posthumous Letters from Various Celebrated Men* ; Addressed to Francis Colman and George Colman the Elder, with Annotations and Occasional Remarks by G. Colman, the Younger. London, 1820.

— see Peake, R. B.

COOPERSMITH, JACOB MAURICE : A List of Portraits, Sculptures, etc., of G. F. Händel. (*Music & Letters*, April 1932.) London.

— Handelian Lacunae : a Project. (*Musical Quarterly*, April 1935.) New York.

— An unpublished Drawing of Georg Friederich Händel (*Music & Letters*, April 1935). London.

— The Libretto of Handel's " Jupiter in Argos " (*Music & Letters*, October 1936.) London.

— Four unpublished letters of G. F. Händel. (*A Birthday Offering for Carl Engel.*) New York, 1943.

COVENTRY, HENRY (pseud. Talbot) : *Philemon to Hydaspes*. London, 1736.

COWPER, MARY COUNTESS : *Diary* (1714–20). Edited by John Murray. London, 1864.

COXE, WILLIAM : see Anonymous : *Anecdotes of George Frederick Handel*, etc., 1799.

CRESCIMBENI, GIOVANNI MARIO : *Storia dell' Accademia degli Arcadi istituita in Roma l' anno 1690 . . . pubblicata l' anno 1712*. (Edited by Lariso Salaminio.) Londra, 1804.

CROFT-MURRAY, EDWARD : John Devoto. A Baroque Scene Painter. (*The Society of Theatre Research. Pamphlet Series ; no. 2, 1952.*) London, 1953.

CULWICK, JAMES C.: *Handel's Messiah : Discovery of the Original Word-Book used at the First Performance in Dublin, April 13, 1742 ; with Some Notes*. Dublin, 1891.

CUMMINGS, WILLIAM HAYMAN : Handel Myths. (*Musical Times*, January and February 1885.) London.

— God save the King. *The Origin and History of the Music and Words of the National Anthem*. London, 1902.

— Handel. London, 1904.

— Muzio Scevola. (*Musical Times*, January 1911.) London.

— Dr. Arne and Rule Britannia. London, 1912.

CUMMINGS, WILLIAM HAYMAN : The Lord Chamberlain and Opera in London, 1700–1740. (*Proceedings of the Musical Association, 1913–1914.*) London, 1914.

— *Handel, the Duke of Chandos, and the Harmonious Blacksmith.* London, 1915.

CUTLER, EDWARD : see Armstrong, B. J.

DACIER, ÉMILE : Une danseuse française [Mlle. Sallé] à London. (*Mercure Musicale et Bulletin français de la S.I.M.*, Paris section, May–July 1907.) Paris.

— *Une danseuse de l'opéra sous Louis XV. Mlle Sallé.* Paris, 1909.

DEFOE, DANIEL : *Tour Thro' the Whole Island of Great Britain, etc.* By a Gentleman. 3 vols. London, 1724–27. Edited by G. D. Cole. 2 vols. London, 1927.

— *see also* Periodicals : *The Daily Post.*

DELANY, MARY : *Autobiography and Correspondence of Mary Granville, Mrs. Delany.* Edited by Lady Llanover. 6 vols. London, 1861–2.

DEMOCRITUS (pseud.) : *Democriti Antwort auf Hans Sachsens Schreiben, und Einfältige Critique, der Opera Julius Caesar in Aegypten. Nebst einer Wiederlegung der abgeschmackten Reflexion des sogenannten Idorythmi.* [Altona ?], Anno 1725.

DENBIGH, EARL OF : *The Manuscripts of the Earl of Denbigh.* Part V. (Historical Manuscripts Commission.) London, 1911.

DENT, EDWARD JAMES : *Handel.* (Great Lives.) London, 1934.

— *Händel in England. Gedächtnis-Rede anlässlich der 250. Geburtstagsfeier in Halle am 24. Februar 1935.* Halle, 1936.

DEUTSCH, OTTO ERICH : 200 Years of the *Messiah.* (*The Antique Collector*, November–December 1941.) London.

— Handel's Will. (Ditto, January–February 1942.) London.

— Handel and Cambridge. (*The Cambridge Review*, 25 April 1942.) Cambridge.

— Handel's Hunting Song. (*Musical Times*, December 1942.) London.

— Purcell and Handel in Bickham's Musical Entertainer. (*The Harrow Replicas*, no. 2.) Cambridge, 1942.

— Selection from *Messiah*, etc. (*The Harrow Replicas*, no. 8.) Cambridge, 1945.

— Poetry preserved in Music. Bibliographical Notes on Smollett and Oswald, Handel and Haydn. (*Modern Language Notes*, February 1948.) Baltimore.

— Burney, Handel and the Barrel Organ. (*Musical Times*, July 1949). London.

— Review of Wm. C. Smith's book, "Concerning Handel". (*Music & Letters*, July 1949.) London.

DÖRING, GOTTFRIED : Die Musik in Preussen im 18. Jahrhundert. (*Monatshefte für Musikgeschichte*, vol. I.) Berlin, 1869.

DRAWCANSIR, SIR ALEXANDER (pseud. for Henry Fielding) : *The Covent-Garden Journal.* Edited by Gerard Edward Jensen. 2 vols. New Haven, 1915.

DREYHAUPT, JOHANN CHRISTOPH VON : *Pagus Neletici et Nudzici . . . Beschreibung des . . . Saal-Kreises, . . . Insonderheit der Städte Halle, etc.* 2 vols. Halle, 1749–50.

DU BOC(C)AGE, ANNE-MARIE : *see* Fiquet du Bocage.

EDWARDS, FREDERICK GEORGE : The Foundling Hospital and its Music. (*Musical Times*, May–June 1902.) London.

— Handel's *Messiah.* Some Notes on its History and First Performance. (ditto, November 1902.) London.

H.-28 a

874 BIBLIOGRAPHY

EDWARDS, FREDERICK GEORGE : Dublin Handeliana and a Hospital [Mercer's]. (ditto, October 1903.) London.

— Dr. Charles Burney . . . A biographical Sketch. (ditto, July–September 1904.) London.

— Handel's Last Days. (ditto, April 1909.) London.

EGMONT, JOHN EARL OF : Manuscripts of the Earl of Egmont. Diary of Viscount Percival, etc. (Historical Manuscripts Commission.) 3 vols. London, 1920–23.

EINSTEIN, ALFRED : Ein Beitrag zur Lebensbeschreibung Händels. (Zeitschrift der Internationalen Musikgesellschaft, vol. VIII.) Leipzig, 1906/7.

— Italienische Musiker am Hofe der Neuburger Wittelsbacher, 1614–1716. (Sammelbände der Internationalen Musikgesellschaft, vol. IX.) Leipzig, 1907/8.

EISENSCHMIDT, JOACHIM : Die szenische Darstellung der Opern Händels auf der Londoner Bühne seiner Zeit. 2 vols. (Schriftenreihe des Händelhauses in Halle, Heft 5 und 6.) Wolffenbüttel, 1940–41.

ENGEL, CARL : Musical Myths and Facts. 2 vols. London, 1876.

FARMER, HENRY GEORGE : Music Making in the Olden Days. The Story of the Aberdeen Concerts, 1748–1801. London, (1950).

FASSINI, SESTO : Il ritorno de [Paolo] Rolli dall' Inghilterra. Perugia, 1908.

— Gli albori del melodramma italiano a Londra. (Giornale storico, vol. LX.) Torino, 1912.

— Il melodramma italiano a Londra ai tempi del Rolli. (Rivista musicale italiana, vol. XIX.) Torino, 1912.

— Il melodramma italiano a Londra nella prima metà del settecento. Torino, 1914.

FIELDING, HENRY : The History of Tom Jones. 3 vols. Dublin, 1749.

— The History of Amelia. 1751.

— see Drawcansir, Sir Alexander (1752).

FIQUET DU BOCAGE (de Boccage), ANNE-MARIE, née Lepage : Letters concerning England . . . Translated from the French. 2 vols. London, 1770.

FISCHER, GEORG : Opern und Concerte im Hoftheater zu Hannover bis 1866. Hannover, 1899.

— [Second edition as :] Musik in Hannover. Hannover, 1903.

FLOOD, W. H. GRATTAN : Music in Dublin 1730–54. (Sammelbände der Internationalen Musik-Gesellschaft, April–June 1910.) Leipzig.

— Handel and the Earl of Egmont. (Musical Times, 1 November 1924.) London.

FLOWER, DESMOND : Handel's Publishers. (English Review, January 1936.) London.

FLOWER, SIR NEWMAN : Catalogue of a Handel Collection formed by Newman Flower. Sevenoaks, [1921].

— George Frideric Handel: his Personality and his Times. London, 1923. (Translated into German by Alice Klengel, Leipzig, 1925.) Revised Edition, 1947.

— A Handel First Night. First world performance of Handel's Mystery Opera [Jupiter in Argos, as] Perseus and Andromeda. (Radio Times, 4th October 1935.) London.

FOERSTEMANN, KARL EDUARD : G. F. Händels Stammbaum, nach Original-Quellen und authentischen Nachrichten aufgestellt und erläutert. Leipzig, 1844.

FORTESCUE, MARY TERESA : *History of Calwich Abbey.* Winchester, [1915].

FRANCKE, JOHANN GEORGE : . . . *Der* . . . *Frau Dorotheen Taustin, des* . . . *Herrn George Händels* . . . *Witwe* . . . *Leichen-Sermon, etc.* Halle, [1731].

— G. F. Händel's Mother. Funeral Sermon for Dorothea Händel, *etc.* Edited by Lore Liebenam. Halle, 1939.

FREUND, HANS, and WILHELM REINKING : *Musikalisches Theater in Hamburg.* Hamburg, 1938.

FRIEDLAENDER, ERNST : Einige archivalische Nachrichten über G. F. Händel und seine Familie. (*Mitteilungen für die Berliner Mozart-Gemeinde,* vol. II.) Berlin, 1902.

FULLER-MAITLAND, JOHN ALEXANDER, and WILLIAM BARCLAY SQUIRE : George Frederick Handel. (*Dictionary of National Biography,* XXIV. 277-291.) London, 1890.

FÜRSTENAU, MORITZ : G. F. Händel in Dresden. (*Dresdner Journal,* 16 February 1860.) Dresden.

— *Zur Geschichte der Musik und des Theaters am Hofe der Kurfürsten von Sachsen.* 2 vols. Dresden, 1861-2.

GAY, JOHN : *Trivia* : or, *The Art of Walking the Streets of London.* London, [1716].

— *Poems on Several Occasions.* 2 vols. London, 1720. 1731 (revised), 1737, 1745, 1757.

GENEST, JOHN : *Some Account of the English Stage from* . . . *1660 to 1830.* 10 vols. Bath, 1832.

GODDARD, SCOTT : Handel article in Grove's *Dictionary of Music and Musicians,* 3rd edition, London, 1927. Vol. II, pp. 504-15. (Cf. Marshall, Julian.)

GOLDSMITH, OLIVER : On the Different Schools of Music. (*The British Magazine,* February and April 1760.) London.

GRANVILLE, MARY : *see* Delany, Mary.

GRAY, THOMAS : *Correspondence.* Edited by Paget Thoynbee and Leonard Whibley. 3 vols. Oxford, 1935.

GRUNERT, JOHANN FRIEDRICH : *see* Heineck, J. M., and Rotth, M. C. A.

HADDEN, J. CUTHBERT : Charles Jennens and *The Messiah.* (*Musical Opinion,* August 1910.) London.

HANBURY, WILLIAM : *The History of the Rise and Progress of the Charitable Foundations at Church-Langton.* London, 1767.

HANDEL : *The Letters and Writings of George Frideric Handel.* Edited by Erich H. Müller. London, 1935.

— *Briefe und Schriften* (together with John Mainwaring's *Handel Biography,* translated by Johann Mattheson). Herausgegeben von Hedwig und E. H. Mueller von Asow. Lindau, 1949. Wien, 1949.

Handel Society (London) : Prefaces to the twelve volumes of Handel's works, edited by William Crotch, Charles Lucas, Ignaz Moscheles, Thomas M. Mudie, Felix Mendelssohn, William Sterndale Bennett, Sir George Smart, George A. Macfarren, Edward Francis Rimbault, and Henry T. Smart. London, 1843-55.

HARE, FRANCIS : *Hare Manuscripts.* (Historical Manuscripts Commission, 14th Report, Appendix, Part IX.) London, 1895.

HARLAND, JOHN : *Manchester Concerts in 1744* [*and 1745*] *in* : *Collectanea relating* to *Manchester*, etc. (Publications of the Chetham Society, vol. 72.) Manchester, 1867.

HARRIS, DAVID FRASER : *Saint Cecilia's Hall in the Niddry Wynd, a Chapter in the History of the Music of the Past in Edinburgh.* [Second Edition.] Edinburgh, 1911.

HARRIS, JAMES : *Three Treatises. The First Concerning Art. The Second Concerning Music, Painting, and Poetry. The Third Concerning Hapiness.* London, 1744. (Translated into German by J. G. Müchler, Danzig, 1756.) Second edition, revised and corrected, London, 1765. (Further editions : 1772, 1783, 1792.)

HAWKINS, SIR JOHN : *An Account of the Institutions and Progress of the Academy of Ancient Music.* London, 1770.

— *A General History of the Science and Practice of Music.* 5 vols. London, 1776.

HAYES, WILLIAM : *The Art of Composing Music by a Method Entirely New, Suited to the Meanest Capacity*, etc. London, 1751.

— *Remarks on Mr. Avison's Essay on Musical Expression.* London, 1753.

— *Anecdotes of the Five Music Meetings at Church-Langton.* Oxford, 1768.

HAYWOOD, ELIZA : *Epistles for the Ladies.* 2 vols. London, 1749.

HEARNE, THOMAS : *Reliquiae Hearnianae : The Remains of Thomas Hearne.* Collected by Philip Bliss. 2 vols. Oxford, 1857.

— *Remarks and Collections.* Edited by C. E. Doble and H. E. Salter. 11 vols. Oxford, 1885-1921. (Oxford Historical Society, vols. 2, 7, 13, 34, 42, 43, 48, 50, 65, 67, 72.)

HEINECK, JOHANN MICHAEL : *Der Hertzens-Trost . . . Bey . . . Beerdigung der . . . Frauen Dorotheen Sophien gebohrnen Händelin, Des . . . Herrn Michael Dietrich Michaelssen . . . Frau Ehe-Liebsten Am 11. August 1718 . . . Der . . . Verstorbenen Frau Doctorin Hinterlassenen Herrn Wittwer, Liebsten Kindern, Frau Mutter, Herrn Bruder . . . übergiebt diese Leich-Rede . . . Johann Grunert,* Universitäts-Buchdrucker. Halle, 1718.

HERBAGE, JULIAN : *Messiah. (The World of Music,* vol. 1.) London, 1948.

HERTFORD, LADY FRANCIS : *The Gentle Hertford : Her Life and Letters.* Edited by Helen Sard Hughes. New York, 1940.

HERVEY, LORD JOHN : *Memoirs of the Reign of George the Second.* Edited by John Wilson Croker. 2 vols. London, 1848.

— *Some Materials towards Memoirs,* etc. Edited by Romney Sedgwick. 3 vols. London, 1931.

— *Lord Hervey and His Friends, 1726-38.* Edited by the Earl of Ilchester. London, 1950.

— *see also* Bristol.

HEYWOOD, ELIZA : *see* Haywood.

HILL, AARON : *The Works of the late Aaron Hill.* 4 vols. London, 1753.

— *The Dramatic Works of Aaron Hill.* 2 vols. London, 1760.

Historical Manuscripts Commission : *see* Royal Historical Manuscripts Commission.

HITZIG, WILHELM : *Georg Friedrich Händel, 1685-1759. Sein Leben in Bildern.* Leipzig, 1935.

HODGKIN, JOHN ELIOT : *The Manuscripts of J. Eliot Hodgkin, F.S.A., of Richmond, Surrey.* (Historical Manuscripts Commission, 15th Report, Appendix, Part II.) London, 1897.

Högg, E. R. Margarete : *Die Gesangskunst der . . . Faustina.* Königsbrück i.Sa., 1931.

Hughes, John : *Poems on Several Occasions.* Edited by William Duncombe. 2 vols. London, 1735.

— *Letters by several eminent Persons deceased, including the Correspondence of John Hughes.* 2 vols. London, 1772.

Hughes, William : *The Efficacy and Importance of Musick. A Sermon Preach'd in the Cathedral-Church of Worcester at the Annual Meeting of the Three Choirs . . . September 13, 1749.* London.

— *Remarks upon Musick ; to which are added Several Observations upon Some of Mr. Handel's Oratorios, and other Parts of his Works.* By a Lover of Harmony. Worcester, 1758.

Huntingdon, Selina Countess of : *The Life and Times of Selina Countess of Huntingdon.* [Edited by A. C. H. Seymour.] 2 vols. London, 1839–40.

Husk, William Henry : *An Account of the Musical Celebrations on St. Cecilia's Day in the Sixteenth, Seventeenth, and Eighteenth Centuries.* London, 1857.

Idorythmus (pseud.) : *Idorythmi Reflexion über . . . die . . . Opera [Julius Caesar in Aegypten].* See Sachs, Hans (pseud.).

James, Robert Rutson : Handel's Blindness. (*Music & Letters,* April 1932.) London.

Johnson, Hurlothrumbo (pseud.) : *see* Anonymous : *Harmony in an Uproar,* etc.

Johnson, Samuel : *Hurlothrumbo, or, The Super-Natural,* see Byrom, *Epilogue,* etc.

— *The Blazing Comet ;* or, *The Mad Lovers ;* or, *The Beauties of the Poets,* see Anonymous : *To the Poets of Future Ages.*

Kelly, Michael : *Reminiscences . . . of the King's Theatre,* etc. Second edition. 2 vols. London, 1826.

Kennan, D. W. : The *Messiah* in Dublin (*Music Book,* Volume VII of *Hinrichsen's Musical Year Book,* ed. by Max Hinrichsen). London, (1952).

Ketton, R. W. : *Manuscripts of R. W. Ketton, Esq.* (Historical Manuscripts Commission, 12th Report, Appendix, Part 9.) London, 1891.

Kidson, Frank : Handel's Publisher, John Walsh, his Successors and Contemporaries. (*Musical Quarterly,* July 1920). New York.

— *British Music Publishers, Printers and Engravers.* London, (1900).

Kielmannsegg, Erich Graf : *Familien-Chronik der Herren, Freiherren und Grafen von Kielmannsegg.* 2. Auflage. Wien, 1910.

Kitzig, Berthold : Zwei Briefe Händels an Telemann. (*Zeitschrift für Musikwissenschaft,* vol. IX.) Leipzig, 1927.

Krause, Christian Gottfried : *see* Anonymous : *Lettre à Mons. le Marquis de B.,* etc.

Lacy, Michael Rophino : *see* Schoelcher, V.: *Catalogue of Handel's Works.*

La Mara (pseud. for Marie Lipsius) : *Musikerbriefe aus fünf Jahrhunderten.* 2 vols. Leipzig, (1886). I. 167–9.

Latimer, John : *The Annals of Bristol in the Eighteenth Century.* (Frome), 1893.

Lawrence, William John : Handeliana. Some Memorials of the Dublin Charitable Musical Society. (*Musical Antiquary,* January 1912.) London.

— The Early Years of the First English Opera House. (*Musical Quarterly,* January 1921.) New York.

— Early Irish Ballad Opera and Comic Opera. (*Musical Quarterly,* July 1922.) New York.

LEICHTENTRITT, HUGO : *Händel.* Stuttgart, 1924.

LEUX, IRMGARD : Über die "verschollene" Händel-Oper "Hermann von Balcke". Ein Beitrag für Elbinger Musikgeschichte. (*Archiv für Musikwissenschaft,* vol. VIII.) Leipzig, 1926.

LEWIS, LAWRENCE : *The Advertisements of The Spectator.* London, 1909.

LIPSIUS, MARIE : see La Mara.

LOCKMAN, JOHN : *Rosalinda. A Musical Drama* : To which is Prefixed an Enquiry into the Rise and Progress of Operas and Oratorios. London, 1740.

LODER-SYMONDS, F. C. : *Manuscripts.* (Historical Manuscripts Commission, 13th Report, Appendix, Part IV.) London, 1892.

LOEWENBERG, ALFRED : *Annals of Opera 1597–1940.* Cambridge, 1943.

LUSTIG, JACOB WILHELM : *Inleiding tot de Muziekkunde.* Groningen, 1751.

— *Samenspraaken over muzikaale beginselen.* Antwerp, 1756.

LUXBOROUGH, LADY : *Letters written by the late Right Honourable Lady Luxborough to William Shenstone, Esq.* London, 1775.

LYNHAM, DERYCK : *Ballet Then and Now.* (London, 1947.)

LYSONS, DANIEL : *History of the Origin and Progress of the Meeting of the Three Choirs of Gloucester, Worcester, and Hereford, etc.* Gloucester, 1812. (Subsequently revised and enlarged by John Amott, 1865, Charles Lee Williams, 1895, Harry Godwin Chance, 1922, and Theodore Hannam-Clark, 1931.)

MACFARREN, SIR GEORGE A.: *A Sketch of the Life of Handel, etc.* London, (1859).

MACKY, JOHN : *A Journey through England, in Familiar Letters from A Gentleman Here to His Friend Abroad.* 2 vols. London, 1714 and 22.

MAINWARING, JOHN : *Memoirs of the Life of the late G. F. Handel. To which is added a Catalogue of his Works and Observations upon them.* London, 1760. Translated into German by Johann Mattheson, Hamburg, 1761 ; new editions, by Bernhard Paumgartner, Zürich 1947, and by Hedwig und E. H. Mueller von Asow, Lindau and Wien 1949. Translated into French, in a shortened version, by Jean-Baptiste Antoine Suard. (Abbé François Arnaud and J.-B. A. Suard : *Variétés littéraires ou Recueil de pièces tant originales que traduites concernant la philosophie, la littérature et les arts.* 4 vols. Paris, 1768–9, I. 346–74 ; 1770, ditto ; 1804, I. 302-26, signed S. = Suard.)

MALCOLM, ALEXANDER : *A Treatise of Musick, Speculative, Practical, and Historical.* Edinburgh, 1721.

MALCOLM, JAMES PELLER : *Anecdotes of the Manners and Customs of London during the Eighteenth Century.* London, 1808. 4°. The Second Edition. 2 vols. 8°. London, 1810.

MALMESBURY, EARL OF : *A Series of Letters of the First Earl of Malmesbury, his Family and Friends, from 1745 to 1820.* Edited by the Earl of Malmesbury. 2 vols. London, 1870.

— Some Anecdotes of the Harris Family. (*The Ancestor,* April 1902.) London.

MANN, ARTHUR HENRY : *Manuscripts and Sketches by G. F. Handel* [in the Fitzwilliam Museum], pp. 157-227 of : J. A. Fuller-Maitland and A. H. Mann, *Catalogue of the Music in the Fitzwilliam Museum,* Cambridge. London, 1893.

MANSFIELD, ORLANDO A.: Librettists of Handel's Choral Compositions. (*Musical Opinion,* May, July, September 1935.) London.

MARCH, CHARLES H. G. L., EARL OF : *A Duke and his Friends ; the life and letters of the second Duke of Richmond.* 2 vols. London, 1911.

MARPURG, FRIEDRICH WILHELM : *Abhandlung von der Fuge*, etc. 2 vols. Berlin, 1753–4. (I. 20, 76, 91, 133, and Table XXXIII.)
— *Historisch-Kritische Beyträge zur Aufnahme der Musik.* 5 vols. Berlin, 1754–1778.
— *Kritische Briefe über die Tonkunst*, etc. [Periodical.] 3 vols. Berlin, 1759–63. (In book form, 1760–64).
MARSHALL, JULIAN : Handel article in Grove's *Dictionary of Music and Musicians.* London, 1879. Vol. I, pp. 647-57. (Cf. Goddard, Scott.)
— Articles on Handel's singers in the first edition of Grove's *Dictionary*, passim.
MARTIN, BENJAMIN (editor) : *Miscellaneous Correspondence, in Prose and Verse.* (Monthly.) London, 1755–59.
MARTINELLI, VINCENZIO : *Lettere familiari e critiche.* London, 1758.
MASON, WILLIAM : *Essays, historical and critical on English Church Music.* York, 1795.
MATTHESON, JOHANN : *Das Neu-Eröffnete Orchestre*, etc. Hamburg, 1713.
— *Das Beschützte Orchestre*, etc. Hamburg, 1717.
— *Exemplarische Organisten-Probe.* Hamburg, 1719.—*See* Niedt, F. E. (1721).
— *Critica Musica*, etc. Hamburg, 2 vols. 1722–5.
— *Der Musicalische Patriot*, etc. Hamburg, 1728. (*See also* Chrysander, 1877.)
— *Ode Auf des S. T. Hrn. Capellmeister Heinichen schönes neues Werk Von General-Bass.* Hamburg, 1728.
— *Die Wol-klingende Finger-Sprache, in Zwölff Fugen, mit zwey biss drey Subjecten, entworffen ; und . . . Herrn Georg Friedrich Händel . . . zugeeignet . . . Erster Theil.* Hamburg, 1735. *Zweyter Theil.* 1737.
— *Kern Melodischer Wissenschaft, bestehend in den . . . Haupt- und Grund-Lehren der musikalischen Setz-Kunst oder Composition*, etc. Hamburg, 1737.
— *Der Vollkommene Capellmeister*, etc. Hamburg, 1739.
— *Grundlage einer Ehren-Pforte*, etc. Hamburg, 1740.
— *Georg Friderich Händels Lebensbeschreibung, nebst einem Verzeichnisse seiner Ausübungswerke*. . . übersetzet [nach Mainwaring], auch mit einigen Anmerkungen, absonderlich über den hamburgischen Artikel, versehen.* Hamburg, 1761.
MEE, JOHN HENRY : *The Oldest Music-Room in Europe. A Record of Eighteenth-Century Enterprise at Oxford.* Oxford, 1911.
MEIKLE, HENRY W. : New Smollett Letters—I. (*The Times Literary Supplement*, 24 July 1943.) London.
MERBACH, PAUL ALFRED : Das Repertoire der Hamburger Oper von 1718 bis 1750. (*Archiv für Musikwissenschaft*, vol. VI.) Leipzig, 1924. (Contains Wilhelm Willers's diary.)
MICHAEL, WOLFGANG : Die Entstehung der Wassermusik von Händel. (*Zeitschrift für Musikwissenschaft*, August-September 1922.) Leipzig.
— Die Anfänge des Hauses Hannover. (*Englische Geschichte im 18. Jahrhundert*, Band I.) Zweite Ausgabe. Berlin, 1921. Translated by L. B. N. as : *The Beginnings of the Hanoverian Dynasty.* (England under George I.) London, 1936.
MILLER, JAMES : *Harlequin-Horace* ; or, *The Art of Modern Poetry.* London, 1731.
MILLER, SANDERSON : *An Eighteenth Century Correspondence.* Edited by Lilian Dickins and Mary Stanton. London, 1910.

MILNES, KEITH : *Memoir Relating to the Portrait of Handel by Francis Keith.* London, 1829.

MITCHELL, JOSEPH : *Ode on the Power of Musick.* London, 1721.

MIZLER (VON KOLOF), LORENZ CHRISTOPH : *Neu eröffnete Musikalische Bibliothek.* 4 vols. Leipzig, 1736–54.

MONTAGU, ELIZABETH (*née* ROBINSON) : *Elizabeth Montagu. The Queen of the Blue-Stockings. Her Correspondence from 1720 to 1761.* Edited by Emily J. Climenson. 2 vols. London, 1906.

MONTAGU, LADY MARY WORTLEY : *Letters and Works.* Edited by Lord Wharncliffe. 3 vols. London, 1837.

MONTAGUE, JOHN DUKE OF : *The Montague Papers.* See Buccleuch.

MOSER, R.-ALOYS : *Annales de la Musique et des Musiciens en Russie au XVIIIᵐ siècle.* Tome I. Genève, (1948).

MUELLER VON ASOW, HEDWIG UND E. H.: *Georg Friedrich Händel, Biographie von Mainwaring* [translated by Mattheson, and] *Briefe und Schriften.* Herausgegeben im Auftrage des Internationalen Musiker-Brief-Archivs. Lindau and Wien (1949).

MÜLLER, ERICH H.: see Handel, Letters and Writings.

MÜLLER-BLATTAU, J. : *Georg Friedrich Händel.* (Die grossen Meister der Musik.) Potsdam, 1933.

MYERS, CLARA L. : *Opera in England from 1656 to 1728.* Cleveland (Ohio), 1906.

MYERS, ROBERT MANSON : *Early Moral Criticism of Handelian Oratorio.* Williamsburg, Virginia, 1947.

— Neo-Classical Criticism of the Ode for Music. (*Publications of the Modern-Language-Association of America,* June 1947.) New York.

— *Handel's Messiah. A Touchstone of Taste.* New York, 1948.

NARES, GORDON : Adlington Hall, Cheshire. The Home of Mrs. [Cynthia] Legh (*Country Life,* 28 November, 5 and 12 December 1952). London.

NICHOLS, JOHN : *Literary Anecdotes.* 9 vols. London, 1812–15.

NICHOLS, REGINALD HUGH, and FRANCIS ASLETT WRAY : *The History of the Foundling Hospital.* London, 1935.

NICOLL, ALLARDYCE : Italian Opera in England. The first five years. (*Anglia,* vol. XLVI.) Halle an der Saale, 1922.

— *A History of Early Eighteenth Century Drama, 1700–1750.* Cambridge, 1925.

NIEDT, FRIEDERICH ERHARD : *Musicalische Handleitung* [*Anderer Theil*] *zur Variationen Des General-Basses . . . Die Zweyte Auflage, . . . mit . . . Anmerckungen . . . versehen durch J. Mattheson.* Hamburg, 1721.

NORTH, ROGER : *Memoirs of Musick* [1728]. Edited by Edward F. Rimbault. London, 1846.

— *The Musicall Gramarian* [c. 1728]. Edited by Hilda Andrews. Oxford, (1925).

OELRICH, JOHANN CARL CASPAR : *Historische Nachricht von den akademischen Würden in der Musik.* Berlin, 1752.

OPEL, J. O.: Der Kammerdiener Georg Händel und sein Sohn Georg Friedrich. (*Zeitschrift für allgemeine Geschichte,* etc., February, 1885.) Stuttgart.

— Mitteilungen zur Geschichte der Familie des Tonkünstlers Händel, nebst einigen sich auf den letzteren beziehenden Briefen. (*Neue Mitteilungen aus dem Gebiete historisch-antiquarischer Forschungen.*) Halle, 1885.

PAUMGARTNER, BERNHARD : *John Mainwaring, G. F. Händel. Nach Johann Matthesons deutscher Ausgabe von 1761 mit anderen Dokumenten herausgegeben.* Zürich, (1947).

PEAKE, RICHARD B.: *Memoirs of the Colman Family.* 2 vols. London, 1841.

PEARCE, ERNEST HAROLD : *The Sons of the Clergy, 1655–1904.* London, 1904. Second edition, London, 1928.

PENNINGTON, MONTAGU : *Memoirs of the Life of Mrs. Elizabeth Carter.* London, 1807.

PILKINGTON, M. LAETITIA : *Memoirs.* 3 vols. Dublin, 1748–54.

PÖLLNITZ, KARL LUDWIG FREIHERR VON : *Mémoires . . . Contenant Les Observations qu'il a faites dans en Voyages,* etc. Liège, 1734. 3 vols.—*The Memoirs, . . . being The Observation He made in his late Travels from Prussia thro' . . . England, &c. In Letters to his Friend,* etc. 2 vols. London, 1737.

POPE, ALEXANDER : *Epistel to the Right Honourable Richard Earl of Burlington.* London, 1731.

— *The Dunciad.* 4 vols. London, 1728–42.

— *See* Warton, J. (1756).

— *Additions to the Works of Alexander Pope,* etc. London,.1776.

— *Works.* Edited by J. Warton and others. 9 vols. London, 1797.

— *Works.* Edited by W. Elwin and W. J. Courthope. 10 vols. London, 1871–89.

PORTLAND, DUKE OF : *Manuscripts.* Vol. VI. (Historical Manuscripts Commission.) London, 1901.

POWNEY, RICHARD : *Templum Harmoniae.* London, 1745.

PRAT, DANIEL : *An Ode to Mr. Handel, On his Playing on the Organ.* London, 1722.

PRÉVOST D'EXILES, ANTOINE-FRANÇOIS (editor) : *Le Pour et Contre.* 20 vols. Paris, 1733–40.

PULITI, LETO : *Cenni storici della vita del serenissimo Ferdinando dei Medici.* Firenze, 1874.

QUADRIO, FRANCESCO SAVERIO : *Della Storia, e della Ragione d' ogni Poesia.* 5 vols. (in 7 parts). Bologna (vol. I) and Milano, 1739–52.

QUANTZ, JOHANN JOACHIM : *Quanzens Lebenslauf, von ihm selbst beschrieben :* see Marpurg, F.: *Historisch-Kritische Beiträge zur Aufnahme der Musik* (vol. I, 1754).

RALPH, JAMES : *The Touch-Stone :* or, *Historical, Critical, Political, Philosophical and Theological Essays on the Reigning Diversions of the Town . . . By a Person of some Taste and some Quality.* London, 1728. Reissued with new title as : *The Taste of the Town :* or, *a Guide to all Publick Diversions.* London, 1731.

RANKE, LEOPOLD VON : *Sämtliche Werke.* 54 vols. Leipzig, 1868–90.

REES, ABRAHAM : *The Cyclopaedia ;* or, *Universal Dictionary of Arts, Sciences, and Literature.* 39 vols. London, 1819.

REICHARDT, JOHANN FRIEDRICH : *Georg Friederich Händels Jugend.* Berlin, 1785.

RENAUD, FRANK : *Adlington, and Legh of Adlington;* in : *Contribution towards a History of the Ancient Parish of Prestbury in Cheshire.* (Publications of the Chetham Society, vol. 97.) Manchester, 1876.

RICHMOND, CHARLES, second Duke of : *see* March, Earl of.

RIMBAULT, EDWARD FRANCIS : Handel's Firework-Music. A historical Sketch. (*The Leisure Hour*, 11 August 1877.) London.

ROBINSON, JOHN R.: *The Princely Chandos. A Memoir of James Brydges . . . afterwards the First Duke of Chandos*. London, 1893.

ROBINSON, PERCY : *Handel and His Orbit*. London, 1908.

— Handel's Journeys. (*Musical Antiquary*, July 1910.) London.

— Handel's Early Life and Mainwaring. (*Musical Times*, September 1925.) London.

— Handel's Music-Paper : with other Notes. (ditto, 1 June 1928.) London.

— Handel up to 1720 : a New Chronology. (*Music & Letters*, January and October 1939.) London.

— Was Handel a Plagiarist ? (*Musical Times*, August 1939.) London.

ROCKSTRO, WILLIAM SMITH : *The Life of G. F. Handel*. London, 1883.

ROGERS, FRANCIS : Handel and five Prima Donnas. (*Musical Quarterly*, April 1943.) New York.

ROLLAND, ROMAIN : Haendel. (*La Revue de Paris*, vol. XVII, no. 8.) Paris, 15 April 1910.

— *Haendel*. Paris, 1910. Translated by A. Eaglefield Hull. London, 1916.

ROTTH, CHRISTIAN AUGUST : *An . . . George Friedrich Händel* [zum Tode seiner Mutter]. Halle, [1730].

— *Ode* [zu Händel's Geburtstag]. Halle, 1750. [No copy known.]

Royal Historical Manuscripts Commission : see Anonymous (Report), Buccleuch, Carlisle, Denbigh, Egmont, Hare, Hodgkin, Ketton, Loder-Symonds, Portland, Throckmorton, and Townshend.

RYLANDS, W. HARRY (editor) : *The Book of the Fundamental Constitutions and Orders of the Philo Musicae et Architecturae Societas*. London, 1725–1727. (*Quatuor Coronatorum Antigrapha*. Masonic Reprints of the Quatuor Coronati Lodge, No. 2076, London, vol. IX.) Margate, 1900.

SACHS, HANS (pseud.) : *Hans Sachsens Schreiben aus dem Reiche der Todten an den geschickten Übersetzer der Opera Julius Caesar in Aegypten. Welchem noch beygefüget ist : Idorythmi Reflexion über eben dieselbe Opera*. [Hamburg,] 1725.

SALZA, ABD-EL-KADER : Paolo Rolli. Note biografiche e bibliografiche intorno. (*Bollettino della Reale Deputazione di Storia Patria per l' Umbria*, vol. XIX, Fasc. I-III.) Perugia, 1915.

SAUSSURE, CÉSAR DE : *Lettres et Voyages . . . en Allemagne, en Hollande et en Angleterre, 1725–1729*. Lausanne, 1903.

— *A Foreign View of England in the Reigns of George I & George II*. The Letters of Monsieur C. de S. to his Family. Translated by Mad. van Muyden. London, 1902.

SCHEIBE, JOHANN ADOLPH : *Der critische Musikus*. Leipzig, 1737–40.

— ditto. Vermehrte Auflage. Leipzig, 1745.

SCHMIDT, GUSTAV FRIEDRICH : *Neue Beiträge zur Geschichte der Musik und des Theaters in Braunschweig*. Wolffenbüttel, 1929.

SCHOELCHER, VICTOR : *The Life of Handel*. (Translated from the French by James Lowe.) London, 1857. Boston, 1858. The first four chapters of the original, but revised and augmented, version printed in *La France musicale*, Paris, 19 August 1860—2 November 1862. (The original manuscript of the whole is preserved in the Library of the Conservatoire, Paris.)

SCHUELLER, HERBERT M.: " Imitation " and " Expression " in British Music Criticism in the 18th Century. (*Musical Quarterly*, October 1947.) New York.

SCHULZE, WALTER : Die Quellen der Hamburger Oper 1678–1738. (*Mitteilungen aus der Bibliothek der Hansestadt Hamburg*, vol. 4.) Hamburg-Oldenburg, 1938.

SERRÉ DE RIEUX, JEAN DE : *Les Dons des Enfans de Latone : La Musique et la Chasse du Cerf. Poèmes dédiés au Roy.* Paris, 1734.

SHEDLOCK, JOHN SOUTH : Handel and his Librettist [Thomas Morell]. (*Musical Times*, August 1897.) London.

SHENSTONE, WILLIAM : *Letters.* Edited by Marjorie Williams. Oxford, 1939.

— *Letters.* Edited by Duncan Mallam. Minneapolis, 1939.

SHERBURN, GEORGE : Timon's Villa and Cannons. (*The Huntington Library Bulletin*, vol. VIII.) Cambridge, Mass., 1935.

SHERIDAN, THOMAS : *British Education* ; or, *The Source of the Disorders of Great Britain.* London, 1756.

SIBLEY, J. CHURCHILL : *Handel at Cannons : with a Description of the Church of St. Lawrence, Whitchurch.* London, [1918].

SMITH, WILLIAM C.: Bibliography [of Handel literature]. In Newman Flower : *G. F. Handel.* London, 1923, 1947.

— George III, Handel, and Mainwaring. (*Musical Times*, September 1924.) London.

— The Earliest Editions of Handel's Messiah. (*Musical Times*, November 1925 ; December 1941.) London.

— Handel's First Visit to England. (*Musical Times*, March 1935.) London.

— Handel's " Rinaldo " : An Outline of the Early Editions. (*Musical Times*, August 1935.) London.

— Handel's First Song on the London Stage. (*Music & Letters*, October 1935.) London.

— Handel's Failure in 1745. New Letters of the Composer. (*Musical Times*, July 1936.) London.

— Recently discovered Handel Manuscripts. (*Musical Times*, April 1937.) London.

— Samson : the Earliest Editions. (*Musical Times*, August 1938.) London.

— The Earliest Editions of Handel's " Water Music ". (*Musical Quarterly*, January 1939.) New York.

— *Concerning Handel, his Life and Works.* London, 1948 [or rather, 1949]. Contains, besides revised reprints of the articles of 1925, 1936, and 1939, the following new essays : *Handel the Man, Finance and Patronage in Handel's Life, Some Handel Portraits reconsidered, Gustav Waltz : was he Handel's cook ?,* and *Acis and Galatea in the Eighteenth Century.*

— *A Bibliography of the Musical Works published by John Walsh .* . 1695–1720. London, 1948.

— Handeliana. (*Music & Letters*, April 1950.) London.

— More Handeliana. (ditto, January 1953.)

— Catalogue of [Handel's] Works. (Gerald Abraham : *Handel. A Symposium.* London, 1954, pp. 275-310.)

SMOLLETT, TOBIAS : *Advice.* London, 1746.

SMOLLETT, TOBIAS (editor) : *The British Magazine*. London, 1760.
— *Continuation of the Complete History of England*. 5 vols. London, 1760–5.
SOLA, ERCOLE : Curiosità storico—artistico—letterarie, tratte dal carteggio dell' inviato estense Giuseppe Riva con Lodovico Muratori. (*Atti e Memorie delle R.R. Deputazioni di Storia patria per le provincie modenesi e parmenesi*, Ser. 3, vol. 4.) Modena, 1886.
SONNECK, OSCAR G. T. : *Early Concert-Life in America*. Leipzig, 1907.
— Library of Congress. *Catalogue of Opera Librettos printed before 1800*. Washington, 1914.
SPITTA, PHILIPP : Händel's Vater als Leibchirurg beim Herzoge Johann Adolph zu Sachsen-Weissenfels. (*Allgemeine Musikalische Zeitung*, IV. 286.) Leipzig, 1869.
— *Johann Sebastian Bach*. 2 vols. Leipzig, 1873 and 1880.
SQUIRE, WILLIAM BARCLAY : Handel in 1745. (*Riemann-Festschrift*.) Leipzig, 1909.
— Handel in Contemporary Song-Books. (*Musical Antiquary*, January 1913.) London..
— Handel's Clock Music. (*Musical Quarterly*, October 1919.) New York.
— A lost Handel Manuscript [*Acis and Galatea*]. (*Musical Times*, 1 October 1921.) London.
— Handel's Water Music. (ditto, 1 December 1922.) London.
— *Catalogue of the King's Music Library*. Part I. The Handel Manuscripts. London, 1927.
— see also Fuller-Maitland, J. A.
STEVENSON, ROBERT ALAN MOWBRAY : Handel and His Portraits. (*Magazine of Art*, Vol. VIII.) London, 1885.
STILLINGFLEET, BENJAMIN : *Literary Life and Select Works*. (Edited by W. Coxe.) 2 vols. London, 1811.
STOPFORD-SACKVILLE, MRS. : *Report on the MSS. of* ——. Vol. I. London, 1904.
STÖSSEL, JOHANN CHRISTOPH and JOHANN DAVID (publ.) : *Kurzgefasstes Musikalisches Lexikon*. Chemnitz, 1737. New edition, 1749.
STREATFEILD, RICHARD ALEXANDER : Handel in Italy, 1706–10. (*Musical Antiquary*, October 1909.) London.
— *Handel*. London, 1909.
— Handel's Journey to Hanover in 1716. (*Musical Antiquary*, January 1911.) London.
— The Granville Collection of Handel Manuscripts. (*Musical Antiquary*, July 1911.) London.
— *Handel, Canons and the Duke of Chandos*. London, 1916.
— Handel, Rolli, and Italian Opera in London in the Eighteenth Century. (*Musical Quarterly*, July 1917.) New York.
STUKELEY, WILLIAM : *The Family Memories, and the Antiquarian and Other Correspondence of William Stukeley, Roger and Samuel Gale*, etc. Edited by W. C. Lukis. 3 vols. (Surtees Society, vols. 73, 76, 80.) Durham, 1882–87.
— *Memoirs of Sir Isaac Newton's Life*. Edited by A. Hastings White. London, 1936.
SUNDON, CHARLOTTE CLAYTON, VISCOUNTESS : *Memoirs . . . including Letters . . .* Edited by Katherine Thomson. 2 vols. London, 1847.

SWIFT, JONATHAN : *Miscellanies in Prose and Verse*. 3 vols. London, 1728–33.
— *Directions for a Birth-day Song*, 1729.
— *Works*, etc. Edited by Walter Scott. 19 vols. Edinburgh, 1814.
— *The Correspondence of Jonathan Swift, D.D.* Edited by F. E. Ball. 6 vols. London, 1910–14.
— *Poems*. Edited by Harold Williams. Oxford, 1937.

TALBOT (pseud.) : see Coventry, H.

TALBOT, CATHERINE : see Carter, Elizabeth.

TAUT, KURT : Verzeichnis des Schrifttums über G. F. Händel. (*Händel-Jahrbuch*, 1933.) Leipzig.

TAYLOR, JOHN, senior : *The History of the Travels and Adventures of the Chevalier John Taylor, Ophthalmiater*. London, 1761.
— junior : *Records of My Life*. 2 vols. London, 1832.

TAYLOR, SEDLEY : *The Indebtedness of Handel to Works by other Composers*. Cambridge, 1906.

TELEMANN, GEORG PHILIPP : *Autobiography* [1739] : see Mattheson, J. *Grundlage einer Ehren-Pforte* (1740).

THOMSON, GLADYS SCOTT : *The Russells in Bloomsbury*. London, 1940.

THROCKMORTON, SIR N. WILLIAM : *The Throckmorton Manuscripts*. (Historical Manuscripts Commission, Third Report, Appendix), London, 1872.

TOLLET, ELIZABETH : *Poems on Several Occasions, etc.* London, 1755.

TOWNSEND, HORATIO : *An Account of the Visit of Handel to Dublin : with Incidental Notices of his Life and Character*. Dublin, 1852.
— *The History of the Mercer's Charitable Hospital in Dublin, to the end of the year 1742*. Dublin, 1860.

TOWNSHEND, MARQUESS : *The Manuscripts of the Marquess Townshend*. (Historical Manuscripts Commission, 11th Report, Appendix, Part IV.) London, 1887.

VALLESE, TARQUINIO : *Paolo Rolli in Inghilterra*. Milano, 1938.

VERTUE, GEORG : *Anecdotes of Painting in England*. Edited by Horace Walpole. With addition by James Dallaway. 5 vols. London, 1826–8. Newly edited by Ralph N. Wornum. 3 vols. London, 1849 ; and 1862.
— *Note Books*. Vol. III. (The Walpole Society, vol. 22.) Oxford, 1934.

VETTER, THEODOR : *Johann Jakob Heidegger, ein Mitarbeiter G. F. Händels*. (Neujahrsblatt, herausgegeben von der Stadtbibliothek Zürich, No. 258,) Zürich, 1902.

VICTOR, BENJAMIN : *Original Letters, Dramatic Pieces, and Poems*. 3 vols. London, 1776.

VINCENT, RICHARD : see Bickham, G.

VOGEL, EMIL : Händel-Portraits. (*Jahrbuch der Musikbibliothek Peters*, vol. III.) Leipzig, 1897.

WALPOLE, HORACE, 4TH EARL OF ORFORD : *Anecdotes of Painting in England*. See George Vertue.
— *Memoirs of the Reign of King George the Second*. Edited by Lord Holland. 3 vols. London, 1846.
— *Letters*. Edited by Peter Cunningham. 9 vols. London, 1891.
— *Letters*. Edited by Mrs. Paget Toynbee. 16 vols. Oxford, 1903–5.
— *Correspondence*. Edited by W. S. Lewis, etc. New Haven, 1937 ff. London 1937 ff.

WALTHER, JOHANN GOTTFRIED : *Musicalisches Lexikon ; oder Musikalische Bibliothec, etc.* Leipzig, 1732.

WARTON, JOSEPH : *An Essay on the Genius and Writings of Pope.* 2 vols. London, 1756–82.

WEINSTOCK, HERBERT : *Handel.* New York, 1946.

WEISSENBORN, B. : *Das Händelhaus in Halle.* Wolfenbüttel, 1938.

WEND(T), CHRISTIAN GOTTLIEB : *Triumph der Grossmuth und Treue, oder Cleofida, Koenigin von Indien.* [Translation of *Poro.*] Hamburg, 1732.

WENTWORTH, THOMAS, EARL OF STRAFFORD : *The Wentworth Papers.* 1705–39. Edited by James J. Cartwright. London, 1883.

WESLEY, JOHN : *The Journal of the Rev. John Wesley, A.M.* Edited by Nehemiah Curnock. Standard Edition. 8 vols. New York, 1909–16.

— *Letters.* Edited by John Telford. 8 vols. London, 1931.

WHINCOP, THOMAS : *Scanderbeg :* or *Love and Liberty. A Tragedy.* See Anonymous : An Account of all the Plays, *etc.*

WHITLEY, WILLIAM T.: *Artists and their Friends in England.* 2 vols. London, 1928.

WIEL, TADDEO : I teatri musicali di Venezia. (*Nuovo Archivio Veneto*, vol. XIX.) Venezia, 1891.

WILLERS, WILHELM : see Merbach.

WILLIAMS, BASIL : *The Whig Supremacy, 1714–1760.* Oxford, 1939.

WILLIAMS, C. F. ABDY : *Handel, his Life and Works.* (The Master Musicians, edited by Frederick J. Crowest.) London, 1901. Revised and edited by Eric Blom. London, 1935.

WRAY, FRANCIS ASLETT : see Nichols, R. H.

WRIGHT, REGINALD WILBERFORCE MILL : George Frederick Handel : his Bath Associations. (*Musical Opinion*, July, August, 1935.) London.

WROTH, WARWICK : *The London Pleasure Gardens of the Eighteenth Century.* London, 1896.

WYNDHAM, HENRY SAXE : *The Annals of Covent Garden Theatre from 1732 to 1897.* 2 vols. London, 1906.

YOUNG, PERCY M. : *Handel.* (The Master Musicians, edited by Eric Blom.) London, 1947.

ZACHARIAE, FRIEDRICH WILHELM : *Die Tageszeiten.* Rostock, 1756. Second, augmented edition, 1757. New, revised edition, 1767.

INDICES

INDEX OF HANDEL'S WORKS
MENTIONED IN THIS BOOK

GENERAL INDEX OF NAMES, PLACES, TITLES AND SELECTED SUBJECTS

H.-29

H.-29 a